R. Gupta's®

POPULAR MASTER GUIDE

National Testing Agency **(NTA)**

UGC-NET/JRF

Junior Research Fellowship & Assistant Professor Eligibility Exam

YOGA

PAPER II

- Specialised Study Material with Solved Previous Years' Paper
- Numerous Solved Multiple Choice Questions (MCQs)

by

RPH Editorial Board

2027
EDITION

RAMESH PUBLISHING HOUSE, NEW DELHI

Published by

O.P. Gupta *for* Ramesh Publishing House

Admin. Office

12-H, New Daryaganj Road, Opp. Officers' Mess,
New Delhi-110002 ✆ 23275224, 23245124

E-mail: info@rameshpublishinghouse.com

For Online Shopping: www.rameshpublishinghouse.com

Showroom

- Balaji Market, Nai Sarak, Delhi-110006 ✆ 23282525 📱 9354373464
- 4457, Nai Sarak, Delhi-110006

Book Code: R-1902

ISBN: 978-93-87604-58-2

Price: ₹ 620

Printed at: B.K. Offset, Delhi

CONTENTS

Previous Years' Paper

National Testing Agency (NTA)

UGC-NET Junior Research Fellowship & Assistant Professor Eligibility Exam

YOGA, JANUARY-2026

(Exam held on 02-01-2026)

PAPER-II

1. Types of Pratyaksha according to Buddha philosophy:

1. 10
2. 8
3. 4
4. 2

2. Bhavya and Abhavya are parts of which according to Jaina philosophy?

1. Jiva
2. Ajiva
3. Shradha
4. Mithya

3. Which Cow's milk is prohibited according to yajnavalkyasmriti?

1. Cow who's calf died
2. Donkey coloured cow
3. 12 day after delivery
4. Pet cow

4. 'Having interest on stories of God is called Bhakti' according to:

1. Parashara
2. Shandilya
3. Narada
4. Garga

5. Who is Sarvasankalpa Sanyasi?

1. Yogarudha
2. Aruruksha
3. Yunjana
4. Prathamika

6. Father of Bhrugu according to Taittariyopanishad:

1. Varuni
2. Varuna
3. Indra
4. Prajapati

7. Bhokta according to Kathopanishad is:

1. Synchronized with Atma, Manas and Indriyas
2. Synchronized with Manas and Indriyas
3. Synchronized with Atma and Manas
4. Synchronized with Manas, Indriyas and Prana

8. Who is always self contented?

1. Atmajnani
2. Yogi
3. Sthitaprajna
4. Jnani

9. How many days will it take to Nirguna dhyani to attain Samadhi according to Yogatattvopanishad?

1. 10
2. 15
3. 12
4. 20

10. How many parts of body kept extended during Asana by Dhyana-yogi according to shvetasvatar Upanishad?

1. Four
2. Three
3. One
4. Five

11. In Trishikhibrahmanopanishad karma yoga is:

1. Liberation of mind
2. Chitta indulge in worldly objects
3. Dettachment of chitta from worldly action
4. Continuous Indulgence of mind

12. Tools of antahkaran according to Dhyanabindu-upanishad, Pranava is:

1. Bow 2. Arrow
3. Target 4. Archer

13. Which purity leads to kaivalya?

1. Sattva and Purusha
2. Manas and Sattva
3. Prakriti and Ahamkara
4. Chittah and Purusha

14. Method to restrain chitta-vritti according to yogasutra:

1. Isvarapranidhana 2. Jnana yoga
3. Karma yoga 4. Hatha yoga

15. "Tato dvandvanabhighatah" what 'Tath' means in the yogasutra reflects?

1. Success in Niyama
2. Success in Dhyana
3. Success in Asana
4. Success in Pranayama

16. Which Guna dominates in 'Mudha' chittabhumi?

1. Rajoguna
2. Sattvaguna
3. Suddha Sattvaguna
4. Tamoguna

17. According to Hathayoga pradlipika, how many years it will take to attain yoga success through siddhasana practice along with moderate diet?

1. 15 years 2. 12 years
3. 7 years 4. 13 years

18. How much food should intake by House holder according to Vashishta Samhita?

1. 10 Grasa 2. 20 Grasa
3. 32 Grasa 4. 16 Grasa

19. Which bandh promotes prana for its upliftment within sushumana according to Hatharatnavali?

1. Uddiyana Bandha
2. Mahabandha
3. Mahavedha
4. Moolbandha

20. According to Shiva Samhita Manipura Chakra is denoted by which letters?

1. Ta to Pa 2. Da to Fa
3. Dha to Ba 4. Ka to Ma

21. People who share characteristics as shyness, social withdrawal and a tendency not to talk much are characterised as:

1. Extrovert 2. Introvert
3. Sanguine 4. Choleric

22. Cytokinesis is separation of:

1. cytoplasma
2. duplicate chromosomes
3. centrioles
4. spindle fibers

23. Which muscle doesn't belongs to shoulder?

1. Supraspinatus 2. Trapazius
3. Levator scapulae 4. Gluteus Minimus

24. Lipids are absorbed/assimilated in the human body through:

1. Capilaries 2. Veins
3. Lacteals 4. Arteries

25. Which kosha is related with vegetative domain of human existence according to taittiriya Upanishad?

1. Annamaya kosha
2. Pranamaya kosha
3. Manomaya kosha
4. Anandmaya kosha

26. Which one of the following is klesha according to Yogasutra?

1. Disease 2. Doubtfullness
3. 'I'ness (Ego) 4. Instability

27. Which one is **not** the characteristic of Pitta-dosha?

1. Untuousness 2. Hotness
3. Sharpness 4. Heavyness

28. Which vayu regulates physiological activities of body uniformaly?

1. Prana Vayu 2. Udana Vayu
3. Samana Vayu 4. Apana Vayu

29. The characteristics of Asana is:
1. Attaining specific posture forcefully
2. Attaining specific posture effortfully
3. Attaining specific posture effortlessly with synchronization of breath
4. Attaining specific posture with external support

30. Keval Kumbhaka is characterized as:
1. State of equal atmospheric and intra-pulmonaric pressure
2. State of increased intrapulmonaric pressure
3. State of decreased intrapulmonaric pressure
4. State of unequal atmospheric intra-pulmonaric pressure

31. Which Asana eliminates hazardous diseases according to Hathayagapradipika?
1. Padmasana 2. Bhujangasana
3. Matsyendrasana 4. Paschimottanasana

32. Which kriya eliminates all types of diseases according to Hathapradipika?
1. Jalavasti 2. Sthalavasti
3. Vastradhauti 4. Trataka

33. Understanding the complex composition of body can be attained by contemplating:
1. On Dhruva
2. On Nabhichakra
3. On Kurma Nadi
4. In Murdha Jyoti

34. The measurement of Sutra for Sutraneti practice according to Hathayogapradipika:
1. Eka Hasta 2. Eka Vitasti
3. Three Vitasti 4. Eka Pada

35. Which system is not the part of disciple approach to the Guru for receiving knowledge according to Bhagvadgita?
1. Pranipata 2. Pariprashna
3. Gyana Vinmaya 4. Seva

36. What should be done if there if fatigue while practicing Asanas?
1. Continue Asana Practice
2. Relax in shavasana
3. Practice pranayama
4. Stop Asana practice

37. How many steps involved in Mind Sound Resonance Technique (MSRT)?
1. 3 2. 5
3. 6 4. 8

38. Practicing method in Vrikshasana according to Gherand Samhita is:
1. Placing Right sole of the foot in thigh root of Left leg
2. Placing Left sole of the foot is thigh root of Right leg
3. Placing Right sole of the foot in middle thigh of Left leg
4. Placing Left sole of the foot in the middle thigh of Right leg

39. Another name of Ugrasana according to shiva-samhita is:
1. Pascimottanasana 2. Swastikasana
3. Padmasana 4. Siddhasana

40. Types of Nadishuddhi according to Gherand Samhita are:
1. 2 2. 1
3. 4 4. 3

41. Given below are two statements: one is labelled as Assertion (A) and the other is labelled as Reason (R).

Assertion (A): Yoga can overcome all the sufferings.

Reason (R): Yoga is having all aspects of physical, mental, social and spiritual wellbeing. Yogi accepts only moderate food proper living, proper effort and proper sleep.

In the light of the above statements, choose the ***most appropriate*** answer from the options given below:
1. Both (A) and (R) are correct and (R) is the correct explanation of (A)
2. Both (A) and (R) are correct, but (R) is NOT the correct explanation of (A)
3. (A) is correct, but (R) is not correct
4. (A) is not correct, but (R) is correct

42. Given below are two statements: one is labelled as Assertion (A) and the other is labelled as Reason (R).

Assertion (A): Prana is Annamayakosa.

Reason (R): Annamayakosa is outcome of Anna. Prana exists in Anna.

In the light of the above statements, choose the ***most appropriate*** answer from the options given below:

1. Both (A) and (R) are correct and (R) is the correct explanation of (A)
2. Both (A) and (R) are correct, but (R) is NOT the correct explanation of (A)
3. (A) is correct, but (R) is not correct
4. (A) is not correct, but (R) is correct

43. Given below are two statements: one is labelled as Assertion (A) and the other is labelled as Reason (R).

Assertion (A): 'A' Kara is right feather and 'U' kara is left feather of the swan of OM-kara.

Reason (R): Om-kara feather of Swan gets destroyed with rajoguna and tamoguna.

In the light of the above statements, choose the ***most appropriate*** answer from the options given below:

1. Both (A) and (R) are correct and (R) is the correct explanation of (A)
2. Both (A) and (R) are correct, but (R) is NOT the correct explanation of (A)
3. (A) is correct, but (R) is not correct
4. (A) is not correct, but (R) is correct

44. Given below are two statements: one is labelled as Assertion (A) and the other is labelled as Reason (R).

Assertion (A): Hathayoga Pradeepika is text of Hathayoga, preacher is yogi swatmarama.

Reason (R): Knowledge of Hathayoga attained himself to yogi swatmaram without Guru's preach.

In the light of the above statements, choose the ***most appropriate*** answer from the options given below:

1. Both (A) and (R) are correct and (R) is the correct explanation of (A)
2. Both (A) and (R) are correct, but (R) is NOT the correct explanation of (A)
3. (A) is correct, but (R) is not correct
4. (A) is not correct, but (R) is correct

45. Given below are two statements: one is labelled as Assertion (A) and the other is labelled as Reason (R).

Assertion (A): Food along with Milk and Ghee is good for pranayama practitioner at the initial stages of practice.

Reason (R): No such rules and regulations regarding food once the practioner is established in pranayama practice.

In the light of the above statements, choose the ***most appropriate*** answer from the options given below:

1. Both (A) and (R) are correct and (R) is the correct explanation of (A)
2. Both (A) and (R) are correct, but (R) is NOT the correct explanation of (A)
3. (A) is correct, but (R) is not correct
4. (A) is not correct, but (R) is correct

46. Given below are two statements: one is labelled as Assertion (A) and the other is labelled as Reason (R).

Assertion (A): Meaning of Hatha is to unite H-kar and Tha-kar.

Reason (R): Hatha yoga is the ladder for achieving Rajyoga. Aim of Raj Yoga is to achieve Kaivalya.

In the light of the above statements, choose the ***most appropriate*** answer from the options given below:

1. Both (A) and (R) are correct and (R) is the correct explanation of (A)
2. Both (A) and (R) are correct, but (R) is NOT the correct explanation of (A)
3. (A) is correct, but (R) is not correct
4. (A) is not correct, but (R) is correct

47. Given below are two statements: one is labelled as Assertion (A) and the other is labelled as Reason (R).

Assertion (A): All arteries carry oxygenated blood.

Reason (R): Artery carries oxygenated blood from heart to all body parts but pulmonary artery carry deoxygenated blood from heart to lungs.

In the light of the above statements, choose the ***most appropriate*** answer from the options given below:

1. Both (A) and (R) are correct and (R) is the correct explanation of (A)
2. Both (A) and (R) are correct, but (R) is NOT the correct explanation of (A)
3. (A) is correct, but (R) is not correct
4. (A) is not correct, but (R) is correct

48. Given below are two statements: one is labelled as Assertion (A) and the other is labelled as Reason (R).

Assertion (A): Locomotion of body is only because of bones and joints.

Reason (R): Skeletal Muscles are attached with bones, contraction and relaxation of muscles leads bones to move across the joints resulting to locomotion.

In the light of the above statements, choose the ***most appropriate*** answer from the options given below:

1. Both (A) and (R) are correct and (R) is the correct explanation of (A)
2. Both (A) and (R) are correct, but (R) is NOT the correct explanation of (A)
3. (A) is correct, but (R) is not correct
4. (A) is not correct, but (R) is correct

49. Given below are two statements: one is labelled as Assertion (A) and the other is labelled as Reason (R).

Assertion (A): Neti cleanse nasal sinus and other cranial disorders.

Reason (R): The procedure and benefits of Jalanet, has been detailed in Hathapradipika and Gherand Samhita.

In the light of the above statements, choose the ***most appropriate*** answer from the options given below:

1. Both (A) and (R) are correct and (R) is the correct explanation of (A)
2. Both (A) and (R) are correct, but (R) is NOT the correct explanation of (A)
3. (A) is correct, but (R) is not correct
4. (A) is not correct, but (R) is correct

50. Given below are two statements: one is labelled as Assertion (A) and the other is labelled as Reason (R).

Assertion (A): Susumna has been termed as yogivallabha.

Reason (R): Siva samhita explains 14 nadis and emphasised Susumna has been considered as most important among all.

In the light of the above statements, choose the ***most appropriate*** answer from the options given below:

1. Both (A) and (R) are correct and (R) is the correct explanation of (A)
2. Both (A) and (R) are correct, but (R) is NOT the correct explanation of (A)
3. (A) is correct, but (R) is not correct
4. (A) is not correct, but (R) is correct

51. Sequence these According to NET yoga syllabus:

A. Yajnavalkya Smriti
B. Prasthanatrayee
C. Maharshi patanjali
D. Tulasids
E. Gorakshanath

Choose the ***correct*** answer from the options given below:

1. A, B, C, D, E 2. B, A, C, E, D
3. A, B, E, C, D 4. C, D, E, B, A

52. Sequence these yogis according to their Birth in descending order:

A. Swami Rama of Himalaya
B. Tirumala Krishnamacharya
C. Maharshi Mahesh Yogi
D. Shri Ram Sharma Acharya
E. Swami Sivananda Saraswathi

Choose the ***correct*** answer from the options given below:

1. B, E, C, A, D 2. D, E, B, C, A
3. E, B, D, C, A 4. A, C, D, B, E

53. Sequence Mantra according to kotopanishad:

A. Buddhim tu Saarathim
B. Viddh
C. Atmanam Rathinam Viddh
D. Manah Pragrahmeva cha
E. Sariram Rathameva cha

Choose the ***correct*** answer from the options given below:

1. C, E, A, B, D 2. E, B, A, C, D
3. D, B, C, A, E 4. C, D, E, B, A

54. Sequence ujjayi benefits according to yogakundali upanishad:

A. Sarvaroghar
B. Sleshmahar
C. Dhatugata dosha vinasana
D. Dehanala vivardan
E. Jalodhar

Choose the ***correct*** answer from the options given below:

1. A, B, C, D, E 2. E, C, B, D, A
3. B, A, D, E, C 4. C, B, A, D, E

55. Sequence according to Shrimad Bhagvadgita:

A. Akrodha B. Ahimsa
C. Satya D. Daya
E. Santi

Choose the ***correct*** answer from the options given below:

1. B, C, D, A, E 2. C, B, A, E, D
3. B, C, A, E, D 4. B, C, E, A, D

56. Order in sequence according to Shrimad Bhagavadgita:

A. Soumyatva B. Manahprasad
C. Mouna D. Bhavasansuddhi
E. Atmavinigraha

Choose the ***correct*** answer from the options given below:

1. A, B, C, D, E 2. B, A, C, E, D
3. C, D, A, B, E 4. E, C, D, A, B

57. Order the yogasutras:

A. Tasya Bhumishu Viniyogah
B. Te Vyaktasukshmah Gunatmanah
C. Heyam Dukhmanagatam
D. Tajja Sanskaro-Anya-Sanskar-Pratibandhi
E. Drastri-Drishyopraktam Chittam Sarvartham

Choose the ***correct*** answer from the options given below:

1. D, C, A, B, E 2. C, D, B, A, E
3. E, C, D, A, B 4. A, D, B, C, E

58. Sequence this sloka according to Hathayogapradipika:

A. Doshanam
B. Medasleshmadhikah Purvam
C. Samabhavatah
D. Shatkarmani Samacharet
E. Anyastu Nacharettani

Choose the ***correct*** answer from the options given below:

1. C, A, E, D, B 2. B, D, E, A, C
3. D, B, C, A, E 4. C, A, B, D, E

59. Sequence of neurological conduction within multi-polar neuron:

A. Synaptic terminals
B. Axon
C. Dendrite
D. Dendritic branches
E. Initial Segment of Axon

Choose the ***correct*** answer from the options given below:

1. B, E, C, D, A 2. D, C, E, B, A
3. D, C, B, E, A 4. E, B, D, C, A

60. Sequence of urine formation with respect to anatomical structure is:

A. Collecting Duct
B. Proximal Convoluted Tubule (PCT)
C. Glomerulus
D. Henelis loop
E. Distal Convoluted Tubule (DCT)

Choose the ***correct*** answer from the options given below:

1. C, D, E, A, B 2. C, B, D, A, E
3. C, B, D, E, A 4. C, D, A, B, E

61. Sequence of Antarayas:

A. Bhrantidarshan B. Sanshaya
C. Alasya D. Avirati
E. Styana

Choose the ***correct*** answer from the options given below:

1. E, B, C, D, A 2. B, C, D, E, A
3. B, D, E, C, A 4. E, B, D, C, A

62. Arrange the followings from superior to inferior order:

A. Lumber B. Thoracic
C. Cervical D. Coccygeal
E. Sacral

Choose the ***correct*** answer from the options given below:

1. D, C, A, B, E 2. A, B, C, E, D
3. E, A, B, C, D 4. C, B, A, E, D

63. Sequence these samadhi types according to Gheranda Samhita:

A. Nadayoga B. Bhakti yoga
C. Dhyana yoga D. Layasiddhi yoga
E. Rasananda yoga

Choose the ***correct*** answer from the options given below:

1. C, A, E, D, B 2. B, C, A, D, E
3. C, B, D, E, A 4. A, B, C, D, E

64. Sequence as per teaching Methodology in Yoga:

A. Verbal Introduction of Practice
B. Demonstration of Practice
C. Sitting Arrangement
D. Emphasis on salient point
E. Individual Group practice

Choose the ***correct*** answer from the options given below :

1. C, B, D, A, E 2. C, D, A, E, B
3. C, A, B, D, E 4. C, A, E, B, D

65. The sequence of bija mantra in Surya Namaskar are:

A. Om Hraam B. Om Hreem
C. Om Hroom D. Om Hraum
E. Om Hraim

Choose the ***correct*** answer from the options given below:

1. A, B, C, D, E 2. A, B, C, E, D
3. C, B, A, D, E 4. B, A, E, D, C

66. According to Tulasidas, dipping into prayaga makes:

A. Crows turn into Cuckoos
B. Donkey becomes Cow
C. Herons becomes Swans
D. Human becomes God
E. Snakes become poison free

Choose the ***correct*** answer from the options given below:

1. A, C only 2. B, C only
3. C, E only 4. D, C only

67. Satvic people like foods:

A. Affectioned food items
B. Saline food
C. Unctuous food
D. Dried food
E. Vital foods

Choose the ***correct*** answer from the options given below:

1. A, D, E only 2. B, C, A only
3. A, C, E only 4. A, D, B only

68. Initial siddhis of yoga practices according to shwetashwatar-upanishad are:

A. Sweetness of voice
B. Lightness of body
C. Brightness of eyes
D. Absence from desires
E. Bindu jaya

Choose the ***correct*** answer from the options given below:

1. B, C, E only 2. A, C, E only
3. C, E, D only 4. A, B, D only

69. Attaining of udana vayu, leads to non-attachment of following with body:

A. Prithvi B. Jala
C. Vayu D. Mud
E. Thorns

Choose the *correct* answer from the options given below:

1. D, E, C only 2. A, D, E only
3. B, C, A only 4. B, D, E only

70. Characteristics of parashakti according to sidhasidhantapadhati:

A. Aprameyata B. Nishchalata
C. Abhinnata D. Spharata
E. Anantata

Choose the *correct* answer from the options given below:

1. A, B, C only 2. B, C, D only
3. A, C, E only 4. C, D, E only

71. Gliding movements occurs between the surfaces of articulating:

A. Carpal bone B. Tarsal bone
C. Sternum D. Elbow joint
E. Hip joint

Choose the *correct* answer from the options given below:

1. A, B, D only 2. A, B, C only
3. B, C, E only 4. A, D, E only

72. According to shivsamhita chakras are:

A. Muladhara Chakra
B. Kundalini Chakra
C. Soma Chakra
D. Visudhi Chakra
E. Manipura Chakra

Choose the *correct* answer from the options given below:

1. A, B, C only 2. A, D, E only
3. A, C, D only 4. B, C, E only

73. Saptasadhana according to Gheranda samhita are:

A. Shodhanam B. Dridhata
C. Moksha D. Dhairyam
E. Samadhi

Choose the *correct* answer from the options given below:

1. A, B, C only 2. B, C, D only
3. A, B, D only 4. C, D, E only

74. Characteristics of Hathasiddhi:

A. Vapu kristwam
B. Nadi-visudhihi
C. Laulyam
D. Dhatu posham
E. Agni dipnam

Choose the *correct* answer from the options given below:

1. A, B, C only 2. A, B, E only
3. A, B, D only 4. A, D, E only

75. Obstacles of yoga according to Hatha Yoga Pradipika:

A. Loitering
B. Excessive eating
C. Tattava Gyan
D. Talkative
E. Excessive sleeping

Choose the *correct* answer from the options given below:

1. A, C only 2. A, B only
3. B, D only 4. D, E only

76. Match the List-I with List-II.

List-I	List-II
A. Shri Shyama Charan Lahri	I. Chitradurg, Karnataka
B. Tirumalai Krishnamacharaya	II. Garhwal, Uttarakhand
C. Swami Rama	III. Nadia, Bengal
D. Shriram Sharma Acharya	IV. Agra, Uttar Pradesh

Choose the *correct* answer from the options given below:

1. A-II, B-I, C-III, D-IV
2. A-I, B-III, C-II, D-IV
3. A-III, B-I, C-II, D-IV
4. A-IV, B-II, C-I, D-III

77. Match the List-I with List-II.

List-I	List-II
A. Jagaritsthan	I. Tajas
B. Swapnasthan	II. Vaisvanar
C. Sushuptasthan	III. Chaturtha
D. Amatra	IV. Prajna

Choose the ***correct*** answer from the options given below:

1. A-II, B-I, C-IV, D-III
2. A-I, B-II, C-III, D-IV
3. A-IV, B-I, C-III, D-II
4. A-I, B-IV, C-II, D-III

78. Match the List-I with List-II.

List-I	List-II
A. Daivi Sampat	I. Kama
B. Asuri Sampat	II. Saucha
C. Narakadwar	III. Ajnana
D. Tamas	IV. Mantraheena

Choose the ***correct*** answer from the options given below:

1. A-I, B-II, C-III, D-IV
2. A-II, B-IV, C-I, D-III
3. A-II, B-III, C-I, D-IV
4. A-III, B-II, C-IV, D-I

79. Match the List-I with List-II.

List-I	List-II
A. Sodasadhara Bandan	I. Brahmagranthi
B. Ajnachakra	II. Vishnugranthi
C. Atisunya	III. Rudragranthi
D. Anahata chakra	IV. Madhyachakra

Choose the ***correct*** answer from the options given below:

1. A-IV, B-III, C-II, D-I
2. A-II, B-III, C-IV, D-I
3. A-I, B-II, C-III, D-IV
4. A-III, B-II, C-IV, D-I

80. Match the List-I with List-II.

List-I	List-II
A. Agneyee	I. Dvitiya matra
B. Vayavyaa	II. Ardha matra
C. Bhanumandal Sankasa	III. Prathama matra
D. Varuni	IV. Tritiyamatra

Choose the ***correct*** answer from the options given below:

1. A-III, B-I, C-IV, D-II
2. A-I, B-II, C-III, D-IV
3. A-IV, B-III, C-II, D-I
4. A-I, B-III, C-II, D-IV

81. Match the List-I with List-II.

List-I	List-II
A. Samsaya	I. Daurmanasya
B. Tapa	II. Niyama
C. Santosh	III. Antaraya
D. Vikshepasahabhu	IV. Kriyayoga

Choose the ***correct*** answer from the options given below:

1. A-I, B-II, C-III, D-IV
2. A-II, B-III, C-IV, D-I
3. A-IV, B-III, C-II, D-I
4. A-III, B-IV, C-II, D-I

82. Match the List-I with List-II.

List-I	List-II
A. Vibhutipada	I. Teevrasam-vegaanamasannah
B. Kaivalyapada	II. Dhyanaheyas-tadvrittayah
C. Sadhanapada	III. Pratyayasya Parachittajnanam
D. Samadhipada	IV. Tatra dhyanajamanasayam

Choose the ***correct*** answer from the options given below:

1. A-IV, B-I, C-II, D-III
2. A-III, B-II, C-I, D-IV
3. A-IV, B-III, C-II, D-I
4. A-III, B-IV, C-II, D-I

83. Match the List-I with List-II.

List-I	List-II
A. Muladhara	I. Lakini
B. Svadisthana	II. Kakini
C. Manipura	III. Rakini
D. Anahata	IV. Dakini

Choose the ***correct*** answer from the options given below:

1. A-IV, B-III, C-I, D-II
2. A-III, B-IV, C-II, D-I
3. A-I, B-II, C-III, D-IV
4. A-II, B-I, C-IV, D-III

84. Match the List-I with List-II.

List-I	List-II
A. Bhulok	I. Kukshi
B. Bhuvarlok	II. Guhyasthan
C. Svarlok	III. Lingasthan
D. Vishnulok	IV. Nabhisthan

Choose the *correct* answer from the options given below:

1. A-I, B-II, C-III, D-IV
2. A-III, B-IV, C-II, D-I
3. A-II, B-III, C-IV, D-I
4. A-IV, B-III, C-I, D-II

85. Match the List-I with List-II.

List-I	List-II
A. Aparmpara	I. Lolata
B. Paramapada	II. Anupamatva
C. Sunya	III. Asamkhytva
D. Niranjan	IV. Sahajatva

Choose the *correct* answer from the options given below:

1. A-II, B-III, C-I, D-IV
2. A-IV, B-III, C-II, D-I
3. A-I, B-II, C-III, D-IV
4. A-III, B-II, C-IV, D-I

86. Match the List-I with List-II.

List-I	List-II
A. Cell	I. Circumduction
B. Neck	II. Actin and Myosin
C. Skeletal Muscle	III. Phagocytosis
D. Brain	IV. Thalamus

Choose the *correct* answer from the options given below:

1. A-II, B-IV, C-III, D-I
2. A-III, B-I, C-II, D-IV
3. A-III, B-IV, C-I, D-II
4. A-II, B-I, C-III, D-IV

87. Match the List-I with List-II.

List-I	List-II
A. Prohibited food for yogi	I. Snigdha
B. Recommended food for yogi	II. Rasayukta
C. Satvik food	III. Utkat Shak
D. Rajsik food	IV. Teekshan Ahar

Choose the *correct* answer from the options given below:

1. A-III, B-I, C-II, D-IV
2. A-IV, B-III, C-I, D-II
3. A-I, B-II, C-III, D-IV
4. A-IV, B-II, C-I, D-III

88. Match the List-I with List-II.

List-I	List-II
A. Musculo skeletal disorder	I. Epilepsy
B. Cardiovascular disorder	II. Spondylosis
C. Neurological disorder	III. Phobia
D. Psychiatric disorder	IV. Angina

Choose the *correct* answer from the options given below:

1. A-IV, B-III, C-II, D-I
2. A-III, B-I, C-IV, D-II
3. A-III, B-I, C-II, D-IV
4. A-II, B-IV, C-I, D-III

89. Match the List-I with List-II.

List-I	List-II
A. Moksa sanyasa yoga	I. Jainadarshan
B. Kaivalyapada	II. Srimadbhagavodgita
C. Aparigrahavrata	III. Patanjala Yogadarshan
D. Vinayapitak	IV. Bauddhadarshan

Choose the *correct* answer from the options given below:

1. A-IV, B-III, C-II, D-I
2. A-II, B-III, C-I, D-IV
3. A-II, B-I, C-III, D-IV
4. A-IV, B-II, C-I, D-III

90. Match the List-I with List-II.

List-I	List-II
A. Viparitakarani	I. Dhauti
B. Vahnisara	II. Satkarma
C. Lauliki	III. Kumbhaka
D. Murcha	IV. Mudra

Choose the *correct* answer from the options given below:

1. A-IV, B-II, C-I, D-III
2. A-III, B-II, C-I, D-IV
3. A-IV, B-I, C-II, D-III
4. A-IV, B-III, C-II, D-I

Directions (Qs. No. 91 to 95): *Read the following passage and answer the questions:*

Rishis determined four ashrama for human life i.e. Brahmacharya, Grihastha, Vanprastha and Sanyasa. Life span of human age was assumed to be hundred years, accordingly every ashrama span was divided equally into twenty five years. After upanayana samskara upto age of twenty five years pupil reside in Gurukula. This period of life was dedicated for accumulation of knowledge from veda, vedanga and every aspect of knowledge including power as well. After competition of Gurukula stage of life pupil enters into Grihastha. Knowledge attained during Brahmacharya ashrama life was applicable for social behaviour, to serve people and gaining punya samchaya by Grihastha. After Grihastha ashrama one goes to vana and lived there for mastery over senses. This life was dedicated for mental purushartha and self realization practices. After completing twenty five year's in vana they leave home and family permanently for sanyasa. This life was dedicated for moksha and liberation of soul and guiding grihastha with his experiences. These four asharama related with life stages of childhood, Adolescence, adulthood and elederly. The four ashrama were directly related with Purushạstha Chatushtya i.e. Dharma, Artha, Kama and Moksha. Brahmacharya was related with Dharma Grihashth was related with Artha and Kama. Vanprastha was related with Nivriti and preparation for moksha. Sanyasa was related with Moksha. Ashramopnishad explain four ashrama Brahmacharya, Grihastha, Vanprastha and Sanyasa. Further Brahmachari were classified as Gayatri, Brahman, Prjapatya and Brihan. Grihastha were classified as Vartakvriti, shaleen Vritti, yayavar and Ghar Sannyasik. Vanprastha were classified as - Vaikhanas, Udumbar, Balkhilya Fenap. Sanyasi were classified as kuteechak, Bahoodak hamsa and Paramhamsa.

91. Which of the following is related to 'Artha' Purushartha?

1. Vanprastha 2. Grihastha
3. Brahmacharya 4. Sanyasa

92. Which of the following is related to Ghor Sannyasika?

1. Sanyasi 2. Grihastha
3. Vanprasthi 4. Brahmachari

93. Vanprastha ashrama has been for How many years?

1. 30 2. 25
3. 100 4. 50

94. Mansik (Mental) Purusharth has been practiced in which ashrama?

1. Brahmacharya 2. Grihastha
3. Vanprastha 4. Sanyasa

95. "Bahoodak" is related with which of the following?

1. Childhood 2. Elderly
3. Adulthood 4. Adolescence

Directions (Qs. No. 96 to 100): *Read the following passage and answer the questions:*

Chakras are the most important component of Pranamayakosa as well as the whole subtle body. The central channels of Prana are known as 'Chakaras'. These centres and channels receives Prana and distributes its potential to Annamayakosa through Pranamayakosa. Chakras are beyond senses and body and centres, of prana can transform the psychic energy to spiritual energy. These centres are not the component of body however part of subtle body. These are circular in nature thats why termed as Chakras. According to Swami Satyanand Saraswati with reference to his yogic references chakras are accepted as 'whirlpool' and 'movable circlet'. Sri Aravinda has accepted chakras as conscious centres. He stated that chakras are the centres and sources of all movable energies of our existence. These energies executes various activities and systematically distributed within the body to flow from higher spiritual centres to lower one. According to Baile chakras are component of Pranamayasarir. The Pranic body is composed of various energy channels and the location where channels cross each other are termed as 'Energy Centres' or 'Chakras' these energy channels are known as 'Nadis'. These energy channels also called as yoganadis. These nadis gets collected within the Spinal column and gets bunched. These bunches of Nadis resembles likes flower petals so these Nadibunches may also called Padma or Lotus which are termed as Chakra. Chakras are the centres of inner consciousness and basically related to subtle body. Opening of these centre led to promote yogic inner consciousness otherwise a common man remains entanyled within simple external consciousness only. The context of chakras are referred with yoga and its practices only.

96. Which of the following receives Prana and distributes its potential?

1. Nadi 2. Pranamayakosa
3. Sukshmasarira 4. Chakra

97. Swami Satyananda referred chakra as:

1. Movable Circlet 2. Consciousness
3. Energy Centres 4. Vital Area

98. Chakras are accepted as conscious centres by whom:

1. Swami Sathyananda
2. Sri Aravinda
3. Baile
4. Swami Niranjanananda

99. Inner consciousness arise by:

1. Opening of chakras
2. Closing chakras
3. By Lotus flower
4. Spinalcord knowledge

100. Energy channels cross each other at:

1. Physical body 2. Water body
3. Keval body 4. Pranic body

ANSWERS

1	2	3	4	5	6	7	8	9	10
3	1	1	4	1	2	1	3	3	2
11	**12**	**13**	**14**	**15**	**16**	**17**	**18**	**19**	**20**
4	1	1	1	3	4	2	3	1	2
21	**22**	**23**	**24**	**25**	**26**	**27**	**28**	**29**	**30**
2	1	4	3	1	3	4	3	3	1
31	**32**	**33**	**34**	**35**	**36**	**37**	**38**	**39**	**40**
3	1	2	2	3	2	4	1	1	1
41	**42**	**43**	**44**	**45**	**46**	**47**	**48**	**49**	**50**
1	4	3	3	2	2	4	4	3	1
51	**52**	**53**	**54**	**55**	**56**	**57**	**58**	**59**	**60**
2	4	1	3	3	2	1	2	2	3
61	**62**	**63**	**64**	**65**	**66**	**67**	**68**	**69**	**70**
1	4	1	3	2	1	3	4	4	3
71	**72**	**73**	**74**	**75**	**76**	**77**	**78**	**79**	**80**
2	2	3	2	3	3	1	3	1	1
81	**82**	**83**	**84**	**85**	**86**	**87**	**88**	**89**	**90**
4	4	1	3	1	2	1	4	2	3
91	**92**	**93**	**94**	**95**	**96**	**97**	**98**	**99**	**100**
2	2	2	3	2	4	1	2	1	4

EXPLANATORY ANSWERS

1. According to Buddhist philosophy, Pratyaksha is generally classified into four types, so option 3 is the fitting answer. These are commonly understood as sense perception, mental perception, self-cognition, and yogic perception. In Buddhist epistemology, Pratyaksha is direct and non-conceptual knowledge, meaning it is not dependent on verbal construction or inference. Since the question asks for the number of types of Pratyaksha according to Buddha philosophy, "4" fits best among the given options. Therefore, the correct answer is option 3: 4.

2. Bhavya and Abhavya are divisions of Jiva according to Jaina philosophy. In Jainism, Jiva means a living soul or conscious substance, and souls are classified according to their capacity for liberation. Bhavya Jiva means a soul capable of attaining moksha, while Abhavya Jiva means a soul not capable of attaining moksha. These terms do not belong to Ajiva because Ajiva refers to non-living substances. Therefore, the correct answer is option 1: Jiva.

3. According to Yajnavalkya-smriti, the milk of a cow whose calf has died is prohibited, so option 1 is the best fitting answer. The rule also mentions avoidance of milk from certain other conditions of cows, but among the given options, "cow whose calf died" directly matches the stated prohibition. The option "12 day after delivery" does not fit exactly because the traditional rule is connected with the early post-delivery impurity period, commonly stated as ten days, not twelve. "Donkey coloured cow" and "pet cow" do not fit the rule asked in the question. Therefore, the correct answer is option 1: Cow who's calf died.

4. "Having interest in stories of God is called Bhakti" is according to Garga. In the discussion of Bhakti, different sages define devotion in different ways. Garga's view connects Bhakti with deep love and interest in hearing divine stories and accounts of God's deeds. This differs from Shandilya's and Narada's broader definitions of devotion as supreme attachment or intense love for God. Therefore, the correct answer is option 4: Garga.

5. Sarvasankalpa Sanyasi is Yogarudha. In the Bhagavad Gita's yogic terminology, a person who has renounced all sankalpas, or mental desires and self-willed resolutions, is considered established in yoga. Yogarudha refers to one who has already ascended or become firmly established in the path of yoga. Arurukshu is only the beginner or one who wants to climb toward yoga, so it does not fit the phrase Sarvasankalpa Sanyasi. Therefore, the correct answer is option 1: Yogarudha.

6. In the Taittiriya Upanishad, Bhrigu is described as Bhrigu Varuni, which means Bhrigu, the son of Varuna. The teaching section is known as Bhrigu Valli, where Bhrigu approaches his father Varuna and asks him to teach Brahman. Varuna then guides Bhrigu through the method of tapas and gradual realization of Brahman through food, prana, mind, knowledge, and bliss. The word "Varuni" is not the father's name here, but it is a patronymic form meaning "belonging to Varuna" or "son of Varuna." Therefore, among the given options, the father of Bhrigu according to Taittiriya Upanishad is option 2: Varuna.

7. According to Kathopanishad, Bhokta is connected with Atma, Manas, and Indriyas. The relevant idea is that the enjoyer or experiencer is understood when the self is associated with mind and senses. Here, Atma is the conscious principle, Manas is the inner instrument coordinating experience, and Indriyas are the sense organs through which objects are contacted. The question asks specifically about Bhokta, and the option containing Atma, Manas, and Indriyas fits the Kathopanishadic expression best. The other options are incomplete because they either omit Atma or add Prana where the asked formulation does not require it. Therefore, the correct answer is option 1: Synchronized with Atma, Manas and Indriyas.

8. The one who is always self-contented is Sthitaprajna. In the Gita-based philosophical description, Sthitaprajna is the person of steady wisdom who is satisfied in the Self by the Self. This condition is not ordinary satisfaction,

but complete inner contentment independent of external objects, pleasures, praise, or worldly gain. Atmajnani and Jnani may also indicate a knower, but the technical expression of being self-contented is most directly attached to Sthitaprajna. A Yogi may be disciplined and absorbed in practice, but the specific state of permanent self-contentment is the mark of Sthitaprajna. Therefore, the correct answer is option 3: Sthitaprajna.

9. According to Yoga-tattvopanishad, a Nirguna Dhyani attains Samadhi within twelve days. The text distinguishes Saguna Dhyana and Nirguna Dhyana, where Nirguna Dhyana is meditation without attributes and is directed toward the attributeless reality. In this context, the attainment of Samadhi is stated in relation to the practitioner of Nirguna Dhyana. Among the given options, 10, 15, and 20 do not match the stated period. The correct numerical answer asked in the question is therefore twelve days. Therefore, the correct answer is option 3: 12.

10. According to Shvetashvatara Upanishad, three parts of the body are kept extended or erect during the meditative posture of the Dhyana-yogi. The instruction refers to keeping the body properly aligned in a threefold erect position during meditation. This is generally understood as the alignment of the chest, neck, and head, so that the posture remains steady and suitable for concentration. The purpose of this bodily arrangement is to support control of mind and senses during inward meditation. Among the given options, "Three" directly matches this Upanishadic yogic instruction. Therefore, the correct answer is option 2: Three.

11. In Trishikhibrahmanopanishad, Karma Yoga is explained through the idea of constant binding or continuous engagement of the mind. The relevant meaning is not ordinary worldly attachment, but keeping the mind continuously connected with prescribed duty and the higher good. Therefore, "continuous indulgence of mind" fits the given options when it is understood as continuous mental engagement or binding of the mind in the proper object. Option 2 is not correct because it says indulgence in worldly objects, which would create bondage rather than Karma Yoga. Option 3 is also not the exact answer because the Upanishadic expression emphasizes continuous binding or engagement of the mind, not merely detachment from worldly action. Therefore, the correct answer is option 4: Continuous Indulgence of mind.

12. According to Dhyanabindu Upanishad, Pranava is described as the bow. In this symbolic yogic teaching, Pranava or Om is used as the means by which the seeker directs consciousness toward the highest reality. The arrow represents the individual self or inner consciousness, while the target represents Brahman or the supreme reality. Since the question specifically asks what Pranava is among the tools of antahkarana, "bow" is the exact fitting answer. Therefore, the correct answer is option 1: Bow.

13. The purity of Sattva and Purusha leads to Kaivalya. This is a direct Yoga philosophical idea where liberation is attained when there is complete purity and distinction between Sattva, the pure aspect of buddhi or prakriti, and Purusha, the conscious self. Kaivalya means absolute isolation or independence of Purusha from Prakriti and its modifications. When Sattva becomes as pure as Purusha and no confusion remains between the two, final liberation becomes possible. Therefore, option 1: Sattva and Purusha is the correct answer.

14. According to Yogasutra, Isvarapranidhana is one of the methods for restraining chitta-vritti. The main definition of Yoga is chitta-vritti-nirodha, meaning restraint of the modifications of the mind. Patanjali primarily gives abhyasa and vairagya as the general means, but among the given options, Isvarapranidhana is the only Yogasutra-based direct method. Isvarapranidhana means dedication or surrender to Ishvara, and it is accepted as a powerful means for concentration and samadhi. Therefore, option 1: Isvarapranidhana is the correct answer.

15. In the Yogasutra phrase "Tato dvandvana-bhighatah," the word "Tatah" refers to success in Asana. This sutra comes immediately after the description of Asana, where Asana is perfected through relaxation of effort and meditation on the infinite. After that perfection of Asana, the yogi is no longer disturbed by pairs of opposites such as heat and cold, pleasure and pain, or comfort and discomfort. So "Tatah" means "from that," and "that" refers to Asana-siddhi or successful mastery of posture. Therefore, option 3: Success in Asana is the correct answer.

16. In Mudha chittabhumi, Tamoguna is dominant. Mudha means a dull, ignorant, confused, and inactive state of mind. This condition is marked by sleepiness, delusion, heaviness, lack of discrimination, and inability to move toward higher knowledge. These qualities directly belong to Tamas, because Tamas produces darkness, inertia, ignorance, and obstruction. Rajoguna produces restlessness, Sattvaguna produces clarity, and Suddha Sattvaguna represents a much higher purified condition. Therefore, the correct answer is option 4: Tamoguna.

17. According to Hathayoga Pradipika, Yoga success through Siddhasana practice along with moderate diet takes twelve years. The text connects Siddhasana with great importance among asanas and says that a yogi practicing it properly becomes successful. The condition includes steady practice, moderation in food, and disciplined yogic conduct. Among the given options, fifteen years, seven years, and thirteen years do not fit this statement. The exact period asked in the question is twelve years. Therefore, the correct answer is option 2: 12 years.

18. According to Vashishta Samhita, a householder should take thirty-two grasas of food. Grasa means a morsel or mouthful of food, and such rules describe measured eating according to the stage and discipline of life. For a householder, the prescribed quantity is higher than that of more renounced or stricter ascetic conditions. Among the options given, 10, 20, and 16 grasas do not match the householder's prescribed intake. The fitting answer for the householder is thirty-two grasas. Therefore, the correct answer is option 3: 32 Grasa.

19. According to Hatharatnavali, Uddiyana Bandha promotes prana for its upliftment within Sushumna. The very meaning of Uddiyana is connected with flying upward or rising upward. In yogic practice, this bandha is described as helping the movement of prana upward through the central channel, Sushumna nadi. Mahabandha combines locks, Mahavedha is a related mudra-like practice, and Moolbandha mainly concerns the root lock and upward control of apana. The specific bandha named for lifting prana upward in Sushumna is Uddiyana Bandha. Therefore, the correct answer is option 1: Uddiyana Bandha.

20. According to Shiva Samhita, Manipura Chakra is denoted by the letters from Da to Fa. Manipura Chakra is described as a ten-petalled chakra, and its petals are associated with a set of ten Sanskrit letters. The sequence is commonly represented from the retroflex "a" group onward up to "pha," which is often written in simplified form as Da to Fa. The other options do not correctly cover the full Manipura letter range as asked in the question. Since the option uses "Fa" for "Pha," option 2 is the closest and correct form among the given choices. Therefore, the correct answer is option 2: Da to Fa.

21. People who show shyness, social withdrawal, and a tendency not to talk much are characterised as introverts. Introversion refers to a personality orientation in which a person is more inward-looking and less socially expressive. Such people may prefer quiet surroundings, limited social interaction, and careful thinking before speaking. Extroverts are generally outgoing and socially active, so option 1 does not fit the characteristics given in the question. Sanguine and choleric are temperament types, but the features mentioned in the question most directly indicate introversion. Therefore, the correct answer is option 2: Introvert.

22. Cytokinesis is the separation of cytoplasm. During cell division, karyokinesis divides the nucleus, while cytokinesis divides the cytoplasm of the parent cell. This process results in the formation of two daughter cells after nuclear division has already taken place. Duplicate chromosomes separate during anaphase of mitosis or meiosis, not during cytokinesis specifically. Centrioles and spindle fibers assist in cell division, but they are not what cytokinesis mainly separates. Therefore, the correct answer is option 1: cytoplasma.

23. Gluteus minimus does not belong to the shoulder. Supraspinatus is a shoulder muscle and is one of the rotator cuff muscles. Trapezius helps move and stabilize the scapula and is functionally related to the shoulder girdle. Levator scapulae also acts on the scapula and is associated with shoulder girdle movement and posture. Gluteus minimus is a hip muscle located in the gluteal region, so it is not a shoulder muscle. Therefore, the correct answer is option 4: Gluteus Minimus.

24. Lipids are absorbed in the human body through lacteals. After digestion, most dietary fats are converted into fatty acids and monoglycerides and then reassembled into triglycerides inside intestinal cells. These fats are packed into chylomicrons, which enter the lymphatic vessels of intestinal villi called lacteals. Capillaries mainly absorb water-soluble nutrients like glucose and amino acids, but larger lipid particles enter lymph first. Veins and arteries carry blood, but the specific structure for lipid absorption in the intestine is the lacteal. Therefore, the correct answer is option 3: Lacteals.

25. The vegetative domain of human existence is related with Annamaya kosha according to the Taittiriya Upanishad-based Panchakosha concept. Annamaya kosha is the food sheath and represents the gross physical body that is born from food, sustained by food, and dependent on food. The vegetative level refers to the bodily, food-based, organic, and physical layer of existence rather than the mental, intellectual, or blissful layers. Pranamaya kosha is the vital-energy sheath, but the question specifically uses "vegetative domain," which fits the food-dependent physical organism of Annamaya kosha more directly. Therefore, the correct answer is option 1: Annamaya kosha.

26. According to Yogasutra, 'I'ness or ego is a klesha and is called Asmita. Patanjali describes five kleshas: Avidya, Asmita, Raga, Dvesha, and Abhinivesha. Asmita means the false identification of the seer with the instruments of seeing, especially buddhi or mind. Disease, doubtfulness, and instability are obstacles or disturbances in yoga practice, but they are not counted among the five kleshas. Therefore, the correct answer is option 3: 'I'ness (Ego).

27. Heaviness is not a characteristic of Pitta-dosha. Pitta is generally associated with qualities such as hotness, sharpness, slight unctuousness, liquidity, spreading nature, and intensity. Hotness and sharpness clearly belong to Pitta because Pitta is connected with fire-like transformation, digestion, metabolism, and heat. Unctuousness can also be accepted as a Pitta quality in the form of slight oiliness or smoothness. Heaviness is more characteristically related to Kapha, not Pitta. Therefore, the correct answer is option 4: Heavyness.

28. Samana Vayu regulates physiological activities of the body uniformly. The word Samana itself indicates balancing, equalizing, and harmonizing functions. It is mainly located around the digestive region and supports digestion, assimilation, separation, and proper distribution of nutritive essence. It also helps coordinate Prana and Apana, maintaining internal balance in bodily activities. Prana Vayu is mainly related to inward movement and respiration, Udana to upward movement and expression, and Apana to downward elimination. Therefore, the correct answer is option 3: Samana Vayu.

29. The characteristic of Asana is attaining a specific posture effortlessly with proper stability, comfort, and breath awareness. In yogic understanding, Asana should not be forceful or full of strain, because the ideal posture is steady and comfortable. Effort gradually becomes relaxed, and the practitioner maintains the posture with ease and control. Synchronization of breath helps the body and mind become stable during the posture. Forceful, effortful, or externally supported posture does not represent the essential yogic characteristic of Asana. Therefore, the correct answer is option 3: Attaining specific posture effortlessly with synchronization of breath.

30. Keval Kumbhaka is characterized as the state of equal atmospheric and intra-pulmonaric pressure. Keval Kumbhaka refers to spontaneous suspension of breath, where inhalation and exhalation naturally cease. When there is no active flow of air into or out of the lungs, pressure difference is not driving respiration. Thus, the atmospheric pressure and intra-pulmonary pressure are in a balanced or equal state. Increased, decreased, or unequal intra-pulmonary pressure would produce movement of air, which does not fit the state of Kumbhaka. Therefore, the correct answer is option 1: State of equal atmospheric and intra-pulmonaric pressure.

31. According to Hathayogapradipika, Matsyendrasana is described as an asana that destroys dangerous or severe diseases. This asana is praised because it stimulates digestive fire and has a strong purifying and health-promoting effect in Hatha Yoga. The expression connected with Matsyendrasana refers to the removal of grave diseases, so it fits the wording "hazardous diseases" most directly. Paschimottanasana is also highly praised and is said to remove many diseases, but the phrase indicating severe or hazardous diseases is more specifically connected with Matsyendrasana. Therefore, the correct answer is option 3: Matsyendrasana.

32. According to Hathapradipika, Jalavasti is the kriya that eliminates all types of diseases. Basti is described as a cleansing process that removes disorders arising from Vata, Pitta, and Kapha. Since the practice is performed in water in the classical Hathapradipika description, it corresponds to Jalavasti among the given options. Sthalavasti is a dry form mentioned in later classifications, while Trataka is mainly connected with eye purification and removal of laziness. Vastradhauti is a cleansing kriya, but the Hathapradipika statement about removing all diseases fits Jalavasti more accurately. Therefore, the correct answer is option 1: Jalavasti.

33. Understanding the complex composition of the body can be attained by contemplating on Nabhichakra. In yogic concentration, meditation on different inner centres produces different kinds of knowledge. Contemplation on the navel centre gives knowledge of the arrangement, structure, and composition of the body. Dhruva is connected with knowledge of stars, Kurma Nadi with steadiness, and Murdha Jyoti with vision of higher beings. Therefore, the correct answer is option 2: On Nabhichakra.

34. According to Hathayogapradipika, the measurement of the sutra for Sutraneti practice is Eka Vitasti. Sutraneti is performed by passing a smooth thread through the nasal passage for purification. The text gives the length of the thread as one vitasti, which means one span. Eka Hasta, Three Vitasti, and Eka Pada do not match the classical measurement given for this practice. Therefore, the correct answer is option 2: Eka Vitasti.

35. Gyana Vinmaya is not part of the disciple's approach to the Guru for receiving knowledge according to Bhagavadgita. The Bhagavadgita describes the proper approach as Pranipata, Pariprashna, and Seva. Pranipata means humble prostration or surrender before the teacher. Pariprashna means sincere and proper questioning to remove doubt and gain understanding. Seva means service to the Guru, showing humility and readiness to receive knowledge. Therefore, the correct answer is option 3: Gyana Vinmaya.

36. If there is fatigue while practicing Asanas, the practitioner should relax in Shavasana. Shavasana is used to remove tiredness, normalize breathing, and bring the body and mind back to a balanced state. Continuing asana practice during fatigue may increase strain and reduce the benefit of practice. Practicing pranayama immediately in a fatigued condition is also not the best answer because the body first needs relaxation. Stopping the whole asana practice is not necessary when simple relaxation in Shavasana can restore energy. Therefore, the correct answer is option 2: Relax in shavasana.

37. Mind Sound Resonance Technique, or MSRT, involves eight steps. These steps include beginning with prayer, sound resonance practices, inner awareness of sound, silence, resolve, and closing prayer. MSRT is a structured relaxation and meditation technique using sound vibration and mental resonance. The purpose of these steps is to move the mind gradually from audible sound to subtle inner silence. Among the given options, 3, 5, and 6 do not match the standard step count of MSRT. Therefore, the correct answer is option 4: 8.

38. According to Gheranda Samhita, the practicing method in Vrikshasana is placing the right sole of the foot at the root of the left thigh. The practitioner stands steadily like a tree after placing the foot in this position. The key point in this classical description is the placement at the thigh root, not merely the middle of the thigh. Therefore, options mentioning the middle thigh do not fit the Gheranda Samhita description. Among the given choices, the option with the right sole placed in the thigh root of the left leg is the exact fitting answer. Therefore, the correct answer is option 1: Placing Right sole of the foot in thigh root of Left leg.

39. According to Shiva Samhita, another name of Ugrasana is Pascimottanasana. The posture described as Ugrasana is identified with the seated forward-stretching posture known as Paschimottanasana. In this asana, the legs are extended and the practitioner bends forward, holding the feet and placing the head near the knees. Swastikasana, Padmasana, and Siddhasana are separate seated postures and are not the alternate name of Ugrasana here. Therefore, the correct answer is option 1: Pascimottanasana.

40. According to Gheranda Samhita, there are two types of Nadishuddhi. These two types are Samanu and Nirmanu Nadishuddhi. Samanu is performed with mental process, mantra, and regulated pranayama. Nirmanu is associated with physical cleansing processes that purify the nadis through external or practical purification. Since the question asks the number of types of Nadishuddhi according to Gheranda Samhita, the correct number is two. Therefore, the correct answer is option 1: 2.

41. Assertion (A) is correct because Yoga is accepted as a means for overcoming sufferings by disciplining body, mind, senses, conduct, and inner awareness. Reason (R) is also correct because Yoga includes physical, mental, social, and spiritual wellbeing. The Reason also correctly includes the yogic discipline of moderate food, proper living, proper effort, and proper sleep. Such moderation is directly connected with reducing sorrow, imbalance, and suffering in yogic life. Therefore, Reason (R) properly explains why Yoga can overcome sufferings. Hence, the correct answer is option 1: Both (A) and (R) are correct and (R) is the correct explanation of (A).

42. Assertion (A) is not correct because Prana is not Annamayakosa. Annamayakosa is the food sheath, while Prana is related to Pranamaya kosha, the vital-energy sheath. Therefore, identifying Prana itself as Annamayakosa is incorrect. Reason (R) is correct because Annamayakosa is formed from Anna or food, and the body maintained by food also supports vital life-functions. The Reason explains the food-based nature of Annamayakosa, but it does not make Prana identical with Annamayakosa. Hence, the correct answer is option 4: (A) is not correct, but (R) is correct.

43. Assertion (A) is correct because in the symbolic description of Om-kara as a swan, 'A' kara is described as the right feather and 'U' kara as the left feather. This symbolic structure belongs to the yogic and Upanishadic explanation of Pranava or Om. Reason (R) is not correct because the feathers of the Om-kara swan are not described as being destroyed by Rajoguna and Tamoguna. Rajoguna and Tamoguna may be connected with lower qualities or bondage, but they do not correctly explain the stated feather-symbolism of A-kara and U-kara. Thus, the Assertion stands correct independently, while the Reason is incorrect. Hence, the correct answer is option 3: (A) is correct, but (R) is not correct.

44. Assertion (A) is correct because Hathayoga Pradipika is a classical text of Hatha Yoga and its teacher or author is Yogi Swatmarama. The text itself presents Hatha Yoga as a traditional teaching system. Reason (R) is not correct because Swatmarama did not claim to receive Hatha Yoga knowledge independently without Guru's teaching. Hathayoga Pradipika begins by saluting Adinatha and follows the Guru-parampara tradition of Hatha Yoga. Therefore, the text and its preacher are correctly stated in the Assertion, but the Reason is wrong. Hence, the correct answer is option 3: (A) is correct, but (R) is not correct.

45. Assertion (A) is correct because food along with milk and ghee is prescribed as suitable for a pranayama practitioner in the initial stages of practice. This supports strength, nourishment, steadiness, and safe progress during early pranayama discipline. Reason (R) is also correct because after the practitioner becomes established in pranayama, strict food regulations are no longer emphasized in the same way. However, Reason (R) does not explain why milk and ghee are useful in the initial stage. The Assertion deals with early-stage diet, while the Reason deals with the later stage after establishment in practice. Hence, the correct answer is option 2: Both (A) and (R) are correct, but (R) is NOT the correct explanation of (A).

46. Assertion (A) is correct because Hatha is traditionally explained as the union of "Ha" and "Tha." "Ha" is commonly associated with Surya, Prana, or Pingala, while "Tha" is associated with Chandra, Apana, or Ida. Reason (R) is also correct because Hatha Yoga is described as a ladder or means for attaining Raja Yoga. The aim of Raja Yoga is the highest yogic state, ultimately leading to Kaivalya or liberation. However, this Reason explains the purpose and role of Hatha Yoga, not the meaning of the word Hatha as union of Ha-kara and Tha-kara. Hence, the correct answer is option 2: Both (A) and (R) are correct, but (R) is NOT the correct explanation of (A).

47. Assertion (A) is not correct because all arteries do not carry oxygenated blood. Most systemic arteries carry oxygenated blood from the heart to body tissues. However, the pulmonary artery is an exception because it carries deoxygenated blood from the right ventricle of the heart to the lungs. Reason (R) correctly states the general rule and also gives the pulmonary artery exception. Therefore, the Reason is correct, but the Assertion becomes incorrect due to the word "all." Hence, the correct answer is option 4: (A) is not correct, but (R) is correct.

48. Assertion (A) is not correct because locomotion of the body is not only because of bones and joints. Bones and joints provide the framework and points of movement, but they cannot produce movement by themselves. Skeletal muscles are essential because their contraction and relaxation pull bones across joints. Reason (R) correctly explains that skeletal muscles are attached to bones and their activity produces movement at joints. Therefore, locomotion depends on bones, joints, and muscles together, not bones and joints only. Hence, the correct answer is option 4: (A) is not correct, but (R) is correct.

49. Assertion (A) is correct because Neti is a Shatkarma cleansing practice that purifies the nasal passage and the region above the neck. Classical Hatha Yoga description connects Neti with cleansing the cranial region, removing disorders of the upper region, and improving clarity of vision. Reason (R) is not correct because the classical texts describe Sutra Neti, not Jalaneti, in the original procedure. Hathapradipika and Gheranda Samhita give the method of passing a smooth thread or sutra through the nasal passage. Jalaneti is a later water-based variation and is not the specific classical Neti procedure detailed in those texts. Hence, the correct answer is option 3: (A) is correct, but (R) is not correct.

50. Assertion (A) is correct because Sushumna has been termed Yogivallabha, meaning beloved or especially important for yogis. Sushumna is central to yogic practice because it is the main channel connected with the rise of prana and higher spiritual awakening. Reason (R) is correct because Shiva Samhita explains the nadis and gives special importance to Sushumna among them. Among the nadis, Sushumna is treated as the most important because yogic attainment depends on prana entering and moving through it. Thus, the Reason correctly explains why Sushumna is called Yogivallabha. Hence, the correct answer is option 1: Both (A) and (R) are correct and (R) is the correct explanation of (A).

51. According to NET Yoga syllabus sequence, the correct order is:

B. Prasthanatrayee: It comes under the introductory foundation of Yoga along with Vedas, Upanishads and Purushartha Chatushtaya. Therefore, it is placed before Smriti-based and later individual tradition-based topics.

A. Yajnavalkya Smriti: It appears under the topic of Smriti and Yoga in Smritis. So it comes after Prasthanatrayee in the syllabus arrangement.

C. Maharshi Patanjali: Maharshi Patanjali is mentioned under yogic contribution and tradition. His tradition is placed before the later Hatha and medieval saint traditions.

E. Gorakshanath: Guru Gorakshanath is connected with the Hatha Yoga tradition. In the NET syllabus sequence, he comes after Maharshi Patanjali.

D. Tulasids: Tulasidas belongs to the literature of saints and medieval Bhakti tradition. Therefore, he comes after Patanjali and Gorakshanath in this syllabus sequence.

52. In descending order of birth, the correct sequence is:

A. Swami Rama of Himalaya: Swami Rama of Himalaya was born later than the other given yogis. So he comes first in descending order of birth.

C. Maharshi Mahesh Yogi: Maharshi Mahesh Yogi was born after Shri Ram Sharma Acharya, Krishnamacharya and Swami Sivananda. Therefore, he comes second in descending order.

D. Shri Ram Sharma Acharya: Shri Ram Sharma Acharya was born before Maharshi Mahesh Yogi but after Krishnamacharya and Swami Sivananda. So he is placed third in the descending sequence.

B. Tirumala Krishnamacharya: Tirumala Krishnamacharya was born earlier than Shri Ram Sharma Acharya, Maharshi Mahesh Yogi and Swami Rama. But he was born after Swami Sivananda, so he comes fourth.

E. Swami Sivananda Saraswathi: Swami Sivananda Saraswathi was the earliest born among the given names. Hence, in descending order of birth, he is placed last.

53. According to Kathopanishad mantra, the correct sequence is:

C. Atmanam Rathinam Viddh: The mantra begins with "Atmana rathina viddhi," meaning know the Self as the lord of the chariot. So this is the first part of the sequence.

E. Sariram Rathameva cha: After the Self is described as the chariot-owner, the body is described as the chariot. Therefore, "Sarira ratham eva ca" comes second.

A. Buddhim tu Saarathim: Then the intellect or Buddhi is described as the charioteer. So "Buddhi tu sarathi" comes after the body-as-chariot statement.

B. Viddh: The word "viddhi" completes the phrase about Buddhi being the charioteer Therefore, it follows "Buddhim tu Saarathim."

D. Manah Pragrahmeva cha: Finally, the mind is described as the reins of the chariot. So "Mana pragraham eva ca" comes at the end of the given sequence.

54. According to Yogakundali Upanishad, the correct sequence of Ujjayi benefits is:

B. Sleshmahar: Ujjayi is first described as removing phlegm or kapha-related impurity from the throat region. So "Sleshmahar" comes first among the given benefit-terms.

A. Sarvaroghar: After that, Ujjayi is stated to remove all diseases. Therefore, "Sarvaroghar" comes after "Sleshmahar."

D. Dehanala vivardan: Ujjayi is also described as increasing the bodily fire or digestive fire. So "Dehanala vivardan" comes after the disease-removing statement.

E. Jalodhar: Then the benefit connected with removing Jalodara is mentioned. Jalodara refers to dropsical or abdominal fluid-related disorder, so it comes before dhatu-related dosha destruction.

C. Dhatugata dosha vinasana: At the end, Ujjayi is stated to destroy defects situated in the dhatus. Therefore, "Dhatugata dosha vinasana" comes last in this sequence.

55. According to Shrimad Bhagavadgita, the correct sequence is:

B. Ahimsa: In the Daivi Sampad sequence, Ahimsa comes before Satya and Akrodha. So among the given terms, Ahimsa is placed first.

C. Satya: Satya follows Ahimsa in the Bhagavadgita's listing of divine qualities. Therefore, Satya is placed second in this sequence.

A. Akrodha: Akrodha comes after Satya in the order of these qualities. It means absence of anger and is placed before Shanti in the sequence.

E. Santi: Shanti comes after Akrodha in the listed order. It represents peace or calmness and therefore comes fourth here.

D. Daya: Daya comes after Shanti in the sequence of these given items. So it is placed last among the options included in this question.

56. According to Shrimad Bhagavadgita, the correct sequence is:

B. Manahprasad: Manahprasad comes first in the sequence of mental austerity. It means serenity, purity, and pleasantness of mind.

A. Soumyatva: Soumyatva comes after Manahprasad in the same sequence. It means gentleness, calmness, and pleasing nature.

C. Mouna: Mouna comes after Soumyatva. It means disciplined silence and restraint of unnecessary speech.

E. Atmavinigraha: Atmavinigraha comes after Mouna. It means self-control or control over the inner self.

D. Bhavasansuddhi: Bhavasansuddhi comes last in this sequence. It means purity of intention, feeling, and inner disposition.

57. According to the order of Yogasutras, the correct sequence is:

D. Tajja Sanskaro-Anya-Sanskar-Pratibandhi: This sutra belongs to the Samadhi Pada. Therefore, it comes earliest among the given sutras.

C. Heyam Dukhmanagatam: This sutra belongs to the Sadhana Pada. So it comes after the Samadhi Pada sutra.

A. Tasya Bhumishu Viniyogah: This sutra belongs to the Vibhuti Pada. Therefore, it comes after the Sadhana Pada sutra.

B. Te Vyaktasukshmah Gunatmanah: This sutra belongs to the Kaivalya Pada. It comes after the Vibhuti Pada sutra.

E. Drastri-Drishyopraktam Chittam Sarvartham: This also belongs to the Kaivalya Pada but occurs after "Te Vyaktasukshmah Gunatmanah." Therefore, it is placed last among the given sutras.

58. According to Hathayogapradipika, the correct sequence of the sloka is:

B. Medasleshmadhikah Purvam: The verse begins with the condition of excess fat and phlegm. Therefore, this phrase comes first.

D. Shatkarmani Samacharet: After mentioning excess meda and slema, the text prescribes the practice of shatkarmas. So this phrase comes second.

E. Anyastu Nacharettani: Then the verse says that others should not practise them. Therefore, this phrase comes after the instruction for shatkarmas.

A. Doshanam: This word begins the reason related to the condition of doshas. So it comes after "Anyastu Nacharettani."

C. Samabhavatah: The verse ends by saying that those whose doshas are balanced should not practise them. Therefore, "Samabhavatah" is the last part of the sequence.

59. The sequence of neurological conduction within a multipolar neuron is:

D. Dendritic branches: Impulse reception begins at the dendritic branches. These branches receive signals from other neurons.

C. Dendrite: The impulse then passes through the dendrite. Dendrites carry the received signal toward the cell body region.

E. Initial Segment of Axon: The impulse then reaches the initial segment of the axon. This is the region where the nerve impulse is initiated for axonal conduction.

B. Axon: The impulse then travels along the axon. The axon conducts the signal away from the neuron body.

A. Synaptic terminals: Finally, the impulse reaches the synaptic terminals. These terminals transmit the signal to the next neuron or effector cell.

60. The sequence of urine formation with respect to anatomical structure is:

C. Glomerulus: Urine formation begins with filtration at the glomerulus. Blood plasma is filtered here to form glomerular filtrate.

B. Proximal Convoluted Tubule (PCT): The filtrate then passes into the proximal convoluted tubule. Maximum reabsorption of useful substances occurs here.

D. Henelis loop: After PCT, the filtrate passes through the loop of Henle. This part helps in water and salt regulation.

E. Distal Convoluted Tubule (DCT): The filtrate then moves into the distal convoluted tubule. Further selective reabsorption and secretion take place here.

A. Collecting Duct: Finally, the filtrate enters the collecting duct. The collecting duct carries urine toward the renal pelvis for further passage.

61. The sequence of Antarayas according to Yogasutra is:

E. Styana: Styana comes after Vyadhi in the list of obstacles. It means mental dullness, stagnation, or lack of active effort in practice.

B. Sanshaya: Sanshaya comes after Styana. It means doubt, uncertainty, or lack of firm conviction in the yogic path.

C. Alasya: Alasya comes after Pramada in the full list, and among the given items it follows Sanshaya. It means laziness or physical and mental unwillingness to practise.

D. Avirati: Avirati comes after Alasya. It means inability to withdraw from sense enjoyment and worldly attachment.

A. Bhrantidarshan: Bhrantidarshan comes after Avirati. It means false perception, wrong understanding, or mistaken knowledge.

62. The superior to inferior anatomical order is:

C. Cervical: Cervical region is the uppermost part of the vertebral column. It is present in the neck region.

B. Thoracic: Thoracic region comes below the cervical region. It is related to the chest and rib area.

A. Lumber: Lumbar region comes below the thoracic region. It forms the lower back portion of the vertebral column.

E. Sacral: Sacral region comes below the lumbar region. It forms the posterior part of the pelvis.

D. Coccygeal: Coccygeal region is the lowest part of the vertebral column. It forms the tailbone region.

63. According to Gheranda Samhita, the sequence of these Samadhi types is:

C. Dhyana yoga: Dhyana Yoga Samadhi is mentioned first in the sequence. It is connected with meditative absorption.

A. Nadayoga: Nadayoga Samadhi comes after Dhyana Yoga Samadhi. It is connected with absorption through inner sound.

E. Rasananda yoga: Rasananda Yoga Samadhi comes after Nadayoga. It is connected with blissful inner experience through rasa.

D. Layasiddhi yoga: Layasiddhi Yoga Samadhi follows Rasananda. It refers to absorption through dissolution of mind.

B. Bhakti yoga: Bhakti Yoga Samadhi comes after Layasiddhi Yoga in the given sequence. It is connected with devotional absorption.

64. As per teaching methodology in Yoga, the correct sequence is:

C. Sitting Arrangement: The class begins with proper sitting arrangement. This creates discipline, visibility, comfort, and readiness for practice.

A. Verbal Introduction of Practice: After arrangement, the teacher gives a verbal introduction of the practice. This explains the name, purpose, precautions, and basic idea of the practice.

B. Demonstration of Practice: Demonstration comes after verbal introduction. The teacher shows the correct method so learners can observe the proper technique.

D. Emphasis on salient point: After demonstration, the teacher emphasizes the important points. This helps students avoid mistakes and understand key alignments and precautions.

E. Individual Group practice: Finally, students perform the practice individually or in group form. At this stage, the teacher observes, corrects, and guides the learners.

65. The sequence of Bija Mantras in Surya Namaskar is:

A. Om Hraam: Om Hraam comes first in the Bija Mantra sequence. It is the first seed sound used in the Surya Namaskar mantra order.

B. Om Hreem: Om Hreem comes after Om Hraam. It is the second Bija Mantra in the sequence.

C. Om Hroom: Om Hroom comes after Om Hreem. It is the third Bija Mantra in the order.

E. Om Hraim: Om Hraim comes after Om Hroom. It is the fourth Bija Mantra in the sequence.

D. Om Hraum: Om Hraum comes after Om Hraim. It is the fifth Bija Mantra among the given options.

66. According to Tulasidas, dipping into Prayaga makes:

A. Crows turn into Cuckoos: This is correct because Tulasidas uses the example that even a crow becomes like a cuckoo by the greatness of Prayaga. It shows the purifying and transforming power of Prayaga.

C. Herons becomes Swans: This is also correct because Tulasidas states that a heron becomes like a swan by bathing in Prayaga. It again shows the symbolic transformation from ordinary or impure nature to refined and pure nature.

67. Satvic people like foods:

A. Affectioned food items: This is correct because Sattvic food is described as pleasing, agreeable, and increasing inner satisfaction. Such food supports calmness, purity, and harmony of mind.

C. Unctuous food: This is correct because Sattvic food is snigdha, meaning slightly oily, smooth, nourishing, and unctuous. It supports strength, stability, and health.

E. Vital foods: This is correct because Sattvic foods increase life, vitality, strength, health, happiness, and satisfaction. Therefore, life-promoting or vital foods are liked by Sattvic people.

68. Initial siddhis of yoga practice according to Shwetashwatar Upanishad are:

A. Sweetness of voice: This is correct because one of the first signs of progress in yoga is pleasantness or sweetness of voice. It indicates refinement of the body and pranic system through yoga practice.

B. Lightness of body: This is correct because lightness of the body is mentioned as an initial sign of yoga progress. It shows reduction of heaviness, dullness, and bodily impurity.

D. Absence from desires: This is correct because freedom from greed or desire is counted among the early signs of yogic progress. It indicates inner purification and control over craving.

69. Attaining Udana Vayu leads to non-attachment of the following with body:

B. Jala: This is correct because mastery over Udana gives non-contact or non-attachment with water. The body is not affected in the ordinary way by water.

D. Mud: This is correct because mastery over Udana also gives non-attachment with mud. The yogic text includes mud or mire among the things that do not cling to the body.

E. Thorns: This is correct because mastery over Udana gives non-contact with thorns also. It shows special control and lightness produced by Udana-jaya.

70. Characteristics of Parashakti according to Siddhasiddhantapaddhati are:

A. Aprameyata: This is correct because Aprameyata, meaning immeasurability, is one of the characteristics of Parashakti. Parashakti cannot be limited or measured by ordinary means.

C. Abhinnata: This is correct because Abhinnata, meaning non-difference or indivisibility, is a characteristic of Parashakti. It shows that Parashakti is not separate from the supreme principle.

E. Anantata: This is correct because Anantata, meaning endlessness or infinitude, is included among the characteristics of Parashakti. Parashakti is limitless and not confined by finite boundaries.

71. Gliding movements occur between the surfaces of articulating:

A. Carpal bone: This is correct because intercarpal joints are plane synovial joints. They allow small sliding or gliding movements between adjacent carpal bones.

B. Tarsal bone: This is correct because intertarsal joints are also plane-type joints. They permit gliding movements between the flat articular surfaces of tarsal bones.

C. Sternum: This is correct because certain articulations related to the sternum permit gliding-type movement. Elbow and hip joints are not examples of gliding joints because elbow is mainly hinge and hip is ball-and-socket.

72. According to Shiva Samhita, the chakras are:

A. Muladhara Chakra: This is correct because Muladhara is one of the principal chakras described in yogic texts. It is the root centre and is included in the chakra system.

D. Visudhi Chakra: This is correct because Vishuddhi Chakra is one of the classical chakras. It is located in the throat region and is included in the Shiva Samhita chakra description.

E. Manipura Chakra: This is correct because Manipura Chakra is one of the principal chakras. It is located at the navel region and is included in the classical chakra sequence.

73. Saptasadhana according to Gheranda Samhita are:

A. Shodhanam: This is correct because Shodhanam, or purification, is the first of the seven means. It is achieved through Shatkarma in the Gheranda Samhita system.

B. Dridhaṭa: This is correct because Dridhata, or firmness, is one of the seven results or means of practice. It is connected with Asana practice.

D. Dhairyam: This is correct because Dhairyam, or steadiness and patience, is included in the sevenfold discipline. It is connected with Pratyahara in the Gheranda Samhita sequence.

74. Characteristics of Hathasiddhi are:

A. Vapu kristwam: This is correct because leanness or lightness of the body is counted as a sign of Hatha-siddhi. It shows purification and proper progress in Hatha Yoga practice.

B. Nadi-visudhihi: This is correct because purification of the nadis is a direct sign of success in Hatha Yoga. Nadi-shuddhi shows that pranic flow has become clear and balanced.

E. Agni dipnam: This is correct because kindling of digestive fire is mentioned as a sign of Hatha-siddhi. It indicates strengthened internal fire and improved yogic health.

75. Obstacles of yoga according to Hatha Yoga Pradipika are:

B. Excessive eating: This is correct because Atyahara, or excessive eating, is clearly listed as an obstacle to Yoga. It increases heaviness and disturbs discipline, health, and practice.

D. Talkative: This is correct because Prajalpa, or excessive talking, is also listed as an obstacle to Yoga. It wastes energy, disturbs concentration, and weakens inner discipline.

76. Match the columns:

A. Shri Shyama Charan Lahri — III. Nadia, Bengal: Shri Shyama Charan Lahiri, also known as Lahiri Mahasaya, is associated with Nadia in Bengal. Therefore, A correctly matches with III.

B. Tirumalai Krishnamacharaya — I. Chitradurg, Karnataka: Tirumalai Krishnamacharaya was born in the Chitradurga region of Karnataka. Therefore, B correctly matches with I.

C. Swami Rama — II. Garhwal, Uttarakhand Swami: Rama of the Himalayas is associated with Garhwal in Uttarakhand. Therefore, C correctly matches with II.

D. Shriram Sharma Acharya — IV. Agra, Uttar Pradesh: Shriram Sharma Acharya was born in Anwalkheda near Agra in Uttar Pradesh. Therefore, D correctly matches with IV.

77. Match the columns:

A. Jagaritsthan — II. Vaisvanar: In Mandukya Upanishad, the waking state is connected with Vaishvanara. Therefore, Jagaritsthan correctly matches with Vaishvanar.

B. Swapnasthan — I. Tajas: The dream state is connected with Taijasa. Therefore, Swapnasthan correctly matches with Tajas.

C. Sushuptasthan — IV. Prajna: The deep sleep state is connected with Prajna. Therefore, Sushuptasthan correctly matches with Prajna.

D. Amatra — III. Chaturtha: Amatra refers to the fourth state beyond the three measurable matras. Therefore, Amatra correctly matches with Chaturtha.

78. Match the columns:

A. Daivi Sampat — II. Saucha: Saucha, meaning purity, is included among divine qualities. Therefore, Daivi Sampat correctly matches with Saucha.

B. Asuri Sampat — III. Ajnana: Ajnana, meaning ignorance, belongs to the demoniac or asuric tendency. Therefore, Asuri Sampat correctly matches with Ajnana.

C. Narakadwar — I. Kama: Kama is one of the gates leading to hell according to the Bhagavadgita. Therefore, Narakadwar correctly matches with Kama.

D. Tamas — IV. Mantraheena: Mantraheena is connected with tamasic form of sacrifice or action. Therefore, Tamas correctly matches with Mantraheena.

79. 1: A-IV, B-III, C-II, D-I: Match the columns:

A. Sodasadhara Bandan — IV. Madhyachakra: Sodasadhara Bandan is matched here with Madhyachakra in the given yogic classification. Therefore, A correctly matches with IV.

B. Ajnachakra — III. Rudragranthi: Ajnachakra is associated with Rudragranthi in the upward yogic path. Therefore, B correctly matches with III.

C. Atisunya — II. Vishnugranthi: Atisunya is connected with the stage related to Vishnugranthi. Therefore, C correctly matches with II.

D. Anahata chakra — I. Brahmagranthi: Anahata chakra is matched with Brahmagranthi in this given option set. Therefore, D correctly matches with I.

80. Match the columns:

A. Agneyee — III. Prathama matra: Agneyee is connected with the first matra in the given Omkara-related classification. Therefore, A correctly matches with III.

B. Vayavyaa — I. Dvitiya matra: Vayavyaa is connected with the second matra. Therefore, B correctly matches with I.

C. Bhanumandal Sankasa — IV. Tritiyamatra: Bhanumandal Sankasa is connected with the third matra. Therefore, C correctly matches with IV.

D. Varuni — II. Ardha matra: Varuni is connected with the Ardha matra. Therefore, D correctly matches with II.

81. Match the columns:

A. Samsaya — III. Antaraya: Samsaya means doubt and is one of the Antarayas mentioned in Yogasutra. Therefore, Samsaya correctly matches with Antaraya.

B. Tapa — IV. Kriyayoga: Tapa or Tapas is one of the three parts of Kriyayoga. Therefore, Tapa correctly matches with Kriyayoga.

C. Santosh — II. Niyama: Santosh is one of the five Niyamas in Yogasutra. Therefore, Santosh correctly matches with Niyama.

D. Vikshepasahabhu — I. Daurmanasya: Daurmanasya is one of the conditions accompanying chitta-vikshepa. Therefore, Vikshepasahabhu correctly matches with Daurmanasya.

82. Match the columns:

A. Vibhutipada — III. Pratyayasya Parachittajnanam: This sutra belongs to Vibhutipada of Yogasutra. Therefore, Vibhutipada correctly matches with Pratyayasya Parachittajnanam.

B. Kaivalyapada — IV. Tatra dhyanajamanasayam: This sutra belongs to Kaivalyapada of Yogasutra. Therefore, Kaivalyapada correctly matches with Tatra dhyanajamanasayam.

C. Sadhanapada — II. Dhyanaheyastadvrittayah: This sutra belongs to Sadhanapada of Yogasutra. Therefore, Sadhanapada correctly matches with Dhyanaheyastadvrittayah.

D. Samadhipada — I. Teevrasamvegaanamasannah: This sutra belongs to Samadhipada of Yogasutra. Therefore, Samadhipada correctly matches with Teevrasamvegaanamasannah.

83. Match the columns:

A. Muladhara — IV. Dakini: Dakini is associated with Muladhara chakra. Therefore, Muladhara correctly matches with Dakini.

B. Svadisthana — III. Rakini: Rakini is associated with Svadhisthana chakra. Therefore, Svadisthana correctly matches with Rakini.

C. Manipura — I. Lakini: Lakini is associated with Manipura chakra. Therefore, Manipura correctly matches with Lakini.

D. Anahata — II. Kakini: Kakini is associated with Anahata chakra. Therefore, Anahata correctly matches with Kakini.

84. Match the columns:

A. Bhulok — II. Guhyasthan: Bhulok is matched with Guhyasthan in this yogic bodily-location classification. Therefore, Bhulok correctly matches with Guhyasthan.

B. Bhuvarlok — III. Lingasthan: Bhuvarlok is matched with Lingasthan. Therefore, Bhuvarlok correctly matches with Lingasthan.

C. Svarlok — IV. Nabhisthan: Svarlok is matched with Nabhisthan. Therefore, Svarlok correctly matches with Nabhisthan.

D. Vishnulok — I. Kukshi: Vishnulok is matched with Kukshi. Therefore, Vishnulok correctly matches with Kukshi.

85. Match the columns:

A. Aparmpara — II. Anupamatva: Aparmpara is associated with Anupamatva, meaning incomparability. Therefore, Aparmpara correctly matches with Anupamatva.

B. Paramapada — III. Asamkhytva: Paramapada is associated with Asamkhytva, meaning innumerability. Therefore, Paramapada correctly matches with Asamkhytva.

C. Sunya — I. Lolata: Sunya is associated with Lolata in the given Siddha-siddhanta classification. Therefore, Sunya correctly matches with Lolata.

D. Niranjan — IV. Sahajatva: Niranjan is associated with Sahajatva, meaning naturalness or innate state. Therefore, Niranjan correctly matches with Sahajatva.

86. Match the columns:

A. Cell — III. Phagocytosis: Phagocytosis is a cellular process in which a cell engulfs solid particles, microbes, or foreign material. Therefore, Cell correctly matches with Phagocytosis.

B. Neck — I. Circumduction: Circumduction is a circular movement possible in regions such as the neck and certain freely movable joints. Therefore, Neck correctly matches with Circumduction.

C. Skeletal Muscle — II. Actin and Myosin: Skeletal muscle contraction occurs through actin and myosin filaments. Therefore, Skeletal Muscle correctly matches with Actin and Myosin.

D. Brain — IV. Thalamus: Thalamus is an important part of the brain that acts as a sensory relay centre. Therefore, Brain correctly matches with Thalamus.

87. Match the columns:

A. Prohibited food for yogi — III. Utkat Shak: Utkat Shak, meaning strong or unsuitable leafy vegetable preparation, is counted among foods avoided by a yogi. Therefore, Prohibited food for yogi correctly matches with Utkat Shak.

B. Recommended food for yogi — I. Snigdha: Snigdha food is smooth, unctuous, nourishing, and suitable for yogic practice when taken moderately. Therefore, Recommended food for yogi correctly matches with Snigdha.

C. Satvik food — II. Rasayukta: Rasayukta food is juicy, pleasing, and nourishing, which fits the nature of Sattvic food. Therefore, Satvik food correctly matches with Rasayukta.

D. Rajsik food — IV. Teekshan Ahar: Teekshan Ahar means sharp, pungent, or strongly stimulating food, which belongs to Rajasic food. Therefore, Rajsik food correctly matches with Teekshan Ahar.

88. Match the columns:

A. Musculo skeletal disorder — II. Spondylosis: Spondylosis is a disorder affecting the spine and musculoskeletal system. Therefore, Musculo skeletal disorder correctly matches with Spondylosis.

B. Cardiovascular disorder — IV. Angina: Angina is chest pain caused by reduced blood supply to heart muscle and belongs to cardiovascular disorders. Therefore, Cardiovascular disorder correctly matches with Angina.

C. Neurological disorder — I. Epilepsy: Epilepsy is a neurological disorder characterized by recurrent seizures due to abnormal brain activity. Therefore, Neurological disorder correctly matches with Epilepsy.

D. Psychiatric disorder — III. Phobia: Phobia is an anxiety-related psychiatric disorder involving excessive irrational fear. Therefore, Psychiatric disorder correctly matches with Phobia.

89. 2: A-II, B-III, C-I, D-IV: Match the columns:

A. Moksa sanyasa yoga — II. Srimadbhagavodgita: Moksha Sanyasa Yoga is the eighteenth chapter of Shrimad Bhagavadgita. Therefore, Moksa sanyasa yoga correctly matches with Srimadbhagavodgita.

B. Kaivalyapada — III. Patanjala Yogadarshan: Kaivalyapada is the fourth pada of Patanjala Yogadarshan. Therefore, Kaivalyapada correctly matches with Patanjala Yogadarshan.

C. Aparigrahavrata — I. Jainadarshan: Aparigraha-vrata is an important vow in Jainadarshan. Therefore, Aparigrahavrata correctly matches with Jainadarshan.

D. Vinayapitak — IV. Bauddhadarshan: Vinayapitaka is one of the major canonical collections of Bauddhadarshan. Therefore, Vinayapitak correctly matches with Bauddhadarshan.

90. Match the columns:

A. Viparitakarani — IV. Mudra: Viparitakarani is classified as a mudra in Hatha Yoga. Therefore, Viparitakarani correctly matches with Mudra.

B. Vahnisara — I. Dhauti: Vahnisara is included under Dhauti-related cleansing practices. Therefore, Vahnisara correctly matches with Dhauti.

C. Lauliki — II. Satkarma: Lauliki, also known as Nauli, is one of the Shatkarmas or cleansing practices. Therefore, Lauliki correctly matches with Satkarma.

D. Murcha — III. Kumbhaka: Murcha is a type of Kumbhaka or pranayama practice. Therefore, Murcha correctly matches with Kumbhaka.

91. According to the passage, Grihastha ashrama is related to Artha Purushartha. The passage clearly states that Brahmacharya is related with Dharma, while Grihastha is related with Artha and Kama. Grihastha life is the stage where knowledge gained in Brahmacharya is applied in society, service, family life, and earning punya. Artha means material prosperity, livelihood, and responsible worldly support, which properly belongs to the householder stage. Therefore, among the given options, Grihastha is the correct answer.

92. Ghor Sannyasika is related to Grihastha according to the passage. The passage classifies Grihastha into Vartakvriti, Shaleen Vritti, Yayavar, and Ghar Sannyasik. So Ghor Sannyasika or Ghar Sannyasik is given as a type within Grihastha classification. It is not listed under Sanyasi, Vanprasthi, or Brahmachari in the given passage. Therefore, among the given options, Grihastha is the correct answer.

93. Vanprastha ashrama has been for twenty-five years according to the passage. The passage states that the total human life span was assumed to be one hundred years. It also says that the four ashramas were divided equally into twenty-five years each. After the Grihastha stage, a person goes to vana and lives there for mastery over the senses. Therefore, among the given options, 25 is the correct answer.

94. Mansik or mental Purushartha has been practiced in Vanprastha ashrama according to the passage. The passage clearly says that after Grihastha, one goes to vana and lives there for mastery over senses. It further states that this life was dedicated to mental Purushartha and self-realization practices. This directly connects Vanprastha with mental discipline and inner spiritual preparation. Therefore, among the given options, Vanprastha is the correct answer.

95. Bahoodak is related with the elderly stage according to the passage. The passage places Bahoodak under the classification of Sanyasi. It also explains that Sanyasa comes after Brahmacharya, Grihastha, and Vanprastha, and belongs to the last stage of life. The four ashramas are related to childhood, adolescence, adulthood, and elderly stages respectively. Since Bahoodak is a type of Sanyasi, it is related with the elderly stage. Therefore, among the given options, Elderly is the correct answer.

96. According to the passage, Chakras receive Prana and distribute its potential. The passage states that these centres and channels receive Prana and distribute its potential to Annamayakosa through Pranamayakosa. Since the question asks which receives Prana and distributes its potential, the most direct answer from the passage is Chakra. Nadis are energy channels, Pranamayakosa is the vital sheath, and Sukshmasarira is the subtle body, but the passage specifically describes Chakras as the central centres of Prana. Therefore, among the given options, Chakra is the correct answer.

97. Swami Satyananda referred to Chakra as movable circlet. The passage states that according to Swami Satyanand Saraswati, chakras are accepted as "whirlpool" and "movable circlet." Among the given options, "Movable Circlet" directly matches the wording used in the passage. The other options such as consciousness, energy centres, and vital area are not the specific terms attributed to Swami Satyananda in the passage. Therefore, among the given options, Movable Circlet is the correct answer.

98. Chakras are accepted as conscious centres by Sri Aravinda. The passage clearly says that Sri Aravinda has accepted chakras as conscious centres. It also states that he described chakras as centres and sources of all movable energies of our existence. Swami Satyananda is associated in the passage with "whirlpool" and "movable circlet," while Baile is associated with Pranamayasarir. Therefore, among the given options, Sri Aravinda is the correct answer.

99. Inner consciousness arises by opening of chakras. The passage says that chakras are centres of inner consciousness and are basically related to the subtle body. It further states that opening of these centres promotes yogic inner consciousness. A common person remains entangled in external consciousness when these centres are not opened. Therefore, among the given options, Opening of chakras is the correct answer.

100. Energy channels cross each other in the Pranic body. The passage states that according to Baile, chakras are components of Pranamayasarir or Pranic body. It further explains that the Pranic body is composed of various energy channels. The locations where these channels cross each other are called energy centres or chakras. Therefore, among the given options, Pranic body is the correct answer.

Previous Years' Paper

National Testing Agency (NTA)

UGC-NET Junior Research Fellowship & Assistant Professor Eligibility Exam

YOGA, JUNE-2025

(Exam held on 27-06-2025)

PAPER-II

1. Upanisad related to pipaladi branch of Arthavaveda:
1. Ishavasyopnisad
2. Kenopnisad
3. Prashnopnisad
4. Mundakopnisad

2. According to Tulsidas ji, siddha cannot visualize God inside them, without:
1. Radha Krishna
2. Sitaram
3. Bhavani Shankar
4. Lakshmi Vinayaka

3. How many types of Vipashyna are there according to Sandhinirmochan?
1. 2
2. 4
3. 3
4. 5

4. Which one is dependent on each other as per Narad Bhakti Sutra?
1. Karma & Jnana
2. Jnana & Bhakti
3. Laya & Jnana
4. Bhakti & Karma

5. What can not be attained with buddhi and listening as per Kathopnisad?
1. Atman
2. Jiva
3. Dharma
4. Adharma

6. By whom one can overcome through Avidhya, according to Ishavasyopnisad?
1. Karma
2. Mrityu
3. Amrit
4. Dharma

7. Which question of Prashnopanisad describes "Prana originates from what and how it enters in the body"?
1. First
2. Second
3. Third
4. Fourth

8. Tapa for achieving 'Satkara' is
1. Satvik
2. Rajas
3. Tamas
4. Baudhik

9. Which one is subtle Prapanchabhidhayaka in Pranava?
1. Akaar
2. Ukaar
3. Makaar
4. Ardhamatra

10. How many stages of Yoga are there according to Yogatattvoupnisad?
1. 3
2. 4
3. 5
4. 6

11. Dhyanayoga diminishes biggest .... like a mountain:
1. Karma
2. Adharma
3. Paapa
4. Punya

12. Which one is not a Pranayama, according to Yogkundalyoupnisad?

1. Seetkari 2. Sheetali
3. Ujjayi 4. Kevala

13. Good characteristics of human body according to Patanjal Yoga Sutra are-

1. Compact built like Vajra, Roopa, Deh, Bala
2. Compact built like Vajra, Roopa, Lavanya, Bala
3. Deh, Roop, Lavanya, Bala
4. Buddhi, Roop, Lavanya, Bala

14. In absence of Trishna in the Guna of Prakrtiti from the khyati of purusha known as .... according to patanjal-yoga-sutra.

1. Kaivalya 2. Abhyasa
3. Vairagya 4. Ekatatva

15. Ability of self (body) and ability of self-regulation (soul) according to Patanjal Yoga Sutra is due to:

1. Samyoga 2. Sahyoga
3. Drishya 4. Maya

16. A Yogi can diminish his Kleshas and Karmas through:

1. Vidya
2. Jnana
3. Vairagya
4. Dharma-megha Samadhi

17. According to Gheranda Samhita, how many times umblicus should be in contracted towards back, for Agnisara?

1. 50 2. 100
3. 200 4. 150

18. Which one is the correct sequence of 12 petalled lotus according to Gheranda Samhita?

1. Ha Ksha Ma La Va Ra Ha Sa Kaha Fre Yun La
2. Ksha Ha Ma La Va Sa Ha Fre Yun La Ra Ham
3. Ha Sa Ksha Ma La Va Ra Yun Ha Sa Kha Fren
4. Ha La Ksha Ma Sa Ra Va Yun Ha Sa Kha Fren

19. The sequence of Mahamudra practice as per Hatharatnavali is:

1. Bend left leg, hold right leg, raise your head.
2. Straight left leg, bend right leg, Jalandhar bandh.
3. Bend left leg, straight right leg, Jalandhar bandh.
4. Bend right leg, straight left leg, Mahabandha.

20. Which Pranayama eliminates Kapaha Roga & induces gastric fire according to Hathayogpradipika?

1. Surya Bhedana
2. Sheetali
3. Ujjayi
4. Sheetkaari

21. Which pro-vitamin is converted into Vitamin A inside the body?

1. Carotene 2. Beta-Carotene
3. Thiamine 4. Cyanocobalamine

22. Junction between two neurons is called as:

1. Nephron
2. Nerve
3. Neurotransmitter
4. Synapse

23. Functional Residual Capacity of Lungs is:

1. Minimal Volume+ Residual Volume
2. Expiratory Reserve Volume + Residual Volume
3. Inspiratory Reserve Volume + Tidal Volume
4. Expiratory Reserve Volume + Tidal Volume

24. How many stages are there in Non-Rapid Eye Movement (NREM) sleep?

1. I 2. II
3. III 4. IV

25. Which Vayu regulates physiological activities in relation to Vishudhi Chakra?

1. Prana Vayu
2. Udana Vayu
3. Samana Vayu
4. Vyana Vayu

26. Regulation of which Chakra controls emotions?

1. Muladhar Chakra
2. Swadishthana Chakra
3. Manipur Chakra
4. Anahata Chakra

27. Which green vegetable is not edible (Pathya) in Hatha Yoage pradipika?

1. Jiwanti-shaka
2. Sarson-shaka
3. Punarnava-shaka
4. Meghnad-shaka

28. Accumulation, vitiation and normalization of Vata respectively takes place in which season?

1. Summer, Rainy, Autumn
2. Rainy, Autumn, Spring
3. Winter, Spring, Rainy
4. Rainy, Autumn, Winter.

29. Which dhauti regulates Pitta and Kapha?

1. Varisar-dhauti
2. Vanhisaar-dhauti
3. Hrid-dhauti
4. Mula-shodhana

30. Parasympathetic activation results in:

1. Increased Metabolic rate
2. Activation of energy reserve
3. Increased secretion of digestive juices
4. Increased mental alertness

31. Smallest functional unit of muscle fiber is:

1. Ligament
2. Tendon
3. Sarcomere
4. Actin

32. Voluntary control of breathing during pranayama is done by:

1. Cerebral Cortex
2. Cerebral Medulla
3. Medulla Oblongata
4. Cerebellum

33. Position of ankle joint and feet during Bhujangasana:

1. Dorsi Flexion
2. Planter Flexion
3. Eversion
4. Inversion

34. In which Mudra, Ida and Pingla become inactive according to Hathayoga?

1. Khechari Mudra
2. Vipreetakarni Mudra
3. Mahaveda
4. Maha Mudra

35. How much should be the length of dhauti according to Hatharatnavali?

1. Ten hands
2. Twenty hands
3. Thirty hands
4. Twelve hands

36. Danda Dhauti destroys .... according to Gheranda.

1. Brain Disease
2. Throat Disease
3. Heart Disease
4. Stomach Disease

37. What can be done first during the practice of Gaumukhasana, according to Hathayogapradipika?

1. Right heel near left pelvis.
2. Left heel near right pelvis.
3. Right knee over the left knee.
4. Left knee over the right knee.

38. What helps to siddha (accomplish) yoga as per Hathayogapradipika?

1. Courage
2. overeating
3. Exertion
4. Ficklemindedness

39. Positioning of body from toe to naval region during Bhujangasana, according to Gheranda Samhita should be:

1. Keep straight.
2. To place on the ground.
3. To lift and place over the head.
4. To see the heel.

40. Which one is not a characteristic of a good lesson plan?

1. Generalised for all yoga practices
2. Detailed lesson plan
3. Specify materials required
4. Should take cognizance of individual difference

41. Arrange the symptoms of Bhakti in sequence according to Narad Bhakti Sutra:

A. According to dumb's taste
B. Only few eligible can receive this illumination
C. The nature of love is undescribed
D. Free from desire
E. Free from Gunas

Choose the correct answer from the options given below:

1. C, A, B, E, D
2. D, C, B, A, E
3. A, B, C, D, E
4. E, D, C, B, A

42. Sequence according to birth time:

A. T. Krishnamacharya
B. Swami Shivananda Saraswati
C. Maharshi Mahesh Yogi
D. Swami Ram
E. Shree Shyamacharan Lahari

Choose the correct answer from the options given below:

1. D, A, B, C, E
2. E, A, D, C, B
3. E, B, A, C, D
4. A, C, B, D, E

43. Arrange according to Shrimadbhagvadgita:

A. Darpa
B. Agyan
C. Dambha
D. Krodha
E. Abhimaan

Choose the correct answer from the options given below:

1. C, A, E, D, B
2. C, A, D, E, B
3. B, C, A, D, E
4. E, B, C, A, D

44. Arrange according to Prashnopanisad:

A. Union of Pran and Rai
B. Questions of Ashwalayan related to origin of Prana
C. Questions of Satyakama related to Omkar Prayer
D. Questions of Gargya Muni related to Jiwatma and Parmatma
E. Question of Bhargav related to people.

Choose the correct answer from the options given below:

1. A, B, C, D, E
2. E, B, D, C, A
3. A, E, B, D, C
4. D, C, A, B, E

45. Arrange in sequence the first five matras of Omkar according to Nadabindoopanisad:

A. Naamdheya
B. Patangini
C. Ghoshini
D. Vidhunmatra
E. Vayuvegini

Choose the correct answer from the options given below:

1. C, D, B, E, A
2. A, B, C, D, E
3. E, D, A, B, C
4. C, A, B, E, D

46. Arrange these in sequence according to Yogasutra:

A. Ishwar
B. Chittavriti
C. Panchaklesha
D. Chitta Parinaam
E. Dharna

Choose the correct answer from the options given below:

1. B, A, C, E, D
2. A, B, C, E, D
3. A, C, B, D, E
4. C, A, B, D, E

47. Arrange these in sequence according to Gheranda:

A. Trataka
B. Varisara
C. Vatkarma
D. Vaman Dhauti
E. Dantmool Dhauti

Choose the correct answer from the options given below:

1. E, B, A, D, C
2. A, B, D, E, C
3. B, E, D, A, C
4. C, B, A, E, D

48. Arrange the suitable place for the practice of Hathayoga according to Hathayogapradipika Sloka:

A. Free from stone and fire
B. Availability of Donation (Subhiksha)
C. Religious
D. Good Province
E. Silent Place

Choose the correct answer from the options given below:

1. A, B, C, D, E
2. D, A, E, C, B
3. D, C, B, A, E
4. D, E, C, B, A

49. Sequence of hearing through hearing organs:

A. Chochlea
B. Tympanic Membrane
C. Ossicles
D. Auricle
E. Vestibule

Choose the correct answer from the options given below:

1. E, D, A, B, C
2. C, D, E, A, B
3. A, E, C, B, D
4. D, B, C, E, A

50. What is the sequence of psychosexual developmental stages according to Sigmund Freud?

A. Genital Stage
B. Phallic Stage
C. Latency Stage
D. Oral Stage
E. Anal Stage

Choose the correct answer from the options given below:

1. D, E, B, C, A
2. D, E, C, B, A
3. E, A, D, B, C
4. A, E, D, C, B

51. Arrange the following in sequence according to Gheranda Samhita Shloka:

A. Onion
B. Lemon
C. Horse gram
D. Kapitha
E. Curd

Choose the correct answer from the options given below:

1. A, C, B, E, D
2. E, C, D, B, A
3. C, E, D, B, A
4. B, C, D, E, A

52. Arrange bones from head to feet:

A. Mandible
B. Scapula
C. Frontal
D. Femur
E. Tarsal

Choose the correct answer from the options given below:

1. B, E, D, A, C
2. C, A, B, D, E
3. C, A, B, E, D
4. A, B, E, D, C

53. Arrange in sequence according to lesson plan:

A. Salient Points
B. Verbal Introduction
C. Advantages
D. Demonstration
E. Question Answer

Choose the correct answer from the options given below:

1. B, D, E, A, C
2. B, D, A, C, E
3. B, D, C, A, E
4. A, B, D, C, E

54. Arrange the subject of Shiv Samhita according to chapter.

A. Four stages of Yoga
B. Description of 10 Mudras
C. Philosophical Principles
D. Tattvagyan Prakaran
E. Self-realisation

Choose the correct answer from the options given below:

1. C, D, A, B, E
2. C, A, B, E, D
3. C, B, A, D, E
4. A, B, C, D, E

55. Sequence the mudra according to shloka written in Gheranda Samhita.

A. Kaki
B. Ashwini
C. Vipreetkarni
D. Uddiyana
E. Mahaveda

Choose the correct answer from the options given below:

1. D, E, C, B, A
2. A, B, C, D, E
3. D, E, A, B, C
4. E, A, B, C, D

56. Which among the following do not come under creation of elements according to Samkhya?

A. Mahat
B. Sattva
C. Ahankaar
D. Mahabhoot
E. Raj

Choose the correct answer from the options given below:

1. A, B & D Only
2. B & C Only
3. B & E Only
4. A & E Only

57. Which options do not come under the seven stages of knowledge according to Yoga Vashistha?

A. Shubheccha
B. Tanumansa
C. Ashubheccha
D. Asattvapatti
E. Sansakti

Choose the correct answer from the options given below:

1. C, D, E Only
2. A, B, C Only
3. B, C, D Only
4. D, E, A Only

58. What is the solution of conquering Chitta according to Yoga Vashistha?

A. Company of saints
B. Avoidance of food
C. Avoidance of lust (vasana)
D. Inhale fast
E. Attainment of Spirituality

Choose the correct answer from the options given below:

1. A, C, E Only
2. B, C, D Only
3. C, D, E Only
4. D, E, A Only

59. Which options are not characteristics of soul according to Kathopanisad:

A. It is an effect
B. It is a cause
C. It does not take birth
D. It does not die
E. It is ancient

Choose the correct answer from the options given below:

1. B, E Only 2. C, D Only
3. B, C Only 4. A, B Only

60. How Bhrama is mentioned in Mundakopanisad according to Paravidya?

A. Draeshya B. Adraeshya
C. Asarvagat D. Agraheya
E. Nitya

Choose the correct answer from the options given below:

1. A, C, E Only 2. C, D, E Only
3. B, D, E Only 4. A, D, E Only

61. Which options are not a limb of yoga, according to Yogachudamani Upanisad?

A. Yama B. Asana
C. Pranavirodha D. Pratyahara
E. Asamadhi

Choose the correct answer from the options given below:

1. A, B, C Only 2. C, D, E Only
3. B, D, A Only 4. A, C, E Only

62. What can be attained through the means of Grahitrivishayaka Samadhi?

A. Pratibha B. Sthoolawastha
C. Sravan D. Mahima
E. Adarsa

Choose the correct answer from the options given below:

1. B, C, D Only 2. A, C, D Only
3. A, C, E Only 4. A, B, D Only

63. Describe the Karma according to Hatharatnavali:

A. Chakri B. Nauli
C. Gajkarni D. Mastakbhranti
E. Shankha Praksalana

Choose the correct answer from the options given below:

1. A, B, C, D Only
2. E, A, B, C Only
3. B, C, D, E Only
4. B, C, E Only

64. Which options are the part of Shatkarma according to Gheranda?

A. Vatsara
B. Chakri
C. Dantmool Dhauti
D. Sheetkrama
E. Gajkarni

Choose the correct answer from the options given below:

1. A, B, C Only
2. A, C, D Only
3. A, C, E Only
4. A, C, B Only

65. Which of the following are not Kumbaka according to Hathayogapradipika?

A. Sahita B. Suryabheda
C. Kevala D. Seetkaari
E. Plawani

Choose the correct answer from the options given below:

1. A, B Only 2. B, D Only
3. A, C Only 4. E, A Only

66. Which are not mentioned under the 12 traditions of Gorakshnath?

A. Dharmanathi B. Krishnanathi
C. Vairag Panthi D. Yamunanathi
E. Dhaj-Panthi

Choose the correct answer from the options given below:

1. A, C Only 2. B, C Only
3. B, D Only 4. D, E Only

67. The supreme divided himself in the following parts according to Brihadranykopnisad:

A. Fire B. Water
C. Air D. Sun
E. Colour

Choose the correct answer from the options given below:

1. A, B, E Only 2. A, C, D Only
3. A, D,. E Only 4. A, C, E Only

68. .... are the appropriate for Dhyana according to Swetaswataropanisad.

A. Free from stones, fire and sand
B. Soothing for eyes
C. In water
D. Sit on tiger's leather
E. Purified from all

Choose the correct answer from the options given below:

1. B, C, A Only
2. C, D, E Only
3. A, C, D Only
4. A, B, E Only

69. Which Asana are not mentioned in Hathyogapradipika?

A. Siddhasana
B. Bakasana
C. Matasyasana
D. Virabhadrasana
E. Dhanurasana

Choose the correct answer from the options given below:

1. A, B, D Only
2. B, C, D Only
3. A, C, E Only
4. B, C, E Only

70. Stages of personality development according to Jung.

A. Childhood
B. Early Childhood
C. Young Adulthood
D. Middle Age
E. Maturity

Choose the correct answer from the options given below:

1. A, C, D Only
2. B, C, D Only
3. B, C, E Only
4. C, D, E Only

71. Which of the following are the types of Joint?

A. Gliding
B. Inversion
C. Condylar
D. Protraction
E. Saddle

Choose the correct answer from the options given below: –

1. A, D Only
2. B, C, D Only
3. B, E, D Only
4. A, C, E Only

72. Which of the following have an ill effect on mental and emotional health?

A. Pramad
B. Karuna
C. Bhranti Darshan
D. Avirati
E. Mudita

Choose the correct answer from the options given below:

1. A, E, D Only
2. A, C, E Only
3. A, C, D Only
4. B, C, D Only

73. Types of Yogic Breathing are:

A. Deep Breathing
B. Abdominal Breathing
C. Thoracic Breathing
D. General Breathing
E. Thoraco-abdominal Breathing

Choose the correct answer from the options given below:

1. A, D Only
2. A, C, D Only
3. B, C, E Only
4. D, C, E Only

74. The advantages of a written lesson plan are:

A. It helps the teacher to organize his thinking.
B. It should be prepared shortly before use.
C. It increases the teacher's confidence.
D. It serves as an aid for future plans.
E. It should be specific and detailed.

Choose the correct answer from the options given below:

1. B, C, E Only 2. A, C, D Only
3. E, B, A Only 4. C, B, E Only

75. Which statement is not correct for Tadagi Mudra?

A. To sit in Paschimottanasana.
B. By doing this hair never becomes grey.
C. Wrinkles do not come over the body.
D. This mudra overcomes old age.
E. This mudra overcomes death.

Choose the correct answer from the options given below:

1. A, D Only 2. D, E Only
3. B, C Only 4. A, E Only

76. Match List-I and List-II according to Fundamentals of Yoga.

List-I	List-II
A. Purusharth	I. Hathayoga
B. Gorakshasanhita	II. Veda
C. Trayee	III. Aranyakanda
D. Ramayana	IV. Four

Choose the correct answer from the options given below:

1. A-II, B-III, C-IV, D-I
2. A-IV, B-I, C-II, D-III
3. A-I, B-II, C-III, D-IV
4. A-IV, B-III, C-I, D-II

77. Match List-I and List-II according to Sidhasidhant-Paddhati.

List-I	List-II
A. Sadacharpalana	I. Shreeshail
B. Skin	II. Ksharsamudra
C. Urine	III. Brahmana
D. Forehead	IV. Kraunchdweep

Choose the correct answer from the options given below:

1. A-III, B-IV, C-I, D-II
2. A-III, B-IV, C-II, D-I
3. A-I, B-IV, C-II, D-III
4. A-IV, B-III, C-I, D-II

78. Match List-I and List-II according to Mandukyopnisad.

List-I	List-II
A. Vashvanara	I. Third
B. Praagya	II. Akaar
C. Antahapragya	III. Saptanga
D. Jagratisthan	IV. Tejas

Choose the correct answer from the options given below:

1. A-I, B-II, C-III, D-IV
2. A-II, B-I, C-IV, D-III
3. A-III, B-I, C-IV, D-II
4. A-III, B-II, C-I, D-IV

79. Match List-I and List-II according to Shrimad-bhagvadgita.

List-I	List-II
A. Purusha	I. Rajas
B. Katu	II. Satvik
C. Snigdha	III. Chetan
D. Tapa	IV. Swadhyaya

Choose the correct answer from the options given below:

1. A-II, B-I, C-IV, D-III
2. A-III, B-II, C-I, D-IV
3. A-I, B-III, C-IV, D-II
4. A-III, B-I, C-II, D-IV

80. Match List-I and List-II according to Nadabindoopnisad.

List-I	List-II
A. Akaar	I. Uttar Paksha
B. Ukaar	II. Dakshin Paksha
C. Makaar	III. Puccha
D. Ardhamatra	IV. Mastaka

Choose the correct answer from the options given below:

1. A-II, B-I, C-III, D-IV
2. A-I, B-II, C-III, D-IV
3. A-IV, B-III, C-II, D-I
4. A-IV, B-II, C-III, D-I

81. Match List-I and List-II according to Yogadarshan.

List-I	List-II
A. Vikshepsahbhuvah	I. Punyatma
B. Chittaprasadanam	II. Bhoga
C. Pramana	III. Daurmanasya
D. Karmashaya	IV. Shabda (Agama)

Choose the correct answer from the options given below:

1. A-II, B-I, C-IV, D-III
2. A-III, B-I, C-IV, D-II
3. A-I, B-III, C-II, D-IV
4. A-IV, B-II, C-III, D-I

82. Match List-I and List-II according to Siddha-siddhantpaddhati.

List-I	List-II
A. Matsarya	I. Prakriti
B. Udyog	II. Vaak
C. Asha	III. Kriya
D. Para	IV. Maya

Choose the correct answer from the options given below:

1. A-IV, B-III, C-I, D-II
2. A-III, B-II, C-I, D-IV
3. A-III, B-IV, C-II, D-I
4. A-I, B-II, C-IV, D-III

83. Match List-I and List-II according to Hathyoga.

List-I	List-II
A. Hridyakash	I. Mahasunya
B. Visuddhiakash	II. Atisunya
C. Brumadhyakash	III. Sunya
D. Kanthasthan	IV. Madhyachakra

Choose the correct answer from the options given below:

1. A-III, B-II, C-I, D-IV
2. A-I, B-III, C-II, D-IV
3. A-II, B-III, C-IV, D-I
4. A-IV, B-III, C-II, D-I

84. Match List-I and List-II according to vegetables and phytochemicals.

List-I	List-II
A. Orange Colored Vegetables	I. Lycopene
B. Red Colored Vegetables	II. Betalines
C. Deep Red Colored Vegetables	III. Beta-carotine
D. Blue & Purple Colored Vegetables	IV. Anthocynins

Choose the correct answer from the options given below:

1. A-I, B-II, C-III, D-IV
2. A-II, B-IV, C-III, D-I
3. A-III, B-I, C-II, D-IV
4. A-IV, B-II, C-III, D-I

85. Match List-I and List-II according to the Yogic diet.

List-I	List-II
A. Snigdha	I. Apathya
B. Til	II. Satvik
C. Sauth	III. Rajsik
D. Amal Ras	IV. Pathya

Choose the correct answer from the options given below:

1. A-II, B-I, C-IV, D-III
2. A-III, B-IV, C-I, D-II
3. A-IV, B-I, C-III, D-II
4. A-III, B-II, C-I, D-IV

86. Match List-I and List-II as per endocrine glands and respective hormones.

List-I	List-II
A. Adrenal Medulla	I. Cortisol
B. Pituitary Gland	II. Estrogen
C. Adrenal Cortex	III. Epinephrine
D. Ovaries	IV. Oxytocin

Choose the correct answer from the options given below:

1. A-II, B-IV, C-III, D-I
2. A-II, B-IV, C-I, D-III
3. A-III, B-I, C-II, D-IV
4. A-III, B-IV, C-I, D-II

87. Match List-I and List-II according to question type and its example.

List-I	List-II
A. Introductory Questions	I. What are the differences between Asana and Pranayama?
B. Thought provoking Questions	II. What are the Principles of Pranayama?
C. Questions of Comprehension	III. What is the relationship of muscular system and doing Asana?
D. Comparison Question	IV. Why do you want health?

Choose the correct answer from the options given below:

1. A-IV, B-III, C-II, D-I
2. A-IV, B-III, C-I, D-II
3. A-IV, B-I, C-III, D-II
4. A-III, B-I, C-II, D-IV

88. Match List-I and List-II according to Leshya Dhyan.

List-I	List-II
A. Center of enlightenment	I. Green colour
B. Center of bliss	II. Blue colour
C. Center of purification	III. White colour
D. Eyebrow center	IV. Pink colour

Choose the correct answer from the options given below:

1. A-I, B-III, C-IV, D-II
2. A-III, B-II, C-I, D-IV
3. A-III, B-I, C-II, D-IV
4. A-II, B-I, C-IV, D-III

89. Match List-I and List-II according to Gheranda Samhita.

List-I	List-II
A. Shodhan	I. Pratyahaar
B. Sthairya	II. Shatkarma
C. Laghav	III. Mudra
D. Dhairya	IV. Pranayama

Choose the correct answer from the options given below:

1. A-I, B-III, C-II, D-IV
2. A-II, B-III, C-IV, D-I
3. A-II, B-IV, C-III, D-I
4. A-I, B-III, C-IV, D-II

90. Match List-I and List-II according to anatomy and physiology of the human eye.

List-I	List-II
A. Rhodopsin	I. 3
B. Oculomotor Muscles	II. Opsin
C. Image	III. 6
D. Cones	IV. Retina

Choose the correct answer from the options given below:

1. A-I, B-II, C-III, D-IV
2. A-II, B-III, C-IV, D-I
3. A-III, B-I, C-IV, D-II
4. A-IV, B-III, C-I, D-II

Directions (Qs. No. 91 to 95): *Read the following passage carefully and answer the questions.*

Our respiratory system has the special feature that it is both voluntary and involuntary, therefore, we can move from the voluntary (conscious control of body physiology) to the involuntary system (lesser control of body physiology). The higher centers of brain are the instruments through which prana and mind work. As far as the physical body is concerned, the area of the brain centers in which highest creativity and intelligence are seen governs the lower brain, as well as total body physiology. Normally the higher centers work through mid-brain but have the control even to change the functions of the lower brain. The hypothalamus which is situated above the midbrain is the master of lower brain, governing and controlling all autonomic functions of the body. It works through Autonomic Nervous System and Endocrine System to change the physiology of entire body. The connection between voluntary nervous system and hypothalamus is essentially through the higher centers of brain and is very feeble in normal human beings. The respiratory system is innately connected by the nerves of this voluntary nervous system. Hence, we can change voluntarily the breathing rates, pattern, rhythm, etc. by directing our will towards the same essentially bringing the voluntary nervous system to override the hypothalamic autonomic control.

91. Breathing is a:
1. Voluntary process
2. Involuntary process
3. Voluntary and involuntary process
4. Neither voluntary nor involuntary process

92. Brain center that has highest creativity is controlled by:
1. Hypothalamus
2. Medulla
3. Medulla Oblongata
4. Cerebellum

93. Example of voluntary regulation of breath:
1. Increased breath rate while running.
2. Gasping during Asthmatic attack.
3. Holding of breath under water.
4. Passive exhalation during Kapalbhati.

94. Hypothalamus regulates:
1. Endocrine System & Autonomic Nervous System
2. Endocrine System & Peripheral Nervous System
3. Autonomic Nervous System and Peripheral Nervous System
4. Sensory and motor nerves

95. Pranayama results in:
1. Regulation of higher brain centers by lower brain.
2. Overcome autonomic control of breathing.
3. Regulation of oxygen.
4. Regulation of haemoglobin.

Directions (Qs. No. 96 to 100): *Read the following passage carefully and answer the questions.*

The syllable 'OM' is first uttered by Udgata priest in the sacrifice. Here it explained the meditation on the Udgitha. The essence of all creatures and objects in the earth. The essence of earth is water. The essence of water is plants. The essence of plants is Mann. The essence of Mann is speech. The essence of speech is Sama (chant). The essence of Sama is Udgith. This is supreme essence among all essences. This is the symbol of supreme self.

Speech itself is the Rik, the prana is the Sama, and the syllable 'OM' is Udgitha. That pair consisting of speech in the form of Rik and prana is the form of Sama is well known. Just as the union of male and female fulfills each other's desires, similarly from the conjunction of this pair the Omkara is produced.

It is through the syllable 'OM' that the threefold Vedic knowledge becomes active in ritual. By saying 'OM' the 'Hotr' priest begins his recitation and the Udgata priest begins the Sama chant. All sacrificial rites are performed for the worship of this very syllable 'OM'.

96. Omkar helps to attain:
1. Brahm
2. Ishwar
3. Desires
4. Purusha

97. Recitation of Veda mantra has been initiated with:
1. Shre OM
2. OM
3. Hari OM
4. OM Gum

98. Which one is the fifth rasa as per the given paragraph?
1. Prithvi
2. Vaak
3. Jala
4. Sama

99. Which pair constitutes Udgeetha?
1. Vaak & Prana
2. Jala & Aushadi
3. Purush & Vaak
4. Female & Male

100. Omkar is the rasa of:
1. Prithvi
2. Rika
3. Vaak
4. Sama

ANSWERS

1	2	3	4	5	6	7	8	9	10
3	3	3	2	1	2	3	2	2	2
11	**12**	**13**	**14**	**15**	**16**	**17**	**18**	**19**	**20**
3	1	2	3	1	4	2	3	3	3
21	**22**	**23**	**24**	**25**	**26**	**27**	**28**	**29**	**30**
2	4	2	3,4	2	4	2	1	3	3
31	**32**	**33**	**34**	**35**	**36**	**37**	**38**	**39**	**40**
3	1	2	3,4	3	3	1	1	2	1
41	**42**	**43**	**44**	**45**	**46**	**47**	**48**	**49**	**50**
1	3	1	3	1	1	3	3	4	1
51	**52**	**53**	**54**	**55**	**56**	**57**	**58**	**59**	**60**
2	2	2	1	1	3	1	1	4	3
61	**62**	**63**	**64**	**65**	**66**	**67**	**68**	**69**	**70**
4	3	1	2	3	3	2	4	2	1
71	**72**	**73**	**74**	**75**	**76**	**77**	**78**	**79**	**80**
4	3	3	2	3	2	2	2,3	4	1
81	**82**	**83**	**84**	**85**	**86**	**87**	**88**	**89**	**90**
2	1	1	3	1	4	1	3	2	2
91	**92**	**93**	**94**	**95**	**96**	**97**	**98**	**99**	**100**
3	1	1,3	1	2	3	2	2	1	4

Explanatory Answers

1. The Mundakopanishad is one of the principal Upanishads associated with the Atharvaveda, specifically its Shaunaka branch, but it is also connected with the Pippalada school of the Atharvaveda, alongside the Prashnopanishad. The Prashnopanishad explicitly mentions the sage Pippalada, from whom the Upanishad gets its name and lineage.

2. According to Goswami Tulsidas Ji, in the invocatory verse of Ramcharitmanas, he pays obeisance to Bhavani and Shankar (i.e., Parvati and Shiva), describing them as the embodiment of Shraddha (faith) and Vishwas (trust). The verse:

"भवानीशंकरौ वन्दे श्रद्धाविश्वासरूपिणौ ।
याभ्यां विना न पश्चन्ति सिद्धाः स्वान्तःस्थमीश्वरम् ।।"

clearly states that without Bhavani and Shankar, even siddhas (perfected beings) cannot realize or visualize the Lord dwelling within their own hearts. This emphasizes the indispensability of both faith and trust on the spiritual path.

3. In the Sandhinirmochana Sutra, a Mahayana Buddhist text, Vipashyana (insight meditation) is categorized into three types. These are explained in the context of three natures (trisvabhava) — imagined, dependent, and perfected — and how insight leads to realization.

4. In the Narada Bhakti Sutra, there is a clear indication that Bhakti and Jnana (devotion and knowledge) are interrelated. Specifically, it states that Jnana (knowledge) is dependent on Bhakti (devotion) for liberation and realization. Jnana without Bhakti is considered incomplete in the path of true realization.

5. As per the Kathopanishad (Katha Upanishad), the Self (Atman) cannot be attained merely by intellect (buddhi) or hearing (shravana). The text emphasizes that Atman is only realized by the one whom it chooses — through grace, deep yearning, and sincere seeking beyond the faculties of the mind.

6. In the Ishavasyopanishad, particularly verse 11, it is said:

   "Vidyam cavidyam ca yas tad vedobhaya saha, avidyaya mrityu tirtva vidyayamatam asnute."

   This means: One who knows both vidya (knowledge) and avidya (ignorance or ritualistic action) together overcomes mrityu (death) through avidya, and attains immortality (amritam) through vidya.

   So, through avidya one overcomes death — that is, the cycle of mrityu.

7. In the Prashnopanishad, six disciples ask six questions to Sage Pippalada.

   The third question, asked by Kausalya Asvalayana, is:

   "O Master! Whence is this Prana born? How does he enter this body? How does he abide dividing himself into five parts? By what passage does he go out? How does he uphold the external world and how the internal (body)?"

   This clearly describes the origin of Prana and its entry into the body.

   Sage Pippalada answers that Prana originates from the Self (Atman) and enters the body at birth to fulfill the desires of the mind.

8. In spiritual literature including the Bhagavad Gita, Tapa (austerity) performed with the intent of gaining Satkara (respect), honor, or recognition is considered Rajasika Tapa — motivated by ego and desire for reward.

   Hence, tapas done for satkara is not sattvic, but rajasik in nature.

9. In the interpretation of Pranava (AUM) in the Mandukya Upanishad and other Vedantic texts:

   - Akaar (A) - Waking state (Jagrat) → Gross body (Sthula sharira)
   - Ukaar (U) - Dream state (Svapna) → Subtle body (Suksma sharira)
   - Makaar (M) - Deep sleep state (Susupti) → Causal body (Karana sharira)

   Here, Ukaar corresponds to the subtle world or Taijasa, and thus, it is the subtle Prapanchabhidhayaka, i.e., the one associated with the subtle manifestation of the cosmos.

10. According to the Yogatattvopanishad, there are four stages of Yoga. These are:

    1. **Arambha (The Beginning):** The yogi starts with chanting the Pranava (Om) mantra to overcome the obstacles of mind, speech, and body.
    2. **Ghata (The Effort):** The yogi makes deliberate effort to unite Prana, Apana, Manas, Buddhi, Jivatma and Paramatma.
    3. **Paricaya (The Familiarity):** With consistent practice, the yogi becomes familiar with the process. Prana along with the inner fire enters the Susumna channel, awakening Kundalini and becoming steady.
    4. **Nispatti (The Perfection):** The final stage where the yogi becomes a Jivanmukta (liberated soul) and transcends the waking, dreaming, and deep sleep states.

    These are the four recognized stages of Yoga according to this Upanishad.

11. In Dhyana Yoga, meditation leads to the purification of the mind and soul. According to yogic texts, especially in commentaries and Upanishadic teachings, Dhyana Yoga is so powerful that it can destroy even the biggest sin (Paapa) — just like a mountain is reduced to dust.

    Thus, Paapa (sin) is described as the biggest obstacle that is diminished by Dhyana Yoga.

12. According to the Yogakundalya Upanishad (Chapter 1, Verse 21), four main types of Kumbhaka (breath retention) are listed under Sahita Kumbhaka (Pranayama with techniques):

    1. Suryabhedana (Surya Bheda)
    2. Ujjayi
    3. Sitali (Sheetali)
    4. Bhastrika (Bhastri)

In Verse 20, Kevala Kumbhaka is mentioned separately as the spontaneous, advanced stage of breath retention, not as one of the named techniques.

The Upanishad does not mention Seetkari as one of these principal techniques — Seetkari is often confused with Sheetali but is not in this specific list.

Thus, Seetkari is not one of the Pranayamas named in this Upanishad.

13. According to Patanjali Yoga Sutra (Chapter 3 – Vibhuti Pada), the good characteristics of the human body resulting from the practice of Yoga are:

- Roopa (beauty/form)
- Lavanya (grace)
- Bala (strength)
- Vajra-samhananatva (compactness like a thunderbolt)

So, the correct set is: Compact built like Vajra, Roopa, Lavanya, Bala

14. According to Patañjali's Yoga Sutras (1.16):

"तत्परं पुरुषख्यातेर्गुणवैतृष्ण्यम्"

Tatparam purusa-khyater guna-vaitrsnyam

This verse describes Para Vairagya — the supreme non-attachment or dispassion.

It is defined as the absence of Trishna (craving/thirst) for the Gunas of Prakrti due to the realization (Khyati) of the Purusa (Self).

Thus, the highest state of Vairagya arises when one truly discerns the Self (Purusa) apart from Nature (Prakrti).

15. As per Patanjali Yoga Sutra, the interaction between Purusha (soul) and Prakriti (body/mind) is known as Samyoga (association or conjunction).

This Samyoga is responsible for the apparent sense of doership, self-regulation, and bodily abilities. Liberation comes from breaking this mistaken association.

16. According to Patanjali's Yoga Sutras, especially in the final stages of practice, it is through Dharma-Megha Samadhi (cloud of virtue samadhi) that all Kleshas (afflictions) and Karmas (past actions) are destroyed.

This is considered the penultimate stage before Kaivalya (liberation).

Dharma-Megha Samadhi is so named because it "rains" down virtue and washes away even latent impressions, leading to freedom from suffering.

17. In the Gheranda Samhita, under the section on Shatkarmas, specifically in the instructions for Agnisara Kriya, it is stated that the navel (umbilicus) should be contracted backward 100 times during the practice.

This practice activates the digestive fire and clears abdominal blockages.

18. In the Gheranda Samhita (6.9–6.10), a 12-petalled luminous lotus is described inside the pericarp of the Sahasrara Chakra, not to be confused with the Heart (Anahata) Chakra which also has 12 petals but a different syllabic sequence in other texts.

The relevant verses state:

सहस्रारे महापद्मे कर्णिकायां विचिन्तयेत्।
विलग्नसहितं पद्मं द्वादशैर्दलसंयुतम्॥
शुक्लवर्णं महातेजो द्वादशैर्बीजीभाषितम्।
ह स क्ष म ल व र युं ह स ख फ्रें यथाक्रमम्॥

So, the correct sequence of syllables is:

Ha Sa Ksha Ma La Va Ra Yun Ha Sa Kha Fren

19. According to Hatharatnavali, the proper sequence of Mahamudra is:

- Bend the left leg
- Straighten the right leg
- Apply Jalandhara Bandha (chin lock)

This sequence ensures proper pranic flow and activation of the internal locks.

20. While Suryabhedana Pranayama is praised for stimulating Kundalini, removing worms, and cleansing the skull, it primarily targets Vata dosha and not specifically Kapha.

The verse on Ujjayi Pranayama in Hathayogapradipika (2.52) explicitly states:

"कण्ठादिगतं वातपित्तश्लेष्महरं भवेत्।
कार्यते जठराग्निं च सर्वदोषनिवारणम्॥"

Meaning:

- "It destroys disorders of Vata, Pitta, and particularly Slesma (Kapha) in the throat and beyond."
- "It also kindles the digestive fire (Jatharagni) and removes all doshas."

Thus, Ujjayi is directly associated with both eliminating Kapha disorders and inducing gastric fire.

21. The pro-vitamin that is converted into Vitamin A (Retinol) in the body is Beta-Carotene, which is found abundantly in carrots, sweet potatoes, and other colorful vegetables.

Among the types of carotene, Beta-Carotene is the most efficient precursor to Vitamin A.

22. The junction between two neurons is called a Synapse.

At the synapse, neurotransmitters are released from the presynaptic neuron and bind to receptors on the postsynaptic neuron, allowing nerve impulse transmission.

23. Functional Residual Capacity (FRC) is the volume of air remaining in the lungs after a normal expiration.

It is the sum of:

- Expiratory Reserve Volume (ERV)
- Residual Volume (RV)

Thus, the correct combination is: Expiratory Reserve Volume + Residual Volume

24. Non-Rapid Eye Movement (NREM) sleep is traditionally divided into Third and forth stages:

1. Stage I – Light sleep
2. Stage II – Onset of sleep
3. Stage III – Deep sleep
4. Stage IV – Very deep sleep (slow-wave sleep)

So, there are four distinct stages in NREM.

25. Udana Vayu is the upward-moving energy associated with the Vishuddhi Chakra (throat chakra).

It governs speech, expression, and growth, and is vital for regulating physiological activities in the head and neck region, including the throat.

26. The Anahata Chakra (Heart Chakra) is primarily responsible for regulating emotions, such as love, compassion, forgiveness, and empathy.

It is the center of emotional balance in the yogic system. While Swadishthana governs desire and creativity, and Manipura governs willpower, it is the Anahata that directly governs emotional experiences.

27. According to Hatha Yoga Pradipika (1.59), Apathya (unwholesome) foods for a yoga practitioner include items that are too pungent, heating, or stimulating.

Among them, Sarshapa (mustard greens) are explicitly listed as to be avoided due to their pungent and heating qualities, which can disturb the doshas and hinder yogic progress.

While Jiwanti-shaka, Punarnava-shaka, and even Meghnad-shaka are counted among the generally accepted or neutral green vegetables in yogic literature, Sarson-shaka is clearly marked Apathya.

28. According to Ayurveda, each Dosha undergoes a natural cycle of:

- Sanchaya (Accumulation)
- Prakopa (Aggravation)
- Prashamana (Pacification)

For Vata Dosha, the correct seasonal sequence is:

1. Accumulation (Sanchaya) – in Summer (Grishma Ritu)

   Due to dryness and heat, Vata begins to accumulate.

2. Vitiation (Prakopa) – in Rainy Season (Varsha Ritu)

   The cool, wet, and unstable nature of the monsoon aggravates Vata further.

3. Normalization (Prashamana) – in Autumn (Sharad Ritu)

   The cool, balanced climate of autumn naturally soothes Vata.

Thus, the correct chronological flow is: Summer, Rainy, Autumn

29. Among the Shatkarmas, Hrid-Dhauti (cleansing of the heart region) is known for its impact on Pitta (fire element) and Kapha (water element) regulation.

It purifies the upper digestive tract and respiratory passages, directly affecting Pitta and Kapha doshas.

30. The parasympathetic nervous system (PNS) is associated with the "rest and digest" state. Its activation results in:

- Increased secretion of digestive juices
- Slowed heart rate
- Relaxation of muscles
- Energy conservation

Hence, the increased secretion of digestive juices is a hallmark of parasympathetic activation.

31. The smallest functional unit of a muscle fiber is the sarcomere. It is the repeating structural unit within myofibrils, bordered by Z-lines, and is responsible for muscle contraction through the sliding filament mechanism involving actin and myosin.

32. Voluntary control of breathing, as done during pranayama, is regulated by the Cerebral Cortex, particularly the motor areas of the frontal lobe. While Medulla Oblongata manages automatic breathing, the Cerebral Cortex enables conscious, voluntary modifications of breath patterns.

33. In Bhujangasana (Cobra Pose), the feet are extended backward, and the ankle joint is in plantar flexion — meaning the top of the foot is pressed downward and the sole faces away from the shin.

34. According to the Hatha Yoga Pradipika and other traditional texts, both Mahaveda Mudra and Maha Mudra are instrumental in deactivating the Ida and Pingala Nadis.

- In Mahaveda Mudra, by applying the three bandhas and striking the perineum (yoni-sthan), the prana is forced into the Sushumna Nadi, causing Ida and Pingala to become inactive.
- Similarly, Maha Mudra balances the upward and downward flowing energies (prana and apana) through bandhas and kumbhaka, enabling the withdrawal of energy from Ida and Pingala, thus allowing the awakening of Kundalini and the flow through Sushumna.

Therefore, both Mudras are correctly associated with Ida and Pingala becoming inactive.

35. According to the Hatharatnavali, the length of the cloth used for practicing dhauti should be thirty hands (approximately 15–18 feet). In this practice, a thin, soft, and clean cloth is taken and slowly swallowed through the mouth and then expelled. The purpose is to purify the pharynx, stomach, and esophagus. This length of cloth is kept sufficient to cleanse the entire tract. With regular practice, this practice removes phlegm, bile, and toxins and strengthens digestion.

36. In the Gheranda Samhita (1.19–20), Danda Dhauti is described as a form of Hrid Dhauti (cleansing of the chest/heart region). The practice involves inserting a smooth stalk (such as plantain, turmeric, or cane) into the throat and gently drawing it out.

This kriya clears phlegm, bile, and impurities lodged in the chest and esophagus. The text explicitly states that by practicing it, a yogi becomes free from heart diseases (Hrid-roga) and disorders of the gullet.

Thus, the benefit of Danda Dhauti is not for the stomach but specifically for the heart region.

37. The Hatha Yoga Pradipika (1.22) explains the method of Gomukhasana (Cow-Face Pose). The verse says:

"Place the right heel near the left buttock (pelvis) and the left heel near the right buttock."

Thus, the first step in the sequence is placing the right heel near the left pelvis before aligning the knees. This is the traditional starting point of the asana.

38. In Hatha Yoga Pradipika (1.16), the text states that the success of yoga (Siddhi in Yoga) depends on six factors:

1. Utsaha (Courage/zeal)
2. Sahas (Perseverance/steadfastness)
3. Dhairya (Firmness/patience)

4. Tattva-jnana (Knowledge of truth)
5. Nishchaya (Determination/faith)
6. Tyaga (Renunciation of excesses)

On the other hand, failure in yoga is caused by overeating, exertion, fickleness, talkativeness, and lack of faith.

Therefore, courage (Utsaha) is one of the key qualities that help a yogi attain accomplishment in yoga.

39. The Gheranda Samhita (2.42–43) describes Bhujangasana (Cobra Pose). It says:

"Lie prone on the ground, keep the palms below the shoulders, lift the upper part of the body like a cobra, but the portion of the body from the toes up to the navel should remain on the ground."

This posture strengthens the spine, tones abdominal organs, and stimulates prana, but the instruction is clear that the lower body stays grounded.

40. A good yoga lesson plan must be specific and systematic. According to principles of yoga pedagogy:

- It should not be generalized for all practices, but instead tailored to the objective and the group.
- It should be detailed, with step-by-step flow.
- It must list necessary materials (like mats, props, cleansing tools).
- It should account for individual differences, as every practitioner has unique abilities and limitations.

Thus, the option "Generalised for all yoga practices" does not fit the qualities of a good lesson plan.

41. Arrange the symptoms of Bhakti according to Narad Bhakti Sutra

The sequence in Narada Bhakti Sutra goes like this:

C. The nature of love is undescribed (cannot be put into words)

A. According to dumb's taste (it is like the indescribable experience of a dumb person tasting something sweet)

B. Only few eligible can receive this illumination (Bhakti is rare and bestowed by grace)

E. Free from Gunas (transcends sattva, rajas, tamas)

D. Free from desire (selfless love for God without worldly motive)

42. Sequence according to birth time of saints/yogis

E. Shree Shyamacharan Lahiri (Lahiri Mahasaya) – 1828–1895

B. Swami Shivananda Saraswati – 1887–1963

A. T. Krishnamacharya – 1888–1989

C. Maharshi Mahesh Yogi – 1918–2008

D. Swami Ram (Swami Rama of the Himalayas) – 1925–1996

So, the correct chronological order is: E, B, A, C, D

43. Arrange according to Shrimadbhagavad Gita

The sequence of enemies of spiritual progress described (esp. Ch. 16 on Daivasura Sampad Vibhaga Yoga):

C. Dambha (hypocrisy)

A. Darpa (arrogance/pride)

E. Abhimaan (ego, self-conceit)

D. Krodha (anger)

B. Agyan (ignorance)

44. Arrange according to Prashnopanishad (six disciples, six questions to Sage Pippalada):

A. Union of Pran and Rai (first question by Sukesha — origin of creation: Prana and Rai)

E. Question of Bhargava (second question — about people and sustenance: how many deities uphold the body)

B. Question of Ashwalayan (third question — origin of Prana)

D. Question of Gargya (fourth question — difference between Jivatma and Paramatma)

C. Question of Satyakama (fifth question — meditation on Om)

So sequence: A, E, B, D, C

45. The Nadabindu Upanisad describes a sequence of inner sounds (matras of Omkara) heard in meditation. The first five are:

C. Ghosini – buzzing sound

D. Vidhunmatra – bell-like

B. Patangini – lute-like

E. Vayuvegini – rushing wind

A. Naamdheya – flute-like resonance

Thus, the correct order is: C, D, B, E, A

46. Arrange according to Yogasutra

The flow of concepts in Patanjali's Yoga Sutras is:

B. Chittavatti – Yoga is defined as cessation of the modifications of mind.

A. Ishwar – Introduction of Ishwar as a special Purusha.

C. Panchaklesha – The five afflictions (Avidya, Asmita, Raga, Dvesha, Abhinivesha).

E. Dharana–Ashtanga Yoga limb of concentration.

D. Chitta Parinama – Transformations of Chitta (Nirodha, Samadhi, Ekagrata, etc.).

47. In the Gheranda Samhita, the Shatkarmas (six purificatory acts) are taught in sequence:

1. Dhauti (internal and external cleansing)
2. Basti (yogic enema)
3. Neti (nasal cleansing)
4. Nauli (abdominal churning)
5. Trataka (gazing)
6. Kapalbhati (frontal cleansing)

Within Dhauti, the subcategories are:

- Antar Dhauti (internal cleansing) → includes Varisara (B)
- Danta Dhauti (teeth cleansing) → includes Dantmool Dhauti (E)
- Hrida Dhauti (chest cleansing) → includes Vaman Dhauti (D)

So, the correct sequence becomes:

1. Varisara (B) – Antar Dhauti
2. Dantmool Dhauti (E) – Danta Dhauti
3. Vaman Dhauti (D) – Hrida Dhauti
4. Trataka (A) – the fifth Shatkarma
5. Vatkarma (C)–Kapalbhati, the sixth Shatkarma

Thus, the proper order is: B, E, D, A, C.

48. In the Hathayogapradipika (1.12–13), Svatmarama describes the ideal environment for Hatha Yoga practice. The yogi should live in solitude, in a hermitage, within a safe and supportive environment. The verse specifies:

D. Good Province (Surajye) – The place should be in a well-administered, peaceful kingdom/region.

C. Religious (Dharmike Dese) – It should be a virtuous and dharmic land where righteousness is upheld.

B. Availability of Donation (Subhiksa) – There should be easy availability of alms or food, ensuring simple sustenance for the yogi.

A. Free from stone and fire (Silagni-jala-varjite) – The immediate environment should be free from rocks, fire hazards, and water disturbances.

E. Silent Place (Ekante Mathikamadhye) – The yogi should stay alone in a quiet hut/hermitage, conducive to seclusion and silence.

Thus, the correct arrangement is: D, C, B, A, E.

49. The process of hearing follows this order:

D. Auricle (Pinna) – Collects sound waves from the environment.

B. Tympanic Membrane (Eardrum) – Vibrates when struck by sound waves.

C. Ossicles (Malleus, Incus, Stapes) – These small bones in the middle ear amplify and transmit the vibrations.

E. Vestibule (Oval window region of the inner ear) – The stapes pushes vibrations into the fluid-filled vestibule.

A. Cochlea – The vibrations travel through cochlear fluid, stimulating hair cells, which then convert mechanical signals into nerve impulses that go to the brain.

So, the correct sequence is: D, B, C, E, A.

50. According to Sigmund Freud's theory of psychosexual development, there are five stages in fixed chronological sequence:

D. Oral Stage (0–1 year) – Infant's pleasure centers on the mouth (sucking, swallowing).

E. Anal Stage (1–3 years) – Pleasure focuses on elimination (toilet training).

B. Phallic Stage (3–6 years) – Focus on genitals; Oedipus/Electra complex arises.

C. Latency Stage (6–12 years) – Sexual feelings are repressed; focus on learning/socialization.

A. Genital Stage (12+ years) – Mature sexual interests develop during puberty.

Thus, the correct sequence is: D, E, B, C, A.

51. In the Gheranda Samhita (Chapter 5, Agrahya Ahara section), a sequence of prohibited foods (Agrahya Ahara – unwholesome foods for yogic practice) is clearly given. Among them are curd, horse gram, wood apple, lemon, and onion.

The order in which they appear is:

E. Curd (Dadhi) – listed early among dairy foods to be avoided.

C. Horse gram (Kulattha) – appears after dairy in the section of legumes/vegetables.

D. Kapitha (Wood apple) – mentioned after legumes and gourds.

B. Lemon (Jambira) – found in the later group of sour fruits.

A. Onion (Lasuna/Palandu) – comes near the end of the prohibited list.

Thus, the correct sequence is: E, C, D, B, A.

52. Correct sequence is:

C. Frontal – Forehead bone (skull, head region).

A. Mandible – Lower jawbone (face, still head region but below the frontal).

B. Scapula – Shoulder blade (upper body).

D. Femur – Thigh bone (longest bone in the leg).

E. Tarsal – Ankle bones (feet).

So, the correct sequence from head to feet is: C, A, B, D, E.

53. Correct order is:

B. Verbal Introduction – Start the lesson with a brief introduction and context.

D. Demonstration – Show the practice/exercise to provide clarity.

A. Salient Points – Highlight the key aspects/ important details while or after demonstrating.

C. Advantages – Explain the benefits of the practice to motivate learners.

E. Question Answer – End with Q&A to clarify doubts.

Thus, the correct order is: B, D, A, C, E.

54. The Siva Samhita has five chapters, and their content flows like this:

C. Philosophical Principles – Chapter 1 deals with Vedantic philosophy, nature of reality, bondage, and liberation.

D. Tattvagyan Prakaran – Chapter 2 discusses the tattvas (principles of creation), cosmology, and knowledge of the body.

A. Four stages of Yoga – Chapter 3 outlines yoga practice, describing four stages (arambha, ghata, paricaya, nispatti).

B. Description of 10 Mudras – Chapter 4 describes the practice of ten mudras, bandhas, and pranayama.

E. Self-realisation – Chapter 5 focuses on meditation, awakening of kundalini, and realization of the Self.

So, the correct sequence is: C, D, A, B, E.

55. From the order in Gheranda Samhita:

- Uddiyana (D) – appears very early in the Mudra section (GS 3.7).
- Mahaveda (E) – described soon after Mahamudra and Mahabandha (GS 3.17).
- Viparitakarani (C) – appears later among higher Mudras (GS 3.32).
- Asvini (B) – described towards the end along with Vajroli etc. (GS 3.55).
- Kaki (A) – appears near the last of the list of Mudras (GS 3.59).

So, the correct sequence is: D, E, C, B, A.

56. According to Samkhya Philosophy, the process of cosmic evolution (Sarga) begins from the primordial matter (Prakrti) and unfolds into twenty-three subsequent principles (Tattvas).

- Mahat (A) – the first product of Prakrti, representing cosmic intelligence.

- Ahankara (C) – evolves from Mahat, representing ego or the sense of individuality.
- Mahabhutas (D) – the five gross elements (earth, water, fire, air, ether) that arise at the final stage of evolution.

Thus, Mahat, Ahankara, and Mahabhutas are all part of the creation process.

However,

- Sattva (B) and Rajas (E) are not created elements; they are two of the three Gunas (Sattva, Rajas, and Tamas) that constitute Prakrti itself.
- These Gunas are eternal, inherent qualities of Prakrti and not products of evolution.

Hence, the principles not included in the creation of elements are Sattva and Rajas.

57. Checking options:

A. Shubheccha – Included in the seven stages.

B. Tanumansa – Included in the seven stages.

C. Ashubheccha – Not included; it means "evil or impure desire," the opposite of Shubheccha.

D. Asattvapatti – Not included; the correct term is Sattvapatti, not Asattvapatti.

E. Sansakti – Not included; it means attachment, which contradicts the stage Asamsakti (detachment).

Hence, Ashubheccha, Asattvapatti, and Sansakti do not come under the seven stages of knowledge.

58. According to the Yoga Vashistha, the conquest of Chitta (mind) — the restless and fluctuating nature of consciousness — is achieved through a combination of spiritual wisdom, right association, and control over desires (Vasanas).

The text emphasizes that the mind (Chitta) is the cause of bondage as well as liberation. When the mind is controlled and purified, liberation (Moksha) is naturally attained. To conquer the mind, Yoga Vashistha prescribes the following methods:

A. Company of saints (Satsanga): Association with wise and holy persons purifies the mind and strengthens detachment from worldly illusions.

C. Avoidance of lust (Vasana): Desires and cravings bind the mind; their removal leads to peace and mastery over Chitta.

E. Attainment of Spirituality: The cultivation of spiritual knowledge and realization (Atma-jñana) leads to stillness and control of the mind.

The text does not advocate extreme fasting (B) or rapid breathing (D) as primary means for conquering Chitta.

Hence, the combination of Satsanga, Vasana-nivrtti, and Atma-jñana is the true method prescribed in the Yoga Vashistha for mastering the mind.

59. According to the Kathopanisad (particularly Chapter 2, Section 18–19), the Atman (Soul) is described as eternal, unborn, undecaying, and indestructible. It is not an effect or a product of anything; rather, it is the ultimate cause and eternal reality. The key characteristics of the Soul as described are:

- It does not take birth (na jayate).
- It does not die (na mriyate).
- It is unborn, eternal, and ancient (ajah nityah sasvato 'yam puranah).
- It is not an effect (A) — meaning it is not produced by any cause.
- It is not a cause (B) in the material sense — because it transcends cause and effect altogether.

Therefore, among the given options, "It is an effect" (A) and "It is a cause" (B) are not characteristics of the Soul.

60. According to the Mundakopanisad (1.1.5–6), Paravidya (Higher Knowledge) is that by which one realizes the imperishable Brahman — described with qualities that negate all sensory and material attributes. The Upanisad characterizes Brahman as:

- Adrsya (B) – Invisible, beyond perception by the senses.
- Agraheya (D) – Incomprehensible, not graspable by the intellect or senses.
- Nitya (E) – Eternal, unchanging, and beyond time.

These qualities show that Brahman is transcendental, beyond physical perception and comprehension.

Hence, the correct combination is Adrsya, Agraheya, and Nitya.

61. According to the Yoga Chudmani Upanisad, the system of Yoga is described in terms of six limbs (Sadanga Yoga) — not the eight limbs (Astanga Yoga) mentioned in the Patañjala Yoga Sutras.

The six limbs of Yoga as per the Yoga Chudamani Upanisad are:

1. Asana - Posture
2. Pranayama - Regulation of breath
3. Pratyahara - Withdrawal of the senses
4. Dharana - Concentration
5. Dhyana - Meditation
6. Samadhi - Absorption or union

Hence, the limbs Yama and Niyama (which appear in Astanga Yoga) are not included here. Additionally, Pranavirodha (restriction of breath) and Asamadhi (non-absorption) are not recognized limbs of Yoga in this Upanisad.

Therefore, the options A. Yama, C. Pranavirodha, and E. Asamadhi do not come under the limbs of Yoga according to the Yoga Chudamani Upanisad.

62. According to the Yoga Sutras of Patañjali (Book III - Vibhuti Pada), Grahitrivisayaka Samadhi refers to deep concentration or absorption related to the triplet of perception — the perceiver (Grahita), the process of perception (Grahana), and the perceived object (Visaya).

Through mastery of this form of Samadhi, a yogi attains Prajña (intuitive wisdom), leading to special psychic or spiritual powers (Siddhis) such as:

- Pratibha (A) - Intuitive or spontaneous knowledge.
- Sravana (C) - Divine hearing.
- Adarsa (E) - Divine vision or clairvoyance.

Thus, the states attained through Grahitrivisayaka Samadhi are Pratibha, Sravana, and Adarsa.

63. According to the Hatharatnavali by Srinivasa Yogi, eight Karmas (Asta Karma) are prescribed as cleansing and preparatory practices essential for purifying the body before engaging in higher stages of yoga. These Karmas remove physical and energetic impurities and promote internal balance.

The text mentions the following as part of the eight Karmas:

A. **Chakri** - A circular abdominal movement similar to Nauli, explicitly mentioned as one of the eight Karmas.

B. **Nauli (Lauliki)** - The churning of the abdominal muscles, essential for internal purification.

C. **Gajkarni (Gajakarani)** - A cleansing practice involving drawing water or air upward through the rectum; listed as one of the eight Karmas.

D. **Mastakbhranti** - A term sometimes used to describe Kapalabhati or Bhastrika-like cleansing of the cranial region; since Kapalabhati is part of the eight Karmas, this is included.

E. **Sankha Praksalana** - Although an important intestinal cleansing technique, it is not listed among the Asta Karmas in Hatharatnavali.

Therefore, the Karmas that belong to the Hatharatnivali's eight-fold cleansing process are Chakri, Nauli, Gajkarni, and Mastakbhranti.

64. According to the Gheranda Samhiti (Chapter 1), the six cleansing techniques known as Shatkarma are:

1. Dhauti - Internal cleansing
2. Basti - Yogic enema
3. Neti - Nasal cleansing
4. Trataka - Gazing practice
5. Nauli - Abdominal churning
6. Kapalabhati - Purification of the skull

Within these, specific subtypes are mentioned.

- **Vatsara (A)** - A type of Dhauti where air is swallowed and expelled, hence part of Shatkarma.
- **Dantmool Dhauti (C)** - A type of Dhauti focusing on cleansing the teeth roots; part of Shatkarma.

- **Sitkrama (D)** - A variation of Kapalabhati involving drawing water through the nose and expelling it through the mouth; part of Shatkarma.
- **Gajkarni (E)** - Though mentioned as a cleansing act in Hatharatnavali, it is not listed as a Shatkarma in Gheranda Samhita.
- **Chakri (B)** - Not part of Shatkarma in Gheranda Samhita.

Thus, the practices that belong to Shatkarma according to Gheranda Samhita are Vatsara, Dantmool Dhauti, and Sitkrama.

65. According to the Hathayogapradipika (Chapter 2), there are two main kinds of Kumbhaka —

1. **Sahita Kumbhaka:** Retention with inhalation and exhalation (Puraka and Rechaka).
2. **Kevala Kumbhaka:** Spontaneous retention without effort, attained after mastering Sahita Kumbhaka.

The text then mentions eight specific Sahita Kumbhakas — Suryabheda, Ujjayi, Sitali, Sitkari, Bhastrika, Bhramari, Murccha, and Plavini.

Here,

- A. Sahit and C. Kewali are categories or stages of Kumbhaka, not part of the eight specific types.
- B. Suryabheda, D. Seetkaari, and E. Plawani are explicitly included among the eight.

Hence, Sahit and Kewali are not counted as the eight specific Kumbhakas.

66. According to the traditions of Goraksanatha, the Nath Sampradaya is divided into twelve main sects (Dvadasa Pantha), each founded by a chief disciple of Guru Goraksanatha. These twelve are commonly recognized across traditional Nath texts and oral lineages.

Among the given options:

A. **Dharmanathi** - Yes, this is one of the twelve principal Nath traditions.

B. **Krishnanathi** - No, this name is not listed among the twelve.

C. **Vairag Panthi** - Yes, this corresponds to the Vairagi Panth, one of the traditional Nath orders.

D. **Yamunanathi** - No, this is not among the twelve Nath Panths.

E. **Dhaj-Panthi** - Yes, also known as Dhwaj Panth, one of the accepted twelve.

Hence, the Krishnanathi and Yamunanathi Panths are not part of the recognized twelve Nath traditions.

67. According to the Brhadaranyaka Upanisad (I.2.3–I.2.4), the Supreme Being (Atman or Brahman), in the process of creation, divided Himself into three fundamental forms — Fire (Agni), Air (Vayu), and Sun (Aditya).

A. **Fire (Agni):** Yes, Fire is the first among the triad formed during the division.

B. **Water (Apah):** Although Water appears earlier in the sequence of creation, it is not part of the final threefold division of the Supreme.

C. **Air (Vayu):** Explicitly mentioned as one of the three divisions.

D. **Sun (Aditya):** Also part of the triad, representing the luminous principle.

E. **Colour (Rupa):** This is symbolic and not part of the threefold division in this specific context.

Thus, the Supreme divided Himself into Fire, Air, and Sun, representing the three elemental essences of existence — energy, motion, and illumination.

68. According to the Svetasvatara Upanisad (Chapter 2, Verse 10), certain environmental conditions are prescribed as suitable for meditation (Dhyana). The verse recommends choosing a place that is:

- Free from stones, fire, and sand (A) - ensuring safety and comfort.
- Soothing for eyes (B) - a serene and visually calm environment.
- Purified from all impurities (E) - a clean and sanctified spot conducive to focus and inner stillness.

It does not suggest meditating in water (C) or necessarily on a tiger's skin (D), which is mentioned in other yoga texts like the Hathayogapradipika, but not in the Svetasvatara Upanisad.

Hence, the most appropriate environment for Dhyana according to this Upanisad is one that is pure, visually pleasant, and free from disturbances.

69. According to the Hatha Yoga Pradipika (Chapter 1, Verses 33–41), only 15 asanas are mentioned. These include Siddhasana, Padmasana, Simhasana, Bhadrasana, Muktasana, Mayurasana, Kukkutasana, Uttanakurmasana, Dhanurasana, Matsyendrasana, Pascimottanasana, Mayurasana, Savasana, etc.

Let's analyze each option:

A. **Siddhasana:** Mentioned — one of the most important asanas.

B. Bakasana: Not mentioned in Hatha Yoga Pradipika.

C. Matsyasana: Not mentioned; Matsyendrasana (different) is included, not Matsyasana.

D. Virabhadrasana: Not mentioned; this asana appears in modern yoga texts.

E. Dhanurasana: Mentioned in Hatha Yoga Pradipika (1.27).

Hence, Bakasana, Matsyasana, and Virabhadrasana are not mentioned in the Hatha Yoga Pradipika.

70. According to Carl Jung, personality develops through several stages of life, reflecting the process of individuation (the unfolding of the self). The main stages are:

A. **Childhood:** The stage of unconscious existence and ego formation.

C. **Young Adulthood:** A stage of adaptation to external life — career, relationships, social responsibilities.

D. **Middle Age:** A period of inner transformation and self-realization (turning inward).

E. **Maturity:** The stage of integration of the conscious and unconscious — true individuation.

B. **Early Childhood:** Not treated as a separate stage in Jung's framework (unlike Freud's model).

Thus, the stages of personality development according to Jung are Childhood, Young Adulthood, and Middle Age.

71. In human anatomy, joints (articulations) are classified based on their structure and movement type. Among the given options:

A. **Gliding joint:** Yes, it is a type of synovial joint allowing sliding movements (e.g., between carpal bones).

B. **Inversion:** Not a joint; it is a movement of the foot.

C. **Condylar joint:** Yes, a biaxial synovial joint (e.g., wrist joint).

D. **Protraction:** Also a movement (forward movement of jaw or shoulder).

E. **Saddle joint:** Yes, a type of synovial joint allowing angular movement (e.g., thumb joint).

Therefore, the types of joints are Gliding, Condylar, and Saddle.

72. The factors that have ill effects on mental and emotional health are those that disturb clarity, balance, and restraint of the mind, according to Yogic philosophy and Patanjali's teachings.

A. **Pramad (negligence or carelessness):** Causes dullness and imbalance — harmful.

B. **Karuna (compassion):** A positive quality; improves emotional health.

C. **Bhranti Darshan (false perception):** Causes delusion and confusion — harmful.

D. **Avirati (non-restraint or indulgence):** Leads to attachment and restlessness — harmful.

E. **Mudita (joy in others' happiness):** A positive emotion that supports mental well-being.

Hence, the qualities that negatively affect mental and emotional health are Pramad, Bhranti Darshan, and Avirati.

73. The types of Yogic Breathing (Pranayamic Breathing) are usually classified based on the part of the respiratory system that predominates in the breathing process. The main types are:

B. **Abdominal Breathing:** Involves diaphragmatic movement; improves oxygen exchange and relaxation.

C. **Thoracic Breathing:** Involves expansion of the rib cage; increases lung capacity.

E. **Thoraco-abdominal Breathing:** A combination of thoracic and abdominal movements — the most balanced and efficient form of yogic breathing.

A. Deep Breathing and D. General Breathing are descriptive terms, not distinct yogic types.

74. The advantages of a written lesson plan are linked to clarity, structure, and confidence in teaching. Let's analyze:

A. **It helps the teacher to organize his thinking:** True — provides structure and flow.

B. **It should be prepared shortly before use:** Incorrect — proper planning requires adequate time.

C. **It increases the teacher's confidence:** True — allows smooth and assured delivery.

D. **It serves as an aid for future plans:** True — provides a record for improvement or reuse.

E. **It should be specific and detailed:** While true in general, it describes a quality of a good plan, not an advantage per se.

Hence, the main advantages are A, C, and D.

75. Checking options:

A. **To sit in Paschimottanasana:** Incorrect — Tadagi Mudra is done in Dandasana, not Paschimottanasana.

B. **Hair never becomes grey:** Traditional benefit mentioned in yogic texts.

C. **Wrinkles do not appear:** Claimed anti-aging effect.

D. **Overcomes old age:** Symbolic of slowing aging and maintaining vitality.

E. **Overcomes death:** Incorrect — yoga seeks liberation, not physical immortality.

Hence, A, E Only.

76. Matching options:

A. **Purusharth – IV (Four):** The four Purusharthas are Dharma, Artha, Kama, and Moksha — the four aims of human life.

B. **Goraksha Samhita – I (Hathayoga):** This text is one of the foundational scriptures of Hathayoga, attributed to Guru Gorakshanath.

C. **Trayee – II (Veda):** The term Trayee refers to the threefold Vedas — Rig, Yajur, and Sama — symbolizing scriptural wisdom.

D. **Ramayana – III (Aranyakanda):** Aranyakanda is one of the seven sections (Kandas) of the Ramayana.

Hence, correct matching is: A-IV, B-I, C-II, D-III.

77. According to Siddha-Siddhanta Paddhati of Gorakshanath, the microcosm (body) is compared to the macrocosm (universe), where human body parts correspond to cosmic regions and sacred sites:

- A. Sadacharpalana – III (Brahmana): Upholding good conduct (Sadachara) represents the Brahmana quality — purity, discipline, and moral foundation.
- B. Skin – IV (Kraunchdweep): The skin corresponds to Kraunchdweep, one of the mythical islands described in Yogic cosmology.
- C. Urine – II (Ksharsamudra): Urine is compared to Ksharsamudra, the ocean of alkaline essence.
- D. Forehead – I (Shreeshail): The forehead represents Shreeshail, a sacred spiritual center or mountain symbolizing higher consciousness.

Hence, correct matching is A-III, B-IV, C-II, D-I.

78. According to the Mandukya Upanisad, the states of consciousness and their corresponding aspects are clearly defined as follows:

A. **Vaisvanara** – Represents the Waking state (Jagrat Sthana), described as having Saptanga (seven limbs) and Ekonavimsati Mukha (19 mouths). → **III. Saptanga**

B. **Prajña** – Represents the Deep Sleep state (Susupti), referred to as the Third (Trtiya Pada) stage of consciousness. → **I. Third**

C. **Antahprajña** – Represents the Dream state (Svapna), illuminated by the inner light of Tejas. → **IV. Tejas**

D. **Jagrat Sthana** – The waking plane of consciousness corresponds to the first sound of Om, A-kara. → **II. Akaar**

Hence, the correct matching is A–III, B–I, C–IV, D–II

79. According to the Srimad Bhagavad Gita, the following associations can be made:

- **A. Purusa – III (Chetan):** The Purusa is the conscious principle or sentient being, distinct from Prakrti (matter).
- **B. Katu – I (Rajas):** Foods that are Katu (pungent, bitter, sour) are associated with Rajasic qualities (stimulating and restless).

- **C. Snigdha – II (Sattvik):** Snigdha (unctuous, smooth, pleasant) foods are Sattvik, promoting clarity and calmness.
- **D. Tapa – IV (Svadhyaya):** In the context of Tapas (austerity), the Gita mentions Svadhyaya (self-study) as part of spiritual discipline.

Hence, the correct matching is: A–III, B–I, C–II, D–IV

80. According to the Nadabindu Upanisad, the components of Om (Pranava) are symbolically related to different parts of a bird:

- **A. Akaar – II (Daksina Paksa):** Represents the right wing (southern side).
- **B. Ukaar – I (Uttara Paksa):** Represents the left wing (northern side).
- **C. Makaar – III (Puccha):** Represents the tail of the bird.
- **D. Ardhamatra – IV (Mastaka):** Represents the head (the supreme consciousness aspect).

Hence, the correct matching is A–II, B–I, C–III, D–IV

81. According to Yoga Darsana (Patañjali Yoga Sutras):

- **A. Vikshepsahbhuvah – III (Daurmanasya):** Distractions of the mind arise from grief, despair, laziness, etc.
- **B. Chittaprasadanam – I (Punyatma):** Calmness of mind comes from being virtuous and pure (Punya).
- **C. Pramana – IV (Sabda/Agama):** Valid knowledge arises from direct perception, inference, and verbal testimony (Sabda or Agama).
- **D. Karmasaya – II (Bhoga):** The storehouse of karmas leads to experience (Bhoga).

Hence, the correct matching is A–III, B–I, C–IV, D–II

82. According to Siddha-Siddhanta Paddhati of Gorakshanatha:

- **A. Matsarya – IV (Maya):** Jealousy arises due to Maya (illusion).
- **B. Udyoga – III (Kriya):** Effort or activity corresponds to Kriya (action).
- **C. Asa – I (Prakrti):** Desire originates from Prakrti (nature).
- **D. Para – II (Vak):** Para Vak is the supreme, subtle form of speech.

Hence, the correct matching is A–IV, B–III, C–I, D–II

83. According to Hatha Yoga texts, various akasas (spaces or inner centers) are associated with different levels of consciousness and subtle locations in the body:

- **A. Hridyakas – III (Sunya):** The heart-space represents Sunya (the inner void).
- **B. Visuddhyakas – II (Atisunya):** The throat-space or Visuddhi Chakra is described as Atisunya (beyond void).
- **C. Bhrumadhyakas – I (Mahasunya):** The space between the eyebrows, representing the Mahasunya (great void).
- **D. Kanthasthan – IV (Madhyachakra):** The region of the throat corresponds to Madhya Chakra.

Hence, the correct matching is A–III, B–II, C–I, D–IV

84. Phytochemicals are natural compounds that give vegetables their distinctive colors and health benefits:

- **A. Orange-colored vegetables – III (Beta-carotene):** Found in carrots, pumpkin, etc.
- **B. Red-colored vegetables – I (Lycopene):** Found in tomatoes and red peppers.
- **C. Deep red-colored vegetables – II (Betalains):** Found in beetroot.
- **D. Blue & purple-colored vegetables – IV (Anthocyanins):** Found in eggplant, purple cabbage, berries.

Hence, the correct matching is A–III, B–I, C–II, D–IV

85. According to the concept of a Yogic diet, foods are classified based on their effect on the body and mind:

- **A. Snigdha – II (Sattvik):** Unctuous and nourishing foods are considered Sattvik, promoting calmness and balance.

- **B. Til – I (Apathya):** Sesame seeds are heavy and heat-producing, hence Apathya (not suitable) in excess for yogic practice.
- **C. Sauth – IV (Pathya):** Dry ginger aids digestion and is beneficial, thus Pathya (wholesome).
- **D. Amal Ras – III (Rajsik):** Sour foods stimulate the senses and are classified as Rajsik.

Hence, correct matching is A–II, B–I, C–IV, D–III.

86. According to the endocrine glands and their respective hormones:

- **A. Adrenal Medulla – III (Epinephrine):** The adrenal medulla secretes epinephrine and norepinephrine, responsible for the fight-or-flight response.
- **B. Pituitary Gland – IV (Oxytocin):** The posterior pituitary secretes oxytocin, which plays a role in childbirth and lactation.
- **C. Adrenal Cortex – I (Cortisol):** The adrenal cortex secretes cortisol, a glucocorticoid hormone regulating metabolism and stress response.
- **D. Ovaries – II (Estrogen):** The ovaries produce estrogen, the main female sex hormone.

Hence, correct matching is A–III, B–IV, C–I, D–II.

87. According to the types of questions and examples:

- **A. Introductory Question – IV (Why do you want health?):** Opens discussion or topic introduction.
- **B. Thought-provoking Question – III (What is the relationship of muscular system and doing Asana?):** Stimulates deeper reflection.
- **C. Question of Comprehension – II (What are the principles of Pranayama?):** Tests understanding of learned material.
- **D. Comparison Question – I (What are the differences between Asana and Pranayama?):** Seeks comparison between two topics.

Hence, correct matching is A–IV, B–III, C–II, D–I.

88. According to Leshya Dhyan (color meditation centers):

- **A. Center of Enlightenment (Jyoti Kendra) – III. White Colour:** Represents tranquility, purity, and the calming of anger and agitation.
- **B. Center of Bliss (Anand Kendra) – I. Green Colour:** Symbolizes peace and freedom from negative attitudes.
- **C. Center of Purification (Vishuddhi Kendra) – II. Blue Colour:** Aids in purification and self-control of desires and impulses.
- **D. Eyebrow Center (Darshan Kendra) – IV. Pink Colour:** Associated with intuition and inner awakening.

Hence, correct matching is A–III, B–I, C–II, D–IV.

89. According to Gheranda Samhita, the following relationships exist between the practices (limbs) and their outcomes:

- **A. Shodhan (Purification) — II. Shatkarma:** The six cleansing acts purify the body and mind.
- **B. Sthairya (Steadiness) — III. Mudra:** The practice of mudras develops firmness and control.
- **C. Laghav (Lightness) — IV. Pranayama:** Breath control brings lightness and vitality.
- **D. Dhairya (Patience/Calmness) — I. Pratyahara:** Sense withdrawal leads to mental calmness and endurance.

Hence, correct matching is A–II, B–III, C–IV, D–I.

90. According to the anatomy and physiology of the human eye:

- **A. Rhodopsin – II (Opsin):** Rhodopsin is formed by opsin and retinal, responsible for vision in dim light.
- **B. Oculomotor Muscles – III (6):** There are six oculomotor muscles controlling eye movement.
- **C. Image – IV (Retina):** Image formation occurs on the retina.
- **D. Cones – I (3):** There are three types of cones for color vision (red, green, blue).

Hence, correct matching is A–II, B–III, C–IV, D–I.

91. Breathing is unique because it can be both voluntary (under conscious control) and involuntary (automatic). The passage clearly states that the respiratory system "has the special feature that it is both voluntary and involuntary," meaning we can consciously alter our breath (like during Pranayama), but it also continues automatically when we are not paying attention.

92. According to the passage, the hypothalamus, located above the midbrain, acts as the "master of the lower brain" and governs all autonomic functions of the body. It connects the voluntary and involuntary systems and controls overall body physiology through the Autonomic Nervous System and Endocrine System. Therefore, it is the brain center that regulates the functions even of the higher creative regions indirectly.

93. Increased breathing rate while running is generally an involuntary physiological response to increased oxygen demand, but even here, higher brain centers (hypothalamus and medulla) are involved, adjusting respiration according to body activity.

On the other hand, holding the breath underwater is an example of completely voluntary control, where the person voluntarily stops or regulates the breathing process.

Thus, both situations involve voluntary control of respiration – one indirect (activity-dependent adjustment) and the other direct (voluntary cessation).

94. The hypothalamus, located above the midbrain, is described as the "master of the lower brain," controlling all autonomic functions through the Autonomic Nervous System (ANS) and Endocrine System. It regulates functions like heartbeat, temperature, and hormones.

95. Through Pranayama, one can consciously control breathing patterns, thus allowing the voluntary nervous system to influence and even override the autonomic (involuntary) control normally managed by the hypothalamus. This leads to better regulation of body and mind.

96. The passage mentions that "from the conjunction of this pair the Omkara is produced, just as the union of male and female fulfills each other's desires."

Hence, Omkara is associated with fulfilling desires.

97. Recitation of Veda mantra has been initiated with –

The passage clearly states, "By saying 'OM' the Hotr priest begins his recitation and the Udgata priest begins the Sama chant."

Therefore, Vedic recitation starts with OM.

98. Which one is the fifth rasa as per the given paragraph?

The sequence of essences is: Earth → Water → Plants → Mann → Speech (Vaak) → Sama → Udgith.

Thus, the fifth rasa is Vaak (Speech).

99. Which pair constitutes Udgeetha?

The passage explains: "Speech is the Rik, prana is the Sama... from the conjunction of this pair the Omkara (Udgitha) is produced."

Hence, Vaak and Prana form Udgitha.

100. Omkar is the rasa of:

According to the text, "The essence of speech is Sama. The essence of Sama is Udgith (Om)."

Therefore, Omkar is the rasa (essence) of Sama.

Previous Years' Paper

National Testing Agency (NTA)

UGC-NET Junior Research Fellowship & Assistant Professor Eligibility Exam

YOGA, JANUARY-2025

(Exam held on 07-01-2025)

PAPER-II

1. According to Sankhya Darshan which Karika of Sankhya Karika consists of reasons (logics) for the siddhi of Purusha.

1. Fifteenth
2. Sixteenth
3. Seventeenth
4. Eighteenth

2. "Svatmanyavasthanam Mokshah" means of Atman (goal) in its true form is Moksha-has been mentioned in following book (text):

1. Sankhya Karika
2. Taittiriyopanishad Shankar Bhasya
3. Nyaya Sutra
4. Yoga Sutra

3. *Mudit Manasi Aayasu Chale Ban Matu Pita Ko. Dharam Dhurandar Dheerdhur gun-seel-jita ko.*

has been mentioned in:

1. Beejak   2. Sakhi
3. Vinay Patrika   4. Dohawali

4. 'Marganamastangiko Shrestha': This sentence finds mention in which of the Buddhist Book.

1. Dhammapada
2. Madhyamikkarikavritti
3. Mahanidansutra
4. Abhikosha

5. According to Chhandogya Upanishad, which of the following worship by Asuras' in the form of udgeeth could not make them free of sins?

1. Mana (Mind)
2. Pramukh Prana (Main Prana)
3. Srotra (Ear)
4. Vani (Speech)

6. The exact reference of 'Purusoyamyev Sa Yoayamatmedamamritamidam Brahmeda Sarvam' is:

1. Brihdaranyak Upanishad 2 |2 |1
2. Brihdaranyak Upanishad 2 |3 |2
3. Brihdaranyak Upanishad 3 |4 |2
4. Brihdaranyak Upanishad 2 |5 |2

7. According to Brihdaranyak Upanishad, the sixteenth phase (Solahawi kala) is:

1. Mana (Mind)
2. Dhan (Wealth)
3. Atma (Soul)
4. Prana

8. According to Yoga Vashistha, the fourth stage among seven stages of knowledge enabling self realization is:

1. Asamsakti
2. Padarthabhavini
3. Turyaga
4. Satvapatti

9. Who was first to receive the knowledge of Vedas by Parmatma according to Shwetashwatar Upanishad?

1. Indra 2. Rudra
3. Vishnu 4. Brahma

10. Whom should we meditate upon while doing Rechak according to Dhyan Bindu Upanishad?

1. Vishnu 2. Shiva
3. Brahma 4. Surya

11. According to Yogachudamanyupnishad which of the following remains intact in the body even after death.

1. Chitta
2. Krikal
3. Dhananjay
4. Indriyan (Sense organ)

12. According to Nadbindu Upnishad, which of the following loka is attained in the eleventh matra of omkar?

1. Brahm Lok 2. Mahah Lok
3. Tapo Lok 4. Rudra Lok

13. 'Sarvarthtaikagratayoh Kshyodayau' is which parinam of chitta?

1. Ekagrata Parinam
2. Nirodh Parinam
3. Samadhi Parinam
4. Lakshan Parinam

14. Where is the description of Mahavrata in Yogasutra found?

1. 2/29 2. 2/31
3. 2/32 4. 2/33

15. According to Patanjal Yogasutra, the following is attained in the purest stage of Nirvichar Samadhi.

1. Control on abstract subjects
2. Control on Trigunatmak Prakriti (Nature having three qualities)
3. Adhyatm Prasad
4. Attainment of Sabeej Samadhi

16. According to Yogasutra how many main types (categories) of Vitark are there?

1. Five 2. Three
3. Two 4. Seven

17. In which chapter of Vasisth Samhita has Dharana been described?

1. First 2. Second
3. Third 4. Fourth

18. From which of the following text has below shloka been extracted?

'Urdhuvadho Bhramate Yadvat Ghatiyantram Gavam Vashat.

Tadvat Karmvashajjivo Bhramate Janmmrityubhih'.

1. Hathyoga Pradipika
2. Yoga Bija
3. Gherand Samhita
4. Shiv Samhita

19. Which Shloka and which updesha of Hatha Pradipika has the statement 'Manomani state is the only state'?

1. 1/60 2. 2/55
3. 3/53 4. 4/72

20. The nine types of Kumbhak have been described in which of the following texts?

1. Hatha Pradipika
2. Gherand Samhita
3. Hatha Ratnavali
4. Yoga Bija

21. Who is the founder of Stimulus-Organism Response model (S-O-R model) of psychology?

1. Skinner 2. Thorndike
3. Kerlinger 4. R.S. Woodworth

22. The food groups which favour slow release of sugar into small intestine and its absorption into blood are known as:

1. Low G.I. foods
2. Medium G.I. foods
3. High G.I. foods
4. Nil G.I. foods

23. The structure in the muscular tissues which is responsible for the contraction of muscles is:

1. Acetylcholine
2. Actin-Myosin Filaments
3. Tendons
4. Neuromuscular Junction

24. The types of Personality which Friedman and Rosenman described after their experiments on the personality traits and coronary Heart disease are:

1. Introvert-Extrovert
2. Pyknic-Asthenic-Athletic-Dysplastic
3. Type A-Type B
4. Endomorphy-Mesomorphy-Ectomorphy

25. Rasya, Snigdha, Sthira are the characteristics of what type of diet according to Shrimad Bhagwad Gita?

1. Satwik Diet only
2. Rajsik Diet only
3. Tamsik Diet only
4. Satwik and Rajsik Diet Both

26. Purification of which chakra results in sharpness of hearing power through ears and mind?

1. Ajna Chakra
2. Vishuddhi Chakra
3. Manipura Chakra
4. Swadhishthana Chakra

27. Which Chakra acts as the control center for distribution of Prana?

1. Mooladhara Chakra
2. Manipura Chakra
3. Vishudddhi Chakra
4. Ajna Chakra

28. Which of the following Chakra is associated with the symbol of "KALPATARU":

1. Mooladhara Chakra
2. Manipura Chakra
3. Anahata Chakra
4. Swadhishthana Chakra

29. Which type of ulcer occurs in the wall of first part of small intestine?

1. Gastric Ulcer
2. Jejenum Ulcer
3. Duodenal Ulcer
4. Perineal Ulcer

30. Which yogic mudra is recommended for hemorrhoids?

1. Pashinee Mudra
2. Ashwini Mudra
3. Vipareet Karni
4. Prana Mudra

31. Practice of Nadi Shodan pranayama along with Jalandhara and Moola bandh, antar and bahir Kumbhaka is recommended for:

1. Hemorrhoids 2. Colitis
3. Heartburn 4. Tonsillitis

32. Recommended meditation practice for constipation.

1. Antar Mouna
2. Ahata-anahata Sadhana
3. Swas-Prasvas sadhana
4. Kaya Sthairayam

33. According to 'Teaching Methods for Yogic Practices' Book. Yama and Niyama are also known as:

1. Culture training practices
2. Emotion training practices
3. Attitude training practices
4. Perception training practices

34. Which objective is emphasized by every school of yoga?

1. Improve understanding of yoga
2. Spread different yoga practices for health
3. Deal with mind directly
4. Highest level of integration through the control of modification of mind

35. Which practice does not have an exhalatory retention phase:

1. Uddiyana 2. Agnisara
3. Nauli 4. Kapalabhati

36. According to 'Teaching Methods for Yoga Practices' Book, Social Scientists Theory is covered by:

1. Sources of teaching methods
2. Means of teaching
3. Art and science
4. Teaching methods

37. In Danta Dhauti, one should rub the root of teeth with the extract of:

1. Hariddandam
2. Cane Plant
3. Stalk of Plantain
4. Khadira Plant

38. Agnisar Kriya is not recommended for people suffering from:

1. Poor appetite
2. Dull and depressive
3. Low blood pressure
4. Hyperthyrodism

39. Most appropriate Mudra for inducing the state of Pratyahara:

1. Kaki mudra
2. Pashini Mudra
3. Shanmukhi mudra
4. Bhoochari mudra

40. From the following which one is the variation of Moolabandasana:

1. Bhadrasana
2. Brahmacharyasana
3. Vrischikasana
4. Lolasana

41. Arrange the parts of Astang Marg of Buddhists in sequence.

A. Samyak Vyayam
B. Samyak Smriti
C. Samyak Karm
D. Samyak Vak
E. Samyak Sankalp

Choose the **correct** answer from the options given below:

1. D, C, B, A, E
2. E, D, C, A. B
3. A, B, D, E, C
4. C, A, B, D, E

42. Sequence the five Avayavas of Nyaya Darshan.

A. Hetu
B. Upanay
C. Udaharan
D. Pratijna
E. Nigaman

Choose the **correct** answer from the options given below:

1. A, C, D, B, E
2. D, A, C, B, E
3. B, C, D, E, A
4. C, B, D, A, E

43. According to Bhagavad Gita, arrange the following in sequence on the basis of Sristi Chakra and Yajna.

A. Yajna
B. Vihit Karma (Prescribed Duty)
C. Sampoorna Prani (All Creatures)
D. Anna ki utpatti (origin of gram)
E. Vrishti

Choose the **correct** answer from the options given below:

1. A, B, C, E, D
2. B, A, E, D, C
3. B, C, D, E, A
4. C, D, E, B, A

44. Arrange the Udgeeth Upasana by dieties in sequence as per Chhandogya upanishad:

A. Chakshu roop ki (of eyes form)
B. Nasika sttit Prana roop ki (of Prana reform situated in nose)
C. Vani roop ki (of tongue form)
D. Mana roop ki (of mind form)
E. Srotra roop ki (of ear form)

Choose the **correct** answer from the options given below:

1. B, A, C, D, E
2. B, C, A, E, D
3. A, C, B, D, E
4. C, A, B, E, D

45. Arrange the Chakras in order according to Yograjopnishad.

A. Brahmarandha Chakra
B. Vyoma Chakra
C. Taluka Chakra
D. Kanth Chakra
E. Bhu Chakra

Choose the **correct** answer from the options given below:

1. E, A, B, D, C
2. D, C, E, A, B
3. A, B, C, D, E
4. C, E, B, A, D

46. According to Patanjal Yogsutra, arrange inner purification in sequence:

A. Concentration of Chitta
B. Purification of Antahkaran (inner-self)
C. Ability of self-realization
D. Happiness (joy) in mind
E. Control over senses

Choose the **correct** answer from the options given below:

1. A, B, D, C, E
2. B, D, A, E, C
3. C, D, B, A, E
4. D, E, B, C, A

47. Arrange in order the Niyamas as described in shloka of Vashisth Samhita.

A. Santosh　　B. Ishwar pujan
C. Astikta　　D. Daan
E. Lajja

Choose the **correct** answer from the options given below:

1. A, C, D, E, B
2. A, C, D, B, E
3. B, D, C, E, A
4. C, D, B, A, E

48. Arrange the following Mudras in order according to the shloka mentioned in Hatha Pradipika:

A. Moola Bandh
B. Uddiyan Bandh
C. Vajroli
D. Maha Bandh
E. Mahavedh

Choose the **correct** answer from the options given below:

1. D, E, B, A, C
2. A, B, D. E, C
3. B, C, E, D, A
4. A, E, B, C, D

49. Choose the correct sequence of events with reference to the conducting system of the heart.

A. Stimulus reaches AV node and initiates atrial contraction
B. Completion of atrial contraction and initiation of ventricular contraction
C. Initiation of SA node activity
D. Impulses reaches to ventricular myocardium through purkinje fibres
E. Spread of impulses through purkinje fibres on right ventricle

Choose the **correct** answer from the options given below:

1. A, E, D, C, B
2. D, C, A, E, B
3. C, D, A, B, E
4. C, A, E, D, B

50. Arrange the unhealthy non-recommended food items according to Hatha Pradipika shloka:

A. Asfoetida　　B. Green vegetable
C. Curd　　D. Garlic
E. Mustard

Choose the **correct** answer from the options given below:

1. B, C, A, E, D
2. B, E, C, A, D
3. A, B, D, C, D
4. C, A, B, D, E

51. Arrange the recommended practices if a person has acute asthmatic attack progression.

A. Jalaneti and Kapalabhati
B. Om Chanting
C. Laghoo Shankhaprakshalana
D. Kunjal Kriya
E. Pranayama

Choose the **correct** answer from the options given below:

1. C, D, A, E, B
2. B, E, A, D, C
3. A, D, C, E, B
4. E, C, B, A, D

52. Arrange the sequence of purification areas to the be done by cleansing practice according to book 'Teaching Methods for Yogic Practices'.

A. Kapal B. Grasani
C. Mouth D. Stomach
E. Nose

Choose the **correct** answer from the options given below:

1. B, C, D, E, A
2. C, D, B, A, E
3. E, B, C, A, D
4. A, C, D, B, E

53. Choose the correct sequence of muscle movements during a normal inhalation process.

A. Rectus abdominis
B. Short inter costal muscles
C. External inter costal muscles
D. Internal inter costal muscles
E. Abdominal muscles

Choose the **correct** answer from the options given below:

1. B, C, D, E, A
2. D, C, B, E, A
3. D, B, C, E, A
4. A, E, B, D, C

54. The following is included in seven stages of knowledge in Yoga Vashistha.

A. Vivek B. Subhechha
C. Titiksha D. Vicharana
E. Tanumanasa

Choose the **correct** answer from the options given below:

1. A, B, C only 2. B, C, D only
3. C, D, E only 4. B, D, E only

55. Triratnas of Buddhists from the following are:

A. Samyak Darshan
B. Prajna
C. Sheel
D. Samyak Jnana
E. Samadhi

Choose the correct answer from the options given below:

1. B, C, E only 2. A, B, C only
3. C, A, D only 4. D, E, A only

56. According to Bhagavad Gita, the following is not the lakshan (attribute) of Tamas Ahara (food).

A. Lavanyukt (Salty)
B. Amedhyam
C. Ruksha
D. Teekshna
E. Paryushitama

Choose the **correct** answer from the options given below:

1. A, B, C only
2. A, C, D only
3. B, C, E only
4. C, D, E only

57. According to Bhagavad Gita, the karma (duty) of Kshatriya is not:

A. Damah B. Tejah
C. Dhritih D. Arjavam
E. Vijnanam

Choose the **correct** answer from the options given below:

1. A, B, C only 2. B, C, D only
3. A, D, E only 4. C, D, E only

58. The sadhak reaches to which of the following states by practising uttam pranayama according to Trishikhbrahmanopanishad:

A. Alpa Nidra
B. Laghu Sharir
C. Complete elimination of sins
D. Alpahari
E. Elimination of all diseases

Choose the **correct** answer from the options given below:

1. A, B, D only
2. B, D, E only
3. B, C, E only
4. A, C, E only

59. What are the limbs of Yoga according to Dhyan Bindu Upnishad?

A. Pranayama B. Shathkarma
C. Yama D. Dharana
E. Samadhi

Choose the **correct** answer from the options given below:

1. A, B, C only 2. B, C, D only
3. D, C, E only 4. A, D, E only

60. According to Yogasutra, describe the stages of Samyama for Indriya Jaya (Senses conquering) are:

A. Asmita B. Manojavitwa
C. Grahan D. Vikaranbhav
E. Anvava

Choose the **correct** answer from the options given below:

1. C, D, E only 2. B, C, D only
3. A, C, E only 4. A, D, E only

61. According to Yogasutra, the attributes of Vivek Jnana is ....

A. Tarakam
B. Pradhanjaya
C. Sarvathavishayam
D. Akramam
E. Antanvachhedat

Choose the **correct** answer from the options given below:

1. A, B, E only 2. A, C, D only
3. B, D, E only 4. C, D, E only

62. What are the benefits of Neti karm as described in Gherand Samhita?

A. Increasing of Appetite
B. Eradication of Cough
C. Cleanliness of Nadis
D. Khechari Siddhi
E. Handsome like cupid

Choose the **correct** answer from the options given below:

1. A, D only 2. B, D only
3. C, E only 4. A, E only

63. What are the benefits of rubbing the sweat on body generated out of efforts done in pranayam as described in Hathyoga Pradipika.

A. Sthirta B. Dridhta
C. Dhirta D. Laghuta
E. Shodhan

Choose the **correct** answer from the options given below:

1. A, E only 2. A, C only
3. C, E only 4. B, D only

64. Choose the correct option with reference to the body tissues.

A. Tendon connects bone to bone
B. Epithelial tissues cover body surface and inner cavities
C. Smooth muscle tissues is present in the heart
D. Blood and lymph are connective tissues with distinctive collection of cells
E. A Neuron or Nerve tissue is **made up** of cell body and axon

Choose the **correct** answer from the options given below:

1. A and C only
2. D and E only
3. B and D only
4. A and E only

65. According to Sigmund Freud, the biological component of Personality structure or Id can be identified by:

A. It is determined by pleasure principle
B. It is considered as the executive branch
C. It is controlled by reality principle
D. It is ethical branch of personality
E. It is absolutely unconscious

Choose the **correct** answer from the options given below:

1. A and E only
2. B and E only
3. C and A only
4. C and D only

66. According to WHO, the quality of life results from factors which determine:-

A. Comfort in the physical environment and health
B. Freedom of expression and action
C. Longevity of life
D. High paying jobs
E. Intellectual educational and social attainment

Choose the **correct** answer from the options given below:

1. A, D, C only
2. B, D, C only
3. A, B, E only
4. C, D, E only

67. According to Hatha Pradipika which of the following is prohibited for health improvement:

A. More sour B. Shashtik
C. More salty D. Re-heated food
E. Prescribed Diet

Choose the **correct** answer from the options given below:

1. A, D, E only
2. A, C, D only
3. B, C, E only
4. D, C, E only

68. The symptoms of thyrotoxicosis include:

A. Tremulous
B. Hysterical
C. Hoarseness
D. Rapid shallow respiration
E. Slowing of movement

Choose the **correct** answer from the options given below:

1. A, C, E only
2. B, D, E only
3. A, B, D only
4. B, C, E only

69. Anti-inflammatory Nutrients include:

A. Quercetin B. Vitamin A
C. B-Complex D. Omega 3 fatty acid
E. Potassium

Choose the **correct** answer from the options given below:

1. A, C, D only
2. B, D, E only
3. C, D, E only
4. B. C, E only

70. What is required in oral teaching?

A. Observation method of teaching
B. Recitation
C. Cultivation of good memory
D. One to one basis teaching
E. Demonstration

Choose the **correct** answer from the options given below:

1. B and C only
2. A and B only
3. C and E only
4. B and D only

71. Select the most specific benefits of Shat Kriya:

A. Control over static reflex
B. Control over different reflexes
C. Increase the adaptability of tissues formation
D. Reduce the adaptability of tissue formation
E. Establish Psychosomatic balance

Choose the **correct** answer from the options given below:

1. B, C, E only 2. A, B, D only
3. B, D, E only 4. A, C, D only

72. Fundamental methods of teaching are:

A. Direction-responsive method
B. Individual Direction method
C. Environment
D. Project method
E. Correction method

Choose the **correct** answer from the options given below:

1. A, B, C only
2. A, B, D only
3. B, C, D only
4. C, D, E only

73. According to Siddh Siddhanta Padhahati, Shakti Panchak consists of:

A. Iccha B. Vasana
C. Maya D. Nischaya
E. Yak

Choose the **correct** answer from the options given below:

1. B, D, E only
2. A, C, E only
3. B, C, E only
4. A, D, E only

74. Vasa-dhauti cures which of the following diseases:

A. Gulma B. Jvara
C. Pliha Roga D. Kosthakathinya
E. Kustha

Choose the **correct** answer from the options given below:

1. A, B, C, E only
2. A, B, D, E only
3. B, C, D, E only
4. A, C, D, E only

75. Match the definitions with books

List-I	List-II
A. Kathopanishad	I. Yoga is union of Shiva and Shakti
B. Bhagvad Gita	II. The way of calming 'mana' (mind) is yoga
C. Mahopanishad	III. Concentrated state of senses is yoga
D. Shiva Samhita	IV. Separation of the association of miseries is yoga

Choose the **correct** answer from the options given below:

1. A-III, B-IV, C-II D-I
2. A-II, B-I, C-III, D-IV
3. A-IV, B-III, C-I, D-II
4. A-I, B-II, C-III, D-IV

76. Match the List-I with List-II according to Bhagvat Gita:

List-I	List-II
A. Gunebhyashch param vetti	I. Satvikam Nirmalam falam
B. Karmanah Sukratsyahuh	II. Rajsah
C. Madhye Tishthanti	III. Adhogacchanti tamasah
D. Jaghanyagun-vrittistha	IV. Madbhavam Soadhigacchati

Choose the **correct** answer from the options given below:

1. A-I, B-II, C-III, D-IV
2. A-II, B-III, C-IV, D-I
3. A-IV, B-I, C-II, D-III
4. A-III, B-II, C-IV, D-I

77. Match the List-I with List-II according to Nadabindu Upanishad:

List-I	List-II
A. Tritiya (Third) Matra	I. Brahmi
B. Chhathvin (Sixth) Matra	II. Dhriti
C. Dasvin (Tenth) Matra	III. Aindri
D. Barahvin (Twelfth) Matra	IV. Patangi

Choose the **correct** answer from the options given below:

1. A-III, B-IV, C-I, D-II
2. A-IV, B-III, C-II, D-I
3. A-I, B-II, C-IV, D-III
4. A-II, B-III, C-I, D-IV

78. Match the List-I with List-II according to Yogkundalyupunishad:

List-I	List-II
A. Suryabhedan, Ujjayi, Shitali, Bhastrika	I. Mitigating gulm, Pitta, Trisha etc.
B. By practicing shitali Pranavam	II. Penetrating all the three granthis originated from three gunas
C. By practicing kapal shodhan kriya	III. Doing Rechan slowly
D. By practicing Bhastrika	IV. Have been called Kumbhak

Choose the **correct** answer from the options given below:

1. A-I, B-II, C-III, D-IV
2. A-III, B-IV, C-II, D-I
3. A-IV, B-I, C-III, D-II
4. A-II, B-III, C-I, D-IV

79. Match the List-I with List-II according to Yogsutra:

List-I	List-II
A. Parinamtray Sanyamat	I. Purvajati-jnanam
B. Samskar Sakshat karanat	II. Tatah prakasha varankshayah
C. Bahirkalpita Vrittirmahavideha	III. Punaranista prasangat
D. Sthanyupanimantrane sangsmayakaranam	IV. Atitanagat jnanam

Choose the **correct** answer from the options given below:

1. A-I, B-II, C-IV, D-III
2. A-III, B-II, C-I, D-IV
3. A-IV, B-I, C-II, D-III
4. A-II, B-III, C-IV, D-I

80. Match the List-I with List-II according to Yoga Sutra:

List-I	List-II
A. Mridumadhyadhi-matritwatttoapi vishesha	I. Vibhuti Pada
B. Te hladparitapphalah Punyaapunayahetutwat	II. Kaivalyad Pada
C. Tadvairagyadapi Doshbij Kshaye Kaivalyam	III. Samadhi Pada
D. Hanmesham Kleshvaduktam	IV. Sadhan Pada

Choose the **correct** answer from the options given below:

1. A-II, B-III, C-IV, D-I
2. A-IV, B-III, C-II, D-I
3. A-III, B-IV, C-I, D-II
4. A-II, B-III, C-I, D-IV

81. Match the List-I with List-II according to Vasisth Samhita:

List-I	List-II
A. Yama	I. Tej
B. Niyama	II. Shunyata
C. Dharna	III. Souch
D. Samadhi	IV. Astikta

Choose the **correct** answer from the options given below:

1. A-I, B-IV, C-III, D-II
2. A-IV, B-I, C-II, D-III
3. A-III, B-II, C-I, D-IV
4. A-IV, B-II, C-III, D-I

82. Match the List-I with List-II:

List-I (Nutrient)	List-II (Signs and symptoms of deficiency)
A. Niacin	I. Subcutaneous bleeding
B. Ascorbic acid	II. Tetany
C. Magnesium	III. Polyneuritis
D. Thiamine	IV. Diarrhoea, dementia and dermatitis

Choose the **correct** answer from the options given below:

1. A-I, B-IV, C-III, D-II
2. A-IV, B-I, C-II, D-III
3. A-III, B-II, C-I, D-IV
4. A-IV, B-II, C-III, D-I

83. Match the List-I with List-II:

List-I (Factors)	List-II (Functions)
A. Adaptive immunity	I. Genetically determined
B. T cell immunity	II. Production of antibodies
C. Innate immunity	III. Regional inflammation and local defense in tissues
D. B cell immunity	IV. Immunity to a specific antigen on exposure

Choose the **correct** answer from the options given below:

1. A-I, B-II, C-III, D-IV
2. A-IV, B-III, C-I, D-II
3. A-III, B-I, C-II, D-IV
4. A-II, B-IV, C-III, D-I

84. Match the type of Samadhi with the yoga practice leading to it as per Gherand Samhita:

List-I	List-II
A. Nada Samadhi	I. Shambhavi
B. Dhyana Samadhi	II. Yoni Mndra
C. Laya Siddhi Samadhi	III. Khechari
D. Rasananda Samadhi	IV. Bhramari

Choose the **correct** answer from the options given below:

1. A-IV, B-II, C-III, D-I
2. A-I, B-IV, C-III, D-II
3. A-II, B-III, C-I, D-IV
4. A-IV, B-I, C-II, D-III

85. Match the List-I with List-II according to Hathpradipika:

List-I	List-II
A. Kulatth	I. Matsyendrasana
B. Rain water	II. Mayurasana
C. Destroys even the poisons	III. Apathya
D. Increases the digestive fire	IV. Pathya

Choose the **correct** answer from the options given below:

1. A-IV, B-III, C-I, D-II
2. A-III, B-I, C-II, D-IV
3. A-III, B-IV, C-II, D-I
4. A-I, B-II, C-III, D-IV

86. Match the List-I with List-II according to Siddhasiddhanta paddhati:

List-I	List-II
A. Kala	I. Internally aroused sound
B. Anahata	II. Rich sensation felt over the body
C. Nada	III. Internally enkindled light
D. Bindu	IV. Listening ceaseless sound

Choose the **correct** answer from the options given below:

1. A-IV, B-I, C-II, D-III
2. A-III, B-IV, C-II, D-I
3. A-I, B-III, C-IV, D-II
4. A-II, B-IV, C-I, D-III

87. Match the List-I with List-II:

List-I (Common complications of cold)	List-II (Symptoms)
A. Secondary Bacterial Infection	I. Swelling, congestion and thick purulent discharge
B. Sinusitis	II. Tracheitis, laryngitis, bronchitis and lobular pneumonia
C. Middle ear infection	III. Secretion become thick and purulent
D. Lower respiratory infection	IV. Bacterial infection spreads from the nasopharynx up the eustachatian tube

Choose the **correct** answer from the options given below:

1. A-II, B-IV, C-I, D-III
2. A-III, B-I, C-IV, D-II
3. A-III, B-IV, C-II, D-I
4. A-IV, B-II, C-I, D-III

88. Match the following according to 'Teaching methods for Yogic Practices' Book:

List-I	List-II
A. Teaching Method	I. Seating arrangements
B. Class Management	II. Audio-visual
C. Teaching Aids	III. Anotomico-Physiological Principle
D. Successful lesson plan	IV. Analyzing the practice

Choose the **correct** answer from the options given below:

1. A-I, B-III, C-II, D-IV
2. A-II, B-IV, C-III, D-I
3. A-III, B-I, C-II, D-IV
4. A-IV, B-III, C-I, D-II

89. Match the List-I with List-II in reference to Surya Namaskar:

List-I (Mantra)	List-II (Position)
A. Om Bhaskaraya Namah	I. Position 5
B. Om Khagaya Namah	II. Position 11
C. Om Marichaye Namah	III. Position 12
D. Om Arkaya Namah	IV. Position 8

Choose the **correct** answer from the options given below:

1. A-III, B-I, C-IV, D-II
2. A-II, B-I, C-III, D-IV
3. A-IV, B-II, C-I, D-III
4. A-III, B-II, C-IV, D-I

90. Match the List-I with List-II:

List-I (Mudra)	List-II (Relation)
A. Bhairava	I. Manas
B. Nasikagra Drishti	II. Adhara chakra
C. Tadagi	III. Hasta
D. Ashwini	IV. Udar

Choose the **correct** answer from the options given below:

1. A-III, B-I, C-IV, D-II
2. A-IV, B-I, C-II, D-III
3. A-III, B-IV, C-I, D-II
4. A-IV, B-II, C-III, D-I

Directions (Qs. No. 91 to 95): *Read the following passage carefully and answer the questions.*

Prana is one such subtle energy through which the entire universe is being governed. Prana has been differentiated into two types, namely Samasti Prana and Vyashti Prana. Every particle of the creation is being resonated by Samashti Prana. In the same way, our Vyashti Body is also being regulated by Prana. Prana maintains the dynamicity of this body as vital energy. The flow of prana in the body is through Nadis. The activities of all the cells of the body are controlled by Nadis. Obstruction to flame of prana results in accumulation of toxic matters in the body. As soon as the flow of prana is corrected, the toxic matters get eliminated from the body. As a result, all the systems of the body restore the state of health. When the flow of prana in the body is corrected, its flexibility improves as a result of which, yogic practices become easy to perform. This is also accompanied by improvement in stability and suppleness in the body. Therefore, prana only is the basis of life and has been considered as an elder brother, friend etc by the traditional texts.

91. Which of the following prana is responsible for resonance of each and every atom of the creation?

1. Samashti Prana 2. Vyashti Prana
3. Samana Prana 4. Vyana Prana

92. The activities of cells is controlled by which of the following:

1. By Prana
2. By Nadis
3. By Samashti Prana
4. By Vayus

93. Obstruction to whose flow results in accumulation of toxic matters in the body:-

1. Food 2. Blood
3. Prana 4. Vayu

94. Whose correction results in production of flexibility in the body:

1. Asana 2. Prana
3. Pranayama 4. Blood (Rakta)

95. What is the basis of life?

1. Atma 2. Paramatma
3. Prana 4. Yoga

Directions (Qs. No. 96 to 100): *Read the following passage carefully and answer the questions.*

When the Chitta is detached from sensory pleasures, it becomes capable of moving everywhere. Such Sadhak can successfully use his chitta as means to attain the goal by employing Purusharth. Control of chitta leads to attainment of the miseryless stage. The main method for controlling chitta is Ashtang yoga which when practiced can lead to attainment of Nirvikalp Samadhi and Kaivalya. Various siddhis are attained by practicing Ashtang Yoga. On worldly level, it provides physical health. Physical health is basis for mental health. When the body and mind are healthy, one can attain stress free and blissful life. A stress free mind can help to achieve the goal. Yoga practice is essential in student life. Regular yoga practice with belief can help to attain firm determination, self-confidence and sharp intellect. These attributes are greatest achievement of student life. A yogi attains Kaivalya while the worldly beings successful life by the practice of Ashtang yoga.

96. What kind of chitta is capable of moving everywhere?

1. Detached from sensory objects
2. When devoid of lust
3. When devoid of sensory objects and purusharth
4. Detached from sensory pleasures

97. Ashtang Yoga is main method of:

1. Controlling mind
2. Controlling Chitta
3. Controlling Kaivalya
4. Controlling Samadhi

98. Several Siddhis can be attained by practicing-

1. Purusharth
2. Samyam
3. Ashtang Yoga
4. Samadhi

99. Which of the following is attained when body and mind are healthy?

1. Goal
2. A blissful life
3. A successful life
4. Target

100. What is helpful in attaining goal?

1. Stress free mind
2. Practice of yoga
3. Sharp intellect
4. Self confidence

ANSWERS

1	2	3	4	5	6	7	8	9	10
3	2	3	1	1	4	3	4	4	2
11	**12**	**13**	**14**	**15**	**16**	**17**	**18**	**19**	**20**
3	3	3	2	3	2	4	3	3	3
21	**22**	**23**	**24**	**25**	**26**	**27**	**28**	**29**	**30**
4	1	2	3	1	2	4	3	3	2
31	**32**	**33**	**34**	**35**	**36**	**37**	**38**	**39**	**40**
1	1	3	4	4	1	4	4	3	1
41	**42**	**43**	**44**	**45**	**46**	**47**	**48**	**49**	**50**
2	2	2	2	2	2	2	1	4	2
51	**52**	**53**	**54**	**55**	**56**	**57**	**58**	**59**	**60**
1	3	1	4	1	2	3	3	4	3
61	**62**	**63**	**64**	**65**	**66**	**67**	**68**	**69**	**70**
2	2	4	3	1	3	2	3	1	1
71	**72**	**73**	**74**	**75**	**76**	**77**	**78**	**79**	**80**
1	2	2	1	1	3	2	3	3	3
81	**82**	**83**	**84**	**85**	**86**	**87**	**88**	**89**	**90**
*	2	2	4	3	4	2	3	1	1
91	**92**	**93**	**94**	**95**	**96**	**97**	**98**	**99**	**100**
1	2	3	2	3	4	2	3	2	1

Explanatory Answers

1. The seventeenth Karika of the *Samkhya Karika* presents the logical reasons for establishing the existence of **Purusa**. It provides five classic arguments: (*i*) *Sanghata-pararthatvat*—the composite world exists for the sake of another, implying a distinct conscious experiencer; (ii) *Trigunadi-viparyayat*—the three gunas undergo transformations, so there must be an unchanging witness perceiving these changes; (iii) *Adhisthanat*—there must be a substratum or support for the changing phenomena; (iv) *Bhoktr-bhavat*—the presence of an enjoyer who experiences pleasure, pain, and delusion proves Puruna's distinctness; (v) *Kaivalyartha-pravrtteh*—the striving for liberation indicates a conscious principle separate from Prakrti. These reasons collectively affirm the independent reality of Purusa.

2. The statement **"Svatmanyavasthanam Moksah"**—"Abiding in one's own Self is Moksha"—is cited by Sankaracarya in his commentary on the *Taittiriya Upanisad*. In Advaita Vedanta, Moksha is not traveling to another place but realizing and resting in the true nature of the Self, identical with Brahman. Sankara explains that liberation is attained when the Self, freed from ignorance and false identification with body and mind, abides in its pure essence. Thus, Moksha is intrinsic self-realization, not an external achievement.

3. The verse **"Mudit Manasi Aayasu Chale Ban Matu Pita Ko. Dharam Dhurandar Dheerdhur Gun-seel-jita Ko."** is found in

Tulsidas's devotional work *Vinay Patrika*. In this passage, Tulsidas poetically praises the departure of parents to the forest with joyful hearts, portraying them as upholders of Dharma, endowed with patience, virtue, and noble character. This reflects Tulsidas's humility and reverence for moral ideals, showing his devotional tone and ethical admiration.

4. The phrase **"Marganamastangiko Shreshtha"**—"Of all paths, the Eightfold Path is supreme"—appears in the Buddhist text *Dhammapada*. The Buddha declares that among all possible paths, the Noble Eightfold Path (Right View, Right Intention, Right Speech, Right Action, Right Livelihood, Right Effort, Right Mindfulness, Right Concentration) is the highest way to end suffering. This underscores the centrality of the Eightfold Path as the practical guide to liberation in Buddhist teaching.

5. **Mana (Mind):** In the *Chandogya Upanishad*, the Asuras worshiped **Mind (Mana)** as the udgitha (sacred chant) in hopes of gaining freedom from sin. However, because the mind is fickle and susceptible to faults, their worship did not free them from sin. The Upanishad narrates a series of attempts—first speech, then breath, sight, hearing, and mind—each tested by the Asuras. The failure of mind worship illustrates that liberation cannot be secured by relying on the unstable mental faculty but requires higher realization, ultimately leading to the worship of Prana (vital breath).

6. The phrase **"Puruso 'yam eva sa yo 'yam atma—idam amrtam, idam brahma, idam sarvam"** is found in *Brhadaranyaka Upanishad* 2.5.2. This passage belongs to the Madhu Brahmana section, where the unity of the individual self and the cosmic principle is explained. It declares that this very Purusa (Person) is none other than the inner Self, and that this Self is immortal (amrta), Brahman (the ultimate reality), and all that exists. The mantra highlights the Advaitic view that Atman and Brahman are identical, affirming the oneness of the individual and the universe.

7. **Atma (Soul):** In the *Brihadaranyaka Upanishad* (specifically verse 1.5.15), the **sixteenth phase (Sodasi Kala)** is described as **Atman**, the Soul. The Upanishad explains that Prajapati (the cosmic person) consists of sixteen parts, representing all aspects of manifested existence. Among these phases—such as speech, mind, senses, and prana—the final and supreme one is the immutable Self, Atman. This Self is unchanging, eternal, and present in every being. The teaching emphasizes that while the other fifteen parts are transient and perishable, Atman alone remains permanent and indestructible, forming the essence of all beings and the ultimate reality. Thus, according to Brihadaranyaka Upanishad 1.5.15, the sixteenth phase is Atman, the imperishable soul.

8. *Yoga Vasistha* outlines seven stages of knowledge (sapta jñana-bhumis) leading to self-realization: (1) Subheccha—noble desire for truth, (2) Vicarana—philosophical inquiry, (3) Tanumanasi—attenuation of the mind, **(4) Sattvapatti–attainment of purity and direct experience of Reality**, (5) Asamsakti—detachment from worldly objects, (6) Padarthabhavani—seeing Brahman everywhere, and (7) Turyaga—transcendental absorption. Sattvapatti, as the fourth stage, marks the moment when the aspirant abides steadily in Truth, achieving inner clarity and equanimity.

9. According to the *Shvetashvatara Upanishad* (6.18), the Supreme Being—often described in this Upanishad as Rudra or Shiva—**first imparted the knowledge of the Vedas to Brahma** at the beginning of creation. The verse explicitly states: *"He who in the beginning of creation produced Brahma and delivered to him the Vedas..."* This highlights

that Brahma, the creator deity, was the first recipient of Vedic wisdom, which he then transmitted to the sages and the world. It underscores the concept that ultimate knowledge originates from the Supreme and flows through Brahma to all beings.

10. In the *Dhyan Bindu Upanishad*, specific deities are prescribed for contemplation during pranyama. For **Rechaka (exhalation)**, the text instructs meditation on **Siva**. This practice signifies releasing impurities and aligning the practitioner's consciousness with the auspicious Lord Siva. By meditating on Siva during exhalation, the yogi purifies the mind, stabilizes awareness, and moves closer to liberation, reflecting the Upanisadic method of uniting breath control with divine contemplation.

11. In the *Yogachudamani Upanishad*, it is stated that among the five vital airs (Pranas)—Prana, Apana, Vyana, Udana, and **Dhananjaya**—the **Dhananjaya Prana** remains in the body even after death. It lingers to prevent immediate decomposition and is said to cause post-mortem phenomena like sounds or slight movements. This teaching illustrates the subtle physiological and metaphysical role assigned to Dhananjaya in yogic and Upanishadic literature.

12. According to the *Nadabindu Upanishad*, the **eleventh matra** (intonation or division) of Omkara is called **Nari**. The text states that meditating upon Om at this eleventh matra or departing the body while fixed in this state leads to the attainment of **Tapoloka**. This teaching forms part of the Upanishadic mapping of spiritual progress through the progressive matras of Om, each corresponding to a different cosmic realm. The twelfth matra (Brahma) is said to lead to Brahmanhood, the highest realization. The sequence indicates a gradual ascent: earlier matras correspond to lower lokas, while higher matras lead to subtler and more exalted planes. Thus, the eleventh matra specifically leads to Tapoloka.

13. The phrase **"Sarvarthataikagratayoh Ksayodayau"** refers to **Samadhi Parinama** as described in *Patañjali's Yoga Sutra* (III.11). Samadhi Parinama is the transformation of the mind where distractions (sarvarthata) are reduced and one-pointedness (ekagrata) arises. This marks the shift of the citta into a deeply concentrated, absorptive state, an essential step in higher yogic practice.

14. The description of **Mahavrata** in *Yoga Sutra* is found in **2.31**. Here Patañjali explains that the five yamas—Ahimsa (non-violence), Satya (truthfulness), Asteya (non-stealing), Brahmacharya (celibacy), and Aparigraha (non-possession)—are to be observed universally, irrespective of time, place, birth, or circumstance. When practiced unconditionally, these are called Mahavratas, or great vows, forming the ethical foundation of yoga.

15. According to *Patañjali's Yoga Sutra* (I.47), in the **purest stage of Nirvichara Samadhi**—a state of meditation free from conceptualization—the yogi attains **Adhyatma Prasada**, meaning inner clarity or spiritual peace. This serene transparency of consciousness allows direct insight into the nature of reality and prepares the practitioner for even deeper stages of Samadhi.

16. In the *Yoga Sutras of Patanjali*, vitarka is understood in **three main categories**—gross reasoning (connected with external objects), subtle reasoning (connected with more refined perceptions), and the transcendence into non-conceptual awareness. These are often spoken of as gradations within samprajñata samadhi. By classifying them into three, the text distinguishes how the mind engages with objects first at the level of names and forms, then in subtler aspects, and finally dissolves into pure awareness.

17. In the *Vasistha Samhita*, the practice of **dharana** (concentration) is described in the **fourth chapter**. This chapter elaborates on fixing the mind steadily on a chosen support—such as a sacred symbol, a deity, or a subtle inner point. Dharana here is the preparatory stage before dhyana (meditation) and samadhi, and the text outlines it systematically so that practitioners can progress from external fixation to inner absorption.

18. The shloka **"Urdhvadho bhramate yadvat ghatiyantram gavamvasat, tadvat karma-vasaj jivo bhramate janmamrtyubhih"** is found in the *Gheranda Samhita*. The verse compares the bound soul to a water wheel turned endlessly up and down by oxen; in the same way, the jiva revolves through birth and death under the power of karma. This metaphor strongly emphasizes the bondage of karmic action and the cycle of samsara, urging the yogi to strive for liberation.

19. In the *Hatha Yoga Pradipika*, the statement about **manonmani**—the state where the mind dissolves into transcendence—is presented in **Chapter 3, verse 53**. Here, the text declares that the manonmani state is the true and highest condition of yoga, beyond fluctuations of thought and mental constructions. By reaching this state, the yogi transcends ordinary consciousness and enters into union with the supreme reality.

20. The enumeration of the **nine types of kumbhaka** is given in the *Hatha Ratnavali*. These include methods such as Suryabhedana, Ujjayi, Sitkari, Sitali, Bhastrika, Bhramari, Moorchha, Plavini, and Kevali. The text explains their techniques, effects on the body and mind, and their importance for purifying the nadis and awakening higher yogic states. The listing of nine kumbhakas is distinctive to the Hatha Ratnavali tradition.

21. The **Stimulus-Organism-Response (S-O-R) model** was proposed by **Robert S. Woodworth**. Unlike the earlier S-R (Stimulus-Response) theory, Woodworth emphasized the role of the "organism" as an active mediator between stimulus and response. This means that internal factors such as needs, drives, and cognitive processes influence how a person responds to external stimuli. The S-O-R model broadened psychology by recognizing human behavior as not purely mechanical but also shaped by internal states.

22. Foods that cause a **slow release of sugar** into the small intestine and gradual absorption into the blood are known as **low glycemic index (Low G.I.) foods**. These include whole grains, legumes, fruits, and vegetables. Because they prevent rapid spikes in blood sugar levels, they are recommended for maintaining steady energy and for conditions like diabetes management.

23. Muscle contraction occurs due to the sliding mechanism of **actin and myosin filaments** within the sarcomere, the basic unit of muscle tissue. When stimulated, myosin heads attach to actin filaments and pull them inward, shortening the muscle fiber. This cross-bridge cycle, powered by ATP, is the fundamental process responsible for voluntary and involuntary muscular contractions.

24. Cardiologists **Friedman and Rosenman** identified **Type A and Type B personalities** in relation to coronary heart disease risk. Type A individuals are competitive, impatient, aggressive, and more prone to stress, which was found to increase the risk of heart problems. Type B individuals are more relaxed, patient, and less stressed, with a lower risk. Their research linked psychological patterns to physiological health outcomes.

25. In the *Shrimad Bhagavad Gita*, a **Sattvic diet** is described as **rasya (juicy), snigdha (unctuous), and sthira (stable or nourishing)**. Such foods promote vitality, health, and clarity of mind. They include fresh fruits, milk, grains, and vegetarian preparations that are wholesome and

moderate. Rajasic foods are described as excessively bitter, sour, salty, or spicy, while Tamasic foods are stale, impure, or heavy; hence these qualities—rasya, snigdha, sthira—belong solely to the Satwik diet.

26. The **Vishuddhi Chakra**, located at the throat, governs communication, sound, and purification. When this chakra is purified, the practitioner gains **sharpness of hearing power not only through the physical ears but also through the subtle mind**. Yogic texts describe that the Vishuddhi chakra refines the faculty of sound perception, leading to heightened auditory sensitivity and even clairaudient abilities.

27. The **Ajna Chakra**, situated between the eyebrows, functions as the **control center for the distribution of prana** throughout the body. While the **Mooladhara Chakra** at the base of the spine is considered the generator or reservoir of pranic energy, it is the Ajna Chakra that governs, channels, and directs this energy to the various centers and nadis. Yogic texts often describe this dynamic as Mooladhara awakening the dormant energy (Kundalini) and Ajna guiding and distributing it under the command of higher will. Hence, Ajna is recognized as the master chakra for pranic regulation and control.

28. The **Anahata Chakra**, located at the heart center, is symbolically associated with the **Kalpataru (wish-fulfilling tree)**. This imagery represents the infinite potential and compassion that arises when the heart chakra is awakened. The Kalpataru symbolism conveys that from the heart, all desires can be harmonized and fulfilled in alignment with divine will, making it a central point for emotional balance and spiritual love.

29. An ulcer that occurs in the wall of the **first part of the small intestine (duodenum)** is called a **duodenal ulcer**. Unlike gastric ulcers, which form in the stomach lining, duodenal ulcers arise due to excess acid secretion, H. pylori infection, or irritation of the mucosal layer of the duodenum. They are among the most common peptic ulcers and typically present with burning pain relieved by eating.

30. For **hemorrhoids (piles)**, yogic practice recommends the **Ashwini Mudra**. This involves repeated contraction and relaxation of the anal sphincter muscles, improving blood circulation in the rectal region and strengthening pelvic muscles. By stimulating energy flow in the lower body, it alleviates congestion and supports healing in cases of hemorrhoids, while also enhancing control over the apana vayu.

31. The practice of **Nadi Shodhana Pranayama** combined with **Jalandhara Bandha, Moola Bandha, and both Antar (internal) and Bahir (external) Kumbhaka** is especially recommended for **hemorrhoids (piles)**. These techniques together improve blood circulation in the abdominal and pelvic regions, reduce venous congestion, and strengthen the anal and pelvic muscles. By balancing pranic flow and relieving strain, this practice helps in both the management and prevention of hemorrhoids, supporting overall rectal health and reducing discomfort.

32. For **constipation**, the recommended meditation practice is **Antar Mouna (inner silence meditation)**. This technique develops heightened awareness of thoughts, sensations, and inner processes, which helps release psychosomatic tensions contributing to constipation. By calming the nervous system and improving the harmony between mind and body, Antar Mouna indirectly enhances peristalsis and eases bowel functioning.

33. In the book *Teaching Methods for Yogic Practices*, **Yama and Niyama** are described as **attitude training practices**. Yama regulates external social behavior (e.g., non-violence, truth, non-stealing), while Niyama refines internal discipline (e.g., purity, contentment, self-study). Together, they shape the practitioner's attitudes, preparing the foundation for deeper yogic practices by cultivating correct mental and emotional orientation.

34. Every school of yoga ultimately emphasizes the **highest level of integration (samadhi)**, achieved by controlling the **modifications (vrittis) of the mind**. Whether through bhakti (devotion), jnana (knowledge), karma (action), or raja (meditation), all paths converge on this goal. The cessation of mental fluctuations leads to union with the higher Self, which is recognized as the supreme objective across traditions.

35. Among the listed practices, **Kapalabhati** does not involve an **exhalatory retention phase**. It is a rapid, forceful exhalation kriya where inhalation is passive, and exhalation is active. Unlike Uddiyana, Agnisara, and Nauli, which involve exhalation followed by holding out the breath (bahir kumbhaka), Kapalabhati is a continuous cleansing process without retention, focusing on energizing and purifying the respiratory system.

36. In the book *Teaching Methods for Yoga Practices*, the **Social Scientists Theory** is placed under the **sources of teaching methods**. This theory highlights how individuals learn and interact in social contexts, providing insights into group dynamics, motivation, and learning styles. By identifying it as a source, the book emphasizes that theories from social sciences serve as foundational knowledge for shaping yoga pedagogy. These theoretical underpinnings inform the design of teaching methods, though they themselves are not the methods but the base on which methods are built.

37. In **Danta Dhauti**, a yogic practice for oral cleansing, the gums and teeth are rubbed with twigs or extracts of the **Khadira plant (Acacia catechu)**. Khadira is valued for its astringent, antimicrobial, and strengthening qualities, which make it effective in maintaining oral hygiene and gum health. Traditional yoga texts recommend this practice for cleansing impurities and energizing the oral cavity, while other options like plantain or cane are not prescribed for this specific technique.

38. **Agnisar Kriya**, involving rapid abdominal contractions, stokes the digestive fire (Agni) and stimulates metabolism. While this practice is beneficial for conditions like poor appetite, low digestive power, or dullness, it is **not suitable for people with hyperthyroidism**. In hyperthyroidism, the thyroid is already overactive and metabolism excessively high; performing Agnisar can aggravate this imbalance. Hence, the practice is contraindicated for such individuals to avoid worsening the condition.

39. The most suitable mudra for inducing **pratyahara (withdrawal of the senses)** is **Shanmukhi Mudra**. In this practice, the practitioner uses the fingers to close the ears, eyes, nostrils, and mouth—symbolically shutting out the external world. This deliberate sensory withdrawal turns awareness inward, quiets the mind, and prepares it for dharana (concentration) and dhyana (meditation). Other mudras like Kaki or Bhoochari are primarily linked to pranayama or concentration, but Shanmukhi directly leads to pratyahara.

40. Among the options, **Bhadrasana (Gracious Pose)** is considered a **variation of Moolabandhasana**. In both postures, the heels are positioned close to the perineum, encouraging activation of the pelvic floor and facilitating the practice of Moola Bandha (root lock). Because of its anatomical similarity and emphasis on the same region, Bhadrasana is treated as a closely related form, making it a supportive or alternative practice to Moolabandhasana. The other options—Brahmacharyasana, Vrischikasana, and Lolasana—belong to different categories and do not directly connect with Moolabandha practice.

41. The *Astanga Marga* (Eightfold Path) of Buddhism is a progressive system of discipline beginning with the correct orientation of thought and culminating in mindfulness and meditation. From the given parts, the correct sequence is:

- **Samyak Sankalpa (E)** – right intention, which sets the moral foundation.
- **Samyak Vak (D)** – right speech, purifying communication.
- **Samyak Karma (C)** – right action, ensuring ethical conduct.
- **Samyak Vyayam (A)** – right effort, sustaining discipline.
- **Samyak Smrti (B)** – right mindfulness, leading to awareness and concentration.

This arrangement reflects how mental resolve flows into speech and action, and then strengthens through effort and mindfulness.

Hence, correct sequence is E, D, C, A, B.

42. The *Nyaya Darsana* system employs a five-step logical process called the *pañcavayava nyaya* (five-member syllogism). The sequence is:

- **Pratijña (D)** – the proposition or statement of what is to be proven.
- **Hetu (A)** – the reason that supports the proposition.
- **Udaharana (C)** – a general example demonstrating the rule or relation.
- **Upanaya (B)** – application of the rule to the specific case.
- **Nigamana (E)** – the conclusion, restating the proposition as established.

This orderly progression ensures logical reasoning moves from assertion to evidence and final inference.

Hence, correct sequence is D, A, C, B, E.

43. In the *Bhagavad Gita*, the **srsti-cakra (cosmic cycle of creation and sustenance)** is described as a chain of dependence. The sequence is:

- **Vihita Karma (B)** – prescribed duties performed in harmony with dharma.
- **Yajña (A)** – sacrificial acts maintained through karma, pleasing the gods.
- **Vrsti (E)** – rainfall that comes as a result of yajña, ensuring fertility.
- **Anna Utpatti (D)** – production of food grains through the rain.
- **Sampurna Prani (C)** – all living beings nourished by food.

This cycle illustrates how duties, sacrifice, natural order, and sustenance of life are interlinked.

44. In the *Chhandogya Upanisad*, the **Udgitha Upasana** (meditation on Om) is described as a progressive contemplation on different deities or faculties, each representing a stage of inner refinement. The correct order is:

- **Nasika-sthita Prana (B)** – meditation begins with **Prana**, the vital force located in the nose, symbolizing breath as the foundation of life.
- **Vak-rupa** (C) – the focus then shifts to the **tongue** as the seat of speech, since sound and chanting are essential for Udgitha.
- **Chaksu-rupa** (A) – next is the **eye**, representing sight and perception of form, connecting outer reality to awareness.
- **Srotra-rupa (E)** – meditation continues with the **ear**, the organ of hearing, which is most directly related to Om as sound vibration.
- **Manas-rupa (D)**–the practice culminates in the **mind**, the inner instrument that governs and integrates all senses, considered the highest field of meditation.

This sequence illustrates a movement from the breath to speech, then to perception (sight and hearing), and finally to the mind, showing how Udgitha Upasana integrates both sensory and mental faculties into spiritual realization.

45. According to the *Yogaraja Upanishad*, chakras are arranged in a distinct order not identical with the more commonly known tantric system. The progression is:

- **Kantha Chakra (D)** – situated in the throat, governing sound and vibration.

- **Taluka Chakra (C)** – located at the palate, associated with subtle taste and nectar.
- **Bhu Chakra (E)** – the earth center, symbolizing grounding and stability.
- **Brahmarandhra Chakra (A)** – located at the crown, the opening to higher consciousness.
- **Vyoma Chakra (B)** – the space or ether center, representing the expansion into the infinite.

This ordering reflects a metaphysical ascent from bodily and elemental centers to the crown and finally into cosmic space.

46. Checking options:

B. Purification of Antahkaran (inner-self): From inner cleanliness (sauca) arises clarity of mind (sattva-suddhi).

D. Happiness (joy) in mind: A purified inner instrument yields calm cheerfulness (saumanasya).

A. Concentration of Chitta: Joyful clarity stabilizes into one-pointedness (ekagrata).

E. Control over senses: A concentrated mind naturally masters the senses (indriya-jaya).

C. Ability of self-realization: Fitness for direct Self-seeing (atma-darsana-yogyata) completes the sequence.

Hence, correct order is B, D, A, E, C.

47. Checking options:

A. Santosha (contentment): Grounds the mind in sufficiency.

C. Astikta (faith): Steadies conviction in the higher truth.

D. Daan (charity): Purifies grasping by giving.

B. Ishwar pujan (worship of the Divine): Directs devotion and surrender.

E. Lajja (modesty): Cultivates humility and restraint.

Hence, correct order is A, C, D, B, E.

48. Checking options:

D. Maha Bandh: Taught among the first major locks after the classic preliminaries.

E. Mahavedh: The dynamic "piercing" practice performed with the great lock.

B. Uddiyan Bandh: Abdominal lock drawing prana upward.

A. Moola Bandh: Root lock stabilizing apana and the pelvic floor.

C. Vajroli: Later instruction on sublimation and conservation of vital energy.

Hence, correct order is D, E, B, A, C.

49. Checking options:

C. Initiation of SA node activity: Natural pacemaker fires.

A. Stimulus reaches AV node: Atria conduct toward AV node as atrial contraction begins.

E. Spread through Purkinje fibres on right ventricle: Conduction enters ventricular pathways.

D. Impulses reach ventricular myocardium via Purkinje fibres: Ventricular muscle depolarizes.

B. Completion of atrial contraction and initiation of ventricular contraction: Ventricles contract in a coordinated beat.

Hence, correct order is C, A, E, D, B.

50. Checking options:

B. Green Vegetable: Certain coarse or overly fibrous greens are discouraged in *Hatha Pradipika* as they may create wind (vata) and disturb the body's harmony during yogic practice.

E. Mustard: Mustard is considered too pungent and heating, which can upset digestion and agitate the mind.

C. Curd: Curd is heavy and phlegm-forming, which can produce mucus and sluggishness, hindering advanced pranayama and meditation.

A. Asfoetida: Its intense, heating nature can imbalance the doshas and disturb pranic flow.

D. Garlic: Garlic is classified as rajasic (stimulating) and tamasic (dulling) in yogic texts, believed to agitate the senses and distract from higher concentration.

This sequence—B, E, C, A, D—matches the *Hatha Pradipika* listing of non-recommended foods for yogic discipline.

51. Checking options:

C. Laghoo Shankhaprakshalana: Begin with gentle intestinal cleansing to remove toxins and relieve digestive strain that can worsen asthma.

D. Kunjal Kriya: Next, perform stomach cleansing by induced vomiting to clear mucus and ease breathing passages.

A. Jalaneti and Kapalabhati: Then, practice nasal cleansing and rapid exhalations to open nasal passages and strengthen respiratory muscles.

E. Pranayama: Follow with controlled breathing exercises to stabilize airflow and expand lung capacity.

B. Om Chanting: Conclude with chanting to relax the nervous system and calm breathing rhythm.

52. Checking options:

E. Nose: Start purification through the nose to ensure clear nasal pathways.

B. Grasani (throat): Then cleanse the throat area to remove phlegm and impurities.

C. Mouth: Purify the mouth to maintain oral hygiene and prepare for deeper practices.

A. Kapal (forehead/sinuses): Cleanse the sinus region for better breathing and concentration.

D. Stomach: Finish with stomach cleansing for internal detoxification.

53. Checking options:

B. Short intercostal muscles: Activate first to initiate rib movement.

C. External intercostal muscles: Expand the chest cavity, drawing air in.

D. Internal intercostal muscles: Assist in fine control of rib spacing during inhalation.

E. Abdominal muscles: Stabilize the trunk and adjust pressure for diaphragm movement.

A. Rectus abdominis: Engages lightly at the end for maintaining posture and support.

54. Checking options:

B. Subhechha (noble desire): The initial yearning for truth and liberation.

D. Vicharana (inquiry): Deep investigation and reasoning into reality.

E. Tanumanasa (attenuation of mind): Reduction of mental distractions leading to steadiness.

These three belong to the seven stages of knowledge (*sapta jñana-bhumi*) in *Yoga Vashistha*.

55. Checking options:

B. Prajna (wisdom): Represents insight and understanding of truth.

C. Sheel (morality): Stands for ethical conduct and discipline.

E. Samadhi (concentration): Denotes deep meditative absorption.

Together, these three—**Prajna, Sheel, and Samadhi**—are the **Triratnas (Three Jewels)** in Buddhism.

56. Checking options:

A. Lavanyukt (Salty): Salty food is considered **Rajasic**, not Tamasic. Rajasic foods are stimulating and excite passion.

C. Ruksha (Dry/rough): Dry and rough foods belong to the Rajasic category, not Tamasic.

D. Teekshna (Pungent/very sharp): Pungent and excessively spicy foods are also Rajasic.

B. Amedhyam: Unclean or impure food is Tamasic.

E. Paryushitama: Stale or decomposed food is Tamasic.

Hence, the foods **not** attributes of Tamasic ahara are A, C, and D.

57. Checking options:

A. Damah (self-restraint): This is listed among **Brahmana** qualities, not Kshatriya karma.

D. Arjavam (straightforwardness): This is also a Brahmana attribute.

E. Vijnanam (discriminative knowledge): This belongs to higher wisdom attributes, not Kshatriya duty.

B. Tejah (valor) and **C. Dhritih (steadfastness)** are part of Kshatriya dharma in the Gita.

Thus, the qualities **not** of Kshatriya duty are A, D, and E.

58. Checking options:

B. Laghu Sharir (light body): The sadhak gains a light and energized body.

C. Complete elimination of sins: Practicing **uttama pranayama** burns impurities and past karma.

E. Elimination of all diseases: Mastery of breath purifies nadis and eradicates ailments.

A. Alpa Nidra (little sleep) and **D. Alpahari (eating little)** are related to discipline but not the direct state described here. Hence, the states attained are **Laghu Sharir, Complete elimination of sins, and Elimination of all diseases.**

59. Checking options:

A. Pranayama: Breath control is a key limb.

D. Dharana: Concentration of the mind is included.

E. Samadhi: Deep absorption or union is listed.

B. Shatkarma is a cleansing process, and **C. Yama** is not counted in Dhyan Bindu's shorter list here. So, the limbs of Yoga according to Dhyan Bindu Upanishad are **Pranayama, Dharana, and Samadhi**.

60. Checking options:

A. Asmita: In samyama practice, understanding of ego-sense or individuality is involved in conquering the senses.

C. Grahan: Perception or grasping of sensory objects must be mastered.

E. Anvava: Subtle following or tracing of sensory impressions is the final refinement.

B. Manojavitwa (speed of mind) and **D. Vikaranbhav** (change of form) are separate siddhis, not stages of samyama for Indriya Jaya.

Therefore, the stages are **Asmita, Grahan, and Anvava**.

61. Checking options:

A. Tarakam: This discriminative knowledge is **transcendent**—it "carries across" the yogi from bondage to liberation, saving one from worldly suffering.

C. Sarvatha Visayam: It is **all-comprehensive**, covering **all objects and phenomena** completely without limitation, signifying perfect discernment.

D. Akramam: It is **instantaneous and non-sequential**, arising as a whole rather than through step-by-step reasoning.

Incorrect options:

B. Pradhanajaya: Mastery over primordial matter is a *result* of yoga, not itself a direct attribute of Vivek Jñana.

E. Antanvachhedat (Anantan vacchedat): Refers to cessation of sorrows but is not classified as an attribute of Vivek Jñana.

62. Checking options:

B. Eradication of Cough: *Gheranda Samhita* states Neti removes mucus and clears phlegm, helping respiratory health.

D. Khechari Siddhi: Regular practice is said to aid in attaining Khechari Siddhi by purifying pathways and stimulating vital energy.

The other options—**A. Increasing of Appetite**, **C. Cleanliness of Nadis**, and **E. Handsome like Cupid**—are not mentioned in *Gheranda Samhita* for Neti Karma.

63. Checking options:

B. Dridhta (Firmness): Rubbing sweat back into the body after pranayama effort is said to give firmness and strength.

D. Laghuta (Lightness): It also imparts a sense of lightness and agility.

Other choices like **Sthirta**, **Dhirta**, or **Shodhan** are not specified benefits in *Hatha Yoga Pradipika* for this action.

64. Checking options:

B. Epithelial tissues cover body surface and inner cavities: Correct—epithelial tissue provides protective and functional lining inside and outside the body.

D. Blood and lymph are connective tissues with distinctive collection of cells: Correct—both are classified as connective tissues due to their cellular composition and fluid matrix.

A. Tendon connects bone to bone is incorrect (tendons connect muscle to bone; ligaments connect bone to bone).

C. Smooth muscle tissue is present in the heart is incorrect (cardiac muscle is found in the heart, not smooth muscle).

E. A neuron statement is incomplete (a neuron also includes dendrites).

65. Checking options:

A. Determined by pleasure principle: Freud's Id operates solely on the pleasure principle, seeking immediate gratification.

E. Absolutely unconscious: The Id is fully unconscious, housing instinctual drives.

B. Executive branch refers to the Ego.

C. Reality principle is controlled by the Ego.

D. Ethical branch describes the Superego.

Thus, only A and E fit the Id.

66. Checking options:

A. Comfort in the physical environment and health: WHO defines quality of life as including physical comfort and good health.

B. Freedom of expression and action: Social and psychological freedom directly influence life quality.

E. Intellectual, educational, and social attainment: Opportunities for learning and social participation shape well-being.

Incorrect: C. Longevity of life and **D. High paying jobs** are outcomes or socio-economic factors but not directly listed as WHO determinants of quality of life.

67. Checking options:

A. More sour: Excessively sour foods are prohibited in *Hatha Pradipika* for maintaining health.

C. More salty: Highly salty foods are also discouraged as they disturb doshic balance.

D. Re-heated food: Reheated or stale foods are considered harmful for health improvement.

Incorrect: B. Shashtik (a wholesome rice variety) and **E. Prescribed Diet** are actually recommended, not prohibited.

68. Checking options:

A. Tremulous: Tremor is a key sign of thyrotoxicosis due to excess thyroid hormone.

B. Hysterical: Emotional instability or nervousness can be seen in thyrotoxic states.

D. Rapid shallow respiration: Increased metabolism speeds up breathing.

Incorrect: C. Hoarseness and **E. Slowing of movement** are not characteristic; slowing is more typical of hypothyroidism.

69. Checking options:

A. Quercetin: A plant flavonoid with anti-inflammatory effects.

C. B-Complex: Certain B vitamins modulate inflammation and immune function.

D. Omega-3 fatty acid: Well-known for strong anti-inflammatory action.

Incorrect: B. Vitamin A and **E. Potassium** are important nutrients but not primarily classified as anti-inflammatory.

70. Checking options:

B. Recitation: Oral teaching relies heavily on repetition and verbal recitation to transmit knowledge.

C. Cultivation of good memory: Strong memory skills are essential for retaining orally transmitted material.

Incorrect: A. Observation method, **D. One-to-one teaching**, and **E. Demonstration** can be useful but are not fundamental requirements for oral teaching as traditionally practiced.

71. Checking options:

B. Control over different reflexes: Shat Kriyas cleanse internal pathways, giving mastery over multiple reflexes such as gag or cough.

C. Increase the adaptability of tissues formation: Regular cleansing increases the body's adaptability and resilience at a tissue level.

E. Establish psychosomatic balance: By harmonizing body and mind, Shat Kriyas stabilize psychosomatic functioning.

Incorrect: A. Control over static reflex is too limited, and **D. Reduce adaptability of tissue formation** contradicts yogic benefits.

72. Checking options:

A. Direction-responsive method: A core teaching approach where learners respond to guidance actively.

B. Individual Direction method: Focuses on personalized instruction, tailoring methods to each student.

D. Project method: Encourages experiential learning through projects and is considered a fundamental method.

Incorrect: C. Environment and **E. Correction method** are important factors or techniques but not listed as fundamental teaching methods.

73. Checking options:

A. Iccha (will): Part of the fivefold Shakti, representing intention and desire.

C. Maya: The power of illusion or manifestation within Shakti Panchaka.

E. Yak: Included in traditional enumeration of five powers in *Siddha Siddhanta Paddhati*.

Incorrect: B. Vasana and **D. Nischaya** are not part of the Shakti Panchaka described in this text.

74. Checking options:

A. Gulma (abdominal tumors or lumps): Vasa-dhauti helps in clearing obstructions affecting digestion.

B. Jvara (fever): Purification assists in balancing doshas, reducing fever.

C. Pliha Roga (spleen disorders): Cleansing benefits spleen-related conditions.

E. Kustha (skin diseases): Internal purification aids in managing chronic skin issues.

Incorrect: D. Kosthakathinya (constipation) is not a primary condition cited for vasa-dhauti.

75. Matching List-I to List-II

A. Kathopanishad - III: Defines yoga as the **concentrated state of senses**, highlighting control over sense organs.

B. Bhagavad Gita - IV: States yoga as the **separation from association with miseries**, emphasizing detachment from suffering.

C. Mahopanishad - II: Describes yoga as **the way of calming the mind (mana)**.

D. Shiva Samhita - I: Declares yoga as **the union of Shiva and Shakti**, symbolizing ultimate cosmic unity.

76. Matching List-I to List-II

A. Gunebhyashch param vetti - IV. Madbhavam Soadhigacchati: One who knows the gunas as beyond themselves attains the divine state (*mad-bhavam*).

B. Karmanah Sukratsyahuh - I. Satvikam Nirmalam Falam: Actions performed in sattva give pure and stainless results.

C. Madhye Tishthanti - II. Rajsah: Those of rajasic nature remain in the middle plane, striving but unsettled.

D. Jaghanyagun-vrittistha - III. Adhogacchanti tamasah: Those abiding in tamasic qualities sink downward.

This matching reflects how the Gita classifies conduct and destiny according to the three gunas.

77. Matching List-I to List-II

A. Tritiya (Third) Matra - IV. Patangi: The third division of Omkara is called *Patangi*.

B. Chhathvin (Sixth) Matra – III. Aindri: The sixth matra is *Aindri*, signifying connection to the power of Indra.

C. Dasvin (Tenth) Matra – II. Dhriti: The tenth matra is *Dhriti*, representing steadiness.

D. Barahvin (Twelfth) Matra – I. Brahmi: The twelfth matra is *Brahmi*, leading to Brahman-consciousness.

This sequence aligns with the Nadabindu Upanishad's enumeration of the twelve divisions of Om meditation.

78. Matching List-I to List-II

A. Suryabhedan, Ujjayi, Shitali, Bhastrika – IV. Have been called Kumbhak: These four pranayamas are grouped as classic kumbhakas.

B. By practicing Shitali Pranavam – I. Mitigating gulm, pitta, trisha etc.: Shitali cools the system, reduces thirst, pacifies pitta, and relieves abdominal disorders.

C. By practicing Kapal Shodhan Kriya – III. Doing Rechan slowly: This kriya cleanses the skull region and is linked with controlled exhalation.

D. By practicing Bhastrika – II. Penetrating all the three granthis originated from three gunas: Bhastrika is described as forceful enough to pierce the three knots, purifying pranic channels.

79. Matching List-I to List-II

A. Parinamtray Sanyamat – IV. Atitanagat Jnanam: Mastery over the three transformations (parinamas) brings knowledge of past and future.

B. Samskar Sakshatkaranat – I. Purvajati-jnanam: Through direct perception of impressions, one knows previous births.

C. Bahirkalpita Vrittirmahavideha – II. Tatah Prakasha Varankshayah: By great disembodied concentration, obstacles to illumination are removed.

D. Sthanyupanimantrane Sangsmaya-karanam – III. Punaranista Prasangat: Acceptance of invitations from higher beings can lead to undesirable consequences.

This order aligns each sutra's concept with its corresponding outcome or description.

80. Matching List-I to List-II

A. Mridumadhyadhimatritwatttoapi Vishesha – III. Samadhi Pada: Variation among mild, medium, and intense aspirants is discussed in the *Samadhi Pada*.

B. Te hladparitapphalah Punyaapunaya-hetutwat – IV. Sadhan Pada: Karmic fruits bringing pleasure or pain are explained in the *Sadhana Pada*.

C. Tadvairagyadapi Doshbij Kshaye Kaivalyam – I. Vibhuti Pada: Through supreme dispassion and destruction of defect-seeds, Kaivalya is reached, explained in the *Vibhuti Pada*.

D. Hanmesham Kleshvaduktam – II. Kaivalyad Pada: The perpetual cause of suffering and its removal is discussed in the *Kaivalya Pada*.

This matching shows which chapters of Patanjali's Yoga Sutra contain each doctrinal point.

81. NONE: None of the provided options correctly match the teachings of the *Vasistha Samhita*.

A. Yama and IV. Astikta: Astikta (faith) is described in *Vasistha Samhita* as a **Niyama**, not a Yama. Pairing Yama with Astikta is incorrect.

B. Niyama and I. Tej: There is no direct correspondence between Niyama and Tej in the text. Tej is a general yogic quality, not specifically assigned to Niyama.

C. Dharana and II. Shunyata: Dharana is defined as focused concentration on specific points or elements, not as Sunyata (emptiness).

D. Samadhi and III. Souch: Saucha (purity) is listed as a **Niyama**, not as an attribute or result of Samadhi.

Because all four answer choices rely on incorrect or misapplied associations, **none of the options accurately reflect *Vasistha Samhita*.**

82. Matching List-I to List-II

A. **Niacin – IV. Diarrhoea, dementia, and dermatitis:** Classic pellagra triad caused by niacin deficiency.

B. **Ascorbic acid – I. Subcutaneous bleeding:** Vitamin C deficiency leads to scurvy, causing bleeding gums and subcutaneous bleeding.

C. **Magnesium – II. Tetany:** Magnesium deficiency results in neuromuscular irritability and tetany.

D. **Thiamine – III. Polyneuritis:** Thiamine deficiency produces beriberi, marked by peripheral neuritis.

83. Matching List-I to List-II

A. **Adaptive immunity – IV. Immunity to a specific antigen on exposure:** Acquired immunity develops after encountering a particular antigen.

B. **T cell immunity – III. Regional inflammation and local defense in tissues:** T cells mediate cellular immunity and trigger local immune responses.

C. **Innate immunity – I. Genetically determined:** Present from birth, not dependent on exposure.

D. **B cell immunity – II. Production of antibodies:** B cells are responsible for humoral immunity through antibody production.

84. Matching List-I to List-II

A. **Nada Samadhi – IV. Bhramari:** Nada Samadhi arises through internal sound (nada) practice like Bhramari.

B. **Dhyana Samadhi – I. Shambhavi:** Shambhavi mudra leads to meditative absorption (dhyana).

C. **Laya Siddhi Samadhi – II. Yoni Mudra:** Yoni Mudra aids dissolution of the mind (laya).

D. **Rasananda Samadhi – III. Khechari:** Khechari mudra produces blissful taste (rasananda).

85. Matching List-I to List-II

A. **Kulatth – III. Apathya:** Horse gram (Kulatth) is considered unsuitable (apathya) in *Hatha Pradipika*.

B. **Rain water – IV. Pathya:** Rain water is recommended (pathya) as wholesome.

C. **Destroys even the poisons – II. Mayurasana:** Mayurasana is credited with neutralizing toxins and improving digestion.

D. **Increases the digestive fire – I. Matsyendrasana:** Matsyendrasana stimulates digestive fire and abdominal organs.

86. Matching List-I to List-II

A. **Kala – II. Rich sensation felt over the body:** Kala refers to the sensation or vibration perceived throughout the body during deep yogic states.

B. **Anahata – IV. Listening ceaseless sound:** Anahata is the "unstruck sound," an endless internal resonance heard without external cause.

C. **Nada – I. Internally aroused sound:** Nada represents the subtle inner sound current experienced in meditation.

D. **Bindu – III. Internally enkindled light:** Bindu is described as a concentrated point of internally enkindled light and consciousness.

87. Matching List-I to List-II

A. **Secondary Bacterial Infection – III. Secretion becomes thick and purulent:** Indicates bacterial superinfection following a cold.

B. **Sinusitis–I. Swelling, congestion, and thick purulent discharge:** Sinusitis produces congestion and pus-filled discharge.

C. **Middle Ear Infection – IV. Bacterial infection spreads from the nasopharynx up the eustachian tube:** Pathogens ascend to the middle ear, causing otitis media.

D. **Lower Respiratory Infection – II. Tracheitis, laryngitis, bronchitis, and lobular pneumonia:** Lower airway complications of a cold involve these conditions.

88. Matching List-I to List-II

A. **Teaching Method – III. Anatomico-Physiological Principle:** Teaching should align with bodily mechanics and physiology.

B. **Class Management – I. Seating arrangements:** Proper seating supports orderly class flow.

C. **Teaching Aids – II. Audio-visual:** Audio-visual tools enhance understanding and retention.

D. **Successful Lesson Plan – IV. Analyzing the practice:** Evaluating and analyzing practice ensures lesson effectiveness.

89. Matching List-I to List-II

A. **Om Bhaskaraya Namah – III. Position 12:** Final position saluting Bhaskara (Sun).

B. **Om Khagaya Namah – I. Position 5:** Fifth position, Khaga signifies movement like a bird in the sky.

C. **Om Marichaye Namah – IV. Position 8:** Eighth position invokes Marichi, ray of light.

D. **Om Arkaya Namah – II. Position 11:** Eleventh position honors Arka, another name for Sun.

90. Matching List-I to List-II

A. **Bhairava – III. Hasta:** Bhairava mudra is a **hand** gesture symbolizing unity of Shiva and Shakti.

B. **Nasikagra Drishti – I. Manas:** Nose-tip gaze steadies the **mind** and enhances concentration.

C. **Tadagi – IV. Udar:** Tadagi mudra involves creating a hollow **abdomen** for pranic control.

D. **Ashwini – II. Adhara Chakra:** Ashwini mudra stimulates the **root chakra** through anal contraction.

91. Samashti Prana is described in the passage as the universal prana that resonates within **every particle of creation**. It governs all atoms and cosmic functions, making it the prana responsible for universal resonance.

92. The passage states that **"The activities of all the cells of the body are controlled by Nadis."** These subtle channels distribute pranic energy to every cell, regulating bodily activities and vitality.

93. It is clearly mentioned that **obstruction to the flow of prana** leads to the **accumulation of toxic matter** in the body. When pranic flow is blocked, toxins build up, affecting health.

94. The text explains that **"When the flow of prana in the body is corrected, its flexibility improves."** Proper pranic flow restores suppleness and stability, making yogic practices easier.

95. The passage concludes that **"Prana only is the basis of life and has been considered as an elder brother, friend etc. by the traditional texts."** Hence, **prana** is the fundamental basis of life.

96. The passage states, **"When the Chitta is detached from sensory pleasures, it becomes capable of moving everywhere."** Detachment from pleasures allows the mind to move freely and be used as a tool for Purusharth (purposeful effort).

97. It is clearly mentioned, **"The main method for controlling chitta is Ashtang Yoga."** Ashtang Yoga provides discipline and practice that stabilize and direct chitta.

98. The passage notes, **"Various siddhis are attained by practicing Ashtang Yoga."** These spiritual powers arise as by-products of sustained yogic practice.

99. The text explains, **"Physical health is basis for mental health. When the body and mind are healthy, one can attain stress free and blissful life."** Healthy body and mind lead to blissful living.

100. It is stated, **"A stress free mind can help to achieve the goal."** Maintaining a calm, stress-free state of mind is directly linked to achieving one's objectives.

Previous Years' Paper

National Testing Agency (NTA)

UGC-NET Junior Research Fellowship & Assistant Professor Eligibility Exam

YOGA, SEPTEMBER-2024

(Exam held on 04-09-2024)

PAPER-II

1. The concept that *Purak* is *Brahma*, *Kumbhak* is *Vishnu* and *Rechak* is *Rudra*, is mentioned in:
1. *Yoga Kundalyopanishad*
2. *Yoga Tattvopanishad*
3. *Dhyan Bindu Upanishad*
4. *Shvetashwatar Upanishad*

2. *Kayadivishvati Gargah* is mentioned in:
1. *Shandilya Bhakti Sutra*
2. *Narad Bhakti Sutra*
3. *Bhakti Rasayan*
4. *Shrimad Bhagwad*

3. In which of the following is mentioned that the disciple obtained knowledge from his *Guru* with the help of *Pranipat* (Surrender), service and questioning?
1. *Bhagavad Gita 6.34*
2. *Yoga Sutra 3.32*
3. *Hath Pradipika 4.22*
4. *Bhagavad Gita 4.34*

4. According to *Yoga Sutra*, on which of the following should be kept under restraint (*samyam*) in order to gain the knowledge of Human anatomy?
1. Heart
2. *Kanthkupa*
3. *Kurma Nadi*
4. *Nabhichakra*

5. Who among the following said, Consciousness is the most miraculous thing of creation, its depth and pervasiveness knows no limit?
1. James Hastings
2. Swami Shivanand Saraswati
3. Dr. David Frawley
4. Adi Guru Shankaracharya

6. Who among the following is one of the famous disciples of Shri Shyama Charan Lahiri?
1. Yoganand Saraswati
2. Niranjanand Saraswati
3. Paramhans Yoganand
4. Swami Shivanand

7. Who among the following gave birth to personal Psychology?

1. Carl Jung 2. Adler
3. Eric Fram 4. Abraham Maslow

8. The Principle of emotions is:
1. Cannon-Bard Principle
2. Ecological Principle
3. James lange Principle
4. Both (1) and (3)

9. Which of the following restraint (*Samyam*) results into the knowledge of *Purvajanam* according to Yoga Philosophy?

1. Sun 2. Moon
3. Star 4. Samskara

10. According to *Yoga Vashishtha*, which of the following is the sixth Bhumi of knowledge?
   1. *Tanumanasa*
   2. *Vicharna*
   3. Devoid of Sensuality (*Asansakti*)
   4. *Padarthabhavna*

11. Which of the following processes helps a teacher in understanding necessary teaching methods and objectives?
   1. Classroom management
   2. Lesson plan
   3. Teaching method sources
   4. Teaching aids

12. In which of the following diseases, *Shitkari Pranayam* is Beneficial?
   1. Asthma 2. Bronchitis
   3. Colitis 4. Arthritis

13. According to *Samkhya* Philosophy, *Tushti* is __________ to Yogic practices.
   1. *Sadhak*
   2. *Badhak*
   3. Phases of Yoga (*Yoga avastha*)
   4. Accomplishments (*Siddhiyan*)

14. Number of Shlokas in *Mandukyopnishad*.
   1. 8 2. 11
   3. 12 4. 24

15. According to Yoga Philosophy which of the following causes disturbances in one's consciousness (*chittavikshepa*)?
   1. *Raga* (Attachment)
   2. *Dvesh* (Apathy)
   3. *Avirati* (lack of renunciation)
   4. *Viparyay*

16. According to Yoga Philosophy which of the following sequences of *Animadi Ashta Sidhhis* is correct?
   1. *Laghima, Anima, Mahima, Garima*
   2. *Anima, Mahima, Laghima, Garima*
   3. *Garima, Prapti, Prakramya, Vashitva*
   4. *Mahima, Garima, Prapti, Vashitva*

17. According to Shrimad Bhagwad Gita, which of the following sorts of food is liked by the person having the attribute of *Tamas*?
   1. Enhancing Age, Intelligence and strength
   2. Very hot, stringent, Acidic
   3. Bitter, sour, dry
   4. Half baked, devoid of Juice, leftover

18. Which of the following Upanishads tells about knowing both *Sambhuti* and *Asambhuli* together?
   1. *Chhandogyopnishad*
   2. *Ishavashyopnishad*
   3. *Yogchudamanyupanishad*
   4. *Dhyanbindopanishad*

19. Which of the following asanas helps in soothing sphincters in the digestive system and pushes the water having drink towards the *Anus*?
   1. *Naukasan* 2. *Bhunamanasan*
   3. *Tadasan* 4. *Padmasan*

20. According to Ramayan, which of the following is **not** a part of *Navadha Bhakti*?
   1. Singing (*Gayan*)
   2. Contentment (*Santosh*)
   3. Satsang
   4. *Padasevan*

21. The practice of which of the following subtle exercise relieves from deteriorating intelligence, forgetting, disturbances scepticism etc.?
   1. *Smaran Shakti Vikasak*
   2. *Medha Shakti Vikasak*
   3. *Buddhi tatha Dhritishakti Vikasak*
   4. Prayer (*Prarthna*)

22. Short processes that receive and carry incoming action potential towards the cell body.
   1. Axon
   2. Microglia
   3. Dendrites
   4. Neurotransmitter

23. According to Yoga Sutra, which of the following is the main cause of the Union of *Drashta* and *Drishya*?

1. Five *virittis*
2. Five *kleshas*
3. Five *mahabhutas*
4. Five *Tanmatras*

24. According to *Vasishtha Samhita*, ... is contemplation of outer space (*Bahyakasha*) with inner space (*Antarakash*) in Heart.

1. Meditation (*Dhyana*)
2. *Samadhi*
3. *Dharna*
4. *Akash Gaman*

25. According to whom, dream is the highway of the unconscious:

1. Abraham Maslow
2. Swami Vivekananda
3. Swami Satyanand Saraswati
4. Freud

26. According to *Trishikobrahamanopnishad*, absolute detachment towards body and sense organs is:

1. *Yama* 2. *Niyam*
3. *Dharna* 4. None of the above

27. According to *Yog Kundalyopnishad Sahita Kumbhak* is:

1. *Suryabhedan, Ujjayi, Sheetali, Shitkaari*
2. *Suryabhedan, Ujjayi, Sheetali, Bhastrika*
3. *Suryabhedan, Ujjayi, Shitkaari, Bhastrika*
4. *Suryabhedan, Ujjayi, Shitkaari, Bhramari*

28. Which of the following harmful foods (*Apathya Ahar*) is mentioned neither in *Hathpradipika* nor in *Gherand Samhita*?

1. Buttermilk 2. Kulath
3. Hing 4. Jambira

29. In which of the patals of *Shiv Samhita, Vayu* has been mentioned?

1. First Patal 2. Second Patal
3. Third Patal 4. Fourth Patal

30. According to *Gherand Samhita Rasanand Samadhi* is related to:

1. *Yoni mudra*
2. *Khechari mudra*
3. *Shambhavi mudra*
4. *Bhramri mudra*

31. The disease related to hallucination is called:

1. Stress
2. Depression
3. *Vatadosha* borne kind of Frenzy (unmad)
4. Insomnia

32. *Trividham Narakasyedam Dwaram Nashnamatmanah Kamah Krodhstatha Lobhastasmadettryam Tyajet*

Identify the chapter and number of this Shloka:

1. Bhagwadgita 6.12
2. Bhagwadgita 16.13
3. Bhagwadgita 18.4
4. Bhagwadgita 7.14

33. '*Asanen Rujam Hanti*' pertains to:

1. *Samadhi*
2. Recovery from disease
3. Concentration and Stability
4. Physical strength

34. During *Yoga Nidra* the physical points of the body become:

1. Extrovert (*Bahirmukhi*)
2. Introvert (*Antarmukhi*)
3. Six faced (*Shadmukhi*)
4. Oriented (*Unmukhi*)

35. The hormone released from Hypothalamus is:

1. Growth hormone (GH)
2. Adrenocorticotropic hormone (ACTH)
3. Corticotropin releasing hormone (CRH)
4. Luteinising hormone (LH)

36. In which *Pranayam*, during breathing obstruction is created in inhalation and exhalation?

1. *Nadishodhan Pranayam*
2. *Laya Pranayam*
3. *Bhramari Pranayam*
4. *Viloma Pranayam*

37. With reference to *Shatachakra Nirupan* scripture, *Sahasrar Chakra* is situated at the peak of which *Nadi*?

1. *Ida* 2. *Pingala*
3. *Sushumna* 4. *Shankhini*

38. Which of the following is not the Physical symptoms of menopause?

1. Hot flushes
2. Vaginal Atrophy
3. Irritability
4. Night Blindness

39. Allergic rhinitis also known as:

1. Bronchitis 2. Hay Fever
3. COPD 4. CAD

40. Which type of disease is Rheumatoid Arthritis?

1. Degenerative Disease
2. Inflammatory and Autoimmune Disease
3. Infectious Disease
4. Renal Disease

41. The correct order of the bones from top to bottom in human body is:

(A) Fibula
(B) Mandible
(C) Patella
(D) Sphenoid
(E) Hyoid

Choose the **correct** answer from the options given below:

1. (B), (D), (E), (C), (A)
2. (D), (B), (E), (C), (A)
3. (D), (B), (E), (A), (C)
4. (B), (E), (D), (A), (C)

42. In Need-hierarchy model, arrange the following in bottom to top order.

(A) Need of Safety
(B) Physical Need
(C) Need for self attainment (*Atmasiddhi*)
(D) Need to get membership and affection
(E) Need for respect

Choose the **correct** answer from the options given below:

1. (A), (E), (B), (D), (C)
2. (B), (C), (D), (E), (A)
3. (B), (D), (A), (E), (C)
4. (B), (A), (D), (E), (C)

43. According to *Siddhasiddhant Paddhati* text arrange the body bases (*Adhar*) in order of bottom to top:

(A) *Talvadhare*
(B) *Ghantikadhare*
(C) *Oudyanadhar*
(D) *Hridayadhar*
(E) *Nabhyadhar*

Choose the **correct** answer from the options given below:

1. (C), (E), (D), (B), (A)
2. (A), (B), (C), (D), (E)
3. (C), (D), (E), (A), (B)
4. (B), (C), (D), (E), (A)

44. Arrange the yoga practices used in yoga therapy in relation to the body from top to bottom:

(A) *Kapalrandhra Dhauti*
(B) *Dantamool Dhauti*
(C) *Sheetkram Kapalbhati*
(D) *Basti*
(E) *Agnisar*

Choose the **correct** answer from the options given below:

1. (A), (B), (C), (D), (E)
2. (B), (C), (D), (A), (E)
3. (A), (B), (C), (E), (D)
4. (B), (D), (A), (C), (E)

45. According to *Gherand Samhita*, the correct order of the features of the diet of a yogi:

(A) Oily (*Snigdha*)
(B) Favourite (*Priya*)
(C) Half cooked (*Laghupak*)
(D) Appealing (*Manonokul*)
(E) Nourishing (*Dhatuposhak*)

Choose the **correct** answer from the options given below:

1. (A), (B), (E), (D), (C)
2. (A), (D), (C), (B), (E)
3. (C), (B), (A), (E), (D)
4. (B), (A), (C), (D). (E)

46. The normal order of the Lesson-plan as defined by *Kaiwalyadham* Lonawala.

(A) Beginning of lesson
(B) Beginning of the Activity (*kriya-vidhi*)
(C) Verbal introduction of the Exercise
(D) Partial and full presentation
(E) Individual and collective exercise

Choose the **correct** answer from the options given below:

1. (A), (C), (B), (D), (E)
2. (A), (B), (C), (E), (D)
3. (A), (B), (C), (D), (E)
4. (A), (B), (E), (C), (D)

47. According to *Gherand Samhita* choose the correct order of Yoga practices from the following:

(A) *Uddiyan Bandha*
(B) *Nabhomudra*
(C) *Jalandhar Bandha*
(D) *Maha bandha*
(E) *Mool bandha*

Choose the **correct** answer from the options given below:

1. (B), (A), (C), (D), (E)
2. (B), (C), (A), (D), (E)
3. (A), (B), (C), (D), (E)
4. (B), (A), (C), (E), (D)

48. According to *yogachudamanya upnishada Mahamudra* treats the following diseases respectively:

(A) Leprosy (*Kushtha*)
(B) Thicket (*Gulma*)
(C) Tuberculosis (*Kshaya*)
(D) Gudavarta (*Gudavart*)
(E) Indigestion (*Ajirna*)

Choose the **correct** answer from the options given below:

1. (A), (B), (D), (C), (E)
2. (C), (B), (D), (A), (E)
3. (A), (C), (B), (E), (D)
4. (C), (A), (D), (B), (E)

49. As per the '*Yagyavalkya Smriti*', arrange the restraint of senses in correct order:

(A) *Dhairya*
(B) *Lazza*
(C) *Asteya*
(D) *Akrodh*
(E) *Vivek*

Choose the **correct** answer from the options given below:

1. (A), (B), (C), (D), (E)
2. (B), (C), (D), (E), (A)
3. (C), (D), (B), (E), (A)
4. (C), (D), (E), (B), (A)

50. According to *Nadbindupnishad*, the correct order of the *Kalayen* of 'Omkar' is:

(A) *Vayu Vegini*
(B) *Patangi*
(C) *Ghoshini*
(D) *Vidyunmatra*
(E) *Namdheya*

Choose the **correct** answer from the options given below:

1. (A), (B), (D), (C), (E)
2. (B), (A), (C), (D), (E)
3. (D), (C), (B), (E), (A)
4. (C), (D), (B), (A), (E)

51. The correct order of the practice of *Yoganidra* is:

(A) Awareness of Breathing
(B) Revolving the consciousness to different parts of the body
(C) Resolution
(D) To feel and Sensitivity
(E) Preparing for the practice

Choose the **correct** answer from the options given below:

1. (E), (B), (C), (A), (D)
2. (E), (C), (B), (A), (D)
3. (E), (D), (B), (A), (C)
4. (C), (E), (B), (A), (D)

52. The correct order of the virtues of a man born with divine properties (*Daivi Sampada*).

(A) *Shaucha* (B) *Tej*
(C) *Kshama* (D) *Dhriti*
(E) *Adroh*

Choose the **correct** answer from the options given below:

1. (B), (C), (D), (E), (A)
2. (C), (D), (A), (B), (E)
3. (B), (C), (D), (A), (E)
4. (D), (A), (B), (C), (E)

53. The correct order of the five types of stages:

(A) *Swarupawastha*
(B) *Sookshmawastha*
(C) *Sthoolawastha*
(D) *Arithvatva-awastha*
(E) *Anway-awastha*

Choose the **correct** answer from the options given below:

1. (C), (A), (E), (B), (D)
2. (C), (A), (B), (E), (D)
3. (A), (C), (B), (D), (E)
4. (B), (E), (D), (A), (C)

54. According to Jain Philosophy, the parts of the '*Aabhyantar Tapa*' in correct order is:

(A) Remorse (*Prayaschit*)
(B) Self-study (*Swadhyay*)
(C) Humility (*Vinaya*)
(D) *Vaiyavratya*
(E) *Vyutsarg*

Choose the **correct** answer from the options given below:

1. (A), (B), (C), (D), (E)
2. (B), (A), (C), (D), (E)
3. (A), (C), (D), (B), (E)
4. (B), (C), (A), (E), (D)

55. In *Bhriguvalli* of *Taittiriyopanishad*, Dev Varun says that these all are the means of attaining Brahma, Arrange them in correct order?

(A) *Prana* (B) *Chakshu*
(C) *Anna* (D) *Mana*
(E) *Shrota*

Choose the **correct** answer from the options given below:

1. (C), (A), (B), (E), (D)
2. (A), (B), (C), (D), (E)
3. (C), (B), (A), (D), (E)
4. (D), (C), (A), (B), (E)

56. The external means of *Gyana Yoga* are:

(A) *Shravana*
(B) *Viveka*
(C) *Vairagya*
(D) *Mumukshutva*
(E) *Nididhyasana*

Choose the **correct** answer from the options given below:

1. (A), (B), (C) only
2. (B), (C), (D) only
3. (A), (C), (D) only
4. (B), (C), (D), (E) only

57. In *Bahya Abhyantar* and *Stambh Vritii Pranayama*, which of the following is/are correct?

(A) It depends on the particular place
(B) It depends on the particular time
(C) It depends on particular number
(D) It depends on the particular individual
(E) It depends on the particular circumstances

Choose the **correct** answer from the options given below:

1. (A), (D), (C) only
2. (A), (B), (C) only
3. (C), (B), (D) only
4. (B), (D), (E) only

58. The hormones released from Adrenal Cortex.

(A) Glucocorticoids
(B) Melatonin
(C) Gonadocorticoid
(D) Prolactin
(E) Mineralocorticoid

Choose the **correct** answer from the options given below:

1. (A), (C), (D) only
2. (B), (A), (D) only
3. (A), (D), (E) only
4. (A), (C), (E) only

59. '*Ten Tyaktena Bhunjitha*' means:

(A) Penance (*Tapa*)
(B) Truth (*Satya*)
(C) *Aparigrah*
(D) *Mitvyayta*
(E) *Tyaga*

Choose the **correct** answer from the options given below:

1. (A), (C), (D) only
2. (B), (D), (E) only
3. (C), (D), (E) only
4. (B), (C), (D) only

60. Which of the following is/are the parts of five-afflictions (*Panch-Klesh*)?

(A) *Prasupta* (B) *Kshipt*
(C) *Vicchinna* (D) *Udar*
(E) *Avidya*

Choose the **correct** answer from the options given below:

1. (A), (E), (B) only
2. (B), (E), (C) only
3. (A), (C), (D) only
4. (B), (C), (D) only

61. The main characteristic of *Nauli* is the development.

(A) Concentration
(B) The development of sub atmospheric pressure inside the abdomen
(C) Maintaining acid base balance in the body
(D) Abdominal organs - stomach and colon
(E) Controlling the blood volume

Choose the **correct** answer from the options given below:

1. (A) and (B) only
2. (B) and (C) only
3. (B) and (D) only
4. (D) and (E) only

62. According to *Hath Pradeepika* the practice included in *Singhasana* are:

(A) *Moolbandh*
(B) *Jalandhar Bandh*
(C) *Uddiyan Bandh*
(D) *Mahabandh*
(E) *Shambhavi mudra*

Choose the **correct** answer from the options given below:

1. (A), (B), (E) only
2. (A), (B), (C) only
3. (A), (B), (D) only
4. (A), (C), (E) only

63. According to *Yoga Vasishtha* following process is adopted for attaining *Turiyavastha*:

(A) *Manolaya*
(B) *Vicharna*
(C) *Pran Nirodh*
(D) Strong feeling of unity (*Ekatva*)
(E) *Asansakti*

Choose the **correct** answer from the options given below:

1. (A), (B), (C) only
2. (A), (C), (E) only
3. (D), (B), (E) only
4. (A), (C), (D) only

64. The component of ill mental healths are:

(A) Happiness (*Prasannta*)
(B) *Styana*
(C) Satisfaction (*Santosh*)
(D) *Pramada*
(E) *Daurmanasya*

Choose the **correct** answer from the options given below:

1. (B), (D), (E) only
2. (A), (B), (C) only
3. (B), (C), (D) only
4. (D), (E), (A) only

65. The *Asanas* described in *Yogatatvopanishad* are:

(A) *Swastikasana* (B) *Siddhasana*
(C) *Padmasana* (D) *Simhasana*
(E) *Ugrasana*

Choose the **correct** answer from the options given below:

1. (A), (B), (E) only
2. (B), (C), (D) only
3. (B), (A), (D) only
4. (A), (B), (C) only

66. In which of the following Shlokas of Bhagwadgita we find description of food?

(A) Chapter 2/15
(B) Chapter 6/13
(C) Chapter 6/17
(D) Chapter 6/12
(E) Chapter 17/4

Choose the **correct** answer from the options given below:

1. (A) and (B) only
2. (B) and (C) only
3. (C) and (E) only
4. (D) and (E) only

67. What happened when *Paschimmottanasana* is practised like isometric exercise?

(A) Heart rate decreases
(B) Heart rate increases
(C) Reduce the burden on the cardio respiratory system
(D) Increase the burden on the cardio respiratory system
(E) Blood pressure decreases

Choose the **correct** answer from the options given below:

1. (B) and (D) only
2. (A) and (B) only
3. (C) and (D) only
4. (D) and (E) only

68. According to *Yogatatvopnishad* what happens with reciting *pranav* having *Plutmatra*?

(A) Destruction of sins of previous birth
(B) *Siddhiya* are attained
(C) *Kapalasuddhi*
(D) Improves digestion
(E) efforts like a frog

Choose the **correct** answer from the options given below:

1. (B) and (C) only
2. (A) and (E) only
3. (A) and (B) only
4. (C) and (D) only

69. For *Staunch Yoga* Practitioner which kind of flood are suggested to be abandoned?

(A) Juicy fruits
(B) Spicy (*Tez*)
(C) Pudding (*Madhur*)
(D) Sour food
(E) Panch shak

Choose the **correct** answer from the options given below:

1. (A) and (B) only
2. (C) and (D) only
3. (B) and (D) only
4. (D) and (E) only

70. According to *Kathopnishad*, Human achieves *Parampada* through the following:

(A) *Sanyam*
(B) *Pran-nirodh*

(C) *Guru-bhakti*
(D) *Pavitrata*
(E) *Yoga-nidra*

Choose the **correct** answer from the options given below:

1. (A) and (B) only
2. (B) and (C) only
3. (A) and (D) only
4. (B) and (E) only

71. According to *yoga darshan* lack of which of the following causes lack of lust?

(A) *Phal* (Fruit)
(B) *Hetu*
(C) *Viparyay*
(D) *Ashraya*
(E) *Vikalp*

Choose the **correct** answer from the options given below:

1. (C), (E), (A) only
2. (A), (B), (D) only
3. (C), (D), (E) only
4. (A), (B), (C) only

72. Kinds of Declarative memory are:

(A) Episodic Memory
(B) Iconic Memory
(C) Echoic Memory
(D) Semantic Memory
(E) Short-term Memory

Choose the **correct** answer from the options given below:

1. (A) and (D) only
2. (A) and (B) only
3. (A) and (C) only
4. (D) and (E) only

73. According to *Hathpradeepika, Ujjayi Kumbhak* is useful in:

(A) For disorder of *Kapha*
(B) For disorder of *Vata*
(C) For disorder of *Dhatu*
(D) For Apetite (*Kshudha*)
(E) For disorder of *Pitta*

Choose the **correct** answer from the options given below:

1. (B) and (D) only
2. (C) and (E) only
3. (A) and (C) only
4. (A) and (D) only

74. The treatment as advised by Swami Kuwalayanand for holistic health.

(A) Prevention from infections
(B) Using the proper medicines
(C) Formulating the light Psychological view point
(D) Emphasis on healthy food
(E) Resorting to modern medicine system

Choose the **correct** answer from the options given below:

1. (A) and (B) only
2. (C) and (D) only
3. (D) and (E) only
4. (E) and (A) only

75. Which of the following do/does not come under *Shatsampatti*?

(A) *Titiksha* (Endurance)
(B) *Shraddha* (Faith)
(C) *Vivek* (Prudence)
(D) *Samadhan* (Solution)
(E) *Vairagya*

Choose the **correct** answer from the options given below:

1. (A) and (B) only
2. (C) and (A) only
3. (B) and (D) only
4. (C) and (E) only

76. Match List-I with List-II.

List-I (Posture of *Surya Namaskar*)	List-II (Meditation of *Chakra*)
(A) *Padhastassan*	(I) *Manipur Chakra*
(B) *Ashwasanchalan*	(II) *Vishuddhi Chakra*
(C) *Parvatasan*	(III) *Swadhishthan Chakra*
(D) *Ashtanga Namaskar*	(IV) *Ajna Chakra*

Choose the **correct** answer from the options given below:

1. (A)-(I), (B)-(II), (C)-(III), (D)-(IV)
2. (A)-(III), (B)-(II), (C)-(I), (D)-(IV)
3. (A)-(III), (B)-(IV), (C)-(II), (D)-(I)
4. (A)-(III), (B)-(IV), (C)-(I), (D)-(II)

77. Match List-I with List-II. In the specific context of *Shiv Samhita*.

List-I (Name of Yoga practice)	List-II (Description of Effect)
(A) *Mahamudra*	(I) Penetration of *Brahmagranthi*
(B) *Mahabandha*	(II) Gets devoid of idleness
(C) *Mahabedha*	(III) *Kashayas* being burnt
(D) *Khechari*	(IV) The different *rasas* flow towards *murdha*

Choose the **correct** answer from the options given below:

1. (A)-(III), (B)-(IV), (C)-(I), (D)-(II)
2. (A)-(I), (B)-(II), (C)-(III), (D)-(IV)
3. (A)-(III), (B)-(II), (C)-(I), (D)-(IV)
4. (A)-(II), (B)-(III), (C)-(I), (D)-(IV)

78. Match List-I with List-II. According to the chronology of birth.

List-I	List-II
(A) Swami Shivanand	(I) 1893
(B) Shri Aurobindo	(II) 1863
(C) Paramhans Yoganand	(III) 1887
(D) Swami Vivekanand	(IV) 1872

Choose the **correct** answer from the options given below:

1. (A)-(II), (B)-(IV), (C)-(III), (D)-(I)
2. (A)-(I), (B)-(IV), (C)-(II), (D)-(III)
3. (A)-(III), (B)-(II), (C)-(I), (D)-(IV)
4. (A)-(III), (B)-(IV), (C)-(I), (D)-(II)

79. Match List-I with List-II. According to the names of chapters.

List-I	List-II
(A) *Mumukshu Prakaran*	(I) First part
(B) *Utpatti Prakaran*	(II) Second part
(C) *Vairagya Prakaran*	(III) Fifth part
(D) *Upsham Prakaran*	(IV) Third part

Choose the **correct** answer from the options given below:

1. (A)-(II), (B)-(IV), (C)-(I), (D)-(III)
2. (A)-(II), (B)-(IV), (C)-(III), (D)-(I)
3. (A)-(I), (B)-(II), (C)-(III), (D)-(IV)
4. (A)-(I), (B)-(IV), (C)-(III), (D)-(II)

80. Match List-I with List-II.

List-I	List-II
(A) Process of adjustment through works	(I) Teacher
(B) Process regarding methods	(II) Teaching
(C) Directing processes	(III) Student
(D) Adjusts itself through works	(IV) Learning

Choose the **correct** answer from the options given below:

1. (A)-(IV), (B)-(II), (C-(I), (D)-(III)
2. (A)-(IV), (B)-(II), (C)-(III), (D)-(I)
3. (A)-(I), (B)-(II), (C)-(III), (D)-(IV)
4. (A)-(II), (B)-(IV), (C)-(I), (D)-(III)

81. Match List-I with List-II.

List-I (Diseases)	List-II (Symptoms)
(A) Diabetes Mellitus	(I) Inflammation of glands
(B) Tonsillitis	(II) Falling out of place
(C) Arteriosclerosis	(III) Disorder in metabolism of sugar
(D) Prolapse	(IV) Degeneration of blood vessels

Choose the **correct** answer from the options given below:

1. (A)-(III), (B)-(I), (C)-(II), (D)-(IV)
2. (A)-(III), (B)-(II), (C)-(I), (D)-(IV)
3. (A)-(III), (B)-(I), (C)-(IV), (D)-(II)
4. (A)-(I), (B)-(II), (C)-(III), (D)-(IV)

82. Match List-I with List-II. According to *Vasishtha Samhita*.

List-I	List-II
(A) Air	(I) य
(B) Water	(II) र
(C) Fire (*Tez*)	(III) ल
(D) Earth	(IV) व

Choose the **correct** answer from the options given below:

1. (A)-(I), (B)-(III), (C)-(IV), (D)-(II)
2. (A)-(IV), (B)-(II), (C)-(III), (D)-(I)
3. (A)-(I), (B)-(IV), (C)-(II), (D)-(III)
4. (A)-(III), (B)-(II), (C)-(IV), (D)-(I)

83. Match List-I with List-II.

List-I	List-II
(A) *Chitta* delving into spiritual upliftment	(I) *Niyama*
(B) Detachment towards sense organs	(II) *Jnanyoga*
(C) Love for *Parmatma Tatva*	(III) *Asana*
(D) Indifferences towards objects	(IV) *Yama*

Choose the **correct** answer from the options given below:

1. (A)-(II), (B)-(I), (C)-(IV), (D)-(III)
2. (A)-(II), (B)-(IV), (C)-(I), (D)-(III)
3. (A)-(III), (B)-(II), (C)-(I), (D)-(IV)
4. (A)-(I), (B)-(III), (C)-(II), (D)-(IV)

84. Match List-I with List-II.

List-I (Vitamins)	List-II (Disease)
(A) Thiamin	(I) Pelagra
(B) Niacin	(II) Dermatitis
(C) Biotin	(III) Pernicious Anaemia
(D) Cyanocobalamin	(IV) Beri beri

Choose the **correct** answer from the options given below:

1. (A)-(I), (B)-(III), (C)-(IV), (D)-(II)
2. (A)-(IV), (B)-(I), (C)-(III), (D)-(II)
3. (A)-(IV), (B)-(II), (C)-(I), (D)-(III)
4. (A)-(IV), (B)-(I), (C)-(II), (D)-(III)

85. Match List-I with List-II.

List-I (Components)	List-II (Sub components)
(A) Fat	(I) Triptophan
(B) Monosaccharide	(II) Sucrose
(C) Disaccharide	(III) Fructose
(D) Protein	(IV) Linolenic Acid

Choose the **correct** answer from the options given below:

1. (A)-(IV), (B)-(III), (C)-(II), (D)-(I)
2. (A)-(IV), (B)-(II), (C)-(III), (D)-(I)
3. (A)-(I), (B)-(III), (C)-(II), (D)-(IV)
4. (A)-(I), (B)-(II), (C)-(IV), (D)-(III)

86. Match List-I with List-II.

List-I (Sukti)	List-II (Name of the Scripture)
(A) *Mitaharaschasanam Cha Shaktichalak tritiya*	(I) *Shrimad Bhagwad Gita*
(B) *Bhujyate Shiv Samprityai Mitaharssa uchyate*	(II) *Yoga Kundaly-upnishad*
(C) *Bhujyate Sursampritya mitaram imam Viduh*	(III) *Hathyoga-pradipika*
(D) *Yuktaharviharasya Yuktacheshtasya Karmasu*	(IV) *Gheranda Samhita*

Choose the **correct** answer from the options given below:

1. (A)-(II), (B)-(III), (C)-(I), (D)-(IV)
2. (A)-(II), (B)-(III), (C)-(IV), (D)-(I)
3. (A)-(I), (B)-(II), (C)-(III), (D)-(IV)
4. (A)-(IV), (B)-(II), (C)-(III), (D)-(I)

87. Match List-I with List-II.

List-I	List-II
(A) *Vishesh*	(I) Intelligence (*Buddhi*)
(B) *Lingmatra*	(II) Ego (*Ahankar*)
(C) *Avishesh*	(III) Mind (*man*)
(D) *Alinga*	(IV) Nature (*Prakriti*)

Choose the **correct** answer from the options given below:

1. (A)-(II), (B)-(IV), (C)-(I), (D)-(III)
2. (A)-(III), (B)-(IV), (C)-(I), (D)-(II)
3. (A)-(IV), (B)-(III), (C)-(I), (D)-(II)
4. (A)-(III), (B)-(I), (C)-(II), (D)-(IV)

88. Match List-I with List-II.

List-I	List-II
(A) *Kenopanishad*	(I) *Shukla Yajurved*
(B) *Aitareya Upanishad*	(II) *Krishna Yajurvediya Shakha*
(C) *Kathopanishad*	(III) *Samvediya Shakha*
(D) *Brihadaranyaka Upanishad*	(IV) *Shukla Rigvediya Shakha*

Choose the **correct** answer from the options given below:

1. (A)-(III), (B)-(IV), (C)-(I), (D)-(II)
2. (A)-(III), (B)-(IV), (C)-(II), (D)-(I)
3. (A)-(IV), (B)-(II), (C)-(III), (D)-(I)
4. (A)-(I), (B)-(II), (C)-(IV), (D)-(III)

89. Match List-I with List-II.

List-I (Concept)	List-II (Scripture)
(A) Concept of *Trigunas*	(I) *Tattirayopanishad*
(B) Concept of *Punch Koshas*	(II) *Yogvasishtha*
(C) Concept of *Punch Pranas*	(III) *Sankhyakarika*
(D) Concept of *Adhi-vyadhi*	(IV) *Sidhasidhant Padhati*

Choose the **correct** answer from the options given below:

1. (A)-(III), (B)-(IV), (C)-(I), (D)-(II)
2. (A)-(IV), (B)-(I), (C)-(III), (D)-(II)
3. (A)-(III), (B)-(I), (C)-(IV), (D)-(II)
4. (A)-(III), (B)-(II), (C)-(IV), (D)-(I)

90. Match List-I with List-II.

List-I	List-II
(A) Glucometer	(I) Brain waves
(B) Sphygnomanometer	(II) Diabetes
(C) EEG	(III) Blood pressure
(D) ECG	(IV) Heartbeat

Choose the **correct** answer from the options given below:

1. (A)-(II), (B)-(III), (C)-(IV), (D)-(I)
2. (A)-(II), (B)-(IV), (C)-(I), (D)-(III)
3. (A)-(II), (B)-(III), (C)-(I), (D)-(IV)
4. (A)-(III), (B)-(II), (C)-(I), (D)-(IV)

Directions (Qs. No. 91-95): *Read the passage carefully and answer the questions that follow:*

The person (*Jivatma*) who has attributes (*gunas*), acts seeking results and consumes the fruits of *Karma* performed by him, he goes through the three routes while bearing different forms and the three attributes. The *Jivatma* who is master the *Pranas*, goes through different form of species according to his *Karmas* he undertakes. This soul i.e. *Jivatma* has the quantum of *Angushtha* only, he is enlightened like the sun and cherishes intelligence alongwith Determination and ego. He is as subtle as the tip of the saw, having existence different from the *Parmatma*. The quantum of *Jiva* is the hundredth part of the hundredth part of the tip of a hair, his form is as subtle as the imaginary part the subtlest part of the hair, but this very soul is capable of expanding in infinite form. This *Jivatma* gets attached with the body he imbibes. As the body get nourishment from food and water, so the soul derives its birth and expansion from determination, touch, vision and attachment.

The *Jivatma* bears different places and different bodies according to the *Karmas* undertaken by him. *Jivatma* assumes Gross, subtle and many forms of life according to his internal attributes. In this vast world, *Jivatma* gets: redemption from all sorts of bondages after he attains knowledge of the supreme soul who is eternal, infinite, creator of the world, having many forms alone pervades the entire world with own existence.

91. Our body gets nourishment from:

1. Food and water (*Anna-Jala*)
2. Touch (*Sparsh*)
3. *Karma*
4. Determination (*Sankalpa*)

92. Which of the following has existence different from God?

1. Body (*Sharir*)
2. Determination (*Sankalpa*)
3. Attachment (*Moha*)
4. *Jivatma*

93. The imaginary form *Jivatma* is equivalent to:

1. Hundredth part of a hair
2. Ten thousandth part of a hair
3. One thousandth part of a hair
4. One thousand one hundredth part of a hair

94. What is the cause *Jivatma's* assuming different bodies?

1. Karma
2. Vision (*Drishti*)
3. Touch (*Sparsha*)
4. All of the above

95. Who among the following has determination and ego?

1. Supreme soul (*Parmatma*)
2. Mind (*Mann*)
3. *Jivatma*
4. All of the above

Directions (Qs. No. 96-100): *Read the passage carefully and answer the questions that follow:*

The whole human race is going through a serious crisis of physical and mental health. With the scientific progress the blind race and limelight of materialistic world has made the things worse.

The basic subject of the nature and properties of the mind are not yet clear in the modern Psychology. In the yoga Psycho-analysis the unconscious is the major fact. In this way many new facts are emerging, which are thinking over it in their own way. The materialistic thinkers have committed the mistake on accepting the mind as originated from the non-living existence of brain.

As with the mind, even the personality remains deprived of the wholistic personality. Behaviourists define personality around the behaviour. The basic defect of Psychology is not accepting the existence of soul and being ignorant and confused about the super conscious stage of mind. While yoga is opposite to it.

Psychology defines mental health mainly in form of psychological adjustment at a practical level. Yet as per its various criteria he/she who is not sick, is normal. According to various views the behaviour arised from the socially invalid, painful and distorted knowledge is called abnormal. On the basis of *Sat, Raj* and *Tam* Virtues normality and abnormality have been eventually viewed. It is the beauty of yoga.

The spiritual system of Indian Rishis that studies the human nature wholistically presents a preface in form of a light of hope. As with the mind, in Indian thought process personality is considered wholistically. The focal point of personality is the soul which is equivalent to Brahma. Due to ignorance it considers itself limited to the body and mind.

96. What is the main reason of mental diseases in modern time?

1. Physical tiredness
2. Mental fatigue
3. Limelight of materialism
4. Social challenges

97. According to Yoga, what is the basis of the nature of mind?

1. Conscious
2. Unconscious
3. Subconscious
4. Mind

98. What is the nature of wholistic personality in Yoga?

1. *Jeevatma*
2. *Paramatma*
3. *Vishwatma*
4. Soul

99. What is the Yogic concept of Mental health?

1. Earth - Water - Fire
2. *Vata - Pitta - Kapha*
3. *Sata - Raja - Tama*
4. *Shabd - Rasa - Gandha*

100. What is the Central idea of Indian Thought?

1. *Jeeva*
2. *Brahma*
3. *Prakriti*
4. *Purush*

ANSWERS

1. **(3):** *Purak* is *Brahma*, *Kumbhak* is *Vishnu* and *Rechak* is *Rudra*-this concept is found in the *Dhyan Bindu Upanishad*.

   This Upanishad is one of the minor Yoga Upanishads of the *Krishna Yajurveda* and focuses extensively on the process of meditation *(dhyana)* and breath control *(pranayama)*.

   It identifies *Puraka* (inhalation) with Brahma (creator), *Kumbhaka* (retention) with *Vishnu* (preserver), and *Rechaka* (exhalation) with *Rudra/Shiva* (destroyer).

   This metaphor emphasizes the *cosmic significance of breath control*, linking the three fundamental aspects of pranayama to the three main deities of the Hindu trinity (*Trimurti*).

   It highlights the spiritual importance of breathing as a method of aligning oneself with universal energies.

2. **(2):** *Kayadivishvati Gargah* is mentioned in *Narad Bhakti Sutra*. The phrase *"Kayadivishvati Gargah"* refers to the idea that *Bhakti* (devotion) can manifest through all activities of life, including bodily actions.

   In the *Narada Bhakti Sutra*, a key text on the philosophy of *Bhakti Yoga*, Sage Narada gives a universal and inclusive view of devotion, accepting that sages like *Gargah* engaged in devotion through the body *(kaya)*, senses *(indriya)*, and intellect *(buddhi)*.

   The mention of Garga *(Kayadivishvati Gargah)* underscores that even through worldly actions, the divine can be approached when done with devotion.

   This *Sutra* promotes the idea that *Bhakti* is not limited to renunciation but is available to householders and active participants in the world.

3. **(4):** The disciple obtained knowledge from his *Guru* with the help of Pranipat (Surrender), service and questioning-is mentioned in *Bhagavad Gita 4.34*.

   The exact verse is:

   "tad viddhi pranipatena pariprasnena sevaya upadeksyanti te jñana- jñaninas tattva-darsinah"

   Meaning: "Know that by long prostration, by question, and by service, the wise who have realized the Truth will instruct you in that knowledge."

   The threefold approach to learning:

   - ***Pranipat***: Total surrender at the feet of the Guru.
   - ***Pariprashna***: Asking sincere, intelligent, and humble questions.
   - ***Seva***: Serving the Guru selflessly.

   This verse defines the ideal student-teacher relationship in the Guru-Shishya *Parampara*, stressing humility and service as prerequisites for true knowledge.

4. **(4):** According to *Yoga Sutra*, restraint *(samyam)* on *Nabhichakra* gives knowledge of human anatomy.

   In *Patanjali's Yoga Sutras*, *Samyam* refers to the combined practice of *Dharana* (concentration), *Dhyana* (meditation), and *Samadhi* (absorption).

   Yoga Sutra 3.30 states: *"Nabhi cakre kaya-vyuha-jñanam"*, meaning: "By performing *Samyama* on the navel center *(nabhichakra)*, knowledge of the organization of the body is obtained."

   Nabhi (navel) is considered a central energy center connected with the distribution of energy and the mapping of bodily systems.

   The practitioner gains deep intuitive and experiential knowledge of the internal structure and functions of the human body-including organs, systems, and their interconnections.

5. **(3):** "Consciousness is the most miraculous thing of creation, its depth and pervasiveness knows no limit"-this statement is attributed to Dr. David Frawley.

Dr. David Frawley (also known as Vamadeva Shastri) is a renowned Vedic scholar and author of numerous works on *Ayurveda, Yoga,* and *Vedanta*. He has emphasized the primacy of consciousness *(Chit)* in all aspects of creation, often highlighting that modern science is only beginning to uncover what ancient rishis already understood.

According to his teachings:

- Consciousness is not a byproduct of the brain, but the substratum of all existence.
- It is infinite, pervasive, and the true essence of the individual and the cosmos.

This view resonates with Vedantic philosophy, especially the Advaita Vedanta, which identifies *Brahman* with pure consciousness *(Sat-Chit-Ananda)*.

6. (3): Paramhans Yoganand is one of the famous disciples of Shri Shyama Charan Lahiri, also known as Lahiri Mahasaya.

Lahiri Mahasaya was a renowned householder *yogi* and *Kriya Yoga* master, and he played a pivotal role in reviving *Kriya Yoga* in modern times.

Among his illustrious disciples was Sri Yukteswar Giri, who later became the guru of Paramhans Yogananda. Though Yogananda did not receive direct instruction from Lahiri Mahasaya (who passed away in 1895), he is regarded as part of the spiritual lineage or parampara of Lahiri Mahasaya. In his famous work *"Autobiography of a Yogi"*, Yogananda acknowledges Lahiri Mahasaya as one of his Gurus and deeply reveres him.

Therefore, in the *Kriya Yoga* tradition, he is often counted as a disciple in a spiritual sense, maintaining the *Guru-Shishya* tradition through the lineage.

7. (2): Alfred Adler is considered the founder of Personal Psychology, also known as Individual Psychology. He broke away from Freud's psychoanalytic school and emphasized the importance of the individual as a whole.

Key principles of Adler's Personal Psychology include:

- **Striving for superiority** as a core motive in human behaviour.
- **Social interest** as essential for mental health.
- Focus on birth order, lifestyle, and early childhood experiences in shaping personality.

Adler introduced the idea that each person has a unique way of seeking significance and belonging, hence the term "Individual Psychology". His work laid the foundation for Humanistic Psychology and strongly influenced later thinkers like Abraham Maslow and Carl Rogers.

8. (4): The Principles of emotions are explained by both the Cannon-Bard Principle and the James-Lange Principle.

James-Lange Theory (Option 3):

- Proposed by William James and Carl Lange.
- States that physiological arousal precedes emotional experience.
- For example, *we feel afraid because we tremble*.

Cannon-Bard Theory (Option 1):

- Developed by Walter Cannon and Philip Bard.
- States that emotional and physiological responses occur simultaneously and independently.
- For example, upon seeing a threat, we feel fear and our heart races at the same time.

Both theories offer foundational understanding in psychology about how emotions are processed in the human mind and body.

Hence, the correct option is Both (1) and (3).

9. (4): According to Yoga Philosophy, restraint *(Samyam)* on *Samskara* results in the knowledge of *Purvajanma* (past lives).

In *Patanjali's Yoga Sutra 3.18*, it is stated: *"Samskara-saksatkaranat purvajati-jñanam"*, meaning: By performing Samyam (concentration-meditation-absorption) on

Samskaras (impressions), knowledge of previous births arises.

Samskaras are deep-seated mental impressions formed by past experiences and actions *(karma)*. These impressions remain stored in the subtle body *(sukshma sharira)* and influence our present behavior, desires, and tendencies.

Through deep yogic practices, when one restrains the mind and focuses on these latent impressions, intuitive knowledge of previous incarnations can be accessed. This is a key concept in Yoga and *Sankhya* philosophies, which accept the existence of reincarnation and karma.

10. (4): According to *Yoga Vashishtha*, *Padarthabhavana* (contemplation of objects) is the sixth *Bhumi* (stage) of knowledge.

Yoga Vashishtha, an important Vedantic text, outlines seven *Bhoomis* or stages of knowledge *(Jnanabhumi)* in the process of spiritual evolution.

The stages are:

- *Subheccha* (good desire)
- *Vicharana* (inquiry)
- *Tanumanasa* (subtlety of mind)
- *Sattvapatti* (attainment of purity)
- *Asamsakti* (detachment from worldly objects)
- *Padarthabhavana* (contemplation of reality)
- *Turiya* (final liberation)

In *Padarthabhavana,* the aspirant perceives the truth or essence of objects *(Padarthas),* understanding the non-dual *Brahman* behind the apparent diversity.

This stage signifies deep intellectual realization and discrimination *(Viveka)*, where *maya* or illusion is transcended, and reality is perceived directly. It is a highly advanced state leading directly to final liberation.

11. (2): Lesson plan helps a teacher in understanding necessary teaching methods and objectives. A lesson plan is a structured guide created by a teacher to outline the instructional strategy for a particular class or topic.

It includes:

- **Learning objectives:** what the students are expected to learn.
- **Teaching methods:** the approach or methodology to be adopted (e.g., lecture, demonstration, discussion).
- **Sequence of activities:** step-by-step instructions to deliver content effectively.
- **Assessment and evaluation** methods.

A well-prepared lesson plan ensures effective classroom delivery, helps the teacher remain goal-oriented, and also helps in time management. It reflects the pedagogical strategy, aligning teaching with curriculum requirements and student needs.

12. (3): *Shitkari Pranayama* is beneficial in the treatment of Colitis. Colitis refers to inflammation of the colon and is often associated with symptoms like abdominal pain, bloating, and irregular bowel movements. *Shitkari Pranayama* is a cooling breathing technique in which air is inhaled through the teeth with a slight hissing sound and exhaled through the nose.

Benefits of *Shitkari* in Colitis:

- **Cooling effect** on the digestive system, which helps reduce intestinal inflammation.
- Promotes **parasympathetic nervous response,** aiding in digestion and relaxation.
- Balances *Pitta dosha*, which is often aggravated in inflammatory bowel conditions like colitis.

It also improves metabolism, reduces acidity, and brings calmness to the gut.

13. (2): According to *Samkhya Philosophy, Tushti* is *Badhak* (an obstacle) to Yogic practices. In *Samkhya, Tushti* refers to a sense of false contentment or complacency, arising from partial knowledge or superficial achievements. Types of *Tushti* include:

- Satisfaction with limited progress.
- Feeling accomplished after minor practices without striving for deeper realization.

Badhak means something that hinders or blocks progress.

Tushti becomes an obstacle because:

- It halts further inquiry or sadhana, leading to stagnation.
- It creates mental inertia, preventing one from reaching higher stages of liberation or purusha-jnana.

Therefore, a true seeker must transcend *Tushti* by cultivating *viveka* (discrimination) and continuous effort in *Yogic* discipline.

14. (3): The *Mandukyopanishad* contains 12 shlokas. The *Mandukya Upanishad* is the shortest of all the major *Upanishads* but holds immense philosophical depth. It belongs to the *Atharvaveda* and consists of only *12 mantras* (verses). Despite its brevity, it deals with profound concepts such as:

- The nature of AUM *(Om)*.
- Four states of consciousness—waking *(jagrat)*, dreaming *(svapna)*, deep sleep *(sushupti)*, and the transcendental *(turiya)*.
- The non-dual *(Advaita)* nature of *Atman* and *Brahman*.

It forms the foundation of *Gaudapada's Karikas* and is highly revered in *Advaita Vedanta* philosophy espoused by *Adi Shankaracharya*. Because of its concise yet comprehensive nature, it is considered one of the most profound spiritual texts.

15. (3): According to *Yoga Philosophy, Avirati* or lack of renunciation causes *Chitta-vikshepa* (disturbance in consciousness). In *Patanjali's Yoga Sutras*, chitta vikshepa are mental distractions that hinder concentration and meditative absorption. *Sutra* 1.30 lists *Avirati* as one of the nine obstacles *(Antarayas)* to Yoga:

- *Vyadhi, Styana, Samsaya, Pramada, Aalasya, Avirati, Bhranti-darshana, Alabdha-bhumikatva, Anavasthitatva.*

Avirati refers to the inability to withdraw the senses or renounce worldly pleasures and indulgences. This creates mental restlessness, attachment, and an inability to focus inward. Without *Vairagya* (dispassion), the mind remains entangled in raga-dvesha (likes and dislikes), obstructing the path to *samadhi*.

Thus, overcoming *Avirati* through discipline *(tapas)*, dispassion, and self-control is essential for progress in Yoga.

16. (3): According to Yoga Philosophy, the correct sequence among the *Animadi Ashta Siddhis* (eight supernatural powers) includes *Garima, Prapti, Prakramya,* and *Vashitva*. The *Ashta Siddhis* are mentioned in various yogic texts including the *Yoga Vashishtha, Hatha Yoga Pradipika*, and *Bhagavata Purana*.

The complete list of the eight Siddhis is:

- *Anima*–the power to become minute.
- *Mahima*–the power to expand infinitely.
- *Garima*–the power to become infinitely heavy.
- *Laghima*–the power to become weightless.
- *Prapti*–the ability to reach anywhere.
- *Prakamyam*–the ability to achieve any desired thing.
- *Ishitva*–lordship or absolute control.
- *Vashitva*–power to subjugate all.

The option *Garima, Prapti, Prakramya, Vashitva* presents a sequence that correctly includes four of these eight siddhis in appropriate progression of physical, spatial, volitional, and commanding abilities.

17. (4): According to *Shrimad Bhagavad Gita,* a person dominated by the *Tamas guna* prefers food that is half baked, devoid of juice, and leftover.

This is stated in *Bhagavad Gita,* Chapter 17, Verse 10:

"Yata-yamam gata-rasam puti paryusitam ca yat, ucchistam api camedhyam bhojanam tamasam priyam".

Characteristics of *Tamasic* food:

- *Yata-yamam:* overcooked or kept for long.
- *Gata-rasam:* tasteless, devoid of natural juices.

- *Puti:* foul-smelling or decayed.
- *Paryushitam:* stale or old food.
- *Ucchishitam:* leftovers.
- *Amedhyam:* impure or unhygienic.

Such food causes lethargy, delusion, mental dullness, and supports ignorance *(tamas)* in the body and mind.

18. **(2):** The *Ishavashyopanishad* speaks about the knowledge of *Sambhuti* and *Asambhuti* together.

Verse 11 of the *Isha Upanishad* states:

"Vidyam cavidyam ca yas tad vedobhayam saha, avidyaya mrtyum turtva vidyayamrtam asnute".

It later differentiates *Sambhuti* (manifest creation) and *Asambhuti* (unmanifest or supreme *Brahman*).

Verse 14 emphasizes:

"Sambhutim ca vinasam ca yas tad vedobhayam saha..."

indicating one must understand both the manifest and the unmanifest to attain complete knowledge.

The text teaches that exclusive pursuit of only *Vidya* (knowledge) or *Avidya* (ignorance or ritualism) is incomplete. Both must be realized together for true liberation.

Hence, *Isha Upanishad* uniquely bridges material and spiritual knowledge in its non-dualistic approach.

19. **(3):** *Tadasan* helps in soothing the sphincters in the digestive system and assists the downward movement of consumed water toward the anus. *Tadasana*, or Palm Tree Pose, is a basic standing posture that stretches the spine and creates alignment in the digestive tract.

Benefits relating to digestion:

- Helps in stretching and toning abdominal muscles, easing tension in intestinal sphincters.
- Promotes peristaltic motion in intestines, aiding bowel movement.
- Enhances fluid movement downward due to gravitational alignment, useful after water cleansing kriyas like *Varisara Dhauti*.

In *Shatkarmic* and yogic detox techniques, *Tadasana* is often practiced after drinking large amounts of water to assist in elimination through the colon.

20. **(4):** According to *Ramayan, Padasevan* is not one of the *Navadha Bhakti* (nine forms of devotion) listed by *Lord Rama* in the discourse to *Shabari*.

The *Navadha Bhakti,* as described in *Ayodhya Kanda* of *Ramcharitmanas*, are:

- *Satsang*–Association with holy people.
- *Katha Shravan*–Listening to divine stories.
- *Guru Seva*–Serving the Guru with humility.
- *Japa*–Chanting the divine name with faith.
- Rules and ethics *(Niyam Palan)*–Following righteousness.
- *Vairagya*–Detachment and contentment.
- Seeing the world as God's play–*Bhav Drishti*.
- Contentment *(Santosh)*–Inner satisfaction.
- Unshakable faith and surrender.

Padasevan (serving the feet of the Lord) is part of *Bhagavata Purana's* version of *Navadha Bhakti*, not of *Ramayan's* version.

Thus, among the options, *Padasevan* does not belong to the *Navadha Bhakti* as described in the *Ramayana*.

21. **(3):** *Buddhi tatha Dhritishakti Vikasak* (Development of intellect and determination) is the subtle exercise that helps in relieving problems like deteriorating intelligence, forgetfulness, disturbances, and scepticism.

This practice aims at enhancing the cognitive faculties — especially *Buddhi* (intellect) and *Dhriti* (determination or mental steadiness).

Benefits include:

- Improved memory retention and recall abilities.
- Better decision-making and discrimination *(viveka)*.
- Mental clarity and focus, reducing doubts and inner conflicts.

Yogic and subtle mental practices *(sookshma vyayama)* such as *trataka,* specific *mudras, pranayama,* and guided contemplation are often included in this category.

When practiced regularly, they activate the *Ajna chakra* (third-eye center), associated with mental insight and intellectual sharpness.

It is particularly effective for students and practitioners facing intellectual fatigue or indecisiveness.

22. (3): Dendrites are short processes that receive and carry incoming action potentials toward the cell body. In a neuron (nerve cell), the dendrites function as the receptive regions. They receive chemical and electrical signals from other neurons and transmit them towards the soma (cell body).

Characteristics:

- Highly branched extensions increasing surface area for communication.
- Covered with synapses, where neuro-transmitters from other neurons bind.
- Act as input sites, whereas the axon functions as the output structure.

Dendrites play a crucial role in neural communication, learning, and memory processing.

Damage or degeneration of dendrites can lead to neurological issues like memory loss and cognitive impairment.

23. (2): According to *Yoga Sutra,* the main cause of the union (apparent identification) of *Drashta* (seer) and *Drishya* (seen) is the presence of the Five *Kleshas.*

Patanjali in *Yoga Sutra 2.17* says: *"Drashtr-drsyayoh samyogo heya-hetuh"*, meaning: *"The cause of suffering is the identification of the seer (Purusha) with the seen (Prakriti)."*

This identification is rooted in *Kleshas* (afflictions) mentioned in *Sutra 2.3*:

- *Avidya*–ignorance of the true Self.
- *Asmita*–egoism or false identification.
- *Raga*–attachment.
- *Dvesha*–aversion.
- *Abhinivesha*–clinging to life or fear of death.

These *kleshas* cloud the consciousness, causing the *Purusha* to misidentify with the body, mind, and senses.

Removal of *kleshas* is essential to separate *Drashta* from *Drishya*, leading to *kaivalya* (liberation).

24. (3): According to *Vasishtha Samhita, Dharna* is the practice involving contemplation of outer space *(Bahyakasha)* with inner space *(Antarakash)* in the heart.

Dharna is the sixth limb of *Ashtanga Yoga,* defined as concentration or holding the mind in a single direction. In the context of *Vasishtha Samhita,* this dharana practice is described as:

- Meditating on *Bahyakasha* (external space), such as the sky or infinite expanse.
- Simultaneously connecting it with *Antarakasha,* the inner subtle space experienced within the *hridaya* (heart center).

The union of the two develops a state of spacious awareness, leading the practitioner towards inner stillness and oneness.

This technique prepares the mind for *Dhyana* (meditation) and *Samadhi* (absorption) by eliminating distractions and expanding inner perception.

25. (4): According to Sigmund Freud, dream is the highway of the unconscious.

Freud, the father of psychoanalysis, believed that dreams are the royal road to the unconscious mind.

In his seminal work, *"The Interpretation of Dreams" (1899)*, he proposed that:

- Dreams are symbolic expressions of unconscious desires, particularly repressed wishes, often of a sexual or aggressive nature.
- The manifest content (what is remembered) masks the latent content (true unconscious meaning).
- Dreams serve as psychic safety valves, allowing unconscious material to surface without disturbing the conscious mind.

Through dream analysis, Freud aimed to uncover hidden aspects of the unconscious psyche, leading to therapeutic insights. His theory laid the foundation for modern depth psychology and dream interpretation.

26. (1): According to ***Trishikhi Brahmana Upanishad,*** absolute detachment towards the body and sense organs is referred to as *Yama.*

In this *Upanishad, Yama* is not just moral restraint, but a deeper renunciation or absolute dispassion *(Vairagya)* towards bodily and sensory pleasures.

It emphasizes that the first step of Yoga is internal detachment from *deha* (body) and *indriyas* (senses).

The purpose of this detachment is:

- To prevent the identification with the physical body.
- To control *indriya-vrttis* (fluctuations due to senses).
- To prepare the aspirant for higher Yogic states such as *Dharana* and *Samadhi.*

Thus, unlike *Patanjali* who lists *Yama* as moral disciplines, here it is described as complete detachment, making it the first spiritual foundation.

27. (2): According to *Yogakundalyopanishad, Sahita Kumbhaka* comprises *Suryabhedan, Ujjayi, Sheetali,* and *Bhastrika.*

The Upanishad classifies *Kumbhaka* (breath retention) into two types:

1. *Sahita Kumbhaka*–practiced with effort and pranayama techniques.
2. *Kevala Kumbhaka*–the effortless spontaneous retention that comes after mastery.

Sahita Kumbhaka involves preparatory methods using four types of pranayama:

- *Suryabhedan*–stimulates the nervous system and removes excess wind.
- *Ujjayi*–calms the mind and regulates body heat.
- *Sheetali*–cools the body and reduces pitta.
- *Bhastrika*–energizes and clears the nadis.

These are practiced with breath retention *(kumbhaka)* to awaken *Kundalini* and purify the *Nadis* (energy channels).

This classification is unique to *Tantric* and *Hatha Yogic* literature like the *Yoga Kundalini Upanishad.*

28. (4): *Jambira* (lemon or citrus fruit) is the food item that is not mentioned as harmful *(Apathya Ahar)* in *Hatha Pradipika* or *Gheranda Samhita.*

Both texts provide lists of wholesome *(Pathya)* and unwholesome *(Apathya)* foods for yogic practitioners.

Foods explicitly listed as *Apathya* include:

- *Kulath* (horse gram)–causes gas and heaviness.
- *Hing* (asafoetida)–pungent, increases rajasic tendencies.
- *Buttermilk*–especially when sour or old, is restricted in some contexts.

Jambira is not mentioned in either *Hatha Pradipika* or *Gheranda Samhita* as harmful. In fact, it is often considered helpful in detoxification and digestion when used appropriately.

Therefore, among the given options, *Jambira* is the correct answer as it is not listed as *Apathya* in either text.

29. (3): In *Shiva Samhita, Vayu (Prana)* is described in detail in the Third Patal. The Third Patal (Chapter) focuses on *Prana*, its types, functions, and the movement of *Vayu* in Nadis.

Key topics include:

- The five major pranas: *Prana, Apana, Samana, Udana, Vyana.*
- The ten *Vayus,* including sub-pranas like *Naga, Kurma,* etc.
- How *Vayu* affects bodily functions, health, and consciousness.
- Techniques to control and direct *Prana* through *Pranayama.*

It also explains the role of *Prana* in *Kundalini* awakening, and how through mastering *Vayu,* a *Yogi* can reach higher states of awareness. Hence, the Third Patal is the section dedicated to the science of *Vayu* in *Shiva Samhita*.

30. (2): According to *Gherand Samhita, Rasananda Samadhi* is related to *Khechari Mudra.*

Khechari Mudra is the yogic technique of curling the tongue back to touch the soft palate or enter the nasal cavity.

Gherand Samhita (Chapter 3) explains that this *mudra* leads to *Rasananda,* the bliss of divine taste.

Effects of *Khechari Mudra:*

- Enables the yogi to experience *Amrit* or nectar flowing from the *bindu* point at the top of the head.
- Results in immense bliss *(Ananda)*, hence the term *Rasananda Samadhi*.
- Suppresses hunger and thirst, extends life, and leads to *Samadhi*.

The mudra facilitates withdrawal from sensory distractions and helps reach a deep meditative state, where divine nectar is savoured mentally and energetically.

31. (3): *Vatadosha* borne kind of Frenzy *(Unmad)* is the condition most closely related to hallucination in traditional yogic and Ayurvedic psychology.

Unmad is described in Ayurvedic texts like *Charaka Samhita* as a mental disorder arising from imbalances in *Doshas,* especially *Vata.* Hallucination, characterized by false perceptions without external stimuli, is commonly a symptom of *Unmad.*

When *Vata dosha* becomes aggravated, it affects the *manas* (mind) and nervous system, leading to symptoms such as:

- Auditory or visual hallucinations
- Delusions and irrational speech
- Extreme fear, anxiety or behavioural instability

This condition is not mere stress or insomnia but a pathological disturbance of mental faculties, hence categorized under *Vatika Unmad.*

32. (*): *Trividham Narakasyedam Dwaram Nashnamatmanah Kamah Krodhas Tatha Lobhas Tasmad Etat Trayam Tyajet* is from *Bhagavad Gita* Chapter 16, Verse 21, not any of the options provided.

The correct reference is: *Bhagavad Gita* 16.21 *"Trividham narakasyedam dvaram nasanam atmanah, kamah krodhas tatha lobhas tasmad etat trayam tyajet."*

Meaning: "There are three gates to this hell—desire *(kama)*, anger *(krodha)*, and greed *(lobha)*; therefore one should abandon all three."

This *shloka* is part of the *Daivasura Sampad Vibhaga Yoga* (Chapter 16), which discusses divine and demoniac qualities. It warns that these three qualities destroy the soul's evolution and should be renounced by sincere seekers. Since none of the given options correspond to Chapter 16, Verse 21, the correct answer is NONE.

33. (2): *'Asanen Rujam Hanti'* translates to "By *Asana,* disease is destroyed", hence it pertains to Recovery from disease.

This phrase appears in *Hatha Yoga* texts, particularly *Hatha Pradipika,* to stress the therapeutic benefit of asanas.

The purpose of *asana,* beyond posture, includes:

- Strengthening the body
- Purifying the *nadis* (energy channels)
- Balancing *doshas (Vata, Pitta, Kapha)*
- Promoting internal healing

Especially in *Hatha Yoga,* it is said that disease *(rujam)* is driven out through regular and correct asana practice, making the body fit for higher yogic practices like *Pranayama, Dharana,* and *Samadhi.*

Therefore, this phrase directly supports the view of asana as a tool for recovery and prevention of illness.

34. (2): During *Yoga Nidra,* the physical points of the body become introvert *(Antarmukhi).*

Yoga Nidra is a systematic method of inducing deep relaxation, often referred to as "psychic sleep".

In this state:

- The mind withdraws from external sensory input *(Pratyahara)*.
- The awareness is guided to internal bodily sensations, *chakras,* and breath.
- The body remains still, but the consciousness is directed inward.

This *Antarmukhi avastha* is a meditative inward state, where healing, transformation, and subconscious access become possible. *Yoga Nidra* practices by Swami Satyananda Saraswati emphasize this introversion of awareness as essential for entering deeper states of inner awareness and subconscious reprogramming.

35. (3): The hormone released from the Hypothalamus is Corticotrophic Releasing Hormone (CRH). The hypothalamus is a key brain region responsible for maintaining homeostasis and regulating endocrine functions. It secretes releasing hormones that stimulate the anterior pituitary to release its own hormones. Among them:

- CRH (Corticotrophic Releasing Hormone) stimulates the release of ACTH (Adrenocorticotropic Hormone) from the pituitary gland.
- ACTH, in turn, signals the adrenal glands to produce cortisol, a stress hormone.
- CRH plays a critical role in the HPA axis (Hypothalamic-Pituitary-Adrenal axis), which is central to the body's stress response.

Therefore, CRH is correctly identified as the hormone originating from the hypothalamus, not GH, ACTH, or LH which are secreted by the pituitary gland.

36. (4): In *Viloma Pranayam,* obstruction (pause) is intentionally created during both inhalation and exhalation.

The term *'Viloma'* means "against the natural order".

In this *pranayama,* the breath is interrupted at specific intervals:

- **Viloma-1:** Interrupted inhalation—inhale for a few seconds, pause, inhale again, and repeat until lungs are full.
- **Viloma-2:** Interrupted exhalation—exhale in stages with pauses.

The pauses simulate controlled breathing and help train the lungs and mind.

Benefits include:

- Improved breath control and lung capacity.
- Calming of the nervous system.
- Promotes awareness and mindfulness during breathing.

This type of *pranayama* is especially useful in managing anxiety, hypertension, and breath irregularities.

37. (4): With reference to the *Shatchakra Nirupan* scripture, the *Śahasrara Chakra* is situated at the peak of the *Shankhini Nadi.*

Shatchakra Nirupan, a classical tantric text attributed to Purnananda Swami, describes the location and functions of the *chakras* and associated *nadis.*

While *Sushumna Nadi* is traditionally known as the central energy channel, *Shankhini Nadi* is mentioned in tantric texts as extending to the uppermost point of the head, where *Sahasrara Chakra* (the thousand-petaled lotus) resides.

Sahasrara Chakra is described as:

- The seat of pure consciousness and ultimate union with the Divine (Shiva).
- Located at the crown of the head, it is beyond the six *chakras* of the body.

Though most *Hatha Yoga* texts associate *Sahasrara* with *Sushumna, Shatchakra Nirupan* specifically mentions *Shankhini* as the terminus nadi at *Sahasrara.* It symbolizes the culmination point of *Kundalini Shakti's* journey.

38. (4): Night Blindness is not a physical symptom of menopause.

Menopause marks the end of a woman's reproductive cycle and is accompanied by a drop in estrogen and progesterone levels.

Common physical symptoms of menopause include:

- Hot flushes
- Vaginal atrophy (dryness and thinning of vaginal walls)

- Sleep disturbances
- Joint pains

Irritability is common, but it is considered more of a psychological or emotional symptom, though hormonally influenced.

Night Blindness (Nyctalopia) is not related to menopause, but is usually caused by Vitamin A deficiency or retinal disorders.

Therefore, among the options listed, Night Blindness is not associated with menopause.

39. (2): Allergic Rhinitis is also known as Hay Fever. It is an allergic reaction caused by exposure to airborne allergens such as pollen, dust mites, animal dander, or mold.

Symptoms include:

- Sneezing, runny nose, nasal congestion
- Itchy eyes, throat, or ears
- Watery eyes

Though called "fever", there is no actual increase in body temperature. It can be seasonal (pollen-related) or perennial (dust, mold).

Conditions like Bronchitis (1) and COPD (3) are chronic respiratory disorders, while CAD (4) refers to coronary artery disease, unrelated to allergic symptoms.

Hence, Hay Fever is the correct and commonly used alternative name for Allergic Rhinitis.

40. (2): Rheumatoid Arthritis (RA) is an inflammatory and autoimmune disease. RA is a chronic condition where the body's immune system mistakenly attacks the synovial lining of joints.

It causes:

- Joint inflammation and swelling
- Pain and stiffness
- Eventual joint deformity if untreated

It is systemic and can also affect lungs, heart, and blood vessels.

Autoimmunity involves autoantibodies, particularly rheumatoid factor (RF) and anti-CCP antibodies. Unlike degenerative arthritis (like osteoarthritis), RA involves immune-mediated inflammation, making it autoimmune in nature.

Therefore, the correct classification is Inflammatory and Autoimmune Disease.

41. (2): The correct order of the bones from top to bottom in the human body is: (D) Sphenoid → (B) Mandible → (E) Hyoid → (C) Patella → (A) Fibula

- **Sphenoid:** A butterfly-shaped bone located at the base of the skull, behind the eyes. It is one of the deepest bones in the cranium.
- **Mandible:** The lower jawbone, located below the sphenoid. It is the only movable bone of the skull.
- **Hyoid:** A U-shaped bone in the neck that supports the tongue, situated below the mandible but above the larynx.
- **Patella:** Commonly known as the kneecap, located in front of the knee joint.
- **Fibula:** A long, thin bone located on the lateral side of the lower leg, below the patella.

Therefore, this sequence correctly follows the descending anatomical order of these bones.

42. (4): In Maslow's Need-Hierarchy Model, the correct bottom-to-top order is: (B) Physical Need → (A) Need of Safety → (D) Need to get membership and affection → (E) Need for respect → (C) Need for self attainment (Atmasiddhi)

Maslow's pyramid of human needs, from basic to advanced, is as follows:

- **Physiological Needs**–food, water, air, shelter (B)
- **Safety Needs**–security, stability, health (A)
- **Love and Belongingness**–friendship, intimacy, affection (D)
- **Esteem Needs**–self-respect, recognition, achievement (E)
- **Self-Actualization**–personal growth, realization of potential (C)

This model is foundational in humanistic psychology, explaining motivational priorities in human behaviour.

43. **(1):** According to the *Siddha Siddhanta Paddhati,* the correct order of body bases *(Adhars)* from bottom to top is: (C) *Oudyanadhar* → (E) *Nabhyadhar* → (D) *Hridayadhar* → (B) *Ghantikadhare* → (A) *Talvadhare*

- ***Oudyanadhar***–Located in the pelvic region, associated with *Muladhara.*
- ***Nabhyadhar***–Navel center, linked to *Manipura Chakra.*
- ***Hridayadhar***–Heart region, associated with *Anahata Chakra.*
- ***Ghantikadhare***–Located in the throat, corresponds to *Vishuddha Chakra.*
- ***Talvadhare***–At the palate/top of the throat cavity, associated with Ajna or higher centers.

These *Adhars* represent energy centers or support points for consciousness within the yogic subtle body map.

44. **(3):** Yoga practices used in yoga therapy arranged from top to bottom of the body: (A) *Kapalrandhra Dhauti* → (B) *Dantamool Dhauti* → (C) *Sheetkram Kapalbhati* → (E) *Agnisar* → (D) Basti

- ***Kapalrandhra Dhauti***–Cleansing of the cranial cavity area (top of the head/skull).
- ***Dantamool Dhauti***–Cleansing near the roots of the teeth and gums.
- ***Sheetkram Kapalbhati***–Involves nasal cleansing, drawing water from the mouth and expelling from nostrils.
- ***Agnisar***–Intestinal and abdominal stimulation through rapid abdominal flapping.
- ***Basti***–Yogic colon cleansing through the rectum, involving the lowest part of the body.

This sequence respects the physical location and direction of cleansing from head to lower digestive organs.

45. **(3):** According to *Gherand Samhita,* the correct order of the features of a yogi's diet is: (C) Half cooked *(Laghupak)* → (B) Favourite *(Priya)* → (A) Oily *(Snigdha)* → (E) Nourishing *(Dhatuposhak)* → (D) Appealing *(Manonukul)*

As per *Gherand Samhita* Chapter 5, the diet of a yogi should be:

- **Lightly cooked** *(Laghupak)* for easy digestion.
- **Pleasant and preferred** *(Priya)* to ensure acceptance.
- **Moderately oily** *(Snigdha)* to maintain vata balance.
- **Nutritious** *(Dhatuposhak)* to replenish bodily tissues.
- **Mentally satisfying** *(Manonukul)* to maintain sattvic mental state.

This structured dietary recommendation ensures both physical nourishment and mental equanimity essential for yogic progress.

46. **(3):** The normal order of the Lesson Plan as defined by *Kaiwalyadham,* Lonawala is: (A) Beginning of lesson → (B) Beginning of the Activity *(Kriya-vidhi)* → (C) Verbal introduction of the Exercise → (D) Partial and full presentation → (E) Individual and collective exercise

(A) Beginning of Lesson: This includes establishing rapport, mental preparation, and setting the intent of the session.

(B) Beginning of Activity: Introduction of the physical part of the session *(asana, kriya,* etc.).

(C) Verbal Introduction: Explaining the technique, benefits, precautions, and alignments.

(D) Partial and Full Presentation: Demonstration in parts and then in complete form by the instructor.

(E) Individual and Collective Exercise: Practice by students individually or in a group, with corrections and observations.

This sequential model promotes progressive understanding, structured instruction, and maximum student engagement in yoga education.

47. **(4):** According to *Gherand Samhita,* the correct order of Yoga practices (*Bandhas* and *Mudras*) is: (B) *Nabhomudra* → (A) *Uddiyan Bandha* → (C) *Jalandhar Bandha* → (E) *Mool Bandha* → (D) *Maha Bandha*

(B) ***Nabhomudra***: Tongue placement practice to direct energy upward and stabilize breath.

(A) ***Uddiyan Bandha***: Abdominal lock; it pulls prana upward.

(C) ***Jalandhar Bandha***: Throat lock; directs energy and prevents downward flow.

(E) ***Mool Bandha***: Root lock at the perineum; foundational for internal energy control.

(D) ***Maha Bandha***: The combined practice of the above three bandhas, performed after mastering each individually.

This progression reflects the safe and effective approach to energy control as described in traditional *Hatha Yoga* manuals, particularly in *Gherand Samhita,* Chapter 3.

48. **(4):** According to *Yogachudamani Upanishad, Mahamudra* treats the following diseases in this specific order: (C) Tuberculosis *(Kshaya)* → (A) Leprosy *(Kushtha)* → (D) *Gudavarta (Gudavart)* → (B) Thicket (*Gulma*) → (E) Indigestion *(Ajirna)*

The Upanishad emphasizes therapeutic aspects of *Mahamudra,* highlighting it as a cure for difficult and chronic diseases.

(C) ***Kshaya***–Respiratory wasting disease (often interpreted as Tuberculosis).

(A) ***Kushtha***–Chronic skin conditions such as leprosy.

(D) ***Gudavarta***–Disturbance in apana vayu leading to pain and improper bowel movement.

(B) ***Gulma***–Abdominal tumour-like growths or hardness.

(E) ***Ajirna***–Indigestion or poor digestion.

This order reflects the depth of impact *Mahamudra* has on various bodily systems, progressing from severe systemic to digestive issues.

49. **(3):** As per *Yajnavalkya Smriti*, the correct order of restraints of senses *(Indriya Nigrah)* is: (C) *Asteya* → (D) *Akrodh* → (B) *Lajja* → (E) *Vivek* → (A) *Dhairya*

(C) ***Asteya***–Non-stealing or not desiring others' possessions; fundamental for ethical restraint.

(D) ***Akrodh***–Absence of anger; controlling emotional responses.

(B) ***Lajja***–Modesty or shame; essential to preserve personal discipline.

(E) ***Vivek***–Discrimination or wisdom; knowing right from wrong.

(A) ***Dhairya***: Patience and perseverance; the stabilizing force in practice.

These values build upon one another to establish complete mastery over sensory impulses, as emphasized in traditional *dharma-shastra* literature.

50. **(4):** According to the *Nadabindu Upanishad,* the correct order of *Kalayen* (phases or modifications) of *Omkar* is: (C) *Ghoshini* → (D) *Vidyunmatra* → (B) *Patangi* → (A) *Vayu Vegini* → (E) *Namdheya*

These are progressive stages of sound perception during deep *Nada Yoga* or inner sound meditation.

(C) ***Ghoshini***–The first audible inner sound, like a reverberating bell.

(D) ***Vidyunmatra***–Like a flash of lightning; sharp and penetrating inner sound.

(B) ***Patangi***–Resembles the fluttering of a butterfly; more subtle than earlier.

(A) ***Vayu Vegini***–Like rushing wind; subtler vibrational awareness.

(E) ***Namdheya***–The final soundless sound (Anahata Nada) leading to absorption in the Self.

This sequence corresponds to progressive refinement of auditory perception through the stages of deep *Nada Sadhana,* culminating in *Samadhi*.

51. **(2):** The correct order of the practice of Yoga Nidra is: (E) Preparing for the practice → (C) Resolution *(Sankalpa)* → (B) Revolving the consciousness to different parts of the body → (A) Awareness of Breathing → (D) To feel and Sensitivity

(E) Preparing for the Practice: The practitioner lies in *Shavasana*, adjusts posture, and prepares mentally for complete stillness.

(C) Resolution: A *Sankalpa* (affirmation or intention) is silently repeated with faith and clarity.

(B) Revolving the Consciousness: Awareness is rotated through specific body parts in a pre-defined sequence to induce *Pratyahara* (withdrawal of senses).

(A) Awareness of Breathing: Attention is directed to natural breath to deepen relaxation and enhance focus.

(D) To Feel and Sensitivity: Includes experiencing opposite sensations (hot-cold, heavy-light), promoting emotional release and deep meditative awareness.

This sequence ensures a gradual withdrawal from external awareness leading to subconscious and unconscious access.

52. **(3):** The correct order of the virtues of a person born with *Daivi Sampada* (Divine qualities) is: (B) *Tej* → (C) *Kshama* → (D) *Dhriti* → (A) *Shaucha* → (E) *Adroh*

As described in *Bhagavad Gita* Chapter 16, divine virtues are essential for liberation and spiritual progress.

(B) *Tej*: Spiritual radiance or energy from inner purity and *tapas*.

(C) *Kshama*: Forgiveness; tolerance of faults or harm by others.

(D) *Dhriti*: Fortitude; the ability to stay stable in difficulty.

(A) *Shaucha*: Cleanliness; both external and internal purity.

(E) *Adroh*: Absence of malice or hatred toward others.

This progression reflects a natural unfolding of character from inner strength to moral and social virtues.

53. **(2):** The correct order of the five types of stages *(Avasthas)* is: (C) *Sthoolawastha* → (A) *Swarupawastha* → (B) *Sookshmawastha* → (E) *Anway-awastha* → (D) *Arithvatva-awastha*

(C) *Sthoolawastha*: Gross state-physical existence and sensory engagement.

(A) *Swarupawastha*: State of identity with one's own nature-developing awareness of inner self.

(B) *Sookshmawastha*: Subtle state-mental and pranic awareness beyond the senses.

(E) *Anway-awastha*: Analytical connection-realization of the link between self and universe.

(D) *Arithvatva-awastha*: Ultimate meaning or essence-understanding the absolute truth *(Brahma Jnana)*.

This sequence depicts the spiritual journey from physical reality to ultimate realization.

54. **(3):** According to Jain Philosophy, the correct order of *Aabhyantar Tapa* (internal austerities) is: (A) *Prayaschit* → (C) *Vinaya* → (D) *Vaiyavratya* → (B) *Swadhyay* → (E) *Vyutsarg*

The six internal tapas in *Jain Darshan* are methods to purify the soul:

(A) *Prayaschit*: Repentance; purification through remorse for past actions.

(C) *Vinaya*: Humility; respecting spiritual elders and teachers.

(D) *Vaiyavratya*: Selfless service to monks and the virtuous.

(B) *Swadhyay*: Self-study; deep reflection on scriptures.

(E) *Vyutsarg*: Detachment from the body and ego.

(F) *Dhyana*: It develops concentration.

This order shows a progression from moral purification to intellectual and spiritual renunciation, forming the core of inner discipline in *Jain Yoga*.

55. **(1):** In *Bhriguvalli* of *Taittiriya Upanishad*, the correct order of means of attaining *Brahman* as taught by *Dev Varuna* is: (C) *Anna* → (A) *Prana* → (B) *Chakshu* → (E) *Shrota* → (D) *Mana*

The Upanishad shows *Bhrigu's* journey of discovering *Brahman* through successive realizations:

(C) ***Anna***–Food is *Brahman* (first realization).

(A) ***Prana***–Life-force is *Brahman.*

(B) ***Chakshu***–Vision (sensory power) is *Brahman.*

(E) ***Shrota***–Hearing is *Brahman.*

(D) ***Mana***–Mind is *Brahman.*

Ultimately, *Bhrigu* realizes that *Ananda* (Bliss) is the supreme *Brahman*. This layered discovery reveals progressive layers of existence, from the gross to the subtle, guiding the seeker inward.

56. (2): The external means of *Gyana Yoga* include: (B) *Viveka* → (C) *Vairagya* → (D) *Mumukshutva*

These are foundational preliminary qualifications described in *Advaita Vedanta* under *Sadhana Chatushtaya* (fourfold discipline).

(B) ***Viveka***: Discrimination between the real (eternal) and unreal (temporary).

(C) ***Vairagya***: Dispassion or detachment from the pleasures of this world and the next.

(D) ***Mumukshutva***: Intense yearning for liberation (moksha).

These three are considered external or preparatory disciplines, unlike *Shravana* and *Nididhyasana,* which are internal or direct means practiced after qualification is attained. Therefore, only (B), (C), and (D) belong to the external sadhanas of *Gyana Yoga.*

57. (2): In *Bahya* (external), *Abhyantar* (internal), and *Stambh Vritti Pranayama,* the correct factors on which the practice depends are: (A) Particular place → (B) Particular time → (C) Particular number

(A) Place: Yogic texts mention that certain locations (e.g., calm, sacred, clean environments) are more conducive for pranayama practice.

(B) Time: Specific times of day like Brahma Muhurta (early morning) or evening are ideal, and duration also matters.

(C) Number: Number of breaths or cycles (e.g., matra count in inhalation, retention, exhalation) is vital for structuring the practice.

(D) and (E), i.e., individual and circumstance, are secondary and not explicitly part of classical determinants for *Vritti* types of *Pranayama.*

Hence, the correct set is (A), (B), (C).

58. (4): The hormones released from the Adrenal Cortex are: (A) Glucocorticoids → (C) Gonadocorticoid → (E) Mineralocorticoid

The Adrenal Cortex, the outer region of the adrenal glands, produces three major types of steroid hormones:

(A) Glucocorticoids–e.g., cortisol, regulate metabolism and stress response.

(E) Mineralocorticoids–e.g., aldosterone, regulate electrolyte and water balance.

(C) Gonadocorticoids–weak sex hormones like androgens.

(B) Melatonin– is secreted by the pineal gland.

(D) Prolactin is secreted by the anterior pituitary gland, not the adrenal cortex.

Thus, only (A), (C), and (E) are relevant to the adrenal cortex.

59. (3): The phrase *'Ten Tyaktena Bhunjitha',* from *Ishavasyopanishad* (verse 1), means: (C) *Aparigrah* → (D) *Mitvyayta* → (E) *Tyaga*

Meaning: *"Enjoy through renunciation, do not covet what belongs to others."*

(E) ***Tyaga***: Core message—renunciation of ownership and doership.

(C) ***Aparigrah***: Non-possessiveness or not hoarding beyond basic needs, aligns with the essence of renunciation.

(D) ***Mitvyayta***: Moderation in use and enjoyment—a lifestyle of balance and restraint.

This shloka instructs on simple, detached living while being fully engaged in life.

Therefore, these three—C, D, and E—capture the spirit of the verse accurately.

60. **(3):** Among the listed options, the correct ones related to the *Panch Kleshas* (five afflictions) in Yoga Philosophy are: (A) *Prasupta* → (C) *Vicchinna* → (D) *Udar*

The five *Kleshas* described in *Patanjali Yoga Sutra* (2.3) are:

1. *Avidya*–Ignorance
2. *Asmita*–Egoism
3. *Raga*–Attachment
4. *Dvesha*–Aversion
5. *Abhinivesha*–Clinging to life/fear of death

Each Klesha exists in four stages (avasthas):

- ***Prasupta*** (latent)
- ***Tanu*** (attenuated)
- ***Vicchinna*** (intermittent)
- ***Udar*** (active or fully expressed)

These stages show how deeply a *Klesha* influences the mind at different times.

Options B *(Kshipt)* and E *(Avidya)* don't fit here:

- ***Kshipt*** refers to one of the five mental states *(Chitta Bhumi)*, not a Klesha stage.
- ***Avidya*** is a *klesha* itself, not a stage of *Klesha.*

Therefore, the correct answer is (A), (C), and (D).

61. **(3):** The main characteristic of *Nauli* is the development of: (B) The development of sub-atmospheric pressure inside the abdomen and (D) Abdominal organs–stomach and colon.

Nauli Kriya is a classical *Shatkarma* (cleansing technique) in *Hatha Yoga.* In this practice, the rectus abdominis muscles are churned rhythmically, creating a negative pressure in the abdominal cavity.

This sub-atmospheric pressure stimulates:

- Stomach and intestines, improving digestion.
- Colon movement, aiding in detoxification and elimination.

It helps tone the abdominal muscles and massage internal organs, particularly the digestive system, making it a unique internal cleansing technique.

Hence, only (B) and (D) directly relate to Nauli's core effects.

62. **(2):** According to *Hatha Pradipika,* the practices included in *Singhasana* (Lion Pose) are: (A) *Moolbandh*, (B) *Jalandhar Bandh*, and (C) *Uddiyan Bandh.*

In *Hatha Pradipika* Chapter 1, Verse 52-53, *Singhasana* is described as a pose that includes *Bandhas* (locks) to regulate *prana*:

- ***Moolbandha***–contraction of the perineum, locks *apana vayu.*
- ***Uddiyan Bandha***–abdominal retraction to lift *prana* upwards.
- ***Jalandhar Bandha***–chin lock to prevent upward escape of *prana.*

These *bandhas* are used in combination with the pose to stimulate the energy channels *(nadis).*

The other options like *Mahabandha* and *Shambhavi Mudra* are not part of the *Simhasana* practice as described in *Hatha Pradipika.*

Hence, the correct set is (A), (B), (C).

63. **(4):** According to *Yoga Vasishtha*, the process adopted for attaining *Turiyavastha* includes: (A) *Manolaya,* (C) *Pran Nirodh,* and (D) Strong feeling of unity *(Ekatva).*

Turiyavastha is the fourth state of consciousness beyond waking, dreaming, and deep sleep.

Yoga Vasishtha, a profound philosophical scripture, outlines steps for its attainment:

(A) *Manolaya*–dissolution of mind, where thoughts become still.

(C) *Pran Nirodh*–cessation of breath or pranic restraint to withdraw life force from external awareness.

(D) *Ekatva Bhava*–intense experience of oneness with all existence; leads to Advaitic realization.

Though *Vicharna* and *Asansakti* are also important, they are supportive states, not primary means to *Turiyavastha.*

Hence, the correct trio is (A), (C), (D).

64. (1): The components of ill mental health are: (B) *Styana*, (D) *Pramada*, and (E) *Daurmanasya*.

In *Patanjali's Yoga Sutra* (1.30-31), obstacles *(Antarayas)* and their symptoms are described, leading to *chitta-vikshepa* (disturbances of the mind).

(B) ***Styana***–mental stagnation or lack of enthusiasm.

(D) ***Pramada***–carelessness or lack of mindfulness.

(E) ***Daurmanasya***–depression or mental anguish.

These are signs of disturbed mind states, which obstruct yogic progression.

Prasannata (A) and *Santosh* (C) are indicators of good mental health, mentioned in *Yama/ Niyama* contexts.

Therefore, only (B), (D), and (E) are valid components of mental ill-health.

65. (2): The asanas described in the *Yoga Tattva Upanishad* include: (B) *Siddhasana*, (C) *Padmasana*, and (D) *Simhasana*.

In *Yoga Tattva Upanishad*, only a few essential meditative asanas are described, specifically those helpful for *pranayama* and *dhyana*.

(B) ***Siddhasana***–considered the most important for spiritual practices.

(C) ***Padmasana***–ideal for long meditation and breath control.

(D) ***Simhasana***–included for its energetic benefits and throat *chakra* stimulation.

Swastikasana (A) and ***Ugrasana*** (E) are found in other texts like *Hatha Yoga Pradipika*, but not explicitly in *Yoga Tattva Upanishad*.

Hence, the correct group is (B), (C), (D).

66. (*): None of the given shloka references — (A) Chapter 2/15, (B) 6/13, (C) 6/17, (D) 6/12, (E) 17/4 — accurately describe food in the context of *Bhagavad Gita*.

The correct section describing food in *Bhagavad Gita* is Chapter 17, Verses 7–10, where *Sattvic, Rajasic,* and *Tamasic* foods are clearly classified.

For example:

- **Verse 17.7:** *"aharas tvapi sarvasya..."* — Food is classified according to guna.
- **Verse 17.8:** *Sattvic* food—increases longevity, virtue, strength.
- **Verse 17.9–10:** *Rajasic* and *Tamasic* foods—very spicy, stale, impure, etc.

Option (E) is 17/4 which discusses the types of faith based on gunas, not food.

Hence, none of the options correctly refer to food-specific shlokas.

67. (1): When *Paschimottanasana* is practiced like an isometric exercise, it causes: (B) Heart rate increases and (D) Increase the burden on the cardio-respiratory system.

Isometric contraction refers to muscle tension without visible movement, which increases internal pressure.

In such a case:

- Muscles are held under tension, especially abdominal and spinal muscles in Paschimottanasana.
- This sustained contraction leads to increased heart rate (B).
- Respiratory muscles may also be restricted, increasing demand on the cardio-respiratory system (D).

Therefore, when not practiced in a relaxed yogic manner but held forcefully, this posture can cause sympathetic nervous activation, raising cardiovascular load.

68. (3): According to *Yoga Tattva Upanishad*, reciting *Pranava (Om)* with *Plutmatra* leads to: (A) Destruction of sins of previous birth and (B) Siddhis are attained.

Plutmatra means the prolonged pronunciation of "Om" with deep vibrational resonance.

The *Upanishad* states:

- The intense and sincere chanting purifies the subtle body and *karma*.
- *Siddhis* (spiritual powers) like heightened perception, subtle vision, and inner clarity arise naturally.

This method is both purificatory and spiritually empowering, forming a key part of *Nada Yoga* (sound-based yoga).

Therefore, (A) and (B) correctly reflect the scriptural benefits of *Plutmatra Pranava* recitation.

69. **(3):** For a staunch yoga practitioner, the following foods should be abandoned: (B) Spicy (Tez) and (D) Sour food.

Classical *Hatha Yoga* texts like *Hatha Pradipika* (1.63) advise yogis to avoid:

- Very spicy *(tikshna)* and sour *(amla)* items, as they:

  Aggravate *pitta dosha,* leading to restlessness.

  Disturb pranic balance, obstructing *pranayama* and meditation.

- These foods are considered rajasic, increasing agitation, passion, and emotional turbulence.

Juicy fruits (A) and pudding (C) in moderation are sattvic and often encouraged.

Panch Shak (E) varies by text but is not universally rejected.

Hence, correct eliminations are (B) and (D).

70. **(3):** According to *Kathopanishad*, one achieves *Parampada* (Supreme State) through: (A) *Sanyam* (control) and (D) *Pavitrata* (purity).

In *Kathopanishad* (1.3.7–1.3.10):

- Emphasis is laid on *Sanyam* (self-restraint) over senses and mind.
- Purity of mind and conduct (*Pavitrata*) is vital for realization of the *Atman.*

It is stated that the wise, pure, and disciplined can perceive the Self that is subtle and hidden in the heart.

Though *Pran-nirodh* and *Guru-bhakti* are important in broader yogic literature, the *Kathopanishad* specifically highlights restraint and purity.

Thus, (A) and (D) are the correct pair as per the text.

71. **(2):** According to *Yoga Darshan (Patanjali Yoga Sutras),* lack of lust *(Raga)* arises from the absence of the following: (A) *Phal* (Fruit) → (B) *Hetu* (Cause) → (D) *Ashraya* (Support/Base)

In *Yoga Sutra* 2.7, *Raga* is defined as attachment or attraction towards pleasurable experiences.

In *Sutra* 2.18 and commentaries by *Vyasa*, it is mentioned that desire or lust arises due to the presence of:

(A) ***Phala***–expectation of result or enjoyment.

(B) ***Hetu***–the underlying cause of desire.

(D) ***Ashraya***–the support or substratum (usually the senses or mind).

Therefore, if fruit, cause, and base are absent, lust doesn't arise.

The options (C) *Viparyaya* and (E) *Vikalpa* are mental modifications *(vrittis)*, not directly linked as preconditions of lust.

Hence, the correct set is (A), (B), and (D).

72. **(1):** The kinds of Declarative Memory are: (A) Episodic Memory and (D) Semantic Memory.

Declarative (explicit) memory is a type of long-term memory that involves conscious recall of facts and experiences. It includes:

(A) Episodic Memory—memory of personal experiences/events (e.g., your last birthday).

(D) Semantic Memory—memory of general facts and knowledge (e.g., capital of India).

The remaining options are not part of declarative memory:

(B) Iconic and (C) Echoic memory are sensory memory types (visual and auditory, respectively).

(E) Short-term memory is a separate component that holds information temporarily before encoding.

Thus, only (A) and (D) are correct as declarative memory types.

73. (3): According to *Hatha Pradipika, Ujjayi Kumbhaka* is useful for: (A) Disorders of *Kapha* and (C) Disorders of *Dhatu* (tissues).

In *Hatha Pradipika,* Chapter 2, Verse 51, it is mentioned that *Ujjayi:*

- Removes phlegm (*Kapha dosha*-related disorders).
- Promotes internal heat, improving metabolic function and balancing *dhatus* (tissues).

It is also known for cleansing the throat, regulating *prana*, and removing obstructions in *Nadis*. Though it improves digestion and affects hunger, the text does not directly emphasize *Vata* or *Pitta* correction in context of *Ujjayi*.

Therefore, the suitable benefits listed are (A) and (C).

74. (2): The treatment advised by *Swami Kuvalayananda* for wholistic health includes: (C) Formulating the light psychological viewpoint and (D) Emphasis on healthy food.

As the founder of *Kaivalyadhama, Swami Kuvalayananda* emphasized that true health includes mental and dietary aspects:

(C) Psychological approach: Cultivating a balanced and optimistic mindset as a healing tool.

(D) Diet: Following a *sattvic* diet, based on moderation, freshness, and nutrition.

Though he acknowledged modern medicine (E), he emphasized yogic therapy as a primary system, not dependency on drugs.

Thus, the essential tools for maintaining wholistic health as per his guidance are (C) and (D).

75. (4): (C) *Vivek* and (E) *Vairagya* do not come under *Shatsampatti* (Sixfold Wealth).

In *Advaita Vedanta*, the *Sadhana Chatushtaya* (Fourfold Qualifications) for the attainment of liberation *(Moksha)* are:

1. ***Viveka*** (C)–Discrimination between the eternal *(Nitya)* and the non-eternal *(Anitya)*.
2. ***Vairagya*** (E)–Dispassion or detachment from enjoyment of the fruits of action here and hereafter.
3. ***Shatsampatti***–The sixfold inner wealth or mental disciplines.
4. ***Mumukshutva***–Intense yearning for liberation.

The *Shatsampatti*, i.e., six inner virtues, include:

- ***Shama***–Calmness or control of the mind.
- ***Dama***–Restraint of the senses.
- ***Uparati***–Withdrawal from worldly activities.
- **(A) *Titiksha***–Endurance of pain and pleasure without resistance.
- **(B) *Shraddha***–Faith in the Guru and the scriptures.
- **(D) *Samadhan***–One-pointed concentration of mind.

Thus, while *Titiksha, Shraddha,* and *Samadhan* are components of *Shatsampatti,* the qualities (C) *Viveka* and (E) *Vairagya* are distinct qualifications that precede the practice of *Shatsampatti* in *Vedantic sadhana.*

Therefore, the correct answer is 4: (C) and (E), as both do not belong to *Shatsampatti*.

76. (3): Matching of *Surya Namaskar* postures with *Chakra* meditation:

(A) *Padhastasana*–(III) *Swadhishthan Chakra*: In the forward bend posture, attention is drawn to the pelvic region, which activates the *Swadhishthan Chakra* associated with creativity and fluidity.

(B) *Ashwa Sanchalan*–(IV) *Ajna Chakra*: In this posture, the gaze is forward and the spine is extended, aligning awareness with the *Ajna Chakra* (third eye), enhancing focus and intuition.

(C) *Parvatasana*–(II) *Vishuddhi Chakra*: In the inverted V-shaped position, the throat is extended and open, stimulating the *Vishuddhi Chakra*, related to communication and purification.

(D) ***Ashtanga Namaskar*–(I)** ***Manipura Chakra:*** With the chest and abdominal region close to the floor, pressure and focus fall on the navel center, activating the *Manipura Chakra*, which governs willpower and energy.

Hence, the correct sequence is: (A)-(III), (B)-(IV), (C)-(II), (D)-(I).

77. **(1):** Matching of Yogic practices in *Shiv Samhita* with their effects:

(A) ***Mahamudra*–(III)** ***Kashayas*** **being burnt:** *Mahamudra* purifies the *nadis* and helps in burning *kashayas* (impurities of the mind and *vasanas*).

(B) ***Mahabandha*–(IV) Different rasas flow towards** ***murdha*:** This practice facilitates upward flow of *rasas* (subtle essences) towards the head (*murdha*), supporting higher states of consciousness.

(C) ***Mahabedha*–(I) Penetration of** ***Brahmagranthi*:** This *kriya* is aimed at piercing *Brahma granthi*, an energetic knot blocking *Kundalini's* ascent.

(D) ***Khechari*–(II) Gets devoid of idleness:** Practicing *Khechari mudra* is said to remove laziness and leads to inner alertness and spiritual awakening.

Hence, the correct matching is: (A)-(III), (B)-(IV), (C)-(I), (D)-(II).

78. **(4):** Matching the spiritual personalities with their chronological year of birth:

(A) Swami Shivanand–(III) 1887

(B) Shri Aurobindo–(IV) 1872

(C) Paramhans Yogananda–(I) 1893

(D) Swami Vivekananda–(II) 1863

This is the correct chronological order of their births. Thus, (A)-(III), (B)-(IV), (C)-(I), (D)-(II) is accurate.

79. **(1):** Matching chapters *(Prakarans)* of spiritual progression:

(A) ***Mumukshu Prakaran*–(II) Second part:** Deals with the desire for liberation (*Mumukshutva*), logically placed after *Vairagya.*

(B) ***Utpatti Prakaran*–(IV) Third part:** Refers to the origination of spiritual awakening or creation of spiritual energy.

(C) ***Vairagya Prakaran*–(I) First part:** Dispassion is the foundation of spiritual progress, thus introduced first.

(D) ***Upsham Prakaran*–(III) Fifth part:** Refers to quietening of mind and realization, usually the culmination of the stages.

Thus, the correct order is: (A)-(II), (B)-(IV), (C)-(I), (D)-(III).

80. **(1):** Matching educational concepts with their descriptions:

(A) Process of adjustment through works–(IV) Learning: Learning is the process where the student adjusts and grows through experience.

(B) Process regarding methods–(II) Teaching: Teaching involves the use of strategies and methods to impart knowledge.

(C) Directing processes–(I) Teacher: The teacher directs the learning process, facilitates understanding, and guides students.

(D) Adjusts itself through works–(III) Student: The student learns and evolves through action and experience (*karma*-based learning).

Thus, the correct match is: (A)-(IV), (B)-(II), (C)-(I), (D)-(III).

81. **(3):** Matching of Diseases with their correct Symptoms:

(A) Diabetes Mellitus–(III) Disorder in metabolism of sugar: Diabetes is characterized by high blood glucose levels due to either insulin deficiency or resistance, which directly affects sugar metabolism.

(B) Tonsillitis–(I) Inflammation of glands: Tonsillitis is the inflammation of the tonsils, which are lymphoid glands located in the throat.

(C) Arteriosclerosis–(IV) Degeneration of blood vessels: Arteriosclerosis refers to the thickening and loss of elasticity of arterial walls, often leading to narrowed and hardened arteries.

(D) Prolapse–(II) Falling out of place: Prolapse is a condition where an organ slips or falls from its normal position, such as uterine or rectal prolapse.

Thus, the correct match is: (A)-(III), (B)-(I), (C)-(IV), (D)-(II).

82. (3): According to *Vasishtha Samhita*, the *Panchamahabhutas* (five great elements) are associated with specific *Sanskrit* phonemes or letters, which symbolize their vibrational essence in metaphysical and phonetic contexts. These mappings are based on *Tantric* and *Yogic* sound science where certain sounds are intrinsically linked to cosmic elements.

Here is the correct match as per Option 3:

(A) Air–(I) य (Ya): The element Air *(Vayu)* is subtle and associated with movement and expansion. The sound "Ya" (य) is traditionally linked to the *Vayu Tattva* in *Yogic* traditions. It symbolizes mobility and the life force (*Prana Vayu*).

(B) Water–(IV) व (Va): Water (Apas) is fluid, cohesive, and essential for life. The sound "Va" (व) resonates with fluidity and emotion, which are dominant qualities of water.

(C) Fire–(II) र (Ra): Fire (*Tejas* or *Agni*) is transformative and radiant. The syllable "Ra" (र) signifies energy, heat, and transformation. It is often used in *Bija Mantras* for Agni-related deities.

(D) Earth–(III) ल (La): Earth (*Prithvi*) is solid, grounded, and stable. The phoneme "La" (ल) represents stability and grounding—the essential nature of the Earth element.

This match corresponds accurately to Option 3, as per *Vasishtha Samhita* and supported by classical *yogic* and *tantric* metaphysical phonology.

83. (2): Matching *Yogic* qualities or tendencies with respective *Yogic* paths or limbs:

(A) *Chitta* delving into spiritual upliftment–(II) *Jnana Yoga*: The mind *(chitta)* focused on self-knowledge and discrimination aligns with *Jnana Yoga*.

(B) Detachment towards sense organs–(IV) *Yama*: Detachment and restraint from sensory pleasures come under *Yama*, the first limb of *Ashtanga Yoga*.

(C) Love for *Parmatma Tatva*–(I) *Niyama*: Devotion, surrender, and purity directed toward the Supreme Self are part of *Niyama* practices like *Ishwar Pranidhana*.

(D) Indifference towards objects–(III) *Asana*: Stability and indifference toward comfort or discomfort are cultivated through asana, allowing the practitioner to remain unaffected.

Thus, correct match: (A)-(II), (B)-(IV), (C)-(I), (D)-(III).

84. (4): Matching Vitamins with Deficiency Diseases:

(A) Thiamin–(IV) Beriberi: Vitamin B1 (Thiamin) deficiency leads to Beriberi, affecting the nervous and cardiovascular systems.

(B) Niacin–(I) Pellagra: Niacin (Vitamin B3) deficiency causes Pellagra, with symptoms like diarrhea, dermatitis, and dementia.

(C) Biotin–(II) Dermatitis: Biotin deficiency can lead to skin disorders like dermatitis, fatigue, and neurological symptoms.

(D) Cyanocobalamin–(III) Pernicious Anaemia: Vitamin B12 (Cyanocobalamin) deficiency results in pernicious anemia, a condition where the body can't make enough healthy red blood cells.

Therefore, the accurate match is: (A)-(IV), (B)-(I), (C)-(II), (D)-(III).

85. (1): Matching Nutrients with their sub-components:

(A) Fat–(IV) Linolenic Acid: Fats include essential fatty acids like Linolenic acid (Omega-3).

(B) Monosaccharide–(III) Fructose: Fructose is a simple sugar, a monosaccharide found in fruits.

(C) Disaccharide–(II) Sucrose: Sucrose (table sugar) is a disaccharide made of glucose and fructose.

(D) Protein–(I) Tryptophan: Tryptophan is an essential amino acid, which is a building block of proteins.

So, correct sequence is: (A)-(IV), (B)-(III), (C)-(II), (D)-(I).

86. **(2):** Matching *Suktis* (quotes) with their respective scriptures:

(A) ***Mitaharaschasanam Cha Shaktichalak tritiya*–(II) *Yoga Kundalyupanishad:*** This *sukta* emphasizes moderation in food *(Mitahara)*, mentioned in the *Yoga Kundalyupanishad*, highlighting it as an essential foundation before awakening kundalini.

(B) ***Bhujyate Shiv Samprityai Mitaharssa uchyate*–(III) *Hatha Yoga Pradipika*:** Found in *Hatha Yoga Pradipika* (1.58), it describes the nature of a yogi's diet that pleases *Shiva* — moderate, light, and suitable for practice.

(C) ***Bhujyate Sursamprityа mitaram imam Viduh*–(IV) *Gheranda Samhita:*** In *Gheranda Samhita* (Chapter 5), this verse outlines the significance of proper eating in physical and spiritual cleansing.

(D) ***Yuktaharviharasya Yuktacheshtasya Karmasu*–(I) *Shrimad Bhagavad Gita:*** From *Bhagavad Gita* (Chapter 6, Verse 17), this verse emphasizes a balanced life — moderation in food, sleep, activity, and discipline, essential for a yogi.

Hence, the correct pairings are: (A)-(II), (B)-(III), (C)-(IV), (D)-(I).

87. **(4):** Matching *Tattva* terms with corresponding principles from *Samkhya Philosophy:*

(A) ***Vishesh*–(III) Mind *(Manas):*** Vishesh refers to particulars, and includes mind *(manas)* and other specific elements that interact with the senses.

(B) ***Lingmatra*–(I) Buddhi (Intelligence):** *Lingamatra* or *Mahattattva* is another term for buddhi, emerging directly from *prakriti*, and is the first evolute.

(C) ***Avishesh*–(II) Ego *(Ahankara)*:** *Avishesh* denotes undifferentiated forms like *ahankara*, which connects intellect to identity and individuality.

(D) ***Alinga*–(IV) Nature *(Prakriti)*:** *Alinga* refers to unmanifested prakriti, the root cause of all creation, without any distinguishing mark (linga).

So the correct order is: (A)-(III), (B)-(I), (C)-(II), (D)-(IV).

88. **(2):** Matching *Upanishads* with their *Vedic Shakhas*:

(A) ***Kenopanishad*–(III) *Samvediya Shakha*:** *Kena Upanishad* belongs to the *Sama Veda,* dealing with the nature of *Brahman* and mind.

(B) ***Aitareya Upanishad*–(IV) *Shukla Rigvediya Shakha*:** *Aitareya* is from the *Rigveda*, discussing *Atman* and creation, often quoted in *Vedantic* studies.

(C) ***Kathopanishad*–(II) *Krishna Yajurvediya Shakha*:** It comes under *Krishna Yajurveda*, and is known for the dialogue between *Nachiketa* and *Yama*.

(D) ***Brihadaranyaka Upanishad*–(I) *Shukla Yajurved*:** One of the oldest and most profound *Upanishads*, part of the *Shukla Yajurveda*, focuses on ***neti-neti*** (not this, not this) philosophy.

Thus, the correct matching is: (A)-(III), (B)-(IV), (C)-(II), (D)-(I).

89. **(3):** Matching Philosophical Concepts with Scriptures:

(A) Concept of *Trigunas*–(III) *Sankhya Karika*: *Sankhya Karika* expounds on *Sattva, Rajas,* and *Tamas,* the three gunas that bind the soul to material existence.

(B) Concept of *Panch Koshas*–(I) *Taittiriya Upanishad*: This Upanishad outlines the five sheaths *(Annamaya, Pranamaya, Manomaya, Vijnanamaya, Anandamaya)* enveloping the Self.

(C) Concept of *Panch Pranas*–(IV) *Siddha Siddhanta Paddhati:* This Nath text elaborates on the five major pranas *(Prana, Apana, Samana, Udana, Vyana)* and their role in yogic physiology.

(D) Concept of *Adhi-vyadhi*–(II) *Yoga-vasishtha*: This epic text describes *Adhi* (mental stress) as the root of *Vyadhi* (physical disease) and provides yogic methods to overcome both.

Correct order: (A)-(III), (B)-(I), (C)-(IV), (D)-(II).

90. (3): Matching Diagnostic Devices with their respective functions:

(A) Glucometer–(II) Diabetes: A glucometer measures blood glucose levels, widely used for managing diabetes.

(B) Sphygmomanometer–(III) Blood pressure: This device is used to measure systolic and diastolic pressure, crucial in assessing hypertension.

(C) EEG–(I) Brain waves: Electroencephalogram (EEG) detects and records electrical activity in the brain, commonly used in diagnosing seizures, sleep disorders, etc.

(D) ECG–(IV) Heartbeat: Electrocardiogram (ECG) measures the electrical impulses of the heart to monitor cardiac rhythms and abnormalities.

Thus, correct match: (A)-(II), (B)-(III), (C)-(I), (D)-(IV).

91. (1): According to the passage, "As the body gets nourishment from food and water, so the soul derives its birth and expansion from determination, touch, vision and attachment." This clearly shows that while the *soul (Jivatma)* gains its development from subtle elements like determination and attachment, The *body* specifically derives its *nourishment* from *food and water* (Anna-Jala).

Therefore, among the options provided, Option 1 is the most accurate choice for what nourishes the physical body.

92. (4): The passage states: *"He (the Jivatma) is as subtle as the tip of the saw, having existence different from the Parmatma."* This makes it explicitly clear that *Jivatma* has a distinct existence from *Parmatma* (Supreme Soul). It possesses its own characteristics such as intelligence, determination, ego, and subtle form. Unlike the all-pervading *Parmatma, Jivatma* is bound by *karma* and undergoes rebirths. Hence, Option 4, *Jivatma*, is the correct answer.

93. (2): The passage says: *"The quantum of Jiva is the hundredth part of the tip of a hair, his form is as subtle as the imaginary part the subtlest part of the hair."* Interpreting this, ancient texts often elaborate that the *Jivatma* is even subtler than a hundredth part of the tip of a hair. This is metaphorically explained in many *Upanishadic* texts to be one ten-thousandth part (1/10,000) of the tip of hair in subtlety.

Therefore, based on metaphysical scriptures and textual interpretation, Option 2 is the correct one — *Jivatma* is *ten thousandth part of a hair* in subtle form.

94. (4): From the passage: *"As the body gets nourishment from food and water, so the soul derives its birth and expansion from determination, touch, vision and attachment."* Also stated: *"The Jivatma bears different places and different bodies according to the Karmas undertaken by him."* Here, *Karma* is directly responsible for the rebirths or assuming new bodies.

However, the factors like *Touch (Sparsha), Vision (Drishti)*, and *Determination (Sankalpa)* also play a role in the *Jivatma's* development and attachment.

Thus, *Karma* is the primary cause, but the others influence the nature and journey of the soul. So, Option 4: All of the above is the most comprehensive and correct answer.

95. (3): The passage clearly states: *"This soul i.e. Jivatma... like the Sun and cherishes intelligence along with determination and ego."*

Here, it is directly mentioned that *Jivatma possesses Determination (Sankalpa)* and *Ego (Ahankara)*. These qualities are part of the *Jiva's* subtle body and form the basis of its individuality and action.

Parmatma, being beyond attributes, is free from ego or determination. Therefore, Option 3: Jivatma is the accurate answer.

96. **(3):** The passage states: ***"With the scientific progress the blind race and limelight of materialistic world has made the things worse."***

This suggests that the increasing focus on material gains and scientific achievements, without spiritual or emotional balance, has created a crisis in physical and mental health.

The "blind race" for material success leads to stress, dissatisfaction, and mental fatigue, thereby becoming a major cause of mental diseases in modern times.

Thus, the limelight of materialism is identified as the *main reason* behind today's mental health issues.

97. **(2):** The passage highlights: ***"In the yoga Psycho-analysis the unconscious is the major fact."***

This directly indicates that *Yoga* psychology gives prime importance to the unconscious mind in understanding mental processes and disorders.

Unlike Western psychology, which often emphasizes the conscious and observable behaviour, *Yoga* delves deeper into unconscious tendencies *(Sanskaras, Vasanas)*.

Therefore, the basis of the nature of mind according to *Yoga* is the Unconscious.

98. **(4):** The passage says: ***"In Indian thought process personality is considered wholistically. The focal point of personality is the soul which is equivalent to Brahma."***

Here, it is clearly stated that the soul *(Atman)* is the central focus or base of holistic personality in *Yogic* and Indian spiritual thought.

The soul is believed to be the eternal, unchanging essence of the being, beyond body and mind.

Therefore, *Yoga* views holistic personality as centered on the soul, not just physical or psychological traits.

99. **(3):** From the passage: ***"On the basis of Sat, Raj and Tam Virtues normality and abnormality have been eventually viewed. It is the beauty of yoga."***

This clearly refers to the three *Gunas* (qualities):

- ***Sattva***–purity, harmony
- ***Rajas***–activity, restlessness
- ***Tamas***–inertia, ignorance

According to *Yoga,* mental health is seen through the balance of these *Gunas*. An imbalance leads to psychological disturbance.

Hence, the *Yogic* concept of mental health is based on *Sata (Sattva), Raja (Rajas),* and *Tama (Tamas)*.

100. **(2):** As per the passage: ***"The focal point of personality is the soul which is equivalent to Brahma."***

In Indian philosophy, especially *Vedanta,* the ultimate reality or truth is *Brahma (Brahman)*, the all-pervading supreme consciousness.

The central idea of Indian thought is that the individual soul *(Atman)* is not different from *Brahma*.

Due to ignorance *(Avidya)*, it seems separate, but true realization comes when the soul knows its identity with *Brahma*.

Thus, the central idea of Indian Thought is *Brahma*, making Option 2 correct.

Previous Years' Paper

National Testing Agency (NTA)

UGC-NET Junior Research Fellowship & Assistant Professor Eligibility Exam

Yoga, December-2023

(Exam held on 08-12-2023)

PAPER-II

1. Where is the definition of yoga 'manah prashamanopayo yoga ityabhidheeyate' given in the Mahopanishad?
A. The Mahopanishad 1/13
B. The Mahopanishad 2/47
C. The Mahopanishad 4/41
D. The Mahopanishad 5/42

2. 'Asadkarnadupangrahanat sarvasambhavaa-bhaavaat

Skatasya shakyakarnat kaaranbhavachch Satkaryam'

To which philosophy the above lines are associated?
A. Nyay Philosophy
B. Vaisheshik Philosophy
C. Sankhya Philosophy
D. Meemansa Philosophy

3. In which prakaran of yagyavlakyasmriti, the technique of meditation of karmendriyas place of pranas and atma is described?
A. Brahmachari Prakaran
B. Snatak Dharma Prakaran
C. Divya Prakaran
D. Yati Dharma Prakaran

4. To which part of yoga sadhna mumukchhatva is associated?
A. Bhakti yoga
B. Raja yoga
C. Gyan yoga
D. Karma yoga

5. Aitareya upanishad is related to:
A. Yajurveda B. Samveda
C. Atharva veda D. Rigveda

6. According to chhandogya upanishad udgeeth is:
A. Shrotra B. Netra
C. Prana D. Vani

7. According to Aitareya upanishad, 'Fire' (agni) emanated from:
A. The mouth (mukha)
B. Vocal Chord (vak)
C. Eyes (Netra)
D. Vision (Chakshu)

8. According to the Bhagavadgita "samah sarveshu bhuteshu madbhaktim labhate param" bears **correct** reference to:
A. 18/54 B. 18/56
C. 11/54 D. 12/04

9. In accordance with yoga tatvopanishad the region ranging from heart zone to the eyebrows has been referred to be belonging to:
A. Fire (Agni) B. Air (Vayu)
C. Earth (Prithvi) D. Sky (Akash)

10. In accordance with yoga chudamani Upanishad, 'A' kar where ingrained in Omkara in Jagrat state among all organisms:
A. Netra B. Kantha
C. Hridaya D. Naabhi

11. According to yoga tatvopanishad, which regular practice of mudra increases Jatharagni:
A. Mahamudra B. Viparitkarni
C. Khechari D. Tadagi

12. According to yoga sutra which knowledge (Buddhi) is different from the knowledge acquired through listening and inference:
A. Adhyatm Prasad
B. Ritambhara Pragya
C. Savichar
D. Ekagra Avastha

13. Where has Drishya been described in yoga sutra?
A. 1/17 B. 2/18
C. 3/21 D. 4/12

14. Lack of Avidya leads to lack of samyoga. This has been described in yogsutra in which of the following terms?
A. Kaivalya
B. Samadhi
C. Vivekkhyati
D. Dharmmegha Samadhi

15. Nirmanchitta emanates from Asmita. Where has it been described in patanjal yogsutra?
A. 1/30 B. 2/15
C. 3/9 D. 4/4

16. According to Hatha yoga pradipika, which musical instrument sound is heard in the parichayaavastha of Nadaanusandhan?
A. Veena B. Mardal
C. Bheri D. Kwanak

17. How many marma sthanas have been described in Vasistha Samhita?
A. Fifteen B. Eighteen
C. Twenty five D. Thirty four

18. Which of the following Pranayamas does not mention in Hatharatnavali?
A. Kewali B. Moorchha
C. Plavini D. Sitkaari

19. In Hatha Pradipika which of the Bandhas has been prescribed to be carried out at the end of poorak?
A. Jalandhar Bandha
B. Uddiyan Bandha
C. Mool Bandha
D. Maha Bandha

20. Which is not an essential Amino Acid?
A. Tryptophan B. Valine
C. Agrinine D. Xylene

21. Those persons who are not able to maintain the social relationship with the people and not have interest in these relations that means they lack of social skills. This indicates which personality disorder?
A. Paranoid personality disorder
B. Schizoid personality disorder
C. Anti-social personality disorder
D. Border line personality disorder

22. In which year American Psychological Society (APS) was established for the strengthen of teachers and practitioners of psychology
A. 1892 B. 1988
C. 1992 D. 1997

23. 'Gestalt Approach' is known for the explanation of which concept
A. Theory of Perception
B. Theory of Connectionism
C. Stimulus - Response approach
D. Theory of Learning

24. Eyes shine and one appear impressive due to which prana vayu?
A. Samana
B. Koorma
C. Kirikal
D. Devadatta

25. Which step in pranayama initiates powerful parasympathetic and sympathetic reflexes?

A. Rechak B. Purak

C. Kumbhaka D. Normal breathing

26. What is the location of Apas tattwa in the body?

A. Naval and knee

B. Head and chest

C. Knee and Ankle

D. Stomach and Naval

27. Which virtue should be cultivated for vice people?

A. Gladness B. Compassion

C. Friendliness D. Indifference

28. Which set of asanas are recommended for cardiac patients?

A. Vajrasana, shashankasana, sarpasana, yoga mudra and bhunamanasana

B. Adhomukha vrikshasrana, padahastasana, sarvargasana and vajrasana

C. Shashankasana, karnapidasana, sarpasana, yoga mudra and bhunamanasana

D. Virkshasana, padahastasana, halasana, and yoga mudra

29. Which hormone control the emotional and Instinct sexual behaviour in human?

A. Hypothalamus releasing hormone

B. Testosterone

C. Thyroxin

D. Cortisol

30. Which type of high level hormones are responsible for cardiac damage?

A. Androgenic hormones

B. Thyroid hormones

C. Pancreatic hormones

D. Hormones of pineal gland

31. Which yoga practices are most appropriate for the patient suffering from goiter?

A. Sarvangasana with pashini mudra

B. Vipreetkarni mudra with ujjayi pranayama

C. Halasana with yoga mudra

D. Sarvangasana with yoga mudra

32. 'Assignments for extra practice of selected yogic practices out of class hours enhance skill and performance levels of the students' is resembling which type of teaching method?

A. Project Method

B. Demonstration Method

C. Directed-Practice Method

D. Response-to-Instruction Method

33. In the yoga sutra, which of the following is 'Prachchhardana vidharanabhyam va pranasya' means of chitha prashadan?

A. First B. Second

C. Third D. Fourth

34. In the current scenario, which teaching approach is getting emphasis in education system?

A. Teacher Centred Approach

B. Student Centred Approach

C. Universities Centred Approach

D. Technology Centred Approach

35. A person who is desirous of adjusting his whole organization to a new situation organized and guided by the educator is called:

A. Teacher

B. Student

C. Curriculum

D. Education Organization

36. How many Pranayamas are mentioned in the Vashishtha samhita?

A. Three B. Four

C. Six D. Eight

37. According to yogbeeja, the method of sheetali pranayama is:

A. Inhale air through the rounded tongue exhale it through the nostrils

B. Inhale air through the mouth and exhale it through the nostrils

C. Inhale air from both the nostrils and exhale it through the left nostril

D. Inhale air through the mouth and exhale it through the mouth itself

38. According to the Hathratnawali, while practicing khechari mudra, the term 'Gomansbhakshan' means:

A. Activate the sushumna nadi
B. Practicing Shakti chalan
C. Touch the palate with the tongue
D. Movement of the tongue

39. According to the Hathapradipika, which asana is required for practising Nadanusandhan:

A. Muktasana B. Swastikasana
C. Sukhasana D. Padmasana

40. According to the Kathopanishada, through which of the following Atma cannot be known:

(*a*) By discourse (pravachan)
(*b*) By grace of the god
(*c*) By Discussion
(*d*) By Studies of scriptures
(*e*) By Yajna

Choose the **correct** answer from the options given below:

A. (*a*), (*c*) and (*d*) only
B. (*b*), (*e*) and (*d*) only
C. (*c*), (*d*) and (*b*) only
D. (*b*), (*a*) and (*d*) only

41. According to the Vaisheshik philosophy which of the following are matter (padarth):

(*a*) Prameya (*b*) Dravya
(*c*) Prayojana (*d*) Guna
(*e*) Karma

Choose the **correct** answer from the options given below:

A. (*a*), (*b*) and (*c*) only
B. (*b*), (*c*) and (*d*) only
C. (*b*), (*d*) and (*e*) only
D. (*c*), (*d*) and (*e*) only

42. Which of the following are the parts of the Dwadas Nidana as per the Buddhist ideology?

(*a*) Jalpa (*b*) Jati
(*c*) Trishna (*d*) Vigyan
(*e*) Guna

Choose the **correct** answer from the options given below:

A. (*a*), (*b*) and (*c*) only
B. (*b*), (*c*) and (*d*) only
C. (*c*), (*d*) and (*e*) only
D. (*a*), (*c*) and (*e*) only

43. In accordance with Ishavasyopanishad 'Mrityumteertva' pertains to:

(*a*) Vidya (*b*) Avidya
(*c*) Sambhuti (*d*) Vinash
(*e*) Samsara

Choose the **correct** answer from the options given below:

A. (*a*) and (*c*) only
B. (*b*) and (*d*) only
C. (*b*) and (*e*) only
D. (*d*) and (*e*) only

44. In accordance with the Bhagavadgita which of the following are not the characteristics of Rajasik Ahaar:

(*a*) Laced with salt (Lavonayukta)
(*b*) Snigdha
(*c*) Very hot
(*d*) Long-lasting
(*e*) Delicious (Rasayukta)

Choose the **correct** answer from the options given below:

A. (*a*), (*b*) and (*c*) only
B. (*b*), (*c*) and (*d*) only
C. (*b*), (*d*) and (*e*) only
D. (*c*), (*d*) and (*e*) only

45. According to Dhyanbindu Upanishad supreme soul (parmatma) has been referred to as:

(*a*) Trividh Brahma (*b*) Triguna
(*c*) Trayakshar (*d*) Ardha matra
(*e*) Vedajna

Choose the **correct** answer from the options given below:

A. (*a*), (*b*) and (*c*) only
B. (*a*), (*c*) and (*d*) only
C. (*c*), (*e*) and (*b*) only
D. (*c*), (*d*) and (*e*) only

46. Which ones of the following are the means for the awakening of kundalini (Kundalini Jagran) in yoga kundlupanishada?

(*a*) Saraswati chalan

(*b*) Pranayam

(*c*) Pratyahar

(*d*) Kriya

(*e*) Asana

Choose the **correct** answer from the options given below:

A. (*a*) and (*b*) only

B. (*b*) and (*c*) only

C. (*c*) and (*d*) only

D. (*d*) and (*e*) only

47. The attainment of Janana in the stage of Dharmmagh Samadhi has been described in yoga sutras as:

(*a*) Klesh-karm Nivritti

(*b*) Anantyaat

(*c*) Gyeam Alpam

(*d*) Chittam Sarvartham

(*e*) Hanmesham Kleshvaduktam

Choose the **correct** answer from the options given below:

A. (*a*) and (*b*) only

B. (*b*) and (*c*) only

C. (*c*) and (*d*) only

D. (*d*) and (*e*) only

48. What are the kinds of Drishya according to yagsutra?

(*a*) Vishesh

(*b*) Pratyayanupashya

(*c*) Avishesh

(*d*) Aling

(*e*) Drishimatra

Choose the **correct** answer from the options given below:

A. (*a*), (*b*) and (*c*) only

B. (*a*), (*c*) and (*d*) only

C. (*a*), (*b*) and (*e*) only

D. (*b*), (*c*) and (*e*) only

49. According to Hatha pradipika, the benefits of mool bandha described are:

(*a*) Nadi Shuddhi

(*b*) Union of Apaan and Prana

(*c*) Deficiency of defecation

(*d*) Even the old becomes akin to the youth

(*e*) The stage of contentment is attained

Choose the **correct** answer from the options given below:

A. (*a*), (*b*) and (*c*) only

B. (*b*), (*c*) and (*d*) only

C. (*c*), (*d*) and (*e*) only

D. (*a*), (*c*) and (*e*) only

50. According to Vasishtha samhita, the physical location of Apaanvayu in human body are:

(*a*) Janu

(*b*) Jangha

(*c*) Toe

(*d*) Centre of the Navel (Nabhimoola)

(*e*) Kantha

Choose the **correct** answer from the options given below:

A. (*a*), (*b*) and (*d*) only

B. (*b*), (*c*) and (*d*) only

C. (*c*), (*d*) and (*e*) only

D. (*a*), (*c*) and (*e*) only

51. According to Hatha pradipika, the benefits of Ujjayi pranayam are:

(*a*) Cure of naadi-disorder

(*b*) Cure of vatta disorder

(*c*) Cure of cough-borne disorder

(*d*) Cure of ascites disease

(*e*) Cure of hunger and thirst

Choose the **correct** answer from the options given below:

A. (*a*), (*c*) and (*d*) only

B. (*b*), (*c*) and (*e*) only

C. (*c*), (*d*) and (*e*) only

D. (*b*), (*c*) and (*d*) only

52. Due to deficiency of proteins, which diseases can occure in childhood?

(*a*) Marasmus

(*b*) Kwashiorkor
(*c*) Rickets
(*d*) Kerato-Malacia
(*e*) Xerophthalmia

Choose the **most appropriate** answer from the options given below:
A. (*a*) and (*b*) only
B. (*b*) and (*c*) only
C. (*c*) and (*d*) only
D. (*d*) and (*e*) only

53. Which bones are not the part of appendicular skeleton?
(*a*) Clavicle
(*b*) Scapula
(*c*) Cervical Vertebra
(*d*) Pelvis
(*e*) Sternum

Choose the **most appropriate** answer from the options given below:
A. (*a*) and (*b*) only
B. (*b*) and (*c*) only
C. (*c*) and (*e*) only
D. (*a*) and (*e*) only

54. If a person is lifting his left leg towards left side and return it while this movement, the knees are straight. These both movements are known as:
(*a*) Flexion
(*b*) Extension
(*c*) Abduction
(*d*) Adduction
(*e*) Inversion

Choose the **correct** answer from the options given below:
A. (*a*) and (*b*) only
B. (*b*) and (*e*) only
C. (*c*) and (*d*) only
D. (*d*) and (*e*) only

55. Which sufferings (Dukh) saddens the mind and in which pada of the yogsutra it has been mentioned?
(*a*) Vartman Dukh
(*b*) Anagat Dukh
(*c*) Sadhan Pada
(*d*) Vibhuti Pada
(*e*) Atit Dukh

Choose the **most appropriate** answer from the options given below:
A. (*b*) and (*c*) only
B. (*a*), and (*b*) only
C. (*c*) and (*d*) only
D. (*d*) and (*e*) only

56. According to the Hatha pradipika, food that adversely affect health are:
(*a*) Reheated
(*b*) Parwal
(*c*) Excessive Salt
(*d*) Butter
(*e*) Excessive Sour substances

Choose the **correct** answer from the options given below:
A. (*a*), (*b*) and (*c*) only
B. (*a*), (*c*) and (*e*) only
C. (*b*), (*d*) and (*e*) only
D. (*c*), (*d*) and (*e*) only

57. According to the yogsutra, what are the essentials for positive aptitude?
(*a*) simplicity
(*b*) compassion
(*c*) disregard
(*d*) kindness
(*e*) friendliness

Choose the **correct** answer from the options given below:
A. (*b*), (*c*) and (*e*) only
B. (*a*), (*b*) and (*d*) only
C. (*c*), (*d*) and (*e*) only
D. (*e*), (*b*) and (*a*) only

58. Major causes of indigestion are:
(*a*) Mineral salts deficiency in diet
(*b*) Have hot tea with heating spices
(*c*) Mental and emotional disturbances
(*d*) Taking too much vitamins and Minerals
(*e*) Habit of swallowing air and gluttony

Choose the **correct** answer from the options given below:

A. (*a*), (*b*) and (*d*) only
B. (*a*), (*c*) and (*e*) only
C. (*b*), (*c*) and (*d*) only
D. (*c*), (*d*) and (*e*) only

59. Which particular mudra is recommended to alleviate premenstrual tension?

(*a*) Maha mudra
(*b*) Nabho Mudra
(*c*) Mahabheda mudra
(*d*) Chinmaya mudra
(*e*) Pashini Mudra

Choose the **correct** answer from the options given below:

A. (*a*) and (*d*) only
B. (*a*) and (*c*) only
C. (*b*) and (*e*) only
D. (*c*) and (*d*) only

60. Which asanas help to restore valvular competence after traumatic accidents?

(*a*) Paschimottansana
(*b*) Parvatasana
(*c*) Sarvangasana
(*d*) Garudasana
(*e*) Gomukhasana

Choose the **most appropriate** answer from the options given below:

A. (*a*), (*c*) and (*d*) only
B. (*b*), (*c*) and (*e*) only
C. (*b*), (*d*) and (*e*) only
D. (*a*), (*c*) and (*e*) only

61. In the yogsutra the sampadas (perfections) of bodies are mentioned as:

(*a*) Form (Roop)
(*b*) Mahima
(*c*) Beauty (Lavanys)
(*d*) Vashitva
(*e*) Strength (Bala)

Choose the **correct** answer from the options given below:

A. (*a*) and (*b*) only
B. (*a*) and (*c*) only
C. (*b*) and (*d*) only
D. (*a*) and (*c*) only

62. Which are not the misconceptions for yoga?

(*a*) Yoga is not meant for the ordinary person
(*b*) Yoga can boost our physical and mental health
(*c*) Yoga is a journey towards inner world
(*d*) Yoga is only a physical exercise
(*e*) Yoga is associated with idea of the miracles.

Choose the **correct** answer from the options given below:

A. (*a*) and (*b*) only
B. (*b*) and (*c*) only
C. (*c*) and (*d*) only
D. (*d*) and (*e*) only

63. Which are not the characteristics for a good teacher?

(*a*) A genuine interest in communication
(*b*) Incompetence in elaboration of topic
(*c*) A willingness to share interest and experiences with others
(*d*) Inability to set a good example through lifestyle and behaviour
(*e*) A sense of professional responsibility towards the students

Choose the **correct** answer from the options given below:

A. (*a*) and (*b*) only
B. (*b*) and (*d*) only
C. (*c*) and (*d*) only
D. (*d*) and (*e*) only

64. According to the Gherand Samhita, for practicing Mahamudra, it is instructed to:

(*a*) Pull the navel backward
(*b*) Press the anal region with the left ankle
(*c*) Shrink the throat
(*d*) Keep the tongue at the cavity of the upper palate
(*e*) Keep the eyes on the eyebrow centre

Choose the **correct** answer from the options given below:

A. (*b*), (*c*) and (*e*) only
B. (*a*), (*b*) and (*c*) only
C. (*b*), (*c*) and (*d*) only
D. (*c*), (*d*) and (*e*) only

65. In Hatha pradipika, the method of Trataka is described as:

(*a*) Focussed vision
(*b*) Eyes should focused on the eye-brow centre
(*c*) Concentrate on micro goal
(*d*) Focused on the tip of the nostril
(*e*) Till the Tears come down from the eyes

Choose the **correct** answer from the options given below:

A. (*b*), (*d*) and (*e*) only
B. (*a*), (*b*) and (*d*) only
C. (*a*), (*c*) and (*d*) only
D. (*a*), (*c*) and (*e*) only

66. According to the yogsutra while describing about the Pranav, there is delineation of:

(*a*) Recitation of Pranav
(*b*) Concentration on Pranav
(*c*) Meaning of Pranav
(*d*) Recitation of Soaham
(*e*) Feel the meaning of Pranav

Choose the **correct** answer from the options given below:

A. (*a*), (*c*) and (*e*) only
B. (*b*), (*c*) and (*d*) only
C. (*c*), (*d*) and (*e*) only
D. (*a*), (*d*) and (*e*) only

67. Match List-I with List-II.

List-I	List-II
(*a*) Maharshi Dayanand Saraswati	I. Jyoti Shakti or Pragya
(*b*) Tulsidas	II. Arya bhivinay
(*c*) Shri Aurobindo	III. Vinay Patrika
(*d*) Swami Shivanada Saraswati	IV. Life Divine

Choose the **correct** answer from the options given below:

	(*a*)	(*b*)	(*c*)	(*d*)
A.	II	III	IV	I
B.	I	II	III	IV
C.	III	I	II	IV
D.	IV	III	I	II

68. According to the Bhagvadgita, Match List-I and List-II.

List-I	List-II
(*a*) Bandham Moksham Cha ya vetti	I. Rajsi dhriti
(*b*) Prasangen Dharmakamarthan Dharayate	II. Sattvik Sukha
(*c*) Na vimunchati Durmedha	III. Sattviki buddhi
(*d*) Abhyasadramate yatra dukhantam cha nigachhati	IV. Tamasi dhriti

Choose the **correct** answer from the options given below:

	(*a*)	(*b*)	(*c*)	(*d*)
A.	III	I	IV	II
B.	II	IV	I	III
C.	III	II	I	IV
D.	IV	II	III	I

69. According to yoga chudamani upanishad, Match List-I and List-II.

List-I	List-II
(*a*) Conversion of food from unsavoury to savoury	I. Khecharimudra
(*b*) Chanting all through the day and night	II. Sukra and maharaj
(*c*) Being free from disease, death, hunger-thirst and faint	III. Practice of mahamudra
(*d*) White and red two colours (Varna)	IV. Twenty-one Thousand Six hundred mantras

Choose the **correct** answer from the options given below:

	(a)	(b)	(c)	(d)
A.	III	IV	I	II
B.	IV	III	II	I
C.	III	IV	II	I
D.	II	I	III	IV

70. Match List-I with List-II.

List-I	List-II
(a) Mahavrat	I. Vibhutipada
(b) Suksham vishyatvam chaaling paryavasaanam	II. Sadhan Pada
(c) Kshantatkramyoh Samyamadvivekajam jnananam	III. Keivalya Pada
(d) Parinamaiktvat vastu-tattvam	IV. Samadhi Pada

Choose the **correct** answer from the options given below:

	(a)	(b)	(c)	(d)
A.	II	IV	I	III
B.	I	II	III	IV
C.	II	IV	III	I
D.	III	I	IV	II

71. As per Vasishtha samhita, Match List-I and List-II.

List-I	List-II
(a) Yama	I. Bhadra
(b) Niyama	II. Koorma
(c) Aasana	III Japa
(d) Upa-prana	IV. Daya

Choose the **correct** answer from the options given below:

	(a)	(b)	(c)	(d)
A.	IV	III	I	II
B.	I	II	III	IV
C.	II	I	III	IV
D.	III	IV	II	I

72. Match List-I with List-II.

List-I	List-II
(a) Thorndike	I. Operant conditioning chamber
(b) Skinner	II. Experiments of stick & box problem
(c) Kohler	III. Theory of Connectionism
(d) Pavlov	IV. Classical conditioning theory

Choose the **correct** answer from the options given below:

	(a)	(b)	(c)	(d)
A.	IV	II	I	III
B.	II	I	III	IV
C.	II	III	I	IV
D.	III	I	II	IV

73. Match List-I with List-II.

List-I	List-II
(a) Mooladhar	I. Six petals
(b) Avirati	II. Klesh
(c) Swadhishthan Chakra	III. Antraya
(d) Abhinivesh	IV. Four Petals

Choose the **correct** answer from the options given below:

	(a)	(b)	(c)	(d)
A.	II	I	III	IV
B.	III	II	I	IV
C.	IV	III	I	II
D.	IV	III	II	I

74. Match List-I with List-II.

List-I (Five Elements)	List-II (Koshas)
(a) Fire	I. Pranamaya
(b) Earth	II. Anadamaya
(c) Ether	III. Manomaya
(d) Water	IV. Anamaya

Choose the **correct** answer from the options given below:

	(a)	(b)	(c)	(d)
A.	I	IV	III	II
B.	III	IV	II	I
C.	IV	III	I	II
D.	I	II	IV	III

75. Match List-I with List-II.

List-I (Yogasutras)	List-II (Related Topic)
(*a*) Tatra niratishayam sarvagyabeejam	I. After getting vivekgyan
(*b*) Tasya saptadha prantbhumih pragya	II. Kaivalya Pada
(*c*) Dharnasu cha yogyata mansah	III. God
(*d*) Jatyantar parinamah prakrityapurat	IV. Pranayam

Choose the **correct** answer from the options given below:

	(*a*)	(*b*)	(*c*)	(*d*)
A.	III	I	IV	II
B.	I	II	III	IV
C.	II	III	IV	I
D.	IV	III	II	I

76. Match List-I with List-II.

List-I (Mudras)	List-II (Technique)
(*a*) Shambhavi	I. Pressing perinium region with the heels of the legs
(*b*) Khechari	II. Patting hips on the ground
(*c*) Mahavedha	III. Eyes focussed on the eyebrow centre
(*d*) Mahamudra	IV. Insert the tongue in the cavity of the upper palate

Choose the **correct** answer from the options given below:

	(*a*)	(*b*)	(*c*)	(*d*)
A.	III	IV	II	I
B.	II	III	I	IV
C.	I	II	III	IV
D.	IV	I	II	III

77. Give the correct sequence of evolution as per the sankhya philosophy:

(*a*) Mahat
(*b*) Ahankar
(*c*) Prakriti
(*d*) Panchmahabhoot
(*e*) Panchtanmatra

Choose the **correct** answer from the options given below:

A. (*a*), (*b*), (*c*), (*d*), (*e*)
B. (*c*), (*a*), (*b*), (*e*), (*d*)
C. (*a*), (*c*), (*d*), (*e*), (*b*)
D. (*b*), (*a*), (*c*), (*d*), (*e*)

78. In accordance with yoga vashishtha, the correct sequence of the stages of Jnana:

(*a*) Sattvapatti
(*b*) Tanumanasa
(*c*) Shubhechha
(*d*) Vicharana
(*e*) Asamsakti

Choose the **correct** answer from the options given below:

A. (*c*), (*d*), (*b*), (*a*), (*e*)
B. (*a*), (*b*), (*d*), (*c*), (*e*)
C. (*b*), (*a*), (*c*), (*d*), (*e*)
D. (*e*), (*b*), (*a*), (*c*), (*d*)

79. Identify the correct sequence of the following as per slokas figuring in yogtatvopanishad:

(*a*) Mahabandh
(*b*) Khechari Mudra
(*c*) Deergh Pranav sandhan
(*d*) Sahjoli
(*e*) Jalandhar Bandh

Choose the **correct** answer from the options given below:

A. (*b*), (*c*), (*d*), (*e*), (*a*)
B. (*a*), (*b*), (*e*), (*c*), (*d*)
C. (*a*), (*b*), (*c*), (*e*), (*d*)
D. (*a*), (*e*), (*d*), (*c*), (*b*)

80. Arrange the following in a sequence according to pada of yogsutras:

(*a*) Kramanyatvam Parinamanyatve Hetuh
(*b*) Pratyayasya Parachittanjanam
(*c*) Tadarth eva Drishyasyatma
(*d*) Tivra Samveganamasannh
(*e*) Drishtra drishyo parktam chittam Sarvartham

Choose the **correct** answer from the options given below:

A. (*d*), (*c*), (*a*), (*b*), (*e*)
B. (*a*), (*b*), (*d*), (*c*), (*e*)
C. (*a*), (*b*), (*c*), (*e*), (*d*)
D. (*d*), (*c*), (*b*), (*a*), (*e*)

81. As per shlokas mentioned in Hatha pradipika, the correct sequence of the ailments (disorders) caused in the event of vayu turning hostile is:

(*a*) Breath disorder (shuras)
(*b*) Headache (shirvedana)
(*c*) Hiccups (Hichaki)
(*d*) Cough
(*e*) Auricular pain (Karna vedana)

Choose the **correct** answer from the options given below:

A. (*c*), (*a*), (*d*), (*b*), (*e*)
B. (*a*), (*b*), (*d*), (*e*), (*c*)
C. (*b*), (*a*), (*c*), (*d*), (*e*)
D. (*c*), (*b*), (*e*), (*d*), (*a*)

82. Arrange the mentioned body organs in sequence of blood flow.

(*a*) Tricuspid Value
(*b*) Pulmonary Aorta
(*c*) Pulmonary Vena cava
(*d*) Right Auricle
(*e*) Bicuspid Valve

Choose the **correct** answer from the options given below:

A. (*d*), (*c*), (*b*), (*a*), (*e*)
B. (*d*), (*e*), (*b*), (*c*), (*a*)
C. (*d*), (*a*), (*b*), (*c*), (*e*)
D. (*d*), (*a*), (*c*), (*b*), (*e*)

83. According to the Hatha pradipika, what is the correct sequence of edible food:

(*a*) Honey
(*b*) Five kinds of vegetables
(*c*) Lentil (Moong)
(*d*) Khand
(*e*) Soonth

Choose the **correct** answer from the options given below:

A. (*a*), (*c*), (*d*), (*e*), (*b*)
B. (*d*), (*a*), (*e*), (*b*), (*c*)
C. (*b*), (*c*), (*d*), (*e*), (*a*)
D. (*e*), (*a*), (*b*), (*c*), (*d*)

84. According to book 'Teaching Methods for Yoga Practices' the correct sequence for a lesson plan is:

(*a*) Setting the Atmosphere
(*b*) Introduction to the Practice
(*c*) Demonstrating Practices
(*d*) Students Individual Practice Time
(*e*) Group Practice

Choose the **correct** answer from the options given below:

A. (*a*), (*b*), (*c*), (*d*), (*e*)
B. (*b*), (*a*), (*c*), (*d*), (*e*)
C. (*a*), (*b*), (*c*), (*e*), (*d*)
D. (*b*), (*a*), (*c*), (*e*), (*d*)

85. The correct sequence of the procedure of the kukkutasan:

(*a*) Perform padmasan
(*b*) Sitting on the Dandasan
(*c*) Place both the hands between the knees and thighs and keep the plams firmly on the ground
(*d*) Pressing the plams; the body should be put on the ground
(*e*) Pressing the plams, the body should be lifted upward (towards the sky)

Choose the **correct** answer from the options given below:

A. (*b*), (*c*), (*e*), (*d*), (*a*)
B. (*a*), (*c*), (*b*), (*e*), (*d*)
C. (*b*), (*a*), (*c*), (*e*), (*d*)
D. (*d*), (*b*), (*a*), (*c*), (*e*)

86. Given below are two statement, one is labelled as Assertion (A) and the other is labelled as Reason (R).

Assertion (A): Rishi Vashishtha referred to king Dasaratha to be equipped with the sublime traits of patience as well as the observer of uttam vrata.

Reason (R): King Dasarath Sent his son Lord Shri Rama and Lakshmana accompanying Sage Vishwamistra for the attainment of yajna Siddhi.

In the light of the above statement, choose the **correct** answer from the options given below:

A. Both (A) and (R) are true and (R) is the correct explanation of (A)

B. Both (A) and (R) are true and (R) is NOT the correct explanation of (A)

C. (A) is true, but (R) is false

D. (A) is false, but (R) is true

87. Given below are two statement: one is labelled as Assertion (A) and the other is labelled as Reason (R).

Assertion (A): Vishnu's highest position (Parampada) is attained through the dissolution of manas.

Reason (R): One ought to meditate on Maha Vishnu laced with luminiscence akin to the one existing in the Moon.

In the light of the above statement, choose the **correct** answer from the options given below:

A. Both (A) and (R) are true and (R) is the correct explanation of (A)

B. Both (A) and (R) are true and (R) is NOT the correct explanation of (A)

C. (A) is true, but (R) is false

D. (A) is false, but (R) is true

88. Given below are two statement: one is labelled as Assertion (A) and the other is labelled as Reason (R).

Assertion (A): According to yogsutra, in the higher state of yoga there should be no attachment on the invocation of Lokpal Deities.

Reason (R): Accepting the invocation of Deities creats the chances of sinister again.

In the light of the above statement, choose the **correct** answer from the options given below:

A. Both (A) and (R) are true and (R) is the correct explanation of (A)

B. Both (A) and (R) are true and (R) is NOT the correct explanation of (A)

C. (A) is true, but (R) is false

D. (A) is false, but (R) is true

89. Given below are two statement, one is labelled as Assertion (A) and the other is labelled as Reason (R).

Assertion (A): In case of Kapha aggravation Shatkarma should be practiced. One should keep secret these cleansing practices which clean the body.

Reason (R): Shatkarma is not essential in case of balanced Vatta, Pitta and Kapha.

In the light of the above statement, choose the **correct** answer from the options given below:

A. Both (A) and (R) are true and (R) is the correct explanation of (A)

B. Both (A) and (R) are true and (R) is NOT the correct explanation of (A)

C. (A) is true, but (R) is false

D. (A) is false, but (R) is true

90. Given below are two statement.

Statement I: Dysmenorrhoea and menorrhagia are the medical terms for problems of painful, irregular or excessively heavy menstruation.

Statement II: Menstrual difficulty spawns as much wretchedness as the common cold and medical insight into this problem is equally limited.

In the light of the above statement, choose the **correct** answer from the options given below:

A. Both Statement I and Statement II are true
B. Both Statement I and Statement II are false
C. Statement I is true, but Statement II is false
D. Statement I is false, but Statement II is true

Directions (Qs. No. 91-95): *Read the following passage carefully and answer the questions.*

Practicing asanas can promote smooth flow of energy in nadis. Further, chakras also can be activated. It enables the attainment of control over the body, mind and energy. Practicing yoga asana is the main tool of achieving high state of awareness.

Pawan muktasan is an important practice in the galaxies of practices which not only have positive effect on body and mind, but it also contributes significantly in treating physical and mental diseases and our health is protected.

These days most of the diseases are psychosomatic. Practicing asanas, coordinated breathing with awareness and thus mind can be vigilant and spontaneous. Appropriate practice of asanas relax our mind and secretion of hormones which bring positive harmonizing effect in internal organs.

Pawanmuktasn is divided in three groups: (1) anti-rheumatic group, (2) the digestive/ abdominal group, (3) shaktibandh. These three are complementary to each other and the practice of which intensifies the independent impact of energy.

91. The practice of Asanas is capable of making smooth flow of energy in nadis and activating which of the following?
A. Kundalini
B. Chakara
C. Pran-urja
D. Self-realization

92. Which of the following is useful for prevention of health and treatment of physical and mental diseases?
A. Practising Asana
B. Prictising Pawan Muktasan
C. Practising Pranayama
D. Self awareness

93. In which of the following can be brought out awareness and ease by practising asana?
A. Mind
B. Body
C. Breath
D. Soul

94. What is the second group of pawan muktasan called?
A. Shakti bandh
B. Digestive/Abdominal practice
C. Anti-rheumetic
D. Vayumukt Practice

95. Which of the practice intensifies the free flow of energy?
A. First Group of Pawan muktasan
B. Second group of Pawan muktasan
C. Third group of Pawan muktasan
D. All the groups of Pawan muktasan

Directions (Qs. No. 96-100): *Read the following passage carefully and answer the questions.*

Today everyone is aware about one's health. The society believes that yoga is the only method to achieve holistic health. Consequently, everyone wants yoga to be a part of one's lifestyle. But diet plays a very important role in the practice of yoga and every practitioner should keep it in his mind. Diet is the primary need of life. One body receives the energy from the rasa obtained after digestion of edible foods taken as a diet, to perform our daily activities. If the diet is not balanced the disorders emerge in the body such as lack of nutrients in the food results in malnutrition. Some way if the food does not have nutrients according to age and need of the body, it results in undernutrition. In view of the importance of nutrition, the government is also emphasising to include coarse grains in the diet. Consequently, the year 2023 has been termed as the "year of millet" by honorable prime minister.

96. What is the only method to achieve Holistic health?

A. Yoga
B. Diet
C. Balanced diet
D. Millet

97. Every yoga practitioner should give importance particularly:

A. Pace of breathing
B. Yama-Niyama
C. Diet
D. God

98. The year 2023 has been termed as ______.

A. The year of disaster
B. The year of yoga
C. The year of Millet
D. The year of health

99. It the diet does not have nutrients according to the age and need of the person, it results in ________ .

A. Malnutrition
B. Wellnutrition
C. Hypernutrition
D. Undernutrition

100. The government is emphasising to include ________ in the diet.

A. Coarse grain
B. Milk products
C. Salad
D. Nutritious pulses

ANSWERS

1. (D): The definition of yoga from The Mahopanishad 5/42, 'manah prashamanopayo yoga ityabhidheeyate', highlights yoga as the method or practice aimed at calming the mind. This definition underscores the fundamental purpose of yoga as a means to achieve inner peace and tranquility by quieting the fluctuations of the mind. It suggests that through specific practices and techniques, one can attain a state of mental equilibrium and spiritual well-being. This definition aligns with the traditional understanding of yoga as a path toward self-realisation and harmonious existence.

2. (C): The lines "Asadkarnadupangrahanat sarvasambhavaa-bhaavaat Skatasya shakyakarnat kaaranbhavachch Satkaryam" are from the Sankhya Karika, a foundational text of Sankhya philosophy. This statement reflects a key tenet of Sankhya philosophy, which is the concept of prakriti and purusha. Prakriti is the material cause of the universe, while purusha is the conscious principle. According to Sankhya, prakriti is composed of three gunas, or qualities: sattva (purity), rajas (activity), and tamas (inertia). These gunas are in a constant state of flux, and their interactions give rise to the manifest universe.

3. (D): The technique of meditation of karmendriyas (organs of action), place of pranas (vital energy), and atma (soul) is described in the Yati Dharma Prakaran of the Yagyavalkya Smriti. This prakaran deals with the duties and practices of yatis, or renunciants who have renounced worldly life. The meditation technique involves focusing the mind on the various parts of the body, starting with the karmendriyas and moving inward to the pranas and atma.

4. (C): Gyan yoga, the path of knowledge, emphasises attaining liberation through self-realization and understanding the true nature of reality. Mumukshutva, the burning desire for liberation, is a fundamental prerequisite for embarking on the path of Gyan yoga. Through study, reflection, and meditation, the Gyan yogi seeks to remove the veil of ignorance (avidya) that keeps them trapped in the cycle of samsara (birth and death).

By attaining true knowledge of the Self (Atman) and its ultimate unity with Brahman (the Absolute), liberation becomes possible.

5. (D): The Aitareya Upanishad is one of the oldest and most important Upanishads, and it is associated with the Rigveda, the oldest and most important of the four Vedas. The Upanishad is embedded within the Aitareya Aranyaka, which is a part of the Rigveda. The Aitareya Upanishad deals with a variety of philosophical topics, including the nature of reality, the soul, and the relationship between the individual and the universe. The Upanishads are philosophical and spiritual texts that form the concluding portions of the Vedas, the ancient sacred scriptures of Hinduism.

6. (B): The Chandogya Upanishad udgeeth is a Hindu scripture that explains the internal features of Netra. It is one of the oldest and most revered Hindu scriptures and is a Sanskrit text that is part of the Chandogya Brahmana of the Sama Veda. The Chandogya Upanishad's central theme is Brahman, the supreme principle of the universe, and its relationship to the individual self. It also explores the path to spiritual liberation.

7. (B): According to the Aitareya Upanishad, 'Fire' (agni) is indeed associated with Vocal Chord (vak). In this Upanishad, the term "vak" refers to the faculty of speech or the organ of speech, particularly emphasising the power of speech in the act of creation. The Upanishad describes a cosmogonic process where various elements and entities, including fire (agni), emerge from the primal being through the manifestation of speech (vak). This highlights the significance of sound, speech, and the creative potential of vocal expression in the context of creation as depicted in the Aitareya Upanishad.

8. (A): The reference "samah sarveshu bhuteshu madbhaktim labhate param" from the Bhagavad Gita corresponds to 18/54.

In Chapter 18, Verse 54 (18/54) of the Bhagavad Gita, Lord Krishna says:

"brahma-bhutah prasannatma na socati na kanksati samah sarveshu bhutesu mad-bhaktim labhate param"

This verse emphasises the qualities of a devotee who is established in transcendental consciousness, free from material desires and unaffected by dualities. Such a devotee sees all living beings equally and attains supreme devotion (madbhaktim) to the Supreme (param).

9. (B): In accordance with the Yoga Tattva Upanishad, the region ranging from the heart zone to the eyebrows has been referred to as belonging to Air (Vayu).

The Yoga Tattva Upanishad associates different elements (bhutas) with specific regions or areas within the subtle body (sukshma sharira). According to this Upanishad:

The heart (hridaya) is associated with the element of air (vayu).

The region between the heart and the eyebrows (kantha to shiras) is attributed to the element of air (vayu).

Therefore, based on the teachings of the Yoga Tattva Upanishad, the answer is Air (Vayu) for the region ranging from the heart zone to the eyebrows. This highlights the subtle energy centers and their elemental associations as described in yogic philosophy and metaphysical teachings.

10. (A): In the Yoga Chudamani Upanishad, the specific placement of the 'A' sound of Omkara (Omkara) in the waking state (Jagrat) is associated with the eyes (Netra), symbolising the awakening and clarity of perception that occurs during the waking state of consciousness. Therefore, based on the teachings of the Yoga Chudamani Upanishad, the correct answer is Netra for the location of the 'A' kar within Omkara in the waking state among all organisms. This highlights the subtle and symbolic associations between sound, consciousness, and the organs of perception in yogic philosophy.

11. (B): According to the Yoga Tattva Upanishad, the regular practice of Viparitkarani mudra is said to increase Jatharagni (digestive fire). Viparitkarani mudra, also known as Viparita Karani or Legs-Up-the-Wall Pose, is a yoga posture where the legs are elevated vertically against a wall while lying down. This posture is known for its therapeutic benefits, including improving blood circulation, calming the nervous system, and aiding digestion. In the context of the Yoga Tattva Upanishad, Viparitkarani mudra is recommended as a practice to enhance Jatharagni (digestive fire) and promote overall health and vitality.

12. (B): Ritambhara Pragya is a state of higher or transcendental knowledge that transcends ordinary perception and inference. It is a direct intuitive knowledge that arises from a deep state of meditation and spiritual realisation. In the context of the Yoga Sutra, Patanjali explains different levels and states of consciousness (pragya) that can be attained through yoga practice. Ritambhara Pragya represents a profound and direct form of knowledge that is beyond the usual methods of acquiring knowledge through sensory perception and logical reasoning.

13. (B): In Yoga Sutra 2.18 (2/18), Patanjali discusses the nature of the seen (Drishya) and emphasizes that everything that is perceived or experienced through the senses and mind falls into the category of Drishya. This sutra is part of Patanjali's teachings on the path of yoga, specifically focussing on the distinction between the seer (Purusha) and the seen (Prakriti), which includes all objects, thoughts, emotions, and sensations. The sutra highlights the importance of understanding the nature of Drishya and its relationship to the seer (Purusha) as essential for the practice of yoga and the attainment of inner liberation (Kaivalya).

14. (A): In the Yoga Sutra of Patanjali, Kaivalya refers to the state of ultimate liberation or isolation, where the practitioner achieves complete independence and detachment from the fluctuations of the mind and the effects of ignorance (Avidya). The concept of samyoga (union or connection) is intertwined with Avidya, as ignorance leads to the identification of the seer (Purusha) with the seen (Prakriti), resulting in bondage (samadhi). By eliminating Avidya through the cultivation of self-awareness (Viveka) and spiritual practices, the practitioner breaks free from this bondage and attains the state of Kaivalya, characterised by ultimate liberation and transcendence.

15. (D): In Yoga Sutra 4.4 (4/4), Patanjali explains the relationship between Asmita (ego-sense) and Nirmanchitta (imaginations or projections). In this sutra, Patanjali explains that the imaginations or projections (Nirmanchitta) created by the mind originate from the identification with the ego (Asmita). These mental creations dissolve or cease when one realises their true nature (swarupa) beyond the egoic identity. This sutra emphasizes the process of transcending ego-driven mental activities through self-realization and understanding of one's true nature.

16. (B): According to the Hatha Yoga Pradipika, the musical instrument sound that is heard in the parichaya avastha (initial stage) of Nadaanusandhana (the practice of inner sound meditation) is Mardal.

The Hatha Yoga Pradipika describes the stages of Nadaanusandhana where the practitioner attunes to the inner sound (Nada) during meditation. The text mentions that in the initial stages (parichaya avastha), the practitioner may perceive various sounds resembling musical instruments. The sound of the mardala (a type of drum) is specifically referenced in this context.

17. (B): The Vasistha Samhita describes Eighteen marma sthanas. Marma sthanas are vital points in the body according to Ayurveda and traditional Indian medicine. These points are considered areas where veins, arteries, tendons, bones, and joints meet, making them crucial for health and well-being. The Vasistha Samhita, a classical Ayurvedic text, provides detailed descriptions of these marma points and their significance in diagnosis, treatment, and therapeutic practices.

18. (C): Plavini kumbhaka is not mentioned in Hatha Ratnavali, a 17th-century Hatha yoga text written by Srinivasa. However, Hatha Ratnavali does mention a new kumbhaka called bhujangakarani kumbhaka, which is similar to the hissing of a snake. Hatha Ratnavali is divided into four chapters and covers topics such as mahayoga, body purifying techniques, mudras, kumbhakas, and nadis.

19. (A): According to Hatha Yoga Pradipika, Jalandhara Bandha should be performed at the end of Puraka. Puraka is the process of filling the lungs with air from outside. Jalandhara Bandha is a chin bandha that involves contracting the throat and pressing the chin onto the chest. It is said to eliminate pain in the throat and old age. The contracted throat veins are thought to receive liquid from the sky, which is why the bandha is also known as Jalandhar Bandha, which means "destroyer of throat pain".

20. (C & D): Arginine and Xylene is not an essential amino acid. The nine essential amino acids are: histidine, isoleucine, leucine, lysine, methionine, phenylalanine, threonine, tryptophan, and valine.

Essential amino acids are vital for bodily functions such as protein synthesis, tissue repair, and nutrient absorption. The body cannot produce these amino acids, so they must be obtained through diet. Arginine can sometimes be synthesised by the body, but not always, depending on the circumstances. Xylene is a completely different type of molecule and is not involved in protein synthesis.

21. (B): Schizoid personality disorder is characterised by a persistent pattern of detachment from social relationships and a limited range of emotional expression. Individuals with schizoid personality disorder often prefer solitary activities and have little desire for close relationships, including both family and friendships. They tend to be introverted, emotionally cold, and detached from social norms and conventions. This detachment can stem from a fear of intimacy or a feeling of indifference towards social experiences. They may appear emotionally cold or aloof to others, and they often have a limited social network or none at all.

22. (B): The Association for Psychological Science (APS) was founded in 1988 with the goal of advancing scientific psychology and representing the interests of psychologists in various fields, including research, teaching, and practice. APS promotes the dissemination of psychological knowledge, fosters collaboration among researchers and educators, and advocates for the application of psychological science to improve human welfare.

23. (A): The 'Gestalt Approach' is known for its explanation of Theory of Perception. The Gestalt psychology movement emerged in the early 20th century as a reaction against the prevailing reductionist approaches to psychology. Gestalt psychologists emphasised the idea that the whole of an experience is different from the sum of its parts. They focused on studying perception as a holistic process, emphasising how individuals perceive patterns, organization, and structure in sensory input. Key concepts associated with the Gestalt Approach include:

- **Principle of Totality:** The whole is different from the sum of its parts.
- **Figure-Ground Relationship:** Perception involves distinguishing between a figure (the object of focus) and its background.
- **Law of Similarity, Proximity, and Closure:** Gestalt psychologists identified principles governing how elements are perceived as organised wholes.

24. (B): Koorma vayu is associated with the eyes and blinking in yogic philosophy. Koorma vayu is considered a minor prana vayu (upa prana vayu) that specifically governs the movement of the eyelids and provides nourishment to the eyes. The role of Koorma vayu in influencing the eyes could indeed contribute to their brightness and clarity, which are often seen as signs of good health and vitality. Additionally, the connection between Koorma vayu and focus or willpower aligns with the aspect of appearing impressive. A strong focus and steady gaze, facilitated by the influence of Koorma vayu, can project confidence and command attention.

25. (C): Kumbhaka refers to the practice of holding the breath after inhalation (Antara Kumbhaka) or after exhalation (Bahya Kumbhaka) during pranayama. This breath retention phase is crucial in pranayama techniques as it influences the autonomic nervous system, which includes both the sympathetic and parasympathetic branches. During Kumbhaka (breath retention):

Inhalation activates sympathetic responses, leading to increased alertness and arousal. Exhalation activates parasympathetic responses, promoting relaxation and calmness. The interplay between these phases of breath retention (Kumbhaka) helps regulate and balance the autonomic nervous system, eliciting powerful physiological effects and reflexes associated with both sympathetic (fight-or-flight) and parasympathetic (rest-and-digest) responses.

26. (*)

27. (D): The concept of indifference is typically considered a virtue in the context of fostering positive interpersonal relationships or personal growth. Indifference generally refers to a lack of interest, concern, or empathy toward others, which may not contribute to positive personal or social development. It is important to engage with others with empathy and understanding, seeking to cultivate virtues that promote connection and support rather than detachment or indifference.

28. (A): The recommended set of asanas for cardiac patients includes Vajrasana (Thunderbolt Pose), Shashankasana (Rabbit Pose), Sarpasana (Snake Pose), Yoga Mudra (Yogic Seal), and Bhunamanasana (Spinal Flexion and Extension). Vajrasana improves digestion and calms the mind, benefiting blood circulation. Shashankasana and Sarpasana stretch the spine and chest, enhancing lung capacity and promoting relaxation. Yoga Mudra relieves stress and stimulates blood flow, while Bhunamanasana improves spinal flexibility and circulation. Together, these gentle poses focus on relaxation, stress reduction, and improved circulation, supporting cardiovascular health.

29. (A): The hypothalamus is involved in regulating many fundamental programs, including sexual behaviour and emotions. Stimulation of the hypothalamus can increase sexual activity and cause violent anger. The hypothalamus also triggers the release of other hormones such as dopamine, oxytocin, and vasopressin, when feelings grow. Stimulation of certain areas of the hypothalamus can indeed increase sexual activity and influence emotions such as anger and aggression. Additionally, the hypothalamus is involved in regulating the release of neurotransmitters and hormones that are crucial for emotional responses and social bonding.

30. (A): High levels of androgens have significant implications for cardiovascular health. Excessive androgens contribute to cardiac hypertrophy, fibrosis, and apoptosis, potentially leading to impaired heart function over time. Elevated androgen levels have also been associated with an increased risk of cardiovascular diseases such as stroke, heart attack, high blood pressure, and heart failure. Additionally, high doses of testosterone can negatively impact HDL ("good") cholesterol levels, further affecting cardiovascular health.

31. (B): The yoga practice of Vipreetkarni mudra with ujjayi pranayama is beneficial for individuals suffering from goiter or thyroid disorders. Vipreetkarni mudra involves lying on the back with the legs elevated, promoting improved blood circulation to the neck area and stimulating the thyroid gland. Ujjayi pranayama, characterised by deep, controlled breathing with a slight constriction of the throat, helps reduce stress, calm the mind, and regulate thyroid function. Together, these practices can support thyroid health by enhancing circulation, reducing stress, and promoting balance in the endocrine system.

32. (C): The Directed-Practice Method involves assigning specific practice tasks or exercises to students outside of regular class hours to enhance their skills and performance. In the context of yoga instruction, this method would involve instructors providing students with specific yoga practices to practice independently outside of scheduled class sessions. By engaging in directed practice assignments, students can reinforce their learning, improve their technique, and enhance their overall proficiency in yoga. This teaching method emphasises active engagement and practice outside of formal instruction time, allowing students to apply and refine their skills independently.

33. (B): The phrase "Prachchhardana vidharanabhyam va pranasya" from the Yoga Sutra is associated with the second aspect of chitta prashadan. This phrase refers to the regulation of the breath (pranasya) through specific techniques such as "prachchhardana" (exhalation) and "vidharana" (retention or holding) to calm and clarify the mind (chitta prashadan). Chitta prashadan is a process of calming or clearing the mind, and in the context of yoga practices outlined in the Yoga Sutra, it involves various techniques including breath regulation (pranayama) to achieve mental clarity and tranquility. The specific technique described in this phrase focuses on the regulation of breath to facilitate this mental calming.

34. (B): In the current educational landscape, the Student Centred Approach is receiving significant emphasis in the education system. This approach places the learner at the center of the educational process, focusing on individual student needs, interests, and learning styles. Student-centred learning encourages active participation, collaboration, critical thinking, and problem-solving skills among students. It shifts away from traditional teacher-centred approaches where the teacher is the primary source of knowledge and instruction. Instead, the student-centred approach promotes personalized learning experiences, student engagement, and self-directed learning, often facilitated by teachers who act as guides or facilitators.

35. (B): In educational contexts, a student is an individual who actively engages in the learning process, seeking to acquire knowledge, skills, and understanding under the guidance of educators or instructors. Students play a central role in education as they navigate new information, concepts, and experiences to adapt and grow intellectually and personally. While educators (teachers) facilitate and guide the learning process, it is ultimately the student who undergoes the process of learning and development. Students actively participate in educational activities, respond to instruction, and strive to adjust and adapt their thinking, behaviours, and capabilities based on the guidance and support provided by educators.

36. (A): The Vashishtha Samhita, which is a yoga text, mentions three main pranayamas:

- **Suryabheda Pranayama:** This pranayama involves inhaling through the right nostril and exhaling through the left nostril. It is believed to stimulate energy and generate heat in the body.
- **Ujjayi Pranayama:** Ujjayi pranayama is characterised by deep, controlled breathing with a slight constriction at the back of the throat, creating a soft ocean-like sound. It promotes relaxation, concentration, and internal heat.
- **Sheetali Pranayama:** Sheetali pranayama involves inhaling through the curled tongue (or between the teeth) and exhaling through the nostrils. This practice is cooling and calming, beneficial for reducing body heat and calming the mind.

37. (B): Sheetali Pranayama is a yogic breathing technique where you inhale air through the mouth and exhale it through the nostrils. To practice Sheetali Pranayama, sit comfortably in a meditative posture and inhale slowly and deeply through the mouth, drawing in cool air. Then, close your mouth and exhale the breath slowly and steadily through the nostrils. This pranayama technique has a cooling effect on the body and helps reduce body heat, calm the mind, and promote relaxation. It is especially beneficial during hot weather or when feeling stressed or overheated.

38. (C): Khechari Mudra is an advanced yogic technique where the practitioner rolls the tongue backward to touch and stimulate the soft palate in the roof of the mouth. This action is known as Gomansbhakshan, which literally means "eating the flesh (or nectar) of the cow" in Sanskrit. The practice involves touching the tongue to the upper palate to activate specific energy points and facilitate the awakening of higher states of consciousness. It is considered as a profound and transformative practice in certain yoga traditions.

39. (A): According to the Hathapradipika, the asana required for practicing Nadanusandhan (meditation on inner sound or Nada) is Muktasana. Muktasana, also known as the Liberated Pose, is a seated posture recommended for meditation practices in yoga texts like the Hathapradipika. It involves sitting with the legs loosely crossed, similar to Sukhasana (Easy Pose) but with the heels placed directly below the perineum. Muktasana helps to stabilise the body and create a steady and comfortable foundation for meditation.

40. (A): According to the Kathopanishad, the Atma (Self) cannot be known solely through certain conventional means. The verse implies that the Self cannot be realised through mere discourse (pravachan), discussions, or the study of scriptures alone. While these activities are important in spiritual pursuits, they are considered insufficient for attaining true self-knowledge. The Kathopanishad suggests that realising the Self requires a deeper, more experiential understanding that transcends intellectual discussions and scholarly pursuits. It emphasizes the need for direct personal experience and inner realisation, which goes beyond external methods of learning or discourse.

41. **(C):** Vaisheshika philosophy, an ancient Indian school of thought, delves into the nature of reality by proposing six fundamental categories called padarthas. Among these categories, the ones considered fundamental matter are Dravya (substance), Guna (quality), and Karma (action). Dravya is the fundamental category in Vaisheshika, representing the basic substances that make up the universe. Examples include earth, water, fire, air, space, time, self (atman), and mind. Guna are qualities that inhere in dravya (substances) and give them their properties. For example, colour, taste, and smell are gunas. Karma refers to action or deeds, which are not considered material substances in Vaisheshika.

42. **(B):** The Twelve Nidanas represent the chain of causation explaining the cycle of birth, suffering, and rebirth (samsara) in Buddhism. The parts of the Dwadasa Nidana corresponding to the options are:

(*b*) Jati (birth): This nidana refers to the process of birth or existence, which is a fundamental part of the cycle of rebirth (samsara).

(*c*) Trishna (craving): This nidana represents craving or desire, which is considered the root cause of suffering (dukkha) and leads to further rebirth.

(*d*) Vigyan (consciousness): This nidana refers to consciousness or awareness, which plays a crucial role in the continuity of existence and rebirth.

43. **(B):** The phrase "Mrityumteertva" indeed pertains to transcending death or overcoming mortality. In the context of the options provided:

(*b*) Avidya (ignorance): This refers to the state of ignorance or spiritual unawareness that keeps individuals bound to the cycle of birth and death (samsara).

(*d*) Vinash (destruction or death): This relates directly to the concept of transcending death or achieving immortality as suggested by "Mrityumteertva."

This indicates the transcendence of ignorance (avidya) and the concept of overcoming death (vinash) or achieving immortality.

44. **(C):** The characteristics that are NOT associated with Rajasik Ahaar (food influenced by the quality of Rajas) according to the Bhagavadgita include being oily or unctuous (snigdha), having a stimulating and long-lasting effect on the body and mind, and being delicious or gratifying to the senses (rasayukta). These qualities reflect the nature of Rajas, which is associated with passion, restlessness, and desire. Rajasik foods are typically spicy, hot, and rich, appealing to the senses and leading to increased activity and attachment.

45. **(B):** The supreme soul (Paramatma) in the Dhyanbindu Upanishad is associated with the concepts of Trividh Brahma, Trayakshar, and Ardha matra.

(*a*) Trividh Brahma: This refers to the three aspects of Brahman (the ultimate reality) - Satyam (Truth), Jnanam (Knowledge), and Anantam (Infinity), which are associated with the supreme soul.

(*c*) **Trayakshar:** This term refers to the supreme soul (Paramatma) represented by the three syllables (AUM) in the Dhyanbindu Upanishad.

(*d*) **Ardha matra:** This term signifies half a matra or the duration of the short vowel sound in Sanskrit, symbolising the essence or subtlety of the supreme soul.

46. **(A):** Based on the teachings of the Yoga Kundalini Upanishad, the means for awakening Kundalini include Saraswati chalan and Pranayama.

(*a*) **Saraswati chalan:** This refers to the practice of awakening the Kundalini energy through the movement of the Saraswati Nadi, which is associated with the flow of consciousness and spiritual awakening.

(*b*) **Pranayama:** This involves breath control techniques that can help awaken and channel the Kundalini energy through the manipulation of prana (vital energy).

47. **(B):** Based on the teachings of the Yoga Sutras, the attainment of Jnana in the stage of Dharmamegha Samadhi is characterised by Anantyaat (limitlessness) and Gyeam Alpam (subtle knowledge).

(*b*) **Anantyaat:** This term refers to limitlessness or infinity, signifying the expensive and boundless nature of the knowledge attained in Dharmamegha Samadhi.

(*c*) **Gyeam Alpam:** This term signifies that the knowledge gained in this state is subtle and minimal, indicating a profound yet concise understanding of reality.

48. **(B):** In the context of the Yoga Sutras, the kinds of Drishya (objects of perception) are classified based on their nature and perceptibility. "Vishesh" refers to specific objects that are clearly perceived through the senses. "Avishesh" denotes general or indistinct objects that lack specific characteristics. "Aling" signifies subtle entities or aspects that are imperceptible to the senses but can be inferred or contemplated through deeper awareness. These classifications highlight the varying degrees of perceptibility and subtlety in our perception of objects and phenomena, reflecting the complex nature of perception as described in the Yoga Sutras.

49. **(B):**

(*b*) **Union of Apana and Prana:** Moola Bandha facilitates the union of Apana (downward energy) and Prana (upward energy), helping to balance and harmonize these vital energies in the body.

(*c*) **Deficiency of defecation:** Moola Bandha can help regulate bowel movements and address issues related to constipation or irregularity.

(*d*) **Even the old becomes akin to the youth:** This benefit suggests that practicing Moola Bandha may contribute to rejuvenation and vitality, promoting a youthful and energetic state.

50. **(A):** According to the Vasishtha Samhita, Apaan Vayu is associated with specific physical locations in the human body. The knee (Janu) and thigh (Jangha) are mentioned as areas influenced by Apaan Vayu, indicating its role in these regions. Additionally, the center of the navel (Nabhimoola) is highlighted as a significant location where Apaan Vayu is active. This implies that Apaan Vayu plays a role in functions related to these body parts, such as movement and energy regulation. Understanding the localisation of Apaan Vayu helps in comprehending its physiological significance and its impact on various bodily processes as described in the Vasishtha Samhita.

51. (A):

(*a*) **Cure of naadi-disorder:** Ujjayi Pranayama is believed to help in correcting and balancing the flow of energy through the nadis (energy channels) in the body, promoting overall energetic balance and health.

(*c*) **Cure of cough-borne disorder:** Ujjayi Pranayama involves a gentle constriction of the throat, which can help in managing respiratory issues, including cough-related disorders.

(*d*) **Cure of ascites disease:** Ascites refers to the accumulation of fluid in the abdominal cavity. Ujjayi Pranayama is thought to aid in improving circulation and fluid dynamics in the body, potentially benefiting conditions like ascites.

52. (A):

(*a*) **Marasmus:** Marasmus is a form of severe malnutrition characterised by energy deficiency in the form of calories, proteins, and other essential nutrients. It typically occurs in young children and infants due to inadequate intake of food, including proteins.

(*b*) **Kwashiorkor:** Kwashiorkor is another form of severe malnutrition resulting from a deficiency of protein in the diet. It often affects children between the ages of one and three years old, particularly when they are weaned from breast milk to a diet that lacks sufficient protein.

53. (C):

(*c*) **Cervical Vertebra:** The cervical vertebrae are part of the axial skeleton, which includes the bones of the skull, vertebral column (spine), and rib cage. The cervical vertebrae specifically belong to the vertebral column (spine), which is considered part of the axial skeleton.

(*e*) **Sternum:** The sternum, also known as the breastbone, is also part of the axial skeleton. It is located in the center of the chest and connects to the ribs via cartilage. The sternum plays a crucial role in protecting the heart and lungs and supporting the rib cage.

54. (C):

(*c*) **Abduction:** Abduction refers to movement away from the midline of the body. In this case, when the person lifts their left leg towards the left side, they are moving the leg away from the midline of their body. This movement of lifting the leg sideways (away from the midline) is called abduction.

(*d*) **Adduction:** Adduction is the opposite of abduction. It refers to movement towards the midline of the body. When the person returns their left leg back to its original position (moving it towards the midline of the body), this movement is called adduction.

55. (A): In the Yoga Sutras of Patanjali, the concept of "Anagat Dukha" refers to future suffering or pain that has not yet occurred but is anticipated or feared. This type of suffering can deeply affect the mind and lead to mental distress or anxiety. Patanjali discusses Anagat Dukha in the context of understanding and addressing the causes of suffering to achieve mental equanimity and liberation from suffering. This concept is discussed in the Sadhan Pada (second pada) of the Yoga Sutras, which focuses on the practices (sadhana) required to attain the state of yoga or union of the individual self with the universal consciousness. Understanding and overcoming Anagat Dukha is essential in the yogic path to cultivate inner peace and liberation from mental anguish.

56. (B): According to the Hatha Pradipika, certain types of foods can adversely affect health due to specific reasons outlined in yogic dietary principles.

(*a*) **Reheated:** Foods that are repeatedly reheated can undergo chemical changes and lose their nutritional value, potentially affecting health adversely.

(*c*) **Excessive Salt:** Consuming foods with excessive salt (sodium) can lead to health problems such as high blood pressure (hypertension) and cardiovascular issues.

(*e*) **Excessive Sour Substances:** Consuming excessive sour substances can disrupt the digestive system and lead to acidity or other gastrointestinal issues.

57. (A): According to the Yoga Sutras, cultivating positive aptitude involves several essential qualities. Compassion is emphasised as a foundational attribute for fostering empathy and understanding towards others. Disregard likely refers to maintaining a sense of detachment or non-attachment, allowing individuals to stay balanced and unaffected by external influences. Friendliness is vital for promoting positive relationships and creating a sense of goodwill in interactions. These qualities collectively contribute to a positive attitude conducive to personal growth and harmonious social interactions, aligning with the principles outlined in the Yoga Sutras for cultivating a balanced and compassionate mindset.

58. (B): Indigestion can be caused by various factors, including mineral salts deficiency in the diet, which impacts the body's ability to digest food efficiently. Mental and emotional disturbances, such as stress or anxiety, can also affect digestion negatively. Additionally, habits like swallowing air and overeating can lead to discomfort and indigestion. These factors highlight the interconnectedness of physical health with mental and emotional well-being in maintaining optimal digestion. Addressing these aspects holistically, including balanced nutrition, stress management, and mindful eating habits, can help prevent indigestion and promote overall digestive health.

59. (B): Premenstrual tension, characterised by physical and emotional symptoms before menstruation, can be alleviated through specific yoga mudras like Maha Mudra and Mahabheda Mudra. Maha Mudra involves a combination of posture, breath control, and concentration techniques to balance the body's energy and calm the mind. This can help reduce stress and discomfort associated with PMS. Similarly, Mahabheda Mudra focusses on breath control and body movements to harmonise energy flow, promoting relaxation and easing PMS symptoms. These yoga practices can be effective complementary approaches to managing premenstrual tension, providing relief and promoting overall well-being during this phase of the menstrual cycle.

60. (C): These specific yoga asanas—Parvatasana (Mountain Pose), Garudasana (Eagle Pose), and Gomukhasana (Cow Face Pose)—are recommended for restoring valvular competence after traumatic accidents due to their beneficial effects on cardiovascular health and circulation. Parvatasana helps improve blood flow and overall circulation, which can support heart health and valve function. Garudasana strengthens muscles in the legs, arms, and shoulders, indirectly benefiting cardiovascular health. Gomukhasana stretches and strengthens muscles around the chest and shoulders, which can contribute to better posture and cardiovascular well-being.

61. (D): In the context of the Yoga Sutras, the perfections (sampadas) of bodies referred to as form (Roop) and beauty

(Lavanys) emphasise the importance of physical appearance and aesthetics in yoga practice. "Form" relates to the outward appearance or structure of the body, which can be refined and perfected through yogic discipline. "Beauty" encompasses the grace, attractiveness, and harmony of the body, reflecting inner balance and vitality cultivated through yoga. These perfections are not just superficial qualities but are seen as manifestations of deeper spiritual progress and alignment with the principles of yoga, highlighting the interconnectedness of physical and spiritual well-being.

62. (B):

(b) **Yoga can boost our physical and mental health:** Numerous studies and anecdotal evidence support the positive effects of yoga on physical and mental well-being, including improved flexibility, strength, stress reduction, and emotional regulation.

(c) **Yoga is a journey towards inner world:** Yoga practices often focus on introspection, self-awareness, and connecting with the inner world. This inward journey can help us understand our thoughts, emotions, and motivations better. Through yoga practices like meditation and mindfulness, we can cultivate a sense of inner peace and calmness.

63. (B):

(b) **Incompetence in elaboration of topic:** A good teacher should have a strong understanding of the subject matter and the ability to explain it clearly and effectively at a level appropriate for the students' age and learning abilities. This includes being able to break down complex concepts into manageable pieces, using clear and concise language, and providing examples or illustrations to aid comprehension.

(d) **Inability to set a good example through life style and behaviour:** Teachers serve as role models for their students, and their behavior and lifestyle choices can have a significant impact on students' development. A good teacher should strive to embody the values they aim to instill in their students, such as honesty, respect, responsibility, and a positive work ethic.

64. (A): According to the Gherand Samhita, the instructions for practicing Mahamudra involve specific actions:

(b) **Press the anal region with the left ankle:** This action is part of the physical alignment and engagement required for Mahamudra practice.

(c) **Shrink the throat:** This refers to a subtle internal action involving the throat area, likely to facilitate the flow of energy (prana) during the practice.

(e) **Keep the eyes on the eyebrow center:** This gaze direction, known as Shambhavi mudra, helps to focus the mind and can facilitate deeper states of concentration and meditation.

65. (D): Trataka, as described in Hatha Pradipika, is a meditation technique that involves focused vision, where practitioners concentrate their gaze on the eyebrow center (bhrumadhya) with unwavering attention.

This practice is continued until tears naturally flow from the eyes, signifying the deepening of concentration and internal absorption. The steady gaze on the eyebrow center helps in cultivating inner focus and calming the mind, leading to heightened awareness and meditative states. Trataka is a powerful method for enhancing concentration, purifying the mind, and progressing in the path of meditation and self-discovery.

66. (A): In the context of the Yoga Sutras, the delineation of Pranava (Om) involves several aspects: first, the recitation of Pranava itself, which is the vocalisation or chanting of the sacred sound "Om"; second, the contemplation or concentration on the meaning of Pranava, which pertains to understanding the significance and symbolism behind the sound Om; and finally, the experiential aspect where one feels the meaning of Pranava, implying a deep internalisation or realisation of its spiritual essence. These practices collectively deepen the practitioner's understanding and experience of Pranava within the context of yoga philosophy and meditation.

67. (A):

(*a*) Maharshi Dayanand is associated with "Arya Bhivinay," which refers to his teachings and principles related to the Arya Samaj movement and the revival of Vedic traditions.

(*b*) Tulsidas is known for his work "Vinay Patrika," which is a devotional composition in praise of Lord Rama and is highly respected in Hindu culture.

(*c*) Shri Aurobindo is the author of "The Life Divine," a comprehensive philosophical and spiritual treatise that explores various aspects of consciousness, evolution, and the divine nature of existence.

(*d*) Swami Shivananda Saraswati's "Jyoti Shakti or Pragya" refers to the illumination of spiritual wisdom and the inner light of consciousness.

68. (A):

(*a*) Bandham Moksham is correctly paired with Sattviki Durmedha buddhi, indicating the discernment between bondage and liberation through a pure, enlightened intellect.

(*b*) Prasangen is matched with Rajsi dhriti, reflecting the determination driven by passion in actions related to righteousness and pursuit of goals.

(*c*) Na vimunchati is appropriately matched with Tamasi dhriti, signifying the determination rooted in ignorance and delusion that leads to inaction and further suffering.

(*d*) Abhyasadramate corresponds to Sattvik Sukha, indicating the contentment derived from persevering through difficulties and experiencing the joy of righteousness.

69. (A):

(*a*) Conversion of food from unsavoury to savoury is paired with Practice of mahamudra, suggesting a transformative process related to inner purification and refinement.

(*b*) Chanting all through the day and night corresponds twenty-one thousand six hundred mantras (Varna), indicating the extensive recitation and practice of specific mantras.

(*c*) Being free from disease, death, hunger-thirst, and faint is correctly matched with Khecharimudra, emphasising a state of spiritual freedom and transcendence over physical limitations.

(*d*) White and red two-colour is appropriately paired with Sukra and maharaj, representing the association with specific deities or practices related to subtle energy and spiritual transformation.

70. (A):

(*a*) Mahavrat is matched with Sadhan Pada, indicating a significant principle or vow related to the path of practice in yoga.

(*b*) Suksham vishyatvam chaaling parya-vasaanam corresponds with Samadhi Pada, suggesting subtle focus and concentration leading towards profound meditative absorption.

(*c*) Kshantatkramyoh Samyamadvivekajam jnananam is paired with Vibhutipada, highlighting the discriminative knowledge and mastery gained through the practice of Samyama.

(*d*) Parinamaiktvat vastu-tattvam is appropriately matched with Keivalya Pada, emphasising the understanding of the nature of existence and the state of absolute liberation (Kevala).

71. (A):

(*a*) Yama is matched with Daya, which relates to ethical principles and practices including compassion (Daya).

(*b*) Niyama corresponds with Japa, emphasising observances and personal disciplines such as the practice of mantra repetition (Japa).

(*c*) Asana is appropriately paired with Bhadra, suggesting auspicious and beneficial postures for physical and mental well-being (Bhadra).

(*d*) Upa-prana is matched with Koorma, indicating supplementary or supporting vital energy practices related to the tortoise (Koorma) pose or breath control.

72. (D):

(*a*) Thorndike with The Theory of Connectionism, which emphasises learning as the formation of neural connections based on trial-and-error.

(*b*) Skinner with Operant Conditioning Chamber, reflecting Skinner's development of the Skinner Box for studying operant conditioning.

(*c*) Kohler with Experiments of Stick & Box Problem, referring to Kohler's experiments with chimpanzees demonstrating insight learning.

(*d*) Pavlov with Classical Conditioning Theory, representing Pavlov's work on classical conditioning, focusing on the association of stimuli to elicit responses.

73. (C):

(*a*) Mooladhar with Four Petals, referring to the Muladhara chakra located at the base of the spine, associated with four petals in its depiction.

(*b*) Avirati with Antraya, representing the hindrance or obstacle (klesha) that can impede progress in yoga practice.

(*c*) Swadhishthan with Six Petals, corresponding to the Swadhisthana chakra located at the sacral region, traditionally depicted with six petals.

(*d*) Abhinivesh with Klesh, indicating the concept of clinging to life or fear of death, one of the kleshas (afflictions) in yoga philosophy.

74. (B):

(*a*) Fire with Manomaya, aligning the element of fire with the mental sheath (Manomaya Kosha), which represents thoughts and emotions.

(*b*) Earth with Anamaya, associating the element of earth with the physical sheath (Anamaya Kosha), which encompasses the physical body.

(*c*) Ether with Anandamaya, connecting the element of ether (or space) with the bliss sheath (Anandamaya Kosha), representing deep joy and contentment.

(*d*) Water with Pranamaya, linking the element of water with the vital energy sheath (Pranamaya Kosha), which pertains to the flow of life force or prana.

75. (A):

(*a*) Tatra niratishayam sarvagyabeejam with Yogyata mansah, aligning the concept of supreme seed of omniscience with the qualification of mind for concentration (Dharnasu cha yogyata mansah).

(*b*) Tasya saptadha prantbhumih pragya with After getting vivekgyan, indicating the sevenfold stages leading to wisdom (pragya) and higher knowledge (vivekgyan).

(*c*) Dharnasu cha yogyata mansah with Pranayam prakrityapurat, connecting the qualification of mind for concentration (Dharnasu cha yogyata mansah) with the practice of pranayama (Pranayam prakrityapurat).

(*d*) Jatyantar parinamah with Kaivalya Pada, associating the transformation of one's birth or life circumstances (Jatyantar parinamah) with the stage of liberation (Kaivalya Pada) in Yoga Sutras.

76. (A):

(*a*) Shambhavi with Eyes focussed on the eyebrow center, aligning the Shambhavi mudra with the technique of focusing the eyes on the eyebrow center.

(*b*) Khechari with Insert the tongue in the cavity of the upper palate, connecting the Khechari mudra with the technique of inserting the tongue into the upper palate.

(*c*) Mahavedha with Patting hips on the ground, associating Mahavedha mudra with the technique of patting hips on the ground.

(*d*) Mahamudra with Pressing perineum region with the heels of the legs, matching the Mahamudra mudra with the technique of pressing the perineum region with the heels of the legs.

77. (B):

(***c***) **Prakriti:** This is the primal, unmanifested substance from which all material phenomena arise. It is the source of all potentialities and contains the three gunas (qualities) of sattva, rajas, and tamas.

(***a***) **Mahat:** Also known as "Mahat-tattva" or cosmic intelligence, Mahat is the first evolute of Prakriti and represents the universal intellect or cosmic mind.

(***b***) **Ahankar:** Ahankar is the principle of individuation or ego. It is the sense of "I" or individual identity that arises from Mahat's differentiation.

(***e***) **Panchtanmatra:** These are the five subtle elements—sound (shabda), touch (sparsha), form (rupa), taste (rasa), and smell (gandha)—which emerge from Ahankar. They are the basic essences or qualities that give rise to the gross elements.

(***d***) **Panchmahabhoot:** Finally, the Panchtanmatras transform into the five gross elements—ether (akasha), air (vayu), fire (agni), water (jala), and earth (prithvi)—which constitute the material world.

78. (A):

(***c***) **Shubhechha:** This stage marks the initial longing for spiritual growth and understanding, where one seeks deeper meaning and purpose beyond mundane existence.

(***d***) **Vicharana:** In this stage, there is a deliberate process of intellectual inquiry and discrimination, where the seeker examines the nature of reality, existence, and the self.

(***b***) **Tanumanasa:** As the inquiry deepens, the mind becomes more refined and subtle. This stage involves cultivating a highly focused and clear state of mind conducive to deeper understanding.

(***a***) **Sattvapatti:** Sattvapatti represents the attainment of true knowledge or realization. It is a transformative stage where the seeker gains direct insight into the nature of reality and transcends ignorance.

(***e***) **Asamsakti:** Finally, in the stage of Asamsakti, the seeker achieves a state of non-attachment or dispassion towards worldly phenomena. This stage reflects a profound sense of inner freedom and liberation from material desires.

79. (B):

(*a*) **Mahabandh** involves contracting specific muscles and controlling breath to redirect prana through the body, considered an advanced yoga practice.

(*b*) **Khechari Mudra** entails touching the tongue to the soft palate, stimulating energy centres.

(*e*) **Jalandhar Bandh** involves tucking the chin to regulate prana flow and aid concentration.

(*c*) **Deergh Pranav Sandhan** likely refers to extended pranayama for breath control.

(*d*) **Sahjoli** involves contracting genital muscles to control prana flow, associated with lower energy centres.

These practices, outlined in the Yogatattva Upanishad, are aimed at harnessing prana and enhancing spiritual development through focused techniques, breath control, and energy redirection. Each method serves a specific purpose in the yogic tradition, facilitating deeper states of meditation and inner awakening within a comprehensive framework of yoga practice.

80. (A):

(*d*) **Tivra Samveganamasannh:** This statement relates to the intensity of the practice and the steadiness of the mind during yoga, particularly emphasising the need for strong commitment and focus.

(*c*) **Tadarth eva Drishyasyatma:** This statement highlights the relationship between the seer (drashta) and the seen (drishya), suggesting that the true nature of the self (atma) is perceived through objects that are observed or experienced.

(*a*) **Kramanyatvam Parinamanyatve Hetuh:** This statement discusses the causal relationship between the sequence of events (krama) and the transformation (parinama), indicating that sequence leads to transformation.

(*b*) **Pratyayasya Parachittanjanam:** This statement refers to the modification of the mind (chitta) by external perceptions or knowledge (pratyaya), emphasising the impact of external influences on the mind.

(*e*) **Drishtra drishyo parktam chittam Sarvartham:** This statement suggests that the entire meaning (artha) of the object lies in its relationship with the seer (drashta) and the seen (drishya), indicating the significance of perception in understanding the nature of reality.

81. (A):

(*c*) **Hiccups (Hichaki):** This refers to sudden, involuntary contractions of the diaphragm, causing a sound like "hic." It is considered an ailment related to vayu disturbance.

(*a*) **Breath disorder (shuras):** This indicates a disorder in breathing, likely caused by vayu imbalance affecting the respiratory system.

(*d*) **Cough:** A cough is another symptom associated with vayu imbalance affecting the respiratory passages.

(*b*) **Headache (shirvedana):** Headache can be a result of vayu aggravation affecting the head and nervous system.

(*e*) **Auricular pain (Kama vedana):** This refers to pain in the ear, potentially caused by vayu disturbance affecting the ear region.

82. (C): The journey of blood flow starts in the right auricle (right atrium), where deoxygenated blood from the body returns to the heart. From the right auricle, blood passes through the tricuspid valve into the right ventricle. From the right ventricle, blood is pumped out through the pulmonary aortas the lungs for oxygenation. Oxygenated blood returns from the lungs to the heart via the pulmonary veins, specifically the pulmonary venae cavae (plural form of vena cava). Finally, oxygenated blood enters the left ventricle through the bicuspid valve (mitral valve) from the left atrium.

83. (B):

(*d*) **Khand:** Khand refers to raw or unrefined sugar, which is recommended as the first item in the sequence. This type of sugar is considered less processed and may have more natural nutrients compared to refined white sugar.

(*a*) **Honey:** Honey is mentioned next in the sequence after khand. Honey is a natural sweetener and is valued for its health benefits, including its antioxidant and antimicrobial properties.

(*e*) **Soonth:** Soonth refers to dried ginger powder. Ginger is known for its digestive properties and is often used in Ayurvedic cooking to aid digestion. Soonth adds a warming and aromatic flavor to dishes.

(*b*) **Five kinds of vegetables:** The Hatha Pradipika recommends consuming a variety of vegetables. The specific mention of "five kinds" likely indicates a diverse selection of seasonal vegetables, providing a range of vitamins, minerals, and fiber.

(*c*) **Lentil (Moong):** Lentils, particularly moong dal (green gram), are mentioned last in the sequence. Lentils are a good source of plant-based protein and are easy to digest, making them a common ingredient in vegetarian diets.

84. (A):

(*a*) **Setting the Atmosphere:** This can involve creating calm and clean environment, adjusting lighting, and playing soothing music or using aromatherapy to enhance relaxation.

(*b*) **Introduction to the Practice:** Provide an overview or introduction and explain the objectives, benefits, and any precautions or modifications that students should be aware of.

(*c*) **Demonstrating Practices:** Demonstrate the yoga practices, postures (asanas), breathing techniques (pranayama), or meditation methods that are part of the lesson.

(*d*) **Students Individual Practice Time:** This stage allows students to apply what they have learned, refine their techniques, and receive personalised feedback or adjustments as needed.

(*e*) **Group Practice:** Conclude the lesson with a group practice session where students perform the yoga practices together. This encourages unity, synchronisation, and a sense of shared experience among participants.

85. (C):

(*b*) **Sitting on the Dandasan:** Begin by sitting in Dandasana (Staff Pose), which is a seated posture with legs extended straight in front.

(*a*) **Perform padmasan:** Next, perform Padmasana (Lotus Pose) by placing each foot on the opposite thigh, bringing the feet close to the groin.

(*c*) **Place both the hands between the knees and thighs and keep the palms firmly on the ground:** Position the hands between the knees and thighs, placing the palms firmly on the ground.

(*e*) **Pressing the palms; the body should be lifted upward (towards the sky):** Press down with the palms to lift the body upward towards the sky, engaging the core and arms.

(*d*) **Pressing the palms, the body should be put on the ground:** Finally, while maintaining the lift from the palms, lower the body back down towards the ground.

86. (B): The assertion (A) states that Rishi Vashishtha referred to King Dasaratha as possessing sublime traits of patience and being observant of uttam vrata (supreme vows), indicating his noble character and devotion to righteous conduct. The reason (R) mentions an event where King Dasaratha sent his sons, Lord Rama and Lakshmana, with Sage Vishwamitra for the successful completion of a yajna (sacrificial ritual). While both (A) and (R) are true statements about King Dasaratha, (R) does not directly explain why Rishi Vashishtha admired King Dasaratha's virtues of patience and observance of vows.

87. (B): The assertion (A) posits that Vishnu's highest state (Parampada) is achieved through the dissolution of the mind (manas), indicating the need for transcending mental states to attain a state of divine realisation or consciousness. Meanwhile, the reason (R) advises meditating on Maha Vishnu with a visualisation resembling the luminosity of the Moon, highlighting the importance of focused and radiant imagery during meditation. While both assertions are valid in their respective contexts, they address different aspects of spiritual practice and do not directly explain or relate to each other.

88. (A): Assertion (A): The Yoga Sutras by Patanjali do discuss achieving a state beyond desires and attachments, which could include attachment to deities. In the pursuit of liberation (Kaivalya), the ultimate goal, focusing on external entities is seen as a distraction.

Reason (R): The Yoga Sutras acknowledge the potential for desires to return, even in the context of devotion to deities. This can be because some might see the deity as a source of worldly fulfillment rather than a path to self-realisation.

Therefore, both Assertion (A) and Reason (R) align with the teachings of the Yoga Sutras. Reason (R) explains why detachment from deities, including Lokpal Deities (protectors of the worlds), might be sought in the higher state of yoga.

89. (B): Assertion (A) correctly suggests that Shatkarma practices are recommended in Ayurveda for addressing Kapha aggravation, emphasizing the need to keep these cleansing practices confidential due to their purifying nature. Reason (R) is also true in stating that Shatkarma may not be essential when Vata, Pitta, and Kapha are balanced, but it does not serve as a direct explanation for Assertion (A). The reason oversimplifies the role of Shatkarma, which can be beneficial for overall health maintenance and targeted therapy even when doshas are balanced, as they contribute to cleansing and detoxification of the body.

90. (A): Statement I correctly defines dysmenorrhoea and menorrhagia as medical terms used to describe specific menstrual issues—painful menstruation and abnormally heavy or prolonged bleeding, respectively. This statement is factual and aligned with medical terminology. Statement II makes a subjective comparison between the distress caused by menstrual difficulties and the common cold, suggesting a level of impact that may vary widely among individuals. Additionally, it implies that medical insight into menstrual problems is limited, which can depend on various factors and advancements in medical research and practice.

91. **(B):** The practice of asanas (yoga postures) is mentioned to promote a smooth flow of energy in nadis (subtle energy channels) and can activate chakras (energy centers in the body). Chakras are integral to the yogic understanding of energy and consciousness.

92. **(B):** The passage highlights the significance of practicing Pawan Muktasan (a specific type of yoga posture) for the prevention and treatment of physical and mental diseases. Pawan Muktasan is noted to have positive effects on the body and mind, contributing significantly to overall health.

93. **(A):** According to the passage, practicing asanas (yoga postures) can bring about awareness and ease in the mind. Asanas are known for their calming and centering effects on the mind, promoting mindfulness and relaxation.

94. **(B):** The passage divides Pawan Muktasan into three groups: (1) anti-rheumatic group, (2) digestive/abdominal group, and (3) shaktibandh. The second group of Pawan Muktasan is specifically referred to as the "digestive/abdominal group," focusing on practices beneficial for digestive health and abdominal function.

95. **(D):** The passage mentions that all three groups of Pawan Muktasan (anti-rheumatic group, digestive/abdominal group, shaktibandh) intensify the free flow of energy. This implies that each group of practices contributes to enhancing the flow of prana (life force energy) and improving overall vitality.

96. **(A):** The passage states that society believes yoga is the only method to achieve holistic health. Holistic health refers to overall well-being encompassing physical, mental, and spiritual aspects. Yoga is considered as a comprehensive practice that promotes health and wellness in all these dimensions.

97. **(C):** According to the passage, every yoga practitioner should give importance particularly to diet. Diet plays a crucial role in supporting the practice of yoga and maintaining overall health. Proper nutrition from a balanced diet supports the body's energy needs and helps optimise the benefits of yoga practice.

98. **(C):** The passage mentions that the year 2023 has been termed as the "year of millet" by the honorable prime minister, emphasising the importance of including coarse grains like millet in the diet. This initiative highlights the significance of nutrition and dietary choices in promoting health and well-being.

99. **(D):** The passage explains that if the diet lacks nutrients appropriate for the age and needs of the individual, it results in undernutrition. Undernutrition occurs when the body does not receive sufficient essential nutrients, leading to health problems and deficiencies.

100. **(A):** The passage mentions that the government is emphasising the inclusion of coarse grains (such as millet) in the diet. Coarse grains are rich in essential nutrients and dietary fiber, contributing to a balanced and nutritious diet. This initiative reflects efforts to improve public health and nutrition awareness.

CHAPTER

1

Foundation of Yoga : History, Evolution of Yoga and Schools of Yoga

INTRODUCTION

Yoga is a way of life. It is predominantly concerned with maintaining a state of equanimity at all costs. All yoga schools of thought emphasize the importance of the mind remaining calm, because as the saying goes, only when the water is still can you see through it. Yoga Darshan or Yoga Philosophy also happens to be a valid discipline of Indian metaphysics (Brahma Vidya). It is the result of human wisdom and insight on physiology, psychology, ethics and spirituality collected together and practiced over thousands of years for the well being of humanity.

The basic idea of yoga is to unite the atma or individual soul with the paramatma or the Universal Soul. According to Yoga philosophy, by cleansing one's mind and controlling one's thought processes one can return to that primeval state, when the individual self was nothing but a part of the Divine Self. This is the sense encapsulated in the term samadhi. The aim of the yogi is to be able to perceive the world in its true light and to accept that truth in its entirety.

In Sanskrit, the term 'yoga' stands for 'union'. A yogi's ultimate aim is to be able to attain this 'union' with the Eternal Self with the help of certain mental and physical exercises. It is often said that Hiranyagarbha (The Cosmic Womb) Himself had originally advocated the traditional system of yoga, from which all other yoga schools have evolved. But for all extant knowledge of yoga and its practices, such as yogasanas and pranayama, the entire credit goes to Maharishi Patanjali.

Patanjali systematized the various yogic practices and traditions of his times by encapsulating them in the form of aphorisms in his Yoga Sutra. In this momentous work, he describes the aim of yoga as knowledge of the self and outlines the eight steps or methods of achieving it. These are:

- Amas or eternal vows,
- Niyamas or observances,
- Yogasanas or yoga postures,
- Pranayama or breath control exercises,
- Pratyahara or withdrawal of the senses from distractions of the outside world,
- Dharana or concentration on an object, place or subject,
- Dhyana or the continuance of this concentration-meditation and
- Samadhi or the ultimate stage of yoga meditation.

A Universal Practical Discipline

Yoga is a psychological, physiological and spiritual discipline that has been an integral part of our Indian culture for centuries. Yoga is a complete science of life that originated about thousands of years ago in India and still been practiced in India for centuries.

Process

Yoga is a process or system that maintains not only the health but also generates a sense of happiness and fulfillment. It also encourages personal growth and development. Yoga brings the mind and body into a mutual state of well-being, balance, ease and vibrant alertness.

Positive Approach to Health

The health of the human being is influenced by various factors. Yoga is one of the systems that include all these factors. These factors are regular exercise in the form of physical postures, proper breathing, sufficient rest and relaxation, meditation, positive thinking and balanced diet. Thus Yoga is an important, natural, preventive measure to ensure good health.

Self Therapy

Yoga is a self therapy. It is a self therapy in the sense that one can perform this discipline on his own. Yoga involves different breathing techniques and postures which are known as Asanas or postures. Postures, Proper Breathing, Relaxation and meditation are an important part of Yoga.

Yoga Philosophy

The Patanjali Yoga philosophy, which is one of the six systems constituting Vedic philosophy, is also known as Ashtanga Yoga (the yoga of eight parts or limbs) and is closely related to Sankhya and Vedantic philosophy. Ashtanga Yoga is the practical manifestation of both these philosophies. This practical system attempts to understand the nature of the elusive element we know as 'mind'—its different states of being, impediments to growth, afflictions and the methods of harnessing it for the achievement of absolute self realization.

While Sankhya philosophy assigns three functions to the mental body - mind (mana), intelligence (buddhi) and false knowledge (mithya jnana) - Vedanta adds a fourth element to this - chitta or conditioned consciousness. But ancient yoga teachers collapse the category of the mental body with the mind and assigns intelligence and false ego as aspects of that mind with the chitta denoting the various states of the mana or mind. Yoga likens mana and chitta with a lake, which is essentially calm and peaceful but whose basic tranquility is obscured by various insubstantial surface waves. According to the philosophy, there are only two ways of disturbing this serenity and engendering patterns of thought - through sense perceptions (pramana) and when our memory (smriti) gets triggered off.

All other sources of mental activity lead to false knowledge. To quote the most venerable among yoga teachers, Sage Patanjali, who said in his Yoga Sutra: "...when the persons possessing a body mistake by their erring intellect, this very body for the soul (atman), this kind of bondage is wrought by ignorance (avidya); its annihilation is emancipation (moksha)."

The central doctrine of Yoga philosophy is that nothing exists beyond the mind and its consciousness, which is the only ultimate reality. The objective of this philosophy is to uproot misconceptions about the existence of external 'realities' from the minds of men. It believes that it is possible to reach this stage of self realization through regular practice of certain yogic meditative processes that bring a complete withdrawal or detachment from all false sources of knowledge and inculcates an inner sense of balanced calm and tranquility.

Five States of Mind

Depending on the degree of distraction, Yoga philosophy categorizes the mind under five stages of being:

- Kshipta or disturbed,
- Mudha or stupefied,
- Vikshipta or distracted,
- Ekagra or concentrated and
- Niruddha or the absolutely balanced state of mind.

While the first three stages are negative and cause impediments to the healthy growth of the mind and its horizons, the following two are the desired states of being. When the mind is in its earliest stage of disturbance, it lacks judgement and is generally hyperactive, unable to ignore external stimuli. The next stage of the mudha or stupefied state of mind is distinguished by inertia, lethargy, sluggishness, vice, ignorance and sleep. The state of vikshipta is an advanced stage of the kshipta mind, when it still lacks consistency and is unable to quieten down or reflect.

Ekagra and niruddha are the mental levels at which, the mind almost ceases to be affected by the pains and miseries of mortal existence. They are the calmest and most peaceful states of mind. Ekagra or the tranquil state of mind is as near to inner stillness as one is ever likely to get. This state of mind is highly conducive to concentration and meditation, which is why the yoga system aims at maintaining and developing it as consistently as possible through various yogic meditational practices.

The last stage or niruddha is that rare state of being, where the mind is totally undisturbed and purified by the flow of positive energy. Niruddha is the ultimate desired mental stage in yogic practices. It is at this pristine state alone that we are able to realize the true nature of our souls. These last two states of mind are positive and conducive to meditation. Various yogic practices such as certain yogasanas, pranayama, dhyana, dharana and samadhi are designed for achieving the niruddha state of mind.

Five Modifications of The Mind

The yoga system categorizes the vrittis or forms of thought into five sections:

- Comprehension or Pramana,
- Misapprehension or Viparyaya,
- Conceptualization or Vikalpa,
- Deep Sleep or Nidra and
- Memory or Smriti.

All our thoughts, emotions and psychological states fall within either of these sections. These five are again further subdivided into two mental types:

- Klista and
- Aklista.

While the first type causes afflictions, the next does not. Misapprehension, conceptualization and deep sleep are considered to be the three main causes of various afflictions while the categories of comprehension and memory (of certain kinds) are viewed more positively. These two categories of pramana and smriti are also conducive to meditation and the attainment of kaivalya or detachment from the material world.

Pramana or comprehension is the awareness of one's true state of existence. The three epistemologies or valid means of knowledge for this category are:

- Pratyaksha or Direct Perception,
- Anumana or Inference and
- Shabda Pramana or Verbal Testimony.

The knowledge gained from either sensory or inner perception, inference and verbal authority are all considered to be true knowledge according to yoga.

Viparyaya or misapprehension is equivalent to ignorance (avidya) in Yoga philosophy. And knowledge borne out of misconceptions such as mistaking a rope for a snake and vice versa are false, leading to afflictions of the greatest kind. Viparyaya gives rise to the following kleshas or obstacles to meditation:

- Avidya or Ignorance,
- Asmita or Egoism,
- Raga or Attachment,
- Dvesa or Hatred and
- Abhinivesa or the sense of self-preservation.

The viparyaya category of comprehension is taken to be correct until more favourable conditions reveal the actual nature of the object of comprehension.

Vikalpa or conceptualization is also considered to be a source of avidya or ignorance because it is the comprehension of an object based only on words and expressions, even though the object is absent. This includes beliefs such as the existence of horned rabbits or winged fairies. It is possible to conceive of such imaginary and purely linguistic categories but nevertheless they are all erroneous knowledge and do not correspond with anything in existence.

Deep sleep or nidra is also thought to be a negative modification of the mind. During this mental state the mind is overcome with heaviness and no other activities are present. This state is virtually a withdrawal from the external world, when one is left without any control over one's consciousness. It is important to note at this point that the dream state and the conscious state are not modifications because while dreaming, our minds are occupied with vikalpa and while awake, the mind is concerned with the categories of pramana and viparyaya.

Smriti or memory is concerned with the evocation of stored impressions, or rather the mental retention of conscious experiences. All these categories are present in the kshipta, mudha and vikshipta states of mind. Ekagra and niruddha are above all such modifications.

Nine Impediments

The above modifications are primarily caused by the nine impediments to a healthy growth and development of the mind. These are:

- Sickness,
- Incompetence,
- Doubt,
- Delusion,
- Fatigue,
- Over-indulgence,
- Confusion,
- Lack of perseverance and
- Regression.

These nine conditions are the greatest causes of all sorrows, miseries and pain, which disturb the mind and result in distractions and loss of mental tranquility. All these interruptions produce symptoms such as, mental discomfort, negative thinking, the inability to be at ease in different body postures, and difficulty in controlling one's breath. The yoga of Patanjali prescribes abhyasa or regular practice and vairagya or detachment as the sole means of conquering such impediments and achieving kaivalya (absoluteness) or self realization. Abhyasa in this case is basically the correct effort required to move toward, reach, and maintain the state of yoga.

MEANING AND CONCEPT OF YOGA

Maharshi Patanjali has given a new dimension to the orthodox yoga philosophy. He collected, coordinated and illustrated the basic principles of yoga in his classical work *Yoga Sutras.* He explained yoga as **'Chitta Vritti Nirodha',** which means to free mind from any kind of modifications.

According to Upanishads, yoga is the higher state of consciousness in which the activities of mind and intellect ceases to a stationary state and wisdom comes to a stand.

Yoga is a system of living with sense and science, of the realization of ultimate values and altruistic mission of life. Yoga involves a harmonious order of mind, matter and man.

Thus Swami Satyananda explains yoga in general term and its place in modern time. **J.P.N. Misra** points out more clearly linguistic meaning as 'Yoga' is derived from the Sanskrit dhatu (root) 'Yuj', which means 'to join' or 'to bind', 'to attach'. It also means 'to direct' and 'to concentrate on a particular point of thought', 'to work in full attention of mind and body'. It is a true union of 'Atma' (Soul) with almighty 'Parmatma' (God). This union also includes physical, mental, intellectual and spiritual faculties of a human being. Further Mishra cited the words of Mahadev Desai as, *'it is the yoking of all the powers of body, mind and soul to God'.* He says "this means the disciplining of the intellect, the mind, the emotions, the will, that yoga presupposes; it means a poise of the soul which enables one to look at life in all its aspects evenly."

As stated in *Sri Bhagvad Gita,* yoga is the freedom from sorrows. It has also been defined as **'Yoga Karmasu Kushalam'.** By a reference as narrated in *Bhagvad Gita,* yoga has been described as **Samatvam Yoga Uchchyate,** which means Yoga is equanimity in success and failure or to act without greed for result and to remain unmoved after both success and failure.

"In *Bhagavad Gita,* Lord Shri Krishna explains to Arjuna that deliverance from contact with pain and sorrow is called yoga. It is mentioned that when mind, wisdom and self are under well control, freedom from desires prevails, only then one can understand the real meaning of eternal joy and that will be condition beyond explanation. In such a condition the person abides by the real feeling and does not move even a bit. He will be free from the greatest state of agonies and sorrows. This is the real yoga." Thus, in *Bhagavad Gita* various definitions are provided because for different states of mind evolution and types of person there exist a particular type of yoga suitable for them respectively.

Few more definitions from different text are very conclusive provided as under:

(*i*) According to **Katha Upanishad:** "Yoga is the firm holding back of the senses."

(*ii*) According to **Maitri Upanishad:** "Union with the deity in the fire, in the sun, in heart is yoga."

(*iii*) According to **Rigveda:** "It implies an attitude, an effort which brings the individual (microcosm) in identity and affirmation with the whole (macrocosm)."

(*iv*) According to **Markande Purana:** "Yoga removes ignorance and impurities and thus leads one's mind to enlightenment as to the true nature of self."

(*v*) According to **Vishnu Purana:** "It is union of mind with the spirit of life, in the river of world's problems and pains."

(*vi*) According to **Darshan Mala:** "Yoga is the union of the seer and the Seeri."

(*vii*) According to **Yoga Vashishta:** "Yoga is method travelling with happiness."

We can define yoga as the science of consciousness, the science of creativity, the science of personality development, the science of self, and the science of body and mind. Actually its meaning, definition and explanation may differ from person to person in view of varied nature of an individual's feelings and experiences. But one thing is perfectly clear that yoga is always concerned with three integrated components of self - body, mind and consciousness.

CONCEPT OF YOGA

The word *yoga* comes from the root use to yoke, to unite, or mixed act. Hence the word means to get united or attached. Normally with what who gets united is a question? It is said in the *sastras* that; the individual self *(jivatma)* gets united with the supreme self *(paramatma).* There is a process involved in this connection because the union does not come automatically. There are many ways through which the union takes place. They are called as *Karma yoga, Bhakti yoga, Jnana yoga, Raja yoga, Hatha Yoga, Tantra Yoga, Mantra yoga, Laya yoga, Kundalini yoga, Dhyana yoga* and so on. Accordingly also there are many definitions which are given in various textes: the *Bhagavad Gita* define *yoga* the skilled manner in performing onces duty.

Patanjali in his *yoga sutra* defines *yoga* as: The cessation of the function of mind. Further on this *sutra,* the communicator *Vyasa* gives that yoga is nothing but *samadhi. Yajnavalkya* defines yoga as: The conjunction of the individual soul and the supreme soul is called *yoga.*

Hence, *yoga sastras* are for the union of individual self and the supermen self. For this there are various doctrine in our system analyses. There by we have got a tremendous horde of literature connecting the important subject called yoga.

The two systems of integral *yoga* practice, that of the *Buddha* and that of *Patanjali* are culmination's of yoga endeavours, trends and traditions stretching from the remote past and pursued for centuries out side the official stream of the *Brahmanic* culture. But when they reached their peaks, they became very conspicuous and consequently, visible to all, including ordinary people whose religious loyalty became diverted from *Brahmans* to *yogis* and wandering ascetics.

As a result, in the subsequent movement of *Brahmanic* revivalism. Some of the yogic methodical principles and guidelines to spiritual life as well as aim of *yoga* direct experience of the ultimate reality - became generally accepted as the higher strata of religious life open to anybody who wanted to tread such a path.

The best codification of the popularised *yoga* path at the end of which lies union with god is the *Bhagavad Gita*. The *Bhagavad Gita* has implanted the seed of *yoga*, over many centuries, in the minds hearts of vast multitudes that otherwise would not have been touched by it. These multitudes no doubt grasped the message of *yoga* only practially.

The appeal of yoga of *Bhagavad Gita* is perhaps due to the way in which it is presented with various aspects of *yoga* being treated almost as separate types yoga. The most important ones are four number:

(*i*) *Karma yoga*

(*ii*) *Dhyana yoga*

(*iii*) *Jnana yoga*

(*iv*) *Bhakti yoga*

(*v*) *Raja yoga.*

(i) *Karma yoga*

Karma is three fold—*kiyaka* (bodily) *vicika* (verbal) and *manasika* (mental). There are two kinds of *karma* or *karma vibhaga*—(*a*) *sakama karma* (*b*) *niskama karma*. *Sakama karma* includes all spiritual sacrifies and other duties enjoined on man for the attainment of *swarga* and other worlds. It is attended with birth and death and rebirth called the wheel of *samsara* or *avagamana.*

Niskama karma yoga leads to *Chitta suddhi* or purification of the mind and prepares the aspirant for the reception of the light of knowledge. The *niskama karma yogi* is one whose goal of life is freedom from the wheel of birth and death. *Nishkama karma* is the *sadhana* for the attainment of this freedom.

Karma is of three kinds namely, (*a*) *sanchita* (*b*) *prarabdha* & (*c*) *agami*. *Prarabdha* is one's own previous *karmas,* which gave rise to the present incarnation. They are three fold—*iccha, anicchha* and *paraeccha*. *Sanchita* is the accumulated *karmas* which are yet to bear fruit, of which *prarabdha* forms a part. *Agami karma* is the current actions, which will fructify in future. The actions performed by a *juvanmukta* after his realization is also termed *agami karma.*

There is a further general classification of karma which falls under five heads—*Satkarma* (good deeds), *Dushkarma* or *Kukarma* (bad deeds), *Akarma* (inaction), *Misrita karma* (mixed deeds) and *Vikarma* (perverted actions). By *satkarma* one attains the world of Devas; by *dushkarma*, *vikarma* and *akarma* one attains the lower births and by *misrita karma* one attains the human birth. *Karma* has been further classified under the following particular heads– *nityakarma, naimittika karma, prayaschitta, kamya karma, nisiddha karma.*

Two fold is the nature of *karma* which concerns an individuals:

(*i*) *swadharma* is one's own duty as ordinated by the scriptures.

(*ii*) *paradharma* is the duties prescribed for another.

The duties vary according to one's own *varna* and *ashrama.* Four *varnas* (castes) are *Brahmana, Kshatriya, Vaisya* and *Shudra.* Four *ashramas* (orders) are *Brahmacharya, Grihastha, Vanaprastha* and *Sannyasa,* Duties of the four varnas are given in Bhagavad Gita, (xviii-42,43 and 44). There are certain universal laws governing *karma* law of cause and effect, law of action and reaction, law of compensation, law of reincarnation, law of retribution, law of resistance.

The remedy that *karma yoga* offers lies in the renunciation of personal aims when acting to live for satisfaction based on sensual pleasure are external achievements is to live in vain. Such a life is entirely and contentment in one self (for there is nothing one has to do exclusively for one's own interest).

(ii) *Dhyana yoga*

Dhyana yoga is a path of meditation. It is made clear that the spiritual path of mediation does not necessarily lead to withdrawal from engagement in actions in the normal day-to-day affairs. But the quietude which the *yogi* usually seeks in renouncing life in the world is, in fact, won more safely by renouncing the aim *(sankalpa)* of life in the world, while remaining active in it. For what really counts is the mental attitude. One can renounce the world and involvement in its affairs externally and yet remain bound by worldly affairs in one's mind, it only negatively by fighting and suppressing the memories or fresh opportunities of worldly involvement. But if one succeeds, in one's mind, in giving up personal benefit or expectations there of as motivation for one's actions. No involvement in active life in the world will disturb one's inner balance needed for successful meditation.

The *Bhagavad Gita* even gives methodical advice for the *dhyana* practice of *yoga* while remaining in the world.

(iii) *Jnana yoga*

Jnana yoga is one type of self-realisation. This process involved the higher type of knowledge. This knowledge becomes wisdom or the final direct realisation of the essential unity of existence. At the same time, however, the eternal existance of the person *(Purusa)* of the *yogi* is maintained even in liberation. This is mystery that *jnana yoga* process to solve by direct experience, not by knowing the result conceptually. That is why the *Bhagavad Gita* does not really claim to expound the final knowledge but only advises that every thing should be seen as arising from the divine, which is therefore to be sought as the changeless essence behind changing forms.

The age of science has made man rational being. Intellectual sharpness is eminent. Analysis from the tool, the path of philosophy *(Jnana yoga)* is apt for the keen intellectuals and is centered around the analysis of happiness the vital contribution of *Upanishads.* Also many other fundamental questions regarding mind, the world outside and inside, and reality are taken up. Basic questions are raised even involving the intellect itself to reach the very basic of intellect. Thus the *jnana yoga* too reaches that some supra-state in which he becomes identified with all the living beings amidst which he lives and moves about, he becomes a light house for illuminating the path for the ship of human life caught in the turbulent sea of endless conflicts and tensions, to the safe anchorage of limitless peace and bliss.

Jnana yoga is the path of intellect. The way of logical faculty called the *Buddhi.* We use the power of discrimination in *jnana yoga* to get at the reality. The way of modern science having its objectives as the search for reality. If science started in the west nearly 4 centuries ago, this quest started in India thousands of year's back. If modern science has fathomed the structure and laws of this physical universe with such bewildering accuracy, *Jnana yoga* in its store the knowledge of the whole universe.

Where is this knowledge base found in *Vedas.* The treasure house of knowledge as the world means *Vedas* form the foundation of Indian culture, one classification of *vedas* is in its four-fold contribution. *Rigveda, Yajurveda, Samveda* and *Atharva Veda.* An another way of classification is two-fold one *Purva Mimansa* and *Uttara Mimansa.* The first describes, the details of all rituals *yajnas, Havanas, homas, pujas, vratas* etc. It is something like modern technology. In modern manufacturing industry we describe in detail the methods for the manufacture of a part like bolts and nuts, individuals parts of the product in the form of check list.

The workers have to follow these instruction meticulously without going into way of it. You only know that we are manufacturing say, a car. In the same way the *Purva Mimansa* prescribes a set of do and don't. The results of *yajnas* would bring the describe results of the participants.

The second part of *Vedas* called *Uttara Mimansa* is like modern science. It has for its aim search for reality. It is also called *Vedanta,* the science of reality. It is contained in the books called *Upanisadas.* Nearly 800 *Upanishadas* are available in print. Among them the following ten are the most important ones.

1. *Isavasya Upanishad*
2. *Kena Upanishad*

3. *Katha Upanishad*
4. *Mundaka Upanishad*
5. *Mandukya Upanishad*
6. *Aitareya Upanishad*
7. *Taittariya Upanishad*
8. *Prasna Upanishad*
9. *Chhandogya Upanishad*
10. *Brhadaranyaka Upanishad*

The smallest among these is the *Mandukya Upanishad* with only 16 *mantras* or *verses* and the biggest is the *Brahadaranyaka Upanishad.* The style of the *Upanishads* are given of modern science. It is an experimental and experimental in nature. The presentations are in the form of questions and answers by the student called the disciple and the teacher called *guru*. The content of the *Upanishads* is essential two-fold. Search for realities as in modern science and the quest for happiness.

If modern science has understood that the whole of this physical universe has been made as of energy *Jnana yoga* and had understood that the base of this whole universe is consciousness. If classical mechanics of newtonian laws and quantum mechanics fathomed the laws of this physical universe *Upanishads* described the laws of the whole universe at the physical, *pranic,* mental, emotional and intellectual and *anandamaya kosa* levels they are called as *artha* (laws related to economics) and *kama* (laws related to sense pleasures) at the physical level *dharma* at the *pranic,* mental and emotional levels. *Satya* (the laws of truth at the intellectual level and (the comsic laws of creation) at the highest level of *anandamaya kosa.*

We line a satisfying happy life. That is the yoga way of life. Thus, the *Upanishads*, provide the basic for yoga a process to calm down the mind and quiet in it fully.

Thus, it is seen that both the search for reality and quest for happiness lead us to the same state silence. This is our real home which we all should return to get freed from all bondage in our lives. This state of perfection and total freedom is called *moksa*—the goal of human life.

(iv) Bhakti Yoga

The control of emotions is the key in the path of worship *(Bhakti yoga).* In the modern world man is tossed up and down due to emotional on slaughts. The path of *Bhakti* is a boon to gain control over emotional instabilities by properly harnessing the energy involved in it. The elimination of distractions from the mind is also achieved through the path of *Bhakti* towards God in the form of one's chosen deity.

Bhakti is the state where there is no *vibhakti* where there is no separation of his thoughts, feelings and actions from God consciousness, such a constant communion with God naturally makes the individual imbibe the same goodly attributely described above. Mentally offering every one of this physical intellectual and mental actions to him is prescribed as the process of achieving such constant communication with God. Which, in turn removes to egoistic consciousness of deership in him and reveals the truth that he is just an instrument in the hands of God. Further on even this sense of being on instrumental given place to a state where in constant god awareness takes over all the functions of his existence.

Bhakti yoga is prescribed for this age. By following this path on comes to God more easily than by following the others. One can undoubtedly reach god by following the paths of *Jnana* and *Karma,* but they are very difficult paths. It is to keep the mind on God by chanting his name and glories. An image can not be impressed on bare glass, but only on glass stained with a black solution, as in photography. The blame solution is devotion to God.

Purification of *prema* takes us to the shrine of *Bhakti.* In prema, we give material things food, comforts and wealth. It is *tyaga* of material possessions if we give up our ego, and our attachment, then we rise to the level of *Bhakti.* Therefore, *Bhakti* is prema plus saranagati or prapati prema plus surrender. Then there is surrender our *prema* gets purified.

In *Bhakti* we surrender ourselves totally, and intellectually, we surrender in totally. Surrender to homes? Surrender to a personal god *saguna bhakti* or to reality pure consciousness itself to *nirguna bhakti*. Our limitations vanish. All over shortcomings vanish. We get expanded to cosmic all pervasive eternal divinity. We turn ourselves to that supreme *satchidananda*. Therefore, we more, losing our individuality and reach that state of more existence, consciousness and bliss. Many time we shudder to think of losing our individuality (our identity). We can not show our ego. Many of rationalise research schools condemn *Bhakti* for this reasons. They even condemn *saranagati* because it kills individuality. By killing individuality we lose our creativity and therefore, we lose our confidence. That is their objection. But actually, exactly the reverse happens when we surrender. By surrendering we surrender our limitations, we surrender our strong likes and dislikes. We surrender our obsessions. Then automatically we get purified. We expand, we become more powerful we start imbibbing the qualities of our *istadevata* (god of choice) by tuning ourselves to that level in, *saguna bhakti*. In *nirguna bhakti*, we reach that deep state of silence, the above of freedom, creativity, knowledge and bliss, become that ultimate itself.

To be egoistic is to be constricted. To be individualistic is contraction. To be selfish is contration: to be limited is contraction. Surrender is the opposite. The ego is to be surrendered. Individual likes and dislikes are to be given up. Selfishness is to be relinquished. That is the path of *Bhakti*. In *Bhakti* we topple the entire tree of ego by cutting the very root, because, the root is the attachment. Root is the 'I-ness'. If we can give up that ego, which is not very easy then the whole tree of ignorance is toppled down. In *raja yoga*, we cut the branches, in *jnana yoga*, we cut the trunk, but in *bhakti yoga*, we uproot the entire tree. That is the specialist of the science of emotions culture. Operating on our emotions, purifying our emotion, raising ourselves from more *kama* to *prema*, from *prema* raising ourselves to *Bhakti*, culminating in realisation *sakshatkara*, is total attainment to that God, *Ista devata*, divinity to reality itself. That is the path of the science of emotions culture. Do we have people in this modern day and age who have followed the path of *Bhakti*, trodden this path of emotions culture? yes, we have. There is the great example of *Sri Ramakrisna Paramahansa*, a man, who was a true scientist, a man, who had that deep thirst for knowledge and realisation, and who as able to constructour entire *sanatana dharma* by his personal efforts, understanding and experiencing through the path of *bhakti*. A brief study of his life is an illustration of this path of *bhakti yoga* our emotions culture.

Let us look at eight main steps *Bhakti* :

(*a*) Incidents in life and the inner touch.

(*b*) Curiousity based practices start, good results.

(*c*) Problems and hurdles arise, most people stop practices, but a rare few march ahead.

(*d*) The real journey starts.

(*e*) Intensification and deeper problems physical, mental and emotional.

(*f*) Solutions leading to greater bliss.

(*g*) Intensification and relinquishing the "I" through or attachment to life itself.

(*h*) *Sakshatkara* - God realization.

Bhakti separated 9 types but that is based on five *bhavas* called *pancha mahabhavas*.

(*a*) *Santa Bhava*

(*b*) *Madhura Bhava*

(*c*) *Sakhya Bhava*

(*d*) *Vatsalya Bhava*

(*e*) *Dasya Bhava*

In tune with the five main *bhavas*, there are nine types of *Rasas* associated in the *bhakti* path. These nava (nine rasas are)

	Navarasas	***Example***
(*i*)	*Sringar Rasa*	*Radha, Krishna*
(*ii*)	*Vira Rasa*	*Bhima, Arjuna*
(*iii*)	*Bhakti Rasa*	*Mira, Sura Dasa*
(*iv*)	*Vatsalaya Rasa*	*Yasodha*
(*v*)	*Bibhatsa Rasa*	*Kali, Bhairavi*
(*vi*)	*Karuna Rasa*	*Buddha*
(*vii*)	*Hasya Rasa*	*Tenali Rama*
(*viii*)	*Raudra Rasa*	*Shiva (Tandava Avastha)*
(*ix*)	*Santa Rasa*	*Shiva (Dhyana Avastha)*

(v) Kundalini Yoga

This is another type of *yoga.* An occult super structure to which *Hatha yoga* may lead those who fell inclined to go that way is called *kundalini yoga. Kundalini yoga* possesses a clear knowledge of the six *chakras.* A detailed knowledge of *nadis* psychic nerves or astral tubes for carrying *prana* and *chakras* (lotuses of spiritual centres of energy or psychic nerve-centres) is necessary for a student who is treading the path of *kundalini yoga. Kundalini* is the family woman. She belongs to a chaste and noble family. Just as a respectable lady is well protected. So, also *kundalini* is well-protected in the *muladhara* by the veil of *avidya. Kundalini yoga* is that yoga which treats of *Kundalini sakti,* the six centres of spiritual energy *(shat chakras).* The arousing of the sleeping *kundalini sakti* and its union which Lord siva in *Sahasrara* at the crown of the head. While practising the rousing of *kundalini sakti* is attended by intense heat. One should not be unnecessarily alarmed by the heat and other symptoms. One should be brave, courageous and cheerful. By doing so, ones inner eye will be opened.

It is basic, is an elaborate and complicated teaching that describes in great detail the physiology of man's subtle body, which is supposed to be the vehicle of the cosmic life-force *(prana).* While practising *Kundalini yoga* one should not bother much about awakening it. Let it awaken by itself spontaneously. Premature awakening is not desirable. Perform *sadhana* and *tapas* systematically and regularly just as the gardener who waters the trees daily gets the fruits when the time comes. So also one will enjoy the fruits of one's *sadhana* when the time comes. Purify the *nadis* in a regular manner without any time gap. Do proper *sadhana. Kundalini* will take care of itself and the inflow of the energy will occur in its normal way.

As the serpent *(Sheshanaga)* upholds the earth and its mountains and woods, so *kundalini* is the support of all the *yoga* practices. The phenomenon of *kundalini* is the basis of *tantra* and *yoga. Kundalini yoga* is the process of bringing together the two opposite poles of energy in the body so that they meet in the nucleus of matter, *mooladhara chakra,* and release the inner potential energy. That energy is called *kundalini sakti. Tantra* is made up of two syllables *tan* 'to expand' *tra* 'to liberate'. *Tantra* is the process of expanding consciousness and liberating energy, and is the oldest science known to man. It has been, and still is, practised even among illiterate and common man. *Kundalini,* the inherent power in every individual, is only just coming to be investigated and accepted by modern science. However, the ancient *Rishis* understood *kundalini* and explained it through the scientific and systematic process of *tantra.*

Kundalini is said to be the coiled like snake. Without a doubt, one who makes that *sakti* flow obtains liberation. While *kundalini* is asleep in *mooladhara,* she is depicted as a snake, usually a cobra, coiled three and a half times around a smoky grey *sivalingam (dhumralingam).* The three and a half coils present the form of the *om mantra.* These three coils are the three states of existence and experience, conscious, subconscious and unconscious, *jagrat, swapna* and *susupti i.e.,* waking, dream and deep sleep objective experience, subjective experience and non experience, past, present and future. The three coils also represent the three qualities of nature. *Prakrti* or *sakti - tamas, rajas* and *sattva.* The half coil represents that which is beyond the play of nature, *turiya* of the fourth dimension, which includes any other dimension beyond the third. The smoky *sivalingam* around which *kundlaini* is coiled the subtle body or *sukshma sarira,* also known as the astral body, but its all defined, smoky quality indicates that the inner consciousness is obscured in the changing realities of the three realms of experience.

In an unaware individual the kundlaini has her head downward, but in the *yogi* the head is lifted up as she begins to awaken. When the *kundalini* serpent wakes up she should rise through *susumna,* until she is perfectly straight from the tip of her tail, anchored in *mooladhara,* to the top of the head which fills the skull. It indicates pervading çonsciousness which is not limited by any influene or subject to any modification.

While *kundalini* lies dormant in *mooladhara* the connection to *ajna-chakra* takes place through *ida* or *pingla, nadis.* Sometimes the connection does not even take place as there is a blockage. Once *kundalini* has risen up so that the head is completely immersed in the brain, the connection is direct *(susumna),* the three states of experience merge into the fourth (transcendental) as the coils of the *kundalini* are straightened. Then there is no separate existence of any of the *gunas,* there is no longer separation of anything. It all becomes one eternal cosmic experience.

(vi) Hatha Yoga

Prostrating first to the *guru, yogi Swatmarama* instructs the knowledge of hatha only for *(raja yoga)* the highest state of yoga. By first prostrating to the *guru, yogi Swatmarama* indicates that he is only a tool of transmission for the knowledge which is to be imparted. It is also emphasized that *Hatha yoga* is to be practiced for the sole purpose of preparing oneself for the highest state of *raja yoga i.e.* Samadhi.

The main *nadis* in *Hatha yoga* are *Ida, Pingala* and *Susumna.* There are five distinct practices in *hatha yoga, asana, pranayama, bandhas, mudras* and *kriyas.* Purificatory *kriyas* are six kinds: *dhauti, bhasti, neti, tratak, nauli* and *kapalabhati.* The classification of *asana* is made in six groups: *topsy-turvy*, forward-bending, backward-bending, sideway bending, spinal-twist and meditative poses.

Dhauti is of five kinds–*varisara, vatasara, agnisara, bahishkriya* and *vamana dhautis. Bhasti* is of two varieties: *Sthala bhasti* and *Jala bhasti.* The *pranas* are five: *pranas, apana, vyana, udana* and *samana.* The *chakras* are six: *muladhara, swadhishtana, manipura, anahata, visuddha* and *ajna chakras.* The deities presiding over the *chakras* are *Brahma* and *Ganapati , Visnu, Rudra, Sadasiva* and *Sambhu.*

The two states of *kundalini* are–*supta* (dormant) and *jagrata* (awakened). The triple combination of *bandhas* or the *bandh-traya* are composed of *Mula-bandha jalandhara-bandha* and *uddiyana-bandha.* The *chakras* above the *ajha-chakra* are: *guru chakra, some-chakra, manaschakra* are *lalana-chakra. Triveni* is the plaited knot made by three *nadis— Ida, pingala* and *susumna* at the *ajna chakra* centre in the *trikuti. Merudanda* is the back-bone column through the middle of which the central canal for the *susumna nadi* passes from *muladhara* up to *sahasrara. Nauli kriya* is three fold in variety–*madhyama nauli, vama nauli* and *daksina nauli.* Granthis or knots that obstruct the upward ascent of the *kundalini sakti* are three in number *i.e., Brahmagranthi, visnu-granthi* and *Rudragranthi.*

Location of the *granthis* are three–*Visuddha Chakra (Rudra), Manipura Chakra (Visnu)* and *muladhara (Brahma). Pranayamas* in *Hatha yoga* are of eight kinds–*bhastrika, bhramari, plavini, seetali, sitkari, surryabheda, vjjayi and murchha.* The ninth *pranayama* for daily practice is the *sukha-purvak i.e.* an easy, comfortable *panayama* consisting of inhalation, retention and exhalation. The stages in the practice of *yoga* are four *arambha avastha, ghata avastha, parichaya-avastha* and *niipatti-avastha. Nada* or the mystic inner sounds heard by the *yogi* are of twelve different kinds: *Vina* (lute) tinkling of bells, flute, hum of bees, *mridanga,* horn, conch, cymbal, drum, thunder and the roar or ocean sings of perfection in *Hatha yoga* are eight. The body becomes slim, speech becomes cloquest, inner sounds are distinctly heard, eyes are clear and bright, body is free from all diseases, seminal fluid is transmuted, digestive power is increased and the *nadis* become purified. The things to be avoided by the *Hatha yoga* practitioners are bad company, basking near the fire (in winter), sensual contract, bathing very early in the morning, fasting too much, and exhausting physical work. The four dangerous things that bring downfall to the *yogi* are over eating, too much talk, impure company and greed. The six things that bring success to the *yogi* are–cheerfulness, perseverance, courage, right knowledge, firm belief in the words of the guru and avoidance of intimacy with anybody, *yama* according to *Hath yoga* is ten fold–*ahimsa* (harmlessness), *satya* (truthfulness), *aiteya* (non-stealing), *brahmacharya* (continence) *kshma* (forbearance), *dhariti* (fortitude), *daya* (mercy), *aarjava* (straight forwardness), *mitahara* (moderation in diet), and *suchi* (purity).

Niyama is also tenfold–*tapas* (austerity), *santosa* (cheerful bearing), *shraddha* (faith), *dana* (Charitable disposition), *satsahga* (good company), *lajja* (modesty), *mati* (sound mind), *japa* (repetittion or divine name), *Ishwarar cana* (worship of God) and *vrata* (observances of vows).

Hatha yoga may be viewed as a further elaborate extension of the third and fourth parts of *Patanjali's yoga system,* namely that concerned with the bodily posture *(asana)* and that dealing with the control of breathing *(pranayam).*

(vii) Raja Yoga

All the processes of *Hatha yoga* and *Laya yoga* are but the means to attain *raja yoga (samadhi).* One who attains *raja yoga* is victorious over time death. *Raja yoga* means realisation of, or being, *Shiva, Brahman Atma,* the self, cosmic consciousness. *Hatha yoga* is the same experience but from the reflection on the primordial. *Sakti, i.e.,* before *samadhi.* In the highest state of *raja yoga* there is no reflection in *Sakti, Siva* and *Sakti* are in equanimity, *Hatha yoga* is the means to experience this, *Sakti* or *tattwa* is the tool.

According to the *sloka,* through *Hatha yoga* and absorption of mind and *prana, i.e. laya, unmani, avastha* is attained. *Unmani* is the condition when finite mind ceases to function. *Avastha* is a state or condition achieved through effort but it is impermanent. It means that Hatha yoga will arouse the condition of *unmani* but until it becomes an established condition or natural state, *sthiti,* one will remain at the level of *Hatha yoga* and not attain *raja yoga. Hatha yoga* culminates in the union of *ida, pingala* and *susumna* in *anja chakra,* whereas *raja yoga* culminates beyond this, when the *kundalini* reaches *sahasrara–chakra.* The supreme is neither state, experience nor condition. There are really no words to express it exactly, although the *Upanishads* and various other scriptures do attempt to go so. It is just beingness.

The earth without *raja yoga,* night without *raja yoga,* even the various *mudras* without *raja yoga* are useless *i.e.,* not beautiful. Without *raja yoga* the value of this life can not be had. The final stage of *samadhi* is *raja yoga,* and it is the only purpose of existence on this earth, without that experience, the real nature of this empirical world can not be grasped. *Samadhi* can be had by following any path or *yoga-karma, Jnana* and *bhakti yoga* etc. They all terminate in the experience of a totally one-pointed mind, *i.e. samadhi. Raja yoga* means not only the particular system of *Patanjali's ashtanga yoga,* but it means the complete absorption in *dhyana* by any means. Without withdrawing the sensory awareness and experiencing the inner world in meditation it is impossible to appreciate the external. Without striving for the inner experience it is meaningless to live for the external experience because that is limited by the sense. The internal world is vast and limitless. Through *dhyana* the external experience expands and becomes part of the internal. The deeper one can go into *dharana* and *dhyana* the more one can appreciate the purpose and beauty of life.

According to *Patanjali raja yoga samadhi* is of two kinds–*Samprajnata* or *(savikalpa)* and *Asamprajnata* or *(nirvikalpa).* In the former, the seeds of *samskaras* are not destroyed. In the latter, the *samskaras* are fried or annihilated in toto. That is the reason why the former is called *sabija samadhi* (with seed) and the latters as *nirbija samadhi* (without seed or *samskaras*) *samprajnata samadhi* leads to *asamprajnata samadhi.*

Savikalpa samadhi is of six kinds—*Savitarka* (with argumentation), *nirvitarka* (without argumentation), *savichara* (with deliberation), *nirvichara* (without deliberation), *sananda* (blissful), and *sasmita* (with individual consciousness).

This is highest from of *samadhi.* This comes after *viveka-khyati* or the final discrimination between *prakriti* and *purusha.* All the seeds or impressions are burnt by the fire of knowledge. This *samadhi* brings *kaivalya* or absolute independence.

One can enter the *raja yoga samadhi* into *asamprajnata samadhi* (*nirvikalpa* state) all the *samskaras* and *vasanas* which bring on rebirths are totally fried up. All *vrittis* or mental modifications that arise from the mind-lake come under restraint. The five afflictions, viz, *avidya* (ignorance), *asmita* (egoism), *raga-dvesa* (love and hatred) and *abhinivesa* (clinging life) are destroyed and the bonds of *karma* annihilated.

Maharsi Patanjali has prescribed the practiced of various kinds of lower *samadhis.* There must be gradual ascent in the ladder of *yoga.* One should pass through successive stages before one attains the highest *asamprajnata* or *nirvikapla samadhi.*

Eventually, the *purusha* realises his own native state of divine glory, Isolation or absolute indepenence *(kaivalya).* He has completely disconnected himself from the *prakriti* and its effects. He feels his absolute freedom and attains *kaivalya,* the highest goal of *raja yoga.* The *gunas* having fulfilled their objects of *bhoga* and *apavarga* now entirely cease to act. The sum total of all knowledge of the three worlds, of all secular science is nothing, nothing but mere husk when compared to the infinite knowledge of a *yogi* who has attained *kaivalya.*

Five *Kleshas*

The five *klesha* afflictions which disturb the equilibrium of consciousness are: ignorance of lack of wisdom, ego, pride of the ego or the sense of "I", attachment to pleasure, aversion to pain, fear of death and clinging in life. Afflictions are of three levels, intellectual, emotional and instinctive. *Avidya* and *asmita* belong to the field of intelligence; here lack of spiritual knowledge combined with pride or arrogance inflates the ego, causing conceit and the loss of one's sense of balance. *Raga* and *dvesa* belong to emotions and feelings. *Raga* is desire and attachment, *dvesa* is hatred and aversion. Succumbing to excessive desires and attachments or allowing oneself to be carried away by expressions of hatred, creates disharmony between body and mind, which may lead to psychosomatic disorders. *Abhinivesa* is instinctive; the desire to prolong one's life, and concern for one's own survival. Clinging to life makes are suspicious in dealings with others, and causes one to become selfish and self-centred.

The root causes of these five afflictions are the behavioural functions and thoughts of the various spheres of the brain. *Avidya* and *asmita* are connected with the conscious front brain, and the top brain is considered the seat of the 'I' consciousness. *Raga* and *dvesa* are connected with the base of the brain, the hypothalamus. *Abhinivesa* is connected with the 'old' brain or back brain which is also known as the unconscious brain, as it retains past subliminal impressions, *samskaras.* The *sadhaka* must learn to locate the sources of the afflictions, in order to be able to nip them in the bud through his *yogis* principles and disciplines.

H!STORY AND EVOLUTION OF YOGA

The history of yoga spans from four to eight thousand years ago to the current days. From hints of its practice in pre-vedic time, the first elucidations and detailed collaborations in Hindu texts, absorption into Buddhist and Jain philosophies up to its modern suffusion into secular life, its applicability has stood the test of time. History books ciria 3000 B.C. and more importantly link it to the great Indus-Sarasvati civilization. The Indus-Sarasvati was the largest civilization in the ancient world and exceptionally modern for its time. Named after the two rivers that flowed through India, the Indus-Sarasvati was maritime society, exporting goods throughout the Middle East and Africa. A triangular amulet seal uncovered at the Mohanjo-daro archaeological excavation site depicts a male figure sitting cross-legged on a low platform, with arms outstretched. His head is crowned with the horns of a water buffalo. He is surrounded by animals (a fish, an alligator and a snake) and diverse symbols. The likeness on the seal and understanding of the surrounding culture have led to its widely accepted identification as "Pashupati", Lord of Beasts, a prototype and predecessor of the modern day Hindu God Shiva. The pose is very familiar one to yogic representing Shiva much as he is seen today, the meditating ascetic contemplating divine truth in "yoga posture".

Another seal found at the Mohanjo-daro site shows a figure standing on its head, which may depict the practice of yoga. As such the history of yoga may go back to eight thousand years, depending on the perspective of all the historian and interpretation of Mohanjo-daro seals.

Feuerstein described complex socio-cultural process of India by organizing it into nine periods, expressing distinguishable cultural styles:

1. Pre-Vedic Age (6500-4500 B.C.E.)
2. Vedic Age (4500-2500 B.C.E.)
3. Brahmanical Age (2500-1500 B.C.E.)
4. The Post-Vedic / Upanishadic Age (1500-1000 B.C.E.)
5. The Pre-Classical Age or Epic Age (1000-100 B.C.E.)
6. The Classical Age (100 B.C.E. – 500 C.E.)
7. The Tantric / Puranic Age (500 - 1300 B.C.E.)
8. The Sectarian Age (1300 -1700 C.E.)
9. Modern Age (1700 – Present)

Pre Vedic

Though yoga's origin is shrouded, evidence links the earliest yoga tradition back at least 5000 years to the beginning of human civilization. Scholars believe that yoga grew out of Stone Age - Shamanism, because of the cultural similarities between modern Hinduism and Mehrgarh, a Neolithic settlement (in what is now Afghanistan). In fact, much of Hindu ideas, rituals and symbols of today appear to have their roots in this shamanistic culture of Mehrgarh. Early yoga and archaic shamanistic had much in common as both sought to transcend the human condition. The primary goal of shamanism was to heal members of the community and act as religious mediators. Archaic yoga was also community oriented, as it attempted to discern the cosmic order through inner vision, then to apply that order to daily living. Later, Yoga evolved into a more inward experience, and yogis focused on their individual enlightenment and salvation.

Vedic

The Indus-Sarasvati civilization also gave birth to the ancient texts known as Vedas, the oldest scriptures in the world. The Vedas is a collection of hymns that praises a Higher power; it contains the oldest recorded yogic teachings and is considered divine revelation. Vedic yoga is characterized by ritualistic ceremonies, from which, the yoga practice that requires yoga practitioners to transcend the limitations of the mind originated. David Frawley, a Vedic scholar writes, "Yoga can be traced back to the Rig Veda, itself, the oldest Hindu text, which speaks about yoking our mind and insight to the Sun of Truth. Great teachers of early yoga include the names of many famous Vedic sages like Vasisth, Yajanavalkya and Jaigishavya".

The earliest term for yoga – like endeavours in India is 'Tapas'. Literally this ancient Sanskrit word means 'heat'. It is derived from the verbal root 'tap' meaning 'to burn' or to 'glow'. The term is often used in the Rigveda to describe the quality and work of the solar or the superficial fire. Yoga spiritualized the orientation of the earlier tradition of 'Tapas' by emphasizing self-transdence over the acquisition of magical powers. At the same time, the 'yogins' adopted and adapted many of the techniques and practices of the older tradition of 'Tapas'. Chasity remained central to its practice, as is clear from the eight-lobed path outlined in the 'yoga-sutra'.

Pre Classical Yoga

(i) Upanishadic

Sometimes between 1800-1500 B.C., Gnostic text called the Upanishads appeared. The 200 or so scriptures comprising the Upanishads explained the transcendental self (atman) and its relation to the ultimate reality (Brahman). The Karma doctrine is believed to have originated with the Upanishads as well. Just as the New Testament rests upon, but furthers the old testament, so too, the Upanishads further expounds upon the scriptures of the Vedas. The teachings of the Upanishads dawned the era of Pre-Classical yoga.

Around 1400 B.C., great sage named Vyasa, categorized the Vedic hymns in four Vedic texts we know today: Rig Veda (knowledge of Praise), Yajur Veda (knowledge of Sacrifice), Sama Veda (knowledge of Chants) and Atharva Veda (knowledge of Atharvan). In 1200 BC, the great enlightened teacher Rishabha started the tradition known as Jainism, which is also dedicated to the liberation of spirit. Then in 100 B.C., a second urbanization began along the banks of Ganges river (the former Indus-Sarasvati civilization). Later, in the sixth century B.C., Lord Buddha spread the teachings of Buddhism, which stresses the importance of meditation and ethics over Physical Postures. Buddhism had some similarities with Hinduism, however, yoga sages saw the limitations of ignoring the physical purification process. Siddhartha Gautama, who was skilled in meditation and also the first Buddhist, who studied yoga, attained enlightenment.

Explicit examples of the concept and terminology of yoga appears in the Upanishads text of the Vedanta, that are the culmination of all vedic philosophy. In the Maitrayaniya Upanishad (200-300 BCE), yoga surfaces as: "Shadanya-Yoga—the uniting discipline of the six limbs (Shad-anga), as expounded in Maitrayaniya Upanishada: (1) breath control (pranayama); (2) sensory inhibition (pratyahara); (3) meditation (dhyana); (4) concentration (dharana); (5) examination (tarka); and (6) ecstasy (samadhi)".

The doctrine propounded in the 'Katha-Upanishad' is called 'adhyatma-yoga' – the yoga of deep self". Its target is the supreme being, which lies hidden in the "cave" of the human heart.

Of the 108 Upanishads of Muktika canon, 17 are considered yoga Upanishads.

(ii) Bhagavad Gita

This ancient text was written about 500 B.C. and is the first scripture devoted entirely to yoga. This Bhagavad Gita confirms that yoga was quite ancient by the time of its writing. Only 700 verses long, the Gita is a conversation between Prince Arjuna and the God-man Krishna. The Gita's message is to oppose evil in the world. The Gita earned its relevance because of its attempt to blend Jnana-yoga, Bhakti yoga, and Karma yoga together unifying these various yogic traditions. Many schools during this era taught way of reaching deep levels of meditation in order to surpass the mind and body system to achieve one's true, limitless self. Feuerstein describes that in Bhagavad Gîtâ, Krishna taught yoga of wisdom (Jnâna-yoga) and yoga of action (Karma-yoga).

Jaina yoga resembles its Hindu counterpart in its higher aspect. Jaina writers like Harichandra Suri (c 750 C.E.) have made use of some of the codifications of Patanjali. In his 'Yoga Bindu', he praises yoga by saying it 'wishfilling tree'. Like Pitanjali's yoga, the yoga of the Buddha comprises eight distinct members or "limbs" which is known as the 'noble eightfold path'. The first two members of the eightfold path are said to deal with understanding, the next three deal with behaviour and the last three with concentration. The first five can also be grouped under the heading of socio-ethical regulations, while the remaining three members are specifically yogic.

Classical Yoga – Patanjali's yoga sutras

After the turn of the millennium, the spread of Yoga in its different forms gave rise to the need for standardization. Thus, in the second century C.E., Patanjali composed a seminal text, 'Yoga-Sutras' and defined classical yoga. The 195 aphorisms or sutras that comprise the yoga-sutras, expound upon Raja-Yoga (the eightfold yoga path). The yoga sutra is meant to be memorized as means of internalizing its wisdom. The eight limbs of classical yoga (Ashtang Yoga) are: (1) Yama or restraint; (2) Niyama, or observance of purity, tolerance and study; (3) Asana, or physical postures/exercises; (4) Pranayama or breath control; (5) Pratyahara, or preparation for meditation; (6) Dharana, or concentration; (7) Dhayana or meditation, and (8) Samadhi or absorption in the sublime. Patanjali advocates studying the sacred scriptures as part of the yoga practice, which became classical yoga's distinct feature.

Patanjali, whose own life is virtually unknown, had the impact of further spreading in compact form the essence of Raja-Yoga. Some legends speak of his being Adinaga, the first snake, the lower half of his body being that the snake, upon which the great Hindu God Vishnu reclines. Many say that he was the same Patanjali, who wrote commentaries on Panini's singular masterwork on Sanskrit grammar. Other speak of the legends of his birth. A few even dispute his existence and attribute the yoga sutras to many authors, but this is highly unlikely due to the structural, linguistic and stylistic uniformity of the short work. His base is Hindu Samkhya philosophy and shows itself to have been highly influenced by Upanishadas.

The real ground breaking characteristic of yoga-sutra, however, is its percept philosophical dualism. Patanjali believed that separation of the matter (prakriti) and spirit (purusha) were necessary to cleanse the spirit to absolute purity. This is in stark contrast to Pre-classical and Vedic yoga, which adopts the unification of the body and the spirit. The teachings of Patanjali represent a departure from traditional non-dualistic yoga and laid the groundwork for Post-classical yoga. For centuries after Patanjali, the dualism of yoga was predominant. Yogis focussed almost exclusively on meditation and neglected the Asans. They were attempting to exit the mortal coil and merge with the ultimate reality through contemplation. But with the advent of alchemy, a precursor to chemistry, the yoga masters rekindled their belief in the body as a temple. Contemporary thought shifted to health, longevity and maintenance. As such, the yoga masters attempted to demonstrate that new yoga techniques fundamentally alter the body's biochemistry and make it immortal. This led back to the Pre-classical and Vedic Yoga belief about the primacy of the Asans and to the beginning of Post-classical Yoga.

Post Classical Yoga

The era of Post-classical Yoga gave rise to prolific literature, the different branches of yoga, which are Hatha and the Tantras and to many holistic schools for yoga. Post-classical yoga can best be defined as an appreciation of the present moment. Practitioners no longer aspired to liberation from this reality, rather to accept it and live at the moment.

Hatha Yoga

In the west, outside of Hindu culture, "yoga" is usually understood to refer to "hatha yoga". Hatha Yoga is, however, a particular system propagated by Swami Swatamarama, a yogic sage of the 15th century in India. Hatha yoga, also known as the yoga of physical discipline, is a form of Raja Yoga, which has recently become extremely popular in the west. The techniques of Hatha Yoga place particular emphasis on physical breathing and concentration methods for regulation of the body's energy.

After the Bhagavad Gita and Yoga sutras, the most fundamental text in Yoga is the Hatha Yoga, written by Swami Swatamarma. It lists all the main asanas, pranayama, mudra and bandha in great detail that are familiar to today's yoga student. It runs in the line of Hindu yoga (to distinguish from Buddhist and Jain Yoga) and is dedicated to Lord Adi Nath, a name of Lord Shiva (the Hindu God of destruction), who is alleged to have imparted the secrets of Hatha Yoga to his divine consort Parvati. It is common for yogins and tantriks of several disciplines to dedicate their practices to a deity under the Hindu ishta-devata concept while always striving to achieve beyond that Brahman. Hindu philosophy in the Vedanta and Yoga streams, views only one thing as being ultimate real : Satchidananda Atman, the Existence-Consciousness-Blissful self. Very Upanishadic in its notions, worship of Gods is a secondary means of focus on the higher being a conduit to realization of the Divine Ground. Hatha yoga follows in that vein and thus successfully transcends being particularly grounded in any one religion.

Hatha is a Sanskrit word meaning 'sun (ha) and 'moon' (tha) representing opposing energies: hot and cold, male and female, positive and negative, similar but not completely analogous to yin and yang. The term Hatha Yoga also has a more specific measuring, to connote a special set of internal cleansing methods, known as "Shat Karmas". Hatha yoga attempts to balance mind and body via physical exercise, or "asanas", controlled breathing, and the calming of the mind through relaxation and meditation. Asanas teach poise, balance and strength and these were originally (and still) practiced to improve the body's physical health and clear the mind in preparation for meditation in the pursuit of enlightenment. "Asanas" means "immovable", *i.e.*, static, and often confused with the dynamic 108 natya karanas described in the Natya Shastra and along with the elements of Bhakti Yoga, is embodied in the contemporary form of Bharatnatyam. Asanas are physical postures, which stretch and strengthen different parts of body, massaging and bringing fresh blood to internal organs while rejuvenating the nervous system and lubricating joints, muscles and ligaments.

By balancing two streams, often known as ida (mental) and pingala (bodily) currents, the sushumana nadi (current of the self) is said to rise, opening various chakras (cosmic power points within the body, starting from the base of the spine and ending right above the head) until Samadhi is attained. Ida and pingala are represented in dynamism of natya yoga by lasya (female) and tandava (male) aspect, and bear direct reference to the Taoist dualism.

By forging a powerful depth of concentration and mastery of the body and mind, Hatha yoga practices seek to still the mental waters and allow for apprehension of oneself as that which one always was, Brahman. Hatha yoga is essentially a manual for scientifically taking one's body through stages of control to a point at which one-pointed focus on the unmanifested Brahman is possible; it is said to take its practitioner to the peaks of Raja Yoga.

Yoga in modern era

Modern Yoga arrived in the United States during the late 1800's. It can be attributed to many gurus, including Swami Vivekananda, and their apostolic works. Vivekananda was a student of Ramakrishna, and he attended the Parliament of Religions in Chicago of 1893. Vivekananda was well accepted and later travelled all around the United States to spread yoga tradition.

Most of the longer established postural yoga schools in United Kingdom (U.K.) have gone through similar developmental phases from the 1950's onwards. These are: Popularization (1950's to mid 1970's), consolidation (mid 1970's to late 1980's) and Acculturation (late 1980's to date). B.K.S. Iyengar brought Iyengar Yoga in Britain during 1954, whereas, British wheel of yoga (known as BWY) got established in 1962. Since early 1990s, Pattabhi Jois' Astanga yoga has also gained popularity (Michelis, 2005). It was estimated that about 15 million Americans now practice Hatha Yoga, and the figure is rising in Australia as well.

Another yoga guru, who is perhaps the most popular, was Swami Paramhansa Yogananda, who founded the Self-Realization Fellowship. Yogananda wrote 'Autobiography of yogi' and his teachings enjoy immense popularity even today. Other yoga gurus include Krishnamurti and Maharishi Mahesh yogi. Krishnamurthi travelled widely, drawing large crowds and expounded upon Jnan-Yogi. It was Maharishi Mahesha Yogi, who popularized Transcendental Meditation (TM) in the 1960's.

Other most prominent yoga guru is Swami Sivananda, who served as a doctor in Malaysia and opened schools in America and Europe in 1960's and 1970's. Swami Sivananda's work is based on modified Five Principles of Yoga: (1) Proper relaxation (savasna), (2) Proper exercise (asanas), (3) Proper breathing (pranayama), (4) Proper diet (vegetarian) and (5) Positive thinking and Meditation (dhyana). Swami Sivananda is the founder of the International Sivananda Yoga Vendanta Centres through his disciple Swami Vishnu-devananda. Swami Vishnu-devananda also wrote the illustrated book on yoga.

Swami Sivananda's other notable disciples include Swami Satchidananda, who introduced chanting and yoga to Woodstock; Swami Sivananda Radha, the woman who explored the connection between psychology and yoga, and ; Yogi Bhajan, who started teaching Kundalini Yoga in the 70's. He also founded the 3H organization (Healthy, Happy, Holy), which now has around 200 centres worldwide. There was also the great Sri Krishnamacharya, who taught Viniyoga Hatha Yoga. The Viniyoga tradition is continued by his son, Desikachar. Desikachar's brother in law, B.K.W. Iyenger also continued teaching Viniyoga Hatha yoga and had quite a large number of followers. Living yoga masters today include Sathya Sai Baba, who has millions of followers; Swami Satyananda, follower of Bihar School of Yoga ; Sri Sri Ravi Shankar, whose centres naming 'Art of Living' are working in India and abroad. "Bhartiya Yog Samsthan", New Delhi, established in 1967 under the guidance of Shri Parkash Lal ji renders selfless service to the society in the field of yoga. 'Sahaja

Yoga' is also made popular by Shri Mata Ji Nirmala Devi during 1970 and various schools are established under the name 'Sahaja yoga International Schools' where students learn 'Sahaja yoga' alongwith their general education. In India, one of their schools is situated in Naddi, Hamachal Pradesh. Swami Ramadev ji, the founder of Patanjali Yogpeeth, has brought a revolutionary awakening among people to realize the relevance of yoga in modern stress prone times.

Shad-Darshanas

Indian Philosophical systems have been divided into two classes viz, *Astika* (orthodox) and *Nastika* (heterodox). The word *Astika* means theist and *Nastika* means an atheist. The first group belong the six chief philosophical systems, it is known as *Shad-darshana,* namely, *Samkhya, Yoga, Nyaya, Vaisesika, Mimamsa* and *Vedanta.* Beside these *Astika* Schools, there are other two types of *Astika* schools which *Madhavacharya* has mentioned in his philosophy. These two systems are known as grammarian school and medical school. Heterodox or *Nastika* philosophy includes the *Charvaka, Jaina* and *Buddha* philosophy. These systems do not believe the authority of the *veda.* They owe their origin to the reaction against vedic traditions. These systems do not believe in the testimony of the *Vedas.* The *Charvaka* philosophers have openly criticize the *Vedas.* According to them, the *Vedas* are full of lies and repetitions. The Jainism also do not believe in the *Vedas*. Jainas believe in the words of tirthankaras instead of Vedas. The Buddhist philosophers have also condemned blind faith in the Vedas.

Astika or orthodox systems include six systems namely *Samkhya, Yoga, Nyaya, Vaisesika* and *Vedanta.* Among these systems *Mimamsa* and *Vedanta* directly based on vedic texts. *Mimamsa* emphasizing the ritualistic aspect of the *Vedas,* and *Vedanta* emphasizing the speculative aspect of the Vedas. The *Samkhya* and the *Mimamsa* are atheists. But other four systems are theists. The *Samkhya* advocates dualism of *Prakrti* and *Purusa.* The *Vedanta* advocates spiritualistic monism and recognizes the reality of *Brahman.* The *Nyaya* and *Vaisesika* advocate the reality of God, Plurality of individual souls and the world of diverse objects. The Mimamsa recognizes the reality of individual selves and the self-existent material world, and rejects the concept of God as the creator of the world. The yoga grafts the notion of God on the *Samkhya* dualism of *Prakrti* and *Purusa,* and makes it theistic. So, the other name of yoga philosophy is theistic *Samkhya.*

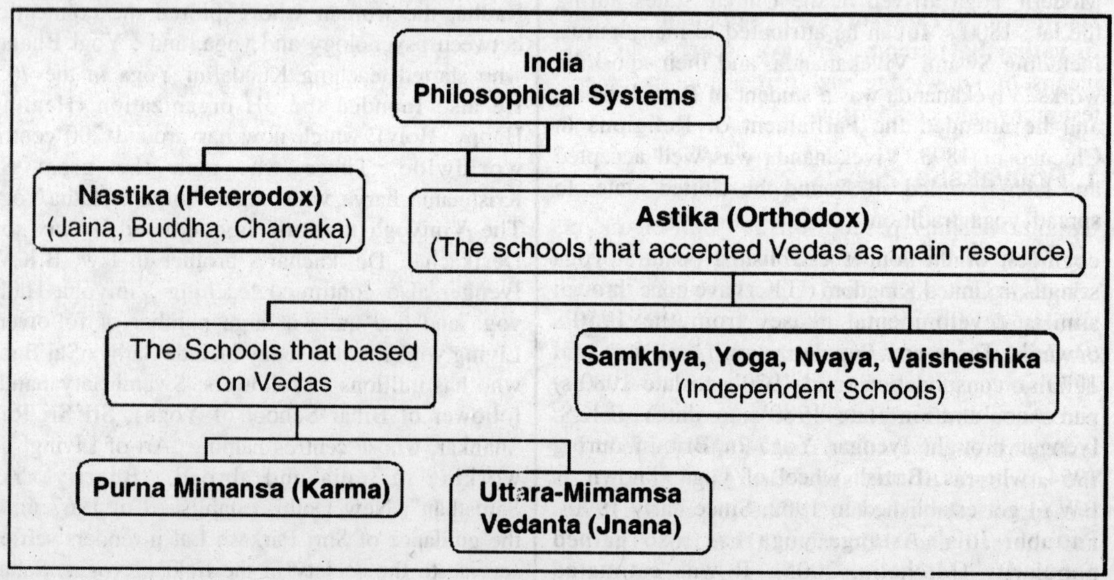

NYAYA PHILOSOPHY

The sage Gotama (*Gautama* or *Akshapada*) is the founder of *Nyaya* school of Indian philosophy. The word *nyaya* means argumentation. *Tarkashastra, Pramanashastra, Vadavidya, Hetuvidya* and *Anvikshiki* are the other names used to denote Nyaya.

Important texts - Gotama's *Nyaya sutra* is the basic text of *nyaya philosophy. Vatsyayana's Nyaya bhashya, Udyotakaras nyayavartika* and *Vachaspati's Tatparyatika* are the other important commentaries and subcommentaries. *Udayana's Nyaya Kusumanjali, Jayanta's Nyaya Manjari* and *Ganesha's Tattvachinthamani* are some of the important texts of this school.

Theory of knowledge

Knowledge, according to Nyaya, reveals both the subject and the object which are quite distinct from itself. This is the reason why Nyaya is called as realist system. Knowledge or cognition is defined as apprehension or consciousness. Knowledge may be valid or invalid. Valid knowledge is called prama and, is defined as the right apprehension of an object. Nyaya maintains the theory of correspondence (Paratah Pramanya.) Non - Valid knowledge is known as aprama. Pramana is valid means of knowledge. **"(Pramakaranam Pramanam – Prama tu yathartha jnanam.)"** Nyaya accepts four valid means of knowledge viz. perception, inference, testimony and comparison.

1. Pratyaksha

Gotama defines perception as 'non-erroneous cognition which is produced by the contact of the sense-organs with the objects, which is not associated with a name and which is well-defined. ***"Indriyartha sannikarsha janyam jnanam."*** This definition includes ordinary as well as extra-ordinary perception and excludes inference, comparison and testimony. Perception is a kind of knowledge and is the attribute of the self. Ordinary perception presupposes the sense-organs, the objects, the manas and the self and their mutual contacts. The self comes into contact with the manas, the manas with the sense-organs and the senseorgans with the objects. The contact of the sense-organs with the objects is not possible unless the manas first comes into contact with the sense-organs, and the contact of the manas with the sense-organs is not possible unless the self comes into contact with the manas. Hence sense-object contact necessarily presupposes the manas-sense contact and the self-manas contact. The sense-organs are derived from the elements whose specific qualities of smell, taste, colour, touch and sound are mani-fested by them. The manas is the mediator between the self and the sense-organs. The external object, through the senses and the manas, makes an impression on the self. The theory, therefore, is realistic.

The Two Stages in Pratyaksha (Savikalpa and Nirvikalpa)

The Nyaya maintains two stages in perception. The first is called inderminate or nirvikalpa and the second, determinate or savikalpa. They are not two different kinds of perception, but only the earlier and the later stages in the same complex process of perception.

All perception is determinate, but is necessarily preceded by an earlier stage when it is indeterminate. Bare sensation or simple apprehension is nirvikalpa perception; perceptual judgement or relational apprehension is savikalpa perception. Perception is a complex indeterminate perception forms the material out of which determinate perception is shaped, but they can be distinguished only in thought and not divided in reality. Nirvikalpa perception is the immediate apprehension, the bare awareness, the direct sense-experience which is undifferentiated and non-relational and is free from assimilation, discrimination, analysis and synthesis. When nirvikalpa perception presents the bare object without any characterization, Savikalpa perception relates the substance with its attributes.

The two kinds of Pratyaksha (Luakika and Alaukika)

Again, according to Nyaya, Pratyaksha is of two kinds, namely, *laukika* (ordinary) and *alaukika* (extraordinary). When the sense-organs come into contact with the object present to them in the usual way, we have Laukika Perception. And if the contact of the sense-organs with the objects is in an unusual way, *i.e.,* if the objects are not ordinarily present to the senses but are conveyed to them through an extraordinary medium, we have Alaukika perception. Ordinary perception is of two kinds - internal (manasa) and external (bahya). In internal perception, the mind (manas) which is the internal organ comes into contact with the psychical states and processes like cognition, affection, conation, desire, pain, pleasure, aversion etc. External perception takes place when the five external organs of sense organs of sight, sound, touch, taste and smell respectively when they come into contact with the external object. The external sense-organs are composed of material elements of earth, water, fire, air and ether and therefore each sense the particular quality of its element. Thus the sense-organ of smell is composed of the atoms of earth and perceives smell which is the specific quality of earth and so on.

Extra-ordinary perception is of three kinds - samanyalakshana, Jnanalakshana and Yogaja. Samanyalakshana perception is the perception of the universals. Jnanalakshana perception is the 'Complicated' perception through association. Sometimes different sensations become associated and form one integrated perception. Here an object is not directly presented to a sense-organ, but is revived in memory through the past cognition of it and is perceived through representation. The theory of illusion accepted by Nyaya called 'Anyata khyati' is based on this kind of perception. The third kind of extra-ordinary perception is called Yogaja perception. This is the intuitive and immediate perception of all objects, past, present and future, possessed by the Yogis through the power of meditation. It is intuitive, supra-sensuous and supra-relational.

2. Anumana

The second kind of knowledge is *anuma* or inferential or relational and its means is called *anumana* or inference. It is defined as that cognition which presupposes some other cognation. It is mediate and indirect and arises through a 'mark', the 'middle term' ***(linga or hetu)*** which is invariably connected with the 'Major term' ***(Sadhya).*** It is knowledge ***(mana)*** which arises after ***(anu)*** other knowledge. ***"Paramarsha janyam jnanam anumitih, Vyaptivishishtapakshadharmata jnanam paramarshah."*** Invariable concomitance ***(vyapti)*** is the nerve of inference. The presence of the middle term in the minor term is called ***pakshadharmata.*** The invariable association of the middle term with the major term is called ***vyapti.*** The knowledge of ***Pakshadharmata*** as qualified by ***vyapti*** is called ***Paramarsha, i.e.,*** the knowledge of the presence of the major in the minor through the middle which resides in the minor (pakshadharmata) and is invariably associated with the major (Vyapti). The major, the minor and the middle are here called ***sadhya, paksha*** and ***linga*** or ***hetu*** respectively.

We know that smoke is invariably associated with fire (Vyapti) and if we see smoke in a hill we conclude that there must be fire in that hill. Hill is the minor term; fire is the major term; smoke is the middle term. We can prove this by explaining the five steps in Nyaya syllogism. The first is called Pratijna or proposition. It is the logical statement which is to be proved. The second is Hetu or the establishment of the proposition. The third is called Udaharana which gives the universal concomitance to the present case. And the fifth is Nigamana or conclusion drawn from the preceding propositions. These five propositions of the Indian Syllogism are called 'Members' or avayavas. The following is a typical Nyaya Syllogism.

1. This hill has fire (Pratijna) ***(Parvatovah-niman).***
2. Because it has smoke (hetu) ***(Dhumat).***
3. Whatever has smoke has fire, e.g., an oven (udaharana) ***yatra yatra dhoomah, tatra tatra vahnih).***
4. This hill has smoke which is invariably associated with fire (upanaya) ***(Tatha chaasau)***
5. Therefore this hill has fire (nigamana) ***(Tasmat tatha).***

Indian logic does not separate deduction from induction. Inference is a complex process involving both.

Classification of Anumana

Inference is generally classified into svartha and parartha. In svartha anumana we do not require formal statements of the members of inference. It is a psychological process. And the pararth anumana, has to be done only to convince other.

Gotama speaks of three kinds of inference - purvavat, sheshavat and samanyatodrshta. The first two are based on causation and the last one on mere coexistence. A cause is the invariable and unconditional antecedent of an effect and an effect is the invariable and unconditional consequent of a cause. When we infer the unperceived effect from a perceived cause we have purvavat inference. When we infer the unperceived cause from a perceived effect we have sheshavat inference. when inference is based not on causation but on uniformity of co-existences; it is called samanyatodrshta.

Another classification of inference gives us the Kevalanvayi, kevalavyatireki and anvayavyatireki inferences. It is based on the nature of Vyapti and on the different methods of establishing it. The methods of induction by which universal casual relationship is established may be anvaya, vyatireka or both. We have kevalanvayi inference when the middle term is always positively related to the major term. The terms agree only in presence, there being no negative instance of their agreement in absence. We have kevala vyatireki inference when the middle term is the differentium of the minor term and is always negatively related to the major term. The terms agree only in absence, there being no positive instance of their agreement in presence. We have anvaya vyatireki inference when the middle term is both positively and negatively related to the major term. The Vyapti between the middle and the major is in respect of both presence and absence.

Hetvabhasa

In Indian logic a fallacy is called Hetvabhasa. It means that middle term appears to be a reason but is not a valid reason. All fallacies are material fallacies. There are five characteristics of a valid middle term. They are the following:

1. It must be present in the minor term (Pakshadharmata); *e.g.*, smoke must be present in the hill.
2. It must be present in all positive instances in which the major term is present; *e.g.*, smoke must be present in the kitchen where fire exists (sapakshasattva).
3. It must be absent in all negative instances in which the major term is absent; *e.g.*, smoke must be absent in the lake in which fire does not exist (vipaksha asattva).
4. It must be non-incompatible with the minor term; *e.g.*, it must not prove the coolness of fire (abaadhita).
5. It must be qualified by the absence of counteracting reasons which lead to a contradictory conclusion; *e.g.*, 'the fact of being caused' should not be used to prove the 'eternality' of sound (aviruddha).

When one of the above mentioned characteristics are violated, we have fallacies.

Five kinds of fallacies are recognized:

1. **Asiddha :** This is the fallacy of the unproved middle. The middle term must be present in the minor term (pakshadharmata). If it is not, it is unproved. It is of three kinds.
   (*a*) **Ashraya asiddha:** The minor term is the locus of the middle term. If the minor term is unreal, the middle term cannot be present in it; *e.g.*, 'the sky-lotus is fragrant, because it is a lotus, like the lotus of a lake'.
   (*b*) **Svarupa asiddha:** Here the minor term is not unreal. But the middle term cannot be its very nature be present in the minor term; *e.g.*, 'sound is a quality, because it is visible'. Here visibility cannot belong to sound which is audible.
   (*c*) **Vyapyatva asidda :** Here Vyapti is conditional (sopadhika). We cannot say, *e.g.*, 'wherever there is fire there is smoke'. Fire smokes only when it is associated with wet fuel. A red-hot iron ball or clear fire does not smoke. Hence 'Association with wet fuel' is a condition necessary to the aforesaid vyapti. Being conditioned, the middle term becomes fallacious if we say: 'The hill has smoke because it has fire'.

2. **Savyabhichara or Anaikantika:** This is fallacy of the irregular middle. It is of three kinds.
   (*a*) **Sadharana:** Here the middle term is too wide. It is present in both the sapaksha (positive) and the vipaksha (negative) instances and violates the rule that the middle should not be present in the negative instances (vipaksha asattva); *e.g.,* 'the hill has fire because it is knowable'. Here 'knowable' is present in fiery as well as non-fiery objects.
   (*b*) **Asadharana:** Here the middle term is too narrow. It is present only in the paksha and neither in the sapaksha not in the vipaksha. It violated the rule that the middle term should be present in the sapaksha (sapakshasattva); *e.g.,* 'sound is eternal, because it is audible'. Here audibility belongs to sound only and is present nowhere else.
   (*c*) **Anupasamhari:** Here the middle term is non-exclusive. The minor term is all-inclusive and leaves nothing by way of sapaksha or vipaksha; *e.g.,* 'all things are non-eternal, because they are knowable'.
3. **Satpratipaksha:** Here the middle term is contradicted by another middle term. The reason is counter-balanced by another reason. And both are of equal force; *e.g.,* 'sound is eternal, because it is audible' and 'sound is non-eternal, because it is produced'. Here 'audible' is counter-balanced by 'produced' and both are of equal force.
4. **Badhita:** It is the non-inferentially contradicted middle. Here the middle term is contradicted by some other pramana and not by inference. It cannot prove the major term which is disproved by another stronger source of valid kowledge; *e.g.,* 'fire is cold, because it is a substance'. Here the middle term 'substance' is directly contradicted by perception.
5. **Viruddha:** It is the contradictory middle. The middle term, instead of being pervaded by the presence of the major term is pervaded by the absence of the major term. Instead of proving the existence of the major term in the minor term, it proves its non-existence therein; e.g., 'sound is eternal, because it is produced'. Here 'Produced', instead of proving the eternality of sound, proves its non-eternality.

Upamana (comparison)

The third kind of valid cognition is Upamiti and its means is called ***Upamana. Samjna-samjnii Sambandhajnanam Upamitih, Tatkaranam Upamanam.*** It is knowledge derived from comparison and roughly corresponds to analogy. It has been defined as the knowledge of the relation between a word and its denotation. It is produced by the knowledge of resemblance or similarity. For example, a man who has never seen a *gavaya* or a wild cow and does not know what it is, is told by a person that wild cow is an animal like a cow, subsequently comes across a wild cow in a forest and recognizes it as the wild cow, then his knowledge is due to upamana.

He has heard the word 'gavaya' and has been told that it is like a cow and now he himself sees the object denoted by the word 'gavaya' and recognizes it to be so. Hence upamana is just the knowledge of the relation between a name and the object denoted by that name. It is produced by the knowledge of similarity because a man recognizes a wild cow as a 'gavaya' when he perceives its similarity to the cow and remembers the description that 'a gavaya is an animal like a cow'.

Shabda (Verbal testimony)

Shabda is valid source, of knowledge in all the systems of Indian Philosophy. Also in the Nyaya system, the fourth kind of valid knowledge is shabda. It is defined, as the statement of a trustworthy person (aptavakya) and consists in understanding its meaning. A sentence is defined as a collection of words and a word is defined as that which is potent to convey its meaning. The power in a word to convey its meaning comes, according to ancient

Nyaya, from God, and according to later Nyaya, from long established convention. Testimony is always personal. It is based on the words of a trustworthy person, human or divine. Testimony is of two kinds - Vaidika and secular (laukika). The Vaidika testimony is perfect and infallible because the Vedas are spoken by God; secular testimony, being the words of human beings who are liable to error, is not infallible. Only the words of trustworthy persons who always speak the truth are valid; others are not. A word is a potent symbol which signifies an object and sentence is a collection of words. But a sentence in order to be intelligible must conform to certain conditions.

These conditions are four - ***akanksha, yogyata, sannidhi*** and ***tatparya.*** The first is mutual implication or expectancy. The words of a sentence are interrelated and stand in need of one another in order to express a complete sense. A mere aggregate of unrelated words will not make a logical sentence. It will be sheer non-sense, e.g., 'cow horse man elephant'. The second condition is that the words should possess fitness to convey the sense and should not contradict the meaning. 'Water the plants with fire' is a contradictory sentence. The third condition is the close proximity of the words to one another. The words must be spoken in quick succession without long intervals. If the words 'bring', 'a' and 'cow' are uttered at long intervals they would not make a logical sentence. The fourth condition is the intention of the speaker if the words are ambiguous. For example, the word 'saindhava' means 'salt' as well as a 'horse'. Now, if a man who is taking his food asks another to bring 'saindhava', the latter should not bring a horse.

GOD

Nyaya accepts the metaphysics of the Vaisheshika School and the accounts of matter, soul and God are almost the same as those in Vaisheshika. The categories, the doctrine of Asatkaryavada, the account of creation and destruction, the nature of atoms and souls, the account of bondage and liberation, the authority of the Veda, the nature and function of God, the Unseen Power - all these are accepted by Nyaya.

Proofs for existence of God

While Kanada himself has not specifically mentioned God, the later Vaisheshikas and particularly the later Naiyayikas have given and elaborate account of God and the latter have made God's Grace and essential thing for obtaining true knowledge of the realities which alone leads to liberation. They refer to God as the creator, maintainer and destroyer of this world and introduce the element of devotion. Nyaya and Vaishika systems give the following nine arguments to prove the existence of God:

1. The world is an effect and hence must have and efficient cause. This intelligent agent is God.
2. The atoms being essentially inactive cannot form the different combinations unless God gives motion to them. The Unseen Power, the Adrshta, requires the intelligence of God. Without God it cannot supply motion to the atoms (Ayojanat).
3. The world is sustained by God's will. Unintelligent Adrshta cannot do this. And the world is destroyed by God's will.
4. A word has a meaning and it signifies an object. The power of words to signify their objects comes from God (Padat).
5. God is the author of the infallible Veda (Pratyayatah).
6. The Veda testifies to the existence of God (sruteh).
7. The Vedic sentences deal with moral injunctions and prohibitions. The Vedic commands are the Divine commands. God is the creator and promulgator of the moral laws.
8. According to Nyaya-Vaisheshika the magnitude of a dyad is not produced by the infinitesimal magnitude of the two atoms each, but by the number of the two atoms. Number 'one' is directly perceived, but other numbers are conceptual creations. Numerical conception is related to the mind of the perceiver. At the time of creation, the souls are unconscious. And the atoms and the Unseen Power and space, time, minds are all

unconscious. Hence the numerical conception depends upon the Divine Consciousness. So God must exist (Sankhyavisheshat)

9. We reap the fruits of our own actions. Merit and demerit accrue from our actions and the stock of merit and demerit is called Adrshta, the Unseen Power. But this Unseen Power, being unintelligent, needs the guidance of a supremely intelligent God (Adrshtat).

SOUL

The law of causation is subservient to the law of Karma. The Nyaya like the Vaisheshika, believes in teleological creation. The material cause of this universe is the eternal atoms of earth, water, fire and air and the efficient cause is God. The infinite individual souls are co-eternal with atoms. And God is co-eternal with atoms and souls and external to both. Nyaya advocates atomism, spiritualism, theism, realism, and pluralism. Creation means combination of atoms and destruction means dissolution of these combinations through the motion supplied to or withdrawn from the atoms by the unseen power working under the guidance of God.

The individual soul is regarded as the substratum of the quality of consciousness which is not the essence God but only an accidental potency. The soul is a real knower, a read enjoyer and a real active agent and an eternal substance. It is not transcendental consciousness and it is different from God who is the supreme soul. Cognitions, affections and conations are the attributes of the soul which is one, part less and all pervading. Each soul has its manas during its empirical life. It is distinct from the body, the senses and the mind. Bondage is due to ignorance and karma. Liberation is due to knowledge and destruction of karma.

VAISHESHIKA PHILOSOPHY

The word Vaisheshika is derived from the word 'Vishesha' which means particularity or distinguishing feature or distinction. The Vaisheshika philosophy, therefore, is pluralistic realism which emphasizes that diversity is the soul of the universe. In origin it comes next to Samkhya and is of greater antiquity than Nyaya. The category of Vishesha or particularity is dealt with at length in this system, and is regarded as the essence of things. The founder of this system is Kanada who is also known as Kanabhuk, Uluka and Kashyapa. He was called Kanada because he used to live as an ascetic on the grains picked up from the fields. Kana (in addition to the meaning grain) also means a particle or a particular and the word Kanada suggests one who lives on the philosophy of particularity - Vishesha.

This system of philosophy was, later on, fused together with the Nyaya which accepts the ontology of the former and developed it in the light of its own epistemology.

Important texts — Kanada's Vaisheshikasutra is the basic text of Vaisheshika philosophy. On this work Prasasta pada has written Padartadharmasamgraha commentary. It is really considered as a valuable independent treatise hence is commented upon by Udayana and Shridhara. The Vaisheshika was later on, fused together with the Nyaya which accepted the ontology out the former and developed it in the light of its epistemology. Thus Shivaditya, Laugakshi Bhaskara, Viswanatha and Annambhatha treat the two systems together.

Padartha

In Vaisheshika philosophy, a category is called padartha and the entire universe is reduced to six or seven padarthas. Padartha literally means 'the meaning of a word' or 'the object signified by a word'. All objects which can be thought (jneya) and named (abhidheya) come under the term padartha.

Originally the Vaisheshika believed in the six categories and the seventh, that of abhava or negation, was added later on. Though Kanada himself speaks of abhava, yet he does not give it the status of a category to which it was raised only by the later Vaisheshikas. The Vaisheshika divides all existent reals which are all objects of knowledge into two classes - bhava or being and abhava or non-being. Six categories come under bhava and the seventh is abhava. All knowledge necessarily points to an object beyond and independent of it.

All that is real comes under the object of knowledge and is called a padartha. The seven Padarthas are :

1. Substance (Dravya)
2. Quality (Guna)
3. Action (Karma)
4. Generality (Samanya)
5. Particularity (Vishesha)
6. Inherence (Samavaya), and
8. Non-being (Abhava).

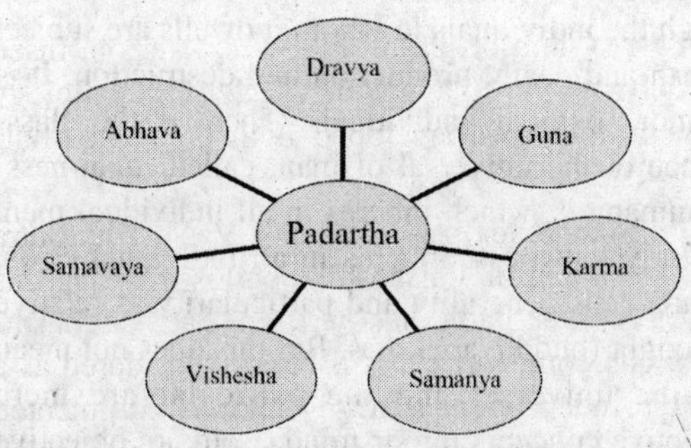

Substance (Dravya)

Substance (dravya) signifies the self-subsistence, the absolute and independent nature of things. Therefore, it is defined as the substratum of actions and qualities and which is the co-existent material cause of the composite things produced from it. Without substance, we cannot have qualities and actions for they cannot hang loose in the air, but must be contained somewhere. Substance is the basis of qualities and actions. Ultimate substances are eternal, independent and individual and are either infinite or infinitesimal. All compound substances (avayavidravya) which are made of parts and arise out of the simple ultimate substance are necessarily transient and impermanent and subject to production and destruction. But simple ultimate substances which are the material causes of the compound substances are eternal and not subject to production and destruction. The dravyas are nine and include material as well as spiritual substances. The Vaisheshika philosophy is pluralistic and realistic but not materialistic since it admits spiritual substances.

The nine substances are:

1. Earth (Prithivi)
2. Water (Ap)
3. Fire (Tejas)
4. Air (Vayu)
5. Ether (Akasha)
6. Time (Kala)
7. Space (Dik)
8. Spirit (Atman) and
9. Mind or the internal organ (Manas).

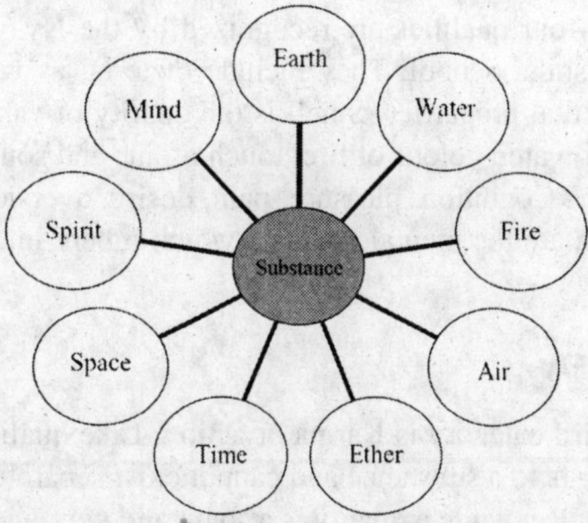

All of them are objective realities. Earth, water, fire, air and manas are atomic and eternal. The first four produce composite things; manas does not. Earth, water, fire, air and ether are the five gross elements. These and manas are physical. Soul is spiritual. Time and space are objective and not subjective forms of experience. Ether, space, time and soul are all - pervading and eternal. Atoms, minds and souls are infinite in number. Ether, space and time are one each.

GUNA

Quality or guna is the second category of Vaisheshikas. Unlike substance, it cannot exist independently by itself and possesses no quality or action. It depends for its existence on the substance and is not a constitutive cause of anything. It is called and independent reality because it can be conceived (Prameya), thought (jneya) and named (abhidheya) independently of a substance where it dwell in. The qualities are therefore called objective entities. They are not necessarily eternal. They include both material and mental qualities. They are a static and permanent feature of a substance, while action is a dynamic and transient feature of a substance. A quality therefore is different from both substance and action. It is defined by Kanada as 'that which dwells in a substance, which does not possess quality of action, which does not produce any composite thing, and which is not the cause of conjunction and disjunction like and action'.

Kanada mentions seventeen qualities to which seven more are added by Prashastapada. These twenty-four qualities are recognized by the Nyaya-Vaisheshika School. They include material as well as spiritual properties. Smell is the quality of earth; taste of water; colour of fire; touch of air; and sound of ether. Cognition, pleasure, pain, desire, aversion, volition are the mental qualities which inhere in the self.

KARMA

The third category is Karma or action. Like quality, it belongs to a substance and cannot exist separately from it. But while a quality is a static and permanent feature of a substance, an action is a dynamic and transient feature of it. Unlike a quality, and action is the cause of conjunction and disjunction. Action is said to be of five kinds: (1) upward movement (Utkshpana), (2) downward movement (Avakshepana), (3) contraction (Akunchana), (4) expansion (Prasarana), and (5) locomotion (Gamana).

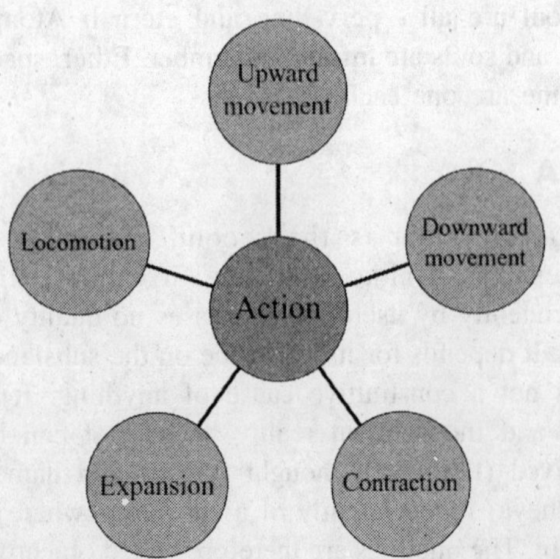

SAMANYA

The fourth category is Samanya or generality. It is class-concept, class-essence or universal. It is the common character of the things which fall under the same class. The Samanya stands for the common characteristic of certain individuals and does not include the sub-classes. It is the universal by the possession of which different individuals are referred to as belonging to one class. It is called eternal, one and residing in many. It is one, though the individuals in whom it resides are many. It is eternal, though the individuals in whom it dwells are subject to birth and death, production and destruction. It is common to many individuals. There is the class-essence of the universal of man, called 'man-ness' of 'humanity', which inheres in all individual men. Similarly 'cowness' inheres in all individual cows. Kanada calls generality and particularity as relative to thought (buddhyapeksha). But this does not mean that the universal and the particular are mere subjective concepts in our mind. Both are objective realities. The universals reside in substances, qualities and action. They are of two kinds, higher and lower.

The Nyaya-Vaisheshika School is an advocate of realism. It believes that both the particulars and the universals are separately real.

VISHESHA

The fifth category is Vishesha or Particularity. It enables us to perceive things as different from one another. Particularity is exclusive. Generality form the basis of assimilation; particularity forms the basis of discrimination. It is very important to remember that the composite objects of this world which we generally call 'particular' objects, are not real 'particulars' according to Nyaya-Vaisheshika. The category of Vishesha or particularity is invented to defend this position. Each part less ultimate substance has an original peculiarity of its own, and underived uniqueness of its own which is called 'particularity' or Vishesha. Vishesha, therefore, is the distinguishing factor (vyavartaka) of ultimate eternal substances (nitysdravyavrtti) which are otherwise alike. There are innumerable eternal Visheshas. They distinguish the substances where they inhere from other substances and they also distinguish themselves from other particularities. Though they, like qualities and actions, inhere in the substances, yet they are a distinct category. The Vaisheshika emphasizes realistic pluralism. Atoms, souls, space, time and manas all have their particularities.

SAMAVAYA

Samavaya is different from conjunction or samyoga which is a separable and transient relation and is a quality (guna). Samavaya is an independent category (padartha) which means an inseparable eternal, relation or inherence. Kanada calls it the relation between cause and effect. Prashastapada defines it as 'the relationship subsisting among things that are inseparable, standing to one another in the relation of container and the contained, and being the basis of the idea, "this is in that". The things related by samavaya are inseparably connected (ayutasiddha). It is inseparable relationship'. It is eternal because its production would involve infinite regress. It is imperceptible and inferred from the inseparable relation of two things. The things which are inseparably connected are these: the part and whole, the quality and the substance, the action and the substance, the particular and the universal, the Vishesha and the eternal substance. Samavaya is found in these. The whole inheres in the parts; a quality inheres in its substance; an action inheres in its substance; the universal inheres in the individual members of the same class; the particularity (vishesha) inheres in its eternal substance. Samavaya is one and eternal relationship subsisting between two things inseparably connected.

ABHAVA

The seventh category is Abhava or non-existence. Kanada does not mention this as a separate category. It is added afterwards. The first six categories are positive. This is negative. The other categories are regarded as absolute, but this category is relative in its conception. Absence of an object and knowledge of its absence are different. Non-existence is of four kinds:

1. Antecedent non-existence (pragabhaava),
2. Subsequent non-existence (pradhvamsaabhaava),
3. Mutual non-existence (anyonyaabhaava) and
4. Absolute non-existence (atyantaabhaava).

The first is the non-existence of a thing before its production. The second is the non-existence of a thing after its destruction. The third is the non-existence of a thing as another things which is different from it. The fourth is the absence of a relation between two things in the past, the present and the future. Antecedent negation has no beginning, but has no end. It begins when the things is destroyed and has no end since the same thing cannot be produced again. Mutual negation is exclusion and is opposed to identity. It is both beginnings and endless. Absolute negation is a pseudo-idea. It is both beginningless and endless. Hare's horn, barren woman's child, sky-flower etc. are its classical examples. Mutual negation or anyonyaabhva means non-existence of a thing as another thing. The other three negations-antecedent, subsequent and absolute - are called non-existence of correlation or Samsargaabhaava which implies the non-existence of something in something else. If antecedent negation is denied, then all things would become beginningless; if subsequent negation is denied, then all things would become eternal; if mutual negation is denied, then all things would become indistinguishable; and if absolute negation is denied, then all things would exist always and everywhere.

PARAMANUVADA OR ATOMISM

According to Nyaya-Vaisheshika philosophy, the effect does not pre-exist in its cause (Asatkaryavada), but, is a new beginning, a fresh creation (Arambhvada). Of course, the effect presupposes a cause. But it is, not contained implicitly in the cause nor is it identical with the cause. The doctrine is also known as Paramanukaranavada. We find that the material object of the world are composed of parts and are subject to production and destruction. They are divisible into smaller parts and the latter are further divisible into still smaller parts. By this logic we have to accept the minutest particle of matter which may not be further divisible. This indivisible, part less and eternal particle of matter is called an atom (paramanu).

All physical things are produced by the combination of atoms. Creation, therefore, means the combination of atoms in different proportions and destruction means the dissolution of such combinations. The material cause of the universe is neither produced nor destroyed, it is the eternal atoms. It is only the atomic the essential nature of the atoms nor do they pre-exist in them. Hence the Nyaya-Vaisheshika advocates Asatkaryavada.

The atoms are said to be of four kinds — of earth, water, fire and air. These atoms combine in geometrical progression and not in arithmetical one. They increase by multiplication and not by mere addition. When motion is imparted to them by the Unseen Power, they begin to vibrate (parispanda) and immediately change into combination. A dyad is produced by the combination of two atoms. The atoms are its inherent cause; conjunction is its non-inherent cause; and the Unseen Power is its efficient cause. An atom is indivisible, spherical and imperceptible. A dyad (dvyanuka) is minute (anu), short (hrasva), and imperceptible. Three dyads form a triad (tryanuka) which is great (mahat), long (dirgha) and perceptible. And so on by geometrical progression till the gross elements of earth, water, fire and air arise.

The Vaisheshika Atomism is not materialistic because the Vaisheshika School admits the reality of the spiritual substances - souls and God - and also admits the Law of Karma. The atoms are the material cause of this world of which God, assisted by the Unseen Power, is the efficient cause. The physical world presupposes the moral order. Evolution is due to the Unseen Power consisting of merits and demerits of the individual souls which want to bear fruits as enjoyments or sufferings to be experienced by the souls.

CAUSATION (ASATKARYAVADA)

A cause is defined as an unconditional and invariable antecedent of an effect and an effect as an unconditional and invariable consequent of a cause. The same cause produces the same effect and the same effect is produced by the same cause. Plurality of causes is ruled out. The first essential characteristic of a cause is its antecedence; the fact that it should precede the effect (Purvavarti). The second is its invariability; it must invariably precede the effect (Ananyathasiddha). Unconditional antecedence is immediate and direct antecedence and excludes the fallacy of remote cause.

An effect (karya) is defined as the 'counter-entity of its own prior non - existence' (Pragabhaava-pratiyogi). It is the negation of its own prior-negation. It comes into being and destroys its prior non-existence. It was non-existent before its production. It did not pre-exist in its cause. It is a fresh beginning, a new creation. This Nyaya-Vaisheshik view of causation is directly opposed to the Samkhys - Yoga and Vedanta view of satkaryavada. It is called asatkaryavada or arambhavada. The effect is distinct from its cause and can never be identical with it. It is neither an appearance nor a transformation of the cause. It is newly brought into existence by the operation of the cause.

There are three kinds of causes - **Samavayi, Asamavayi** and **Nimitta.** The first is the Samavayi or the inherent cause, also called as the upadana or the material cause. It is the substance out of which the effect is produced. For example, the threads are the inherent cause of the cloth and the clay is the inherent cause of a pot. The effect inheres in its material cause. The cloth inheres in the threads. The effect cannot exist separately from its material cause, though the cause can exist independently of its effect. The material cause is always a substance (dravya). The second kind of cause is asamavayi or non-inherent. It inheres in the material cause and helps the production of the effect. The conjunction of the threads (tantusamyoga) which inheres in the threads is the non-inherent cause of the cloth of which the threads are the material or the inherent cause. The colour of the threads (tanturupa) is the non-inherent cause of the colour of the cloth. The cloth itself is the inherent cause of its colour. The effect as well as its non-inherent cause both co-inhere in the material cause. The non-inherent cause is always a quality or an action (guna or karma). The third kind of cause is nimitta or efficient. It is the power which helps the material cause to produce the effect. The weaver is the efficient cause of the cloth. The efficient cause includes the accessories (sahakari), e.g., the loom and shuttle of the weaver or the staff and wheel of the potter. The efficient cause may be a substance, a quality or an action.

GOD

The Vaisheshika believes in the authority of the veda and in the moral law of Karma. Kanada himself does not openly refer to God. His aphorism - The authority of the Veda is due to its being His (or their) word ***(tadvachanad aamnaayasya Pranamyam)*** has been interpreted by the commentators in the sense that the Veda is the word of God. But the expression 'Tadvachana' may also be meaning that the Veda is the word of the seers. But all great writers of the Nyaya-Vaisheshika systems including Prasastapada, Shridhara and Udayana are openly theistic and some of them give classical arguments to prove the existence of God. God is omniscient, eternal and perfect. He is the Lord. He is guide by the law of Karma representing the unseen power is unintelligent and needs God as the Supervisor or controller. He is the efficient Cause of the world of which the eternal atoms are the material Cause.

BONDAGE AND LIBERATION

The Vaisheshika also regards bondage as due to ignorance and liberation as due to knowledge. The soul, due to ignorance, performs actions. Action leads to merits and demerits. These merits and demerits of the individual souls make up the unseen moral power, the adrshta. According to the law of Karma, one has to reap the fruits of actions he has performed. The Adrshta, guided by God, imparts motion to the atoms and leads to creation for the sake of enjoyment or suffering of the individual souls.

As long as the soul will go on performing actions, it will be bound. To get rid of bondage, the soul must stop actions. Liberation comes through knowledge. Liberation is the cessation of all life; all consciousness, all bliss, together with all pain and all qualities. It is quality less, indeterminate, pure nature of the Individual soul as pure substance devoid of all qualities. The liberated soul remains its own peculiar individuality and particularity and remains as it is.

Atomic pluralism proposed by the Vaisheshika School can be cited as an important stage of the development of Indian philosophy. It emphasizes the scientific thinking and is an advance on the materialistic standpoint. The acceptance of negation as a separate category, and the recognition of inherence are the two real advances made by the vaisheshika system.

SAMKHYA PHILOSOPHY

Samkhya is undoubtedly one of the oldest systems of Indian Philosophy. It occupies a unique place among the six systems of Indian Philosophy. All most all branches of literature like Srutis, Smritis and Puranas reflect the influence of Samkhya Philosophy. This system is sometimes, described as the 'atheistic Samkhya' as distinguished from Yoga Philosophy, which is called 'theistic Samkhya'. This system is accepted as the main opponent (pradhana malla) of vedantha philosophy.

Tradition regards Kapila as the founder of this System. Kapila, Asuri, and Panchashikha were the earlier acharyas of this system. Kapila certainly flourished before Buddha and he must have composed Samkhya-Sutra, which was unfortunately lost long ago. Samkhya pravachana sutra attributed to Kapila is assumed to have a later origin. Ishwarakrishna's Samkhyakarika seems to be the earliest available and the most popular work of this system.

Guadapada's SamkhyKarikabhashya, Vachaspati Misra's SamkhyaTattva-kaumudi and Vijnabikshu's Samkhyapravachana Bhashya are the other important works of the system.

The Word Samkhya is derived from the word 'Samkhya' which means right knowledge as well as number. The Bhagavad Gita used the word in the sense of knowledge. Samkhya is also the philosophy of the numbers, because it deals with twenty five categories. Samkhya maintains a clear-cut dualism between purusha and prakrti and further maintains the plurality of Purusha, and is silent on God. It is a pluralistic spiritualism and an atheistic realism and uncompromising dualism.

Theory of Causation - Satkarya Vada

The Samkhya theory of causation is 'Parinama Vada'. The Samkhya system believes in Satkarya Vada that the effects is not a new creation, it pre-exists in its material cause. The effect is only an explicit manifestation of that which was implicitly contained in its material cause. According to Samkhya theory the effect is a real transformation of its cause and it is called Parinama Vada. (Parinama - Real Modification). The view of Samkhya- Yoga is called Prakrtiparinama Vada.

Samkhya believes in Satkarya Vada. All the material effects are the modifications (parinama) of Prakrti. They pre-exist in the eternal bosom of Prakrti and simply come out of it at the time of creation and return to it at the time of dissolution. There is neither new production nor utter destruction. Production means development or manifestation (avirbhava); destruction means envelopment or dissolution (tirobhava). Samkhya gives five agreements in support of Satkaryavada.

1. If the effect does not pre-exist in its cause, it becomes a mere non-entity like the hare's horn or the sky-flower and can never be produced ***(Asadakaranat).***
2. The effect is only a manifestation of its material cause, because it is invariably connected with it ***(Upadanagrahanat).***
3. Everything cannot be produced out of everything. This suggests that the effect, before its manifestation, is implicit in its material cause ***(Sarvasambhavabhavat).***
4. Only an efficient cause can produce that for which it is potent. This again means that the effect, before its manifestation, is potentially contained in its material cause. Production is only an actualization of the potential ***(saktasya sakyakaranat.)*** Were it not so, then curd should be produced out of water, and cloth out of reeds, and, oil out of sand particles.
5. The effect is the essence of its material cause and as such identical with it. When the obstructions in the way of manifestation are removed, the effect naturally flows out of its cause. The cause and the effect are the implicit and the explicit stages of the same process. The cloth is contained in the threads, the oil in the oil-seeds, and the curd in the milk. The effect pre-exists in its material cause ***(Karanabhavat).***

PRAKRTI

The system of Samkhya accepts Prakrti as the root-cause of the world of objects. All worldly effects are latent in this uncaused cause, because infinite regress has to be avoided. It is the potentiality of nature, 'the receptacle and nurse of all generation'. As the uncaused root-cause, it is called Prakrti; as the first principle of this Universe, it is called Pradhana; as the unmanifested state of all effects, it is known as Avyakta; as the extremely subtle and imperceptible thing which is only inferred from its products, it is called Anumana; as the unintelligent and unconscious principle, it is called Jada; and as the ever-active unlimited power, it is called shakti. The products are caused, dependent, relative, many and temporary as they are subject to birth and death or to production and destruction; but Prakrti is uncaused, independent, absolute, one and eternal, being beyond production and destruction. Prakrti alone is the final source of this world of objects which is implicitly and potentially contained in its bosom.

Samkhya gives five proofs for the existence of Prakrti as follows:

1. All individual things in this world are limited, dependent, conditional and finite. The Finite cannot be the cause of the

universe. Logically we have to proceed from the finite to the infinite, from the limited to the unlimited, from the many to the one. And it is this infinite, unlimited, eternal and all pervading Prakrti which is the source of this universe ***(Bhedanam parimanat).***

2. All worldly things possess certain common characteristics by which they are capable of producing pleasure, pain and indifference. Hence there must be a common source composed of three Gunas, from which all worldly things arise ***(Samanvayat).***
3. All effects arise from the activity of the potent cause. Evolution means the manifestation of the hitherto implicit as the explicit. The activity which generates evolution must be inherent in the world-cause. And this cause is Prakrti ***(Karyatah Pravrttescha).***
4. The effect differs from the cause and hence the limited effect cannot be regarded as its own cause. The effect is the explicit and the cause is the implicit state of the same process. The effects, therefore, point to a world-cause where they are potentially contained ***(Karanakaryavibhagat)***
5. The unity of the universe points to a single cause. And this cause is Prakrti. ***(Avibhagat vaishvarupyasya).***

Prakrti is said to be the unity of the three Gunas held in equilibrium (gunanam samyavastha). The three Gunas are Sattva, Rajas and Tamas. When these gunas are held in a state of equilibrium, that state is called Prakrti. Evolution of worldly objects does not take place at this state. These gunas are said to be ever-changing, they cannot remain static even for a moment. Change is said to be of two kinds-homogeneous or Sarupa-parinama and heterogeneous or Virupa-parinama. During the state of dissolution (pralaya) of the world, the gunas change homogeneously, *i.e.,* sattva changes into sattva, rajas into rajas and tamas into tamas. This change does not disturb the equilibrium of the gunas and unless the equilibrium is disturbed and one predominates over the other two, evolution cannot take place. Evolution starts when there is heterogeneous change in the gunas and one predominates over the other two and brings about terrific commotion in the bossom of Prakrti.

The Evolutes

The first product of the evolution is called Mahat, the great. It is the germ of this vast world of objects including intellect, ego and mind. It is cosmic in its nature. But it has a psychological aspect also in which it is called buddhi or intellect. Buddhi is distinguished from consciousness. Purusha alone is pure consciousness. Buddhi or intellect, being the evolute of Prakrti, is material. Its functions are said to be ascertainment and decision. It arises when sattva predominates. Its original attributes are virtue (dharma), knowledge (jnana), detachment (vairagya) and power (aishvarya). When it gets vitiated by tamas these, attributes are replaced by their opposites. Memories and recollections are stored in buddhi.

Mahat produces Ahankara. It is the principle of individuation. Its function is to generate self sense (abhimana). It Produces the notion of the 'I' and the 'mine'. It is the individual ego-sense. Purusha wrongly identifies himself with this ego and knows himself as the agent of actions, desirer of desires and striver for ends, and possessor and enjoyer of ideas, emotions and volitions and also of material objects. Ahankara is said to be of three kinds:

1. Vaikarika or sattvika, when sattva predominates.
2. Bhetadi or tamasa, when tamas predominates.
3. Taijasa or rajasa, when rajas predominates.

Manas or mind which arises from the Sattvika Ahankara is the subtle and central sense-organ. It can come into contact with the several sense organs at the same time. The Sattvika Ahankara produces, besides manas, the five sensory and the five motor organs. The five sensory organs (jnanendriya) are the function of sight, smell, taste, touch and sound. Buddhi, Ahankara and manas represent the three psychological aspects of knowing, willing and feeling or cognition, conation and affection respectively. Samkhya calls them material and derives them from Prakrti. From the Tamasa Ahankara arise the five subtle essences which are called Tanmatras or 'things-in-themselves'. These are the essences of sight, smell, taste, touch and sound. From these tanmatras five Mahabhutas of earth, water, fire, air and ether are produced. Evolution is the play of these twenty-four principles which, together with the Purusha who is a mere spectator and outside the play of evolution, are the twenty-five categories of Samkhya.

Out of these twenty-five principles, the Purusha is neither a cause nor an effect; Mahat, Ahankara and the five subtle essences are both causes and effects; while the five sensory and the five motor organs and the five gross elements and manas are effects only. The whole process of evolution can be represented as follows.

The Steps of Evolution

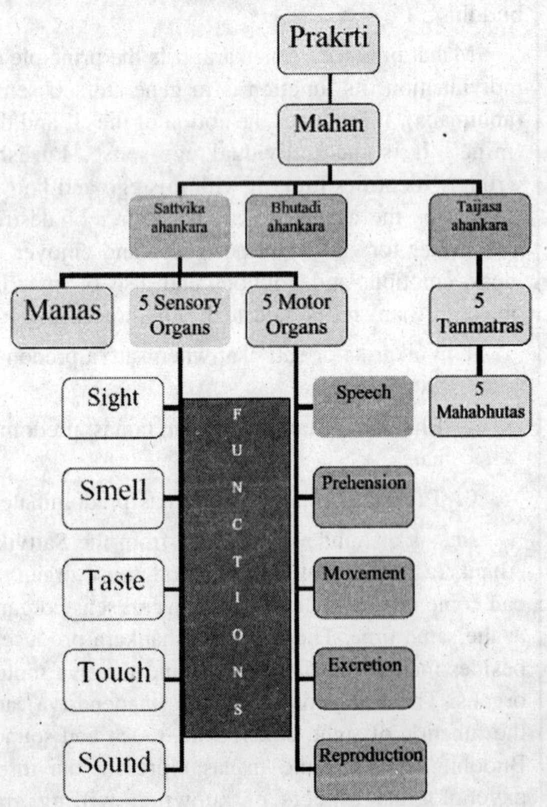

Purusha

The other of the two co-present co-eternal realities of Samkhya is the Purusha, the Principal of pure consciousness. Purusha is the soul, the self, the spirit, the subject, the knower. It is neither body nor senses nor brain nor mind (manas) nor ego (ahankara) nor intellect (buddhi). It is not a substance which possesses the quality of Consciousness. Consciousness is the essence. It is itself pure and transcendental Consciousness. It is ultimate knower which is the foundation of all knowledge. It is the pure subject and as such can never become an object of knowledge. It is the silent witness, the emancipated alone, the neutral seer, the peaceful eternal. It is beyond time and space, beyond change and activity. It is self-luminous and self-proved. It is uncaused, eternal and all pervading. It is the indubitable real, the postulate of knowledge, and all doubles and denials pre-suppose its existence. It is called nistraigunya, udasina, akarta, kevela, madhyastha, saksi, drashta, sadaprakashasvarupa, and Jnata.

The Samkhya believes in the plurality of the Purusha. The selves are all essentially alike; only numerically are they different. Their essence is consciousness. Bliss is regarded as different form consciousness and is the product of the sattvaguna.

Proofs for the existence of Purusha

Samkhya gives the following Proofs for the existence of the Purusha

1. All compound objects exist for the sake of the Purusha. The body, the senses, the mind and the intellect are all means to realize the end of the Purusha. The three gunas, the Prakrti, the subtle body - all are said to serve the purpose of the self. Evolution is teleological or purposive. Prakrti evolves itself in order to serve the Purusha's end. This proof is teleological ***(Samghataparar-thatvat).***
2. All objects are composed of the three gunas and therefore logically presuppose the existence of the Purusha who is the witness of these gunas and is himself beyond them.

The three gunas imply the conception of a nistraigunya - that which is beyond them. This proof is logical ***(Trigunadiviparyayat).***

3. There must be a transcendental synthetic unity of pure consciousness to co-ordinate all experience. All knowledge necessarily presupposes the existence of the self. The self is the foundation **(Adhishthanat).**
4. Non-intelligent Prakrti cannot experience its products. So there must be an intelligent principle to experience the worldly products of Prakrti. Prakrti is the enjoyed (bhogya) and so there must be an enjoyer (bhokta), *i.e.,* Purusha ***(bhoktrbhavat).***
5. There are persons who toy to attain release from the sufferings of the world. The desire for liberation implies the existence of a person who can try for liberation. ***(Kaivalyartham Pravrtteh).***

Proofs for the plurality of Purusha

Samkhya gives the following three arguments for proving the plurality of the Prursha.

1. The souls have different sensory and motor organs and undergo separate births and deaths. Had there been only one Purusha, the birth or death of one should have meant the birth or death of all and any particular experience of pleasure, pain or indifference by one should have been equally shared by all. Hence the souls must be many.
2. If the self were one, bondage of one should have meant bondage of all and the liberation of one should have meant the liberation of all. The activity of one should have made all persons active and the sleep of one should have lulled into sleep all other persons.
3. Though the emancipated souls are all like and differ only in number as they are all beyond the three gunas, yet the bound souls relatively differ in qualities. Also, since in some sattva predominates, while in others rajas, and in still others tamas.

Purusha and Prakrti

The evolution is teleological; everything works to serve the purpose of the Purusha though unconsciously. Just as non-intelligent trees grow fruits, or water flows on account of the declivity of the soil, or iron filings are attracted towards a magnet, or mils flows through the udders of the cow in order to nourish the calf, everything unconsciously tends to serve the purpose of the Purusha, whether it is enjoyment or liberation. Prakrti is the benefactress of Purusha. Though Purusha is inactive and indifferent and devoid of qualities, the virtuous and the generous Prakrti which is full of qualities and goodness ceaselessly works through various means in a spirit of detachment for the realization of the Purusha. Without any benefit to herself, Prakrti works to liberate the Purusha. There is immanent teleology in Prakrti. Though Purusha is neither a cause nor an effect, yet relatively it is he who should be regarded as the efficient cause as well as the final cause of evolution, though Samkhya regards Prakrti as both the material and the efficient cause. He is the unmoved mover who is beyond evolution. He is the end towards which the creation moves. And the creation moves by his mere presence.

The gunas, which mutually differ and yet always cooperate, work like the oil, wick and flame of a lamp and illuminate the entire purpose of the Purusha and present it to the buddhi or the intellect. All the organs work for the realization of the Purusha's end and for no other end. The subtle body too works for the sake of the Purusha's end. Thus the whole creation unconsciously tends towards the realization of the purpose of the Purusha. And creation will continue till all the Purusha are liberated. The entire evolution of Prakrti, therefore, right from the first evolute, the Mahat, up to the last evolutes, the gross elements, is for the purpose of liberating each individual Purusha.

Bondage and liberation

The earthly life is full of three kinds of pain. The first kind, called adhyatmika, is due to intra-organic psychophysical causes and includes, all mental and bodily sufferings. The second, adhibhautika, is due to extra-organic natural causes like men, beasts, birds, thorns etc. The third, adhidaivika, is due to supernatural causes like the planets, elemental agencies, ghosts, demons etc. Wherever there are gunas, there are pains. Even the so-called pleasures lead to pain. Even the life in heaven is subject to the gunas. The end of man is to get rid of these kinds of pain and sufferings. Liberation means complete cessation of all sufferings which is the summum bonum, the highest end of life (Apavarga or Purushartha).

Purusha is free and pure consciousness. It is inactive, indifferent and possesses no attributes. Really speaking, it is above time and space, merit and demerit, bondage and liberation. It is only when it mistakes its reflection in the buddhi for itself and identifies itself wrongly with the internal organ the intellect, the ego and the mind, that it is said to be bound. It is the ego, and not the Purusha, which is bound. When the Purusha realizes its own pure nature it gets liberated which in fact it always was. Hence bondage is due to ignorance or non-discrimination between the self and the not-self. Liberation cannot be obtained by means of actions. Karma, good or bad or indifferent, is the function of the gunas and leads to bondage and not to liberation. Good actions may lead to heaven and bad actions to hell but heaven and hell alike, like this worldly life, are subject to pain. It is only knowledge which leads to liberation because bondage is due to ignorance and ignorance can be removed only by knowledge.

Samkhya admits both Jivanmukti and Vedehamukti. The moment right knowledge dawns, the person becomes liberated here and now, even though he may be embodied due to prarabdha Karma.

The final and the absolute emancipation, the complete disembodied isolation automatically results after death. Samkhya liberation is a state of complete isolation, freedom from all pain, a return of the Purusha to its pure nature is consciousness. There is no pleasure or happiness or bliss here, for pleasure presupposes pain and is relative to it. Pleasure is the result of sattva guna and liberation transcends all gunas.

Samkhya believes that bondage and liberation alike are only phenomenal. The bondage of the Purusha is a fiction. It is only the ego, the product of Prakrti, which is bound. And consequently it is only the ego which is liberated. Purusha, in its complete isolation, is untouched by bondage and liberation. If Purusha were really bound, it could not have obtained liberation even after hundred births, for real bondage can never be destroyed. It is Prakrti which is bound and Prakrti which is liberated.

God

The Original Samkhya was monistic and theistic. But the classical Samkhya, perhaps under the influence of Materialism, Jainism and Early Buddhism, became atheistic. It is orthodox because it believes in the authority of the Veda. It does not establish the non-existence of God. It only shows that Prakrti and Purusha are sufficient to explain this universe and therefore there is no reason for postulating a hypothesis of God. But some commentators have tried to repudiate the existence of God, while the later Samkhya writers like Vijnanabhikshu have tried to revive the necessity for admitting God. Those who repudiate the existence of God give the following arguments: if God is affected by selfish motives, he is not free; if He is free, he will not create this world of pain and misery.

Either God is unjust and cruel or He is not free and all-powerful. If he is determined by the law of Karma, he is not free; if not, he is a tyrant. Again, God being pure knowledge, this material world cannot spring from Him. The effects are implicitly contained in their cause and the material world which is subject to change requires an unintelligent and ever-changing cause and not a spiritual and immutable God. Again, the eternal existence of the Purusha is inconsistent with God. If they are the parts of God, they must have some divine power, if they are created by God, they are subject to destruction. Hence there is no God.

YOGA PHILOSOPHY

Patanjali is the traditional founder of the Yoga System and is regarded as the complement of Samkhya. The word 'Yoga' literally means 'Union', *i.e.,* spiritual union of the Individual soul with the universal soul and is used in this sense in the Vedantha. The Bhagavad Gita defines Yoga as that state in which there is nothing higher or worth realizing and firmly rooted in which a person is never shaken even by the greatest pain; that state free from all pain and misery is yoga. According to Patanjali, Yoga does not mean union, but spiritual effort to attain perfection through the control of the body, senses and mind, and through right discrimination between Purusha and Prakrti.

Yoga is intimately allied to Samkhya. Yoga means spiritual action and Samkhya means knowledge. Samkhya is theory; Yoga is practice. For all practical purposes, Samkhya and Yoga may be treated as the theoretical and the practical sides of the same system. Yoga mostly accepts the metaphysics and the epistemology of Samkhya. It shows the practical path by following which one may attain Viveka-Jnana which alone leads to liberation.

Yoga accepts three pramanas—Perception, inference and testimony of Samkhya and also the twenty-five metaphysical principles. Yoga believes in God as the highest self distinct from otherselves. Hence it is sometimes called. (Seshwara Samkhya) or 'theistic Samkhya' as distinct from classical Samkhya which is nirishwara or atheistic.

The Yoga Sutra of Patanjali is the first authoritative text in this system and is divided into four parts. The first is called Samadhi Pada which deals with the nature and aim of concentration. The Second, Sadhanapada, explains the means to realize this end. The third, Vibhutipada deals with the supra -normal powers which can be acquired through Yoga. The fourth, Kaivalya pada, describes the nature of liberation and the reality of the transcendental self. The Yoga Sutras of Patanjali were believed to have been written in the second century B.C. A commentary of this text was prepared by Vyasa, and later on was followed by a number of learned interpretations of it, all of which help to explain the Yoga Philosophy.

Psychology of Yoga

The Path of Yoga is based on sound psychological foundation. Hence to appreciate this path, the psychology of Yoga must first be understood. The most important element in the psychology of Yoga is Chitta. Chitta is the first modification of Prakrti in which there is the predominance of Sattva over rajas and tamas. It is material by nature, but due to the closest contact with the self it is enlightened by its light. It assumes the form of anything in whose contact it comes. Due to the modifications of the Chitta according to objects, the self knows these objects.

According to Yoga Sutra, though there is no modification in the self, except as the reflection of the changing Chitta Vrttis (modifications of Chitta), there is an appearance of change in it, just as the moon reflected in the river seems to be moving. When true knowledge is attained, the self ceases to see itself in these modifications of the Chitta and gets rid of attachment and aversion to the worldly pleasures and sufferings. This attachment and aversion is bondage. The only way to get rid of this bondage is to control the modification of the chitta. This control is the result of Yoga. In the words of Patanjali, "Yoga is the cessation of the modification of Chitta. (Yogah Chittavrttinirodhah)

Stages of Chitta

Chitta has five stages which are known as Chittabhumi. These five stages are as follows:

1. **Kshipta.** This is the stage in which the chitta is very much disturbed and remains loitering after the worldly objects.
2. **Mudha.** When there is preponderance of tamas, just as when one is overpowered by sleep, the stage of the chitta is known as Mudha.
3. **Vikshipta.** This is the state in which in spite of preponderance of the sattva guna, the

chitta is oscillating between the tendencies of success and failures created by the rajas. The Chitta of the gods and that of beginners in yoga is of this sort. This differs from the Kshipta stage because due to the preponderance of sattva sometimes there is temporary ceasing of the modifications of the chitta in this stage.

4. **Ekagra.** The stage of the chitta when it is fixed on someone subject due to the preponderance of the sattva is known as the ekagra stage, just as the flame of the burning lamp remains always pointing to one side and does not flicker hither and thither.
5. **Niruddha.** When only the impressions remain in chitta after the cessation of the modifications, the stage is known as the niruddha stage. It is this stage which is known as Yoga.

Of the above-mentioned five stages, the first three are harmful in Yoga and may be removed by practice. The last two stages are useful in Yoga.

Forms of Chitta

Because chitta is of the nature of three gunas, it always remains changing due to the preponderance of one or the other of the gunas. With this preponderance, three main forms of Chitta can be noticed which are under.

1. **Prakhya.** In this stage, the chitta is predominated by sattva guna and tamas remain in subordination. In this form, the chitta aspires for different powers of Yoga, *e.g.,* anima, etc.
2. **Pravritti.** When the tamas becomes weak, and the chitta is predominated by the rajas, it appears to be enlightened and full of dharma, knowledge renunciation, etc.
3. **Sthiti.** As the rajas is subordinated, the chitta, predominated by the sattva element, gets established in its own form and attains the discriminating reason. This form of the chitta is known as sthiti.

Modifications of Chitta

As has already been pointed out, the Chitta, in spite of its being material, seems to be living entity due to the reflection of the self in it. It is these changes in the chitta which are known as its Vrittis or modifications. These modifications are due to ignorance and their result is bondage. These modifications are of five types which are as follows:

1. **Pramana** (Right cognition) : Like Samkhya philosophy. Yoga has also accepted three Pramanas of perception, inference and testimony. By going outside through the sensation, the Chitta attains the form of object. This is known as pramana.
2. **Viparyaya** (Wrong cognition) : The false knowledge of anything is known as viparyaya. Vachaspati Mishra has included doubt (Samsaya) also in viparyaya.
3. **Vikalpa** (Verbal cognition or imagination): This is knowledge in which the object which is known does not exist, *e.g.,* in the knowledge that consciousness is the form of the Purusha, a distinction is made between the consciousness and the Purusha which actually does not exist. The conception of the two as distinct is vikalpa.
4. **Nidra** (Absence of cognition or sleep) : The modification of the chitta which is the substratum of the knowledge of absence of anything is known as nidra or sleep. Due to the preponderance of tamas in its vritti, there is absolute absence of the waking and dreaming modifications. But this stage should not be conceived as the total absence of knowledge because after arising from sleep the person has the consciousness that he had slept well. Hence, sleep is also a modification.
5. **Smriti** (Memory) : Smriti or memory is the remembering of the experience. The above-mentioned modifications cause samskaras or predispositions in the inner instrument *i.e.,* Chitta and due course these predis-positions again take the form of modi-fications. Thus, the cycle goes on for ever.

According to Yoga Philosophy, there are several causes of disturbance (vikshepa) in the chitta. These are: Disease, inactivity, doubt, carelessness, attachment with object, false knowledge, non-attainment of the stage of samadhi, absence of concentration, etc.

The Yoga prescribes the practice of concentration to check the above mentioned causes of the distraction of chitta. Together with concentration, there should be friendliness towards living beings, sympathy towards sufferers, aversion towards evil doers and pleasant attitude towards the good persons.

Kinds of Kleshas

Avidya or ignorance breeds false knowledge and false knowledge breeds kleshas. These are of five types:

1. **Avidya** (ignorance) : The seeing of self which is eternal and pure in non-eternal, impure and painful not-self is avidya or ignorance.
2. **Asmita** (egoism) : Asmita is the false conception of identify between purusha and Prakrti and the absence of distinction between them.
3. **Raga** (attachment) : Raga is the acute thirsting for worldly pleasures.
4. **Dwesha** (aversion) : Dwesha is anger in the means of suffering.
5. **Abhinivesha :** It is fear of death.

Eight-fold Path of Yoga

Yoga advocates control over the body, the senses and the mind. It does not want to kill the body; on the other, it recommends its perfection. A sound mind needs a sound body. Sensual attachment and passions distract the body as well as the mind. They must be conquered. To overcome them, Yoga gives us the Eight-fold path of Discipline (Ashtanga Yoga).

1. **Yama:** It means abstention and includes the five vows of Jainism. It is abstention from injury through thought, word or deed (ahimsa), from falsehood (satya), from stealing (asteya), from passions and lust (brahmacharya), and from avarice (aparigraha).
2. **Niyama :** It is self-culture and includes external and internal purification (Shaucha), contentment (Santosha), austerity (Tapas), study (Svadhyaya) and devotion to God (Ashvarapranidhana).
3. **Asana :** It means steady and comfortable posture. There are various kinds of postures which are a physical help to meditation. This is the discipline of the body.
4. **Pranayama:** It means control of breath and deals with regulation of inhalation, retention and exhalation of breath. It is beneficial to health and is highly conductive to the concentration of the mind. But it must be performed under expert guidance otherwise it may have bad after-effects.
5. **Prathyahara:** It is the control of the senses and consists in with drawing the senses from their objects. Our senses have a natural tendency to go to outward objects. They must be checked and directed towards the internal goal. It is the process of introversion.

These five are called external aids to Yoga (bahiranga sadhana), while the remaining three which follow are called internal aids (antaranga Sadhana).

6. **Dharana:** It is fixing the mind on the object of meditation like the tip of the nose or the midpoint of the eyebrows or the lotus of the heart or the image of the deity. The mind must be steadfast like the unflickering flame of a lamp.
7. **Dhyana:** It means meditation and consists in the undisturbed flow of thought round the object of meditation (pratyayaikatanata). It is steadfast contemplation without any break.
8. **Samadhi:** It means concentration. This is the final step in Yoga. Here the mind is completely absorbed in the object of meditation. In dhyana the act of meditation and the object of meditation remain separate.

But here they become one. It is the highest means to realize the cessation of mental modifications which is the end. It is the ecstatic state in which the connection with the external world is broken and through which one has to pass before obtaining liberation.

Samadhi is of two kinds: Conscious or Samprajnata and supraconscious or Asamprajnata. In the former consciousness of the object of meditation persists, in the latter it is transcended. The former is Ekagra, the latter is Niruddha. In the former the mind remains concentrated on the object of meditation. The meditator and the object of meditation are fused together, yet the consciousness of the object of meditation persists. This state is said to be of four kinds:

(*a*) **Savitarka:** When the Chitta is concentrated on a gross object of meditation like the tip of the nose or the mind-point of the eyebrows or the image of the deity.

(*b*) **Savichara:** When the Chitta is concentrated on a subtler object of meditation like the tanmatras.

(*c*) **Sananda :** When the Chitta concentrated on a still subtler object of meditation which produces joy, like the senses.

(*d*) **Sasmita :** When the Chitta is concentrated on the ego substance with which the self is generally identified. Here we have conscious ecstasy where individuality persists.

Asamprajnata Samadhi is that supra-conscious concentration where the meditator and the object of meditation are completely fused together and there is not even consciousness of the object of meditation.

Here no new mental modifications arise. They are checked (niruddha), though the latent impressions may continue. It is the highest form of Yoga which is divine madness, perfect mystic ecstasy difficult to describe and more difficult to attain. Even those who attain it cannot retain it longer. Immediately or after very short time, the body breaks and they obtain complete liberation.

Eight Siddhis

According to Yoga Philosophy, the Yogis attain various siddhis by practising the path of Yoga. These powers are mainly of eight types and hence are called Ashta Siddhis or Ashta Aishhwaryas.

1. **Anima:** This is the power to become small like an atom and to be invisible.
2. **Laghima:** This is the power to become light like cotton and so to be able to fly away.
3. **Mahima:** This is the power to become big like mountains.
4. **Prapti:** This is the power to secure whatever is desired.
5. **Prakamya:** This is the power by which all the impediments in the will power are removed.
6. **Vashitva:** This is the power by which all the living beings may be conquered.
7. **Eshitva:** This is the power by which one attains absolute mastery over all the physical objects.
8. **Yatrakamavashayitva:** This is the power by which all the desires are fulfilled.

The powers attained through the above-mentioned eight siddhis may be used according to the wish of the Yogi. But in the Yoga philosophy the pursuance of the path of Yoga for attainment of these powers has been vehemently decried because that results in deflecting the aspirant from the path of Yoga. The ultimate end of Yoga is not the attainment of these powers, but the realization of liberation.

God

Yoga accepts the existence of God. The interest of Patanjali himself in god seems to be practical, but later Yogins have taken also a theoretical interest in him and have tried to prove. His existence as necessary philosophical speculation. Patanjali defines God as special kind of Purusha, who is always free from pains, actions, effects and impressions - ***Kleshakarmavipakashayair***

aparamrstah purushavishesa Ishowarah - says Yogasutra. He is eternally free and was never bound nor has any possibility of being bound. He is above the law of Karma. He is omniscient and omnipotent and omnipresent. He is perfection incarnate. He is purest knowledge. He is the teacher of rishis, and teacher of Veda. 'Aum' is his symbol. Devotion to God is one of the surest means of obtaining concentration. He cannot grant liberation. He can only remove the obstacles in the upward progress of the devotees. Directly he has nothing to do with the bondage and the liberation of the Purusha. Ignorance binds the discrimination between Prakrti and Purusha liberates. The end of human life is not the union with God but only the separation of Purusha from Prakrti.

PURVA MIMAMSA

The word *'Mimamsa'* literally means 'revered thought' *(Poojito vicharah)* and was originally applied to the interpretation of the vedic rituals which commanded highest reverence. The word is now used in the sense of critical investigation. *Mimamsa* deals with the earlier portion of the Veda *i.e.,* the *Mantra* and the *Brahmana* portion and is therefore called *Purva - Mimamsa* and also *Karma mimamsa.* It also deals with Dharma as the main subject and hence is also called *Dharma mimamsa.*

Mimamsa and Vedantha are treated as allied systems of thought. Both are based on and both try to interpret the Veda. The earlier portion of the Veda, *i.e.,* the Mantra and the Brahmana portion, is called *Karmakanda*, while the later portion, *i.e.,* the Upanishads is called *Jnanakanda,* because the former deals with action with the rituals and the sacrifices and the latter with the knowledge of reality. Mimamsa deals with the earlier portion of the Veda and is therefore called Purva-Mimamsa and also Karma-Mimamsa. Jaimini was the founder of Purva-mimamsa.

Literature

The earliest work of this system is the *Mimamsa sutra* of Jaimini, which begins with an enquiry into the nature of Dharma. It is the biggest of the entire philosophical Sutras and discusses about one thousand topics. Shabara Swamin has written a great commentary on this work and his commentary has been explained by Prabhakara and Kumarika Bhatta, who differ from each other in certain important aspect and gave rise to two principle schools of Mimamsa. Prabhakara's commentary Brhati has been commented up on by Shalikanatha who has also written another treatise Prakarana Panchika. Kumarila's huge commentary on Mimamsa bhashya is divided into three parts - *Slokavartika, Tantra Vartika* and *Tuptiika,* the first of which has been commented upon by Parthasarathy Misra who has also written his Shastradipika. Tradition makes Prabhakara a pupil of Kumarila who nicknamed him as 'guru' on account of his great intellectual powers.

Sruti and its importance

The aim of the Mimamsa is to ascertain the nature of Dharma. Dharma is not a physical existent, and so it cannot be apprehended through the senses. The other pramanas are of no use, since they all presuppose the work of perception. Perception, inference and such other sources of knowledge have nothing to say on the point that the performer of the Agnishtoma sacrifice will go to heaven. This knowledge is derived only from the Vedas. Though the Pramana of the Veda is the only source of our knowledge of dharma, the others are considered, since it is necessary to show that they cannot give rise to knowledge of dharma. They are also found useful in repudiating wrong views.

The Vedas are eternal, since the words of which they are composed are eternal. The relationship between the word and its meaning is natural and not created by convention. The cognitions brought about by Vedic injunctions cannot be set aside at any time or place or under any conditions. It is a self contradiction to assert that the injunction expresses something which is not true. The Vedas manifest their own validity. Words used by us denote things that can be cognized by other means of knowledge; and, if we cannot know them through other means, then those who utter them must be of unquestionable authority. So, non-Vedic utterances do not possess any inherent validity. Prabhakara holds that non-Vedic verbal cognition is of the nature in inference. Only the verbal cognitions afforded by the Veda is strictly verbal, but it is not in consistency with the other theory of the self-validity of all cognitions. Since there is no author of Vedic texts, there is no possibility of defects, and so the non-authoritativeness of the Vedas is inconceivable. As the utterances of human beings are valid, if their authors are trustworthy, Kumarila considers them also to be sabdapramana.

Classification of Srutivaktas (Vidhi, Nishedha and Arthvada)

Vedas are broadly divided into the *Mantras* and the *Brahmanas.* The contents of the Veda are also classified into

1. *Injunctions (vidhi),*
2. *Hymns (mantras),*
3. *Names (namadheya),*
4. *Prohibitions (nishedha),* and
5. *Explanatory passages (arthavada).*

Injunction which impel one to action in expectation of certain results, such as "One who is desirous of heaven is to sacrifice" (svargakamo yajeta), are the most important. There are subsidiary injunctions which describe the details of the sacrifice, the order in which several parts of it are to be carried out, as well as the persons who are entitled to perform them. The *mantras* are largely useful in reminding the sacrificer of the different matters connected with the sacrifice, such as the deities to whom oblations are to be made. Some of the mantras are said to possess a mystical or super sensuous effect and to contribute directly to the transcendental result, Apurva. Names indicate the results to be obtained by the sacrifices. Nishedhas are only vidhis in disguise. *Arthavadas* comprise the sentence which contains either praise of the things enjoined (prashamsa), or a censure of things prohibited (ninda), as well as description of the doings of others (parakrti) and instances from history (Purakalpa) (Arthasamgraha).

Sabdanityavada

The Mimamsakas propound the theory that words (sabdas) are not really the perceived sounds (dhvanis). The sound produced by the speaker and perceived by the hearer and only the revealers of the words which are not themselves produced. Words are really the letters which are part less and uncaused. Though these letter-sounds vary, we recognize that the same letter is pronounced by all of them. This identity of the letter shows that it is not produced at any time and place, but transcends them. So the words as letters may be regarded as eternal, that is, as having existence, but being uncaused. This Mimamsaka's theory is known as *shabdanityavada.*

Jaimini sets forth positive considerations in support of this view. The words are ever present, since the utterance of it is only for the purpose of manifesting it to others. There cannot be any effort manifest a non-existing thing. For non-eternal things, cause of destruction is found, but we do not find causes for the destruction of words. The sound produced from air is distinct from the word which it serves to manifest. Besides, we have many Vedic texts insisting on the eternal nature of words.

Jatishaktivada

Mimamsakas' theory of jatishaktivada states that universals (Jati) are eternal and have potency (shakti) to manifest akritis and seem as different kinds of individuals. Words denote classes and not individuals. When we say "bring a cow", we do not mean a particular cow, but any animal possessing the features of a cow. The word denotes the class or form, since it has action for its object. If individuals are denoted by words, a generic idea like "cow" would be impossible. Again, a word cannot denote all the individuals, since then it would possess as much potency as there are individuals. I cannot denote a collection of individuals, since then it would be undergoing changes, as some individuals die out and others get in. Again, if the word means a single individual only, there cannot be an eternal connection between word and meaning, and action would be impossible, as it would be difficult to decide which individual is meant. If individuals are object denoted, then since they are not omnipresent, there cannot be a relation between a word and its meaning. Akrti is eternal, and is therefore capable of relationship with the eternal word.

Dharma and Bhavana

Dharma is the subject of inquiry in Mimamsa. The Purvamimamsa sutra begins with the enquiry about the nature of dharma. ***"Athatodharma jijnasa"*** Jaimini defines dharma as a command or injunction which impels men to action. Chodanalakshanartho dharmah. It is the supreme duty, the 'ought' the 'categorical imperative'. Artha and Kama which deal with ordinary common mortality are learnt by worldly intercourse. But Dharma and Moksha which deal with true spirituality are revealed only by the Veda. Dharma is supra-sensible and consists in the commands to do certain acts and to refrain from doing certain other acts. The authoritativeness of the Veda is supported by social consciousness as well as by individual conscience.

Dharma and adharma deal with happiness and pain to be enjoyed or suffered in the life beyond. Actions performed here produce an unseen potency (apurva) in the soul of the agent which yields fruit when obstructions are removed and time becomes ripe for its fructification. The apurva is the link between the act and its fruit. It is the causal potency (shakti) in the act which leads to its fructification. **Actions are first divided into three kinds — obligatory** (which must be performed, for their violation results in sin though their performance leads to no merit); **optional** (which may or may not be performed; their performance leads to merit, though their non-performance does not lead to sin); and **prohibited** (which must not be performed, for their performance leads to sin, though their non-performance does not lead to merit).

The earlier Mimamsaka believed only in dharma (and not in moksha) and their ideal was the attainment of heaven (svarga). But later Mimamsakas believe in moksha and substitute the ideal of heaven by that of liberation (apavarga). Prabhakara and Kumarila both believe that the goal of human life is liberation. The soul is chained to Samsara on account of its association with the body, the senses, the mind and the understanding. Through this association, the soul becomes a knower, an enjoyer and an agent. This association is due to karma which is the cause of bondage. When the cause is removed, the effect also ceases to exist. So abstention from karma automatically leads to the dissolution of the 'marriage-tie' of the soul with the body. The senses, the mind etc. and consequently to the return of the soul to its pure nature as a substance rid of all qualities and modes including consciousness and bliss also.

Validity of Knowledge

Mimamsakas uphold the theory of svatah pramanyavada or the self validity or intrinsic validity of knowledge. All knowledge is valid by itself. Truth is normal and error is abnormal. Both in respect of its origin and ascertainment knowledge is valid. A valid cognition therefore must fulfill these four conditions. **Firstly,** it must not arise from defective causes (karanadosarahita). **Secondly,** it must be free from contradiction. It must be self-consistent and should not be set aside by subsequent knowledge (badhakajnanarahita). **Thirdly,** it must apprehend an object which has not already been apprehended. Novelty is an essential feature of knowledge (agrhitagrahi). Thus memory is excluded from valid knowledge by Kumarila also. **Fourthly,** it must truly represent the object (yathartha).

Pramanas

Jaimini regards knowledge itself as pramana or means of knowledge and admits three pramanas—**perception, inference** and **testimony.** Prabhakara adds two more—comparison and implication. Kumarila further adds non-apprehension.

Perception

Knowledge is of two kinds—immediate and mediate. Perception is immediate and there are two stages in perception viz indeterminate and determinate. In agreement to the Nyaya theory Mimamsakas believe that the process of perception proceeds as follows - the self comes into contact with the mind (manas);

the mind comes into contact with the sense-organ; and the sense-organ comes into contact with the external object.

Inference

The Mimamsa account of inference also generally agrees with that of the Nyaya. Only difference is that the Mimamsa recognizes only three members of a syllogism, either the first three or the last three.

Comparison

Comparison, according to Mimamsa, apprehends the similarity of the remembered cow to the perceived wild cow. This knowledge is like this: 'the remembered cow is like the perceived wild cow' (gavayasadrshi gauh). It is the cow as possessing similarity with the wild cow that is known by comparison. A person need not be told by anybody that a wild cow is similar to a cow. Any person who has seen a cow and happens to see a wild cow himself remembers the cow as similar to the wild cow he perceives. This knowledge of similarity is comparison. It is distinguished from inference because the vyapti or the invariable concomitance is not needed here.

Testimony

Shabda-pramana has got the greatest importance in Mimamsa. Testimony is verbal authority. It is the knowledge of supra-sensible objects which is produced by the comprehension of the meanings of words. Kumarila divides testimony into personal (pauruseya) and impersonal (apaurusheya). The former is the testimony of the trustworthy persons (aptavakya). The latter is the testimony of the Veda (Vedavakya). It is valid in itself. It has intrinsic validity. But the former is not valid in itself. Its validity is inferred from the trustworthy character of the person.

Arthapatti or implication

It is the assumption of an unperceived fact in order to reconcile two apparently inconsistent perceived facts. If Devadatta is alive and he is not in his house, we presume that he is elsewhere. 'Being alive' and 'not being in the house' are two perceived facts which appear to be inconsistent. Their apparent inconsistency is removed when we presume the fact of 'being elsewhere'. The element of doubt distinguishes presumption or implication from inference.

Anupalabdhi (Non-apprehension)

Kumarila admits non-apprehension (anupalabdhi) as the sixth independent pramana. The Naiyayika and Prabhakara reject it. In response to the criticism Kumarila opines that negation cannot be perceived, for there is no sense-object-contact. Negation cannot be inferred for the invariable concomitance is not known here. Negation cannot be known by testimony, for there is no verbal cognition here. Nor can it be known from comparison or presumption. Negation which is an independent category is known by an independent pramana called non-apprehension.

Realism

The Mimamsaka is a pluralistic realist. He believes in the reality of the external world and of the individual souls. There are innumerable individual souls, as many as there are living bodies, plus the bodiless liberated souls. There are also innumerable atoms and the other eternal and infinite substances. Mimamsa believes in the Law of Karma, in Unseen Power (apurva), in heaven and hell, in liberation and in the ultimate authority of the eternal authorless Veda. God is ruled out as an unnecessary hypothesis, though the later Mimamsakas like Apadeva and Laugaksi try to bring in God. Mimamsa does not admit the periodic creation and dissolution of this world. The conception of the categories and the substances etc. in Mimamsa is generally the same as in the Nyaya-Vaishesika.

The concept of self and knowledge

Mimamsa admits the plurality of the individual souls and regard the self as an eternal (nitya), omnipresent (sarvagata), ubiquitous (vibhu), infinite (vyapaka), substance (dravya) which is the substratum (ashraya) of consciousness and which is a real knower (jnata), enjoyer (bhokta) and agent (karta). The self is different from the body, the senses, the mind and the understanding. Self-luminous knowledge, reveals the self as the subject and the known thing as the object simultaneously with itself.

The concept of Dharma

Dharma is the subject of inquiry in Mimamsa. Jaimini defines dharma as a command or injunction which impels men to action. It is the supreme duty, the 'ought', the 'categorical imperative'. Artha and Kama which deal with ordinary common morality are learnt by worldly intercourse. But Dharma and Moksha which deal with true spirituality are revealed only by the Veda. The authoritativeness of the Veda is supported by social consciousness as well as by individual conscience.

Dharma and adharma deal with happiness and pain to be enjoyed or suffered in the life beyond. Actions performed here produce an unseen potency (apurva) in the soul of the agent which yields fruit when obstructions are removed and time becomes ripe for its fructification. The apurva is the link between the act and its fruit. It is the causal potency (shakti) in the act which leads to its fructification. Actions are first divided into three kinds—obligatory (which must be performed, for their violation results in sin, though their performance leads to no merit); optional (which may or may not be performed; their performance leads to merit, though their non-performance does not lead to sin); and prohibited (which must not be performed, for their performance leads to sin, though their non-performance does not lead to merit). Obligatory actions are of two kinds—those which must be performed daily (nitya) like daily prayers (sandhyavandana) etc., and those which must be performed on specified occasions (naimittika). Optional actions are called kamya and their performance leads to merit, *e.g.*, he who wants to go to heaven should perform certain sacrifices (svargakamo yajeta). Prohibited actions are called pratisiddha and their performance incurs sin and leads to hell. Then, there are expiatory acts (prayashchitta) which are performed in order to ward off or at least mitigate the evil effect of the performed prohibited actions.

Differences between the Prabhakara and Kumarila schools of Mimamsa

Prabhakara school	Kumarila school
Defines valid knowledge as apprehension (anubhuti). All apprehension is direct and immediate and valid per se.	Defines valid knowledge as apprehension of an object which is produced by causes free from defects and which is not contradicted by subsequent knowledge.
Accepts five pramanas - Perception, Inference, Testimony, Comparison and Implication.	Accepts six pramanas—Perception, Inference, Testimony, Comparison, Implication and non-apprehension.
Defines perception as direct apprehension (sakshat pratitih pratyaksham).	Defines perception as direct knowledge produced by the proper contact of the sense-organs with the presented objects, which is free from defects.
Holds the inference involves a previous knowledge of the general relation and refers to things already known.	Makes novelty an essential feature of inference. The object of the inferential cognition is something that is not already known.
The facts observed by implication remain inconsistent or doubtful until the assumption is made. In inference there is no room for any element of doubt.	Arthapatti helps us to reconcile two apparently inconsistent facts. There is no such inconsistency between well-ascertained facts in inference.

Does not accept non-apprehension as an independent source of knowledge.	Accepts non-apprehension as an independent source of knowledge.
Prabhakara's theory of error is known as Akhyativada.	Kumarila's theory of error is Viparitakhyati.
Consciousness is only an accidental quality of soul.	Consciousness is modal change in the self.
Advocates the theory of simultaneous revelation of knower, known and knowledge (triputi-pratyakshavada).	Advocates the theory of cognizedness of objects (jnatatavada).
Accepts self as a subject of every knowledge.	Accepts self as the object of self-consciousness.
Does not regard liberation as a state of bliss. (According to Parthasarathi).	Regard liberation as the state of bliss. (According to Narayana Bhatta)
Accepts the theory of Anvitabhidhanavada.	Accepts the theory of Abhihitanvayavada.

Triputipratyakshavada

Prabhakara's theory of knowledge is known as triputipratyaksavada. It regards knowledge as self-luminous (svaprakasha). It manifests itself and needs nothing else for its manifestation. Though self-luminous, is not eternal. It arises and vanishes. Knowledge reveals itself and as does so, it also simultaneously reveals its subject and its object. In every knowledge-situation we have this triple revelation. The subject and the object both are manifested by knowledge itself simultaneously with own manifestation. The triputi of the jnata, jneya and jnana is simultaneously revealed in every act of cognition. The self and the object both depend on knowledge for their manifestation. The self is not cognized in deep sleep because there is no knowledge to manifest it. Every knowledge has a triple manifestation—the cognition of the self as the knower (ahamvritti), the cognition of the object as the known (visayavritti) and the self-conscious cognition (svayamvritti).

Jnatatavada

Kumarila's theory of knowledge is known as jnatatavada. Kumarila regards knowledge as a mode of the self and it is essentially an act (kriya) or a process (vyapara). It cannot reveal itself nor can it be revealed by another cognition. It can only be inferred. And it is inferred from the cognizedness (jnatata) of its object. Cognition relates the self to the object and enables it to know the object. Cognition manifests the object and is inferred by this fact. It cannot manifest itself nor can be manifested by any other cognition.

Akyativada

This is Prabhakara's theory of error. According to him, Error is only partial truth. It is imperfect knowledge. It is a composite of two cognitions which really fall apart unrelated. Error is due to non-discrimination between these two cognitions and their separate objects. It is a mere non-apprehension of the distinction between the two cognitions and their objects. Error arises when we forget the fact that instead of one cognition there are really two cognitions denoting two separate objects and further forget the fact that these two cognitions as well as their objects are distinct and unrelated. Two factors are involved in error. One is positive and the other is negative. The positive factor consists in the presence of two cognitions which reveal their respective objects only partially. The negative factor consists in overlooking the distinction between these two cognitions and their objects. It is called vivekakhyati or bhedagraha or asamsargagraha.

Viparitakhyati

It is the theory of error accepted by Kumarila. He recognizes error as such and regards it as misapprehension and not as mere non-apprehension. He maintains that there is a positive wrong synthesis of these two elements—the perceived and the remembered, and that error is not due merely to the non-apprehension of the distinction between them. The two elements are not united in fact. But they appear to be so in error. Error is partial misrepresentation. Error is not akhyati or non-apprehension but viparita-khyati or misapprehension. It is not due to non-discrimination between two imperfect cognitions, but it is due to a positive wrong synthesis of the two imperfect cognitions which, though in fact unrelated, are welded together as a unitary knowledge in error (samsarga-graha or viparitagraha). Thus error becomes a single psychosis, a unitary cognition, a positive misapprehension and therefore one of commission.

Anvitabhidhanavada

According to Prabhakara, who accepts the theory of Anvitabhidhanavada, the meaning of the words can be known only when they occur in a sentence enjoining some duty, and so words denote objects only as related to the other factors of such sentence. If they are not related to an injunction, but simply remind us of meanings, it is case of remembrance, which is not valid cognition.

Since the potency of the word originates from the separate potencies of the letters, the latter are said to be the direct cause of verbal cognition. The cognition of the meaning of the word is not obtained through sense-perception. The senses present the letters which possess the power to bring about the words have naturally denotative powers by which they refer to objects whether we understand their meanings or not.

Abhihitanvayavada

According to the Abhihitanvayavada accepted by Kumarila's followers, the knowledge of meanings is due to words; but this knowledge is not due to recollection or apprehension, but to denotation. Words denote meanings which, when combined, give rise to a knowledge of there is such a relationship between the word and its meaning is directly cognisable. If one does not recognise it, when one hears the word for the first time, it only means that the accessories are absent, but that does not makes the relationship non-existent. If the eye cannot see without light, it does not mean that the eye is incapable of seeing altogether. The accessory is the knowledge that such - and such a word denotes such - and - such- and object, which is gained from experience. The expressiveness of the word belongs to it by its very nature. This is absolutely true of common names like jar and the like, where the relation of the words to their meanings is independent of any convention.

UTTARAMIMAMSA (VEDANTA)

The system of philosophy based on the Upanishads is called the *Vedanta Darshana.* It is called *Vedanta,* firstly because they are the literally the concluding portion, the end of the Vedas, secondly because they are the essence, the cream, the height, of the vedic philosophy. The system itself is based on three canonical works *(Prasthana thraya),* the Upanishads, the Brahma Sutra and the Bhagavad Gita. The passages in the Upanishads are manifold. Some of them clearly speak of the identity of the individual soul with the Supreme Being, while there are passages which appear to speak of the difference between the individual soul, the God and the matter. Such passages have given rise to the different interpretations and Vyasa *(Badarayana)* wrote the *Brahmasutras* in order to clear the apparent contradictions of the *Upanishad* passages and show that the fundamental doctrine of all the *Upanishads* is the identification of the individual soul *(Jiva)* with the Supreme soul *(Brahma).* The evidence of experience which show a multiplicity of phenomena and the statements of the Vedas which speak of souls are only true till true knowledge of the *Brahman* is required. The Ultimate cause of all false impressions is *Avidya* or ignorance. The illusion caused by the *Avidya* vanishes through the acquisition of true knowledge.

The Upanishads

The *Upanishads* are the concluding portion as well as the cream of the Veda and are therefore rightly called *'Vedanta'*. The word *Upanishad* is derived from the root 'Sad' which means—(1) to sit down (2) to destroy and (3) to loosen. (Gati, Avasadanam and Visharanam) 'Upa' means nearby 'and 'ni' means devotedly. The word therefore means the sitting down of the disciple near his teachers in a devoted manner to receive instruction about the reality which loosens all doubts and destroys all ignorance of the disciple. Gradually the word comes to signify any secret teaching about reality and it is used by the *Upanishads* in this sense *(Rahasya vidya)*. The *Muktikopanishad* gives the number of the Upanishads as 108. But ten or eleven *Upanishads* are regarded as important and authentic, on which Sankarcharya has commented.

These are:

1. *Ishavasyopanishad*
2. *Kenopanishad*
3. *Kathopanishad*
4. *Prashnopanishad*
5. *Mundakopanishad*
6. *Mandukyopanishad*
7. *Taittiriyopanishad*
8. *Aitareyopanishad*
9. *Chandogyopanishad and*
10. *Brhadaranyakopanishad.*

The *Upanishads* contain the quintessence of Vedic religion and philosophy. The six systems of Indian Philosophy derive their strength and inspiration from them. The Vedanta Systems are entirely an outcome of their, study. The idea of *Moksha* and the primary goal of life, which has permeated the Indian religions and culture of the succeeding centuries, owe its origin entirely to the *Upanishads* and they are the basis of *Prastanatraya.*

Brahma Sutra

The *Brahma Sutra* claims to be an aphoristic summary of the *Upanishads.* The work derives its name from the fact that it deals chiefly with *Brahman* as described in the *Upanishads,* in all its aspects.

It is also known by other names as:

(*a*) The *Vedantasutras,*

(*b*) The *Sariraka Sutras,*

(*c*) The *Uttara Mimamsa Sutras* and

(*d*) The *Bikshu-Sutras.*

Tradition accepts, *Badarayana,* as the author of this work.

The work Brahma Sutra is divided into four chapters called *adhyayas.* Each *adhyaya* is divided into four *padas. Padas* are further divided into *adhikaranas* and *sutras.* The total number of *adhikaranas* and *sutras* are 191 and 555 respectively. Each *pada* of the various *adhyayas* comprises several *adhikaranas.*

An *adhikarana* must have five parts and they are:

1. *Vishaya* (topic),
2. *Samshaya* (doubt),
3. *Purvapaksha* (opponent's view),
4. *Siddhantha* (established conclusion) and
5. *Samgati* (connection between the different sections).

The four *adhyayas* in *Brahma Sutra* are

1. *Samanvayadhyaya,*
2. *Avirodhadhyaya,*
3. *Sadhanadhyaya and*
4. *Phaladhyaya.*

The first *Adhyaya* attempts to harmonize *(Samanvaya)* the principles dealt with in the various *Upanishads.* The second *Adhyaya* applies itself to dispel any *Virodha* or contradiction that many confront the philosophy of Vedanta. *Sadhanadhyaya* discusses the various *Vidyas* or meditations mentioned in the *Upanishads.* The fourth one, *Phaladhyaya* discusses the outcome of the study of Vedanta.

The *Brahmasutra* of Badarayana has attracted the attention of the distinguished scholars over the years as a result they have enriched the *Brahmasutra* literature by their brilliant commentaries. Of the several *bhashyas* or commentaries available today *Sankaracharya's bhashya* is the earliest. Ramanuja's *Sribhashya,* Madhva's *Anubhashya* are also important. *Bhaskaracharya, Nimbarka, Vallabha* and *Baladeva* have also commented on this work.

Sankaracharya wrote bhashya in Advaita point of view. Padmapada, the direct disciple of Sankara wrote *Panchapadika* on *Brahmasutra Sankarabhashya.* This was commented up on Prakasatman in his *Panchapadika Vivarana.* There is a gloss on this called Tattvadipanam by Akhandananda Muni. All these commentaries collectively have created the *Vivarana Prastana* in Advaita Vedanta in the post-Sankara period. As opposed to this *Bhamatiprastana* was developed by Vachaspatimisra by writing a commentary called *Bhamati* on *Brahmasutra Sankarabhashya.* Amalananda's *'Kalpataru'* and Appayyadikshita's *'Parimalam'* are also famous commentaries in their School of thought. *Sankshepa Sarirakam* of Sarvajnatma and *'Vivarana Prameya'* of Vidyaranya are also important Brahmasutra commentaries.

Bhagavad Gita

Bhagavad Gita literally means 'The Lord's song' *i.e.,* the philosophical discourse of Lord Krishna to persuade the reluctant Arjuna to fight. It is included in the great epic *Mahabharata's* Bhishma Parva. The book itself, comprising eighteen chapters called Yogas. It is a poetical work, composed in Anushtup Vritta in the form of a dialogue between Krishna and Arjuna on the battle field of Kurukshetra. Arjuna, the recipient of the teachings, though himself a great warrior, is a typical representative of the humans, liable to be upset or confused during periods of crisis. The questions and doubts he rises and the solutions that Krishna offers are not only relevant but also valid even today. The fundamental metaphysical teaching of the Gita is that of the unreal there is no being; and the real there is no non-being. The Gita represents a unique Synthesis of Action, Devotion and Knowledge. Gita teaches *Jnana, Bhakti, Karma,* and *Dhyana* - yogas to attain moksha. Gita is a practical treatise of the teachings of the Upanishad.

Pre-Sankara Advaita Vedanta

Gaudapada is regarded as the systematic expounder of Advaita philosophy. His *Mandukya Karika* or *Gaudapada Karika* also known as the *Agama-sastra* is the first available systematic treatise on Advaita Vedanta. Tradition says Gaudapada was the teacher of Govindapada who was the teacher of Srisankara. Sankara himself most respectfully salutes Gaudapada as his grand-teacher (paramaguru).

The fundamental doctrine of Gaudapada is the Doctrine of No-Origination *(Ajadivada).* It means that the world being only an appearance is in fact never created. Absolute being self existent is never created (Aja). The doctrine of *Asparshayoga or Amanibhava or Vaisharadya* is Gaudapada's own contribution to Advaita Philosophy.

Sankaracharya

Sankara of the 8th centrury A.D, played a prominent part in the cultural history of India as a mystic philosopher, commentator of *prastanatraya,* great teacher and a systematic propounder of Advaita Vedanta Philosophy. Sankara was born in Kaladi. His parents are Sivaguru and Aryamba. Sankara lived barely for 32 years, but that short span of life was full of tremendous constructive activity and dynamic universal thought. Sankara expounded Advaita Philosophy in his monumental Bhashya on Prastanatraya and also many minor works such as *Vivekachudamani, Atmabodha, Dakshinamurti-stotra, Upadesa Sahasri, Dasasloki, Satasloki, Bhaja Govindam, Soundaryalahari* etc.

Philosophy of Sankaracharya

Ultimate reality, according to *Sankara* is *Atman* or *Brahman* which is pure consciousness. *(Jnana Swarupa)* which is devoid of all attributes *(Nirguna)* and all categories of the intellect *(Nirvishesha).* Brahman associated with its potency maya appears as qualified Brahman *(Saguna Brahma or Ishwara),* who is the creator of this world. *Jiva* or the individual self is a subject- object complex. *Avidya* is the root cause of the individuality. In liberation *avidya* is destroyed by *jnana* and the *Jiva* is realized as the

Brahma which it always is. *Maya* or *Avidya* is not pure illusion. It is not only the absence of knowledge; it is also positive wrong knowledge. It is indescribable and positive. When right knowledge dawns and the essential unity of the *jiva* with *Brahman* is realized, *Maya* vanishes. *Sankaracharya* emphasizes that from the phenomenal point of view the world is quite real. It is not an illusion. The world is quite real so long as the true knowledge of the nature of *Jagat* is not dawn *Brahma satyam jagan mithya jivo brahmaiva naaparah* is the summary of *Sankara's* teachings. *Advaita Vedanta* may be summerised in this verse: *Brahman* is the only reality; the world is ultimate false; and the individual soul is not different from *Brahman.* This oneness of *Jiva* and *Brahma* can be attained by manana of the *Upanishads* and the *Mahavakyas* like *Prajnaanam brahma (Aitareyopanishad) Ayamaatmaa brahma (Mandukyopanishad) Tattvamasi (Chandogyopanishad)* and *Aham brahmaasi (Brhadaranyakopanishad). Sankara* maintains *Brahma karana* vada as he recognizes that *Brahmam* is the cause of the world. The theory is also called *vivarta vada* because it takes the world to be only a phenomenal appearance of *Brahman-Sankara's* theory of illusions is called *Vivarta Vada. Advaitins* believe in *Anirvachaniyakhyati vada* also.

Padmapada, Sureswara, Totaka and *Hastamalaka* are the four direct disciples of *Sankara,* who constitute four mathas in Sringeri, Puri, Dwaraka and Badarinath to establish the Advaita Philosophy and spread its message to the future generations.

The Philosophy of Advaita Vedanta

Brahman

From the objective side this ultimate reality is called *Brahman,* The word is derived from the root *'Brh'* which means to grow or to evolve. Brahman is that which spontaneously bursts forth as nature and soul. It is the ultimate cause of this universe. In the Chandogya, it is cryptically described as *'Tajjalan'* - as that *(tat)* from which world arises *(ja),* into which it returns *(la),* and by which it is supported and it lives *(an).* In the Taittiriya, Brahman is defined as that from which all these beings are born, by which they live, and into which they are reabsorbed. Brahman is the only reality. It is absolutely indeterminate and non duel. It is beyond speech and mind. It is indescribable because no description of it can be complete. The best description of it is through the negative formula *'neti, neti'*. The basic cause of the universe and the cause of all causes is called Brahman by the Upanishads. Atman, Sat, Aksharam, Akasa, are the other appellations used for Brahman. The world rises out of him, is supported by him and gets dissolved back in to him. Yato vaa imaani bhutaani jaataani, yena jaataani jiivanti, yam prayanthyabhinivishanti tam vijijnaasasva tat brahmeti. The Swarupalakshana of Brahma is Satyam jnaanam anantam brahma. Atman is the same as Brahma. It is pure consciousness. It is the self which is self-luminous and which transcends the subject-object duality. It is the unqualified absolute. It is the only reality. There is no duality and no diversity at all. It is self proved or original *(Svayam Siddha).* All means of cognitions *(pramanas)* are founded on it and he who knows Brahman becomes Brahman.

Ishwara

The Brahman reflected in or conditioned by Maya, is called *Ishwara.* Ishwara is the personal aspect of the impersonal Brahma. Ishwara is known Saguna Brahman. Ishwara is the perfect personality. He is the lord of Maya. He is imminent in the whole universe which he controls from within. He is called *Antaryamin* (immanent inner ruler). He is the creator, sustainer and destroyer of the Universe.

Srisankara says that there is no multiplicity here that one who sees the many here is doomed to death. In explanation of the unity of all things, which appear to be many, examples like these are cited: Just as different articles made of gold are all really one, gold is the only real substance in them and the different names and forms *(nama-rupa)* which make them appear as many, are merely matters of verbal distinction, similarly in all objects there is the same Reality, and their differences are merely verbal. The objects of the world are denied separate, individual existences. Brahman (or Atman) is also described not as Creator, but as a Reality which is indescribable, being not only unspeakable but even unthinkable. Difference or multiplicity seen in this world is only due to Maya, Maya is also as avidya, ajnana, adhyasa etc.

Adhyasa

It is self-evident, says Sankara, that the Subject and the object are absolutely opposed to each other like light and darkness. The subject is pure Consciousness; the object is Unconsciousness. The one is the ultimate. 'I'; the other is the 'non-I'. Neither these two nor their attributes can, therefore, be identified. Yet it is the natural and common practice of people that they wrongly superimpose the object and its attributes upon the subject and error, this coupling of the real and the unreal is called superimposition *(adhyasa)* or error *(bhrahma)* or illusion *(maya)* or ignorance *(avidya)*. All definitions of error agree in maintaining that error is the superimposition of one thing on another, *e.g.,* the superimposition of silver on shell or the illusion of the moons on a single moon. This superimposition the learned call 'ignorance', and the realization of the true nature of reality by discarding error, they call 'knowledge'. This transcendental Ignorance is the presupposition of all practices of this phenomenal world. Superimposition, therefore, is the notion of a thing is something else *(atasmin tadbuddih)*. This unreal beginning less cycle superimposition goes on leading to the false notions of the agent and the enjoyed and to all phenomenal practices. The study of the Vedanta texts is undertaken in order to free oneself from this false notion of superimposition and thereby realize the essential unity of the Self.

Maya

Brahman is the only Reality; the world is ultimately false; and the individual soul is non-different from Brahman. Brahman and Atman or the Supreme Self are synonymous terms. The world is a creation of Maya. The individual selves on account of their inherent Avidya imagine themselves as different from Brahman and mistake Brahman as this world of plurality, even as we mistake a rope as a snake. Avidya vanishes at the dawn of knowledge-the supra-relational direct and intuitive knowledge of the non - dual self which means liberation. The words Maya, Avidya, Ajnana, Adhyasa, Adhyaropa, Akshara, Bijashakti, etc, are recklessly used in Vedanta as very nearly synonymous. Of these Maya, Avidya, Adhyasa and Vivarta are very often used as interchangeable terms. There are two schools among later Advaitins divided on the question whether Maya and Avidya are identical or different. The general trend of the Advaitins including Sankara himself has been to treat these two terms as synonymous and to distinguish between the two aspects of Maya or Avidya which are called avarana and vikshepa, the former being the negative aspect of concealment and the latter the positive aspect of projection.

Maya or Avidya is not pure illusion. It is not only absence of knowledge. It is also positive wrong knowledge. It is a cross of the real and the unreal (satyanrte mithuni krtya). In fact it is indescribable. For the appearance of Brahman as the world, it cannot be both existent and non-existent for this conception is self-contradictory. It is called neither real nor unreal (sadasadvilalkshāna). It is false or mithya. But it is not a non-entity like a hare's horn (tuchchha). It is positive (bhavarupa). It is potency (shakti). It is also called superimposition (adhyasa). A shell is mistaken as silver. The shell is the ground on which the silver is superimposed. When right knowledge (prama) arises, this error (bhranti or bhrama) vanishes. The relation between the shell and the silver is neither that of identity nor of difference nor of both. It is unique and is known as non-difference (tadatmya). Similarly, Brahman is the ground on which the world appears through Maya. When right knowledge dawns and the essential unity of the jiva with the Paramatman is realized, Maya or Avidya vanishes.

Three grades of satta

The world possesses three different grades of existence. The first kind of facts possesses only ephemeral existence (pratibhasika satta or apparent existence); the second empirical or virtual existence, the sort of existence necessary for ordinary life and practice (vyavaharika satta or practical existence) and the third absolute existence (paramarthika satta or supreme existence). The world is thus not a homogeneous conception; and if, in spite of this one insists on being told what such a world (as a whole) is, the fairest reply can only be, what Sankara gives, namely that it is indescribable (anirvachaniya) either as real or as unreal. But if the word, world, is confined only to the second aspect, it would be again fair to say, that the world is real only for practical purpose, more real than the first and less real than the third kind of existence. But if the word is taken in the third sense, Sankara would emphatically assert that the world is eternally real. As he puts it: "As the cause, Brahman, does not lack existence at any time, past, present or future, so does the world not lack existence in any of three periods of time". Again, "all particular modes of existence with different names and forms are real as existence, but unreal as particulars".

Jiva

Jiva or the individual self is a subject-object complex. Its subject-element is Pure Consciousness and is called the Sakshin. Its object-element is the internal organ called the antah karana which is bhautika as it is composed of all the five elements, with the predominance of tejas which makes it always active except in deep sleep or states like swoon or trance. The source of the internal organ is Avidya which causes individuality. In perception, the internal organ, when a sense-organ comes into contact with an object, assumes the 'form' of that object. It is the vrtti or the mode of the internal organ.

This vrtti inspired by the Sakshin takes the form of empirical knowledge. In waking state, the internal organ is aided by the senses; in dream state, it functions by itself; and in deep sleep it is lost in its cause Avidya. In this state too individuality persists because the Sakshin is associated with Avidya. In liberation, Avidya is destroyed by jnana and the Sakshin is realized as the Brahman which it always is.

Jivanmukti

Sankara repeatedly asserts that the Absolute can be realized through knowledge and knowledge alone; karma and upasana are subsidiary. They may help us in urging us to know reality and they may prepare us for that knowledge by purifying our mind (sattvashuddhi), but ultimately it is knowledge alone which, by destroying ignorance, the root-cause of this world, can enable us to be one with the Absolute. The opposition of knowledge and action stands firm like a mountain. They are contradictory (viparite) and are poles apart. Those who talk of combining knowledge with action, says Sankara, have perhaps not read the Brhadaranyaka nor are they aware of the glaring contradiction repeatedly pointed out by the Shruthi and the Smrti. Knowledge and action are opposed like light and darkness. Actions are prescribed for those who are still in ignorance and not for those who are enlightened. Knowledge only removes ignorance and then reality shines forth by itself. A liberated sage, however, performs actions without any attachment and works for the uplift of humanity. Sankara's own life bears ample witness to this fact.

Vivartavada

Illusory modification of any substance, as of the rope into the snake is called vivarta. Sankara's theory of creation is known as vivartavada.

The other Schools of Vedanta

The following are some of the well-known Schools of Vedanta.

1. *Sankara* - *Advaita*
2. *Bhaskara* - *Bhedabheda*
3. *Yadavaprakasa* - *Bhedabheda*
4. *Ramanuja* - *Vishistadvaita*
5. *Madhva* - *Dvaita*
6. *Nimbarka* - *Dvaitadvaita*
7. *Srikandha* - *Saiva-Vishishtadvaita*
8. *Sripati* - *Bhedabhedatmaka*
9. *Vallabha* - *Suddhadvaita*
10. *Suka* - *Bhedavada*
11. *Baladeva* - *Achintyabhedaabheda*

These schools are well-known in India but Vishishtadvaita of Ramanuja and Dvaita of Madhva are more well-known and gained precedence over the others.

Vishishtadvaita

The Vishishtadvaita Schools was founded by Ramanuja who wrote Sribhashyam on Brahma Sutra. Ramanuja accepts the Pancharatra and Vaikhanasa Agamas in addition to the Sutras and Upanishads. According to this School the world is real, not an illusion. Souls and matter are many. They are the body of the Supreme Being. The absolute is Visishta or qualified by Chit and Achit says this School. The animate beings and the inanimate matter are all modes of the Supreme Being. They exist only for him. Hence they are Sesha and the God is Seshi. Vishishtadvaita accepts that there are many Souls and objects which are mutually different. It is through Bhakti and Prapatti (devotion and surrender) that the Jiva ultimately attains the supreme self. Ramanuja believes in the Parinama vada form of Satkarya Vada.

Dvaita

Ananda Tirtha or Madhvacharya is the founder of Dvaita School of Vedanta. He wrote Prastanatraya Bhashyas and other independent works on Dvaita Philosophy. His Brahmasutra bhashya is known as Anubhashya. He has also written commentary on Bhagavatam. According to this school, matter, souls and God are all eternal and are different from each other.

Bhakti is the means adopted by the followers of this School for obtaining the salvation through the grace of Vishnu (Hari) the Supreme Lord. According to Madhva, Brahman, identified with Vishnu is the Supreme reality. Madhava proclaims the theory of Panchabhedas between Jagat, Jeeva and Ishwara.

Multiple Choice Questions

1. What is *Pudgala* according to the *Jaina* philosophy?
A. The physical world in which souls live
B. Matter which etymologically means 'that which is liable to integration and disintegration'
C. The soul which is a conscious substance
D. None of the above

2. According to the *Jaina* philosophy, the smallest parts of matter which cannot be further divided, being partless are called:
A. *Anu*
B. *Sthavara*
C. *Trasa*
D. None of the above

3. According to *Jainism*, the whole universe is brought under the two everlasting, uncreated, eternal and co-existing categories called:
A. *Kala* and *Akasha*
B. *Jiva* and *Ajiva*
C. Both A and B
D. None of the above

4. In the Jainism, the category of *Ajiva* is divided into *Akasha, dharma, adharma, kala* and:
A. *Pudgala*
B. *Trasa*
C. *Sthavarna*
D. None of the above

5. In the *Vaisesika*, system, the six positive categories are:
A. *Samavaya, Samanya, Samyoga, Dravya, Guna, Karma*
B. *Atman, Manas, Visesa, Dravya, Guna, Karma*
C. *Samavaya, Samanya, Visesa, Dravya, Guna, Karma*
D. None of the above

6. In Jaina ethics, *Tri-ratna* refers to:
A. *Samyag Smriti, Samyag-Jnana, Samyag-darsana*
B. *Samyag Charitra, Samyag-darsana, Samyag-Smriti*

C. *Samyag-Jnana, Samyag-Smriti, Samyag Charitra*
D. *Samyag darsana, Samyag-Jnana, Samyag-Charitra*

7. Match List-I with List-II and select the correct answer using the code given below the list:

List-I	***List-II***
(*a*) *Vedanta*	1. Clinging to enjoyment
(*b*) *Upadana*	2. Six-sence organs including mind
(*c*) *Sadayatara*	3. Initial consciousness of the embryo
(*d*) *Vijnana*	4. Sense-experience

Codes:

	(*a*)	(*a*)	(*c*)	(*d*)
A.	1	2	3	4
B.	2	1	4	3
C.	3	4	1	2
D.	4	1	2	3

8. According to Buddhism the criterion of the existence (*Satta*) of a thing is its:
A. Capacity to produce some effect
B. Non-permanent existence
C. Capacity to produce both cause and effect
D. None of the above

9. Man is only conventional name for a collection of different constituents, the material body (*Kaya*), the immaterial mind (*mana* or *chitta*), the formless consciousness (*Vijnana*), just as a chariot is a collection of wheels, axles, shafts etc. This view is held by:
A. *Buddhism* B. *Jainism*
C. *Advaita Vedanta* D. *Earraka*

10. The *pancha-skandha* of Buddhism are:
A. *Rupa, Vedana, Sanjna, Samskaras, Vijnana*
B. *Avidya, Rupa, Vedana, Samskaras, Vijnana*
C. *Avidya, Sadayatana, Sparsa, Samskaras, Vijnana*
D. None of these

11. According to *Nyaya-Vaisesika,* there is no Universal subsisting in another Universal because there is/are:
A. No Universals which can be intermediate
B. One single Universal for one class of objects
C. Two or more universals in the same class of things
D. None of the above

12. According to *Vaisesika*, in respect to their scope or extent, universals may be distinguished into para and:
A. *Parapara*
B. *Apara*
C. Both A and B
D. None of the above

13. According to *Vaisesika* 'being hood' (*Satta*) is the:
A. *Parapara* or the intermediate Universal
B. *Apara* or the lowest Universal
C. *Para* or the highest Universal
D. None of the above

14. Substantiality or *dravyatva* is regarded in *Nyaya Vaisesika* system as the:
A. *Apara* or the lowest Universal
B. *Para* or the highest Universal
C. *Parapara* or the intermediate Universal
D. None of the above

15. According to *Nyaya*-Vaisesika, jar-ness (*ghatatva*) as the Universal present in all jars is the:
A. *Para* or the highest Universal
B. *Parapara* or the intermediate Universal
C. *Apara* or the lowest Universal
D. None of the above

16. *Svatantra Yogachara* school is also called the school of Buddhism:
A. Illogical B. Logical
C. Conventional D. Modern

17. According to *Svatantra Yogachara, Buddhism* in order to differentiate similar individuals of a so-called community from individuals of other communities, the wise persons resorted to conventional names and coined the:
A. Quality
B. Substance
C. Inherence
D. Universal

18. Reality is the unique and absolutely, dissimiler particular thing-in-itself. Intellect, words, names concepts cannot even touch it. This view is given by:
A. *Jainas* B. *Naiyayikas*
C. *Buddhists* D. None of the above

19. What is the conception of the reflection in cognition which is wrongly grasped as 'an object' according to Svatantra Yogachara Buddhism?
A. *Apoha* B. *Nisedha*
C. Potency D. All of the above

20. Things in themselves are neither unified nor diversified; it is only the conceptual content that appears as diverse. This view is given by:
A. *Buddhists* B. *Naiyayikas*
C. *Mimamsakas* D. None of the above

21. Svatantra Yogachara Buddhists suggest that when a thing excludes another, it is called its:
A. *Apoha* B. Difference
C. Negation D. None of the above

22. From the .... standpoint, Apohas are recognised as positive and so they cannot be taken to be mere non-entities by the Buddhists:
A. Logical B. Ethical
C. Phenomenal D. None of the above

23. Ramanuja attempts a harmonious combination of absolutism with:
A. *Shaivism* B. *Shaktism*
C. Personal theism D. None of the above

24. Match List-I with List-II and select the correct answer from the codes given below the lists:

List-I (Main sects)	***List-II (Name of the Philosophers)***
(*a*) *Shrisampradaya*	1. Visnusvami
(*b*) *Brahmasampradaya*	2. Nimbarka
(*c*) *Rudra sampradaya*	3. Madhva
(*d*) *Sanakasampradaya*	4. Ramanuja

Codes:

	(*a*)	(*a*)	(*c*)	(*d*)
A.	1	2	3	4
B.	4	3	1	2
C.	3	4	1	2
D.	1	3	4	2

25. The *Vaisnavas*, the *Shaivas* and the *Shaktas* all have their different sacred literature called the:
A. *Agamas* B. *Samhita*
C. *Tantra* C. Real *vedas*

26. Shri-bhasya, Gita-bhasya, Vedanta-sara, Vedantadipa etc. were written by:
A. Ramanuja B. Madhva
C. Sankara D. Vallabha

27. Ramanuja recognises three things as ultimate and real (*tattva-traya*), viz.
A. *Avidya*, matter, soul
B. Matter, Soul, God
C. World, matter, soul
D. None of the above

28. Mahatma Buddha discovered which type of dhyana?
A. Sthula dhyana B. Sukshama dhyana
C. Vipassana dhyana D. Jyotirmaya dhyana

29. Who is the writer of 'Ashtanga Yoga Grantha'?
A. Shri Shyamacharana
B. Swami Charandas
C. Shri Aurobindo
D. Swami Shivananda

30. The word 'yoga' is derived from the sanskrit word:
A. Yuj B. Yog
C. Yogeya D. Yoja

31. What is the correct sequence of the limbs of saptanga yoga sadhna as described by Maharishi Gheranda?
A. Asana, Mudra, Pranayama, Pratyahara, Dharna, Dhyana, Samadhi
B. Shatkarma, Asana, Mudra, Pratyahara, Pranayama, Dharna, Dhyana
C. Shatkarma, Asana, Mudra, Pratyahara, Pranayam, Dhyana, Samadhi
D. Asana, Shatkarma, Mudra, Pranayama, Pratyahara, Dhyana, Samadhi

32. In which text the discourse between king Chandakapali and Maharishi Gheranda is mentioned?
A. Hatha Yoga Pradipika
B. Ashtanga Yoga Grantha
C. Yoga Chintamani
D. Gheranda Samhita

33. How many limbs of hatha yoga are described by Maharishi Gheranda?
A. 4 B. 6
C. 7 D. 8

34. How many mudras are considered important by Maharishi Gheranda?
A. 10 B. 15
C. 20 D. 25

35. Which mudra is related to dhyana yoga samadhi?
A. Khechari B. Yoni
C. Shambhavi D. Shaktichalini

36. Which of the following match is incorrect?
A. Dhyana yoga samadhi - Shambavi mudra
B. Nad yoga samadhi - Khechari mudra
C. Laya yoga samadhi - Yoni mudra
D. Bhakti yoga samadhi - Kaki mudra

37. Which of following is not considered as a element by Buddhism?
A. Fire B. Space
C. Air D. Water

38. Which chakra is most described in Bhagavad Gita?
A. Sahashara B. Ajna
C. Manipura D. Anahata

39. Who is the author of 'Yoga Vartika'?
A. Maharishi Vyasa B. Vigyanbhikshu
C. Kapila muni D. Gorakshanath

40. According to ....– 'Yoga is to redirect the mind and body towards soul'.
A. Shiva purana B. Vishnu purana
C. Buddhism D. Jainism

41. Who is known as the founder of Yoga?
A. Maharishi Patanjali
B. Matseyandranath
C. Hiranyagarbha
D. Maharishi Vyasa

42. According to Jain philosophy, how many types of parmana vrittis are there?
A. 1 B. 3
C. 4 D. 5

43. According to Gautam rishi the total number of padarthas are ...., while according to Kanada rishi the total number of padarthas are ....
A. 6, 16 B. 16, 6
C. 6, 18 D. 18, 12

44. Who compiled the yoga first time in a systematic way?
A. Maharishi Gheranda
B. Matseyandranath
C. Gorkashanath
D. Maharishi Patanjali

45. According to yoga philosophy the kaivalya is attained when sadhaka gets the stage of .... samadhi.
A. Sabija B. Abija
C. Nirbija D. None

46. In bhakti yoga the 'bhakti' word is derived from which word?
A. Bhaj B. Bhagaj
C. Bhagad D. Bhajag

47. Whose opinion is this? – 'A deep faith in God is bhakti'.
A. Narad sutra B. Shandilya sutra
C. Bhagavad Gita D. Yoga Vashistha

48. To dedicate everything to God is known as:
A. Sakha bhava B. Dasya bhava
C. Pada shevana D. Atamanevadana

49. How many types of bhakti is told by Acharya Ramanuja?
A. 4 B. 5
C. 7 D. 9

50. By means of external objects the worship of deity is called as:
A. Para bhakti B. Apara bhakti
C. Ragatamika bhakti D. Vedik bhakti

51. When the sadhaka adores the almighty Brahma, the type of bhakti is known as:
A. Para bhakti B. Apara bhakti
C. Vediki bhakti D. None

52. To redirect the senses towards Brahma by withdrawling from external objects is known as:
A. Shama B. Dama
C. Titiksha D. Vairagya

53. To bear the endurance by sadhaka is known as ....

A. Sama B. Dama
C. Viveka D. Titiksha

54. Deattachment from wordly objects by not desiring for the results and to dedicate all the acts to almighty god, is known as ....

A. Shraddha B. Shama
C. Dama D. Uprati

55. To attain the stage of Brahma bhava is the main aim of .... yoga.

A. Jnana yoga B. Kriya yoga
C. Laya yoga D. Raja yoga

56. To concentrate mind on Brahma and to serve his master is known as:

A. Bhakti B. Vairagya
C. Viveka D. Samadhana

57. Which of the following are parts of shatasampati?

A. Shama, Dama
B. Shraddha, Samadhana
C. Titiksha, Uprati
D. All the above

58. To purify mana, buddhi, chitta in jnana yoga by means of four ways (viveka, vairagya, shatsampati, mumukshtava) is known as:

A. Bahiranga sadhna
B. Antaranga sadhna
C. Chatustaya
D. None

59. For bahiranga sadhna 4 means are mentioned, for antaranga sadhna how many means are mentioned?

A. 3 B. 4
C. 5 D. 6

60. In jnana yoga sadhna .... is considered as a false element.

A. Jagat B. Prakriti
C. Chitta D. Brahma

61. To concentrate on Brahma by listening shruti vakyas and understanding the meaning of these vakyas is known as:

A. Nidhidhyasana B. Manana
C. Shradha D. Uprati

62. What was the time period of bhakti yoga?

A. 11th-13th century
B. 12th-16th century
C. 9th-11th century
D. 14th-18th century

63. The main aim of Raja yoga is:

A. To control emotions
B. To control mind
C. To control organs
D. To control senses

64. 'Bhakti yoga is to realize the God honestly'– Whose opinion is this?

A. Shri Aurovindo
B. Swami Vivekananda
C. Acharya Shankara
D. Acharya Ramanuja

65. 'Bhakti yoga sadhna' is suitable for which type of sadhakas?

A. Emotional
B. Rational
C. Rajasguna dominant
D. Sattvaguna dominant

66. Which guna is dominant in medium category sadhakas?

A. Tamas guna B. Rajas guna
C. Sattva guna D. Both B and C

67. 'Tapo Davindav Sahanam' line is related to which yoga?

A. Jnana yoga B. Bhakti yoga
C. Kriya yoga D. Hatha yoga

68. Which yogic sadhna is suggested for medium category sadhaka?

A. Ashtanga yoga B. Kriya yoga
C. Hatha yoga D. Raja yoga

69. Which of the following is not bahiranga sadhana of jnana yoga sadhna?

A. Mumukshutava B. Shravana
C. Viveka D. Vairagya

70. Who was the proponent of Bhakti yoga?

A. Shri Krishna
B. Swami Vivekananda
C. Chaitanya Mahaprabhu
D. Shiva

71. By practice of mantra yoga sadhna:
A. Concentration of mind increases
B. Conscience becomes pure
C. Negative thoughts get eliminated
D. All of the above

72. Match the correct:

(*a*) Nyaya philosophy		1. Kapila	
(*b*) Vaisesika philosophy		2. Gautam	
(*c*) Mimamsa philosophy		3. Jamini	
(*d*) Samkhya philosophy		4. Kanada	

Codes:

	(*a*)	(*b*)	(*c*)	(*d*)
A.	1	2	3	4
B.	2	4	3	1
C.	2	4	1	3
D.	3	2	1	4

73. Which of the following is not a antaranga sadhana of jnana yoga sadhna?
A. Nidhidhyasana B. Samadhi
C. Manana D. Shatsampati

74. Who is the author of 'Adresses on Bhakti yoga'?
A. Annie Bessant
B. Shri Aurobindo Ghosh
C. Swami Vivekanand
D. Swami Shivanand

75. Who is the author of 'Rajamartanda'?
A. Sankaracharya B. Ramanujacharya
C. Bhojdeva D. Gorakshnath

76. Who is writer of the book 'Rebirth and Karma'?
A. Shri Aurobindo Ghosh
B. Annie Besant
C. Swami Vivekanand
D. Dr. David Frawley

77. Shri Aurobindo preached mainly which type of yoga?
A. Integral yoga B. Ashtanga yoga
C. Raja yoga D. Bhakti yoga

78. Who is the writer of the text "Yoga Sutra Bhasya"?
A. Maharishi Vyasa B. Acharya Ramanuja
C. Acharya Sankara D. Swami Charandas

79. Which is the most ancient systematic text of yoga?
A. Patanjali Yoga Sutra
B. Shri Bhagavad Gita
C. Shiva Samhita
D. Hatha Yoga Pradipika

80. Which of the following is work of Swami Vivekananda?
A. Karma yoga
B. Raja yoga
C. Vedanta Darshan
D. All of the above

81. Which hatha yoga tradition was prominent during medieval period?
A. Natha dhara B. Tantra dhara
C. Bhakti dhara D. All of the above

82. Which of the following match is correct?
A. Dvaitavada – Madvacharya
B. Dvaitadvaitavada – Nimbarkacharya
C. Vishistadvaitavada– Ramanujacharya
D. All of the above

83. Who was the author of 'Ashtanga Yoga Grantha'?
A. Swami Shivananda
B. Swami Brahmdasa
C. Swami Parmananda
D. Swami Charandas

84. Who is known as 'The Father of the Indian medicine'?
A. Acharya Charak
B. Maharishi Shusrut
C. Maharishi Patanjali
D. None of these

85. The term 'the fruit has arisen out of the action and action out of the fruit' is related to .... :
A. Concept of Karma
B. Concept of Bhakti
C. Concept of Moksha
D. Concept of Nishkamakarma

86. The philosophy of Vivekananda is related to ....
A. Advaita B. Dvaita
C. Visistadvaita D. None of these

87. The philosophy of Sri Aurobindo is known as:
A. Integral Yoga B. Jnana yoga
C. Karma yoga D. Bhakti yoga

88. The concept of Supermind is associated with the philosophy of:
A. Sri Aurobindo
B. Swami Vivekananda
C. Patanjali
D. Sri Narayana Guru

89. The process of Ascent through Descent means:
A. Existence B. Consciousness
C. Integration D. Bliss

90. Creation according to Sri Aurobindo is nothing but an:
A. Expression of Joy
B. Expression of Sorrow
C. Expression of Nothingness
D. None of these

91. Ascent according to Sri Aurobindo means:
A. Involution B. Evolution
C. Destruction D. Combination

92. Sri Aurobindo claims that his Yoga is Integral or ....
A. Synthetic B. Analytic
C. Descriptive D. None of these

93. .... is known as Father of Renaissance.
A. Kumaranasan
B. Ayyankali
C. Sreenarayana Guru
D. Chattambiswamikal

94. According to Swami Vivekananda, Raja Yoga means
A. Chitta vrtti nirodha
B. Mental concentration
C. Physical concentration
D. None of the above

95. Yoga literally means
A. modification B. action
C. union D. sacrifice

96. According to Swami Vivekananda, a Karma yogi should work ....
A. Physically B. Spiritually
C. Consciously D. Incessantly

97. According to Swami Vivekananda, Self-Abnegation means:
A. attachment B. self-determination
C. non-attachment D. non-existence

98. According to Swami Vivekananda, the Highest ideal in a Karma yogi is ....
A. self-abnegation B. self-discipline
C. self-determined D. self-satisfied

99. The word Karma means ....
A. to do B. to think
C. to learn D. to visualize

100. A jnana-yogi identifies Ultimate reality as:
A. Existence B. Knowledge
C. Bliss D. All of the above

101. Vivekananda was the disciple of:
A. Sree Narayana Guru
B. Mahaveera
C. Buddha
D. Sri Ramakrishna

102. Swamiji's Chicago speech held on:
A. 1894 B. 1895
C. 1892 D. 1893

103. Whose birthday is celebrated as National Youth Day?
A. Gandhiji
B. Aurobindo Ghosh
C. Vivekananda
D. Chattambiswamikal

104. Which day is celebrated as National Youth Day?
A. 12 December B. 12 January
C. 12 February D. 13 January

105. .... of realization accepted by Vivekananda.
A. 3 ways B. 5 ways
C. 4 ways D. 2 ways

106. Vivekananda's philosophy commonly known as.............. .
A. Dvaita Vedanta
B. Vishistadvaita Vedanta
C. Practical Vedanta
D. None of these

107. Bhakti-Yoga means realization through:
A. Action B. knowledge
C. Yoga D. Devotion

108. The aim of Bhaktiyoga:
A. Physical realization
B. Spiritual realization
C. Mental realization
D. None of these

109. By religion Vivekananda means:
A. Universal Religion
B. Hindu Religion
C. Christianity
D. Islam

110. The active who wants to work is known as:
A. Bhakti yogi B. Raja yogi
C. Karma yogi D. Jnana yogi

111. .... follow the path of Raja Yoga.
A. Worker B. Emotional man
C. Mystic D. Philosopher

112. Those who follow the path of intellect to know the truth is known as:
A. Karma yoga B. Jnana yoga
C. Bhakti yoga D. Raja yoga

113. A karma yogi should practice ....
A. Kamyakarma B. Nishkamakarma
C. Bhaktimarga D. Jnanamarga

114. Bhaktiyoga is the yoga of .... and ....
A. Love and Devotion
B. Love and Desire
C. Emotion and Desire
D. None of these

115. In Jnana yoga 'Kshetrajna' is:
A. Body B. Soul
C. Knowledge D. Emotion

116. A Karma yogi should practice ....
A. Pravritti marga B. Ashtanga marga
C. Nivritti marga D. None of these

117. How many days Swami Vivekananda meditated on the rock of Kanyakumari
A. 3 days B. 2 days
C. 4 days D. 5 days

118. Swami Vivekananda delivered lecture on Raja yoga and Jnana yoga in
A. Washington B. Canada
C. Chicago D. New York

119. In which year Government of India decided to observe the birthday of Swamiji as the National Youth Day?
A. 1980 B. 1910
C. 1984 D. 1985

120. Who is the master in Sister Nivedhida's book "The master As I saw Him"?
A. Sri Ramakrishna
B. Vivekananda
C. Brahmananda Shivayogi
D. Sankaracharya

121. Which society established by Swami Vivekananda in New York?
A. Ramakrishna Mission
B. Advaita Mission
C. Vedanta Society
D. Advaita Ashram

122. When did Swami Vivekananda take 'Maha-samadhi'
A. 4th July 1902
B. 4th July 1903
C. 2nd Auguhst 1900
D. 12th January 1863

123. According to Swami Vivekananda, the genuine search after the God is known as
A. Karma yoga B. Jnana yoga
C. Bhakti yoga D. Raja yoga

124. .... describes the true nature of man as Soul-Force or Atman.
A. Aurobindo B. Vivekananda
C. Radhakrishnan D. Tagore

125. The Life Divine was written by
A. Dr. S. Radhakrishnan
B. Tagore
C. Sri Aurobindo
D. Narayana Guru

126. Sri Aurobindo's Yoga is otherwise known as:
A. Hatha Yoga B. Karma Yoga
C. Raja Yoga D. Purna Yoga

127. Sri Aurobindo's concept of Absolute is:
A. Existence B. Consciousness
C. Bliss D. All of the above

128. According to Sri Aurobindo, the transformation from Inconsciousness to knowledge is known as:
A. Psychic change
B. Spiritual change
C. Supramental change
D. None of these

129. According to Sri Aurobindo, the progress from Life to Mind is completed:
A. Mind descends into Life
B. Mind descends into Matter
C. Mind descends into Psyche
D. None of these

130. According to Sri Aurobindo, the Gnostic being is governed by the power of:
A. Morality B. Rationality
C. Spirituality D. None of the above

131. According to Sri Aurobindo Evolution presupposes:
A. Involution B. Illusion
C. Maya D. None of these

132. Creation according to Sri Aurobindo is nothing but an:
A. Expression of Sorrow
B. Expression of Nothingness
C. Expression of Joy
D. None of these

133. According to Sri Aurobindo, which is the root of birth, the cause of remaining in existence and that into which creation ceases:
A. Brahman B. Delight/Ananda
C. Ignorance D. Maya

134. According to Sri Aurobindo, the Delight of world process in relation to the Sachchidananda is called
A. Maya B. Adhyasa
C. Lila D. Prakriti

135. According to Sri Aurobindo, the realm of reality has been divided into two hemispheres are ....
A. Higher & Lower B. North & South
C. Upper & Lower D. None of the above

136. According to Sri Aurobindo Evolution is possible only because .... has already taken place.
A. Destruction B. God
C. Involution D. None of the above

137. Evolutionary growth according to Sri Aurobindo is a:
A. Four-fold process
B. Triple process
C. Two-fold process
D. None of the above

138. According to Sri Aurobindo, the Triple process of Evolutionary growth involves a process of:
A. Widening, Heightening and Integration
B. Widening, Heightening and Destruction
C. Widening, Heightening and Combination
D. Widening, Heightening and Differentiation

139. According to Sri Aurobindo, the most important character of Evolutionary process is:
A. Widening B. Heightening
C. Integration D. Combination

140. The difference between Mind and Supermind, according to Sri Aurobindo, consists in the difference between their
A. Manner of apprehending the Reality
B. Appearance
C. Structures
D. None of the above

141. The Supermind is described by Sri Aurobindo by calling it:
A. Omnipotent, Omniscient, Omnipresent
B. Superconscious entity
C. Creator, The Real Idea, and the Supreme Truth Consciousness
D. None of the above

142. According to Sri Aurobindo, which of the following belong to Lower Hemisphere?
A. Matter, Life, Mind, Psyche
B. Matter, Life, Mind, Supermind
C. Mind, Supermind
D. Matter

143. According to Sri Aurobindo, the Triune principle of Sachchidananda is:
A. Existence, Consciousness, Bliss
B. Matter, Life, Mind
C. Psyche, Mind, Supermind
D. None of the above

144. Ascent according to Sri Aurobindo means:
A. Evolution B. Involution
C. Destruction D. Construction

145. The Three steps of Integral Yoga are:
A. Psychicisation
B. Spiritualization
C. Supramentalization
D. All of the above

146. Yoga according to Sri Aurobindo is the effort to move the mind along the path of ascend towards ....
A. Highermind B. Supermind
C. Illumined mind D. None of the above

147. According to Sri Aurobindo, Mind is the Subordinate power of
A. Supermind B. Life
C. Psyche D. Matter

148. According to Sri Aurobindo, which of the following belong to Higherhemisphere?
A. Existence, Consciousness-force, Bliss, Supermind
B. Mind, Psyche, Life, Matter
C. Existence, Mind, Psyche, Supermind
D. Existence, Bliss, Supermind, Mind

149. Sri Aurobindo founded Ashram at ....
A. Pondichery B. Madras
C. Hyderabad D. None of the above

150. Sri Aurobindo claims that his Yoga is Integral or ....
A. Synthetic
B. Analytic
C. Descriptive
D. None of the above

151. The guiding principle of Sri Aurobindo's metaphysics is:
A. Reconciliation B. Renunciation
C. Self-abnegation D. None of these

152. According to Sri Aurobindo, Yoga means Union with the Divine. This union is:
A. Transcendental
B. Cosmic
C. Individual
D. All the three together

153. Sri Aurobindo describes creation as the plunge of the Spirit into ....
A. Ignorance B. Maya
C. Adhyasa D. Non existence

154. According to Sri Aurobindo, ... is the power that creates the world.
A. Maya B. Nothingness
C. Avidhya D. God

155. According to Sri Aurobindo, Maya created this world for the sake of ....
A. Sorrow B. Joy
C. Unhappiness D. Destruction

156. Who was the Author of the work 'The Integral Theory of Evolution'?
A. Sri Aurobindo
B. K.C. Bhattacharya
C. Swami Vivekananda
D. None of the above

157. How many kinds of ignorance are mentioned by Sri Aurobindo?
A. Three B. Five
C. Six D. Seven

158. Theories of Existence accepted by Sri Aurobindo are:
A. One B. Two
C. Three D. Four

159. The philosophy of Sri Aurobindo is described as ....
A. Purna-advaita B. Visista-advaita
C. Dvaita D. Advaita

160. According to Sri Aurobindo, ... is the root principle of creation.
A. Chhita B. Psyche
C. Matter D. Existence

161. Which chakra is activated by practise of bhadrasana?
A. Muladhara B. Swathisthana
C. Manipura D. All of the above

162. Which kriya activates the manipura chakra?
A. Vayusara B. Varisara
C. Agnisara D. Vahnisara

163. By practise of which mudra fear of death is lost and ajna chakra is activated?
A. Mahabandha B. Vajroli
C. Mahabheda D. Shaktichalini

164. In which kosha 'kriya shakti' exists?
A. Anandamaya B. Vijyanamaya
C. Pranamaya D. Manomaya

165. Which of the following match is not correct?
A. Yama – Muladhara chakra
B. Niyama – Swathisthana chakra
C. Pratyahara – Visudhi chakra
D. Pranayama – Manipura chakra

166. Which kosha is related to will power?
A. Anandamaya B. Manomaya
C. Vijyanamaya D. Pranamaya

167. Which of the following is not a part of yama?
A. Ahimsa B. Satya
C. Asteya D. Swadhyaya

168. Pratyahara is a
A. Physical activity B. Mental activity
C. Part of dhyana D. Part of dharna

169. How many types of sahita kumbhaka are there?
A. 2 B. 4
C. 6 D. 7

170. In the first stage during the practice of nigarbha sahita kumbhaka, the sadhaka feels
A. Vibration in body
B. Coldness in body
C. Sweating in body
D. Lightness in body

171. Which of the following are parts of kriya yoga?
A. Socha, Santosha, Tapa, Pranidhana
B. Santosha, Tapa, Swadhyaya
C. Tapa, Swadhyaya, Pranidhana
D. Tapa, Swadhyaya, Aprigraha

172. At which chakra a sadhaka should concentrate while performing vrikshasana?
A. Manipura B. Visudhi
C. Anahata D. Muladhara

173. Which chakra is awakened by the practice of mulbandha?
A. Swasthisthana B. Visudhi
C. Muladhara D. Both A and C

174. Ajapa japa is related to which pranayama?
A. Sahita B. Murchha
C. Kevali D. Palavini

175. Which of the following is not a part of kriya-yoga?
A. Swadhyaya B. Tapa
C. Santosha D. Ishwar pranidhana

176. Which of the following is antaranga sadhana of yoga sadhna?
A. Asana B. Pranayama
C. Pratyahara D. None

177. Which is the main element of visudhi chakra?
A. Earth B. Water
C. Fire D. Space

178. Which is the bija mantra of visudhi chakra?
A. Lam B. Yam
C. Ram D. Ham

179. Which vayu is related to visudhi chakra?
A. Prana B. Udana
C. Apana D. Sarana

180. What is bija mantra of anahata chakra?
A. Earth B. Water
C. Air D. Space

181. Which is the main element of anahata chakra?
A. Earth B. Water
C. Air D. Space

182. How many petals does visudhi chakra have?
A. 10 B. 12
C. 16 D. 14

183. How many petals does anahat chakra have?
A. 12 B. 14
C. 16 D. 18

184. Apana vayu is related to which chakra?
A. Anahata B. Manipura
C. Muladhara D. Visudhi

185. Samana vayu is related to which chakra?
A. Anahata B. Muladhara
C. Manipura D. Visudhi

186. Prana vayu is related to which chakra?
A. Visudhi B. Muladhara
C. Anahata D. Ajana

187. Udana vayu is related to which chakra?
A. Sahashra B. Anahata
C. Ajna D. Visudhi

188. Which vayu controls sensory organs?
A. Udana B. Apana
C. Samana D. Vayana

189. Which vayu exists in body as the reserved energy?
A. Prana B. Vyana
C. Samana D. Apana

190. Who is the deity of ajna chakra?
A. Vishnu B. Varuna
C. Shiva D. Maheswar

191. Who is the deity of mooladhara chakra?
A. Ganesha B. Shiva
C. Vishnu D. Varuna

192. Which of the following match is incorrect?
A. Space – Middle finger
B. Earth – Ring finger
C. Fire – Index finger
D. Water – Little finger

193. Who is the deity of manipura chakra?
A. Brahma B. Shrigura
C. Shiva D. Vishnu

194. Who is the deity of anahata chakra?
A. Shiva B. Vishnu
C. Brahma D. Mahesha

195. Activation of which chakra provides second sight to a sadhaka?
A. Visudhi B. Ajna
C. Anahata D. Muladhara

196. How many petals does muladhara chakra have?
A. 4 B. 6
C. 8 D. 10

197. Which chakra is related to digestive system?
A. Svathisthana B. Manipura
C. Visudhi D. Muladhara

198. What is bija mantra of muladhara chakra?
A. Lam B. Yam
C. Ham D. Ram

199. What is bija mantra of manipura chakra?
A. Yam B. Ram
C. Ham D. Lam

200. How many petals does manipura chakra have?
A. 4 B. 6
C. 8 D. 10

201. Practise of mudras stengthen which kosha?
A. Anandmaya B. Anamaya
C. Manomaya D. None

202. Which upa-prana regulates our hunger and thirst?
A. Krikala B. Dhanajaya
C. Devadatta D. Kurma

203. Burping is caused due to which upa-prana?
A. Krikala B. Naga
C. Dhanajaya D. Devadatta

204. Which practise should be performed to purify samana vayu?
A. Kunjal, Neti
B. Mulbandha, dhauti
C. Jalandharbandha, Ujjayi pranayam
D. Uddiyana bandha, Kapalbhati kriya

205. What is the direction of samana vayu in body?
A. Towards center B. Towards outside
C. Upwards D. Downwards

206. In the body samana vayu is located at
A. From heart to navel
B. From throat to kapala
C. From naval to feet
D. From heart to throat

207. What is the main element of samana vayu?
A. Air B. Water
C. Fire D. Earth

208. Which vayu helps in digestion?
A. Apana B. Samana
C. Vyana D. Udana

209. Deterioration of which vayu causes kidney disorders?
A. Samana B. Vyana
C. Udana D. Apana

210. In the body apana vayu is located at:
A. From heart to throat
B. From heart to navel
C. From throat to skull
D. From navel to feet

211. What is the main element of apana vayu?
A. Earth B. Air
C. Fire D. Water

212. Which vayu helps in reproduction?
A. Samana B. Prana
C. Udana D. Apana

213. In the body five types of vayus are the constituent of which kosha?
A. Ananmaya B. Manomaya
C. Pranamaya D. Anandmaya

214. Which vayu helps in urination?
A. Samana B. Apana
C. Vyana D. Udana

215. What is the main element of vyana vayu?
A. Earth B. Fire
C. Air D. Water

216. What is the direction of apana vayu in body?
A. Upwards B. Downwards
C. Towards centre D. None

217. Vyana vayu is related to which chakra?
A. Manipura B. Anahata
C. Visudhi D. Swathisthana

218. Which chakra creates equability in human?
A. Visudhi B. Manipura
C. Anahata D. Ajna

219. Vishnu is related to which chakra?
A. Muladhara B. Manipura
C. Anahata D. Ajna

220. Which chakra is also known as third eye?
A. Visudhi B. Ajna
C. Anahata D. Manipura

221. Which upa-prana is related to yawning and sleep?
A. Naga B. Krikala
C. Kurma D. Devdatta

222. Which vayu helps in word utterance?
A. Udana B. Samana
C. Apana D. Prana

223. What is the direction of udana vayu in body?
A. Towards centre B. Towards outside
C. Upwards D. Downwards

224. Udana vayu in body is located at:
A. From throat to navel
B. From throat to skull
C. From throat to feet
D. From navel to skull

225. What is the main element of udana vayu?
A. Earth B. Fire
C. Air D. Water

226. Which dosha causes migraine?
A. Vatta B. Pitta
C. Kapha D. None

227. Which dosha causes obesity?
A. Vatta B. Pitta
C. Kapha D. None

228. Vatta is related to which elements?
A. Space, air B. Water, fire
C. Water, earth D. Water, air

229. Pingla nadi is related to which part of brain?
A. Left B. Right
C. Middle D. Front

230. Pingla nadi provides us:
A. Coldness B. Heat
C. Pleasure D. Patience

231. PIngla nadi is related to:
A. Left nostril B. Right nostril
C. Left part of brain D. Both B and C

232. Ida and Pingla nadis join together at:
A. Sahashra chakra B. Ajna chakra
C. Anahata chakra D. Visudhi chakra

233. Pingla nadi originates from which chakra?
A. Swathisthana B. Muladhara
C. Ajna D. Visudhi

234. Ida nadi originates from which chakra?
A. Muladhara B. Swathisthana
C. Ajna D. Visudhi

235. Where the three nadis (ida, pingla, sushumna) joins each other?
A. Ajna chakra B. Sahasra chakra
C. Muladhara chakra D. Visudhi chakra

236. Which vayu joins samasti prana to vayasti prana?
A. Samana B. Udana
C. Apana D. Prana

237. Which element is related to kurma upa-prana?
A. Air B. Fire
C. Space D. Earth

238. Which element is related to dhanjaya upa-prana?
A. Earth B. Water
C. Fire D. Air

239. Which element is related to krikala upa-prana?
A. Earth B. Water
C. Air D. Fire

240. Which vayu helps in formation of sapta-dhatus in body?
A. Apana B. Udana
C. Samana D. Vayana

241. Vyana vayu in the body is located at:
A. Heart to navel B. Throat to skull
C. Mouth to heart D. Whole body

242. Diabetes is caused by deactivation of which chakra?
A. Muladhara B. Visudhi
C. Anahata D. Manipura

243. Deactivation of which chakra creates the possibility of paralysis in the body?
A. Muladhara B. Sahashara
C. Anahata D. Ajna

244. The meaning of word 'nad' is:
A. Energy B. To flow
C. Prayer D. To supply

245. 'Nadi' word is derived from which sanskrit word?
A. Nadi B. Nad
C. Nadh D. Nadhya

246. Pitta dosha is related to which elements?
A. Space, air B. Water, fire
C. Water, earth D. Water, air

247. Vatta dosha is related to which elements?
A. Space, air B. Water, fire
C. Water, earth D. Water, air

248. Pingla nadi represent which river?
A. Ganga B. Yamuna
C. Saraswati D. Krishana

249. What is colour of pingla nadi?
A. Yellow B. Green
C. Red D. White

250. Which element is related to muladhara chakra?
A. Water B. Earth
C. Fire D. Air

251. What is the main element of manipura chakra?
A. Earth B. Water
C. Fire D. Air

252. What is the main element of swasthisthana chakra?
A. Air B. Earth
C. Water D. Fire

253. Budhi and gyanendriyas are parts of which kosha?
A. Manomaya B. Anandmaya
C. Ananmaya D. Vijyanmaya

254. Which pranayama purifies causal body?
A. Suryabhedi B. Nadi shodhan
C. Bhastrika D. Ujjayi

255. Space element is related to which chakra?
A. Muladhara B. Visudhi
C. Anahata D. Manipura

256. Yellow colour is related to which chakra?
A. Visudhi B. Muladhara
C. Anahata D. Manipura

257. Red colour is related to which chakra?
A. Anahata B. Manipura
C. Muladhara D. Visudhi

258. What is the colour of swathisthana chakra?
A. Green B. Orange
C. Red D. Yellow

259. What is the colour of anahata chakra?
A. Red B. Yellow
C. Green D. Blue

260. What is the colour of visudhi chakra?
A. Pink B. Sky blue
C. Violet D. Black

261. What is the colour of ajna chakra?
A. Red B. Indigo
C. Yellow D. Green

262. What is the main element of sahashra chakra?
A. Earth B. Water
C. Fire D. None

263. Violet colour is related to which chakra?
A. Anahata B. Visudhi
C. Ajna D. Sahashra

264. How many petals does swathisthana chakra have?
A. 4 B. 6
C. 8 D. 10

265. Who is the deity of swathisthana chakra?
A. Shiva B. Vishnu
C. Brahma D. Mahesh

266. In the body prana vayu is located at:
A. Mouth to heart B. Heart to navel
C. Throat to skull D. Navel to feet

267. What is the main element of prana vayu?
A. Space B. Air
C. Earth D. Fire

268. Deterioration of which vayu causes disorders of heart and lungs?
A. Samana B. Apana
C. Vyana D. Prana

269. Deterioration of which vayu causes different types of diseases in the body?
A. Udana B. Apana
C. Samana D. Vyana

270. Which of the following match is incorrect?
A. Manipura Chakra – Wisdom
B. Ajna Chakra – Creativity
C. Muladhara Chakra – Stability
D. Swathisthan Chakra – Happiness

271. By awakening of which chakra one can control his chittavrittis and ignorance?
A. Sahashra B. Anahata
C. Ajana D. Manipura

272. Ajna chakra is located at:
A. The middle of eyebrow
B. The middle of heart
C. The middle of throat
D. The middle of navel

273. What is bija mantra of ajna chakra?
A. Ohm B. Ham
C. Yam D. Ram

274. Awakening of which chakra makes a person hardworking?
A. Manipura B. Visudhi
C. Anahata D. Swathisthana

275. Which of the following match is incorrect?
A. Anahata chakra – Pranayama
B. Manipura chakra – Asana
C. Visudhi chakra – Pratyahara
D. Ajna chakra – Samadhi

276. Which vayu regulates digestive system?
A. Apana B. Samana
C. Vyana D. Udana

277. Which of the following creates relation between causal and gross body?
A. Consciousness B. Soul
C. Prana D. Samadhi

278. Which asana connects prana-vayu to apana vayu?
A. Padmasana B. Shavasana
C. Sidhasana D. Shirshasana

279. Which chakra is related to excretory system?
A. Muladhara B. Swathisthana
C. Manipura D. Anahata

280. Where is dhanjaya up-prana located in body?
A. Heart B. Mouth
C. Brain D. Whole body

281. How many types of 'Dhatu agins' are there in body?
A. 5 B. 6
C. 7 D. 9

282. Which of the following is the quality of earth element?
A. Taste B. Form
C. Smell D. Touch

283. Which vayu in human body flows downwards?
A. Samana B. Vyana
C. Prana D. Apana

284. Which gland is activated by practise of gyana mudra?
A. Thymus B. Thyroid
C. Pituitary D. Pineal

285. Ham is the bija mantra of which chakra?
A. Anahata B. Visudhi
C. Ajna D. Muladhara

286. Which of the following upa-prana is related to yawning?
A. Naga B. Kurma
C. Devdatta D. Dhanjaya

287. Which upa-prana helps in creating speech sound?
A. Kurma B. Dhanjaya
C. Naga D. Devdatta

288. In the body introvert flow of prana is maintained by which of the following?
A. Panch-kosha B. Panch-tatva
C. Karmendriya D. Gyanendriyas

289. Enthusiasm and patience in human is due to:
A. Tamas guna B. Satva guna
C. Rajas guna D. All of the above

290. Niddhidhyasana means:
A. Self analysis
B. Daily meditation
C. To perform asanas daily
D. Self determination

291. Which of the following is a characteristics of fire element?
A. Heat B. Minim
C. Light D. All of the above

292. Which vayu exists between apana and prana vayu?
A. Samana B. Vyana
C. Udana D. None

293. Anger, anxiety and fear in humans are caused due to deterioration of which vayu?
A. Prana B. Samana
C. Udana D. Apana

294. Which klesha is known as 'moha' in samkhya philosophy?
A. Avidya B. Asmita
C. Raga D. Dwesha

295. Which klesha is known as 'mahavega' in samkhya philosophy?
A. Avidya B. Asmita
C. Raga D. Dwesha

296. How many types of yoga are described in 'Charaka Samhita'?
A. 4 B. 6
C. 7 D. 8

297. How many number of substances and qualities are described by vaisheshika philosophy?
A. 6, 12 B. 7, 16
C. 9, 24 D. 11, 25

298. Who is the founder of vaisheshika philosophy?
A. Kapila muni B. Maharishi Vyasa
C. Gautam rishi D. Kanada rishi

299. Which philosophy is useful in perception of the real nature of padarthas?
A. Nyaya B. Samkhya
C. Vaishesika D. Yoga

300. Into how many books vaisheshika philosophy is divided?
A. 4 B. 6
C. 8 D. 10

301. How many total sutras are there in vaisheshika philosophy?
A. 350 B. 356
C. 370 D. 376

302. In vaishesika philosophy the description of sutras begins with the explanation of:
A. Religion B. World
C. Consciousness D. Yoga

303. According to vaisheshika philosophy the total number of objects of experience are:
A. 4 B. 6
C. 7 D. 8

304. Who is the founder of nyaya philosophy?
A. Gautam B. Kapila
C. Kanada D. Jamini

305. Nyaya philosophy is divided into how many books?
A. 5 B. 6
C. 7 D. 8

306. The total numbers of sutras in nyaya philosophy are
A. 2643 B. 2243
C. 2143 D. None of these

307. The total number of pramanas according to nyaya philosophy are:
A. 2 B. 4
C. 6 D. 8

308. The total number of padarthas according to nyaya philosophy are:
A. 12 B. 14
C. 15 D. 16

309. Who is the founder of purva mimamsa philosophy?
A. Kanada B. Kapila
C. Jamini D. Ved Vyasa

310. Who is the founder of uttara mimamsa philosophy?
A. Ved Vyasa B. Kanada
C. Jamini D. Kapila

311. The total number of books in mimamsa philosophy are:
A. 7 B. 8
C. 10 D. 12

312. The total number of sutras in mimamsa philosophy are:
A. 2623 B. 2633
C. 2643 D. 2653

313. Which of the following is not a type of yagya?
A. Brahma yagya B. Deva yagya
C. Sadha yagya D. Atithi yagya

314. Nyaya philosophy has considered .... pramanas, whereas vaisheshika philosophy has considered .... pramanas.
A. 2, 4 B. 4, 2
C. 4, 6 D. 6, 4

315. Who is the founder of samkhya philosophy?
A. Kapila B. Jamini
C. Kanada D. Gautam

316. The total number of chapters in samkhya philosophy are:
A. 4 B. 6
C. 7 D. 8

317. The total number of sutras in samkhya philosophy are:
A. 648 B. 1848
C. 1740 D. None of these

318. The total number of Aranyakas are:
A. 4 B. 5
C. 6 D. 7

319. 'Brahma is the chetna'–This is the opinion of which text?
A. Upanishad B. Rigveda
C. Samveda D. Samkhya

320. Who said?– 'Consciousness is the foremost characteristic of body'.
A. Mimamsa B. Charvaka
C. Vedanta D. Nyaya

321. Prakriti is known by which another name?
A. Jada tatva B. Alinga
C. Both A and B D. None of the above

322. The total number of prameya according to vaisheshika philosophy are:
A. 8 B. 10
C. 12 D. 16

323. 'Arthhathho Dharma Jigyasa'–lines are related to which philosophy?
A. Nyaya B. Samkhya
C. Vedanta D. Mimamsa

324. According to ....– 'Yoga is to get skill by which one can get rid off his sorrow.'
A. Patanjali Yoga Sutra
B. Yoga Vashistha
C. Shri Bhagavad Gita
D. Yoga Darshana

325. Which of the following is characteristic of six Indian philosophies?
A. Behavioural aspect
B. Optimistic aspect
C. Moral aspect
D. All of the above

326. What is the meaning of word 'purana'?
A. To know B. To understand
C. Knowledge D. Ancient

327. According to samkhya philosophy which of the following is characteristics of 'Purusha'?
A. Purusha is passive
B. Purusha is multifold
C. Purusha is witness
D. All of the above

328. According to which philosophy, 'Consciousness is eternal and purusha is indestructible'.
A. Samkhya B. Yoga
C. Mimamsa D. All of the above

329. Charvaka does not consider which of following as a element?
A. Water B. Space
C. Air D. Earth

330. According to Ramanujacharya consciousness is:
A. A characteristic of soul
B. A form of prakriti
C. A mental activity only
D. None of the above

331. Which philosophy shows consciousness in the form of gyata, gayeya and gyana?
A. Samkhya
B. Vedanta
C. Mimamsa
D. Nyaya

332. 'Prakriti is not independent while it underlet almighty God'–this opinion belongs to which philosophy?
A. Samkhya B. Nyaya
C. Vedanta D. Mimamsa

333. Charvak represents:
A. Aatmvada
B. Partyavada
C. Padarthavada
D. Shunyavada

334. Who is founder of Charvaka philosophy?
A. Acharya Ramanuja
B. Acharya Shankara
C. Shridhara
D. Acharya Brihaspati

335. The total number of elements according to Samkhya philosophy are:
A. 26 B. 25
C. 22 D. 21

336. Samkhya philosophy has explained how many karmendriyas (active instruments) in human?
A. 4 B. 5
C. 7 D. 10

337. Samkhya philosophy has explained how many gyanendriyas (cognitive senses) in human?
A. 4 B. 5
C. 6 D. 7

338. What does word 'grahaya' mean?
A. Objects of senses
B. Past experiences
C. Preserved qualities
D. Hard austerity

339. Prana shakti exists in:
A. All the living things
B. All the non-living things
C. Only in humans
D. Both A and B

340. According to samkhya philosophy what is the characteristic of 'prakriti'?
A. Prakriti is independent
B. Prakriti is agamous
C. Prakriti is infinite
D. All of the above

341. According to samkhya philosophy what characteristic does 'purusha' not have?
A. Purusha is trigunatmika
B. Purusha is cognizable
C. Purusha is subject
D. All of the above

342. 'The cause of sorrows and sufferings of human are the wrong deeds done due to ignorance'. This opinion belongs to which philosophy?
A. Samkhya philosophy
B. Yoga philosophy
C. Nyaya philosophy
D. Vedanta philosophy

343. Who was the proponent of dvaita-advaita (dualistic non-dualism)?
A. Nimbarkacharya B. Madhvacharya
C. Ramanujacharya D. Sankaracharya

344. According to Charvaka philosophy the number of parmana vritis are:
A. 2 B. 3
C. 4 D. None

ANSWERS

1	2	3	4	5	6	7	8	9	10
B	A	B	A	C	D	D	A	A	A
11	12	13	14	15	16	17	18	19	20
B	C	C	C	C	B	D	C	A	A
21	22	23	24	25	26	27	28	29	30
A	C	C	B	A	A	B	A	B	A
31	32	33	34	35	36	37	38	39	40
C	D	C	D	C	D	B	B	B	D
41	42	43	44	45	46	47	48	49	50
C	A	B	D	C	A	B	D	B	D
51	52	53	54	55	56	57	58	59	60
A	B	D	D	A	D	D	A	B	A
61	62	63	64	65	66	67	68	69	70
B	B	D	D	A	D	C	B	B	C
71	72	73	74	75	76	77	78	79	80
D	B	D	C	C	A	A	B	A	D
81	82	83	84	85	86	87	88	89	90
D	D	D	A	C	A	A	A	C	A
91	92	93	94	95	96	97	98	99	100
B	A	C	A	C	D	C	A	A	D
101	102	103	104	105	106	107	108	109	110
D	D	C	B	C	C	D	B	A	C
111	112	113	114	115	116	117	118	119	120
C	B	B	A	B	C	A	D	C	B
121	122	123	124	125	126	127	128	129	130
C	A	C	B	C	D	D	B	A	C
131	132	133	134	135	136	137	138	139	140
A	C	B	C	A	C	B	A	C	A
141	142	143	144	145	146	147	148	149	150
C	A	A	A	D	B	A	A	A	A
151	152	153	154	155	156	157	158	159	160
A	D	A	A	B	A	D	D	A	A
161	162	163	164	165	166	167	168	169	170
D	C	A	C	D	B	D	B	A	C
171	172	173	174	175	176	177	178	179	180
C	C	D	C	C	D	D	D	B	C
181	182	183	184	185	186	187	188	189	190
C	C	A	C	D	C	D	A	B	D

191	192	193	194	195	196	197	198	199	200
A	C	D	A	B	A	D	A	B	D
201	202	203	204	205	206	207	208	209	210
C	A	B	D	A	A	C	B	D	D
211	212	213	214	215	216	217	218	219	220
A	D	C	B	D	B	D	B	B	B
221	222	223	224	225	226	227	228	229	230
D	A	C	B	D	B	B	A	A	B
231	232	233	234	235	236	237	238	239	240
D	B	A	A	A	B	D	B	D	C
241	242	243	244	245	246	247	248	249	250
D	D	D	B	B	B	A	B	C	B
251	252	253	254	255	256	257	258	259	260
C	C	D	B	B	D	C	B	C	B
261	262	263	264	265	266	267	268	269	270
B	D	D	B	C	A	B	D	C	B
271	272	273	274	275	276	277	278	279	280
C	A	A	D	D	B	C	A	A	D
281	282	283	284	285	286	287	288	289	290
C	C	D	C	B	C	B	D	B	D
291	292	293	294	295	296	297	298	299	300
D	A	A	B	C	A	C	D	C	D
301	302	303	304	305	306	307	308	309	310
C	A	B	A	A	A	B	D	C	A
311	312	313	314	315	316	317	318	319	320
D	C	C	B	A	B	D	A	A	B
321	322	323	324	325	326	327	328	329	330
C	C	D	C	D	D	D	D	B	A
331	332	333	334	335	336	337	338	339	340
C	C	C	D	B	B	B	A	D	D
341	342	343	344						
D	C	A	A						

●●●

CHAPTER

2

Basic Yoga Texts : Principal Upanishads Bhagavad Gita, Yoga Vasishtha

It is in the *Upanishads* that we find a real basis for the system of *Yoga*. The age of the *Upanishads* was a peak period of Indian thought and *Yoga* forms a very solid part of the same. Most of the early *Upanishads* have been certainly revealed in the highest trans-psychic *Yogic* state of mind. The powerful words of the *Upanishads* cannot be explained on any other basis. Amongst the *Upanishads*, the earliest ones are the *Chhandogya* and the *Brahadaranyaka*. We find a very powerful description of the *Yogic* mystic experiences in these *Upanishads* also. It seems that *Prana* was considered to be the self and *Vayu* to be the supreme reality or Brahman in the age of these *Upanishads*.

In the *Samvargavidya* of the *Chhandogya*, *Prana* has been extolled as the internal absorbent (*Adhyatmika Samvarga*) and *Vayu* as the external absorbent (*Adhi-Daivika Samvarga*). It has been stated that all internal activities are absorbed in *Prana* during sleep and arise again out of *Prana* during the waking state. Similarly all external principles are absorbed in *Vayu* and they reoriginate from *Vayu*. The essential unity of these absorbents is implied in this description.

In the famous dialogue between Aruni and his son Svetaketu, constituting the sixth chapter of the *Chhandogya Upanishad*, it has been stated that three elements, viz., light, water and earth were produced from the absolute Reality. It is thus indicated that *vayu* and *air*, is the unproduced ultimate Reality. In another famous dialogue between Sanat Kumara and Narmada consisting the seventh chapter of the *Chhandogya Upanishad*, *Prana* has been declared as the ultimate principle or the supreme *Bhuman* and the trans psychic-non-dual realization of the same has been very graphically described. In the *Brahadaranyaka Upanishad*, *Vayu* or *Prana* is said to be the non-concrete form of *Pranava*. In the famous controversy in Janaka's court included in the third chapter of the *Brahadaranyaka Upanishad*, Yajnavalkya declares *Vayu* or air to be the basic principle behind the universe, while answering the question put by Aruni. However, while answering Gargi's question, Yajnavalkya describes the ultimate immutable reality as transcending ether also. The realization of this supreme principle as one's own self is the summum bonum of human life: According to the *Upanishad*, this realization cannot be achieved by any action or by means of wealth, etc., but only by means of knowledge.

We can also find the basis for Kriya Yoga as also of the *Yamas* and the *Niyamas* in these two oldest *Upanishads*. There is no specific description of *Asana* in these *Upanishads*. *Pranayama* too has not been directly described in these *Upanishads*. But *Prana* forms a very important topic of discussion. The *Chhandogya* describes *Prana, Vyana, Apana* and *Samana* as forming respectively the Eastern, Southern, Western and Northern gates of the heart, whereas *Udana* is said to be the upper gate. The different *Nadis* of the heart have also been described in both these *Upanishads*. The colours of these *Nadis* have also been mentioned. It is worth noting in this connection that, the *Nadi* of tawny (*pingala*) colour has been called *Aditya* or the Sun. We find here the root of the Yogic concept of *pingala* or the *Surya-nadi*. These *Nadis* are said to be thinner than the thousandth part of a hair. The *Nadi* going to the head is said to be the most important one and it has been declared that one gets immortality by going upwards through this Nadi. Here, we find the root of the *Yogic* concepts of *Susumna* and *Kundalini* or serpent power. The idea that human body is a microcosm, in miniature containing everything in the macrocosm, can also be found in this *Upanishad*. It has been stated that the inner space is as vast as the outer space and that it contains the Sun, Moon, Earth, etc. However, we do not come across the idea of concentration on the *Nadis* or vital regions of human body, in these *Upanishads*. The *Chhandogya* uses the word *Dhyana* at one place and the root *Dhyai* quite often. However, we do not find the word *Yoga* and *Yogin* used in their technical sense in these early *Upanishads* also.

Yoga in the Aitareya and Taittiriya Upanishads

In the two prose *Upanishads* falling in the next chronological strata—*Taittiriya* and *Aitareya*, we do not come across any important concepts from the viewpoint of growth of the system of *Yoga*. However, in both these *Upanishads*, *Vayu* or air has been included amongst the gross elements and the ultimate non-dual reality is said to be beyond air and ether. Similarly in human body also, the self is said to be beyond *Prana*, in the *Taittiriya Upanishad*. In the description of the *Vijnanamaya Kosa*, we come across the word *Yoga*, which may be interpreted in its technical sense. *Yoga Kshema* is said to be the technical name for *Prana* and *Apana*, in the *Taittiriya Upanishad*.

Yoga in the Isa, Kena and Katha Upanishads

The three *Upanisads, viz.*, the *Isa*, *Kena* and *Katha* fall in the next chronological strata. In this very period a firm basis for the system of *Yoga* was formed. The *Isa* and *Kena*, though small in size, are rich with philosophical implications. It is here that we find the basis of the *Karma-Yoga* that was elaborated later on in the *Bhagavad Gita*. Renunciation and enjoyment, knowledge and actions are judiciously combined in the teachings of these *Upanishads*.

The *Kenopanishad* also indirectly hints at such a *Karma-yoga*. In the first section of this *Upanishad*, the trans-psychic nature of self-realization has been explained. Paradoxically it has been stated that one who knows, does not know, whereas he alone knows who does not know.

In the fourth section, we find description of mystic experience for which purpose penance, control on senses, actions, study of scriptures and truth, are said to be very essential. These form the basis of the *Yogic* concepts of the *Yama* and the *Niyamas*. However, the words *Yoga* and *Yogin* do not occur even in these *Upanishads*.

It is in the *Katha Upanishad*, that the word *Yoga* has been used in its technical sense. We also find quite elaborate discussion of *Yoga* in this *Upanishad*. Nachiketa and Yama have been presented here as the ideal disciple and preceptor respectively. Yama explains the necessity of a proper preceptor and explains that the *Adhyatma* Yoga is the only means of self-realization. He also opens the house of Supra-conscious experience for the sake of Nachiketa by means of the transfer of power.

After this initiation, the nature of the self has been explained in detail and the syllable 'Om' has been recommended as the best object for meditating on the self. The *Adhyatma-Yoga* mentioned in the second chapter has been explained in the third chapter by resorting to the metaphor of a chariot. Herein, the self is said to be the owner of the chariot, body the chariot, intellect the charioteer, mind the reigns, senses the horses and sense-objects the paths on which the chariot moves. The chariot reaches its proper goal if the horses are properly controlled by the charioteer keeping full control over the reigns. The goal is said to be the highest abode of Lord Vishnu. Of course, if the horses are not properly controlled, the chariot naturally goes astray. After this, the relative importance of senses, etc., has been explained and *Purusa* or self has been said to be the Supreme Reality. For reaching this Reality, it has been recommended that a practicant should absorb the speech within the mind, the mind within the intellect, the intellect within the cosmic intellect and finally the cosmic intellect within the tranquil self. This can be said to be the core of the *Adhyatma Yoga*, which includes the accessories of *Yoga* such as *Pratyahara, Dharana, Dhyana* and *Samadhi*. In the fourth chapter, it has been stated that the senses have been fashioned out by the creator in such a way that they naturally run outwards. It is only a rare sage who turns them inwards with efforts, with a desire for immortality and realizes the self. This is of course the process of *Pratyahara* and *Sanyama*. Mind is said to be the most important thing for getting this experience. The mystic experiences of *Raja Yoga* have also been described here. In the fifth chapter *Pranayama* has also been described indirectly. However, it is in the last chapter that we get a detailed description and also a scientific definition of *Yoga*. Here we find how the word *Yoga*, originally used in connection with *Yoking* horses came to mean metaphorically holding the senses steady and calm. As we have already seen, the senses have been described as the horses yoked to the chariot of body. The *Kathopanishad* states here that the transcendental state of experience in which mind stops functioning, together with the sense organs and even the intellect does not function is supposed to be the *Yoga*. Then we get a scientific definition of *Yoga*, as *Yoga* is the rising and the setting of the sense-functions without ignorance.

Yoga is that trans-psychic experience in which a person voluntarily stops the activities of senses, mind and intellect and gets himself merged in pure consciousness. This is exactly the state of samadhi or absorbing tranquillity. Thus, we see how at the time of this Upanishad, the word '*Yoga*' has acquired its technical meaning viz *Samadhi*. In the last chapter of the *Kathopanishad*, the 'granthis' and the nadis have also mentioned and raising of the serpent power is also indicated as in the *Chhandogya Upanishad*. In the concluding portion, the Yoga vidhi together with the vidya is said to be the gist of the teaching. These words are the equivalents of Yoga sastra and Brahma Vidya which we come across in the colophon of the *Bhagavad Gita*.

Yoga in the Prasna and Mundaka Upanishads

In the next chronological strata fall the *Prasna* and the *Mundaka Upanishad* in which we find further development of *Yoga*. The *Prasnopanishad* mainly deals with the *Prana Vidya*. Praying to *Prana*, sage Pippalada asks for glory and intellectual brilliance. It is in this *Upanishad*, that we get a clear mention of the places and function of vital airs within the human body. The organ of excretion and sex is said to be the place of *Apana*. *Prana* resides in eyes, ears, mouth and nostrils. *Samana* stays in between these two. *Vyana* is said to move in seventy two thousand channels within human body and the *Udana* is said to carry the life through the upward channel at the time of death. Similarly, in the macrocosm, the sun is said to be the place of *Prana*, Earth the place of *Apana*, the middle space, the place of *Samana*, Breeze, the place of *Vyana*, whereas Light, the place of *Udana*. The *Upanishad* promises immortality through correct knowledge of these vital airs. This detailed description certainly indicates a developed stage of *Yoga*. In this *Upanishad*, we also come across a detailed, description of meditation on the syllable 'Om'. Syllable 'Om' is described as a symbol of both the lower as well as the higher *Brahman*. The *Mundakopanishad* represents a further development of the philosophy of the *Kathopanishad* and we come across many common ideas in these two *Upanishads*. *Meditation* and *yoga* can be said be to the main topics of this *Upanishad*.

We also get here a description of the mystic experiences of *Raja Yoga* for this purpose. Truth, austerity, study of scriptures and continence have been recommended as the preliminary practices. These can be said to be the basic *Yamas* and *Niyamas*. This *Upanishad* also mentions the *Sanyasa Yoga* or the *Yoga* of renunciation. Thus it represents further development of *Raja Yoga*.

Yoga in the Mandukya, Svetasvatara and Kaushitaki Upanishads

The *Mandukya Upanishad* consisting just of twelve mantras is the shortest of all the *Upanishads*. It deals with the symbolism of syllable 'Om'.

In the *Kaushitaki Upanishad*, the main topic of discussion is the *Prana Vidya*, which is borrowed mainly from the *Chhandogya* and *Brahadaranyaka Upanishads*. The dialogue between Balaki and Ajatshatru has been borrowed from the *Brahadaranyaka Upanishad* in which the *Nadis* have been described. However, there is nothing new as far as the development of *Yoga* is concerned.

The *Svetasvatara Upanishad* is perhaps the most important one from the viewpoint of *Yoga*. This *Upanishad* has, for the first time, described in detail the posture useful for meditation. The other accessories of *Yoga* are also hinted at. The place useful for *yogic* practice has also been described fully. The sequence of the accessories - *Asanas*, *Pratyahara* and *Pranayama* is the one that has been maintained in the *Hatha Yoga* and *Raja Yoga* treatise. The sequence in Patanjali's *Astanga Yoga* is obviously different. Patanjali has also described the place for practice *Yoga* and also the physiological changes brought in by the *Yogic* practice. This *Upanishad* has described them in detail.

Yoga and Samkhya

All the systems of thought have passed through various earlier stages before assuming their final forms in which they are available to us today. This early history of Indian thought is shrouded in mystery and we get only a few gleanings through the references in the works like the *Mahabharata*. However, from the available sources, it can be safely assumed that *samkhya* and *yoga* were the earliest systems getting their individual forms. These two systems have been very frequently referred to in the *Mahabharata* and early Sanskirt literature. Even the *Nirukta* seems to refer to these systems.

सांख्य योगं संमभ्यस्ते् पुरुषं वा पञ्चविंशकम्।

...........(Nirukta XIV).

Several scholars have tried to study these references and have formed different theories as regards the nature of the original *Samkhya* and *Yoga*. Different views are current as regards the founders of these two systems. From the age of the *Upanishads* itself, we find the words *Samkhya* and *Yoga* going hand in hand. From the very ancient time, these two have been regarded as the allied systems and some have gone to the extent of considering these two as the aspects of one and the same system.

Such a view has been staunchly expressed by Swami Hariharananda Aranya in his commentary on the *Yoga-Sutra* called *Bhasvati*. He states therein that Hiranyagarbha who is supposed to be the first founder of *Yoga* was just another name of Kapila the founder of the *Samkhya* system. According to him, Hiranyagarbha was the first born Lord of the Universe and Kapila too was born with same knowledge and powers and hence, the sages gave this title Hiranyagarbha to Kapila. This great sage Kapila himself was the founder of both the Samkhya as well as the Yoga systems. He has tried to quote a passage from the *Mahabharata* in support of this view:

सांख्यस्य वक्ता कपिलः परमार्षिः स उच्यते।

हिरण्यगर्भो योगस्य वेत्ता नान्यः पुरातनः॥

.... M.Bh. XII 337.60

Thus, it is clear from the above that *Samkhya* and *Yoga* were related to each other and were complimentary to each other.

Yoga in the age of the Epics and the Puranas

A further development of the *Yoga-Sastra* can be seen mainly in the *Mahabharata* itself. Of course, the *Mahabharata* being an epic of growth, we are required to study the different portions separately.

The case of the *Ramayana* is somewhat different, although the *Ramayana* is also an epic of growth. The main kernel of the same has come almost from one pen. This main kernel consists of mostly books (Kandas) second to sixth. A large portion of the *Bala Kanda*, as also the whole of the *Uttara Kanda* are evidently a later addition. Again, the *Ramayana* does not include lengthy didactic portions as does the *Mahabharata*. As such, we do not get much information as regards the development of *Yoga* in the *Ramayana*. However, it can certainly be said that different kinds of *yogic* practices were current in the age of the *Ramayana*. This age can be said to be synchronous with the earliest portions of the *Mahabharata*. The *Puranas* in their present form are chronologically much later. However, the mention of the *Purana* type of literature can be found even in the *Brahmanas* and the *Upanishads*. A portion of this early literature must have been preserved to the extent of *Puranas* as well. This portion can be again said to be synchronous with the earliest portion of the *Ramayana* and the *Mahabharata*. We mean this early age, when we are speaking here of the age of the Epics and the *Puranas*.

Yoga in the Ramayana

According to tradition, the famous *Vasishtha Ramayana* or the *Yoga Vasishtha*, has been composed by Valmiki, the author of the original *Ramayana*. In the original *Ramayana*, we get only casual references to *Yoga* and *Yogic* practices have been referred to in the *Aranya Kanda* of the *Ramayana*. In the sixth chapter of this epic, several types of ascetics have been mentioned and all of them are said to be firmly resorting to *Yoga*. Casual mention of several accessories of *Yoga* and also other *Yogic* concepts can also be found in the *Ramayana*. From all these references, it can safely be assumed that *Yoga* as a discipline and also a system of thought was quite popular in the age of this great Epic.

Yoga in the Bhagavad Gita

Amongst different sections of the *Mahabharata* dealing with *Yoga*, the oldest and by far the most important one is the famous *Bhagavad Gita* from the *Bhisma Parvan*. This small treatise of seven hundred verses has become one of the most important and popular scriptures of the world.

The *Bhagavad Gita* has been called the *Yoga Sastra* along with the *Brahma-vidya* in the colophan. It can be said to be the *Yoga Sastra* par excellence, dealing with different kinds of *Yoga*, suitable for people from all walks of life and in different stages of life, belonging to different faiths and climes. The message of the *Bhagavad Gita* can be summed up in just two words "Yogi Bhava" or be a "Yogin". But the connotation and implications of the word *Yogin* are very wide indeed. Certainly the goal of *Yogins* or of the paths of *Yoga* is just the same but the means are very much different. Three lines from the *Bhagavad Gita* are understood as the definition of Yoga. The first and the most important being "Equality is called Yoga".

समत्वं योग उच्चयते। .... (BG, II, 48)

Another sentence appearing just after two verses is "Yoga is skill in action".

योगः कर्मसु कौशलम्। .... (BG, II, 50)

From the context, it can easily be seen that this skill lies in equality or maintaining the balance of mind. The third sentence appearing in the sixth chapter declaring that 'dissociation from association with grief may be known to be what is called Yoga' also culminates into equality or equanimity, with which one becomes able to achieve such dissociation.

तं विद्यादुःखसंयोग वियोगं योगसंज्ञितम्।

.... (BG, VI, 23)

Thus, *Samatva* is the main meaning of the word yoga in the *Bhagavad Gita*. This *Samatva* has varied implications including social equality and equity, as also balance and evenness of mind. lt is in this state of mind that one enjoys union. Secondarily, however, the word *Yoga* means the path leading to such a union or equality and equanimity. The *Gita* accepts variety of paths. It is in this secondary sense that every chapter of the *Gita* is also called *Yoga*. The *Gita* recognizes four main paths suitable for people of different temperaments and different capacities. These four main paths are the *Karma Yoga* or the *Yoga* of Action, the *Jnana Yoga* or the *Yoga* of Knowledge, the *Dhyana Yoga* or the *Yoga* of Meditation and the *Bhakti Yoga* or the Yoga of Love and Devotion. Here, let us see in brief, the exposition of these four paths as given by the *Bhagavad Gita*.

BHAGAVAD GITA

The 700 *slokas* of the *Gita* are divided into 18 chapters—

Chapter 1

The *Gita* contains the authoritative teachings of the Supreme Soul - Lord Sri Krishna to his beloved friend and disciple Arjuna, right in the middle of the battlefield of Kurukshetra, when the greatest war was about to begin between Pandavas and Kauravas, the first cousins in Kuru dynasty. Incidentally, Sanjaya, an aid of the blind Kaurava King Dhritarashtra was bestowed with a divine vision by Lord Sri Krishna to enable him to describe the goings on in the battlefield to the blind king, whose everything was at stake in the war. The King was not only blind literally but also even metaphorically because he could not see anything that comes in the way of his evil son Duryodhana's pleasure and prosperity.

Arjuna Vishada Yoga deals with the agonising dilemma of Arjuna who had to choose between fighting a war, killing his own brothers, elders and teachers, or commit the sin of dereliction of duty. In this dilemma, compassion overtaking valour, Arjuna felt completely debilitated. He put forward numerous arguments against the righteousness of fighting the war and finally dropped his great bow Gandiva and arrows. With tears in his eyes he pleaded with Lord Krishna who was his charioteer, the futility and his inability to fight the war.

Chapter 2

In the chapter on *Samkhya Yoga* and those ahead, Lord Krishna makes a strong bid to educate and enlighten the mighty and invincible warrior Arjuna, who at the crucial moment of starting a sacred war against evil and evildoers, collapses like a weakling and a coward. Krishna says one should not grieve for the unworthy. The wise grieve neither for the living nor for the dead.

Lord Sri Krishna says that there are essentially two paths in life for the people. One is the *Samkhya Yoga*, the path of transcendental knowledge and the other is the *Karma Yoga*, the path of action. According to the former, all objects being unreal, the sense of doership should be lost and all consciousness should be lost of everything except that of God, who is an embodiment of Truth, Knowledge and Bliss.

In *Karma Yoga*, everything is regarded as belonging to God and one practises renunciation of attachment as well as the fruit of action by surrendering to God. *Samkhya Yoga* is a preferred path for monks while *Karma Yoga* is recommended for the normal people.

Lord Krishna tries to dispel the myth of life and death, about assigning to Arjuna himself, action or inaction, about the unreal, which never exists and the real that never ceases to exist. He tells Arjuna about the difference between the perishable body and the imperishable Soul. The Soul never borns or dies. Unchangeable is *Sat* and Soul. Changeable is *Asat* the body. He further explains to Arjuna the futility of owning responsibility for the forthcoming deaths in the battlefield and grieving for the inevitable.

Krishna tells that comprehensive knowledge about the Soul is difficult to acquire even to the most knowledgeable. Birth and death apply only to the body and not to the Soul. Boyhood, youth and old age are the manifest forms of body development. So is death. These things do not apply to the unmanifest Soul which is inside. The contact between the senses and their objects, which gives rise to feelings and emotions, is transitory and fleeting. It needs to be ignored. By not fighting the war, Arjuna is told that he will incur the sin of dereliction of duty. Krishna further says that everybody has a right to work but not to its fruit. Renouncing the fruits of action will free us from all bondage and gives us Supreme Bliss.

A stable mind is that which is unperturbed by sorrow, does not crave for pleasures and is free from attachment, fear and anger. The intelligent should rise above the pairs of opposites and renounce attachment and attain equipoise. This attitude can be developed by practising *Yoga.*

Samatvam Yoga Utchyate : The evenness of temper is called *Yoga*. One attains *Yoga* by discarding the confusing arguments and when one's mind settles on the Supreme. Treating victory and defeat, gain and loss, pleasure and pain alike, will not attract any negative effects. Action is the duty of all human beings. Action with the awareness that body and Soul are different is *Karma Yoga*, the *Yoga* of selfless action. The intelligent focus their action towards one goal, while the ignorant actions are unfocussed and undecided. Those who chase worldly pleasures and rewards arising out of the *Vedic* knowledge and rituals cannot attain the determinate intellect concentrated in God. A stable mind is also one that dismisses all cravings and is thoroughly satisfied in the joy of self. A person free from passion, fear and anger has no thirst for pleasures. An unattached mind has the ability to withdraw its senses like a tortoise. Senses always try to distract man.

Always dwelling on sense objects develops attachment, which rakes up desires. Unfulfilled desires lead to frustration and anger. This leads to infatuation, confusion of memory, loss of reason and complete ruin. So to control the mind one should sit for meditation. The self controlled mind, while enjoying the sense objects does not get stuck with them and enjoys peace. Such a mind is firmly established in God. Like an Ocean, which does not react to the mighty inflow from rivers or the lack of it, a stable mind attains peace, being free from desire, attachment, ego and thirst for enjoyment. Even if such a state is attained at a late stage in life or last minute also, one attains Brahminic Bliss.

Chapter 3

The third chapter deals with *Karma Yoga*, the *Yoga* of Action. The choice of path of knowledge or action is to be determined by the person. A man should choose a path that is easy of practice and in which he can excel. Lord Krishna asks Arjuna to opt for the path of action, with an attitude of sacrifice. Pleasing Gods through sacrifice gets the reward of the highest good. Upon the investment of this good again in sacrifice, one gets back more of it. Enjoying the fruits of righteous action does not attract any sin or remorse.

All beings are evolved from food, which is produced from rain, which is in turn caused by sacrifice or *Yajna*. And sacrifice is caused only by action. This is the wheel of Creation and must be obeyed. Action without attachment leads to the Supreme. But to maintain the World Order action is essential. However, he who finds gratification in the self has no duty and has no use for dependence on anything worldly.

Ordinary people try to emulate the great ones and follow the standards set by them. A wise man established in the Self should not unsettle the mind of the ignorant attached to action but should get them to perform all their duties, duly performing his own duties. In fact it is the Nature's qualities that are responsible for all actions but not the doer himself. All actions are performed by the modes of Prakriti, the primordial matter. The fool thinks he is the doer. So dedicating all actions to Him, one can be free from fear and hope. Also one's own duty however lowly is superior to another's even if it is well performed. The former brings blessedness even in death while the latter is fraught with fear and danger.

What is the force that propels man to commit sin even involuntarily? It is the Rajoguna that creates desire and leads to sins. Knowledge is covered by desire, which is insatiable like fire. It sits on the senses, mind and intellect, which shroud the embodied soul. The body is controlled by senses, which is controlled by the mind, which in turn is controlled by intellect that is again controlled by the Soul. So one has to kill the enemy in the form of desire, which is no doubt tough.

Chapter 4

In *Jnana Yoga*, Lord Krishna says that when righteousness is on the decline and evil dominates, He comes down in human form or Avatara to protect the good and exterminate the evil forces.

Lord Krishna explains the difference between action, inaction and prohibited action. He who sees inaction in action and action in inaction is wise among men, a *Yogi* who has performed all actions.

He who has given up attachments to actions and their fruits is ever satisfied and is involved in no sin. The *Karma Yogi*, the one free from the dualities, is not bound by action. He acts merely for sacrifice. For him everything is Brahman, the act of offering, the oblation, the doer, the fire.

All things, in any form and any action can be converted into sacrifice. Those who do this, attain the eternal Brahman. The *Vedas* give many such sacrifices involving the action of mind, senses and body. All actions culminate in knowledge. On earth there is no purifier as great as knowledge. This knowledge, which is imparted only through a Guru, will carry us through all sins.

He who masters the senses attains knowledge and truth leadings to Supreme peace. A person devoid of faith and possessed by doubt is happy neither in this world nor hereafter.

Chapter 5

In *Karma Sanyasa Yoga*, Lord Krishna further explains that *Jnana Yoga* and *Karma Yoga* can both independently take us to salvation but the latter is superior. A *Karma Yogi*, to get rid of the effects of past actions, does *Yoga* of action with the help of body, mind, intellect and senses, leading to self-purification. The Soul has no fixed body and can enter any body depending on the actions, which are body related. The Soul has no shape and is the same in a *Brahmin*, a *Chandala* or a dog.

Knowledge gets shrunken due to past actions, which create attachment to the body. Without *Yoga* of action, it is diffiult to practice Yoga of knowledge. The *Samkhya Yogi* thinks that things happen and he is not doing or undoing. The omnipresent God does not receive the virtue or sin of any one. He is a disinterested friend of all beings. The wise look with the same eye a holy man or an outcast. Meditation gives *Sattvik* joy, which leads to eternal Bliss. Pleasures attached to senses are time bound and not worthy. So wise people do not indulge in them. He, who is free from lust and anger and subdues the mind, realises God and is eternally peaceful.

Chapter 6

Explaining the *Atma Sanyama Yoga*, Lord Krishna says that he who does his duty without expecting the fruits is a *Sanyasi* and *Yogi, i.e.*, a *Samkhya Yogi* and a *Karma Yogi* both. One's own self is his friend, if the senses are under control and his enemy, if they are not controlled. To God realized Soul, gold, clay and stone are alike. He who looks upon friends and foes, the virtuous or the sinful with the same eye and is devoid of selfish motive, is said to have attained *yogic* perfection. Such an attitude is acquired only by moderate eating, action, sleep and through *Yoga*.

Yoga requires a firm seat, with sacred Kusha grass, deer-skin and a cloth spreaa there on, mind free from distraction and body held straight, fixing the gaze on the tip of the nose. Fearless and calm, the mind should be fixed on Him constantly, steady like a light that does not flicker in a windless place. Having obtained that state, one does not reckon on any other gain. The state of *yoga* is free from contact of sorrow. One should, through gradual practice, attain tranquillity. Such *Yogi* sees Self in all beings and all beings in the Self. He can feel the pain and pleasure of others as his own.

Mind can be controlled by repeated practice of meditation. None who strives for self redemption meets with evil destiny. He who fails in attaining perfection in *Yoga* does not fall down. He takes birth in pious and wealthy family or in the family of enlightened *Yogis*. In that birth he strives harder for self-realization. Even a thought towards self-realization transcends the fruits of action. The *Yogi* is superior to the ascetics, scholars and ritualists.

Chapter 7

In the *Jnana Vignana Yoga* Lord Krishna says that the Universal Soul is the repository of all power, strength, glory and other attributes. The absolute knowledge of the formless and the qualified God is given in this chapter. Only one in millions among those who strive to know, knows this.

The eight-fold material nature representing lower energy of God or *Prakriti* comprises the earth, water, fire, air, Ether, mind, intellect and ego, and is under His control. The spiritual nature of higher energy involving *Purusha* or *Jiva*, the life principle is the one that sustains life in the universe. From this two fold nature all creation is born and disappears into. This *Purusha* is the sapidity in water, light in the moon and sun, the sacred symbol Om, the sound in Ether, the manliness in men, pure odour of the earth, brilliance in fire, life in all beings, austerity in men of ascetics, intelligence of the intelligent, might in the mighty, glory of the glorious. Free from the passion. He is also the sexual desire that does not conflict with scriptural injunctions. The *Trigunas* of *Sattva*-knowledge, *Rajas*-activity and *Tamas*-inertia, evolve from him.

Lord Krishna says that four types of devotees of noble deeds worship Him. These are (*i*) the seeker of worldly possessions, (*ii*) the afflicted, (*iii*) the seeker of knowledge and (*iv*) the man of wisdom. Although all of them are noble, the best among them is the man of wisdom, ever established in identity with Him and possessed of exclusive devotion. Such a man is extremely dear to Him and vice-versa. In the very last of all births the enlightened Soul worships Him only and realises that everything is God. Conversely when one reaches such a stage one may consider it to be his last birth.

The delusion created by the dualities of Nature borne of desire and hatred is responsible for people falling a prey to infatuation. But this can be broken only by constant adoration of him.

Chapter 8

The eighth chapter called *Akshara Para Brahma Yoga* is all about *Brahman* the Supreme indestructible, whose various manifestations are explained here. *Adhyatma* is the individual soul or *Jeevatma. Adhibhuta* is all perishable objects that is matter. *Adhidaiva* is the shining *Purusha* representing the divine intelligence. *Adhiyajna* is the inner witness dwelling in the body. Constant engagement and contemplation on Him makes one attain the supremely effulgent divine *purusha*. He, who holds the life breath between the two eyebrows even at the time of death and contemplates God on saying Om, reaches Him. The last thoughts on the deathbed decide what one attains.

Those who reach him thus have no rebirths. All worlds from *Brahmaloka* downwards are time bound and thus transitory. But not He. All embodied beings emanate from the unmanifest *Brahman's* subtle body by day and merge into it by night. Far beyond this there is another unmanifest existence, the Supreme Divine, who does not perish. That supreme goal is his abode. The wise man discards all the fruits, of studying the *Vedas*, performing *yagjnas*, charity and all other actions, just for Him and the supreme position. Some people constantly chant His names and glories and strive for realisation. Some offer their knowledge as one with themselves. And some others worship Him in universal form and in many ways.

Those who are not reborn, travel along the path presided by fire god, daylight, bright fortnight of the moon and six months northward course of the Sun. Those people who return to earth tread the path, which is presided by smoke, night, dark fortnight of the moon, the six months southward course of sun.

Chapter 9

In the *Raja Vidya Raja Guhya Yoga*, the most secret and sovereign science, the knowledge of Nirguna and Saguna aspects of Divinity, *i.e., Brahman* is explained by Lord Krishna. The whole universe is pervaded by Him, the unmanifest *Brahman*. All beings abide in him. During final dissolution, all beings enter his *prakriti* and at the beginning of the creation are sent out. But He is not touched by *Karma*. Nature brings forth the whole creation consisting of sentient and insentient beings. It is due to this cause the wheel of creation is going round.

Lord Krishna says he is the *Veda* and the *Vedic* ritual as well as sacrificial offering to the departed.

He is the herbage and foodgrain. He is the sacred fire and also the act of offering oblations into the fire. He is the sustainer, ruler of the universe, father, mother, the one worth knowing, the purifier, the sacred symbol Om. He is the origin and end. He is immortality as well as death. He is being and non-being both. People who worship Him without expecting any return are completely taken care of by Him.

Lord Krishna says that He delightfully accepts any offering a leaf, a flower, a fruit or even water given to Him, without expecting any return. He is equally present in all beings. None is hateful or dear. Even the vilest sinner, who worships Him with exclusive devotion, is considered a saint. Such a person speedily becomes virtuous and secures lasting peace. All classes of people taking refuge in Him attain the supreme goal. He obliges the bargainers also so that they do not turn to atheists.

Chapter 10

The *Vibhuti Yoga* says that the supreme consciousness represents the best of everything in the world. Reason, right knowledge, clear understanding, forbearance, veracity, non-violence, equanimity, contentment, austerity, charity, control over senses and mind arise from him. Joy and sorrow, evolution and dissolution fear and fearlessness, fame and infamy, all these diverse traits of creatures emanate from him alone.

Lord Krishna says that the entire creation is born of his will. He is the universal self seated in the hearts of all beings. He is the sun among stars, moon in the night sky, mind among the organs, and consciousness among living beings.

He is Om among words, Himalaya among the immovable, king among men, thunderbolt among weapons, Yama the god of death among rulers, time among reckoners, shark among fishes and Ganges among the streams. He is the beginning, middle and end of all creations. He is the science of soul among sciences, endless time and sustainer. He is death and birth. Among women, He is *Kirti* the glory as well as *Kshama* the forbearance. He is *Gayatri* among hymns, spring among seasons, fraud of the gambler, splendor of the splendid, resolution among the resolute, good among goodness. He is silence among secrets and wisdom of the wise. No creature moving or inert exists without Him.

Lord Krishna says that the entire universe is held by a fraction of his magical power.

Chapter 11

Now Arjuna's delusion is dispelled. Having heard of the mind boggling attributes of the Supreme, in this *Viswarupa Sandarsana Yoga*, Arjuna pleads to see the Universal form of Lord Krishna which the latter shows it in all its blinding, flaming and scorching brilliance. This form of Him contains everything that was said earlier, everything that is conceivable and imaginable in the universe. Hundreds of thousands of multifarious divine forms decorated with divine ornaments and equipped with divine weapons. On the whole, it is the form of hair raising supreme indestructible. It is a stupendous and dreadful form. Arjuna finds all the warriors of enemy camp rushing into the several mouths of this mighty destroyer just as moths rush into a great fire.

It is the supreme Effulgent, primal and infinite cosmic body. No beginning, no end. He is *kala* the eternal time spirit. He is the progenitor of *Brahma* himself, Primal Deity, and infinite Lord of the celestials. He is *Sat* the existent and *Asat* the non existent and that which is beyond both.

The worlds, including Arjuna, are terror struck looking at the form. His body starts trembling and voice choked, Arjuna pleads for mercy. He begs Lord Krishna to come back to his charming self, which the latter obliges. Lord Krishna says that this universal form of His is impossible to be seen by anybody except by single minded devotion.

Chapter 12

In the *Bhakti Yoga* or the *Yoga* of Devotion, Arjuna asks Lord Krishna, about the best knowers of Yoga among those who worship Him in form and attributes and those who adore Him as the unmanifest Brahman.

Lord Krishna replies that the practice of fixing the mind on the unmanifest is more difficult than to concentrate on the manifest form, with attribute. So he tells Arjuna, Focus the mind on me and let the intellect dwell on me. If that is not possible, seek to reach me by practice of spiritual discipline or Sadhana. If Sadhana is also not possible be intent on performing duty for me.

If even this is not possible, with a subdued mind, renounce the fruits of all work. He further says that knowledge is better than mere ritualistic practice. Meditation on God is superior to knowledge. Renunciation of fruits of action is even superior to meditation as peace immediately follows.

Lord Krishna says that the dearest devotee to Him is the one who loves all living organisms, is rid of 'I' and 'Mine', is balanced in joy and sorrow, is forgiving by nature, is ever contented, is internally and externally pure, renounces doership in all undertakings, both good and evil, is balanced in pleasure and pain, honour and ignominy and other contrary experiences, and is free from attachments to people and objects.

Chapter 13

In the *Kshetra Kshetragjna Vibhaga Yoga* or The Yoga of the creation and the creator, the body is compared with 'Field' or creation and the enriched soul as the 'Fieldman' or the creator.

The body is made up of five elements, the 'I' consciousness or ego, intellect, unmanifest primordial matter or Prakriti, five organs of perception, five organs of action, mind and the five sense objects, a total of twenty four components.

This field is also associated with desire and aversion, pleasure and pain, the physical body, consciousness and resolve. Only the true understanding of the creator and the creation is considered knowledge, which is defined by humility in spite of higher learning, wealth or pedigree, absence of hypocrisy, concurrence in thought, word and action, realisation of the perils of birth, death and disease, attachment to soul and supreme soul, minimum and essential attachment with wife, son, house and the like, living in sacred and secluded places, aversion to the company of greedy and lazy people and lastly knowledge that the rest is all ignorance. The *purusha* or the soul associated with the *prakriti* or matter enjoys and also suffers the *gunas* or qualities of *prakriti*. But pre soul unaffected by such *prakriti* has no birth or death. It has a brilliant wisdom called *Brahman*, but when it is attached to the body, it loses its wisdom. The formless wisdom of soul can do everything without apparently having the organs or perception and action. Except for worldly attachments a pure soul is as great as the supreme soul. Soul can enter any living organism - man, animal or plant. But all actions done by body are impossible to be done without the presence of soul in it. Soul is clearly visible to the knowledgeable whereas for others it is invisible like a distant object. While actions are done by the body, result is felt by the soul. The soul takes rebirth only to fulfil its desires in the previous births. The attachment to the *Gunas* due to ignorance caused by previous actions is the cause of rebirth in good or eveil wombs. He who knows the *purusha* the spirit and *prakriti* the nature together with the *gunas* or qualities, even though performing his duties in everyway, is never born again. This is achieved by some people by the intellect through meditation, some through discipline or *yoga* of knowledge, some by discipline of action and some by just hearing with sacred interest about the above classes of people.

Every *human* is born of matter and spirit. The moment man perceives that all the diversified existence of beings, animate or inanimate, is rooted in one supreme spirit, he attains *Brahman*, who is truth, consciousness and bliss solidified. Thus the self is not affected by the attributes of the body due to its attributeless character. This one spirit illuminates the whole creation.

Chapter 14

In the *Gunatrahya Vibhagya Yoga*, Lord Krishna says that for the entire creation, matter, the *prakriti* is the conceiving mother and spirit, the *purusha* is the seed giving father.

The three qualities of *Sattva, Rajas* and *Tamas* born of Nature tie the imperishable soul to the body. *Sattva* binds through joy and wisdom. *Rajas* binds through attachment to the fruits of action. *Tamas* binds through error and sleep. Sattva drives one to joy while *Rajas* drives one to action and Tamas incites one to error. For one quality to excel, the other two qualities have to be overpowered. If *Sattva* is predominant, light and discernment dawn on the body.

With preponderance of *Rajas*, greed, activity based on self interest, restlessness, and thirst for enjoyment dominate. When *Tamas* overpowers, there will be a disinclination to perform one's obligatory duties. At the time of death, preponderance of *Sattva* takes one to the heaven, *Rajas* takes one to action oriented births and *Tamas* takes a person to a birth of insects and beasts. Reward of *Sattva* is joy due to wisdom, *Rajas* is sorrow due to greed and *Tamas* is stupor and error due to ignorance. The *Sattvikas* rise, the *Rajasikas* get caught in the sub routine of birth and death in the middle while the *Tamasikas* sink to abject levels of filth.

He who transcends all the three *Gunas* attains supreme bliss or *Brahman*. Such a person does not hate either light due to *Sattva*, action due to *Rajas* or even stupor due to *Tamas*, when prevalent nor longs for them when they cease to exist. Sitting like a witness and undisturbed by the *Gunas*, he remains established in God and never falls from that state.

Chapter 15

In *Purushottama Prapti Yoga*, Lord Krishna explains as how to attain perfection. He says he who can visualize the creation in the form of an imperishable, inverted Pipal tree, with the trunk represented by *Brahman* at the top and branches by lower worlds and the leaves as the actions born of desires, is considered a knower of the *Vedas*.

Propelled by the three qualities and sense objects for their tender leaves, the branches extend both upwards and downwards and its roots bind the soul according to the actions in the human body and spread all round. This mythical tree of creation actually has no beginning, no end and no stability. Felling this deep rooted tree is possible only with formidable axe of dispassion. Only after that one can reach one's supreme abode, from which there is no return. And that place cannot be illuminated any more by sun, moon or fire because they are all part of his light.

It is he who digests the four kinds of food we eat and sits in the hearts of all creatures and controls their memory, knowledge and reasoning. The entire purpose of the *Vedic* knowledge is only to realise Him. The imperishable Supreme Being or *purushottama*, who is beyond the perishable matter and above the *Trigunas*, upholds and maintains the entire world. By understanding the philosophy behind this most esoteric teaching, man becomes wise and his life's mission accomplished.

Chapter 16

The characteristics of the angelic and demonic people are explained in this chapter called *Daivasura Sampadvibhaga Yoga*. While divine qualities are said to be conducive to liberation, the demonic qualities lead to bondage. It is to be remembered that scriptures alone are the guide for a man to distinguish between good and evil.

Men born with divine qualities possess absolute fearlessness, perfect purity of mind, charity in the *Sattvik* form, control of senses and absence of attachment to sense objects. They practise non violence in thought, word and deed, geniality of speech, sense of shame in transgressing against scriptures, enmity to none and absence of self esteem. Men born of demonic qualities show hypocrisy, annoyance, pride, anger, sternness, and ignorance. They believe that the world is only brought forth by male female union propelled by lust. Intoxicated with wealth and power, they are self conceited and haughty men who even hate the God inside them as well as in others. They fall into the foulest hell and cast again into demonical wombs and sink lower and lower, leading to ruination of their soul.

Chapter 17

In this *Shraddhatraya Vibagha Yoga*, *i.e.*, the *Yoga* of Three fold faith, Lord Krishna says that people are divided into three types depending on their faith, *Sattvik, Rajasik* and *Tamasik*.

These three types of people have typically distinguished habits of food, attitude and behaviour. The *Sattviks* worship Gods, learned *Brahmins*, elders and wise men while the *Rajasiks* worship demigods and demons and lastly the *Tamasiks* worship spirits of the dead and group of ghosts.

The *Sattviks* eat foods, which are sweet, bland, natural and substantial that promote longevity, intelligence, vigour, wealth, happiness and cheerfulness. The *Rajasiks* eat bitter, acid, salty, pungent, dry and burning foods that cause suffering, grief, sickness. The *Tamasiks* eat half cooked, half ripe, insipid, putrid, stale polluted, impure foods that cause error and inertia.

The *Sattviks* make sacrifices without expecting return; the Rajasiks make sacrifices for show and expect return and the *Tamasiks* devoid of faith, make sacrifices against scriptural instruction. The penance of the *Sattviks* involves the study of scriptures, purity, harmlessness and straightforwardness. The *Rajasiks* make penance for the sake of renown, honour and selfish gains while austerity practised by the *Tamasiks* involves perversion, self mortification and harm to others.

While the Sattviks bestow gifts with a sense of duty to the right people at the right and on right occasion, the *Rajasiks* bestow gifts grudgingly and expecting returns. The gifts by the *Tamasiks* are always bestowed out of place, to the wrong persons and in a humiliating manner.

Acts of sacrifice, charity and austerity are the great purifiers and hence must be followed by people. OM TAT SAT has been declared as the threefold name of *Brahman,* the Absolute. All acts of charity start with Om. All acts are done without seeking any reward and uttering *Tat*, which means 'He is all'. Action for the sake of God is truly termed as *Sat*.

Chapter 18

The final chapter is called *Moksha Sanyasa Yoga* or Liberation through Renunciation. *Sanyasa* is renunciation of any selfish work. *Tyaga* is renunciation of the fruits of action. To practise this *Yoga* it is necessary for one to develope the Sattvik qualities. All acts of sacrifice, charity and austerity should be done with complete faith.

Possessing a body, one cannot completely renounce action but one can renounce fruits of action. The five factors responsible for the accomplishment of all actions are

1. Body the seat of *karma*
2. Soul driven by the *gunas*
3. Five organs of action
4. Various bio-impulses of the body
5. The destiny or the presiding deity.

These are the contributory factors for whatever actions, right or wrong performed through mind, speech and action. So he who thinks that only 'he' is the doer, is totally wrong. He has only a fraction of responsibility in any act, which also can be passed on to one of other four factors, if he is wise. The knower, knowledge and the object of knowledge motivate action. The practical elements of all actions are again threefold — the doer, the deed and the instrument. The fruits of action due to unrenouncing are threefold — welcome, unwelcome and mixed. Sacrifice, charity and penance are the purifiers of wise men. No creature can escape from these three *gunas* born of nature.

The four-fold division of labour in the society was made based on the intrinsic qualities and talents of the people. These are

1. Study and teaching of scriptures
2. Ruling and protecting the land and the people
3. Agriculture and business, and finally
4. Service to the society.

Sticking to such a division would not only help perfecting one's own craft but also provides an assured employment to the people. Even the present society would benefit if people of whatever origin and in whatever profession perform their duties in the way such duties are recommended to be performed by the scriptures.

There is no being, human or divine, either on the earth or in any other world who is free from the material nature borne of these three *Gunas* of *Prakriti*. Lord Krishna explains the difference between the three types of knowledge, duty, action, intellect, firmness and joy of these people. The *Sattvik* knowledge recognizes one imperishable divine existence in all living beings while the *Sattvik* duty is done without attachment and receiving fruit. A *Sattvika* does the right thing at the right time and is firm in his resolve. The *Sattvik* joy looks like poison in the beginning but tastes like nectar at the end.

The *Rajasik* knowledge accepts the presence of divine but distinguishes various forms of life from one another. A *Rajasika's* actions are ego based and done with a lot of strain and expecting return. His actions are greedy and he is highly reactive to success and failure. He cannot correctly perceive between right and wrong, not firm and his sense oriented joy finally turns to poison. The *Tamasik* knowledge is irrational, trivial and harmful to others. The *Tamasika* abandons duties through ignorance. His actions are undertaken foolishly or irresponsibly, causing a lot of hurt to himself and / or others. He is uncultured, arrogant, deceitful and slothful. He thinks right to be wrong and vice versa. He uses firmness only to cling to sleep, sorrow, vanity and fear. He is haunted by a false sense of joy out of ignorance. One can attain perfection and attain the Supreme by doing one's natural duties well, whatever they be. The final consummation of all knowledge is realizing *Brahman* by completely following the *Sattvik* way of life. He who has attained unison with *Brahman* neither desires nor grieves. The *Karma yogi* also attains *Brahman* by performing all actions without attachment. When you concentrate on the *Brahman*, be devoted to Him, worship Him and bow to Him, then you go to Him only.

YOGA VASHISHTHA

Highlight of Yoga Vashishtha

Yoga Vashishtha, written by Sage Valmiki, is the spiritual teaching imparted by Sage Vashishtha to Sri Rama. In *Balakand* of the *Ramayana* there is also a reference that Rama received spiritual instructions and guidance from his *guru* Vashishtha. While the *Ramayana* relates Sri Rama's adventures and the meaning of the different stages of his life, *Yoga Vashishtha* relates the teachings which he received and describes the different chapters in his spiritual evolution. *Yoga Vashishtha* is also known as the *Maha Ramayana*, the *Uttar Ramayana* and the *Vashishtha Ramayana*. We can also call it the 'Behind the scenes Ramayana', because it describes how Rama's knowledge, wisdom and understanding evolved and progressed throughout the different stages of his life.

Yoga Vashishtha is an elaborate work, consisting of 32,000 verses and 64,000 lines. It has been divided into six main chapters, which are the different stages of spiritual evolution in the life of Sri Rama. The chapters are called *Prakaranas*. The first chapter is *Vairagya Prakarana*, in which Sri Rama experiences a very deep and intense dispassion and distaste for all worldly objects and pleasures.

Although in Sri Rama's case the desire for worldly objects was never described as being very intense, still it is the first stage of Sri Rama's spiritual evolution and the first requirement in spiritual life. The second chapter is *Mumukshu Prakarana*, which describes the intense desire for *Self-realization* that Sri Rama experiences.

After achieving *vairagya*, after attaining the state of being different from the world, of not being involved but being more of an observer, then the next stage is changing the quality of the desires from worldly to spiritual. That is the second stage of Sri Rama's evolution.

The third chapter is *Utpatti Prakarana* in which Sri Rama learns from his *guru* the origins of the world. It is deepening the understanding of why we get caught up and involved with worldly objects and pleasures, and how those outside objects are identified in the mind.

The fourth chapter is *Sthiti Ramayana* in which, after having attained that firm understanding of the origin of the world process, Sri Rama sustains himself in the Self, in *Brahman*. That is the time of spiritual enlightenment. The fifth chapter is *Upasana Prakarana*, which describes the deep peace that emerged from having attained that spiritual enlightenment. The sixth chapter is *Nirvana Prakarana*, which is the final liberation.

Waking up from the dream

The main theme of *Yoga Vashishtha* is that the soul is undergoing a dream from which it must awake. This dream represents our association and identification with the world. The fact that it is described as being a dream means that whatever is in it has to be false. Nothing in a dream can be true. Waking up from that dream is the ultimate goal, *Self-realization*.

Yoga Vashishtha has been written, not as straight dialogue between Sage Vashishtha and Sri Rama, but in the form of a story within a story. It is not a standard scriptural textbook. Our lives are also rather like a story within a story. For example, a desire arises for a particular object. Then there is a pursuit to obtain that object. If the object is attained, there is an elation, a happiness, that doesn't last very long, as we know. Then there is a further desire for what we consider to be a better object. Again there is another pursuit after that object. But if the object is not obtained, there is frustration, anger, loss of mental balance, and then, all of a sudden, out of nowhere guilt arises - "Why was I pursuing this object in the first place?" But the desire for that object still remains along with the guilt. The mind that is feeling guilty for pursuing that object is the same mind that wants to obtain that object. So there is a mental conflict, confusion and no clarity.

The first chapter has been called *Vairagya Prakarana* because until one cuts that identification with and desires for worldly objects, that fogginess will remain. Not until the fogginess disappears will mental clarity prevail and will one be able to evaluate, analyze and reflect on what the true aspiration is. While we are involved in that desire, we cannot see what the real aspirations are and what we really want to obtain, and there will be no real transformation in the quality of that desire. That is why *Vairagya Prakarana* has been described as the first chapter in Sri Rama's spiritual evolution, and of course it applies to all aspirants. Once there is clarity, then comes the second chapter, *Mumukshu Prakarana,* which is changing the quality of that desire to a higher nature, which is *Self-realization.*

Sri Rama describes this in a very beautiful and simple way. If you pour water into a basket made out of straw, what will happen? The water will not remain in the basket. All the water will permeate through and the basket will remain empty. The basket symbolizes the drive to indulge and involve oneself in worldly objects and pleasures because there is a need for happiness and peace, the desire to obtain something, to achieve something, and to be stable in that happiness and inner peace. The pouring of water into the basket represents the effort, the *purushartha*, that one makes in one's life to obtain that something. But what happens? The fact that the water permeates through the basket and leaves it empty means that no matter how much water you pour in, no matter how deep you go in that dream, the basket will always remain empty. That is the transitory, short term and temporary nature of the happiness and contentment derived from worldly objects.

Imagine you are having a nightmare in which people are chasing you and you are running away. Suddenly the road splits into two. On one side people are still chasing you, so you say, "I'd better not go in that direction and I cannot go back." So what do you do? You either turn to the right and continue running in the same circle, or you simply wake up and put an end to the dream. This waking up from the dream, which is described in *Yoga*

Vashishtha, is the opening of the third eye. The third eye is a symbol which represents discrimination and wisdom. It is that discrimination and wisdom which ultimately leads one to the experience of *vairagya*, of dispassion.

Discrimination means knowing what is right and what is wrong, being able to differentiate and to guide one's life and efforts towards something everlasting, not something temporary which will disappear the moment you touch it. Applying that discrimination then becomes a dispassion. Dispassion is not something that can be applied as an intellectual concept, rather it is a gradual process of transformation of the mind and of the nature of the mind, transformation of the desires and the quality of these desires. So, *Yoga Vashishtha* describes the spiritual aim as being the waking up from that dream that we are going through.

Sutikshna and Agastya

The first story in the *Vairagya Prakarana* does not begin with Sage Vashishtha speaking to Sri Rama, but with a very humble and modest *Brahmin* named Sutikshna who has gone to his *guru*, Sage Agastya, for spiritual guidance. When Agastya, knowing his disciple very well, asked him the cause of his confusion and grief, Sutikshna said, "Tell me, is it the performance of one's duty that will lead one to liberation, to *nirvana*, to *moksha*, or it is the renunciation of everything, going to the Himalayas and forgetting everybody and everything?"

Sage Agastya replied, "Just as a bird flies on two wings, in the same way the aspirant flies up to the goal of self-realization, to liberation, on the two wings of *karma* and wisdom. So it is neither one nor the other but the blending of the two. That is the art which one has to learn to evolve in spiritual life." Seeing that Sutikshna was still confused, Agastya said, "I will tell you another story to help you understand better."

Agnivesya and Karunya

The second story is about Karunya and his father Agnivesya. Once upon a time there was a boy named Karunya. He went to the *gurukul* at an early age and mastered the *Vedas* and the *Puranas* and became a very knowledgeable person. After finishing his training, he returned to his father's home. Suddenly, one day he too became depressed and fell into a state of grief. Agnivesya went to him and said, "Tell me the cause of your grief." Karunya replied, "I have been studying all this time, but still I have one question. It is mentioned in the scriptures that one will attain liberation, that one will free oneself from the cycle of births and deaths, through the performance of one's duties. But at the same time it says that only through renunciation will one attain this freedom. So what should one do?" Agnivesya replied, "I will tell you a story which will help you to understand this point perfectly."

Suruchi and Devadutta

So here is the third story, and the dialogue between Sage Vashishtha and Sri Rama has still not yet begun. Agnivesya began, "Once upon a time a beautiful damsel named Suruchi was sitting on a mountain peak in the Himalayas, reflecting on life. All of a sudden she saw a messenger of Lord Indra's flying by, so she called him and asked, "Where are you going?" He replied, "That is a very good question, let me tell you a story."

Devadutta and Arishtanemi

Once upon a time there was a king named Arishtanemi. After having performed his kingly duties and having ruled the kingdom with authority, according to the scriptures, he had retired and passed on his kingdom to his son. For hundreds and hundreds of years he had practised severe austerities and meditations in the forest. Lord Indra was so impressed that he sent his messenger Devadutta to invite Arishtanemi to the heavens. So Devadutta went off in a chariot full of the most beautiful damsels and the most learned scholars to invite King Arishtanemi on a first class flight to the heavens.

Devadutta arrived in the forest where Arishtanemi was practising his meditation, and passed on Lord Indra's invitation. Arishtanemi understood that he was being offered a reward for his good deeds, the fruits of his karmas. He said, "Tell me what kind of fruits I will enjoy from these *karmas* in the heavens?" Devadutta replied,

"According to the *karmas* one has performed in one's life, the quality of the fruit will vary. Due to this variety, there is a jealousy amongst the enjoyers of the fruits. Therefore, once the bonus is consumed, you have to go back and pass through another stage of birth."

King Arishtanemi said very firmly, "No, I am not going with you. I am performing these austerities to experience everlasting happiness and peace within, and to know that source, not to go through the same thing. Therefore, I'm not going with you."

Arishtanemi and Valmiki

So Devadutta returned in an empty flight, first class, and told Lord Indra what Arishtanemi had said. Lord Indra said, "Go back and take him to Sage Valmiki. Tell Sage Valmiki to instruct Arishtanemi in spiritual knowledge, to guide him and lead him towards liberation, which is the reason why he is here."

Devadutta took King Arishtanemi to Sage Valmiki and when Arishtanemi saw Valmiki, he understood that he had come to the right place. He said, "I wish you to instruct and guide me, so that I can become free from these sorrows and miseries which I am unable to separate myself from alone." At this point, Sage Valmiki begins to tell King Arishtanemi the story of *Yoga Vashishtha*, the dialogue between Sage Vashishtha and Sri Rama.

From intellect to intuition

So the introduction to *Vairagya Prakarana* contains many stories within stories. These stories have a twofold meaning. There is always a superficial meaning and at another level a more spiritual and deeper understanding.

In the first story Sutikshna approaches Agastya for spiritual guidance. Sutikshna means subtle, sharp, and Agastya means the effulgent sun. The movement of Sutikshna towards Sage Agastya represents the move of the intellect towards intuition. An aspirant with the ability to move from intellect to intuition is considered to be the highest type of aspirant. The scriptures say that intellect is considered to be a barrier in spiritual life, but this has to be understood properly. As the absence of intellect is not the key to overcome this barrier, the key has to be something associated with intellect.

Intellect begins with the letter 'I'. The purpose of intellect is also to serve 'I', so if intellect is not the barrier directly, it is this 'I-ness' associated with the intellect which becomes the barrier. Intellect and ego, 'I-ness', have a very intimate relationship, even more intimate than the relationship between a husband and wife. The way to transcend this barrier is therefore not to create an absence of intellect, but to change the purpose and application of intellect. Instead of applying the intellect for ourselves, we apply the intellect for others.

The *guru*-disciple relationship is described as the way to transcend this barrier. In all these stories there is a *guru* and a disciple. In the *guru*-disciple relationship there is acceptance, faith and surrender: one is undergoing training, one is 'intuition'. This ability to move from intellect to intuition is considered to be a quality of the highest type of aspirant, because while letting go off family and possessions is not considered so difficult, letting go off that 'I-ness' is considered to be one of the toughest and rarest abilities.

Purification of the mind

The second story is between Karunya and Agnivesya. Karunya means one who is full of grief, confusion, and Agnivesya is an embodiment of fire. The movement of Agnivesya towards Karunya represents the need of the *chitta* to be purified by the superconsciousness, the need of the mind to be purified through *raja yoga*. Karunya is considered to be the second best type of aspirant on the spiritual path. In the first story Sutikshna approached Agastya for spiritual guidance, but here Agnivesya had to approach Karunya in order to relieve him of his grief and confusion.

Spiritual inclination

The third story is between Suruchi, a damsel, and Devadutta, Lord Indra's divine messenger. Suruchi means good taste. Her calling out to Devadutta is a sign of spiritual inclination, because even though it may have been a mental diversion initially, it becomes the source of her being led to spiritual heights, as Devadutta then tells the story which eventually leads to the dialogue between Sage Vashishtha and Sri Rama. Suruchi also represents the integration of sentiments required in an aspirant on the path of *bhakti*. She is considered to be the third best type of aspirant on the spiritual path.

From rajas to sattva

In the next story, Arishtanemi approaches Sage Valmiki, not directly, but after having refused a first class invitation to the heavens. The movement of Arishtanemi towards Valmiki therefore symbolizes the movement of *rajas* towards *sattva*, Arishtanemi representing *rajas*, the destroyer of evil, and Valmiki representing the divine purity, *sattva*.

Sri Rama and Sage Vashishtha

In the next story revealed by Sage Valmiki to Arishtanemi, Sri Rama represents the embodied divine Self and Sage Vashishtha represents the Self in the highest state of liberation. This depicts the movement of the soul towards *Self-realization*. It is the waking up of the soul from the world, which is the theme of *Yoga Vashishtha*. Sri Rama is the ideal disciple, the best that one can find.

In this teaching, Sage Valmiki expands on each and every aspect of spiritual evolution. These stories, therefore, are not only stepping stones leading into *Yoga Vashishtha*, but also describe the different types of aspirants on the spiritual path and the internal processes and movements they undergo as the personality is transformed. They also emphasize the need for a *guru*-disciple relationship.

Multiple Choice Questions

1. How many parts of 'yama' are described in upanishads?
A. 10 B. 12
C. 8 D. 7

2. How many parts of 'niyama' are described in upanishads?
A. 10 B. 12
C. 8 D. 7

3. Which two methods are mentioned in 'Yoga Vashistha' to make control over chitta?
A. Dhyana, samadhi
B. Pranayama, pratyahara
C. Yama, asana
D. Niyam, asana

4. Which is the first limb of Sadhanga yoga?
A. Yama
B. Niyama
C. Asana
D. Shatkarma

5. Which yogic sadhna is suggested for high category sadhaka?
A. Ashtanga yoga
B. Kriya yoga
C. Bhakti yoga
D. Abhyasa and vairagya

6. Chakras and nadis are related to which kosha?
A. Pranamaya
B. Manomaya
C. Anandmaya
D. Ananmaya

7. Will power is related to _____ kosha.
A. Pranamaya B. Manomaya
C. Anandmaya D. Ananmaya

8. Koshas related to subtle body are:
A. Anandmaya, pranamaya, manomaya
B. Anandmaya, pranamaya, vijyanmaya
C. Ananmaya, pranamaya, manomaya
D. Pranmaya, manomaya, vijyanmaya

9. Koshas related to causal body is:
A. Ananmaya B. Anandamaya
C. Pranamaya D. Manomaya

10. Which kosha is related to gross body?
A. Ananmaya B. Anandamaya
C. Pranamaya D. Manomaya

11. Manna, buddhi, chitta and ahamkara are related to which kosha?
A. Manomaya B. Pranamaya
C. Vijyanmaya D. Ananmaya

12. Anandmaya kosha is strengthened by:
A. Yama, niyama, dharna
B. Yama, niyama, asana
C. Abhyasa and vairagya
D. Asana and pranayama

13. Ananmaya kosha is strengthened by:
A. Asana B. Pranayama
C. Pratyahara D. Dharna

14. Pranamaya kosha is strengthened by:
A. Dhyana B. Dharna
C. Pranayama D. Shatkarma

15. Manomaya kosha is strengthened by:
A. Yama, niyama, pratyahara
B. Yama, niyama, dharna, dhyana
C. Mudra, bandha, asana
D. All of the above

16. Vijyanmaya kosha is strengthened by:
A. Yama, niyama
B. Asana, pranayama
C. Japa, dhyana
D. Mudra, bandha

17. 'Panch-Karmendriyas' (active instruments) are most effected by:
A. Soul B. Sanskara
C. Outer environment D. Panch Koshas

18. Which of the following strengthen the manomaya kosha?
A. Yama, niyama B. Dharna
C. Dhyana D. All of the above

19. Weakening of which kosha results in mental disorders?
A. Anandamaya B. Anamaya
C. Pranamaya D. Manomaya

20. Changing the body size to minimum by a sadhaka is called as:
A. Prakamya B. Mahima
C. Anima D. Sukshama

21. Which of the gunas relates the senses to external objects?
A. Sattva B. Tamas
C. Rajas D. Both A and B

22. ______ is dominant during active state of body.
A. Sattva guna B. Tamas guna
C. Rajas guna D. All of the above

23. In which state tamas guna becomes dominant?
A. Parlyavastha B. Swapanavastha
C. Susuptavastha D. Jagritavastha

24. Anxiety and suffering in humans is due to:
A. Tamas guna B. Sattva guna
C. Rajas guna D. All of the above

25. Idleness and poverty in humans is due to:
A. Tamas guna B. Rajas guna
C. Sattva guna D. None of these

26. Which of the following guna represents pleasure and lightness?
A. Tamas B. Rajas
C. Sattva D. Both A and B

27. Which guna corresponds to sufferings and activeness in humans?
A. Tamas B. Rajas
C. Sattva D. Both A and B

28. Which of the following match is correct?
A. Tamas guna – Fear, illusion
B. Rajas guna – Sorrow, sufferings
C. Sattva guna – Pleasure, prosperity
D. All of the above

29. During susuptavastha which guna makes perception of existence of blankness?
A. Tamas B. Rajas
C. Sattva D. Both B and C

30. Which guna is eliminated by practise of vairagya?
A. Tamas B. Rajas
C. Sattva D. Both A and B

31. Which guna is dominant during sleepness?
A. Rajas B. Tamas
C. Sattva D. None of these

32. _________ is given more importance by upanishadas.
A. Shatkarma B. Pranayama
C. Trataka D. Bandha

33. In which upanishad is illustrated that– "By attaining first stage of yoga the mind of sadhaka becomes light, body becomes healthy and vrittis of chitta get eliminated."
A. Svetasvatara upanishad
B. Yogasikho upanishad
C. Yogatatva upanishad
D. Chhandogya upanishad

34. Which is the most ancient philosophy?
A. Mimamsa B. Vedanta
C. Samkhya D. Yoga

35. Panch-kosha siddhanta is explained in which upanishad?
A. Savetasvatara upanishad
B. Chhandogya upanishad
C. Tetraiya upanishad
D. Shandilya upanishad

36. Panch-kosha are explained in which of the following Upanishads?
A. Savetasavtara and Tetraiya upanishad
B. Etraiya and Tetraiya upanishad
C. Shandilya and Chhandogya upanishad
D. All of the above

37. The total number of main puranas are:
A. 12 B. 16
C. 18 D. 22

38. Brahmana granthas are included in which part of Vedas?
A. Karma kanda B. Upasna kanda
C. Gyana kanda D. All of the above

39. Which Maharishi was considered supreme by Shri Krishna?
A. Jamini B. Patanjali
C. Gautam D. Kapila

40. Literatures written in forests are called as:
A. Upanishad B. Aranayaka
C. Veda D. Shruti literature

41. Which stage of consciousness is considered as most important?
A. Jagritavastha B. Susuptavastha
C. Turiyavastha D. Both A and B

42. The total number of upanishadas are:
A. 18 B. 28
C. 108 D. 118

43. Which type of yoga is explained in Bhagavad purana?
A. Karma yoga B. Laya yoga
C. Raja yoga D. Bhakti yoga

44. Which type of karma is explained in Vedanta philosophy?
A. Sanchita karma B. Prarabadha karma
C. Kriyamana karma D. All of the above

45. Which topic is explained in fifth chapter's sixth saloka (stanza) of Shri Bhagavad Gita?
A. Niskama karma yoga
B. Elements of success in yoga
C. Elements of failure in yoga
D. Attaining of salvation

46. Vedas are composed of which of the following four parts?
A. Samhitas, Upanishads, Purana, Gita
B. Samhitas, Brahmanas, Aranyakas, Upanishads
C. Upanishads, Puranas, Samhitas, Aranyakas
D. Rigveda, Upanishads, Purana, Samhitas

47. What is the meaning of word 'Ved'?
A. Knowledge B. To understand
C. To know D. Consciousness

48. Which of the following is also known as shruti grantha?
A. Upanishads B. Vedas
C. Gita D. Yoga Vashistha

49. Which upanishad has considered the Puranas as fifth Veda?
A. Chhandogaya B. Brahdaranyaka
C. Yogsikho D. Shandilya

50. In Gita, samkhya has been called by which another name?
A. Laya yoga B. Tatva yoga
C. Dhyana yoga D. Gyana yoga

51. Which philosophy do not consider nindra as a vritti?
A. Samkhya B. Nyaya
C. Yoga D. Vedanta

52. Pratyahara, dharna and dhyana are explained in which 'purana'?
A. Shiva purana
B. Vishnu purana
C. Vraha purana
D. Vayu purana

53. According to yoga philosophy how many stages of chitta bhumis are there?
A. 4 B. 5
C. 6 D. 7

54. How many total chapters are there in Shri Bhagavad Gita?
A. 12 B. 16
C. 18 D. 22

55. According to whom? – 'Consciousness is originated from the union of soul, objects and senses'.
A. Acharya Ramanuja
B. Kapila muni
C. Shri Krishna
D. Shridhara

56. In which text prakriti is called as 'aditi'?
A. Rigaveda B. Atharvaveda
C. Samaveda D. Upanishads

57. Which of the following are the two main parts of vedas?
A. Karma kanda, Marma kanda
B. Karma kanda, Jnana kanda
C. Gyana kanda, Marma kanda
D. Marma kanda, Upasana kanda

58. How many total stanzas are there in Shri Bhagavad Gita?
A. 400 B. 500
C. 600 D. 700

59. The explanation of practice of various yogic activities is described in which upanishads?
A. Savetasavtara upanishads
B. Amritnada upanishads
C. Amritbindu upanishads
D. Shandilya upanishads

60. 'Samatvam Yoga Uchayate'–line is illustrated in which text?
A. Shri Bhagavad Gita
B. Patanjali Yoga Sutra
C. Ashtanga Yoga Grantha
D. Yoga Vashishtha

61. What is the meaning of word "ju" in Yajurveda?
A. Consciousness B. Akash
C. Bramha D. Prithvi

62. According to samkhya philosophy the intelligence is _______ guna.
A. Rajas B. Sattva
C. Tamas D. All the above

63. According to samkhya philosophy ahamkara is _______ guna dominant.
A. Rajas B. Sattva
C. Tamas D. All the above

64. 'Gyani Tvatamevame Matam' –line have been pointed out from which text?
A. Patanjali Yoga Sutra
B. Narada Sutra
C. Shri Bhagavad Gita
D. Samkhya philosophy

65. In which upanishad body nadis were explained first?
A. Chhandogya B. Svetasavtara
C. Yogatatva D. Yogasikho

66. According to Gita 'Vikarma' is:
A. Lack of action
B. Prohibited action
C. Action of virtue
D. Selfless action

67. Which of the following is a 'Neimitika karma'?
A. To perform yajna for victory
B. To perform worship daily
C. To do act of charity
D. To perform act of shradha

68. In Bhagavad Gita which type of karma are not explained?
A. Akarma B. Krishna karma
C. Karma D. Vikarma

69. Ashtanga yoga and Brahma vidya are described in which upanishad?
A. Chhandogya B. Amritbindu
C. Amritnada D. Shandilya

70. According to 'Shri Bhagavad Gita' which of the following are elements of success in yoga?
A. Moderate sleep
B. Moderate recreation
C. Moderate working
D. All the above

71. According to 'Shri Bhagavad Gita' which of the following are elements of failure in yoga?
A. Ego, wealth
B. Depression, confusion
C. Carelessness, doubt
D. All the above

72. Who is the author of 'Yoga Bhasya'?
A. Ved Vyasa B. Vachaspati Misra
C. Panini D. Valmiki

73. To concentrate on Brahma is known as:
A. Shunya dhyana B. Jyotira dhyana
C. Sukshama dhyana D. Brahma dhyana

74. What does the antraya 'vyadi' mean?
A. Kalesha B. Disease
C. Vikshepa D. Accident

75. What does the antraya 'avriti' mean?
A. Doubt B. Desire
C. Carelessness D. Vikshepa

76. The adorer who does bhakti for wealth is known as:
A. Kami B. Aarta
C. Arthatho D. Lobhi

77. The adorer who does bhakti for getting rid off wordly sorrows and sufferings is known as:
A. Arthatho B. Aarta
C. Partha D. Aarthatha

78. 'Yoga Vashisttha' is related to mainly which type of yoga?
A. Bhakti yoga B. Laya yoga
C. Gyana yoga D. Raja yoga

79. Which of the following is described in the text 'Yoga Taravali' by Adi Shankaracharya?
A. Kundalini yoga B. Tantra yoga
C. Raja yoga D. Hatha yoga

80. In which stage the sattvaguna becomes dominant completely?
A. Sampragyata samadhi
B. Jagritavastha
C. Vivekakhyati
D. All the above

81. Which of the following is correct?
A. During swapanavastha the sattva guna remains supressed
B. During jagritavastha the sattva guna remains supressed
C. During susuptavastha the sattva guna remains mainly supressed
D. All the above

82. Which yogic sadhna is suggested for sadhaka of lower category?
A. Ashtanga yoga
B. Kriya yoga
C. Dhyana yoga
D. Bhakti yoga

83. To continue doing niskāma karmas by a person results in which stage of chitta?
A. Ekagratavastha
B. Kshiptavastha
C. Vikshiptavastha
D. Nirudhavastha

84. The perception arised due to words of siddha purushas and veda vakyas is:
A. Agama parmana
B. Partyaksha parmana
C. Upmana parmana
D. Shasvata parmana

85. 'The yoga backsliders also get rebirth at the home of benevolent souls'. Whose opinion is this?
A. Bhagat Prahlada
B. Maharishi Narada
C. Maharishi Ved Vyasa
D. Shri Krishna

86. The higher stage of ragatamika bhakti is known as:
A. Para bhakti
B. Apra bhakti
C. Gauni bhakti
D. Atmanivedana bhakti

87. What is the higher stage of Ragatamika bhakti?
A. Apara bhakti
B. Para bhakti
C. Aatmanivedan bhakti
D. Dasya bhakti

88. To worship the God by means of vedic hymns, is called as which type of bhakti?
A. Vandana bhakti B. Kirtana bhakti
C. Shravana bhakti D. Manana bhakti

89. Who is known as "The father of Modern Yoga"?
A. T. Krishnamacharya
B. K. Patabhi Jois
C. Swami Kuvalyananda
D. Shri Shri Ravi Shankar

90. How many total number of verses are there in "Yoga vashistha"?
A. 22,000 B. 32,000
C. 25,000 D. 35,000

91. How many types of yoga is described in the text 'Charak Samhita'?
A. 4 B. 5
C. 6 D. 7

92. Who is the compiler of the text 'Yoga Vashistha'?
A. Maharishi Vyasa B. Maharishi Valmiki
C. Maharishi Narad D. None of these

93. The text 'Yoga Vashistha' is also known by which another name?
A. Maha-Ramayana B. Aarsha-Ramayana
C. Jana-Vashistha D. All of the above

94. How many total verses are there in 'Yoga Vashistha'?
A. 22,000 B. 26,000
C. 29,000 D. 32,000

95. Vashistha rishi gave the teachings of spiritual knowledge to which king?
A. Shri Krishna B. Shri Rama
C. Vikramaditya D. Ashoka

96. How many types of mantra japa are there in mantrayoga?
A. 12 B. 13
C. 14 D. 16

97. The japa that persist continuously is called as:
A. Bharmara japa B. Ajapa japa
C. Manas japa D. Chala japa

98. Which is the second limb of sadanga yoga sadhna?
A. Asana B. Niyama
C. Pranayama D. Pratyahara

99. Which of the following is not a part of Brahdaranyaka upanishad?
A. Madhu Khanda B. Khila Khanda
C. Abha Khanda D. Muni Khanda

100. Which of the following match is incorrect?
A. Taitiriya Upanishad - Yajurveda
B. Chhandogya Upanishad - Samveda
C. Aetaireya Upanishad - Rigveda
D. Mundoka Upanishad - Ayurveda

101. 'Nachiketa' is a character in which upnishad?
A. Chhandogya B. Katha
C. Amrit-nada D. Swetasavtara

102. How many total chapters are there in Bhagavad Gita?
A. 12 B. 16
C. 18 D. 21

103. Which is the last chapter of Bhagavad Gita?
A. Samyasa Yoga B. Vibhaga Yoga
C. Bhakti Yoga D. Darsana Yoga

104. Karma Yoga is explained in which chapter of 'Bhagavad Gita'?
A. 2 B. 3
C. 4 D. 5

105. Samkhya Yoga is described in which chapter of Bhagavad Gita?
A. 2 B. 3
C. 4 D. 5

106. Ashtanga Yoga is described in which chapter of Bhagavad Gita?
A. 5 B. 6
C. 7 D. 8

107. The most number of verses are described in which chapter of Bhagavad Gita?
A. Sanyasa yoga B. Bhakti yoga
C. Karma yoga D. Samkhya yoga

108. How many total number of verses are described in last chapter, sanyasa yoga of Bhagavad Gita?
A. 66 B. 77
C. 78 D. 88

109. The Bhagavad Gita is also known by which other name?
A. Geetopanishad B. Kathopanishad
C. Shruti Granth D. None of these

110. How many verses did Shri Krishna tell to Arjuna during Gita upadesha?
A. 474 B. 574
C. 674 D. 700

111. How many verses did Arjuna speak during Gita upadesha?
A. 65 B. 75
C. 85 D. 95

112. For how many days the war of Kurukshetra had been fought between Kauravas and Pandavas?
A. 12 B. 16
C. 18 D. 22

113. Which type of yoga is described in Bhagavad Gita?
A. Bhakti yoga B. Karma yoga
C. Jnana yoga D. All of the above

114. The Bhagavad Gita is a part of which chapter of Mahabharata?
A. 4th B. 5th
C. 6th D. 7th

115. When was the Bhagavad Gita composed?
A. 4th Century B. 6th Century
C. 8th Century D. 9th Century

116. The verses of Bhagavada Gita are described in which of the following chapter of Mahabharata?
A. 6.25 - 42 B. 6.27 - 42
C. 6.28 - 43 D. 6.29 - 43

117. In the position of which of the following asana the pranayama can be done?
A. Savasana
B. Trikonasana
C. Kukkutasana
D. None of these

118. Which of the following subject is described in 'Yoga Vashistha'?
A. The art of self realization
B. The nature of Brahma
C. The super consciousness
D. All of the above

119. How many total number of hymns are there in four Vedas?
A. 15,416 B. 18,416
C. 20,416 D. 22,416

120. Which philosophy is also known as 'moksha shastra'?
A. Vedanta B. Samkhya
C. Mimansa D. Nyaya

121. Out of six Indian philosophies which is the largest?
A. Mimamsa B. Samkhya
C. Nyaya D. Vedanta

122. Which of the following yogic activity was most popular during vedic period?
A. Trataka B. Sun salutation
C. Kunjala D. Kapalbhati

123. The author of Brahmasutras is ______ .
A. Badarayana B. Gautama
C. Kapila D. Jaimini

124. The concept of Panchabedha is held by ______.
A. Advaita B. Dvaita
C. Visistadvaita D. Dvaitadvita

125. The term Pranayama in Yoga refers to ____.
A. withdrawal of senses
B. fixed attention
C. control of breathing
D. bodily posture

126. ______ is the founder of Nyaya school.
A. Kanada B. Gautama
C. Patanjali D. Kapila

127. According to Samkhya system, Prakriti is constituted of ______ gunas.
A. Five B. Three
C. Four D. Six

128. Jamini is the founder of ______ system.
A. Nyaya B. Samkhya
C. Mimamsa D. Vaisesika

129. Prastanatraya includes Upanishads, Bhagavad Gita and ______ .
A. Brahmasutras
B. Samkhyakarika
C. Nyaya sutras
D. Yoga sutra

130. The Mantras and Brahmanas are called the ______ of the Vedas.
A. Jnana Kanda B. Karma Kanda
C. Upasana Kanda D. Aranya Kanda

131. The author of the Yoga Sutra is ______ .
A. Patanjali B. Gautama
C. Prabhakara D. Kanada

132. Abhava as a metaphysical category is accepted by ______ .
A. Vaisesika B. Samkhya
C. Purva Mimamsa D. Jainism

133. In Yoga philosophy, Samprajnata and Asamprajnata are the stages of ______ .
A. Samadhi B. Dhyana
C. Asana D. Dharana

134. The negative expression 'neti, neti' defines ______ .
A. Brahman B. Perception
C. Maya D. Manas

135. The invariable association of the middle term with the major term is called ______ .
A. Vyapti B. Anumana
C. Cognition D. Sadhya

136. ______ means non-cognition.
A. Anumana B. Pratyaksha
C. Anupalabdhi D. All of these

137. ______ is regarded as the founder of Samkhya system.
A. Kanada B. Kapila
C. Patanjali D. Jaimini

138. Chitta means the three internal organs of Samkhya, they are ______ .
A. manas, jnanendriyas and karmendriyas
B. manas, ego and jnanendriyas
C. buddhi, ahmakara and manas
D. Jnanendriya, karmendriya and tanmatras

139. Pragabhava means ______ .
A. Absolute non-existence
B. Mutual non-existence
C. Antecedent non-existence
D. Subsequent non-existence

140. Nyaya maintains the theory of ______ .
A. Paratahpramanyavada
B. Svatahpramanyavada
C. Intrinsic validity of knowledge
D. None of the above

141. The fourth member of Nyaya syllogism is called ______ .
A. Pratijna B. Hetu
C. Upanaya D. Nigamana

142. The view of karma-jnana-samuchaya is advocated by ______ .
A. Prabhakara B. Kumarila
C. Sankara D. Ramanuaja

143. The Nyaya category of Hetvbhasa refers to ______ .
A. instances B. fallacious reasons
C. purpose D. None of these

ANSWERS

1	2	3	4	5	6	7	8	9	10
A	A	B	C	D	A	B	D	B	A
11	**12**	**13**	**14**	**15**	**16**	**17**	**18**	**19**	**20**
A	C	A	C	B	C	C	D	D	C
21	**22**	**23**	**24**	**25**	**26**	**27**	**28**	**29**	**30**
C	C	C	C	A	C	B	D	B	B

31	32	33	34	35	36	37	38	39	40
B	B	A	C	C	B	C	A	D	B
41	**42**	**43**	**44**	**45**	**46**	**47**	**48**	**49**	**50**
C	C	D	D	A	B	A	B	B	D
51	**52**	**53**	**54**	**55**	**56**	**57**	**58**	**59**	**60**
B	D	B	C	D	A	B	D	A	A
61	**62**	**63**	**64**	**65**	**66**	**67**	**68**	**69**	**70**
C	B	A	C	A	B	D	B	D	D
71	**72**	**73**	**74**	**75**	**76**	**77**	**78**	**79**	**80**
D	A	B	B	B	C	B	C	D	C
81	**82**	**83**	**84**	**85**	**86**	**87**	**88**	**89**	**90**
D	A	C	A	D	A	B	A	A	B
91	**92**	**93**	**94**	**95**	**96**	**97**	**98**	**99**	**100**
A	B	D	C	B	C	B	C	C	D
101	**102**	**103**	**104**	**105**	**106**	**107**	**108**	**109**	**110**
B	C	A	B	A	B	A	C	A	B
111	**112**	**113**	**114**	**115**	**116**	**117**	**118**	**119**	**120**
C	C	D	C	A	A	A	D	C	B
121	**122**	**123**	**124**	**125**	**126**	**127**	**128**	**129**	**130**
A	B	A	B	C	B	B	C	A	B
131	**132**	**133**	**134**	**135**	**136**	**137**	**138**	**139**	**140**
A	A	A	A	A	C	B	C	C	A
141	**142**	**143**							
C	D	B							

●●●

CHAPTER 3

Patanjali Yoga Sutras

Patanjali Yoga Sutras, written by Maharshi Patanjali in 2000 BC are considered to be the basic texts of *Yoga*.

All *yoga* as practised today is based on *Yoga Sutras*, a collection of aphorisms offered more than 2000 years ago by the Indian sage, Patanjali. *Yoga Sutras* by Maharshi Patanjali are known as the *Patanjali Yoga Sutras* and is the foundational text for *Yoga*. Historically, it is believed that Maharshi Patanjali lived in around 500 BC to 2000 BC and wrote on mainly three subjects, viz., grammar, medicine and *yoga*. Patanjali's three works together deal with man's development as a whole in thought, speech and action.

The teachings and practices of the *Yoga Sutras* are based on three principles:

1. Suffering is not caused by forces outside of us but by our faulty and limited perception of life and of who we are.
2. The unwavering peace we seek is realized by experiencing the unlimited and eternal peace that is our true identity. Though hidden by our ignorance, it exists within us, waiting to be revealed.
3. Self-realization is attained by mastering the mind. Only a single-pointed, calm mind can reveal the true self.

Patanjali Yoga Sutras consists of 196 *sutras* which are divided into four chapters or *padas*. Each *sutra* consists of Sanskrit words that are written in one or two lines. The 196 *sutras* are precise, reflective and pious in approach. Each of the *sutras* contains a wealth of ideas and wisdom towards full knowledge of his real nature. The *Patanjali Yoga Sutras* states that, through proper practice one can radiate grace, disposition and compassion. The four chapters or *padas* of the Yoga Sutras correspond to the four stages of life. The ultimate achievement of following the path of *Patanjali Yoga Sutras* is to experience the effortless, indivisible state of the prophet.

The four chapters of *Patanjanli Yoga Sutras* include, *Samadhi Pada, Sadhana Pada, Vibhuti Pada* and *Kaivalya Pada.*

Pada 1: Concentration (*Samadhi Pada*)

Pada 2: Practice (*Sadhana Pada*)

Pada 3: Experiences (*Vibhuti Pada*)

Pada 4: Absolute Freedom (Kaivalya Pada)

Samadhi Pada (51 Sutras) is the first chapter of *Patanjanli Yoga Sutras* that defines *yoga* and the movement of the Chitta (loosely known as mind) and how to reach samadhi state. It is directed towards the individuals who were already highly evolved to enable them to uphold their advanced state of cultured, mature aptitude and wisdom. It is assumed that Patanjali's aim, in beginning was to attract those rare souls who were already on the brisk of self-realisation. In *Samadhi Pada*, Patanjali defines the *yoga* as "Chitta Vritti Nirodha", meaning to stop the movement of *Chitta* (loosely called as mind). But it is not possible to stop fluctuation or movement of *Chitta*. *Chitta* is imbued by three qualities (*gunas*), viz., *Sattva, Rajas* and *Tamas*. Patanjali also explains that through *abhyasa* and *vairagya*, a person will be able to experience *Samadhi*.

In this *pada*, Patanjali comes to the level of those who are not spiritually evolved. Here he coins the word *Kriya Yoga*. *Kriya* means action and *Kriya Yoga* emphasizes the energetic effort to be made by the aspirant. This *pada* is composed using the eightfold paths of *yoga*. All the eight disciplines are compressed into a three-tier format. The tier formed by the first two pairs, *yama* and *niyama, asana* and *pranayama*, comes under *tapas* (religious spirit in practice). The second tier, *pratyahara* and *dharana*, is self-study (*svadhyaya*). The third, *dhyana* and *samadhi*, is *Isvara pranidhana*, the surrender of the individual self to God. In this way, Patanjali covers the three great paths of Indian philosophy in the *Yoga Sutras*. In the *Sadhana pada* the seeker is taught to perform *asana* (postures) so that he becomes familiar with his body, senses and intelligence. He develops alertness, sensitivity and the power concentration.

Sadhana Pada (55 Sutras) is the second chapter of *Patanjali Yoga Sutras*, where Patanjali comes down to the level of those who are not spiritually evolved. Patanjali in this chapter identifies *Avidya* or spiritual ignorance as the source of all sorrow and unhappiness. Here he coins the word, *Kriya Yoga*. *Kriya* means action and *Kriya Yoga* emphasizes the energetic effort to be made by the aspirant. First, he explains the concept of *Kriya Yoga*, which is the yoga of action and has three tiers, viz., *tapas, svadhyaya* and *Isvara pranidhana*. *Tapas* means burning desire, *Savadhyaya* means self study and *Isvara pranidhana* means surrender to God. When these three aspects of *kriya yoga* are followed earnestly, life's sufferings are overcome and *Samadhi* is experienced. He also explains causes of sufferings and how to minimise them; followed with the eightfold path of *Yoga* to achieve freedom for common man. This eightfold path is known as *Astanga Yoga* which is suitable for all. These eight steps are the *yama, niyama, asana, pranayama, pratyahara, dharana, dhyana and samadhi.*

Yamas are social moral conduct; while *Niyamas* are to be observed for self-development. *Asana* is a comfortable, steady and peaceful posture to make the physical body strong and ready for inner journey and *Pranayama* is the controlling of bio-energy. The first four steps are external supports called *Bahiranga* and last three are internal aid called *Antaranga*. *Pratyahara* is the connection between external and internal. It consists of controlling of five sense organs. In the chapter of *Sadhana pada*, Patanjali explains the journey from *yama* to *pratyahara*.

Vibhuti Pada (56 Sutras) is the next chapter of *Patanjali Yoga Sutras*. *Vibhuti* is the Sanskrit word for "power" or "manifestation". This chapter speaks of the divine effects of *yoga sadhana*. When a *sadhaka* attains expertise in the steps of the first five steps, he acquires the eight supernatural powers or *siddhis*. However, Patanjali cautions that the temptation of these powers should be avoided and the attention should be fixed only on liberation. Patanjali then explains *Dharana* or concentration, *Dhyana* or meditation, which comes from repeated concentration and *Samadhi*, which comes from deep absorption.

Kaivalya Pada (34 Sutras) is the fourth chapter of *Patanjali Yoga Sutras*. *Kaivalya* literally means "isolation", but as used in the *Sutras* depicts the idea of liberation or *moksha* (liberation), which is the intention of *Yoga*. The *Kaivalya Pada* describes the nature of liberation and the reality of the transcendental self. In this chapter, Patanjali distinguishes *Kaivalya* from *Samadhi*. In *Samadhi Pada*, the aspirant experiences a passive state where he can see his soul and in *Kaivalya* he lives above the *tamasic*, *rajasic* and *sattvik* influences of the three *gunas* of Nature (the primary qualities of Nature). The ultimate aim of *Yoga* is to achieve *Kaivalya* that can be achieved by birth, through use of drugs, by repetition of *mantra*, by *tapas* and through *Samadhi*. Of these, only the last two develop to matured intelligence and lead to stable growth.

Patanjali Yoga Sutras explains that the soul is pure and divine provided it is unblemished by action. Man may make or mar his progress through good action or bad action. *Yogic* action leads to religious life and non-*yogic* actions bind one to the world. With *yogic* practices the *sadhaka* is freed from the reactions of his actions and engrossed in *Kaivalya*. The *Patanjali Yoga Sutra* states, through proper practice one can radiate goodwill, friendliness and compassion. The four chapters or *padas* of the *Yoga Sutras* correspond to the four stages of life. The ultimate achievement of following the path of *Patanjali Yoga Sutras* is to experience the effortless, indivisible state of the prophet. *Patanjali Yoga Sutras* stands as the non-theistic doctrine of *Yoga Sutra*.

Pada 1 of the Yoga Sutras: Concentration (Samadhi Pada)

The first part of the *Sutras (Pada One)* introduces the main themes and practices that are expanded on in the rest of the text. This section gives us the basic definition of *yoga*. It presents the five categories of mental modifications (*vrittis*). It also introduces the idea of non-attachment, and it discusses obstacles to our *yoga* practice and to non-attachment and ways to overcome or prevent these obstacles. It finally examines specific practices for quieting the mind.

What is Yoga? (Yoga Sutras 1.1-1.4)

The first section of *Pada One* defines what *yoga* is. That definition is expanded upon in the other *sutras*. In a systematic process of meditation, you gradually move your attention further inward. There is a fundamental simplicity to the process of *Yoga* that is outlined in the *Yoga Sutras*. While the process might appear very complicated *while* reading the *Yoga Sutras*, the central theme is one of removing, transcending or setting aside the obstacles, or false identities. The many suggestions in the *Yoga Sutras* are the details or refinements of how to go about doing this. By being ever mindful of this core simplicity it is much easier to systematically progress on the path of *Yoga*.

1.1 : Now, after having done prior preparation through life and other practices, the study and practice of *Yoga* begins.

1.2 : *Yoga* is the control (nirodhah, regulation, channeling, mastery, integration, coordination, stilling, quieting, setting aside) of the modifications (gross and subtle thought patterns) of the mind field.

1.3 : Then the Seer abides in Itself, resting in its own True Nature, which is called Self-realization.

1.4 : At other times, when one is not in Self-realization, the Seer appears to take on the form of the modifications of the mind field, taking on the identity of those thought patterns.

Un-colouring your thoughts (Yoga Sutras 1.5-1.11)

This section of *Pada One* explains the different kinds of thoughts a person may have, and how to gain correct knowledge. While *Yoga* was defined in *sutras* 1.1-1.4, the process of experiencing the goal of *Self-realization* begins in this section. It looks at the idea that many of our thoughts are coloured by our judgments and expectations. For example, when we are driving down the street, we may think that we see a squirrel run in front of the car, so we step on the brake. But, then it turns out to just be some dry leaves blowing across the street. Things aren't always as we think they are. We also tend to think of things as "mine" or "yours" and Patanjali would say that there is nothing that really belongs to any one person and that by releasing our attachments, we find more peace.

To observe the colouring of thoughts simply means that when a thought and its corresponding emotions arise, you simply say that, "This is coloured," or "This is not coloured." Basically saying if it is a fact or a mental concept. For example, saying that a car is driving down the street is a fact, while saying that the car driving down the street is mine, or I want it to be mine, is a concept. Similarly, to notice whether some decision or action is useful or not useful brings great control over your habits of mind. It is simply observing, and saying to yourself, "This is useful," or "This is not useful."

1.5 : Those thought patterns (*vrittis*) fall into five varieties, of which some are coloured (*klishta*) and others are uncoloured (*aklishta*).

1.6 : The five varieties of thought patterns to witness are: (1) knowing correctly, (2) incorrect knowing, (3) fantasy or imagination, (4) deep sleep (*nidra*), and (5) recollection of memory.

1.7 : Of these five, there are three ways of gaining correct knowledge (*pramana*): (1) perception, (2) inference, and (3) testimony or verbal communication from others who have knowledge.

1.8 : Incorrect knowledge or illusion (viparyaya) is a false knowledge formed by perceiving a thing as being other than what it really is.

1.9 : Fantasy or imagination (*vikalpa*) is a thought pattern that has verbal expression and knowledge, but for which there is no such object or reality in existence.

1.10 : Dreamless sleep (*nidra*) is the subtle thought pattern which has as its object an inertia, blankness, absence, or negation of the other thought patterns (*vrittis*).

1.11 : Recollection or memory (*smriti*) is a mental modification caused by the inner reproducing of a previous impression of an object, but without adding any other characteristics from other sources.

Practice and non-attachment (Yoga Sutras 1.12-1.16)

This section of *Pada One* explains how, with sustained practice, one can reach the state of non-attachment. Practice (*abhyasa*, 1.13) and non-attachment (*vairagya*, 1.15) are the two core principles on which the entire system of *Yoga* rests (1.12). It is through the cultivation of these two that the other practices evolve, by which mastery over the mind field occurs, and allows the realization of the true Self.

In *yoga*, our daily inner practice should include the following: (1) being careful never to hurt others, (2) learning to meditate, and (3) exploring the question of where things really come from. We start by giving up our attachments to things, then to distractions (experiences) and to people. While we will still enjoy and love certain things, people, or experiences, through *yoga* practice we can learn to let go of our attachment, which is the cause of pain.

1.12 : These thought patterns (*vrittis*) are mastered (regulated, coordinated, controlled, stilled, quieted) through practice and non-attachment.

1.13 : Practice (*abhyasa*) means choosing, applying the effort, and doing those actions that bring a stable and tranquil state (*sthitau*).

1.14 : When that practice is done for a long time, without a break, and with sincere devotion, the practice becomes a firmly rooted, stable and solid foundation. *Yoga* practice should be steady and without gaps.

1.15 : When the mind loses desire even for objects seen or described in a tradition or in scriptures, it acquires a state of utter non-desire that is called non-attachment (*vairagya*). This is the ability to give up the attachment to distractions.

1.16 : Indifference to the subtlest elements, constituent principles, or qualities themselves (*gunas*), achieved through a knowledge of the nature of pure consciousness, is called supreme non-attachment (*paravairagya*). We should enjoy life, but we should also enjoy finding deeper meaning in life, and not lose our life in little distractions and attachments.

Sometimes the first sixteen *sutras* are referred to as the "Sweet Sixteen," since they present the fundamentals of the *Yoga Sutras*. It introduces the idea that true happiness comes from within and not through any thing, experience or person outside ourselves.

Types of concentration (Yoga Sutras 1.17-1.18)

In this section of *Pada One*, we learn of the different types of concentration and the definition of *samadhi*. Building upon practice and non-attachment, the meditator systematically moves inward, through four levels or stages of concentration on an object, and then progresses to the stage of objectless concentration. You can think of it in terms of listening to a song. First you only note that a song is being played, then you begin to examine the words or melody, then a feeling of pleasure washes over you as you enjoy the song, and finally you begin to lose yourself in the song completely.

1.17 : The deep absorption of attention on an object is of four kinds, (1) gross (*vitarka*), (2) subtle (*vichara*), (3) bliss accompanied (*ananda*), and (4) with oneness (*asmita*). This last stage is called *samprajnata samadhi*.

1.18 : The other kind of *samadhi* is *asamprajnata samadhi*, and has no object in which attention is absorbed, wherein only latent impressions remain; attainment of this state is preceded by the constant practice of allowing all of the fluctuations of mind to recede back into the field from which they arose. We stop "seeing" things in the wrong way.

Efforts and commitment (Yoga Sutras 1.19-1.22)

This section of the *Pada* examines how different people reach *samadhi* in different ways and in different time frames. Level of intensity and commitment to practise can determine how quickly someone reaches *samadhi*. It introduces the idea of the "five powers" which include: belief, effort, awareness, meditation and wisdom. Belief is the knowing or belief in our own power to reach enlightenment. Awareness has different stages; from the ability to be present in the moment to the ability to keep our mind on where the things that happen to us really come from. Being able to objectively examine our thoughts and the factors that shape those thoughts is part of mediation. We begin to understand that we create our own world through our mental projections.

1.19 : Some who have attained higher levels (*videhas*) or know unmanifest nature (*prakritilayas*), are drawn into birth in this world by their remaining latent impressions of ignorance, and more naturally come to these states of *samadhi*.

1.20 : Others follow a five-fold systematic path of (1) faithful certainty in the path, (2) directing energy towards the practices, (3) repeated memory of the path and the process of stilling the mind, (4) training in deep concentration, and (5) the pursuit of real knowledge, by which the higher *samadhi* (*asamprajnata samadhi*) is attained.

1.21 : Those who pursue their practices with intensity of feeling, vigour, and firm conviction achieve concentration and the fruits thereof more quickly, compared to those of medium or lesser intensity.

1.22 : Because the methods may be applied in slow, medium, or speedy ways, even among those who have such commitment and conviction, there are differences in the rate of progress, resulting in nine grades of practice.

Direct route through AUM (Yoga Sutras 1.23-1.29)

Through remembering the meaning of OM (AUM), our connection with the universe is more quickly developed. Remembering the sound vibration of AUM (or OM) brings both the realization of the individual Self and the removal of obstacles that normally block that realization. In a sense, this practice is like a short cut, in the sense that it goes directly to the heart of the process. These *sutras* also encourage people to find a living master from whom they can learn.

1.23 : From a special process of devotion and letting go into the creative source from which we emerged (*ishvara pranidhana*), the coming of *samadhi* is imminent.

1.24 : That creative source (*ishvara*) is a particular consciousness (*purusha*) that is unaffected by colourings (*kleshas*), actions (*karmas*), or results of those actions that happen when latent impressions stir and cause those actions.

1.25 : In that pure consciousness (*ishvara*) the seed of omniscience has reached its highest development and cannot be exceeded.

1.26 : From that consciousness (*ishvara*) the ancient-most teachers were taught, since it is not limited by the constraint of time.

1.27 : The sacred word designating this creative source is the sound OM, called *pranava*.

1.28 : This sound creates deep feeling for the meaning of what it represents.

1.29 : From that remembering comes the realization of the individual Self and the removal of obstacles.

Obstacles and solutions (Yoga Sutras 1.30-1.32)

This section of *Pada One* explains the major obstacles to reach *samadhi*, as well as the consequences of these obstacles and how to prevent or deal with them. There are a number of predictable obstacles that arise on the inner journey, along with several consequences that grow out of them. While these can be a challenge, there is a certain comfort in knowing that they are a natural, predictable part of the process. Knowing this can help to maintain the faith and conviction that were previously discussed as essential.

Predictable Obstacles

Illness	Dullness	Doubt
Negligence	Laziness	Cravings
Misperceptions	Failure	Instability

Companions to those Obstacles

Mental and physical pain	Sadness and frustration
Unsteadiness of the body	Irregular breath

One-pointedness is the solution: There is a single, underlying principle that is the antidote for these obstacles and their consequences, and that is the one-pointedness of mind.

1.30 : Nine kinds of distractions come. Those are: obstacles naturally encountered on the path, and are physical illness, tendency of the mind to not work efficiently, doubt or indecision, lack of attention to pursuing the means of *samadhi*, laziness in mind and body, failure to regulate the desire for worldly objects, incorrect assumptions or thinking, failing to attain stages of the practice, and instability in maintaining a level of practice once attained.

1.31 : From these obstacles, there are four other consequences that also arise. These are: (1) mental or physical pain, (2) sadness or dejection, (3) restlessness, shakiness, or anxiety, and (4) irregularities in the exhalation and inhalation of breath.

Our unhappy thoughts can cause physical problems, which can then cause more unhappy thoughts.

Stabilizing and clearing the mind (Yoga Sutras 1.32-1.39)

These *sutras* examine how the mind can maintain a state of peace regardless of the situation. They provide practical steps for finding inner peace. *Sutra* 1.33 is especially important in shaping our attitude towards peace. It suggests that we should have infinite kindness, which is the desire to bring happiness to all living things. We should use kindness, compassion, joy and equanimity in our thoughts and dealings with others. This group of *sutras* places importance on not only serving others, but really thinking about what others want and focusing on their needs, so we can stop obsessing about our own lives. Helping others and thinking about how other people are feeling and what they want, helps us eliminate our own unending wanting which leads to a life of pleasure and pain rather than true happiness. Once we are free from attachment to our own desires, we can find true and lasting happiness.

1.32 : To prevent or deal with these nine obstacles and their four consequences, the recommendation is to make the mind one-pointed.

1.33 : In relationships, the mind becomes purified by cultivating feelings of friendliness towards those who are happy, compassion for those who are suffering, goodwill towards those who are virtuous, and indifference or neutrality towards those we perceive as wicked or evil.

1.34 : The mind is also calmed by regulating the breath, particularly attending to exhalation and the natural stilling of breath that comes from such practice.

1.35 : The inner concentration on the process of sensory experiencing, done in a way that leads towards higher, subtle sense perception; this also leads to stability and tranquillity of the mind. The physical practice of *yoga* can help unblock our inner energy channels.

1.36 : Or concentration on a painless inner state of lucidness and luminosity also brings stability and tranquillity.

1.37 : Or contemplating on having a mind that is free from desires, the mind gets stabilized and tranquil.

1.38 : Or by focusing on the nature of the stream in the dream state or the nature of the state of dreamless sleep, the mind becomes stabilized and tranquil.

1.39 : Or by contemplating or concentrating on whatever object or principle one may like, or towards which one has a predisposition, the mind becomes stable and tranquil.

Results of stabilizing the mind (Yoga Sutras 1.40-1.51)

These *sutras* focus on the results of having a tranquil mind. It looks at the wisdom and peace gained from having an objective, clear and unbothered mind. Once the mind is reasonably stabilized and clear, the deeper process of *Yoga* can begin. The mind eventually becomes like a transparent crystal, and is a purified tool for the subtler explorations of the gross and subtle levels. Such a mind can explore the whole range of objects, even the smallest or the largest.

Four levels of meditation on an object: There are only four levels of meditation on an object. These are systematically experienced, all the way to the level of un-manifest matter:

1. With gross thoughts, *savitarka samapattih*
2. Without gross thoughts, *nirvitarka samapattih*
3. With subtle thoughts, savichara samapattih
4. Without subtle thoughts, *nirvichara samapattih*

1.40 : When, through such practices, the mind develops the power of becoming stable on the smallest size object as well as on the largest, the mind truly comes under control.

1.41 : When the modifications of mind have become weakened, the mind becomes like a transparent crystal, and thus can easily take on the qualities of whatever object observed, whether that object be the observer, the means of observing, or an object observed, in a process of engrossment called *samapatti*.

1.42 : One type of such an engrossment (*samapatti*) is one in which there is a mixture of three things, a word or name going with the object, the meaning or identity of that object, and the knowledge associated with that object.

1.43 : When the memory or storehouse of modifications of mind is purified, the mind appears to be devoid of its own nature and only the object on which it is contemplating appears to shine forward.

When we communicate briefly with the ultimate reality, we begin to understand how we see things wrong, how we attach opinions and feelings to things that don't need it.

1.44 : In the same way that these engrossments operate with gross objects in *savitarka samapatti*, the engrossment with subtle objects also operates, and is known as *savichara* and *nirvichara samapatti*.

1.45 : Having such subtle objects extends all the way up to un-manifest *prakriti*.

1.46 : These four varieties of engrossment are the only kinds of concentrations (*samadhi*) which are objective, and have a seed of an object. We begin to understand that our thoughts are merely that – just thoughts, and are not reality unless we decide to experience them.

1.47 : As one gains proficiency in the undisturbed flow in *nirvichara*, a purity and luminosity of the inner instrument of mind is developed.

1.48 : The experiential knowledge that is gained in that state is one of essential wisdom and is filled with truth.

1.49 : That knowledge is different from the knowledge that is commingled with testimony or through inference, because it relates directly to the specifics of the object, rather than to those words or other concepts. Once all negativity is gone we progress through the final stages to total purity.

1.50 : This type of knowledge that is filled with truth creates latent impressions in the mind-field, and those new impressions tend to reduce the formation of other less useful forms of habitual latent impressions.

1.51 : When even these latent impressions from truth filled knowledge recede along with the other impressions, there is an objectless concentration. We can be in this state at any time and feel the connection to everything around us, and feel no limitations.

Pada Two of the Yoga Sutra: Practice (Sadhana Pada)

While *Pada One* focuses more on the theoretical aspects of *raja yoga*, the focus in *Pada Two* is on motivation for regular practice, while offering clear, comprehensive instructions for *yoga* practice. It outlines specific tools of attention that are used to systematically carve out, or cut away the obstacles of the inner mental shield that is blocking the light of the Self within. In *sutra* 2.29, we are introduced to the eight limbs of *yoga*, which are then elaborated on throughout the remainder of *Pada Two*.

Minimizing gross colouring (Yoga Sutras 2.1-2.11)

These *sutras* explain the role of active *yoga* in the dissipation of wrong thinking or wrong attitudes. They describe the different types of problem thinking that the practice of *yoga* can help eliminate. There are four principles that help stop our pain (the four higher truths). These *sutras* look at the first truth; the truth of where our pain comes from. Our pain comes from our ignorance – which allows our minds to turn around the truth. We look for pleasure in things that will eventually end and cause pain, rather than realize that everything we really want, or see "out there" is within us, and is everlasting.

2.1 : *Yoga* in the form of action (*kriya yoga*) has three parts: (1) training and purifying the senses (*tapas*), (2) self-study in the context of teachings, and (3) devotion and letting go into the creative source from which we emerged.

2.2 : That *Yoga* of action (*kriya yoga*) is practised to bring about *samadhi* and to minimize the coloured (or mistaken) thought patterns (*kleshas*).

2.3 : There are five kinds of colouring (*kleshas*): (1) forgetting, or ignorance about the true nature of things, (2) I-ness, individuality, or egoism, (3) attachment or addiction to mental impressions or objects, (4) aversion to thought patterns or objects, and (5) love of these as being life itself, as well as fear of their loss as being death.

2.4 : The root forgetting or ignorance of the nature of things (*avidya*) is the breeding ground for the other of the five colorings (*kleshas*), and each of these is in one of four states: (1) dormant or inactive, (2) attenuated or weakened, (3) interrupted or separated from temporarily, or (4) active and producing thoughts or actions to varying degrees.

2.5 : Ignorance (*avidya*) is of four types: (1) regarding that which is transient as eternal, (2) mistaking the impure for pure, (3) thinking that which brings misery to bring happiness, and (4) taking that which is not-self to be self.

2.6 : The colouring (*klesha*) of I-ness or egoism (asmita), which arises from the ignorance, occurs due to the mistake of taking the intellect (*buddhi*, which knows, decides, judges, and discriminates) to itself be pure consciousness.

2.7 : Attachment (*raga*) is a separate modification of mind, which follows the rising of the memory of pleasure, where the three modifications of attachment, pleasure, and the memory of the object are then associated with one another.

2.8 : Aversion (*dvesha*) is a modification that results from misery associated with some memory, whereby the three modifications of aversion, pain, and the memory of the object or experience are then associated with one another.

2.9 : Even for those people who are learned, there is an ever-flowing, firmly established love for continuation and a fear of cessation, or death (*abhinivesa*), of these various coloured modifications (*kleshas*).

2.10 : When the five types of colourings (*kleshas*) are in their subtle, merely potential form, they are then destroyed by their disappearance or cessation into and of the field of mind itself.

2.11 : When the modifications still have some potency of colouring, they are brought to the state of mere potential by meditation (*dhyana*).

Breaking the alliance of karma (Yoga Sutras 2.12-2.25)

These *sutras* focus on the idea that the choices we make in life determine whether our experiences are of happiness or suffering. It argues that the key to breaking the cycle of *karma* is to set aside the connection between "observer" and that which is "observed." You have thoughts in your mind, but who is listening to those thoughts? Two people can have the same thought, but have very different reactions to that thought. Why is that?

2.12 : Latent impressions that are coloured, result from other actions (*karmas*), that were brought about by colourings (*kleshas*), and become active and experienced in a current life or a future life. All of our actions are stored in our minds as seeds. When we do good deeds and have good thoughts of others, we eventually create better experiences for ourselves.

2.13 : As long as those colourings (*kleshas*) remain at the root, three consequences are produced: (1) birth, (2) span of life, and (3) experiences in that life.

2.14 : Because of having the nature of merits or demerits (virtue or vice), these three (birth, span of life, and experiences) may be experienced as either pleasure or pain.

2.15 : A wise, discriminating person sees all worldly experiences as painful, because of reasoning that all these experiences lead to more consequences, anxiety, and deep habits (*samskaras*), as well as acting in opposition to the natural qualities.

2.16 : Because the worldly experiences are seen as painful, it is the pain, which is yet to come, that is to be avoided and discarded. Our thoughts and actions come back to us eventually. So, if we have kind, loving thought and do kind actions without thought of what's in it for us, eventually that same kindness returns to us. If we have thoughts of fear, doubt, or anger, those same aspects will eventually show up in our lives. You have to guard your thoughts and keep them kind and positive, and really desire happiness for other people as much as you would want it for yourself.

2.17 : The uniting of the seer (the subject, or the experiencer) with the seen (the object, or that which is experienced) is the cause or connection to be avoided.

2.18 : The objects are by their nature of: (1) illumination or sentience, (2) activity or mutability, or (3) inertia or stasis; they consist of the elements and the powers of the senses, and exist for the purpose of experiencing the world and for liberation or enlightenment. Our perceptions of all things are coming from the seeds in our minds. We can either blindly consume what we've been conditioned to believe, or begin planting new seeds in our minds for a perfect world of freedom.

2.19 : There are four states of the elements (*gunas*). These are: (1) differentiated, (2) undifferentiated, unspecialized, (3) indicator only (mere signs), and (4) without indicator (beyond all signs).

2.20 : The Seer is but the force of seeing itself, appearing to see or experience that which is presented as a cognitive principle. There are two realities. In the first level, things seem different from each other. On the second level, we realize that all things are one thing in the sense that they all come from our mental seeds, from our mind. If we understand this, we can build a new world free of pain.

2.21 : The essence or nature of the knowable objects exists only to serve as the objective field for pure consciousness.

2.22 : Although knowable objects cease to exist in relation to one who has experienced their fundamental, formless true nature, the appearance of the knowable objects is not destroyed, for their existence continues to be shared by others who are still observing them.

2.23 : Having an alliance, or relationship between objects and the Self is the necessary means by which there can subsequently be realization of the true nature of those objects by that very Self.

2.24 : *Avidya* or ignorance (2.3-2.5), the condition of ignoring, is the underlying cause that allows this alliance to appear to exist.

2.25 : By causing a lack of *avidya*, or ignorance there is then an absence of the alliance, and this leads to a freedom known as a state of liberation or enlightenment for the Seer.

Reason for the Eight rungs (Yoga Sutras 2.26-2.29)

These *sutras* explain that there are specific steps in *yoga*, a certain order of steps, that leads to enlightenment. It is here that the eight fold path is introduced. The eight rungs include:

1. **Yama:** Codes of restraint, abstinences (self-control)
2. **Niyama:** Observances, self-training (self-study, purity)
3. **Asana:** Meditation posture
4. **Pranayama:** Expansion of breath and *prana*
5. **Pratyahara:** Withdrawal of the senses
6. **Dharana:** Concentration (fixation)
7. **Dhyana:** Meditation (focus)
8. **Samadhi:** Deep absorption (wisdom)

2.26 : Clear, distinct, unimpaired discriminative knowledge is the means of liberation from this alliance. We understand that things happen *from* us – not *to* us.

2.27 : Seven kinds of ultimate insight come to one who has attained this degree of discrimination.

2.28 : Through the practice of the different limbs, or steps to *Yoga*, whereby impurities are eliminated, there arises an illumination that culminates in discriminative wisdom, or enlightenment.

2.29 : The eight rungs, limbs, or steps of *Yoga* are the codes of self-regulation or restraint (*yamas*), observances or practices of self-training (*niyamas*), postures (*asana*), expansion of breath and *prana* (*pranayama*), withdrawal of the senses (*pratyahara*), concentration (*dharana*), meditation (*dhyana*), and perfected concentration (*samadhi*).

The first five rungs of the eight limb path are externally oriented, where our progress is easier. The final three are inwardly focused practices.

Yamas & Niyamas, #1-2 of Eight rungs (Yoga Sutras 2.30-2.34)

These *sutras* explain the specifics of *yamas* (self control) and *niyamas* (cleanliness of mind and body).

2.30 : Non-injury or non-harming (*ahimsa*), truthfulness (*satya*), abstention from stealing, walking in awareness of the highest reality, and non-possessiveness (or non-grasping with the senses), are the five *yamas* (codes of self-regulation), and are the first of the eight steps of *Yoga*.

2.31 : These codes of self-regulation or restraint become a great vow when they become universal and are not restricted by any consideration of the nature of the kind of living being to whom one is related, nor in any place, time or situation.

2.32 : Cleanliness and purity of body and mind, an attitude of contentment, training of the senses (*tapas*), self-study and reflection on sacred words, and an attitude of letting go into one's source, are the observances or practices of self-training (*niyamas*), and are the second rung on the ladder of *Yoga*.

2.33 : When these codes of self-regulation (*yamas*) and practices of self-training (*niyamas*) are inhibited from being practised due to perverse, unwholesome, troublesome, or deviant thoughts, principles in the opposite direction should be cultivated. Develop the habit of pure thoughts.

2.34 : Actions arising out of such negative thoughts are performed directly by oneself, or caused to be done through others. These actions may be preceded by, or performed through anger, greed or delusion, and can be mild, moderate or intense in nature. Therefore, it is a reminder to oneself that, oneself that these negative thoughts and actions are the causes of unending misery and ignorance is the principle in the opposite direction that was recommended in the previous *sutra*.

Remind yourself that anger, jealousy and judgment directed towards another person only eventually hurts you.

Benefits from Yamas & Niyamas (Yoga Sutras 2.35-2.45)

These *sutras* provide the motivation for practising the *yamas* and *niyamas* by illustrating the benefits of such practice. Ideas such as loss of hostility, improved concentration and contentment, are some of the benefits mentioned. However, it is important to note that, while these are benefits, they really result from the opening of what is already there, by the removal of obstacles.

2.35 : As a *Yogi* becomes firmly grounded in non-injury (*ahimsa*), other people who come near will naturally lose any feelings of hostility. If you make it a way of life never to hurt others, then in your presence all conflict comes to an end.

2.36 : As truthfulness (*satya*) is achieved, the fruits of actions naturally result according to the will of the *Yogi*.

2.37 : When non-stealing is established, all jewels, or treasures present themselves, or are available to the *Yogi*.

2.38 : When walking in the awareness of the highest reality is firmly established, a great strength, capacity, or vitality is acquired.

2.39 : When one is steadfast in non-possessiveness or non-grasping with the senses, there arises knowledge of the why and wherefore of past and future incarnations.

2.40 : Through cleanliness and purity of body and mind (*shaucha*), one develops an attitude of distancing, or disinterest towards one's own body, and becomes disinclined towards contacting the bodies of others.

2.41 : Also through cleanliness and purity of body and mind (*shaucha*) comes a purification of the subtle mental essence, a pleasantness, goodness and gladness of feeling, a one-pointedness with intentness, the conquest or mastery over the senses, and a fitness, qualification, or capability for self-realization.

2.42 : From an attitude of contentment (*santosha*), unexcelled happiness, mental comfort, joy, and satisfaction are obtained. Rather than having never ending wanting and grasping, happiness comes from an attitude of contentment with what is.

2.43 : Through training of the senses (*tapas*), there comes a destruction of mental impurities, and an ensuing mastery or perfection over the body and the mental organs of senses and actions.

2.44 : From self-study and reflection on sacred words (svadhyaya), one attains contact, communion, or concert with that underlying natural reality or force.

2.45 : From an attitude of letting go into one's source, the state of perfected concentration (*samadhi*) is attained.

Asana, #3 of Eight rungs (Yoga Sutras 2.46-2.48)

These *sutras* focus on the proper form for *asana* practice. They emphasize that postures should be held in an effortless manner, so that one can merge with the moment. The posture (*asana*) for *Yoga* meditation should be steady, stable, and motionless, as well as comfortable, and this is the third of the eight rungs of *Yoga*. By learning to control the body and keep it in balance, avoiding lethargy and hyperactivity, we learn to control the mind and keep it in balance.

2.46 : The posture (*asana*) for *Yoga* meditation should be steady, stable, and motionless, as well as comfortable, and this is the third of the eight rungs of *Yoga*.

2.47 : The means of perfecting the posture is that of relaxing or loosening of effort, and allowing attention to merge with endlessness, or the infinite.

2.48 : From the attainment of that perfected posture, there arises an unassailable, unimpeded freedom from suffering due to the pairs of opposites (such as heat and cold, good and bad, or pain and pleasure).

The physical part of *yoga* (*asana*) helps to release blockages in our bodies and in the way we see things.

Pranayama, #4 of Eight rungs (Yoga Sutras 2.49-2.53)

These *sutras* explain the practice of *pranayama* and the benefits of this practice. *Pranayama* is the mastery of *prana*, the universal life force, through the breath. The fourth of the eight rungs of *Yoga* is *Pranayama*, which is regulating the breath, leading to the experience of the steady flow of energy (*prana*). While *asana* works from the outside in, *pranayama* works from the inside out.

2.49 : Once that perfected posture has been achieved, the slowing or braking of the force behind, and of unregulated movement of inhalation and exhalation is called breath control and expansion of *prana* (*pranayama*), which leads to the absence of the awareness of both, and is the fourth of the eight rungs.

2.50 : That *pranayama* has three aspects, viz., external or outward flow (exhalation), internal or inward flow (inhalation), and the third one, which is the absence of both during the transition between them, is known as fixedness, retention, or suspension. These are regulated by place, time, and number, with breath becoming slow and subtle.

2.51 : The fourth *pranayama* is that continuous *prana* which surpasses, is beyond, or behind those others that operate in the exterior and interior realms or fields.

2.52 : Through that *pranayama* the veil of *karma* (2.12) that covers the inner illumination or light is thinned, diminishes and vanishes.

2.53 : Through these practices and processes of *pranayama*, which is the fourth of the eight steps, the mind acquires or develops the fitness, qualification, or capability for true concentration (dharana), which is itself the sixth of the steps.

Pratyahara, #5 of Eight rungs (Yoga Sutras 2.54-2.55)

These *sutras* explain the state of *pratyahara*. The senses do not function independently of the mind. Therefore, when the attention is pulled inward, they disconnect from their objects and also go within.

2.54 : When the mental organs of senses and actions cease to be engaged with the corresponding objects in their mental realm, and assimilate or turn back into the mind-field from which they arose, this is called *pratyahara*. It is the fifth step.

2.55 : Through that turning inward of the organs of senses and actions also comes a supreme ability, controllability, or mastery over those senses inclining to go outward towards their objects.

Pada 3 of the Yoga Sutras: Experiences (Vibhuti Pada)

Chapter 3 starts by presenting the last 3 of the 8 rungs of *Yoga*, which are concentration, meditation, and *samadhi*, collectively known as *samyama*. The rest of the chapter explains how *samyama* is used as the finer tool to remove the subtler veils of ignorance. *Pada Three* lists the accomplishments that can result from the practice of *yoga*. In this *Pada*, Patanjali also examines the nature of the material world and its relationship to the mind. The powers listed in this *Pada* seem extraordinary because we do not see the true nature of our world. It also explains how these abilities can actually hinder our path to self-realization, if we don't learn to control the ego. We must let go of any attachments to these new abilities. This *Pada* ends with a description of the final stages that lead to self-realization (or direct experience with the Absolute).

Dharana, Dhyana, & Samadhi, #6, 7, and 8 of Eight rungs (Yoga Sutras 3.1-3.3)

These three *sutras* complete the concepts presented in *Pada Two*. Even brief concentration is success: It is also easy to think that a meditation session was "not good" because it did not bring some deep sense of bliss. Actually, when one understands the tremendous value of simple concentration training, even the brief, shallower practices are seen in a proper context of having a positive value.

3.1 : Concentration (*dharana*) is the process of holding or fixing the attention of mind onto one object or place, and is the sixth of the eight rungs.

3.2 : The repeated continuation, or uninterrupted stream of that one point of focus is called absorption in meditation (*dhyana*), and is the seventh of the eight steps.

3.3 : When only the essence of that object, place, or point shines forth in the mind, as if devoid even of its own form, that state of deep absorption is called deep concentration or *samadhi*, which is the eighth rung.

Samyama and the final practices (Yoga Sutras 3.4-3.8)

These *sutras* present the major stages of mental mastery that practitioners will experience. *Samyama* is the collective practice of concentration (*dharana*), meditation (*dhyana*), and *samadhi*, which are the sixth, seventh, and eighth of the eight rungs of *Yoga*. These stages can be described as fixation, focus, and wisdom. Once you master these stages, you have the ability to put your mind on a single point and keep it there. At the same time, you really understand where the thing you're focused on is really coming from – that everything comes from you.

Purpose of the first five rungs: The primary purpose of all the preparation work and the first five rungs of *Yoga* is to build this tool called *samyama*.

3.4 : The three processes of *dharana, dhyana*, and *samadhi*, when taken together on the same object, place or point are called *samyama*.

3.5 : Through the mastery of that three-part process of *samyama*, the light of knowledge, transcendental insight, or higher consciousness (*prajna*) dawns illumines, flashes, or is visible.

3.6 : That three-part process of *samyama* is gradually applied to the finer planes, states, or stages of practice.

3.7 : These three practices of concentration (*dharana*), meditation (*dhyana*), and *samadhi* are more intimate or internal than the previous five practices.

3.8 : However, these three practices are external, and not intimate compared to *nirbija samadhi*, which is *samadhi* that has no object, nor even a seed object on which there is concentration.

Witnessing subtle transitions (Yoga Sutras 3.9-3.15)

This section provides a more detailed description of the progression from *dharana* to *dhyana* and finally to *samadhi*. It is the process that leads to self realization. In this section, it looks at our thoughts as *objects*. However, the thoughts in the mind field not only interact with one another; but also come and go. Just imagine for a moment that you had mastery over that process of the coming and going of the thoughts, the *transitions*. With mastery over the *transition process* itself, you would gain tremendous insight and mastery over the thoughts themselves, as well as the *subtlest* inner transitions of mental process. Those subtle *transitions* are also *objects* themselves, subject to exploration and witnessing, as well as to setting aside through non-attachment. The mind doesn't stop, but it becomes connected with everything and becomes clear. Being in this state can eliminate certain negative thoughts for good.

3.9 : That high level of mastery called *nirodhah-parinamah* occurs in the moment when there is a convergence of the rising tendency of deep impressions, the subsiding tendency, and the attention of the mind field itself.

3.10 : The steady flow of this state (*nirodhah-parinamah*) continues by the creation of deep impressions (*samskaras*) from doing the practice.

3.11 : The mastery called *samadhi-parinamah* is the transition whereby the tendency to all-pointedness subsides, while the tendency to one-pointedness arises.

3.12 : The mastery called *ekagrata-parinamah* is the transition whereby the same one-pointedness arises and subsides sequentially.

3.13 : These three transition processes also explain the three transformations of form, time, and characteristics, and the way these relate to the material elements and senses.

3.14 : There is an unmanifest, indescribable substratum or existence that is common or contained within all the other forms or qualities.

3.15 : Change in the sequence of the characteristics is the cause for the different appearances of results, consequences, or effects.

Experiences from Samyama (Yoga Sutras 3.16-3.37)

These *sutras* explain that *samyama* is a way of obtaining knowledge through experience. It is a direct perception of the highest order because it is just the mind confronting objects head-on. The suggestion is to set aside as not-self all the levels of our physical being and levels of discovery, by a process of discrimination and non-attachment. This section describes some seemingly remarkable feats that can be obtained through the practice of *yoga* (such as psychic abilities – knowing what others are thinking, predicting future events, etc). It suggests that by performing *samyama* on desirable characteristics, we can obtain those characteristics for ourselves. However, some people may use these powers to further their ego identity. The true *yogi* realizes this and sets aside feelings of pride. When reading the *sutras*, it is important to not feel as though you must attain all the experiences to progress on the path to self-realization.

People who meditate very regularly, even if it is just to chill out for a bit, will gain more power simply because in any deep state of meditation, we can not commit the negative actions and thoughts towards others that keep us from these powers.

3.16 : By *samyama* on the three-fold changes in form, time, and characteristics, there comes knowledge of past and future.

3.17 : The name associated with an object, the object itself implied by that name, and the conceptual existence of the object, all three usually interpenetrate or commingle with one another. By *samyama* on the distinction between these three, the meaning of the sounds made by all beings becomes available.

3.18 : Through the direct perception of the latent impressions (*samskaras*) comes the knowledge of previous incarnations.

3.19 : By *samyama* on the notions or presented ideas comes knowledge of another's mind. (This is the idea of being able to "read" another person).

3.20 : But the underlying support of that knowledge (of the other person's mind, in 3.19) remains unperceived or out of reach.

3.21 : When *samyama* is done on the form of one's own physical body, the illumination or visual characteristic of the body is suspended, and is thus invisible to other people. (It is said, *yogis* can intercept the light that reflects off their bodies, making it seem they have disappeared).

3.22 : In the same way as described in relation to sight (3.21), one is able to suspend the ability of the body to be heard, touched, tasted, or smelled.

3.23 : *Karma* is of two kinds, either fast or slow to manifest; by *samyama* on these *karmas*, comes foreknowledge of the time of death.

3.24 : By *samyama* on friendliness (and the other attitudes of 1.33), there comes great strength of that attitude. (By performing *samyama* on a desirable quality, such as friendliness, we can attain its benefits).

3.25 : By *samyama* on the strength of elephants comes a similar strength.

3.26 : By directing the flash of inner light of higher sensory activity, knowledge of subtle objects, those hidden from view, and those very distant can be attained.

3.27 : By *samyama* on the inner sun, knowledge of the many subtle realms can be known.

3.28 : By *samyama* on the moon, knowledge of the arrangement of the inner stars can be known.

3.29 : By *samyama* on the pole-star, knowledge of the movement of those stars can be known.

The next *sutras* discuss the idea of the *chakras* and gaining knowledge of the *chakras* (energy channels in the body).

3.30 : By *samyama* on the navel centre, knowledge of the arrangement of the systems of the body can be known.

3.31 : By *samyama* on the pit of the throat, hunger and thirst leave.

3.32 : By *samyama* on the tortoise channel, below the throat, steadiness is attained.

3.33 : By *samyama* on the coronal light of the head, visions of the *siddhas*, the masters can come.

3.34 : Or, through the intuitive light of higher knowledge, anything might become known.

3.35 : By practising *samyama* on the heart, knowledge of the mind is attained.

3.36 : The having of experiences comes from a presented idea only when there is a commingling of the subtlest aspect of mind and pure consciousness, which are really quite different. *Samyama* on the pure consciousness, which is distinct from the subtlest aspect of mind, reveals knowledge of that pure consciousness.

3.37 : From the light of the higher knowledge of that pure consciousness or *purusha* (3.36) arise higher, transcendental, or divine hearing, touch, vision, taste, and smell. You develop super-normal abilities of the senses.

These *sutras* are also saying that we often put limitations on ourselves based on what we are conditioned to think is possible. But we are often capable of more than we imagine.

What to do with experiences (Yoga Sutras 3.38)

This *sutra* explains that the powers gained from *samyama* are expressions of great mental power, but still exist in the realm of relativity and can actually be obstacles to self realization. When under the influence of attachment, these powers can tempt the ego to "perform" and become obstacles to *samadhi*.

3.38 : These experiences resulting from *samyama* are obstacles to *samadhi*, but appear to be attainments or powers to the outgoing or worldly mind.

More from Samyama (Yoga Sutras 3.39-3.49)

These *sutras* discuss how a *yogi* gains knowledge of the way mind-stuff moves into and interacts with the body. It examines how *samyama* helps to break the false identification with the body.

3.39 : By loosening or letting go of the causes of bondage and attachment, and by following the knowledge of how to go forth into the passages of the mind, there comes the ability to enter into another body.

3.40 : By the mastery over *udana*, the upward flowing *prana vayu*, there is a cessation of contact with mud, water, thorns, and other such objects, and this ensures the rising or levitation of the body.

3.41 : By mastery over *samana*, the *prana* flowing in the navel area, there comes effulgence, radiance, or fire.

3.42 : By *samyama* over the relation between space and the power of hearing, the higher, divine power of hearing comes.

3.43 : By *samyama* on the relationship between the body and space (*akasha*) and by concentrating on the lightness of cotton, passage through space can be attained.

3.44 : When the formless thought patterns of mind are projected outside of the body, it is called *maha-videha*, a great disincarnate one. By *samyama* on that outward projection, the veil over the spiritual light is removed.

3.45 : By *samyama* on the five forms of the elements (*bhutas*), viz., gross form, essence, subtleness, interconnectedness, and its purpose, mastery over those *bhutas* is attained.

3.46 : Through that mastery over the elements, comes the abilities of making the body atomically small, perfect, and indestructible in its characteristics or components, as well as bringing other such powers.

3.47 : This perfection of the body includes beauty, gracefulness, strength, and adamantine hardness in taking the blows that come.

3.48 : By *samyama* on the process of perception and action, essence, I-ness, connectedness, and purposefulness of senses and acts, mastery over those senses and acts (*indriyas*) is attained.

3.49 : By that mastery over the senses and acts (*indriyas*), there comes quickness of mind, perception with the physical instruments of perception, and mastery over the primal cause out of which manifestation arises.

Renunciation that brings liberation (Yoga Sutras 3.50-3.52)

These *sutras* say that to attain liberation, a *yogi* must let go of everything – even of the desire to know everything or to be a more powerful *yogi*. In the preceding *sutras*, many types of experience were described. As these are encountered, the *yogi* goes ever deeper into the levels of his or her own being. Each is encountered, explored, experienced, and set aside, so as to go still deeper.

3.50 : To one well established in the knowledge of the distinction between the purest aspect of mind and consciousness itself, there comes supremacy over all forms or states of existence, as well as over all forms of knowing.

3.51 : With non-attachment or desirelessness even for that supremacy over forms and states of existence and the omniscience (3.50), the seeds at the root of those bondages are destroyed, and absolute liberation is attained.

3.52 : When invited by the celestial beings, no cause should be allowed to arise in the mind that would allow either acceptance of the offer, or the smile of pride from receiving the invitation, because to allow such thoughts to arise again might create the possibility of repeating undesirable thoughts and actions.

Higher discrimination through Samyama (Yoga Sutras 3.53-3.56)

This section discusses discrimination, as in the ability to distinguish between that which changes and that which is changeless. This allows us to distinguish between the individual self and the universal self. Moments and succession: Experience usually comes like a movie. It only *appears* to be an unfolding process, whereas it is actually independent events. It is like the movie film being many independent frames, all of which coexist on the same reel. However, when you look at those frames sequentially, there is the appearance of a uniform and unfolding event or process. Beyond moments and succession: When *samyama* is done on the moments and the process of succession, the higher knowledge of what is *really* going on is revealed. One comes to see the nature of movie production of the mind and virtually the whole of the creation process. This opens the door to the realization of the Truth.

3.53 : By *samyama* over the moments and their succession, there comes the higher knowledge that is born from discrimination.

3.54 : From that discriminative knowledge (3.53) comes awareness of the difference or distinction between two similar objects, which are not normally distinguishable by category, characteristics, or position in space.

3.55 : That higher knowledge is intuitive and transcendent, and is born of discrimination; it includes all objects within its field, all conditions related to those objects, and is beyond any succession.

3.56 : With the attainment of equality between the tranquil individual mind and the purity of the universal mind (pure consciousness), there comes absolute liberation, and that is the end.

Pada 4 of the Yoga Sutras: Absolute Freedom (Kaivalya Pada)

Chapter 4 of the *Yoga Sutras* is entitled *Kaivalya Pada,* which means the chapter on final liberation. *Pada Four* covers different subjects, all of which lead to enlightenment. The causes of evolution (or change) are addressed, as well as the inner workings of subconscious impressions. Patanjali also contrasts the individual mind with the universal mind (or pure consciousness). Chapter 4 explains how the mind is constructed and veils the inner light of the Self. It describes how the *yogi* deals with the natural breaches in enlightenment, and how the primal building blocks of the mind resolve back into their cause, allowing final liberation.

Means of attaining experience (Yoga Sutras 4.1-4.8)

The first eight *sutras* address evolution, paying particular attention to the role that our actions play in the process of change.

4.1 : The subtler attainments come with birth or are attained through herbs, *mantra*, austerities or concentration.

4.2 : The transition or transformation into another form or type of birth takes place through the filling in of their innate nature.

4.3 : Incidental causes or actions do not lead to the emergence of attainments or realization, but rather, come by the removal of obstacles, much like the way a farmer removes a barrier (sluice gate), so as to naturally allow the irrigation of his field.

4.4 : The emergent mind fields springs forth from the individuality of I-ness (*asmita*).

4.5 : While the activities of the emergent mind fields may be diverse, the one mind is the director of the many.

4.6 : Of these mind fields, the one that is born from meditation is free from any latent impressions that could produce *karma*.

4.7 : The actions of *yogis* are neither white nor black, while they are threefold for others.

4.8 : Those threefold actions result in latent impressions that will later arise to fruition only corresponding to those impressions.

Being careful with your thoughts allows you to take back control of your life. It means understanding how your thoughts and actions now will affect your future.

Subconscious impressions (Yoga Sutras 4.9-4.12)

These *sutras* examine the idea that what we picture in our minds and what we would consider a real experience are not that much different. *Yogis* understand that the mental images you play over and over will become your experience. These *sutras* also suggest that there is a continuous thread of individuality that links lifetimes or personalities.

4.9 : Since memory and the deep habit patterns (*samskaras*) are the same in appearance, there is an unbroken continuity in the playing out of those traits, even though there might be a gap in location, time, or state of life.

4.10 : There is no beginning to the process of these deep habit patterns (*samskaras*), due to the eternal nature of the will to live.

4.11 : Since the impressions (4.10) are held together by cause, motive, substratum, and object, they disappear when those deep impressions disappear.

4.12 : Past and future exist in the present reality, appearing to be different because of having different characteristics or forms.

Objects and the 3 gunas (Yoga Sutras 4.13-4.14)

These *sutras* look at how the three *gunas* (*sattva, rajas, tamas*) are present within every object.

Sattvas: The aspect of the subtlest primordial matter, which has the nature of existence, light, illumination, sentience, harmony, or clearing.

Rajas: The aspect of matter, which has the nature of activity, motion, energy, movement, or changing.

Tamas: The aspect of matter, which has the nature of stability, stasis, darkness, dullness, heaviness, insentience, obstructing, and veiling.

Equilibrium between the gunas: When there is perfect equilibrium between the three *gunas*, there is no manifestation of the universe. It is only when there are fluctuations or modifications among them that there begins to be manifestation. *Gunas* are at all levels, including the subtlest: The principles of the three *gunas* operate at all levels. For example, one might eat: (1) *sattvic* (light) food, which will lead to a clear state of mind, (2) *rajasic* (spicy) food, which will lead to a restless state of mind, or (3) *tamasic* (heavy) food, which will lead to a lethargic state of mind. However, this *sutra* (4.13) relates mostly to the *subtlest* operation of the three *gunas*, which is to say that the subtlest, subconscious impressions are all entirely constituted of *only* these three *gunas*.

4.13 : Whether these ever-present characteristics or forms are manifest or subtle, they are composed of the primary elements called the three *gunas*.

4.14 : The characteristics of an object appear as a single unit, as they manifested uniformly from the underlying elements.

Mind perceiving objects (Yoga Sutras 4.15-4.17)

These *sutras* look at how different minds (different people) perceive the same object in different ways. Some people feel that we can never totally see the truth because our minds are ultimately defective. *Yogis* say that we can see the truth if we work by way of our self awareness. By keeping a little independent corner of our mind that watches and observes the rest of the mind, even though the mind itself never sees anything correctly, we can become aware of this and get closer to the truth.

4.15 : Although the same objects may be perceived by different minds, they are perceived in different ways, because those minds manifested differently.

4.16 : However, the object itself does not depend on any one mind, for if it did, what would happen to the object if it were not being experienced by that mind?

4.17 : Objects are either known or not known according to the way in which the colouring of that object falls on the colouring of the mind observing it.

Illumination of the mind (Yoga Sutras 4.18-4.21)

The activities of the mind are always known by the pure consciousness (*purusha*), because that pure consciousness is superior to, support of, and master over the mind.

4.18 : The activities of the mind are always known by the pure consciousness, because that pure consciousness is superior to, support of, and master over the mind.

4.19 : That mind is not self-illuminating, as it is the object of knowledge and perception by the pure consciousness.

4.20 : Nor can both the mind and the illuminating process be cognized simultaneously.

4.21 : If one mind were illumined by another, as its master, then there would be an endless and absurd progression of cognitions, as well as confusion.

Buddhi and liberation (Yoga Sutras 4.22-4.26)

These *sutras* explain the foundation of individual consciousness. The countless minds of the universe are born of the reflection of the one universal mind. Thus, we have the potential to understand all minds (or all other objects).

4.22 : When the unchanging consciousness appears to take on the shape of that finest aspect of mind-field (4.18), the experience of one's own cognition process is possible.

4.23 : Therefore, the mind field, which is coloured by both seer and seen, has the potential to perceive any and all objects.

4.24 : That mind field, though filled with countless impressions, exists for the benefit of another witnessing consciousness, as the mind field is operating only in combination with those impressions.

4.25 : For one who has experienced this distinction between seer and this subtlest mind, the false identities and even the curiosity about the nature of one's own self come to an end.

4.26 : Then the mind is inclined towards the highest discrimination, and gravitates towards absolute liberation between seer and seen.

Breaches in enlightenment (Yoga Sutras 4.27-4.28)

These *sutras* mention the final obstacles to self-realization.

4.27 : When there are breaks or breaches in that high discrimination, other impressions arise from the deep unconscious mind.

4.28 : The removal of those interfering thought patterns is by the same means by which the original colourings were removed.

This is when the physical practices of *yoga* are very important, working from the outside in, as well as the inside out. So first the negative emotions go for good, and then gradually all the seeds that created those negative emotions go as well.

Perpetual enlightenment (Yoga Sutras 4.29-4.31)

These *sutras* look at how the *yogi* moves from discrimination between the mind and the universal mind, now is purified of ignorance and moves toward union with the absolute (self-realization). We learn to keep the mind focused on the distinction of what seems real and what is real. We release anything related to old negative thoughts and actions.

4.29 : When there is no longer any interest even in omniscience, that discrimination allows the *samadhi*, which brings an abundance of virtues like a rain cloud brings rain.

4.30 : After that *dharma-meghah samadhi*, the colourings of the *kleshas* and the *karmas* are removed.

4.31 : Then, by the removal of those veils of imperfection, there comes the experience of the infinite, and the realization that there is almost nothing to be known. As a culture, we tend to think that we know more than people in the past because we know more things. But there is also the idea of knowing one thing really well; knowing how things really work. Once we understand our connection to all things, all knowledge is right there.

Liberation (Yoga Sutras 4.32-4.34)

This section examines how the gunas provides us with lessons we need to go beyond ignorance. The yogi then "sees" the true nature of existence and is completely free of all limitation and pain.

4.32 : Also resulting from that *dharma-meghah samadhi* (4.29), the three primary elements or *gunas* (4.13-4.14) will have fulfilled their purpose, cease to transform into further transformations, and recede back into their essence.

4.33 : The sequencing process of moments and impressions corresponds to the moments of time, and is apprehended at the end point of the sequence.

4.34 : When those primary elements involve, or resolve themselves back into that out of which they emerged, there comes liberation, wherein the power of pure consciousness becomes established in its true nature.

CHITTA AND CHITTA-VRTTI

According to Patanjali tradition yoga is defined as *"yogah chittvrtti nirodhah"* which means *yogah*-union or integration from the outer most layer to the innermost self, that is, from the skin to the muscles, bones, nerves, mind, intellect, will, consciousness and self.

Chitta: Consciousness, which is made up of three factors: mind (*manas*), intellect (*buddhi*) and ego (*ahamkara*). *Chitta* is the vehicle of observation, attention, aims and reason. It has three functions, cognition, volition, and motion.

Vrtti: State of mind, fluctuations in mind, course of conduct, behaviour, a state of being, mode of action movement, function and operation.

Nirodhah : Obstruction, stoppage, opposition, annihilation restraint, control and cessation.

Yoga is the cessation of movements in the consciousness. *Yoga* is defined as restraint of fluctuations in the consciousness. It is the art of studying the behaviour of consciousness, which has three functions. Cognition, conation or volition, and motion.

Yoga shows way of understanding the functionings of the mind, and helps to quieten their movements, leading one towards the undisturbed state of silence which dwells in the very seat of consciousness. *Yoga* is thus the art and science of mental discipline through which the mind becomes cultured and matured.

Chitta has two causes, *vasana* and *prana* when one of the two is destroyed or inactivated the other also will become immobile.

This vital *sutra* contains the definition of *yoga;* the control or restraint of the movement of conciousness, leading to their complete cessation. *Chitta* is the vehicle which takes the mind *(manas)* towards the soul *(atma). Yoga* is the cessation of all vibration in the seat of consciousness. It is extremely difficult to convey the meaning of the word *chitta* because it is the subtlest form of cosmic intelligence *(mahat). Mahat* is the great principle, the source of the material world of nature *(Prakriti),* as opposed to the soul, which is an offshoot of nature. According to *Samkhya* philosophy, creation is effected by the mingling of *prakriti* with *purusha,* the cosmic soul. This view of cosmology is also accepted by the *yoga* philosophy. The principles of *purusha* and *prakriti* are the source of all action, volition and silence.

Words such as *chitta, buddhi* and *mahat* are so often used interchangeable that the student can easily become confused. One way to structure one's understanding is to remember that every phenomenon which has reached its full evolution or individuation has a subtle or cosmic counterpart. Thus, we translate *buddhi* as the individual discriminating intelligence, and consider *mahat* to be its cosmic counterpart. Similarly, the individuated consciousness, *chitta,* is matched by its subtle from *chit.* For the purpose of self-realization, the highest awareness of consciousness and the most refined faculty of intelligence have to work so much in partnership that it is not always useful to split hairs by separating them.

The thinking principle, or conscience *(antahkarana)* links the motivating principle of nature *(mahat)* to individual consciousness which can be thought of as a fluid enveloping ego *(ahamkara),* intelligence *(buddhi)* and mind *(manas).* This 'fluid' tends to become cloudy and opaque due to its contact with the external world via its three components. He *sadhaka's* aim is to bring the consciousness to a state of purity and transluence. It is important to note that consciousness not only links evolved or manifest nature to non-evolved or subtle nature, it is also closest to the soul itself, which does not belong to nature, being merely immanent in it.

Buddhi possesses the decisive knowledge which is determined by perfect action and experience. *Manas* gathers and collects information through the five senses of perception, *jnanendriyas,* and the five organs of action, *karmendriyas.* Cosmic intelligence, ego, individual intelligence mind, the five senses of perception and the five organs of action are the products of the five elements of nature—earth, water, fire, air and ether *(prithvi, ap, tejas, vayu and akasha)* with their infra-atomic qualities of smell, taste, form or sight, touch and sound *(gandha, rasa, rupa, sparsa and sabda).*

In order to help man to understand himself, the sages analysed humans as being composed of five sheaths, or *kosas*

Sheath	***Corresponding Eement***
Anatomical *(annamaya)*	Earth
Physiological *(pranamaya)*	Water
Mental *(manomaya)*	Fire
Intellectual *(vijnanamaya)*	Air
Blissful *(anandamaya)*	Ether

The first three sheaths are within the field of the elements of nature. The intellectual sheath is said to be the layer of the individual soul *(Jivatman),* and the blissful sheath the layer of the universal soul *(paramatman).*

In effect, all five sheaths have to be penetrated to reach emancipation. The innermost content of the sheaths, beyond even the blissful body, is *purusa,* in indivisible, non-manifest one, the 'void which is full'. This is experienced in *nirbija samadhi,* whereas *sabija samadhi* is experienced at the level of the blissful body.

If *Ahamkara* (ego) is considered to be one and of a thread, then *anataratma* (universal self) is the other end. *Antah karana* (conscience) is the unifier of the two. The practice of *yoga* integrates a person through the journey of intelligence and consciousness from the external to the internal level. It unifies him from the intelligence of the skin to the intelligence of the self, so that his self merges with the cosmic self. This is the merging of one half of one's being *(prakriti)* with the other *(purusha)*. Through *yoga*, the practitioner learns to observe and to think, and to intensify his effort until eternal joy is attained. This is possible only when all vibrations of the individual *chitta* are arrested before they emerge. Mind and *prana* are mixed like milk and water. Both of them are equal in their activities where there is *pranic* movement or activity there is mind (consciousness). Where there is consciousness there is *prana.*

Yoga, the restraint of fluctuating thought, leads to a *Sattvic* state. But in order to restrain the fluctuations, force of will is necessary: hence a degree of *rajas* is involved. Restraint of the movements of thought brings about stillness, which leads to deep silence, with awareness. This is the *sattvic* nature of the *chitta.*

Stillness is concentration *(dharana)* and silence is meditation *(dhyana)*. Concentration needs a focus or a form, and this focus is *ahamkara,* one's own small, individual self. When concentration flows into meditation that self loses its identity and becomes one with the great self. Like two sides of coin, *ahamkara* and *atma* are the two opposite poles in man.

The *sadhaka* is influenced by the self on the one hand and by objects perceived on the other. When he is engrossed in the object, his mind fluctuates. This is *vrtti.* His aim should be to distinguish the self from the objects seen, so that it does not become engrossed by them. Through *yoga,* he should try to free his consciousness from the temptations of such objects, and bring it closer to the seer.

Restraining the fluctuations of the mind is a process, which leads to an end *samadhi.* Initially, *yoga* acts as the means of restraint. When the *sadhaka* has attainted a total state of restraint, *yogic* discipline is accomplished and the end is reached: the consciousness remains pure. Thus, *yoga* is both the means and the end.

NATURE OF PRAMANA IN YOGA

All philosophers obey *pratyaksa pramana.* Among the *pramanas, pratyaksa pramana* is the first *pramana.*

Through this *praman* one can see the thing directly and he derives the direct knowledge. So this *pramana* is faithful and dependable.

Patanjali like other philosophers also accept three *pramanas* in *yoga darsana: pratyaksa, anuman* and *agama. Patanjali's sutras* are : *Pratyaksa numanagamah pramanani.* In Sanskrit literature the word *yoga* has been described in many meanings. In *Amarkosa* the word *yoga* has been described in *Samhana, Upaya, Dhyana, Sangti, Yukti* etc. In Gita, the word *yoga* has been defined as *karmasu kausalam.*

In Mahabharata the word *yoga* has been used to means *Upaya.* In the tradition we have description regarding *Patanjali* as:

yogen chittasaya padena vaacham
malam sarirasya ca vaidyakena /
yoapakarottam pravaram muninam
Patanjalim pranjaliranato'smi //

According to this sloka, it is said that Patanjali is the author of *charaka samhita, mahabhasya* and *yoga sutra.* The author of *Yoga darsana* is Patanjali Maharshi. After his name, this has been named as *Patanjali yogadarsana.* There are many different views on his birthplace and time. But his birthplace is said to be the Gonarda in Kashmir state and time to be the 2nd century. *Patanjali* has divided *yoga darsana* into four padas.

(*i*) *Samadhi pada*
(*ii*) *Sadhana pada*
(*iii*) *Vibhuti pada* and
(*iv*) *Kaivalya pada.*

The number of *sutras* in these four *padas* are, 295 in *samadhi pada,* 55 in *sadhana pada,* 55 in *vibhuti pada* and 34 in *kaivalya pada.* In *yoga paribhasa Patanjali* has written *yogah chitta vrtti nirodhah.*

Pratyaksa Pramana

In the views of *yoga,* the define knowledge based on the relationship with *padartha* is called *pratyaksa pramana,* or the evolution of *sannikarsa i.e.,* knowledge of sense organs and *padartha* is called *pratyaksa pramana.* Each sense organ (nose, tongue, eyes, skin, ears) and *grahya rupa* and their material *(gandha, rasa, rupa, sparsa, iabda)* accordingly develop from a single reason. For this, there is an attractive force between these two *e.g.,* the eyes come in contact with a pot, the rays from the eyes fall on the pot, as the mind gets drowned by the *padartha* (pot).

This reaches the region of *padartha* by the eyes and assumes the shape of a pot. The result of the mind assuming the shape of a pot is called *pratyaksa pramana* meaning *"aham ghatam janami"* or I know a pot which is called *pratyaksa pramana.*

As the *pramana* is the result of *vrtti,* this is also called *phala prama.* This is *Pauruseya* knowledge because it is known by a human being. The views of *Samkhya* and *yoga* for *pratyaksa pramana* is almost same, *saksi cheta kevalo nirgunasca.* That is to say a *chetana purusha i.e.,* a conscious person being *nirguna* is only remaining as a *saksi.* Again too Vijnana viksu has written about *pratyaksa pramana e.g., kalpitam darsan arttrtvam vastutastu budhe saksekapurusa.*

Regarding *pratyaksa pramans,* the concept like *pramana, prameya, prama, pramata* and *saksi* these five objects have been accepted. *Purusastu samasakseva na pramata. Vijnana viksu* has also told that *purusha* is the *saksi* of *prama,* not *pramata.* All philosphers agree to *pratyaksa pramana.*

Pratyaksa pramana is the basis of all the *pramanas.* So, this *pramana* is given much importance. Then other *pramanas* are considered. All the philosophers believe in *pratyaksa.* In *pratyaksa* the eyes see the object and one gains knoweldge *i.e. "aham ghatam janami".*

In other word, I know the *ghata.* For this, out side knowledge is required. Again, there is no need for inner knowledge. Because, eye sees the objects directly. Hence, for *pratyaksa,* there is a need for the contact of sensory organ with chitta. For that, there is no need for *smriti.* Therefore, it has been further described in yoga *varttika* as:

ananta rasmaya-stasya dipadyah sthito hrdi/
bahusakha hyanantasca buddhayo vyasyavinam//

For the production of this outside knowledge is required.

Anumana Pramana

That which has been engendered by *linga* is called *anumana pramana* or the real knowledge, which is gained in relation to *linga-linga, sadhana-sadhya, karya-karana* is called *anumana pramana.*

It is necessary to know about the *anumana* that the relationship between *dhrama videsha,* and *linga-lingi* as *sadhana-sadhya* what is called *vyapti.* So when a person gains knowledge from this relationship is called *vyapti-jnana.*

After seeing the *linga* dirctly the *anumana* of indirect *lingi* generally is done through the knowledge of a person. From the knowledge of the relationship between smoke and fire, specifically seeing smoke this can be deduced that where smoke is seen, it can never exist without viz : *yatra yatra dhuma tatra tatra vahnih.*

From his knowledge of *vyapti,* the knowledge arises about *apratyaksa* fire from the *pratyaksa* smoke through a process which is called *anumana.* The *anumana pramana* of *Samkya* is the same as the *anumana pramana* of *Yoga.* In the *Samkya* also *anumana* has been divided into three categories. In *yoga* also *anumana* has been divided into three categories viz: *(i) purvavat (ii) sesavat* and *(iii) samanyatodrgta.*

(i) ***purvavat:*** where the effect is imagined from the cause it is *purvavat i.e.,* imagining rain by seeing the clouds.

(ii) ***sesavat :*** where the cause is imagined from the effect it is *sesavat i.e.,* imagining the first rains by seeing the muddy water of the river.

(iii) ***Samanayatodrsta:*** This is seen in a general manner but not in a special manner *e.g.*, imagining the potter by looking at the pot.

The origin of *anumana* is *pratyaksa* because *anumana* is generated from the prior *pratyaksa.* Sometimes *pratyaksa* is wrongly assumed because of many *dosas* which are as follows:

(a) ***Visaya dosa :*** Sometimes the object is at a great distance. Real knowledge is not gained from that. If a glass comes between the observer and the observed object, the object can not be known in its true form.

(b) ***Indriya dosa :*** For example, everything looks yellow to a joundice patient.

(c) ***Mano dasa :*** True knowledge can not be gained because of fickleness of mind.

These above dosas create problem for the perceptual knowledge, hence, it is necessary to remove them for true knowledge. It is the second one in the list of *pramana.* According to *yoga, anumiti* is gained through *anumana pramana.* In other words, *anuman* is defined as *laksayati anumeyasyeti. Anumana* is based on *pratyaksa* which is establised through *vyapti.* In this, eyes have not seen the objects directly. For this, it is said in *yogavattika* that: *sadhya visistah faksenumeyah.* One has the experience of the object regularly before he proceeds for *anumana.* So, he has acquired the prior knowledge of the relationship between a *sadhya* and *sadhana.* He also knows that prior relationship establishes truth of that object. Therefore, it is said in *yoga varttika* that

sambandha iti pathe api sambandhata iti sambandha.

When one sees same type of object from a distance, at that time he recalls the previous knowledge. In other words, he thinks about the relationship of the earlier one with that object. After establishing the relationship, he as certains that this object is also of that type which already existed earlier through a relationship. And after that confirmation he inferes accordingly and the knowledge of *anumiti* arises. All theist philosophers accept *anumana pramana.*

Agama Pramana

In *alaukika* matters, *veda* can be the proof. For this reason, this *pramana* is known as *agama pramana.* That which is *apta vakya* or is originated by *sabda pramana* is known as *sabda pramana* or *agama pramana.* All the sentenes of *Munis, Risis* and *Acharyas* based on *veda* is inlcuded in this type of *pramana.* In *laukika* matters also *apta purusha* can only become a *pramana.* Those who are devoid of any mistakes in knowing and saying, in other words those whose knowledge is not afflicted by *bhranti dosa* and are free from *vipralipsa.* The knowledge gained by a man through this *pramana* is called *agama pramana* or *phala-prama.* This *phala-prama* is also of three kinds like *chitta-vrtti-rupa pramana e.g pratyaksa prama, anumiti prama* and *sabda prama.* Among the theist philosophers the *Vaisesikas* only do not accept *sabda pramana,* but other philosopher accept *sabda pramana.*

According to the view of *yoga,* the words which come from the long tradition are called *agama.* The yoga school accept God. As per their views: *mulavag-abhiprayena srute veti noktah tada pyupa laksaniyam.* This means the God who tells *aptavakya,* no body has seen him. He is almighty and omnipresent and never tell lie. As it is described in the text: *brahma pramada vipralipsa karana-ptavadi dosa rahite netyarthah.* Which means that he tells those statements, those are not false, and imaginary.

The word he says are truth full which leads to *agama pramana.* No body can disobey that. The word which an ordinary person tells may be false sometimes. As per yoga these words are faulty. They believe in the authority of the *vedas* because this is enunciated by God. For this ground it is said in *yoga varttika,* that

yah kaschid kasyachiddharmo manuna-parikirtitah/

sa sarvo abhihito vede sarva jnana mayo hi sah//

They believe in God only. Hence, *agama* is *pramana* based on words which lead one to get a verbal knowledge.

PRAMANA AND KNOWLEDGE

The concept of *samadhi* is dominant in *yoga* but also in other systems too. *Samkhya* and *yoga* basically aim at suggesting the way for liberation through analysing the reality. Such an analysis presupposes some epistemological stand, through it is not duly stressed and sufficiently explained. The above exposition brings out the salient features of the epistemology of *Samkhya-yoga.* Knowledge means modification of *buddhi* in the form of the object known and is thus located in *buddhi,* and is insentient in nature. The verbal expression of such a theory:

However, involves many technicalities and is severely criticised by other systematists. The pivot around which all explanations revolve is the cause of confusion of identity of *buddhi* and *purusha.* According to *Patanjali* and *Isvarakrsna* it is the contact of *purusha* with *buddhi. Vyasa* understands the contact in the form of more proximity due to which *purusha* starts developing feeling of ownership towards *buddhi.* Vachaspati Mishra understands the contact as the capability of *purusha* and *buddhi* to be enjoyer and the object if enjoyment respectively.

When the movement of *prana* is completed annihilated, then mind is reabsorbed and then, samadhi is considered attained. He develops his theory of single reflection to explain the point further. *Vijnabhiksu* is not satisfied with Vachaspati Mishra's explanation and develops his theory of double reflection as an advance over it. The explanation given by *Samkhya-yoga* has provoked reaction of the other systems. However, it apparent consciousness in *buddhi* is understood to be caused by the proximity of *purusha* to it, the theory can be explained more logically.

The *Samkhya-yoga* concept of nature of valid knowledge and the means there of is peculiar and does not seem to the influenced by other systems. The validity in knowledge is characterised by certainty, correspondence to object and novelty. Knowledge is the function of *buddhi* or *chitta.* When the two-fold nature of the individual soul and cosmic soul becomes one, all desires ideations are destroyed and that is considered *samadhi.* It is the state of *buddhi* in which *sattva* dominates. Knowledge is, however, falsely attributed to *purusha* when the *purusha* is stated to be *jna* (knower). *Purusha* is the knower, bound and liberated only from empirical point of view; from transcendent point of view it is of the nature of pure consciousness. Since *buddhi* is one, *pramana* is actually one, but it is said to be three-fold through limiting adjuncts in form of other factors, viz., sense object contact, etc. It further involves the distinction between means of knowledge and the knowledge. The former is of the nature of ascertainment of object and is located in *buddhi* while the latter is the favour rendered to purusha. Due to which *purusha* falsely appears to have knowledge.

Both of these can be called *prama* also in so far as they refer to the knowledge but the former may be called means of knowledge because of its being the means of the latter. This is made clear by *Vijnana-bhiksu* through interpreting *prama* in both the ways, though he favours the idea of considering *prama* as located in *purusha.* In this way, the *Samkhya-yoga* could retain the immutable nature of *purusha* and the non-eternal nature of knowledge. The other systems have criticized *Samkya-yoga* concept mainly due to assigning knowledge to the non-sentient object. However, they ignore the fact that due to the contact with *purusha buddhi* becomes sentient for all practical purposes.

Samkhya-yoga accepts three independent means of knowledge perception, inference and verbal testimony. The additional means admitted by other systems are included in these only. They do not reject the process involved in them but are not prepared to allot the status of a means of knowledge independent of the three admitted by *samkhya-yoga.* As regard *upmana,* the views of the *Naiyayikas* and the *Mimamsakas* are different with reference to the means and the resultant knowledge. As regards the *Nyaya* view the *Yuktidipika* followed by *Gaudapada* includes it under verbal testimony or inference, and Mathara, the *Samkhyachandrika* and *Vijnanabhiksu* under inference. The Mimamsa view is included under perception. Presumption which is in turn included under inference. Mathara, the Jayamangala and Vachaspati Mishra include it under inference without the middle step of presumption; *Gaudapada* and the *Samkhya chandrika* include it under verbal testimony. Negation is interpreted by the *Yuktidipika* in terms of presumption and is included under inference. Vachaspati Mishra, the *Jayamangala* and *Vijnanabhiksu* consider it a case of perception. The *Samkhyachandrika* holds that it assists perception and is not an independent means of knowledge *Gaudapada* includes it under verbal testimony. Gesture is included under inference. Rumour or tradition is included under verbal testimony by the *Yuktidipika, Gaudapada,* the *Jayamangala, Samkhyachandrika* and *Vijnanabhiksu,* and under inference by Mathara. As regards imagination the *Yuktidipika* states that the object cognised through it can be cognised through any of perception, inference and verbal testimony, while Mathara includes it under interference, and *Gaudapada* under verbal testimony. As regards the scope of means of knowledge, *Samkhya-yoga* believes indefinite adjustment of means of knowledge with their objects.

The *Samkhya karika* mentions the scope of the means of knowledge, which is interpreted in two ways. According to one, the objects apprehensible through the senses are cognised through perception, the non-perceptible objects through inference and those which are not cognised even through inference are cognised veral testimony. According to the other inter rotation, the ordinary objects are known through *samanyatodrsta* type of inference, and those having no probans and are absolutely imperceptible are cognised through verbal testimony.

Perception is the most authentic means of knowledge. The oldest definition in *Samkhya-yoga* was forwarded by *Vindhyavasin* as function of cognitive organs ear and the rest free from imagination, which was later on revised by some follower of *Varsaganya* by dropping the condition 'free from imagination. Isvarakrisna's definition as 'ascertainment of individual object, is also quite old and peculiar as it has no reference to sense-object contact.

The commentator of the *Samkhyakarika,* however, interpret it in their own way introducing various technicalities in it. A more comprehensive definition of perception is offered by *Vyasa* as function of *chitta* with reference to ascertaining the specific nature of an object possesing both the generic and specific nature after being coloured with the form of external object through the medium of senses. The definition given by the *Samkhyasutra* as 'knowledge which portrays the form of the object coming in contact with it, is of late character. *Chitta* has two causes, *vasana* and *prana.* When one of the two is destroyed or inactivated the other also will become immobile.

Vijnanabhiksu explains it in the light of the definition of *Advaita vedanta.* Perception is of two kinds—normal *(laukika)* and abonormal *(alaukika).* The former is again of two kinds: determinate and indeterminate in accordance with the stages in perception. Vyasa holds that chitta goes to the external object and assumes the form of that Vachaspati Mishra describes the process of sense object contact, etc, on the analogy of Nyaya, while Vijnanabhiksu describes it in terms of *Advaita Vedanta. Vijnanabhiksu* further maintains that the senses can yield the determinate perception as well. Perception is again of two kinds: internal and external in accordance with the object cognised. The *Samkhya* view that the organ of hearing also travels to the sounding object has provoked much criticism at the hands of the *Naiyayikas* and *Mimamsakas. Samkhya-yoga* provides details about psychic apparatus in context of perception.

The karanas are thirteen: three internal, viz., *manas, ahamkara* and *buddhi,* and ten external located in marks of body and classified into two: the organs of knowledge and the organs of action. *Buddhi* is defined as 'definite cognition' or as 'resolution to act'. It is a determining faculty and the definition is coined so to suggest non-difference between action and substratum. Similarly, *ahamkara,* is defined as egoism in the form of 'I' and 'Mine'. *Manas* is also defined in term of its characteristic function of *samkalpa* which may mean desire or reflection over specific properties of an object and, in this way, to turn in determinate perception offered by senses into determinate.

It is considered to be an *Indriya* also and partakes the nature of both the organ of action and organ of sense. It is of medium size and partite in nature. Where mind is stilled, then the *prana* is suspended there, and where *prana* is suspended there the mind is still. *Manas* and term external organs come out of *ahamkara.* Each of the senses has its own field of activity and, thus, the plurality of senses does not bring about chaos. Their activities are prompted by mutual intention. The internal organs are considered more important than the external. Among the internal organs also chief importance is attached to *buddhi.*

The functions performed by organs are of three kinds: seizing, retaining and illuminating. *Yoga* lays more stress on physical discipline and postulates the concept of chitta which is another name of *buddhi* or the totality of internal organs. The *Samkhya-yoga* concept of nature and composition definition, and number of the senses is peculiar and has invited criticism from all directors: *brahmanical* and *non-brahmanical*, which is valuable to clarify the *Samkhya-yoga* fully. The *Samkhya-yoga* concept of perceptual error was not crystalized in the early texts of the *Samkhya-yoga.* The *Samkhyakarika* implies the theory resembling *akhyati* while dealing with the attitude towards erroneous perception. The *Samkhya-yoga* view is found mentioned in the *Samkhya-sutra* as *sadasatkhyati* according to which the earliar knowledge is partly sublated by the right knowledge arising later.

Vijnanabhiksu further introduces the idea of commission as against the factor of omission of the *samkhyakarika* thus bringing the view nearer to the *anyathakhyati* or *viparitakhyati* held by the *Naiyayikas, Vaisesikas* and the Bhatta school of *purvamimamsa.* Yoga system, however, explicitly believes in *anyathakhyati* for explaining the erroneous perception. This conclusion is drawn by Vijnana bhiksu from the description of *Avidya* in *yoga sutras* that *Avidya,* is not lack of knowledge. But a positive misconception loading a perverted knowledge. *Prabhachandra* a Jaina logician, however, believes that the *Samkhyas* hold *Prasiddhartha-khyati* as the theory of perceptual error according to which the real object itself is apprehended in case of erroneous knowledge also.

The *Samkhya-yoga* works dealing with the details of inference might have been lost to us. The extent works of *Samkhya-yoga* contain only scanty informations about inference. Inference must be accepted as an independent source of knowing ignorance, doubt or wrong knowledge of the one to whom the philosophical doctrines are to explained. The earliest *Samkhya-yoga* view on the nature of inference is quoted by *Uddyotakara* as 'establishment of some residual fact on the basis of relation perceived earlier'. The *Samkhya karika* offers a different definition as 'knowledge derived from (the knowledge of) sign and signate'. Vachaspati Mishra explains the definition in away yielding the idea of the condition of application of probans or subject; while the *Samkhyasandrika* traces in it the idea of *paramarsa.* It is also understood to give scope to the thinking that sometimes the *linga,* through it is not warranted by the terminology in inference.

The *Samkhya sutra* defines inference as the knowledge of invariable association. *Vyasa* also defines inference in terms of invariable concomitance as the cause in it. Thus, the early *Samkhya-yoga* text considers invariable concomitance as leading to inference, while the commentators introduce the idea of probans and its existence on the subject. Vachaspati Mishra's discussion of *Vyapti* implies that vyapti means natural and unconditional relation. The *samkhya sutra* defines vyapti as the invariable concomitance of properties in the case of one or the two, and gives scope to the division of *vyapti* into *sama* and *visama. Vyapti* is not an independent category defferent from co-existence of properties. Here, the *Samkhya sutra* informs of the view of *Panchasikha.* The *vyapti* is ascertained through appropriate confutation. In addition to the division into *sama* and *visama vyapti* the *samkhya-yoga* admits the *anvaya* and *vyatireki* kind of *vyapti* also. The *Yuktidipika* considers the components in inferential syllogism. *Mathara* records two traditions of considering three and five of them.

As regards the kinds of inference, the *Samkhyakarika* refers to a tradition of considering the three: *purvavat, sesvat* and *samanyato drasta. Aniruddha* mentions another additional division into *kevalanvayi, kevala vyatireki* and *anvayavyatireki. Mathara* in the *Yuktidipika* imply the division into *svartha* and *parartha.* The idea of seven fold inference is the peculiarity of *Samkhya-yoga.* The division into *vita* and *avitas* rooted in the kinds of probans. Such a division seems to be devised by the *Samkhyas.* The extant *Samkhya yoga* texts do not discuss the fallacies and we are left to understand them in the light of Nyaya system.

The extent texts of *Samkhya-yoga* discuss only a few aspects of verbal testimony. Vachaspati Mishra refutes the contention of the *vaisesikas* and the *Bauddhas* who favour the inclusion of verbal testimony under inference. The form of syllogism devised for this purpose will not satisfy the condition of inference. Verbal testimony is the statements of a reliable person. Vachaspati Mishra restricts reliability to the *vedas* while the *Yuktidipika* includes the statements of worldly authority also in it. The *samkhyasutra* further states that the Vedas are not eternal yet are not created by some human agency. They come out of the self-born spontaneously. The validity of the *vedas* is intrinsic and natural. The relation between a word and its meaning is that of expressive and expressed. Such a relation is infered through observing someone acting according to the instructions of others. Such an activity is possible by understanding an individual as donetation of a word. The yoga, however, seems to consider that a word denotes generality of which particularity lies as subordinate through forming the nature of an object. It further provides scope to an understanding that *Samkhya-yoga* holds that the sense is expressed by correlated words in a sentence.

The *Samkhyas-yoga* believes in information by a reliable man and association of a word with another already known word as the additional means for knowing denotative relation. The further discussion of the mode of understanding the meaning of a word and a sentence implies the national acceptance of the theory of *sphota.*

ASTANGA YOGA

The practice of yoga consists of the eight subservients known as *astanga yoga.* Of these, the first five are external observances and the last three, mental disciplines. With the practice of these eight, the impurity of mind consisting of five-fold Error is eliminated, through which true knowledge becomes manifest.

The eight subservients of *yoga* are as follows:

1. Yamas

Yamas are five rules of behaviour which purify one's mind and behaviour. They also have social relevance.

(*i*) The first Yama is **Ahimsa** *i.e.,* not to hurt anyone including animals, plants and the so called non-living being like things you use. You must learn to respect everyone and everything around you. Jainism and Buddhism give great importance to Ahimsa. Mahatma Gandhi was a worshipper of Ahimsa. Angulimal – a seasoned murderer underwent magical transformation when he came in contact with Buddha. Christ, when he was crucified, said, 'God forgive them for they do not know what they are doing.' Only brave people can observe Ahimsa. Cowards can not practice it.

(*ii*) The second Yama is **Satya** *i.e.,* to speak truth. We should mean what we say. Our words should be gentre and free from deception. They should be uttered with the desire to do good to others. We see many types of deception in society. It takes the form of corruption and adulteration. Malpractices in Medicine can cause deaths of innocent people. Selling the secrets of our country to enemy countries – all these are the forms of Asatya behaviour. It is socially harmful and individually dangerous to one's integrity. So all Asatya – in speech and behaviour is to be avoided.

(*iii*) The third yama is **Asteya** *i.e.,* not to steal. Sometimes there is temptation to grab money which does not belong to you. There is tendancy in some people to take bribes. They take money for what they are already paid. Some people steal credit of others, happiness of others. All this is Steya *i.e.,* theft. To keep away from all these temptations is Asteya or non stealing. Sometimes one tends to steal the credit of the other person. A senior research officer takes the credit of the discovery made by his junior researcher. That also is Steya. To give everyone his or her due share of credit is also Asteya. When Vikram Sarabhai space center sent a satellite in space, the whole world congratulated the leader. But he gratefully recognized the indebtedness to the last man on the ladder. That is Asteya.

(*iv*) The fourth Yama is **Brahmacharya** *i.e.,* As there are temptations of money, there are temptations of indulging into joys related to opposite sex. Wasting time in seeing provocative movies, thinking of and dreaming about opposite sex by dresses, talk and behaviour consumes a lot of one's energy. In fact this energy can be fruitfully used for one's personality development *i.e.,* development of one's physical prowess and mental faculties. This is Brahmacharya. This way you channelize your energy for individually satisfying and socially useful purposes. Marriage and householder's life can be equally pure if its sanctity is taken care of. Husband and wife should be loyal to each other. Thoughtless sex can invite incurable diseases like AIDS and some youths in our country are falling prey to this dreadful disease. So, sage Patanjali very rightly emphasizes the importance of Brahmacharya – restraint in sex behaviour.

(*v*) The fifth yama is **Aparigraha** *i.e.,* keeping away from receiving money or things from people. All kinds of receiving limits your freedom, you become obliged to those who give you money or things, even emotional support. There is nothing wrong in healthy giving and receiving but when receiving makes you obliged to please the giver then it soils your soul. Aparigraha also means not to store more than what you need, because by doing that you may be depriving those who are in genuine need of the object. We often see that grocers hoard sugar, oil and other eatables and sell them at high cost when a festival approaches. He certainly has his fair share. But unfair hoarding is against Aparigraha. At the time of natural calamities helps pours in from all directions. But it hardly reaches the grassroot level. But there are generous souls who are ready to spend the last Paisa in their hands for the calamity-stricken. This is Aparigraha.

2. Niyamas

Niyamas are mainly for purifying the body and mind. They are practiced on individual basis. The first Niyama is **Shauch** *i.e.,* keeping your body and mind clean. Taking bath everyday, cleaning your teeth, drinking pure water helps you keep your body clean. Healthy food including grains, fresh green vegetables provide all the necessary ingredients like starch, fats, vitamins, salts and minerals give stamina and strength to your body. So Yoga advises to each healthy food. It also expects you to be regular in your toilet habits so that your body is free of toxins (harmfull substances).

Shauch also means purity of mind. Our sages have recognized six enemies that make our minds impure. *Kama* – excessive desire, *Krodha* – anger, *Lobha* – greed, *Moha* – temptation, *Meda* – ego, *Matsar* – jealousy. *Shauch* means keeping away from these six enemies and filling one's mind with noble thoughts.

The second Niyama is **Santosh** which means contentment. You should do your best in every undertaking and be happy with that. There are certain factors which are beyond your control so if you achieve the expected success, that is fine and if you do not achieve the expected success that also is fine. Joy is in doing the work itself and not in its outer fruit. Inner fruit is Santosh.

When Gita says कर्मण्येवाधिकारस्ते मा फलेषु कदाचन। it means the same. The inner fruit, Santosh is always ours. We should not expect the outer fruit. Suppose you are playing a match with a strong team. You do your level best but lose the game. Be sport and congratulate the captain of the other team. A real winner never loses. It is the winning spirit that matters. The heart which is full of hope is the contented heart. It knows to strive hard but its joy does not rest in the result of the game.

The third Niyama is **Tapa.** The literal meaning of Tapa is penance. When our exams approach we generally give up seeing movies and T.V. We do not waste time in chatting with friends. To achieve a goal we have to make hard effort, and give up certain pleasures. This is Tapa. While treading the path of Yoga we have to control our desires and concentrate our mind on the Yogic practices which is Tapa. Gita recognizes three types of Tapa.

1. **Kayik Tapa :** The Tapa we do with our body. Fasting is basically is Kayik Tapa. Regular exercise is also Kayik Tapa.
2. **Vachik Tapa :** Here we control our speech, we do not talk unnecessarily, and do not use language in a wrong way. We speak truth and the expression of truth is gentle.
3. **Manasik Tapa :** This Tapa is for purification of mind. Our mind gets clouded by negative, depressing thoughts. They have a weakening effect on mind. Selfishness makes mind narrow. Only noble thoughts can purify and strengthen the mind. Keeping away negative and narrow thoughts and learning to see the whole world as our family is Manasik Tapa.

The forth Niyama is **Swadhyayay** which literally means self-study. Here it means studying the principles related to Yoga. If we do not understand it all by ourself, we may seek guidance from experts. Swadhyaya not only means reading literature related to Yoga but also includes contemplating on the principles of Yoga and go into the depths of their meaning. Unless we engage with learning and Yogic experiencing, we will not be able to understand it.

The fifth and the last Niyama is **Ishwar Pranidhan** which means being in constant contact with God by chanting or by keeping in mind all the time that this whole creation – everything we see is created by God. Everything we do is the worship of the Lord. Lord is the witness of everything we see, do and experience. Chaitanya Mahaprabhu, when he would see ocean, would start dancing with joy saying that the blue waters of the ocean depicted his Lord Krishna.

3. Asana

Sage Patanjali defines Asana as *that posture in which we can sit comfortably for the Yogic practices, with our head, neck and back in a straight line.* Since Yoga is vitally related to our nervous system, our spinal chord should be in the right position. Squatting on a mat or sitting on your knees usually prescribed for yogic practice (Sukhasan, Sahajasan or Vajrasan).

The yogic tradition gives us 84 Asanas to keep our body and nerves supple. Yoga sees body as an instrument to achieve union with God. As we take care of our vehicles and instruments, so we must take care of body. We must give it proper exercise. Hence, the need to do Asanas. They build our resistance to diseases and keep us fit.

4. Pranayama

Pranayama is getting control on our Pranic energy through the control on our breathing. Inhaling air is called as *Purak* in Yoga. Exhaling air out is called as *Rechak.* Stopping for a few seconds before exhalation is called *internal Kumbhak* and stopping after exhalation is called *external Kumbhak*. Kumbhak should not be done for more than five seconds. Pranayama should be done under expert guidance. Otherwise, instead of being useful, it can become harmful. Alongwith air we also take in the vital energy in the atmosphere which is called Prana or the life-force, Breathing rhythmically improves your blood circulation and circulation of Pranic or vital energy in our body.

5. Pratyahara

Pratyahara literally means withdrawing. In Pratyahara we withdraw the senses from their external objects and turn them inward. We have five main senses which are sight, smell, hearing, touch and taste. Our eyes see, our nose smells, our ears hear, our skin touches and our tongue tastes. Visible things are sense objects for eyes. Fragrant things are objects for nose. Sounds are sense objects for ears, soft, hard and other materials are for skin and different tastes are for tongue. In Yoga we train our sense organs to remain quiet without outer stimulation. Yama, Niyama, Asana, Pranayam and Pratyahara are called external aids to Yoga. For the next steps you have go still deeper. So they are called as internal aids.

6. Dharana

Dharana is focussing of mind on a particular object. The object may be a part of our body like the midpoint of our eye-brows or it may be outside our body like a flame of a candle or moon or an image of the Lord or a saint. Our attention should be focussed on either internal or external object. This practice improves concentration which helps in studies and also helps in improving our memory.

7. Dhyana

When one learns to maintain Dharana or attention on a single object for relatively longer periods, that steady contemplation is called Dhyana or meditation. In Dhyana, we are aware that we are a witness to what is happening in our mind. But we are not emotionally or intellectually involved in what our mind is doing. This is also called Meditation.

8. Samadhi

In Samadhi, the mind is so deeply absorbed in the object of contemplation that it loses itself in the object and has no awareness of itself. Only when one comes out of Samadhi one realizes that it was a state of Samadhi where sense of time and place was totally absent.

A person who progresses along this eight-fold path of Yoga successfully and becomes one with the supreme reality becomes an evolved kind of human being. He or she is free from anger, lust and other vices. S/he becomes a lover of the entire humanity. S/he does his/her own duty with great excellence but is not at all proud of his/her achievements. S/he becomes an instrument in the hands of the Lord. This eight-fold path is not for a chosen few. Everybody can tread on it and sooner or later he or she can reach the ultimate goal of Yoga that is union with God or the supreme energy that mobilizes us and the cosmos.

Multiple Choice Questions

1. How many parts of Ashtanga yoga are described by Maharishi Patanjali?
   A. 6 B. 7
   C. 8 D. 10
2. Which are the first five parts of Ashtanga yoga?
   A. Yama, Niyama, Asana, Dharana, Dhyana
   B. Yama, Niyama, Pratyahara, Asana, Dharana
   C. Yama, Niyama, Asana, Pratyahara, Dharana
   D. Yama, Niyama, Asana, Pratyahara, Pranayama
3. According to ashtanga yoga how many parts there of yama?
   A. 4 B. 5
   C. 6 D. 7
4. Which of the following are parts of yama?
   A. Ahimsa, Satya, Asteya, Brahamcharya, Aprigraha
   B. Ahimsa, Satya, Santosha, Tapa, Aprigraha
   C. Ahimsa, Satya, Santosha, Brahamcharya, Aprigraha
   D. Saucha, Santosha, Tapa, Swadhyaya, Pranidhana

5. "Sthira Sukham Asanam" - this definition is given by:
A. M. Vedvyasa B. M. Patanjali
C. M. Gheranda D. Shri Krishna

6. The main types of samadhi are:
A. 2 B. 4
C. 6 D. 3

7. How many parts of yama are described in 'Patanjali Yoga Sutras'?
A. 5 B. 6
C. 8 D. 10

8. Who gave the definition – 'Yoga Chitta Vritti Nirodha'?
A. Maharishi Vyasa
B. Maharishi Patanjali
C. Shri Krishna
D. Maharishi Gheranda

9. Practise of asanas eliminates:
A. Rajas guna B. Tamas guna
C. Sattva guna D. Both A and B

10. What is the meaning of word 'Bhati' in 'Kapalbhati'?
A. Shine B. Hard
C. Light D. None of these

11. Which of the following is not a pranayama?
A. Murchha B. Kevali
C. Nabho D. Sahita

12. Which of the eleventh posture is performed during suryanamaskara?
A. Parvatasana B. Hasta-uttanasana
C. Bhujangasana D. Sastang namaskara

13. Practise of kapalbhati kriya awakens which chakra?
A. Sahashara B. Muladhara
C. Anahata D. None of these

14. Trataka kriya done by gazing at a candle flame is known as
A. Antarika trataka B. Bahriya trataka
C. Madhya trataka D. Bindu trataka

15. Which bandha should be practised before nauli kriya?
A. Jalandhara bandha B. Mulabandha
C. Uddiyana bandha D. All of the above

16. Jalavasti kriya mainly cleans which organ?
A. Small intestine B. Large intestine
C. Stomach D. All of the above

17. Which asana is useful in controlling the anger?
A. Singhasana B. Utkatasana
C. Matasyasana D. Kurmasana

18. Kapalbhati is useful in eliminating disease caused by which doshas?
A. Vata B. Pitta
C. Kapha D. Both A and B

19. 'Deshbandhaschitsaya Dharana' line is described in which chapter of 'Patanjali Yoga Sutra'?
A. Samadhi pada B. Kevalya pada
C. Sadhna pada D. Vibhuti pada

20. Which is the tenth posture during surya namaskara?
A. Uttanasana B. Bhujangasana
C. Hasta Uttanasana D. Hasta Padasana

21. Which of the following are considered as the means to block the chitta vritti?
A. Abhyasa and Pranayama
B. Asana and Mudra
C. Dharana and Dhyana
D. Abhyasa and Vairagya

22. Withdrawling of the senses from external objects and reversing their direction towards soul is known as ________.
A. Pratyahara B. Asteya
C. Dharana D. Ishwar Pranidhan

23. Which mudra destroys all the kleshas?
A. Mahamudra
B. Mahabheda mudra
C. Shaktichalini mudra
D. Vajroli mudra

24. How many types of kapalbhati kriya are there?
A. 2 B. 3
C. 4 D. 5

25. Which of the following statement is incorrect?
A. Trataka provides second sight
B. Trataka removes depression
C. Trataka removes migraine
D. Trataka improves memory power

26. During the practice of which asana the three bandhas occur naturally?
A. Mayurasana B. Siddhasana
C. Salabhasana D. Bhadrasana

27. Pranayama means:
A. To expand prana
B. To control prana
C. To unite prana with apana
D. Both A and B

28. Shambhavi mudra is performed during the practice of which samadhi?
A. Dhyana yoga samadhi
B. Bhakti yoga samadhi
C. Laya yoga samadhi
D. Nada yoga samadhi

29. Which of the following match is incorrect?
A. Raja yoga samadhi - Kumbhaka
B. Laya yoga samadhi - Yoni mudra
C. Nada yoga samadhi - Bhramari pranayama
D. Bhakti yoga samadhi - Khechari mudra

30. Pratyahara is:
A. To withdraw senses from external objects
B. To be introvert
C. To control over the senses
D. All of the above

31. Which type of karma is not described in 'Patanjali Yoga Sutra'?
A. Sukla karma
B. Akarma
C. Krishna karma
D. Sukla-krishna karma

32. The karmas by which one passes to hell are called as:
A. Akarma
B. Sukla karma
C. Krishna karma
D. Sukla-krishna karma

33. Which of the following is not a type of anumana-pramana?
A. Purvavata
B. Aagama
C. Shesvata
D. Samanya drishto

34. How many sutras are there in samadhi pada?
A. 45 B. 55
C. 51 D. 61

35. How many sutras are there in sadhna pada?
A. 45 B. 55
C. 61 D. 51

36. How many sutras are there in vibhuti pada?
A. 45 B. 55
C. 34 D. 51

37. How many sutras are there in kevalaya pada?
A. 45 B. 55
C. 34 D. 51

38. In which pada the ways to eliminate the kleshas are described?
A. Samadhi pada B. Sadhna pada
C. Vibhuti pada D. Kevalya pada

39. Which yogic sadhna is considered suitable for medium category sadhaka?
A. Kriya yoga B. Bhakti yoga
C. Raja yoga D. Nada yoga

40. Davesha occur due to:
A. Ignorance B. Asmita
C. Raga D. Abhinivesha

41. To concentrate on a object is known as:
A. Pratyahara B. Samadhi
C. Dharana D. Dhyana

42. How many types of sampragyata samadhi are:
A. 2 B. 3
C. 4 D. 5

43. In which type of samadhi the thoughts also disappear?
A. Anandanugata samadhi
B. Asmitanugata samadhi
C. Vitarkanuagata samadhi
D. Vicharanugata samadhi

44. In which type of samadhi the pleasure also disappears only the feeling of the selfness remains and all the other feelings disappear?
A. Anandanugata samadhi
B. Asmitanugata samadhi
C. Vitarkanugata samadhi
D. Vicharannugata samadhi

45. In which stage a person is influenced by lethargy, depression, and sleepness?
A. Viksiptavastha B. Nindravastha
C. Ksiptavastha D. Mudhavastha

46. Which is the fifth chitta vritti?
A. Vikalpa B. Nindra
C. Smriti D. Vipraya

47. Which vritti shows false perception?
A. Parmana vritti B. Nindra vritti
C. Vikalpa vritti D. Vipreya vritti

48. What is yoga-antraya?
A. Elements of success
B. Elements of failure
C. Low stage of yoga
D. Upper stage of yoga

49. How many total chitta vrittis are there according to 'Patanjali Yoga Sutra'?
A. 4 B. 5
C. 6 D. 7

50. Maharishi Patanjali is also known by which another name?
A. Ahipati B. Shesha avatara
C. Naganatha D. All of the above

51. Which of the following is not a kalesha?
A. Asmita B. Ignorance
C. Abhinivesha D. Vikalpa

52. Krishna karmas are:
A. Good karmas B. Bad karmas
C. Shradha karmas D. Virtuous karmas

53. The karmas performed by yogis are called as:
A. Sukla-krishna karmas
B. Krishna karmas
C. Shukla karmas
D. Ashukla-akrishna karmas

54. Sampragyata samadhi is also known as ________ samadhi.
A. Sabija B. Abija
C. Nirbija D. Vabija

55. Which of the following is a pramana vritti?
A. Pratyaksha
B. Anumana
C. Aagama
D. All of the above

56. In which type of samadhi the soul recognizes his real form?
A. Asampragyata
B. Sampragyata
C. Jnana yoga samadhi
D. Laya yoga samadhi

57. In which type of samadhi there remains the real knowledge of the subject?
A. Sampragyata
B. Asampragyata
C. Both the above
D. None of the above

58. In which pada of 'Patanjali Yoga Sutra' the different types of samadhis are explained?
A. Samadhi pada B. Vibhuti pada
C. Sadhana pada D. Kaivalya pada

59. Raga-dvesha give rise to which stage of chitta?
A. Mudhavastha B. Kshiptavastha
C. Vikshiptavastha D. Nirudhavastha

60. Rajas guna is dominant in which stage of chitta?
A. Vikshiptavastha B. Mudhavastha
C. Kshiptavastha D. Nirudhavastha

61. Satvaguna is dominant in which stage of chitta?
A. Mudhavastha B. Kshiptavastha
C. Vikshiptavastha D. Nindravastha

62. Tamasguna is dominant in which stage of chitta?
A. Mudhavastha B. Kshiptavastha
C. Vikshiptavastha D. Nirudhavastha

63. Which stage is known as the sampragyata samadhi?
A. Nirudhavastha B. Ekagratavastha
C. Vikshiptavastha D. None of the above

64. Which of the following samadhi is ekanugata?
A. Anandanugata B. Vicharanugata
C. Asmitanugata D. Vitarkanugata

65. Which of the following samadhi is triyakanugata?
A. Asampragyata B. Vicharanugata
C. Bhavapratya D. Vitarkanugata

66. The vritti which shows nil object knowledge is known as:
A. Pramana vritti B. Smriti vritti
C. Vipreya vritti D. Vikalpa vritti

67. The vrittis which causes sorrows and sufferings are known as:
A. Akalista vritti B. Kalista vritti
C. Pramana vritti D. Both A and B

68. Which of the following is not a vritti?
A. Nindra vritti B. Smriti vritti
C. Vikalpa vritti D. Mudha vritti

69. The knowledge of objects arised due to attachment of senses to external objects is called as which type of vritti?
A. Pratyaksha pramana
B. Agama pramana
C. Shakshata pramana
D. Apratayksha pramana

70. The perception of a rope as a snake is the result of which type of vritti?
A. Pramana vritti B. Vipraiya vritti
C. Vikalpa vritti D. Nindra vritti

71. The perception arised due to vipraiya vritti is always:
A. Stable B. Unstable
C. Real D. None of these

72. Which of the following is a vikalpa vritti?
A. Anuvritti B. Abhivritti
C. Anhavritti D. Nindravritti

73. Which of the following statement is incorrect?
A. The chittavastha of yogis is known as ekagravastha
B. The chittavastha of seekers is known as vikshiptavastha
C. The chittavastha of lower category people known as mudhavastha
D. The chittavastha of higher category people is known as nirudhavastha

74. Which of the following is a stage of nirbija samadhi?
A. Ekagratavastha
B. Shunyavastha
C. Siddhavastha
D. Niruddhavastha

75. Whose statement is this? - 'Yoga means samadhi'?
A. Gorakshanath
B. Swami Vivekananda
C. Maharishi Vyasa
D. Maharishi Patanjali

76. To maintain concentration on a minute object is a type of which samadhi?
A. Vitarka B. Vichara
C. Ananda D. Asmita

77. The main cause of all the kleshas is:
A. Raga B. Davesha
C. Avidya D. Ahamkara

78. In bhava-prataya samadhi what is the meaning of word 'bhava'?
A. Present B. Past
C. Ignorance D. Asmita

79. Which of the following is not a anumana pramana?
A. Puravavata B. Sakshyavata
C. Sheshavata D. Both A and B

80. By influence of prejudice when a person percepts about a thing, it is known as ______ vritti.
A. Pramana vritti B. Vipreya vritti
C. Nindra vritti D. Vikalpa vritti

81. The perception arised due to the words of a siddha purusha is called as:
A. Pratyaksha pramana B. Yathartha
C. Agama-pramana D. Satya-pramana

82. To percept a thing in the influence of any other famous thing or scene is known as ______ pramana.
A. Agama B. Yathartha
C. Vipreya D. Upmana

83. Which of the following statement is correct?
A. In vikshiptavastha the sattvic vrittis are influenced by the rajastic vrittis.
B. In vikshiptavastha the rajasic vrittis are influenced by tamasic vrittis.
C. In kshiptavastha the sattvic vrittis are influenced by rajasic vrittis.
D. In kshiptavastha tamasic vrittis are influenced by rajasic vrittis.

84. Which of the following is not a vritti?
A. Pramana B. Vikalpa
C. Abhinivesha D. Smriti

85. Dharana, dhyana, and samadhi are means of bahiranga sadhana of ______ Samadhi.
A. Sabija B. Nirbija
C. Bhakti yoga D. Nada yoga

86. What is the meaning of word abhinivesha?
A. Fear of accident
B. Fear of death
C. Fear of disease
D. Fear of kleshas

87. Which of the following is stage of 'Chitta bhumis'?
A. Kshipta, mudha B. Vikshipta, ekagra
C. Ekagra, Niruddha D. All of the above

88. Kshiptavastha arises due to dominance of which guna?
A. Rajas B. Tamas
C. Sattva D. Both A and C

89. In kshiptavastha chitta becomes ______
A. Stable B. Unstable
C. Calm D. Pure

90. Meaning of Heya is:
A. What is the form of sorrow?
B. What is the reason of sorrow?
C. What is the state of sorrow?
D. What are the means to eradicate sorrow?

91. According to Maharishi Patanjali which of the following are elements of success in yoga?
A. To help the needy people
B. To ignore the wicked people
C. To cultivate favour of people
D. All of the above

92. According to Maharishi Patanjali which of the following are elements of failure in yoga?
A. Disease doubt, carelessness
B. Laziness, false perception, excitement
C. Lack of concentration, back sliding
D. All of the above

93. In vikshiptavastha the chitta becomes:
A. Stable B. Unstable
C. Rajoguni D. Both A and B

94. Which guna is dominant during ekagratavastha?
A. Rajas guna
B. Sattva guna
C. Tamas guna
D. All in balanced state

95. Which pramana is based on linga and lingi?
A. Pratayksha B. Aagama
C. Anumana D. None of the above

96. Which type of dhyana includes concentrating on brahma randra and to purify the chitta, by passing the chakras?
A. Pindasatha dhyana
B. Sthula dhyana
C. Sukshma dhyana
D. Padastha dhyana

97. Maharishi Patanjali was the contemporary of:
A. Pushyamitra
B. Chandragupta Maurya
C. Kanishka
D. Shrigupta

98. According to Maharishi Patanjali, pranayama is the ______ limb of ashtanga yoga.
A. Second B. Third
C. Fourth D. Fifth

99. Which of the following is not a kleshas?
A. Avidya B. Raga
C. Vyadi D. Abhinivesha

100. According to the text 'Patanjali Yoga Sutra' how many antrayas are there?
A. 6 B. 7
C. 8 D. 9

101. Which of the following is not a pranayama according to 'Patanjali Yoga Sutra'?
A. Bahyavritti B. Kumbhakavritti
C. Aphyantakavritti D. Stambhavritti

102. According to Maharishi Patanjali the virtous deeds are:
A. Krishna karma B. Shukla karma
C. Kamya karma D. Sanchita karma

103. How many types of sampragyata samadhi are there?
A. 2 B. 3
C. 4 D. 5

104. To concentrate mind on a object or panchmahabhuts and adoring these is known as:

A. Vitarkanugata samadhi
B. Vicharanugata samadhi
C. Anandanugata samadhi
D. Asmitanugata samadhi

105. 'Raga arises due to attachment, and it causes all the sorrows'. Whose opinion is this?

A. Shri Bhagavad Gita
B. Patanjali Yoga Sutra
C. Yoga Vashistha
D. Narada Sutra

106. What is correct sequence of chapters of the text 'Patanjali Yoga Sutra'?

A. Sadhanapada – Samadhipad – Vibhutipada – Kaivalyapada
B. Samadhipada – Sadhnapada – Vibhutipada – Kaivalyapada
C. Samadhipada – Sadhnapada – Kaivalyapada – Vibhutipada
D. Sadhanapada – Samadhipad – Kaivlyapada – Vibhutipada

107. The siddhi by which a sadhaka changes the size of his body to maximum is known as:

A. Mahima B. Anima
C. Mudrima D. Rudrima

108. 'Aamni dasha' arises during which samadhi?

A. Asampragyata B. Sampragyata
C. Vicharanugata D. Anandanugata

109. 'Yoga Chitta Vritti Nirodha' – is explained in which pada of 'Patanjali Yoga Sutra'?

A. Samadhipada B. Sadhnapada
C. Vibhutipada D. Kaivalyapada

110. Panch kleshas are described in which part of 'Patanjali Yoga Sutra?'

A. Samadhi pada B. Sadhana pada
C. Vibhuti pada D. Kaivalya pada

111. The main cause of nindra vritti is:

A. Sattva guna
B. Rajas guna
C. Tamas guna
D. All of the above

112. "Chatuvayurahvada" is described in which part of 'Patanjali Yoga Sutra'?

A. Samadhipada B. Sadhanapada
C. Vibhutipada D. Kaivalyapada

113. False perception is:

A. Pramana vritti B. Nindra vritti
C. Vipreya vritti D. Vikalpa vritti

114. To attain the goal by enduring the sufferings happily, is known as which type of Sadhana?

A. Dama B. Uparati
C. Titiksha D. Samadhana

115. Which is the second chapter of the text 'Patanjali Yoga Sutra'?

A. Sadhanapada B. Kaivalyapada
C. Vibhutipada D. Samadhipada

116. Upper category sadhakas can attain samadhi by means of which sadhana?

A. Abhyasa and vairagya
B. Ishwarpranidhana
C. Kriya yoga
D. Both A and B

117. Medium category sadhakas can attain samadhi by means of which sadhana?

A. Tapa B. Swadhyaya
C. Ishwarpranidhana D. All of the above

118. Low category sadhakas can attain samadhi by means of which sadhana?

A. Kriya yoga B. Jnana yoga
C. Ashtanga yoga D. Prana yoga

119. What does 'Deshbandhachitsyadharna' mean:

A. To control chitta by senses is dharana
B. To control the chitta at a point is dharana
C. To perform bandhas to fix chitta in dharana
D. To control chitta by performing bandhas is dharana

120. In which pada of 'Patanjali Yoga Sutra', karmas are explained?

A. Samadhipada B. Sadhanapada
C. Vibhutipada D. Kaivalyapada

121. How many types of karma are explained by Maharishi Patanjali?

A. 2 B. 3
C. 4 D. 5

122. The total number of sutras in 'Patanjali Yoga Sutra' are:
A. 155 B. 175
C. 185 D. 195

123. How many types of samadhi are explained in 'Shaiva tradition'?
A. 4 B. 5
C. 6 D. 7

124. Which is the last chapter of 'Patanjali Yoga Sutra'?
A. Sadhanapada
B. Samadhipada
C. Kaivalyapada
D. Vibhutipada

125. Kalista vrittis are dominant in:
A. Tamas guna
B. Rajas guna
C. Sattva guna
D. All of the above

126. Akalista vrittis are dominant in:
A. Tamas guna B. Rajas guna
C. Sattva guna D. All of the above

127. Who among the following is also known as 'Nagnath'?
A. Gorakshnath
B. Matseyandranath
C. Maharishi Patanjali
D. Shri Krishna

128. Who is known as 'The father of Yoga"?
A. Matseyandranath
B. Shiva
C. Maharishi Patanjali
D. Maharishi Gherand

129. Who is the author of the text "Patanjali Rahasya"?
A. Swami Shivananda
B. Swami Vivekananda
C. Raghvananda Saraswati
D. Acharya Shankar

130. 'Sanyam' is described in which chapter of 'Patanjali Yoga Sutra'?
A. Sadhanapada B. Samadhipada
C. Vibhutipada D. Kaivalyapada

131. Which philosophy considers consciousness as a activity of chitta?
A. Vedanta B. Nyaya
C. Yoga D. Samkhya

132. According to Charvaka philosophy, how many types of pramana vritti are there?
A. 2 B. 3
C. 4 D. None of these

133. Bhramari pranayama is performed during which type of samadhi?
A. Bhaktiyoga samadhi
B. Layayoga samadhi
C. Dhyanayoga samadhi
D. Nadayoga samadhi

134. Asanas should be performed daily because they provide us:
A. Health B. Steadiness
C. Lightness D. All of the above

ANSWERS

1	2	3	4	5	6	7	8	9	10
C	C	B	A	B	A	A	B	D	A
11	**12**	**13**	**14**	**15**	**16**	**17**	**18**	**19**	**20**
C	B	C	C	C	B	D	C	D	A
21	**22**	**23**	**24**	**25**	**26**	**27**	**28**	**29**	**30**
D	A	A	B	C	A	D	A	D	D
31	**32**	**33**	**34**	**35**	**36**	**37**	**38**	**39**	**40**
B	C	B	C	B	B	C	B	A	C

41	42	43	44	45	46	47	48	49	50
C	C	A	B	D	C	D	B	B	D
51	**52**	**53**	**54**	**55**	**56**	**57**	**58**	**59**	**60**
D	B	D	A	D	A	A	D	B	C
61	**62**	**63**	**64**	**65**	**66**	**67**	**68**	**69**	**70**
C	A	B	C	B	D	B	D	A	B
71	**72**	**73**	**74**	**75**	**76**	**77**	**78**	**79**	**80**
B	C	D	D	C	B	C	C	B	D
81	**82**	**83**	**84**	**85**	**86**	**87**	**88**	**89**	**90**
C	D	A	C	B	B	D	A	B	A
91	**92**	**93**	**94**	**95**	**96**	**97**	**98**	**99**	**100**
D	A	D	B	C	A	A	C	C	D
101	**102**	**103**	**104**	**105**	**106**	**107**	**108**	**109**	**110**
B	B	C	A	C	B	A	A	A	B
111	**112**	**113**	**114**	**115**	**116**	**117**	**118**	**119**	**120**
C	B	C	C	A	D	D	C	B	D
121	**122**	**123**	**124**	**125**	**126**	**127**	**128**	**129**	**130**
C	D	C	C	A	C	C	C	C	C
131	**132**	**133**	**134**						
C	D	D	D						

●●●

CHAPTER 4

Hatha Yoga Texts

Introduction to Hatha Yoga

Hatha Yoga is one of the first types of *yoga* with which people become acquainted. However, it is not a separate system of *yoga* as many people seem to think. It is one of the eight steps of *raja yoga*. Nonetheless, it can be used separately if only for helping keep the body and mind fit and in shape.

The word *hatha* consists of two *bija* or seed mantras, viz., *ha* (*prana*) and *tha* (the mind or mental energy). *Ha* means the *prana* or energy flowing within the body and that associated with the sun, while *tha* means the mind or mental energy, or that associated with the moon. Thus, *hatha* means to bring in balance the energies of the sun and moon, or unify the vital energy of the body with the mental. This opens the door to higher consciousness, which culminates in samadhi during meditation. With the use of yoga, the body can become more subtle, or what is called a yoga body.

Hatha yoga is described in such early texts as the *Hatha Yoga Pradipika* by Yogi Swatmarama, the *Gheranda Samhita* by the sage Gherand, and the *Shiva Samhita*. Lord Shiva is said to be the originator of the system found in the *Hatha Yoga Pradipika*. This is highly regarded by the Nath tradition founded by Gorakhnath and his teacher Matsyendranath, who was accepted to be a disciple of Lord Shiva. Yogi Gorakhnath wrote the *Gorakha Samhita*. A later text on yoga is known as the *Hatharatnavali* by Srinivasabhatta Mahayogindra. Of course, most people are aware of the *Yoga Sutras* by Patanjali in which he codified the steps of *yoga*.

The mind naturally has to become purified of all materialism or attraction to material and sensual desires. But in order for that to happen, the body must also be cleansed of all impurities. That is the purpose of *hatha yoga*, to help purify the body and align it and the energies within for meditation. Therefore, the preliminary step in all such *yogas*, like *raja yoga, kundalini yoga, tantra yoga,* or *kriya yoga,* must be *hatha yoga*. Thus, *hatha yoga* is not a system of its own, but is merely a step for reaching something higher. If the impurities of the body are not removed, then these will adversely affect the ability to meditate, or even bring abnormal experiences or difficulties in some *yoga* systems.

Hatha yoga is known as the time when there is a union with the *Ida, Pingala*, and *Sushumna* channels of subtle energy. It is this union that is the awakening in *kundalini* and *raja yogas*. However, it is no longer *hatha yoga* when the *kundalini* or *prana* moves to the *Sahasrara chakra*, when it then becomes *yoga*. *Yoga* means union, and in *raja yoga* it is when the *pranic* force unites with *Brahman* at the *Sahasrara chakra*, or when the *kundalini shakti* rises to the *Sahasrara* and unites with *Shiva*.

As it states in the *Hatha Yoga Pradipika* (1:76) "There can be no perfection if *hatha yoga* is without *raja yoga*, or *raja yoga* without *hatha yoga*. Therefore, through practice of both, perfection is attained."

In any case, *hatha yoga* is one of the most popular forms of *yoga*, which can be done by anybody, regardless of how serious he or she may be about attaining higher levels of spiritual development. Although it is a part of a spiritual process, when taken as an isolated exercise technique it can be completely secular as well. Thus, it is practically non-denominational and non-sectarian. Anyone from any background can use it and acquire its benefits.

Hatha yoga involves maneuvering the body through particular *asanas* or exercises, along with breathing techniques for controlling the life airs within the body. This is the *prana*, the universal energy that flows through the body. *Prana* is divided into certain bodily airs that function in different ways. *Prana* is the incoming and outgoing breath; *apana* is the air which expels bodily waste; *vyana* assists in the power of physical movement; *samana* distributes nutrition through the body; and *udana* is the air in the *Sushumna* channel. The main goal of *hatha yoga* is to help keep the body in shape and free from disease, the mind peaceful and steady for spiritual pursuits, and the inner energy balanced and flowing. This, however, is very useful in whatever spiritual process we pursue because if our body is too diseased, and if our mind is too restless and unsteady, they become a hindrance in our quest for spiritual awareness for perfection. Thus, with the practice of *hatha yoga*, the body and mind become healthier and our spiritual practice can continue with fewer impediments to higher levels of realizations. Thus, it is beneficial regardless of what one's spiritual discipline is, or even when there is no spiritual interest at all.

In the following section we will narrate some of the significant classical texts on *Hatha Yoga*:

HATHAPRADIPIKA

The *HathaYoga Pradipika* (HP) "the Light on *Hatha Yoga*" was composed by *Svatmarama* (as *Atmarama*) *Yogindra* in the middle of the fourteenth century. This is undoubtedly the classical manual on Hatha-Yoga. It comprises 38 stanzas organized into four chapters viz. *Upudesa. Svatmarama,* a follower of the *Saiva Yoga* tradition of Andhra, mainly expounds Hatha-Yoga as a means to Raja Yoga. The first chapter is dedicated primarily to a description of the principal postures *(asanas),* the second chapter speaks of the cleansing practices as well as the life force *(Prana)* and its regulation through breath-control *(Pranayama).* In the third chapter, *Svatmarama* introudces us to the subtle physiology and techniques, such as the *mudras* and *bandhas,* by which the life force can be properly continued in the body and the *Kundalini* is awakened. The concluding chapter deals with the higher stages of Yogic practices, including the ecstatic condition *(Samadhi),* which is understood in Vedantic terms. The HP has an excellent commentary entitled *Jyotsana ("Light")* by *Brahmananda* of mid-eighteenth century.

The systems of Yoga are differentiated according to their methods and they are known as *Astanga, Laya, Dhyana, Mantra, Bhakti, Taraka, Karma* etc. All these are classified into two broad divisions viz. *Hathayoga* and *Rajayoga.* These two are interdependent either of them being impracticable without the other. It is suggested in the HP that each yoga viz. the *Laya,* the *Taraka,* the *Dhyana,* etc. has its beginning in the *Hathayoga,* consciously or unconsciously and ends in *Rajayoga.* The regulation of breath for the purpose of checking the modification of the thinking principle *i.e.,* the mind is called the *Hathayoga,* under which the *Astanga,* Mantra, etc. naturally fall. *Rajayoga* begins where *Hathayoga* properly followed. As the *Hathayoga* begins the power to remove diseases, bodily or mental, its practices regulates the action of the heart, the lungs, and the circulation of the blood. It even bestows the gift of putting off death indefinitely although it is rarely exercised by the true Yogin who knows the consequences of interfering with the laws of nature. The HP, mainly, describes the intimate relation between the mind and the *Prana.* That relation is proved by our daily experience of life; when we absorbed in deep thought, the process of breathing becomes slow. The suspension of the mental activity increases in proportion to the slowness of the breath; in case of asphyxia, mental activity ceases altogether until respiration is revived and complete disappearance of mental activity takes place with the death of the body. These considerations prove that mind and *Prana* are interdependent, each unable to act independently of the other.

Thus, both the *Hathayoga* and the *Rajayoga* are necessary counterparts of each other. Either of them cannot be successfully followed to the exclusion of the other. Moreover, without the directions of a competent *Guru,* benefits are not secured and no one can be a perfect Yogi without the knowledge of the practices of both.

Updesa

According to the tradition of Yoga, the HP, mainly emphasizes on the right place known as Matha for the practice of Yoga as well as the obstacles, before describing the *asanas.*

Monastery (Matha)

It is a small room, situated in a solitary place, being 04 cubits square. It should be free from stones, fire, water and all kinds of disturbances. It should be in place where justice is properly administrated, where good people live and food can be obtained easily and plentifully. The room should have a small door, be free from holes, hollows, neither too high nor too low, well plastered with cowdung and free from dirt, filth and insects. On its outside, there should be bowers, raised platform, a well and a compound. Having seated in such a room and free from all anxieties, *Hathayogi* should practise Yoga, as instructed by *Guru.*

To depict the obstacles in the practice of the *Hathayoga,* the HP discloses the six causes, which destroy the Yoga, viz. over-eating, exertion, talkativeness, adhering to rules, promiscuous company and unsteadiness. But Yoga succeeds by six viz. zeal, bold determination, perseverance *(dhairya),* discriminative knowledge, faith and aloofness from company.

Yama and Niyama

The 10 yamas viz. non-injuring, truth, non-stealing, continence, forgiveness, endurance, compassion, rectitude, temperance in food and cleanliness; as well as the 10 *Niyamas* viz. penance, contentment, belief in God, donation, worship of God, study of establish truth, modesty, faith, austere *(tapa)* and sacrificial rites *(hutam)* – are listed in the HP.

Asanas

As the HP depicts - the asanas should be practised for gaining steady posture, health and lightness of body, they are described 15 in number.

1. The Svastikasana

Technique: Having kept both the legs under both the thighs with the body straight; calmly sitting in this way is called *Svastikasana.*

2. The Gomukhasana

Technique : Placing the right ankle on the left side and the left ankle on the right side, makes the *Gomukhasana* which appears like the face of a cow.

3. The Virasana

Technique : Placing one foot on the thigh of the opposite side, so also the other foot on the opposite thigh, makes the *Virasana.*

4. The Kurmasana

Technique : Placing the right ankle on the left side of the anus and the left ankle on the right side of it, make the *Kurmasana.*

5. The Kukkutasana

Technique : Taking the posture of the *Padmasana* and carrying the hands under the thighs, when the Yogi raises himself above the ground, with his palms resting on the ground, it becomes the *Kukkutasana.*

6. The Uttanakurmasana

Technique : Having assumed the *Kukkutasana*, when one grasps his neck by crossing his hands behind his head, and lies in this posture with his back, touching the ground, it becomes *Uttana kurmasana,* which appears like a tortoise.

7. *The Dhanurasana*

Technique : Having caught the toes of the feet with both the hands and carried them to the ears by drawing the body like a bow, it becomes *Dhanurasana.*

8. *The Matsyasana*

Technique : Having placed the right foot at the root of the left thigh, grasping the toe with the right hand passing over the back. One should place the left foot at the root of the right thigh, and it should be grasped with the left hand passing behind the back.

Benefits:

(*i*) It increases gastric fire.

(*ii*) It destroys the group of the most deadly diseases.

(*iii*) Its practice awakens the *Kundalini.*

(*iv*) It makes the moon steady in men.

9. *The Paschimotanasana*

Technique : Having stretched the feet on the ground like a stick and grasping the toes of both the feet with both the hands, one should sit with his forehead resting on the thighs - it becomes the *Paschimotanasana.*

Benefits:

(*i*) It carries the air from the front to the back part of the body *i.e.,* to the *Susumna.*

(*ii*) It kindles gastric fire.

(*iii*) It reduces obesity and cures all diseases of men.

10. *The Mayurasana*

Technique : Placing both the palms on the ground and the navel on both the elbows, balancing thus, one should stretch his body backward like a stick– this is *Mayurasana.*

Benefits:

(*i*) It soon destroys all diseases.

(*ii*) It removes abdominal diseases arising from irregularities of phlegm, bile and wind.

(*iii*) It digests unwholesome food taken in excess.

(*iv*) It increases the gastric fire and destroys the most deadly poison.

11. *The Savasana*

Technique : Lying down on the ground like a corpse; is called Savasana, which removes fatigue and gives rest to the mind.

12. *The Siddhasana*

Technique:

* Press firmly the heel of the left foot against the perineum and the right heel above the male organ.
* With the chin pressing on the chest, sit calmly.
* Restrain the senses and gaze steadily the space between the eyebrows.

Benefits:

(*i*) It opens the door of salvation.

(*ii*) It cleanses the impurities of 72,000 nadis.

Importance:

This *asana* is also known as the *Vajrasana,* the *Muktasana* or the *Guptasana.* Just as the importance of the temperance in food is among *yamas,* that of non-injuring among the *niyamas,* similarly, the *Siddhasana* is the chief of all the *asanas.* By practising this *asanas* simultaneously with contemplating on oneself and being temperance in food, the yogi, obtains success. Without knowing this *asana,* other postures are of no use, if success has been achieved in this *asana, Prana vayu* becomes calm and becomes restrained by *Kevala Kumbhaka.* By getting success in this posture, one gets *Unmani* state at once and three bandhas are accomplished of themselves.

Lastly, it praises this posture by saying that there is no *asana* like the *Siddhasana,* no *kumbhaka* like *kevala,* no *mudra* like *khechari* and no *laya* like *nada i.e.,* the *Anahata Nada.*

13. *The Padmasana*

Technique :

* Place the right foot on the left thigh and left foot on the right thigh.

* Grasp the toes with the hands crossed over the back.
* Press the chin against the chest, and
* Gaze on the tip of the nose. This is the destroyer of the diseases.

It also mentions the another way—"Placing the feet on the thighs with the sole upwards and hands on the thigh with the palm upwards, one should gaze on the tip of the nose. One should keep the tongue pressing against the root of the teeth of the upper jaw. Pressing the chin against the chest one should raise the air up slowly *i.e.,* raise the *apana vayu* gently upward." This posture, destroyer of all diseases, is difficult to attain by everybody but can be learnt by intelligent people.

The another way is—Having kept both the hands together in the lap, performing the *padmasana* firmly, keeping the chin fixed to the chest and contemplating on Him in the mind, by drawing the *Apanavayu* up and pushing down the air after inhaling it. Joining thus, the *prana* and the *Apana* in the navel, one gets the highest intelligence by awakening the *Sakti (Kundalini).* One who can control breathing, sitting with *padmasana,* is free from bondage.

14. The Simhasana

Technique : Press the heels on both sides of the seam of perineum, so that the left heel touches the right side and the right heel touches the left side of it.

* Place the hands on the thighs with stretched fingers.
* Keep the mouth open and the mind concentrated.
* Gaze on the tip of the nose. This effects the completion of the three *bandhas.*

15. The Bhadrasana

Technique :

* Place the heels on either sides of the seam of the perineum, keeping the left heel on the left side and the right one on the right side.
* Hold the feet firmly joined to one another with both the hands.

According to the HP, the expert yogis call it ***Goraksasana,*** which removes fatigue.

The temperance in food *(mitahara)*

The temperance in food is that in which the food well cooked with ghee and sweets, leaving a fourth part of his stomach, should be eaten with the offering of it to *siva,* according to the HP.

Now, the food injurious as well as suitable to a Yogi is mentioned in the HP.

(*a*) **Food injurious to a Yogi**—Bitter, sour, saltish, hot, green vegetables, oily, mixed with til seed, rape seed, intoxicating liquors, fish, meat, curds, butter milk, plums *(Kulattha),* oil cake, asafotida, garlic, onion etc. should not be eaten. Moreover, food heaten again, dry, too much saltish, sour, minor grands and vegetables that cause burning sensation should not be eaten. Fire, women, travelling, etc. should be avoided. Further the view of *Goraksa* is represented here one should keep aloof from the society of the evil-minded, fire, women, travelling, early morning bath, fasting and all kinds of bodily exertion.

(*b*) **Food beneficial to a Yogi**—Wheat, rice, barley, sastik, good corns, milk, ghee, sugar, butter, sugarcandy, honey, dried ginger, parval, moong, pure water are very beneficial to a Yogi. A yogi should eat tonics, well sweetened, greasy, milk, butter etc that may increase humors of the body, according to his desire.

To complete the first *Upadesa* of the HP, *Svatmarama* discloses the way how to attain success in the practice of yoga—whether the young, old or too old, sick or lean if he discards the laziness, he gets success by practising Yoga. Success comes to him who is engaged in the practice. By merely reading books on Yoga, one can never get success. Not by adopting a particular dress, not by telling tales, but practice alone is the means to success. Moreover, it is stated that by regular and close attention to *Nada* in *Hathayoga,* a *brahmachari,* sparing in diet, unattached to objects of enjoyment, and devoted to Yoga, gains success within a year. And *asanas,* various *kumbhakas,* and other divine means should be practised till the fruit is obtained.

The six purificatory practices *(Satkarmas)*

In the II - *Upadesa* of the HP, which mainly explains about the breath control *(pranayama),* the six purificatory practices are mentioned briefly and clearly. The HP opines that these six practices are necessary only if there are impurities in the *Nadis* in other words if there is excess of fat or phlegm in the body, these six should be performed before performing the breath control. But those who are not suffering from the excess of these, should not perform them. The six practices are as follow:

1. The *Dhauti*—A strip of cloth, moist with warm water, about 03 inches wide and 15 cubits long, is swallowed through the passage shown by the *Guru,* and is taken out again—this is known as *Dhauti karma.* By practising it, cough, asthma, enlargement of the spleen, leprosy and 20 kinds of diseases born of phlegm are disappeared.
2. The *Basti*—Squatting in navel -deep water and inserting a pipe, open at both ends, six inches long, smooth piece of ½ inch diameter pipe, half inside the anus, the anus should be contracted and expelled. This is known as a *Bastikarma,* by practising which, colic, enlarged spleen, dropsy arising from the disorders of *vata, pitta* and *kapha*—are all cured. Secondly, the *Dhatus,* the sense organs and the mind become calm. It gives glow and tone to the body and increases the gastric fire. All the disorders disappear.
3. The *Neti*–A string *(sutra)* about six inches long should be passed through the passage of the nose and the end of a string is taken out in the mouth—this is the *Neti karma* by which all the diseases of the cervical and scapular regions are destroyed. It is the cleaner of the brain and giver of divine sight.
4. The *Trataka*—Being calm one should gaze steadily at a small mark, till eyes are filled with tears—this is *trataka* which destroys the eye-diseases and removes sloth etc.
5. The *Nauli*—Sitting on the toes with heels raised above the ground, resting the palms on the ground and in this bent pasture, the belly is moved forcibly from left to right just as in vomiting - this is *Nauli Karma* which removes dyspepsia, increases the gastric fire dries up all the disorders and causes happiness. It is like the goddess of creation and known as the excellent exercise in *Hatha yoga.*
6. The *Kapalabhati*—To perform the inhalation and the exhalation very quickly like a pair of bellows of a blacksmith, is known as *kapalabhati* which dries up all the disorders from the excess of phlegm.

Thus, one can easily attain success if the breath-control is performed after being free from the phlegmatic disorders, impurities etc. by above mentioned six practices.

Moreover, the additional practice viz. the *Gajakarani* is mentioned. By carrying the *Apanavayu* up to the throat, the food etc. in the stomach are vomited. Practising it, by degrees, the system of *Nadis* become known (or controlled).

The Breath-control *(Pranayama)*

As suggested in the HP, having established the posture, and eating salutary and moderate food, a yogi should practice the breath-control, as instructed by his *Guru* purpose *of* performing *pranayama:* To get steadiness of mind, a yogi should restrain the vital air because the vital air being disturbed, the mind becomes disturbed. So long the vital air stays in the body, it is called life and death consists in the passing out of the air. Therefore, it is necessary to restrain the breath. Moreover, to attain success in the non-mindedness state *(Unmani-avastha)* the vital air should be passed through the middle channel, *i.e., Susumna,* which is not possible owing to the impurities of the *nadis.* So, when the whole system of *nadis* is cleaned a yogi becomes able to control the *prana*. Therefore, *pranayama* should be performed daily with *sattvic buddhi* in order to drive out the impurities of *susumna*.

Method of Performing *Pranayama*

At first, a yoga should pertain the following two practices

(*a*) Sitting in the *Padmasana*, a yogi should fill in the air through the left nostril, keeping it confined according to his ability, it should be expelled slowly through the right nostril. Then,

(*b*) Drawing in the air through the right nostril slowly, belly should be filled keeping it confined *(i.e., kumbhaka)* as before, it should be expelled slowly through the left nostril.

These two practices of *pranayama* are known as *Anuloma* and *pratilomapranayama* respectively.

Thus, one should inhale through at the nostril through which it was expelled, and having restrained it there till possible, it should be expelled through the other, slowly not forcibly. By practising in this way, through the right and the left nostrils alternately, the collection of the *nadis* of a *yogi* becomes clean *i.e.,* becomes free from impurities after three months and over.

Importance of *Pranayama*

Brahma and other deities were also engaged in the exercise of the breath control by which they got rid of the fear of death. Therefore, one should practise it. So long as the mind is undisturbed and so long as the gaze is between the eyebrows there is no fear of death. Moreover, by properly controlling the *prana,* the systems of *Nadis* become clear of the impurities, then the air, piercing the entrance of the *susumna*, enters it easily.

Retaining the breath *(Kumbhaka)*

As suggested by the HP, to accomplish the *manonmani* state various *kumbhakas* are performed by those who are expert in the method. The *manonmani* state is the steadiness of mind which comes when the air moves freely in the middle, *i.e.,* in the *Susumna,* and when the mind becomes calm. The eight kinds of *Kumbhakas* are described.

1. **The *Suryabhedana:*** Taking any comfortable posture the *yogi* should drawn in the air slowly through the right nostril. Then it should be confined within, so that it fills from the nails to the tips of the hair, then expelled through the left nostril slowly. This excellent *Suryabhedana* cleanses forehead, destroys the disorders of *vata,* removes the worms, hence, it should be performed again and again. Before mentioning this process it informs that - at the end of *puraka, jalanadhara bandha* should be perfomed at the end of *kumbhaka,* and at the beginning of *rechaka, Uddiyana bandha* should be performed. By drawing up from below and contracting the throat, by pulling back the middle of the front portion of the body, *i.e.,* beltly, the *prana* goes to the *Brahma nadi i.e.,* the *Susumna.* By pulling up the *Apana vayu* and by forcing the *prana vayu* down the throat, the *yogi* liberated from old age, becomes young as it were 16 years old.
2. **The *Ujjayi kumbhaka*:** Having closed the mouth, the air should be drawn in such a way that it touches from the throat to the chest and makes noise while passing. It should be retained within so that it fills from the nails to the tips of the hair and expelled it through the left nostril. This *ujjayi kumbhaka* removes phlegm in the throat and increases the gastric fire. It destroys the defects of the *nadis* dropsy and disorders of humours. It should be perfomed in all condition of life even while walking or sitting.
3. **The *Sitkari kumbhaka* :** The air should be drawn in through the mouth, making a hissing noise and exhale it only through the nostrils. By practising this *kumbhaka,* one's beauty becomes like that of the God of Love. He is regarded adorable by the yogins and becomes destroyer of the cycle of creation.

He is not afflicted with hunger, thirst sleep or lassitude. The goodness *(sattvik)* of his body becomes free from all the disturbances, and really, he becomes the lord of the yogis in this world.

4. **The *Sitali* :** Protruding the tongue, a little, outside the lips, one should inhale the air with the tongue and perform *Kumbhaka* as the air, holds within, from the nail to the tip of the hair. Then, the air is expelled slowly through the nostrils. This cures colic, enlarged spleen, fever, disorders of bile, hunger, thirst and counteracts poisons.
5. **The *Bhastrika* :** It is elaborated with the physical and spritual benefits. Crossing the feet and placing them on both the thighs, one assumes *Padmasana,* the destroyer of all sins. Keeping the body straight, closing the mouth carefully, the air should be expelled through the nose. It should be filled up to the lotus of the heart by drawing it in, with force, making noise and touching the throat, the chest and the head. It should be expelled again and filled again and again as before, just as a pair of bellows of the blacksmith is worked. In the same way, the air of the body should be moved intelligently, filling it through the right nostril when fatigue is experienced. The air is drawn in through the right nostril by pressing the thumb against the left side of the nose, to close the left nostril. When the nostril is filled to the full, it should be closed with the fourth finger and kept confined properly. Then, it should be expelled through the left nostril. This destroys wind, bile and phlegm and increases the digestive power. It quickly awakens the *Kundalini*, purifies the system, gives pleasure, and is beneficial. It destroys phlegm and the impurities, accumulated at the entrance of the *Susumna nadi.*

   This *Bhastrika* should be performed plentifully, for it breaks the three knots viz. *Brahma granthi* in the chest, *Visnu granthi* in the throat and *Rudra granthi* between the eyebrows.
6. **The *Bhramari* :** By filling the air with force, making noise like wasp *(bhringi)* and expelling it slowly, making noise in the same way - this practice causes a sort of ecstacy in the minds of *Yogindras.*
7. **The *murccha kumbhaka* :** Closing the passages with *Jalandhara Bandha* firmly at the end of puraka and expelling the air slowly, is called *Murccha.* It causes the mind to swoon and giving comfort.
8. **The *Plavini* :** When the belly is filled with the air and the inside of the body is filled to its utmost with air, the boat floats in the deepest water, like the leaf of a lotus.

Any YU does not utter a single word about it, now both the HP and the SDU states thus - breath-control is broadly classified in the two viz. *Sahita* and *Kevala.* Considering the inhaling, the expelling and the holding, *pranayama* is of three kinds. And considering it accompanied by the inhaling and the expelling, it is *Sahita* and without these it is called *Kevala.* The practice of *Sahita* should be continued till success in *Kevala* is gained. *Kevala* is simply confining the air with ease, without the inhaling and the expelling. For him who is able to keep the air confined according to pleasure, by means of the *kevala kumbhaka,* everything is possible to obtain in the three worlds. This detail about *kevala kumbhaka* is also found in the YTU, He obtains the position of *Rajayoga* undoubtedly, *kundalini* awakens by *kumbhaka* by which *susumna* becomes free from impurities. On the complition of *kumbhaka,* the mind should be given rest. Thus, one is raised to the position of *Rajayoga,* when the indications of success in the practice of *HathaYoga* is found in the body of a yogi.

1. The body becomes lean.
2. The face glows with delight.
3. The *Anahata nada* manifests.
4. Ears are clear.
5. Body becomes healthy.

6. *Bindu* is under control.
7. The gastric fire is increased, then one should know that the *Nadis* are purified and success in *Hathayoga* is approaching.

According to the HP, there is no success in *Rajayoga* without *Hathayoga* and no success in *Hathayoga* without *Rajayoga*. One should, therefore, practise both these, well, till complete success is gained.

Mudras

The whole III Upadesa of the HP is pertaining to the description of *Mudras*.

The purpose for practising *mudra* and its importance: Just as the chief of the snakes is the support of the earth with the mountains and forests on it, so all the yoga practices rest on the *kundalini*. And by awakening the sleeping *kundalini* by favour of a *guru,* all the lotuses and the knots are pierced through. Therefore, in order to awaken this goddess, sleeping at the entrance of *Brahmadvara, mudras* should be practised. These *mudras* should be kept secret by every means, as one keeps one's box of jewellery, and just as husband and wife keep their dealings secret. These all have been explained by *Adinath i.e.,* the lord *Shiva,* they give eight kinds of divine wealth *(aisvarya) viz. Anima, Garima, Mahima, Prapti, Ladhima, Prakamya, Isata and Vasitva.*

There are ten *mudras* which annihilate old age and death:

1. The Mahamudra

Pressing the perineum *(yoni)* with the heel of the left foot and stretching forth the right foot, one should grasp its toe by the thumb and first finger by stopping the throat, the air is drawn in from the outside and carried down. Just as a snake, stuck with a stick, becomes straight like a stick, similarly, *kundalini sakti* becomes straight at onces. Then, *Ida* and *pingala* becomes lifeless; leaving them, *kundilini* enters the *susumna.* Then, the air should be expelled slowly and not violently, for this very reason, it is known as *Mahamudra,* propounded by great maters, Great evils and pains, death are destroyed by it, hence it is called the *Mahamudra.* Having practised with the left nostril, it should be practiced with the right one. When the number of both sides becomes equal, the *mudra* should be discontinued.

There is nothing wholesome or injurious because it destroys the injurious effect of all the chemicals *(rasas).* Even the deadliest of poisons, if taken, act like nectar. Consumption, leprosy, prolepsus anus celoic and the diseases due to indigestion - all these irregularities are removed by the practice of the *mudra,* moreover, it is the giver of great success to men. Hence, it should be kept secret by every effort and not revealed to any and everyone.

2. The Mahabandha

Pressing the left heel to the perineum and placing the right foot on the left thigh, one should fill in the air. Keeping the chin firm against the chest and having pressed the air, the mind should be fixed on the middle of the eyebrows or in the *susumna.* Having confined it so long as possible, it should be expelled slowly. Thus, having practised on the left side, it should be practised on the right side, the another view is that the closing of throat is not necessary here for keeping the tongue pressed against the root of the upper teeth which makes a good *bandha* (stop), this practice stops the upward motion of all the *nadis*.

This *mahabandha,* the giver of great *siddhis,* is the most skillful means for cutting away the snares of death. It brings about the conjunction of *Ida, pingala* and *susumna.* Then it carries the mind to *kedara i.e.,* the space between the eyebrows which is the sect of *shiva.*

3. The Mahavedha

As the beauty and loveliness do not avail a woman without husband so the *maha-mudra* and the *maha-bandha* are useless without the *mahavedha.* Such is the value of practising the *maha-vedha.*

Sitting with the *Mahabandha,* the *yogi* should fill in the air and keep his mind concentrated. The movements of the vital air should be stopped by closing the throat. Resting both the hands equally on the ground, he should raise himself a little and strike his buttocks against the ground gently leaving both the passages *i.e.*, *Ida* and *pingala* the air moves into the middle one. The union of the *Ida (soms) pingala, (surya)* and *susumna (agni)* brings immortality. When the air becomes as it were dead, the air should be expelled. This *mahavedha,* the given of great *siddhis,* destroys old age and death grey hair and shaking of the body. The three viz. the *mahamudra* the *mahabandha* and the *mahavedha* destroy old age and death, increase the gastric fire, confer the accomplishment of *Anima* etc. These three should be practised in eight different ways daily and hourly, they increase collection of good actions and lessen the evil ones. People instructed well, should begin their practise by little, first.

4. The Khechari

The mind and the tongue reach *akasa* by its practice, so it is known as *Khechari mudra* by *siddhas.*

The *khechari mudra* is accomplished by thursting the tongue into the gullet by turning it over itself and keeping the eyesight in the middle of the eyebrows.

To accomplish this, the tongue is lengthened by cutting the fraenum lingual moving and pulling it. Taking a sharp, smooth and clean instrument of the shape of a cactus leaf, the fraenum of the tongue should be cut a little, at a time. Then, rock salt and yellow myrobalan should be rubbed on the seventh day, it should again be cut a hair's breadth. This should be done regularly for six months. At the end of six months, the freanum of the tongue will be completely cut. Turning the tongue upwards, it is fixed on the three ways *(tripathe)* known as *Vyomachakra* that makes it the *khechari mudra.*

Thus, the *yogi* who sits for a minute turning his tongue upwards, is saved from posions, diseases, death, old age etc. He is not afflicted with diseases death, sloth, sleep, hunger, thirst and swooning. He is not stained with *karmas* and not snared by time.

If the hole behind the palate is stopped with *khechari* by turning the tongue upwards, *bindu* cannot leave its place even if a woman was embraced.

By sitting with the tongue turned backwards and concentrated mind, if the yogi drinks *somarasa,* he conquers death within 15 days. And his body, full of *Somarasa* even if beaten by *taksaka,* its poison cannot permeat his body, The soul does not leave the body which is full of nectar exuding from the *soma.*

The word *Gobhaksanam* means cutting the *'go'* means the tongue, which means thrusting the tongue in the gullet which destroys great sins. *Amaravaruni* (immortal liquor) is the nectar exuding from the moon. It is produced by the fire which is generated by thrusting the tongue. If the tongue can touch with its end the hole from which falls the juice *(rasa)* which is saltish, bitter, sour, milky and similar to ghee and honey, one can drive away diseases, destroy old age, can evade an attack of arms, become immortal and can attract fairies.

He who drinks the clear stream of liquor of the moon falling from the brain to the sixteen-petalled lotus in the heart, obtained by means of *prana,* by applying the tongue to the hole of the pendient in the palate, and by meditating on the great power *kundalini,* becomes free from disease and tender in body like the stalk of a lotus. The *yogi* lives a very long life.

On the top of the *Meru* (vertebral column), concealed in a hole, there is the *somarasa* and there is the universal spirit *i.e., atma* in it. It is the source of the down going *Ida, pingala* and *susuman nadis* which are the *Gangas, yamuna* and the *sarasavati* from that *chandra* is shed the essence of the body which causes death of men. Therefore, it should be stopped from shedding.

This *Khechari mudra* is a very good means for this purpose. There is no other means of achieving this end. This hole is the generator of knowledge and is the source of the five streams *i.e., Ida, pingala* etc. In that colourless vaccum, *khechari mudra* should be established. There is only one seed germinating the whole universe from it, there is only one without any one's support and there is one condition called *manonmani,* similarly, there is only one *mudra* called *khechari.*

5. The Uddiyanabandha

By practising it, *prana* flies in the *susumna* or it may be said that the *prana,* the great bird tied to it flies without being fatigued, therefore it is known as the *Uddiyanabandha.*

According to the HP, of all the *bandhas, uddiyana* is the best, for by the binding it firmly, liberation comes spontaneously.

6. The Mulabandha

It is made by pressing perineum *(Yoni)* with the heel contracting up the anus and by drawing the *Apana.* During the practice, the *Apana* naturally inclined downward, goes up, by force hence, by constriction of the anus *i.e.,* the seat of the *Muladhara,* the *mulabundha* is so known. Further, pressing the heel well against the anus, one should draw up the air by force, again and again till it goes up. This is *mulabandha.*

Result: *Prana, Apana, Nada* and *Bindu* uniting into one in this way, give success in yoga undoubtedly. By the purfication of *Prana* and *Apana* urine and excrements decrease. And even an old man becomes young by constantly practising *Mulabandha.*

Moreover, going up the *Apana* enters the zone of fire *i.e.,* the stomach. The flame of fire struck by the air is thereby lengthened. These, fire and *Apana,* go to the naturally hot *prana* which becomes inflamed thereby and causes burning sensation in the body.

Then, the sleeping *kundalini* becomes well heated and awakens well. It becomes straight like a serpent, struck dead with a stick. It enters the *Brahmanadi* just as a serpent enters its hole. Therefore, the yogi should always practise the *mulabandha.*

7. The Jalandhara bandha

By contracting the throat, one should press the chin firmly against the chest. This *Jalandhara bandha* destroys old age and death.

Result: The HP describes that this *bandha* stops the opening of the group of the *Nadis,* through which the juice from the sky (the *soma* in the brain) falls down. It is, therefore, called the *Jalandhara bandha* - the destroyer of a hosts of diseases of the throat. In this *bandha,* the indications of a perfect contraction of throat are the nectar which does not fall into the fire and the air is not distrubed. The two *nadis* viz. *Ida* and the *pingala,* should be stopped, firmly by contracting the throat, and the middle centre *i.e.,* the *visuddhi chakra* stops the 16 vital parts *(adharas).* The usuage of the three *bandhas.*

By drawing up the anus *(mulasthana), Uddiyana bandha* should be performed by closing the *Ida* and the *pingala,* the flow of the air should be directed to the *susumna.* The *Prana* becomes calm and latent by this means. Thus there is no death, old age, and disease, etc. These three *bandhas* are the best of all and have been practised by the masters.

The nectar, possessing divine qualities, which exudes from the soma is devoured by the surya in the stomach, owing to this, the body becomes old. To remedy this, the opening of the *surya* is avoided by excellent means, and it should be learnt best by instruction from a *guru,* but not by even a million discussion.

8. The Viparitakarani

Placing the head on the ground and the feet up into the sky, for a second only the first day, one should increase that period daily. After six months, the wrinkles and grey hairs are not seen. He who practises it daily, even for two hours, conquers death. It increases the gastric fire, so, one who practises it, should eat more food otherwise it will burn him at once. The HP suggests that this exercise should be learnt from the *Guru's* instruction, because there are *surya* and the *chandra* above the navel and below the palate respectively.

9. The Vajroli

For the practise of the *vajroli,* two things are necessary which are difficult to get for the ordinary people – milk and a woman behaving as desired.

By practising to draw in *bindu,* discharged during cohabitation, one obtains success in the practice of *Vajroli.* By means of pipe, one should blow air slowly into the passage in the male organ: The *bindu* that is about to fall into the genital organ of a woman should be drawn up by practice of the *vajroli-mudra.* If already fallen, he should draw up his own semen *(bindu)* and preserve it.

The *yogi,* who can protect his *bindu,* thus, overcomes death because death comes by discharging *bindu* and life is prolonged by its preservation. By preserving the *bindu,* the body of the yogi emits a pleasing smell. There is no fear of death, so long as the *bindu* is well-established in the body. The *bindu* is under the control of the mind and life is dependent on the *bindu.* Hence mind and *bindu* should be protected by all means. If one lives wayward life without observing any rules of *yoga,* by performing *vajroli,* he deserves success and is a *yogi.*

Now, according to the HP, *Sahajoli* and *Amaroli* are only the different kinds of *vajroli.* Hence, being together these there, it is described as one *mudra* among 10.

(*a*) **Sahajoli:** Being free from the exercise of *vajroli,* man and woman should rub the ashes on their bodies, the ashes should be made from burnt up cowdung mixed with water. This is called *sahajoli.* It gives liberation. It is achieved by courageous wise men who are free from sloth.

(*b*) **Amaroli:** It is the drinking of the mid-stream of *'Amari'* leaving the first flow, as it is the mixture of too much bile and the last flow which is usuless.

This is the doctrine of the sect of the *kapalikas.* He who drinks *Amari,* snuffs it daily and practises *vajroli,* is called practising *Amaroli.* Moreover, it is stated that the *bindu* discharged in the practice of *vajroli* should be mixed with ashes, and rubbing it on the best parts of the body, gives divine sight.

10. The Sakticalana

Place and form: It means to awaken the *sakti (kundalini).* Various epithets are there in the HP-*Kulilangi, Kundalini, Bhujangi, Sakti, Isvari, Kundali, Arundhati, Paramesvari Balaranda, Tapasvini.*

Kundali is of a bent shape and has been described to be like a serpent.

As a door is opened with a key so the yogi opens the door of Liberation by rousing *kundalini* by means of *Hathayoga.* This sleeping *kundalini* sleeping covers the hole of the passage by which one can go the seat of *Brahma,* free from pains. She sleeps on the knot *(Kanda)* for giving liberation to yogis and bondage to the ignorant.

This knot *(Kanda)* is above the anus, twelve fingers long and four fingers in extent, it is soft and white and appears as if a folded cloth.

Ida is called goddess *Gange, pingala* is goddess *yamuna* in the middle of these two there is *kundalini,* it should be caught hold by force, to get the highest position.

The sleeping serpent, should be awakened by catching hold of her tail. Then, the *Sakti,* leaving her sleep, rises up with force, she should be caught and moved daily, morning and evening, for 1.5 hours, by filling with air through *pingala* by the *paridhana* method. The commentator adds that the process of *paridhana* should be learnt from a *guru.* The process is the movement of the abdominal muscle from left to right and right to left in a spiral.

Sitting in the *vajrasana,* holding firmly, with the hands, the feet near the ankles, one should put pressure on the *kanda.* Then, having caused the *kundalini* to move, one should perform the *Bhastrika kumbhaka* the *kundalini* awakes. By contracting the navel (*surya* near the navel) a yogi should cause *kundalini* to move. There is no fear for him, even if he has entered the mouth of death. By moving this, for two *muhurtas,* it is drawn up a little by entering the *susumna.* By this process, *kundalini* certainly leaves the mouth of the *susumna.* Therefore *prana* goes naturally through the *susumna,* so this sleeping *kundalini* should always be moved so that the *yogi* gets rid of diseases.

The *yogi* who has been able to move the *sakti,* deserves success, and conquers death playfully.

Observing continence *(brahmacharya)* being temperance in food, a *yogi* gets success within 40 days by practice with *kundalini.* If plenty of *Bhastrika* should be performed after moving the *kundalini,* he has no fear from death. This practice of *kundalini* is the only way washing away the impurities of 72,000 *nadis.*

By steady practice of postures, breath-control and *mudras,* the middle *nadi,* becomes straight. All these practices relating to the air should be performed with concentrated mind, a wisemen should not allow his mind to wander away. He is really the *Guru* and to be considered as *Isvara* in human form who teaches the *mudras* as handed down from *guru* to *guru.* Engaging in practice, by putting faith in his words, one gets the *siddhis* of *Anima* etc. as also evades death.

Samadhi

The whole IV *upadesa* describes about the *Samadhi* as a means for obtaining *Brahmananda,* and destroying death. *Rajayoga, Samadhi Unmani, Manonmani, Amarava, Laya, Tattva, Sunya Asunda, Purama pada Amanaska Advaita, Niralamba, Niranjana, Jivanamukti, Sahaja, Turya* are all synonymous.

Necessity of a *Guru:* By instructions from a *guru* alone, knowledge *mukti* and *siddhis* can be learnt. As indifference to worldly enjoyments, the knowledge of Realities, and the condition of *Samadhi* is very difficult to obtain without the favour of a true *guru.*

The *Susumna*

After awakening *Sakti* and renouncing all actions, the *Yogi* attains the condition of *Samadhi,* without any effort. When the *prana* flows in the *susumna* and the mind has entered *unya yogi* becomes free from the effects of *karmas.* So *Amaroli, Vajroli* and *Sahajoli* are accomplished when the mind becomes calm and *prana* has entered the middle one. *i.e.,* the *susumna;* because so long as the *prana* flows through *Ida* and *pingala* and the mind has not left its functions, knowledge can not be possible, no one can get liberation. Aways living in a good locality and having known the secret of the susumna making the air move in it, the *yogi* should restrain the vayu in the *Brahmarandhra.* Then death can be conquered by him.

Among 72,000 openings of *nadis,* only the *Susumna* is the important. It has *sambhavi sakti.* The sun and the moon create Time in the form of day and night. The *prana* moves in the *Ida* (moon) for about an hour, then in the *pingala* (sun). So two hours form a day and night for the yogin. The ordinary day consists of twelve such days when the *prana* leaves remains in the *susumna,* there is no time, so *susumna* is said to consume time. Hence, the *vayu* should be made to enter the *susumna* without restraint, after practising the control of breathig and the awakening *kundalini* by the gastric fire. Thus, the *prana,* flowing through the *Susumna,* brings about the *manonmani* state.

The Relation between *Prana* and *Mana*

It is explained in the HP that by controlling the breathing, the activities of the mind have been controlled, and conversely by controlling the activities of the mind, the breathing has been controlled, There are two causes of the activities of the mind (1) Desires *(vasana)* and (2) the respiration *(prana),* of which by destroying one, the other is destroyed. When the mind becomes absorbed, the breathing is lessened, and when the *prana* is restrained, the mind becomes absorbed. Both the mind and the breath are united together like milk and water and both are equal in their activities. Mind begins its activities where there is the breath. By the suspension of the one, there comes the suspension of the other, and by the operation of the one, there brings about that of the other. When they are present, the sense organs remain engages in their proper functions, and when they become latent, there is liberation. Having compared both the mind and the breath with mercury, it is stated that everything is possible in this world by making the mind and mercury steady and when mercury and breathing are made steady they destroy diseases and the death, himself comes to life by their means.

When the mind becomes steady and calm, the breathing is calmed hence there is the preservation of *Bindu*. Mind is the master of the senses, the breath is the master of the mind, the breath depends on the *Laya* which depends on the *Nada*. And this Absorption *(laya)* is called Liberation. Thus, when the mind becomes absorbed, a sort of ecstacy is experienced.

Dissolution *(Laya)*

Laya is simply the forgetting of the objects of senses when the desires *(vasana)* do not rise into existence again. When all thoughts and activities are destroyed, the *laya* stage is produced, the description of which is beyond the power of speech. By the suspension of respiration and the annihilation of the enjoyments of the senses, when the mind becomes devoid of all the activities and remains changeless, the *yogi* attains the *Laya* stage.

Sambhavi Mudra

The HP praises this *mudra* by saying that the *vedas* and the *sastras* are like ordinary public woman. *Sambhavi mudra* is the one which secluded like a respectable lady. Introspecting inwardly, and keeping the sight directed to the external objects without blinking eyes, is called the *sambhavi mudra*. It is explained thus when the *yogi* remains inwardly attentive to the *Brahman,* keeping the mind and *prana* absorbed and the sight steady as if seeing everything while, in reality, seeing nothing outside-that is known as the *sambhavi mudra*. It should be learnt by the favour of a *guru*. Whatever, wonderful, *sunya* or *Asunya* is perceived, it should be regarded as the manifestation of that great *sambhu (Jiva)*.

Both, the *Sambhavi* and the *Khechari Mudras* cause happiness for the mind becomes absorbed in the *Chitta-sukha Rupa-atman* which is void. Both are different because of their seats *i.e.,* being the heart, the seat of the *sambhavi* and the space between the eyebrows that of the *khechari*.

The *Unmani*

Fix the gaze on the light, seen on the tip of the nose and raise the eyebrows a little, with the mind contemplating inwardly thinking of *Brahma,* but apparently looking outside. This creates the *unmani* state at once. It is the *Taraka i.e.,* enables on to cross the ocean of existence.

With steady and calm mind and half-closed eyes, fixed on the tip of the nose, stopping the *Ida* and the *pingala,* without blinking, he who sees the light which is the seed, the entire brilliant, great *tatvam,* approaches to the great object *i.e., parama pada*. Thus, one should meditate on the *Atma (linga)* neither in the day nor in the night (when *Ida* and *pinlgala* is working) but should always contemplate after restraining both.

The *Khechari*

When the air has ceased to move in the right and the left nostrils, and has begun to flow in the *susumna, khechari mudra* is accomplished there. The *prana* being motionless there, the *khechari mudra* can truely became steady there. It is perfomed in the supportless space between the *Ida* and the *pingala* and called *vyomachakra* thus, this is called *khechari*.

The *Khechari* which causes the stream to flow from the *chandra* is beloved of *Shiva*. The incomparable divine *Susumna* should be closed by the tongue drawn back. It can be closed from the front also, then surely it becomes the *khechari*. By practice, this *khechari* leads to *Unmani*. The mind becomes absorbed between the eyebrows which is the seat of *Shiva*. This condition is known as *Turya;* death has no access there.

This *mudra* should be practised till there is *yoga-nidra-(Samadhi)* because having induced *yoga-nidra* one can not fall a victim to death. Freeing the mind from all thoughts and thinking of nothing, one should sit firmly like a pot in the space. As the air, in and out of the body, remains unmoved, so the breath with mind becomes steady in its place *i.e.,* in the *Brahmarandhra*. By practising thus night and day, the breathing is brought under control and as the practice increases, the mind becomes calm and steady. By rubbing the body over with the nectar exuding from the moon, from head to foot, one gets great strength and energy.

End of Khechari

Placing the mind into the power *(Kundalini)* getting the latter into the mind, by looking upon the intellect with mind, the *paramapada* should be attained.

Keeping the *atma* inside the *kha (Brahma)* and placing *Brahma* inside the *atma,* he should made everything pervading *kha i.e., Brahma,* and should not think else. One should become void in and void out and void like a pot in the space. Full in and full outside, like a jar in the ocean, he should be neither of his inside nor of outside world. Leaving all thoughts, he should think of nothing.

Here, the state of the *khechari mudra* is mentioned as a means of attaining *Samadhi i.e.,* the *Unmami* state, though this *mudra* is described before among 10 *mudras.*

The Practice of *Anahata Nada*

This practice mentioned here is propounded by *Goraksa Natha.* This is for those people who are unable to understand the principle of knowledge. The HP believes this practice as the chief one. *Adinatha* propounded 1.1/4 crore methods of trance which are extant.

Process: Sitting in *Muktasana* with the *sambhavi mudra,* the *yogi* should hear the sound inside his right ear with concentreted mind. Having closed the ears, the eyes, the nose and the mouth one hears the clear sound in the passage of the *susumna* which has been cleansed of all its impurities.

In all the *forms of yogas,* there are four states—

1. The preliminary state (The *Arambhavastha*): When the *Brahmagranthi* in the heart is pierced through by *Pranayama,* a sort of happiness is experienced in the heart and the *anahata* sound like various tinkling sounds of ornaments are heard. In this state, a *yogi's* body becomes divine, glowing, healthy and emits a divine smell. The heart become void.
2. The state of jar (The *Ghatavastha*): The airs are united into one and begin moving in the middle *i.e.,* the *susumṇa.* The posture of a *yogi* becomes firm and he becomes wise like a God. By this means, the *Vishnu granthi* in the throat is pierced which is indicated by highest pleasure experienced then the *Bheri* sound (like the beating of a kettle drum) is evolved in the throat.
3. The known state (The *parichayavastha*): The sound of the drum is known to arise in the *Sunya* between the eyebrows. Then the *Nada* goes to the *Mahasunya,* the home of all the *Siddhis.* Conquering the pleasures of the mind, ecstacy *(Sahajananda)* is spontaneously produced which is devoid of evils, pains, old age, disease, hunger and sleep.
4. The Consumate State (The *Nispatti avastha*): When the Rudra granthi is pierced and the air enters the seat of the Lord *i.e.,* the space between the eyebrows the perfect sound like that of a flute is produced.

Thus, the union of the mind and sound is called *Rajayoga* (*i.e., Samadhi*). Consequently the real yogi becomes the creator and the destroyer of the universe, like God. The perpetual happiness resulting from absorption, is obtained by means of *Rajayog.* Without knowing the *Rajayoga,* only the practice of the *Hathayogas* wastes the energy of a person fruitlessly.

The contemplation on the space between the eyebrows is best for accomplishing the *unmani* state, it is very easy method for obtaining perfection in the *Raja yoga.* This absorption *(Laya)* produced by *nada* gives experience.

The yogi who has gained success in *Samadhi* by means of attention to the *Nada* (*Nadanu-samdhana*), becomes happy which is beyound description.

The *Nadanusamdhana*

The contemplative man, having closed his ears with his fingers, should hear the sound, till the mind becomes steady in it. By practising it, all other external sounds are stopped and the *yogi* becomes happy by overcoming all distraction within 15 days.

In the beginning, the sounds heard are of great variety and very loud, but by increasing the practice, they become more and more subtle. In the first stage, the sounds are surging, thundering like the beating of kettle drums and jingling ones. In the intermediate stage, they are like those produced by conch, mridang, bells etc. In the last stage, the sounds resemble those from tinklets, flute bee etc. These various sounds are heard as being produced in the body. Leaving the loudest, one should take up the subtle are, and leaving the subtle are, one should take up the loudest, by practising thus, the distracted mind does not wander elsewhere, wherever the mind attaches itself first, it becomes steady there, then it becomes absorbed in it. Just as a bee, drinking sweet juice, does not care for the smell of the flower, So the mind, absorbed in the *Nada* does not desire the objects of enjoyment.

The mind, like an elephant habituated to wander in the garden of enjoyments can be controlled by the sharp goad of *anahata nada*. Then, captivated in the snares of *nada*, the mind gives up all its activity, like a bird with clipped wings it becomes calm at once. Thus, *Nada* is the snare for catching the mind. When it is caught like a deer it can be killed also like it. A yogi should determine to practise constantly in the hearing of the *Nada* sounds.

The mind gets the *properties* of calcined mercury when deprived of its unsteadiness it is calcined. Combined with the sulphur of *Nada,* it raams like it, in the supportless *akasa i.e., Brahman.* The mind is like a serpent. Forgetting all its unsteadiness by hearing the *Nada,* it does not run away anywhere. The mind working with the *nada,* becomes latent alongwith it.

The knowable interpenetrates the *anahata* sound which is heard and the mind interpenetrates the knowable. The mind becomes absorbed in almigthy Lord, the seat of the all-pervading.

So long as the sounds continue, there is the idea of *akasa,* after disappearance of the sounds, it is called *para Brahma,* paramatman. Whatever is heard in the form of *Nada,* is the final state of the *Tattvas,* is the Paramesvara. Those desirous of the kingdom of yoga should take up the practice of hearing *Anahata Nada,* with concentrated mind and free from all cares.

All the methods of *Hatha* are meant for gaining success, in the *Rajayoga Tattva* is the seed, *Hatha* is the field, the non-attachment *(vairagya)* is the water: by the action of these three, the creeper *Unmani* thrives very rapidly. Sins are destroyed by practising with the Nada, the mind and the airs certainly become latent in the *Paramatman.*

GHERANDA SAMHITA

The *Gheranda Samhita i.e.,* the collections of Sage *Gheranda,* probably composed towards the end of the seventeenth century, is one of the best known works on *Hatha-Yoga.* The author of the GS followed the *Vaisnava Yoga* tradition of Bengal. This work has seven chapters with 317 verses in all, though some manuscripts have additional stanzas. It describes no fewer than 102 Yogic practices, including 21 hygienic techniques, 32 postures and 21 seals *(Mudras).* It speaks of seven subservients of Yoga and curiously treats breath-control *(Pranayama)* after sense-withdrawal *(Pratyahara).* Generally, the breath control is the fourth and the sense withdrawal, the fifth limb.

This Tantrik text, in the form of dialogue between the Sage *Gheranda* and an inquirer *Chandakapali,* teaches Yoga under seven heads or *(Sadhanas).* Hence, the system of Yoga described in GS is said to be *Saptasadhana* or *'Saptanga Yoga'* as distinguished from *Goraksa's 'Sadanga Yoga'* or *Patanjali's 'Astanga Yoga'.*

It is an important manual of Yogic practices, as it describes more than 100 Yogic practices of various nature.

- The first *Sadhana* gives direction for the purification of the body (inside & outside)
- The second *Sadhana* relates to Postures (*asana*)
- The third relates to *Mudras*
- The fourth relates to *Pratyahara*
- The fifth relates to *Pranayama*
- The sixth deals with *Dhyana*
- The seventh deals with *Samadhi.*

It widely differs from other texts on *Hathayoga* since the word *'Hatha'* is found in the form of *Ghatastha Yoga,* which can not find in any other treatises on Yoga. The word *'Ghata'* refers to the body and *Ghatastha Yoga* means Yoga based on the approach through the body.

Satkarmas

The *Satkarmas* or six purificatory practices is the first *Sadhana* by which the purification of the body is acquired. They are:

(*a*) *Dhauti*,
(*b*) *Basti*,
(*c*) *Neti*,
(*d*) *Laukiki*,
(*e*) *Trataka* and
(*f*) *Kapalabhati*.

Dhautis

Dhautis are of four kinds which clear away the impurities of the body.

Antardhauti

Antardhauti is sub-divided into four parts:

1. *Vatasara-Dhauti:*

Method

- Having contracted the mouth like the beak of a crow,
- Drinking the air slowly,
- Filling the stomach slowly with it,
- Moving it therein,
- Then slowly force it out through the lower passage.

It is a very secret process which causes the purification of the body, destroys all diseases and increases the gastric-fire.

2. *Varisara-Dhauti:*

Method

- Filling the mouth with water down to the throat,
- Drinking it slowly, then moving it through the stomach,
- Forcing it downwards,
- One should expel it through the rectum.

This process purifies the body and by practising it with care, one gets a luminous body. It is said to be the highest *Dhauti.* He who practises it with ease, purifies his filthy body and turns it into a shining one.

3. *Agnisara-Dhauti*

Method

- To press the navel knot or intestines towards the spine for one hundred times is the fire process *i.e, Agnisara.*
- It gives success in the practice of Yoga, it cures all the diseases of the stomach and increases the internal fire. It should be kept very secret and it is hardly to be attained even by the gods, and by this alone, one certainly gets a luminous body.

4. *Bahiskrita-Dhauti:*

Method

- By crow-bill *mudra*, filling the stomach with air,
- Holding it there for one hour and a half,
- Then one should force it down towards the intestines.

5. *Praksalanam*

Method

- Standing in navel-deep water,
- Drawing out the *sakti nadi. i.e.,* long intestines,
- Washing the *nadi* with hand, so long as its filth is not all washed away.
- Washing it with care, one should draw it in again into the abdomen.

Simply by this *Dhauti,* one gets Godlike body. As long as a person has not the power of retaining the breath for an hour and a half, so long he can not achieve this grand *Bahiskrita Dhauti.*

Danta Dhauti

It is of five kinds:

1. **Purification of the teeth *(Danta-mula-Dhauti)* :** One should rub the teeth with catechu-powder or with pure earth, so long as dental impurities are not removed. It is an important process in the practice of Yoga for the Yogis. It should be done daily in the morning by the Yogis in order to preserve the teeth.

2. ***Jihva Sodhana***

   Method

   - Join together the three fingers viz. index, the middle and the ring finger,
   - Put them into the throat,
   - Rub well and clean the root of the tongue,
   - By washing it again throwout the phlegm,
   - Having thus washed it, rubbed it with butter, and milk it again and again,
   - Then holding the tip of the tongue with an iron instrument, pull it out slowly and slowly.

   One should do this daily with diligence before the rising and setting sun; thus the tongue becomes elongated.

3 & 4. **Purification of the two holes of the ear (*Karna Dhauti*):** One should Clean the two holes of the ears by the index and the ring fingers. By practising it daily, the mystical sounds are heard.

5. ***Kapala-randhra-Dhauti:*** One should rub with the thumb of the right hand the depression in the forehead near the bridge of the nose. By this practice, diseases arising from derangements of phlegmatic humorous are cured. The *nadis* become purified and clairvoyance is induced. It should be practised daily after awakening from sleep, after meals and in the evening.

Hrid-Dhauti

It means the purification of the heart which of three kinds:

1. ***Danda-Dhauti***

   Method

   - Take either a plaintain stalk or a stalk of termeric or a stalk of cane,
   - Thrust it slowly into the aesophagus,
   - Then draw it out slowly.

   By this process, all the phlegm, bile and other impurities are expelled, out of the mouth, and every kind of heart diseases are surely cured.

2. ***Vamana-Dhauti***

   Method

   - After meal, one should drink water full up to the throat,
   - Then looking for a short while upwards,
   - He should vomit it out.

   By daily practising it, disorders of phlegm and bile are cured.

3. ***Vastra-Dhauti:*** Having swallowed slowly a thin cloth, which is four-fingers wide, he should draw it out again. This process cures abdominal diseases, fever, enlarged spleen, leprosy and other skin diseases and disorders of phlegm and bile. Day by day, one gets health, strength and cheerfulness.

4. ***Mula-Sodhana :*** By the stalk of the root of turmeric or the middle finger, the rectum should be carefully cleansed with water over and over again. This destroys constipation, indigestion, dyspepsia and increases the beauty and vigour of the body and enkindles the sphere of the fire. The *Apana Vayu* does not flow freely so long as the rectum is not purified, therefore, one should practise it carefully.

Basti

It is the second purificatory practice among the six *i.e.,* Satkarmas. It is of two kinds:

(i) ***Jala Basti:*** It is done in water. Entering into water upto the navel and assuming the posture called *Utkatasana,* one should

contract and dilate the sphincter-muscle of the anus. This is called *Jala-Basti.* It cures urinary disorders *(Prameha),* disorders of digestion and that of the wind. The body becomes free from all diseases and becomes as beautiful as that of the God Cupid.

(ii) *Sthala-Basti*

Method

- Assuming the posture called *Paschimottanasana*
- Moving the intestines slowly downwards,
- Then contract and dilate the sphincter muscle of the anus with the *Aswinimudra.*

By this practice, constipation never occurs, it increases gastric fire and cures flatulence.

Neti Method

- Take a thin thread, measuring half a cubit,
- Insert it into the nostrils,
- Passing it through, pull it out by the mouth.

This is called *Neti Kriya,* by practising which, one obtains *Khechari Siddhi.* It destroys the disorders of phlegm and produces clairvoyance or clear sight.

Laukiki Yoga

With great force, to move the stomach and intestines from one side to the other, that is called *Laukiki Yoga.* This destroys all diseases and increases the bodily fire.

Trataka

Gazing steadily without winking at any small object until tears begin to flow, that is called *Trataka.* By practising it, *Sambhavi Siddhis* are obtained and certainly all diseases of the eye are destroyed and clairvoyance is induced.

Kapalabhati

It is of three kinds:

(i) *Vamakrama :* It is the practice of drawing the wind through the left nostril, expelling it through the right, drawing it again through the right and expelling it through the left. This inspiration-expiration must be done without any force, it destroys disorders of phlegm.

(ii) *Vyutkrama* : It is the practice of drawing the water through the nostrils, expelling it through the mouth slowly and slowly. It destroys the disorders of phlegm.

(iii) *Sitkrama :* It is the practice of sucking the water through the mouth and expelling it through the nostrils. By this practice, one becomes like the God Cupid; old age never comes to him and decrepitude never disfigures him. The body becomes healthy, elastic and disorders of phlegm are destroyed:

It is found that the GS is, perhaps, the only text which elaborates the practices of *Dhauti* and the like. The 21 *Kriyas* have been described in this text under *Satkarmas.*

Dhauti	13
Bastis	02
Neti	01
Trataka	01
Nauli	01
Kapalabhatis	03
	21 *Kriyas*

Having purified his body by the practice of *Satkarmas,* one becomes free from diseases. Thus, the body becomes a fit receptacle for the attainment of Liberation.

Asanas

The thirty-two asanas are explained among number of *asanas,* which are good for health and for peace of mind, though they are not of equal efficacy or importance.

Asanas in GS are:

1. The Perfect Posture (*Siddhasana*)

Technique:

- Having subdued one's passions, one should place one's heel at the anal aperture,

- He should keep the other heel on the root of the generative organ,
- Afterwards, he should affix his chin upon the chest,
- Being quiet and straight, gaze at the spot between the two eye-brows.

This is called *Siddhasana* which leads to emancipation.

2. The Lotus Posture (*Padmasana*)

Technique:

- Place the right foot on the left thigh, similarly the left one on the right thigh,
- Cross the hands behind the back, firmly hold the great toes of feet so crossed.
- Place the chin on the chest and fix the gaze on the tip of the nose.

According to the GS, this posture destroys all diseases.

3. The Gentle Posture (*Bhadrasana*)

Technique:

- Place the heels crosswise under the testes attentively,
- Cross the hands behind the back and take hold of the toes of the feet,
- Fix the gaze on the tip of the nose having adopted the *Jalandhara Mudra.*

According to the GS, it destroys all sorts of diseases.

4. The Free Posture (*Muktasana*)

Technique:

- Place the left heel at the root of the organ of generation and the right heel above that,
- Keep the head and the neck straight with the body.

This posture gives *Siddhi* according to the GS.

5. The Adamant Posture (The *Vajrasana*)

Technique:

- Make the thighs tight like adamant, and
- Place the legs by the two sides of the anus.

This is the *Vajrasana* which gives psychic powers to the Yogi.

6. The Prosperous Posture (The *Svastikasana*)

Technique:

- Drawing the legs and thighs together,
- Placing the feet, underneath them,
- Keeping the body in its easy condition and sitting straight.

This will constitute the *Svastikasana.*

7. The Lion Posture (The *Simhasana*)

Technique:

- Place the two heels under the scrotum contrariwise,
- Keep open the mouth,
- Practice the *Jalandhara Mudra,* and
- Fix the gaze on the tip of the nose.

8. The Cow-mouth Posture (The *Gomukhasana*)

Technique:

- Place the two feet on the ground,
- Place the heels contrariwise under the buttocks,
- Keep the body steady and mouth raised,
- Sit equably.

9. The Heroic Posture (The Virasana)

Technique:

- Place one leg on the other thigh,
- Turn backwards the other foot.

10. The Bow Posture (The *Dhanurasana*)

Technique:

- Spread the legs on the ground, straight like a stick,
- Catch hold of the feet *i.e.*, the toes, with the hands,
- Make the body bent like a bow.

11. The *Paschimottanasana*

Technique:

- Spread the two legs on the ground, stiff like a stick,

- Place the forehead on the two knees,
- Catch with the hands the toes.

12. The Peacock Posture (The *Mayurasana*)

Technique:

- Place the palms of the two hands on the ground,
- Place the umbilical region on the two elbows,
- Stand upon the hands, being raised the legs in the air.

According to the GS, it destroys the effects of unwholesome food, it produces heat in the stomach, it destroys the effect of deadly poison, it easily cures diseases like *Gulma* and fever.

13. The Cock Posture (The *Kukkutasana*)

Technique:

- Sit on the ground,
- Cross the legs in the *Padmasana*,
- Thrust down the hands between the thighs and the knees,
- Stand on hands, supporting the body on the elbows.

14. The Tortoise Posture (The *Kurmasana*)

Technique:

- Place the heels contrariwise under the scrotum,
- Stiffen the head, neck and body.

15. The *Uttanakurmasana*

Technique:

- Assume the Cock Posture,
- Catch hold of the neck with the hands and stand stretched like a tortoise.

16. The Yoga-posture (The *Yogasana*)

Technique:

- Turn the feet upwards,
- Place them on the knees,
- Place the hands on the ground with the palms turned upwards,
- Inspire and fix the gaze on the tip of the nose.

It is assumed by the *Yogis* when practising Yoga.

Remaining 16 *asanas* as follow:

17. The Corpse Posture (The *Mritasana*)

18. The Hidden Posture (The *Guptasana*)

19. The Fish Posture (The *Matsyasana*)

20. The *Matsyendrasana*

21. The *Goraksasana*

22. The Hazardous Postures (The *Utkatasana*)

23. The Dangerous Posture (The *Sankatasana*)

24. The Frog Posture (The *Mandukasana*)

25. The *Uttanamandukasana*

26. The Tree Posture (The *Vriksasana*)

27. The Eagle Posture (The *Garudasana*)

28. The Bull-Posture (The *Vrisasana*)

29. The Locust Posture (The *Salabhasana*)

30. The Dolphin Posture (The *Makarasana*)

31. The Camel Posture (The *Ustrasana*)

32. The Serpent-Goddess (*Kundalini* Force) Posture (The *Bhujangasana*)

Mudras

The GS describes the group of 25 *mudras* as the third *Sadhana* of the *Ghatastha Yoga.* It marks a transition from the physical to the psychological.

1. The *Mahamudra*

Technique:

- Press carefully the anus by the left heel,
- Stretch the right leg and take hold of the great toe by the hand,
- Contract the throat and fix the gaze between the eye-brows.

Benefit: According to the GS, this *Mudra* cures consumption, the obstruction of the bowels, the enlargement of the spleen, indigestion and fever. Infact, it cures all diseases.

2. **The *Nabho Mudra***

Technique: Keep the tongue turned upwards (*Urdhvajihvah*), in whatever business a Yogi may be engaged, wherever, he may be; and restrain the breath. It destroys all diseases of the *Yogi.*

This *mudra* is different from the *Khechari,* since *Urdhvajihva* does not mean that the tongue is to be forced into the nasal opening but simply to be turned upwards towards the palate. It may be considered that it is the preliminary exercise for *Khechari.*

3. **The Mahavedha**

Technique: To perform the *Mahavedha,* the practice of *Mahabandha* is necessary.

Technique:

- Close the anal orifice by the left heel,
- Press that heel with the right foot carefully,
- Move slowly and slowly the muscles of the rectum,
- Slowly contract the muscles of the *Yoni,*
- Restrain the breath by *Jalandhara bandha.*

This is called *Mahabandha.*

After sitting in *Mahabandha* posture, mentioned above, restrain breath by *Uddana Kumbhaka.*

This is known as *Mahavedha* - the giver of success to the *Yogies.*

Benefits : It is mentioned, in the GS, that the *Yogi* who practises *Mahabandha* accompanied with *Mahavedha* is the best for the *yogies.* There is no fear of death and decay for the yogin.

4. **The *Khechari Mudra***

The GS states the preliminary action *i.e.*, to lengthen the tongue, to perform the *Khechari Mudra.*

Technique

- The lower tendon of the tongue is cut down so that the tongue moves constantly,
- Rub it with fresh butter and draw it out with an iron instrument,
- By such practice, the tongue becomes long; when it reaches the space between the two eye-brows; the *Khechari* is accompanied.
- Practise, turning the tongue upwards and backwards so as to touch the palate, till at length it reaches the holes of the nostrils opening into the mouth.
- Close the holes with the tongue, stopping inspiration, and fix the gaze on the space between the two eye-brows.

This is called *khechari.*

Benefits : The GS mentions thus:

- There is neither fainting, nor hunger, nor thirst, nor laziness, neither diseases, nor decay, nor death.
- The body becomes divine, and beautiful, it can not be burnt by fire, nor dried up by the air, nor wetted by water, nor bitten by snakes.
- *Samadhi* is verily attained.
- The tongue, touching the holes, obtains various juices, day by day the man experiences the new sensations— (*a*) he experiences a saltish taste, (*b*) the taste of alkaline, (*c*) that of bitter, (*d*) that of astringent, (*e*) then that of butter, then ghee, milk, curd, whey, honey, palm juice and lastly the taste of nectar.

5. **The *Viparitakarni*:** According to the GS the technique to perform this *mudra* is as follows:

- Placing the head on the ground with hands spread,
- Raising the legs up, one remains steady; by which the sun dwelling at the root of the navel is brought upward and the moon dwelling at the root of the palate is carried downward.

This is called *Viparitakarani.*

By the constant practice of this *mudra,* decay and death are destroyed and one becomes an adept, one does not perish even at *Pralaya.*

6. The *Yonimudra*

According to the GS, the process of this *mudra* is thus:

- Sitting in *Siddhasana,* one closes the two ears with the two thumbs, the eyes with the index fingers, the nostrils with the middle fingers, the lips with the fore fingers and the little fingers.
- Draw in the *Prana Vayu* by *Kaki mudra* and join it with the *Apana Vayu.*
- Contemplating the six *chakras* in their order, the wise men should awaken the sleeping serpent (Goddess *Kundalini*), by repeating the *mantra 'Hun'* and *'Hamsa'*.
- Raising the *Kundalini* with the *Jiva,* place them at the thousand petalled lotus.
- Being himself full of *Shakti* and being joined with the great *Shiva,* one should think of the various pleasures and enjoyments.
- One should contemplate on the union of *Shiva* and *Shakti* in this world.
- He realises that he is *Brahman* being himself Blissful.

This is known as *Yonimudra,* a great secret and difficult to be attained even by *Devas;* by obtaining perfection in its practice, one enters verily into *Samadhi.*

Benefits:

- One is never polluted by the sins of killing a *Brahman,* killing a foetus, drinking liquor, or polluing the bed of the preceptor.
- All the moral sins and the venal sins are completely destroyed by the practice of this *mudra.*

7. *Vajronimudra*

Technique : Placing the palms on the ground, raise the legs in the air upward and the head not touching the earth. This awakes the *Shakti* and causes long life.

Benefits:

- It causes emancipation and gives perfection to the yogis.
- The *Bindu-Siddhi* (retention of seed) is obtained.
- Though immersed in manifold pleasures, if he practises this *mudra,* he attains verily all perfections.

The text of GS, edited by *Digambarji* and M.L. Gharote, this *mudra* is named *Vajroli.*

8. *Sakticalani Mudra*

It is explained thus in the GS : Self *i.e.*, the *Atmashakti,* having three coils and a half in the form of serpent, sleeps in the *Muladhara.* So long as she is asleep in the body, the knowledge does not arise.

Technique:

- Encircling the loins with a piece of cloth, one should practise it in a secret room. The cloth should be long, four finger (3 inches) wide, soft, white and of a fine texture.
- Join the cloth with the string *(kati-sutra)*
- Rub the body with ashes.
- Sitting in *Siddhasana*, drawing the *Pranavayu* with the nostrils, forcibly join it with the *Apana.*
- Contract the rectum slowly by the *Ashvini mudra* so long as the *Vayu* does not enter the *Susumna.*
- Having restrained the breath by *Kumbhaka,* the serpent power, feeling suffocated, awakes and rises upwards to the *Brahmarandhra.*

Benefits : It destroys decay and death, so the yogi, desirous of perfection, should be practise it. One acquires adeptship, attains *Vigrahasiddhi* and all his diseases are cured. It is informed that without this *mudra*, the *yonimudra* is not perfected *i.e,* at first, one should practise this, then the *yonimudra* should be learnt. It should be kept carefully concealed.

9. *Tadagi Mudra*

Technique: Sitting in *Paschimottana*-posture, one makes stomach like a tank. This *Mudra* destroys decay and death.

10. The *Manduki Mudra*

Technique : Closing the mouth, one moves the tip of the tongue towards palate and tastes slowly the nectar. This is Frog *Mudra.*

Benefits :

- The body never sickens or becomes old.
- It retains perpetual youth.
- The practitioner's hair never grows white.

11. *Sambhavi Mudra*

Technique: Fixing the gaze between the two eye-brows, one beholds the self-existent. It is secret in all the *Tantra.*

Importance: The *Vedas,* the scriptures, the *Puranas* are like public women but this *Sambhavi* should be guarded as if it were a lady of a respectable family. The knower of this *mudra* is like the *Adinatha,* he is *Narayana* and he is *Brahma.*

12. The *Ashvini Mudra*

Technique : Contract and dilate the anal aperture again and again, this practice is known as *Ashvini Mudra.*

Benefits:

- It awakens the *Shakti* (*Kundalini*).
- It destroys all diseases of the rectum.
- It gives strength and vigours, and
- It prevents premature death.

13. The *Pasini Mudra*

Technique:

- Throw the two legs on the neck towards the back,
- Hold them strongly together like a noose (Pasha).

Benefits:

- It awakens the *Kundalini Shakti.*
- It gives strength and nourishment.
- Those who wants to attain achievements (*Siddhikanksibhih*) practise it with care.

14. The *Kaki Mudra*

Technique:

- Contract the lips like the beak of a crow,
- Drink (draw in) the air slowly and slowly.

This *Kaki Mudra,* should be kept secret in all *Tantras.*

Benefits :

- It destroys all diseases.
- One becomes free from diseases like a crow.

It is used in the *Sitali Kumbhaka* and *Sunmukhimudra,* mentioned in the YU.

15. The *Matangini Mudra*

Technique:

- Stand in neck-deep water,
- Draw in the water through the nostrils and throw it out by the mouth,
- Then draw in the water through the mouth and expel it through the nostrils,
- One should repeat this again and again.

This *mudra* should practise with fixed attention in a solitary place, free from human intrusion.

Benefits:

- It destroys decay and death.
- One becomes strong like elephant. The *yogi* enjoys great pleasure, hence this *mudra* should be practised with great care.

16. The *Bhujangini Mudra*

Technique:

- Extend the neck a little forward,
- Draw in the air through the aesophagus.

Benefits:

- It destroys decay and death,

- It quickly destroys all stomach diseases, especially indigestion, dyspepsia etc.

Further, the five *Dharanas*, generally known as the sixth subservients among well-known eight, are included and explained under the group of *mudras*, they are in sequence:

17. *Parthivi*,
18. *Ambhasi*,
19. *Agneyi*,
20. *Vayavi* and
21. *Akasidharana*.

These five concentrations (*dharana*) upon the material elements involve focussing the life force and the mind on each respective elements for five *ghatikas* while imaging the various symbolic forms associated with each presiding deity of each element, its seed mantra *(bija)* and so on. The inclusion of these concentration practices under the heading of *mudra* is curious but it illustrates the close relationship between physical practice and mental focus.

Benefits :

1. By the practice of the *Parthivi dharana mudra,* one conquers the Earth, no earthy elements can injure him. It causes steadiness. One becomes like the conqueror of death. As an adept he walks over this earth.
2. The *Ambhasi dharana mudra* is the destroyer of all sorrow. Water can not injure the practitioner. He never meets death even in the deepest water. This great *mudra* should be kept carefully concealed; by revealing it success is lost.
3. The *Agneyi dharana mudra* is the destroyer of the fear of dreadful death. Fire cannot injure the practitioner.
4. The *Vayavi dharana mudra* destroys decay and death. The practitioner never killed by any aerial disturbances. He walks in the air; one should not be taught to the wicked person of those devoid of faith, otherwise success is lost.
5. The *Akashi dharana mudra* opens the gates of emancipation. Death does not approach him, nor does he perish at *pralaya.* One becomes a real yogi.

These above mentioned five *dharana-mudras* are described in brief in the GS (III. 68-81), with their benefits.

The Five *Dharana Mudra*

Mudra	***Tattva***	***Colour***	***Letter (bya)***	***Form***	***Deity***	***Place***	***Period of Concentration***
1. *Parthivi*	Earth	Yellow	*Lakara*	Four-sided form	*Brahma*	The heart	Five *Ghatikas*
2. *Ambasi*	Water	White like a conch or the moon	*Va Kara*	Circular like the moon	*Vishnu*	The heart	Five *Ghatikas*
3. *Agneyi*	Fire	Red like Indragop insect	*Ra Kara*	Triangular	*Rudra*	The Navel	Five *Ghatikas*
4. *Vayavi*	Air	Black like collinum	*Ya Kara*	-	*Ishvara*	-	Five *Ghatikas*
5. *Akashi*	Ether	Pure Sea water	*Ha Kara*	-	*Sadashiva*	-	Five *Ghatikas*

More benefits of *mudras:*

1. *Mudrds* destroy decay and death.
2. They give happiness and emancipation.
3. They destroy all diseases.
4. They increase the gastric fire of the practitioner.
5. Cough, *asthma*, enlargement of spleen, leprosy, being diseases of twenty sorts, are verily destroyed by the practice of these *Mudras.*
6. In short, there is nothing in this world like the *mudras* for giving quick success.

Moreover, *mudras* should not be taught indiscriminately, nor to a wicked person, nor to a devoid of faith. This should be preserved secret with great care; it is difficult to be attained even by the *Devas*. These *mudras* should be taught to a guileless, calm and peace-minded person, who is devoted to his Teacher and comes of good family.

Summing up, according to the GS, there are 25 mudras. Since the list contains what are called *Bandhas* as also the five kinds of *Dharanas.* The nature of these *mudras* is more physiological at one end and more psychological at the other. By the inclusion of *Panchadharana, mudras,* the third *Sadhana* of *Ghatastha Yoga,* mark a transition from the physical to the psychological. Alongwith the qualities of *mudras* leading to destroying of diseases and bestowing of *siddhis,* in case of some *mudras*, emancipation *(mukti)* is added, which indicates that the aim is never lost sight of.

Bandha

The GS speaks of the four types of *Bandha.* They are mentioned at follows:

1. The Uddiyana Bandha

In the practice of this *bandha,* one contracts the bowels equably above and below the navel towards the back so that the abdominal viscera may touch the back. The Great bird *i.e.,* breath is instantly forced up into the *Susumna* and flies *(Uddiyate)* constantly therein only.

Benefits: The practitioner conquers death without ceasing, and the complete practice makes emancipation easy.

In the GS, there is no mention about the stage of respiration. Traditionally, when the practice is taken independently, it is done under exhalatory condition. When accompanied with *pranayama,* it is practised under inhalatory conditions.

2. The Jalandhara Bandha

Contracting the throat, to place the chin on the chest, is called *Jalandhara bandha,* the success-giving and well-tried *bandha.*

Benefits: By this *bandha,* the sixteen *adharas* are closed. It destroys death. Practising it for six months, one becomes an adept without doubt.

3. The Mulabandha

According to the GS, the process is thus -

- Press the region between the anus and the scrotum, with the heel of the left foot and contract the rectum,
- Carefully press the intestines near the navel on the spine,
- Put the right heel on the organ of generation.

Benefits : It destroys decay, the *Vayu* is controlled undoubtedly. By practising it in secrecy one crosses the ocean of existence.

4. The Maha bandha

According to the GS, the process is as follows -

- Close the anal orifice *(payumulam)* by the left heel and press the heel with the right foot carefully.
- Move slowly and slowly the muscles of the rectum and slowly contract the muscles of the perineum *(Yoni) i.e.*, the space between anus and organ.
- Restrain breath by *Jalandhara.*

Benefits: It destroys decay and death and one accomplishes all his desires.

Summing up, In the GS both *dharana* and *bandha* are included under the group of *mudra* because both give the result, as an outcome of the practice, physiological and psychological benefit which is useful to *achieve* the *siddhis.*

Pratyahara

Pratyahara means sense-withdrawal the fourth *Sadhana* of *Ghatastha-Yoga,* consists in withdrawing attention from external, sensory objects. This practice is placed before breath control, which indicates that yogic breathing presupposes a great measure of mental discipline, according to the GS.

In *pratyahara,* one should bring the *Chitta* (thinking principle) under his control by withdrawing it wherever it wanders away, drawn by the various objects of sight. Secondly, one should withdraw his mind from praise or censure, good or bad speech and bring it under the control of the Self. Thirdly, one should withdraw the mind from sweet smell or bed smell by wherever odour the mind may be attracted; and should bring under the control of his self. Fourthly, one should withdraw it from sweet or acid tastes, from bitter or astringent tastes by whatever taste the mind may be attracted; one should bring under the control of his self.

Pranayama

The Breath-control *(Pranayama)* is the careful regulation of the life-force in its different forms. Before describing the various techniques of breath-control, sage *Gheranda* stresses the importance of place, proper environment, proper diet and purifying the veins *(nadis).*

(a) Place

One should erect a small hut, raising walls around it, at the place where food is easily and abundantly procurable, and there are no disturbance. This hut should be in a country whose king is just; in the centre of the enclosure, one should sink a well and dig a tank. The hut should be neither very high nor very low. It should be free from insects and be completely plastered over with cow-dung. One should practise *pranayama* in this hut, built and situated in such a hidden place.

The practice of yoga should not be attempted in a far off country from home, nor in a forest, nor in a capital city, nor in the midst of a crowd, otherwise one loses success. Because in a distant country, one loses faith; in a forest, one is without protection and in the midst of thick population, there is a danger of exposure, then the curious will trouble him. Therefore, one should avoid these three.

(b) Time

A beginner should commence the practice of yoga in spring *(vasanta)* and autumn *(sharada),* seasons for success is attained without much trouble. The practice of yoga should not be commenced in the remaining four seasons viz. Winter *(hemanta),* cold *(sisira),* hot *(grishma),* rainy *(varsha)* otherwise one will contract diseases.

It mentions the six seasons in their order, in the twelve month beginning with Chaitra and ending with *phalguna.* It states the experiencing of seasons—

Sanskrit Months	*Season*	*English*
1. *Magha* to *Vaisakha*	*Varshanubhava*	January to April
2. *Chaitra* to *Asadha*	*Grishmanubhava*	March to June
3. *Asadha* to *Ashvina*	*Varshanubhava*	June to September
4. *Bhadra* to *Agrahayana*	*Sharadanubhava*	August to November
5. *Kartika* to *Magha*	*Hemantanubhava*	October to January
6. *Agrahayana* to *Phalguna*	*Sisiranubhava*	November to February

(c) Food

As proper environment is necessary, sage *Gheranda* emphasises the importance of diet. One who practises yoga without moderation of diet, *(mitahara)* incurs various diseases and obtains no success. That is known as moderation of diet in which pure, sweet and cooling food should be eaten to fill half the stomach; eating sweet juices with pleasure, one should leave the other half of the stomach empty. Moreover, half the stomach should be filled with food, one quarter with water and one quarter should be kept empty for practising *pranayama.*

A fairly long list of fruits and vegetables recommended and prohibited, are given elaborately in the GS.

Recommended Food: Rice, barley, *Mudga* beans, *Masa* beans, gram, patol, jack fruit, *manakachu, Kakkola,* the jujube, the bonduc nut, cucumber, plantain, fig, the unripe plaintain the small plaintain, the plaintain stem and roots, brinjal, medicinal roots and fruits, Green fresh vegetables, black vegetables, the leaves of *patola,* the *vastuka-saka, hima-lohika saka.* Cardamom, jaiphal, cloves, aphrodisidac, the rose-apple, haritaki, palm dates. Thus, easily digestible, agreeable and cooling foods which nourish the humours of the body, may be eaten by a yogi, according to his desire.

Prohibited Food: One should discard bitter, acid, salt, pungent and roasted things, curd, whey, heavy vegetables, wine, palmnuts and over ripe jack-fruit, *kulattha, masur* beans, *pandu* fruit, pumpkins, vegetable stems, gourds, berries, katha-bel, *kanta-bilva* and *palasa, kadamba, jambira, bimbao, lukuoma,* onions, lotus *kamaranga piyala hinga, salmali, kemuka,* fresh butter, ghee, thickned milk, sugar, date-sugar, ripe, plantain, cocoanut, pomegranate, dates, *lavani* fruit, *amalaki* and everything containing acid juices. A yogi should avoid hard, sinful food, very hot, very stale, as well as very cooling or very much exciting food. A beginner should avoid much travelling, company of women and warming himself by fire. He should avoid early baths, fasting, anything given pain to the body, so also is prohibited to him eating only once a day or not eating at all; but he may remain without food for 3 hours. In the beginning before commencing *pranayama,* he should take a little milk and ghee daily (it is avoided too), and take his food twice daily, once at noon and once in the evening.

Thus, the GS discusses the *mitahara* giving it proper definition, which is easily understood by a *Hathayogin.*

(d) The purification of veins (Nadisuddhi)

The sage *Gheranda* also emphasises the importance of purifying the veins along which the life force flows. The *vayu* does not enter the veins so long as they are full of impurities, e.g. faeces etc. *pranayama* can not be accomplished and there is no knowledge of *Tattvas,* hence the veins should be purified, at first, then *pranayama* should be practised.

The purification process of veins is said to be of two kinds, which are technically known as *Samanu* and *nirmanu.*

1. ***Samanu* Process :** It is a meditative exercise by means of which the presiding deities of the various occult bodily centres *(chakras)* are invoked and 'installed' in the body. This is combined with the recitation of their respective *bija-mantras.* Sitting in the *Padmasana* and performing the adoration of the *Guru,* as taught by the Teacher, one should perform purification of *Nadis* for success in *Pranayama.*
   - (*i*) Contemplating on *Vayu-bija i.e., 'Yam',* full of energy and of a smoke-colour, one should draw in breath by the left nostril, repeating the *bija* sixteen times—this is *puraka.* He should restrain the breath for a period of sixty-four repetitions of the *Mantra*—this is *Kumbhaka.* Then he should expel the air by the right nostril slowly during a period occupied by repeating the *Mantras* thirty-two times.
   - (*ii*) Raising the fire from the root of the navel (the seat of *Agni-Tattva*), join the *Prithivi Tattva* with it, then one should contemplate on this mixed light.

Repeating sixteen times the *Agni-bija i.e.* 'Ram' one should draw in breath by the right nostril and retain it for the period of sixty-four repeatitions of the *Mantras,* he should expel it by the left nostril for a period of thirty-two repeatitions of the *Mantra.*

(*iii*) Fixing the gaze on the tip of the nose, contemplating the luminous reflection of the moon there, one should inhale through the left nostril, repeating the *Bija-Mantra* — *'Tham',* sixteen times. He should retain it by repeating that *Bija* sixty-four times, in the meanwhile imagine that the nectar flowing from the moon at the tip of the nose runs through all the vessels *nadis* of the body, and purifies them; thus, contemplating, one should expel the air by repeating thirty-two times the *Prithivi Bija i.e., 'lam'.*

By these three *pranayamas,* the *nadis* are purified. Then sitting firmly in a posture, one should begin regular *pranayama.* He should sit on a seat of Kusa-grass, or an antelope skin, or tiger skin or a blanket, or on earth, calmly and quietly, facing east or north. And, having purified the nadis, one should begin *pranayama.*

2. ***Nirmanu* Process :** The *Nirmanu* type of purification is the practice of cleansing the physical body *(dhauti),* as described under the *'Satkarmas'.*

Kinds of *Kumbhaka*

1. Sahita Kumbhaka

It is of two sorts — (*a*) The *Sagarbha Kumbhaka* is performed by the repetition of *Bija mantra,* and (*b*) The *Nirgarbha* is done without such repetition of *Bija mantra* and the period of *Puraka, Kumbhaka* and *Rechaka* may be extended from one to hundred *matras.* (The best is twenty *matras i.e., Puraka* 20 seconds, *Kumbhaka* 80 seconds and *Rechaka* 40 seconds. The sixteen *mantras* is middling *i.e.,* 16, 64, 32. The twelve mantras is the lowest *i.e.* 12, 48, 24. It means there is no regid rule for *mantras.*

Result: By practising the lowest *pranayama* for sometime, the body begins to perspire copiously, by the middle, the body begins to quiver, and by the best, one leaves the ground *i.e.,* there is levitation.

These three signs attend the success of three kinds of *pranayama.*

The Sagarbha pranayama : Sitting in *sukhasana,* facing east or north, one should contemplate on *Brahma,* full of *Rajas* quality of a blood-red colour in the form of the letter 'A'. The practitioner inhale by the left nostril, repeating *'Am'* sixteen times. After performing *Uddiyana bandha,* he should retain by repeating 'U' sixty-four times, contemplating on *Hari* of a black colour and of *Sattva* quality. Then he exhales the breath through the right nostril by repeating *'Ma'* thirty-two times, contemplating *Shiva* of a white colour and of *Tamasa* quality. In the same way, one should inhale through *Pingala i.e.,* right nostril, retain by *Kumbhaka* and exhale by left nostrils. Thus, one should practise, alternating the nostrils again and again. After the completion of inhalation, one should close both nostrils *i.e.,* the right one by the thumb and the left one by the ring-finger and little-finger, but never using index and middle-fingers.

Benefit:

1. The power of levitation *(Khechari Shakti)* is attained.
2. Diseases are cured.
3. The spiritual energy is awakened.
4. The calmness of mind and the exhalation of mental powers are obtained. The mind becomes full of bliss. And the practitioner of *pranayama* is happy.

2. The Surya-bheda Kumbhaka

Technique :

- Inspire, with all strength, the external air through the right nostril.
- Retain this air, with the great care, performing the *Jalandhara mudra. Kumbhaka* should be kept up so long as the perspiration does not burst out from the tips of the nails and the roots of the hair.

- Raise up, from the root of the navel, all ten *Vayus* separated by *Suryanadi*.
- Expire them by the left nostril slowly and with unbroken and continuous force.
- He should do this above mentioned practice again and again. In this process, the air is always inspired through the *Suryanadi* which takes the name *Suryabheda Kumbhaka.*

Benefits :

1. It destroys decay and death.
2. It awakens the *Kundalini Shakti* and increases the bodily fire.

3. The Ujjayi Kumbhaka

Technique:

- Closing the mouth, draw in the external air through both the nostrils.
- Pulling up the internal air from the lungs and throat, retain them in the mouth.
- Having washed the mouth *i.e.*, having expelled air through mouth, perform *Jalandhara.*
- Perform *Kumbhaka* with all his might and retain the air unhindered.

Benefits: One never attacked by phlegm diseases, nervous diseases, indigestion, dysentery, consumption, cough, fever and enlarged spleen. One should perform this to destroy decay and death.

The Vital Airs : While describing the ***Suryabheda Kumbhaka,*** the GS informs about the ten vital airs with their seats and functions.

1. The *Prana* moves always in the heart,
2. The *Apana* moves in the sphere of anus,
3. The *Samana* in the navel region,
4. The *Udana* moves in the throat,
5. The *Vyana* pervades the whole body.

These five principal vayus are known as *Pranadi.* They belong to the inner body. The following *Nagadi* five *vayus* belong to the outer body—

6. The *Naga* performs the function of eructation. It gives rise to consciousness.
7. The *Kurma* opens the eye-lids and causes vision.
8. The *Krkara* causes sneezing, hunger and thirst.
9. The *Devadatta* does yawning.
10. The *Dhananjaya* pervades the whole body, it does not leave the body even after death, by *Dhananjaya,* sound is produced.

4. The Sitali Kumbhaka

Technique:

- Draw in the air through the mouth, with the contracted lips and tongue thrown out.
- Fill the stomach only.
- Retain it there for a short time.
- Exhale it through both the nostrils.

This *Kumbhaka,* giver of bliss will destroy indigestion, phlegm and bilious disorders.

5. The Bhastrika Kumbhaka

Just as the bellows of the ironsmith constantly dilate and contract, similarly one should slowly draw in the air by both the nostrils and expand the stomach. Then throw it out quickly, making sound like bellows. Having thus inspired and expired quickly twenty times, one should perform *Kumbhaka.* Then one expels it by the previous method. Performing this *Kumbhaka* thrice, one will never suffer any disease and will be always healthy.

6. The Bhramari Kumbhaka

That is known as *Bhramari Kumbhaka* in which the yogi practises *Puraka* and *Kumbhaka,* closing the ears by the hands. This practice should be in a place where there are no sounds of any animals etc. at past midnight.

Benefits: He will hear various internal sounds in the right ear, during the daily practice of this *Kumbhaka.*

1. Like that of crickets,
2. The sound of a lute,

3. That of a thunder,
4. That of a drum,
5. That of a beetle,
6. That of bells,
7. Those of gongs of bell-metal, trumpets, kettle-drums, *mridanga,* military drums and *dundubhi* etc.

Lastly, the *Anahata* sound rising from the heart, is heard; of this sound, there is a resonance in which there is a light. In that light, the mind should be immersed. After the absorption, the mind reaches the Highest seat of *Vishnu.* By success in this *Kumbhaka,* one gets success in *Samadhi.*

7. The Murchha Kumbhaka

Having performed *Kumbhaka* with comfort, one withdraws the mind from all objects and fix it in the space between the two eye-brows. This causes fainting of the mind and gives happiness. Thus, by joining the *Manas* with *Atman,* the bliss of Yoga is certainly obtained.

8. The Kevali Kumbhaka

It is simply retention of the breath for as long as possible. It should be performed five to eight times a day, with one to sixty-four repetitions per session.

While describing this *Kumbhaka,* the GS informs about the *Ajapa Mantra,* the body of *Vayu* etc. — The breath of every person in entering, makes the sound of *'Sah'* and in coming out, that of *'ham'* – thus the sound becomes *'Soham'* means 'I am that' or *'Hamsa'*. Throughout a day and a night, there are twenty-one thousand and six hundred respirations, *i.e.,* 15 respirations per minute. The *Jiva* performs this *japa* unconsciously, but constantly. This is called *Ajapa Gayatri.*

According to the GS, this *Ajapa Japa* is performed in three places *i.e.*, in the *Muladhara* in the *Anahata* lotus and in the *Ajna* lotus.

The body of *Vayu* is ninety-six digits length as a standard. The ordinary length of the air-current is twelve digits, when expired; its length becomes sixteen digits while singing; it is twenty digits while eating; it is twenty four digits while walking; it is thirty digits while sleeping; it is thirty-six digits while copulation;— and while taking physical exercise, it is more than that. By decreasing the natural length of the expired current from twelve digits to less and less, there takes place increase of life and by increasing the current there is decrease of life. So long as breath remains in the body, there is no death.

When the full length of the wind is all confined in the body, nothing being allowed to go-out, it is *Kevala Kumbhaka.*

All *Jivas* are constantly and unconsciously reciting the *Ajapa Mantra,* only for a fixed number of times everyday. But a *yogi* should recite this consciously and counting the numbers. By doubling the number of *Ajapa i.e.,* by 30 respirations per minute, the state of *Manonmani* is attained. There are no regular *Rechaka* and *Puraka* in this process, it is only *Kumbhaka.* In the practice of *Keval Kumbhaka,* one should inspire the air by both nostrils and retain breath from one to sixty-four times. Once, it should be performed eight times a day in every three hours, or one may do it five times a day— *i.e.,*

1. in the early morning,
2. at noon,
3. in the twilight,
4. at midnight and
5. in the fourth quarter of the night.

Or one may do it thrice a day *i.e.*, in the morning, noon and evening.

One should increase the length of *Ajapa japa* every day, one to five times so long as success is not obtained in *Kevali.* He who knows *pranayama* and *Kevali,* is the real *yogi.* One can accomplish everything in this world who has acquired success in *Kevali Kumbhaka.*

Dhyana Yoga

The sixth *Sadhana* deals with *Dhyana,* of three kinds. Some elements of *Dhyana* was already introduced in the earlier *Sadhanas.* Generally in *Hatha-Yoga, Dhyana* is characteristically understood as visualization. The GS speaks of three kinds of *dhyana*

1. Sthula Dhyana

When a particular figure, such as one's *Guru* or Deity is contemplated it is *sthula dhyana.*

Process: Having closed the eyes, one should contemplate a sea of nectar in his heart in the midst of which, there is an island of precious stones, the very sand of which is pulverised diamonds and rubies. On all sides of it, there are *Kadamba* trees, laden with sweet flowers. Like a rampart, next to those trees, there is a row of flowering trees, such as *malati, mallika, jati, kesara, champaka, parijata* and *padmas,* the fragrance of these flowers is spread all round in every quarters. In the middle of this garden, the *yogi* should imagine a beautiful *kalpa* tree, having four branches representing the four vedas and full of flowers and fruits. Insects are humming there and cuckoos are singing. Beneath that tree, one should imagine a rich platform of precious gems, on that costly throne inlaid with jewels on which there is one's particular Deity, as taught to him by his *Guru.* And one should contemplate on the appropriate form, ornaments and vehicles of that Deity. The constant contemplation of such a form is *Sthula Dhyana.*

The another process is thus— In the pericarp of the great thousand petalled lotus *i.e.,* the brain, the *yogi* should imagine a smaller lotus having twelve petals, having twelve *bija* letters *viz. Ha, Sa, Ksa, Ma, La, Va, Ra, Yam, Ha, Sa, Kha, Phrem.* Its colour is white, highly luminous. In the pericarp of this small lotus, there are three lines forming a triangle– *A, Ka, tha;* having three angles called *Ha, La, Ksa.* In the middle of this triangle, there is the *Pranava, 'Om'.* There, one should contemplate a beautiful seat having *Nada* and *Bindu.* On that seat, there are two swans and a pair of wooden shoes. There, one should contemplate his *Guru* deva having two anns, two eyes, dressed in pure white, anointed with white sandal-paste wearing garlands of white flowers, to the left of whom stands *Sakti* of white colour. Thus, by contemplating the *Guru,* the *Sthula Dhyana* is attained.

2. The Jyotirdhyana

It is known as *Jyotirdhyana* when *Brahma* or *Prakriti* is contemplated as a mass of light.

Process : In the *Muladhara,* there is *Kundalini* having the form of a serpent and the *Jivatma* is there like the flame of a lamp. To contemplate on this flame as the luminous *Brahma* is known as the *Jyotirdhyana.*

Another process is thus : In the middle of the two eye-brows, above the *Manas,* there is a light consisting of *Om.* To contemplate on this flame is the another method of the *Jyotirdhyana.*

Thus, in this type of *dhyana,* the aspirant meditates upon the *Tejomaya Brahma i.e.,* the *Jivatman* resembling the flame in the *Muladhara* or the *Pranavatmaka* flame between the two eye-brows.

3. The Suksma Dhyana

When the Absolute *(Brahma)* in the form of the transcendental point-origin *(bindu)* and *Kundalini* force are contemplated, it is known as *Suksma Dhyana.*

If, by a great good fortune, the *Kundalini* is awakened, it joins with the *Atman* and leaves the body through the portals of the two eyes. It enjoys itself by walking in the royal road *i.e.,* the astral light. It can not be seen on account of its subtleness and great changeability—this success is attained by performing *Sambhavi Mudra i.e.* by gazing fixedly at space without winking. This is *Suksma Dhyana,* difficult to be attained by the *Devas,* as it is a great mystery.

In this *dhyana,* the attention is simply introverted upon the inner essence *i.e.,* the self. Sage *Gheranda* explains this process in terms of the awakened *Kundalini* uniting with the self and rising to the centre at the crown of head.

Importance: The contemplation of light *(Jyotirdhyana)* is a hundred times better than *Sthula dhyana.* And the *Suksma dhyana,* the greater of all is a hundred-thousand times better than the contemplation of light.

The *Sthula dhyana* and the *Jyotirdhyana* are the forms of *Saguna Dhyana,* while the *Suksma dhyana* is a form of *Nirguna dhyana.*

Samadhi

The seventh *Sadhana* of the *Ghatastha Yoga* is *Samadhi* which is the last subservient of well-known eight subservients of *Rajayoga.*

The *Samadhi* is a great yoga. The Yogi who (1) has confidence in knowledge, (2) has faith in his own *Guru,* (3) has faith in his own self and (4) whose mind awakens to intelligence from day to day, quickly attains this most beautiful practice of *Samadhi.* Among some practices leading to *Samadhi,* the importance of service to the *Guru,* his blessings and one's fortune are also recognised here.

Separating the *Manas* from the body and unite it with the *Paramatma* is known as *Samadhi. Samadhi* also means *mukti* from all states of consciousness.

The GS describes the six-fold *Samadhi:*

1. *Dhyanayoga Samadhi* : Performing the *Sambhavi mudra,* one perceives the *Atma.* Having seen once the *Brahman* in a *Bindu i.e.,* point of light, one should fix the mind in that point. Further, one brings the *Atma* in Ether and should bring the Ether in the *Atma.* Thus, seeing the *Atma* full of Ether, nothing will obstruct him. And being full of perpetual bliss, the man enters *Samadhi.*
2. *Nada Yoga Samadhi* : One should turn the tongue upwards closing the wind-passages by performing the *Khechari-mudra.* By so doing, *Samadhi* will be induced.
3. *Rasananda Yoga Samadhi* : Having performed *Bhramari Kumbhaka,* drawing in air slowly, one should expel the air slowly and slowly with a buzzing sound like that of a beetle. And the *Manas* should be placed in the centre of this sound of humming beetle. By so doing, there will be *Samadhi.* Consequently, the knowledge of *'Soham'* is arised and a great happiness takes place.
4. *Laya-Siddhi Yoga Samadhi* : Performing the *Yonimudra,* one should imagine himself as *Shakti* and *Parmatma* as *Purusha,* both have been united in one. Thus, the union of *Shakti*-and *Purusha* results in *Samadhi.* Consequently, one becomes full of bliss and realises *"Aham Brahma"* which conduces to *Advaita Samadhi.*
5. *Bhakti Yoga Samadhi* : Having contemplated within his heart his special deity, one should be full of ecstasy and shed tears of happiness. Consequently, he will become entraced *(dashabhava)* which leads to *Samadhi* and *Manonmani.*
6. *Raja Yoga Samadhi* : Performing the *Manomurccha Kumbhaka,* one should unite the *Manas* with the *Atma* by this which is obtained the *Raja Yoga Samadhi. Raja Yoga Samadhi, Unmani, Sahajavastha,* are all synonyms.

Praise of Samadhi

Samadhi leads to emancipation. It describes that *Vishnu* is in water, in the earth and on the peak of the mountain, in the midst of volcanic fires and flames. Thus, the whole universe is full of *Vishnu.* All living and animate creation, trees, shrubs, roots etc., ocean and mountains— all are to be known as *Brahman.* And one should see them all in *Atma.* The *Atma* confined in the body is consciousness *(chaitanya),* without a second, the Eternal, the Highest, knowing it separate from body, one becomes free from desires and passions.

Thus *Samadhi,* free from all desires, free from attachment to his own body, to son, wife, riches, kinsmen is obtained, thus, one obtains fully the *Samadhi.*

Siddha-siddhanta-paddhati

This is perhaps the only book elaborating on the philosophical doctrine on which the *Hatha cult* of the *Natha Yogis* is built. Therefore, this assumes significance.

It is a very systematically written text having 350 verses distributed over six chapters. Authorship of this book goes to *Gorakhanatha.*

- The first chapter describes the process of evolution originating from *Anama* (the nameless).

- The second chapter discusses the human body which has *Chakras, Adharas,* etc.
- A deep insight into the human body is developed in the third chapter. It is said that body is a replica of the macrocosm, the cosmos.
- The fourth chapter talks about the support of the body or *Pindadhara* and aiso of the universe. *Shakti* is substratum.
- The fifth chapter describes the process by which the individual self can strike an equipoise with the Absolute.
- The sixth chapter discusses the nature and characteristics of an *Avadhutayogi* and much more on the similar line.

Goraksa Sataka

It is a small book on *Hatha Yoga* extending to approximately hundred verses. It speaks of *Yoga* of six components *(Sadanga Yoga)* while omitting *Yama* and *Niyama.* It follows the *Upanisadic* ideal of unity (*Advaita*) and suggests the means to achieve such an objective.

It lays emphasis on *Sidhasana* and *Kamalasana (Padmasana)* among all the eighty-four *Asanas.*

Chakras, Nadis and various *Pranas* are described well. Certain techniques of *Pranayama* are elaborated upon. Process of *Prana* to be raised to *Mahapadma (Sahasrara)* through the passage of *Susumna* is described.

One of its special features is a lucid description of five *Dharanas* practised on five basic elements with visualision, *Bija, Yantra,* etc., so that one can gain control on these elements.

Kumbhakapaddhati

This is authored by Raghuvira who was a resident of *Kasi.* It is devoted to featuring a host of techniques of *Pranayama* and various levels of consciousness that a spiritual aspirant would pass through during his inbound journey. There are about 72 techniques of *Pranayama* many of which are hitherto unknown. Most of them are unique in nature. Names of these techniques are not found in any other of the published texts of *Hatha Yoga. Kumbhaka* has been divided into two segments—one *Meru Kumbhaka* (may be compared to *Kevala Kumbhaka*) and the other *Ameru Kumbhaka.* There is another classification, *Antah Kumbhaka* (internal *Kumbhaka*), *Bahya Kumbhaka* (external *Kumbhaka*) and *Stambhavritti (Kevala Kumbhaka).*

Hatharatnavali

It is authored by *Srinivasayogi.* This book is not as popular as *Hathapradipika.* It is also known as *HathaYogaratnasarani* or *Ratnavali.* The contents are divided into four chapters. The distribution of various topics is as follows:

1st chapter: *Mantra, Laya, Raja* and *Hatha Yoga* are described under *Maha Yoga.* Eight processes of purification are described (instead of usual six). These are to purify not only fat and toxins but also the *Chakras.*

2nd chapter: Elaborate description of nine *Kumbhakas* is provided; the additional ninth *Kumbhaka* is *Bhujangikarana.*

3rd chapter: In this chapter we get a complete list and description of eighty-four *Asanas.*

4th chapter: *Samadhi* is described in this chapter along with *Nadanusandhana.* Four progressive states of *Hatha* such as *Arambha, Ghata, Paricaya* and *Nispatti* are the topics of this chapter.

The characteristic feature of the commentary is its language and style which is clear, and flowing as if he is explaining the contents to a common man.

The explanation about the topics discussed reflects on his experience and rational outlook.

Hathatatvakaumudi

It is perhaps the largest compendium on *Yoga* available in published form which spans over 56 chapters. Author of this voluminous text of *Yoga* is one Sundaradeva who was living in *Kasi* (*Benaras*). Almost all information on *Hatha Yoga* techniques is available in this book. There are plenty of original quotations cited by the author to support his viewpoint. Most of the quotations are taken from classical authentic sources. This lends value to this work.

Shiva Samhita

This is one more work on *Hatha Yoga*.

In addition to these above mentioned texts, there are many more classical texts on *Hatha Yoga* critically edited and published by many *Yoga* institutions. Most of these works are brought to the *Yoga* fraternity for the first time and many of these are also rare books. Those who want to go to the further depth on the subject may study the same.

Some of these are:

1. *Yuktabhavadeva* of Bhavadeva Mishra
2. Critical Edition of Selected *Yogopanishads*
3. *Mandalabraahmanopanishad* and *nadabind-upanishad*
4. *Amanaska Yogah* a treatise on Laya Yoga
5. *Amritavakyam*
6. *Dattatreya Yogasastram*
7. *Sivasvarodaya*

HATHA YOGIC PRACTICES

There is a large number of practices suggested in the *Hatha Yogic* texts. We are presenting a brief description on the major groups of these practices:

Asanas

Hatha Yoga considers that *Asanas* are the forerunners of the practices of *Yoga*.

Asanas are body postures adopted consciously, held for some time and then coming to the original position. Certain *Asanas* such as *Sukhasana, Siddhasana*, etc., can be maintained for a long time.

There are hundreds of such *Asanas*. Some of these could be difficult to adopt and maintain. Some are easier. Practice of *Asanas* make the body supple and energetic. Mind feels relaxed. Breathing flows smoothly.

Most of the *Hatha texts* mentioned above do give some description of *Asanas*. It is commonly held that *Asanas* are eighty-four in number. The text of *Hatharatnavali* mentions the name of all eighty-four *Asanas*. This list seems to be a complete one.

Pranayama, eight kumbhakas

Hatha Yoga assigns a great lot of emphasis on the practice of *Pranayama*. Cleansing of the *Nadis*, relaxing the mind, managing emotions, managing various physical ailments, withdrawal of senses, entering into the state of meditation, doing *Dharana*, undertaking *Pratyahara,* practising *Dhyana* and achieving the state of *Samadhi, Hatha Yoga* says that *Pranayama* is the practice basic to reaching the stage of *Samadhi.*

There are more than seventy techniques of *Pranayama* described in the book of Kumbhaka. Such a large number is not seen in any book of *Yoga*. *Hathapradipika* gives a set of eight techniques of breathing which are known as *Kumbhakas*.

There are two broad sections of *Pranayama (Kumbhaka),* one *Sahita* and the other *Kevala. Kevala Kumbhaka* is the natural outcome of *Sahita Kumbhaka. Kevala Kumbhaka* is equated with the state of *Samadhi.*

However, purification of the *Nadis (Nadisudhi)* forms the prerequisite for all advanced methods of *Pranayama*. One more significant aspect of *Pranayama* is to send the flow of *Prana* through the central passage of *Susumna* and to take it to the top of the head known as *Sahasrara Chakra*, the seat of Pure Consciousness. Thus *Pranayama* serves a sublime purpose.

A few of the practices such as *Nadisodhana Pranayama*, *Ujjayi* and *Suryabhedana* are quite popular and widely practised. Here are the techniques:

- ***Nadisodhana pranayama:*** One inhales through the left nostril, holds it and exhales through the other (after retention) and again inhales through the right nostril and holds the breath before exhalation. Consistently and frequently following this technique through alternate nostrils, one gets his/her *nadis* purified in three months.

- ***Ujjayi:*** Close the mouth. Inhale through both nostrils fully with frictional sound felt from the throat to the chest. Hold the breath and then exhale through left nostril. This is *Ujjayi Kumbhaka.* This should be practised all the time.
- ***Suryabhedana:*** One sits comfortably in *Padmasana*, slowly draws the external air in through the right nostril and retains it as long as the sensations are felt at the tips of the hair and nails. Thereafter, (to the fullest of capacity) slowly exhales through the left nostril. This *Surya-Bhedana* should be practised quite frequently.
- ***Eight kumbhakas of hatha tradition are:*** *Surya-bhedana, Ujjayi, Sitkari, Sitạli, Bhasrika, Bhramari, Murchha* and *Kevala.*

Dharana on five elements

Dharana makes advanced techniques. The text of *Hathapradipika* gives the description on five *Dharanas* on five elements which are as follows:

- ***Bhuvo-dharana:*** The earth element which has deep golden yellow colour, having 'la' (as the *bija*), and is presided over by Brahma as the deity, having four corners, placed in the heart, one should concentrate upon with the *prana* raised there and retained for five *ghatikas*. This is *bhuvo-dharana,* which brings restraint and by which one conquers earth element.
- ***Varini-dharana:*** The water element, which is as white as crescent moon and *kunda* flower (jasmine) is located in the throat, having *'va'* as bija and is presided over by Vishnu as deity. One should take the *prana* there and hold it for five *ghatikas* with one-pointed mind. This is *Varini-Dharana,* which digests even severe poisons.
- ***Vaisvanari-dharana:*** The fire element, which is located in the palate and is as deep red as *indra-gopa* insect (cochineal), having three shining corners, 'ra' as *bija*, as brightly red as coral, which is presided over by *rudra* as deity. One should take the *prana* there and hold it for five *ghatikas* with rapt attention. This is *Vaisvanari-Dharana,* by which one controls fire element.
- ***Vayavi-dharana:*** The element of air is situated between the two eye-brows, bright like a heap of collyrium, round in shape, consisting of *vayu* and associated with the letter *'ya'* (as *bija*) and *Isvara* as presiding deity. One should bring the *prana* there and maintain it for five *ghatikas* with one-pointed mind. This *Vayavi-Dharana* enables a *Yogi* to move in the space.
- ***Nabho-dharana:*** The *akasa* element, which is placed in the *brahma-randhra,* which is as pure as water. It bears that *anahata* (unheard) *nada*, having *Sadasiva* as presiding deity and embedded with '*ha*' (as *bija*). One should take the *prana* there accompanied with mind for five *ghatikas.* This *Nabho-Dharana* brings liberation to the *Yogis.*

Mudras and bandhas

Mudras: There seems to have been great influence of *Mudras* in the literature of medieval times.

Limiting our discussion only on the *Mudras* of *Hatha Yoga*, we find that *Hathapradipika* describes ten *Mudras*. *Gheranda Samhita* speaks of 25 *Mudras.* In all these texts *Mudras* occupy a larger space for description.

The purpose of *Mudras,* according to *Gheranda Samhita*, is to establish equilibrium or *'sthirata'*, while according to *Hathapradipika* is 'awakening of *kundalini shakti*'.

Ten *Mudras* of *Hathapradipika* are:

Mahamudra, Mahabandha, Mahavedha, Khechari, Uddiyana, Mulabandha, Jalandhara-bandha, Viparita-karani, Vajroli and Sakti-calana.

We describe only *Uddiyana* and *Mulabandha* below:

Uddiyana (it is also a *Mudra*): Retract the abdomen above the navel towards the back. This is *Uddiyana,* which overcomes death, like a lion killing an elephant.

Mulabandha (it is also a *Mudra*): Press the perineum with the heel, contract the anus and raise the *apana* upwards. This is called *Mula-bandha.*

Bandhas: These are essentially *Mudras* and are very few in number. They are usually practised as an essential part of the *Pranayama* in *Hathayogic* tradition. Some of them are otherwise practised independently. We may say that those *Mudras* practised in the technique of *Pranayama* are called *Bandhas*, because they bind the current of *Prana* in a particular region and channelize the *pranika* currents in a particular direction. The commonly practised *Bandhas* and their locations are as under:

	Bandha	***location***
(i)	Jalandhara	throat
(ii)	Uddiyana	abdomen
(iii)	Mulabandha	anus
(iv)	Jihva	mouth

All the above *bandhas* are applied during the performance of *abhyantara kumbhaka,* meaning holding the breath inside. Use of *bandhas* during *Pranayama* seems to be a special technique of *Hathayogika Pranayama.* The idea behind this seems to be to intensify the sensations of *pranika* currents through the channel of *Susumna* by increasing the pressure in the middle path. The total effect of the application of the three *bandhas* is to regulate the working of *Ida* and *Pingala* and to activate *Susumna nadi.*

Satkarma, the set of six cleansing techniques

These techniques of cleansing the body from inside form a special feature of *Hatha.* For this purpose, various odd methods are applied. Some of the *Hatha* texts consider these to be pre-requisites for undertaking the practice of *Pranayama.* It is so because by application of such practices, the body is rendered free of excess fat and toxicity. Thus *Prana* can be easily and smoothly channelized through *Nadis,* especially through *Susumna.* If *nadis* are not pure, how can *Prana* flow through the central channel to reach the *Brahmarandhra?* And without this happening, how can one experience the state of non-mind (*Unmani Bhava*)?

Based on such rationale, *Hatha* tradition suggests *Satkarmas.*

The set of *sat-karmas* are *Dhauti, Basti, Neti, Trataka, Nauli* and *Kapalabhati.*

Here we indicate the techniques of *Neti* and *Kapalabhati:*

Neti: One inserts a smooth sheaf of cotton, measuring (approximately) 23 cms. in length, in the nose and pulls it out through the mouth. This is *neti.*

Kapalabhati: One imitates the movements of the bellows of a blacksmith, using the left and right nostrils. This famous *Kapalabhati* removes phlegmatic disorders.

Multiple Choice Questions

1. How many types of kumbhakas are described in 'Hatha Yoga Pradipika'?

A. 6 B. 7
C. 8 D. 9

2. Which of the following kumbhaka is not described in book 'Gheranda Samhita'?

A. Shitli B. Suryabhedi
C. Sahita D. Shitkari

3. Suryabhedi pranayama is very useful because:

A. It takes digestive system strong
B. It takes away the fear of death
C. It eliminates vata dosha
D. All of the above

4. Which of the bandh is performed during the practice of vajroli mudra?

A. Mulbandha B. Jalandhara bandh
C. Uddiyanbandha D. Mahabandha

5. By practice of which mudra the effect of poison is lost?
A. Mahamudra B. Mahabheda mudra
C. Khechari mudra D. Kaki mudra

6. According to the text 'Gherand Samhita' which is the first step of hatha yoga?
A. Shatkarma B. Asana
C. Surya namaskara D. Pranayama

7. Which kriya should be performed before nauli kriya?
A. Vatsara B. Varisara
C. Agnisara D. None of the above

8. The fear of death is lost due to practice of which mudra?
A. Pashini B. Manduki
C. Kaki D. Mahabandha

9. In the position of which asana murchha pranayama can be done?
A. Padmasana B. Shavasana
C. Makarasana D. All of the above

10. For the emotional development of children which mudra is beneficial?
A. Shambhavi B. Pashini
C. Nabho D. Kaki

11. During practice of vipritkarni mudra the opposite situation occur between:
A. Ananmaya-Pranmaya kosha
B. Surya-Chandra
C. Brain-Heart
D. Prana-Apana vayu

12. Practice of which mudra increases the consciousness and awareness of human being?
A. Mahabheda mudra B. Mahamudra
C. Shambhavi mudra D. All of the above

13. Practice of mulsodhan kriya strengthens which type of vayu?
A. Udana vayu B. Vyana vayu
C. Apana vayu D. Prana vayu

14. According to 'Hatha Yoga Pradipika' which is the first limb of hatha yoga?
A. Shat kriya B. Asana
C. Pranayama D. Surya namaskara

15. Regular practice of which pranayama (kumbhaka) makes a sadhaka to float effortlessly on water?
A. Kevali B. Murchha
C. Palavani D. Sahita

16. According to Swami Savatmarama which bandha is best?
A. Mulbandha B. Uddiyana bandha
C. Jalandhar bandha D. Mahabandha

17. Which mudra should be performed before vajroli mudra?
A. Shambhavi B. Khechari
C. Mahabandh D. Shaktichalini

18. Which chakra is activated by practice of tadagi mudra?
A. Muladhara B. Visuddhi
C. Manipura D. Anahata

19. Which chakra is activated by practice of pashini mudra?
A. Muladhara B. Anahata
C. Visuddhi D. Both A and C

20. Which type of bandha is performed during practice of shaktichalini mudra?
A. Mulabandha
B. Jalandhara bandha
C. Uddiyana bandha
D. Mahabandha

21. Which chakra is activated by practice of Jalandhara bandha?
A. Muladhara B. Visuddhi
C. Manipura D. Anahata

22. Which chakra is activated by practice of Uddiyana bandha?
A. Manipura B. Visuddhi
C. Anahata D. Swathisthana

23. Which mudra is also known as earth element oppressor?
A. Vayu mudra B. Surya mudra
C. Apana mudra D. Sankha mudra

24. Which type of pranayama is not mentioned in the text 'Gheranda Samhita'?
A. Plavani B. Murchha
C. Kevali D. Sahita

25. Which type of pranayama is not mentioned in the text 'Hatha Yoga Pradipika'?
A. Kevali B. Plavani
C. Murchha D. Shitli

26. How many types of dharnas are mentioned in the text 'Gherand Samhita'?
A. 3 B. 4
C. 5 D. 6

27. By practice of mulabandha _____ vayu and _______ vayu starts harmonizing.
A. Apana vayu, Prana vayu
B. Udana vayu, Apana vayu
C. Vyana vayu, Prana vayu
D. Prana vayu, Udana vayu

28. How many mudras are described in 'Shiva Samhita'?
A. 5 B. 6
C. 8 D. 10

29. Practise of mudras leads to:
A. Pratyahara B. Dhyana
C. Dharana D. Samadhi

30. Regular practitioner of which asana do not face problem of naval displacement?
A. Uttanpadasana B. Chakrasana
C. Mandukasana D. Sarvangasana

31. Which type of mudra is useful in eliminating coryza and allergy?
A. Linga B. Prana
C. Surya D. Apana

32. Which mudra is performed by placing tips of ring finger and thumb together?
A. Surya mudra B. Prana mudra
C. Prithvi mudra D. Vayu mudra

33. Which mudra is performed by placing tips of index finger and thumb together?
A. Surya mudra B. Vayu mudra
C. Prana mudra D. Apana mudra

34. Which of the following match is incorrect?
A. Thumb – Fire element
B. Index finger – Air element
C. Middle finger – Space element
D. Ring finger – Water element

35. Which of the following match is correct?
A. Small finger – Water element
B. Ring finger – Earth element
C. Thumb – Fire elements
D. All of the above

36. What is the meaning of letter 'kh' in the word khechari mudra?
A. Earth B. Water
C. Space D. Air

37. Practise of which mudra destroys the panch kaleshas?
A. Maha mudra B. Mahabandh mudra
C. Mahabheda mudra D. Khechari

38. Which asana is related to sathala vasti kriya?
A. Paschimotanassna B. Sidhasana
C. Padmasana D. Singhasana

39. Which bandhas are performed during practice of mahabheda mudra?
A. Jalandhra bandh B. Mulabandha
C. Uddiyana bandha D. All of the above

40. Jalandhara bandha reverses the flow of _____ vayu to downwards.
A. Samana B. Prana
C. Apana D. Vyana

41. Practise of bandhas and mudras leads us towards:
A. Physical world B. Panch koshas
C. Karmendriyas D. Gyanendriyas

42. How many mudras are described in 'Hatha Yoga Pradipika'?
A. 6 B. 8
C. 10 D. 12

43. Which of the following mudra helps in removing wet dream disorder?
A. Yoni mudra B. Vajroli mudra
C. Kari mudra D. Sankh mudra

44. How many flavours does a sadhaka tastes on attaining khechari mudra?
A. 4 B. 5
C. 6 D. 7

45. What is the meaning of word 'kurma' in kurmasana?
A. Turtle B. Crocodile
C. Lizard D. Deer

46. Regular practice of which pranayama brings divine powers to sadhaka?
A. Murchha B. Kevali
C. Bhramari D. Bhastrika

47. Steadiness is related to which part of hatha yoga sadhna?
A. Asana B. Pranayama
C. Mudra D. Dhyana

48. Laghava is related to which part of hatha yoga sadhna?
A. Asana B. Pranayama
C. Dharana D. Dhyana

49. Patience is related to which part of hatha yoga sadhna?
A. Mudra B. Asana
C. Pratyahara D. Dhyana

50. Which mudra should be followed by mahamudra?
A. Mahabheda B. Mahabandha
C. Nabho D. Pashini

51. Which asana is considered as the best asana?
A. Mandukasana B. Trikonasana
C. Siddhasana D. Mayurasana

52. Which asana is known as the 'King of asana'?
A. Bhadrasana B. Shirshasana
C. Sidhasana D. Salabhasana

53. Which kriya is related to khechari mudra?
A. Neti B. Vasti
C. Dhauti D. Tratak

54. During the practice of ujjayi pranayama puraka (inhalation) is done through:
A. Mouth B. Both nostrils
C. Left nostril D. Right nostril

55. Which bandha are performed during practice of ujjayi pranayama?
A. Jalandharbandha
B. Mulabandha
C. Uddiyanabandha
D. All of the above

56. How many mudras are described by Maharishi Gheranda?
A. 22 B. 24
C. 23 D. 28

57. Which bandha is performed during mahamudra?
A. Mulabandha B. Uddiyanbandha
C. Mahabanda D. Jalandarbandha

58. During the practice of which mudra, sadhaka concentrate on kundalini shakti?
A. Shambhavi B. Pashini
C. Kaki D. Ashwini

59. Tridhatu vikaras are eliminated by practice of which kumbhaka?
A. Ujjayi B. Bhastrika
C. Shitli D. Murchha

60. Regular practice of which kumbhaka cures pyrosis?
A. Shitli B. Ujjayi
C. Suryabhedi D. Nadishodhan

61. Practise of which mudra purifies all the nadis of body?
A. Shaktichalini B. Vajroli
C. Vipritkarni D. Khechari

62. Which bandha is considered best by Maharishi Gheranda?
A. Mulabandha B. Uddiyanbandha
C. Jalandharbandha D. Mahabandha

63. Which asana is considered best for students?
A. Gorakshasana B. Siddhasana
C. Shavasana D. Gomukhasana

64. Which mudra is beneficial for people suffering from obesity?
A. Prithvi B. Sankha
C. Prana D. Surya

65. Which mudra is related to nadayoga?
A. Mahabheda B. Mahamudra
C. Kaki mudra D. Yoni mudra

66. How many kumbhakas are described in 'Gheranda Samhita'?
A. 6 B. 8
C. 10 D. 12

67. Which kriya is performed before practice of mulabandha?
A. Varisara B. Vahnisara
C. Ashwini D. Agnisara

68. Which kriya is useful for practice of uddiyana bandha?
A. Kapalabhati B. Vahnisara
C. Agnisara D. Varisara

69. According to 'Hatha Yoga Pradipika' how many limbs are there of hatha yoga?
A. 4 B. 6
C. 7 D. 8

70. Bhastrika pranayama is performed during the practice of which mudra?
A. Mahabheda B. Shaktichalini
C. Khechari D. Vajroli

71. By regular practice of which mudra a sadhaka can get the eight siddhis?
A. Mahabandha B. Khechari
C. Pashini D. Kaki

72. By regular practice of which mudra the fear of death is lost?
A. Vajroli B. Shaktichalini
C. Mahabandha D. Mahabheda

73. How many bandhas are described in Gheranda Samhita?
A. 3 B. 4
C. 5 D. 6

74. Which of the following is not a mudra?
A. Tadagi B. Nabho
C. Sahita D. Pashini

75. The direction of flow of which two vayus in the body is opposite?
A. Apana – Udana
B. Samana – Prana
C. Samana – Udana
D. Vyana – Samana

76. Which mudra suppresses the prithvi-tattva?
A. Surya B. Vayu
C. Prithvi D. Prana

77. "By practice of pranayama one can get illuminated by the light of its soul"–Whose opinion is this?
A. Swami Swatmarama
B. Maharishi Gheranda
C. Maharishi Patanjali
D. Maharishi Vedvyasa

78. What is the correct sequence of asanas performed during the sankhaprakhsalana kriya?
A. Tadasana - kati chakrasana - tryiak tadasana - triyak bhujangasana - udarkarshnasana
B. Tadasana - triyak tadasana - kati chakrasana - triyak bhujangasana - udarkarshnasana
C. Triyak tadasana - tadasana - kati chakrasana - udarkarshanasana - bhujangasana
D. Tadasana - kati chakrasana - bhujangasana - udarkarshnasana - triyak tadasana

79. Which type of doshas are eliminated by practice of shitli pranayama?
A. Vata doshas B. Pitta doshas
C. Kapha doshas D. Both B and C

80. How many limbs of hatha yoga are explained by Gorakshanatha?
A. 4 B. 6
C. 7 D. 8

81. Purifying the body by means of vasti-kriya is known as
A. Abhayantrasocha B. Bahrayasocha
C. Antrikasocha D. Both A and C

82. Which of the following asana is described in both 'Gheranda Samhita' and 'Hatha Yoga Pradipika'?
A. Bhadrasana B. Salabhasana
C. Mandukasana D. Guptasana

83. Which of the following asana is not mentioned in 'Hatha Yoga Pradipika'?
A. Gorakshasana B. Mayurasana
C. Gomukhasana D. Dhanurasana

84. Which of the following mudra is useful for person suffering from lack of concentration, aggression and hyperactivity?
A. Vayu mudra B. Sankha mudra
C. Prithvi mudra D. Surya mudra

85. 'Hakara' is related to
A. Surya nadi B. Chandra nadi
C. Susumna nadi D. All of the above

86. During the practice of which mudra all the three bandhas are performed?
A. Mahabandha B. Mahamudra
C. Shaktichalini D. Pashini

87. Which mudra should not be performed daily by introvert people?
A. Maha mudra B. Yoni mudra
C. Pashini mudra D. Kaki mudra

88. Which of the following statement is correct?
A. By practise of vayaviya mudra a sadhaka attains siddhi of floating on air
B. Practise of bhujangni mudra removes stomach disorders
C. Practise of kaki mudra removes all the types of disorders
D. All of the above

89. Which bandha should be performed during practise of sagarbha sahita pranayama?
A. Mula bandha
B. Jalandhara bandha
C. Uddiyana bandha
D. Maha bandha

90. Which of the following statement is not correct?
A. Jalandhar bandha is performed during practise of ujjayi pranayama
B. Ujjayi pranayama removes insomenia
C. Nigarbha pranayama should be performed with bija mantra
D. During practice of sagarbha pranayama inhalation should be done through left nostril

91. Which vayu is strengthened by practise of uddiyana bandha?
A. Prana B. Vyana
C. Samana D. Udana

92. Which vayu is purified by practise of jalandhara bandha?
A. Samana B. Udana
C. Prana D. Vyana

93. Practise of meditation strengthens which vayu?
A. Samana B. Udana
C. Prana D. Vyana

94. In 'Gheranda Samhita' which type of the dhyana is not mentioned?
A. Sthula B. Jyotira
C. Sukshama D. Pindastha

95. According to 'Hatha Yoga Pradipika' which are the elements of failure in yoga?
A. Overeating, Exertion
B. Talkativeness, Hard rules
C. Company of common people
D. All of the above

96. According to 'Hatha Yoga Pradipika' which are the elements of success in yoga?
A. Enthusiasm, Perseverance
B. Faith, Courage
C. Avoiding company of common people
D. All of the above

97. In yogic sadhna, the time period for dharana is suggested how many nadis?
A. 4 nadis B. 5 nadis
C. 6 nadis D. 7 nadis

98. 1 nadi =
A. 14 minutes B. 18 minutes
C. 24 minutes D. 28 minutes

99. The time period for dhyana is suggested how many nadis?
A. 40 B. 55
C. 60 D. 76

100. Who is the author of 'Tattva Vaisardi'?
A. Vachaspti Mishra B. Charvaka
C. Maharishi Vyasa D. Kapila muni

101. How many types of dhyana are explained by Maharishi Gheranda?
A. 3 B. 4
C. 5 D. 6

102. Who is the author of book 'Yoga Martanda'?
A. Chauranginatha
B. Gorakshanath
C. Adi Shankaracharya
D. Madhvacharya

103. What is the life period of Maharishi Gheranda?
A. 1450–1550 A.D. B. 1550–1650 A.D.
C. 1650–1750 A.D. D. 1150–1250 A.D.

104. Which century is the life period of Swami Swatmaram?
A. 12th century B. 13th century
C. 14th century D. 15th century

105. Who is the author of 'Hatha Ratnavali'?
A. Shankaracharya
B. Swami Dayananda
C. Swami Shivananda
D. Shri Niwas Bhatt

106. Shastanga Yoga (six limbs of yoga) are explained in which book?
A. Goraksha Astakarma
B. Hatha Ratnavali
C. Yoga Chintamani
D. Saundrya Lahiri

107. Saptanga Yoga (seven limbs of yoga) are explained in which book?
A. Hatha Ratnavali
B. Gheranda Samhita
C. Goraksha Samhita
D. Patanjali Yoga Sutra

108. Who is the author of the book 'Tantra Sara'?
A. Goraksha Nath
B. Chaurangi Nath
C. Acharya Ramanuja
D. Nimbarkacharya

109. Which of the following are works of Gorakshanath?
A. Yoga Chintamani, Yoga Martanda, Yoga Bhija, Hatha Yoga
B. Hatha Samhita, Siddha Siddhanta, Amrodha, Gyanamrita Yoga
C. Nadi Gyana, Vivekmartanda, Shrinath Sutra, Gyana Parkash
D. All of the above

110. Who is author of the text 'Hatha Yoga Pradipika'?
A. Maharshi Gherand
B. Swami Swatmaram
C. Maharshi Patanjali
D. None of the above

111. Which type of yoga is explained in 'Shiva Samhita'?
A. Hatha yoga B. Gyana yoga
C. Kriya yoga D. Bhakti yoga

112. Who is known as Yogiraja and Kashibaba?
A. Swami Shivananda
B. Shri Shyama Charan Lahiri
C. Gorakshanath
D. Chauranginath

113. How many total chapters are there in Gherand Samhita?
A. 5 B. 6
C. 7 D. 8

114. Who was the disciple of Matseyandranath?
A. Chauranginath B. Gorakshanath
C. Balaknath D. Golaknath

115. Gorakshanath preached the yoga in which century?
A. 10-11th century B. 12-13th century
C. 14-15th century D. 16-17th century

116. How many total chapters are there in Hatha Yoga Pradipika?
A. 4 B. 5
C. 6 D. 7

117. Who is author of 'Shiva Samhita'?
A. Gorakshanath
B. Matsyendranath
C. Swami Shivananda
D. None of these

118. To percept 'anitya as nitya' is called as:
A. Avidya B. Yoga antraya
C. Kaleshas D. Chitta vikshepa

119. By practise of which mudra the sadhaka gets the power to digest even the poision?
A. Mahamudra
B. Mahabheda mudra
C. Khechari mudra
D. Shaktichalini mudra

120. Which of the following match is correct?
A. Jalandhara bandha – Visuddhi Chakra
B. Uddiyanabandha – Manipura Chakra
C. Mulabandha – Muladhara Chakra
D. All the above

121. What is the colour of udana prana?
A. Sky Blue B. Pale White
C. Yellow D. Dark Blue

122. Which is the second stage of pranayama?
A. Ghata Avastha B. Nishpatti Avastha
C. Visuddhi Avastha D. Parichaya Avastha

123. Which is the fourth stage of pranayama?
A. Nishpatti B. Ghata
C. Visudha D. Nirudha

124. What is the correct sequence of the four limbs of hatha yoga as described in 'Hatha Yoga Pradipika'?
A. Shatkarma - Asana - Pranayama - Mudra
B. Shatkarma - Asana - Pranayama - Nadanusandhana
C. Asana - Pranayama - Mudra - Nadanusandhana
D. Asana - Mudra - Pranayama - Nadanusandhana

125. 'Purusha' word is made up of two words – 'paru + usha', which means
A. Dawn of east B. Dawn of west
C. Perfect dawn D. Shining dawn

ANSWERS

1	2	3	4	5	6	7	8	9	10
C	D	C	A	C	A	C	D	A	A
11	**12**	**13**	**14**	**15**	**16**	**17**	**18**	**19**	**20**
B	B	C	B	C	B	D	C	D	C
21	**22**	**23**	**24**	**25**	**26**	**27**	**28**	**29**	**30**
B	A	B	A	A	C	A	D	A	A
31	**32**	**33**	**34**	**35**	**36**	**37**	**38**	**39**	**40**
A	C	B	D	D	C	A	A	D	B
41	**42**	**43**	**44**	**45**	**46**	**47**	**48**	**49**	**50**
B	C	B	C	A	B	A	B	C	A
51	**52**	**53**	**54**	**55**	**56**	**57**	**58**	**59**	**60**
C	B	A	B	D	C	A	A	B	A
61	**62**	**63**	**64**	**65**	**66**	**67**	**68**	**69**	**70**
A	B	A	D	D	B	B	C	A	B
71	**72**	**73**	**74**	**75**	**76**	**77**	**78**	**79**	**80**
B	A	B	C	A	A	A	B	D	B
81	**82**	**83**	**84**	**85**	**86**	**87**	**88**	**89**	**90**
B	A	A	A	A	A	B	D	C	C
91	**92**	**93**	**94**	**95**	**96**	**97**	**98**	**99**	**100**
C	B	C	D	D	D	B	C	C	A
101	**102**	**103**	**104**	**105**	**106**	**107**	**108**	**109**	**110**
A	B	C	C	D	A	B	B	D	B
111	**112**	**113**	**114**	**115**	**116**	**117**	**118**	**119**	**120**
A	B	C	B	A	A	D	A	A	D
121	**122**	**123**	**124**	**125**					
B	A	A	C	A					

●●●

CHAPTER

5 Allied Sciences—General Psychology, Essential Anatomy and Physiology; Dietetics and Nutrition

GENERAL PSYCHOLOGY

Introduction

Psychology is derived from the Greek words *psyche* and *logos* which means 'study of mind or soul'. It is a science that deals with behaviour and mental processes. Hence, psychology is defined as the scientific study of behaviour and mental processes. It focuses on both biological and social dimensions. The physiological psychologists or psychobiologists focus on relationships between behaviour and mental functioning. As for the social psychologists, they focus on group and social influences on individuals.

Psychologists are interested in every aspect of human thought and behaviour. The different fields of psychology includes developmental psychology, physiological psychology, experimental psychology, personality psychology, clinical psychology, counselling psychology, social psychology, industrial psychology, organizational psychology, etc. In these fields, they study different areas like development, physiological bases of behaviour, learning, perception, consciousness, memory, thought, language, motivation, emotion, intelligence, personality, adjustment, abnormal behaviour, social influences and social behaviours. Psychology is often applied in education, industry, health, clinical, consumer affairs, engineering and many other areas.

Given the wide array of interests, psychologists in various fields are drawn together by their common interests in a number of fundamental issues or questions about behaviour that cut across their areas of specialisation. These enduring issues include the ones related to 'person-situation', 'heredity-environment', 'stability-change', 'diversity' and 'mind-body'.

The 'person-situation' issue focuses on to what extent behaviour is caused by the influence of processes occurring inside a person and external environment or situation. For decades, psychologists have been debating the degree of influence that heredity (genetics) and environment (experiences) have on behaviour. Psychologists are also interested in knowing to what extent people stay relatively unchanged (stability) throughout their lives and how people change. Another enduring issue is the one related to diversity, which inquires to what extent every person is in certain respects like all other people, like some other people and like no other person. Finally, many psychologists are fascinated by the 'mind-body' relationship, *i.e.*, relationship between what we experience (such as thoughts and feelings) and the biological processes (such as activity in the nervous system).

Psychology as Science

Psychology is the science of behaviour and mental processes. Science provides logical guidelines for evaluating evidence and well reasoned techniques for verifying principles. Hence, psychologists rely on the scientific method while searching out answers to psychological questions. Consequently, they follow the scientific method which is essentially an approach to knowledge that relies on systematically collecting data through observation, generating a theory to explain the data, producing testable hypotheses based on the theory and testing those hypotheses empirically to reach valid generalisable conclusions. Thus like all scientists, psychologists use the scientific method to describe, understand, predict and eventually to achieve some measure of control over what they study.

Since psychologists see themselves as scientists, the terms 'psychologist' and 'behavioural scientist' may be used to denote them. The broader label social scientist refers to all who study society or behaviour, and may include psychologists, sociologists, anthropologists, historians and others.

Psychology and Other Social Sciences

Psychology is not alone in applying the scientific method to the study of behaviour. The behavioural sciences like psychology, sociology, anthropology, political science, economics and history are very closely related. However, the questions and hypotheses that guide the research in each field differ, and consequently different methods of research are adopted.

A Brief History of Modern Scientific Psychology

Psychology has a long past but a short history. Human beings or homosapiens appeared on earth about 100,000 years ago and probably ever since they have been trying to understand themselves. Going back to the time of Greek philosophers like Plato and Aristotle, who had wondered about human behaviour and mental process. Aristotle (384-322 B.C) is sometimes called the Father of psychology. But speculation about psychological matters did not begin with the Greek thinker. Hundreds of years before Aristotle, the earliest philosophers on record were dealing with these topics. But not until the late 1800s, did great thinkers like Aristotle began to apply the scientific method to questions that had puzzled philosophers for centuries. Only then did psychology come in to being as a formal scientific discipline separate from philosophy.

The brief history of psychology will be discussed at a much later point in history, *i.e.*, in the last part of the 19th century when the field called psychology emerged. Charles Darwin (1809-1882) who was not a psychologist yet was considered to be responsible for the idea that human behaviour and thinking might be a subject for scientific inquiry. In the 'Origin of Species' (1859) and 'The Descent of Man' (1871), Darwin marshalled evidence that like other forms of life on earth, human beings *evolved* through a process of natural selection. If human beings are a product of evolution, may be we too are subject to laws of nature, and therefore, can be studied, analysed and understood scientifically.

Psychologists were just beginning to use scientific methods to study the brain, nerves and sense organs. Most important was the philosopher and physicist Gustav Fechner (1801-1887) who had shown how scientific methods could be applied to the study of mental processes. Early in the 1850s Fechner became interested in the relationship between physical stimulation and sensation. He was fascinated by the sensitivity of human senses. Fechner devised the necessary techniques to find precise answers to questions like – how bright must a star be, to be seen? How loud must a noise be, to be heard? How heavy must a touch be, to be felt? When Fechner's major work, 'Elements of Psychophysics' was published in 1860, it showed how experimental and mathematical procedures could be used to study the human mind. About twenty years later, a German psychologist Wilhelm Wundt, founded a discipline that he eventually called psychology.

THE MAJOR MOVEMENTS IN MODERN PSYCHOLOGY

Structuralism: Wilhelm Wundt and Edward Bradford Titchener

Wilhelm Wundt (1832-1920) was originally trained as a physician, taught physiology for seven years at the University of Heidelberg in Germany. Early in his career he showed interest in mental processes. During this time, the field of psychology had no domain of its own and its subject matter belonged to philosophy. Wundt's ambition was to establish an independent identity for psychology. With this goal he left Heidelberg to accept chairpersonship of the philosophy department at the University of Leipzig in Germany.

Four years later, in 1979, Wundt founded the first experimental psychology laboratory in the world, thus conferring on psychology a full fledged scientific status. His goal was to develop techniques for uncovering the natural laws of human mind. He believed that psychologists should investigate the elementary process of human consciousness, their combinations and relationships much as chemists study the fundamental elements of matter. Wundt felt that it was also important to study the central mental operations such as attention, intentions and goals.

In order to study the elementary process, Wundt and his followers devised a method called 'analytic or objective introspection', a formal type of self observation. They trained themselves in the art of objective introspection, recording in minute detail, their thoughts, feelings, heart beat and respiration rates, *e.g.*, when listening to a metronome. From this they analysed many kinds of sensation patterns in to their component parts. The most important product of Leipzig was its students who carried the new science to universities around the world. Among them was Edward Bradford Titchener, British by birth, who eventually published the summary of the basic 'sensation qualities' that had been discovered.

In 1892, Titchener migrated to the United States and took charge of a new experimental laboratory at Cornell University. He considered psychology as the science of consciousness. He broke consciousness down into three basic elements: physical sensations (what we see), feelings (such as liking or disliking bananas) and images (memories of other bananas). Even the most complex thoughts and feelings can be reduced to these simple elements. Titchener saw psychology's role as identifying these elements and showing how they can be combined and integrated. Because it stresses the basic units of experience and the combinations in which they occur, this school of psychology is called structuralism. The stucturalists held the following beliefs:

1. Psychologists should study human consciousness particularly sensory experiences.
2. They should use analytic introspective laboratory studies.
3. They should analyse the mental processes in to elements, discover their combinations and connections and locate related structures in the nervous system.

Limitations

1. Emphasised one method of study, *i.e.*, formal analytic introspection, which automatically excluded the experiences of children and animals that could not be properly trained.
2. Considered complex phenomena such as thinking, language, morality and abnormality in appropriate for introspective studies.
3. Structuralists were unwilling to address themselves to practical issues.

Functionalism: William James

William James (1842-1910) was the first American born psychologist. He taught philosophy and psychology at Harvard University for thirty five years. William James did not identify with any movement. His special 'system' of psychology evolved from keen observation of himself and others.

James opposed structuralism because he saw it as artificial, narrow and essentially inaccurate. He held that Wundt's 'atoms of experience' – pure sensation without associations, simply do not exist in real life experiences. According to James, our minds are constantly weaving associations, revising experience, starting, stopping, jumping back and forth in time, perception, emotion and images cannot be separated. He argued, consciousness flows in a continuous stream. If we could not recognise a banana, we would have to figure out what it was each time we saw a banana. Mental associations allow benefiting from previous experience.

William James suggested that when we repeat something, our nervous systems are changed so that each repetition is easier than last. With these insights, James arrived at a functionalist theory of mental behaviour. In the early 1900s, several psychologists at the University of Chicago (including John Dewey) were strongly influenced by James' views.

Functionalist theory goes beyond were sensation and perception to explore how an organism learns to function in its environment. The functionalists held the following beliefs:

1. Psychologists should study the functioning of mental processes and many other topics, including the behaviour of children and simple animals, abnormality and individual differences.
2. Psychologists should use informal introspection (self-observation and self report) and objective methods (those relatively free of bias) such as experimentation.
3. Psychological knowledge should be applied to practical matters such as education, law and business.

Behavourism: John B. Watson

John Watson (1878-1958) completed his doctorate in the field of animal psychology at the University of Chicago. In 'Psychology as Behaviourist Views It' (1913), Watson contented that you cannot define consciousness any more than you can define soul. And if you cannot locate or measure something, it cannot be the object of scientific study. Challenging structuralists, functionalists and psychodynamic theories, Watson argued that the whole idea of mental processes or consciousness could not be tested and reproduced by all trained observers, because they depended on each person's idiosyncratic impressions.

Watson's view of psychology, known as behaviourism, was based on well known experiments conducted by the Russian psychologist Ivan Pavlov. Pavlov concluded that all behaviour is learned response to some stimulus in the environment called conditioning.

Many young American psychologists were attracted to the behaviouris movement. In some form or another it dominated American psychology for about thirty years. The early behaviourists had the belief that:

1. Psychologists should study environmental events (stimuli) and observable behaviour (responses).
2. Experience has a more important influence on behaviour, abilities and traits than heredity.
3. Introspection should be abandoned and objective methods should be used like experimentation, observation and testing.
4. Psychologists should aim at the description, explanation, prediction and control of behaviour.
5. The behaviour of lesser animals should be investigated along with human behaviour because, simple organisms are easier to study and understand than complex ones.

Psychoanalytic Psychology: Sigmund Freud

Sigmund Freud (1856-1939) was a Vienese physician specialised in treating problems of the nervous system, particularly neurotic disorders. Freud noticed that many of his patients' nervous ailments appeared to be psychological rather than physiological in origin. Freud's clinical discoveries led him to develop a comprehensive theory called the psychoanalytic theory. Freud held that human beings were motivated by unconscious instincts and urges that are not available to the rational, conscious part of our mind. To uncover the unconscious, he developed a technique, called psychoanalysis, in which the patient lies on a couch, recounts dreams, and says whatever comes to mind which is termed as free association. The psychoanalyst sorts through half remembered scenes, broken trains of thoughts and the like and attempts to reconstruct the past experiences that shape the patient's present behaviour.

Freud held that personality develops in a series of critical stages during the first few years of life. If we successfully resolve the conflicts that we encounter at each of these stages, we can avoid psychological problems in later life. But if we become 'fixated' at any one of these stages, we may carry related feelings of anxiety or exaggerated fears with us in to adulthood. Freud maintained that many unconscious desires and conflicts had their roots in sexual repression. The view reflects that unconscious conflicts within the individual influence much human thought and the action is known as psychoanalytic psychology.

The psychoanalytic psychologists held the following beliefs:

1. Psychologists should study the laws and determinants of personality (normal and abnormal) and devise treatment methods for personality disorders.
2. The important aspects of personality like unconscious motives, memories, fears, conflicts and frustration are to be brought to consciousness for treatment of personality disorders.
3. Personality is formed during early childhood. Exploring memories of the first five years of life is essential for treatment.
4. Personality is most suitably studied in the context of a long term intimate relationship between patient and therapist.

Psychoanalytic theory as expanded and revised by Freud's colleagues and successors, laid the foundation for the study of personality and psychological disorders and remains influential today.

Gestalt Psychology

While behaviourism was becoming popular in America, Gestalt psychology (gestalt is the German word for whole or pattern of structure) was growing in Germany. As the name suggests, the gestalt psychologists believed that experiences carried with them a quality of wholeness of structure. Just like behaviourism, gestalt psychology arose as a protest against structuralism, particularly the practice of reducing complex experiences to simple elements. Gestalt psychology is that school of psychology that studies how people perceive and experience objects as whole patterns.

The gestalt movement had a number of psychologists like Max Wertheimer, Wolfgang Kohler and Kurt Koffka. Gestalt psychology paved the way for the modern study of perception.

The Views of Modern Psychology

Psychology as a science is continuing to grow in dimensions. Although contemporary psychologists rarely follow specific movements, they disagree on some fundamental philosophical issues and hence approach psychology in different ways. Many behavioural scientists identify themselves to some degree with one of the four major points of view like, psychoanalytic, neo-behaviouristic, cognitive and humanistic. Some follow a combination of these views known as eclectic approach.

1. Psychoanalytic View

The psychoanalytic view holds that behaviour results from psychological dynamics that interact within the individual and is often outside conscious awareness.

2. The Neo-behaviouristic View

The behaviouristic approaches have become broader and flexible today. Modern behaviourists still investigate stimuli, observable responses and learning. They also study complicated phenomena that cannot be directly observed like stress, attribution, motivation and personality. This new type of behaviourism is sometimes called neo-behaviourism, where 'neo' means new. The major characteristic of Neo-behaviouristic position is its insistence on asking precise, well delineated questions, using objective methods and careful research.

3. The Cognitive View

In the early 1960s cognitive psychologists began to rebel against the old behaviouristic model. They insisted that psychologists had to come to understand what was going on inside the human mind, particularly the operations of the mind.

Cognitive psychologists hold the following beliefs:

1. Behaviourist scientists should study the mental processes like thought, memory, perception, attention, problem solving, language, etc.
2. Psychologists should aim at acquiring precise knowledge of how these processes operate and how they are applied in daily life.
3. Informal introspection should be used particularly to develop hypotheses, whereas, objective methods are preferred to confirm these hypotheses.

Thus, cognitive psychology combines various aspects of functionalism, gestalt psychology and behaviourism.

4. The Humanistic View

Humanistically oriented psychologists have the aim of humanising psychology. Abraham Maslow (1908-1970) is an important psychologist in the humanistic movement. Most of the humanistically oriented psychologists share the following beliefs:

1. Psychologists should help people understand themselves and develop to their fullest potential enriching human lives.
2. Behavioural scientists should study living human beings as a whole.
3. Significant human problems should be the subject of investigations.
4. Behavioural scientists should focus on subjective awareness.

Methods in Psychology

Psychology is a scientific study of human behaviour and mental processes. It involves collecting data systematically and objectively. To accomplish this, a variety of research methods are used by researchers. Each method has its own advantages and limitations. The following section gives a brief description about the methods in psychology.

1. Naturalistic Observation

Psychologists and researchers use naturalistic observation to study human behaviour in natural settings. It is essentially a way of perceiving behaviour as it is. This method helps to infer mental processes of others through the observation of their external behaviour. Since there is a minimal interference from the researcher, the behaviour observed is more likely to be accurate, spontaneous and varied than behaviour studied in a laboratory.

Advantages

1. It is a natural and flexible procedure, and hence economical.
2. It is reliable and more accurate.
3. It is verifiable by other researchers.
4. Very useful in developmental psychologies.
5. Very useful for clinical psychologists to gather data required for understanding abnormal behaviour.

Limitations

1. Can be used for observing overt behaviours only.
2. It is very difficult to apply in adults as they can easily manipulate or hide their behaviour.

3. Subjectivity of interpretations on the part of the observer will affect the results.
4. The success of the method depends on the ability to establish cause and effect in a proper manner.
5. The behaviour being observed is dependent on time, place and individual or groups involved.

2. *Case Studies*

Researchers conducting a case study investigate the behaviour of one person or a few persons in depth. The concept of clinical method is included in the concept of clinical psychology which is the art and technology of dealing with the adjustment problems of individuals for achieving optimum social adjustment and welfare. It is a method used for studying the behavioural problems of maladjusted or deviant personalities which is often considered as a case.

Case study is characterised by detailed and realistic description of a case. Data pertaining to the past and present are collected and analysed to locate causes of maladjustment or deviation in order to find remedies to it.

The clinical set up or environment is associated with healthcare and treatment of individuals who undergo treatment of physical and mental disorders. This method can yield a great deal of detailed, descriptive information useful for forming hypotheses.

Advantages

1. It can be used for studying specific behaviour of an individual or a group.
2. It studies the problems indepth, and hence it is intensive yielding better results.
3. It is an efficient and useful method.
4. It helps in finding out the problems and its related causes, and suggests remedies to it.

Limitations

1. The success of this method depends on the efficiency of the researcher.
2. The area covered or the scope of the problem is often limited.
3. It focuses only on individual cases.
4. The findings of case studies cannot be generalised.

3. *Surveys*

Under this method data pertaining to a particular phenomenon are gathered and studied to reach at generalisable results. For this, the phenomena under study are thoroughly analysed in to relevant aspects. Questions are formed and pooled so that the maximum relevant data relating to the phenomenon can be generated for studying. Survey research generates large amount of data quickly and inexpensively by asking a set of questions from a large number of people. The data thus gathered are analysed using techniques that are appropriate for the study.

Advantages

1. Data pertaining to phenomenon can be studied on a fairly large sample or population.
2. Data can be collected from a large number of people using questionnaires.
3. Fairly large detailing of data can be done by including more questions in the questionnaires.
4. Large amount of data can be collected quickly that is economical.
5. The results can be generalised.

Limitations

1. The quality of questions determines the accuracy of data collected. Hence, if the questions are not prepared carefully, it may show wrong results.
2. If the sample is not a representative of population, it may affect the results and will give a wrong picture when generalised to the population.
3. The analysis of large amount of data is often a tedious work.

4. The response of respondents is very crucial. If they wrongly represent their responses, it may affect the study.

4. Correlational Research

Correlational research is used to investigate the relation and correlation between two or more variables. Correlational research is useful for clarifying relationships between pre-existing variables that cannot be examined by other means.

5. Experimental Research

In the experimental method one variable (independent variable) is systematically manipulated and the effects on another variable (dependent variable) are studied, usually using both an experimental group of subjects (participants) and a control group for comparison purposes. By holding all other variables constant, the researcher can draw conclusions about cause and effect. Often a neutral person is used to record data and results, so that experimenter bias does not exist.

Advantages

1. It is a scientific method of inquiry.
2. It follows an objective method of research.
3. It helps in establishing the cause and effect relationship.
4. It helps to identify the problems for remediation.

Disadvantages

1. It is conducted under controlled situations.
2. Specific situation demands specific experiments to understand the problem under study.
3. Specialised knowledge is required to conduct experiments.
4. The skill and efficiency of the researcher is very important in conducting experimental research.
5. The researcher must have the ability to design appropriate experiments for conducting research.

ALTERED STATES OF CONSCIOUSNESS

Any state of awareness which differs from the normally experienced state is called altered state of awareness. Altered state can vary from highly focused attention during working to the sleep state of dreaming and sleep. Each day, we all experience the changing states of consciousness, varying levels of awareness of ourselves, our behaviour, and the environment around us. When we go to sleep at night or take drugs, we may experience shifts in consciousness. This raises the question : What happens when we fall asleep and dream? Following section we will examine shifts in consciousness during sleep, hypnosis, and under the influence of drugs.

Sleep

Sleep is a process in which important physiological changes occur. There is slowing of basic bodily functions, accompanied by major shifts in the levels of consciousness. Let us study what goes on during sleep.

It has been seen that various changes occur as individuals fall asleep and remain asleep. Primarily, three major types of changes occurring in the electrical activity of the brain during sleep are studied—Electroencephalogram (EEG), Electron-myogram (EMG), and Electroculogram (EOG). In addition, changes in heart rate, respiration, and skin conduction are also measured.

Stages of Sleep

Usually people pass through 5 stages of sleep: 1, 2, 3, 4 and REM (Rapid Eye Movement) sleep. These stages progress cyclically from 1 through REM then begin again with stage 1. A complete sleep cycle takes an average of 90 to 110 minutes. The first sleep cycle each night have relatively short REM sleeps and long periods of deep sleep but later in the night, REM periods lengthen and deep sleep time decreases.

Stage 1: This is light sleep where you drift in and out of sleep and can be awakened easily. In this stage, the eye move slowly and muscle activity slows. During this stage many people also experience sudden muscle contractions called hypnic myoclonia, often preceded by a sensation of starting to fall. This sleep lasts only a brief time (5-10 minutes).

Stage 2: This stage lasts for approximately 20 minutes. During this stage eye movement stop and our brain waves become slower, with occasional bursts of rapid waves called sleep spindles.

Stage 3: When a person enters stage 3, extremely slow brain waves called delta waves are interspersed with smaller, faster waves.

Stage 4: The brain produces delta waves almost exclusively and sleep lasts for approximately 30 minutes. Stage 3 and 4 are referred to as deep sleep, and it is very difficult to wake someone from them. In deep sleep, there is no eye movement or muscle activity. This is when some children experience bedwetting, sleepwalking and night terrors.

REM Sleep: In REM period, breathing becomes more rapid, irregular and shallow, eyes jerk rapidly and limb muscles are temporarily paralyzed. Brain waves during this stage increase to levels experienced when a person is awake. Also, heart rate increases, blood pressure rises, males develop penile erections and body loses some of the ability to regulate its temperature. This is the time when most dreams occur and if awoken during REM sleep, a person can remember the dreams. Most people experience 3 to 5 intervals of REM sleep each night.

Infants spend almost 50% of their time in REM sleep. Adults spend nearly half of sleep time in stage 2, about 20% in REM and the other 30% is divided between the other 3 stages. Older adults spend progressively less time in REM sleep.

Disorders of Sleep

A sleep disorder (somnipathy) is a medical disorder of the sleep patterns of a person or animal. Some sleep disorders are serious enough to interfere with normal physical, mental and emotional functioning. A test commonly ordered for some sleep disorders is the polysomnogram.

Common Sleep Disorders

1. **Primary Insomnia:** Chronic difficulties in falling asleep and/or maintaining sleep that cannot be attributed to a medical, psychiatric, or environmental cause (such as drug abuse or medications).
2. **Bruxism:** Involuntarily grinding or clenching of the teeth while sleeping. Bruxism can occur during the day or night. Generally, patients clench their teeth throughout the day and gnash and clench them during sleep.
3. **Delayed Sleep Phase Syndrome (DPSP):** Inability to awaken and fall asleep at socially acceptable times but no problem with sleep maintenance, a disorder of circadian rhythms. Children and adolescents with DSPS may experience depression and other psychiatric problems including behavioural problems as a result of daytime drowsiness and missing school.
4. **Hypopnea:** Abnormally shallow breathing or slow respiratory rate while sleeping. Hypopnea is distinct from apnea in which there is no breathing.
5. **Narcolepsy:** Excessive daytime sleepiness (EDS) often culminates in falling asleep spontaneously but unwillingly at inappropriate times. The daytime sleep attacks may occur with or without warning, and can occur repeatedly in a single day. Persons with narcolepsy often have fragmented night time sleep with frequent brief awakenings.
6. **Cataplexy:** A sudden weakness in the motor muscles that can result in collapse to the floor at times of strong emotion such as during laughter, anger, fear, or surprise. In so collapsing, people with cataplexy may injure themselves.
7. **Night Terror:** Abrupt awakening from sleep with behaviour consistent with terror. Night terrors occur during the transition from stage

3 non-REM sleep to stage 4 non-REM sleep, beginning approximately 90 minutes after the child falls asleep. The sleep disorder of night terrors typically occurs in children aged 3-12 years, with a peak onset in children aged 3½ years.

8. **Parasomnias:** Disruptive sleep related events involving inappropriate actions during sleep stages, sleep walking and night terrors are examples.
9. **Periodic Limb Movement Disorder (PLMD):** Sudden involuntary movement or jerking of arms and/or legs during sleep, for example kicking the legs. It is the only movement disorder that occurs only during sleep, and it is sometimes called periodic leg (or limb) movements during sleep.
10. **Rapid Eye Movement Behaviour Disorder:** People who suffer from REM behaviour disorder (RBD) act out their dreams. They physically move limbs or even get up and engage in activities associated with waking. Some engage in sleep talking, shouting, screaming, hitting or punching.
11. **Sleep Paralysis:** This is characterized by temporary paralysis of the body shortly before or after sleep.
12. **Sleep Walking or Somnambulism:** Is characterized by walking or other activity while seemingly still asleep. Some types of sleep walking are related to seizure disorders, bipolar disorders, or other neurological conditions, but most cases are transitory and due to unknown causes.
13. **Nocturia:** A frequent need to get up and go to the bathroom to urinate at night. It can be troublesome in itself, by disturbing sleep, and can have a significant impact on quality of sleep and quality of life.
14. **Sleep Apnea:** This disorder is potentially very serious and even life threatening. During the episodes of apnea, the person wakes up to breathe again, disrupting sleep, and also suffer from a brief lack of oxygen or a complete stop of breathing during sleep. There are two main types of sleep apnea; obstructive sleep apnea (OSA) and central sleep apnea (CSA). Mixed sleep apnea refers to the combination of both central and obstructive sleep apnea.

Physiological Mechanism of Sleep & Waking

Neural control of arousal/waking

1. **Acetylcholine:** One of the most important neurotransmitters involved in arousal. Two groups of acetycholinergic neurons located in the pons and basal forebrain, produce activation & cortical de-synchrony when they are stimulated.
2. **Norepinephrine:** Norepinephrine is an excitatory neurotransmitter, and it regulates mood and physical and mental arousal.
3. **Serotonin (5-HT):** It is an important inhibitory neurotransmitter, which can have a profound effect on emotion, mood, and anxiety. It is involved in regulating sleep, wakefulness, and eating. It plays a role in perception as well.
4. **Histamine:** A neurotransmitter implicated in control of wakefulness and arousal; a compound synthesized from histidine, an amino acid.
5. **Tuberomammillary nucleus:** A nucleus in the ventral posterior hypothalamus, just rostral to the mammillary bodies consists of, largely, histaminergic neurons (*i.e.*, neurones releasing histamine) and is involved with the control of arousal, sleep and circadian rhythm.
6. **Hypocretin:** Orexin, also called hypocretin, is a neurotransmitter that regulates arousal, wakefulness, and appetite. It is basically Involved in regulating the sleep on/off cells in the ventro lateral preoptic area (VLPA).

Neural Control of Slow Wave Sleep

Ventrolateral Preoptic Area (VLPA): The VLPO is active during sleep, primarily during non-rapid eye movement sleep (NREM sleep), and releases inhibitory neurotransmitters, mainly GABA and galanin, which inhibit neurons that are involved in wakefulness and arousal.

Lesions of the preoptic area produce total insomnia, leading to death, whereas electrical stimulation of the preoptic area induces signs of drowsiness.

Neural Control of REM Sleep

PGO Wave (Pons, Geniculate, Occipital) are most prominent in the period right before rapid eye movement sleep (or REM sleep), and are theorized to be intricately involved with eye movement of both wake and sleep cycles in many different animals.

Dreams

Dreams are cognitive events often vivid, sometimes jumbled but disconnected, that occur during sleep. Most of the dreams take place during the REM sleep. As demonstrated by the EEG recordings during sleep, everyone dreams during sleep. Dreams seem to run on "real time". That is, dreams last for some time. Some people are able to remember the dreams, others are not able to do so.

Sigmund Freud, a psychologist, believed that often dreams reflect our unconscious unfulfilled wishes or impulses. Freud thought that dreams provide useful means for probing the unconscious. He believed that we express the impulses and desires we find unacceptable during our waking hours. For example, one can dream of having sexual experience or murdering someone. However, this view of dream interpretation has not been accepted by other psychologists.

Another explanation of dreams in the terms is physiological process. The dreams are our subjective experience of random-neural activity in the brain during sleep. Dreams, according to the physiological view, simply represent the efforts by our cognitive system to make sense out of the random neural activity.

Closely related to the physiological view is the cognitive view. In the dreams the cortical structures or systems that normally regulate perception and thought have only their own activity as input. In waking state the input for perceptual and thought processes generally comes from outside. Thus, the neural activity of the brain forms the basis of our dreams. Since dreams represent interpretations of neural activity by our own brain, they reflect aspects of our memories and waking experience. Thus, dreams are not meaningless.

Hypnosis

Hypnosis is the state of highest suggestibility. It is an altered state of consciousness. The individual under hypnosis undergoes "deep trans". Hypnosis is a special type of interaction between two persons in which one (the hypnotist) gives suggestions to the other (the hypnotized) and the changes are induced in the hypnotized. The suggestions by the hypnotist is that the person, being hypnotized, is feeling relaxed, is getting sleepy, and is unable to keep the eyes open. Speaking continuously in a calm voice, the hypnotist suggests to the person that she/he is gradually sinking deeper and deeper into a relaxed state.

The person does not go into sleep state, but a state in which he/she will be highly susceptible and open to suggestions by the hypnotist. There are other methods of inducing hypnosis.

In hypnosis, the individual enters into what appears to be an altered state of consciousness that is not sleep. The EEG recording of a hypnotized person resembles those of normal waking state. During the hypnotic trans like state the individual is highly susceptible and carries out the instructions provided by the hypnotist.

The Consciousness-altering drugs

Drugs are compounds that, because of their chemical structure, change the functioning of biological system. These drugs produce changes in person's consciousness. These drugs are, thus, called consciousness-altering drugs. People who take drugs purely to change their moods are said to indulge in drug abuse. Such abuse impairs their behaviour and social functioning and gradually they often develop psychological dependence on those drugs.

Many different drugs affect consciousness. These drugs could be classified as : **depressants, stimulants, opiates, or psychedelics and hallucinogens.** Let us study about them.

Depressants

Drugs that reduce both behavioural output and activity in the central nervous system (CNS) are classified as depressants. Most important and more often used in the world is alcohol. Small doses of alcohol seem to be stimulating, *i.e.*, it induces feelings of excitement and activation. However, larger doses of alcohol act as depressant, dull the senses, in which case feelings of pain, and other kinds of discomfort are not perceived. Large quantity of alcohol affects coordination and normal functioning of our senses. It also lowers social inhibition. Under the heavy usage of alcohol people are more likely to engage in dangerous and socially unacceptable forms of behaviour such as aggression.

Other types of drugs in depressant include barbiturates such as sleeping pills and other relaxants. These drugs depress activity in the CNS and reduce the degree of activation and mental alertness. Initially, high doses of barbiturates produce feelings of relaxation and euphoria. However, they often go on to produce confusion, slurred speech, memory lapses and reduced ability to concentrate. Extremely large doses can be fatal, because they result in paralysis of centres of the brain that regulate breathing. These drugs induce sleep. People often use them to treat sleep disorder.

Stimulants

Stimulants include those drugs that induce feelings of energy and activation. In this category fall Amphatamines and Cocaine. These drugs produce a condition in which neurons, that would otherwise stop firing, continue to respond. These drugs raise blood pressure, heart rate, and respiration. All these are signs of activation. In addition, these drugs yield short periods of pleasurable sensations. However, the effect wears off in a few minutes and the users often experience an emotional crash involving anxiety, depression, and fatigue.

Cocaine is usually consumed through inhalation into each nostril. It is absorbed through the lining of the nose directly into the blood stream. It often produces psychological dependence. Other stimulants in common use are caffeine, found in coffee, tea, and many soft drinks like Coca-Cola, Pepsi, etc. Nicotine is another stimulant that is highly addictive. It is found in tobacco.

Opiates

The most often used and dangerous drugs are opiates. They include opium, morphine, heroin, and related synthetic drugs. Opium is derived from the opium poppy. Morphine is produced from opium, and heroin from morphine. Opiates produce lethargy and pronounce slowing of body functions. These drugs also alter consciouness, producing a dreamlike state. However, these drugs are extremely addictive and withdrawal from these drugs produces agony.

Psychedelics and Hallucinogens

Psychedelics are drugs that alter perception and is considered mind expanding. Hallucinogens are drugs that generate perceptions for which there are no external stimuli. The most widely used psychedelic drug is marijuana. Marijuana increases heart rate (upto 160. beats/minute), changes in blood pressure, and dilation of blood vessels in the eye. Short-term psychological effects include heightened senses of vision and audition.

Marijuana, interferes with the attentional processes, affects memory, and reduces ability to judge distances. Some people report reduction in inhibition, feelings of relaxation, and increased sexual pleasure. It has generally been found that the effects of marijuana are shaped according to users' expectations.

Marijuana, used widely all over the world, produces perceptual distortions and can result in accident. More dramatic effects are produced by hallucinogens, which produce hallucinations and other perceptual shifts. The most infamous drug is LSD (Lysergic Acid Diethylamide) which is produced synthetically. After taking LSD, many people report profound changes in perception of external world. There may be strange blending of sensory experiences. For example, colours produce feeling of warmth or cold, one's own body may seem distorted, one may experience deep sorrow or develop intense fear, etc. The effects of drug are unpredictable, same person may experience radically different effects at different times. LSD is considered the most dangerous drug and can result in permanent brain damage.

BEHAVIORAL PSYCHOLOGY

Models of Human Behaviour

Psychoanalytic Model

Freudian approach depends on conflict model of humans. Using clinical techniques of free association and psychotherapy Freud felt that behaviour is not always consciously explained. "Unconscious" is the major factor which guides the individual's behaviour. Freud felt that the individual's behaviour depends on three factors: (*i*) Id, (*ii*) Ego and (*iii*) Superego.

Id: Id indicates pleasure. To a certain degree of having Id in an individual is constructive but may also lead to destructive tendencies like being aggressive, dominating, fighting and generally destroy. This kind of instinctive is more dominating in childhood. But once individuals develop and mature, they learn to control the id. But it is always unconscious. Throughout life the 'id' becomes an important source of thinking and behaving.

Ego: Ego represents 'conscious' stage in one's behaviour. Though Id comes in conflict with ego, the ego depends on the super ego.

Superego: It represents "conscience". An individual is not aware of the superego's functioning. The conscience is dependent on two factors, *i.e.*, cultural values and moral of a society. Superego's development depends mostly on parents' influence. Once the child grows up, it will unconsciously identifies with parents' value and morals.

There is always tussle between id, ego and superego. The degree of each of them varies from person to person. So the variations in individual's behaviour can be better understood with the help of this model.

But the modern theorists have severely criticised this theory as it is not based on any empirical facts and as such it can not be accepted in totality. But the concept of "unconscious" is a significant contribution in understanding specific behaviour of humans.

Existential Model: This model is not scientifically based. Its base is literature and philosophy.

The existentialists believe that the depersonalising effects of this environment force individuals to make their own destiny. So the individuals shape their own identity and make their "existence" meaningful and worthwhile to themselves.

This is more true and happening in today's urbanisation. Because people have become so materialistic and busy, they do not have time for traditional values and norms and it becomes impractical sometimes to follow them. Existential model is, especially true when you are employed in today's world.

Though this model is not scientific it can be definitely used in understanding human behaviour.

Internal vs. External Determinants of Behaviour

Environment plays a major role in shaping behaviour and genetic endowment and personality development is influenced by our historical heritage.

Personality vs. the Environment

Both personality and situational variables must be taken into account in order to explain an individual's behaviour but a focus on the environment is as important or perhaps slightly more important than focusing on personality traits.

Cognition vs. the Environment

To understand one's behaviour all we have to know is the individual's past responses to similar (stimulus) situations and the rewards or punishments that followed that response.

There are two models which come out of these approaches:

1. **Behaviouristic Model:** In this model the behaviour is dependent on two factors, *viz.*, stimulus and response. Learning occurs with this kind of model. Pavlov and Watson with their research felt that behaviour can be best understood by stimulus and response.

   Behaviourist model is represented as: S-R (Stimulus-Response)

2. **Cognitive Model:** S-OR-R. This model emphasises the positive and free-will factors of human beings and uses concepts such as expectancy, demand and incentive.

   Tolman with his experiments found that the basis of learning as of 'expectancy' is understood as one particular event leading to a particular consequence *i.e.*, goal. Human behaviour is based on these goals.

   The cognitive model is represented as:
   S-O-R (Stimulus-Organism-Response model)

Both approaches see learning and the environment as having a major impact on behaviour. From these different approaches it can be said that:

(*i*) Behaviour is caused by instincts, genetic background and personality traits that are formed at an early age. Change is very difficult for the individual and that one's capacity is severely limited.

(*ii*) Behaviour is mostly learned through our interactions with the environment. Present events rather than past events are important. Even though there are some limitations on one's capacities, one is capable of great amounts of change.

Determinants of Behaviour

Behaviour is determined by attitude, personality, perception, motivation, abilities, self-concept, and socio-cultural set up, reference group, needs and situation. These factors are explained below.

1. **Attitude:** Attitude is a cognitive and affective evaluation that predisposes a person to act in a certain way. Behaviour is an outward expression of a particular attitude. Attitude results in intended behaviour. Attitude influences behaviour. Example: An employee with an attitude 'I like my job'. will behave enthusiastically and extend cooperation on the job.
2. **Personality:** Personality is the sum total of personal characteristics (physical and psychological) of a human being which affects behaviour. Example: introverts are shy; extroverts happen to be outgoing; agreeable people tend to be cooperative and flexible; and a conscientious person reflects thoroughness and dependability.
3. **Perception:** Perception is the unique way each person 'sees' and interprets things. Point of view is perception. Perception discriminates the understanding of one person from another. Different people attach different meaning to the same stimulus and these result in differences in behaviour. For example, a manager may not hire an old person because of his perception that an old person lacks flexibility as compared to a young worker. On the other hand, another may hire an old person giving lots of importance to his experience.
4. **Motivation:** Our inner needs determine behaviour. A person interested in sports would love to arrange sports activity if given a chance.
5. **Ability:** Abilities influence behaviour, in order to do well on job; one needs the abilities to do the same. For example, a typist can type speedily and accurately as compared to someone who has not learned this activity.

6. **Self-Concept:** A person owns perception about himself and his self worth in his eyes shapes his behaviour. People with healthy self concept behave positively.
7. **Self-Efficacy:** An individual's belief about his own capacity to perform a task determines behaviour. Research indicates that self efficacy is associated with high work performance in many work areas like sales, life insurance job, etc.
8. **Socio-Cultural Set Up:** Shared sentiments, feelings, rituals, customs, etc., affect and govern behaviour.
9. **Reference Group:** The reference group with which individuals interact determines behaviour. Compliance is always sought from reference group in case of important decisions.
10. **Needs:** Individual's needs determine behaviour. For example, if a student wants to be successful in exams he will study hard.
11. **Situations:** Situations or external factors also affect behaviour. For example, a student will behave differently in the principal's office, in temple or in an employment interview.

PERSONALITY

Concept of Personality

The term 'personality' often appears in our day-to-day discussion. The literal meaning of personality is derived from the Latin word **persona**, the mask used by actors in the Roman theatre for changing their facial make-up. After putting on the mask, audience expected the person to perform a role in a particular manner. It did not, however, mean that the person enacting the given role necessarily possessed those qualities.

For a layperson, personality generally refers to the physical or external appearance of an individual. For example, when we find someone 'good-looking', we often assume that the person also has a charming personality. This notion of personality is based on superficial impressions, which may not be correct.

In psychological terms, **personality** *refers to our characteristic ways of responding to individuals and situations.* People can easily describe the way in which they respond to various situations. Certain catchwords (e.g., shy, sensitive, quiet, concerned, warm, etc.) are often used to describe personalities. These words refer to different components of personality. In this sense, personality refers to unique and relatively stable qualities that characterise an individual's behaviour across different situations over a period of time.

Definitions of personality

- **N.L. Munn**—'Personality may be defined as the most characteristic—integration of an individual's structure, modes of behaviour, interest, attitudes, capacities, abilities and aptitudes'.
- **C.V. Good**—'The total psychological and social reaction of an individual, the synthesis of his subjective, emotional and mental life'.
- **Valentile**—'Personality is the sum total of innate and acquired dispositions'.

Nature of Personality

Personality is the result of both heredity and environment

Heredity involves all those physiological and psychological peculiarities, which a person inherits from his parents. These peculiarities are transmitted to us through genes. It is indisputable that heredity determines the difference of sex and it is on this basis that some scientists contend that heredity determines personality because it is the difference of sex, which determines the personality of men and women.

Environment has a very significant effect on man. Its effect starts from his birth and continues almost till his death. The status of the child, youth and the old man in the family and in the society is not same and as a result of this difference, a man's roles, temperaments, ways of thinking, tendencies and character are affected; all these determine the personality of men and women. In the same way, the status of the person in places like school, occupation, social situation, etc., affects his personality.

Personality is composed of traits, which are by and large learned or acquired

By the time we become a mature personality, the contribution of learning is so prominent that we often misinterpret personality as the equivalent of learning. It is important to note that learning plays a very important role in the making of one's personality. In order to explain the dynamics of one's personality, it is sometimes convenient to refer to the various types of learning, which a person is able to exhibit in his behavioural range.

Personality implies an integration of various traits

All the elements, which are ultimately identified as parts of personality structure, get integrated rather than assembled together. Thus, the integration of various traits results into a distinct whole which is known as personality of an individual. Personality represents a unique integration of traits so as to differentiate one person from another on the basis of this very quality. The unique way in which we laugh or smile, weep or cry, talk or lecture, greet or salute becomes the watermark of our personality.

Personality is a dynamic process

Personality is the dynamic organization within the individual. Here, dynamic means that personality is undergoing a constant change but is still organized. Personality development is a reciprocal relationship between the ways in which a person views his experiences and his actual social and interpersonal experiences. Development of personality is a continuous growth, which occurs because of the inherent tendency toward self-growth on the one hand and our personal, environmental and social experiences on the other hand. Therefore, we can say that personality is a dynamic process.

Major Approaches to the Study of Personality

Psychologists interested in the study of personality, try to answer certain questions about the nature and origin of individual differences in personality. You may have observed that two children in the same family develop dramatically different personalities. Not only they look physically different, but they also behave differently in different situations. These observations often generate curiosity and force us to ask: "Why is it that some people react differently in a given situation than others do? Why is it that some people enjoy adventurous activities, while others like reading, watching television or playing cards? Are these differences stable all through one's life, or they are just short-lived and situation-specific?"

A number of approaches and theories have been developed to understand and explain behavioural differences among individuals, and behavioural consistencies within an individual. These theories are based on different models of human behaviour. Each throws light on some, but not all, aspects of personality.

Psychologists distinguish between type and trait approaches to personality. The **type approach** attempts to comprehend human personality by examining certain broad patterns in the observed behavioural characteristics of individuals. Each behavioural pattern refers to one type in which individuals are placed in terms of the similarity of their behavioural characteristics with that pattern. In contrast, the **trait approach** focuses on the specific psychological attributes along which individuals tend to differ in consistent and stable ways. For example, one person may be less shy, whereas another may be more; or one person may be less friendly, whereas another may be more. Here "shyness" and "friendliness" represent traits along which individuals can be rated in terms of the degree of presence or absence of the concerned behavioural quality or a trait. The **interactional approach** holds that situational characteristics play an important role in determining our behaviour. People may behave as dependent or independent not because of their internal personality trait, but because of external rewards or threats available in a particular situation. The cross-situational consistency of traits is found to be quite low. The compelling influence of situations can be noted by observing people's behaviour in places like a market, a courtroom, or a place of worship.

Type Approaches

As we explained above, personality types are used to represent and communicate a set of expected behaviours based on similarities. Efforts to categorise people into personality types have been made since ancient times. The Greek physician Hippocrates had proposed a typology of personality based on fluid or humour. He classified people into four types *(i.e. sanguine, phlegmatic, melancholic* and *choleric);* each characterised by specific behavioural features.

In India also, *Charak Samhita,* a famous treatise on *Ayurveda,* classifies people into the categories of *vata, pitta* and *kapha* on the basis of three humoural elements called *tridosha.* Each refers to a type of temperament, called *prakriti* (basic nature) of a person. Apart from this, there is also a typology of personality based on the *trigunas, i.e., sattva, rajas,* and *tamas. Sattva guna* includes attributes like cleanliness, truthfulness, dutifulness, detachment, discipline, etc. *Rajas guna* includes intensive activity, desire for sense gratification, dissatisfaction, envy for others, and a materialistic mentality, etc. *Tamas guna* characterises anger, arrogance, depression, laziness, feeling of helplessness, etc. All the three *gunas* are present in each and every person in different degrees. The dominance of one or the other *guna* may lead to a particular type of behaviour.

Within psychology, the personality types given by Sheldon are fairly well-known. Using body build and temperament as the main basis, Sheldon proposed the **Endomorphic, Mesomorphic,** and **Ectomorphic** typology. The endomorphs are fat, soft and round. By temperament they are relaxed and sociable. The mesomorphs have strong musculature, are rectangular with a strong body build. They are energetic and courageous. The ectomorphs are thin, long and fragile in body build. They are brainy, artistic and introvert.

Let us remember that these body typologies are simple, and have limited use in predicting behaviour of individuals. They are more like stereotypes which people hold.

Jung has proposed another important typology by grouping people into *introverts* and *extroverts.* This is widely recognised. According to this typology, introverts are people who prefer to be alone, tend to avoid others, withdraw themselves in the face of emotional conflicts, and are shy. Extroverts, on the other hand, are sociable, outgoing, drawn to occupations that allow dealing directly with people, and react to stress by trying to lose themselves among people and social activity.

In recent years, Friedman and Rosenman have classified individuals into Type-A and Type-B personalities. The two researchers were trying to identify psychosocial risk factors when they discovered these types. People characterised by **Type-A** *personality* seem to possess high motivation, lack patience, feel short of time, be in a great hurry, and feel like being always burdened with work. Such people find it difficult to slow down and relax. People with Type-A personality are more susceptible to problems like hypertension and coronary heart disease (CHD). The risk of developing CHD with Type-A personality is sometimes even greater than the risks caused by high blood pressure, high cholesterol levels, or smoking. Opposite to this is the **Type-B** *personality,* which can be understood as *the absence of Type-A traits.* This typology has been further extended. Morris has suggested a **Type-C** *personality,* which is prone to cancer. Individuals characterised by this personality are cooperative, unassertive and patient. They suppress their negative emotions (e.g., anger), and show compliance to authority. More recently, a **Type-D** *personality* has been suggested, which is characterised by proneness to depression.

Personality typologies are usually very appealing, but are too simplistic. Human behaviour is highly complex and variable. Assigning people to a particular personality type is difficult. People do not fit into such simple categorisation schemes so neatly.

Trait Approaches

These theories are mainly concerned with the description or characterisation of basic components of personality. They try to discover the 'building blocks' of personality. Human beings display a wide range of variations in psychological attributes, yet it is possible to club them into smaller number of personality traits. Trait approach is very similar to our common experience in everyday life. For example, when we come to know that a person is *sociable,* we assume that she/he will not only be cooperative, friendly and helping, but also engage in behaviours that involve other social components. Thus, trait approach attempts to identify primary characteristics of people. A trait is considered as a relatively enduring attribute or quality on which one individual differs from another. They include a range of possible behaviours that are activated according to the demands of the situation.

To summarise, (*a*) traits are relatively stable over time, (*b*) they are generally consistent across situations, and (*c*) their strengths and combinations vary across individuals leading to individual differences in personality.

A number of psychologists have used traits to formulate their theories of personality. We will discuss some important theories.

Allport's Trait Theory

Gordon Allport is considered the pioneer of trait approach. He proposed that individuals possess a number of traits, which are dynamic in nature. They determine behaviour in such a manner that an individual approaches different situations with similar plans. The traits integrate stimuli and responses which otherwise look dissimilar. Allport argued that the words people use to describe themselves and others provide a basis for understanding human personality. He analysed the words of English language to look for traits which describe a person. Allport, based on this, categorised traits into *cardinal, central,* and *secondary.* **Cardinal traits** are highly generalised dispositions. They indicate the goal around which a person's entire life seems to revolve. Mahatma Gandhi's non-violence and Hitler's Nazism are examples of cardinal traits. Such traits often get associated with the name of the person so strongly that they derive such identities as the 'Gandhian' or 'Hitlerian' trait. Less pervasive in effect, but still quite generalised dispositions, are called **central traits.** These traits (*e.g.*, warm, sincere, diligent, etc.) are often used in writing a testimonial or job recommendation for a person. The least generalised characteristics of a person are called **secondary traits.** Traits such as 'likes mangoes' or 'prefers ethnic clothes' are examples of secondary traits.

While Allport acknowledged the influence of situations on behaviour, he held that the way a person reacts to given situations depends on her/his traits, although people sharing the same traits might express them in different ways. Allport considered traits more like intervening variables that occur between the stimulus situation and response of the person. This meant that any variation in traits would elicit a different response to the same situation.

Cattell: Personality Factors

Raymond Cattell believed that there was a common structure on which people differ from each other. This structure could be determined empirically. He tried to identify the primary traits from a huge array of descriptive adjectives found in language. He applied a statistical technique, called **factor analysis,** to discover the common structures. He found 16 primary or source traits. The **source traits** are stable, and are considered as the building blocks of personality. Besides these, there are also a number of **surface traits** that result out of the interaction of source traits. Cattell described the source traits in terms of opposing tendencies. He developed a test, called **Sixteen Personality Factor Questionnaire (16PF),** for the assessment of personality. This test is widely used by the psychologists.

Eysenck's Theory

H.J. Eysenck proposed that personality could be reduced into two broad dimensions. These are biologically and genetically based. Each dimension subsumes a number of specific traits.

These dimensions are:

1. *Neuroticism vs. emotional stability* : It refers to the degree to which people have control over their feelings. At one extreme of the dimension, we find people who are neurotic. They are anxious, moody, touchy, restless and quickly lose control. At the other extreme lie people who are calm, even-tempered, reliable and remain under control.
2. *Extroversion vs. introversion* : It refers to the degree to which people are socially outgoing or socially withdrawn. At one extreme are those who are active, gregarious, impulsive and thrill-seeking. At the other extreme are people who are passive, quiet, cautious and reserved.

In a later work Eysenck proposed a third dimension, called *Psychoticism vs. Sociability,* which is considered to interact with the other two dimensions mentioned above. A person who scores high on psychoticism dimension tends to be hostile, egocentric, and antisocial. **Eysenck Personality Questionnaire** is the test which is used for studying these dimensions of personality.

The trait approach is very popular and many advances in this respect are taking place. These are beyond the scope of your present studies. A new formulation has also been advanced that provides a novel scheme of organising traits.

Psychodynamic Approach

This is a highly popular approach to study personality. This view owes largely to the contributions of Sigmund Freud. He was a physician, and developed this theory in the course of his clinical practice. Early in his career he used hypnosis to treat people with physical and emotional problems. He noted that many of his patients needed to talk about their problems, and having talked about them, they often felt better. Freud used *free association* (a method in which a person is asked to openly share all the thoughts, feelings and ideas that come to her/his mind), *dream analysis,* and *analysis of errors* to understand the internal functioning of the mind.

Levels of Consciousness

Freud's theory considers the sources and consequences of emotional conflicts and the way people deal with these. In doing so, it visualises the human mind in terms of **three levels of consciousness.** The first level is **conscious,** which includes the thoughts, feelings and actions of which people are aware. The second level is **preconscious,** which includes mental activity of which people may become aware only if they attend to it closely. The third level is **unconscious,** which includes mental activity that people are unaware of.

According to Freud, the unconscious is a reservoir of instinctive or animal drives. It also stores all ideas and wishes that are concealed from the conscious awareness, perhaps, because they lead to psychological conflicts. Most of these arise from sexual desires which cannot be expressed openly and therefore are repressed. People constantly struggle to find either some socially acceptable ways to express unconscious impulses, or to keep those impulses away from being expressed. Unsuccessful resolution of conflicts results in abnormal behaviour. Analysis of forgetting, mispronunciations, jokes and dreams provide us with a means to approach the unconscious. Freud developed a therapeutic procedure, called **psychoanalysis.** The basic goal of psychoanalytic therapy is to bring the repressed unconscious materials to consciousness, thereby helping people to live in a more self-aware and integrated manner.

Structure of Personality

According to Freud's theory, the primary structural elements of personality are three, *i.e.,* **id, ego** and **superego.** They reside in the unconscious as forces, and they can be inferred from the ways people behave (see Fig.). Let us remember that id, ego and superego are concepts, not real physical structures. We will discuss these terms in some detail.

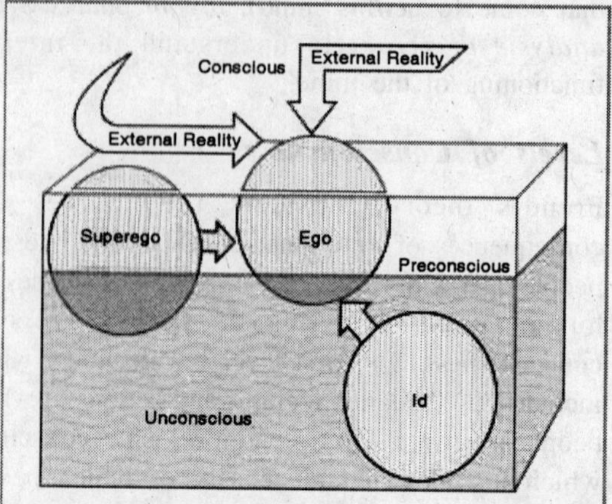

Fig. : *Structure of Personality in Freudian Theory*

Id : It is the source of a person's instinctual energy. It deals with immediate gratification of primitive needs, sexual desires and aggressive impulses. It works on the **pleasure principle,** which assumes that people seek pleasure and try to avoid pain. Freud considered much of a person's instinctual energy to be sexual, and the rest as aggressive. Id does not care for moral values, society, or other individuals.

Ego : It grows out of id, and seeks to satisfy an individual's instinctual needs in accordance with reality. It works by the **reality principle,** and often directs the id towards more appropriate ways of behaving. For example, the id of a boy, who wants an ice-cream cone, tells him to grab the cone and eat it. His ego tells him that if he grabs the cone without asking, he may be punished. Working on the reality principle, the boy knows that the best way to achieve gratification is to ask for permission to eat the cone. Thus, while the id is demanding, unrealistic and works according to pleasure principle, the ego is patient, reasonable, and works by the reality principle.

Superego : The best way to characterise the superego is to think of it as the moral branch of mental functioning. The superego tells the id and the ego whether gratification in a particular instance is ethical. It helps control the id by internalising the parental authority through the process of socialisation. For example, if a boy sees and wants an ice-cream cone and asks his mother for it, his superego will indicate that his behaviour is morally correct. This approach towards obtaining the ice-cream will not create guilt, fear or anxiety in the boy.

Thus, in terms of individual functioning Freud thought of the unconscious as being composed of three competing forces. In some people, the id is stronger than the superego; in others, it is the superego. The relative strength of the id, ego and superego determines each person's stability. Freud also assumed that id is energised by two instinctual forces, called **life instinct** and **death instinct.** He paid less attention to the death instinct and focused more on the life (or sexual) instinct. The instinctual life force that energises the id is called **libido.** It works on the pleasure principle, and seeks immediate gratification.

Ego Defence Mechanisms

According to Freud, much of human behaviour reflects an attempt to deal with or escape from anxiety. Thus, how the ego deals with anxiety largely determines how people behave. Freud believed, people avoid anxiety mainly by developing defence mechanisms that try to defend the ego against the awareness of the instinctual needs. Thus, **defence mechanism** is a way of reducing anxiety by distorting reality. Although some defence against anxiety is normal and adaptive, people who use these mechanisms to such an extent that reality is truly distorted develop various forms of maladjustment.

Freud has described many different kinds of defence mechanisms. The most important is **repression,** in which anxiety-provoking behaviours or thoughts are totally dismissed by the unconscious. When people repress a feeling or desire, they become totally unaware of that wish or desire. Thus, when a person says, "I do not know why I did that", some repressed feeling or desire is expressing itself.

Other major defence mechanisms are projection, denial, reaction formation and rationalisation. In **projection,** people attribute their own traits to others.

Thus, a person who has strong aggressive tendencies may see other people as acting in an excessively aggressive way towards her/him. In **denial,** a person totally refuses to accept reality. Thus, someone suffering from HIV/AIDS may altogether deny her/his illness. In **reaction formation,** a person defends against anxiety by adopting behaviours opposite to her/his true feelings. A person with strong sexual urges, who channels her/his energy into religious fervour, presents a classical example of reaction formation. In **rationalisation,** a person tries to make unreasonable feelings or behaviour seem reasonable and acceptable. For example, when a student buys a set of new pens after doing poorly in an examination, she/he may try to rationalise her/his behaviour by asserting, "I will do much better with these pens".

People who use defence mechanisms are often unaware of doing so. Each defence mechanism is a way for the ego to deal with the uncomfortable feelings produced by anxiety. However, Freud's ideas about the role of defence mechanisms have been questioned. For example, his claim that projection reduces anxiety and stress has not found support in several studies.

Stages of Personality Development

Freud claims that the core aspects of personality which are established early, remain stable throughout life, and can be changed only with great difficulty. He proposed a **five-stage theory** of personality (also called *psychosexual*) development. Problems encountered at any stage may arrest development, and have a long-term effect on a person's life. A brief description of these stages is given here.

Oral Stage : A newborn's instincts are focused on the mouth. This is the infant's primary pleasure seeking centre. It is through the mouth that the baby obtains food that reduces hunger. The infant achieves oral gratification through feeding, thumb sucking, biting and babbling. It is during these early months that people's basic feelings about the world are established. Thus, for Freud, an adult who considers the world a bitter place probably had difficulty during the oral stage of development.

Anal Stage : It is found that around ages two and three the child learns to respond to some of the demands of the society. One of the principal demands made by the parents is that the child learns to control the bodily functions of urination and defecation. Most children at this age experience pleasure in moving their bowels. The anal area of the body becomes the focus of certain pleasurable feelings. This stage establishes the basis for conflict between the id and the ego, and between the desire for babyish pleasure and demand for adult, controlled behaviour.

Phallic Stage : This stage focuses on the genitals. At around ages four and five children begin to realise the differences between males and females. They become aware of sexuality and the sexual relationship between their parents. During this stage, the male child experiences the **Oedipus Complex,** which involves love for the mother, hostility towards the father, and the consequent fear of punishment or castration by the father *(Oedipus was a Greek king who unknowingly killed his father and then married his mother).* A major developmental achievement of this stage is the resolution of the Oedipus complex. This takes place by accepting his father's relationship with his mother, and modelling his own behaviour after his father.

For girls, the Oedipus complex (called the **Electra Complex** *after Electra, a Greek character, who induced her brother to kill their mother)* follows a slightly different course. By attaching her love to the father a girl tries to symbolically marry him and raise a family. When she realises that this is unlikely, she begins to identify with her mother and copy her behaviour as a means of getting (or, sharing in) her father's affection. The critical component in resolving the Oedipus complex is the development of identification with the same sex parents. In other words, boys give up sexual feelings for their mothers and begin to see their fathers as role models rather than as rivals; girls give up their sexual desires for their father and identify with their mother.

Latency Stage : This stage lasts from about seven years until puberty. During this period, the child continues to grow physically, but sexual urges are relatively inactive. Much of a child's energy is channelled into social or achievement-related activities.

Genital Stage : During this stage, the person attains maturity in psychosexual development. The sexuality, fears and repressed feelings of earlier stages are once again exhibited. People learn to deal with members of the opposite sex in a socially and sexually mature way. However, if the journey towards this stage is marked by excessive stress or over-indulgence, it may cause fixation to an earlier stage of development.

Freud's theory also postulates that as children proceed from one stage to another stage of development, they seem to adjust their view of the world. Failure of a child to pass successfully through a stage leads to **fixation** to that stage. In this situation, the child's development gets arrested at an earlier stage. For example, a child who does not pass successfully through the phallic stage fails to resolve the Oedipal complex and may still feel hostile toward the parent of the same sex. This failure may have serious consequences for the child's life. Such a boy may come to consider that men are generally hostile, and may wish to relate to females in a dependable relationship. **Regression** is also a likely outcome in such situations. It takes a person back to an earlier stage. Regression occurs when a person's resolution of problems at any stage of development is less than adequate. In this situation, people display behaviours typical of a less mature stage of development.

Post-Freudian Approaches

A number of theorists further developed their ideas following Freud. Some had worked with him and then moved on to develop their own versions of the psychoanalytic theory. These theorists have been called *neo-analytic,* or *post-Freudian* in order to differentiate their work from Freud's. These theories are characterised by less prominent roles to sexual and aggressive tendencies of the id and expansion of the concept of ego. The human qualities of creativity, competence, and problem solving abilities are emphasised. Some of these theories are briefly described here.

Carl Jung : Aims and Aspirations

Jung worked with Freud in his early stages of career, but later on he broke away from Freud. Jung saw human beings guided as much by aims and aspirations as by sex and aggression. He developed his own theory of personality, called **analytical psychology.** The basic assumption of his theory is that personality consists of competing forces and structures within the individual (that must be balanced) rather than between the individual and the demands of society, or between the individual and reality.

Jung claimed that there was a **collective unconscious** consisting of **archetypes** or primordial images. These are not individually acquired, but are inherited. The God or the Mother Earth is a good example of archetypes. They are found in myths, dreams and arts of all mankind. Jung held that the self strives for unity and oneness. It is an archetype that is expressed in many ways. He devoted much of his efforts to the study of such expressions in various traditions. According to him, for achieving unity and wholeness, a person must become increasingly aware of the wisdom available in one's personal and collective unconscious, and must learn to live in harmony with it.

Karen Horney : Optimism

Horney was another disciple of Freud who developed a theory that deviated from basic Freudian principles. She adopted a more optimistic view of human life with emphasis on human growth and self-actualisation.

Horney's major contribution lies in her challenge to Freud's treatment of women as inferior. According to her, each sex has attributes to be admired by the other, and neither sex can be viewed as superior or inferior. She countered that women were more likely to be affected by social and cultural factors than by biological factors. She argued that psychological disorders were caused by **disturbed interpersonal relationship** during childhood. When parents' behaviour toward a child is indifferent, discouraging, and erratic, the child feels insecure and a feeling called **basic anxiety** results. Deep resentment toward parents or basic hostility occurs due to this anxiety. By showing excessive dominance or indifference, or by providing too much or too little approval, parents can generate among children feelings of isolation and helplessness which interfere with their healthy development.

Alfred Adler : Lifestyle and Social Interest

Adler's theory is known as **individual psychology.** His basic assumption is that human behaviour is purposeful and goal-directed. Each one of us has the capacity to choose and create. Our **personal goals** are the sources of our motivation. The goals that provide us with security and help us in overcoming the feelings of inadequacy are important in our personality development. In Adler's view, every individual suffers from the feelings of inadequacy and guilt, *i.e.,* **inferiority complex,** which arise from childhood. Overcoming this complex is essential for optimal personality development.

Erich Fromm : The Human Concerns

In contrast to Freud's biological orientation, Fromm developed his theory from a social orientation. He viewed human beings as basically **social beings** who could be understood in terms of their relationship with others. He argued that psychological qualities such as growth and realisation of potentials resulted from a **desire for freedom,** and **striving for justice and truth.**

Fromm holds that character traits (personality) develop from our experiences with other individuals. While culture is shaped by the mode of existence of a given society, people's dominant character traits in a given society work as forces in shaping the social processes and the culture itself. His work recognises the value of positive qualities, such as tenderness and love in personality development.

Erik Erikson : Search for Identity

Erikson's theory lays stress on rational, conscious ego processes in personality development. In his theory, development is viewed as a lifelong process, and ego identity is granted a central place in this process. His concept of **identity crisis** of adolescent age has drawn considerable attention. Erikson argues that young people must generate for themselves a central perspective and a direction that can give them a meaningful sense of unity and purpose.

Psychodynamic theories face strong criticisms from many quarters. The major criticisms are as follows:

1. The theories are largely based on case studies; they lack a rigorous scientific basis.
2. They use small and atypical individuals as samples for advancing generalisations.
3. The concepts are not properly defined, and it is difficult to submit them to scientific testing.
4. Freud has used males as the prototype of all human personality development. He overlooked female experiences and perspectives.

Behavioural Approach

This approach does not give importance to the internal dynamics of behaviour. The behaviourists believe in data, which they feel are definable, observable, and measurable. Thus, they focus on learning of stimulus-response connections and their reinforcement. According to them, personality can be best understood as the response of an individual to the environment. They see the development simply as a change in response characteristics, *i.e.* a person learns new behaviours in response to new environments and stimuli.

For most behaviourists, the structural unit of personality is the **response.** Each response is a behaviour, which is emitted to satisfy a specific need. As you know, all of us eat because of hunger, but we are also very choosy about foods. For example, children do not like eating many of the vegetables (e.g., spinach, pumpkin, gourds, etc.), but gradually they learn to eat them. Why do they do so? According to the behavioural approach, children may initially learn to eat such vegetables in anticipation of appreciation (reinforcement) from their parents. Later on they may eventually learn to eat vegetables not only because their parents are pleased with this behaviour, but also because they acquire the taste of those vegetables, and find them good. Thus, the core tendency that organises behaviour is the reduction of biological or social needs that energise behaviour. This is accomplished through responses (behaviours) that are reinforced.

From your study in Class XI, you may recall that there are several different learning principles that involve the use of stimuli, responses, and reinforcement in different ways. The theories of *classical conditioning* (Pavlov), *instrumental conditioning* (Skinner), and *observational learning* (Bandura) are well-known to you. These theories view learning and maintenance of behaviour from different angles. The principles of these theories have been widely used in developing personality theories. For example, observational learning theory considers thought processes extremely important in learning, but these find almost no place in classical or instrumental conditioning theories. Observational learning theory also emphasises social learning (based on observation and imitation of others) and self-regulation, which again is missed out in other theories.

Cultural Approach

This approach attempts to understand personality in relation to the features of ecological and cultural environment. It proposes that a group's 'economic maintenance system' plays a vital role in the origin of cultural and behavioural variations. The climatic conditions, the nature of terrain of the habitat and the availability of food *(flora* and *fauna)* in it determine not only people's economic activities, but also their settlement patterns, social structures, division of labour, and other features such as child-rearing practices. Taken together these elements constitute a child's overall learning environment. People's skills, abilities, behavioural styles, and value priorities are viewed as strongly linked to these features. Rituals, ceremonies, religious practices, arts, recreational activities, games and play are the means through which people's personality gets projected in a culture. People develop various personality (behavioural) qualities in an attempt to adapt to the ecological and cultural features of a group's life. Thus, the cultural approach considers personality as an adaptation of individuals or groups to the demands of their ecology and culture.

Let us try to understand these aspects with a concrete example. As you know, a good proportion of the world's population, even today, lives in forests and mountainous regions with hunting and gathering (economic activities) as their primary means of livelihood. The Birhor (a tribal group) of Jharkhand represent such a population. Most of them live a nomadic life, which requires constant movement in small bands from one forest to another in search of games and other forest products (e.g., fruits, roots, mushrooms, honey, etc.). In the Birhor society, children from an early age are allowed enormous freedom to move into forests and learn hunting and gathering skills. Their child socialisation practices are also aimed at making children independent (do many things without help from elders), autonomous (take several decisions for themselves), and achievement-oriented (accept risks and challenges such as those involved in hunting) from an early age of life.

In agricultural societies, children are socialised to be obedient to elders, nurturant to youngsters, and responsible to their duties. Since these behavioural qualities make people more functional in agricultural societies, they become dominant features of people's personality in contrast to independence, autonomy and achievement, which are more functional (and thus highly valued) in hunting-gathering societies. Because of different economic pursuits and cultural demands, children in hunting-gathering and agricultural societies develop and display different personality patterns.

Humanistic Approach

The humanistic theories are mainly developed in response to Freud's theory. Carl Rogers and Abraham Maslow have particularly contributed to the development of humanistic perspective on personality. We will briefly examine their theories.

The most important idea proposed by Rogers is that of a **fully functioning person.** He believes that fulfilment is the motivating force for personality development. People try to express their capabilities, potentials and talents to the fullest extent possible. There is an inborn tendency among persons that directs them to actualise their inherited nature.

Rogers makes two basic assumptions about human behaviour. One is that behaviour is goal-directed and worthwhile. The second one is that people (who are innately good) will almost always choose adaptive, self-actualising behaviour.

Rogers' theory grew out of his experiences of listening to patients in his clinic. He noted that self was an important element in the experience of his clients. Thus, his theory is structured around the concept of self. The theory assumes that people are constantly engaged in the process of actualising their true self.

Rogers suggests that each person also has a concept of ideal self. An ideal self is the self that a person would like to be. When there is a correspondence between the real self and ideal self, a person is generally happy. Discrepancy between the real self and ideal self often results in unhappiness and dissatisfaction. Rogers' basic principle is that people have a tendency to maximise self-concept through self-actualisation. In this process, the self grows, expands and becomes more social.

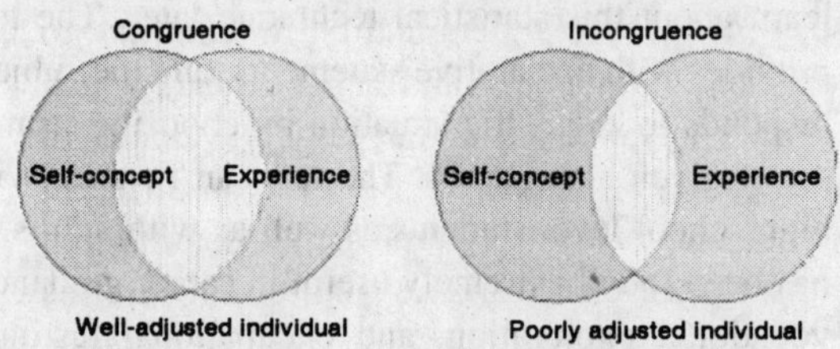

Fig. : *Pattern of Adjustment and Self-concept*

Rogers views personality development as a continuous process. It involves learning to evaluate oneself and mastering the process of self-actualisation. He recognises the role of social influences in the development of self-concept. When social conditions are positive, the self-concept and the self-esteem are high. In contrast, when the conditions are negative, the self-concept and the self-esteem are low. People with high self-concept and self-esteem are generally flexible and open to new experiences, so that they can continue to grow and self-actualise.

This situation warrants that an atmosphere of **unconditional positive regard** must be created in order to ensure enhancement of people's self-concept. The **client-centred therapy** that Rogers developed basically attempts to create this condition.

You are already familiar with the hierarchy of needs propounded by Maslow from your study of motivation in Class XI. Maslow has given a detailed account of psychologically healthy people in terms of their attainment of **self-actualisation,** a state in which people have reached their own fullest potential. Maslow had an optimistic and positive view of man who has the potentialities for love, joy and to do creative work. Human beings are considered free to shape their lives and to self-actualise. Self-actualisation becomes possible by analysing the motivations that govern our life. We know that biological, security, and belongingness needs (called *survival needs*) are commonly found among animals and human beings. Thus, an individual's sole concern with the satisfaction of these needs reduces her/him to the level of animals. The real journey of human life begins with the pursuit of self-esteem and self-actualisation needs. The humanistic approach emphasises the significance of positive aspects of life.

Assessment of Personality

To know, understand and describe people is a task in which everybody is involved in day-to-day life. When we meet new people, we often try to understand them and even predict what they may do before we interact with them. In our personal lives, we rely on our experiences, observations, conversations and information obtained from other persons. This approach to understanding others may be influenced by a number of factors that may colour our judgement and reduce objectivity. Hence, we need to organise our efforts more formally to analyse personalities. A formal effort aimed at understanding personality of an individual is termed as **personality assessment.**

Assessment refers to the procedures used to evaluate or differentiate people on the basis of certain characteristics. The goal of assessment is to understand and predict behaviour with minimum error and maximum accuracy. In assessment, we try to study what a person generally does, or how she/he behaves, in a given situation. Besides promoting our understanding, assessment is also useful for diagnosis, training, placement, counselling, and other purposes.

Psychologists have tried to assess personality in various ways. The most commonly used techniques are **Psychometric Tests, Self-Report Measures, Projective Techniques,** and **Behavioural Analysis.** These techniques are rooted in different theoretical orientations; hence they throw light on different aspects of personality.

Self-report Measures

It was Allport who suggested that the best method to assess a person is by asking her/him about herself/himself. This led to the use of self-report measures. These are fairly structured measures, often based on theory, that require subjects to give verbal responses using some kind of rating scale. The method requires the subject to objectively report her/his own feelings with respect to various items. The responses are accepted at their face value. They are scored in quantitative terms and interpreted on the basis of norms developed for the test. Some of the well-known self-report measures are briefly described below.

The Minnesota Multiphasic Personality Inventory (MMPI)

This inventory is widely used as a test in personality assessment. Hathaway and McKinley developed this test as a helping tool for psychiatric diagnosis, but the test has been found very effective in identifying varieties of psychopathology. Its revised version is available as MMPI-2. It consists of 567 statements. The subject has to judge each statement as 'true' or 'false' for her/him. The test is divided into 10 subscales, which seek to diagnose hypochondriasis, depression, hysteria, psychopathic deviate, masculinity-femininity, paranoia, psychasthenia, schizophrenia, mania and social introversion. In India, Mallick and Joshi have developed the Jodhpur Multiphasic Personality Inventory (JMPI) along the lines of MMPI.

Eysenck Personality Questionnaire (EPQ)

Developed by Eysenck this test initially assessed two dimensions of personality, called **introverted-extroverted** and **emotionally stable-emotionally unstable.** These dimensions are characterised by 32 personality traits. Later on, Eysenck added a third dimension, called **psychoticism.** It is linked to psychopathology that represents a lack of feeling for others, a tough manner of interacting with people, and a tendency to defy social conventions. A person scoring high on this dimension tends to be hostile, egocentric and antisocial. This test is also widely used.

Sixteen Personality Factor Questionnaire (16 PF)

This test was developed by Cattell. On the basis of his studies, he identified a large set of personality descriptors, which were subjected to factor analysis to identify the basic personality structure. You will learn about this statistical technique later. The test provides with declarative statements, and the subject responds to a specific situation by choosing from a set of given alternatives. The test can be used with high school level students as well as with adults. It has been found extremely useful in career guidance, vocational exploration, and occupational testing.

Apart from the few popular tests which use self-report technique which have been described above, there are several others that try to assess specific dimensions of personality (*e.g.*, authoritarianism, locus of control, optimism, etc.). As you proceed further with your study of psychology, you will come to know more about them.

The self-report measures suffer from a number of problems. **Social desirability** is one of them. It is a tendency on the part of the respondent to endorse items in a socially desirable manner. **Acquiescence** is another one. It is a tendency of the subject to agree with items/questions irrespective of their contents. It often appears in the form of saying 'yes' to items. These tendencies render the assessment of personality less reliable.

It is also necessary to sound a note of caution at this stage. Remember that psychological testing and understanding personality requires great skill and training. Unless you have acquired these to an optimum level under careful supervision of an expert, you should not venture into testing and interpreting the personality of your friends who do not study psychology.

Projective Techniques

The techniques of personality assessment described so far are known as direct techniques, because they tend to rely on information directly obtained from the person who clearly knows that her/his personality is being assessed. In these situations, people generally become self-conscious and hesitate to share their private feelings, thoughts, and motivations. When they do so, they often do it in a socially desirable manner.

The psychoanalytic theory tells us that a large part of human behaviour is governed by unconscious motives. Direct methods of personality assessment cannot uncover the unconscious part of our behaviour. Hence, they fail to provide us with a real picture of an individual's personality. These problems can be overcome using indirect methods of assessment. Projective techniques fall in this category.

Projective techniques were developed to assess unconscious motives and feelings. These techniques are based on the assumption that a less structured or unstructured stimulus or situation will allow the individual to project her/his feelings, desires and needs on to that situation. These projections are interpreted by experts. A variety of projective techniques have been developed; they use various kinds of stimulus materials and situations for assessing personality. Some of them require reporting associations with stimuli (*e.g.*, words, inkblots), some involve story writing around pictures, some require sentence completions, some require expression through drawings, and some require choice of stimuli from a large set of stimuli.

While the nature of stimuli and responses in these techniques vary enormously, all of them do share the following features:

1. The stimuli are relatively or fully unstructured and poorly defined.
2. The person being assessed is usually not told about the purpose of assessment and the method of scoring and interpretation.
3. The person is informed that there are no correct or incorrect responses.
4. Each response is considered to reveal a significant aspect of personality.
5. Scoring and interpretation are lengthy and sometimes subjective.

Projective techniques are different from the psychometric tests in many ways. They cannot be scored in any objective manner. They generally require qualitative analyses for which a rigorous training is needed. In the following pages, some of the well-known projective techniques are briefly discussed.

The Rorschach Inkblot Test

This test was developed by Hermann Rorschach. The test consists of 10 inkblots. Five of them are in black and white, two with some red ink, and the remaining three in some pastel colours. The blots are symmetrical in design with a specific shape or form. Each blot is printed in the centre of a white cardboard of about 7" × 10" size. The blots were originally made by dropping ink on a piece of paper and then folding the paper in half (hence called *inkblot test*). The cards are administered individually in two phases. In the first phase, called **performance proper,** the subjects are shown the cards and are asked to tell what they see in each of them. In the second phase, called **inquiry,** a detailed report of the response is prepared by asking the subject to tell where, how, and on what basis was a particular response made. Fine judgement is necessary to place the subject's responses in a meaningful context. The use and interpretation of this test requires extensive training. Computer techniques too have been developed for analysis of data. An example of the Rorschach Inkblot is given in Figure.

Fig. : *An Example of the Rorschach Inkblot*

The Thematic Apperception Test (TAT)

This test was developed by Morgan and Murray. It is a little more structured than the Inkblot test. The test consists of 30 black and white picture cards and one blank card. Each picture card depicts one or more people in a variety of situations. Each picture is printed on a card. Some cards are used with adult males or females. Others are used with boys or girls. Still others are used in some combinations. Twenty cards are appropriate for a subject, although a lesser number of cards (even five) have also been successfully used.

The cards are presented one at a time. The subject is asked to tell a story describing the situation presented in the picture: What led up to the situation, what is happening at the moment, what will happen in the future, and what the characters are feeling and thinking? A standard procedure is available for scoring TAT responses. The test has been modified for children and for the aged. Uma Chaudhury's Indian adaptation of TAT is also available. An example of a TAT card is given in Figure.

Fig. : *An Illustration Showing the Drawing of a Card of TAT*

Rosenzweig's Picture-Frustration Study (P-F Study)

This test was developed by Rosenzweig to assess how people express aggression in the face of a frustrating situation. The test presents with the help of cartoon like pictures a series of situations in which one person frustrates another, or calls attention to a frustrating condition. The subject is asked to tell what the other (frustrated) person will say or do. The analysis of responses is based on the type and direction of aggression. An attempt is made to examine whether the focus is on the frustrating object, or on protection of the frustrated person, or on constructive solution to the problem. The direction of aggression may be towards the environment, towards oneself, or it may be tuned off in an attempt to gloss over or evade the situation. Pareek has adapted this test for use with the Indian population.

Sentence Completion Test

This test makes use of a number of incomplete sentences. The starting part of the sentence is first presented and the subject has to provide an ending to the sentence. It is held that the type of endings used by the subjects reflects their attitudes, motivation and conflicts. The test provides subjects with several opportunities to reveal their underlying unconscious motivations. A few sample items of a sentence completion test are given below.

1. My father————————.
2. My greatest fear is ————.
3. The best thing about my mother is ———— ————————.
4. I am proud of ———————— ————————.

Draw-a-Person Test

It is a simple test in which the subject is asked to draw a person on a sheet of paper. A pencil and eraser is provided to facilitate drawing. After the completion of the drawing, the subject is generally asked to draw the figure of an opposite sex person. Finally, the subject is asked to make a story about the person as if she/he was a character in a novel or play. Some examples of interpretations are as follows:

1. Omission of facial features suggests that the person tries to evade a highly conflict-ridden interpersonal relationship.
2. Graphic emphasis on the neck suggests lack of control over impulses.
3. Disproportionately large head suggests organic brain disease and preoccupation with headaches.

The analysis of personality with the help of projective techniques appears fairly interesting. It helps us to understand unconscious motives, deep-rooted conflicts, and emotional complexes of an individual. However, the interpretation of the responses requires sophisticated skills and specialised training. There are problems associated with the reliability of scoring and validity of interpretations. But, the practitioners have found these techniques quite useful.

Behavioural Analysis

A person's behaviour in a variety of situations can provide us with meaningful information about her/his personality. Observation of behaviour serves as the basis of behavioural analysis. An observer's report may contain data obtained from **interview, observation, ratings, nomination,** and **situational tests.** We will examine these different procedures in some detail.

Interview

Interview is a commonly used method for assessing personality. This involves talking to the person being assessed and asking specific questions. Diagnostic interviewing generally involves in-depth interviewing which seeks to go beyond the replies given by the person. Interviews may be structured or unstructured depending on the purpose or goals of assessment.

In **unstructured interviews**, the interviewer seeks to develop an impression about a person by asking a number of questions. The way a person presents her/ himself and answers the questions carries enough potential to reveal her/his personality. The **structured interviews** address very specific questions and follow a set procedure. This is often done to make objective comparison of persons being interviewed. Use of rating scales may further enhance the objectivity of evaluations.

Observation

Behavioural observation is another method which is very commonly used for the assessment of personality. Although all of us watch people and form impressions about their personality, use of observation for personality assessment is a sophisticated procedure that cannot be carried out by untrained people. It requires careful training of the observer, and a fairly detailed guideline about analysis of behaviours in order to assess the personality of a given person. For example, a clinical psychologist may like to observe her/his client's interaction with family members and home visitors. With carefully designed observation, the clinical psychologist may gain a considerable insight into a client's personality.

In spite of their frequent and widespread use, observation and interview methods are characterised by the following limitations:

1. Professional training required for collection of useful data through these methods is quite demanding and time-consuming.
2. Maturity of the psychologist is a precondition for obtaining valid data through these techniques.
3. Mere presence of the observer may contaminate the results. As a stranger, the observer may influence the behaviour of the person being observed and thus not obtain good data.

Behavioural Ratings

Behavioural ratings are frequently used for assessment of personality in educational and industrial settings. Behavioural ratings are generally taken from people who know the assessee intimately and have interacted with her/him over a period of time or have had a chance to observe her/him. They attempt to put individuals into certain categories in terms of their behavioural qualities. The categories may involve different numbers or descriptive terms. It has been found that use of numbers or general descriptive adjectives in rating scales always creates confusion for the rater. In order to use ratings effectively, the traits should be clearly defined in terms of carefully stated behavioural anchors.

The method of rating suffers from the following major limitations:

1. Raters often display certain biases that colour their judgements of different traits. For example, most of us are greatly influenced by a single favourable or unfavourable trait. This often forms the basis of a rater's overall judgement of a person. This tendency is known as the **halo effect.**
2. Raters have a tendency to place individuals either in the middle of the scale (called **middle category bias**) by avoiding extreme positions, or in the extreme positions (called **extreme response bias**) by avoiding middle categories on the scale.

These tendencies can be overcome by providing raters with appropriate training or by developing such scales in which the response bias is likely to be small.

Nomination

This method is often used in obtaining peer assessment. It can be used with persons who have been in long-term interaction and who know each other very well. In using nomination, each person is asked to choose one or more persons of the group with whom she/he would like to work, study, play or participate in any other activity. The person may also be asked to specify the reason for her/his choices. Nominations thus received may be analysed to understand the personality and behavioural qualities of the person. This technique has been found to be highly dependable, although it may also be affected by personal biases.

Situational Tests

A variety of situational tests have been devised for the assessment of personality. The most commonly used test of this kind is the **situational stress test.** It provides us with information about how a person behaves under stressful situations. The test requires a person to perform a given task with other persons who are instructed to be non-cooperative and interfering. The test involves a kind of role playing. The person is instructed to play a role for which she/he is observed. A verbal report is also obtained on what she/he was asked to do. The situation may be realistic one, or it may be created through a video play.

COGNITIVE PSYCHOLOGY

CONCEPT OF LEARNING

Meaning and Definitions of Learning

Learning, in psychology, is the process by which a relatively lasting change in potential behaviour occurs because of practice or experience. Learning is also a process of acquiring modifications in existing knowledge, skills, habits, or tendencies through experience, practice, or exercise.

Gates and Others "Learning is the modification of behaviour through experience."

Henry, P Smith "Learning is the acquisition of new behaviour or strengthening or weakening of old behaviour as a result of experience."

Crow and Crow "Learning is the acquisition of habits, knowledge and attitudes. It involves new ways of doing things, and it operates in an individual's attempt to overcome obstacles or to adjust to new situations."

Skinner "Learning is the process of progressive behaviour adaptation."

Munn "To learn is to modify behaviour and experience."

M.L. Bigge "Learning may be considered as change in insights, behaviour, perception, motivation or a combination of these."

The above definitions emphasize four attributes of learning:

- **As Process:** the first is that learning is a permanent change in behaviour.
- It does not include change due to illness, fatigue, maturation and use of intoxicant.
- Learning is not directly observable but manifests in the activities of the individual.
- Learning depends on practice and experience.

Characteristics of Learning

Yoakum and Simpson have stated the following general characteristics of learning: Learning is growth, adjustment, organisation of experience, purposeful, both individual and social, product of the environment.

According to W.R Mclaw learning has the following characteristics.

1. Learning is a continuous modification of behaviour continues throughout life.
2. Learning is pervasive. It reaches into all aspects of human life.
3. Learning involves the whole person, socially, emotionally and intellectually.
4. Learning is often a change in the organisation of behaviour.
5. Learning is developmental. Time is one of its dimensions.
6. Learning is responsive to incentives. In most cases positive incentives such as rewards are most effective than negative incentives such as punishments.
7. Learning is always concerned with goals. These goals can be expressed in terms of observable behaviour.
8. Interest and learning are positively related. An individual learns best those things, which he is interested in learning. Most boys find learning to play football easier than learning to add fractions.
9. Learning depends on maturation and motivation.

Types of Learning

Learning has been classified in many ways.

I. *Informal, formal and non-formal learning:* Depending on the way of acquiring it learning may be informal, formal or non-formal.

- Informal learning is incidental. It takes place throughout life. It is not planned.
- Formal learning is intentional and organized. It takes place in formal educational institution.
- Non-formal is also intentional and organized. It is flexible.

II. *Individual or Group learning:* Learning is called either individual or group learning depending upon the number of individuals involved in the learning process.

III. Another classification involves the types of activity involved:

(*a*) **Motor learning:** When learning involves primarily the use of muscles, it is called motor learning, *e.g.*, learning to walk, to operate a typewriter.

(*b*) **Discrimination learning:** Learning which involves the act of discrimination, is called discrimination learning., *e.g.*, infant discriminates between mother and aunt, milk and water.

(*c*) **Verbal learning:** When learning involves the use of words, it is called verbal learning.

(*d*) **Concept learning:** When learning involves the formation of concept, it is called concept learning.

(*e*) **Sensory learning:** When learning is concerned with perception and sense, it is sensory learning.

Nature of Learning

(*a*) **Learning is adaptation or adjustment:** Friends, we all continuously interact with our environment. We often make adjustment and adapt to our social environment. Through a process of continuous learning, the individual prepares himself for necessary adjustment or adaptation. That is why learning is also described as a process of progressive adjustment to ever changing conditions, which one encounters.

(*b*) **Learning is improvement:** Learning is often considered as a process of improvement with practice or training. We learn many things, which help us to improve our performance.

(*c*) **Learning is organizing experience:** Learning is not mere addition of knowledge. It is the reorganization of experience.

(*d*) **Learning brings behavioural changes:** Whatever the direction of the changes may be, learning brings progressive changes in the behaviour of an individual. That is why he is able to adjust to changing situations.

(*e*) **Learning is active:** Learning does not take place without a purpose and self-activity. In any teaching learning process, the activity of the learner counts more than the activity of a teacher.

(*f*) **Learning is goal directed:** When the aim and purpose of learning is clear, an individual learns immediately. It is the purpose or goal, which determines what the learner sees in the learning situations and how he acts. If there is no purpose or goal, learning can hardly be seen.

(*g*) **Learning is universal and continuous:** All living creatures learn. Every moment the individual engages himself to learn more and more. Right from the birth of a child till the death learning continues.

Process of Learning

Learning is a process. It is carried out through steps. Learning process involves–

(*a*) A motive or a drive

(*b*) An attractive goal

(*c*) A block to the attainment of the goal.

Let us see the steps one by one:

(*a*) **A motive or a drive:** Motive is the dynamic force that energizes behaviour and compels an individual to act. We do any activity because of our motives or our needs. When our need is strong enough, we are compelled to strive for its satisfaction. Learning takes place because of response to some stimulation. As long as our present behaviour, knowledge, skill and performance are adequate to satisfy all our needs, we do not feel any necessity to change our behaviour or acquire new knowledge and skills. It is this requirement, which initiates a learner to learn something.

(*b*) **Goal:** Every individual has to set a definite goal for achievement. We should always have a definite goal for achieving anything. If a definite goal is set, then learning becomes purposeful and interesting.

(*c*) **Obstacle/block/barrier:** The obstacle or block or the barrier is equally important in the process of learning. The obstacle or the barriers keep us away from attaining the goal.

Learning Curve

Learning curve is a graphic representation of how learning takes place in a particular situation. In all type of learning situations, the course of learning can be depicted and described graphically by drawing learning curves against *x* and *y* axis.

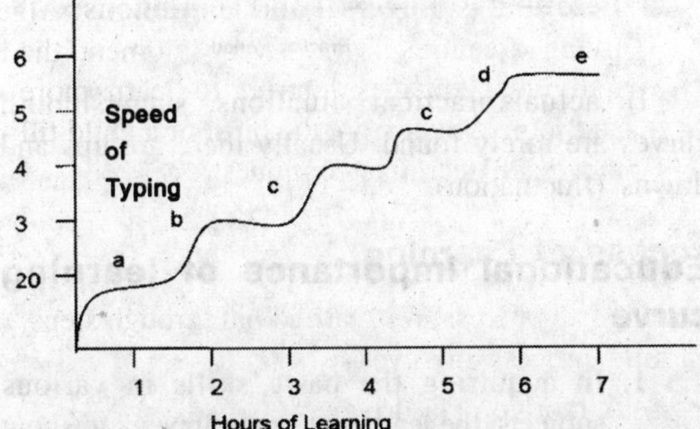

The above figure shows a typical learning curve of many types of learning. The curve consists of a number of irregularities, as the progress is not constant.

For the convenience, the curve is divided into five stages:

(*a*) **Period of slow progress:** Generally, when a person has to start a learning of a given activity from a scratch, his early progress will be slow. For example, an infant's progress in learning to walk is very negligible in the beginning.

(*b*) **Period of rapid progress:** In this stage, the learner's output raises rapidly. For example, in typing once the learner has developed co-ordination of the movement of fingers he shows rapid progress.

(*c*) **Period of no apparent progress:** Learning curves frequently display a period of no apparent progress. It is also known as plateau. A period of no visible learning progress, preceded and followed by improvement is called plateaus. For example, in typing, a person after having made rather consistent progress for some time, may reach a point where perhaps for weeks no further progress is made.

Causes of plateau

(*i*) The learner may be reorganizing the previous learning into a new pattern before further progress is possible.

(*ii*) The learner may have hit upon bad habits.

(*iii*) Lack of progress may be due to decrease in motivation.

(*iv*) The task may not be of uniform difficulty.

(*v*) Loss of interest.

(*vi*) The onset of fatigue is also one of the causes of a plateau.

(*d*) **Period of sudden rise:** At the end of a plateau, there is generally a spurt in achievement. While on the plateau, the learner acquires better techniques, which help him later on to show rapid progress.

(*e*) **Levelling:** All learning will finally slow down to such an extent that it will ultimately reach a period of no improvement. No one can continue to improve indefinitely in any given situation. The learning curve will eventually reach a limit, where no further improvement is possible. This limit is known as physiological limit.

Characteristics of Learning Curve

(*i*) Slow initial progress

(*ii*) Spurt-like learning after some time

(*iii*) Declination in the rate of learning

(*iv*) Plateaus of learning

(*v*) Sudden increase in learning

(*vi*) Gradual levelling at the end.

Types of Learning Curve

We get different types of learning curves depending upon:

(*a*) The nature of the learner

(*b*) The nature of the task/learning material

(*c*) Time available

(*d*) Conditions under which the learning takes place.

It is difficult to classify these learning curves. However, three common types of curves are there:

(*i*) Negatively accelerated learning curve or the convex curve.

(*ii*) Positively accelerated learning curve or the concave curve.

(*iii*) Combination of convex-concave curve.

Convex Curve

It depicts rapid initial improvement in learning that slows down with time. When the task is simple and the learner has previous practice on a similar task, we get this type of learning curve.

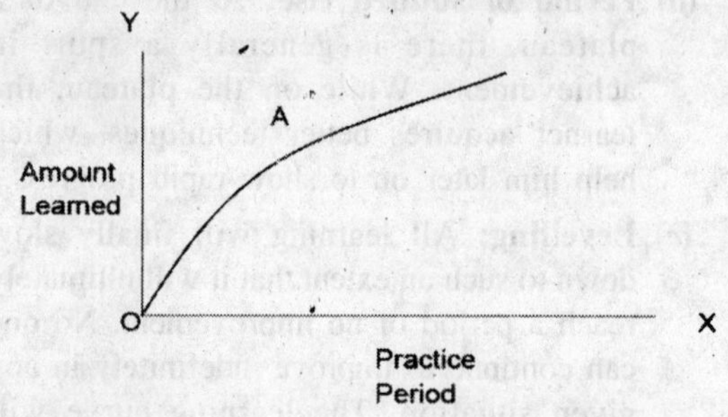

Concave Curve

There is a slow initial improvement and learning increases with time. When the task is difficult we get such type of learning curve.

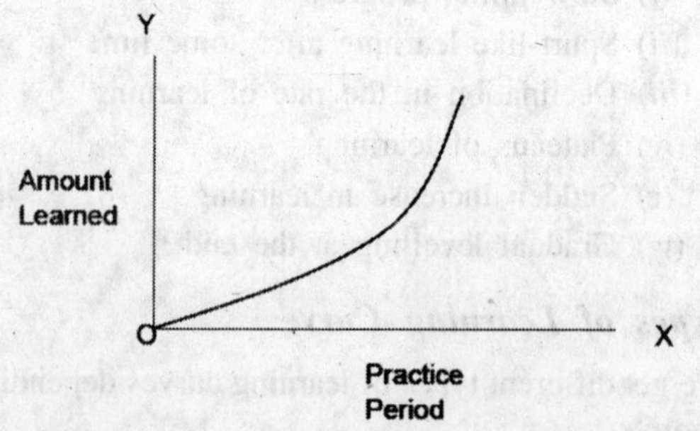

Combination of convex concave curve

It looks like the capital letter 'S'. The curve takes concave or convex shape in the beginning depending upon the nature of the task.

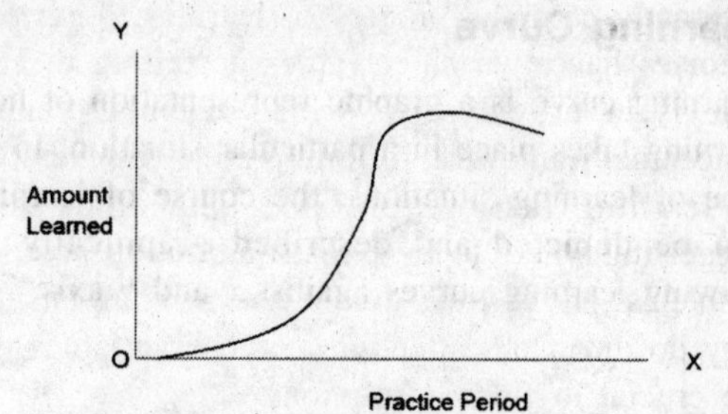

In actual practical situations, such smooth curves are rarely found. Usually there are ups and downs (fluctuation).

Educational importance of learning curve

1. In acquiring the basic skills in various subjects, the learner at times appears to show no progress. At such moments, the teacher can diagnose the reasons for the lack of progress.
2. A student's progress may be arrested because the work is too complex for him. The teacher can observe the student's work and detect the part that gives him trouble. The teacher should see if the student has developed any faulty study habits, which impede his progress.
3. The plateau may be due to the lack of motivation. The teacher should provide encouragement in order to maintain motivation at a high level.
4. The learning curves give a graphic evidence of one's progress, which is an effective motivational device for the learner.
5. Occurrence of plateaus can be minimized using superior teaching methods.

LEARNING THEORIES

Learning as a process focuses on what happens when the learning takes place. Explanations of what happens constitute **learning theories.** A **learning theory** is an attempt to describe how people and animals learn, thereby helping us understands the inherently complex process of learning. **Learning theories** have two chief values according to Hill. One is in providing us with vocabulary and a conceptual framework for interpreting the examples of learning that we observe. The other is in suggesting where to look for solutions to practical problems. The theories do not give us solutions, but they do direct our attention to those variables that are crucial in finding solutions.

The three main categories or philosophical frameworks under which learning theories fall are *behavioural, cognitive,* and *constructivism.* Behaviourism focuses only on the objectively observable aspects of learning. Cognitive theories look beyond behaviour to explain brain-based learning. In addition, constructivism views learning as a process in which the learner actively constructs or builds new ideas or concepts.

We will discuss the behavioural theories under two broad categories: S-R theories.

- S-R (Stimulus-Response) theory with reinforcement
  - E.L. Thorndike—Trial and Error theory
  - B.F. Skinner—Operant Conditioning
- S-R (Stimulus-Response) theory without reinforcement
  - Pavlov—Classical Conditioning

S-R (STIMULUS-RESPONSE) THEORY WITH REINFORCEMENT

(A) E.L. Thorndike—Trial and Error Theory of Learning

Edward Lee Thorndike (1874-1949) was the first American psychologist who put forward the Trial and Error Theory of learning. According to Thorndike, all learning takes place because of formation of bond or connection between stimulus and response. He further says that learning takes place through a process of approximation and correction. A person makes a number of trials, some responses do not give satisfaction to the individual but he goes on making further trials until he gets satisfactory responses. Thorndike conducted a number of experiments on animals to explain the process of learning. His most widely quoted experiment is with a cat placed in a puzzle box.

Thorndike put a hungry cat in a puzzle box. The box had one door, which could be opened by manipulating a latch of the door. A fish was placed outside the box. The cat being hungry had the motivation of eating fish outside the box. However, the obstacle was the latch on the door. The cat made random movements inside the box indicating trial and error type of behaviour biting at the box, scratching the box, walking around, pulling and jumping, etc., to come out to get the food. Now in the course of her movements, the latch was manipulated accidently and the cat came out to get the food. Over a series of successive trials, the cat took shorter and shorter time, committed less number of errors, and was in a position to manipulate the latch as soon as it was put in the box and learnt the art of opening the door.

Thorndike concluded that it was only after many random trials that the cat was able to hit upon the solutions. He named it as Trial and Error Learning. An analysis of the learning behaviour of the cat in the box shows that besides trial and error the principles of goal, motivation, explanation and reinforcement are involved in the process of learning by Trial and Error.

Laws of Learning

Based on Trial and Error Learning Theory, Thorndike gave certain laws of Learning. We shall discuss three fundamental laws of Learning in this section. These laws are:

1. Law of Readiness

This law refers to the fact that learning takes place only when the learner is prepared to learn. No amount of efforts can make the child learn if the child is not ready to learn. The dictum that 'you can lead a horse to the pond but you can't make it drink water unless it feels thirsty' goes very well with this law. In other words, if the child is ready to learn, he/she learns more quickly, effectively and with greater satisfaction than if he/she is not ready to learn. In the words of Thorndike the three stages of this Law of Readiness are :

- For a conduction unit ready to conduct, to conduct is satisfying.
- For a conduction unit ready to conduct, not to conduct is annoying.
- For a conduction unit not ready to conduct, to conduct is annoying.

Thus, the Law of Readiness means mental preparation for action. It is not to force the child to learn if he is not ready. Learning failures are the result of forcing the learner to learn when he is not ready to learn something.

Educational Implications of Law of Readiness: The law draws the attention of the teacher to the motivation of the child. The teacher must consider the psycho-biological readiness of the students to ensure successful learning experiences. Curriculum/Learning experiences should be according to the mental level of maturity of the child. If this is not so, there will be poor comprehension and readiness may vanish.

2. Law of Exercise

This law explains the role of practice in learning. According to this law, learning becomes efficient through practice or exercise. The dictum 'Practice makes a man perfect' goes very well with this law. This law is further split into two parts — Law of use and Law of disuse. The law of use means that a connection between a stimulus and a response is strengthened by its occurrence, its exercise or its use. In other words, the use of any response strengthens it, and makes it more prompt, easy and certain. Regarding the law of disuse, it is said that when a modifiable connection is not made between a stimulus and a response over a length of time, the strength of that connection is decreased. This means that any act that is not practised for some time gradually decays. Anything that is not used exercised or practised for a certain period tends to be forgotten or becomes weak in strength, efficiency and promptness.

Educational Implications: Exercise occupies an important place in learning. Teacher must repeat, give sufficient drill in some subjects like mathematics, drawing, music or vocabulary for fixing material in the minds of the students. Thorndike later revised this law of exercise and accordingly it is accepted that practice does bring improvement in learning but it in itself is not sufficient.

Always practice must be followed by some reward or satisfaction to the learner. The learner must be motivated to learn.

3. Law of Effect

This is most important of Thorndike's laws, which state that when a connection between stimulus and response is accompanied by satisfying state, its strength is increased. On the other hand, when a connection is accompanied by an annoying state of affairs, its strength is reduced or weakened. The saying 'nothing succeeds like success' goes very well with this law. In other words, the responses that produce satisfaction or comfort for the learner are strengthened and responses that produce annoyance or discomfort for the learner are weakened. Thorndike revised this law in 1930 and according to this revision, he stated that reward strengthened the response but punishment did not always weaken the response. Then he placed more emphasis on the reward aspect than on the punishment aspect of Law of Effect.

Educational Implications: This law signifies the use of reinforcement or feedback in learning. This implies that learning trials must be associated with satisfying consequences. The teacher can use rewards to strengthen certain responses and punishment to weaken others. However, the use of reward is more desirable than the use of punishment in school learning. The teacher for motivating the students for learning situations can exploit the use of reward.

(B) B.F. Skinner's Operant Conditioning

What is Operant Conditioning?

Operant conditioning (sometimes referred to as **instrumental conditioning**) is a method of learning that occurs through rewards and punishments for behaviour. Through operant conditioning, an association is made between a behaviour and a consequence for that behaviour.

Behaviourist B.F. Skinner coined the term 'operant conditioning', which is why it is also referred to as Skinnerian conditioning. As a behaviourist, Skinner believed that internal thoughts and motivations could not be used to explain behaviour. Instead, he suggested, we should look only at the external, observable causes of human behaviour.

Skinner used the term *operant* to refer to any "active behaviour that operates upon the environment to generate consequences" (1953). In other words, Skinner's theory explained how we acquire the range of learned behaviours we exhibit each and every day.

Skinner is regarded as the father of Operant Conditioning, but his work was based on Thorndike's law of effect. Skinner introduced a new term into the Law of Effect - Reinforcement. Behaviour that is reinforced tends to be repeated (*i.e.* strengthened); behaviour that is not reinforced tends to die out-or be extinguished (*i.e.*, weakened).

Skinner studied operant conditioning by conducting experiments using animals, which he placed in a "*Skinner Box*" which was similar to Thorndike's puzzle box.

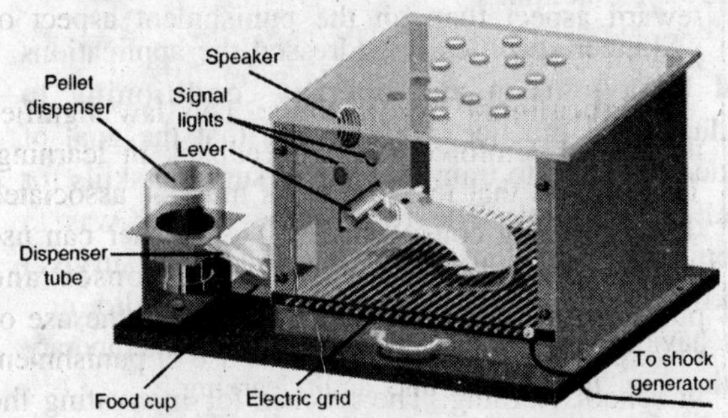

The Skinner box involved placing an animal (such as a rat or a pigeon) into a sealed box with a lever that would release food when pressed. If food was released every time the rat pressed the lever, it would press it more and more because it learnt that doing so gives it food. Lever pressing is described as an operant behaviour, because it is an action that results in a consequence. In other words, it operates on the environment and changes it in some way. The food that is released as a result of pressing the lever is known as a reinforcer, because it causes the operant behaviour (lever pressing) to increase. Food could also be described as a conditioned stimulus because it causes an effect to occur.

Note: There is an important difference between a reward and a reinforcer in operant conditioning.

- A reward is something, which has value to the person giving the reward, but may not necessarily be of value to the person receiving the reward.
- A reinforcer is something, which benefits the person receiving it, and so results in an increase of a certain type of behaviour.

Skinner identified three types of responses or operants that can follow behaviour.

- **Neutral operants:** Responses from the environment that neither increase nor decrease the probability of a behaviour being repeated.
- **Reinforcers** are any event that strengthens or increases the behaviour it follows. There are two kinds of reinforcers.

1. **Positive reinforcers** are favourable events or outcomes that are presented after the behaviour. In situations that reflect positive reinforcement, a response or behaviour is strengthened by the addition of something, such as praise or a direct reward.
2. **Negative reinforcers** involve the removal of unfavourable events or outcomes after the display of a behaviour. In these situations, a response is strengthened by the removal of something considered unpleasant.

In both of these cases of reinforcement, the behaviour *increases*.

- **Punishment** is the presentation of an adverse event or outcome that causes a decrease in the behaviour it follows. Punishment weakens behaviour. There are two kinds of punishment:

1. **Positive punishment,** sometimes referred to as punishment by application, involves the presentation of an unfavourable event or outcome in order to weaken the response it follows.
2. **Negative punishment,** also known as punishment by removal, occurs when a favourable event or outcome is removed after a behaviour occurs.

In both of these cases of punishment, the behaviour **decreases.**

Schedules of Reinforcement

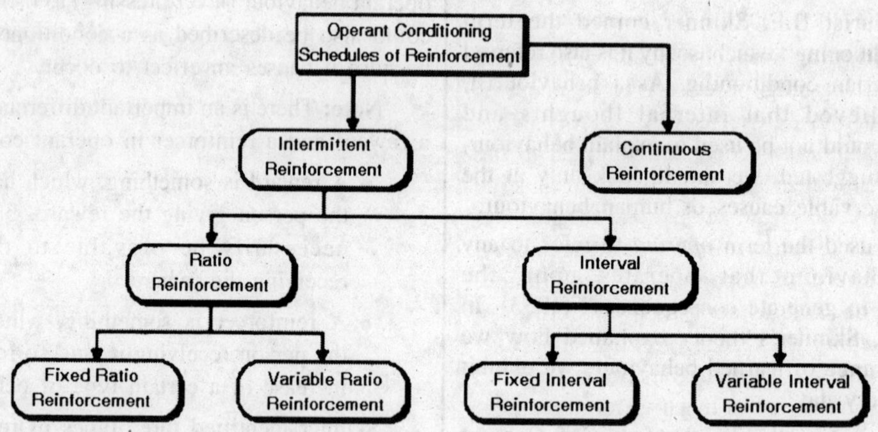

Intermittent reinforcement - reinforcement is given only part of the times the animal gives the desired response.

Continuous reinforcement - reinforcement is given every time the animal gives the desired response.

Ratio reinforcement - a pre-determined proportion of responses will be reinforced.

Fixed ratio reinforcement - reinforcement is given on a regular ratio, such as every fifth time the desired behaviour is produced.

Variable (random) fixed reinforcement - reinforcement is given for a predetermined proportion of responses, but randomly instead of on a fixed schedule.

Interval reinforcement - reinforcement is given after a predetermined period of time.

Fixed interval reinforcement - reinforcement is given on a regular schedule, such as every five minutes.

Variable interval reinforcement - reinforcement is given after random amounts of time have passed.

In animal studies, Skinner found that continuous reinforcement in the early stages of training seems to increase the rate of learning. Later, intermittent reinforcement keeps the response going longer and slows extinction.

Skinner specifically addressed the applications of behaviourism and operant conditioning to educational practice. He believed that the goal of education was to train learners in survival skills for self and society. The role of the teacher was to reinforce behaviours that contributed to survival skills, and extinguish behaviours that did not. Behaviourist views have shaped much of contemporary education in children and adult learning.

Implication of the theory of operant conditioning:

1. **Conditioning study behaviour:** Teaching is the arrangement of contingencies of reinforcement, which expedite learning. For effective teaching teacher should arrange effective contingencies of reinforcement. Example: For Self learning of a student teacher should reinforce student behaviour through variety of incentives such as prize, medal, smile, praise, affectionate patting on the back or by giving higher marks.
2. **Conditioning and classroom behaviour:** During learning process a child acquires unpleasant experiences also. This unpleasantness becomes conditioned to the teacher, subject and the classroom and the learner dislikes the subject and the teacher. Suitable behavioural contingencies, atmosphere of recognition, acceptance, affection and esteem help the child in approaching the teacher and the subject. If the student is not serious in study, the teacher makes use of negative reinforcement like showing negligence, criticising the student, etc., but if the student is serious in study, the teacher makes use of positive reinforcement like prize, medal, praise and smile.
3. **Managing Problem Behaviour:** Two types of behaviour is seen in the classroom, viz., undesired behaviour and problematic behaviour. Operant conditioning is a behaviour therapy technique that shapes students behaviour. For this teacher should admit positive contingencies like praise, encouragement, etc., for learning. One should not admit negative contingencies. Example, punishment (student will run away from the dull and dreary classes – escape stimulation).
4. **Dealing with anxieties through conditioning:** Through conditioning fear, anxieties, prejudices, attitudes and perceptual meaning develop. Examples of anxiety are signals on the road, siren blown during wartime, child receiving painful injection from a doctor. Anxiety is a generalized fear response. To break the habits of fear, a teacher should use desensitization techniques. Initially teacher should provide very weak form of conditioned stimulus. Gradually the strength of stimulus should be increased.
5. **Conditioning group behaviour:** Conditioning makes entire group learn and complete change in behaviour is seen due to reinforcement. It breaks undesired and unsocial behaviour too. Example: Putting questions or telling lie to teachers will make teachers annoyed. In such circumstances students learn to keep mum in the class. Asking questions, active participation in class discussion will make the teacher feel happy – interaction will increase and teaching learning process becomes more effective.
6. **Conditioning and Cognitive Processes:** Reinforcement is given in different form, for the progress of knowledge and in the feedback form. When response is correct, positive reinforcement is given. Example: A student who stands first in the class in the month of January is rewarded in the month of December. To overcome this Programme instruction is used. In this subject matter is broken down into steps. Organizing in logical sequence helps in learning. Each step is built upon the preceding step. Progress is seen in the process of learning. Immediate reinforcement is given at each step.
7. **Shaping Complex Behaviour:** Complex behaviour exists in the form of a chain of small behaviour. Control is required for such kind of behaviour. This extended form of learning is shaping technique. Smallest Behaviour is controlled at initial stage. On behalf of different contingencies, next order of chain of behaviours is controlled. Example: Vocabulary in English. Teaching spelling is mainly a process of shaping complex form of behaviour.

S-R (Stimulus-Response) theory without reinforcement

Pavlov - Classical Conditioning

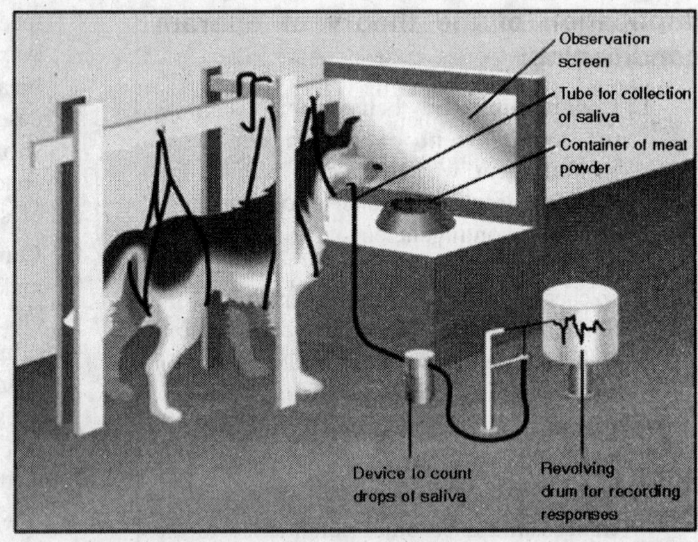

Classical conditioning is a term used to describe learning which has been acquired through experience. One of the best-known examples of classical conditioning can be found with the Russian psychologist Ivan Pavlov and his experiments on dogs.

In these experiments, Pavlov trained his dogs to salivate when they heard a bell ring. In order to do this he first showed them food, the sight of which caused them to salivate.

Later Pavlov would ring a bell every time he would bring the food out, until eventually, he could get the dogs to salivate just by ringing the bell and without giving the dogs any food.

In this simple but ingenious experiment, Pavlov showed how a reflex (salivation, a natural bodily response) could become conditioned (modified) to an external stimulus (the bell) thereby creating a conditioned reflex/response.

Before Conditioning

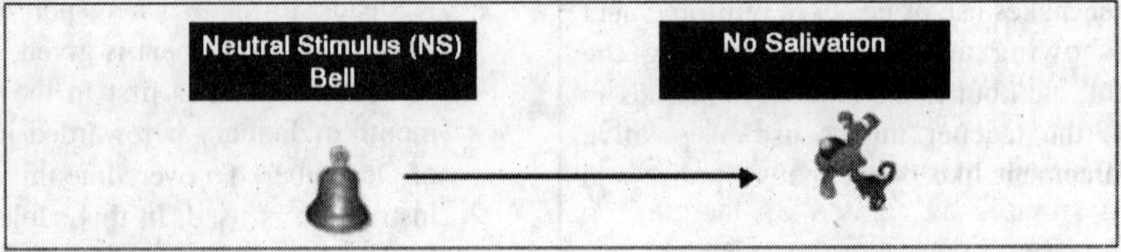

During Conditioning

After Conditioning

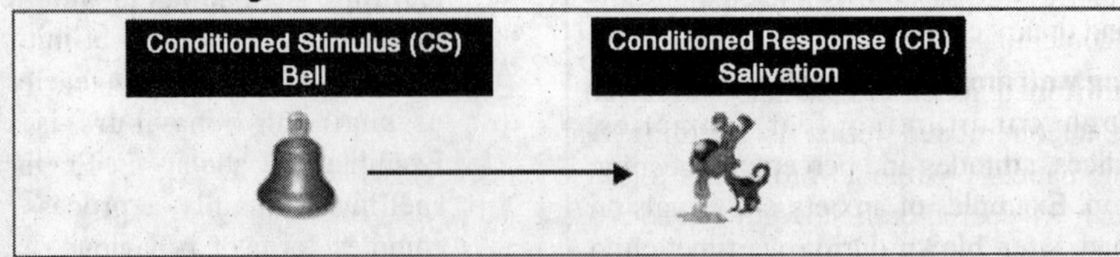

Components Involved in Classical Conditioning: We can gain a better understanding of classical conditioning by looking at the various components involved in his experiment:

- The unconditioned stimulus.(UCS)
- The conditioned stimulus.(CS)
- The unconditioned reflex/response.(UCR)
- The conditioned reflex/response. (CR)

So let's look at each of these classical conditioning components in more detail now.

Note: In its strictest definition classical conditioning is described as a previously neutral stimulus which causes a reflex (stimulus means something which causes a physical response).

The Unconditioned Stimulus (food): (UCS) An unconditioned stimulus is anything, which can evoke a response without prior learning or conditioning.

For example, when a dog eats some food it causes his mouth to salivate. Therefore, the food is an unconditioned stimulus, because it causes a reflex response (salivation) automatically and without the dog having to learn how to salivate.

Unconditioned Stimulus–This causes an automatic reflex response.

Conditioned Stimulus (bell): (CS) The conditioned stimulus is created by learning, and therefore does not create a response without prior conditioning.

For example, when Pavlov rang a bell and caused the dogs to salivate, this was a conditioned stimulus because the dogs learnt to associate the bell with food. If they had not learnt to associate the bell with food, they would not have salivated when the bell was rung.

Conditioned Stimulus – You need to learn first before it creates a response. It is an acquired power to change something.

Unconditioned Reflex/Response (salivation): (UCR) An unconditioned reflex is anything that happens automatically without you having to think about it, such as your mouth salivating when you eat. Unconditioned Reflex – Reflex that happens automatically and you did not have to learn how to do it.

Conditioned Reflex (salivation in response to bell): (CR) A conditioned reflex is a response which you have learnt to associate with something.

For example, the dogs salivated when Pavlov rang a bell, when previously (without conditioning) the bell would not cause the dogs to salivate.

Conditioned Reflex–A reflex that can be evoked in response to a conditioned stimulus (a previously neutral stimulus).

Basic concepts in Classical conditioning

There are several principles that are associated with classical conditioning, some of these are:

- **Extinction:** A conditioned response will disappear over time when the conditioned stimulus is no longer presented.
- **Spontaneous recovery:** Sometimes there is the weak appearance of a previously extinguished response.
- **Stimulus generalization:** This is when individuals respond in this same way to experience stimuli. For example, all fuzzy animals scaring a young child instead of just a fuzzy cat.
- **Stimulus discrimination:** Organisms can learn to discriminate between various stimuli.
- **Higher order conditioning:** This is when a neutral stimulus can cause the conditioned response sense if it had been associated with the conditioned stimulus.

Types of Classical conditioning

Forward conditioning: Learning is fastest in forward conditioning. During forward conditioning the onset of the conditioned stimulus (CS) precedes the onset of the unconditioned stimulus (US). Two common forms of forward conditioning are delay and trace conditioning.

Delay conditioning: In delay conditioning, the conditioned stimulus (CS) is presented and is overlapped by the presentation of the unconditioned stimulus (US).

Trace conditioning: During trace conditioning, the conditioned stimulus (CS) and the unconditioned stimulus (US) do not overlap. Instead, the conditioned stimulus (CS) is presented, a period is allowed to elapse during which no stimuli are presented, and then the unconditioned stimulus (US) is presented. The stimulus-free period is called the *trace interval*. It may also be called the conditioning interval.

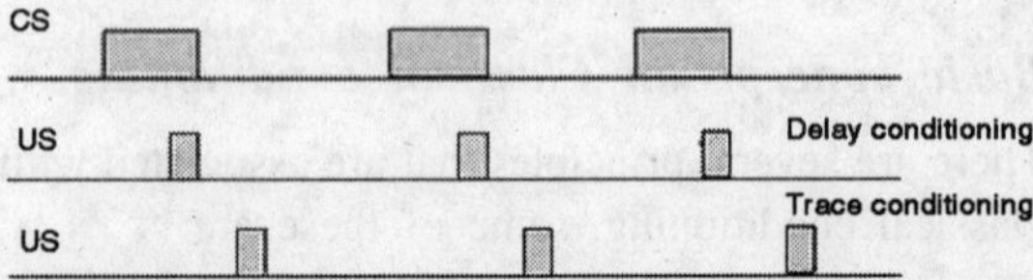

Simultaneous conditioning: During simultaneous conditioning, the conditioned stimulus (CS) and the unconditioned stimulus (US) are presented and terminated at the same time.

Backward conditioning: Backward conditioning occurs when a conditional stimulus (CS) immediately follows an unconditional stimulus (US). Unlike traditional conditioning models, in which the conditional stimulus (CS) precedes the unconditional stimulus (US), the conditional response (CR) tends to be inhibitory. This is because the conditional stimulus (CS) serves as a signal that the unconditional stimulus (US) has ended, rather than a reliable method of predicting the future occurrence of the unconditional stimulus (US).

Temporal conditioning: The unconditioned stimulus (US) is presented at regularly timed intervals, and CR acquisition is dependent upon correct timing of the interval between unconditioned stimulus (US) presentations. The background, or context, can serve as the conditioned stimulus (CS) in this example.

Unpaired conditioning: The conditioned stimulus (CS) and the unconditioned stimulus (US) are not presented together. Usually they are presented as independent trials that are separated by a variable, or pseudo-random interval. This procedure is used to study non-associative behavioural responses, such as sensitization.

CS-alone extinction: The conditioned stimulus (CS) is presented in the absence of the unconditioned stimulus (US). This procedure is usually done after the conditional response (CR) has been acquired through "forward conditioning" training. Eventually, the conditional response (CR) frequency is reduced to pre-training levels. Essentially, the stimulus is presented until habituation occurs.

Implications of Pavlov's Theory to Classroom Situations

1. The theory believes that one must be able to practise and master a task effectively before embarking on another one. This means that a student needs to be able to respond to a particular stimulus (information) before he/she can be associated with a new one.
2. Teachers should know how to motivate their students to learn. They should be versatile with various strategies that can enhance effective participation of the students in the teaching-learning activities.
3. Most of the emotional responses can be learned through classical conditioning. A negative or positive response comes through the stimulus being paired with. For example, providing the necessary school material for primary school pupils will develop good feelings about school and learning in them, while, punishment will discourage them from attending the school.

COGNITIVE PERSPECTIVES OF LEARNING

We have learnt that the behaviourist perspectives of learning and the theories support its insights. The next is the cognitive perspective. Cognitive psychology is the theoretical perspective that focuses on learning based on how people perceive, remember, think, speak, and solve problem. The Cognitive perspective differs from the behaviourist perspective into two distinct ways. First, Cognitive psychology acknowledges the existence of internal mental states discharged by the behaviourists. Examples of these states are belief, desire, ideas and motivation (non-observable states). Secondly, the cognitive psychologists claim that memory structures determine how information is perceived, processed, stored, retrieved and forgotten. Cognitive psychology encompasses perception, categorization, memory, knowledge representation, language and thinking process.

The major cognitive psychologist you should be familiar with includes Jean Piaget who developed Piaget's theory of Cognitive Development and Stages of Cognitive Development. Lev Vygotsky, best known for his Socio Cultural Development theory; Noam Chomsky, referred to as the father of modern linguistics; and Jerome Bruner, who coined the term 'scaffolding'.

Insight Learning - Kohler

This theory is related to the cognitive type of theory of learning. It was developed by Gestalt psychologist. The main exponents are Wolfgang Kohler, Kurt Koffka and Max Wertheimer.

This theory advocates that when a particular situation is being learnt, it does not help to learn it in parts but it helps to learn its whole. Learning is an exploratory, purposive and creative activity but not a trial and error method of activity. Learning means, 'Reorganization of the perceptual field'. Learning is dependent upon intelligence of the individuals.

Experiment

Wolfgang Kohler conducted experiments through chimpanzees in a laboratory at Canary Islands. He conducted the following experiments based upon box-problems and some others on stick problems. He inserted hungry chimpanzees (Sultan) in a cage and hung bananas at the ceiling and placed a stick and a wooden box inside. The hungry chimpanzees tried to catch the banana by standing on the box but it could not. They sat in a corner and tried to grasp the situation by analyzing how to take the bananas. A student insight appeared in its mind and it jumped at the top of wooden box and hit the bananas with the help of stick.

An illustration of Kohler's Insight Learning Theory

Instead of the above method, Kohler also conducted the various experiments by placing the bananas outside the box and placing two sticks inside the box and by removing the wooden box.

The results of the experiment are:

(*i*) Learning is achieved not only by trial and error method but on the chimpanzee's intelligence.

(*ii*) The whole situation has to be understood along with the inner relations involved therein. One can solve the problem through the experience gained.

Classroom Implications

(*i*) Learning and teaching should be in total and not in part.

(*ii*) The learner should be motivated by arousing the interest and curiosity to well acquaint with the specific aims and purposes of the learning process.

(*iii*) The teacher should adhere to inter-disciplinary approach in teaching.

(*iv*) Learning should be in an intelligent form and not in a mechanical form.

Discovery Learning by Bruner

Discovery Learning is the active process of inquiry based instruction that encourages that learners to build on prior knowledge through experience and to search for new information and relationships based on their interests.

Bruner was one of the founding fathers of constructivist theory. Bruner's theoretical framework is based upon the theme that the learners construct new ideas or concepts based upon existing knowledge. Learning is an active process. Bruner's theory emphasises the significance of categorization in learning. "To perceive is to categories, to conceptualize is to categories, to learn is to form categories to make decisions is to categories". Interpreting information and experiences by similarities and differences is a key concept.

Theory

Four features of Bruner's theory of instruction.

1. *Predisposition to learn:* This feature specifically states the experiences which move the learner toward a love of learning in general, or of learning something in particular. Motivational, cultural and personnel factors contribute to this. Bruner emphasized social factor and early teachers and parents influence on this. He believed learning and problem solving emerged out exploration. Part of the task of a teacher is to maintain and direct a child's spontaneous explorations.
2. *Structure of knowledge:* It is possible to structure knowledge in a way that enables the learners to most readily grasp the information. This is a relative feature, as there are many ways to structure a body of knowledge and many preferences among the learners. Bruner offered considerable detail about structuring knowledge.

   Understanding the fundamental structure of a subject makes it more comprehensible. Bruner viewed categorization as a fundamental process in the structuring of knowledge. The discrepancy between beginning and advanced knowledge in a subject area is diminished when instruction centres on a structure and principles of orientation. This means that a body of knowledge must be in a form recognizable to the student's experience.
3. *Modes of representation:* The representations could be visual, words, symbols.
4. *Ellective sequencing:* Every learner adheres to sequencing according to their individual differences in learning. Sequencing can make learning easy and lack of sequencing can make the learning process difficult.

Categorization

Bruner gave much attention to categorization of information in the construction of internal cognitive maps. He believed that perception, conceptualization, learning, decision making, and making inferences all involved categorization.

Bruner suggested a system of coding in which people form a hierarchical arrangement of related categories. Each successively higher level of categories becomes more specific, echoing Benjamin Bloom understands of knowledge acquisition as well as the related idea of instructional scaffolding **(Bloom's Taxonomy).**

Categories are "rules" that specify four things about objects.

1. Critical attributes required characteristics for inclusion of an object category.
2. The second rule prescribes how the critical attributes are combined.
3. The third rule assigns weight to various properties.
4. The fourth rule sets acceptance limits on attributes.

There are several kinds of categories:

Identity categories—categories include objects based on their attributes or features. Equivalent categories provide rules for combining categories. Equivalence can be determined by affective criteria, based on related functions (for example, "car" "truck" "van" could all be combined in an exclusive category called "motor vehicle") or by formal criteria, for example by science, law or cultural agreement. For example, 'an apple' is still 'an apple' whether it is green, ripe, dried, etc. (identity), it is food (functional) and it is a member of a botanical classification group (formal).

Coding systems are categories served to recognize sensory input. They are major organizational variables in higher cognitive functioning. Going beyond immediate sensory data involves making inference on the basis of related categories. Related categories form a "coding system". These are hierarchical arrangements of related categories.

Application:

Burner emphasized four characteristics of effective instruction which emerged from his theoretical constructs.

1. *Personalized:* Instruction should relate to learner's predisposition, and facilitate interest towards learning.
2. *Content structure:* Content should be structured so it can be most easily grasped by the learner.
3. *Sequencing:* Sequencing is an important aspect for presentation of material.
4. *Reinforcement:* Rewards and punishment should be selected and placed appropriately.

Intellectual development

Bruner postulated three stages of intellectual development.

- The first stage he termed "Enactive", when a person learns about the world through actions on physical objects and the outcomes of these actions.
- The second stage was called "Iconic" where learning can be obtained through using models and pictures.
- The final stage was "Symbolic" in which the learner develops the capacity to think in abstract terms. Based on this three-stage notion, Burner recommended using in a combination of concrete and pictorial, then symbolic activates will lead to more effective learning.

Types of Discovery learning

- Experiments
- Exploration
- Simulation-based learning
- Problem-based learning
- Inquiry-based learning
- Web quests

Classroom Implications

- Actively engages students' learning process
- Motivates students to participate
- Encourages autonomy and independence
- Promotes the development of creativity and problem-solving skills
- Provides an individualized learning experience.

Developmental Theory - Piaget

The most influent exponent of cognitivism was Swiss child psychologist Jean Piaget. Piaget rejected the idea that learning was the passive assimilation of given knowledge. Instead, he proposed, "learning is a dynamic process comprising successive stages of adoption to reality during which learners actively construct knowledge by creating and testing their own theories of the world".

Theory

Piaget's theory has two major parts: "ages" and "stages" components that predict what children can and cannot understand at different ages and a theory of development that describes how children develop cognitive abilities. It is the theory of development that will be the focus here because it is the major foundation for cognitive constructivist approaches to teaching and learning.

Piaget's theory of cognitive development proposes that humans cannot be "given" information which they immediately understand and use. Instead, humans must "construct" their own knowledge. They build their knowledge through experience. Experiences enable them to create "Schemas"-mental models in their heads. The schemas are the representation in the mind of a set of perceptions, ideas and actions which go together. These schemas are changed, enlarged and made more sophisticated through two complimentary processes given below:

(*i*) *Assimilation* - The process by which a person takes material into their mind from the environment, which may mean changing the evidence of their senses to make it fit.

(*ii*) *Accommodation* - The difference made to one's mind or concepts by the process of assimilation.

The basic principle underlying Piaget's theory is the principle of equilibration:

All cognitive development including both intellectual and affective development progresses towards increasingly complex and stable levels of organization. Equilibration takes place through a process of adoption, *i.e.*, assimilation of new information to existing cognitive structures and the accommodation of that information through the formation of new cognitive structures.

For example, learners who already have the cognitive structures necessary to solve percentage problems in mathematics will have some of the structures necessary to solve time-rate-distance problems, but they will need to modify their existing structures to accommodate the newly acquired information to solve the new type of problem. Thus, learners adapt and develop by assimilating and accommodating new information into existing cognitive structures. It should be noted that assimilation and accommodation go together.

Piaget suggested that there are four main stages in the cognitive development of children as follows:

(*i*) The Sensory motor stage (0-2 yrs)

(*ii*) The Preoperational stage (2 to 7 yrs)

(*iii*) The Concrete Operational stage (7 to 12 yrs)

(*iv*) The Formal Operational stage (12 yrs and above)

(*i*) The Sensory motor stage (0-2 yrs): In the first two years, children pass through a sensory motor stage during which they progress from cognitive structures dominated by instinctual drives and undifferentiated emotions to more organized systems of concrete concepts, differentiated emotions, and their first external affective fixations. At this stage, children's outlook is essentially egocentric in the sense that they are unable to take into account other's point of view.

(*ii*) The Preoperational stage (2 to 7 yrs) : The second stage of development lasts until around seven years of age. Children begin to use language to make sense of reality. They learn to classify objects using different criteria and to manipulate numbers. Children's increasing linguistic skills open the way for greater socialization of action and communication with others.

(*iii*) The Concrete Operational stage (7 to 12 yrs): Children at this point of development begin to think more logically, but their thinking can also be very rigid. They tend to struggle with abstract and hypothetical concepts. At this point, children also become less egocentric and begin to think about how other people might think and feel. They begin to understand that their thoughts are unique to them and that not everyone else necessarily shares their thoughts, feelings and opinions.

(*iv*) The Formal Operational stage (12 yrs and above) : From the age of twelve to adolescent, the final stage of Piaget's theory involves an increase in logic, the ability to use deductive reasoning and an understanding of abstract ideas. At this point, people become capable of seeing multiple potential solutions to problems and think more scientifically about the world around them.

Educational Implications

- Focus on the process of children's thinking, not just its products.
- Recognition of the crucial role of children's self-initiated, active involvement in learning activities.
- Emphasis on practices aimed at making children adult like in their thinking.
- Acceptance of individual differences in developmental progress.

Social Learning - Bandura

The social learning theory proposed by Albert Bandura has become perhaps the most influential theory of learning and development. While rooted in many of the basic concepts of traditional learning theory, Bandura believed that direct reinforcement could not account for all types of learning. While the behavioural theories of learning suggested that all learning was the result of associations formed by conditioning, reinforcement and punishment, Bandura's social learning theory proposed that learning can also occur simply by observing the actions of others.

His theory added a social element, arguing that people can learn new information and behaviours by watching other people. Known as observational learning (or modelling), this type of learning can be used to explain a wide variety of behaviours.

Theory

There are three concepts at the heart of social learning theory. First is the idea that people can learn through observation. Next is the notion that internal mental states are an essential part of this process. Finally, this theory recognizes that just because something has been learned, it does not mean that it will result in a change in behaviour.

Let us explore each of these concepts in greater depth.

1. People Can Learn Through Observation
2. Observational Learning

In his famous Bobo doll experiment, Bandura demonstrated that children learn and imitate behaviours they have observed in other people. The children in Bandura's studies observed an adult acting violently towards a Bobo doll. When the children were later allowed to play in a room with the Bobo doll, they began to imitate the aggressive actions they had previously observed.

Bandura identified three basic models of observational learning:

1. A live model, which involves an actual individual demonstrating or acting out a behaviour.
2. A verbal instructional model, which involves descriptions and explanations of a behaviour.
3. A symbolic model, which involves real or fictional characters displaying behaviours in books, films, television programs, or online media.

Bandura noted that external, environmental reinforcement was not the only factor to influence learning and behaviour. He described *intrinsic reinforcement* as a form of internal reward, such as pride, satisfaction, and a sense of accomplishment. This emphasis on internal thoughts and cognitions helps connect learning theories to cognitive developmental theories. While many textbooks place social learning theory with behavioural theories, Bandura himself describes his approach as a 'social cognitive theory'.

The Modelling Process

Not all observed behaviours are effectively learned. Factors involve both the model and the learner to play a role in whether social learning is successful. Certain requirements and steps must also be followed. The following steps are involved in the observational learning and modelling process.

(*a*) *Attention:* In order to learn, you need to be paying attention. Anything that distracts your attention is going to have a negative effect on observational learning. If the model is interesting or there is a novel aspect to the situation, you are far more likely to dedicate your full attention to learning.

(*b*) *Retention:* The ability to store information is also an important part of the learning process. Retention can be affected by a number of factors, but the ability to pull up information later and act on it is vital to observational learning.

(*c*) *Reproduction:* Once you have paid attention to the model and retained the information, it is time to actually perform the behaviour you observed. Further practice of the learned behaviour leads to improvement and skill advancement.

(*d*) *Motivation:* Finally, in order for observational learning to be successful, you have to be motivated to imitate the behaviour that has been modelled. Reinforcement and punishment play an important role in motivation. While experiencing these motivators can be highly effective, so can observing other experience some type of reinforcement or punishment. For example, if you see another student rewarded with extra credit for being to class on time, you might start to show up a few minutes early each day.

Classroom Implications

(*i*) Students learn a great deal simply by observing others.

(*ii*) Describing the consequences of behaviour increases appropriate behaviours, decreasing inappropriate ones; this includes discussing the rewards of various behaviours.

(*iii*) Modelling such as attention, retention, motor reproduction and motivation provides an alternative to teaching new behaviours.

(*iv*) Students must believe that they are capable of accomplishing a task; it is important to develop a sense of self-efficacy.

(*v*) Teachers should help students set realistic expectations; ensure that expectations are realistically challenging.

(*vi*) Self-regulation techniques provide an effective method for improving student behaviours.

Social Constructivism Theory - Vygotsky

The psychologist, Lev Vygotsky shared many of Piaget's views about child development, but he was more interested in the social aspects of learning. Vygotsky differs from discovery learning, which is also based on Piaget's ideas, in the sense that the teacher and the older children play important roles in learning. He argued that all cognitive functions originate in, and must therefore be explained as products of social interactions and that learning was not simply the assimilation and accommodation of new knowledge by learners; it was the process by which learners were integrated into a knowledge community.

The teacher is typically active and involved. The classroom should provide a variety of learning materials (including electronic) and experiences and the classroom culture provides the child with cognitive tools such as language, cultural history and social context.

The Zone of Proximal Development (ZPD) is a concept for which Vygotsky is well-known. It refers to the observation that children, when learning a particular task or body of information, start out by not being able to do the task. Then they can do it with the assistance of an adult or older child mentor, and finally they can do it without assistance. The ZPD is the stage where they can do it assisted, but not alone. Thus the teacher often serves to guide a child or group of children as they encounter different learning challenges.

Vygotsky's observations led him to propose a complete relationship between language and thought. He observed egocentric speech and child monologues such as Piaget wrote about, as well as internal speech. He proposed that speech (external language) and thought have different origins within the human individual. He described thought as non-verbal, and speech as having a pre-intellectual stage, in which words are not symbols for the objects they denote, but are properties of the objects. Up to about age two, they are independent. After that thought and speech become connected. At this point, speech and thought become interdependent, and thought becomes verbal. Thus, children's monologues become internalized as internal dialogue.

Vygotsky differed from Piaget in the sense that he considered development after age 2 as at least partially determined by language. He believed, "egocentric speech serves the function of self-guidance, and eventually becomes internalized. It is only spoken aloud because the child has not yet learned how to internalize it". He found that egocentric speech decreased when the child's feeling of being understood diminished, as when there was no listener or the listener was occupied with other matters. These ideas, while intriguing, have never been adequately researched, so it is difficult to evaluate their significance.

Classroom Implications

(*i*) Learning and development is a social, collaborative activity.

(*ii*) The Zone of Proximal Development can serve as a guide for curricular and lesson planning.

(*iii*) Classroom activity should be reality-based and applicable to the real world.

(*iv*) Learning extends to the home and other out-of-school environments and activities and all learning situations should be related.

HUMANIST PERSPECTIVES OF LEARNING

Humanistic "theories" of learning tend to be highly value-driven and hence more like prescriptions (about what ought to happen) rather than descriptions (of what happens). The school is particularly associated with Rogers, Abraham Maslow, John Holt and Malcolm. They emphasize the "natural desire" of everyone to learn. Whether this natural desire is to learn whatever it is you are teaching, however, is not clear.

- It follows from this, they maintain, that learners need to be empowered and to have control over the learning process.
- So the teacher relinquishes a great deal of authority and becomes a facilitator.

Learner-Centred Approach

Learner-centred approach, also known as student-centred approach involves the methods of teaching that shifts the focus of instruction from the teacher to the learner. It aims to develop learner autonomy and independence by putting responsibility for the learning by the learner himself. It focuses on skills and practices that enable lifelong learning and independent problem-solving. This approach and practice are based on the constructivist learning theory that emphasizes the learner's critical role in constructing meaning from new information and prior experiences.

Carl Roger's notions about the formation of the individual also contribute to this learner-centred learning. It means inverting the traditional teacher-centred understanding of the learning process and putting the learners in the centre of the learning process. Roger emphasized that significant learning is acquired through doing. The concept is placing a teacher closer to a peer level to the learner as peer-to-peer interaction can lead to an abundance of knowledge through collaborative thinking.

In learner-centred approach, the learners choose what they will learn, how they will learn and how they will assess their own learning. Here the teacher as a facilitator act the passive role and the learners acts the active role, contrast to the traditional teacher-centred approach.

Classroom Implications

- The learners should be provided with rich educational environment.
- Teacher should be a facilitator of learning, guiding and nurturing the learners in order to build their talent.
- The relationship between the learner and the teacher should be positive.
- Curriculum should be new and modern.
- Teacher should be an active listener.
- Education should nurture rather than construct learners.

Factors Influencing Learning

We have seen that 'learning' is one of the most important functions of our cognitive system which brings about relatively permanent changes in the behaviour of the learner. There are some factors which influence the acquisition of knowledge by perceived information through learning. These factors determine the achievement of desired goals aimed in the learning process. The factors are:

(*a*) Psychological individual differences of learners.

(*b*) Teachers' enthusiasm in classroom learning.

(*c*) Environment and other factors.

(a) Psychological individual differences of learners

The individual differences in the psychological, physical, social and cultural factors influence the quality and quantity of learning. The individual differences in psychological aspects make learners to differ from one another in the learning process.

The psychology of individual differences of learners deals with the intelligence and abilities associated with the personality of learners, learning styles and needs and interests of the learners. The personality of the learners includes their aptitude, attitude, motivation, mental health and aspiration to achieve their goals of life.

Learning is most effective when differences in the learners' language, cultural, and social behaviour are taken into account. Although basic principles of learning, stimulus and effective instructions may apply to all learners, it is necessary to pay attention to language, intelligence, ethnic group, race, belief and socio-economic status of the learners which can influence learning. When learners see that their individual differences in abilities, background, and cultures are valued and respected, the motivation for learning enhances.

(b) Teachers' enthusiasm in classroom learning

The modifications in behaviour of a learner depend on the nature and method of learning experiences gained by that learner. Teachers play an important role in the teaching-learning process as a facilitator of learning. By adopting dynamic and efficient teaching techniques and strategies, a teacher could explore the talents of the learner and could progress quality of teaching-learning process.

Learning of different subjects and area of experiences could be enhanced by adopting pertinent teaching techniques and strategies. The teachers should employ applicable methods such as teacher-centred or learner-centred and a number of good techniques such as memorising, understanding, reflective, interaction, mentoring, etc., to enable the learners to learn their subject and content matter.

A teacher should be able to identify and meet the educational needs of the learners. The awareness in educational psychology could enable a teacher to know the motivational level, abilities, attitude, emotional conditions, interests and intelligence of the learners, and should be aware of the advances in educational psychology.

A teacher should also be sensitive to individual differences, keep in mind the level of intelligence and abilities of the learners and their different cultural attitudes. A teacher should respond in a sensitive way and view the learners positively regardless of their cultural backgrounds.

The developmental needs of the learners could be motivated by a teacher if he or she finds himself or herself passionate towards their profession. In the process of teaching the teachers could counsel the learners using psychometric instruments such as tests, rating scales, checklists, observation and interview. These instruments help the learners to overcome their psychological obstacles in their way to attain their aims of learning.

(c) Environment and other factors

The external environmental factors such as surroundings, cultural and social demands such as relationship with parents, teachers and peer, information factors such as media influence the learners. Surroundings include factors associated

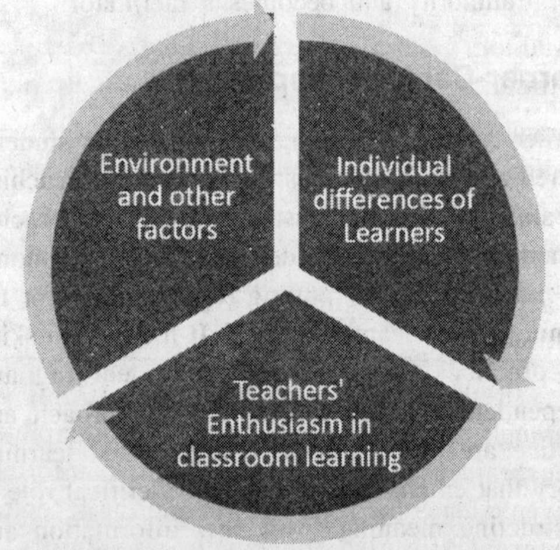

Factors influencing learning

with one's location, weather, and people in the surrounding area, schedules and events. Cultural settings of the learners such as culture of their origin, religion and place influence the learning process. The learners' social relationship with their parents, teachers and peer group and mass media greatly influence the type of learning, intense of learning and time required to learn a need of the learners.

SENSATION

In general, it is necessary that our brain should recognise and interpret what has been happening around us in the environment where we live. It would make us to experience and feel the surrounding around us. Sensation is the process which allows our brain to take in information from the environment through our sensory system which can be then experienced and interpreted by the brain. It is the first step in the acquisition of knowledge in a conscious mind.

Sensation is defined as the "process by which sense organs gather information about the environment and transmit it to the brain for initial processing" - Kowalski & Western. Sensation occurs through our sense organs.

Stimuli	*Sense Organ(s)*	*Sensation*	*Sense*
Visual Stimuli	Eyes	Aural/Visual sensation	Seeing
Auditory Stimuli	Ears	Auditory sensation	Hearing
Fragrance/ odour Stimuli	Nose	Olfactory	Smelling
Taste Stimuli	Tongue	Gustatory sensation	Tasting
Tactile Stimuli	Skin	Tactile sensation	Feeling or touch

In the learning process, the stimuli given through the sense organs would be interpreted in the brain to perceive or realise the information given. Hence the sense organs are the receptors of external stimuli. These sense receptors have specialized cells that respond to environmental stimuli into neural impulse that can be understood by the brain in a process known as transduction. This is the reason for the effectiveness of instructional process in the classroom through sensory learning style.

ATTENTION

Attention is the cognitive process of selectively concentrating on one aspect of the environment while ignoring other things. It is closely related to the immediate experience of the individual; it is a state of current awareness. Within the vast field of potential experiences, an individual focuses upon - or attends to - some limited subset of the whole. This subset constitutes the subjective field of awareness. A person cannot consciously experience all the events and information available at any one time. Likewise, it is impossible to initiate, simultaneously, an unlimited number of different actions. The question becomes one of how an appropriate subset of inputs, intermediate processes, and outputs is selected to command attention and engage available resources.

Attention, then, may be understood as a condition of selective awareness which governs the extent and quality of one's interactions with one's environment. It is not necessarily held under voluntary control. In other words, attention is the first step in the observation. It is focusing the consciousness on a stimulus. It is a process of preferentially responding to a stimulus or a range of stimuli. Sometimes attention shifts to matters unrelated to the external environment, a phenomenon referred to as mind-wandering or "spontaneous thought".

Attention is one of the most intensely studied topics within psychology and cognitive neuroscience. Of the many cognitive processes associated with the human mind (decision-making, memory, emotion, etc.), attention is considered the most concrete because it is tied so closely to perception. As such it is a gateway to the rest of cognition.

Definition

Attention has been commonly referred to as a "general, or universal, characteristic of consciousness".

"Everyone knows what attention is. Focalization, concentration, of consciousness are of its essence. It implies withdrawal from some things in order to deal effectively with others, and is a condition which has a real opposite in the confused, dazed, scatterbrained state." (Principles of Psychology, 1890).

—*William James*

"Attention is a state of sensory clearness with a margin and a focus. Attention is the aspect of consciousness that relates to the amount of effort exerted in focusing on certain aspects of an experience, so that they become relatively vivid".

—*Titchener*

Attention and the Processing of Information

This can be explained using the concept of *filtering*. Since we cannot process all the information in our sensory channels, we filter or partially blackout some inputs. It is hard to pay attention to more than one set of inputs at a time. This is called serial processing, *i.e.*, attending one set of inputs and then another. Whether you process the conversation serially, or listen to only one of them, you are filtering out the unattended conversation. In the filter model of attention, inputs in the margin shift to the focus, when various attending getting features of the environment are present in the filtered input.

Clinical model of attention

Many times clinical models differ from investigation models. One of the most used models for the evaluation of attention in patients with very different neurologic pathologies is the model of Sohlberg and Mateer. This hierarchic model is based in the recovering of attention processes of brain damage patients after coma. Five different kinds of activities are described in the model; connecting with the activities that patient could do as their recovering process advanced.

1. **Focused attention:** This is the ability to respond discretely to specific visual, auditory or tactile stimuli.
2. **Sustained attention:** This refers to the ability to maintain a consistent behavioural response during continuous and repetitive activity.
3. **Selective attention:** This level of attention refers to the capacity to maintain a behavioural or cognitive set in the face of distracting or competing stimuli. Therefore, it incorporates the notion of "freedom from distractibility".
4. **Alternating attention:** It refers to the capacity for mental flexibility that allows individuals to shift their focus of attention and move between tasks having different cognitive requirements.
5. **Divided attention:** This is the highest level of attention and it refers to the ability to respond simultaneously to multiple tasks or multiple task demands.

This model has shown to be very useful to evaluate attention in very different pathologies, correlates strongly with daily difficulties and it is especially helpful to design stimulation programs such as the APT (Attention Process Training); a rehabilitation program for neurologic patients.

Overt and Covert Attention

Attention may be differentiated according to its status as 'overt' versus 'covert'. Overt attention is the act of directing sense organs towards a stimulus source. Covert attention is the act of mentally focusing on particular stimuli. Covert attention is thought to be a neural process that enhances the signal from a particular part of the sensory panorama.

There are studies that suggest the mechanisms of overt and covert attention may not be as separate as previously believed. Though humans and primates can look in one direction but attend in another, there may be an underlying neural circuitry that links shifts in covert attention to plans to shift gaze. For example, if individuals attend to the right hand corner field of view, we want to move eyes in that direction, and have to actively suppress the eye movement that linked to this shift in attention.

The current view is that visual covert attention is a mechanism for quickly scanning the field of view for interesting locations. This shift in covert attention is linked to eye movement circuitry that sets up a slower saccade to that location.

Forms of Attention: Voluntary, Non voluntary, Involuntary and Habitual Attention

1. **Voluntary Attention:** Sometimes an individual will divert his attention towards a particular activity or situation deliberately. Active, or voluntary, attention is precisely what the name implies, attention as the result of definitely self-initiated activity. In its clearest and most unambiguous form it always involves mental strain and effort.

   It is not diverted spontaneously, but after some struggle. For example, while sitting in a class, the students divert their attention towards the lecture even if it is not interesting, because they have to pass the examination.

2. **Non Voluntary Attention:** It requires no extended reflection upon everyday experience to reveal to us the fact that in the course of every twenty-four hours we attend in an effortless way to a great many things to which we have no explicit purpose to direct our thought, to which we cannot, therefore, be said to attend voluntarily in the full sense of the word; but to which we certainly are not attending *against* our will and in spite of ourselves. Such cases constitute what is meant by non-voluntary, or spontaneous attention.

3. **Involuntary Attention:** At times the attention is diverted towards some other activity without the conscious effort, may be against the will of the individual. This is known as involuntary attention. For example, though the student is listening to a lecture with all interest, some loud sound outside the classroom may draw his attention towards it.

4. **Habitual Attention:** In some situations, reaction to a stimulus or attending to a stimulus becomes a habit. So the individual will automatically divert his attention towards that stimulus.

   For example, a musician's attention will automatically be diverted towards the sound of music even if he is busily engaged in talking to somebody.

Factors Affecting Attention

Attention is a selective activity which often depends upon the preference of our mind. Apart from this, there are other factors in the objects as well as in the individual which can influence attention. These factors are divided into two: Objective factors and Subjective factors.

1. Objective Factors

These factors relate to particular aspects of objects which are inherent in the objects one perceives.

1. **Movement:** A moving object draws our attention more easily than a stationary object.
2. **Intensity:** More intense light, sound or smell draws our attention more easily than less intense one.
3. **Novelty:** New kinds of objects draw our attention quickly.
4. **Size:** A bigger or a smaller object draws the attention of people very easily than average level size of any object.
5. **Change:** A change in our environment draws our attention quickly.
6. **Repetition:** When a stimulus is presented repeatedly our attention is diverted.
7. **Clarity:** An object or sound which can be experienced clearly draws our attention than the stimuli which are not clear.

8. **Colours:** Colourful objects draw our attention more easily than black or white objects.
9. **Contrast:** An object that is strikingly different from its background draws our attention.

2. Subjective Factors

These factors refer to factors related to the individual. There are several subjective factors which determine our attention. They are:

1. **Interest:** Objects of our interest draw our attention immediately.
2. **Motives:** Motives are powerful forces which make us to divert our attention.
3. **Mental set:** Mind set or readiness of mind is very important in attending to any stimulus.
4. **Emotional state:** Attention is disturbed during emotional state. It also affects our perception.
5. **Habits:** Our attention is diverted automatically towards the things to which we are habituated.

Major Conditions of Attention

There are four conditions of attention which refer to the duration and degree of attention. They are as follows: (1) Fluctuation of Attention (2) Distraction of Attention (3) Division of Attention (4) Span of Attention/Apprehension.

1. Fluctuation of Attention

It appears for us that our attention can be concentrated on a particular act for more time. But careful observation clearly shows that we cannot concentrate on a single act or stimulus for more than a few seconds.

When we are seeing an object or listening to a sound, after a few seconds, the attention will be shifted towards other stimulus or other area of the stimulus for a fraction of time and will return to the original stimulus. This process is called fluctuation. Here, we will be unable to notice this short shift.

2. Distraction of Attention

When our attention is concentrated on a particular act or stimulus, some other more powerful stimulus may draw our attention and hold it to remain there for more time.

It may or may not return to the earlier stimulus. For example, while reading a book, our concentration will be on the book. Meanwhile if we listen to an attractive music sound, our attention may be shifted towards that under such circumstances, physically we may be reading the book, but we may not follow the contents. Students are much affected by distraction. Hence, they should learn to have concentration of mind on studies.

3. Division of Attention

Attending to more than one act at a time is known as division of attention. In such situations, we will divide our attention towards more than one act. For example, a tailor will be stitching the cloths and also speaking to his customers.

A nurse will be observing the pulse of a patient and also the changes in his face. We ride a scooter while speaking to our friends. In such activities the attention is not divided, but it is possible to perform more than one act because, either our attention is shifted from one act to another rapidly, or our attention is concentrated on only one act and the remaining activities are carried on automatically.

Such activities do not need our attention, because these are almost mechanical. But in some technical jobs, attention has to be divided to perform more than one act at a time. However, under such circumstances, the quality and quantity of the task is affected. This can be proved experimentally using a "Division of attention board".

4. Span of Attention/Apprehension

Span refers to the number of letters or digits or sounds that an individual can grasp within a given period of time. Using an instrument called 'Tachistoscope', it is experimentally proved that an individual can grasp 4-5 digits or letters easily within a fraction of time.

It is also proved that span will be more for meaningful material like words, than digits or non-sense syllables. It may be observed that digits on number plates of automobile vehicles are restricted to four only.

Role of Attention in Perception

During every waking moment enormous numbers of stimuli compete for our attention. Ordinarily, people and other animals select a small trickle of impressions to attend to. The stimuli that lie in the periphery (boundary) of our attention form a background. This selective openness to a small portion of impinging sensory phenomena is called attention.

Currently there is disagreement regarding the nature of attention. Some psychologists see attention as a type of *filter* that screens out information at different points in the perceptual process. Others believe that people simply *focus* on what they wish to perceive by actively engaging themselves with the experience without directly shutting out competing events.

Psychologists are interested in identifying the points in the perceptual process where attention operates. Studies suggest that attention is active at several times like, initially while receiving input from a sense organ and later on while sorting and interpreting sensory data, deciding whether to respond to them and preparing to act. According to Daniel Kahneman an Israeli psychologist, the capacity of attention depends on the resources demanded by the task that are being attempted. Needs, interests and values have been shown to be important influences on attention.

Normally people pay particular attention to events that are novel, unexpected, intense or changing. This perceptual style has important survival value. It helps us to respond to sudden dangers, locate and manipulate objects in space and move about without collisions. If we attended to everything at once, important survival related cues could easily be lost amidst the clutter.

PERCEPTION

The inputs from our senses are elaborately transformed so that we perceive a meaningful and orderly world. Perception is defined as the process of organising and interpreting incoming sensory data (sensations) to develop an awareness of surroundings and self. Perception involves interpretation, whereas sensation does not.

Nature of Perception

Perception is an active complicated operation. The distinct nature of perception is described below.

Perception is not a mirror of reality : People sometimes assume that perception provides a perfectly accurate reflection of reality. Perception is not a mirror. First, our human senses do not respond to many aspects of our surroundings. Secondly, people sometimes perceive stimuli which are not present. Direct electrical stimulation of the brain can cause a person to see vision or hear voices. Thirdly, human perceptions depend on expectations, motives and past experiences.

Perception is a multifaceted cognitive capacity: Perception involves numerous cognitive activities. Early in the perceptual process people decide what to attend to. Consciousness also influences perception. Memory enters in to the perceptual process at several points. Information processing takes place during perception too. Language influences our cognitions, moulding perception indirectly.

While all cognitive processes are highly interconnected, we are beginning with perception because it may be considered as the point where cognition and reality meet and the most basic activity out of which all others emerge. Information must be taken into our minds before anything else can be done with it.

The Psychological Basis of Perception

The complex perceptual process depends on both sensory systems and brain. The sensory system detects information, converts (or transduces) it into nerve impulses, processes some of it, and sends most of it to the brain via nerve fibres. The brain plays the major role in processing sensory data. Perception depends on four operations like detection, transduction (the conversion of energy from one form to another), transmission and information processing.

Detection, Transduction and Transmission

The senses detect, transduce and transmit sensory information. Each sense has a detection element called a receptor. A receptor is a single cell or a group of cells that is particularly responsive to a specific type of energy. Certain cells in the ears are especially designed for registering sound, or vibrations in the air, a form of mechanical energy. Cells in the eyes are very sensitive to light, a form of electromagnetic energy. Pressure or vibrations may stimulate the eye too.

Receptors behave like transducers. The pickup cartridge on a record player is a transducer that you are probably familiar with. The cartridge converts (transduces) the mechanical vibrations of the needle riding in the record groove into electrical signals. After the signals have been amplified, the speaker (another transducer) transforms this electrical energy back into mechanical vibrations that we can hear. Receptors in our senses convert incoming energy into the electrochemical signals that the nervous system uses for communication. If the incoming energy is sufficiently intense, it will trigger nerve impulses that transmit coded information about various features of the stimulus along specific nerve fibres to particular brain regions.

The Organisation of Visual Perception

The data that our senses supply are continually being organised. Ordinarily the process is so rapid and automatic that we are completely unaware of it. People use several processing strategies to interpret visual information about objects. It includes constancy, figure-ground and grouping.

1. Constancy

Constancy means that objects viewed from different angles at various distances or under diverse conditions of illumination are still perceived and retain the same shape, size and colour. Constancy gives a great deal of stability to our perceptual worlds. In ways that are not fully understood, people use knowledge derived from past experience without making any effort or having any awareness of the process, to complement the images that the retina picks up.

2. Figure-ground

Whenever we look around, we tend to see objects (or figures) against a background (or ground). The same object may be seen as figure or ground depending on how you direct your attention. The stimuli that seem figure like appear to own the boundary or contour that is common to figure and ground and to be in front of the ground. Figures are seen as vivid and definitely shaped, as well.

As long as our senses and brain are operating normally, the same stimulus cannot be seen as both figure and ground at the same time. Notice how figure fluctuates. Sometimes we see two faces on a vague white background. At another time we see a vase on the featureless background. The reversals occur spontaneously and are hard to control. Still although we alternate between the two interpretations, only one dominates at any single time.

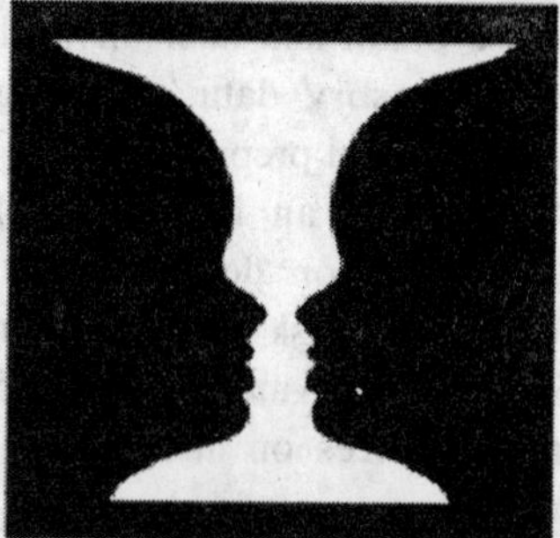

Fig.: *Reversals in perception of figure and ground should occur simultaneously*

The figure-ground principle appears to be basic to all object perception. Something cannot be seen as an object until it has been separated from its background. This particular rule appears to be largely inborn.

3. *Grouping*

The following principles are among those that govern the way we group elements of incoming visual information. See figure for visual elements illustrating the principles of grouping.

1. *Similarity:* Visual elements with similar colour, shape or texture are seen as belonging together. We tend to group elements that move in a similar direction too.
2. *Proximity:* Visual elements near one another are seen as belonging together.
3. *Symmetry:* Visual elements that form regular, simple, well-balanced shapes are seen as belonging together.
4. *Continuity:* Visual elements that permit lines, curves or movements tend to continue in the direction already established as to be grouped together.
5. *Closure:* Incomplete objects are usually filled in and seen as complete, a tendency known as closure.

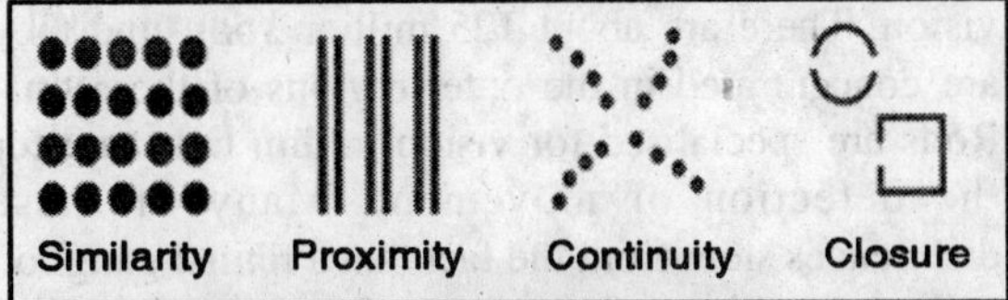

Fig.: *Visual elements with same shape and colour appear to belong together*

4. *Perceiving Depth and Distance*

Like a movie screen retina registers images in two dimensions: left-right and up-down. Yet people and animals perceive a three dimensional world. This is because; we use physiological, motion-related and pictorial cues to see depth and distance.

1. Physiological Cues: Several common physiological depth cues depend on the operation of both eyes, so they are *binocular depth cues.* Because our eyes are located in different positions, each retina records a slightly different visual image. This phenomenon is known as *binocular disparity.*

Convergence provides another binocular physiological depth cue. As our eyes fixate on a nearby object, they turn in towards one another. The resulting kinaesthetic feedback from the eye muscles gives us some idea about how distant the object is. Convergence cues are primarily useful for distances less than about 30 feet.

Even without two eyes, people and other animals still perceive distance. They use *monocular depth cues,* those that require the operation of only one eye. We will describe physiological, motion-related and pictorial monocular depth cues. First consider, *accommodation,* a physiological monocular depth cue. As you look at visual objects in any field, the lens system of the eye automatically focuses the incoming light rays on to the retina. During this process, known as accommodation, the eye muscles make the lens bulge to focus nearby objects or flatten to focus distant ones. In each case, the brain receives different kinaesthetic sensations from the eye muscles. These sensations provide information about distance. Because only minimal changes in accommodation occur beyond a few feet, this monocular depth cue is mainly effective for estimating short distances.

2. Motion-related Cues: Some cues about depth come from the perceiver's own actions. Whenever we move, for example, retina images of the visual field change. Objects that are close to us appear to sweep with great speed than distant ones. This important monocular depth cue is known as *motion parallax.* Motion parallax is vivid while driving. Fences, posts and poles beside the road seem to fly at high speed, while those far away drift past slowly. The relative motion of objects provides reliable information about their distances.

3. Pictorial Cues: A two dimensional retinal image of an actual scene contains a great deal of information about distance. People rely on such picture related, or pictorial cues continually, usually without being aware of doing so. There are six categories of monocular depth cues. They are discussed below:

1. *Familiar Size:* Whenever we see a familiar object, we roughly gauge its distance by

noting the size of our retinal image. When the image is relatively large, we assume that the object is near, and when it is relatively small, we infer that the object is distant.

2. *Linear Perspective:* It is a special case of familiar size. In the given figure, if we measure the cabinets on the photograph, we would find those towards the centre are smaller, closer and higher. Past experience tells us that the actual cabinets are not smaller, closer and higher. We have seen the apparent narrowing of parallel structures in viewing the sides of roads, rails, tracks, steams, etc., often enough to know their funnel shaped appearance signifies distance and not convergence. So every time we see what we believe to be parallel lines converge, we make an interpretation. We assume that the gradually changing retinal image means that the converging end of the structure is farthest away. This cue is called *linear perspective*.

Fig. *A cue for linear perspective*

3. *Light and Shadow:* When light from a specific source such as the sun strikes a three dimensional object, it illuminates the side(s) facing the light source and leaves the other side(s) in shadow. The pattern of light and shadow helps to define contours and gives information about solidity, depth, protrusions and indentations.
4. *Texture gradient:* Objects in visual field show a gradual change in texture with distance. They appear clear, detailed, and coarse nearby and less distinct farther away.
5. *Aerial Perspective:* Haze usually present in the atmosphere, makes distant objects appear bluish as well as blurred and indistinct.
6. *Interposition:* Whenever one object obstructs the view of another, the complete object is seen as closer than the obstructed one.

Colour Perception

There are two main reasons why colour vision is of value to us: *Detection:* Colour vision helps us to distinguish between an object and its background.

Discrimination: Colour vision makes it easier for us to make fine discriminations among objects (*e.g.*, between ripe and unripe fruit).

In order to understand how we can discriminate about five million different colours, we need to start with the retina. There are two types of visual receptor cells in the retina: cones and rods. There are about six million cones, and they are mostly found in the fovea or central part of the retina. The cones are specialised for colour vision and for sharpness of vision. There are about 125 million rods, and they are concentrated in the outer regions of the retina. Rods are specialised for vision in dim light and for the detection of movement. Many of these differences stem from the fact that a retinal ganglion cell receives input from only a few cones but from hundreds of rods. As a result, only rods produce much activity in retinal ganglion cells in poor lighting conditions.

Theories of Colour Vision

There are two major theories that explain and guide research on colour vision: the *trichromatic* theory also known as the Young-Helmholtz theory, and the *opponent-process* theory. These two theories are complementary and explain processes that operate at different levels of the visual system.

1. Trichromatic Theory

Evidence for the trichromatic theory comes from colour matching and colour mixing studies. In 1802,

Thomas Young proposed that all human vision occurred through the combination of sensitivity to red, green, and blue. This theory, modified by Hermann von Helmholtz in 1852, came to be known as the *Young-Helmholtz* or *trichromatic* (*three-colour*) theory of colour vision. The basic idea was that the eye responded to three primary colours, and combining the three primary colours of additive colour mixing formed all the other colours.

Young and Helmholtz carried out experiments in which individuals adjusted the relative intensity of 1, 2, or 3 light sources of different wavelengths so that the resulting mixture field matched an adjacent test field composed of a single wavelength. The finding that there are three types of colour-sensitive cone receptors in the retina supported the three-colour theory. One set of receptors is sensitive to long wavelengths such as red, one to medium wavelengths such as green, and one is sensitive to short wavelengths such as blue.

Individuals with normal colour vision needed three different wavelengths (*i.e.*, primaries) to match any other wavelength in the visible spectrum. This finding led to the hypothesis that normal colour vision is based on the activity of three types of receptors, each with different peak sensitivity. Consistent with the trichromatic theory, we now know that the overall balance of activity in S (short wavelength), M (medium wavelength), and L (long wavelength) cones determines our perception of colour.

So there is some truth to the three-colour theory. However, other aspects of colour vision cannot be accounted for by the trichromatic theory. For example, there is the phenomenon of *colour afterimages*. If you stare at a red dot, then move your gaze to a white wall, you will see a green dot as an afterimage. If you stare at a green dot, you will see a red afterimage. The same thing happens with yellow and blue.

2. Opponent-Process Theory

Ewald Hering put forward an opponent-process theory that handles some findings that cannot be explained by the Young-Helmholtz theory. Hering's key assumption was that there are three types of opponent processes in the visual system. He suggested that colour vision occurred in three channels where "opposite" colours (called *complementary* colours) were in a form of competition. For example, red and green are complementary colours. When you stare at something red, your redness detectors are worn out or fatigued. Their opponents, the green receptors, gain the upper hand, and you see a green afterimage after staring at a red dot. One type of process produces perception of green when it responds in one way and of red when it responds in the opposite way. A second type of process produces perception of blue or yellow in the same fashion. The third type of process produces the perception of white at one extreme and of black at the other.

The modern form of this theory assumes there are three basic channels for vision. One channel is the *red/green* channel; another is the *yellow/blue* channel. A third channel, the *black/white* or *brightness/darkness* channel, may also provide information relevant to colour vision, but that is a complex issue being debated among researchers.

The yellow/blue channel may seem odd, because there are no yellow-sensitive cones in the retina. Yellow light stimulates a *combination* of long-wavelength (red-sensitive) and medium wavelength (green-sensitive) cones. If there is more activity in blue receptors (compared to red plus green receptors) the brain interprets this as blue. If there is more red plus green activity (as compared to blue) the brain interprets this as yellow. The result is a yellow/blue channel. Yellow and blue act as opponent processes just like red and green. If you stare at a blue image, you get a yellow afterimage; if you stare at a yellow dot, you get a blue afterimage.

Monochromat, Dichromat or Trichromat

A person with no colour-sensitive pigments, therefore no colour vision, is called a *monochromat* (one-colour person). To such a person, the world looks like a black-and-white TV picture. Colours are shades of gray. A person with a defect in one channel - either the red/green or yellow/blue channel - is called a *dichromat*. Both colours in a channel are affected; so if the person cannot distinguish red that same person cannot distinguish green. A person who cannot see blue as a distinct colour will also not see yellow as a distinct colour. People with normal colour vision use all three channels (black/ white, red/green, and yellow/blue) and are called *trichromats*.

Theoretical Approach to Perception

There are four major approaches towards a theory of perception. The Gestalt approach heavily stresses nativistic factors of perceptual organisation. The constructionist approach accords greater influence to the factors of learning and memory. The motor approach centres on the role of feedback from the perceiver's motor exploration of his environment. Gibson's ecological approach emphasises the full environmental information inherent in the stimulus pattern.

1. The Gestalt Approach

A small group of experimental psychologists in Germany began to champion what was then a radical view: that we naturally, normally, immediately and directly perceive forms, figures and objects that have properties reflecting the whole stimulus pattern. The movement began by these German psychologists became known as Gestalt psychology. (Gestalt is the German word for 'pattern' or 'whole'). Its intellectual pioneers were Max Wertheimer, Kurt Koffka and Wolfgang Kohier, all of whom later emigrated to the United States.

The Gestaltists believed in inherent or innate laws of brain organisation. This, they argued, accounted for the central phenomena of figure-ground differentiation, contrast, contour, closure, the principles of perceptual grouping, etc. They asserted that any pattern involving greater symmetry, closure, closely knit units and similar units would seem 'simpler' to the observer. The influence of the Gestalt approach on the field of perception has been immense. It has pervaded and covered all modern conceptions of perceptual organisation and functioning. At the same time many limitations have been expressed. It has been objected that the demonstrations of the 'laws' of organisation and the simplicity principle were too heavily based on lines and dots on flat paper, a kind of display that is pictorial and lacks all the rich detail of real objects in a real world. Perhaps under these circumstances, it is said, when the stimulus structure is weak and ambiguous, the gestalt principles do come in to play. But in the densely textured three dimensional solid world we normally move around in a different kind of perceptual process which may occur.

A heavy criticism of the Gestalt approach is that, in its pre-occupation with innate factors of organisation, it has not given appropriate emphasis to factors of prior experience. This leads us next to a brief look at the constructionist approach.

2. The Constructionist Approach

In the constructionist view of perception, central importance is assigned to the role of *memory*. It is suggested that we add remembered residuals of previous experiences to here-and-now stimulus-induced sensations and thus construct a percept. And, the constructionist argue, the processes of selecting, analysing and adding to stimulus information from ones' memory store are the bases of organised perceptions, rather than the Gestaltists' natural operation of innate laws of brain organisation.

The constructionists suggest that memory is highly significant in the perceptual process in the sense that it provides a familiar context for perceiving; but this need not occur by literally adding details to perception.

3. The Motor Approach

Following the direction of Pavlov's early work, modern Russian perceptual research has concentrated on the role of motor behaviour in influencing and guiding perception. These investigators argue that there is a 'motor copy' that controls some of our perception of patterns. They believe that a copy of the movements made in exploring an object is one of the determiners of what will be seen.

Such movements seem to be, at least in part a learned tendency. In the early stages of the development of visual perception, eye movements do not tend to follow the outlines of objects or to concentrate upon their more figural features. Eye movement tracing seems to have an adaptive function; procedures especially designed to induce children and adults to trace the contours of objects visually have been found to aid visual learning and relearning. It is certain that our eye movements are closely related to perception. Indeed, if we do not move our eyes at all, the effect is that the visual scene fades completely.

A motor approach to perception, and its emphasis on effect, may hold in a powerful way for eye movements, but that the approach may not be equally appropriate for all kinds of movement in the perceptual process.

4. Gibson's Ecological Approach

In 1950, American psychologist, J.J. Gibson proposed that perception relies very heavily on a kind of relation that he believed had been overlooked by previous generations of psychologists. According to him, the normal environment is composed of textured surfaces and that a visual system that can detect textures makes important use of gradients of texture in perceiving the world. He believed the texture forms the basis for our perception of surfaces, and called the perception of textured surfaces as normal or ecological perception. He thought that the highly structured world, with its textured surfaces, supplied sufficiently rich and accurate information from which the observer could select. In Gibson's view, our perceptual selection skills get better and better with age.

Underlying Gibson's 'ecological' approach is the belief that in many respects all people see the world in similar ways, clearly and in whole. According to him people generally see the sizes and shapes and locations of objects quite accurately, and the mechanisms for seeing edges and surfaces operate similarly in most people.

Visual Illusions

Visual illusions stimulate us by challenging us to see things in a new way. Some optical illusions trick us because of the properties of light and the way our eyes work, and are addressed by biology and perhaps optics, while other illusions depend on a "higher" level of processing which is better addressed by psychology. Gregory, one of the most well-known researchers of optical illusions, addresses the difficulty in defining "illusion" in such a way that it includes everything that we think of as illusions, but excludes things like movies, which are illusions in the sense that they appear to depict motion while actually being composed of a series of static pictures.

How many triangles are present in the image below?

Answer: There are no triangles. In reality there are only 3 V shapes and 3 shapes that look like Pac-Men.

According to Gregory, many classic visual illusions can be explained by assuming that previous knowledge derived from the perception of three-dimensional objects is applied inappropriately to the perception of two-dimensional figures. For example, people typically see a given object as having a constant size by taking account of its apparent distance.

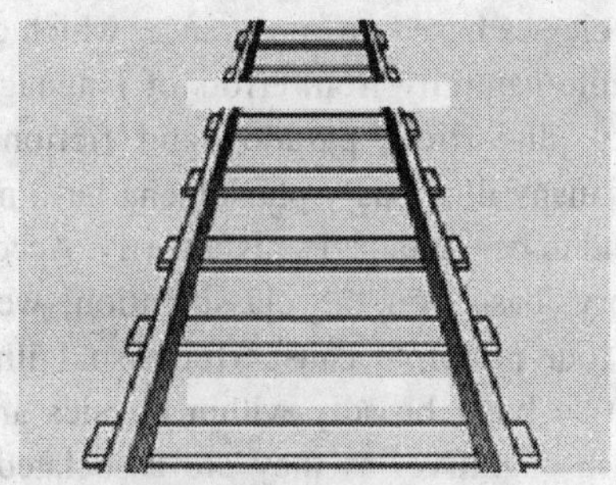

Fig. : *Ponzo illusion*

Size constancy means that an object is perceived as having the same size whether it is looked at from a short or a long distance away. This constancy contrasts with the size of the retinal image, which becomes progressively smaller as an object recedes into the distance. Gregory's misapplied size-constancy theory argues that this kind of perceptual processing is applied wrongly to produce several illusions.

The basic ideas in the theory can be understood with reference to the Ponzo illusion (see figure). The long lines in the Figure look like railway lines or the edges of a road receding into the distance. Thus, the top horizontal line can be seen as further away from us than the bottom horizontal line.

Misapplied size-constancy theory can also explain the Müller-Lyer illusion; (see figure). The vertical lines in the two figures are of the same length. However, the vertical line on the left looks longer than the one in the figure on the right. According to Gregory, the Müller-Lyer figures can be thought of as simple perspective drawings of three-dimensional objects. The left figure looks like the inside corners of a room, whereas the right figure is like the outside corners of a building. Thus, the vertical line in the left figure is in some sense further away from us than its fins, whereas the vertical line in the right figure is closer to us than its fins. Because the size of the retinal image is the same for both vertical lines, the principle of size constancy tells us that the line that is further away (*i.e.*, the one in the left figure) must be longer. This is precisely the Müller-Lyer illusion.

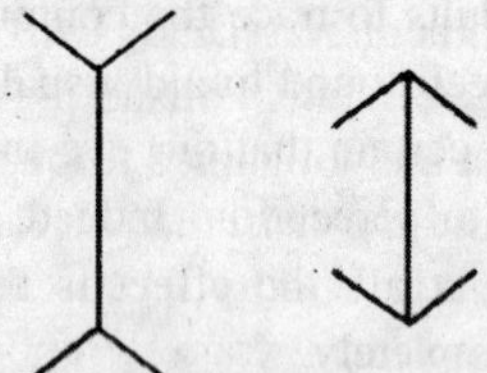

Fig. : *Müller-Lyer illusion*

One of the most complete classification systems of visual illusion that can be found comes from Gregory. He starts with defining a simple division between physical and cognitive illusions. He further divides physical illusions into two categories: those due to optics (disturbance of light between objects and the eyes), and those due to the disturbance of the sensory signals of the eye. He then divides cognitive illusions into those that are due to general knowledge (or "rules"), and those that are due to specific knowledge of objects.

	Physical		Cognitive	
Kinds	Optics	Signal	Rules	Objects
Ambiguity	Mist	Retinal rivalry	Figure-ground	Hollow face
Distortion	Mirage	Cafe wall	Muller-Lyer	Size -weight
Paradox	Mirror	Rotating spiral	Penrose triangle	Magritte mirror
Fiction	Rainbow	After-images	Kaniza triangle	Faces in the fire

From the above table, visual illusion is classified into four classes based on appearance, which can be named quite naturally from errors of language like ambiguity, distortion, paradox and fiction. The causes of many illusionary phenomena have not yet been found to be explained satisfactorily. According to Gregory, based on the classification, we may suppose four principle causes for visual illusion; the first two lying broadly within physics and the last two in cognitive, as they are associated with knowledge.

The first (physical) is the result of optical disturbance intervening between the object and the retina; the second (physical) is due to disturbed physiological signals in the eyes or brain; the third (cognitive) is the application of misleading knowledge of objects; the fourth (cognitive) is the application of misleading general rules.

However, Gregory cautions that "although (physical and cognitive illusions) have extremely different kinds of causes, they can produce some surprisingly similar phenomena," so it may not be wise to put seemingly similar illusions in the same category without looking at the research. In addition, some illusions may have aspects that place them in two or more categories.

Extra Sensory Perception (ESP)

The term 'Extra Sensory Perception (ESP)' was coined by Sir Richard Burton and adopted by J.B. Rhine, a psychologist at Duke University. ESP is used to denote the ability of the psyche to receive information that are not gained through the physical senses; only mind can sense ESP. It includes psychic abilities like telepathy, clairaudience and clairvoyance and their trans temporal operations such as precognition or retrocognition. ESP is sometimes referred to as the sixth sense.

The study of ESP and other paranormal psychic phenomena is termed as parapsychology. Parapsychologis‘s demand evidences for existence of ESP through tests like the Ganzfeld experiment; while the scientific community rejects ESP on the grounds that it lacks evidence base and theoretical base explanations.

Types of Extra Sensory Perception

1. *Clairvoyance:* Clair means 'clear' and voyance means 'vision'. Hence, clairvoyance is the ability of an individual to gain information regarding an object, location or a person through means other than the known human senses. The person having this ability is called as a clairvoyant.
2. *Clairaudience:* Clair means 'clear' and audience means 'hearing'. Clairaudience is the ability of a person to acquire information by paranormal auditory means.
3. *Clairsentience:* Clair means 'clear' and sentience means 'feelings'. Hence the person possessing the ability can feel the vibrations of other people through paranormal perception.
4. *Clairalience:* (clear-smelling) is a form of extra sensory perception wherein a person accesses psychic knowledge through the physical sense of smell.
5. *Claircognizance:* (clear-knowing/knowledge) an ESP in which the individual acquires information by means of intrinsic knowledge.
6. *Clairgustance:* (clear-tasting) a form of ESP in which a person tastes a substance without actually tasting it.

MEMORY

It is said education is a life long process and we are learning all the time. But simply learning without being able to repeat that in another situation or occasion is of no use. Thus we must be able to make use of past experiences. We must be able to reproduce it. Memory is the power of reproduction, or the ability to retain and recall the past events to present consciousness. This implies that memory is the reproduction of past experience even without the presence of the stimulus.

Guilford: "Memory is the retention or storage of information in any form".

Woodworth & Marquis: "Memory consists in learning what was previously learned".

Ryburn: "The power that we have to store our experience and to bring them back into the field of consciousness some time after the experience has occurred is termed as memory".

F'iedsetal: "Memory is the ability to retain and reproduce impressions once perceived".

Memory is the special ability of our mind to store when we learn something to recollect & reproduce it after some time. Memory is the complex process involving learning, retention, recall & recognition. The experiences which we undergo, leaves traces in our minds in the form of 'Schemas'. The length of our retention depends on the strength & quality of the traces.

Types of Memory

1. **Immediate Memory:** This is also known as short term memory. This memory is when the individual has to reproduce immediately after he has learnt something, thus the time

span is very less for the matter to be registered in the consciousness. Hence, the learnt matter is forgotten rapidly, *e.g.*, we may first look at the seat number of our ticket and once we sit down we forget about it. In this type of memory, the retention time is very brief. Immediate memory is needed which helps us to learn a thing immediately with speed and accuracy, remember it for a short duration and forget it rapidly after use.

2. **Short-term memory:** This type of memory is also called temporary memory. It is not short lived as the immediate memory. The information temporarily stored in short-term memory may last as long as thirty seconds even if the material is not being rehearsed. However, some people are able to retain much more information in short-term memories by a process called chunking, which groups information by coding it, *e.g.* the number 143254376 can be remembered by listing under three heads: 143, 254, 376 for better remembering.
3. **Long term memory:** This is also known as Permanent Memory. Here the individual learns and retains the information for a very long period of time. There is an interval of time between learning & recall or reproduction. Thus, permanent memory is involved, *e.g.*, knowing our account number of the bank or the phone number.

Nature of Memory

Memory refers to retaining and recalling information over a period of time, depending upon the nature of cognitive task you are required to perform. It might be necessary to hold an information for a few seconds. For example, you use your memory to retain an unfamiliar telephone number till you have reached the telephone instrument to dial, or for many years you still remember the techniques of addition and subtraction which you perhaps learned during your early schooling. Memory is conceptualised as a process consisting of three independent, though interrelated stages. These are **encoding, storage** and **retrieval.** Any information received by us necessarily goes through these stages.

(*a*) *Encoding* is the first stage which refers to a process by which information is recorded and registered for the first time so that it becomes usable by our memory system. Whenever an external stimulus impinges on our sensory organs, it generates neural impulses. These are received in different areas of our brain for further processing. In encoding, incoming information is received and some meaning is derived. It is then represented in a way so that it can be processed further.

(*b*) *Storage* is the second stage of memory. Information which was encoded must also be stored so that it can be put to use later. Storage, therefore, refers to the process through which information is retained and held over a period of time.

(*c*) *Retrieval* is the third stage of memory. Information can be used only when one is able to recover it from her/his memory. Retrieval refers to bringing the stored information to her/his awareness so that it can be used for performing various cognitive tasks such as problem solving or decision-making. It may be interesting to note that memory failure can occur at any of these stages. You may fail to recall an information because you did not encode it properly, or the storage was weak so you could not access or retrieve it when required.

Information Processing Approach : The Stage Model

Initially, it was thought that memory is the capacity to store all information that we acquire through learning and experience. It was seen as a vast storehouse where all information that we knew was kept so that we could retrieve and use it as and when needed. But with the advent of computer, human memory came to be seen as a system that processes information in the same way as a computer does. Both register, store, and manipulate large amount of information and act on the basis of the outcome of such manipulations. If you have worked on a computer, you would know that it has a temporary memory (random access memory or RAM) and a permanent memory (*e.g.*, a hard disk). Based on the programme commands, the computer manipulates the contents of its memories and displays the output on the screen. In the same way human beings too register information, store and manipulate the stored information depending on the task that they need to perform. For example, when you are required to solve a mathematical problem, the memory relating to mathematical operations, such as division or subtraction are carried out, activated and put to use, and receive the output (the problem solution). This analogy led to the development of the first model of memory, which was proposed by Atkinson and Shiffrin in 1968. It is known as **Stage Model.**

According to Stage Model, there are three memory systems : the **Sensory Memory,** the **Short-term Memory** and the **Long-term Memory.** Each of these systems has different features and performs different functions with respect to the sensory inputs (see fig.). Let us examine what these systems are:

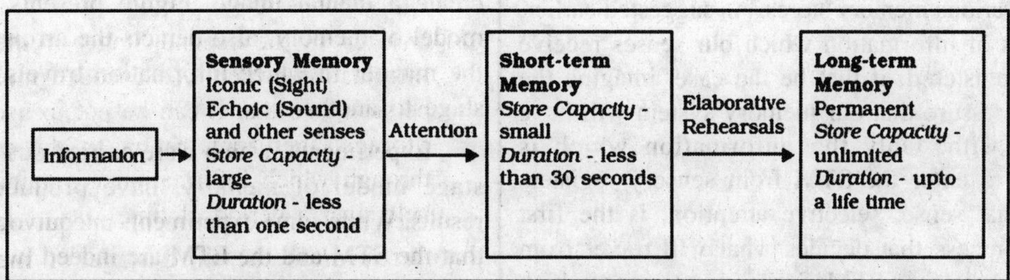

Fig. : *The Stage Model of Momory*

Sensory Memory

The incoming information first enters the *sensory memory*. Sensory memory has a large capacity. However, it is of very short duration, *i.e.*, less than a second. It is a memory system that registers information from each of the senses with reasonable accuracy. Often this system is referred to as sensory memories or sensory registers because information from all the senses is registered here as exact replica of the stimulus. If you have experienced visual after-images (the trail of light that stays after the bulb is switched off) or when you hear reverberations of a sound when the sound has ceased, you are familiar with iconic (visual) or echoic (auditory) sensory registers.

Short-term Memory

Information that is attended to enter the second memory store is called the *short-term memory* (abbreviated as STM). It holds small amount of information for a brief period of time (usually for 30 seconds or less). Atkinson and Shiffrin propose that information in STM is primarily encoded acoustically, *i.e.,* in terms of sound and unless rehearsed continuously, it may get lost from the STM in less than 30 seconds. Note that the STM is fragile but not as fragile as sensory registers where information decays automatically in less than a second.

Long-term Memory

Materials that survive the capacity and duration limitations of the STM finally enter the *long-term memory* (abbreviated as LTM) which has a vast capacity. It is a permanent storehouse of all information that may be as recent as what you ate for breakfast yesterday to as distant as how you celebrated your sixth birthday. It has been shown that once any information enters the long-term memory store it is never forgotten because it gets encoded semantically, *i.e.,* in terms of the meaning that any information carries. What you experience as forgetting is in fact retrieval failure; for various reasons you cannot retrieve the stored information. You will read about retrieval related forgetting later in this chapter.

So far we have only discussed the structural features of the stage model. Questions which still remain to be addressed are how information travel from one store to another and by what mechanisms it continues to stay in any particular memory store. Let us examine the answers to these questions.

How does information travel from one store to another? As an answer to this question, Atkinson and Shiffrin propose the notion of **control processes** which function to monitor the flow of information through various memory stores. As suggested earlier, all pieces of information which our senses receive are not registered; if that be the case, imagine the kind of pressure that our memory system will have to cope with. Only that information which is attended to enter the STM from sensory registers and in that sense, selective attention, is the first control process that decides what will travel from sensory registers to STM. Sense impressions, which do not receive attention, fade away quickly. The STM then sets into motion another control process of **maintenance rehearsal** to retain the information for as much time as required. As the name suggests, these kinds of rehearsals simply maintain information through repetition and when such repetitions discontinue the information is lost. Another control process, which operates in the STM to expand its capacity, is **Chunking**. Through chunking it is possible to expand the capacity of the STM which is otherwise 7±2. For example, if you are told to remember a string of digits such as 194719492004 (note that the number exceeds the capacity of the STM), you may create the chunks as 1947, 1949, and 2004 and remember them as the year when India became independent, the year when the Indian Constitution was adopted, and the year when the tsunami hit the coastal regions of India and South East Asian countries.

From the STM, the information enters the long-term memory through **elaborative rehearsals.** As against maintenance rehearsals, which are carried through silent or vocal repetition, this rehearsal attempts to connect the 'to be retained information' to the already existing information in long-term memory. For example, the task of remembering the meaning of the word 'humanity' will be easier if the meanings of concepts such as 'compassion', 'truth' and 'benevolence' are already in place. The number of associations you can create around the new information will determine its permanence. In elaborative rehearsals one attempts to analyse the information in terms of various associations it arouses. It involves organisation of the incoming information in as many ways as possible. You can expand the information in some kind of logical framework, link it to similar memories or else can create a mental image. Figure presents the stage model of memory, also depicts the arrows to show the manner in which information travels from one stage to another.

Experiments, which were carried out to test the stage model of memory, have produced mixed results. While some experiments unequivocally show that the STM and the LTM are indeed two separate memory stores, other evidences have questioned their distinctiveness. For example, earlier it was shown that in the STM information is encoded acoustically, while in the LTM it is encoded semantically, but later experimental evidences show that information can also be encoded semantically in the STM and acoustically in the LTM.

Shallice and Warrington in the year 1970 had cited the case of a man known as KF who met with an accident and damaged a portion of the left side of his cerebral hemisphere. Subsequently, it was found that his long-term memory was intact but the short-term memory was seriously affected. The stage model suggests that information was committed to the long-term memory via the STM and if KF's STM was affected, how could his long-term memory be normal? Several other studies have also shown that memory processes are similar irrespective of whether any information is retained for a few seconds or for many years and that memory can be adequately understood without positing separate memory stores. All these evidences led to the development of another conceptualisation about memory which is discussed below as the **second model of memory.**

Levels of Processing

The levels of processing view was proposed by Craik and Lockhart in 1972. This view suggests that the processing of any new information relates to the manner in which it is perceived, analysed and understood which in turn determines the extent to which it will eventually be retained. Although this view has undergone many revisions since then, yet its basic idea remains the same. Let us examine this view in greater detail.

Craik and Lockhart proposed that it was possible to analyse the incoming information at more than one level. One may analyse it in terms of its physical or structural features. For example, one might attend only to the shape of letters in a word say *cat* - in spite of whether the word is written in capital or small letters or the colour of the ink in which it is written. This is the first and the shallowest level of processing. At an intermediate level one might consider and attend to the phonetic sounds that are attached to the letters and therefore the structural features are transformed into at least one meaningful word, say, a word *cat* that has three specific letters. Analysing information at these two levels produces memory that is fragile and is likely to decay rather quickly. However, there is a third and the deepest level at which information can be processed. In order to ensure that the information is retained for a longer period, it is important that it gets analysed and understood in terms of its meaning. For instance, you may think of cat as an animal that has furs, has four legs, a tail, and is a mammal. You can also invoke an image of a cat and connect that image with your experiences. To sum up, analysing information in terms of its structural and phonetic features amounts to shallower processing while encoding it in terms of the meaning it carries (the semantic encoding) is the deepest processing level that leads to memory that resists forgetting considerably.

Types of Long-term Memory

There are two types of LTM—**Declarative** and **Procedural** (sometimes called non-declarative) memories. All information pertaining to facts, names, dates, such as a rickshaw has three wheels or that India became independent on August 15, 1947 or a frog is an amphibian or you and your friend share the same name, are part of declarative memory. Procedural memory, on the other hand, refers to memories relating to procedures for accomplishing various tasks and skills such as how to ride a bicycle, how to make tea or play basketball. Facts retained in the declarative memory are amenable to verbal descriptions while contents of procedural memory cannot be described easily. For example, when asked you can describe how the game of cricket is played but if someone asks you how you ride a bicycle, you may find it difficult to narrate.

Tulving has proposed yet another classification and has suggested that the declarative memory can either be **Episodic** or **Semantic.**

Episodic memory contains biographical details of our lives. Memories relating to our personal life experiences constitute the episodic memory and it is for this reason that its contents are generally emotional in nature. How did you feel when you stood first in your class? Or how angry was your friend and what did she/he say when you did not fulfil a promise? If such incidents did actually happen in your life, you perhaps will be able to answer these questions with reasonable accuracy. Although such experiences are hard to forget, yet it is equally true that many events take place continuously in our lives and that we do not remember all of them. Besides, there are painful and unpleasant experiences which are not remembered in as much detail as pleasant life experiences.

Semantic memory, on the other hand, is the memory of general awareness and knowledge. All concepts, ideas and rules of logic are stored in semantic memory. For instance, it is because of semantic memory that we remember the meaning of say 'nonviolence' or remember that 2 + 6 = 8 or the STD code of New Delhi is 011 or that the word *'elaphant'* is misspelt. Unlike episodic memory this kind of memory is not dated; you perhaps will not be able to tell when you learnt the meaning of non-violence or on which date you came to know that Bengaluru is the capital of Karnataka. Since the contents of semantic memory relate to facts and ideas of general awareness and knowledge, it is affect-neutral and not susceptible to forgetting.

Enhancing Memory

There are a number of strategies for improving memory called **mnemonics** (pronounced ni-mo-nicks) to help you improve your memory. Some of these mnemonics involve use of images whereas others emphasise self-induced organisation of learned information. You will now read about mnemonics and some suggestions given for memory improvement.

Mnemonics using Images: Mnemonics using images require that you create vivid and interacting images of and around the material you wish to remember. The two prominent mnemonic devices, which make interesting use of images, are the *keyword method* and the *method of loci.*

(*a*) *The Keyword Method:* Suppose you want to learn words of any foreign language. In keyword method, an English word (the assumption here is that you know English language) that sounds similar to the word of a foreign language is identified. This English word will function as the keyword. For example, if you want to remember the Spanish word for duck which is *'Pato'*, you may choose 'pot' as the keyword and then evoke images of keyword and the target word (the Spanish word you want to remember) and imagine them as interacting. You might, in this case, imagine a duck in a pot full of water. This method of learning words of a foreign language is more superior to any kind of rote memorisation.

(*b*) *The Method of Loci:* In order to use the method of loci, items you want to remember are placed as objects arranged in a physical space in the form of visual images. This method is particularly helpful in remembering items in a serial order. It requires that you first visualise objects/places that you know well in a specific sequence, imagine the objects you want to remember and associate them one by one to the physical locations. For example, suppose you want to remember bread, eggs, tomatoes, and soap on your way to the market, you may visualise a loaf of bread and eggs placed in your kitchen, tomatoes kept on a table and soap in the bathroom. When you enter the market all you need to do is to take a mental walk along the route from your kitchen to the bathroom recalling all the items of your shopping list in a sequence.

Mnemonics using Organisation

Organisation refers to imposing certain order on the material you want to remember. Mnemonics of this kind are helpful because the framework you create while organisation makes the retrieval task fairly easy.

(*a*) *Chunking :* While describing the features of short-term memory, we noted how chunking can increase the capacity of short-term memory. In chunking, several smaller units are combined to form large chunks. For creating chunks, it is important to discover some organisation principles, which can link smaller units. Therefore, apart from being a control mechanism to increase the capacity of short-term memory, chunking can be used to improve memory as well.

(*b*) *First Letter Technique :* In order to employ the first letter technique, you need to pick up the first letter of each word you want to remember and arrange them to form another word or a sentence. For example, colours of a rainbow are remembered in this way (VIBGYOR - that stands for Violet, Indigo, Blue, Green, Yellow, Orange and Red).

Mnemonic strategies for memory enhancement are too simplistic and perhaps underestimate complexities of memory tasks and difficulties people experience while memorising. In place of mnemonics, a more comprehensive approach to memory improvement has been suggested by many psychologists. In such an approach, emphasis is laid on applying knowledge about memory processes to the task of memory improvement. Let us examine some of these suggestions. It is suggested that one must:

(a) *Engage in Deep Level Processing:* If you want to memorise any information well, engage in deep level processing. Craik and Lockhart have demonstrated that processing information in terms of meaning that they convey leads to better memory as compared to attending to their surface features. Deep processing would involve asking as many questions related to the information as possible, considering its meaning and examining its relationships to the facts you already know. In this way, the new information will become a part of your existing knowledge framework and the chances that it will be remembered are increased.

(b) *Minimise Interference :* Interference, as we have read, is a major cause of forgetting and therefore you should try to avoid it as much as possible. You know that maximum interference is caused when very similar materials are learned in a sequence. Avoid this. Arrange your study in such a way that you do not learn similar subjects one after the other. Instead, pick up some other subject unrelated to the previous one. If that is not possible, distribute your learning/practice. This means giving yourself intermittent rest periods while studying to minimise interference.

(c) *Give Yourself enough Retrieval Cues :* While you learn something, think of retrieval cues inherent in your study material. Identify them and link parts of the study material to these cues. Cues will be easier to remember than the entire content and the links you have created between cues and the content will facilitate the retrieval process.

Thomas and Robinson have developed another strategy to help students in remembering more which they called the methods of PQRST. This acronym stands for Preview, Question, Read, Self-recitation and Test. Preview refers to giving a cursory look at the chapter and familiarising oneself with its contents. Question means raising questions and seeking answers from the lesson. Now start reading and look for answers to questions you had raised. After reading try to rewrite what you have read and at the end test how much you have been able to understand.

At the end, a note of caution must be sounded. There is no one method that can solve all problems related to retention and bring about an overnight memory improvement. In order to improve your memory, you need to attend to a wide variety of factors which affect your memory such as your health status, your interest and motivation, your familiarity with the subject matter and so on. In addition, you must learn to use strategies for memory improvement depending upon the nature of memory tasks you are required to accomplish.

INTELLIGENCE

The word 'intelligence' forms part of own ordinary stock of words which we use everyday. In the field of psychology too, the word intelligence finds a fairly comprehensive use. In fact, there are as many definitions of intelligences as there are writers on the subject. On account of the different ways in which intelligence is interpreted, it has become less acceptable and more exposed to criticism by the psychologists. Nevertheless, it is traditionally acknowledged by the parents and teachers that intelligence is the most important single variable which affects success in school and in life. In general terms, intelligence means the manner with which an individual deals with facts and situations. First, intelligence is defined in terms of observable objective behaviour. Secondly, most definitions refer both to an individual's capacity to learn and to knowledge that has already been acquired. Many definitions also suggest that the ability to adapt to the environment is a sign of intelligence.

A variety of definitions on intelligence have been suggested by the psychologists which can be classified into at least four distinct groups as follows.

1. Ability to Adjust

According to this group, intelligence is general mental adaptability to new problems and new situations of life. Some definitions come under this group are as follows.

Binet: "Intelligence is the ability of an individual to direct his behaviour towards a goal".

William James: "It is the ability to adjust oneself successfully to a relatively new situation'.

J. Piagel: "Intelligence is an adaptations to physical and social environment".

F.N. Freeman: "Intelligence is represented in behaviour by the capacity of the individual to adjust himself to new situations to solve new problems to learn."

2. Ability to Learn

This group of definitions of Intelligence stresses the ability to learn. The more intelligent the person, the more readily and extensively he is able to learn and enlarge his field of activity and experience is the key-words of these definitions.

Buckingham: "Intelligence is the learning ability."

Superman: "Intelligence may be though of interns of two abilities *i.e.* "g" or general and 's' or specific."

Thurstone: "Defines intelligence in terms of five primary abilities *i.e.* 'S' or space factor, 'N' or number factor, 'V' or Verbal Comprehension factor, 'W' or word fluency factor and 'M' or memory factor."

3. Ability to do Abstract Reasoning

This group of definitions maintains that intelligence is the ability to carry on abstract thinking. This implies the effective use of ideas and efficiency in dealing with symbols, specially numerical and verbal symbols.

L.M. Termon: "An individual is intelligent in proportion as he is able to carry on abstract thinking."

P.E. Vernon: "Intelligence is an allround thinking capacity or mental deficiency."

E.L. Thorndike: "We may define intelligence in general as the power of good responses from the point of view of truth or fact."

Henry Garrel: "Intelligence is the abilities demanded in the solution of problems which require the comprehension and use of symbols *i.e.* words, numbers diagrams, equations, formula."

4. Operational definition

These categories of definitions are not and perhaps can not be mutually exclusive.

They intersect and overlap at many points.

P.E. Vernon: "Intelligence is what intelligence test measures."

G.D. Stoddard: "Intelligence is the ability to undertake activities."

Boring: "Intelligence is what intelligence tests".

D.W. Wechster: "Intelligence is the aggregate or the global capacity of the individual to act purposefully, to think rationally and to deal effectively with the environment."

Evaluating on the basis of the above definition, we can call a person intelligent in proportion to his being able to use his mental energy in handing his actual life problems and leading a happy and well contented life.

The important nature & characteristics of intelligence are:

1. **Intelligence is inherited:** The amount of intelligence that a person possesses is inherited and fixed. The amount though fixed does not reveal itself at the start of life with the growth of the child, the amount inherited by a child also grows. The general belief is that the growth of intelligence stops and it reaches it's limit at the age of sixteen. But you know and it is also true that a man of forty knows more than he was a boy of sixteen. But this does not mean that the amount of intelligence possessed by him has increased. This may be due to his experience. As regards his intelligence, his positions remains the same.

2. **Intelligence is influenced by environment factors:** Love, affection, concern and generosity judiciously bestowed on growing children, have very desirable effects. Poor environment retard development of intelligence.
3. **Intelligence helps in adjustment & inventions:** An intelligent person has the ability to adjust himself to the changing circumstances with ease, efficiency and speed. He has the capacity to assimilate ideas very quickly and clearly. He can cope with new situations very successfully. All the inventions of the word can be attributed to persons of very high intelligence.
4. **Intelligence has no sex differences :** Various studies have been conducted by the psychologists and the researchers to find out whether women are more intelligent than men or vice versa. The result of these researches hangs in one way or the other. In some of the cases no significant difference has been found. Research studies also show that the average scores of the sense are strongly similar. Therefore, it is proper to think that difference in sex does not contribute towards difference in intelligence.
5. **Intelligence has no racial or cultural differences:** Now, students we will see whether a particular race, caste or cultural group is superior to others in intelligence. This hypothesis is also examined by so many research workers, the results of earlier studies proved that intelligence is not the birth right of particular race of group. The bright and the 'dull' can be found in any race, caste or cultural group. In this regard Franze Boas states. "If we were to select the most intelligent, imaginative, energetic and emotionally stable third of mankind, all races would be represented. "You can also take any study & prove it."

Intelligence can be recognized in three broad areas

According to Thurstone intelligent behaviour can be recognized in three broad areas.

Abstract Intelligence: Abstract intelligence is the ability to understand and manage ideas and symbols. Such as words, numbers, etc. In the case of students this is very close to scholastic aptitude.

Mechanical Intelligence: Mechanical intelligence is the ability to clean, understand and manage things and mechanisms, such as a knife, a gun, a moving machine and automobile etc.

Social Intelligence: Social intelligence is the ability to understand and mange men and women, boys and girls, to act wisely in human relations.

Functions of Intelligence

Intelligence directs one's behaviour towards a goal. It helps one to adjust to a new situation. It helps an individual to adopt to physical and social environment. It helps to learn new things and to solve new problems. It directs the individual to think rationally and act purposefully.

Measurement of Intelligence

It is important to note that intelligence is inferred from a variety of elements, *i.e.,* behaviour and speed of doing things correctly etc. In ancient India intelligence was measured through conversation, physical features, gestures, gait, speech, changes in the eye and facial expression. But today, many intelligence tests are widely which primarily measure abstract intelligence as exemplified by competence in dealing with symbols in a meaningful way. A number of tests measuring social intelligence as well as mechanical intelligence have also been developed. An intelligence test is an objective and a standard measure.

General (or abstract) Intelligence test

The general intelligence test was first designed by the psychologists for use in schools. These were intended to serve primarily as tools in determining a child's ability to carry on school's work, to use symbols and numbers quickly and accurately and to read with comprehension. It is for this reason that tests designed to measure abstract abilities came to be known as general intelligence tests. Another purpose of designing such tests was to measure the abilities that distinguishes the bright child from the dull one. Since this distinction is significant for schools and vocational success and also for social adjustment, the intelligence test is an important tool in psychology.

Types of General Intelligence Test

The general intelligence tests have been classified into three groups — Individual, group and performance tests.

Types of General Intelligence Test

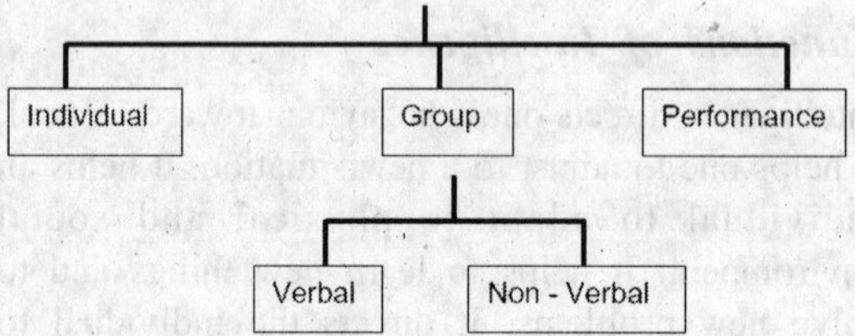

(*a*) **Individual Test:** The individual intelligence test is administered to only one individual at a time. A trained psychologist is expected to administer the test for a definite period of time and interpret the result. These tests cover age group from 2 years to 18 years. These are (*i*) The Binet Simon tests, (*ii*) Revised tests by Terman, (*iii*) Mental scholastic tests of Burt and (*iv*) Weschler test.

(*b*) **Group Test:** The group intelligence tests are meant for assessing the intelligence of a large number of individuals in one sitting. There are two kinds of group intelligence tests: verbal and non-verbal.

(i) **Verbal:** The verbal group test requires an individual to read out certain problems and write out solutions to these problems.

(*ii*) **Non-Verbal:** The non-verbal group tests present similar problems as the verbal test but in a different way. The problems are presented in the form of pictures, diagrams, puzzles and images. It does not require the individual to read or write, but only to be able to make a mark with a pencil.

(c) **Performance Test:** Performance tests are designed to test problem solving ability using certain objects such as pictures and blocks, instead of words. These tests are specially useful with young children, illiterates, persons with speech defects and persons who do not have proficiency in language. Some of the famous tests are (*i*) Koh's Block design test, (*ii*) The cube construction tests and (*iii*) The Pass Along tests.

Group tests had their birth in America when the intelligence of the recruits who joined the army in the First World War was to be calculated. These are: (*i*) The Army Alpha and Beta test, (*ii*) Terman's group tests and (*iii*) Out self administrative tests.

Intelligence tests consist of different types of questions to test the intelligence of individual. These questions are based on the following factors.

Vocabulary : The extent of an individual's vocabulary is one of the most reliable indices of his intelligence. It can be tested through arranging words in difficult order or giving synonym or antonym of a word.

Verbal analogies: In this section questions are asked like branch is to a tree as brook is to a river.

Sentence completion : India has .... states is one of the examples of this type of questions.

Arithmetic reasoning: Simple arithmetical sum increasing in difficulty is included in the test.

Number series: A series of number is given and asked what will the next be. For example 11, 13, 15, 17, 19, 21 ....?

Comprehension: It consists of questions designed to measure general understanding. It includes questions such as, why are coins made of metal?

Digit Span: For testing on memory, digits are spoken and the subject is asked to repeat them in the same or reverse order. For example, if the examiner says 8, 4, 3 the subject is to say 3, 4, 8.

Similarities: The subject is asked to describe the way in which certain objects are similar. In what way cotton and silk are alike?

General Information: It consists of questions from everyday life. Kinds of questions are asked include: How many inches are there in a foot?

Picture arrangement: Each item consists of a collection of cartoon like drawings which make a story when arranged in a proper order.

Picture completion: This test consists of a series of pictures which are presented to the subject one at a time. An important part is missing from each picture and must be identified by the subject.

Block design: The subject must arrange a collection of coloured cubes in such a way that they reproduce certain printed design.

Object assembly test. Three jigsaw type puzzles are presented to the subject one at a time and in order of increasing difficulty.

Digit symbol test: The subject is required to match each one of series of printed digits with an appropriate symbol, using a prescribed code.

These are different verbal and non-verbal factors on which questions are framed to test the intelligence of the individual. But this process of determining the intelligence is a complicated process. It involves a comparison and establishment of a relationship between chronological age (C.A.) and mental age (M.A.). This relationship is expressed by the term I.Q. (Intelligence Quotient). Now we will discuss the concept of mental age, chronological age and intelligence quotient.

Mental Age

In categorizing children of different abilities Binet developed a scale of units. He called it mental age. A child's intelligence was determined by the mental age level which he could attain on the test. A ten years old child who was able to all the tests meant for ten years old children was said to be normal or average. If he could do the test meant for a higher age level his mental age was said to be more than his chronological age and he was described as a bright child. If he was unable to do the tests meant for his own age level, the child's "mental age" was said to be lower than his chronological age and he was described as slow or retarded. Mental age is a simple and useful concept. You can easily interpret it, when deal with children differing in mental ability.

Chronological Age: (C.A.)

Chronological age is nothing but the actual calendar age of the child. The real age of the child in mental into consideration for test is called chronological age.

Intelligence quotient

The intelligence quotient represents the degree of brightness possessed by an individual. It expresses intelligence as the ratio of the mental age of the chronological age. When the mental age is divided by the chronological age and the quotient is multiplied by 100 the result is I.Q. So the formula of finding out I.Q is.

$$\text{I.Q.} = \frac{\text{M.A.}}{\text{C.A.}} \times 100$$

The fraction is multiplied by 100 in order to remove the decimal point and to give the I.Q. a value of 100 when mental age is equal with chronological age. If the M.A. is above the C.A., I.Q. will be above 100. If the M.A. is less than the C.A., the resulting I.Q. will be less than 100. Thus, the scale has the same meaning from one age to another. I.Q. may also be regarded as an index of brightness. The following table shows the relationship between I.Q. and the degree of brightness given by Dr. Merrily based on the studies by Terman Merely Revision.

I.Q. Range	*Classification*
140 and above	Very superior
129 – 139	Superior
110 – 119	High Average
90 – 109	Average
80 – 89	Low Average
70 – 79	Borderline defective
Below 70	Mentally defective

The lowest classification mentally defective is sometimes subdivided into three classes, as:

Moron	I.Q. – 50 – 70
Imbecility	I.Q. – 20 – 50
Idiot	I.Q. – Below 20

PSYCHOPATHOLOGY

Psychopathology is the scientific study of mental disorders, including efforts to understand their genetic, biological, psychological, and social causes; effective classification schemes (nosology); course across all stages of development; manifestations; and treatment. In general Psychopathology derives from two Greek words: 'psyche' meaning 'soul', and 'pathos' means 'suffering'. Currently, 'psychopathology' is understood to mean the origin of mental disorders, how they develop and their symptoms. Traditionally, those suffering from mental disorders have usually been treated by the psychiatric profession, which adheres to the DSM-IV-TR (APA, 2002) or ICD-10 (WHO, 1992) for classifying mental disorders.

Historically, the concept of psychopathology is rooted in the medical tradition. This is where the terms 'diagnosis', 'symptoms', 'aetiology' and 'prognosis' come from (Murphy, 2010). Psychiatrists categorise severe mental distress into psychopathological disorders whose symptoms they can treat with prescribed drugs, and use the word 'patients'. Counselling psychologists, counsellors and psychotherapists favour the term 'clients' over 'patients' (because of the medical connotations of the word 'patients') and use talking, more than anything else, as a therapeutic 'tool'. They also prefer the concept of 'formulation' instead of 'diagnosis, symptoms, aetiology and prognosis'.

The scientific discipline of psychopathology was founded by Karl Jaspers in 1913, whose object of study was "mental phenomena". Many different professions may be involved in studying mental disorders or distress. Psychiatrists in particular are interested in descriptive psychopathology, which has the aim of describing the symptoms and syndromes of mental illness. Before diagnosing a psychological disorder, clinicians must study the themes, also known as abnormalities, within psychological disorders. The most prominent themes consist of: deviance, distress, dysfunction and danger. These themes are known as the four Ds, which define abnormality. The DSM, or Diagnostic and Statistical Manual of Mental Disorders, is an official guideline for the diagnosis of psychological disorders. Clinicians, researchers and psychologists use this manual as a reference guide to diagnose psychological disorders.

Classifying Psychopathology

Mental illness is classified today according to the Diagnostic and Statistical Manual of Mental Disorders, Fourth Edition (DSM IV), published by the American Psychiatric Association (1994). The DSM uses a multiaxial or multidimensional approach to diagnosing because rarely do other factors in a person's life not impact their mental health. It assesses five dimensions as described below:

Axis I: Clinical Syndromes

- This typically includes the diagnosis (*e.g.*, major depressive episode, schizophrenic episode, panic attack, schizophrenia, social phobia).

Axis II: Developmental Disorders and Personality Disorders

- Developmental disorders include the five Pervasive Developmental Disorders (PDDs), also known as Autism Spectrum Disorders (ASDs), as defined by the Diagnostic and Statistical Manual of Mental Disorders - Fourth Edition (DSM-IV). These include the

Autistic disorder, Pervasive developmental disorder, Asperger's Disorder, Rett's Disorder and Childhood Disintegrative Disorder.

- Personality disorders are clinical syndromes which have a more long lasting symptom and encompass the individual's way of interacting with the world. They include Paranoid, Antisocial personality disorder, Avoidant personality disorder, Borderline personality disorders, Narcissistic personality disorder, Obsessive-Compulsive personality disorder and Schizotypal personality disorder.

Axis III : Physical Conditions which play a role in the development, continuance, or exacerbation of Axis I and II Disorders

- Physical conditions such as brain injury or HIV/AIDS that can result in symptoms of mental illness are included here.

Axis IV: Severity of Psychosocial Stressors

- Events in a person's life, such as death of a loved one, starting a new job, college, unemployment, and even marriage can impact the disorders listed in Axis I and II. These events are both listed and rated for this axis.

Axis V: Highest Level of Functioning

- It contains the global assessment of functioning, which is a numerical scale that measures the level of functioning of the client. The scale ranges from 0 (inadequate information) to 100 (high functioning with no symptoms of mental illness present).

Common Clinical Disorders

A Clinical Disorder is a series or group of behaviours that equal or match a list of expected behaviours listed in, "The Diagnostic and Statistical Manual of Mental Disorders (DSM) is the standard classification of mental disorders used by mental health professionals. It is intended to be applicable in a wide array of contexts and used by clinicians and researchers of many different orientations (*e.g.*, biological, psychodynamic, cognitive, behavioural, interpersonal, family/systems). Some of the common mental health disorders include depression, generalised anxiety disorder, panic disorder, obsessive-compulsive disorder, post traumatic stress disorder and social anxiety disorder. Few among them are discussed below:-

1. **Depression:** To be diagnosed as suffering from major depression, a person must have had one or more major depressive episodes—periods that involved more than just "sadness" which includes symptoms like an increase or decrease appetite, altered sleep patterns, loss of interest or pleasure in usual activities, including sex; loss of energy, diminished ability to think and concentrate; feeling of worthlessness or self-reproach; or suicidal thoughts or acts. During depressive episode, the person's mood and thought patterns may be strikingly negative. He/she often appears lost, vulnerable, detached, and unable to find joy in any aspect of daily life. Often the person seems constantly on the verge of tears. The future may seem almost completely hopeless, and this becomes one of the reasons of suicide attacks.

   Life events and changes that may precipitate depressed mood include childbirth, menopause, financial difficulties, job problems, a medical diagnosis (cancer, HIV, etc.), bullying, loss of a loved one, natural disasters, social isolation, relationship troubles, jealousy, separation, and catastrophic injury. Adversity in childhood, such as bereavement, neglect, unequal parental treatment of siblings, physical abuse or sexual abuse, significantly increases the likelihood of experiencing depression over the life course. Certain medications are known to cause depressed mood in a significant number of patients.

   Depressed mood can be the result of a number of infectious diseases, neurological conditions and physiological problems. Depression is associated with abusive drug use.

2. **Generalized Anxiety Disorder:** People with generalized anxiety disorder can't seem to get rid of their concerns, even though they usually realize that their anxiety is more intense than the situation warrants. They can't relax, startle easily, and have difficulty concentrating. Such anxiety can make people thoroughly miserable and even upset their health. Symptoms of generalized anxiety disorder may include trembling, fatigue, breathlessness, insomnia, sweating, nervousness, chest pain, dizziness, faintness, headache, and so on. A sense of foreboding, apprehension, and a feeling of impending doom may also be mixed with the physical symptoms.

3. **Panic Disorder:** Panic disorder involves specific, focused, time-bound attacks of intense fear, even terror. The panic attacks, lasting from a few minutes up to an hour or more. People with panic disorder have panic attacks with feelings of terror that strike suddenly and repeatedly with no warning. Symptoms of a panic attack includes difficulty in breathing, pounding heart or chest pain, intense feeling of dread, dizziness or feeling faint, trembling or shaking, sweating, nausea or stomach-ache, tingling or numbness in the fingers and toes, also may include severe physical symptoms such as choking or smothering sensations. Beyond the panic attacks themselves, a key symptom of panic disorder is the persistent fear of having future panic attacks. The fear of these attacks can cause the person to avoid places and situations where an attack has occurred or where they believe an attack may occur.

4. **Obsessive Compulsive Disorder(OCD):** Obsessive-compulsive disorder (OCD) is an anxiety disorder characterized by uncontrollable, unwanted thoughts and repetitive, ritualized behaviours one feel compelled to perform. Obsessions are recurrent and persistent thoughts, impulses, or images that cause distressing emotions such as anxiety or disgust. Compulsions on the other hand are repetitive behaviours or mental acts that the person feels driven to perform in response to an obsession. The behaviours are aimed at preventing or reducing distress or a feared situation. The Common obsessive thoughts in obsessive-compulsive disorder (OCD) includes - Fear of being contaminated by germs or dirt or contaminating others, fear of causing harm to yourself or others, intrusive sexually explicit or violent thoughts and images, fear of losing or not having things you might need, order and symmetry: the idea that everything must line up "just right", superstitions; excessive attention to something considered lucky or unlucky. Common compulsive behaviours in obsessive-compulsive disorder (OCD) includes - Excessive double-checking of things, such as locks, appliances, and switches, repeatedly checking in on loved ones to make sure they're safe, counting, tapping, repeating certain words, or doing other senseless things to reduce anxiety, spending a lot of time washing or cleaning, ordering or arranging things "just so", praying excessively or engaging in rituals triggered by religious fear etc.

   People with obsessive-compulsive disorder find their obsessions or compulsions distressing and debilitating but feel unable to stop them.

5. **Post traumatic stress disorder:** Post-Traumatic Stress Disorder (PTSD) is an anxiety disorder that may develop after exposure to a terrifying event or ordeal in which severe physical harm occurred or was threatened. Traumatic events that may trigger PTSD include violent personal assaults, natural or unnatural disasters, accidents, or military combat. PTSD can cause many symptoms. These symptoms can be grouped into three categories: Re-experiencing symptoms, Avoidance symptoms and Hyperarousal symptoms.

Re-experiencing symptoms may cause problems in a person's everyday routine. The symptoms include flashbacks-reliving the trauma over and over, including physical symptoms like a racing heart or sweating, bad dreams and frightening thoughts.

The Avoidance symptoms includes feeling emotionally numb, feeling strong guilt, depression, or worry, losing interest in activities that were enjoyable in the past, having trouble remembering the dangerous event and staying away from places, events, or objects that are reminders of the experience. Things that remind a person of the traumatic event can trigger avoidance symptoms.

Hyper arousal symptoms may includes being easily startled, feeling tense or "on edge" and having difficulty sleeping, and/or having angry outbursts. Hyper arousal symptoms are usually constant, instead of being triggered by things that remind one of the traumatic events. They can make the person feel stressed and angry.

PTSD can develop at any age, including in childhood. Symptoms typically begin within 3 months of a traumatic event, although occasionally they do not begin until years later. Once PTSD occurs, the severity and duration of the illness varies. Some people recover within 6 months, while others suffer much longer.

6. **Social Anxiety Disorder:** Social anxiety disorder (SAD), also known as social phobia, is the most common anxiety disorder. It is characterized by intense fear in one or more social situations, causing considerable distress and impaired ability to function in at least some parts of daily life. The physical symptoms includes red face, or blushing, shortness of breath, trembling or shaking, upset stomach, nausea, tightness in chest, sweating and feeling dizzy or faint. People with social phobia tend to show some emotional symptoms such as feeling very anxious about being with other people and have a hard time talking to them, even though they wish they could, they tend to be very self-conscious in front of other people and feel embarrassed, they feel afraid that other people will judge them and worry for days or weeks before an event where other people will be. They have a hard time making friends and keeping friends.

Mental Retardation

Intellectual disability (ID) or learning disability or general learning disability is a generalized disorder appearing before adulthood, characterized by significantly impaired cognitive functioning and deficits in two or more adaptive behaviours. Intellectual disability is also known as mental retardation (MR) and mental handicap, although these older terms are being used less frequently. It was historically defined as an intelligence quotient score under 70. It is manifested through defective perceptual and other thought processes and emotional as well as social development. Those who are mentally retarded are also called mental retardates. They show retardation in acquiring intellectual competence, emotional stability, and social maturity. Even when they are physically grown-up they show such emotional and social behaviours which are appropriate to children of much lower age.

According to H.J Grossman (1983)—"Mental retardation refers to significantly sub average general intellectual functioning existing concurrently with deficits in adaptive behaviour and manifested during the developmental period".

Factors Contributing to Mental Retardation

(*a*) **Problems During Prenatal Period:** Use of alcohol or drugs by the pregnant mother can cause mental retardation. Moreover, prenatal causes include congenital infections such as cytomegalovirus, toxoplasmosis, herpes, syphilis, rubella and human immunodeficiency virus; prolonged maternal fever in the first trimester; exposure to anticonvulsants or alcohol; and untreated maternal phenylketonuria (PKU) (Strømme & Hagberg, 2007). Complications of prematurity, especially in extremely low-birth-weight infants, or postnatal exposure to lead can also cause mental retardation (Piecuch et al., 1997). Physical malformations of the brain and HIV infection originating in prenatal life may also result in mental retardation.

(*b*) **Complications During Child Birth:** Although any birth condition of unusual stress may injure the infant's brain, prematurity and low birth weight predict serious problems more often than any other conditions. Injuries at birth, caused by the use of forceps, often lead to mental retardation.

(*c*) **Accidents or Problems During Infancy and Childhood:** Fall from cots or staircases, knockdowns by older children or fall from the mother's or attendant's lap etc. Besides these Postnatal problems include brain infections such as tuberculosis, Japanese encephalitis, and bacterial meningitis. As well as head injury, chronic lead exposure, severe and prolonged malnutrition and gross under stimulation (Leonard & Wen, 2002; Zoghbi, 2003).

(*d*) **Genetic Defects:** These result from abnormality of genes inherited from parents, errors when genes combine, or from other disorders of the genes caused during pregnancy by infections, overexposure to x-rays and other factors. A number of single-gene disorders result in mental retardation. Many of these are associated with atypical or dysmorphic physical characteristics (Sultana et al.,1995). Such conditions include fragile X syndrome, neurofibromatosis, tuberous sclerosis, Noonan's syndrome and Cornelia de Lange's syndrome (Baraitser & Winter, 1996; Jones & Smith, 1997).

(*e*) **Exposure to certain types of disease or toxins:** Diseases like whooping cough, measles, or meningitis can cause mental disability if medical care is delayed or inadequate. Exposure to poisons like lead or mercury may also affect mental ability (Aicardi, 1998; Daily, Ardinger & Holmes, 2000).

(*f*) **Poverty and cultural deprivation:** Children in poor families may become mentally retarded because of malnutrition, disease-producing conditions, inadequate medical care and environmental health hazards. Also, children in disadvantaged areas may be deprived of many common cultural and day-to-day experiences provided to other youngsters. Research suggests that such under-stimulation can result in irreversible damage and can serve as a cause of mental retardation.

Management of Mentally Retarded

(*a*) **Family Responsibility:** Mentally retarded children need family affection, interaction and peer-group identification. Usually the family of a retarded child often feel guilty about the child which results in over protective behaviour, due to which the child cannot make full advantage of his/her limited abilities by learning easy self help skills. Some families even deny retardation which creates more problems for the child who often fails to meet their expectations.

(*b*) **Accepting the Diagnosis:** Parent's reactions to the diagnosis that their child is mentally retarded are often quite different. There are four types of responses to the diagnosis; guilt, anger, disappointment and denial. Parent's reactions are often confusing about their child. On the one hand they are over protective, loving and caring to their child; on the other hand they feel anger, shame and guilt about him/her.

(*c*) **Institutionalization:** Professionals generally advise to keep the mentally retarded child with the family members if possible, and be responsible for his/her care. However, severely and profoundly retarded children may require institutionalization. Institutionalization, or admission in special institutions or hospitals, is determined mainly of two factors, namely (a) degree of behavioural difficulties in the retarded child, and (b) socio-economic factors related to proper adjustment, accommodation, and maintenance of a retardate's.

Mental Health

Mental health is a level of psychological well-being, or an absence of a mental disorder; it is the "psychological state of someone who is functioning at a satisfactory level of emotional and behavioural adjustment". In other words mental health is defined as a state of well-being in which every individual realizes his or her own potential, can cope with the normal stresses of life, can work productively and fruitfully, and is able to make a contribution to her or his community.

According to World Health Organization (WHO) mental health includes "subjective well-being, perceived self-efficacy, autonomy, competence, intergenerational dependence, and self-actualization of one's intellectual and emotional potential, among others."

Persons with good mental health have the following characteristics:

- They are not overwhelmed by their own emotions—fears, anger, love, jealousy, guilt or worries.
- They can take pleasure in simple, everyday things.
- A sense of contentment with their lives.
- A zest for living, laughing, and having fun.
- Able to deal with stress and to bounce back from adversity.
- They accept their responsibilities.
- They set realistic goals for themselves.
- They welcome new experiences and new ideas.
- They are able to make their own decisions.
- Flexibility to learn new things, and adaptability to deal with change.
- They have personal relationships that are satisfying and lasting.
- They feel a sense of responsibility to fellow human beings.
- Self-confidence and high self-esteem.
- Good balance between work and play.
- A sense of meaning and purpose in life, including activities and relationships.

Factors Affecting Mental Health

Mental health and mental illness are determined by multiple and interacting social, psychological, and biological factors. Among the globe, poverty and low levels of education correlates with mental disorders, irrespective of their level of the development. An individual's mental health state can also influenced by genetic and biological factors; that is, determinants that persons are born or endowed with, including chromosomal abnormalities (*e.g.*, Down's syndrome) and intellectual disability caused by prenatal exposure to alcohol or oxygen deprivation at birth

Factors such as insecurity and hopelessness, rapid social change, and the risks of violence and physical ill-health may explain the greater vulnerability of poor people in any country to mental illnesses (Patel & Kleinman 2003).

Mental health for each person is affected by individual factors and experiences, social interaction, societal structures and resources, and cultural values. It is influenced by experiences in everyday life, in families and schools, on streets, and at work (Lehtinen, Riikonen & Lahtinen 1997; Lahtinen et al. 1999).

Discrimination, social or gender inequality and conflict are some of the examples of adverse structural determinants of mental well-being. Physical health is inextricably linked to mental health. Poor mental health is associated with other priority public health conditions such as obesity, alcohol misuse and smoking, and with diseases such as cancer, cardiovascular disease and diabetes. Poor physical health also increases the risk of mental illness.

Interventions to Promote Good Mental Health

Some low-cost and cost-effective interventions that can raise the level of individual and community mental health are as follows—

1. Intervention to improve parental health - Home visiting programmes, peer support and telephone peer support for women at high risk of depression reduces rates of postnatal depression. Health visitor training to improve detection also reduces levels of postnatal depression.
2. Pre-school and early education interventions - Systematic reviews of pre-school and early education programmes show their effectiveness in enhancing cognitive and skills, school readiness, improved academic achievement and positive effect on family outcomes including for siblings, as well as prevention of emotional and conduct disorder. Home visiting programmes improve child functioning and reduce behavioural problems.
3. Support to children - Such programs may include skills-building or child and youth development.
4. Violence and abuse prevention programs - At a family level, these include parental mental health promotion, parent training and early intervention for child emotional and behavioural disorders. At a school level, they include school-based mental health promotion, violence prevention; bullying prevention and social and emotional mental health promotion, violence prevention, bullying prevention also prevent sexual abuse. Among the benefits of school-based violence prevention programmes are reductions in aggressive behaviour, conduct problems and attention span problems, as well as improvements in social skills and social relationships, school performance, school attendance, and attitudes towards violence and bullying.
5. Housing policies - designed to improve housing.
6. Empowerment of women - Socio-economic programs to improve access to education and credit, for example. Mental health services have a crucial role to play in alleviating suffering associated with psychiatric illnesses, emotional distress, psychological disorders, and behavioural pathology. Abused women, troubled children, those traumatized by political violence, those who have attempted suicide or are addicted to alcohol or narcotics, and especially those who suffer acute or chronic mental illnesses can be helped substantially by competent mental health care.
7. Social support for the elderly - including day and community centres for the aged and so-called "befriending" initiatives.
8. Mental health interventions in the workplace - Interventions aimed at employees' mental health protection include, at the organizational level - working conditions improvement and work schedule changes. At the individual level, stress management and skills training programs may provide the participants with resources helping them to cope with the detrimental impact of work-related problems.
9. Programs targeted for vulnerable groups - These groups may include migrants, minorities, indigenous people, and people.

Still, being mentally and emotionally healthy doesn't mean that people never go through hard times or suffer through some painful situations. Thus to maintain emotional balance in these situations the need of resiliency comes in. Resiliency, according to the American Psychological Association (APA), is not a trait that people either have or don't have. It involves actions, thoughts, and behaviours that can be learned and developed - in anyone. The APA suggests 10 ways to build resilience. They are briefly included here:

1. Accept that change is a part of living. All of life involves change. Accepting that fact, you will be better served by focusing on things that you can change and putting a plan together to do so.
2. Make connections. Good relationships are important: family, friends, co-workers, and others. Accept help if you need it, and don't be afraid to ask for it.
3. Avoid seeing crises as insurmountable problems. You can't change what's happened, but you can look toward the solution and act accordingly.
4. Take decisive actions. Acting decisively, even during stressful or adverse situations, helps build self-confidence and resilience.
5. Move toward your goals. Create realistic goals and take steps to achieve them. Even small steps are a sign of progress. Keep moving forward.
6. Look for opportunities for self-discovery. You can often learn something good from any situation, even tragedies and hardship.
7. Nurture a positive view of yourself. Develop your confidence and problem - solving ability helps to build resilience.
8. Maintain a hopeful outlook. Try visualizing what you want, instead of worrying about how you'll attain it.
9. Take care of yourself. Pay attention to the physical and mental aspects of personal caretaking. This keeps mind and body primed and ready to deal with situations requiring resilience.
10. Keep things in perspective. Try to look at the broader, long-term view and avoid blowing things out of proportion.
11. Find additional ways of strengthening resilience. These may include journal writing, meditation, or spiritual practices.

Psychotherapies

Psychotherapy, or "talk therapy", is a way to treat people with a mental disorder by helping them understand their illness. It teaches people strategies and gives them tools to deal with stress and unhealthy thoughts and behaviours. Psychotherapy helps patients manage their symptoms better and function at their best in everyday life. In general terms psychotherapy helps people with a mental disorder to understand the behaviours, emotions, and ideas that contribute to his or her illness and learning how to modify them. It helps to understand the behaviours, emotions, and ideas that contribute to his or her illness and learning how to modify them. Psychotherapy also regains a sense of control and pleasure in life and helps to learn coping techniques and problem-solving skills.

There are several main broad systems of psychotherapy. Few among them are briefly mentioned below:

Psychodynamic therapy: Psychodynamic therapy helps people gain greater self-awareness and understanding about their own actions. It helps patients identify and explore how their unconscious emotions and motivations can influence their behaviour. Sometimes ideas from psychodynamic therapy are interwoven with other types of therapy, like CBT (Cognitive Behavioural Therapy) or IPT (Interpersonal Therapy), to treat various types of mental disorders.

Behaviour therapy/applied behaviour analysis: Focuses on changing maladaptive patterns of behaviour to improve emotional responses, cognitions, and interactions with others.

Cognitive behavioural: Generally seeks to identify maladaptive cognition, appraisal, beliefs and reactions with the aim of influencing destructive negative emotions and problematic dysfunctional behaviours.

Existential psychotherapy: Is a unique style of therapy that puts emphasis on the human condition as a whole. Existential psychotherapy uses a positive approach that applauds human capacities while simultaneously maintaining a genuine perception of the limitations of the human being, human spirit, and human mind.

Humanistic: Humanistic therapies focus on self-development, growth and responsibilities. They seek to help individuals recognise their strengths, creativity and choice in the 'here and now'.

Interpersonal Therapy: Interpersonal therapy focuses on the behaviours and interactions a patient has with family and friends. The primary goal of this therapy is to improve communication skills and increase self-esteem during a short period of time. It usually lasts three to four months and works well for depression caused by mourning, relationship conflicts, major life events, and social isolation.

Systemic: Seeks to address people not at an individual level, as is often the focus of other forms of therapy, but as people in relationship, dealing with the interactions of groups, their patterns and dynamics (includes family therapy & marriage counseling). Community psychology is a type of systemic psychology.

Transpersonal psychology: Uses positive influences, rather than the diseased human psyche and our defenses, as a model for the realization of human potential. Transpersonal psychology enhances the study of mind-body relations, spirituality; consciousness, and human transformation. Experts disagree as to the specific model and margins of this form of therapy, however the three key areas that are considered through transpersonal psychotherapy are:

1. Combined/holistic and natural psychology
2. Transformative psychology
3. Ego-transcended psychology

Frustration and Conflict

Frustration

We come across many occasions when things go in an unexpected direction and we fail to realise our goal. The blocking of a desired goal is painful, but all of us experience it in life in different degrees. *Frustration occurs when an anticipated desirable goal is not attained and the motive is blocked.* It is an aversive state and no one likes it. Frustration results in a variety of behavioural and emotional reactions. They include aggressive behaviour, fixation, escape, avoidance, and crying. In fact **frustration-aggression** is a very famous **hypothesis** proposed by Dollard and Miller. It states that frustration produces aggression. Aggressive acts are often directed towards the self or blocking agent, or a substitute. Direct aggressive acts may be inhibited by the threat of punishment. **The main sources or causes of frustration are found in:** (*i*) environmental forces, which could be physical objects, constraining situations or even other people who prevent a person from reaching a particular goal, (*ii*) personal factors like inadequacies or lack of resources that make it difficult or impossible to reach goals, and (*iii*) conflicts between different motives.

Conflict

Conflict occurs whenever a person must choose between contradictory needs, desires, motives, or demands. There are three basic forms of conflicts, for example, **approach-approach conflict, avoidance-avoidance conflict,** and **approach-avoidance conflict.**

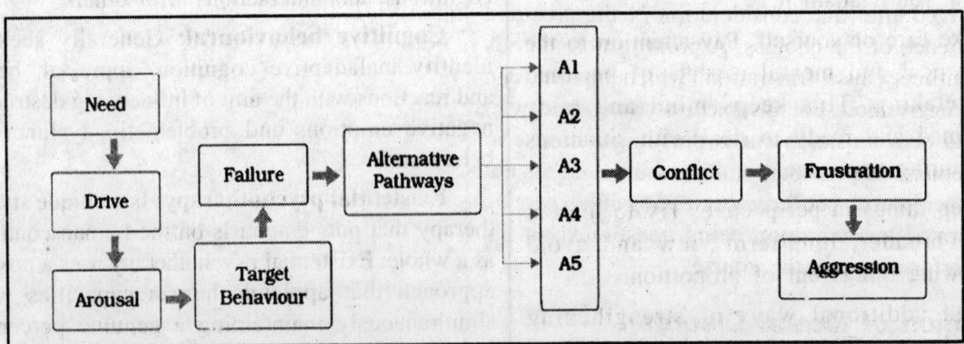

Fig. *Need-Conflict-Frustration Route*

Approach-approach conflict comes from having to choose between two positives and desirable alternatives. Avoidance-avoidance conflict comes from choosing between two negatives, or mutually undesirable alternatives. In real life, these double avoidance conflicts involve dilemmas such as choosing between the dentist and tooth decay, roadside food and starvation, etc. Approach-avoidance conflict comes from being attracted to and repelled by the same goal or activity.

These types of conflicts are also difficult to resolve, as they are more troublesome than avoidance conflicts. A central characteristic of approach-avoidance conflict is ambivalence — a mix of positive and negative conflicts. Some examples of approach-avoidance conflicts are: a person wanting to buy a new motorbike but not wanting to make monthly payments, wanting to eat when one is overweight, and planning to marry someone her/his parents strongly disapprove of. Many of life's important decisions have approach-avoidance dimensions.

A major source of frustration lies in motivational conflict. In life, we are often influenced by a number of competing forces that propel us in different directions. Such situations demonstrate the condition of conflict. Hence, the *simultaneous existence of multiple wishes and needs characterise conflict.*

In all the cases of conflicts, the selection of one option against the other depends on the relative strength/importance of one over the other, and environmental factors. Conflicting situations should be resolved after due consideration of the pros and cons of each of the choices. A point to note here is that conflicts cause frustration, which in turn, can lead to aggression. For instance, a young man who wants to be a musician but is pursuing a course in management due to parental pressure and is not able to perform as per the expectations of his parents may turn aggressive upon being questioned on his poor performance in the course.

Definition of Mental Disorder

The concept of mental disorders is fundamental to the processes of diagnoses and treatment. The authors of the DSM define a mental disorder as "a clinically significant behavioural or psychological syndrome or pattern that occurs in an individual that is associated with present distress (*e.g.*, painful symptom) or disability (*i.e.*, impairment in one or more areas of functioning) or with a significantly increased risk of suffering death, pain, disability, or an important loss of freedom and it is not typical or culturally expected."

Let's understand this definition

- **A mental disorder is clinically significant** - this implies that the symptoms have to be present for a specified period of time and should have a major effect on the person's life. Thus, an occasional low mood or strange behaviour or a sense of instability is a common experience and does not represent a mental disorder.
- **A mental disorder is behavioural or psychological syndrome or pattern** - a syndrome is a collection of defined symptoms. A behavioural or psychological syndrome indicates a set of observable actions and the thoughts and feelings reported by the individual. Accordingly a random thought or behaviour does not constitute a mental disorder. A person has to experience a wide range of defined thoughts, feelings and behaviours in order to be called as having a psychological disorder.
- Further, it is **associated with present distress, disability, impairment or serious risk.** This means that the syndrome sufficiently interferes with the individual's everyday functioning. For example, a woman who compulsively washes hands may be very disturbed by her actions and may not be able to overcome the behaviour. Her productivity at work and social life may also be severely affected by this.

In certain mental disorders the person may not experience any distress but there may be a serious risk to life. For example, a person in a hyper-excited state of mania, having a good time, may believe he can fly and is thus at risk.

- Finally, **the disorder is not a culturally expected or sanctioned pattern.** For example, a woman feeling sad, having difficulty in eating, sleeping, concentrating, etc., for a few days, following the death of her husband, will not be called as suffering from Major Depressive Disorder because it is an expected reaction to this event.

Major Mental Disorders

Anxiety Disorders

We experience anxiety when we wait to take an examination, or visit a dentist, or even give a solo performance. This is normal and expected and even motivates us to do our task well. On the other hand, high levels of anxiety that are distressing and interfere with effective functioning indicate the presence of an anxiety disorder — the most common category of psychological disorders.

Everyone has worries and fears. The term **anxiety** is usually defined as a diffuse, vague, very unpleasant feeling of fear and apprehension. The anxious individual also shows combinations of the following symptoms: rapid heart rate, shortness of breath, diarrhoea, loss of appetite, fainting, dizziness, sweating, sleeplessness, frequent urination and tremors. There are many types of anxiety disorders. They include **generalised anxiety disorder,** which consists of prolonged, vague, unexplained and intense fears that are not attached to any particular object. The symptoms include worry and apprehensive feelings about the future; hypervigilance, which involves constantly scanning the environment for dangers. It is marked by motor tension, as a result of which the person is unable to relax, is restless, and visibly shaky and tense.

Another type of anxiety disorder is **panic disorder,** which consists of recurrent anxiety attacks in which the person experiences intense terror. A panic attack denotes an abrupt surge of intense anxiety rising to a peak when thoughts of a particular stimuli are present. Such thoughts occur in an unpredictable manner. The clinical features include shortness of breath, dizziness, trembling, palpitations, choking, nausea, chest pain or discomfort, fear of going crazy, losing control or dying.

You might have met or heard of someone who was afraid to travel in a lift or climb to the tenth floor of a building, or refused to enter a room if she/he saw a lizard. You may have also felt it yourself or seen a friend unable to speak a word of a well-memorised and rehearsed speech before an audience. These kinds of fears are termed as **phobias.** People who have phobias have irrational fears related to specific objects, people, or situations. Phobias often develop gradually or begin with a generalised anxiety disorder. Phobias can be grouped into three main types, *i.e., specific phobia, social phobia,* and *agoraphobia.*

Specific phobias are the most commonly occurring type of phobia. This group includes irrational fears such as intense fear of a certain type of animal, or of being in an enclosed space. Intense and incapacitating fear and embarrassment while dealing with others characterises **social phobias. Agoraphobia** is the term used when people develop a fear of entering unfamiliar situations. Many agoraphobics are afraid of leaving their home. So their ability to carry out normal life activities is severely limited.

Have you ever noticed someone washing their hands everytime they touch something, or washing even things like coins, or stepping only within the patterns on the floor or road while walking? People affected by **obsessive-compulsive disorder** are unable to control their preoccupation with specific ideas or are unable to prevent themselves from repeatedly carrying out a particular act or series of acts that affect their ability to carry out normal activities. **Obsessive behaviour** is the inability to stop thinking about a particular idea or topic. The person involved, often finds these thoughts to be unpleasant and shameful. **Compulsive behaviour** is the need to perform certain behaviours over and over again. Many compulsions deal with counting, ordering, checking, touching and washing.

Very often people who have been caught in a natural disaster (such as tsunami) or have been victims of bomb blasts by terrorists, or have been in a serious accident or in a war-related situation, experience **post-traumatic stress disorder** (PTSD). PTSD symptoms vary widely but may include recurrent dreams, flashbacks, impaired concentration and emotional numbing.

Somatoform Disorders

These are conditions in which there are physical symptoms in the absence of a physical disease. In somatoform disorders, the individual has psychological difficulties and complains of physical symptoms, for which there is no biological cause. Somatoform disorders include *pain disorders, somatisation disorders, conversion disorders,* and *hypochondriasis.*

Pain disorders involve reports of extreme and incapacitating pain, either without any identifiable biological symptoms or greatly in excess of what might be expected to accompany biological symptoms. How people interpret pain influences their overall adjustment. Some pain sufferers can learn to use active coping, *i.e.,* remaining active and ignoring the pain. Others engage in passive coping, which leads to reduced activity and social withdrawal.

Major Anxiety Disorders and their Symptoms

1. *Generalised Anxiety Disorder :* Prolonged, vague, unexplained and intense fears that have no object, accompanied by hyper-vigilance and motor tension,
2. *Panic Disorder :* Frequent anxiety attacks characterised by feelings of intense terror and dread; unpredictable 'panic attacks' along with physiological symptoms like breathlessness, palpitations, trembling, dizziness, and a sense of losing control or even dying.
3. *Phobias :* Irrational fears related to specific objects, interactions with others, and unfamiliar situations.
4. *Obsessive-compulsive Disorder:* Being preoccupied with certain thoughts that are viewed by the person to be embarrassing or shameful, and being unable to check the impulse to repeatedly carry out certain acts like checking, washing, counting, etc.
5. *Post-traumatic Stress Disorder (PTSD):* Recurrent dreams, flashbacks, impaired concentration, and emotional numbing followed by a traumatic or stressful event like a natural disaster, serious accident, etc.

Patients with **somatisation disorders** have multiple and recurrent or chronic bodily complaints. These complaints are likely to be presented in a dramatic and exaggerated way. Common complaints are headaches, fatigue, heart palpitations, fainting spells, vomiting and allergies. Patients with this disorder believe that they are sick, provide long and detailed histories of their illness, and take large quantities of medicine.

The symptoms of **conversion disorders** are the reported loss of part or all of some basic body functions. Paralysis, blindness, deafness and difficulty in walking are generally among the symptoms reported. These symptoms often occur after a stressful experience and may be quite sudden.

Hypochondriasis is diagnosed if a person has a persistent belief that she/he has a serious illness, despite medical reassurance, lack of physical findings, and failure to develop the disease. Hypochondriacs have an obsessive preoccupation and concern with the condition of their bodily organs, and they are continually worried about their health.

Dissociative Disorders

Dissociation can be viewed as severance of the connections between ideas and emotions. Dissociation involves feelings of unreality, estrangement, depersonalisation, and sometimes a loss or shift of identity. Sudden temporary alterations of consciousness that blot out painful experiences are a defining characteristic of **dissociative disorders.** Four conditions are included in this group: *dissociative amnesia, dissociative fugue, dissociative identity disorder,* and *depersonalisation.*

Dissociative amnesia is characterised by extensive but selective memory loss that has no known organic cause (e.g., head injury). Some people cannot remember anything about their past. Others can no longer recall specific events, people, places, or objects, while their memory for other events remains intact. This disorder is often associated with an overwhelming stress.

Dissociative fugue has, as its essential feature, an unexpected travel away from home and workplace, the assumption of a new identity, and the inability to recall the previous identity. The fugue usually ends when the person suddenly 'wakes up' with no memory of the events that occurred during the fugue.

Dissociative identity disorder, often referred to as *multiple personality,* is the most dramatic of the dissociative disorders. It is often associated with traumatic experiences in childhood. In this disorder, the person assumes alternate personalities that may or may not be aware of each other.

Depersonalisation involves a dreamlike state in which the person has a sense of being separated both from self and from reality. In depersonalisation, there is a change of self-perception, and the person's sense of reality is temporarily lost or changed.

Salient Features of Somatoform and Dissociative Disorders	
Somatoform Disorders	*Dissociative Disorders*
Hypochondriasis : The person interprets insignificant symptoms as signs of a serious illness despite repeated medical evaluations that point to no pathology/disease.	*Dissociative amnesia :* The person is unable to recall important, personal information, often related to a stressful and traumatic report. The extent of forgetting is beyond normal.
Somatisation : The person exhibits vague and recurring physical/bodily symptoms such as pain, acidity, etc., without any organic cause.	*Dissociative fugue :* The person suffers from a rare disorder that combines amnesia with travelling away from a stressful environment.
Conversion : The person suffers from a loss or impairment of motor or sensory function (e.g., paralysis, blindness, etc.) that has no physical cause but may be a response to stress and psychological problems.	*Dissociative identity (multiple personality) :* The person exhibits two or more separate and contrasting personalities associated with a history of physical abuse.

Mood Disorders

Mood disorders are characterised by disturbances in mood or prolonged emotional state. The most common mood disorder is **depression,** which covers a variety of negative moods and behavioural changes. Depression can refer to a *symptom* or a *disorder.* In day-to-day life, we often use the term 'depression' to refer to normal feelings after a significant loss, such as the break-up of a relationship, or the failure to attain a significant goal. The main types of mood disorders include *depressive, manic* and *bipolar disorders.* **Major depressive disorder** is defined as a period of depressed mood and/or loss of interest or pleasure in most activities, together with other symptoms which may include change in body weight, constant sleep problems, tiredness, inability to think clearly, agitation, greatly slowed behaviour, and thoughts of death and suicide. Other symptoms include excessive guilt or feelings of worthlessness.

Factors Predisposing towards Depression : Genetic make-up, or heredity is an important risk factor for major depression and bipolar disorders. Age is also a risk factor. For instance, women are particularly at risk during young adulthood, while for men the risk is highest in early middle age. Similarly gender also plays a great role in this differential risk addition. For example, women in comparison to men are more likely to report a depressive disorder. Other risk factors are experiencing negative life events and lack of social support.

Another less common mood disorder is **mania.** People suffering from mania become euphoric ('high'), extremely active, excessively talkative, and easily distractible. Manic episodes rarely appear by themselves; they usually alternate with depression. Such a mood disorder, in which both mania and depression are alternately present, is sometimes interrupted by periods of normal mood. This is known as **bipolar mood disorder.** Bipolar mood disorders were earlier referred to as manic-depressive disorders.

Among the mood disorders, the lifetime risk of a suicide attempt is highest in case of bipolar mood disorders. Several risk factors in addition to mental health status of a person predict the likelihood of suicide. These include age, gender, ethnicity, or race and recent occurrence of serious life events. Teenagers and young adults are as much at high risk for suicide, as those who are over 70 years. Gender is also an influencing factor, *i.e.*, men have a higher rate of contemplated suicide than women. Other factors that affect suicide rates are cultural attitudes toward suicide. In Japan, for instance, suicide is the culturally appropriate way to deal with feeling of shame and disgrace. Negative expectations, hopelessness, setting unrealistically high standards, and being over-critical in self-evaluation are important themes for those who have suicidal preoccupations.

Suicide can be prevented by being alert to some of the symptoms which include:

- changes in eating and sleeping habits
- withdrawal from friends, family and regular activities
- violent actions, rebellious behaviour, running away
- drug and alcohol abuse
- marked personality change
- persistent boredom
- difficulty in concentration
- complaints about physical symptoms, and
- loss of interest in pleasurable activities.

However, seeking timely help from a professional counsellor/psychologist can help to prevent the likelihood of suicide.

Schizophrenic Disorders

Schizophrenia is the descriptive term for a group of psychotic disorders in which personal, social and occupational functioning deteriorate as a result of disturbed thought processes, strange perceptions, unusual emotional states, and motor abnormalities. It is a debilitating disorder. The social and psychological costs of schizophrenia are tremendous, both to patients as well as to their families and society.

Symptoms of Schizophrenia

The symptoms of schizophrenia can be grouped into three categories, viz., **positive symptoms** (*i.e.*, excesses of thought, emotion, and behaviour), **negative symptoms** (*i.e.*, deficits of thought, emotion and behaviour), and **psychomotor symptoms.**

Positive symptoms are 'pathological excesses' or 'bizarre additions' to a person's behaviour. Delusions, disorganised thinking and speech, heightened perception and hallucinations, and inappropriate affect are the ones most often found in schizophrenia.

Many people with schizophrenia develop **delusions.** A delusion is a false belief that is firmly held on inadequate grounds. It is not affected by rational argument, and has no basis in reality. **Delusions of persecution** are the most common in schizophrenia. People with this delusion believe that they are being plotted against, spied on, slandered, threatened, attacked or deliberately victimised. People with schizophrenia may also experience **delusions of reference** in which they attach special and personal meaning to the actions of others or to objects and events. In **delusions of grandeur,** people believe themselves to be specially empowered persons and in **delusions of control,** they believe that their feelings, thoughts and actions are controlled by others.

People with schizophrenia may not be able to think logically and may speak in peculiar ways.

These **formal thought disorders** can make communication extremely difficult. These include rapidly shifting from one topic to another so that the normal structure of thinking is muddled and becomes illogical *(loosening of associations, derailment),* inventing new words or phrases *(neologisms),* and persistent and inappropriate repetition of the same thoughts *(perseveration).*

Schizophrenics may have **hallucinations,** *i.e.,* perceptions that occur in the absence of external stimuli. **Auditory hallucinations** are most common in schizophrenia. Patients hear sounds or voices that speak words, phrases and sentences directly to the patient *(second-person hallucination)* or talk to one another referring to the patient as she/he *(third person hallucination).* Hallucinations can also involve the other senses. These include **tactile hallucinations** (*i.e.,* forms of tingling, burning), **somatic hallucinations** (*i.e.,* something happening inside the body such as a snake crawling inside one's stomach), **visual hallucinations** (*i.e.,* vague perceptions of colour or distinct visions of people or objects), **gustatory hallucinations** (*i.e.,* food or drink tastes strange), and **olfactory hallucinations** (*i.e.,* smell of poison or smoke).

People with schizophrenia also show **inappropriate affect,** *i.e.,* emotions that are unsuited to the situation.

Negative symptoms are 'pathological deficits' and include poverty of speech, blunted and flat affect, loss of volition, and social withdrawal. People with schizophrenia show **alogia** or poverty of speech, *i.e.,* a reduction in speech and speech content. Many people with schizophrenia show less anger, sadness, joy, and other feelings than most people do. Thus they have **blunted affect.** Some show no emotions at all, a condition known as **flat affect.** Also patients with schizophrenia experience **avolition,** or apathy and an inability to start or complete a course of action. People with this disorder may withdraw socially and become totally focused on their own ideas and fantasies.

People with schizophrenia also show **psychomotor symptoms.** They move less spontaneously or make odd grimaces and gestures. These symptoms may take extreme forms known as **catatonia.** People in a **catatonic stupor** remain motionless and silent for long stretches of time. Some show **catatonic rigidity,** *i.e.,* maintaining a rigid, upright posture for hours. Others exhibit **catatonic posturing,** *i.e.,* assuming awkward, bizarre positions for long periods of time.

Sub-types of Schizophrenia

According to DSM-IV-TR, the sub-types of schizophrenia and their characteristics are:

- **Paranoid type :** Preoccupation with delusions or auditory hallucinations; no disorganised speech or behaviour or inappropriate affect.
- **Disorganised type :** Disorganised speech and bahaviour; inappropriate or flat affect; no catatonic symptoms.
- **Catatonic type :** Extreme motor immobility; excessive motor inactivity; extreme negativism (*i.e.,* resistance to instructions) or mutism (*i.e.,* refusing to speak).
- **Undifferentiated type :** Does not fit any of the sub-types but meets symptom criteria.
- **Residual type :** Has experienced at least one episode of schizophrenia; no positive symptoms but shows negative symptoms.

Behavioural and Developmental Disorders

Apart from those mentioned above, there are certain disorders that are specific to children and if neglected can lead to serious consequences later in life. Children have less self-understanding and they have not yet developed a stable sense of identity, nor do they have an adequate frame of reference regarding reality, possibility, and value. As a result, they are unable to cope with stressful events which might be reflected in behavioural and emotional problems. On the other hand, although their inexperience and lack of self-sufficiency make them easily upset by problems that seem minor to an adult, children typically bounce back more quickly.

We will now discuss several disorders of childhood like **Attention-deficit Hyperactivity Disorder (ADHD), Conduct Disorder,** and **Separation Anxiety Disorder.** These disorders, if not attended, can lead to more serious and chronic disorders as the child moves into adulthood.

Classification of children's disorders has followed a different path than that of adult disorders. Achenbach has identified two factors, viz., *externalisation* and *internalisation,* which include the majority of childhood behaviour problems. The **externalising disorders,** or undercontrolled problems, include behaviours that are disruptive and often aggressive and aversive to others in the child's environment. The **internalising disorders,** or overcontrolled problems, are those conditions where the child experiences, viz., depression, anxiety, and discomfort that may not be evident to others.

There are several disorders in which children display disruptive or externalising behaviours. We will now focus on three prominent disorders, viz., *Attention-deficit Hyperactivity Disorder* (ADHD), *Oppositional Defiant Disorder* (ODD), and *Conduct Disorder.*

The two main features of ADHD are **inattention** and **hyperactivity-impulsivity.** Children who are **inattentive** find it difficult to sustain mental effort during work or play. They have a hard time keeping their minds on any one thing or in following instructions. Common complaints are that the child does not listen, cannot concentrate, does not follow instructions, is disorganised, easily distracted, forgetful, does not finish assignments, and is quick to lose interest in boring activities. Children who are **impulsive** seem unable to control their immediate reactions or to think before they act. They find it difficult to wait or take turns, have difficulty resisting immediate temptations or delaying gratification. Minor mishaps such as knocking things over are common whereas more serious accidents and injuries can also occur. **Hyperactivity** also takes many forms. Children with ADHD are in constant motion. Sitting still through a lesson is impossible for them. The child may fidget, squirm, climb and run around the room aimlessly. Parents and teachers describe them as 'driven by a motor', always on the go, and talk incessantly. Boys are four times more likely to be given this diagnosis than girls.

Children with **Oppositional Defiant Disorder** (ODD) display age-inappropriate amounts of stubbornness, are irritable, defiant, disobedient, and behave in a hostile manner. Unlike ADHD, the rates of ODD in boys and girls are not very different. The terms **Conduct Disorder** and **Antisocial Behaviour** refer to age-inappropriate actions and attitudes that violate family expectations, societal norms, and the personal or property rights of others. The behaviours typical of conduct disorder include aggressive actions that cause or threaten harm to people or animals, non-aggressive conduct that causes property damage, major deceitfulness or theft, and serious rule violations. Children show many different types of aggressive behaviour, such as **verbal aggression** (*i.e.,* name-calling, swearing), **physical aggression** (*i.e.,* hitting, fighting), **hostile aggression** (*i.e.,* directed at inflicting injury to others), and **proactive aggression** (*i.e.,* dominating and bullying others without provocation).

Internalising disorders include **Separation Anxiety Disorder** (SAD) and **Depression**. Separation anxiety disorder is an internalising disorder unique to children. Its most prominent symptom is excessive anxiety or even panic experienced by children at being separated from their parents. Children with SAD may have difficulty being in a room by themselves, going to school alone, are fearful of entering new situations, and cling to and shadow their parents' every move. To avoid separation, children with SAD may fuss, scream, throw severe tantrums, or make suicidal gestures.

The ways in which children express and experience depression are related to their level of physical, emotional, and cognitive development. An infant may show sadness by being passive and unresponsive; a pre-schooler may appear withdrawn and inhibited; a school-age child may be argumentative and combative; and a teenager may express feelings of guilt and hopelessness.

Children may also have more serious disorders called **Pervasive Developmental Disorders.** These disorders are characterised by severe and widespread impairments in social interaction and communication skills, and stereotyped patterns of behaviours, interests and activities. **Autistic disorder** or **autism** is one of the most common of these disorders. Children with autistic disorder have marked difficulties in social interaction and communication, a restricted range of interests, and a strong desire for routine. About 70 per cent of children with autism are also mentally retarded.

Children with autism experience profound difficulties in relating to other people. They are unable to initiate social behaviour and seem unresponsive to other people's feelings. They are unable to share experiences or emotions with others. They also show serious abnormalities in communication and language that persist over time. Many autistic children never develop speech and those who do, have repetitive and deviant speech patterns. Children with autism often show narrow patterns of interests and repetitive behaviours, such as lining up objects or stereotyped body movements such as rocking. These motor movements may be self-stimulatory, such as hand flapping or self-injurious such as banging their head against the wall.

Another group of disorder which is of special interest to young people is **eating disorder.** This includes *anorexia nervosa, bulimia nervosa and binge eating*. In **anorexia nervosa,** the individual has a distorted body image that leads her/him to see herself/himself as overweight. Often refusing to eat, exercising compulsively and developing unusual habits such as refusing to eat in front of others, the anorexic may lose large amounts of weight and even starve herself/himself to death. In **bulimia nervosa,** the individual may eat excessive amounts of food, then purge her/ his body of food by using medicines such as laxatives or diuretics or by vomiting. The person often feels disgusted and ashamed when she/he binges and is relieved of tension and negative emotions after purging. In *binge eating,* there are frequent episodes of out-of-control eating.

Mental Retardation

Mental retardation refers to below average intellectual functioning (with an IQ of approximately 70 or below), and deficits or impairments in adaptive behaviour (*i.e.,* in the areas of communication, self-care, home living, social/interpersonal skills, functional academic skills, work, etc.) which are manifested before the age of 18 years. The Table in the next page describes characteristics of the mentally challenged persons.

Substance-use Disorders

Addictive behaviour, whether it involves excessive intake of high calorie food resulting in extreme obesity or involving the abuse of substances such as alcohol or cocaine, is one of the most severe problems being faced by society today.

Disorders relating to maladaptive behaviours resulting from regular and consistent use of the substance involved are called *substance abuse disorders.* These disorders include problems associated with using and abusing such drugs as alcohol, cocaine and heroin, which alter the way people think, feel and behave. There are two sub-groups of substance-use disorders, *i.e.,* those related to *substance dependence* and those related to *substance abuse.*

In **substance dependence,** there is intense craving for the substance to which the person is addicted, and the person shows tolerance, withdrawal symptoms and compulsive drug-taking. Tolerance means that the person has to use more and more of a substance to get the same effect. Withdrawal refers to physical symptoms that occur when a person stops or cuts down on the use of a psychoactive substance, *i.e.,* a substance that has the ability to change an individual's consciousness, mood and thinking processes.

In **substance abuse,** there are recurrent and significant adverse consequences related to the use of substances. People who regularly ingest drugs damage their family and social relationships, perform poorly at work, and create physical hazards.

Characteristics of Individuals with Different Levels of Mental Retardation

Area of Functioning	Mild (IQ range = 50–70)	Moderate (IQ range = 35–49)	Severe (IQ range = 20–34) and Profound (IQ = below 20)
Self-help Skills	Feeds and dresses self and cares for own toilet needs	Has difficulties and requires training but can learn adequate self-help skills	No skills to partial skills, but some can care for personal needs on limited basis
Speech and Communication	Receptive and expressive language is adequate; understands communication	Receptive and expressive language is adequate; has speech problems	Receptive language is limited; expressive language is poor
Academics	Optimal learning environment; third to sixth grade	Very few academic skills; first or second grade is maximum	No academic skills
Social Skills	Has friends; can learn to adjust quickly	Capable of making friends but has difficulty in many social situations	Not capable of having real friends; no social interactions
Vocational Adjustment	Can hold a job; competitive to semi-competitive; primarily unskilled work	Sheltered work environment; usually needs consistent supervision	Generally no employment; usually needs constant care
Adult Living	Usually marries, has children; needs help during stress	Usually does not marry or have children; dependent	No marriage or children; always dependent on others

We will now focus on the three most common forms of substance abuse, viz., **alcohol abuse and dependence, heroin abuse and dependence,** and **cocaine abuse and dependence.**

Alcohol Abuse and Dependence

People who abuse alcohol drink large amounts regularly and rely on it to help them face difficult situations. Eventually the drinking interferes with their social behaviour and ability to think and work. For many people the pattern of alcohol abuse extends to dependence. That is, their bodies build up a tolerance for alcohol and they need to drink even greater amounts to feel its effects. They also experience withdrawal responses when they stop drinking. Alcoholism destroys millions of families, social relationships and careers. Intoxicated drivers are responsible for many road accidents. It also has serious effects on the children or persons with this disorder. These children have higher rates of psychological problems, particularly anxiety, depression, phobias and substance-related disorders. Excessive drinking can seriously damage physical health. Some of the ill-effects of alcohol on health and psychological functioning are presented in Box.

Heroin Abuse and Dependence

Heroin intake significantly interferes with social and occupational functioning. Most abusers further develop a dependence on heroin, revolving their lives around the substance, building up a tolerance for it, and experiencing a withdrawal reaction when they stop taking it. The most direct danger of heroin abuse is an overdose, which slows down the respiratory centres in the brain, almost paralysing breathing, and in many cases causing death.

Effects of Alcohol : Some Facts

- All alcohol beverages contain ethyl alcohol.
- This chemical is absorbed into the blood and carried into the central nervous system (brain and spinal cord) where it depresses or slows down functioning.
- Ethyl alcohol depresses those areas in the brain that control judgement and inhibition; people become more talkative and friendly, and they feel more confident and happy.
- As alcohol is absorbed, it affects other areas of the brain. For example, drinkers are unable to make sound judgements, speech becomes less careful and less clear, and memory falters; many people become emotional, loud and aggressive.
- Motor difficulties increase. For example, people become unsteady when they walk and clumsy in performing simple activities; vision becomes blurred and they have trouble in hearing; they have difficulty in driving or in solving simple problems.

Cocaine Abuse and Dependence

Regular use of cocaine may lead to a pattern of abuse in which the person may be intoxicated throughout the day and function poorly in social relationships and at work. It may also cause problems in short-term memory and attention. Dependence may develop, so that cocaine dominates the person's life, more of the drug is needed to get the desired effects, and stopping it results in feelings of depression, fatigue, sleep problems, irritability and anxiety. Cocaine poses serious dangers. It has dangerous effects on psychological functioning and physical well-being.

Commonly Abused Substances (Following the *DSM-IV-TR* Classification)

- **Alcohol**
- **Amphetamines:** Dextroamphetamines, metaamphetamines, diet pills
- **Caffeine:** Coffee, tea, caffeinated soda, analgesics, chocolate, cocoa
- **Cannabis:** Marijuana or '*bhang*', *hashish*, sensimilla
- **Cocaine**
- **Hallucinogens:** LSD, mescaline
- **Inhalants:** Gasoline, glue, paint thinners, spray paints, typewriter correction fluid, sprays
- **Nicotine:** Cigarettes, tobacco
- **Opioid:** Morphine, heroin, cough syrup, painkillers (analgesics, anaesthetics)
- **Phencyclidine**
- **Sedative.**

INTRODUCTION TO HUMAN ANATOMY AND PHYSIOLOGY

ANATOMY

Anatomy is the study of structure of human body. Study of anatomy helps in understanding the functions of body. **Herophilus** (335-280 BC) born in Chalcedon in Asia Minor (now Kadiköy, Turkey), and later moved to Alexandria is called the 'Father of anatomy'. **Andreas Vesalius,** a Flemish physician is referred to as the 'Father of modern human anatomy'. Different aspects included in anatomy are Histology, Osteology, Myology, Arthrology and Neurology, etc. Histology is the study of tissues. Osteology is the study of bones. Myology is the study of muscles, Arthrology is the study of joints, Neurology is the study of nerves and nervous system.

Cell

Cell is the basic structural and functional unit of

living matter. It is the smallest unit of life. It is capable of carrying life processes independently. Some organisms such as bacteria are unicellular.

Structure of Cell

There are two types of cells in body. They are: (1) Somatic cells, (2) Gonadal cells.

Somatic cells are diverse cells which make up somatic structure of body. Gonadal cells are gametes which can unite to form new individual.

Cells vary in size and shape. Most of the cells contain similar type of intracellular components. Average size of mammalian cell is 10^{-2} mm in diameter.

Every cell comprises following parts.

1. Cell wall (cell membrane)

2. Protoplasm, consisting of Cytoplasm and Nucleus

Cell Wall

It is also called plamsalemma or plasma membrane or cell membrane. It is the outer protective layer of cell. It isolates cell from neighbouring environment. It cannot be seen by light microscope. It can be seen by electron microscope. It is about 80 Å thick. It has trilaminar structure of phospholipid bilayer sandwitched between two densely stained protein layers.

Phospholipid molecules have two parts. They are: (1) Head (Phosphate) and (2) Tail (Fatty acid) outer surface of cell wall contains pinocytotic vesicles. Inner surface is continuous with endoplasmic reticulum (ER). Functions of cell wall are: (1) Transport of materials (main function), (2) Protection, (3) Reception of external stimuli, (4) Ingestion of nutrients and (5) Excretion of waste products of cellular metabolism.

Cytoplasm

Cytoplasm is the mass of living matter between cell wall and nucleus. It contains stored foods, secretion granules, pigments and crystals. These are called cytoplasmic inclusions. Stored foods are carbohydrates, fats, proteins, minerals and vitamins. Pigments are of two types - endogenous and exogenous. Endogenous pigments are haemoglobin and melanin. Exogenous pigments are carotene from vegetables, dusts (carbon) and minerals (silver, lead, etc.). Cytoplasmic organelles are: Endoplasmic reticulum, Golgi apparatus, Mitochondria, Lysosomes, Ribosomes, Centrosomes, etc.

Endoplasmic reticulum

Endoplasmic reticulum is a system that continues with infoldings of cell membrane and interlaces with the interior of cell. There are two types of endoplasmic reticulum - Smooth ER & Rough ER. Smooth ER is a network of smooth tubules. Functions of smooth ER are metabolism and synthesis of steroids and glycogen. Rough ER consists of ribosomes. It is prominent in Adrenal cortex, liver and striated muscle. Functions of rough ER are: (1) Protein synthesis & (2) Translation of language of nucleic acids.

Golgi apparatus

It is shaped like network of threads. Its functions are (1) Synthesis of various secretions & (2) Storage of enzymes, ascorbic acid and some other substances.

Mitochondria

They are granular, filamentous or rod shaped solid bodies. They vary in size from 0.5 to 5 microns. They are surrounded by trilaminar double membrane. Inner one remains folded to form partitions called cristae mitochondriales. Intramitochondrial space contains fluid called matrix. Number and size of mitochondria of a cell are determined by energy requirements of cell. Cells of liver, kidney and heart possess large amount of mitochondria.

Functions of mitochondria are: (1) They are called power houses of cells. They supply 95% of cell's energy requirement. In presence of oxygen, Kreb's cycle runs in mitochondria with the help of respiratory enzymes - flavoprotein enzymes and cytochrome. These enzymes help in oxidative phosphorylation. They provide site for formation of ATP & (2) Synthesis of RNA and DNA.

Lysosomes

They are digestive organs of cells. They are also called suicide bags of cells. They are digestive organelles of cells. They contain powerful hydrolytic enzymes. Lysosomes are absent in RBC. Functions of lysosomes are: (1) Breaking down of particles taken into cell and digestion, (2) Autolysis, (3) Phagocytosis, (4) Killing of cells (planned way), (5) Cell division, etc.

Ribosomes

They are scattered throughout cytoplasm singly or as groups. They are ribonucleoprotein in nature. Their function is protein synthesis.

Centrosome

Centrosome contains centrioles. Centrioles control polarisation of spindle fibres. Centriole is closely related to spindle formation during cell division (Mitosis).

Plasmosin

Plasmosin is a constant constituent of cytoplasm. They form - Tonofibrils in epithelial cells, myofibrils in muscles and neurofibrils in nerves. They consist of long protein molecules rich in deoxy-ribonucleoprotein.

Vacuoles

They are also cytoplasmic organelles. They are found covered by fat on staining with dilute neutral red solution.

Nissl bodies

They are found in nerve cells.

Secretory granules

They store secretory products of cell and are found in - Golgi apparatus and E.R.

Nucleus

It is the key structure of living cell. Nucleus is covered by nuclear membrane. Nucleus consists of chromatin and nucleolus. Chromatin is a dense chromosomal network. There is usually simple nucleolus or 2-5 nucleoli in a cell. Nucleolus contains nucleolemma. Nuclear material differs from cytoplasm in several ways. Chromosomes seen in interphase nucleus are densely stained portions of chromosomes. Chromatin contains different genes which determine heredity of cell.

Chromosomes

Chromosomes are present as individual bodies in interphase as well as in mitosis. Predominant component in chromosome is DNA. Genes are located in chromosome. They are discrete units of transmission of hereditary characters.

In females, 2X chromosomes and in males 1X and 1Y chromosomes are present.

Properties of Cell

Properties of cell in unicellular organisms like amoeba are —

(*a*) Irritability
(*b*) Conductivity
(*c*) Contractility
(*d*) Absorption
(*e*) Excretion
(*f*) Growth and reproduction
(*g*) Motility
(*h*) Secretion

Tissue

Tissue is defined as group of cells of similarity in structure, function and genesis.

Classification: Human body contains following types of tissues: (1) Epithelial tissue, (2) Connective tissue, (3) Muscular tissue and (4) Nervous tissue.

Epithelial tissue

Epithelial tissue gives covering to other tissues by forming epithelial membrane. Epithelial membrane rests upon *laminapropria*. *Laminapropria* is a loose vascular connective tissue, which supplies requirements to epithelial membrane. Cells of epithelial tissue lie close together cemented by a mucoprotein containing hyaluronic acid and calcium salts.

Functions of epithelial tissue are:

1. Protecting the underlying surfaces
2. Providing surface for absorption
3. Secretory activity
4. Excretion.

Types of Epithelial tissue: Epithelial tissue is majorly classified into:

1. *Simple epithelium* - consisting of single layer of cells.
2. *Compound epithelium* - consisting of multiple layers of cells.

Simple epithelium: Different types of simple epithelial tissues are:

(*a*) *Squamous or pavement epithelium* - consisting of single layer of flat cells.

(*b*) *Cuboidal epithelium* - consisting of single layer of cuboidal cells of same dimensions.

(*c*) *Columnar epithelium* - consisting of single layer of cells which are lengthier in height than breadth.

(*d*) *Ciliated columnar and cuboidal epithelium*- columnar and cuboidal cells containing cilia.

(*e*) *Glandular epithelium* - lining the alveoli and ducts of glands.

Squamous or pavement epithelium : It is found in alveoli of lungs, serous membranes like peritoneum, pleura, nephrons, inner lining of heart etc.

Functions : 1. Dialysis, 2. Passage of liquids and 3. Protection.

Cuboidal epithelium : They are found in inner parts of thyroid gland, salivary glands, digestive glands, etc.

Functions : 1. Protection, 2. Secretion and 3. Storage, etc.

Columnar epithelium: It is supported by basement membrane. It is found in stomach, small intestine, large intestine, alveoli, ducts of glands, etc. In alimentary canal and nephron, it is brush bordered. Goblet cells are another type of columnar epithelium found in large intestine mainly and secrete mucus.

Functions : 1. Absorption and 2. Secretion.

Ciliated columnar and cuboidal epithelium: They are ciliated. Border of cell containing cilia contains basal particles in a row. They are found in trachea, fallopian tubes, CNS, etc.

Functions: 1. Ciliary movement to maintain flow of mucus in one direction; 2. In CNS, its function is suggested to be circulation of CSF.

Glandular-epithelium : They line the alveoli and ducts of glands ex-salivary, sebaceous, mammary and intestinal glands.

Functions : 1. Formation of new substances & 2. Secretion.

Compound epithelium : Compound epithelium is classified into

1. *Transitional epithelium*-consisting of four layers of cells and lying between simple epithelium and many layered stratified epithelium.
2. *Stratified squamous cornified epithelium* - consisting of many layers and horny due to deposition of keratin.
3. *Stratified squamous noncornified epithelium* - consisting of stratified squamous epithelium, not keratinised.
4. *Stratified columnar epithelium* - consisting of several layers of columnar cells.
5. *Stratified columnar ciliated epithelium* - consisting of stratified columnar epithelium containing cilia.

Transitional epithelium : It is found in pelvis of kidney, ureter, urinary bladder and urethra, etc.

Functions:

1. Protection,
2. Prevention of reabsorption,
3. Prevention of drawing water from blood and tissues.

Stratified squamous cornified epithelium : It is found in skin. Hairs, nails, horns, enamel of teeth are modified stratified squamous cornified epithelium.

Functions:

1. Protection from atmosphere
2. Protection from mechanical pressure
3. Protection from injury and friction.

Stratified squamous non-cornified epithelium: It is found in cornea, mouth, pharynx, oesophagus, anal canal, urethra, vagina and cervix, etc.

Function: Mechanical protection.

Stratified columnar epithelium : It is found in conjunctiva, pharynx, epiglottis, cavernous portion of urethra etc.

Stratified columnar ciliated epithelium: It is found in larynx, soft palate, etc.

Connective Tissue

Connective tissue is also called mesenchymal tissue. It is developed from mesoderm. It serves the function of binding two tissues. Cells will be less and intercellular matrix will be abundant.

Several types of connective tissue are:

(*a*) Areolar tissue
(*b*) Adipose tissue
(*c*) White fibrous tissue
(*d*) Yellow elastic tissue
(*e*) Reticular tissue
(*f*) Blood
(*g*) Hemopoietic tissue
(*h*) Cartilaginous tissue
(*i*) Osseous tissue
(*j*) Jelly like tissue
(*k*) Reticuloendothelial tissue.

Areolar tissue : It is a supporting and packing tissue. It is distributed among muscular, vascular and nervous tissues. It is distributed in subcutaneous, subserous and submucous tissues. It is composed of fibres and cells. Spaces in the network of fibres is filled with ground substance. Fibres contained are white or collagenous fibres and yellow elastic fibres.

Types of cells found in areolar tissue are:

(*a*) Fibroblasts
(*b*) Histiocytes
(*c*) Basophilic cells
(*d*) Plasma cells
(*e*) Pigment cells
(*f*) Mast cells
(*g*) Lymphocytes
(*h*) Monocytes.

Adipose tissue : It is also known as loose connective tissue. It contains fat inside fat cells. It is found below skin in mesentery, omentum, etc. It prevents injury to organs. It gives shape to limbs.

It stores energy in the form of fat. It helps in regulation of body temperature.

White fibrous tissue : It is made of white fibres formed by fibroblasts.

These fibres are non-branching and present in bundles. They are present in tendons and ligaments of limbs. It is made of collagen.

Yellow elastic tissue : It is another variety of fibrous tissue. It is yellow in colour. Fibres are thicker, bundles are wavy, but follow a straight course. Fibres appear angular. Fibres are made of elastin. It is most resistant to many chemicals. It is digested by pancreatin.

It is found in areolar tissue throughout body. It is in concentrated form in ligamentum nuchae of the quadrupeds and ligamentum flava of the vertebrae. It is also present in bronchi, larynx, arterial walls, etc. It functions as strong elastic rope. It serves to maintain circulation and blood pressure by its elastic recoil.

Reticular tissue : Reticular tissue is similar to white fibrous tissue with certain differences. Reticular tissue is widely distributed and forms basement membrane of many epithelia. It is found in spleen, liver, lymph and bone marrow, etc.

Blood: Blood is a fluid connective tissue of body.

Haemopoietic tissue: There are two types of haemopoietic tissues. They are:

(*a*) Myeloid tissue (*b*) Lymphatic tissue

Myeloid tissue: Myeloid tissue is a blood forming tissue as well as phagocytic. Myeloid tissue is synonymously used for bone marrow. 'Myelos' means marrow. There are two types of bone marrow:

(*a*) Red bone marrow – Active form

(*b*) Yellow bone marrow – Inactive form.

Red cells are produced in red bone marrow. In foetal life, most of the bones contain red bone marrow. In postnatal life and with advancement of age, red bone marrow is located only in upper ends of humerus and femur, bones of skull, thorax, vertebrae and pelvic innominate bones. Yellow bone marrow occupies the space where red bone marrow will not be present. Although half of the bone marrow (red bone marrow) is active and half is inactive in adult, active half is enormously functional.

Lymphatic tissue: Lymphatic tissue is of two types:

(*a*) Non-capsulated lymphnodules present in loose connective tissue.

(*b*) Capsulated lymph tissue present in lymph organs - lymph node, spleen, thymus, tonsils.

Cartilaginous tissue: It is a connective tissue, which is intermediate between fibrous tissue and osseous tissue in firmness and elasticity. Components of cartilaginous tissue are cartilage cells, chondroblasts, inter cellular ground substance called matrix, fibres and two types of proteins called chondromucoid and chondroalbumoid. Chondromucoid on hydrolysis gives chondroitin sulphate.

Cartilaginous tissue is divided into three classes.

(*a*) Hyaline cartilage, (*b*) Fibrocartilage and (*c*) Elastic cartilage.

Hyaline cartilage: It is made of cartilaginous cells and clear homogenous ground substance. Cartilage cells are also called chondrocytes and occupy small empty spaces in matrix. These small empty spaces in the matrix are called lacunae. Matrix is a solid intercellular substance of cartilage or bone. It is distributed in the articular end of bones.

Fibrocartilage: This type of cartilage has great tensile strength with flexibility and rigidity. It can stand with shearing forces. It is found in intervertebral discs, menisci of knee joints, mandibular joints, pubis symphisis, linings of tendon, grooves in bones etc.

Elastic cartilage: It is in between fibrous tissue and osseous tissue. It is yellow in colour and contains elastic fibres. It differs from hyaline cartilage as it contains large number of elastic fibres in the matrix. It is distributed in external ear, epiglottis, eustachian tube and some laryngeal cartilages.

Elastic cartilage strengthens attached organs.

Jelly like connective tissue: It is an embryonic form of areolar tissue. Cells are large fibroblasts. A few macro phages and lymphocytes are also present. Ground substance is mucin in nature. It is found in umbilical cord. It is called as Wharton's jelly here. Vitreous humour of eye ball is composed of this tissue in adult life.

Reticuloendothelial tissue: It possesses various types of connective tissue cells, widely distributed in body. Main functions are phagocytosis, antibody formation, erythropoiesis, haemolysis, etc.

Osseous tissue : Osseous tissue constitutes skeleton. It is the hardest connective tissue of body. It is made of bone cells and intercellular ground substance. There are three types of bone cells. They are - Osteoblasts, osteocytes and osteoclasts. Organic part of intercellular ground substance is made of osteocollagenous fibres, bound by ossein.

There are two types of bone tissues according to density and hardness.

They are: (1) Compact bone tissue, (2) Spongy bone tissue.

Outer layer of all bones and shaft is compact bone tissue. Inner parts of flat bones, rounded ends of long bones and body of vertebrae possess spongy bone tissue.

Bone is covered with periosteum. Periosteum has two layers - Outer layer and inner layer, called cambium. Cambium is osteogenic in its functions to produce osteoblasts and osteoclasts. Endosteum is the lining membrane of marrow cavity. It possesses osteogenic and haemopoietic functions. Bursae consist of small sacs of connective tissue with synovial fluid. Bursae act like cushions and relieve pressure in moving parts. Bone cavity is the hollow space inside the bone and filled with bone marrow. Bone marrow is of two types - Red bone marrow and yellow bone marrow. Further reference of bone marrow can be had at myeloid tissue.

Transverse section of bone: T.S. of bone under microscope shows haversian system consisting of:

1. Central haversian canal
2. Lamellae
3. Lacunae
4. Canaliculi.

Central haversian canal contains blood vessels, nerves and lymphatic vessels. Lamellae are layers of bone deposited in concentric circles around haversian. Lacunae are interlamellar spaces. Canaliculi are minute canals joining lamellae and communicating with central haversian canal.

Muscular Tissue

It is a type of tissue having contractile ability on excitation. It has also property of conductivity. There are different types of muscular tissues. Their classifications are based on physiological and anatomical aspects.

Types of muscular tissues based on striation : On this basis, they are of two types:

1. Striated muscles
2. Non-striated muscles.

Striated muscles have cross striations. Non-striated muscles do not have cross striations and are plain.

Types of muscular tissues on the basis of control: On this basis, they are of two types

1. Voluntary muscles
2. Involuntary muscles

Voluntary muscles are under volitional control. Involuntary muscles are not under volitional control.

Types of muscular tissues on the basis of distribution:

On this basis, they are:

1. Skeletal muscles, 2. Cardiac muscle and 3. Visceral muscles.

Skeletal muscles are attached to bones. They are under the control of will power. Hence, they are voluntary muscles. Fibres of skeletal muscles show striations. Hence, they are also striated muscles. Epimysium is the outer covering of skeletal muscle. Perimysium is the outer covering for smaller bundles of skeletal muscle. Smaller bundles into which skeletal muscle is divided are called fasciculi. Each fasciculus contains muscle fibres. Each fibre is covered with endomysium.

Histology of skeletal muscle fibres: Skeletal muscle fibres are cylindrical. They are elongated with several nuclei.

Dimensions of skeletal muscle fibres are: $1 - 40 \times 0.01 - 0.1$ mm^2

Sarcolemma is the transparent cell wall of muscle fibre. Myofibrils are bundles of myofilaments embedded in sarcoplasm inside the plasmalemma. Sarcoplasm contains sarcosomes (mitochondria), small Golgi apparatus, myoglobin, lipid glycogen, sarcoplasmic reticulum.

From electron microscopic studies, it is relevant that myofilaments are formed by thread like protein filaments of which, thicker one is myosin filament (100 Å diameter) and thinner one is actin filament (50 Å). They contain multiple flat nuclei in the periphery under sarcolemma.

Cardiac muscle: It is involuntary, striated muscle of heart. It contracts rhythmically and automatically.

Main differences between skeletal and cardiac muscle are

1. Spontaneous nature of rhythmicity and contractility of cardiac muscle.
2. 3-D network of Fibres of cardiac muscle appearing like syncytium under light microscope.
3. Single oval shaped nucleus at the centre of each cell.

Visceral muscles: They are smooth, involuntary and plain muscles of viscera. Visceral muscle fibres are smooth and elongated. They are fusiform with tapering towards periphery. Fine longitudinal striations may be found in special preparation. They contain one oval or rod shaped nucleus at the centre of each cell.

Nervous Tissue

Nervous tissue constitutes nervous system. Nervous tissue is an excitable type tissue receiving and transmitting messages. It is composed of neurons and neuroglia. Nervous system is ectodermal in origin. There are three types of matters in nervous tissue. They are:

1. Grey matter - forming nerve cells
2. White matter - forming nerve fibres
3. Neuroglia - holding nerve cells and fibres together and supporting them.

Histogenesis of nervous tissue: Nervous system develops from ectoderm and neutral plate (also called medullary plate). Medulloblasts give rise to neuroblasts and spongioblasts. Neural cells (Neuroblasts) pass through different stages to give neuron. Spongioblasts are also called glial cells. Spongioblasts give rise to neuroglia.

Neuron: Neuron is the basic functional and structural unit of nervous system.

Parts of neuron are:

1. Nerve cell body (also called perikaryon or neurocyton or soma)
2. Nerve fibres (also called processes of nerve cells)

Nerve cell body: It is the part of neuron containing cell membrane, neuroplasm and nucleus. Neuroplasm contains neurofibrils, nissl bodies, mitochondria, golgi apparatus, superficial reticulum of golgi, ribosome, endoplasmic reticulum, centrosome and inclusions. Neurofibrils are fine filaments passing through neuroplasm from dendrites to axon. Nissl bodies are angular granules stained with basic dyes.

Nerve fibres: Two types of nerve fibres (also called processes of nerve cell) arise from nerve cell. They are:

(*a*) Receptive processes called dendrons (also called dendrites)

(*b*) Discharging processes called axon.

Dendrites carry impulses from other neurons and carry them towards nerve cell body. Axon carries impulses away from nerve cell. Axon consists of three parts - axis cylinder, myelin sheath and neurolemma. Axis cylinder contains axoplasm, neurofibrils and mitochondria. Myelin sheath is absent over nerve fibres within grey matter. It is present over nerve fibres after entering white matter. Myelin sheath is also called medullary sheath. Fibres covered with myelin sheath are called myelinated fibres and fibres not covered with myelin are called non-myelinated fibres. Function of myelin sheath is insulation of nerve fibre. Nodes of Ranvier are points of absence of myelin in the myelinated fibres (medullated fibres). Neurolemma is the homogeneous nucleated covering over somatic and autonomic nerve fibres outside C.N.S. Myelinated fibres in brain and spinal cord do not have neurolemma. Neuroglia is a special type of interstitial tissue giving support and insulation. They are divided into - astrocytes, - oligodendrocytes (or oligodendroglia) and microglia.

Fibres of peripheral nerve trunks are divided into bundles. Individual fibres are held together by loose connective tissue called endoneurium. Each bundle is covered with a sheath called perineurium. Epineurium is the tough enclosure of whole nerve trunk.

RESPIRATORY SYSTEM

It is the system consisting of parts concenred with inhalation and exhalation.

Parts of the Respiratory System

1. Nose
2. Pharynx
3. Larynx
4. Trachea
5. Bronchi
6. Bronchioles

7. Alveolar ducts

8. Alveoli.

Upper respiratory tract extends from upper nares to the vocal cord. Lower respiratory tract extends from vocal cord to the alveoli.

1. Nose

It is the part of respiratory system through which Air is inhaled in and exhaled out.

External nose: It is the visible part of nose. It is formed by the two nasal bones and cartilage. It is covered with skin. There are hairs inside.

Nasal Cavity : It is a large cavity divided by a septum. It is lined with ciliated mucous membrane. It is extremely vascular.

Anterior nares: They are the openings which lead in.

Posterior nares: They are similar openings at the back and lead into pharynx.

Roof : Roof of the nose is formed by ethmoid bone at the base of the skull.

Floor: Floor of the nose is formed by the hard and soft palates at the roof of the mouth.

Paranasal sinuses: They are the hollows in the bones surrounding the nasal cavity, which are lined with mucous membrane and open into nasal cavity. Maxillary sinus lies below the orbit and opens through the lateral wall of the nose.

Frontal sinus lies above the orbit towards the midline of the frontal bone. Ethmoidal sinuses are contained within the part of the ethmoid bone separating the orbit from the nose. They are numerous.

Sphenoidal sinus lies in the body of the sphenoid bone.

2. Pharynx

It lies between nasal cavity and larynx. Pharynx is divided into three parts. They are:

1. Nasopharynx, 2. Oropharynx and 3. Laryngopharynx.

Nasopharynx lies in between nasal cavity and oropharynx. It is lined with ciliated mucous membrane which is continuous with lining of the nose. Oropharynx lies in between nasopharynx and laryngopharynx. Its lateral wall contains collections of lymphoid tissue called tonsils. Laryngopharynx is the lowest part of pharynx. It lies behind larynx.

3. Larynx

It lies below pharynx and above trachea. It is continuous with oropharynx. Muscles of the neck lie in front of larynx. Laryngopharynx and cervical vertebrae lie behind larynx. Lobes of thyroid gland lie on the either side of larynx.

Larynx is composed of several cartilages. They are joined together by ligaments and membranes.

Cartilages of larynx are:

1. Thyroid cartilage
2. Cricoid cartilage
3. Arytenoid cartilages
4. Epiglottis.

Thyroid cartilage: Thyroid cartilage is formed with two flat pieces of cartilage. It is the largest upper part. Thyroid cartilage is lined with stratified epithelium. Lower part is lined with ciliated epithelium.

Cricoid cartilage: It lies below the thyroid cartilage. Its shape is like a signet ring. It is broad at the back. It is lined with ciliated epithelium.

Arytenoid cartilages: They are a pair of small pyramids. They are made of hyaline cartilage. They are located on the broad portion of cricoid cartilage. Vocal ligaments are attached to them. Chink is the gap between vocal ligaments.

Epiglottis: Epiglottis is a leaf shaped cartilage. It is attached to the inside of the front wall of thyroid cartilage. During swallowing, larynx moves upward and forward and its opening is occluded by epiglottis.

4. Trachea

It is also called wind pipe. It is a cylindrical tube. It is about 11 cm. in length. It begins at the lower end of pharynx. It divides into two bronchi at the level of fifth thoracic vertebra. It is made of sixteen to twenty C-shaped incomplete cartilages. They are connected by fibrous tissue at the back. It is lined by ciliated epithelium. Ciliated epithelium contains goblet cells which secrete mucus.

5. *Bronchi*

Trachea divide into right and left bronchi. Trachea and bronchi, combinedly are inverted Y shaped. Right bronchus leads into right lung and left bronchus leads into left lung. Right bronchus is shorter than left bronchus. It is also wider. Bronchi are made up of complete rings of cartilage.

6. *Bronchioles*

Bronchioles are the finest branches of bronchi. They do not have cartilage. They are lined by cuboidal epithelium. Bronchioles become further smaller to form terminal bronchioles. Terminal bronchioles are a single layer of flattened epithelial cells.

7. *Alveolarducts*

Terminal bronchioles divide repeatedly to form minute passages. These minute passages are called alveolar ducts. Alveolar sacs and alveoli open from alveolar ducts.

8. *Alveoli*

Alveoli are the final terminations of each bonchi. They contain a thin layer of epithelial cells. They are surrounded by numerous capillaries. Capillary network is the site of exchange of gases between blood and air in the alveoli.

Lungs

Lungs are the principal organs concerned with respiratory process. They are two in number. They are spongy organs. They lie in the thoracic cavity on either side of heart and great vessels. They extend from roof of the neck to the diaphragm. Ribs, costal cartilages and intercostal muscles lie in front of lungs. Behind them - ribs, intercostal muscles and transverse processes of thoracic vertebrae lie. Mediastinum is a block of tissue in between the two lungs. Within mediastinum lie - heart, great vessels, trachea, oesophagus, thoracic duct and thymus gland.

Lungs are conical in shape with apex above and base below. Apex slightly rises over the clavicle. Base is near the diaphragm. Each lung is divided into lobes by means of fissures. Right lung is bigger than left lung. Right lung is divided into three lobes. Left lung is divided into two lobes. Each lobe is divided into number of lobules. Each lobe contains a small bronchial tube. This tube divides and sub-divides to end in air sacs.

Pleura is a serous membrane covering the lungs. It contains two layers. Inner layer close to the lungs is called visceral layer. Outer layer is called parietal layer. Pleural fluid lies in the space between visceral and parietal layers.

Hilum is a triangular shaped depression on the concave medial surface of the lung. It is a vertical slit on each lung through which structures like blood vessels, nerves and lymphatics pass. Root of the lungs (Hilum) is formed by pulmonary arteries, pulmonary veins, bronchial arteries, bronchial veins, bronchi and lymphatic vessels. Pulmonary arteries carry deoxygenated blood to lungs from heart. Pulmonary veins carry oxygenated blood from lungs to the heart. Bronchial arteries are the branches of thoracic aorta carrying arterial blood to lungs. Bronchial veins are the vessels carrying venous blood of lungs to superior venacava.

Respiratory muscles

Intercostal muscles and diaphram are respiratory muscles. However, during forced respiration sternocleidomastoid, scalenie, mylohyoid, platysma and abdominal muscles also participate.

Intercostal muscles: They are two series of muscles. Thus they are 11 pairs. They are external intercostal muscles and internal intercostal muscles. They are innervated by intercostal nerves.

Diaphragm: It is a large dome-shaped sheath of muscle. It separates thoracic cavity from abdominal cavity. It is innervated by phrenic nerve on each side.

DIGESTIVE SYSTEM

Digestive system consists of gastrointestinal tract and various glands attached. Length of the tract is about 8-10 metres. It starts with mouth and ends with anus.

Various parts of the Digestive Tract

1. Mouth
2. Pharynx
3. Oesophagus
4. Stomach
5. Small intestine
6. Large intestine
7. Rectum
8. Anus.

Accessory organs of the digestive tract:

1. Teeth
2. Three pairs of salivary glands
3. Hepato biliary system
4. Pancreas.

Mouth

It is the first part of the digestive tract. It opens through upper and lower lips. Roof of the mouth is called palate. It is dome-shaped. Front part of the roof is hard palate and back part of the roof is soft palate. Walls of the mouth are formed by muscles of cheeks. Mouth is lined by mucous membrane. It is continuous with skin of lips and mucous lining of pharynx. Lips enclose orbicularis oris muscle. This muscle keeps the mouth closed. Pharyngeal tonsils are on either side at the back of oral cavity. Uvula hangs down from lower border of soft palate.

Tongue

Tongue is at the base of the mouth. It is a musculo-membranous structure. It consists of (1) Stratified and cornified epithelium, (2) Voluntary, cross striated muscle fibres and (3) Glands. Epithelium of tongue is modified into papillae and taste buds. Under surface of the anterior part of tongue is connected to the floor of the mouth by frenulum. Frenulum is a fold of mucous membrance.

Teeth

Man is provided with two sets of teeth in his life. First set is called Deciduous teeth or primary teeth. They are 10 + 10 in number. They erupt through the gums during first and second years of life. Second set starts replacing the first set at about sixth year and process is complete by twenty fifth year. Second set remains upto old age and is called as permanent teeth.

Permanant teeth are 16 + 16 in number. Four types of teeth are there. They are:

1. Incisor teeth (I)
2. Canine teeth (C)
3. Premolar teeth (P)
4. Molar teeth (M).

Upper teeth are attached to upper jaw and lower teeth are attached to lower jaw.

Arrangement of permanent teeth

	M	P	C	I		I	C	P	M
Right upper jaw	3	2	1	2	Left upper jaw	2	1	2	3
Right lower jaw	3	2	1	2	Left lower jaw	2	1	2	3

Structure of tooth: Each tooth consists of three parts. They are : 1. Root; 2. Neck; 3. Crown

Root is embedded in the alveolus of maxilla or mandible. Neck is the constricted part between root and crown. Crown is the part projecting beyond the gum.

Tooth is composed of three substances. They are:

1. Dentine; 2. Enamel; 3. Cementum

Dentine forms major part of tooth. Enamel is the outer covering of crown.

It is the hardest substance. Cementum is in the neck. It is as hard as bone.

Crowns of Incisor teeth are chisel shaped. Crowns of canine teeth are large and conical. Crowns of premolar teeth are bicuspid and almost circular. Crowns of molar teeth are broad and tetra or penta cuspid.

Salivary glands

There are three pairs of salivary glands in the mouth. They are:

1. Parotid
2. Submandibular and
3. Sublingual glands.

1. **Parotid glands:** They are the biggest salivary glands. One gland is present below each ear. Each gland opens on inner side of cheek opposite to the second upper molar teeth through its duct. Ducts of the parotid glands are called Stenson's ducts.
2. **Submandibular glands :** They are also called Submaxillary glands. They are smaller than parotid glands. One on each side lies under the angle of jaw. Each submandibular gland has a duct called Wharton's gland. They open near the mid line under the tongue.
3. **Sublingual glands :** They are the smallest salivary glands. They lie under the tongue. They pour their secretions into the mouth through several openings.

Pharynx

Pharynx lies between mouth and oesophagus. It is divided into (1) Nasopharynx, (2) Oropharynx and (3) Laryngopharynx. It serves commonly for both digestive and respiratory systems. Base of the skull forms its roof. There lies a lymph node called adenoid at the back of nasopharynx.

Oesophagus

It is a muscular tube extending between pharynx and stomach.

Trachea and vertebral column lie in the front and back of oesophasus respectively. It lies in both thoracic and abdominal cavities. It passes from thoracic cavity into abdominal cavity through oesophagal opening of the diaphragm. On each side of upper part of oesophagus, are present - corresponding common carotid artery and part of thyroid gland. Oesophagus begins at the level of 6th vertebra, enters the abdomen at the level of tenth thoracic vertebra and ends at the level of 11th thoracic vertebra.

Cross-section of oesophagus shows similar structure as remainder of alimentary canal. It shows the following layers.

(1) Muscular coat, (2) Submucous coat and (3) Mucous coat.

It is devoid of Serosa. Upper one third of oesophagus consists of striated muscles. Lower one third contains smooth muscles and middle one third contains both types of muscles.

Stomach

Stomach is the most dilated part of digestive tract. It is **J** shaped. It is situated between the end of the oesophagus and begining of the small intestine. It lies below the diaphragm in the abdominal cavity. Its major part is to the left of the mid line. It distends when it is filled with food. Average capacity of stomach is 1.5 L in an adult. Stomach has two surfaces, two curvatures, two ends, three parts and two sphincters. They are as follows.

The two surfaces of stomach are: 1. Anterior surface and 2. Posterior surface.

Two curvatures are: 1. Lesser curvature and 2. Greater curvature.

Three parts of stomach are :

1. Fundus (upper portion) - above the cardiac sphincter.
2. Body (middle portion) - between fundus and pylorus.
3. Pylorus (lower portion) - below incisura angularis. Pylorus is subdivided into pyloric antrum and pyloric canal.

Two ends of stomach are:

1. Cardiac end guarded by cardiac sphincter.
2. Pyloric end guarded by pyloric sphincter.

Two sphincters of stomach are:

1. Cardiac sphincter (at the beginning)
2. Pyloric sphincter (at the ending)

Histologically, it shows

1. Outer serous coat, which is the visceral layer of peritoneum.
2. Muscular coat made of three layers consisting of longitudinal, circular and oblique unstripped muscle fibres.
3. Submucous layer made of loose areolar tissue.
4. Mucous membrane containing numerous folds called as rugae.

Small intestine

It is a coiled tubular structure about 6 metres long. It extends from pyloric sphincter to its junction with large intestine at the ileo-caecal valve. It lies within the curves of large intestine in the central and lower parts of abdominal cavity.

It is divided into three parts. They are:

1. Duodenum, 2. Jejunum and 3. Ileum

Duodenum: It is the first part of small intestine. It is C shaped. Duct from gall bladder, bile duct and pancreatic duct open into duodenum through the hepatopancreatic ampulla. Hepatopancreatic ampulla is guarded by a sphincter like muscle. Head of the pancreas lies in the curve of duodenum.

Jejunum: Jejunum is the upper two fifth part of remainder of the small intestine. It lies in between duodenum and ileum. It is bound behind by a fold of peritoneum called mesentery which carries blood vessels, autonomic nerves and lymphatics to jujunum. It has several glands.

Ileum : It is the distal three fifth of long and coiled up small intestine. It extends between Jejunum and caecum (begining of large intestine). There are number of peyer's patches in ileum. They are minute lymphoid structures. Ileum has similar structure as Jejunum but more villi. Ileum also contains digestive glands. But they are less than in the jejunum.

Structure of small intestine : It contains four layers similarly as the remainder of alimentary tract. They are:

1. Serous coat, formed of peritoneum (Serosa)
2. Muscular coat with a thin external layer of longitudinal fibres and a thick internal layer of circular fibres. (Muscularis externa).
3. Submucous coat containing blood vessels, lymph vessels and nerves (submucosa). It contains Brunner glands.
4. Mucous membrane (Muscularis interna/ Muscularis mucosa)

Structure of small intestine contains goblet cells in addition to villi. They produce mucus.

Lining of the mucous membrane has the following three features. They are

1. Mucous membrane contains circular folds. Unlike the rugae of the stomach, they are permanent. They enhance the surface area available for absorption.
2. It contains fine hair like projections called villi, each contains a lymph vessel called lacteal and blood vessels.
3. It is supplied with glands of simple, tubular type. They secrete intestinal juice.

Small intestine contains lymphoid tissue considerably. Mucous membrane contains solitary lymphatic follicles. They are most numeroues in the lower part of ileum.

Large intestine

Ileum of the small intestine merges into large intestine. There is ileocecal valve at the junction of ileum and large intestine. Colon measures about 1.5 metres in length.

Large intestine consists of the following parts:

1. Caecum
2. Vermiform appendix
3. Ascending colon
4. Transverse colon
5. Descending colon
6. Sigmoid colon.

1. Caecum: It is a short rounded sac. It lies in the right iliac fossa. It begins at the ileocecal valve where ileum and caecum join. It is continuous with ascending colon.

2. **Vermiform appendix:** It springs out from caecum at about an inch from ileocecal valve. Lumen of the appendix communicates with that of caecum. It contains same four layers as intestine but the submucous layer contains lymphoid tissue. It is a vestegeal organ in human body.
3. **Ascending colon:** It ascends upwards from crecum and infront of right kidney. It turns to left below the liver. It forms into transverse colon.
4. **Transverse colon:** It lies transversely below the stomach. It is suspended from its own mesentery from the posterior abdominal wall. It extends to the left and merges with descending colon at the lower surface of spleen. It extends between the lower surfaces of liver and spleen.
5. **Descending colon:** It is situated vertically on the left side of abdomen. It extends from transverse colon and merges with sigmoid colon.
6. **Sigmoid colon:** It lies in the pelvis. Hence it is also called pelvic colon. It is situated at the left. It forms loops. It has a mesentery of its own. It continues below with rectum.

Structure of large intestine: Large intestine has the same structure of small intestine. Difference is - longitudinal muscles are arranged in three bands. Mucous membrane does not contain villi.

Rectum: It is a straight tube lying in lower posterior part of pelvic region. It is 12 cm long and extends from sigmoid colon to anal canal. It is situated behind urinary bladder, prostate and seminal vesicles in males and behind uterus and vagina in females. It lies as a straight tube on the inside of sacrum and coccyx. Mucous coat of rectum has longitudinal and transverse folds. Lower portion of rectum is called rectal ampulla. Rectal ampulla is a dilated part.

Anus : Rectum ends in anus. It is about 1 inch long. It is a small canal guarded by two sphincters. Internal sphincter is involuntary and external sphincter is voluntary.

Peritoneum

Peritoneum is a serous membrane. In males it is a closed sac lining the abdomen. In females, free ends of uterine tubes open into peritoneal cavity.

Peritoneum consists of two layers. They are

1. Parietal layer lining the walls of abdominal cavity.
2. Visceral layer covering the abdominal organs.

Peritoneal cavity: It is the space between parietal and visceral layers of peritoneum.

Omenta: Folds of the peritoneum connected to stomach are called omenta.

Omenta are divided into:

1. Greater omentum
2. Lesser omentum

Greater omentum hangs from lower border of stomach to the front surface of small intestine. Lesser omentum extends from lower border of liver to the lesser curvature of stomach.

Mesentery: Mesentery is the fold of peritoneum which attaches different parts of small intestine to the posterior abdominal wall. Blood vessels, nerves and lymphatics enter the intestines through mesentery.

Pelvic peritoneum: Part of the peritoneum lying in the pelvic region is called pelvic peritoneum.

Peritoneal ligaments: Folds of the peritoneum connecting organs like liver, uterus, etc., to the posterior part of abdominal wall are called peritoneal ligaments.

Pouch of Douglas: Sac of peritoneum between rectum and uterus is called pouch of Douglas.

Regions of abdomen: Abdomen is divided into nine regions.

1. Right hypochondrium
2. Epigastrium
3. Left hypochondrium

4. Right lumbar region
5. Umbilical region
6. Left lumbar region
7. Right iliac fossa
8. Hypo gastrium
9. Left iliac fossa.

Liver

Liver is the largest organ in abdomen. It is the largest gland in the body. It is situated in the upper right part of abdominal equity. It occupies almost entire hypochondrium. It lies below the diaphragm under the cover of lower ribs.

Lobes of liver : Falciform ligament divides it into two lobes. They are:

1. Right lobe
2. Left lobe.

Right lobe of the liver lies over the right colic flexure and right kidney. Left lobe lies over stomach, Right lobe is bigger than left lobe. On the inferior surface two bands are present. They subdivide liver into four compartments.

1. Right lobe
2. Left lobe
3. Quadrate lobe
4. Caudate lobe.

Lobules of liver: Liver consists of large number of hepatic lobules. They are hexagonal in shape. Diameter of each lobule is about 1 mm. Each lobule has a small central intra lobular vein, which is a tributary of a hepatic vein.

Portal canals are present around the edges of lobules. Each portal canal contains:

1. inter lobular vein
2. a branch of hepatic artery, and
3. a small bile duct.

These three structures together are called portal triad. Lobules consist of liver cells. These cells are large cells. Liver cells are arranged in sheets of one cell thickness. They are called hepatic laminae. Spaces between laminae contain small veins with many anastomoses and small bile ducts called canaliculi.

Surfaces of Liver:

1. Superior surface
2. Inferior surface
3. Anterior surface
4. Posterior surface.

Superior surface of liver is in contact with inferior surface of diaphragm.

Inferior surface faces abdominal viscera.

Anterior surface is separated from ribs and costal cartilages by diaphragm.

Posterior surface lies in front of vertebral column, aorta, inferior venacavae and lower end of oesophagus.

Blood supply

Hepatic artery and portal vein carry blood to liver. Hepatic artery supplies oxygenated blood to liver. It is a branch of coeliac plexus. It in turn arises from abdominal aorta. Portal vein brings blood to liver from stomach, spleen and intestines. It divides into inter lobular veins. They subdivide and finally form central veins. One central vein lies in centre of each lobule. These central veins unite to form sublobular veins. Sublobular veins unite to form hepatic veins.

These hepatic veins join with inferior venacava and drain impure blood of liver into inferior venacava.

Biliary system

Biliary system consists of:

1. Common hepatic duct formed by the union of right and left hepatic ducts from liver.
2. Gall bladder
3. Cystic duct from gall bladder
4. Common bile duct formed by union of common hepatic duct and cystic duct.

Gall bladder: Gall bladder is a pear-shaped organ situated at the under surface of right lobe of liver.

It consists of three parts.

1. Fundus, 2. Body and 3. Neck.

Layers of gall bladder: It consists of three layers. They are:

1. Outer serous coat
2. Middle muscular coat
3. Inner mucous coat.

Pancreas

Pancreas is a soft greyish pink-coloured gland. It is about 12 to 15 cm long. It lies transversely across the posterior abdominal wall behind the stomach.

Pancreas has three parts.

1. Head, 2. Body and 3. Tail.

Head of the pancreas lies within the curve of duodenum. Tail extends as far as the spleen. Body lies between head and tail. Pancreatic duct lies within the organ. Pancreatic duct joins bile duct at the head of the pancreas and opens together into duodenum at heptopancreatic ampulla.

Pancreas is composed of lobules. Each consists of tiny vessel. All these tiny vessels lead to the main duct and end in number of alveoli. Alveoli lined with cells secrete the enzymes trypsinogen, amylase and lipase. Collections of cells called Islets of langerhans are present in between the alveoli. Alpha cells constitute 25 per cent of total number of Islets and beta cells constitute 75 per cent of the total number of Islets.

CARDIO VASCULAR SYSTEM

Cardiovascular system consists of Heart and Vascular system. It is a well organised blood transport system of the body. Heart is the central pumping organ. Blood vessels constituting vascular system are arteries, arterioles, capillaries, venules and veins.

Anatomy of Heart

Heart lies on the left upper part of thoracic cavity. It lies between the two lungs under sternum. It is broad above and conical below.

Histology of Heart

Heart consists of three layers. They are:

1. **Pericardium:** Outermost layer consisting of
   (*a*) Visceral pericardium
   (*b*) Parietal pericardium
2. **Myocardium :** Middle layer made of cardiac muscle cells and interstitial cells.
3. **Endocardium :** Innermost layer.

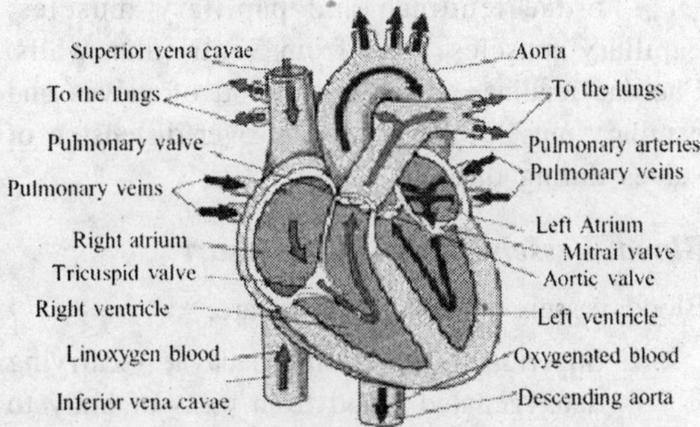

Fig. : *Structure of Heart*

Pericardium forms bag like structure between visceral and parietal layers containing pericardial fluid.

Chambers of Heart

Heart has four chambers. Two of them are upper chambers called atria or auricles. Lower two chambers are called ventricles. The two atria are separated by interatrial septum. The two ventricles are separated by interventricular septum.

Atria are filling chambers and ventricles are pumping chambers. Compared to atria, ventricles are thicker since they are pumping chambers. Of the two ventricles, wall of left ventricle is three times thicker than that of right ventricle since left ventricle pumps oxygenated blood to all parts of body and right ventricle pumps deoxygenated blood to lungs only.

Valves of Heart

Opening between right atrium and right ventricle is guarded by tricuspid valve. It prevents back entry of blood into right atrium from right ventricle at the beginning of ventricular systole. Opening between left atrium and left ventricle is guarded by bicuspid or mitral valve. It prevents back entry of blood into left atrium at the beginning of ventricular systole - Pulmonary trunk is guarded by tricuspid semilunar valve which prevents back flow into right ventricle at the begining of ventricular diastole. Aorta has tricuspid semilunar valve which prevents back flow of blood into left ventricle at the beginning of ventricular diastole.

Chordae tendinae and papillary muscles: Papillary muscles arise from ventricular walls. Chordae tendinae attach apical end of valves and papillary muscles. They prevent over distension of valves during diastole.

Blood Vessels attached to Heart

Blood vessels attached to heart are:

1. Superior and inferior venacavae - carrying deoxygenated blood from parts of body to right atrium.
2. Pulmonary artery carrying venous blood to lungs from right ventricle.
3. Pulmonary veins carrying oxygenated blood from lungs to the left atrium of heart.
4. Aorta carrying oxygenated blood to all parts of body from left ventricle of heart.

Blood vessels supplying oxygenated blood to heart : Right and left coronary arteries arising from Aorta supply oxygenated blood to heart.

Blood vessels draining heart: Coronary veins bring deoxygenated blood of heart into coronary sinus, which opens directly into right atrium.

Ductus arteriosus: Ductus arteriosus is the vestigeal remnant of cord like structure which existed in foetal life between arch of aorta and pulmonary trunk. In foetal life, it bypasses pulmonary circulation. After birth, it closes, becomes obsolete and atrophies.

Septum ovale: It is a crescenteric mark on interatrial septum. It is a closed foramen ovale that existed in foetus.

Foramen ovale : It is the opening in interatrial septum in foetal life. It avoids blood entry into lungs in foetal life. After birth, it closes and forms septum ovale.

Cardiac centres

1. Cardio inhibitory centre is a dorsal motor nucleus of vagus in medulla.
2. Cardio accelerator centre is situated in lateral horn cells of upper thoracic segments of spinal cord.

Nerve supply to Heart

Sympathetic and vagus nerves supply heart.

Conducting System of Heart

System of conducting impulses of cardiac contraction consists of:

1. Sinoatrial node (SA node)
2. Atrioventricular node (AV node)
3. Bundle of His
4. Right and left branches of bundle of His
5. Purkinje fibres.

SA node : It is present at the opening of superior venacava into right atrium. It is called pacemaker of heart. It is made of modified cardiac muscle fibres. It measures about 5 × 20 mm.

AV node : It is present in the right atrium at the posterior part of inter atrial septum. It is close to the opening of coronary sinus. Cells of AV node are cardiac muscle fibres having a few myofibrils. It measures about 2 × 5 mm.

Bundle of His: Main trunk of bundle of His is continuous with AV node. It passes through interventricular septum. It is about 20 mm long.

Right and left branches of bundle of His: Bundle of His is divided into right and left branches. Right branch is longer than left branch. Left branch bifurcates into superior and inferior divisions.

Purkinje fibres: They arise from branches of bundles of His. They spread from interventricular septum directly to papillary muscle and ultimately end in sub endocardial network. Purkinje fibres have larger diameter than ordinary cardiac muscle fibres. Purkinje fibres have diameter of 50-70 μ whereas cardiac muscle fibres have diameter of about 15 μ.

Anatomy of Vascular System

Blood vessels constitute vascular system. There are two types of blood vessels mainly. They are arteries and veins. Arteries are subdivided into arterioles. Arterioles end in capillaries. Capillaries are single layered thin vessels. Capillaries unite to form venules. Venules unite to form veins. Arteries are the vessels carrying oxygenated blood to tissues (except pulmonary arteries). Veins are the vessels carrying deoxygenated blood (except pulmonary veins).

Histology of Arteries and Veins: Arteries and veins consist of three layers

1. **Tunica externa :** The outer layer made of fibrous tissue and elastic tissue and also called tunica adventitia.
2. **Tunica media:** The middle layer of plain muscles and network of elastic fibres.
3. **Tunica interna:** The innermost layer made of endothelial cells and also called tunica intima.

Tunica media in arteries is thicker than in veins.

Valves of Veins: Valves are present in veins (of lower limbs particularly). They prevent back flow of blood from heart. These valves are semilunar pocket like flaps. They are formed by local folding of intima.

Vasavasorum: They are blood vessels supplying blood to large arteries and veins of above 0.1 mm diameter.

Sinusoids: Sinusoids and sinusoidal capillaries are not true capillaries. They have larger size than capillaries. Continuous endothelial lining is absent.

Arteries of the Body

Aorta, arising from left ventricle of heart is the main artery of body. It consists of three parts. They are:

1. **Ascending aorta,** giving off two branches
   (*i*) Right coronary artery
   (*ii*) Left coronary artery. Coronary arteries supply blood to heart.
2. **Arch of aorta:** Giving off three branches and supplying blood to head, neck and upper limb.
   Branches of arch of aorta are:
   (*i*) Innominate artery - dividing into
   (*a*) Common carotid artery
   (*b*) Right subclavian artery
   (*ii*) Left common carotid artery
   (*iii*) Left subclavian artery.
3. **Descending aorta :** divided into
   (*i*) Thoracic aorta - supplying blood to wall of chest cavity and viscera
   (*ii*) Abdominal aorta supplying wall of abdominal cavity and its viscera.

Right and left common carotid arteries are divided into:

(*a*) Internal carotid artery
(*b*) External carotid artery on right and left sides.

Branches of external Carotid artery

(*i*) Facial artery, supplying face
(*ii*) Maxillary artery, supplying jaws
(*iii*) Temporal artery supplying temporal parts in skull.
(*iv*) Occipital artery supplying occipital parts in skull.

Branches of Internal Carotid Artery

(*i*) Anterior cerebral artery supplying brain
(*ii*) Middle cerebral artery supplying brain and
(*iii*) Opthalmic artery, supplying eyes.

Circle of willis: Circle of willis is formed by cerebral arteries and branch of vertebral artery. Branch of vertebral artery is also called basilar artery.

Right and left subclavian arteries, their course and branches:

- Subclavian artery after entering axilla continues as axillary artery.
- It becomes brachial artery at lower boundary of axilla.

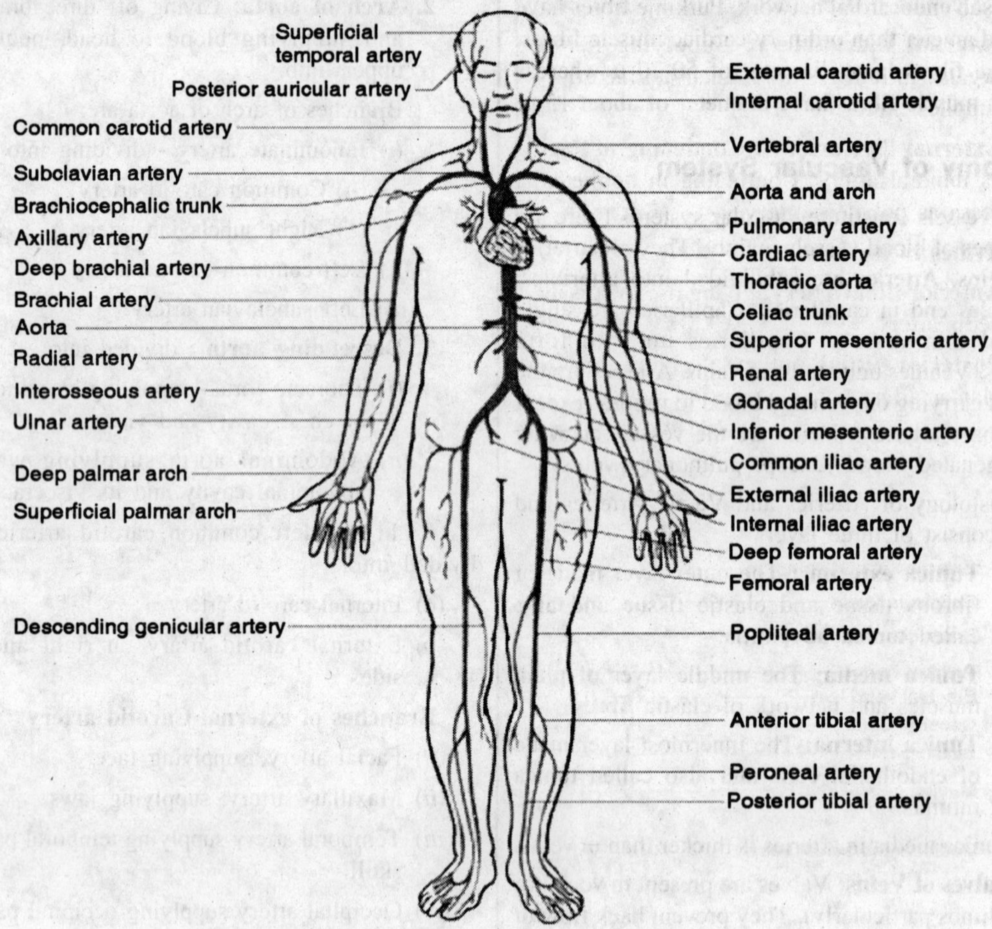

Fig : *Arteries of Human Body*

It runs down the arm and divides into:

(*a*) Radial artery (*b*) Ulnar artery

Palmar arch is formed by union of these two arteries in the palm.

Palmar arch is divided into digital arteries, which supply fingers.

Course of thoracic aorta: Descending aorta continues as thoracic aorta above diaphragm.

It, then continues as abdominal aorta below diaphragm.

Branches of abdominal aorta

They are:

(*i*) Coeliac plexus

(*ii*) Mesenteric arteries

(*iii*) Renal arteries

(*iv*) Final branches.

Coeliac plexus is divided into:

(*i*) Hepatic artery - supplying liver

(*ii*) Gastric artery - supplying stomach

(*iii*) Splenic artery - supplying spleen

Mesenteric arteries are:

(*i*) Superior mesenteric artery

(*ii*) Inferior mesenteric artery

Renal arteries supply kidney

Final branches are:

(*i*) Right common iliac artery

(*ii*) Left common iliac artery

These common iliac arteries are divided into:

(*i*) **Internal iliac artery:** Supplying pelvic organs. In females, its branch uterine artery supplies uterus.

(*ii*) **External iliac artery :** Continuing in thigh as femoral artery. Continuing in poplieteal fossa as polieteal artery.

It divides in leg into:

(*a*) **Anterior tibial artery:** giving rise to dorsalis pedis artery.

(*b*) **Posterior tibial artery :** giving rise to plantar artery.

Plantar arch is formed by union of dorsalis pedis and plantar artery. It is divided into digital branches supplying the toes.

Veins of the body

All the veins of the body join superior and inferior venacavae and drain the collected blood into right atrium of heart.

Superior venacava: Superior venacava is formed by union of right and left brachiocephalic veins collecting blood from head, neck, upper extremities and some part of thorax.

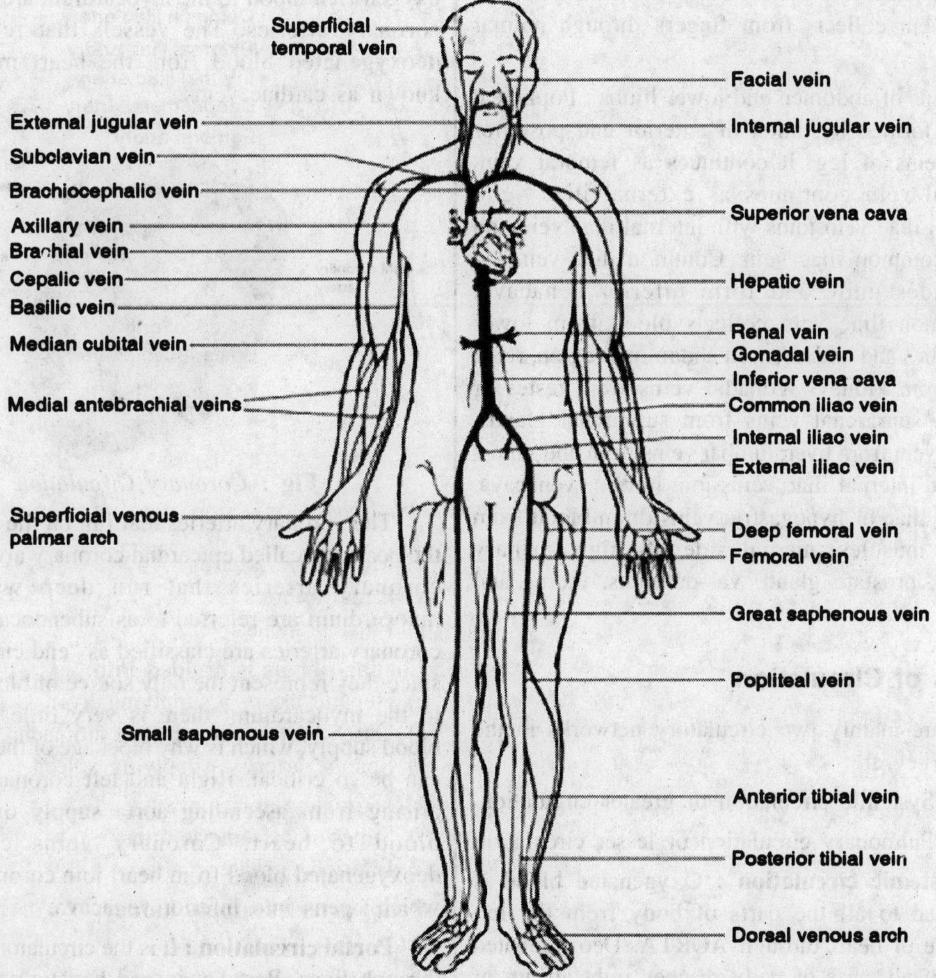

Fig : *Veins of Human Body*

Inferior venacava: Inferior venacava is formed by union of two common iliac veins collecting blood from lower extremities and abdomen. It extends upwards through abdomen and thorax and opens into right atrium.

Veins of the head, neck and upper limbs: Internal and external jugular veins drain head and neck. They join with subclavian veins forming brachiocephalic veins. Subclavian veins collect blood from upper limbs. Subclavian vein is axillary vein in axilla. It is formed by union of brachial, cephalic and basilic veins of upper arm. Radial and ulnar veins of forearms join with those of upper arms. Radial veins collect blood from metacarpals. Ulnar vein collects from fingers through palmar arch.

Veins of abdomen and lower limbs : Poplieteal vein is formed by union of anterior and posterior tibial veins of leg. It continues as femoral vein. Femoral vein continues as external iliac vein. External iliac vein joins with internal iliac vein and forms common iliac vein. Common iliac veins of both sides unite and form inferior venacava. Commmon iliac vein collects blood from lower extremities and abdomen. In abdominal region, renal veins from kidneys, gonadal veins from testes or ovaries, suprarenal veins from suprarenal glands, hepatic vein from liver, lumbar veins from abdominal wall and internal iliac veins join inferior venacava. Internal iliac or hypogastric veins drain blood from gluteal muscles, medial side of thigh, urinary bladder, prostate gland, vas-deferens, uterus and vagina.

Types of Circulation

There are mainly two circulatory networks in the body. They are:

1. Systemic circulation or greater circulation
2. Pulmonary circulation or lesser circulation

Systemic circulation : Oxygenated blood is circulated to all the parts of body from the left ventricle of heart through AORTA. Deoxygenated blood of all parts of body reaches right atrium of heart through SUPERIOR and INFERIOR VENACAVA. This is the major circulatory network of body and called systemic circulation or greater circulation.

Pulmonary circulation : Deoxygenated blood reaching right atrium goes into right ventricle and from here, it reaches lungs through pulmonary artery. After losing CO_2 in lungs, it gets oxygenated and reaches left atrium of heart through PULMONARY VEINS. It is called pulmonary circulation or lesser circulation.

Coronary circulation : Coronary circulation is the circulation of blood in the blood vessels of the heart muscle (myocardium). The vessels that deliver oxygen-rich blood to the myocardium are known as coronary arteries. The vessels that remove the deoxygenated blood from the heart muscle are known as cardiac veins.

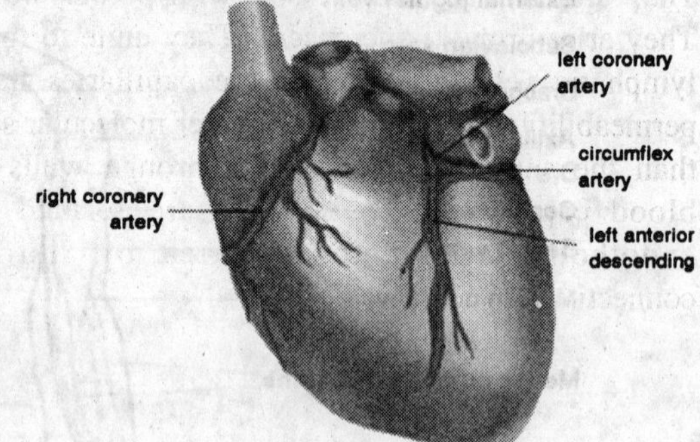

Fig : *Coronary Circulation*

The coronary arteries that run on the surface of the heart are called epicardial coronary arteries. The coronary arteries that run deep within the myocardium are referred to as subendocardial. The coronary arteries are classified as "end circulation", since they represent the only source of blood supply to the myocardium: there is very little redundant blood supply, which is why blockage of these vessels can be so critical. Right and left coronary arteries arising from ascending aorta supply oxygenated blood to heart. Coronary veins collecting deoxygenated blood from heart join coronary sinus, which opens into inferior venacava.

Portal circulation : It is the circulatory network through liver. Portal vein and hepatic artery bring blood to liver. Portal vein carries blood into liver through superior mesenteric and splenic veins. Superior mesenteric vein carries blood from mesenteric bed (stomach, small intestine, part of large intestine and pancreas). Splenic vein carries from spleen. Hepatic artery carries oxygenated blood to liver. Capillaries of portal vein join with capillaries of hepatic artery. Hepatic vein carries blood circulated in liver to right atrium of heart through inferior venacava. This circulatory network of liver is called portal circulation.

LYMPHATIC SYSTEM

Lymphatic system is a closed system consisting of 1. Lymphatic capillaries, 2. Lymphatic vessels 3. Lymph nodes and 4. Lymph ducts.

Lymphatic Capillaries

They are fine hair like vessels with porous walls. They arise in the tissue spaces. They unite to form lymphatic vessels. Walls of the capillaries have permeability to substances of greater molecular size than the substances permeable through walls of blood capillaries. Their walls are formed by endothelial cells and supported by fibrous connective tissues.

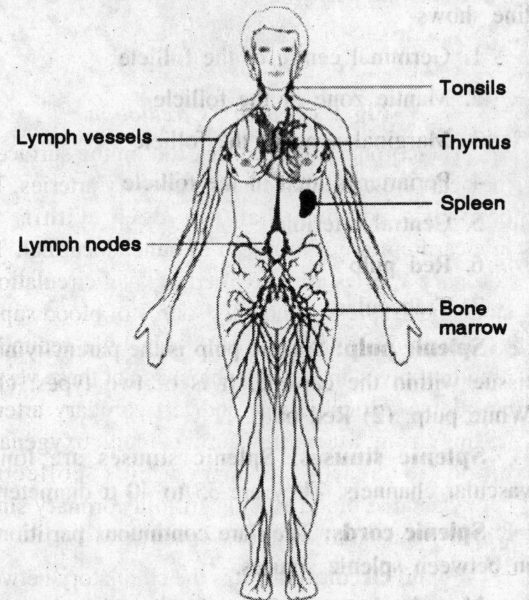

Fig : *Lymphatic System*

Lymphatic Vessels

Lymphatic capillaries unite to form lymph vessels. They have one sided valves. They are superficially and deeply located. They are found in skin, muscles and several visceral organs. Various lymphatic vessels are linked together by free anastamoses. Lymph vessels pass through lymph nodes. They gradually increase in size. Finally lymph collected from the body pours into right lymphatic duct and left lymphatic duct. Left lymphatic duct is also called thoracic duct.

Lymph Nodes

Lymph nodes are small bodies made of lymphatic tissue. They vary in size from pin head to almond. They are important glandular structures spread at all strategic points in the body. They are located both superficially and deeply. Lymphatic vessels bring lymph to lymph nodes. They divide within the node and discharge lymph. Again lymph is gathered into fresh lymphatic vessels which empty lymph into lymphatic ducts after carrying the lymph through more lymph nodes. Lymphatic vessels entering into the lymph node are called afferent lymph vessels. Lymph vessels leaving the lymph nodes are called efferent lymph vessels.

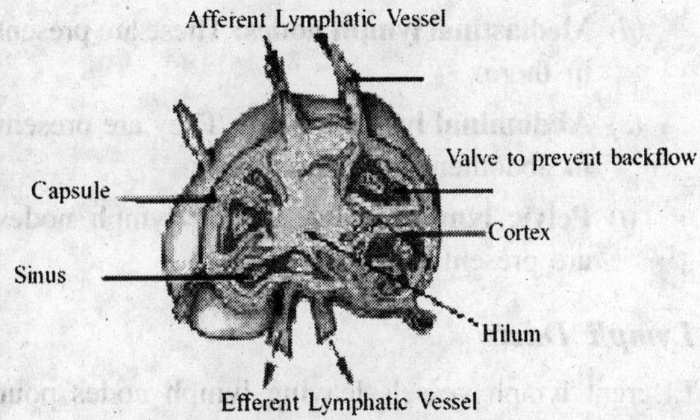

Fig : *L.S. of Lymph node*

Histology of Lymph node : Histology of lymph node shows three parts. They are: Cortex, medulla & hilum.

1. Cortex: Cortex is the outer part of lymph node. It contains lymphatic nodules peripherally and germinal centres in the inner zone. Germinal centres present in the lymph nodes produce lymphocytes. Lymph sinuses separate lymph nodules from capsule.

2. **Medulla:** It is the inner part of lymph node. It is devoid of lymph nodules. It contains reticulo-endothelial cells. It also contains a few giant cells.
3. **Hilum:** It is the depression at one side of lymph node or lymph gland. Through hilum, an artery enters and there is an exit to a vein and an efferent lymphatic vessel. Afferent lymph vessels enter from all sides but efferent lymph vessels leave through hilum. Chief efferent vessel leaving lymph node carries filtered and lymphocyte enriched lymph fluid.

Naming of lymph nodes: Lymph nodes are named accordingly as they are located. They are:

(*a*) **Cubital and axillary lymph nodes:** They are situated in arms.

(*b*) **Poplietal and inguinal:** Lymph nodes situated in legs are named so.

(*c*) **Submaxillary and cervical lymph nodes:** Lymph nodes present in the neck are called submaxillary and cervical lymph nodes.

(*d*) **Mediastinal lymph nodes:** These are present in thorax.

(*e*) **Abdominal lymph nodes:** They are present in abdomen, ex: Mesenteries

(*f*) **Pelvic lymph nodes:** Pelvic lymph nodes are present in pelvic organs.

Lymph Ducts

Efferent lymph vessels leaving lymph nodes pour lymph into right lymphatic duct and left lymphatic duct (thoracic duct). Thoracic duct is comparatively large than right lymphatic duct. It begins at cisterna chyli. Cisterna chyli is a small pouch at the back of the abdomen. Lymphatic vessels from lower limbs, abdominal and pelvic organs empty into this pouch. From cysterna chyli, thoracic duct runs up through mediastinum behind the heart to the root of the neck. Here, it turns to the left where lymphatic vessels from the left side of head, thorax and left upper limp join. Thoracic duct finally empties into left subclavian vein at its junction with left internal jugular vein. It is provided with unidirectional valves to prevent lymph from flowing in wrong direction. Right lymphatic duct is comparatively small. It is formed by joining of lymphatic vessels from right side of head, thorax and right upper limb at the root of neck. It enters into right subclavian vein, where it joins right internal jugular vein. Lymphatic ducts thus gather lymph from all the body and return it to blood stream.

Spleen

Spleen is the largest lymphoid tissue in the body. It is a bean-shaped, fist-sized organ. It is a highly vascular organ. It is located in the left hypochondrium beneath the diaphragm. It is above the left kidney and descending colon and behind the stomach. It weighs about 150 g. in adult human being and does not contain afferent lymphatic vessels. It is haemopoietic.

SPLEEN (follicle), stained with haematoxylin and eosin - lymphoid follicle, circled with dotted line shows-

1. Germinal centre of the follicle
2. Mantie zone of the follicle
3. Marginal zone of the follicle
4. Periarterial area of the follicle
5. Central arteriole
6. Red pulp
7. Trabeculae.

Splenic pulp: Splenic pulp is the parenchymal tissue within the capsule. It is of two types: (1) White pulp, (2) Red pulp.

Splenic sinuses: Splenic sinuses are long vascular channels. They are 35 to 40 μ diameter.

Splenic cords: They are continuous partitions in between splenic sinuses.

Marginal zone: It is the junctional zone between white pulp and red pulp.

Tonsils

Tonsils are well-defined organs of accumulated lymphoid tissue in the mucous membrane at the root of tongue. Tonsils are present at the surrounding of pharynx, where nasal and oral passages unite. Tonsils do not possess afferent lymphatic vessels.

Tonsils can be divided into three groups.

1. **Palantine tonsils:** Covered with stratified squamous epithelium.
2. **Lingual tonsil:** Situated at the root of tongue.
3. **Pharyngeal tonsils:** One on each side in the median posterior wall of nasopharynx.

Thymus

Thymus is partly an endocrine gland and partly a lymphoid structure. It is present in anterior and superior mediastinum of thorax. It extends from pericardium up into neck. It consists of two lobes.

Histology of thymus shows:

1. Capsule
2. Cortex
3. Medulla

BONES AND JOINTS

Bones and Joints form the skeletal system of body. There are about 206 bones in human body. Main functions of skeletal system are:

1. Giving support and protection to soft tissues and vital organs.
2. Giving attachment to muscles and assisting in body movements.
3. Formation of blood cells in the red bone marrow.
4. Storage of mineral salts like calcium and phosphorous.

Composition of Bone

Bone is structurally a complex organ and has the following composition.

Water	:	25%
Ossein, Osseomucoid and Osseo Albumin (organic solids)	:	35%
Inorganic salts of calcium	:	45%

Calcium salts impart hardness to bones.

Functions of bone marrow

Bone marrow performs the following functions:

1. Formation of blood cells (Haemopoeisis)
2. Destruction of old RBC with the help of reticulo endothelial cells (haemolysis)
3. Protection of body against infections by microbes with the help of reticulo endothelial cells against foreign particles (Defence mechanism)
4. Against foreign particles (Defence mechanism).

Ossification

Ossification is the process of bone formation. Development of bones takes place from spindle-shaped cells called osteoblasts. There are two types of ossification. They are:

1. Intra-membranous ossification
2. Intra-cartilaginous ossification

1. **Intra-membranous ossification:** Type of ossification in which, dense connective tissue is replaced by deposits of calcium, forming bone is called as intra-membranous ossification.

   Ex: Bones of skull are formed by this process.

2. **Intra-cartilaginous ossification :** Type of ossification in which, cartilages are replaced by bone is called intra-cartilaginous ossification. Most of the bones of the body are formed by this process.

Types of Bones

Bones are mainly of five types. They are:

1. Long bones

2. Short bones
3. Flat bones
4. Irregular bones
5. Seasmoid bones.

1. **Long bones:** Long bones are found in limbs. A long bone has two ends. Ends of a long bone are called epiphyses. These two ends are connected by shaft, which is called diaphysis. Periosteum is the outer membrane covering the bone. Periosteum is followed by layer of compact bone. Central medullary canal is inside this.

   Through nutrient foramen, arteries enter. Medullary canal contains yellow bone marrow. Extremities consist of mass of spongy bone, which contains red bone marrow. Yellow bone marrow contains fat and blood cells but is not rich in blood supply or red blood cells. Long bones develop from three centres called centres of ossification. Centre of ossification present in shaft is called diaphysis and centres of ossification present at the ends of the bones are called epiphyses. Line of cartilage between epiphysis and diaphysis is called epiphyseal cartilage or epiphyseal plate. Epiphyseal plate separates epiphysis and diaphysis approximately upto 25 years of age. After this age, fusion of diaphysis and epiphysis takes place. After fusion, growth in length of bone becomes impossible. Acromegaly is growth of bone occurrings after fusion of diaphysis and epiphysis by the overactivity of growth hormone. It will be confined mostly to the bones of face and limbs. This growth will be abnormal. Gigantism is growth occurring in immature bones before fusion of diaphysis with epiphysis due to excessive secretion of growth hormone.

2. **Short bones :** Short bones do not have shaft. They contain spongy substance covered by shell of compact bone, ex: small bones of wrist and ankle.

3. **Flat bones:** They contain two layers of compact bone with spongy substance between the two layers. They are found in pelvis and scapula.

4. **Irregular bones:** Bones which do not fall into any category are irregular bones, ex: vertebrae and bones of face.

5. **Seasmoid bones:** They are small bones and develop in tendons of muscles, ex: Patella of knee joint.

Bones of the Human Body

Total 206 bones forming the human skeleton can be divided into

1. **Bones of Axial skeleton:**
   (*i*) *Bones of skull:* Bones of cranium, Bones of face.
   (*ii*) *Bones of trunk:* Sternum, Ribs, Vertebral column
2. **Bones of appendicular skeleton:**
   (*i*) Bones of upper limbs
   (*ii*) Bones of lower limbs

Bones of Axial Skeleton

Bones of skull: Skull is a large bony structure containing cranium and bones of face attached to cranium.

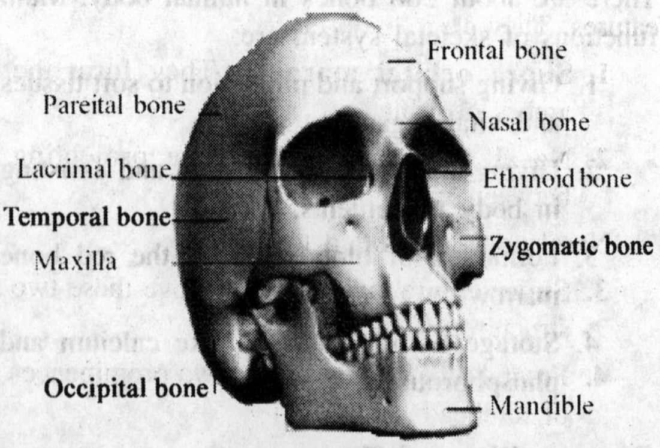

Fig : *Bones of Skull*

Bones of Cranium: Cranium is called brain box. It is a large, hollow bony case. It is formed by fusion of various bones with zigzag edges. Cranium is formed by 8 bones. They are:

1. Frontal bone - 1
2. Parietal bones - 2
3. Temporal bones - 2
4. Occipital bone - 1
5. Sphenoid bone - 1
6. Ethmoid bone - 1

Sutures of the Cranium

Immovable joints of bones of skull are called sutures. Important sutures of cranium are:

1. Coronal suture
2. Sagital suture
3. Lambdoid suture.

Coronal suture: Coronal suture is the immovable joint between frontal bone and parietal bones.

Sagital suture: Sagital suture is the immovable joint between the two parietal bones.

Lambdoid suture: Lambdoid suture is the immovable joint between occipital bone and parietal bones.

Frontal bone: It is in the front central portion of cranium. It is joined with two parietal bones. It extends upto forehead and forms roof of orbital and nasal cavities.

Features of frontal bone: It has the following features. They are:

1. **Supra orbital margins:** They form the arches of orbit.
2. **Nasal notch:** It is the bone projecting between supra orbital margins.

Nasal bones are fitted to this.

3. **Super ciliary arch:** It lies above these two structures.
4. Frontal tuberosities are the two prominences of forehead.

Parietal bones

Parietal bones are two in number. They form the roof and sides of the skull. They are of quadrilateral shape. Prominence of parietal bone is called parietal tuberosity. Inner surface of parietal bone is concave. Superior and inferior temporal lines run parallelly.

A parietal bone has joint with:

—frontal bone anteriorly
—occipital bone posteriorly
—other parietal bone medially and
—temporal bone inferiorly.

Temporal Bones

Temporal bones are two in number. They form lower part of sides of skull.

Temporal bones have joint with:

—sphenoid bone in the front
—parietal bones above
—occipital bone behind.

A temporal bone has the following parts.

(*a*) **Squamous part:** It is flat part having zygomatic process.
(*b*) **Petrous part:** It forms the bone of internal ear.
(*c*) **Mastoid part:** It contains mastoid process.
(*d*) **Tympanic part:** It contains external auditory meatus.

Occipital Bone

Features of occipital bone: An occipital bone has the following features.

(*a*) **External occipital protruberance:** It is a prominence of occipital bone. It gives attachment to muscles.
(*b*) **Foramen magnum:** It is a large oval opening below the external occipital protruberance. Cranial cavity communicates with vertebral canal through this opening.
(*c*) **Occipital condyles:** They are two in number. They lie on each side of foramen magnum. They articulate with atlas. This joint allows nodding movement of head.

Sphenoid Bone

It is one in number. It is situated at the base of the skull infront of temporal bones. It forms large part of middle cranial fossa. It is shaped like a Figat with outstretching.

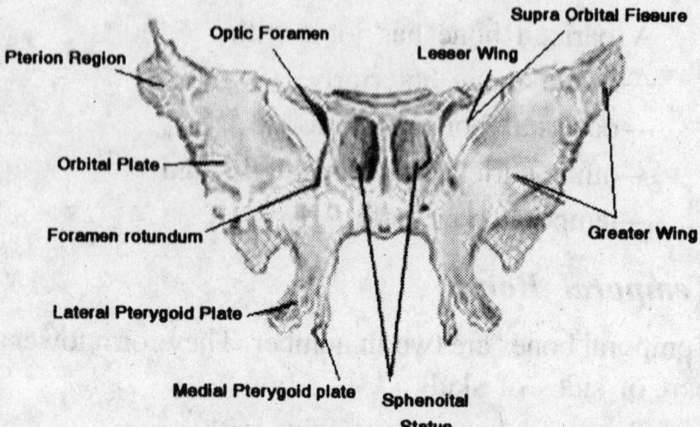

Fig.: Sphenoid Bone

(*a*) **Body:** Body contains two large air sinuses. They communicate with nasal cavity. Body also has a deep depression called hypophyseal fossa, which contains pituitary gland. Hypophyseal fossa is also called sella turica.

(*b*) **Wings:** These wing like structures are called greater and lesser wings. They have many openings for passage of nerves and blood vessels.

Ethmoid bone: It is one in number. It is cubical in shape. It fills the space between orbits. Ethmoid bone consists of three parts. They are:

(*a*) Cribriform plate

(*b*) Perpendicular plate

(*c*) Labyrinths

Cribriform plate is a small horizontal plate perforated with number of fine openings through which branches of olfactory nerve pass from nose to the brain. Perpendicular plate descends from cribriform plate. It forms upper part of nasal septum. Two labyrinths each consisting of a number of ethmoidal sinuses are thin walled and communicate with nasal cavity.

Superior and middle nasal conchae are thin plates of ethmoid bone. Inferior nasal conchae are curved plates of bone which lie in the walls of the nasal cavity below superior and middle nasal conchae of ethmoid bone.

Cranial Fossae

Base of the skull is divided into three fossae.

They are:

1. Anterior cranial fossa
2. Middle cranial fossa
3. Posterior cranial fossa.

Anterior cranial fossa is formed by horizontal plates of frontal bone. Middle cranial fossa is formed by sphenoid bone and petrous portion of temporal bones. Posterior cranial fossa is formed by occipital bone.

Fontanelles

Due to incomplete ossification of skull bones of child at birth, membranes fill the space between bones. These membranes at the angles of bones are called fontanelles. They are:

1. Anterior fontanelle
2. Posterior fontanelle.

Anterior fontanelle: It is the largest fontanelle present at the junction of frontal and two parietal bones where coronal and sagital sutures meet. It closes at the age of 1½ years.

Posterior fontanelle : It is the fontanelle present at the junction of parietal bones and occipital bone. It closes as soon as birth takes place.

Sinuses : Sinuses are the cavities in the bones of skull and communicating with nose. They are

1. Frontal sinuses
2. Maxillary sinuses
3. Ethmoidal and sphenoidal sinuses.

Frontal sinuses are a pair of sinuses present in frontal bones. They are present one on each side of the root of the nose. Maxillary sinuses are a pair of sinuses in maxillary bones - each lying on each side of nose. Ethmoidal and sphenoidal sinuses are also present in skull.

Functions of Sinuses

Functions of Sinuses are:

1. Lightening of bones of face and cranium
2. Giving resonance to voice.

Bones of the face

Bones making the face are 14 in number. They are:

Maxillae - 2 (upper jaw)

Mandible - 1 (lower jaw)

Zygomatic bones - 2 (cheek bones)

Palate bones - 2 (roof of mouth cavity and hard palate)

Lacrimal boness - 2

Nasal bones - 2 (Nasal bridge)

Turbinate bones - 2 (Nasal conchae)

Vomer - 1 (Lower part of nasal septum)

Maxillae

They are two in number.

They form the upper jaw.

Features of Maxillae

1. Body is pyramidal in shape.
2. Zygomatic process, palatine process, alveolar process and frontal process are present. Alveolar process contains upper teeth.
3. Maxillary sinus is present in internal aspect.

Mandible: It forms the lower jaw. It is the only movable bone of skull.

Features of Mandible

1. Body is horizontal part in the centre. It contains lower teeth. It forms chin.
2. Two rami are present one on each side. Each ramus contains coronoid process in the front. Condyle of jaw lies behind.

Zygomatic bones: They are two in number. They are irregular bones forming the prominence of cheek and part of walls of orbit. Each of them contains temporal process which articulates with zygomatic process of temporal bone to form zygomatic arch.

Palate bones: They are two in number. They are irregular bones forming part of the hard palate, lateral wall of nasal cavity and floor of orbit.

Nasal bones: They are two in number. They are small bones situated in between sockets of orbits. They form nasal ridge.

Turbinate bones: They are two in number. They are called nasal conchae.

Lachrymal bones: They are the smallest bones. They are fragile. They form part of walls of orbits. Grooved part of lacrimal bones contains lacrimal sac and nasolacrimal duct.

Vomer: It is one in number. It is a flat bone. It forms lower part of nasal septum. It is a vertical bone.

Hyoid bone: It is a 'U' shaped bone. It has a body and two horns (lesser horn and greater horn). It lies at the base of the tongue. It is attached to the styloid processes of temporal bone by means of ligaments.

Bones of Trunk

Bones of trunk are - Sternum, ribs, vertebral column.

Sternum : It is a long flat bone. It runs down the front of thorax. It is divided into three parts.

(*a*) Manubrium sterni

(*b*) Body - also called mesosternum

(*c*) Xiphoid process

Manubrium sterni: Manubrium sterni is triangular and articulates on either side with clavicle, first and second costal cartilages.

Features of Manubrium sterni

(*a*) Clavicular notches : on both sides for articulation with clavicle.

(*b*) Suprasternal notch : between clavicular notches.

(*c*) Articular surfaces : on both sides for first rib.

Body: Body is longer and narrower than manubrium sterni. There is a small notch where it joins the manubrium.

Xiphoid process: Xiphoid process is small. It is the lowest part of sternum. Diaphragm, linea alba and rectus abdominus muscles are attached to this part of sternum.

Ribs: They are 12 pairs of arched bones attached on back side to thoracic vertebrae.

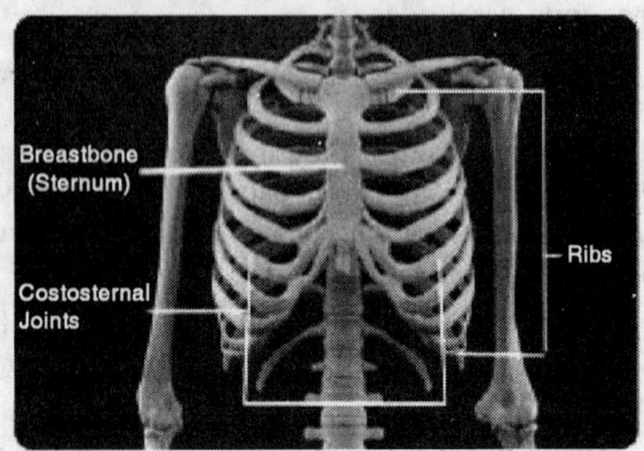

Fig. : *Ribs*

Features of a rib: A rib has (*a*) Anterior end, (*b*) Posterior end and (*c*) Shaft.

(*a*) Anterior or sternal end has depressions for attachment of costal cartilage

(*b*) Posterior or vertebral end - It has three parts: 1. Head, 2. Neck and 3. Tuberclec.

Shaft : It has two surfaces:

1. Inner surface, 2. Outer surface.

It has two borders:

1. Upper border, 2. Lower border.

Sub costal groove contains intercostal vessels and nerve.

Classification of ribs: On the basis of attachment to sternum, they are classified as:

1. *True ribs* - attached to the sternum directly. First seven pairs are true ribs.
2. *False ribs* - attached to the sternum through costal cartilages. Remaining five pairs are false ribs. Of these, last two pairs are known as floating ribs.

Costal cartilages: They are bars of hyaline cartilage connecting ribs and sternum.

Vertebral column: Vertebral column is a powerful and flexible pillar made of a number of irregular bones called vertebrae. There are 33 vertebrae connected to one another. They have limited movement. Vertebral column provides central axis. It provides protection to spinal cord.

Structure of a typical vertebrum: Except atlas and axis, remaining vertebrae have common features. Each vertebra consists of :

(*a*) Body - cylindrical in shape and lying to the front.

(*b*) Vertebral arch (also called neural arch) - posterior part. It encloses vertebral foramen.

(*c*) Vertebral foramen - Spinal cord passes through this foramen.

(*d*) Spinous process - directed backwards and downwards.

(*e*) Two transverse processes - projecting laterally for attachment of muscles and ligaments.

(*f*) Four Articular processes - Two above, Two below. They meet corresponding processes of adjoining vertebrae.

(*g*) Laminae - wide parts of arch carrying spinous process.

(*h*) Intervertebral discs - They are discs of fibrocartilage for connecting one vertebra to another. Each disc has - outer ring of fibrous cartilage and inner core called nucleus pulposus.

Vertebrae are divided into five groups. They are:

1. Cervical vertebrae - 7 in number forming the neck region.
2. Thoracic vertebrae - 12 in number forming back of thorax.
3. Lumbar vertebrae - 5 in number forming lumbar region.
4. Sacral vertebrae - 5 in number forming sacrum.
5. Coccygeal vertebrae - 5 in number forming coccyx.

Cervical vertebrae: They are smallest. First cervical vertebrum is called atlas. Second vertebrum is called axis.

Atlas: It is the first cervical vertebrum.

Features:

1. It does not have body
2. It does not contain spinous process
3. It has two facets on upper surface for articulation with condyles of occipital bone.

Axis: It is the second cervical vertebra.

Features:

1. Odontoid process - upward projection from body.
2. Two facets - on anterior surface for articulation with atlas.
3. Spine - small and bifid part.

Thoracic vertebrae: They are 12 in number. They carry ribs.

Features:

1. Body - heart-shaped
2. Facets - one on each side for attachment of ribs
3. Transverse process
4. Vertebral foramen is not present.

Lumbar vertebrae: They are five in number. They are largest vertebrae.

Features:

1. They have no facets for articulation with ribs.
2. Spinous processes are large and strong. They give attachment to muscles.
3. Body is big and kidney-shaped.

Sacral vertebrae: They are five in number. They are fused forming sacrum. Sacrum is triangular and forms wedge between two hip bones with which it articulates. They have following features:

1. Four sacral foraminae - opening of anterior surface through which nerves pass.
2. Lateral masses on either side - formed by union of transverse processes.
3. Sacral promontory - projection of upper part of sacrum.

Coccygeal vertebrae: They are four in number. They are fused to form coccyx. Coccyx is a triangular bone. It articulates with sacrum.

Main functions of vertebral column are:

1. Supporting spinal cord
2. Protecting spinal cord
3. Cushioning when jumping and landing on feet.

Ligaments: Ligaments holding the vertebrae together are:

1. Anterior and posterior ligaments
2. Ligamenta flava
3. Supraspinous ligaments
4. Intervertebral discs.

Anterior and posterior ligaments connect anterior and posterior aspects of bodies respectively. Ligamenta flava connect vertebral arches. Supraspinous ligaments lie between spines and connect them. Intervertebral discs are made of fibrocartilage and are helpful for connecting vertebrae with one another.

Curves of vertebral column: Vertebral column has four curves when viewed from side.

1. Primary curves: (*a*) Thoracic curves, (*b*) Pelvic curve.

2. Secondary curves: (*a*) Cervical curve, (*b*) Lumbar curve.

Primary curves are present during foetal life - cervical curve appears when child begins to hold up head and sit. Lumbar curve appears when child stands and walks.

Bones of Appendicular Skeleton

Bones of limbs: Appendicular skeleton consists of:

(*a*) Bones of upper limb (Bones of arms)

(*b*) Bones of lower limb (Bones of legs).

Bones of Upper Limb

Upper limb consists of shoulder, upper arm, fore arm, wrist and fingers.

Bones of upper limb are:

(*a*) Bones of shoulder girdle - Scapula, clavicle (1+1) on each side.

(*b*) Bones of upper arm - Humerus (1) on each side.

(*c*) Bones of forearm - Radius, ulna (1+1) on each side.

(*d*) Bones of wrist and palm:

Bones of wrist - carpals (8)

Bones of palm - metacarpals (5)

(8 + 5 = 13) on each side.

(*e*) Bones of fingers:

Phalanges - 3 each for fingers other than thumb (3 × 4 = 12)

- 2 for thumb

Total - (12 + 2 = 14) on each side.

Functions of upper limbs are:

- handling the objects.
- performing various types of work.
- movement.

Functions of lower limbs are: - Locomotion, posture, giving stability to trunk.

Bones of shoulder girdle : Bones forming shoulder girdle are Scapula and Clavicle.

Scapula

Scapula is a large triangular flat bone. It contributes to the wide range of movement of upper limb. It lies over ribs behind thorax. It does not articulate with them. It has two surfaces:

1. Anterior or costal surface – nearest the ribs.
2. Posterior or dorsal surface – divided into two fossae by spine of scapula with ends with acromion process.

The two fossae are:

1. Supraspinous fossa – upper one giving attachment to supraspinatous muscle.
2. Infraspinous fossa – lower one giving attachment to infraspinatous muscle.

It has three borders. They are:

1. Superior border – lying in the upper part.
2. Medial border (vertebral border) – nearest the vertebral column
3. Lateral border (axillary border) – nearest the axilla.

It has three angles. They are:

1. Superior angle - between superior and medial borders.
2. Inferior angle - between medial and lateral borders (lowest point of scapula).
3. Lateral angle (external angle) - It contains glenoid cavity for receiving the head of humerus to form shoulder joint. Coracoid process arises internal to glenoid cavity. It is large and irregular.

Clavicle

It is also called collar bone. It does not contain marrow cavity. It is a long bone at the root of the neck just below the skin. It is a weight bearing bone. It is roughly shaped. It has two ends. They are:

1. Sternal extremity
2. Acromial extremity.

Sternal extremity is inner extremity articulating with sternum. It is roughly pyramidal in shape. Acromial extremity is outer extremity articulating with scapula. It is flatter.

Humerus

It is the bone forming upper arm. It is the long bone of upper limb. It has two extremities and a shaft.

Upper extremity contains:

(*a*) Head - hemispherical in shape
- articulating with glenoid cavity of scapula at shoulder joint.

(*b*) Anatomical neck - below the head.

(*c*) Greater tuberosity - below the anatomical neck
- located in the outer side of upper extremity.

(*d*) Lesser tuberosity - below the anatomical neck
- located at the front.

(*e*) Bicipital groove - lying between the two tuberosities.

(*f*) Surgical neck - narrow point between the two tuberosities.

Lower extremity contains:

(a) Trochlea - pulley shaped surface on inner side articulating with ulna

(*b*) Capitulum - on outer side
- It articulates with radius

(*c*) Coronoid fossa - It is a depression located above articulating surface for ulna.

(*d*) Olecranon fossa - It lies at back and receives olecranon process of ulna.

(*e*) Medial and lateral epicondyle - lying on each side of articulating surfaces.

Shaft contains

(*a*) Deltoid tuberosity - rough tubercle on lateral aspect.

(*b*) Spiral groove - also known as radial groove. Radial nerve passes through it.

Radius

It is the outer bone of forearm. It is a long bone. It contains two extremities and a shaft.

Upper extremity: It contains—

(*a*) Head - It is disc-shaped with hollow upper surface to articulate with capitulum of humerus. It also articulates with ulna.

(*b*) Neck - It lies below the head. It is a constricted portion.

(*c*) Radial tuberosity - On the ulna side, there is a projection, which is called radial tuberosity. Radial tuberosity gives insertion to biceps muscle.

Lower extremity: It is wider part. It forms wrist joint. It has a projection called styloid process.

Shaft: Shaft of the radius has a sharp ridge facing ulna. Interosseous membrane connects radius and ulna.

Ulna: It is the inner bone of forearm. It contains two extremities and a shaft.

Upper extremity: It is shaped like a hook and contains:

(*a*) Olecranon process - upward projection at the back, which fits into olecranon fossa of humerus (when arm is kept straight). Its upper border forms elbow.

(*b*) Coronoid process - It is a smaller projection to the forwards. It fits into coronoid fossa of humerus.

(*c*) Trochlear notch - formed by the above two processes which articulates with trochlear surface of humerus.

(*d*) Radial notch - It is a depression on upper part of coronoid process. It articulates with head of radius.

Shaft: It tapers towards lower end. It carries a sharp ridge for attachment of interosseous membrane lying between ulna and radius.

Lower extremity: It contains:

(*a*) Head - rounded part which articulates with lower extremity of radius.

(*b*) Styloid process - a projection giving attachment to a ligament of wrist joint.

Bones of wrist: Bones of wrist are called carpal bones. They are eight bones arranged in two rows.

—Bones of proximal row are scaphoid, lunate, triquetral and pisiform bones.

—Bones of distal row are trapezium, trapezoid, capitate and hamate bones.

Bones of palm: Bones of palm are called metacarpal bones. They are five miniature long bones each having base and head.

Bases of metacarpal bones articulate with distal row carpal bones and heads articulate with proximal row phalanges.

Bones of fingers: Bones of fingers are called phalanges. They are 14 miniature long bones arranged in rows. Thumb finger has two phalanges and the remaining fingers have three phalanges each. Three phalanges in a finger are called proximal phalange, middle phalange and distal phalange. Proximal row phalanges articulate with metacarpal bones and the joints are called metacarpo phalangial joints. Inter phalangial joints exist between phalangial bones.

Bones of Lower Limbs and Pelvic Girdle

Bones of pelvic girdle: Pelvic girdle forms link between trunk and lower limbs. Pelvic girdle is formed by 2 innominate bones, 1 on each side with sacrum and coccyx behind. Pelvis is divided into Greater pelvis (false) and Lesser pelvis (true) by line-a-terminalis and promontory of sacrum. Greater pelvis is upper expanded portion. It is bounded on each side by Ilium and at back by base of sacrum. Lesser pelvis consists of short curved canal. It is deeper at back than front.

Innominate Bone: It is called pelvic bone or hip bone. Innominate bone is made of ilium, ischium and pubis. Ilium, ischium and pubis are united at deep cavity on outer aspect of bone called acetabulum. Ossification is incomplete among ilium, ischium and pubis between ages of 15-25 years. They are united by cartilage before this.

Differences between male and female pelvis: Female pelvis is shorter than male pelvis. Female pelvis is wider than male pelvis. It is shallower than male pelvis. Sacrum is shorter and wider. Pubic arch forms obtuse angle in females whereas it forms acute angle in males. Sciatic notch is also wider. This variation in female pelvis adapts female pelvis for pregnancy and child birth.

Bones of the lower limb:

Bones of lower limb are:

- Femur (thigh bone) one on each side
- Patella (knee cap) one on each side
- Tibia and fibula (leg bones) two on each side
- Tarsal bones (ankle bones) seven on each side
- Metatarsal bones (instep bones) five on each side
- Phalanges (bones of toes) (3 × 4) + 2 on each side.

Femur: It is the longest and the strongest bone of the body. It resembles humerus of upper arm. Features of femur: It contains

1. Upper extremity, 2. Shaft and 3. Lower extremity.

Upper extremity: It has following features.

(*a*) Head - spherical in shape and covered with hyaline cartilage.

(*b*) Neck - long and flat lying below head.

(*c*) Greater trochanter - located on the outer side where neck and shaft join.

(*d*) Lesser trochanter - located on inner side where neck and shaft join.

(*e*) Anterior and posterior inter trochantric lines - unite greater and lesser trochanters.

Shaft: It has following features.

(*a*) Linea aspera ridge on posterior aspect.

(*b*) Gluteal ridge extending from linea aspera to the back of greater trochanter.

(*c*) Spiral line extending at the inner aspect from linea aspera to lesser trochanter.

Lower extremity: It has following features.

(*a*) Medial and lateral condyles.

(*b*) Inter condylar notch - separating the two condyles.

(*c*) Adductor tubercle - lying above medial condyle.

(*d*) Patellar surface.

(*e*) Poplietal surface.

Patella: It is a small mobile disc located in front of knee joint in the tendon of quadriceps muscle. It forms knee cap. It is a seasmoid bone. It is triangular in shape with its apex facing downwards. Its posterior surface is smooth. It articulates with condyles of femur. Its anterior surface is rough.

Bones of leg: Bones of leg are - Tibia and fibula.

Tibia : It is the inner bone of leg. It is stronger than fibula. It has following features - upper extremity, shaft and lower extremity.

Upper extremity of tibia has: (*a*) Head, containing two condyles. They are (*i*) medial condyle, (*ii*) lateral condyle. Surfaces of these condyles articulate with corresponding condyles of femur.

(*b*) Poplietal notch, separating the two condyles at back.

(*c*) Tubercle below the condyles in the front.

Shaft: Shaft is triangular in shape. It has three borders and three surfaces. Crest of tibia is located at the middle third portion of anterior border. Soleal line is a ridge of bone. It is strong. It is present in the posterior surface.

Lower extremity: It is slightly expanded. Its surface articulates with talus and forms ankle joint.

Fibula: It is the outer bone. It does not participate in weight bearing. It has upper extremity, shaft and lower extremity.

Upper extremity has head and styloid process. Shaft is thin and gives attachment to muscles. Lower extremity has lateral malleolus and malleolar fossa.

Bones of foot: Tarsal bones, meta tarsal bones and phalanges are collectively called bones of foot. Tarsal bones are seven bones in two rows. Tarsal bones are - Talus, calcaneum, navicular, cuboid and 3 cuneiform. Talus and calcaneum are the most prominent bones among tarsals. Talus is the main connecting link between foot and leg. Calcaneum is the largest bone of foot. Navicular is disc shaped. Cuneiform bones are three in number. They are: medial, intermediate and lateral.

Metatarsal bones: They are 5 bones. Their heads articulate with phalanges.

Phalanges: They are 14 in number. Greater toe has two phalanges. Remaining toes have three phalanges each.

Joints

Definition: Joint or articulation is a junction between two or more bones.

Arthrology: Arthrology is a study of joints.

Classification of Joints

Joints are classified depending on the degree of movement allowed. On this basis, there are three types of joints. They are:

1. Fibrous joints (Immovable)
2. Cartilaginous joints (Slightly movable)
3. Synovial joints (Freely movable).

Fibrous Joint: It is the type of joint where there is no movement of bones, fibrous tissue is the connecting medium between the bones.

Ex: 1. Sutures of skull. (*a*) Coronal suture between frontal and parietal bones. (*b*) Sagittal suture between parietal bones 2. Tibiofibular joint between tibia and fibula 3. Joints between teeth and jaws.

Cartilaginous Joints: It is the type of joint where bones forming the joint are slightly movable. Surfaces of the bones at the joint are covered with hyaline cartilage and fibrous cartilage or fibrous ligaments act as connecting medium.

Ex:

1. Intervertebral joints
2. Joint between manubrium sterni and body of sternum.

Synovial Joints: It is the joint between the bones where bones are freely movable. Joint forming bone surfaces are covered with articular hyaline cartilage. Cavity around the joint is called synovial cavity. Fluid in the cavity lubricating the articulating surfaces is called synovial fluid. Joint is completely surrounded by a fibrous capsule lined with synovial membrane, ex: elbow joint.

Types of Synovial joints : On the basis of type of movement, synovial joints are divided into several classes.

They are:

1. Hinge joints
2. Pivot joints
3. Condyloid joints
4. Ball and socket joint
5. Gliding joints
6. Saddle joint.

1. **Hinge Joint:** It is the type of joint allowing unidirectional movement as in knee and elbow.
2. **Pivot Joint:** It is the type of joint allowing rotation only.

   Ex: (*i*) Atlas and axis

   (*ii*) Radius and ulna.
3. **Condyloid joint:** It is the type of joint allowing movement in two planes.

   Ex: Ankle joint, Wrist joint.

4. **Ball and socket joints:** It is the type of joint allowing movement in all directions as a ball in cup-shaped socket cavity.

   Ex: Shoulder joint and hip joint.
5. **Gliding Joints:** It is the type of joint allowing the joint forming surfaces of bones to glide over each other.

   Ex: Carpal joints, Tarsal joints.
6. **Saddle Joint :** It is the type of joint allowing free movement in all directions.

   Ex: Joint between metacarpal bone of thumb and trapezium.

Types of Movements at the Joints

Various types of movements at joints are:

1. Rotation movements
2. Angular movements
3. Gliding movements

Rotation movements: Movements due to one bone moving within another bone are rotation movements.

Ex:

1. Movements of femur in acetabulum of hip bone.
2. Movement of head rotation of radius over ulna.
3. Movement of ball of humerus in shoulder joints.

Angular movements: They are different types.

(*a*) *Flexion:* Bending of parts towards each other.

(*b*) *Extension:* Straightening out of a part from other.

(*c*) *Adduction:* Movement of a part towards medial axis.

(*d*) *Abduction:* Movement of a part away from medial axis.

(*e*) *Pronation:* Bending of ventral surface downwards or turning of palm downwards as in blessing.

(*f*) *Supination:* Turning of palm upwards as in begging.

(*g*) *Circumduction:* Movement involving flexion, abduction, extension and adduction in a sequence.

Ex: Movement in shoulder.

Gliding movements : Gliding movement is a type of movement in which two flat surfaces move on each other.

Ex: 1. Movement of carpal bones in wrist.

2. Movement of tarsal bones in foot.

Joints of Human Body

Joints of human body can be classified on the basis of anatomical location into:

1. Joints of head
2. Joints of trunk
3. Joints of upper limbs
4. Joints of lower limbs.

Joints of Head

The only movable joint in head is temporo-mandibular joint. It lies between temporal bone and head of mandible. Sutures of the skull are immovable joints. Unossified membranous areas at the junctions of bones of skull are called fontanelles.

Joints of trunk: They are:

1. Inter vertebral joints: They are the joints between all vertebrae from second cervical vertebra to sacrum. Joints between vertebral bodies are slightly movable whereas joints between vertebral arches are synovial joints.

2. Costovertebral Joints: Joints between ribs and vertebrae are called costovertebral joints. They allow gliding movements.

3. Sternocostal Joints: Joints between ribs and sternum are sternocostal joints. They also allow gliding movements.

Joints of upper limbs

Joints of upper limbs are:

1. ***Sternoclavicular joint:*** Sternoclavicular joint is a gliding type of joint between sternum and clavicle.

2. ***Acromio-clavicular joint:*** The acromio-clavicular joint, or AC joint, is a joint at the top of the shoulder. It is the junction between the acromion (part of the scapula that forms the highest point of the shoulder) and the clavicle.
3. ***Shoulder joint:*** It is a ball and socket joint between scapula and humerus. Flexion, extension, adduction, abduction, rotation and circumduction occur at this joint.
4. ***Elbow joint:*** It is a hinge joint between humerus and ulna, humerus and radius. Flexion and extension occur at this joint.
5. ***Radio ulnar joints:*** These are pivot joints between radius and ulna. They are superior radio ulnar joint and inferior radio ulnar joint. Pronation and supination movements occur at these joints.
6. ***Wrist joint:*** It is a condyloid joint between radius and carpal bones. It is also known as radiocarpal joint. Flexion, extension, abduction and adduction occur at this joint.
7. ***Intercarpal joints:*** They are gliding joints between carpal bones.
8. ***Carpometacarpal joints:*** Gliding joints between carpal bones and metacarpal bones. Carpometacarpal joint of thumb is a saddle type joint.
9. ***Metacarpo phalangeal joint:*** They are condyloid type of joints between metacarpal bones and proximal row phalanges. Flexion, extension, adduction and abduction occur at these joints.
10. ***Interphalangeal joints:*** Hinge joints between phalanges. Flexion and extension occur at these joints.

Joints of lower limbs

Joints of lower limbs are:

1. ***Hip Joint:*** Ball and socket type joint between hip bone and femur is called hip joint. Flexion, extension, abduction, adduction and circumduction occur at this joint.
2. ***Knee joint:*** Knee joint is a hinge joint between femur and tibia. Patella is present on smooth surface of femur. It helps in gliding movements. Flexion and extension occur at this joint.
3. ***Tibio fibular joints:*** Tibio fibular joints are fibrous joints between tibia and fibula at their lower and upper extremities.
4. ***Ankle joint:*** Ankle joint is a hinge joint between tibia and tarsals. Dorsiflexion and plantar flexion occur at this joint.
5. ***Tarsometatarsal joints:*** They are gliding joints between tarsal bones and metatarsal bones.
6. ***Metatarso phalangeal joints:*** They are gliding joints between metatarsal bones and phalanges.
7. ***Inter phalangeal joints:*** They are gliding joints between phalanges.
8. ***Mediotarsal joints:*** They are joints between talus with navicular and calcaneum with cuboid.
9. ***Talocalcaneal joint:*** It is the joint between talus and calcaneum. It is also called subtalar joint. Movement is rocking type.

NERVOUS SYSTEM – CNS

Nervous system controls and integrates the functions of human body. It is essentially a biological information highway. It consists of the Central Nervous System (CNS), essentially the processing area and the Peripheral Nervous System which detects and sends electrical impulses that are used in the nervous system. Nervous system consists of neurons, its fibres, dendrites and axons.

Nervous Tissue

It is composed of neurons and neuroglia. Neurons are structural and functional units whereas glial cells are supportive cells. Glial cells provide nutrients to neurons. They also protect neurons.

Neuron

It is the structural and functional unit of nervous system. It is made of nerve cell body, dendrites and axons. Nerve cell body consists of large nucleus, neuro fibrils and Nisslgranules, which are present in neuroplasm. Nerve cell body also contains mitochondria and other cell organelles. Dendrites are the receptive fibres receiving impulses and transmiting them to the nerve cell body. Axons carry impulses away from the nerve cell body.

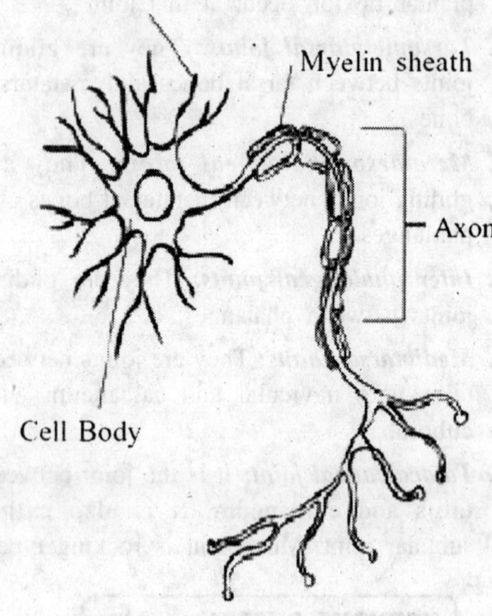

Fig : *Neuron*

Types of neurons

On the basis of number of processes, they are classified into:

(*a*) *Apolarneurons:* Neurons having no processes.

(*b*) *Unipolarneurons:* Neurons having only one process axon.

These two types are found only in foetal life.

(*c*) *Bipolarneurons:* Neurons having one axon at one pole and dendrite at the other pole.

(*d*) *Pseudounipolar neurons:* Neurons, which are typically bipolar at first and spindle shaped, but cell processes converging to meet at one side of the cell body as the devolopment proceeds. They are found in all spinal ganglia and ganglia of cranial nerves except 8th cranial nerve.

(*e*) *Multipolar neurons:* Neurones having most varied form. They are found in cerebral cortex, nuclei of trigeminal nerve and motor neurons of spinal cord.

Types of Nerve Fibres

Histologically there are two types of nerve fibres.

1. Medullated nerve fibres
2. Non-medullated nerve fibres.

In medullated or myelinated nerve fibres, axon is covered with myelin sheath except at the nodes of Ranvier. In non-medullated or non-myelinated nerve fibres, axons are not covered with myelin sheath.

Neuroglia

Neuroglia is a special type of interstitial tissue present both in grey and white matter. There are three types of neuroglia.

1. Astrocytes: (*a*) protoplasmic astrocytes, (*b*) fibrous astrocytes
2. Oligodendroglia or oligodendrocytes (having few processes)
3. Microglia (having small size).

Astrocytes and oligodendrocytes are ectodermal in origin. Microglia is mesodermal in origin.

Synapse

Synapse is the junction where one neuron ends and another neuron begins.

Classification of synapses:

They are:

1. Axosomatic synapse
2. Axo-dendritic synapse
3. Axo-axonic synapse.

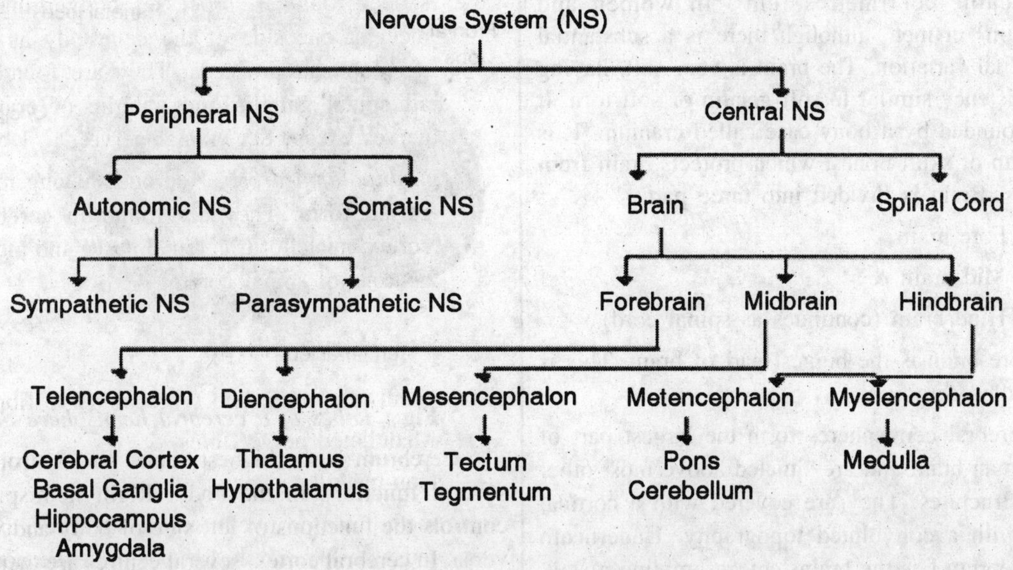

Division of Nervous System

In axosomatic synapses, presynaptic terminal of the axon ends in the cell body of neurone. In axodendritic synapse, presynaptic fibres of any axon end in the dendrites of postsynaptic cell. In axo-axonic synapse, presynaptic fibres of any axon end in the axon of the postsynaptic cells.

Anatomy of the synapse: Microscopic anatomy of a motor neurone of the anterior horn cells of the spinal cord shows the main body of the neuronesoma, dendrites, axon and multiple presynaptic terminals (synaptic knobs) ending in the soma and dendrites. These presynaptic terminals are the ends of the neurofibrils of other neurones. Presynaptic fibres end in an expanded terminal called synaptic knob. Synaptic knob and soma have intact membrane. Membrane of the synaptic knob is called presynaptic membrane. Membrane of the soma is called postsynaptic membrane.

The Central Nervous System (CNS)

The Central Nervous System is effectively the centre of the nervous system. The CNS consists of the brain and spinal cord. This information highway, called the nervous system consists of many nerve cells, also known as neurones. As mentioned in the above table, brain and spinal cord are the components of CNS. They are continuous with each other. Both of them have nerve cells and glial cells. In brain, all cell bodies of neurons are present in the outer layers. The outer layers of brain look dullish gray coloured. Due to this, this matter is called Gray matter. Deeper layers of the brain have the axons of cell bodies present in the top layers. Most of these axons are myelinated. Hence, they appear white coloured and this matter is called white matter. In spinal cord, white matter is on the surface and the gray matter is in deeper layers.

Both brain and spinal cord are covered with three membranes. They are:

1. Dura mater (Outermost layer)
2. Arachnoid membrane (Middle layer)
3. Pia mater (Innermost layer).

A fluid flows between the outer and the middle membranes, which is called cerebrospinal fluid (CSF). This fluid flows from brain to spinal cord and back to brain. It is protective to brain and spinal cord from injuries. It supplies nutrients to the cells in brain and spinal cord.

Brain

The adult human brain weighs on an average about 3 lb (1.5 kg) with a size (volume) of around

1130 cubic centimetres (cm^3) in women and 1260 cm^3 in men, although there is a substantial individual variation. The brain is very soft, having a consistency similar to soft gelatin or soft tofu. It is surrounded by a bony case called cranium. It is made up of skull bones, which protects brain from injuries. Brain is divided into three parts.

1. Fore brain
2. Mid brain &
3. Hind brain (continues as spinal cord).

Fore brain is the biggest part of brain. This is also called cerebrum.

Cerebral hemispheres form the largest part of the human brain and are situated above most other brain structures. They are covered with a cortical layer with a convoluted topography. Underneath the cerebrum lies the brainstem, resembling a stalk on which the cerebrum is attached. At the rear of the brain, beneath the cerebrum and behind the brainstem, is the cerebellum, a structure with a horizontally furrowed surface that makes it look different from any other brain area. Cerebellum is not so large relative to the rest of the brain. As a rule, the smaller the cerebrum, the less convoluted the cortex.

Cerebrum: A deep groove is present in the middle of the cerebrum. It divides cerebrum into two halves. These are called cerebral hemispheres. Right and left hemispheres are connected to each other by a bundle of axons. Outer portion of cerebrum is gray in colour and is called cerebral cortex. There are several ridges on the surface of brain called GYRI. SULCI are the grooves on the brain's surface. They increase the surface of cortex to accommodate more number of neurons. Deep grooves present across a cerebral hemisphere are three in number and they divide a hemisphere into four lobes. They are:

1. Frontal lobe
2. Parietal lobe
3. Temporal lobe
4. Occipital lobe.

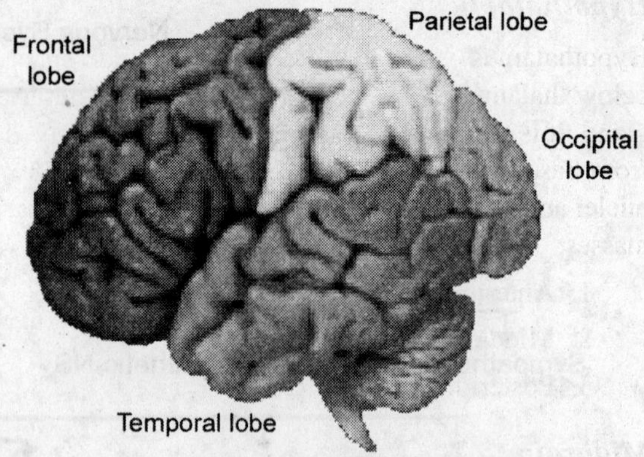

Fig : *Lobes of a cerebral hemisphere*

Cerebrum is the highest centre for controlling several functions in the body. Right hemisphere controls the functions of left side of body and vice versa. In cerebral cortex, several centres are there to receive and analyse information. Some of them are

1. Visual centre for sight
2. Auditory centre for hearing
3. Olfactory centre for smell, etc.

Parts of the brain below the cerebrum are together known as Diencephalon. It has centres controlling emotions like anger, pain and pleasure. This portion connects the fore brain with mid brain. Hypothalamus is present in this section. Pituitary gland is attached to hypothalamus by a stalk.

Thalamus

Thalamus and Hypothalamus are present in Diencephalon. Thalamus is a large, dual lobed mass of gray matter buried under the cerebral cortex located at the top of midbrain. It is involved in sensory perception and regulation of motor functions. Thalamus is a limbic system structure and it connects the areas of the cerebral cortex that are involved in sensory perception and movement with other parts of the brain and spinal cord that also have a role in sensation and movement.

As a regulator of sensory information, the thalamus also controls sleep and awake states of consciousness.

Hypothalamus

Hypothalamus is located at interpeduncular space below thalamus. It has a close relation with Pituitary gland. It is the highest centre for A.N.S. It is derived from basal plate of diencephalon. It forms complex nuclei and fibres. It consists of the following nuclear masses.

1. Anterior group
2. Middle group
3. Posterior group.

Midbrain

Midbrain is the connection between forebrain and hindbrain. Dorsal part of midbrain contains four rounded eminences. These four rounded eminences are called corpora Quadrigemina.

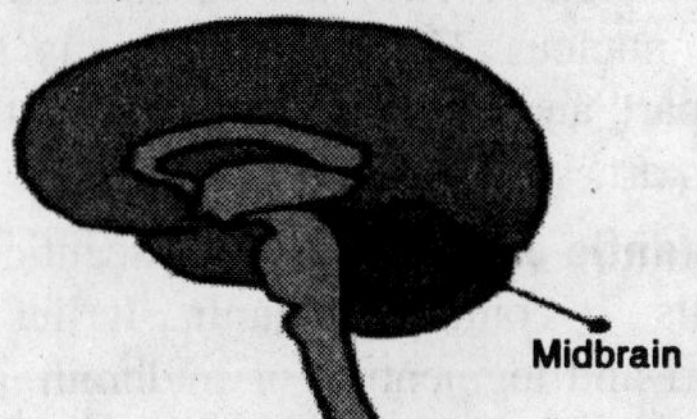

Fig : *Midbrain*

Ventral part of midbrain contains a pair of cerebral peduncles. These are cylindrical bodies. Cerebral peduncles consist of Basis pedunculi, substantia nigra and tegmentum. Rednucleus consists of two groups of cells—nucleus magnocelluforis and nucleus parvocellularis.

Ponsvaroli: It is located above medulla oblongata. Anteriorly, it appears as a bulging mass of transverse fibres, posteriorly, it is separated from cerebellum by fourth ventricle. T.S. of pons varoli shows two main portions.

Hindbrain: Hindbrain consists of two parts.

1. Cerebellum 2. Brain stem.

Cerebellum: Cerebellum is the largest part of hindbrain. It lies behind pons and medulla oblongata. Cerebellum is a separate structure attached to the bottom of the brain, tucked underneath the cerebral hemispheres. Average weight of cerebellum in adults is about 150 gm. It consists of gray matter on the surface and white matter in the deeper layers. The surface of the cerebellum is covered with finely spaced parallel grooves, in striking contrast to the broad irregular convolutions of the cerebral cortex.

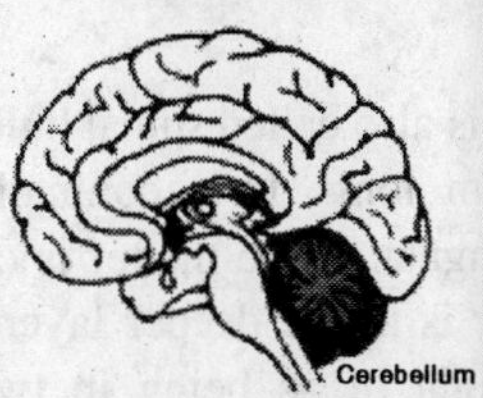

Fig: *Cerebellum*

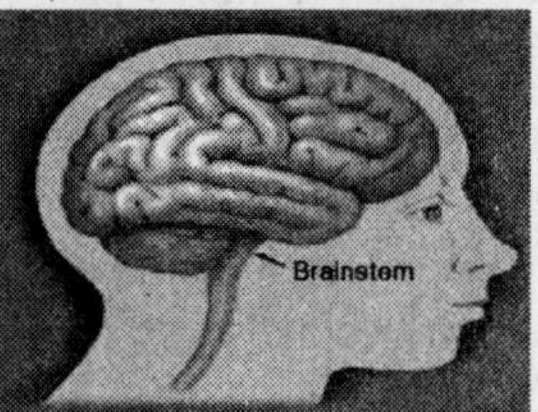

Fig: *Brain stem*

These parallel grooves conceal the fact that the cerebellum is actually a continuous thin layer of tissue (the cerebellar cortex), tightly folded in the style of an accordion. Within this thin layer, there are several types of neurons with a highly regular arrangement, the most important being Purkinje cells and granule cells. This complex neural network gives rise to a massive signal-processing capability, but almost all of its output is directed to a set of small deep cerebellar nuclei lying in the interior of the cerebellum.

Cerebellum consists of right and left cerebellar hemispheres. They are joined by vermis. From functional and morphological point of view, cerebellum consists of two parts. They are

1. Flocculonodular lobe
2. Corpus cerebelli.

Flocculonodular lobe is separated from corpus cerebelli by posterior lateral fissure. Phylogenetically cerebellum is divided into:

1. Archicerebellum
2. Palaeocerebellum
3. Neo cerebellum.

Afferent and efferent fibres connecting the cerebellum with extra cerebellar regions run through three large bundles. They are known as superior, middle and inferior cerebellar peduncles. It is divided into: (*a*) Anterior limb, (*b*) Posterior limb and (*c*) Genu.

Brain stem: Brain stem includes Medulla oblongata and Pons varoli. Medulla oblongata continues as spinal cord. In medulla oblongata there are several centres to control several vital functions of body such as heart beat, respiration, temperature, blood pressure, secretions of salivary glands, etc. All the nerve fibres pass from brain to spinal cord through this part.

Medulla oblongata: It is also called spinal bulb. It is approximately 28 mm long. It is conically expanded. In medulla oblongata, white matter is on the surface and gray matter is in the deeper layers. The medulla is often thought of as being in two parts.

Pituitary and Pineal Glands

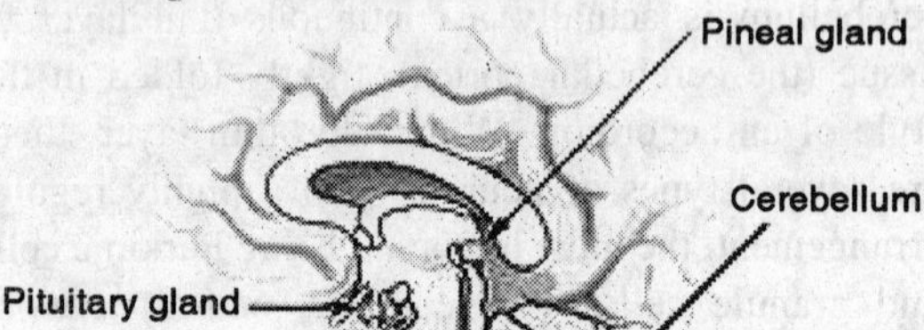

Fig : *Medulla oblongata and Pons Varoli*

1. Open part or superior part where the dorsal surface of the medulla is formed by the fourth ventricle.
2. Closed part or inferior part where the metacoel lies within the medulla oblongata. It extends from foramen magnum to the caudal border of pons. It continues as spinal cord.

Sulci present on surface of spinal cord also continue upward into medulla oblongata.

Pons Varoli: Pons Varoli is a structure located on the brain stem. It is superior to the medulla oblongata, inferior to the midbrain, and ventral to the cerebellum. In humans and other bipeds this means it is above the medulla, below the midbrain, and anterior to the cerebellum. This white matter includes tracts that conduct signals from the cerebrum down to the cerebellum and medulla, and tracts that carry the sensory signals up into thalamus.

The pons measures about 2.5 cm in length. Most of it appears as a broad anterior bulge rostral to the medulla. Posteriorly, it consists mainly of two pairs of thick stalks called cerebellar peduncles. They connect the cerebellum to the pons and midbrain.

Internal capsule: It is a 'V' shaped band of fibres. It is bounded medially by thalamus and caudate nucleus. It is laterally bounded by lentiform nucleus.

Basal ganglia: Basal ganglia includes corpus striatum, claustrum, rednucleus, body of Luys and substantia nigra. Corpus striatum includes caudate nucleus, lobus pallidus and putamen.

Corpus striatum: It is a mass of gray matter lateral and anterior to thalamus. Anterior limb of internal capsule divides corpus striatum into two parts incompletely. They are caudate nucleus and lentiform nucleus. Caudate nucleus is the small anterior part and lentiform nucleus is the larger posterior part.

Substantia nigra: It is a crescentic mass of nerve cells. It contains melanin. It lies between cruscerebri and tegmentum of midbrain.

Body of Luys: It is also called corpus luysi or subthalamic nucleus. It lies laterally and ventrally to red nucleus. It lies dorsal to substantia nigra. It is connected to red nucleus, substantia nigra and globus pallidus, etc.

Subthalamus: It is dorsally bounded by thalamus. It is bounded medially and rostrally by hypothalamus. It is bounded laterally and ventrally by pespedenculi and neighbourhood area of internal capsule.

Reticular Formation: Diffused ill defined mass of nerve cells and fibres form mesh work in the central portion of brainstem. It is collectively called reticular formation. It extends upward into thalamus and subthalamus. It extends downwards into spinal cord. Parts of reticular formation which play roles in wakefulness are called ascending reticular activating system.

Vestibular apparatus: It consists of bony labyrinth lodging membranous labyrinth. Bony labyrinth includes vestibule, semi circular canals and cochlea. These three cavities are filled with perilymph. Perilymph is a clear fluid of high sodium. Membranous labyrinth lies within bony labyrinth. Membranous labyrinth is filled with endolymph. Endolymph contains high potassium content.

Semicircular canals: They are three in number and lying in three planes at right angles to one another. These are lateral, anterior and posterior canals. Lateral canal is horizontal and other two are vertical. Histologically, these canals contain:

1. Outer vascular and fibrous coat.
2. Middle thicker, homogeneous and transparant coat forming basement membrane.
3. Inner layer made up of cubical epithelium.

Otolithic Organ: It consists of saccule and utricle. Histologically it consists of same coats as that of semicircular canals. Both in saccule and utricle, a sense organ is present. It is called 'macula'.

Cerebral Ventricles: These are the cavities in the brain where CSF flows and bathes the whole brain. There are four ventricles—two lateral ventricles, a third ventricle and a fourth ventricle.

Lateral ventricles are present in the cerebrum. Third ventricle lies in between two halves of the thalamus. Fourth ventricle lies in front of cerebellum and behind the medulla oblongata and pons varoli.

Spinal cord

Spinal cord is a long cylindrical structure which passes through vertebral column extending all along the dorsal surface of trunk.

T.S. of spinal cord: T.S. of Spinal cord shows 1. Central canal, 2. Gray matter and 3. White matter.

Central Canal: Central Canal is in the middle of the spinal cord. It is lined by cubical ciliated epithelium. Cerebrospinal fluid (C.S.F) circulates through this canal. The central canal actually pierces through the isthmus (commissure) of the two symmetrical lateral halves of the gray matter. Parts of the gray matter in front of the central canal is known as anterior (ventral) gray commissure and the same on behind the central canal is known as posterior (dorsal) gray commissure.

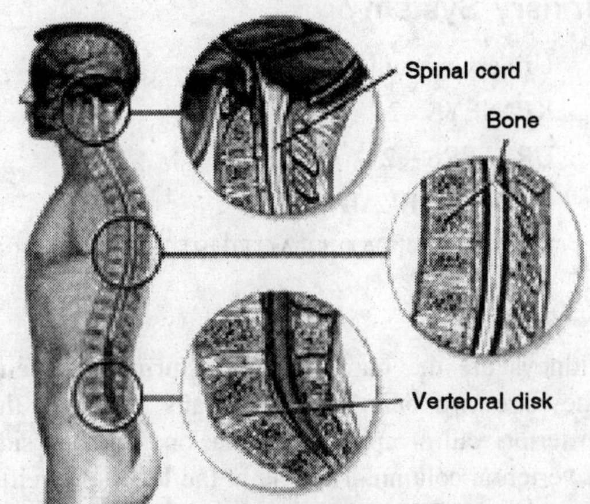

Fig : *Spinal cord*

Gray matter: It is in the form of a rough crescent one on each side. Each crescent has three parts - anterior horn, lateral horn and posterior horn. Gray matter is chiefly composed of three elements - (*a*) nerve cells, (*b*) neuroglia and (*c*) nerve fibres. Lateral horn projects in the thoracic region of spinal cord.

White matter: White matter of the spinal cord surrounds the gray matter and consists of myelinated and unmyelinated fibres. Myelinated fibres are predominating. The lateral half of white matter on each side is divided into three compartments—anterior white column, lateral white column and posterior white column.

EXCRETORY SYSTEM

Excretory system consists of organs concerned with excretion of waste products formed in the cellular metabolism of body. Such channels concerned with excretion are called channels of excretion.

They are:

KIDNEYS - 2

SKIN

LIVER

LUNGS - 2

DIGESTIVE TRACT

SALIVARY GLANDS

Urinary System

Urinary system consists of:

KIDNEYS - 2

URETERS - 2

URINARY BLADDER

URINOGENITAL TRACT/URETHRA

Kidneys

Kidneys are the main organs of urinary system. They are two bean shaped organs lying on the posterior wall of upper abdomen, one on each side of vertebral column. They lie at the level of twelfth thoracic to third lumbar vertebrae. Right kidney is located slightly lower than left kidney. Dimensions of each kidney are 11 × 5 × 3 cm^3. Each kidney weighs 150 g. approximately. On each kidney, an adrenal gland is present.

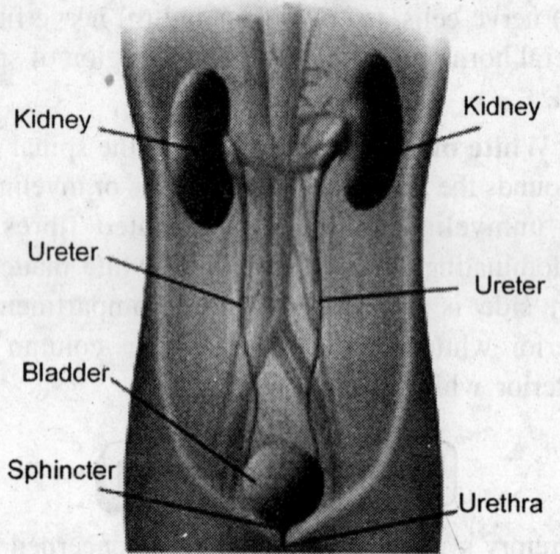

Fig. : *Urinary System*

Each kidney is embedded in fat called perirenal fat. Right kidney bears the impression of part of duodenum on its front. Pancreas crosses the left kidney transversely in its front. Each kidney is convex on its outer border and concave in the centre of its inner border. At this point, blood vessels, nerves and ureter enter and leave kidney. This point of kidney is called Hilus.

Ureters transport urine formed in kidneys to urinary bladder. From urinary bladder, urine is passed to the exterior through urethra. Urethra in males is also a passage for semen. Hence, it is also called urinogenital tract in males. In females, it is independent.

Structure of Kidney

Longitudinal section of Kidney: Kidney is surrounded by a fibrous capsule. It can be stripped off easily. Portion inside this fibrous capsule can be divided into: 1. Cortex, 2. Medulla.

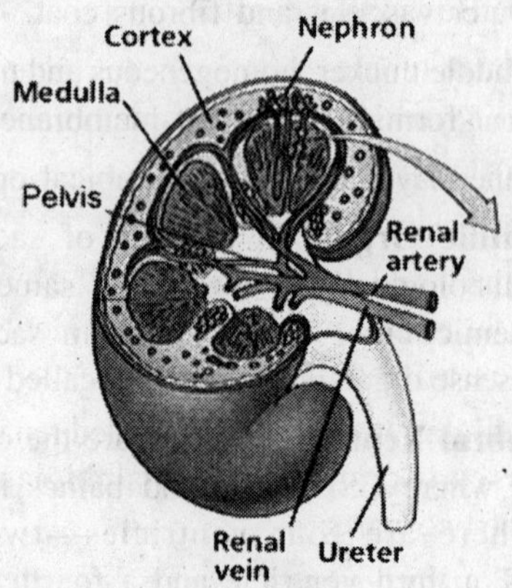

Fig. : *A longitudinal section of right kidney*

Cortex is the outer reddish brown coloured portion and medulla is the inner lighter area.

Medulla is subdivided into 10 to 15 conical areas called renal pyramids. Pyramids have their broad base towards cortex and apex projecting into lumen of minor calyx. Columns of Bertin are the projections of cortex. They form the boundaries of the pyramids.

Microscopic structure of kidney: Kidneys consist of number of minute units called nephrons. They are basic structural and functional units of kidney. There are about one million nephrons in each kidney. Nephrons drain into pelvis of ureter and then into urinary bladder.

Nephrons: Uriniferous tubules consist of two portions: 1. Nephron, 2. Collecting tubule. Nephron is the secretory portion of uriniferous tubule. About 85% of total number of nephrons lie in outer two third portion of cortex. They are called superficial nephrons. About 15% of total number of nephrons occupy inner one-third of cortex and they are called Juxtamedullary nephrons. Superficial nephrons are smaller than Juxtamedullary nephrons. Superficial nephrons are functional in normal conditions whereas Juxtamedullary nephrons are functional in conditions of stress.

Parts of Nephron: Nephron consists of the following parts in succession.

1. Malphigian body
   (*a*) Glomerulus
   (*b*) Bowman's capsule
2. Renal tubule:
   (*a*) Proximal convoluted tubule
   (*b*) Loop of Henle
   (*c*) Distal convoluted tubule

Proximal and distal parts of the convoluted tubule lie in cortex whereas loop of Henle extends from cortex to medulla.

Malphigian body: It is also called renal capsule. It lies in cortex of kidney. Malphigian capsule consists of two parts:

(*a*) Glomerulus and

(*b*) Bowman's capsule

Glomerulus is tuft of about 6-8 renal capillaries invaginating into the end of tubule. Glomerulus has two poles

1. Vascular pole - where blood vessels are attached.
2. Tubular pole - where renal tubule begins.

Afferent arteriole brings blood to glomerular tuft. It is short and wide. This capillary tuft reunites and forms efferent arteriole. It is long and narrow. This arrangement builds up a pressure gradient of 70 mm Hg and facilitates filtration. Bowman's capsule is the dilated end of nephron. It is invaginated by glomerular tuft. It is made of two layers called parietal and visceral layers. It gradually continues with tubule.

Renal tubule: Renal tubule begins at the tubular pole of glomerulus. Renal tubule is about 3 cm long and 20-60 microns wide. Short constricted part of tubule just below the glomerulus is - neck. Parts of the renal tubule after neck are:

Proximal convoluted tubule

Loop of Henle and

Distal convoluted tubule

Proximal convoluted tubule: It is also called pars convoluta. Length is about 14 mm. Outer diameter is 60 microns and inner diameter is 15-25 microns. It is lined by cubical cells arranged in single layers. Free borders of the cells are brush bordered. This portion of nephron lies in cortex of kidney.

Loop of Henle: It is also called as Pars recta. Pars recta is a U shaped loop. It is anatomically divided into:

Descending limb of loop of Henle

Thin walled ascending limb of loop of Henle

Thick walled ascending limb of loop of Henle

Variable length of loop of Henle lies in medulla. It is made of epithelial cells with variable shape in different portions of loop.

Distal convoluted tubule: Average length is about 4.9 mm. Diameter is 20 to 50 microns. It is lined by cubical epithelium.

Collecting tubule: It is the non-secretory portion of uriniferous tubule. It is collecting system. It is about 20 mm long. It is lined by pale cuboidal cells. Several collecting tubules from nephrons join to form duct of Bellini. It opens at apex of renal pyramid. Nephrons ultimately drain into pelvis of ureter. From here urine collects into urinary bladder. Urine is passed out into exterior through urethra.

Renal Circulation: There are two circulations in kidney.

1. Greater circulation 2. Lesser circulation

Greater circulation carries 85% of blood and lesser circulation carries 15% of blood. Renal arteries enter the kidneys through respective hilus. On or before entering the hilus, renal artery on each side divides into anterior and posterior divisions. Primary branches of divisions are called sigmental arteries. Sigmental arteries divide into lobar branches one for each pyramid. Branches passing between pyramids are called inter lobar arteries. Inter lobar arteries divide into arcuate arteries. These arteries subdivide to give small branches called inter lobular arteries. Inter lobular arteries break up into afferent arterioles. Each afferent arteriole forms capillary tuft called glomerulus. This tuft reunites to form efferent arteriole and again breaks up to form second capillary tuft called peritubular network around renal tubule. All these peritubular capillaries drain into venous plexus. From this plexus, blood passes through inter lobular veins. Inter lobular veins reunite to form arcuate veins. Arcuate veins form interlobar veins. Interlobar veins form renal vein.

Nerve supply: Kidneys are mainly supplied by sympathetic nervous system, partly by parasympathetic system.

Ureters

There are two ureters carrying urine from kidneys to urinary bladder.

They are continuous from renal pelvis to urinary bladder and are about 25-30 cm long. Diameter is about 3 mm. Ureter is slightly constricted at three places.

Ureter has three layers. They are:

1. Outer fibrous coat which is continuous with the fibrous coat of kidney.
2. Muscular coat containing outer circular layer and inner longitudinal layer.
3. Lining of mucous membrane continuous with that of bladder.

Urinary bladder

Urinary bladder is sac serving as distensible reservoir of urine evacuating its contents at suitable intervals of time. It lies in pelvic cavity behind symphisis pubis. Urinary bladder consists of two portions.

1. Body - sac of detrussor muscle.
2. Trigone - triangular region connecting the three openings of bladder - two of ureters and one of urethra.

Urinary bladder has two sphincters. They are:

1. Internal sphincter
2. External sphincter.

Internal sphincter is formed by smooth muscles surrounding the opening of urethra. External sphincter is formed by striated muscle of urogenital diaphragm.

Urethra

Urethra is the canal through which urine from bladder is passed to the exterior. It extends from base of the bladder. It has two sphincters. They are:

1. Internal sphincter - involuntary.
2. External sphincter - voluntary.

It has two orifices. They are:

1. Internal urethral orifice in the bladder.
2. External urethral orifice.

Male urethra serves as a common tract for urinary and reproductive systems and thus it is called urinogenital tract. In females it serves for urinary system only.

Male urethra: It is about 20 cm. long. It is divided into three portions.

1. **Prostatic portion:** surrounded by prostate gland and 3 cm long. Prostatic and ejaculatory ducts open into this point.
2. **Membranous portion:** passing through pelvic floor and 1-2 cm long.
3. **Spongy portion:** lying within penis and 15 cm long.

Female Urethra: It is about 4 cm long. It serves for urinary system only. It extends from the base of the bladder. It passes downwards behind symphisis pubis. It opens to the exterior in front of vaginal orifice.

Other Channels of Excretion

Other channels of excretion are Skin, Liver, Lungs, Colon and Salivary Glands.

Skin: Skin excretes water, salts, little urea, etc., in the form of sweat. Fats are also excreted by skin. For more details of anatomy - Refer to Anatomy of Sense organs.

Liver: Liver excretes fatty substances through bile. It also excretes heavy metals. For more details of anatomy refer to - Anatomy of Digestive system and Hepato Biliary system.

Lungs: Lungs excrete CO_2, water vapour, alcohol, ammonia etc. for details of anatomy refer to - Anatomy of Respiratory system.

Colon: It excretes heavy metals.

For more details of anatomy refer to - *Anatomy of Digestive system* and *Hepato Biliary System.adults.*

Salivary Glands: For more details of anatomy, refer to *Anatomy & Hepatobiliary System.*

ENDOCRINE SYSTEM

Endocrine system consists of endocrine glands of body.

There are two types of glands in body. They are:

1. Exocrine glands
2. Endocrine glands

Exocrine glands : They are glands of the body with ducts.

Ex: Mammary glands, sweat glands, lacrimal glands, salivary glands.

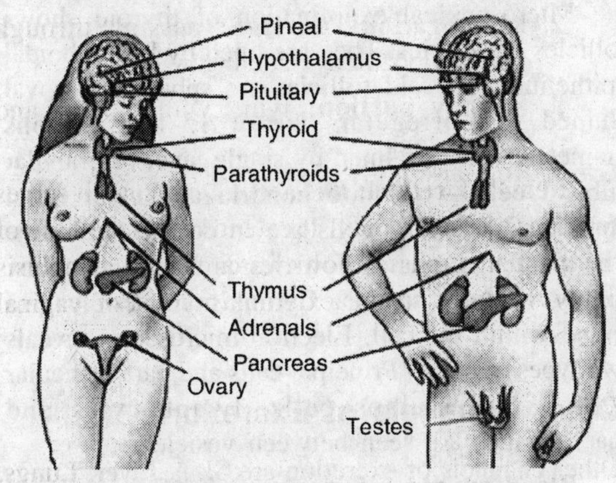

Fig : *Endocrine System*

Endocrine Glands

Endocrine glands are ductless glands which pour their secretions directly into blood circulation from where these secretions reach their site of action. These secretions are called hormones.

Endocrine glands in the human body: Endocrine glands of human body are:

1. Pituitary gland (Master gland)
2. Thyroid gland
3. Parathyroid gland
4. Adrenal glands
5. Pancreas
6. Testes
7. Ovaries
8. Placenta (during pregnancy)

Thymus and pineal body are glands with probable endocrine function. Stomach, small intestine and kidneys also have endocrine activity.

Hypothalamus

Hypothalamus is a complex neurohormonal regulatory part. Diencephalon contains thalamus and hypothalamus. Hypothalamus forms lower part of lateral ventricle. It forms anterior wall of third ventricle. It is situated at the interpudencular space below thalamus. It forms complex nuclei and fibres.

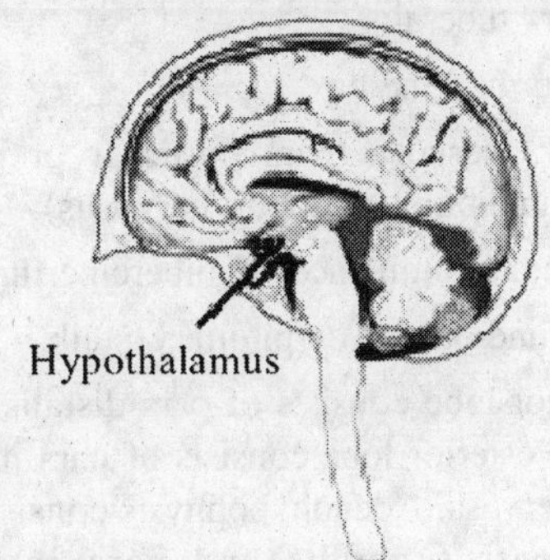

Fig : *Hypothalamus*

Pituitary gland

It is called the master gland of the body. It is substituted by the term 'hypophysis'. It is reddish gray coloured and small oval shaped structure. It is located at the base of the brain in the sellaturica of sphenoid bone. A stalk attaches hypophysis to the floor of third ventricle. Average weight is 0.5 to 0.6 g. In females it weighs from 0.6-0.7 g. Its dimensions are:

- 10 mm (anterio-posteriorly)
- 6 mm (dorsoventrally)
- 13 mm (laterally)

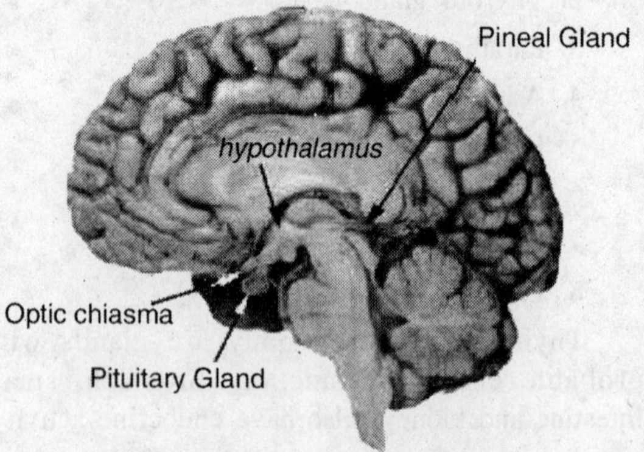

Fig : *Pituitary gland*

Anatomically, it has two lobes:

1. Anterior lobe of pituitary gland
2. Posterior lobe of pituitary gland

Its histology shows 6 parts. They are:

1. Pars distalis (pars anterior)
2. Pars tuberalis
3. Pars intermedia
4. Pars nervosa (pars posterior or processus infundibulis or lobus nervosus)
5. Median eminence of tubercinerium
6. Infundibulum or pituitary stalk.

Anterior lobe consists of pars distalis and pars tuberalis. Posterior lobe consists of pars intermedia and pars nervosa. Adenohypophysis consists of pars distalis, pars tuberalis and pars intermedia. Neurohypophysis consists of pars nervosa (lobus nervosus) and infundibulum (pituitary stalk or neural stalk).

Pars distalis contains acidophils, basophils and chromophobes. Pars intermedia contains basophilic polygonal or prismatic cells. Pars tuberalis contains mainly cuboidal columnar cells.

Blood Supply

Blood supply of anterior lobe: Anterior lobe of pituitary gland is supplied blood by several hypophyseal arteries. These originate from internal carotid artery and circle of willis. There are two sets of blood vessels. One set supplies the lobe directly. Second set reaches capillary plexus of median eminence and infundibular stem. Capillary plexus is drained by a long portal vein.

Blood supply to neural lobe: Neural lobe is supplied blood by inferior hypophyseal arteries. Vessels form capillary network while ending in pars nervosa.

Nerve supply: Few fibres from hypothalamo hypophyseal tract or carotid plexus or from greater superficial petrosal nerves have control over this gland. Probably, they may be vasomotor nerves.

Thyroid

This gland is situated at the root of the throat. It has two fairly lateral lobes, which are symmetrical. Each measures $5 \times 2 \times 2$ cm^3 approximately. These lobes are present one on either side of trachea. They are connected by a thin portion of thyroid tissue called as isthmus. Pyramidal lobe extends upwards from isthmus. Thyroid gland moves upwards during swallowing. Weight in adults is between 20-25 g. It is highly vascular gland.

Microscopical examination of thyroid shows follicles or vesicles. They are lined by low cuboidal epithelium. Thyroid follicles are spherical or oval shaped with irregular size of 15-150 microns diameter. They are lined by single layer of granular cubical cells with mitochondria and clear golgi apparatus. Bases of cells are in contact with fine basement membrane. Follicles are surrounded by highly vascular stroma. Cytoplasmic vesicles are found within the cell. Electron microscopy reveals two types of cells - Principal cells and para follicular cells. Solid clumps cells, lymphocytes and macrophages are seen between vesicles.

Blood supply : Superior and inferior thyroid arteries supply thyroid gland. Internal jugular vein and innominate vein drain the gland.

Lymphatic drainage : Lateral lymph nodes of neck commonly drain lymph. Anterior mediastinal lymph nodes drain to some extent.

Nerve supply: Sympathetic fibres derive from superior, middle and inferior cervical ganglia.

Parasympathetic fibres derive from superior and inferior recurrent laryngeal branches of vagus.

Parathyroid

It consists of four oval bodies embedded in posterior surface of thyroid. Each body measures 6 × 3 × 2 mm^3. Each of the two pairs are present vertically behind each of the two lobes of thyroid. Total weight is about 140 mg. Gland is highly vascular. Superior and inferior thyroid arteries supply blood. Nerve supply is same as for thyroid. There are two types of cells in parathyroid.

1. Chief cells or principal cells
2. Oxyphil cells or eosinophil cells.

Adrenal glands

Adrenal glands are two in number. They are also called suprarenal glands as each of the two glands are located on upper pole of each kidney. Right suprarenal gland is smaller of the two. Left one is large of the two. Dimensions of each gland are 50 × 30-40 × 10 mm^3.

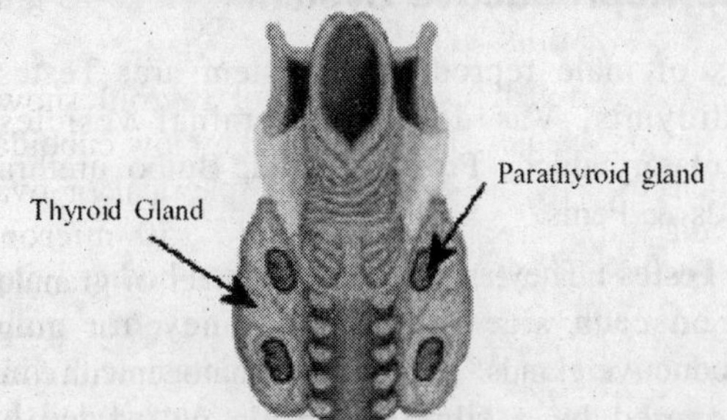

Fig. : *Parathyroid*

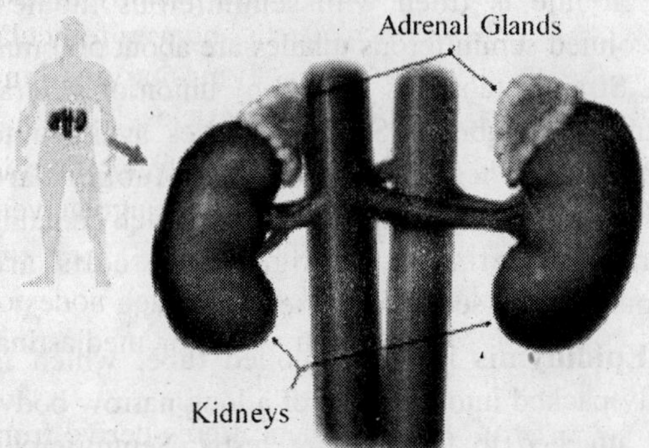

Fig. : *Adrenal Glands*

There are two parts in adrenal gland.

1. **Adrenal cortex:** Outer part consisting of (*a*) Zona glomerulosa (outer), (*b*) Zona fasciculata (middle) and (*c*) Zona reticularis (inner).
2. **Adrenal medulla:** Inner part consisting of irregular masses of polyhedral granular cells.

Pancreas

Human pancreas is large gland which is both exocrine and endocrine in its functions. It lies transversely across posterior abdominal wall behind the stomach at the level of 1st and 2nd lumbar vertebrae. It contains both exocrine cells and endocrine cells. Endocrine cells are distributed all over the gland. They are called as islets of Langerhans. These islets are not connected with duct system of the gland. There are mainly three distinct types of islet cells in human pancreas.

They are:

1. α-cells of islets of Langerhans.
2. β-cells of islets of Langerhans.
3. γ-cells of islets of Langerhans.

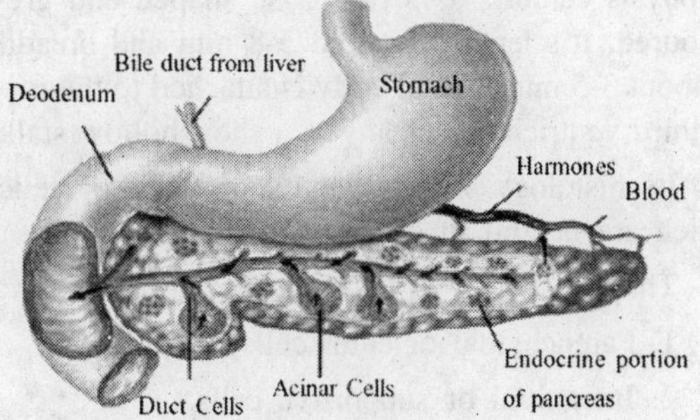

Fig. : *Pancreas*

α-cells are also called A2-cells and constitute 10-15%, β-cells are also called B-cells and constitute 30-40%. γ-cells are also called A1-cells and constitute 5%. In higher vertebrates, ratio of alpha cells and beta cells is 1 : 4 and other cell types are X or F, E & C.

Testes : Testes are the male reproductive organs concerned with spermatogenesis. For anatomy refer to Anatomy of Reproductive system.

Ovaries: Refer to Anatomy of Reproductive system.

Placenta: Refer to Anatomy of Reproductive system.

Thymus: It is both endocrine and lymphoid structure, located in the anterior and superior mediastina of thorax behind sternum. It extends from pericardium upwards upto the lower border of thyroid. There are two lobes in thymus gland. They are fused and asymmetrical. Right lobe is bigger than left lobe. Numerous lobules are present in each lobe. Follicles of lobules have diameter of 1 mm each.

Histology of Thymus shows:

(*a*) *Capsule* - dense connective tissue, rich in macrophages, mast cells, granulocytes and fat cells etc.

(*b*) *Cortex* - which is similar to lymph tissue of ordinary lymph nodes, but deficit of primary follicles.

(*c*) *Medulla* - broad, branched band of thymic tissue.

Pineal body: Pineal body is also called epiphysis cerebri. It is flat, cone shaped and grey coloured. It's length is about 5-8 mm and breadth is about 3-5 mm. Pineal body is attached to the roof of third ventricle by means of a short hollow stalk.

Its histology shows two major types of cells, which are neutral in origin.

They are:

1. Parenchymal or chief cells
2. Interstitial or supportive cells.

GIT as endocrines : Certain localised area of GIT acts as endocrine to secrete gastro intestinal hormones. Cells responsible for endocrine activity in GIT are not known with certainity. Gastrin I and II are produced in modified epithelial cells of glandular mucosa of pyloric part of stomach. Mucosa of upper part of small intestine secretes cholecystokinin - pancreozymin hormone. Duodenal mucosa produces secretin. Wall of stomach and small intestine produce gut glucagon hormone. Human gastric mucosa contains gastrone. Mucosa of upper small intestine produces villikinin. Intestinal lumen secretes enterocrinin.

Refer to digestive system for more anatomy.

Kidneys as Endocrine: Juxtaglomerular cells produce renin. Erythropoietin is largely produced by kidneys. Prostaglandins are also produced by kidneys. Refer to Excretory system for anatomy.

REPRODUCTIVE SYSTEM : MALE AND FEMALE

Continuity of any species is maintained by reproduction. Reproduction is the process of producing same type of offsprings. Mode of reproduction is sexual in human being.

Reproductive System : System consisting sex organs is called reproductive system. Primary sex organs are testes in males and ovaries in females. They are also called as gonads. Remaining structures are called secondary sex organs.

Male Reproductive System

Parts of male reproductive system are: Testes, Epididymis, Vas deferens, Seminal vesicles, Ejaculatory ducts, Prostate gland, Bulbo urethral glands & Penis.

Testes : They are two oval shaped bodies lying one on each side in scrotum. They are male reproductive glands. They are spermatogenic. Testis is covered by a fibrous capsule called tunica albuginea. Each testis consists of 200-300 lobules. Each lobule is filled with seminiferous tubules. Convoluted seminiferous tubules are about 500 mm long. Straight tubule is formed by union of several seminiferous tubules. Straight tubules again unite forming rete testis. Seminiferous tubules are supported by loose connective tissue which contains interstitial cells of Leydig. These cells are responsible for secretion of testosterone.

Epididymis is a fine coiled tube, which is tightly packed into the form of a long narrow body. It is attached to the back of testis. Seminiferous tubules open into it.

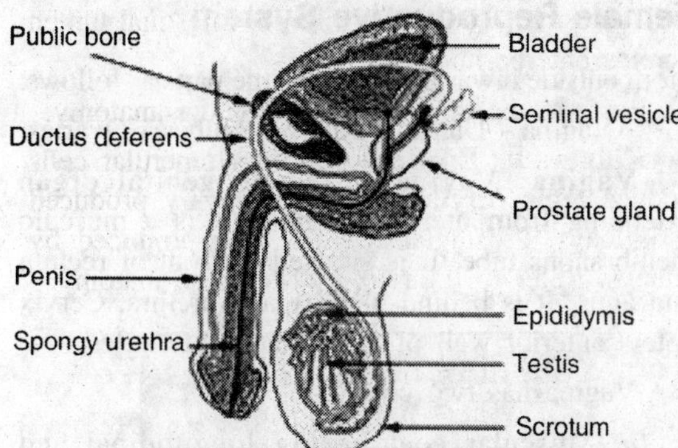

Fig. : *Male Reproductive System*

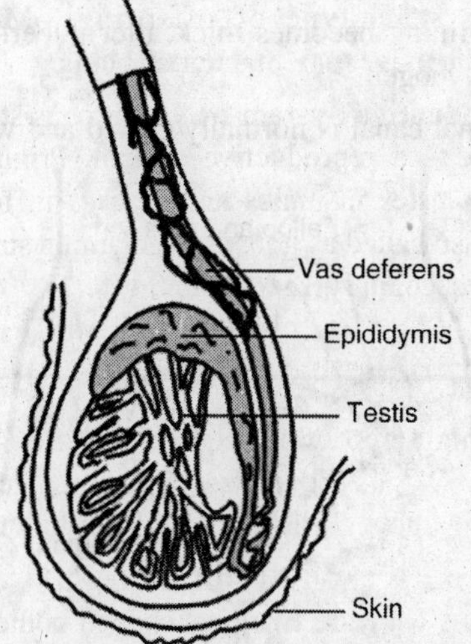

Fig. : *A testis (Testicle) looking from left side*

Vas Deferens: Vas deferens is continuation of epididymis. It enters pelvic part of abdomen and enters into prostatic part of urethra. It joins ejaculatory duct here.

Seminal Vesicles: Seminal vesicles are secretory glands. They are located between base of bladder and rectum. They secrete semen. Spermatozoa produced in testes adds to it. Seminal secretion from prostate also adds to it. Secretion of seminal vesicles is alkaline in nature. It constitutes large part of seminal fluid.

Ejaculatory ducts: Ducts of seminal vesicles and Vas deferens unite to form ejaculatory ducts. They begin at the base of prostate gland and at the opening of prostatic utricle in urethra.

Prostate gland: It is a nut sized secretory gland. It is present at the opening of bladder into urethra. It contains lobes. It consists glandular tissue and involuntary muscular tissue. Prostatic secretion is alkaline in nature and adds to semen. It nourishes spermatozoa. Prostaglandin is also secreted by prostate.

Bulbo urethral glands : They are situated on either side of membranous part of urethra. Ducts open into spongy portion of urethra. Their secretion also forms part of semen.

Penis: Penis is tubular male copulatory organ. Penis is supplied with large venous sinuses, which can fill with blood causing erection of the organ. Tip of penis is enlarged and is called glans penis. Glans penis contains urinary meatus in the centre. Glans penis is covered by loose double fold of skin. It is called prepuce or foreskin.

T.S. of penis shows three cylindrical bodies of erectile tissue. Erectile tissue is also called cavernous tissue. Two of the cylindrical bodies are corpora cavernosa. Third long body of erectile tissue is corpus cavernosum urethra. It contains urethra in it. It is also called as corpus spongiosum. Corpora cavernosa are arranged side by side in the dorsal half of the organ. Corpus spongiosum lies ventral to corpora cavernosa. Tunica albuginea Spongiosum is a stout sheath surrounding each erectile cylindrical body. All the three erectile cylindrical bodies are covered by fascia penis. It is elastic areolar tissue. Epidermis of penis is thin. Hair is absent on epidermis except at the root of penis.

Spermatozoa

It is the last descendent of male germ cell. It is a specialised cell which differs from ordinary cell in many ways. It is about 60 microns in length.

Parts of mature spermatozoon are:

1. Head
2. Tail.

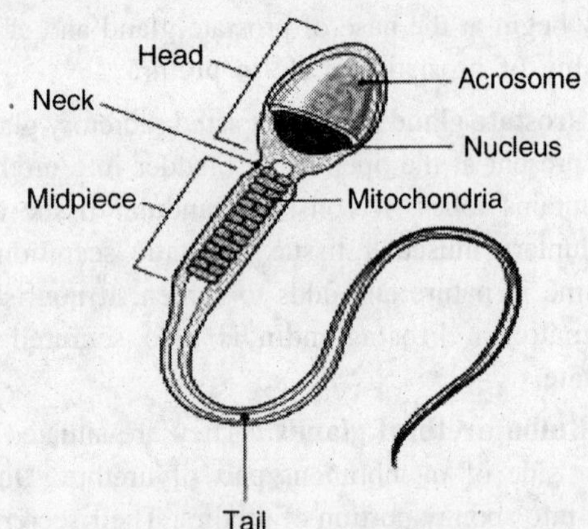

Fig. : *Spermatozoa*

Head

Shape: Oval from surface view. Pear shaped from side view. *Length :* 4.5 microns. *Diameter:* 2.5 - 3.5 microns

Head is nucleus with nuclear membrane surrounded by plasma membrane without cytoplasm in between. Head cap or acrosome covers interior two thirds of nucleus.

Tail: Tail is divided into: 1. Neck, 2. Body, 3. Main piece of tail and 4. End piece of tail.

Neck: It is a short, weak segment connecting head and body. Proximal centriole lies between head and neck whereas distal centriole lies between neck and body.

Body: It is middle piece of tail. It is also called engine room of spermatozoon.

It is cylindrical in shape. It has rings of fibrils with a sheath.

Length - 5-7 μ m Thickness - 1 μ m

Main piece of tail: Length - About 45 μ m Thickness - 1/2 micron at the base. It is tapering towards end piece. It consists of core of longitudinal filaments surrounded by fibrous sheath.

End piece of tail: Length - 5 μ m. Cross section is same as that of a cilium.

Normal sperm count: 40-300 millions/ml. of semen. Count of spermatozoa less than 20 million per ml. of semen is called oligospermia and it can cause infertility.

Female Reproductive System

From outside inwards it contains the parts as follows:

- Vagina - Uterus - Fallopian tubes - Ovaries

Vagina: Vagina is female genital organ extending from uterus to Labia. It is a musculo membranous tube. It is situated in front of rectum and anus. It is behind bladder and urethra. Cervix enters anterior wall of vagina at right angles.

Vagina has two coats:

(*a*) Muscular coat having longitudinal and circular fibres.

(*b*) Inner lining of mucous membrane.

This lining becomes thick after puberty and is rich in glycogen.

Vaginal canal is normally closed and wrinkled.

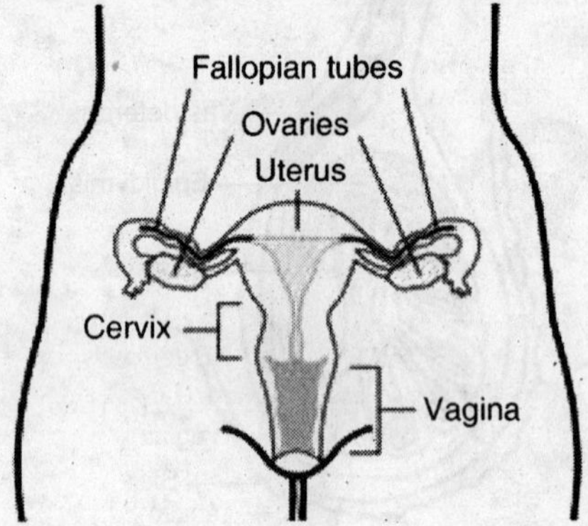

Fig. : *Female Reproductive System*

Uterus: Uterus is a hollow muscular organ. It is thick walled and situated in lesser pelvis between rectum and bladder. It is inverted pear shaped.

Length : about 7.5 cm. *Width :* about 5 cm.

Thickness : about 2.5 cm. *Weight :* about 30 g.

Uterus has two parts. They are:

1. Body and 2. Cervix.

Body : It is the upper broader part. Fallopian tubes open into uterus from sides in the upper part. Part of body above the entrance of fallopian tubes is called fundus.

Cervix : It is the lower part of uterus, narrower and more cylindrical than body.

Cervix has two openings. They are: Internal OS, External OS.

Internal OS is the opening of cervix at its upper end which is continuous with body of uterus (above). External OS is the opening of cervix at its lower end which is continuous with vagina (below). Cervix of uterus protrudes into vagina at right angle.

Uterine wall has two coats.

1. Myometrium and 2. Endometrium.

Myometrium is outer muscular coat. It is made of smooth muscle fibres arranged in three layers. They are inner longitudinal layer, middle thick oblique layer and outer thin longitudinal layer.

Endometrium is inner mucous membrane. It is lined by epithelical cells. Endometrium undergoes cyclic changes during menstrual cycle. Perimetrium is the outer serous coat.

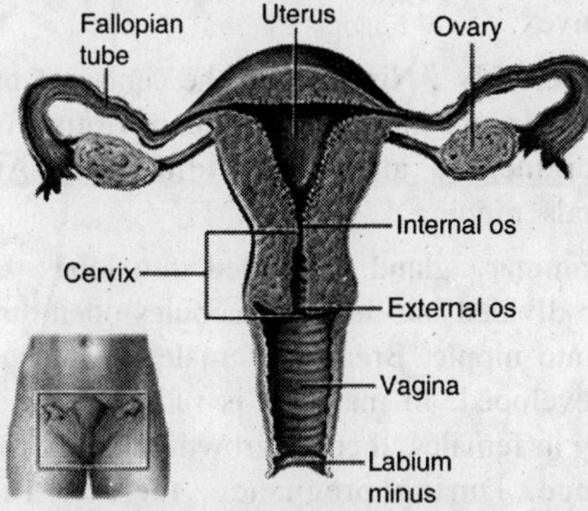

Fig. : *Parts of Uterus*

Fallopian tubes: They are two in number. They are situated in the upper part of broad ligaments of uterus. Length of each uterine tube is about 10 cm.

They transmit ova from ovaries to uterus.

Each tube has the following parts.

1. **Infundibulum** - trumpet shaped expansion, close to the ovary and having number of processes called fimbriae.
2. **Ampulla** - thin walled tortuous part. It forms more than half of uterine tube.
3. **Isthmus** - round and forming one third of tube.
4. **Uterine part** - passes through wall of uterus. It is 1 cm long.

Ovaries: Ovaries are two in number. They are bean shaped bodies lying one on each side at the free end of uterine tube. They hang from broad ligament by a fold of peritonium. This fold of peritonium is called mesovarium. They are supplied richly by blood vessels and nerves. Structure of ovaries shows variations at various stages of life such as childhood, puberty, pregnancy and menopause.

There are six features in the histology of ovaries. They are:

1. Germinal epithelium
2. Tunica albuginea
3. Stroma
4. Graffian follicles
5. Corpus luteum
6. Interstitial cells

Germinal epithelium: Germinal epithelium is the outermost covering. It is single layer of cuboidal cells.

Tunica albuginea: Tunica albuginea is a thin layer of eosinophilic collagenous connective tissue.

Stroma: Stroma is network of connective tissue, continuous with tunica albuginea. It is containing spindle shaped cells.

Graffian follicles: Graffian follicles are also called as vessicular follicles. They are small islands of cells in various stages of developement. They are scattered at the periphery of ovary. Immature follicles are called primordial follicles. Ovum is the central cell. Remaining cells surround ovum in single layer.

Corpus luteum: Corpus luteum develops on ruptured graffian follicle. It is temporary.

Interstitial cells: Interstitial cells are groups of polyhedral cells developed from cells of stroma or unruptured follicles.

- In infancy, follicles do not mature. There is no ovulation. No corpus luteum.

- At puberty, germinal epithelium contains flattened cells, large number of ruptured or unruptured maturing follicles and small size corporalutea.
- In pregnancy, there is large size corpus luteum.
- At menopause, ovaries atrophy, follicles disappear and are replaced by fibrous scars, interstitial cells degenerate and little oestrogen is produced.

Placenta: It is the functional connection between embryo and uterus, which is formed by dilatation and proliferation of maternal blood vessels. It consists of two parts: 1. Maternal part and 2. Foetal part.

External female genitalia: They are:

1. Mons pubis
2. Labia majora
3. Labia minora
4. Clitoris
5. Vestibule
6. Hymen
7. Greater vestibular glands
8. Perineum.

Mons pubis: Mons pubis is a pad of fat covered with skin. It lies over symphisis pubis. Pubic hairs grow here after puberty.

Labia majora: Labia majora are two folds of fatty tissue covered with skin. They extend backwards from mons on either side of vulva. It disappears into perineum behind. They develop at puberty and atrophy after menopause.

Labia minora: Labia minora are two smaller folds within labia majora. These fleshy folds meet in front to form prepuce. Prepuce is a hood like structure protecting clitoris.

Clitoris: Clitoris is small sensitive organ containing elastic tissue. It lies below mons pubis, protected by prepuce.

Vestibule: Vestibule is the cleft between labiae. Vaginal orifice and urethral orifice open into it.

Hymen: Hymen is double fold of mucous membrane blocking vaginal orifice and leaving gap at the front to allow menstrual flow in virgin woman.

Greater vestibular glands: Greater vestibular glands are two small glands lying under labia majora. They secrete a lubricating fluid, which facilitates sexual intercourse.

Perineum: Perineum is expanse of skin from the back of vaginal orifice back to the anus. It is 5 cm. long and bears hair.

Perineal body: Perineal body is a mass of muscular and fibrous tissue, separating vagina from rectum. Perineal skin is covering perineal body. Levatorạni is the name of the muscle of perineal body. It is the chief muscle of pelvic floor.

Mammary glands: They are accessory organs of female reproductive system. They secrete milk after parturition. They are circular in shape. They are convex.

Anteriorly : Nipple is in the centre of breast, projecting from skin. Nipple is pink in virgin woman. It is pigmented after first child birth. Areola surrounds nipple.

Mammary gland is divided into lobes. Lobes are sub divided into lobules. Lobules open through ducts into nipple. Breast of female before puberty is undeveloped. In males, it is rudimentary. After puberty in females, there is growth under hormonal influence. During pregnancy, there is further development and proliferation under hormonal influence. Development of breasts is completed during pregnancy. After parturition, there is lactation.

SENSE ORGANS

Sense organs are the organs of senses of body. They are: Eye, ear, tongue, nose and skin. Of these five organs, first four are organs of special senses. Skin is the organ of general sensations.

Eye

Eye is the organ of special sense of vision. It consists of eyeball accessory structures. Eye ball is almost spherical in shape. It is situated in anterior part of orbital cavity. Accessory structures of eye are: eyebrows, eye lids, lachrymal apparatus and extrinsic muscles of eye.

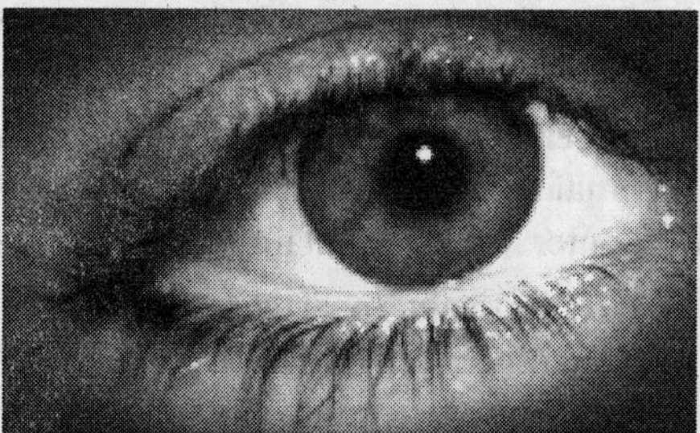

Fig. : *Human Eye*

Eye Ball : Eye ball contains three coats and light transmitting structures.

Layers of eye ball : Layers of eye ball are:

1. **Outer fibrous coat** - containing posterior opaque part called sclera and anterior transparent part called cornea.
2. **Middle vascular coat** - containing choroid, ciliary body and iris.
3. **Inner nervous coat** - also called retina.

- Sclera forms 5/6th of outer fibrous coat.
- Cornea forms 1/6th of outer fibrous coat.
- Choroid is highly vascular. It forms 5/6th of middle coat. It is dark.
- Ciliary body is in between choroid and iris.
- Iris is anterior continuation of ciliary body and is a pigmented membrane. Its central opening is called pupil. Pupil is controlled by circular and radial muscles.
- Circular muscles are pupillary constrictors and radial muscles are pupillary dilators.
- Retina is the innermost nervous coat of eye ball. It contains special structures called 'Rods and Cones'. They are for reception of light. Each retina contains 6 million cones and 120 million rods. Rods are for critical vision and cones for dim vision.

Optic disc: It is the point where optic nerve leaves eye ball. This point does not contain retina and thus it is photo insensitive. It is also called blind spot.

Macula: It is a small area of retina. It is also called yellow spot, situated opposite to the centre of pupil lateral to the entrance of optic nerve. It is for focussing near vision.

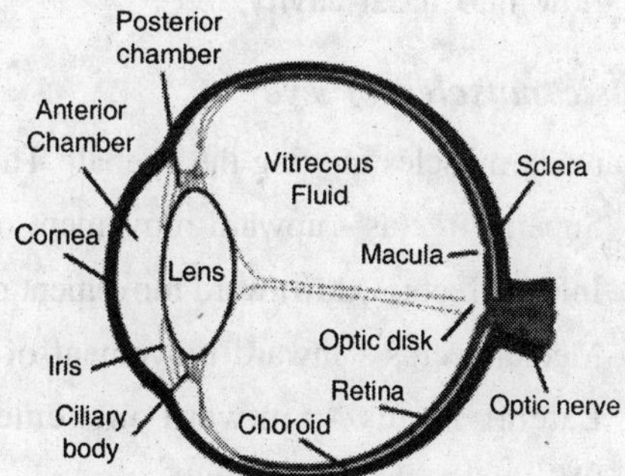

Fig. : *Structure of Human Eye*

Conjuctiva: It is the thin stratified mucous membrane covering the exposed part of eye ball.

Light transmitting structures of Eye ball : They are:

1. Aqueous humour
2. Lens and
3. Vitreous humour

- Aqueous humour is fluid present in anterior chamber of eye.
- Lens is behind iris and pupil. It is the organ of refraction of light onto retina.
- Vitreous humour is jelly like fluid in between lens and retina. It is responsible for maintenance of shape of eye.

Accesory structures of eye: They are eye brows, eyelids, lachrymal apparatus.

Eyebrows: They are arches of thick skin present over the eyes and containing thick hairs.

Eyelids: They are musculocutaneous curtain like structures in front of eye. Upper eyelids are bigger than lower eyelids. Eye lashes are hairs projecting from eyelids.

Lachrymal apparatus: It consists of:

1. Lachrymal gland situated in the lateral end of upper eyelid.
2. Lachrymal duct through which tears come out.
3. Lachrymal sac.
4. Naso lachrymal duct through which tears flow into nasal cavity.

Extrinsic muscles of eye

There are six muscles moving the eyeball. They are

1. Superior rectus - upward movement of eye.
2. Inferior rectus - downward movement of eye.
3. Medial rectus - inward movement of eye.
4. Lateral rectus - outward movement of eye.

These four are straight muscles.

5. Inferier oblique - upward and outward movement of eye.
6. Superior oblique - downward and outward movement of eye.

These two are oblique muscles.

Ear

Ear is the organ of special sense of hearing. It is also responsible for equilibrium. It is divided into three parts.

Parts of ear are:

1. External Ear: Lying outside the skull
2. Middle Ear: Lying inside the skull
3. Internal Ear

External ear: It contains two parts. They are:

- **Pinna** - Funnel shaped organ made of fibroelastic cartilage. It is the organ of collection of sound waves.
- **External auditory meatus** - small channel of about 3 cm length. It is lined with skin and wax creating glands are contained in this part. Hair and wax present in its outer part prevent dust particles. Its inner part is closed by a thin membrane called tympanic membrane or ear drum. This canal is the organ of conveyance of vibrations of sound to the tympanic membrane.

Middle ear: It is a small cavity in the temporal bone, internal to eardrum. *i.e.* tympanic membrane forms its outer wall. It contains air. It contains:

1. Fenestra ovalis (oval window) and fenestra rotundum (round window). Round window is also called fenestra cochleae.
2. Eustachian tube - which communicates with nasopharynx. It helps in equalisation of pressure on both sides of tympanic membrane.
3. Auditus - Channel connecting middle ear posteriorly with mastoid antrum of temporal bone.
4. Auditory ossicles - Malleus, incus and stapes arranged across middle ear.

These are minute bones of middle ear and are bound by ligaments. They vibrate as a single unit when sound waves impinge on tympanic membrane.

Internal ear: It contains:

1. Bony labyrinth - present in petrous portion of temporal bone.
2. Membranous labyrinth - lyeing with the bony labyrinth.

Fluids of Internal ear: Perilymph is the fluid of bony labyrinth. Endolymph is the fluid of membranous labyrinth.

Structures of bony labyrinth: Bony labyrinth contains vestibule, cochlea and semi circular canals. Cochlea is the organ of hearing and semicircular canals for equilibrium.

Vestibule: It is present between vestibule and semicircular canals. Vestibule contains utricle and saccule. Utricle and saccule are parts of membranous labyrinth cochlea. It is a bony spiral canal. These spirals wind round a central bony pillar Modiolus.

Basilar membrane is membranous septum dividing cochlea into two parts. Organ of corti is the neuroepithelium of cochlea. It is auditory receptor resting on basilar membrane. Cochlear nerve fibres enter the organ of Corti. Vestibulocochlear nerve collects sensation of equilibrium from vestibular division. It collects sensation of hearing from cochlear division. Auditory nerve fibres reach special nucleus on the back of thalamus and then cerebral cortex.

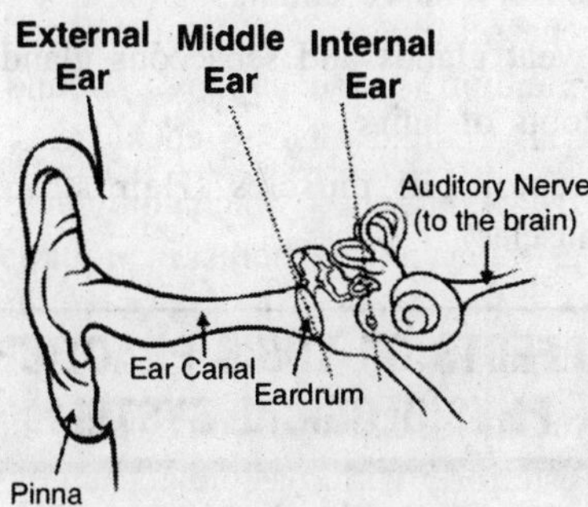

Fig. : *Structure of Ear*

Semicircular Canals: Each ear contains three semicircular canals. They are arranged at right angles to each other. They are superior, posterior and lateral canals. Ampulla is enlarged end of each canal. Vestibular nerve endings are present in ampullae. Ampullae help cerebellum in maintaining equilibrium. Semicircular canals are for informing dynamic equilibrium and otolithic organ for static equilibrium.

Tongue

Tongue is the organ containing taste buds. Taste buds are receptors of special sensation of taste. Epithelium of tongue is modified into papillae and taste buds. Papillae are: 1. Filiform, 2. Fungiform and 3. Circumvallate.

Taste buds are located on the sides of papillae. Taste buds are oval clusters of cells with a small pore on the surface in the epithelial layer. They measure 60-80 microns in length and 40 microns in diameter. Few taste buds are located on soft palate, epiglottis and pharynx.

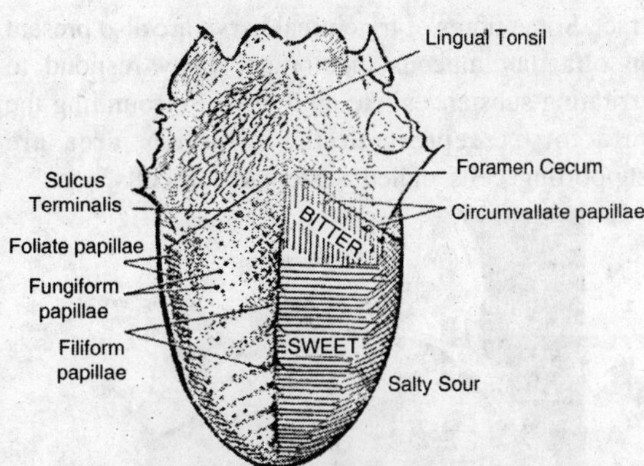

Fig. : *Tongue*

Cells within taste buds are two types. They are: (1) Taste cells or gustatory cells or hair cells, (2) Supporting cells. Nerve fibres arise from hair cells and form nerve plexus near basement membrane. They finally join with glossopharyngeal or facial nerve. Branch of facial nerve innervates anterior 2/3rds of tongue. Glossopharyngeal nerve innervates posterior 1/3rd of tongue. Vagus nerve receives impulses from pharynx and throat. Taste buds are surrounded by stratified squamous epithelium of tongue. These nerves are connected to taste centre present in medulla. It is connected to thalamus and cerebral cortex. There are four types of taste buds based on sensation of taste–bitter, sour, salt and sweet.

Nose

Olfactory Receptors: Olfactory receptors are specialised bipolar nerve cells present in the olfactory area of mucous membrane of upper part of nasal cavity. They are about 10-20 millions in man.

They receive sensation of smell. Total surface area of olfaction on each side in man is about 250 mm^2. Olfactory area in man is comparativly small and man is called microsmotic animal.

Olfactory area in dog being large, it is macrosmotic animal. Ends of olfactory receptors join to form olfactory nerve (1st cranial nerve). Olfactory nerve passes through root of nose and ends in olfactory bulb. Olfactory bulb is connected to olfactory centre in the cerebrum through olfactory tract. Some fibres of trigeminal nerve are also present in olfactory mucous membrane. They respond to irritating substances like ammonia. Surrounding the olfactory receptors in the olfactory area are supporting cells called sustentacular cells.

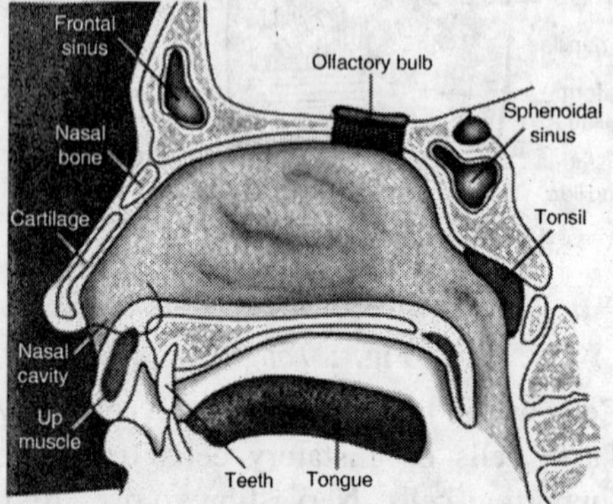

Fig. : *Structure of Nose*

Skin consists of two layers. They are:

1. Epidermis - Outer layer
2. Dermis - Inner layer.

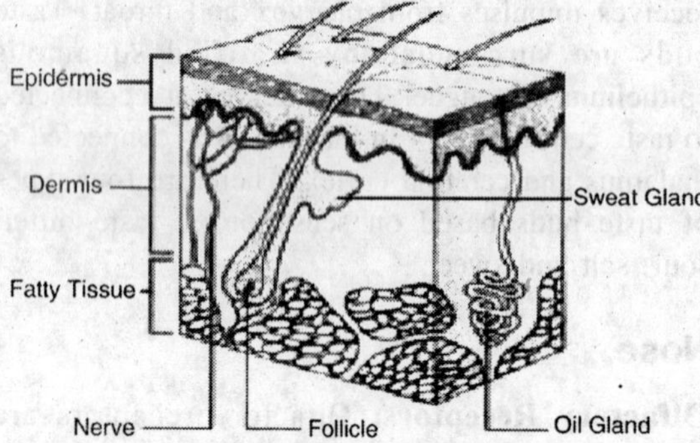

Fig. : *Structure of Skin*

Epidermis is made of stratified epithelium. Layers of epidermis are:

1. Stratum corneum
2. Stratum lucidum
3. Stratum granulosum
4. Stratum germinatum.

- Stratum corneum contains scale like cells. They have keratin protein and these cells are constantly replaced.
- Stratum lucidum is a glistening layer.
- Stratum granulosum is made of spindle shaped cells. They have granules in their cytoplasm.
- Stratum germinatum is made of cuboidal cells. Multiplication of skin cells takes place in this layer.

Dermis: Dermis is inner layer of skin. It contains melanophore cells containing melanin pigment, arterial and venous capillaries and also:

- Sensory nerve endings
- Sweat glands and sebaceous glands
- Roots of hairs
- Erector pili muscles (Hair straightening muscles).

THE EFFECTS OF YOGIC PRACTICES ON PHYSIOLOGICAL SYSTEM

The yogic practices like the Asanas, Pranayamas, Sat-karmas (the six practices for internal purification), and Meditation effect the body systems individually as well as collectively.

The Effects of Asanas

There are three types of Asanas – Meditative, Cultural and Relaxative.

During **Meditative Asanas** *(Dhyanasanas)* the practitioner sits on a particular posture with the spine and head erect, relaxing all the muscles, keeping the hands on the knees in Jnana Mudra. Due to the erect posture of the body, the organs like the heart and lungs in the chest cavity, stomach, intestine, liver, kidney, pancreas and spleen in the abdominal cavity, the sex organs in the pelvic cavity, become free from pressure and are able to work freely, through the free flow of blood to these areas. As a result, they become healthy and strong.

In the **Cultural Asanas,** the spine is bent forward, backward, sideward and twisted. Thereby, the vertebral column becomes flexible. Flexibility removes the difficulty of movement in the body. The body is rejuvenated due to the circulation of sufficient amount of fresh blood to the various parts of the body and thus becomes filled with freshness and vitality.

In the **Relaxative Asanas** the muscles of the body and the mind are relaxed, and thus all the internal organs of the body as well as the mind get rest.

Awareness is the first principle to be observed in practicing yoga. Thus, the practice of Asana increases awareness, stability and endurance.

The Effects of Pranayama

Pranayamas are breathing techniques whereby the prana, the vital energy, is controlled and extended. Oxygen that goes inside our body through breathing is used in the cells of our body for metabolic activities and production of energy. Respiration is a natural process. It is involuntary. In our usual respiration only one third of our lungs is filled up. Pranayama is voluntary; it is a special type of breathing where it tries to fill up the entire lungs. Thereby, more oxygen enters into the lungs which means the cells receive more oxygen for their use and are able to produce more energy.

Due to the uses of all the three lobes in pranayama, they become active and energised. As a result, the vital index goes up and the body of the practitioner becomes full of vitality with strength, agility, cheerfulness and enthusiasm.

The Effects of Meditation

Meditation is keeping the mind fixed on an object or thought for a long period. In meditation, all distractions, stress and anxiety are removed from the mind. When the mind becomes stress-free, the frequency of the brain waves gradually slows down and comes to the minimum possible frequency. At such a stage, the analytical power increases clarity comes to the mind, memory increases and the latent talents start unfolding.

In mediation, the entire mind-body complex is relaxed. As a result, metabolic activities comes to the minimum; hence all the parts of the body get rest. The entire body is rejuvenated with energy and freshness.

The Effects of Sat-Karmas

The Sat-Karmas or the six means of purification helps to keep the internal body clean by removing the residual waste materials from the body. The internal organs, free from accumulated waste materials, are enabled to function efficiently and thus they becomes free from diseases. Sat-karmas not only improve the physical health of the practitioner, but also prepare the body towards practicing various types of higher yogic practices.

NUTRITION AND DIETETICS

Concepts of Food

Food is the basic necessity of man. It is a mixture of different nutrients such as carbohydrate, protein, fat, vitamins and minerals. These nutrients are essential for growth, development and maintenance of good health throughout life. They also play a vital role in meeting the special needs of pregnant and lactating women and patients recovering from illness.

FUNCTIONS OF FOOD

Food may be classified according to their functions in the body.

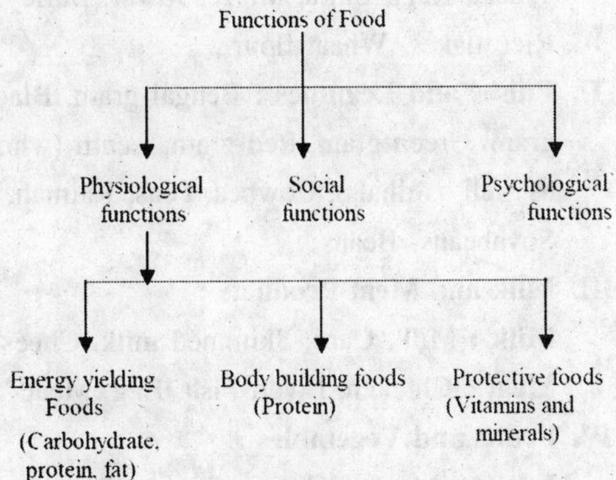

Fig. : *Functions of food*

Physiological functions of food

(*i*) **Energy yielding foods:** Foods rich in carbohydrates and fats are called energy yielding foods. They provide energy to sustain the involuntary processes essential for continuance of life, to carry out various professional, household and recreational activities and to convert food ingested into usable nutrients in the body.

The energy needed is supplied by the oxidation of foods consumed. Cereals, roots and tubers, dried fruits, oils, butter and ghee are all good sources of energy.

(*ii*) **Body building foods:** Foods rich in protein are called body building foods. Milk, meat, eggs and fish are rich in proteins of high quality. Pulses and nuts are good sources of protein but the protein is not of high quality. These foods help to maintain life and promote growth. They also supply energy.

(*iii*) **Protective and Regulatory foods:** Foods rich in protein, minerals and vitamins are known as protective and regulatory foods. They are essential for health and regulate activities such as maintenance of body temperature, muscle contraction, control of water balance, clotting of blood, removal of waste products from the body and maintaining heartbeat. Milk, egg, liver, fruits and vegetables are protective foods.

Social functions of food

Food has always been the central part of our community, social, cultural and religious life. It has been an expression of love, friendship and happiness at religious, social and family get-togethers.

Psychological functions of food

In addition to satisfying physical and social needs, foods also satisfy certain emotional needs of human beings. These include a sense of security, love and acceptance. For example, preparation of delicious foods for family members is a token of love and affection.

Table : *Five Food Group System*

Food Group	Main Nutrients
I. Cereals, Grains and Products : Rice, Wheat, Ragi, Bajra, Maize, Jowar, Barley, Rice flakes, Wheat flour.	Energy, Protein, Invisible fat, Vitamin – B_1, Vitamin – B_2, Folic Acid, Iron, Fibre.
II. Pulses and Legumes : Bengal gram, Black gram, Green gram, Red gram, Lentil (whole as well as dhals), Cowpea, Peas, Rajmah, Soyabeans, Beans.	Energy, Protein, Invisible fat, Vitamin – B_1, Vitamin – B_2, Folic Acid, Calcium, Iron, Fibre.
III. Milk and Meat Products :	
Milk : Milk, Curd, Skimmed milk, Cheese	Protein, Fat, Vitamin – B_{12}, Calcium.
Meat : Chicken, Liver, Fish, Egg, Meat.	Protein, Fat, Vitamin – B_2
IV. Fruits and Vegetables :	
Fruits : Mango, Guava, Tomato Ripe, Papaya, Orange. Sweet Lime, Watermelon.	Carotenoids, Vitamin – C, Fibre.
Vegetables (Green Leafy) : Amaranth, Spinach, Drumstick leaves, Coriander leaves, Mustard leaves, fenugreek leaves.	Invisible Fats, Carotenoids, Vitamin – B_2. Folic Acid, Calcium, Iron, Fibre.

Other Vegetables : Carrots, Brinjal, Ladies fingers, Capsicum, Beans, Onion, Drumstick, Cauliflower.	Carotenoids, Folic Acid, Calcium, Fibre.
V. Fats and Sugars :	
Fats : Butter, Ghee, Hydrogenated oils, Cooking oils like Groundnut, Mustard, Coconut.	Energy, Fat, Essential Fatty Acids
Sugars : Sugar, Jaggery	Energy

CEREAL AND CEREAL PRODUCTS

Cereals form the staple food of the human race. In India wheat, rice, maize (corn), oats, jowar, ragi and bajra are the common cereals and millets used.

Nutritive Value of Cereals

Cereals are an important and economic source of energy. Hundred grams of cereals supply 340 kilo calories of energy. Cereals are also a significant source of proteins (8 – 11 per cent) in the diets of people whose staple food is cereals.

However, cereal protein is incomplete as it lacks an essential amino acid, lysine. This lack is made up when cereals are eaten along with other protein foods such as dhals, pulses and milk.

Wheat flour contains glutelin and gliadin as proteins which are commonly known as gluten. The strength of the wheat flour is based on the quality of gluten used.

Whole grains chiefly furnish starch, proteins, minerals, B-Vitamins and fibre. Refined cereals lose part of the protein, minerals, and B-Complex vitamins in milling. They contain a little more starch than whole cereals.

Whole grains contain more vitamins, minerals and fibre than refined grain and are valuable dietary sources of iron, phosphorus, thiamine and fibre.

Nutrient Content of Ragi, Maize and Jowar

Ragi: Ragi or finger millet is widely consumed without any refining by many people in rural areas. It contains B Vitamins but is poor in thiamine. Ragi is rich in minerals especially calcium. It is also rich in fibre and is a fair source of iron.

Maize or corn: Maize, like any other cereal is rich in calories. It is deficient in amino acid lysine. It is a good source of carotene and contains thiamine and folic acid in appreciable amounts.

Jowar: Jowar or Sorghum is grown in Maharashtra, Karnataka, Madhya Pradesh, Gujarat, Uttar Pradesh and parts of Tamil Nadu. It is rich in carbohydrate, and B-Complex vitamins. It is poor in vitamin-A and rich in dietary fibre. Compared to rice, jowar is richer in protein but the quality is not as good as rice protein.

Advantages of Including A Combination of Cereals in the Menu

Cereals are the main source of energy in Indian diets contributing 70-80 per cent of daily energy intake of majority of Indians. The major cereals consumed in India are rice, wheat, jowar, bajra and ragi.

Rice is the staple diet of South Indians. However, rice among the cereals is a poor source of calcium and iron. Whole wheat is a fair source of protein and fibre.

Although rice contains less protein when compared to other cereals, its protein quality is better than that of other cereals.

Ragi is rich in minerals especially calcium. Millets including ragi are rich in minerals and fibre. Inclusion of millets will help in making up deficiencies of some minerals in the diet besides providing bulk to the diet, particularly rice based ones.

The nutritive value of cereals varies with the part of the grain used. All whole cereals furnish starch, protein, iron, phosphorus, thiamin and fibre but refined cereals lose part of these nutrients during the milling process.

A judicious combination of different cereals in the days diet will help to meet the nutrient requirements.

For example, wheat dosa, rice flakes payasam, ragi adai and broken wheat uppuma can be included in the menu instead of rice-based meals alone. Batters used for idli and dosai and doughs used for chappatis. This can be prepared using a combination of cereal flours. This will contribute different nutrients to the days diet.

PULSES

Pulses are the edible fruits or seeds of pod-bearing leguminous plants. The term pulse in India is used for edible legumes and dhal is used for decuticled split legumes. Bengal gram, red gram, black gram, green gram, lentil, horse gram, peas and kesari dhal are some of the major pulse crops in India. Soyabean is also grown.

Nutrient Content of Pulses

Pulses give 340 calories per 100 gm which is almost similar to cereal calorie. They are a rich source of protein containing about 18-25 per cent protein. Soyabean is an exception containing about 35 to 40 per cent protein. All pulses contain sufficient amount lysine which is deficient in cereals and therefore they can supplement cereal protein. A mixture of cereals and pulses is superior to that of either one. Hence, a combination of cereals and pulses is ideal for human consumption.

Pulses contain 55-60 per cent of carbohydrate including starch soluble sugar and fibre.

They contain 1.5 per cent lipids. Pulses also contain calcium, magnesium, zinc, iron, potassium and phosphorus. They are a poor source of carotene and vitamin C but fairly rich in niacin. Germination increases the vitamin C content of pulses. The thiamine content of pulses is equal to or exceeds that of cereals. Being rich in B-Vitamins, they contribute significantly to B-Vitamin intake.

Toxic Substances In Pulses

Some toxic substances are naturally present in some pulses. These include trypsin inhibitors and haemagglutinins. Trypsin inhibitor, as the name indicates, interferes with digestion of proteins by inhibiting the action of the enzyme trypsin. Haemagglutinins combine with haeme and thus destroy haemoglobin. Fortunately, both of these toxic substances are destroyed by heat, which is used in the normal cooking process.

Broad beans contain some toxic substances. When these beans are consumed raw a disease called favism occurs. This disease is characterized by haemolytic anemia. Since human beings usually do not consume broad beans raw, they are not likely to suffer from favism.

Kesari dhal also contains a toxic substance. This dhal is grown in Madya Pradesh (M.P). It was observed that during the drought conditions, only this dhal is grown and used as a staple food. When this dhal is consumed over a long time paralysis of lower limbs occurs in males. This is known as lathyrism. It is reported that when the intake of kesari dhal is restricted to 30 per cent of the total calorie intake, no adverse effects are observed. Therefore it is important to ensure that the intake of this dhal must be restricted to a maximum of 30 per cent of the total calorie intake.

VEGETABLES AND FRUITS

India with its diverse, but favourable agroclimatic conditions produces a wide range of tropical and temperate fruits and vegetables. The annual production of these crops is about 53 million tonnes.

Vegetables are plants or parts of plants served with the main course of a meal. Apart from the nutritive value, vegetables probably do more than any other group of foods to add appetising colour, texture and flavour to our daily food.

With the wide choice of colour of vegetables, it is possible to select a vegetable with a desired colour to highten the appearance of a meal.

The texture of a vegetable varies depending upon whether it is served raw or cooked. The texture and appearance of meals can then be varied by the way the vegetable is served.

Vegetables contain a wide range of characteristic flavours. By a proper choice of vegetables, the desired flavour of a meal can be obtained.

A fruit is the edible and juicy product of a tree or plant and consists of the matured ovary including its seeds and adjacent parts. Usually fruits are sweet, with a wide range of flavours, colours and textures.

Classification of Vegetables

Vegetables can be classified into three groups according to their nutritive value.

- green leafy vegetables
- roots and tubers
- other vegetables

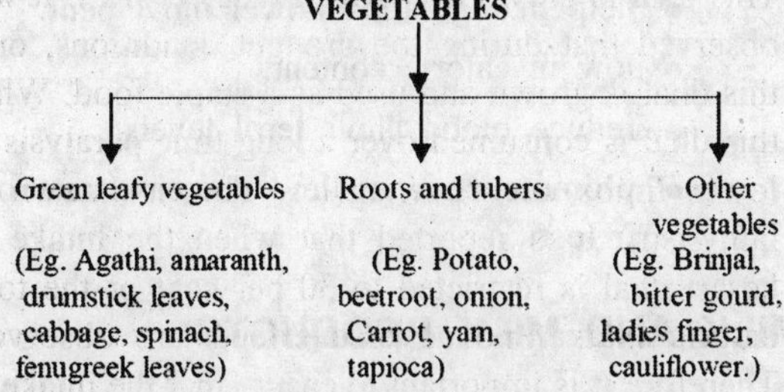

Fig. : *Classification of vegetables*

Nutrient Content of Vegetables and Fruits

Vegetables

(i) **Green Leafy Vegetables:** They are an inexpensive rich source of many nutrients such as β-carotene, ascorbic acid, folic acid, calcium, iron and fibre. They are a poor source of protein.

(ii) **Roots and Tubers:** Roots and tubers are rich in carbohydrates and are a source of energy in the diet. Carrot and yellow varieties of yam are rich in carotene and potato contains Vitamin C. Tapioca and yam are rich in calcium. Roots and tubers are a poor source of iron, protein and a fair source of B-Vitamins.

(iii) **Other Vegetables:** These are a good source of dietary fibre and add variety to the diet. They are a fairly good source of vitamins and minerals. (E.g.) brinjal, ladies finger, cauliflower, cucumber, gourd varieties.

Fruits

A fruit is a mature ovary of a flower. The fleshy portion of the pericarp makes up the chief edible portion of the fruit.

Fruits can be classified as follows:

Berries - Gooseberry, grapes, strawberry.

Citrus - Lemon, lime, orange, sweet lime.

Drupes - Peach, plums, apricot.

Melons - Water melon, musk melon

Pomes - Apple, pear.

Berries

Berries are fruits with layers of pericarp (fruit coat) which are often homogenous, except for the skin on the outside. The pericarp layers are pulpous and juicy, and contain seeds embedded in the pulp mass. The fruits have fragile cell structure that is damaged by rough handling or freezing.

Citrus Fruits

These fruits belong to the genus *Citrus* which contains about 16 species of evergreen aromatic shrubs and trees mostly with thorny branches distributed throughout the tropical and subtropical regions of the world. The common citrus fruits are orange, lemon and lime. The bright colour, pleasing flavour and sweetness make them a favourite fruit. They are served as juice and can be eaten raw.

Drupes

Drupes are edible fruits with a thin skin, and juicy flesh enclosing a single seed (Stone). Apricots, cherries, peaches and plums belong to this group.

Melons

Melons belong to the same family as cucumbers (Cucurbitaceae). Melons are commonly eaten raw. Their flesh consists of about 94% water and only 5% sugars. The seeds stripped of their hard coats may be eaten and also yield an edible oil.

Pomes

Pomes are fruits of apple and pear trees. The receptacle, surrounds the ovaries in the flower, enlarges to become edible and juicy, and encloses the cells containing the seeds.

Fruits particularly citrus varieties and guava are a good source of vitamin C. Yellow fruits like mango and papaya contain β-carotene. Banana is a good source of carbohydrate and hence energy. Fruits are a poor source of protein and fat with the exception of avacado.

Fruits also contain fibre and minerals such as sodium, potassium and magnesium. They are not a good source of calcium. Dry fruits, seethaphal and watermelon contribute appreciable amounts of iron.

Need For Inclusion of Fruits and Vegetables in the Days Menu

1. Fruits and vegetables provide vitamins and minerals required for growth and maintenance of health and are thus termed as protective foods.
2. Roots and tubers provide energy.
3. Vegetables are low in fat and can be used liberally in low calorie diets for weight reduction.
4. Besides providing nutrients they add variety to the diet. They make the diet attractive by their texture, flavour and colour.
5. Fruits and vegetables contain phytochemicals. The term phytochemicals refers to the wide variety of plant compounds naturally produced by plants. They include plant pigments and flavouring substances. Fruits and vegetables with bright colours viz., yellow, orange, red, green, blue, purple contain phytochemicals.

   Beta-Carotene, Vitamin C and Vitamin E are nutrients that function as antioxidants. An antioxidant is a substance that significantly reduces or prevents oxidation of fatty acids and protein thus preventing cell and tissue damage caused by free radicals in the body.

   Free radicals are unstable molecules resulting from normal metabolic processes. During these processes oxygen molecules lose an electron, which creates an unstable (molecule) thereby causing oxidative stress.

   These free radicals attack healthy cells in the body in the hope of finding another electron to stabilize themselves. This process can cause damage to healthy cells.
6. Intake of fibrous fruits and vegetables are important as they:
   - give satiety and thereby decrease food intake.
   - help in regulating bowel movement.
   - low in calorie content.
   - reduce blood cholesterol levels.
   - promote chewing and decrease rate of ingestion.

MILK AND MILK PRODUCTS

The story of milk goes back to the beginning of civilization itself. Cattle were domesticated even in prehistoric times and milk was one of the most essential of all foods. Milk is one of the most complete single foods available in nature for health and promotion of growth.

Milk is the normal secretion of mammary gland of mammals. Its purpose in nature is to provide good nourishment for the young of the particular species producing it. Man has learnt the art of using milk and milk products as a food for his well being and has increased the milk producing function of the animals best adapted as a source of milk for him.

The cow is the principle source of milk for human consumption in many part of the world. Other animals as source of milk for human beings are the buffalo, goat, sheep, camel and mare. In India, more milk is obtained from the buffalo than the cow. Some amount of goat milk is also consumed.

Nutritive Value of Milk

Milk is a complex fluid containing protein, fat, carbohydrate, vitamins and minerals. The main protein in milk is casein and it constitutes 3.0-3.5 per cent of milk.

The fat content of milk varies from 3.5 per cent in cow's milk to about 8.0 per cent in buffalo's milk. Fat is present in the form of fine globules varying in diameter from 1 to 10 μm (micrometers). Milk also contains phospholipids and cholesterol.

Lactose is the sugar present in milk. The important minerals in milk are calcium, phosphorus, sodium and potassium. Milk is an excellent source of riboflavin and a good source of Vitamin A. However, milk is a poor source of iron and ascorbic acid. The small amount of iron present is bio available.

Physical Properties of Milk

Acidity: Milk has a pH of about 6.5 to 6.7. The salts of the minerals – calcium, phosphorus, sodium and potassium help to maintain this pH level.

Viscosity: The viscosity of milk is affected by temperature, amount and nature of dispersion of protein and fat, acidity and the effects of various enzymes and bacteria. Homogenization increases the viscosity of milk.

Freezing Point: The freezing point of milk is –0.55°C.

Boiling Point: Milk boils at 100.2°C.

Pasteurisation of Milk

Milk is a favourable medium for bacterial growth. Pasteurisation destroys all pathogenic bacteria, including those causing typhoid, tuberculosis, diphtheria as well as yeasts and moulds.

Pasteurization is a process which consists of heating milk to a certain temperature for a definite time to ensure destruction of harmful bacteria. There are three methods of pasteurisation.

(*a*) **Holding method or Batch process:** In this method, milk is held at 62.8°C for 30 minutes and then rapidly cooled to prevent multiplication of surviving bacteria.

(*b*) **High temperature short time (HTST) method or continuous process:** Milk is heated to 71.7°C for not less than 15 seconds.

(*c*) **Ultra High temperature method:** Milk is heated to a temperature of 93.4°C for 3 seconds.

Advantages of Pasteurization

- During pasteurization the nutritive value of milk is not altered to a great extent because the temperature employed is not high and cooking time is short. However, there is a slight decrease in heat labile vitamin such as thiamine and ascorbic acid. Proteins are denatured only slightly and minerals are not appreciably precipitated.
- It does not produce an unpleasant cooked flavour.
- Shelf life of milk is increased due to a marked decrease in the total bacterial count.
- Harmful pathogens especially TB bacteria are destroyed.

NUTS AND OIL SEEDS

Nutritive Value of Nuts

Nuts are a rich source of protein and fat and a good source of B-Vitamin and antioxidant vitamin E. They are a concentrated source of energy.

Groundnut, cashewnut, coconut and almonds are the nuts commoly used in India and their nutritive value is given in table.

- Groundnuts are a very rich source of protein and fat. They are exceptionally rich in niacin. Groundnuts are boiled or roasted and consumed.

  It is also used in the preparation of groundnut butter. The chief product is the oil which can be used for cooking. The cake left after the oil is extracted is purified and used in supplementary mixes.

- Cashewnuts are also a rich source of protein and fat and contain appreciable amount of iron. It is widely used in the preparation of sweets and confectionery.

  It can be roasted and eaten. Cashewnuts are also used to garnish dishes such as pulavs and payasam.

- The white flesh of coconut is rich in calories though not a very good source of protein. It is extensively used in cookery in Tamil Nadu and Kerala in the preparation of curries, chutneys, sweets and puddings.

  The white flesh when dried is called copra and has a high content of oil.

- Almonds are expensive and are used in the preparation of badam milk and sweets. It is a rich source of protein that are not of high biological value. Almonds are an excellent source of vitamin E, an antioxidant.

Table : *Nutritive value of nuts per 100 gm.*

Nuts	Energy kcal	Protein g	Fat g	Carbohydrate g	Calcium mg	Iron mg	Thiamine mg	Riboflavin mg	Niacin mg
Groundnut	567	25.3	40.1	26.1	90	2.5	0.90	0.13	19.9
Cashewnut	596	21.2	46.9	22.3	50	5.8	0.63	0.19	1.2
Coconut fresh	444	4.5	41.6	13.0	10	1.7	0.05	0.10	0.8
Almond	655	20.8	58.9	10.5	230	5.1	0.24	0.57	4.4

FATS AND OILS

Fats are an important component of the diet and is present naturally in many foods. Fats are solid at room temperature while oils are liquid. Fats in the diet can be of two kinds viz., the visible and the invisible fat.

Invisible fats are those present inherently in foods. Example of food containing appreciable quantities of invisible fat include meat, poultry, fish, dairy products, eggs, nuts and seeds.

Visible fats are those fats that are made from these products. They are, cooking oils, salad oils, butter, ghee and margarine.

Nutritional Significance

- They are a concentrated source of energy. One gram of fat contributes 9 kilocalories as against 4 kilocalories contributed by carbohydrates and protein.
- They are a good source of vitamin A, D, E and K.
- They provide essential fatty acids which are components of membranes of living cells.
- They impart special flavour and texture to our foods, thus increasing palatability.
- They are also used by the body to make prostoglandins involved in a large variety of vital physiological functions.

SUGAR, JAGGERY AND HONEY

Nutritive Value

Sugar, honey and jaggery are sweetening agents. They are added to beverages and foods to increase palatability. Sugar is made up of glucose and fructose.

It is a source of energy providing 4 kilocalories per gram. Jaggery is made from sugar cane juice after processing it. Jaggery is a fair source of iron. Palmyra palm, date palm or coconut palm is used for it.

Honey is the golden coloured syrup made by bees from the nectar of flowers. It is a mixture of glucose and fructose. The nutritive value of sugar, honey and jaggery are given below:

Table : *Nutritive value per 100 g*

Item	Energy (k cal)	Carbohydrate (g)	Calcium (mg)	Iron (mg)
Sugar	398	99.4	12	0.15
Jaggery	383	95.0	80	2.65
Honey	313	79.5	5	0.69

Nutrition

Nature has provided a variety of foods for man to consume and be healthy. We consume food for maintenance of health, growth and to develop greater resistance against infections.

Foods contain substances called nutrients in varying proportions, which are needed for proper growth and maintenance of life processes. Knowledge of the functions of these nutrients and major food sources is necessary for man to formulate a nutritious diet.

Definition and History of Nutrition

Nutrition is defined as a science concerned with the role of food and nutrients in the maintenance of health. Nutrition as defined by Robinson is "the science of foods and nutrients, their action, interaction and balance in relationship to health and disease, the processes by which the organism ingests, digests, absorbs, transports and utilizes nutrients and disposes of their end product".

Nutrients are the constituents in food that must be supplied to the body in adequate amounts. These include Carbohydrates, Proteins, Fats, Minerals and Vitamins. Nutritional status is the condition of health of the individual as influenced by the utilization of the nutrients.

The science of Nutrition has been developed by using the combined knowledge of the physical and biological sciences. Its application involves the social sciences related to man's behaviour - Psychology, Sociology, Anthropology and Economics.

Until World War I the significance of nutrition was recognized by a relatively small group of scientists and physicians. Since then, a wider awareness has developed on the role of nutrients in health of individuals and the economic development of the nation.

A great number of important discoveries and developments in this field have enabled health care professionals to understand the nutrient needs of people and the means of supplying them. It is difficult to set in a chronological order of events that show the development of nutrition.

Many aspects developed simultaneously or overlapped each other. Some discoveries went unnoticed for several years because scientific attention was occupied with other developments and theories.

Some progresses were stimulated by national emergencies. Others depended on technical development of the supporting sciences. Nutrition research in India, as beri-beri inquiry was started in 1918, under the guidance of Sir Mc Carrison at Coonoor in South India.

It has blossomed into an important national institution, at Hyderabad called National Institute of Nutrition. It is currently engaged in carrying out basic as well as applied research work in nutrition. This national institute comes under the Indian Council of Medical Research (ICMR).

Relation between Good Nutrition and Health

Health is defined by the World Health Organization (WHO) as the "State of complete physical, mental and social well-being and not merely the absence of disease or infirmity".

To maintain good health and nutritional status one must eat a balanced food, which contains, all the nutrients in the correct proportion.

The essential requisites of health would include the following:

1. Achievement of optimal growth and development, reflecting the full expression of one's genetic potential.
2. Maintenance of the structural integrity and functional efficiency of body tissues necessary for an active and productive use.
3. Mental well-being.
4. Ability to withstand the inevitable process of aging with minimal disability and functional impairment.
5. Ability to combat diseases such as
   - resisting infections (immunocompetence).
   - preventing the onset of degenerative diseases.
   - resisting the effect of environmental toxins/pollutants.

Till three decades ago the role of nutrition in growth and development and tissue integrity alone was clear, but now the persuasive role nutrition plays in the other dimensions of health is implicit. Hence, an optimal nutritional status is an indication of good health. This recent advance has brought about a large-scale change in dietary habits and practices of the population.

Concepts of Malnutrition – Under Nutrition and Over Nutrition

Malnutrition as defined by World Health Organisation (WHO) is a pathological state resulting from a relative or absolute deficiency or excess of one or more essential nutrients, this state being clinically manifested or detected only by biochemical, anthropometric or physiological tests.

Four forms can be distinguished:

(*a*) *Undernutrition* – the pathological state resulting from the consumption of an inadequate quantity of food over an extended period of time.

(*b*) *Marasmus* is synonymous with severe undernutrition. Starvation implies total elimination of food and hence the rapid development of under nutrition and marasmus.

(*c*) *Specific deficiency* – the pathological state resulting from a relative or absolute lack of an individual nutrient.

(*d*) *Over nutrition* – the pathological state resulting from a disproportion of essential nutrients with or without the absolute deficiency of any nutrient as determined by the requirement of a balanced diet.

Signs of A Well Nourished Child as Against those of an Ill Nourished Child

Sl. No	*Signs of well nourished child*	*Signs of ill nourished child*
1.	Skin is smooth, pliable and elastic and of a healthy colour.	Lack of colour of skin-paleness
2.	Bright and clear eyes and pink eye membranes.	Pale, dark red, or purple mucous membrane lining the eyes. Failing eye sight.
3.	Firm pink nails	Rigid brittle nails.
4.	The hair is lustrous and firmly attached to the scalp.	Dull hair lacking sheen, dry, and can be easily plucked.
5.	Healthy gums and membranes of the mouth.	Pale, dark red or purple colour of gums.
6.	Reddish pink tongue. Not coated, pink lips.	Sores on skin, lip or tongue, pale lips.
7.	Desirable height for age and desirable weight for height.	Stunted growth and weight deficit.
8.	Good appetite and sound nutrition.	Loss of appetite, digestive disturbances, undernutrition.
9.	Normal body temperature, pulse rate and breathing rate.	Above normal body temperature, shortness of breath while performing normal activity.
10.	Healthy children are alert.	Listless, irritable and depressed.

NEED FOR AND METHODS OF ASSESSING NUTRITIONAL STATUS

Nutritional status is the condition of health of the individual as influenced by the utilization of the nutrients. It can be determined by correlation of information obtained through medical and dietary history, thorough physical examination and laboratory investigation.

Nutritional assessment aids in identifying

(*a*) Under Nutrition.

(*b*) Over Nutrition.

(*c*) Nutritional deficiencies.

(*d*) Individuals at the risk of developing malnutrition.

(*e*) Individuals at the risk of developing nutritional related diseases.

(*f*) The resources available to assist them to overcome nutritional problems.

The nutritional status can be assessed by the following methods:

I. Direct Methods

(*a*) Nutritional Anthropometry

(*b*) Clinical Examination

(*c*) Biochemical tests and

(*d*) Biophysical methods.

II. Indirect Methods

(*a*) Vital statistics of the community

(*b*) Assessment of socio-economic status and

(*c*) Diet surveys

NUTRITIONAL ASPECTS OF CARBOHYDRATES

Carbohydrates are the most important sources of energy. Even though their calorific value at 4 kcal/g is less than half of fats they form the chief source of energy in our body because they are easiest to digest also the most abundant and cheap source of energy.

Brain uses glucose exclusively as a source of energy. Almost 20 to 25% of our total energy intake is used by the brain and almost 50% of our carbohydrate intake.

The main forms of carbohydrate that we consume are:

1. **Starch:** It is the form of carbohydrate we consume the most and hence forms the most important source of energy in our body. It is present in all food grains, pulses, tuberous vegetables etc.
2. **Sugars:** Sugar is a term generally used for disaccharides and monosaccharides. They are present in fruits and vegetables in form of glucose, fructose, sucrose. It is also found in milk in form of lactose. Glucose and fructose are examples of naturally occurring monosaccharides. Lactose, Sucrose, Maltose are naturally occurring disaccharides.
3. **Cellulose:** Cellulose is a polysaccharide which is present in the structural elements of plants. It cannot be digested by humans but it plays a very important role as roughage. Roughage provides bulk to our food. The bulk helps in the movement of food through our digestive system and also has a role to play in digestion. It traps water in the large intestine and helps in its absorption.

Carbohydrates have a protein sparing effect which means that when adequate carbohydrates are taken in diet the amino acids in diet are spared from energy metabolism and used for synthesis of proteins in the body.

All carbohydrates required by our body from other sources hence there are no essential amino acids.

Nutritional Aspects of Lipids

Lipids play many roles in our body. They act as a storage of energy, structural elements of cells and tissues. They act as hormones and vitamins. As a source of energy it has very high calorific value 9 kcal/g.

Lipids as a group is composed of hydrophobic non polar organic compounds that are insoluble in water and soluble in organic solvents. They are composed of trigycerides (fats and oils), cholesterol, cholesterol esters.

Lipids can be divided into saturated, mono unsaturated and poly unsaturated lipids based on the number of double bonds present in the fatty acid. All poly unsaturated fatty acids cannot be synthesized in our body hence certain lipids that have essential fatty acids need to be present in our diet to prevent deficiency disease. Essential fatty acids are alpha-linolenic acid, linoleic acid and arachidonic acid. These essential fatty acids should make up for at least 3% of the energy requirement in adults and 5% to 6% of energy requirements in children. These essential fatty acids are present in plant oils rich in poly unsaturated fatty acids. Fish oil is also a good source of poly unsaturated fatty acids.

Our diet should be rich in poly unsaturated fatty acids and low in saturated fatty acids as saturated fatty acids are linked to atherosclerosis and cardiac disorders.

Lipids also act as carriers of fat soluble vitamins. Certain fats also act as hormones such as steroid hormones.

Cholesterol is also an important component of our diet. It is responsible for the structural integrity of the cell membrane and hence some amount needs to be taken exogenously. The yolk of an egg is a rich source of cholesterol. But excessive cholesterol intake has been linked to atherosclerosis and cardiovascular disorders. The RDA for cholesterol intake in adults and children above four years of age is 300 mg / day.

Nutritional Aspects of Proteins

Proteins form the main building blocks of our body both functionally and structurally. Almost all of our body is composed of proteins. Our muscles, bones, cartilages, blood vessels, connective tissues, skin, hair, nails etc. are all mainly composed of proteins. Apart from these almost all functional elements of our body are also composed of proteins such as the actin myosin involved in movement, the enzymes responsible for all metabolic reactions in our body, the hormones, the cellular channels, the receptors for various signaling molecules etc. In cases of energy deprivation proteins can also be broken down as a source of energy. They have a calorific value similar to carbohydrates, *i.e.,* 4 kcal /g, but their metabolism is much less efficient than that of carbohydrates.

Proteins are composed of amino acids. They are polymers of the 20 amino acids that exist in our body. Of these 11 amino acids can be synthesized in the body from non protein sources and hence are deemed non essential in our diet. The rest 9 amino acids cannot be synthesized in the body and hence need to be taken in food to prevent any deficieny disorder from occurring. They are histidine, isoleucine, leucine, lysine, methionine, phenylalanine, threonine, tryptophan, and valine.

Not all proteins are nutritionally equivalent when it comes to food. Certain proteins such as keratin undergoes almost nil digestion while proteins like albumin present in the egg undergo almost complete digestion. Hence the nutritional quality of proteins has to be decided depending upon the balanced presence of all essential amino acids, their digestibility (% of protein ingested digested known as digestibility coefficient, DC), and the biological value, BV (which is the percentage of protein retained by the body after digestion and absorption).

Net protein utilization (NPU) is a measure of the utilization of ingested protein for protein synthesis inside the body. It is calculated by:

$$NPU = \frac{(DC \times BV)}{100}$$

Animal proteins are superior biologically as they contain all essential amino acids in the needed amount and are better digested and absorbed. They have a high biological value and are termed as first class proteins. While vegetable proteins have a low biological value and are termed as second class proteins as they are generally deficient in one amino acid or the other and they are also more difficult to digest and absorb. While egg protein is taken as a reference protein due to its excellent bioavailability and completeness as far as amino acids are concerned.

This short coming of plant proteins can be overcome are mutual supplementation *i.e.*, taking two kinds of plant proteins together. A perfect example is rice and pulses. This results in a complete protein diet being taken by using two proteins that are deficient in two different amino acids.

Protein requirement is higher in growing years as well as in hyper metabolic states such as pregnancy, fever, infection etc. Protein requirement is expressed in relation to body weight. In infants, upto 3 months of age, the protein requirement is about 2.5 gm per kg body weight. Then post this the protein requirement is between 2 to 1.5 gm/kg body weight up till adolescence. In adulthood, after 18 yrs of age, the protein requirement is about 1gm/kg body weight. During pregnancy and lactation the requirement is higher nearly 2.5 to 2 gm/kg body weight.

Balanced Diet

A balanced diet is a diet that provides all the nutrients in their correct proportion so as to fulfill the biological requirement of an individual. It neither creates a deficiency nor an excess of any of the nutrients. Balanced diet is different for different individuals and is dependent on the biological need of an individual. For example the biological demand for carbohydrates fats proteins as well of the vitamins required for their metabolism will be much higher in an athlete than in a person with a sedentary desk job.

A balanced diet should contain:

(*a*) Cereals

(*b*) Pulses

(*c*) Vegetables and Fruits

(*d*) Milk and milk products

(*e*) Oils and fats

(*f*) Sugars

(*g*) In cases of non vegetarians it should also contain animal proteins and eggs on a regular bases.

A balanced diet should contain all the above said food groups in our daily diet in a balanced manner so that all the nutritional requirements of the body are fulfilled.

The cereals are energy rich and form a major source of carbohydrates in our diet. Their energy yield is about 350 kcal/100g.

They consist of staples such as wheat, rice, maize, sorghum, jowar, bajra etc. The cereals are deficient in proteins and the proteins present in them are generally deficient in one amino acid or another.

They contain adequate minerals but the absorption of minerals from them is inefficient.

Their outer covering is rich in vitamin B complex. But in most cases the outer covering is lost due to milling.

Pulses are a rich source of proteins among vegetarian food. But similar to other vegetable proteins they are deficient in certain amino acids but these deficiencies can be overcome by supplementing them with cereals. They have a energy density of about 350 kcal/100 gm and 20% to 25% of their mass is protein. Germinating pulses are an important source of vitamin C and vitamin B complex.

Vegetables and fruits are the most important source of water soluble and certain fat soluble vitamins in our diet. Apart from that they are also an important source of fibre. They provide minerals and carbohydrates. Their contribution to proteins in our diet is negligible.

Dairy and its products form almost a complete diet. It contains almost all nutrients other than vitamin C and Iron. It is a specially good source of Calcium. Milk is rich in saturated fats.

The protein content of milk can be increased by converting to curd. Also curd can be eaten by those who are lactose intolerant as during the fermentation process most of the lactose is fermented.

Fats and oils form an essential part of our diet. They are obtained from the fats and oils we add to our food during cooking. Other than these lipids they are obtained also from lipids contained in food items such as dairy and its products, lipids present in cereals and pulses and fats present in meats and eggs. We should try to avoid saturated fats in our diet and include unsaturated lipids in form of oils in our diet. Refined sugars are used as flavoring agents in our diet but excess of these sugars should be avoided as they provide empty calories.

Fig. : *Food pyramid showing the servings of various food items in a balanced diet*

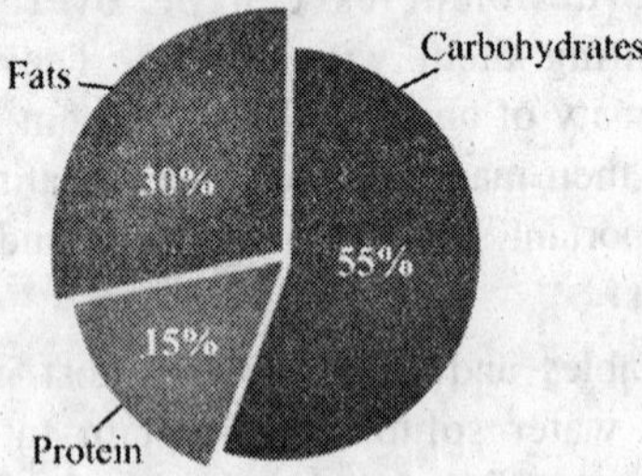

Fig. : *This pie graph shows the percentage of energy that should be provided by the various macro nutrients in a balanced diet.*

Eggs are an excellent source of protein and cholesterol in our diet. An average egg is about 100 k cal in energy value. Similarly, non vegetarian diet such as meat, poultry and fish are an excellent source of high quality proteins. They are also a good source of fat soluble vitamins as well as vitamins of the B complex except for vitamin C.

A balanced diet should take care of the energy and nutrient requirement of the body and these should be provided by a mix of food items.

The energy requirement of an individual has to provide for the energy requirement for the various activities as well as growth and repair of wear and tear of the body. Hence the energy requirement is dependent on the sex, built as well as the life style of an individual. The following are the average energy requirements for various population groups.

Group	*Particulars*	*Body wt. kg*	*Net Energy kcal*
Man	Sedentary	60	2320
	Moderate	”	2730
	Heavy work	”	3490
Woman	Sedentary	55	1900
	Moderate	”	2230
	Heavy work	”	2850
	Pregnancy	55 kg + GWG	+350
	Lactation (0-6 m)	55 kg + WG	+600
	Lactation (6-12 m)	”	+520

Daily energy requirement for an average Indian man and woman as per ICMR guideline.

Energy requirement of infants and children according to ICMR.

Group	*Age*	*Weight*	*Energy requirement (kcal)*
Infants	0-6 months	5.4	500
	6-12 months	8.4	670
Children	1-3 y	12.9	1060
	4-6 y	18.1	1350
	7-9 y	25.1	1690
Boys	10-12 y	34.3	2190
Girls	10-12 y	35.0	2010
Boys	13-15 y	47.6	2750
Girls	13-15 y	46.6	2330
Boys	16-17 y	55.4	3020
Girls	16-17 y	52.1	2440

BASAL METABOLISM

Basal Metabolism is the minimum amount of energy needed by the body for maintenance of life when the person is at post absorptive state, physical and emotional rest.

Basal Metabolic Rate (BMR) is a measure of the energy required by the activities of resting tissue.

The Basal Metabolic rate can be measured directly from the heat produced (using a Respiration Calorimeter and Metabolic Chamber) or indirectly from O_2 intake and CO_2 expenditure when the subject is at rest.

Factors affecting Basal Metabolic Rate (BMR)

The factors affecting Basal Metabolic Rate are listed in table.

Table : *Factors affecting Basal Metabolic Rate (BMR)*

Factor	Effect on BMR
Body Compositon	The more lean body mass higher is the BMR. This is due to greater metabolic activity in these tissues when compared to bones and fat. Men with a high proportion of muscle mass or lean body mass have a higher BMR than women.
Fever	Fever raises the BMR. There is a 7% increase in BMR for each degree rise in temperature in Fahrenheit.
Stress	Stress raises BMR.
Smoking & Caffeine	Increases the BMR.
Hyperthyroidism (Oversecretion of thyroxin)	The basal metabolic rate is elevated as much as 50-70%.
Growth	In children and pregnant women the BMR is higher.
Pregnancy	During the last trimester of pregnancy Basal Metabolic rate is increased by 15-25% as there is a increase in muscle mass of uterus, size of mammary gland, foetal mass and placenta, cardiac work and respiratory rate.
Fasting/Starvation	Lowers BMR.
Hypothyroidism (under secretion of thyroxin)	The basal metabolic rate is decreased by 30%.
Age	Lean body mass diminishes with age slowing the BMR. In tall people the BMR is higher.
Undernutrition	Prolonged undernutrition lowers the BMR.

ENERGY COST OF PHYSICAL ACTIVITIES

Next to Basal Metabolism it is the physical activity, which accounts for the largest energy expenditure. There is a wide variation from individual to individual in occupational activity.

The energy required for the actual physical activity varies depending on the type of occupation of an individual. For computing energy requirements, the occupations have been classified as sedentary, moderate and heavy.

The ICMR classification of activities based on occupation is given in table.

Table : *Classification of activities based on occupation*

Sex	Sedentary (80-180 kcal/hr)	Moderate (170-240 kcal/hr)	Heavy (250-350 kcal/hr)
Male	1. Teacher 2. Tailor 3. Executive	1. Fisherman 2. Potter	1. Stone cutter 2. Mine worker 3. Wood cutter
Female	1. Teacher 2. Executive 3. Nurse	1. Servant maid 2. Weaver	1. Stone cutter

The energy cost of physical activities is expressed in terms of BMR units.

BMR Unit

The energy cost of rest and physical activity is expressed as multiples of BMR which is called the physical activity ratio (PAR).

The physical activity ratio expresses the energy cost of an individual activity per minute as ratio of the cost of BMR per minute. Hence it is advantageous to express the energy expenditure in terms of BMR units.

Table: *Energy cost of some common activities in terms of BMR Units*

Activity	*Energy cost of activities in BMR Units*
Sitting quietly	1.2
Standing quietly	1.4
Sitting at desk	1.3
Walking (3MPH)	3.7

Using factorial method the WHO / FAO expert committee has derived the BMR factors for Indian men and women as 1.6, 1.9 & 2.5 respectively for the three categories of activities namely, sedentary, moderate & heavy as given in table.

Table : *Energy requirements of Indian Adults in terms of BMR Units*

Activity	*Duration (hrs)*	*Rate of energy expenditure in terms of BMR Units*		
		Sedentary	*Moderate*	*Heavy*
Sleep	8	1.0	1.0	1.0
Occupational activity	8	1.7	2.8	4.5
Non-Occupational Activity	8	2.2	2	-
Average for 24 hr		1.6	1.9	2.5

Thermic Effect of Food

Food ingestion stimulates metabolism and requires energy to meet the multiple activities of digestion, absorption and transport of nutrients.

This overall stimulating effect of food is called dietary thermogenesis or thermic effect of food (formerly called as specific dynamic action (SDA). The increase in energy cost because of thermogenesis is 10%.

Estimation of Total Energy Needs

The energy requirement of an individual is the level of energy intake from food that will balance energy expenditure when the individual has a body size and composition and level of physical activity, consistent with long term good health, and that will allow for maintenance of economically necessary and socially desirable activity. In children and pregnant and lactating women, the energy requirement includes the energy needs associated with the deposition of tissues or the secretion of milk at rates consistent with good health. (WHO) Energy requirements are best determined by measurements of energy expenditure.

Energy expenditure from a physiological point of view is made up of three major components:

(*i*) BMR (*ii*) Dietary Thermogenesis (*iii*) Physical activity.

For all practical purposes, the component of energy expenditure related to regulatory energy output or dietary thermogenesis are known to merge into measurements related to the cost of physical activity. Hence energy expenditure has only two principal component: (*i*) BMR & (*ii*) Physical activity.

Calculation of energy requirements.

1. **Predicting BMR :** Equations for predicting BMR (K.cal/24 hrs) as proposed by the ICMR expert committee for Indians is given in table.

Table : *Equations for predicting BMR (Kcal / 24 hr)*

Sex	*Age (yrs)*	*Prediction Equation*
Male	18 – 30	14.5 × B.W (kg) + 645
	30 – 60	10.9 × B.W (kg) + 833
	> 60	12.8 × B.W (kg) + 463
Female	18 – 30	14.0 × B.W (kg) + 471
	30 – 60	8.3 × B.W (kg) + 788
	> 60	10.0 × B.W (kg) + 565

2. **Calculating Daily energy requirement:** Using the computed BMR from body weights and recommended BMR factor for Indians for different levels of physical activity (which is 1.6, 1.9 & 2.5 for sedentary, moderate & heavy activity respectively) the energy requirements are arrived at.

For example:

For an Indian adult man 29 yrs of age, weighing 60 kg and doing moderate activity, the energy requirement is calculated as follows.

1. BMR = 14.5 × 60 + 645
   = 1515 k.cal / 24 hr
2. Energy requirement
   = predicted BMR × BMR units
   for activity = 1515 × 1.9 = 2878.5
   = 2878 k.cal / day.

MINERALS AND VITAMINS

Until the middle of the nineteenth century, the importance of minerals and vitamins was not known. It was observed that carbohydrate, fat, protein alone were incapable of promoting and sustaining growth.

Hence scientists attempted to find out the "g-missing elements", namely minerals and vitamins which are essential for growth and maintenance.

Essential minerals which are inorganic substances are classified as macro and micronutrients based on the amount needed by humans per day.

Macrominerals are those which are vital to health and that are required in the diet by more than 100 mg per day and those required in the diet less than 20 mg per day are called microminerals or trace minerals.

The essential microminerals are Calcium, Phosphorous, Magnesium, Sulphur, Potassium and Chloride. Important microminerals of relevance in human nutrition are Iron, Zinc, Copper, Sodium, Cobalt, Fluoride, Manganese, Chromium, Iodine and Molybdenum.

Functions, Foodsources, Requirements and Effects of Deficiency

Calcium and Phosphorus: Calcium is an essential element required for several life processes. The requirements of Calcium and Phosphorous are considered together as their function and requirement are closely linked.

Over 99% of the Calcium and Phosphorous is present in the bones and the remaining 1% in the body fluids.

The Calcium and Phosphorous are present in the ratio of 2 : 1 in our body. In the skeletal system Ca and P is present in the form of hydroxyapatite crystals.

Hydroxyapatite is a compound made up of calcium and phosphate that is deposited into the bone matrix to give it strength and rigidity.

Functions:

1. **Bone formation:** The major mineral ions of the bone are Calcium, Phosphorous and

Magnesium. For proper calcification of bones, (deposition of minerals on the bone matrix) which occurs during the growing years, adequate supply of these minerals is essential.

2. **Tooth formation:** Calcium and Phosphorous together as a compound is essential for the formation of dentin and enamel.
3. **Physiological Process:**
   (*a*) Calcium is essential for the clotting of blood as it is required for prothrombin activation.
   (*b*) Calcium regulates the permeability of the capillary walls and ion transport across the cell membranes.
   (*c*) It is essential for the contraction of the heart and skeletal muscle.
   (*d*) Calcium regulates the excitability of the nerve fibres.
   (*e*) Calcium acts as an activator for enzymes such as rennin and pancreatic lipase.
4. Phosphorous is essential for the storage and release of adenosine triphosphate (ATP) molecules.
5. Phosphates plays an important role as buffers to prevent changes in acidity of the body fluids.
6. Phospholipids are major components of cell membrane and intra cellular organelles.
7. In the DNA and RNA phosphate is an essential part of the nucleic acids.

Food sources : Among cereals ragi contains large amounts of calcium. Bengalgram whole, gingely seeds, cuminseeds, poppy seeds, agathi, amaranth, drumstick leaves are good sources of calcium. Milk and milk products are good sources of calcium and phosphorous. Only 20-30% of the calcium in the diet is absorbed, which is facilitated by Vitamin D. All foods contain significant amounts of phosphorous.

Requirements: The recommended dietary allowances for Calcium, as suggested by the ICMR is given in table.

Table: *ICMR recommended dietary allowances for Calcium*

	Age Group	*RDA for calcium mg/day*
Infant	0–12 months	500
Children	1–9 years	400
Children	10–15 years	600
Adolesent	16–18 years	500
Adult		400
Pregnant women		1000
Lactating women		1000

Deficiency: Calcium related health problems occur due to inadequate intake, improper absorption or utilization of calcium.

Osteoporosis: Osteoporosis is a condition found primarily among middle aged and elderly woman, where the bone mass of the skeleton is diminished.

It is a condition of multiple origin. It results due to the following reasons:

(*i*) Prolonged dietary inadequacy
(*ii*) Poor absorption and utilization of calcium
(*iii*) Immobility
(*iv*) Decreased levels of oestrogen in post menopausal women.
(*v*) Hyper parathyroidism
(*vi*) Vitamin D deficiency

Osteomalacia: This is a condition in which the quality but not the quantity of bone is reduced. This condition is dicussed in detail under deficiency of Vitamin D.

Tetany: Tetany occurs when Calcium in the blood drops below the critical level. There is a change in the stimulation of nerve cells resulting in increased excitability of the nerve and uncontrolled contraction of the muscle tissue. Hence Calcium and Phosphorous ratio in the diet should be maintained at 1 : 1 for proper utilization of Calcium in the body.

Microminerals: Microminerals are also known as trace elements. The microminerals are Iron, Iodine,

Zinc, Copper, Fluoride, Selenium, Chromium, Manganese, Cobalt and Molybdenum.

However only the deficiency of few of these elements is observed in humans. Iron and Iodine deficiencies are wide spread while deficiency of Cu, Zn, Cr and Se have been reported in recent years.

Iron

The total body iron is 4 g in adults. Iron exists in a complex form in our body. It is present as:

(*a*) **Iron porphyrin compounds:** Haemoglobin in RBC, myoglobin in muscle.

(*b*) **Enzymes:** (*e.g.*) peroxidases, succinase dehydrogenase and cytochrome oxidase.

(*c*) **Transport and storage forms:** (*e.g.*) transferrin and ferritin.

Functions: The chief functions of iron in the body are:

1. Iron forms a part of the protein - haemoglobin which carries oxygen to different parts of the body.
2. It forms a part of the myoglobin in muscles which makes oxygen available for muscle contraction.
3. Iron is necessary for the utilization of energy as part of the cells metabolic machinery.
4. As part of enzymes iron catalizes many important reactions in the body. Examples are

(*a*) Conversion of beta carotene to active form of Vitamin A.

(*b*) Synthesis of carnitine, purines, collagen and neuro transmitters.

(*c*) Detoxification of drugs in the liver.

Food Sources: The iron present in food can be as haem and non-haem iron depending upon the source from which it is obtained. Haem iron – is obtained from animal tissues, non-heam iron – is obtained from plant foods. Sources of non-haem iron are ragi, green leafy vegetables, dried fruits and jaggery. Liver, fish, poultry, meat, eggs, dates are good sources of haem iron.

Haem iron is absorbed and utilized better than the non-haem iron. Iron absorption from Indian diets is only 3 per cent as it is mainly cereal based diet.

Requirement: Iron requirements for various age groups is listed in table.

Table : *ICMR–Recommended dietary Allowances for Iron*

Group	*Iron requirement (mg/day)*
Birth–1 year	1
1–5 year	15–20
6–12 years	15–20
13–18 years	
Boys	25
Girls	35
Men	20
Women	30
Pregnancy	40
Lactation	30

Deficiency: Dietary iron deficiency leads to nutritional anaemia. Nutritional anaemia is defined as the condition that results from the inability of the erythropoetic tissue to maintain a normal haemoglobin concentration.

Anaemia occurs when the haemoglobin level falls below 12 gm/dl in adult man and woman. During pregnancy haemoglobin level below 11 gm/dl is termed anaemia.

Nutritional anaemia is the common form of anaemia affecting women in reproductive years, infants and children which is mainly due to poor intake and absorption.

Iron deficiency anaemia is wide spread in our country. The prevalence varying from 45% in men and 70% in women and children. The major cause of anaemia in India is because of Iron and folic acid deficiency.

Nutritional anaemia is manifested as:

1. Reduced Haemoglobin level. (less than 12 g/dl)
2. Defects in the structure, function of the epithelial tissues.

3. Paleness of skin and the inside of the lower eyelid is pale pink.
4. Finger nails becoming thin and flat and eventually (spoon shaped nails) koilonychia develops.
5. Progressive untreated anaemia results in cardiovascular and respiratory changes leading to cardiac failure. The general symptoms include lassitude, fatigue, breathlessness on exertion, palpitations, dizziness, sleeplessness, dimness of vision, and increased susceptibility to infection.

Iodine

Iodine is an essential constituent of the thyroid hormone produced by the thyroid glands. It occurs as free iodide ions or as protein bound iodine in our body. About 15-23 mg of iodine is present in the adult human body. The body store of iodine is predominantly present in thyroid gland and also in salivary gland, mammary glands, gastric glands and in kidneys to a certain extent.

Function: Iodine is essential for the synthesis of the thyroid hormones T_3 and T_4.

Sources: Richest source of iodine are sea foods like sea fishes and common salt from sea water. Iodine content of vegetables, fruits and cereals depends upon the iodine content of the soil in which they grow. The soil of mountaineous regions contains less iodine.

Requirement: The ICMR recommended dietary allowance for Iodine is 150 μg/day.

Deficiency: Iodine deficiency in the diet, causes enlargement of the thyroid gland called as "goitre". Goitre occurs in people staying in hilly regions where the iodine content of water and soil is comparatively less.

In India goitre is common in hilly districts of Himalaya. Goitre can be treated by administration of iodine. If treatment is given in early stages goitre can be corrected.

Severe iodine deficiency in children leads to hypothyroidism resulting in retarded physical and mental growth. This condition is known as cretinism.

Goitrogens are substances present in foods which cause goitre. These substances react with iodine present in the food making it unavailable for absorption. Foods like cabbage, cauliflower, raddish contain goitrogens.

Zinc

Zinc is primarily intracellular substance. Its total quantity in the body is 2.3 g. Largest stores of Zinc is present in the bones. Zinc forms a constituent of the blood. Zinc is an important element performing a range of function in the body as it is a cofactor for a number of enzymes.

Functions:

1. Zinc is a constituent of enzymes such as carbonic anhydrase, alkaline phosphatase, lactic dehydrogenase.
2. It is a constituent of the hormone insulin.
3. It plays a major role in the synthesis of DNA and proteins.

Sources: Meat, unmilled cereals and legumes are good sources. Fruits and vegetables are poor sources.

Requirements: The daily requirement of Zinc in adults is 15.5 mg/day as recommended by the ICMR expert group.

Apart from iron, iodine, zinc, copper, selenium and fluorine are essential trace elements. Copper is essential element in iron absorption.

Selenium is an essential element along with Vitamin E for maintaining integrity of the liver cells. Fluorine is required in minimum amounts to prevent dental caries. Excessive consumption leads to mottling of teeth.

Vitamins

Vitamins are organic substances present in small amounts in food, they are required for carrying out vital functions of the body. They are involved in the utilization of the major nutrients like proteins, fats and carbohydrates.

Though needed in small amounts, they are essential for health and well being of the body.

When these Vitamins were discovered on the basis of their function and before their chemical nature were elucidated, they were designated as A, B, C, D or in terms of their major functions like, antineuritic, antirichitic Vitamins. Vitamins are classified based on their solubility as fat soluble and water soluble vitamins.

Classification of Vitamins

Vitamins

1. Fat soluble
Vitamin A, D, E, K

2. Water soluble
Vitamin B_1, B_2, B_6, B_{12}
(Niacin) Nicotinic Acid
Folic Acid and Vitamin C

Water soluble vitamins are not accumulated in the body, but are readily excreted while fat soluble vitamins are stored in the body. For this reason excessive intake of fat soluble vitamins, especially Vitamin A and D can prove toxic. Excessive intake leads to the condition called hypervitaminosis.

Functions, food sources, requirements and effects of deficiency

Fat soluble vitamins:

Vitamin A

Vitamin A was the first fat soluble vitamin to be recognized. Three forms of Vitamin A are active in the body, retinol, retinal and retinoic acid. They are collectively called as retinoids.

Beta carotene is the provitamin of Vitamin A. Provitamins are substances that are chemically related to a vitamin but must be changed by the body into the active form of the vitamin. Vitamin A in the diet comes in two forms.

Retenoids (preformed Vitamin A) and carotenoids. Vitamin A is present in vegetable foods which contain yellow pigment called carotenes. It was isolated from carrots hence called carotenoids which are provitamins of Vitamin A.

Functions

1. A well understood function of retinol is in the visual process. The retina of the human eye contains two distinct photo receptors of which one is sensitive to light intensities. Vitamin A is essential for the formation of rhodopsin and normal functioning of the retina for clear vision in dim light. Lack of Vitamin A leads to impaired adaptation to darkness.
2. Participates in protein synthesis and cell differentiation and thereby maintaining the health of the epithelial tissues and skin.
3. Supports reproduction and growth.
4. Vitamin A regulates the antibodies and cellular immune response. It is essential for maintaining the epithelial tissue which is the first line of defence against invading microorganism.
5. Beta carotene acts as an antioxidant capable of protecting the body against disease like cancer, cardiovascular diseases and cataract.

Sources: Vitamin A in the human diet exist as retinol or as retinal or beta carotene which has to be converted to Vitamin A. Foods of animal origin contain retinol.

Plant sources are rich in Beta carotene. Only one third of the dietary beta Carotene is absorbed. Beta Carotene from green leafy vegetables is well utilized than from carrots and papayas. Good sources of Vitamin A are sheep liver, butter, ghee, egg, milk, curds, liver oils of shark and halibut. Good sources of beta carotene are agathi, amaranth, drumstick leaves, green leafy vegetables, mango, papaya, carrot and jack fruit.

Requirements: The ICMR recommended dietary allowance for retinol is given in table.

Table : *ICMR recommended dietary allowance for Retinol*

Group	*Retinol μg/day*
Men	600
Women	600
Pregnant women	600
Lactation	950
Infants	350
Children	400-600

Effects of Deficiency: Deficiency of Vitamin A is manifested as nutritional blindness and increased susceptibility to infection. Nutritional blindness is an important public health problem among young children in India.

Night blindness is an early symptom of Vitamin A deficiency. The individual cannot see in dim light. This can be corrected with adequate supply of Vitamin A. In the absence of adequate Vitamin A intake the outer lining of the eye ball loses its usual moist, white appearance and becomes dry and wrinkled called xerosis.

This condition is followed by raised muddy dry triangular patches on the conjunctiva called the bitots spots. Redness and inflammation of the eye and gradual loss of vision may follow. The central portion of the eye loses its transparency and becomes opaque and soft if not treated and leads to total blindness termed Xeropthalmia. Xeropthalmia encompasses all ocular manifestations of Vitamin A deficiency.

Increased susceptibility to infection occurs because the mucous membrane lining becomes dry and rough which is easily invaded by the micro-organism.

Hypervitaminosis: Intake of large amount of Vitamin A for prolonged periods can lead to toxic symptoms which include irritability, headache, nausea and vomitting.

Vitamin D

Vitamin D can be synthesized in the body in adequate amounts by simple exposure to sunlight, even for 5 minutes per day is sufficient.

It is essential for bone growth and calcium metabolism. It acts as a hormone in the body by facilitating calcium absorption and deposition in the bone.

Functions:

1. Vitamin D helps in the absorption of calcium and phosphorous by increasing the synthesis of calcium binding protein.
2. Vitamin D helps to maintain the calcium and phosphorous levels in the body by stimulating,
   (*a*) Absorption in the gastro intestinal tract.
   (*b*) Retention by the kidney.
3. Vitamin D helps in deposition of calcium in the bones. The bones grow denser and stronger.

Food Sources: The Vitamin D content of food sources from animals varies with the diet, breed and exposure to sunlight of the animal.

The good sources of Vitamin D are cod liver oil, shrimp, liver, butter, yolk, cheese, milk, spinach and cabbage.

Requirements: The expert group of ICMR has not recommended dietary intake of Vitamin D for Indians. Only in those cases where the Vitamin D requirement is not met due to inadequate exposure to sunlight the ICMR recommends 400 μg/day of Vitamin D.

Deficiency: Deficiency of Vitamin D leads to decreased absorption of calcium which is manifested as muscular tetany, rickets in children and osteomalacia in adults.

Due to faulty calcification of bones the following deformities is manifested in children which is called rickets. It is a disease in which there is weakness and abnormalities in bone formation. Rickets primarily affects children.

Manifestations:

(*a*) Faulty deposition of calcium on the bones
(*b*) Bowing of legs
(*c*) Enlargement of ends of long bones
(*d*) Deformities of ribs beading of ribs
(*e*) Delayed closing of frontanel
(*f*) Slow erruption of teeth
(*g*) Malformed, decay prone teeth.

Osteomalacia in Adults: Osteomalacia is a condition where the quality of the bone is reduced. It occurs in women who are not exposed to sunshine and who have depleted mineral reserves resulting from successive pregnancies and prolonged lactation.

Osteomalacia is associated with low phosphorous level but low blood calcium level is the most frequent cause.

The following symptoms occur:

1. softening of the bones.
2. deformities of the limbs, spine, thorax and pelvis.
3. demineralization of the bones.
4. pain in pelvis, lower back and legs.
5. frequent bone fractures.

Hypervitaminosis: As in the case of Vitamin A intake of excessive amounts of Vitamin D leads to toxic symptoms which include irritability, nausea, vomiting and constipation.

Vitamin E

Vitamin E is known as antisterility vitamin because it is required for normal reproduction in animals and men.

Functions

1. Vitamin E is the primary antioxidant in the body and serves to protect polyunsaturated fatty acids (PUFA) from oxidation in cells and maintain integrity of the cell membrane. It also prevents the oxidation of beta carotene and Vitamin A. Vitamin E helps to maintain cell membrane integrity and protect RBC against hemolysis.
2. Vitamin E reduces platelet aggregation.
3. Vitamin E is essential for the iron metabolism and the maintenance of nervous tissues and immune function.
4. Vitamin E has been promoted as an anti-aging vitamin, because as cells age they accumulate lipid breakdown products. Vitamin E prevents this accumulation in maintaining cell health.

Food Sources: Vitamin E is widely distributed in foods. It is present in high concentration in vegetable oils and in cereal grains. Wheat gum, sunflower seeds, almonds, safflower oil, eggs, butter are good sources. Meat, fruits and vegetables contain small amounts. Sesame oil and mustard oil are good sources of Vitamin E.

Requirement: The requirement of Vitamin E is linked to that of essential fatty acids (linoleic and linolenic acids). The requirement of Vitamin E is 0.8 mg/g of essential fatty acid.

Deficiency

1. Prolonged intake of Vitamin E deficient diets produces uncoordinated movement, weakness and sensory disturbances.
2. It causes haemolytic anaemia in low birth weight infants.
3. Defective functioning of the retina leading to permanent blindness in premature infants occurs.
4. It leads to reproductive failure in humans.
5. Vitamin E deficiency is associated with decreased ability of the lymphocytes.

Vitamin K

Vitamin K is recognized as the anti haemorrhagic factor owing to its vital role in blood clotting mechanism.

Functions: Synthesis of blood clotting proteins. Vitamin K is essential for the activation of prothrombin. This gets converted to thrombin, which in turn activates fibrinogen to form fibrin.

The process of blood clotting occurs as follows: Injured tissue releases thromboplastin, which catalyses prothrombin formation. Vitamin K catalyses, conversion of prothrombin to thrombin. This in turn causes conversion of fibrinogen to fibrin which forms the clot.

Food Sources: Dark green leafy vegetables are good sources of vitamin K. Fruits, tubers, seeds, dairy and meat products contain Vitamin K.

Requirements: The ICMR committee considered that no recommendation is needed for this Vitamin, as the synthesis of Vitamin K occurs in the lower intestine by the colonic bacteria and present widely in foods.

Effects of Deficiency: Primary deficiency arises in infants resulting in delayed blood clotting and haemorrhage. This is because the new born babies have a sterile intestinal tract thus lack in the colonic bacterial colonies which produces Vitamin K. Vitamin K deficiency does not occur in adults.

Water soluble Vitamins: Vitamin C (Ascorbic Acid) The chemical name for Vitamin C is ascorbic acid. It was discovered in 1747 by the British physician Lind and demonstrated that citrus fruit juices prevented and cured scurvy.

Functions:

1. Ascorbic Acid is essential for formation of cement substances and collagen which is found in blood vessels, teeth and bones.
2. It helps in the biosynthesis of non-essential amino acids (*e.g.*) hydroxy proline, tyrosin.
3. It is required for absorption of iron as it reduces ferric to ferrous form which is easily absorbed.
4. Vitamin C is essential for the formation of collagen a major structural protein of connective tissues.
5. It is required for normal wound healing because it helps in the formation of connective tissue.
6. Vitamin C is required for carnitine synthesis which aids in the transport of fatty acids in the cell.
7. Vitamin C is essential for the synthesis of norepinephrine a neurotransmitter.
8. It activates hormones (*e.g.*) growth hormone, gastrin releasing peptide, calcitonin, gastrin oxytocin.
9. Drug detoxifying metabolic systems in the body require Vitamin C for its optimal activity.
10. Vitamin C is an excellent anti-oxidant. It combines with free radicals oxidizing them to harmless substances that can be excreted.

Food Sources: Amla, drumstick leaves, guava, cashew fruit, agathi, cabbage, bitter gourd, oranges, tomatoes are good sources of ascorbic acid. Cereals and pulses are poor sources. Vitamin C content of pulses increases on germination.

Requirements: The recommended dietary allowances of ICMR for ascorbic acid is as given in table.

Table: *ICMR Recommended Dietary Allowances for Vitamin C*

Group	*Requirement mg/day*
Adult	40
Pregnant women	40
Lactation	80
Infants	25
Children	40

Effects of Deficiency: Prolonged deficiency of ascorbic acid produces a disease condition called as 'scurvy' in both infants and adults.

Infantile scurvy: There is loss of appetite, failure to gain weight, irritability, palor, defective growth of bones. Haemorrhage occurs under the skin. There is defective formation of teeth and gums are swollen. The ends of the ribs become prominent resulting in beaded appearance called scorbutic rosary.

Adult Scurvy:

1. General manifestation are fever, susceptibility to infection, and delayed wound healing.
2. Anaemia: Microcytic hypochromic anaemia develops due to failure of absorption of iron.
3. Gums become spongy and bleed easily. Gums become swollen and ulcerated.
4. The blood vessels become fragile and porous due to defective formation of collagen. Joints become swollen and tender.
5. Clinical symptoms appear when total body pool of ascorbic acid decreases. Skin becomes rough and dry. There are small petechial haemorrhages around hair follicles.

Thiamine: Thiamine is known as Vitamin B_1. Deficiency of thiamine leads to beri-beri. This condition is widely prevalent among population whose diet contains more of polished cereals.

Functions:

1. Thiamine is converted to thiamine pyrophosphate (TPP), which is an important co enzyme in the carbohydrate metabolism.

2. It is involved in transmission of nerve impulses across the cells.
3. Thiamine as TPP is an essential cofactor for the conversion of amino acid tryptophan to niacin.

Sources: Yeast, whole wheat, millets, hand pounded rice, parboiled rice are good sources of thiamine. The bran contains most of the thiamine in the cereals. Gingelly seeds, groundnut, soyabean, cashewnuts, organ meats, pork, liver and eggs supply thiamine.

Requirements: Thiamine is involved in the carbohydrate metabolism. Its requirement is related to energy derived from carbohydrate. The ICMR expert group recommends an allowance of 0.5 mg per 1000 kcal for adults and for infants 0.3 mg/ 1000 kcal is suggested. The recommended dietary allowance per day is given in table.

Table : *ICMR Recommended Dietary Allowance For Thiamine Per Day*

Group	***Thiamine requirement mg/day***
Men	
Sedentary	1.2
Moderate	1.4
Heavy work	1.6
Women	
Sedentary	0.9
Moderate	1.1
Heavy work	1.2
Pregnant women	+0.3
Lactation	+0.3 – +0.2
Infants	55 mg/kg – 50 mg/kg
Children (1–9 years)	0.6–1.2
Boys (10–18 years)	1.1–1.3
Girls (10–18 years)	1.0

Effects of Deficiency: Deficiency of thiamine is associated with low calorie intake. Severe deficiency of thiamine produces a disease known as beri-beri.

It is manifested as

(*a*) Dry beri-beri

(*b*) Wet beri-beri

(*c*) Infantile beri-beri

(*a*) **Dry beri-beri:** There is loss of appetite, tingling numbness and burning sensation in hands and feet. Calf muscles are tender. Knee and ankle jerks are sluggish. In later stages complete loss of sensation in hands and legs occur. It is characterized by foot and waist drop. Mental depression and confusion occurs.

(*b*) **Wet beri-beri:** In this case there is enlargement of heart and the cardiac output is high. Oedema or accumulation of fluid in legs, face and trunk is observed. Palpitations are marked.

(*c*) **Infantile beri-beri:** It occurs in first few months of life if the diet of the mother is deficient in thiamine. Symptoms are restlessness, sleeplessness, constipation, enlargement of the heart and breathlessness.

Riboflavin: Riboflavin or Vitamin B_2 is the yellow enzyme which is heat stable unlike other B Vitamins. Riboflavin in the combined form with proteins form flavo proteins or yellow enzymes.

This enzyme is of two types FAD — Flavin-di-nucleotide. FMN — Flavin mono-nucleotide.

(*a*) These substances act as coenzymes in many biological reactions primarily in oxidation—reduction, and dehydrogenation reaction

(*i*) Release of energy from glucose, fatty acids and amino acids.

(*ii*) Conversion of vitamin B_6 and folate to active coenzymes.

(*c*) It is essential for the formation of red blood cells.

(*d*) It is required for the synthesis of glycogen.

Food Sources: Rich sources are liver, dried yeast, egg, milk, meat, fish, whole cereals, legumes, and green leafy vegetables.

Requirements: Riboflavin requirement is related to energy intake – 0.6 mg/1000 kcal. The ICMR recommends the following requirement per day as given in table.

Table : *ICMR Recommended Dietary Allowance for Riboflavin*

Group	*Riboflavin mg/day*
Men	
Sedentary	1.4
Moderate	1.6
Heavy work	1.9
Women	
Sedentary	1.1
Moderate	1.3
Heavy work	1.5
Pregnant women	+0.2
Lactation	+0.3
Infants	65 mg/kg – 60 mg/kg
Children (1–9 years)	0.7–1.2
Boys (10–18 years)	1.3–1.6
Girls (10–18 years)	1.2

Effects of Deficiency: Riboflavin deficiency is prevalent mainly among the low income groups particularly the vulnerable group and the elderly adults. Riboflavin deficiency is characterized by

1. Soreness and burning of the mouth and tongue.
2. Lesions at the angles of the mouth called Angular Stomatitis.
3. The inflammation of the tongue called glossitis.
4. Dry chapped appearance of the lip with ulcers termed cheilosis.
5. The skin becomes dry and results in seborehoeic dermatitis.
6. Photophobia, lacrimation, burning sensation of the eyes and visual fatigue.
7. Decreased motor co-ordination.
8. Normocytic anaemia.

Niacin

Niacin or Nicotinamide (amide form) is required by all the cells of our body. Like thiamine and riboflavin it plays a vital role in the release of energy from carbohydrates, protein, fat and alcohol.

Functions:

1. Nicotinamide is essential for tissue metabolism. The active forms of nicotinanide are NAD – Nicotinamide adenine dinucleotide and NADP – Nicotinamide adenine dinucleotide phosphate.
2. NAD and NADP are involved as coenzymes in large number of reversible oxidation reduction reactions.
3. Nicotinic acid enhances stomach secretion
4. NAD is involved in catabolic reactions and NADP is involved in anabolic reaction in our body.

Food Sources: Dried yeast, liver, rice polishing, peanut, whole cereals, legumes, meat, fish, are good sources. Tryptophan present in dietary protein is converted to niacin in humans. 60 mg of tryptophan yields 1 mg of niacin.

Requirements: ICMR recommended dietary allowance of Niacin per day is given in table.

Table: *ICMR Recommended Dietary Allowance for Niacin*

Group	*Niacin requirement mg/day*
Men	16–21
Women	12–16
Pregnant women	+2
Lactation	+4
Infants	710 mg/kg–650 mg/kg
Children (1–9 years)	8–13
Boys (10–18 years)	15–17
Girls (10–18 years)	13–14

Effects of Deficiency: Deficiency of nicotinic acid causes a disease known as pellagra. It is characterized by three D's → Dermatitis, Diarrhoea and Dementia.

1. **Dermatitis:** Name pellagra comes from pelle-skin and agra-rough. Marked changes occur in the skin especially in the skin exposed to sun and friction areas like elbows, surfaces of arms, knees. Lesions are symmetrically distributed, in the affected parts. At first there is reddening, thickening and pigmentation of the skin.

   Later on there is exfoliation leading to ultimately parchment of skin – butterfly like appearance.
2. **Diarrhoea:** Diarrhoea enhances the deficiency state. There are structural and absorptive defects in the small intestine. Tongue appears raw, and mucous membrane of the tongue is inflammed.
3. **Dementia:** There is irritability, depression, poor concentration and loss of memory. Delirium is a common mental disturbance.

Folic Acid

Folic acid was first extracted from dark green leafy vegetables. It forms yellow crystals and is a conjugated substance made up of three acids namely pteroic, para amino benzoic acid and glutamic acid.

Functions:

1. Folic acid coenzyme is essential in bringing about transferring single carbon units for many interconversions. A number of key compounds are formed by these reactions like (*i*) Purines which are essential constituents of living cells, (*ii*) Thymine – this essential compound forms a key part of DNA, (*iii*) the formation of haem group of haemoglobin.
2. The conversion of phenylalanine into tyrosin.

Food Sources: Green leafy vegetables, liver, kidney, gingelly seeds, cluster beans, are rich sources of folic acid.

Requirements: The recommended dietary allowances of Folic acid by ICMR are given in table.

Table: *ICMR Recommended Dietary Allowance for Folic acid*

Group	*Folic acid mg/day*
Men	100
Women	100
Pregnant women	400
Lactation	150
Infants	25
Children (1–9 years)	30–60
Boys & girls (10–18 years)	70–100

Deficiency:

1. Simple folate deficiency results in the bone marrow producing immature cells (megaloblasts cells) and few matured red blood cells. This results in reduced oxygen carrying capacity causing anaemia termed - Megaloblastic anaemia.
2. Folate deficiency during pregnancy causes neural tube disorders of the foetus.
3. Folate deficiency impairs the ability of the immune system to fight infection.

Pyridoxine (B_6)

Pyridoxine is unique among B-complex Vitamins in that it functions primarily in protein metabolism. Pyridoxine denotes related substances such as Pyridoxine, Pyridoxal and Pyridoxamine are three forms in which it is present in our body.

Functions : Vitamin B_6 in the form of pyridoxal phosphate functions as a co-enzyme in many biological reactions:

1. Pyridoxine is essential for the process of
   (*a*) *Transamination:* Transfer of amino group from one amino acid to another.
   (*b*) *Deamination:* Removal of the amino group.
   (*c*) *Decarboxylation:* Removal of the carboxyl group.
2. Vitamin B_6 is involved in several biochemical steps for the conversion of the amino acid tryptophan to niacin.

3. It aids in the formation of elastin, synthesis of messenger RNA and haem part of haemoglobin.
4. It aids in the conversion of linoleic acid to arachidonic acid.
5. In the carbohydrate metabolism it aids in the release of glycogen from liver and muscle.

Food sources: Meat, pulses and wheat are rich sources. Other Cereals are fair sources of this vitamin. Fruits and vegetables are poor sources. Cooking and processing of food causes loss of this vitamin.

Requirement: The ICMR recommended dietary allowance for pyridoxine is given in table.

Table: *The ICMR Recommended Dietary Allowance for Pyridoxine*

Group	*Pyridoxine mg/day*
Adults	2.0
Pregnant women	2.5
Lactation	2.5
Infants	0.1–0.4
Children (1–9 years)	0.9–1.6
Boys & girls (10–18 years)	1.6–2.0

Deficiency: Vitamin B_6 deficiency leads to abnormalities in protein metabolism which is manifested as poor growth, convulsions, anaemia, decreased antibody formation and skin lesions. Severe deficiency leads to microcytic hypochromic anaemia.

Symptoms such as weakness, nervousness, irritability, insomnia and difficulty in walking is predominant.

Vitamin B_{12} (Cyanocobalamin)

Until 1926, pernicious anaemia was a fatal disease of unknown origin with an unknown cure. In 1926 Minot and Murphy found that pernicious anaemia could be cured by feeding a patient atleast 0.3 kg of raw liver per day.

Also in 1926 Castle noted that patients with pernicious anaemia had a low level of gastric secretion. He suggested that the anti-pernicious anaemia factor had two components: an 'extrinsic factor' found in food and an 'intrinsic factor' within normal gastric secretions. The extrinsic factor is now known as vitamin B_{12} – cobalamine.

Functions: Vitamin B_{12} is necessary for normal growth and maintenance of healthy nervous tissue and normal blood formation.

Vitamin B_{12} is involved in DNA synthesis and thus in cell replication.

In the bone marrow the Vitamin B_{12} co-enzymes are essential for the formation of red blood cells. It facilitates the formation of folate co-enzymes needed for nucleic acid synthesis.

Vitamin B_{12} is also required for the synthesis of myelin sheath that surrounds the nerve fiber.

Food sources: Vitamin B_{12} is present only in foods of animal origin. Liver sheep, shrimp, mutton, egg, milk are good sources of Vitamin B_{12}. Vitamin B_{12} is synthesized by the colonic bacteria.

Requirements: The recommended dietary allowance prescribed by ICMR for B_{12} are given in table.

Table : *The ICMR Recommended Dietary Allowance for Vitamin B_{12}*

Group	*Vitamin B_{12} mg/per day*
Man	1.0
Woman	1.0
Pregnancy	1.0
Lactation	1.5
Infants	0.2
Children boys and girls	0.2–1.0

Deficiency: Pernicious anaemia is the major problem arising from an inadequate amount of vitamin B_{12}. Pernicious anaemia is a condition characterized by very large, immature red blood cells with normal amounts of haemoglobin.

WATER

Water is vital for human existence. We can live without food for extended periods of time, but without water will result in death.

Water is colourless, calorie less compound of hydrogen and oxygen that virtually every cell in the body needs to survive. Water is closer being a universal solvent than any other compound.

Water is the largest single compound of the body and it is distributed as follows.

Distribution of water in the body

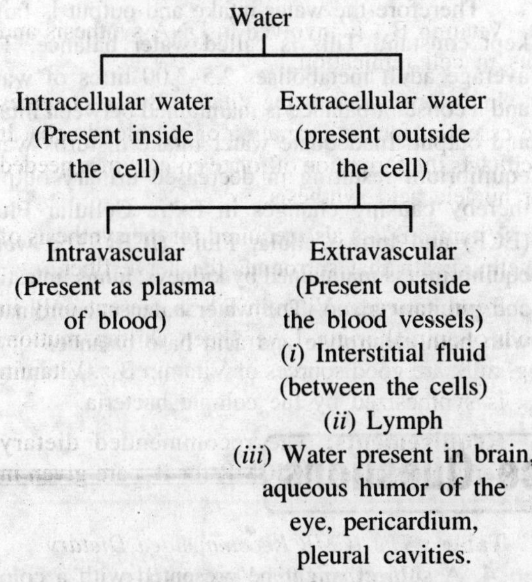

Total body water content is mainly determined by total amount of salt in the body. Salt and water concentration in the body is controlled by the kidneys.

Functions of Water

1. It is an essential constituent of all the cells of the body and the internal environment.
2. Serves as a transport medium by which most of the nutrients pass into the cells and removes excretory products.
3. Water is a medium for most biochemical reactions within the body and sometimes a reactant.
4. It is a valuable solvent in which various substances such as electrolytes, non-electrolytes, hormones, enzymes, vitamins are carried from one place to another.
5. Plays a vital role in the maintenance of body temperature. Heat is produced when food is burnt for energy. Body temperature must be kept at 80°–108° Fahrenheit for higher or lower body temperature will cause death. Body heat is lost through the skin, lungs, urine and faeces.
6. It forms a part of fluids in body tissues; (*e.g.*) the amniotic fluid surrounds and protects the foetus during pregnancy.
7. Saliva is about 99.5 per cent water. In healthy individuals it makes swallowing easier by moistening the food.
8. Water helps in maintaining the form and texture of the tissues.
9. Water is essential for the maintenance of acid base and electrolyte balance. It should be noted that pure water consists of hydrogen ion ($H+$) and hydroxyl ion (OH^-).

Substances dissolve in water as ions with positive and negative charge. They are called electrolytes. The common electrolytes in our body are sodium, potassium and chloride. Changes in electrolyte balance causes accumulation or depletion of water in intracellular and extracellular fluid.

The balance between the positively and negatively charged ions is essential for water flow and maintain osmolarity between the cells. This is called electrolyte balance. Acid base balance is the dynamic state of equilibrium of hydrogen ion concentration. When pH falls below 7 it is termed acidity and when it increases above 7 it is termed alkalinity.

Extremes of both cases results in death. The pH of the body should be maintained near neutrality. Enzymatic action depends on the pH. The digestion, absorption and utilization of nutrients are dependent on pH. Most body fluids are near neutral with the exception of gastric juice.

10. Water forms good source of macro minerals like Calcium, Magnesium, Fluoride, Iron and Iodine.

Requirements

Requirements of water varies with climate, dietary constituents, activities and surface area of the body.

As a rule a person should take enough water to excrete about 1200–1500 ml of urine per day. In tropics because of greater water loss through perspiration increased water intake is required to maintain urine volume. Normal intake of water ranges between 8–10 glasses per day.

Daily Water Input

In tropical countries like India the daily water input amounts to 2400–3000 ml of water through food, as fluid drinks and as metabolic water.

1. As fluid drinks – water, tea, coffee, milk soups	1500 – 1750 ml
2. Water intake through solid food	600 – 900 ml
3. Oxidation of carbohydrate, fat, proteins (metabolic water)	300 – 350 ml
Total	2400 – 3000 ml

Daily output of water

1. Urine	1200 – 1500 ml	→ (kidney)
2. Perspiration	700 – 900 ml	→ (Skin)
3. Respiration	400 ml	→ (lung)
4. Faeces	100 – 200 ml	→ (intestine)
Total	2400 – 3000 ml	

Therefore the water intake and output is fairly kept constant. This is called water balance. The average adult metabolises 2.5–3.00 litres of water and a constant balance is maintained between intake and output. Inadequate water intake disturbs water equilibrium resulting in decreased urinary output, thereby causing changes in Extra Cellular Fluid (ECF) and Intra Cellular Fluid (ICF). The water equilibrium is maintained by kidneys, lungs, intestine and pituitary gland. The water balance coordinates with both electrolyte and acid base balance.

Multiple Choice Questions

1. "Cognitive" was not clearly influenced by_________
A. Structuralism
B. Functionalism
C. Empiricism
D. Associationism

2. The term "Behaviour" in the definition of Psychology is used as ________ .
A. Minds or Thoughts or Feelings
B. Act of a person
C. Mental process
D. Individual's feelings, attitudes, thoughts and other mental processes which may be behind the behaviour

3. Psychologists who are involved in vocational and other forms of counselling are ______.
A. Psychoanalyst
B. Psychiatrist
C. Clinical Psychologist
D. Educational psychologists

4. A subject might be presented with a colour light, a tone, or an odour and asked to describe it as minutely as possible, is:
A. Introspection
B. Perception
C. Sensation
D. Feeling

5. Gestalt Psychology was founded in Germany in 1912 by:
A. Max Wertheimer, Kurt Koffka, Wolfgang Kohler
B. Max Wertheimer, Wolfgang Kohler, William James
C. Kurt-Koffka and Wolfgang Kohler
D. Max Wertheimer only

6. The German word 'Gestalt' means______.
A. Structure
B. Elements
C. Form or Configuration
D. Combination

7. A perspective that focuses on the role of feelings and impulses which are thought to be unconscious is _______.

A. Psychoanalytic B. Humanistic
C. Behavioural D. Biological

8. Finding the causes of behaviour from number of observations is called _____.

A. Inductive reasoning
B. Deductive reasoning
C. Both A and B
D. None of these

9. _______ method is ordinarily used only when people come to psychologists with personal problems.

A. Experimental B. Survey
C. Clinical method D. Interview

10. Empathic inference was one of the main technique used by _____.

A. Piaget B. James
C. Wundt D. Watson

11. Who has defined psychology as the 'scientific study of the behaviour of living creatures in their contact with the outer world'?

A. J.B. Watson B. James Angell
C. Arthur Gates D. Kurt Koffka

12. What is the goal of the structuralist psychologists?

A. To describe our behaviour
B. To find the units, or elements, which make up the mind
C. To analyse the unconscious drive
D. None of the above

13. Diagnosis may be carried out through:

A. Building up a comprehensive history
B. Arranging clinical interview
C. Adequate physical check-up
D. All of the above

14. Psychologists make measurements to discover relationships between events, this is called _______.

A. Correlational method
B. Experimental method
C. Clinical method
D. All of the above

15. The problem of effect of the observer is minimized by ________.

A. Concealing the behaviour
B. Concealing the observer
C. Concealing the observed
D. None of these

16. Which of the following is the function of 'Cytoplasm'?

A. Secretion B. Metabolism
C. Contractibility D. All of the above

17. Which of the following is the example of duct glands?

A. Tear glands
B. Salivary glands
C. Elimination glands
D. All of the above

18. The ________ gland produces one primary hormone, thyroxin, the main constituent of which is iodine.

A. Parathyroid B. Pituitary
C. Thyroid D. Adrenal

19. ______ is usually known as the 'relay station'.

A. Hypothalamus B. Thalamus
C. Cerebrum D. None of the above

20. Which one of the following areas of the brain is involved in controlling movements of the body?

A. Primary B. Secondary
C. Supplementary D. All of the above

21. ________ is the basic unit of the nervous system.

A. Brain B. Neuron
C. Spinal Cord D. Glands

22. ______ lobe of the brain is specialized area for vision.

A. Temporal B. Occipital
C. Frontol D. Parietal
E. All of the above

23. If _______ gland is removed in young animals, their growth is stunted and they fail to develop sexually.

A. Adrenal B. Pituitary
C. Thyroid D. Parathyroid

24. ______ glands are distinguished from the other glands by the fact that they secrete directly into the blood stream.
A. Exocrine B. Endocrine
C. Duct D. None of the above

25. ________ neurologist found that when an area on the right side of left hemisphere is destroyed, the loss of speech occurs
A. Lashley B. Broca
C. Franzy D. Munn

26. The ______ lobe processes auditory information.
A. Occipital B. Temporal
C. Parietal D. Frontal

27. Which of the following are the types of neurons?
A. Sensory neurons B. Inter neurons
C. Motor neurons D. All of the above

28. ________ provide for automatic and rapid responses to specific types of stimulation:
A. Neuron B. Reflex arcs
C. Neurotransmitters D. Hormones

29. ________ vary in shape, size, chemical composition and function.
A. Cell B. Nerves
C. Neurons D. None of the above

30. An adult brain weights about:
A. 1.35 kg B. 1.39 kg
C. 1.41 kg D. 1.33 kg

31. How much neurons does an adult brain contain?
A. 1000 million B. 10 billion
C. 100 billion D. 1 milion

32. __________ is the center for basic life support, breathing, heart beat, walking and sleeping.
A. Pons B. Neuron
C. The Brain stem D. None of the above

33. The _______ region connects to the cerebellum and is involved in dreaming and waking.
A. Pons
B. Medulla Oblongata
C. Thalamus
D. Cerebellum

34. With which of the following is the cerebellum associated?
A. Controlling posture
B. Maintaining equilibrium
C. Coordinating movements
D. All of the above

35. Which of the following has important role in 'aggression'?
A. Hippocampus B. Hypothalamus
C. Amygdala D. Thalamus

36. The _______ regulates higher levels of cognitive and emotional functions.
A. Cerebellum B. Cerebrum
C. Limbic system D. None of the above

37. The ______ is one of the smallest structures in the brain, but plays a vital role in our behaviour.
A. Amygdala B. Hippocampus
C. Hypothalamus D. Thalamus

38. ______ helps in maintaining internal homeostasis by regulating body temperature, blood pressure and blood sugar level.
A. The brain stem B. Cerebral Cortex
C. Limbic system D. None of the above

39. Which of the following is responsible for some simple reflexes that do not involve the brain?
A. Neuron B. Spinal Cord
C. Endocrine system D. None of the above

40. Water forms nearly ______ of the total cell volume.
A. 60% B. 40%
C. 70% D. 90%

41. Which of the following is the part of a neuron?
A. Axon B. Cell body
C. Dendrites D. All of the above

42. Patients with damage to the angular gyrus may be able to communicate with and understand speech, but they cannot read. This is called
A. Aphasia B. Dyslexia
C. Agnosia D. None of the above

43. Which of the following is the major neurotransmitter?
A. Acetylcholine B. Dopamine
C. Epinephrine D. All of the above

44. In most people, the right hemisphere seems to be specialized for the recognition and memory of ______ patterns of stimulation.
A. Visual B. Auditory
C. Tactile D. All of the above

45. The ______ is located towards the top of the head and controls incoming sensory information.
A. Frontal Lobe B. Parietal Lobe
C. Occipital Lobe D. Temporal Lobe

46. Which of the following neurons is directly responsible for all the movements and responses we make?
A. Sensory neuron B. Inter neuron
C. Motor neuron D. None of the above

47. An excess amount of ______ in the females can develop masculine tendencies and aggressive and dominant sex role behaviour in the females:
A. Estrogens B. Androgens
C. Oxytocin D. Vesopressin

48. Which of the following glands secrets serotonin and melatonin hormones?
A. Thyroid B. Thymus
C. Paneal D. Pancreas

49. If the ______ structures in the lower part of the temporal lobe, are damaged, consolidation of short-term memory into long term memory
A. Hippocampus B. Amygdala
C. Both (A) and (B) D. None of the above

50. The ______ is called the "Small brain":
A. Cerebrum B. Limbic system
C. Hypothalamus D. None of the above

51. Which of the following is the symptom of damage to 'Wernicke's area'?
A. Problems with reading and writing
B. Impairment of the ability to repeat a spoken word
C. Difficulty in naming common objects
D. All of the above

52. A ______ is an organ that is specialized for the secretion of various substances.
A. Neuron B. Brain
C. Gland D. Spinal Cord

53. Which one of the following lies between the two cerebral hemispheres and is covered by them?
A. Hypothalamus B. Thalamus
C. Cerebrum D. Limbic system

54. The ______ is a record of the slowly changing electrical activity of millions of nerve cells, all functioning at the same time in the brain.
A. C.T. Scanning
B. E.E.G. or Electroencephalogram
C. MRI or Magnetic Resonana Imaging
D. E.C.G.

55. A narrow gap, called the ______ separates the neurons.
A. Axon tip B. Cell body
C. Synaptic cleft D. None of the above

56. The information is passed from one neuron to another by chemicals known as:
A. Cell membrane B. Neurotransmitters
C. Nerve impulses D. None of the above

57. Which of the following areas of the brain deals with psychological processes like reasoning and memory?
A. Motor B. Premotor
C. Association D. Sensory

58. **Assertion (A) :** Neurons are tremendously varied in appearance.
Reason (R) : Most of the neurons consist of three basic parts.
A. Both A and R are true and R is the correct explanation of A
B. Both A and R are true but R is not a correct explanation of A
C. A is true but R is false
D. A is false but R is true

59. **Assertion (A) :** Graded potential is a basic type of signal within neurons.
Reason (R) : Stimulation of the dendrite produces graded potential.
A. Both A and R are true and R is the correct explanation of A
B. Both A and R are true but R is not a correct explanation of A
C. A is true but R is false
D. A is false but R is true

60. Assertion (A) : Action potential is the most basic signal in the nervous system.

Reason (R) : Action potential is a rapidly moving wave of depolarization that travels along the cell membrane of a neuron.

A. Both A and R are true and R is the correct explanation of A
B. Both A and R are true but R is not a correct explanation of A
C. A is true but R is false
D. A is false but R is true

61. Match List-I with List-II and select the correct answer from the codes given below the lists:

List-I	***List-II***
Brain parts	***Functions***
(*a*) Medulla	1. Concerns with the regulation of vital bodily functions as breathing and heartbeat
(*b*) Pons	2. Sensory and motor information passes through it
(*c*) Reticular	3. Concerns with sleep Activating System and arousal

Codes:

	(*a*)	(*b*)	(*c*)
A.	1	2	3
B.	2	1	3
C.	3	1	2
D.	2	3	1

62. A patient with left parietal lobe damage would have trouble recognizing objects by touch with the:

A. Right hand
B. Left hand
C. Both right and left hand
D. None of the above

63. Many painkillers (analgesics):

A. Occupy receptor sites normally stimulated by endorphins
B. Block pain and produce a temporary high
C. Both A and B
D. None of the above

64. Afferent Nerve Fibers are:

A. Nerve fibers in the spinal cord
B. Nerve fibers carrying information from receptors throughout the body toward the brain
C. Both (A) and (B)
D. None of the above

65. Peripheral Nervous System:

A. Connects internal organs and glands to the CNS
B. Connects voluntary and involuntary muscles to the CNS
C. Disconnects the glands from CNS
D. Both A and B

66. The spinal cord runs through the middle of a bony column of hollow bones known as:

A. Vertebrae
B. Nerve fibers
C. Afferent bone
D. Efferent bone

67. Match List-I suitably with List-II and select the correct answer from the codes given below:

List-I	***List-II***
(*a*) Efferent nerve fibers	1. Sensory nerve fibers
(*b*) Afferent nerve fibers	2. Motor nerve fibers
(*c*) Somatic Nervous System	3. Connects the spinal cord to voluntary muscles
(*d*) Autonomic Nervous System	4. Connects involuntary muscles to the CNS

Codes:

	(*a*)	(*b*)	(*c*)	(*d*)
A.	1	2	3	4
B.	2	1	3	4
C.	3	1	2	4
D.	4	2	1	3

68. ________ hormone, stimulates the outer layer of the adrenal gland causing it to secrete cortisone:

A. ACTH B. TCAH
C. CATH D. HACT

69. Match List-I with List-II and select the correct answer from the codes given below the lists:

List-I *Brain parts*	*List-II* *Functions*
(*a*) Cerebellum	1. Concerns with regulation of basic motor activities
(*b*) Midbrain	2. Contains primitive centres for vision and hearing and visual reflexes
(*c*) Hypothalamus	3. Plays key role in regulating ANS

Codes:

	(*a*)	(*b*)	(*c*)
A.	1	3	2
B.	1	2	3
C.	2	1	3
D.	3	1	2

70. Limbic System plays a role in:
A. Formation of emotional memories
B. Emotional reactions and behaviour
C. Control
D. All of the above

71. Damage to the motor cortex of frontal lobe:
A. Produces total paralysis
B. Results in a loss of control over fine movements, especially of the fingers
C. Produces partial paralysis
D. Both (B) and (C)

72. Match List-I with List-II and select the correct answer from the codes given below the lists:

List-I *Lobes of the brain*	*List-II* *Functions*
A. Parietal Lobe	1. The motor cortex within it controls the body movements
B. Occipital Lobe	2. Skin Senses (touch, temperature and pressure)
C. Temporal Lobe	3. Hearing
D. Frontal Lobe	4. Vision

Codes:

	(*a*)	(*b*)	(*c*)	(*d*)
A.	1	2	3	4
B.	4	2	1	3
C.	2	4	3	1
D.	3	1	2	4

73. _____ is a technique for measuring the electrical activity of the brain via electrodes placed at specified locations on the skull:
A. Electroencephalography
B. Electromonography
C. Electroneurography
D. Magnetic Reasoning Image

74. ERPs stands for:
A. Event-rating potentiality
B. Event-related potentials
C. Event recognizing potentialities
D. All of the above

75. Mongolism is also known as:
A. Down's syndrome
B. Klinefelter's syndrome
C. Turner's syndrome
D. None of the above

76. Most human characteristics are determined by many sets of genes; they are called:
A. Biogenic B. Multigenic
C. Polygenic D. Sociogenic

77. The Autonomic Nervous System is divided into:
A. Sympathetic and parasympathetic divisions
B. Autonomic nervous system and somatic nervous system
C. Peripheral and central nervous system
D. Sympathetic and somatic nervous system

78. When the axon of a nerve cell is stimulated:
A. The electric potential across the membrane is increased
B. The electric potential across the membrane is reduced at the point of stimulation
C. The electric potential across the membrane remains unchanged
D. None of the above

79. The electroencephalograph measures the pattern of electrical activity within the:
A. Brain
B. Body
C. Brain and body
D. None of the above

80. Consider the following statements about Neurons:
1. Neurons are the information carriers of the nervous system.
2. Neurons are of many sizes and shapes.
3. Neurons do have certain features in common.
4. Each neuron has a cell body to keep it alive.

Select the correct answers from the options give below:
A. 1, 2 and 4 B. 3 and 4
C. Only 1 D. 1, 2, 3 and 4

81. Consider the following statements:
1. Spinal cord and brain stem control and regulate many bodily functions.
2. No bodily activity is related to spinal cord.
3. No movement of the body can occur without activation of motoneurons in the spinal cord and brain stem.

Select the answer from the options given below:
A. 1, 2 and 3 B. Only 3
C. Only 2 D. 1 and 3

82. Cerebellum means:
A. Huge brain B. Little brain
C. Mid brain D. Hind brain

83. Consider the following statements about Cerebellum:
1. Receives sensory inputs from the spinal cord, brain stem and forebrain.
2. Processes information.
3. Sends outputs to many parts of the brain.
4. Helps to make our movements smooth.

Choose the correct options:
A. Only 1 B. 1 and 3
C. 1, 2, 3 and 4 D. Only 4

84. Find out the incorrect statements:
A. All behaviour depends upon the interaction between heredity and environment.
B. Heredity and environment are important in shaping behaviour.
C. Researchers are interested to find out how heredity limits the individual's potential and to what degree environmental conditions can change the inherited potential.
D. Heredity is more important than environment because environment can not change the potentiality level set by heredity.

85. ________ is also known as master gland as it directs the activities of most of the glands in our body.
A. Adrenal gland B. Pituitary gland
C. Thyroid gland D. All of the above

86. ________ produces milk in pregnant and nursing mothers.
A. Prolactin hormone B. Growth hormone
C. Insulin D. Oxytocin

87. Growth hormone is related to:
A. Posterior pituitary hormone
B. Anterior pituitary hormone
C. Both A and B
D. None of the above

88. Match List-I with List-II and select the correct answer from the codes given below:

List-I *Hormone*	*List-II* *Functions*
(*a*) Prolactin	1. Controls the release of milk during child birth
(*b*) Oxytocin	2. Prompts the production of milk in pregnant and nursing mothers
(*c*) Thyroxin	3. Helps liver to break down glucose
(*d*) Insulin	4. Influences the body's metabolic rate

Codes:

	(*a*)	(*b*)	(*c*)	(*d*)
A.	1	2	3	4
B.	2	1	3	4
C.	1	3	4	2
D.	2	1	4	3

89. Find out the incorrect statement about thyroxin:
A. It influences body's metabolic rate
B. It is produced by the thyroid gland
C. It influences behaviour
D. It does not play any role in the development of a child

90. Under production of thyroxin leads to:
A. Lethargy B. Weight gain
C. Cretinism D. All of the above

91. Insulin is released by:
A. Adrenal medulla B. Thyroid gland
C. Pancreas D. Pituitary gland

92. Consider the following statements about testosterone:
1. Testosterone prompts physical changes such as growth of body hair, deepening of voice and increase in sexually oriented behaviour.
2. Increased aggression has been linked with testosterone production.
3. Testosterone is produced in both the sexes.
Select the correct answer from the options given below:
A. Only 3 B. 1 and 2
C. Only 2 D. All of the above

93. Endocrine glands are also called ________ glands.
A. Ductless B. Blood
C. Active D. Inactive

94. Epinephrine and norepinephrine are the hormones secreted by:
A. Adrenal gland B. Pituitary glands
C. Thyroid glands D. Pancreas

95. The steroids
A. Help to maintain the normal metabolic processes of the body
B. Promote the release of sugar stored in the liver so the body has energy for quick action
C. Both A and B
D. None of the above

96. The ________ immediately surrounds the cell body which is essential for the generation and conduction of nerve impulses.
A. Cell membrane B. Myelin sheath
C. Neurotransmitters D. None of the above

97. Rapid eye movement (REM) occurs in:
A. Normal sleep B. Deep sleep
C. Beauty sleep D. Paradoxical sleep

98. The chemical substances secreted by the ductless glands are called:
A. Biles B. Hormones
C. Enzymes D. None of the above

99. Under-secretion or over-secretion of hormones can lead to serious physical and:
A. Psychophysical changes in us
B. Behavioural changes in us
C. Psychological changes in us
D. None of the above

100. ________ gland is located below the brain stem and secretes ________ hormones which regulate the other endocrine glands and body functions.
A. Pituitary, nine
B. Pineal, eight
C. Pituitary, five
D. None of the above

101. Early deprivation of ________ leads to cretinism or a type of feeble-mindedness.
A. Hormone B. Thyroxin
C. Melatonin D. None of the above

102. ________ glands are found in the midregion of the body above the kidneys.
A. Adrenal B. Thyroid
C. Parathyroid D. None of the above

103. The hereditary units we receive from our parents and transmit to our offspring are carried by microscopic particles, known as:
A. Genes B. Chromosomes
C. Glands D. None of the above

104. Many behavioural changes that occur in the early months of life are clearly related to maturation of the:
A. Nervous system B. Muscles
C. Glands D. All of the above

105. Which of the following is a significant development in the process of evolution that differentiates human being from other species?
A. Bipedalism
B. Encephalization
C. Language development
D. All of the above

106. Who among the following study the relationship between complex behaviours and processes in the nervous system?

A. Bio-psychologists
B. Neuro-psychologists
C. Physiological psychologists
D. All of the above

107. Between the ages of seven and twelve, the _______ stage, the child masters the various conservation concept and begins to perform still other manipulations.

A. Operational B. Preoperational
C. Sensorimotor D. Concrete

108. In which of the following psychosexual stages of development does normal heterosexual interests arise?

A. Oral B. Anal
C. Latent D. Genital

109. Developmental changes that occur across all stages of life is emphasised by:

A. Cognitive B. Life span approach
C. Ecology D. Genetics

110. Delinquency is often associated with:

A. Low parental support
B. Inappropriate discipline
C. Family discord
D. All of the above

111. To understand the biological foundations of behaviour we need to know something about:

A. Personality
B. Hereditary influence
C. Attitude
D. None of the above

112. Many of our physical characteristics, like, height, bone structure, hair and eye colour are:

A. Inherited
B. Non inherited
C. Secondary qualities
D. None of the above

113. Faulty nutrition leading to wasting and muscular weakness is termed as:

A. Dysrhythmia B. Dystrophy
C. Dysphagia D. Dyslogia

114. Most body cells contain:

A. 46 chromosomes B. 56 chromosomes
C. 36 chromosomes D. None of the above

115. The actual carrier of hereditary information within the genes is a complex nucleic acid called:

A. DNA B. RNA
C. INA D. None of the above

116. At a signal from the hypothalamus, the pituitary gland triggers the growth spurt, and:

A. Youth follows B. Puberty follows
C. Childhood follows D. None of the above

117. Match List-I (Main feature) with List-II (Name of the theory) and select the correct answer using the codes given below the lists:

List-I	*List-II*
(*a*) Grouping people into discrete behavioural categories	1. Social Learning Theory
(*b*) Relative difference between one person and another on a Continuous dimensions	2. Psychoanalysis
(*c*) Emphasis on the Unconscious motives	3. Trait Theories
(*d*) Analysis of the Unconscious motives that direct behaviour	4. Type Theories

Codes:

	(*a*)	(*b*)	(*c*)	(*d*)
A.	4	3	1	2
B.	3	4	2	1
C.	4	3	2	1
D.	3	4	1	2

118. Consider the following stages of personality development:

1. Identification
2. Latency
3. Primary motive satisfaction
4. Genital

According to Freud, the correct sequence of these stages in personality developments is:

A. 1, 3, 4, 2 B. 3, 1, 4, 2
C. 1, 3, 2, 4 D. 3, 1, 2, 4

119. The growth during infancy and childhood follows:
A. Cephalocaudal patterns
B. Proximodistal patterns
C. Both A and B
D. None of the above

120. Developmental psychologists are concerned with:
A. How certain behaviours develop and why they appear when they do
B. What factors produce abnormal development, such as mental illness or retardation
C. How psychological processes of the human adult originate and how they change over time
D. All of the above

121. Many behavioural changes that occur in the early months of life are clearly related to maturation of:
A. The nervous system
B. The muscles
C. The glands
D. All of the above

122. Infants cognitive development is expressed through:
A. Perceptual and motor activity
B. Perceptual activity alone
C. Motor activity alone
D. Motor and thinking activity

123. Misperceptions resulting from misinterpretation of information received by our sensory organs are known as:
A. Delusions B. Illusions
C. Hallucinations D. None of the above

124. Which of the following is the principle of perceptual organization?
A. Closure B. Grouping
C. Contrast D. All of the above

125. Sense organs in the muscles, tendons, and joints tell us about the position of our limbs and the state of tension in the muscles. They serve the sense called:
A. Kinesthesis B. Simulation
C. Receptors D. Transduction

126. During the transduction process, receptor cells convert physical energy into an electric voltage called:
A. Receptor potential B. Receptor activity
C. Receptor organism D. All of the above

127. Match List-I with List-II and choose the correct answer from the codes given below the lists:

***List-I* (*Receptors*)**	***List-II* (*Body parts*)**
(*a*) Meissner corpuscle	1. Areas of the skin with no receptor
(*b*) Basket nerve ending	2. Palms of the hands
(*c*) Free nerve endings	3. Roots of hairs

Codes:

	(*a*)	(*b*)	(*c*)
A.	2	3	1
B.	3	1	2
C.	3	2	1
D.	2	1	3

128. The most important Binocular cue comes from the fact that:
A. The two eyes receive slightly different views of the world
B. The two eyes receive the same view of the world
C. There is retinal parity
D. None of the above

129. Select the incorrect information about a binocular cue for depth perception:
A. The fovea is much more sensitive than the rest of the retina
B. When we look at an object, we fixate our eyes so that the image of the object falls mostly on each fovea
C. Images are more dissimilar when the object is close than when it is far in the distance
D. The image of the object falls only on one eye

130. The stability of the environment as we perceive it is termed as:
A. Perceptual constancy
B. Perceptual stability
C. Perceptual vision
D. Perceptual organization

131. Perceptual-cognitive styles refer to the idea that:
A. People differ in the ways they typically and characteristically process information
B. People process information in the same way
C. People do not process information
D. Informations get processed on their own

132. People whose perceptions are at the constricted end of the flexible constructed dimension:
A. Are dominated by internal needs and motives
B. Have narrow focus of attention
C. Are greatly affected by interfering influences
D. All of the above

133. Factors that influence an individual's perception are
1. Perceptual learning
2. Persons's set
3. Motives and needs
4. Individual's characteristic perceptual Cognitive style.
Select the correct answer from the options given below:
A. Only 1 and 2 B. Only 2 and 3
C. Only 1, 2, 3 and 4 D. Only 4

134. '*Telepathy*' is a form of:
A. Perception
B. Illusion
C. Apparent motion
D. Extrasensory perception

135. Accommodation is a process in the eye where
1. Ciliary muscles attached to the lens flatten it for distant objects.
2. Ciliary muscles attached to the lens thicken for closer objects.
3. Ciliary muscles flatten the lens for closer objects.
4. Ciliary muscles thicken the lens for distant objects.
Select the correct answer from the options given below:
A. 1 and 2 B. 3 and 4
C. 1 and 3 D. 2 and 4

136. Sensory Adaptation is:
A. The reduced sensitivity to unchanging stimuli over time
B. Getting used to a frequently changing stimuli
C. Increased sensitivity to unchanging stimuli
D. A static view

137. Retrieval cues and reconstructive processes are important factors in the:
A. Storage from memory
B. ''Read-out'' from memory
C. Recognise from memory
D. None of these

138. The technique used in the short-term memory is known as:
A. Free recall B. Reconstruction
C. Recognition D. None of the above

139. The .... of rehearsal given to items is important in the transfer of information from short-term to long-term memory.
A. Process B. Amount
C. Clarity D. None of the above

140. The memories of specific things that have happened to a person is called :
A. Episodic memory B. Semantic memory
C. Long-term memory D. None of the above

141. .... refers to the degree to which incoming information is processed so that it can be tied to, or integrated with, existing memories.
A. Perception B. Elaboration
C. Meaning D. None of the above

142. The observation that in memory experiments using a list of items to be remembered, items at the beginning and end of the list are remembered best, is called:
A. Primary effect
B. Recency effect
C. Serial-position effect
D. None of the above

143. Which of the following is a mechanical device for presenting items to be remembered at a constant rate of speed?
A. Memory scheme B. Memory scale
C. Memory drum D. Memory trumpet

144. Heavy drinking over a period of years can result, through vitamin B deficits and other chemical imbalances in irreversible brain damage known as:
A. Korsakoff syndrome
B. Senile dementia
C. Defensive amnesea
D. None of the above

145. Difficulty in writing language is a memory disorder known as:
A. Agnosia B. Apraxia
C. Agraphia D. Aphasia

146. The theory of .... holds that the memories are not recalled because their retrieval would in some way be unacceptable to the person, possibly because of the anxiety they would produce or the guilt they might activate.
A. Recall B. Repression
C. Recognition D. None of the above

147. Memory interference resulting from activities that come after or subsequent to, the events we are trying to remember is called:
A. Proactive interference
B. Retroactive interference
C. Episodic memory
D. None of the above

148. The recovery of childhood memories under hypnosis is an example pointing to the:
A. Permanent nature of memory
B. Retrieval of memory
C. Recall of memory
D. None of the above

149. .... is the process of gaining access to stored, coded information when it is needed.
A. Retrieval B. Encoding
C. Storage D. None of the above

150. .... method involves remembering information learnt earlier and reproducing it.
A. Recall B. Relearning
C. Recognition D. None of the above

151. The processes of memory are an encoding process, a storage process and a:
A. Cognitive process B. Imaginative process
C. Retrieval process D. None of the above

152. The .... method in ordinary learning forces the learner to define and select what is to be remembered.
A. Recall B. Recognition
C. Self-recitation D. None of the above

153. Consider the following stages:
(1) Storage (2) Encoding
(3) Retrieval (4) Recognition
The correct sequence of these stages in the memory information flow is:
A. 2, 1, 4, 3 B. 1, 2, 3, 4
C. 2, 1, 3, 4 D. 1, 2, 4, 3

154. Senile dementia is usually the result of reduction in blood flow to:
A. The heart B. The muscles
C. The brain D. None of the above

155. People with .... may forget their names, where they have come from, who their spouses are and many other details of their past lives.
A. Dementia B. Dream amnesia
C. Defensive amnesia D. None of the above

156. Information in long-term memory is episodic, as well as :
A. Semantic B. Distinct
C. Subjective D. None of the above

157. The term used for a faint copy of the visual input which persists in the visual sensory register for a few seconds before it gradually decays is:
A. Photographic image
B. Normative image
C. Iconic image
D. None of the above

158. The selective dropping of details and the tendency to accentuate certain features of remembered events is called:
A. Retroactive inhibition
B. Systematic distortion
C. Proactive inhibition
D. None of the above

159. In the Atkinson-shiffrin theory, memory starts with a sensory input from the:
A. Brain B. Spinal cord
C. Environment D. None of the above

160. The first level of incoming information for memory is:
A. Environment B. Perception
C. Meaning D. None of the above

161. In the .... method, the total number of items are correctly re-called regardless of their position in the list.
A. Free recall B. Anticipation score
C. Recognition D. None of the above

162. What does the word 'loci' mean?
A. Situation B. Places
C. Home D. None of these

163. Mnemonics mean:
A. The art or system of memory training
B. The art of learning
C. The art of cognition
D. The process of perception

164. Episodic memory deals with:
A. Interpersonal relationships
B. Individual's knowledge about world
C. Individual's personal experiences
D. Word-meaning association

165. Context-Dependent memory refers to the fact that:
A. Information entered into memory in one context or setting is easier to recall in that context than in others
B. Information entered into memory in one context is not easy to recall in that context
C. Information entered into memory in one context can be recalled in any context
D. Information cannot be recalled in any context without the help of a cue

166. The term chunk refers to:
A. The items containing several reparate bits of information
B. The memory procedure
C. Neural network
D. Large mass

167. The sensory register is a:
A. Storage function of the sensory channels
B. Function of nervous system
C. Storage system of memory
D. Sensory organ

168. No memories are reported pertaining to early childhood particularly during the first 4 to 5 years. This is called:
A. Neonate amnesia
B. Childhood amnesia
C. Infancy amnesia
D. Amnesia of the newborn

169. Senile dementia is characterized by deficits in:
A. Memory and abstract thought
B. Attention
C. Judgement
D. All of the above

170. Maintenance rehearsal is useful for maintaining information in the :
A. STM B. LTM
C. Sensory memory D. Procedural memory

171. The models of memory that describe parallel processing of information by numerous neural modules in the brain are called:
A. Parallel Network Models
B. Memory Network Models
C. Neural Network Models
D. The Atkinson and Shiffrin Model

172. A memory system that retains representations of sensory input for brief periods of time is known as:
A. Primary Memory B. Sensory Memory
C. Organic Memory D. Episodic Memory

173. Flash Bulb memories are the memories of:
A. Events that are very arousing or surprising
B. Personal dislikes
C. Word-meaning association
D. Inter personal relationships

174. Riding a bicycle, typing, writing are simple examples of:
A. Semantic Memory
B. Procedural Memory
C. Episodic Memory
D. Symbolic comparison

175. Procedural memory is a kind of memory which:
A. Refers to the way we remember how things are done
B. Includes stimulus-response associations and skilled patterns of responses

C. Is used to acquire and retain different kinds of skills
D. All of the above

176. Which of the following factors can improve memory?
A. Encoding and storing the information
B. Retaining it over a period of disuse
C. Retrieving it at the time of recall
D. All of the above

177. Duration of short-term memory is:
A. 2 seconds B. 20 seconds
C. 1/2 second D. 30 seconds

178. The storage capacity of short-term memory can be increased by a process known as:
A. Cognitive process B. The saurus
C. Chunking D. Retrieved

179. Which of the following is an important characteristics of episodic memory?
A. Holds all kind of knowledge
B. The emotional nature of events
C. Used to acquire different kinds of skills
D. None of the above

180. In psychology, which of the following mental processes provides the basis for all cognitive processes?
A. Thinking B. Learning
C. Memory D. Motivation

181. Which of the following kind of remembering is a common experience, but is a complex and a mysterious process?
A. Recall
B. Recognition
C. Redintegrative memory
D. Relearning

182. When newer memories interfere in the retrieval of old memory it is called:
A. Proactive interference
B. Saving
C. Retroactive-interference
D. Implicit memory

183. Which of the following types of long-term memory deals with individual's personal experiences?
A. Semantic memory B. Episodic memory
C. Procedural memory D. None of the above

184. Which of the following is a symptom of senile dementia, a disease of brain?
A. Personality changes
B. Delusions
C. General disorientation
D. All of the above

185. Programmed learning allows learners to proceed at their own pace and to receive immediate feedback on the correctness of their responses. This is a form of:
A. Punishment B. Reinforcement
C. Stimulus D. Reward

186. The instrumental-conditioning forms of behaviour therapy treat psychological disorders:
A. By contingently reinforcing socially adaptive behaviours
B. By extinguishing maladaptive behaviours
C. Both A and B
D. None of the above

187. Escape learning is an example of instrumental conditioning which is based on:
A. Negative reinforcement
B. Positive reinforcement
C. No reinforcement
D. Reinforcement

188. Which of the following information is/are correct about classical conditioning:
A. During acquisition, the excitatory tendency is dominant
B. During extinction, inhibition builds up to suppress conditioned responding
C. Pavlov thought of conditioning in terms of excitation and inhibition
D. All of the above

189. An increase in the magnitude of a conditioned response after a period of time no explicit training is known as:
A. Spontaneous recovery
B. Reconditioning
C. Extinction
D. Acquisition

190. Which one of the following statements is correct about 'learning'?

A. Learning is a change that takes place through practice or experience

B. Learning is a change in behaviour, for better or worse

C. Learning is a change that must be relatively permanent, it must last a fairly long time

D. All of the above

191. Which of the following statements about the theories of classical conditioning is the correct one?

A. Classical conditioning is concerned with the processes occurring when a conditioned response is acquired

B. They speculate about the nature of the learning that takes place in classical conditioning

C. One version of the theory is the theory of stimulus substitution

D. All of the above

192. Find out the correct statement:

A. Theory of stimulus substitution is an older theory about the nature of classical conditioning

B. Information and Expectation theories are current ideas about the theory of classical conditioning

C. Both A and B

D. None of the above

193. _____ is a schedule of reinforcement in which reinforcement occurs only after a fixed number of responses have been emitted:

A. Fixed-Interval schedule

B. Fixed-Ratio schedule

C. Variable-Ratio schedule

D. Schedules of Reinforcement

194. Operant conditioning was first investigated by:

A. B.F. Skinner

B. Pavlov

C. Thorndike

D. Tolman

195. A _____ is defined as any stimulus or event, which increases the probability of the occurrence of a desired response:

A. Reinforcer

B. Stimulus

C. Response

D. Conditioned stimulus

196. Which of the following statements is correct about observational learning?

A. It is investigated by Bandura

B. It is sometimes called social learning

C. It is a kind of learning where human beings learn social behaviour

D. All of the above

197. A stimulus that may influence operant behaviour is called a:

A. Positive stimulus

B. Negative stimulus

C. Discriminitive stimulus

D. Powerful stimulus

198. The process by which organisms learn to respond to certain stimuli but not to others, is known as:

A. Stimulus Discrimination

B. Response Discrimination

C. Stimulus Generalization

D. Spontaneous Recovery

199. Biological constraints on learning are the tendencies of some species:

A. To acquire some forms of conditioning less readily than other species do

B. To acquire some forms of conditioning more readily than other species do

C. To exhibit nocturnal activity

D. To depend on vision to associate food with illness

200. Which of the following are the areas for application of learning principles?

A. Organisations

B. Maladjustive behaviours

C. School learning

D. All of the above

201. Contemporary psychologists have developed techniques and procedures based on the principles of _____ for improving many aspects of life:

A. Classical learning B. Operant learning
C. Social learning D. All of the above

202. A mental as well as a physiological state, which arouses an organism to act for fulfilling the current need is:

A. Learning B. Motivation
C. Memory D. Emotion

203. Skinner conducted his studies on _____ in specially made boxes called Skinner Box.

A. Rats B. Pigeons
C. Dogs D. Both A and B

204. _____ Conditioning was first investigated by B.F. Skinner

A. Classical B. Operant
C. Both A and B D. None of the above

205. The simplest kind of learning is called :

A. Modelling
B. Conditioning
C. Observational learning
D. Concept learning

206. _____ learning is different from conditioning and is limited to human beings.

A. Concept B. Latent
C. Verbal D. Instrumental

207. The behaviour of children can easily be modified and shaped through the use of the:

A. Classical conditioning
B. Operant conditioning
C. Verbal learning
D. Concept learning

208. Which of the following methods of verbal learning is used to find out how participants learn the lists of verbal items?

A. Paired Association learning
B. Serial learning
C. Free recall
D. None of the above

209. Thorndike put a hungry _____ in a puzzle box for his experiment.

A. Dog B. Rat
C. Cat D. None of the above

210. Which of the following laws of learning propounded by Thorndike on the basis of his theory?

A. The law of readiness
B. The law of effect
C. The law of exercise
D. All of the above

211. _____, the father of behaviourism supported Pavlov's ideas on conditioned responses.

A. Hull B. Johan Watson
C. Tolman D. Skinner

212. _____ technique is based on the interaction between classical and instrumental conditioning.

A. Assertiveness learning
B. Systematic desensitisation
C. Biofeed-back treatment
D. None of the above

213. Which of the following factors influenced the learning?

A. Motivational variables
B. Fatigue
C. Knowledge of result and feed back
D. All of the above

214. Change of behaviour due to fatique drugs or other intoxicants is not considered as:

A. Memory B. Motivation
C. Learning D. Adjustment

215. _____ learning gives evidence of the 'doableness' of the behaviour and encourages the belief that 'I can do it too'.

A. Cognitive B. Observational
C. Perceptual D. None of the above

216. The 'I can' notion has become especially important in theory and research on:

A. Cognitive learning B. Perceptual learning
C. Modelling D. None of the above

217. Now several approaches emphasize cognitive process so heavily that they are often grouped as:

A. Modelling
B. Observational learning
C. Cognitive therapy
D. None of the above

218. Match List-I with List-II and select the correct answer using the codes given below the lists:

List-I	*List-II*
(*a*) Tolman	1. Trial and error learning
(*b*) Guthrie	2. Insightful learning
(*c*) Thorndike	3. Purposive behaviourism
(*d*) Kohler	4. Contiguous conditioning

Codes:

	(*a*)	(*b*)	(*c*)	(*d*)
A.	3	4	2	1
B.	4	3	1	2
C.	3	4	1	2
D.	4	3	2	1

219. Principles of motor learning help in achieving excellence in the field of:
A. Sports B. Education
C. Painting D. Imprinting

220. What may be defined as a behavioural trend in the direction of accuracy of performance?
A. Attitude B. Skill
C. Inclination D. None of the above

221. Verbal skills are generally acquired through:
A. Trial and error learning
B. Memorising
C. Skill learning
D. Both A and B

222. Escape learning means:
A. Learning to escape from dangers in life
B. Learning by negative re-inforcement
C. Learning by positive re-inforcement
D. All of the above

223. Match List-I (Impairment due to focal brain damage) with List-II (Psychological symptoms) and select the correct answer using the codes given below the lists:

List-I	*List-II*
(*a*) Agnosia	1. Difficulty in recognising objects or forms by touch
(*b*) Agraphia	2. Difficulty in writing language
(*c*) Apraxia	3. Difficulty in recognising certain familiar objects
(*d*) Asterognosis	4. Disturbances of memory of movements

Codes:

	(*a*)	(*b*)	(*c*)	(*d*)
A.	3	4	2	1
B.	2	3	1	4
C.	3	2	4	1
D.	1	2	4	3

224. The process of taking in external events and converting them into internal events or thoughts is called:
A. Organisation B. Adaptation
C. Assimilation D. Internalisation

225. Stress is often a factor in ____ disease, the leading causes of death.
A. Heart
B. Cancer
C. Dementia
D. Both A and B

226. ______ are also major stressors.
A. Frustration
B. Conflicts
C. Aggression
D. Both A and B

227. Stressors are able to activate the nerve cells of the ___ so that more corticotropin-releasing factor is sent to the pituitary gland, thus increasing secretion of ACTH into the blood.
A. Thalamus B. Hypothalamus
C. Neuron D. Brain

228. ____are methods for coping with stress.
A. Relaxation training
B. Hypnosis
C. Biofeedback and systematic desensitization
D. All of the above

229. ____arises between a motive and a person's internal standards, rather than between two external goals.
A. Frustration B. Conflict
C. Aggression D. Stress

230. The conflict can be affected by:
A. Religious scruples
B. Loss of self-control
C. Search for companionship
D. All of the above

231. Sometimes an_____conflict is resolved by refusing to select either alternative or in some way evading the choice.
A. Approach-approach
B. Approach-avoidance
C. Avoidance-avoidance
D. Multiple approach-avoidance

232. When circumstances block direct attack on the cause of frustration aggression may be:
A. Repressed B. Displaced
C. Regressed D. Suppressed

233. Freud used the term ______ to refer to unconscious processes that defend a person against anxiety.
A. Libido
B. Defense mechanisms
C. Psychosexual stages
D. None of the above

234. ______ is used to describe the unpleasant emotional state that results from blocked goal-seeking, rather than the event itself.
A. Conflict B. Frustration
C. Aggression D. Regression

235. Any situation that threatens the well being of the organism is assumed to produce a state of:
A. Frustration B. Anxiety
C. Conflict D. Aggression

236. Who among the following psychologists was the first to focus on the importance of anxiety?
A. Jung B. Freud
C. Adler D. Erikson

237. Frustration mainly arises from three important sources which include:
A. Physical B. Social
C. Psychological D. All of the above

238. ____can be defined as an internal state which can be caused by physical demands on the body or by environmental and social situations which are evaluated as potentially harmful, uncontrollable, exceeding our resources for coping.
A. Frustration B. Conflict
C. Stress D. Aggression

239. The physical, environmental, and social causes of the stress state are termed:
A. Stress B. Stressors
C. Distress D. None of the above

240. The term ______ disorders is used when perceived stressors-mental events increase the susceptibility of the body to disease.
A. Psychophysiological
B. Psychosomatic
C. Affective
D. Developmental

241. Which one of the following pairs is correctly matched?

A. Task oriented coping	Refers to examining the problem objectively
B. Emotion focused copying	Aims at controlling and managing emotions
C. Ego defence mechanism	Protects the ego against the impending dangers of hurt.

D. All of the above

242. General Adaptation Syndrome (GAS) is a three-stage model of reactions to stress, proposed by:
A. Hans Selye B. Lazarus
C. Freud D. Maslow

243. Consider the following statements about work-related stress:
1. Being asked to do too much in too short a time, can cause extreme overload.
2. Being asked to do too little can also cause stress.
3. Being the target of conflicting demands on expectations from different groups of people cause stress.

Which of the above statements is correct?
A. 1, 2 and 3 B. Only 3
C. 2 and 3 D. 1 and 2

244. Which one of the following options is correct about stress?
A. Stress plays some role in 50 to 70% of all physical illness
B. Stress upsets our complex internal chemistry

C. Stress interferes with efficient operation of our immune system
D. All of the above

245. Consider the following statements about individual differences in resistance to stress:
1. People who have general expectancies for good outcomes are much more stress-resistant than pessimists.
2. Men are more likely to report work-related problems, whereas women tend to report problems relevant to themselves, parenting and interactions with others.
3. Chang (1996) found that Asian students were more pessimistic and tended to use more problem avoidance and social withdrawal as coping strategies.

Which of the above statements is correct?
A. Only 1 B. Only 3
C. 1, 2 and 3 D. 1 and 2

246. Which one of the following statements is correct?
A. Anxiety and hostility can increase general arousal and facilitate the release of catecholamines
B. Catecholamines stands for a class of neuro transmitters that play an important role in the sympathetic nervous system
C. The release of the catecholamine epinephrine has the effect of boosting a person's overall readiness to act — a rise in blood pressure is a symptom of this
D. All of the above

247. Frustration refers to:
A. The blocking of motive satisfaction
B. The unpleasant emotional state that results from blocked goal-seeking rather than the event itself
C. Thwarting circumstances – the external events rather than their internal consequences
D. All of the above

248. Which one of the following statements is not correct?
A. A major source of frustration is conflict between two opposing motives
B. When two motives conflict the satisfaction of one leads to the frustration of the other
C. Conflict arises between a motive and a person's internal standards
D. Conflict never arises between external goals

249. Consider the following statements about conflicts:
1. Most conflicts involve goals that are simultaneously desirable and undesirable—both positive and negative.
2. The attitude towards a goal at once wanted and not wanted is called an ambivalent attitude.
3. Ambivalent attitudes are very common.
4. Conflicts between motives and internal standards can often be more difficult to resolve than conflicts between external goals.

Select the correct answer from the options given below:
A. 1, 2, 3 and 4 B. 1, 2 and 4
C. 1 and 3 D. 2, 3 and 4

250. The term Hassles refer to:
A. Acute stress
B. The countless minor annoying sources of everyday stress
C. Chronic stress
D. Specific stress

251. ______ is often a factor in two of the leading causes of death, viz, heart disease and cancer.
A. Ill health B. Stress
C. Conflict D. None of the above

252. The hassles of everyday life centring around work, family, social activities, health and finances are important:
A. Conflicts B. Adjustments
C. Stressors D. None of the above

253. In the ______ stage, prompt responses of the body, many of them mediated by the sympathetic nervous system prepare us to cope with the stressor.
A. Alarm reaction B. Resistance
C. Exhaustion D. None of the above

254. During the stage of ____, certain hormonal responses of the body are an important line of defence in resisting the effects of stressors.

A. Alarm reaction B. Resistance
C. Exhaustion D. None of the above

255. The rate of ACTH secretion is, in part, controlled by another hormone - like chemical.

A. CRF B. ACT
C. CRG D. None of the above

256. CRF is mode by certain cells in the brain structure known as the:

A. Pineal gland B. Hypothalamous
C. Pituitary gland D. None of the above

257. The corticotropin-releasing factor flows from the hypothalamus to the ______ gland through a specialized system of blood vessels.

A. Pituitary B. Pineal
C. Thymus D. None of the above

258. ACTH stimulates cells in the outer layers of the:

A. Pineal glands B. Pituitary glands
C. Adrenal glands D. None of the above

259. The outer layer of the adrenal gland is known as:

A. Cortex B. Cortin
C. Cortisoi D. None of the above

260. The adrenal glands secret:

A. Cortex hormones B. Corticoid hormones
C. Cretinin hormones D. None of the above

261. _____ promotes the formation of glucose (blood sugar), a fuel needed for nerve and muscle activity.

A. Corticoid B. Thyroxin
C. Cortisol D. None of the above

262. Cortisol hormone promotes the formation of glucose by breaking down fats and:

A. Minerals B. Carbohydrates
C. Proteins D. None of the above

263. _____ cells are crucial for fighting infection, have a short life-time and must be continuously replaced.

A. Blood B. White blood
C. Red blood D. None of the above

264. The inhibitory action of cortisol on the formation of the infection-fighting proteins are called:

A. Vitamins B. Antibodies
C. Enzymes D. None of the above

265. Sometimes relaxation instructions aim for deep-muscle relaxation and include suggestions of drowsiness or deep sleep which is knwon as:

A. Hypnosis
B. Relaxation
C. Trance like state
D. None of the above

266. ______ is a procedure in which people learn to modify internal responses such as heart rate and body temperature.

A. Hypnosis B. Biofeedback
C. Sublimation D. None of the above

267. Sometimes continual emotional tension can create:

A. Physical disorder
B. Hereditary disorder
C. Psychophysiological disorder
D. None of the above

268. Personality disorders are long standing patterns of _____ behaviour such as drug dependence, alcoholism and psychopathic personality.

A. Abnormal
B. Socially maladaptive
C. Radical
D. None of the above

269. The more severe life-event causing stress for adults is:

A. Pregnancy
B. Marriage
C. Divorce
D. Trouble with in-laws

270. Stressors are calibrated according to which of the following units.

A. Life-change units
B. Readjustment units
C. Conflict units
D. Distress units

271. Stress has which of the following immediate effects?

A. Behavioural B. Physiological
C. Emotional D. All of the above

272. Ways of handling stress so as to respond adaptively is termed as the:

A. Wellness cycle
B. Adjustment cycle
C. Accomodation cycle
D. Life-change cycle

273. Which hormones are a major feature of the stage of resistance?

A. Noradrenalin
B. Acetylcholine
C. Adrenocorticotropic hormone
D. Epinephrine

274. What does the 'Bell' denotes in Pavlov's Classical conditioning experiment?

A. Unconditional Stimulus (UCS)
B. Conditioned Stimulus (CS)
C. Unconditional Response (UCR)
D. Conditioned Response (CR)

275. .... is a chamber that contains a bar or key that an animal can press or manipulate in order to obtain food or water as a type of reinforcement.

A. Skinner Box
B. Thorndike puzzle box
C. Pavlov's Box
D. Both B and C

276. Reconditioning is .... original learning.

A. Slower than B. Equal to
C. Different D. More rapid than

277. .... refers to a procedure whereby an unconditioned stimulus is consistently presented before a neutral stimulus.

A. Forward conditioning
B. Instrumental conditioning
C. Backward conditioning
D. Emotional conditioning

278. Positive and negative punishment tends to:

A. Strengthen behaviour
B. Weaken behaviour
C. Make child stubborn
D. Diminish personality

279. Punishment is most effective in suppressing behaviour when it is:

A. immediate, consistent and intense
B. delayed, consistent and mild
C. immediate, consistent and mild
D. delayed, inconsistent and intense

280. An oil painting itself can include all of the following cues to depth perception except:

A. Linear Perspective
B. Retinal Disparity
C. Texture Gradient
D. Relative Image Size

281. Learning of fears is best explained by:

A. Operant conditioning
B. Classical conditioning
C. Observational learning
D. Latent learning

282. Learning by imitating others' behaviour is called ______ learning. The researcher best known for studying this type of learning is ______

A. Observational; Bandura
B. Secondary; Pavlov
C. Observational; Watson
D. Secondary; Skinner

283. Which theory proposes that memory fades due to the mere passage of time?

A. Motivated forgetting theory
B. Retrieval failure theory
C. Interference theory
D. Trace decay theory

284. When new learning is disturbed by previous learning it is called:

A. Distortion of memory
B. Retroactive inhibition
C. Reconstruction of memory
D. Proactive inhibition

285. When the first learning is disturbed by the new learning, it is called:

A. Retroactive inhibition
B. Proactive inhibition
C. Distortion of memory
D. Reconstruction of memory

286. Which memory system is also sometimes known as working memory?
A. Sensory memory
B. Short-term memory
C. Long-term memory
D. Flashbulb memory

287. Damage to thalamus and hypothalamus structures of brain plays a role in amnesia observed in which type of disease?
A. Alzheimer's disease
B. Depression
C. Korsakoff's syndrome
D. None of the above

288. .... refers to the process through which information is retained and held over a period of time.
A. Storage B. Encoding
C. Retrieval D. Memory

289. Answering a question on a fill-in-the-blank test is a good example of which type of memory retrieval?
A. Recognition B. Recollection
C. Recall D. None of the above

290. Which type of memory retrieval involves reconstructing memory, often utilizing logical structures, partial memories, narratives or clues?
A. Recognition B. Recall
C. Relearning D. Recollection

291. .... is the memory of autobiographical events (times, places, associated emotions, and other contextual knowledge) that can be explicitly stated.
A. Semantic memory
B. Episodic memory
C. Sensory memory
D. Long term memory

292. Which type memory involves memories of body movement and how to use objects in the environment?
A. Declarative memory
B. Procedural memory
C. Episodic memory
D. Semantic memory

293. Which type of memory involves the abstract knowledge and meaning of words, symbols, ideas and rules for relating them?
A. Semantic memory
B. Episodic memory
C. Procedural memory
D. Declarative memory

294. .... is derived from the Greek word icon, which means image, is the name given to visual sensory memory, or the memory of visual sensory information.
A. Episodic memory B. Semantic memory
C. Echoic memory D. Iconic Memory

295. .... is a permanent storehouse of all information and stores a large amount of information over a long period of days, months, years or even a lifetime.
A. Sensory memory B. Short term memory
C. Long term memory D. Episodic memory

296. Match List-I with List-II and indicate your answer with the help of the codes given below:

List-I (Definition)	***List-II (Memory system)***
(*a*) Memory for factual information that we acquire at a specific time	1. Procedural memory
(*b*) Memory for general, abstract knowledge that we cannot remember acquiring at a specific time	2. Episodic memory
(*c*) Memory for information necessary to perform skilled motor activity	3. Autobiographical memory
(*d*) Memory for events in our own life	4. Semantic memory

Codes:

	(*a*)	(*b*)	(*c*)	(*d*)
A.	2	4	1	3
B.	2	1	3	4
C.	3	2	4	1
D.	1	3	2	4

297. .... is the process of putting more than one bit of information into a unit, thereby expanding the capacity of STM.

A. Semantic codes B. Chunking
C. Rehearsal D. Working memory

298. One type of rehearsal in which items in short-term store are simply repeated over and over is called:

A. Elaborative Rehearsal
B. Sensory Register
C. Maintenance Rehearsal
D. Rehearsal Buffer

299. Each of the following is true regarding differences between STM and LTM, except:

A. information in STM is stored in terms of physical qualities
B. information in LTM may be permanent
C. information in LTM is primarily stored in the frontal lobes of the cortex
D. information in LTM is indexed

300. The memory we merely remember as long as it is in our eyes, casting an image in our retina, is:

A. Sensory Memory B. Iconic Memory
C. Episodic Memory D. Semantic Memory

301. Which structure of the working memory model was responsible for storing speech sounds for a limited duration?

A. Phonological loop
B. Short-term memory
C. Episodic memory
D. Long-term memory

302. Which characteristic of long-term memory facilitates the retrieval of information?

A. The chunking of information
B. The organization of material
C. Unlimited capacity
D. All of the above

303. Short term memory is capable of holding approximately how many items of unrelated information?

A. one B. two to four
C. five to nine D. ten to twelve

304. Which type of memory results from conditioning of forced associations?

A. Semantic Memory
B. Iconic Memory
C. Rote Memory
D. Episodic Memory

305. .... is "the aggregate or global capacity of the individual to act purposefully, to think rationally, and to deal effectively with the environment".

A. Thinking B. Learning
C. Remembering D. Intelligence

306. The formula for calculating IQ is:

A. $\frac{MA}{CA} \times 100$ B. $\frac{CA}{MA} \times 100$
C. $\frac{MA}{CA} \div 100$ D. $\frac{CA}{MA} \div 100$

307. The famous book 'Emotional Intelligence' was written by whom?

A. Spearman B. Galton
C. Goleman D. Thurstone

308. Who proposed the two factor theory of intelligence in 1904?

A. Spearman B. Thurstone
C. Goleman D. None of the above

309. Who gave the group factor theory of Intelligence?

A. Wechsler B. Sternberg
C. Thurstone D. Jensen

310. When the Mental Age (MA) and Chronological Age (CA) of a person is same, then the IQ of that person will be:

A. 100 B. 50
C. 75 D. 120

311. Among these who gave the concept of IQ?

A. Alfred Binet B. Lewis Terman
C. William Stern D. None of the above

312. The original Guilford's structure of intellect model suggests:

A. 100 identifiable abilities
B. 120 identifiable abilities
C. 125 identifiable abilities
D. 150 identifiable abilities

313. .... includes those aspects of intelligence that involve drawing on previously learned information to make decisions or solve problems.
A. Fluid intelligence
B. Emotional intelligence
C. Artificial intelligence
D. Crystallized intelligence

314. Who originally developed the Standard-Binet Intelligence Scales in 1905?
A. J.P. Guilford B. Lewis Terman
C. Alfred Binet D. L.L. Thurstone

315. Wechsler intelligence test consists of:
A. Performance items
B. Non-verbal items
C. Verbal items
D. Both verbal and performance items

316. Who developed the 'culture-free' test of intelligence?
A. Wechsler B. Cattel
C. Binet D. Thurstone

317. Guilford's concept of intelligence includes what he calls?
A. Creative Thinking
B. Divergent Thinking
C. Abstract Thinking
D. Convergent Thinking

318. Deterioration Quotient (DQ) was first used in which intelligence tests?
A. Binet-Simon Test
B. Galton-Cattell Test
C. Raven Progressive Matrices
D. Wechsler Adult Intelligence Test

319. Spearman Inferred General Intelligence on the basis of:
1. Positive manifold in intercorrelation matrix.
2. Tetrad differences in equation.
3. Unequal scores of same subjects on intelligence tests.
4. Reports from the subjects.

Codes:
A. 1 & 3 B. 2 & 4
C. 1 & 2 D. 3 & 4

320. The way in which we select, organize and interpret sensory input to achieve a grasp of our surrounding is called:
A. Illusion
B. Perception
C. Delusion
D. Information processing

321. A series of activities by which stimuli are perceived, transformed into information, and stored is called:
A. Attention
B. Selection
C. Perception
D. Information processing

322. The absolute threshold is the smallest magnitude of a stimuli that can be detected:
A. 30 per cent of the time
B. 40 per cent of the time
C. 50 per cent of the time
D. 60 per cent of the time

323. Which of the following stages of the information processing model constitute perception?
A. Exposure and attention
B. Exposure, attention and interpretation
C. Exposure, attention, interpretation and memory
D. Exposure, attention, interpretation, memory and action

324. Who among the following is not a Gestalt psychologist?
A. Kohler B. Koffka
C. Pavlov D. Wertheimer

325. In depth perception retinal disparity represents a:
A. Monocular cues B. Binocular cues
C. External cue D. None of the above

326. The sensations of colour are dependent upon which three basic factors:
A. size, contrast, and hue
B. frequency, intensity, and hue
C. brightness, hue, and saturation
D. None of the above

327. Which combination of sense organs and their process is wrong?
A. Visual - Eyes B. Auditory - Ears
C. Olfactory - Nose D. Cutaneous - Tongue

328. Which type of sensation is responsible for maintaining the equilibrium of the body?
A. Kinesthesis B. Vestibular
C. Gustatory D. Auditory

329. In prosopagnosia disorder a person is not able to:
A. Perceive colour B. Perceive size
C. Perceive shape D. Perceive faces

330. The presumed ability to perceive a stimulus that is below the threshold for conscious experience is called:
A. Perception
B. Subliminal perception
C. Sensation
D. Transduction

331. Negative thinking in pain can increase the perceived intensity of pain is referred to as:
A. Catastrophizing
B. Clairvoyance
C. Delusion
D. None of the above

332. The amount of change in a stimulus required before a person can detect the shift is known as:
A. Difference threshold
B. Just noticeable difference
C. Absolute threshold
D. Subliminal perception

333. The Gestalt perceptual law of common fate is associated with which one of these stimulus properties?
A. Size B. Colour
C. Motion D. Contrast

334. The information surrounding a stimulus is known as the:
A. Adaptation level
B. Context
C. Aura
D. Internal frame of reference

335. In humans, which sensory signals do not go via the thalamus, en route from receptor cells to cortex?
A. Auditory B. Vestibular
C. Visual D. Olfactory

336. The ability to see three-dimensional space and to accurately judge distances is called:
A. Size constancy
B. Shape constancy
C. Depth perception
D. Perceptual organization

337. Misinterpretation of perceptions or experiences in Schizophrenia are known as:
A. Hallucinations B. Misperceptions
C. Delusions D. Illusion

338. The perception of a stimulus that is below the threshold for conscious experience is termed as:
A. Just noticeable difference
B. Differential threshold
C. Signal detection
D. Subliminal perception

339. Match the items of List-I (Theory) with List-II (Description) and mark your answer with the help of the codes given below:

List-I (Theory)	***List-II (Description)***
(*a*) Theory of Signal Detection	1. Sensory subjective magnitude grows in proportion to the intensity of the stimulus raised to a power.
(*b*) The Fechner Law	2. The minimal amount of stimulus energy required for a detection of a stimulus.
(*c*) Absolute Threshold	3. Evaluation of the separate effects of the observer's sensory capacity and response bias.
(*d*) Stevens Power Law	4. Larger and larger inputs in stimulus energy are required to obtain a corresponding sensory effect.

Codes:

	(*a*)	(*b*)	(*c*)	(*d*)
A.	1	2	3	4
B.	1	2	4	3
C.	3	4	2	1
D.	3	2	1	4

340. Closure, nearness, similarity, and continuation are categories of:
A. Perceptual (Gestalt) organization.
B. Cognitive style.
C. Cognitive organization.
D. Perceptual integration.

341. Who developed the 'Retinex Theory' of colour perception?
A. Thomas Young
B. Hermann Von Helmholtz
C. Edward Herring
D. Edwin Land

342. The underlying mechanism for perceptual expectancies is:
A. A misleading perception that distorts or misjudges a stimulus.
B. Top-down processing.
C. The organization of perception by beginning with low-level features.
D. Bottom-up processing.

343. Read the following two statements : Assertion (A) and Reason (R) and indicate your answer using the codes given below:
Assertion (A): A major function of the perceptual system is to keep the appearance of objects the same inspite of change in the stimuli.
Reason (R): The posterior brain system selects objects on the basis of location, shape or colour and the anterior system is responsible for guiding the process.
Codes:
A. Both (A) and (R) are true and (R) is correct explanation of (A).
B. Both (A) and (R) are true, but (R) is not the correct explanation of (A).
C. (A) is true, but (R) is false.
D. (A) is false, but (R) is true.

344. Decreased perceptual response to a repeated stimulus is called:
A. Habituation B. Selective attention
C. Divided attention D. Illusion

345. Perceptive auditory receptors in the cochlea are identified as:
A. Basilar cells B. Hair cells
C. Malleus cells D. Glial cells

346. Sensations are organized into meaningful perceptions by:
A. Perceptual constancies
B. Meaning
C. Perceptual grouping (Gestalt) principles
D. Sensory adaptation

347. Given below are two statements labelled as Assertion (A) and the other labelled as Reason (R). Indicate your answer using the code given below:
Assertion (A): Subliminal or below threshold perception exerts an observable influence on various response parameters is not a controversial question.
Reason (R): Subliminally presented emotional stimuli activate cortical areas that mediate emotional experiences.
Codes:
A. Both (A) and (R) are true and (R) is the correct explanation of (A).
B. Both (A) and (R) are true, but (R) is not the correct explanation of (A).
C. (A) is true, but (R) is false.
D. (A) is false, but (R) is true.

348. The concept of programme learning was introduced by:
A. Hull B. Tolman
C. Skinner D. Thorndike

349. Much learning in human being takes place by:
A. Imitation and insight
B. Insight and conditioning
C. Conditioning and imitation
D. Trial and error

350. Latent learning is said to occur:
A. In the absence of punishment
B. In the absence of shock
C. In the absence of reward
D. All of the above

351. Social learning theory explicitly includes which of the following concepts?
A. Sign learning
B. Behavioural modelling
C. Action learning
D. None of the above

352. Behaviour modification mainly focuses on:
A. The process of sign learning
B. The ways to increase intelligence
C. The environmental contingencies that precede and follow behaviour
D. The ways to increase tacit knowledge

353. A technique in which closer and closer approximations of desired behaviour are required for the delivery of positive reinforcement is known as:
A. Shaping B. Modelling
C. Conditioning D. All of the above

354. Experiments on "Latent Learning" reveal that learning can occur:
A. Without reinforcement
B. With reinforcement
C. Without response
D. Without Stimulus

355. A parent deliberately ignores a child's temper tantrums in an attempt to discourage them. The parent's strategy is in accordance with:
A. Negative reinforcement
B. Extinction
C. Operant escape
D. Operant avoidance

356. Latent-learning studies established that .... is/are not always necessary for learning to occur.
A. experience
B. fixed action patterns
C. reward
D. motivation

357. Which of the following is not a Behaviour Therapy Technique?
A. Flooding
B. Counter transference
C. Counter conditioning
D. Systematic desensitisation

358. Which of the following is NOT an assumption of behavioural theories?
A. Focus on overt behaviours rather than unconscious motivations.
B. Action changes brain patterns.
C. Reliance on empirical data and scientific methods.
D. A valuing of an active, directive, prescriptive role for helpers.

359. Client centred therapy is a type of:
A. Humanistic therapy
B. Psychodynamic therapy
C. Cognitive therapy
D. Behavioural therapy

360. Most human habits are resistant to extinction because these are reinforced:
A. In a constant fashion
B. All the times
C. Every now and then
D. In a variable fashion

361. Some people believe that certain objects bring luck and help them in being successful. Such superstitions may be the result of:
A. insight
B. a program of behaviour modification
C. autoshaping
D. token economy systems

362. Behaviour analysis is based upon the principles of:
A. Classical conditioning
B. Operant conditioning
C. Dream analysis
D. All of the above

363. Behavioural symptoms of learned helplessness include emotional disturbance, cognitive deficits, and:
A. hallucinations
B. suicidal ideation
C. motivational deficits
D. dissociative personalities

364. Client centred therapy is associated with whom?
A. Rollo May B. Victor Frankl
C. Carl Rogers D. Abhram Maslow

365. When a discrepancy exists between the self-concept and the ideal self .... arises.
A. Incongruence
B. Inner tension
C. Actualizing tendency
D. None of the above

366. The humanistic theory of personality was proposed by:
A. Jung B. Allport
C. Maslow D. Frankl

367. Which of the following is NOT one of the four basic types of tools used by psychologists to measure personality?
A. Projective tests
B. Personal interview
C. Aptitude test
D. Self-report inventories

368. Which of the following is correct of the Rorschach Ink Blot Cards?
A. Five chromatic and five achromatic
B. Two chromatic and eight achromatic
C. Three chromatic and seven achromatic
D. Three chromatic, five achromatic and two unstructured

369. Behaviour of individuals with Anti-social Personality Disorder often appears impulsive and unpredictable due to switching quickly and unpredictably between:
A. Dysfunctional memories
B. Dysfunctional schemas
C. Dysfunctional thinking
D. Dysfunctional listening

370. Which personality measuring instrument uses four scales and is derived from the work of Jung?
A. Myers-Briggs Type Indicator
B. Big five personality factors
C. Cattell's 16PF traits
D. None of the above

371. Which is the one that is not a "Big Five" factor of personality?
A. Extraversion
B. Psychoticism
C. Conscientiousness
D. Agreeableness

372. Arousal is linked to which brain structure?
A. The Amygdala
B. The Reticular activating system
C. The Sympathetic nervous system
D. Both B & C

373. .... activity characterizes slow-wave sleep.
A. Delta activity B. Beta waves
C. Alpha waves D. Theta waves

374. What can be used to record eye movement during sleep?
A. EOG B. EGG
C. EEG D. ECG

375. .... is the duration of healthy stages of sleep.
A. 20-50 minutes B. 90-110 minutes
C. 110-120 minutes D. 85-110 minutes

376. Increased parasympathetic activity is a characteristic of ....?
A. Slow wave sleep B. REM sleep
C. Both A & B D. None of the above

377. When we are awake and very alert, the EEG normally shows:
A. Theta waves B. Delta waves
C. Beta waves D. Alpha waves

378. The presence of beta-wave activity in the EEG of an awake person implies that the person is:
A. About to enter the first stage of sleep
B. Drowsy
C. Alert and attentive
D. None of the above

379. An effective performance is more likely if the level of arousal is suitable for the activity, according to the:
A. Performance arousal model
B. Yerkes Dodson law
C. James Lange theory of motivation
D. None of the above

380. The non-REM sleep is commonly associated with:
A. Night terrors
B. Increased blood pressure
C. Frequent dreaming
D. All of the above

381. Nightmares occur in:
A. REM sleep B. NREM-I sleep
C. NREM-II sleep D. NREM-III sleep

382. The .... regulates the sleep wake homeostasis.
A. The circadian clock B. The hippocampus
C. Temporal lobe D. Hypothalamus

383. Homeostatic mechanisms are involved in:
A. Drinking
B. Eating
C. Maintaining body temperature
D. All of the above

384. In which stage of sleep are sleep spindles and K complexes first observed?
A. Stage 3 B. Stage 2
C. Stage 1 D. Stage 4

385. .... is involved with the digestion system and the circulatory system; helps to maintain blood sugar levels.
A. Pancreas B. Hormone
C. Proteins D. Polypeptide

386. Non-REM sleep consists of how many stages?
A. 4 B. 3
C. 1 D. 5

387. Problems of sleep that occurs during slow-wave sleep (stage-4) includes:
A. Urinating while asleep
B. Talking while asleep
C. Walking while asleep
D. All of the above

388. The giant sloth sleeps for about .... each day.
A. 20 hours B. 12 hours
C. 02 hours D. 00 hours

389. The REM phase of sleep is characterized by:
A. A silent EMG record.
B. The presence of gross eye movements
C. An EEG that appears to be of an awake person.
D. All of the above

390. Which gland is one of the largest endocrine glands in the body and is involved in the production of the hormones T3 (triiodo-thyronine) and T4 (thyroxine).
A. The Thyroid gland
B. Pineal gland
C. Pituitary gland
D. Gonad glands

391. .... acts to lower blood sugar levels by allowing the sugar to flow into cells.
A. The pancreas B. Insulin
C. Islet cells D. Glucagon

392. .... is classified as a steroid and is responsible for many of the physical characteristics in males like broad shoulders, muscular body and hair.
A. Testosterone B. Estrogen
C. Progesterone D. Amino Acid

393. Among the options given below, which one of the following locations is for the mechanism that triggers REM-sleep?
A. Amygdala
B. Lateral Hypothalamus
C. Midbrain
D. Pontine reticular formation

394. The pancreas gland has a duct which opens into the:
A. Duodenum B. Kidney
C. Liver D. Large intestine

395. Which gland produces melatonin, a serotonin derived hormone, which affects the modulation of sleep patterns in both seasonal and circadian rhythms?
A. Thyroid gland B. Adrenal gland
C. Pineal gland D. Parathyroid gland

396. Hypnogogic images occur during drowsy state *i.e.*, between .... and ...., whereas hypnopompic images occur between .... and ....
A. waking, sleeping; waking, sleeping
B. sleeping, waking; waking, sleeping
C. waking, sleeping; sleeping, waking
D. sleeping, waking; sleeping, waking

397. Which among these is correct about Insulin?
A. Is secreted by beta cells of pancreas.
B. Increase protein and lipid synthesis.
C. Promotes glycogenesis in liver & muscles.
D. All are correct

398. Which antidiuretic hormone (ADH) mainly targets kidneys & arterioles, stimulates water retention; raises blood pressure by contracting arterioles?
A. Vasopressin B. Estrogen
C. Oxytocin D. Thyroxine

399. Hunger is caused by:
I. Expectation of food
II. Deficiency of energy
III. Homeostatic disturbance
IV. Deficiency of Oxygen
Codes:
A. I B. I, II
C. I, II, III D. I, II, III, IV

400. Antidiuretic hormone acts on the .... and helps regulate ....
A. Liver, blood sugar
B. Kidneys, body water
C. Pancreas, proteins
D. Stomach, body weight

401. The parasomnias include:
A. Somnambulism B. Sleep apnoea
C. Narcolepsy D. Depression

402. Damage to which portion of brain is known to cause insomnia.
A. Preoptic-anterior region of the hypothalamus
B. Posterior hypothalamus
C. Posterior segment of the diencephalons
D. None of the above

403. Insufficiency of thyroxin can lead to:
A. Cretinism B. Myxedema
C. Down syndrome D. Goiter

404. Hormones are chemical messengers secreted by the:
A. Endocrine organs
B. Exocrine organs
C. Both A and B
D. Digestive system

405. Which of the following is a characteristic of slow wave sleep?
A. Increased parasympathetic activity
B. Decreased parasympathetic activity
C. Increased sympathetic activity
D. Decreased sympathetic activity

406. Antidiuretic hormone is synthesized in the:
A. Anterior pituitary
B. Posterior pituitary
C. Thalamus
D. Hypothalamus

407. Which among these options is incorrect about Narcolepsy?
A. There are less hypocretin secreting cells in the body of those with narcolepsy
B. Cause is due to a loss of REM inhibiting mechanism
C. Begins during the middle ages and worsens as the person gets older
D. Shows familial incidence

408. In which of the following pairs, endocrine glands and its primary action is correct?
A. Thyroid - controls physical growth
B. Parathyroid - controls the quantity of calcium
C. Gonad - affects the personality
D. All of the above are correct

409. The hypothalamus regulates ....
A. heart rate B. body temperature
C. water balance D. All of the above

410. Which of the following signs or symptoms are seen in both primary and secondary adrenal insufficiency?
A. Hyperpigmentation B. Weakness
C. Chronic headache D. Both A and C

411. Among these which of the following conditions increase the likelihood of having obstructive sleep apnoea?
A. Obesity B. Hypothyroidism
C. Small airways D. All of the above

412. Each of the following is a cue that helps the hypothalamus regulate eating except:
A. stomach contractions
B. blood sugar levels
C. body fat levels
D. red blood cell levels

413. Which of the following are associated with sleep?
A. GABA B. Raphe nuclei
C. Acetylcholine D. Both A & B

414. The main function of insulin is to:
A. Break down protein
B. Enable glucose to enter body cells
C. To provide sugar free diet to the body
D. Absorb all essential nutrients

415. Which among these is true about Somnambulism?
A. Occurs during REM sleep
B. Is commonly seen between the ages of 5 and 12
C. Is associated with enuresis
D. Both B & C Correct

416. Which one of the followings are male sex hormones?
A. Androgens B. Progesterone
C. Estrogen D. Aldosterones

417. Depressed individuals exhibit which of the following symptoms?
A. Cognitive symptoms
B. Physical symptoms
C. Behavioural symptoms
D. All of the above

418. In which theory of depression, an individuals exhibit an expectation that positive outcomes will not occur, negative outcomes will occur, and that the individual has no responses available that will change this state of affairs.
A. Attribution theory
B. Berne's Humanistic Theory
C. Beck's Cognitive Theory
D. Hopelessness Theory

419. In Major Depression, hippocampus abnormalities are regularly linked with which of the following?
A. High levels of dopamine
B. High levels of cortisol
C. High levels of GABA
D. High levels of acetylcholine

420. .... disorder is an excessive or aroused state characterized by feelings of apprehension, uncertainty and fear.
A. Anxiety B. Mental
C. Depressive D. Phobic

421. Which of the following physical symptoms is not associated with Panic attacks?
A. Choking feeling
B. Heart palpitations
C. Hyperventilating
D. Feelings of helplessness

422. .... is a set of persistent anxiety-based symptoms that occur after experiencing or witnessing an extremely fear-evoking traumatic event.
A. Post Traumatic Stress Disorder (PTSD)
B. Panic Disorder
C. Obsessive Compulsive Disorder
D. None of the above

423. Which of the following is not an anxiety disorder?
A. Bipolar disorder
B. Obsessive-compulsive disorder
C. Post-traumatic stress disorder
D. Panic disorder

424. Which of the following would be classified as a negative symptom of schizophrenia?
A. Delusions
B. Visual hallucinations
C. Social withdrawal
D. Aggressive behaviour

425. Which of the following is considered to be a symptom of Post Traumatic Stress Disorder (PTSD)?
A. Re-experiencing the traumatic event
B. Avoiding reminders of the trauma
C. Increased anxiety and emotional arousal
D. All of the above

426. .... includes phobia, panic disorder, obsessive-compulsive disorder, and post-traumatic stress disorder.
A. Anxiety disorder
B. Mental retardation
C. Anti social behaviour
D. None of the above

427. Which among these is not a symptom of generalised anxiety disorder?
A. Constant worries
B. Inability to tolerate uncertainty
C. Social withdrawal
D. Pervasive feeling of apprehension or dread

428. OCD tends to begin:
A. Between 6 and 15 years of age for both genders.

B. Between 6 and 15 years of age for women and between 20 and 29 years of age for men.
C. Between 6 and 15 years of age for men and between 20 and 29 years of age for women.
D. Between 6 and 18 years of age for both genders.

429. Which of the following is an effective treatment for OCD?
A. Exposure and response prevention (ERP)
B. Group therapy
C. Psychodynamic therapy
D. Medication

430. Anhedonia refers to the:
A. Inability to remember things and persons
B. Inability to sleep
C. inability to gain pleasure from normally pleasurable experiences
D. Both B & C

431. The most common focus of obsessive thoughts is:
A. Repeated doubts
B. Dirt and contamination
C. Sexual impulses
D. All of the above

432. Beck's Cognitive therapy for depression requires the individual to:
A. Alleviate Major negative symptoms
B. Make an objective assessment of their beliefs
C. Set attainable life goals
D. All of the above

433. Systematic desensitisation is an effective therapy for which of the following?
A. Generalised fears or anxieties
B. Specific phobias
C. Depression
D. Schizophrenia

434. Monoamine oxidase inhibitors (MAOIs) are effective for the treatment of:
A. Obsessive compulsive disorder
B. Phobias
C. Schizophrenia
D. Major depression

435. .... is a personality disorder in which individuals show exceptionally perfectionist tendencies including a preoccupation with orderliness and control at the expense of flexibility, efficiency and productivity.
A. Obsessive-Compulsive Personality Disorder
B. Post Traumatic Stress Disorder
C. Generalized Anxiety Disorder
D. Panic Disorder

436. .... therapies focus on self-development, growth and responsibilities.
A. Humanistic
B. Cognitive behavioural
C. Systematic
D. Psychodynamic

437. .... is a psychiatric illness that can occur after experiencing or witnessing a traumatic event, including natural disasters, rape, violent crime, or war.
A. Obsessive-Compulsive Personality Disorder
B. Post-traumatic stress disorder
C. Generalized Anxiety Disorder
D. Panic Disorder

438. According to epidemiology, different types of measures of epidemiology of mental illness are:
1. Prevalence
2. Point prevalence
3. Incidence
4. Percentage

Codes:
A. 1, 2, 4 only
B. 1, 3, 4 only
C. 2, 3, 4 only
D. 1, 2, 3 only

439. Which among these is a specific learning disability characterised by mathematical ability being substantially below norm for chronological age, intelligence, and educational level?
A. Dyscalculia B. Dyslexia
C. Dysphasia D. Dyspraxia

440. DSM-IV classifies which disorder, also known intermittent explosive disorder under 'habit disorders'?
A. Borderline personality disorder
B. Impulsive personality disorder
C. Dissocial personality disorder
D. Histrionic personality disorder

441. Which of the following pairs is not the negative symptom of Schizophrenia?
A. Emotional flattening and Asociality
B. Anhedonia and Amotivation
C. Poverty of speech and Apathy
D. Hallucinations and Bizarre Behaviour

442. Which among these symptoms are related to Narcissistic personality disorder?
A. Increased sense of self-worth
B. Egocentric
C. Sense of superiority
D. All of the above

443. Persistent social inhibition, hypersensitivity to negative evaluation and feelings of inadequacy are the symptoms of which personality disorder?
A. Avoidant personality disorder
B. Dissocial personality disorder
C. Borderline personality disorder
D. Antisocial personality disorder

444. A modern term replacing Mental Retardation to describe the more severe and general learning disabilities is:
A. Behaviour Abnormalities
B. Intellectual Disabilities
C. Distorted Abilities
D. None of the above

445. A child was classified as a case of mental retardation. On DSM IV/ IV (TR), this diagnosis would be recorded on:
A. Axis I B. Axis II
C. Axis III D. Axis IV

446. Which of the following do/does not describe an obsession?
1. Continually reliving a traumatic event.
2. An unwanted thought that a person finds intrusive and distressing.
3. A behaviour or mental act that a person feels compelled to perform.
4. Something a person enjoys doing and talking about constantly.

Codes:
A. 1, 2 and 4 B. 2 and 4
C. 2, 3 and 4 D. 1, 3 and 4

447. .... is an excessive or aroused state characterised by feelings of apprehension, uncertainty and fear.
A. Anxiety disorder
B. Panic disorder
C. Bipolar disorder
D. Post-traumatic stress disorder

448. Given below are two statements—Assertion (A) and Reason (R). Indicate your answer using the code given below.

Assertion (A): In case of anxiety disorder, people become inclined to make negative evaluation of themselves, their world, and their future.

Reason (R): People acquire a relatively stable set of cognitive structures or schemas that contain dysfunctional beliefs.

Codes:
A. Both (A) and (R) are true and (R) is the correct explanation of (A).
B. Both (A) and (R) are true, but (R) is not the correct explanation of (A).
C. (A) is true, but (R) is false.
D. (A) is false, but (R) is true.

449. Among the options given below which are the symptoms of Schizotypal personality disorder:
A. Aloof and isolated
B. Suffer from depersonalization
C. Indulgence in magical thinking
D. All of the above

450. .... is characterized by excessive, unreasonable, persistent fear triggered by a specific object or situation?
A. Anxiety disorder
B. Panic disorder
C. Specific Phobias
D. Obsessive Compulsive Disorder (OCD)

451. Read each of the following two statements—Assertion (A) and Reason (R) and indicate your answer using the codes given below:

Assertion (A): Increased metabolic activity in frontal cortex and the caudate nucleus has been implicated in Obsessive Compulsive Disorder.

Reason (R): Current evidence suggests that increased serotonin activity and increased sensitivity of some brain structures to serotonin are involved in Obsessive Compulsive Symptoms.

Codes:

A. Both (A) and (R) are true and (R) is the correct explanation of (A).
B. Both (A) and (R) are true, but (R) is not the correct explanation of (A).
C. (A) is true, but (R) is false.
D. (A) is false, but (R) is true.

452. Using the multiaxial system of DSM-IV-TR paranoid personality disorder and borderline personality disorder would be coded on:

A. Axis I B. Axis II
C. Axis III D. Axis IV

453. A phobia of heights is known as:

A. Acrophobia B. Claustrophobia
C. Hemophobia D. Glossophobia

454. Match List-I with List-II and indicate your answer using the codes given below:

List-I (Disorder)	***List-II (Explanation)***
(*a*) Depression	1. Classical conditioning
(*b*) Schizophrenia	2. Negative attribution style
(*c*) Phobia	3. Alcoholism
(*d*) Korsakoff's syndrome	4. Dopamine hypothesis

Codes:

	(*a*)	(*b*)	(*c*)	(*d*)
A.	3	2	4	1
B.	2	4	1	3
C.	1	3	2	4
D.	2	1	4	3

455. Match List-I with List-II and indicate your answer with the help of the codes given below:

List-I (Description)	***List-II (Nomenclature)***
(*a*) Number of new cases that occur over a given period of time.	1. Epidemiology
(*b*) Study of the distribution of diseases or health related behaviours in a given population	2. Syndrome
(*c*) Number of active cases in a population in a given period of time.	3. Incidence
(*d*) A group or cluster of symptoms that occur together	4. Prevalence

Codes:

	(*a*)	(*b*)	(*c*)	(*d*)
A.	2	1	3	4
B.	4	2	1	3
C.	3	1	4	2
D.	1	4	3	2

456. The most common cause of mental retardation is:

A. Korsakoffs syndrome
B. Depression
C. Birth asphyxia
D. Kluver-Bucy syndrome

457. Ragi is richest source of:

A. Iron B. Calcium
C. Iodine D. Vitamin B complex

458. Cereals are mainly rich in:

A. Glucose B. Maltose
C. Proteins D. Starch

459. Pulses are a good source of:

A. Carbohydrates B. Fats
C. Proteins D. Vitamins

460. The largest part of most diet is made up of:

A. nucleic acid B. proteins
C. carbohydrates D. lipids

461. Match the following:

List-I	*List-II*
(*a*) Beri-beri	1. Vitamin A
(*b*) Night-blindness	2. Vitamin E
(*c*) Scurvy	3. Vitamin K
(*d*) Haemorrhage	4. Vitamin C
	5. Vitamin B

Codes:

	(*a*)	(*b*)	(*c*)	(*d*)
A.	4	3	5	2
B.	3	4	5	2
C.	4	1	5	3
D.	5	1	4	3

462. Sources of Vitamin B_{12} are:
A. Mushrooms, grains, nuts
B. Dairy products and yeast extracts
C. Bread, rice, broccoli and beans
D. All of these

463. Raw potatoes are not digested in humans because each of the potato granules has an outer coating of:
A. lignin
B. cellulose
C. lignin and cellulose
D. amylopectins

464. In case of cardiac arrest, what should be the most primary step?
A. mouth-to-mouth respiration
B. cardiac massage
C. to call a doctor
D. None of these

465. The blood corpuscles that help to build up resistance against disease are:
A. all leucocytes B. monocytes
C. neutrophils D. lymphocytes

466. Insufficient dietary iodine causes a/an:
A. cretin B. giant
C. enlarged thyroid D. small thyroid

467. Which of the following is a substance abundantly available in the sea and administered in a certain deficiency disease?
A. iodine B. iron
C. vitamin A D. flourine

468. The body loses a huge amount of water when a person suffers from severe diarrhoea. This acute water loss can be made good by:
A. a slow and gradual intravenous administration of sterile distilled water
B. a slow and gradual intravenous administration of 0.1% glucose dissolved in sterile distilled water as a ready source of energy
C. an intravenous drip comprising glucose and normal saline
D. an intravenous drip comprising sodium chloride, potassium chloride, magnesium chloride, calcium chloride and glucose

469. In countries where polished rice is the main cereal in their diet, people suffer from:
A. pellagra B. scurvy
C. beri-beri D. osteomalacia

470. People who consume maize as the main cereal in their diet are susceptible to:
A. beri-beri B. pellagra
C. scurvy D. kwashiorkor

471. The deficiency of vitamin A causes:
A. hair to fall B. dysentery
C. night blindness D. weakness

472. Jaundice results from the malfunctioning of the:
A. kidney B. liver
C. lungs D. stomach

473. Excessive consumption of alcoholic drinks causes damage to the:
A. liver B. kidney
C. heart D. lungs

474. The most important stimulant in tea leaves is:
A. brucine B. caffeine
C. phenylalanine D. theine

475. Half-cooked potatoes, if eaten with food, are not digested. This is because:
A. starch in semi-cooked potatoes is in insoluble form and fails to form a complex with the concerned enzyme
B. Starch granules in semi-cooked potatoes are coated with cellulose which, in turn, is not digested

C. starch granules in semi-cooked potatoes are coated with lignin which, in turn, is not digested
D. insufficient heat does not convert cellulose into starch

476. A doctor advises a patient to take plenty of citrus fruits, guavas, tomatoes and amlas over a period of two months regularly. What do you think is the complaint of the patient?
A. softness and pain in bones, bending of vertebral column
B. gums spongy, swollen and bleed easily
C. blurred vision, burning and dryness of eye and tongue, cracking of skin of angle of mouth
D. extreme weakness, swelling and pain in legs, loss of appetite, headache

477. Ripe mangoes contain:
A. Vitamin A B. Vitamin B_6
C. Vitamin C D. Vitamin E

478. Which one of the following seeds can benefit a patient of diabetes mellitus by normalizing his blood sugar level?
A. Coriander seeds B. Mustard seeds
C. Cumin seeds D. Fenugreek seeds

479. Most food nutrients are absorbed into the blood from the:
A. large intestine B. mouth
C. small intestine D. stomach

480. Chocolates can be bad for health because of a high content of:
A. Cobalt B. Nickel
C. Zinc D. Lead

481. Which of the following vitamins is essential for growth of skin?
A. Vitamin A B. Vitamin B
C. Vitamin C D. Vitamin D

482. Which of the following vitamins is concerned with proper bone formation in the young?
A. Vitamin A B. Vitamin B
C. Vitamin D D. Vitamin E

483. Which one of the following contains both vitamins A and D?
A. Codliver oil B. Mutton
C. Orange D. Wheat

484. Which of the following vitamins aids night vision?
A. Vitamin A B. Vitamin B
C. Vitamin C D. Vitamin D

485. All of the following contain minerals, except:
A. fruits B. jaggery
C. milk D. vegetables

486. Absence or inadequacy of proteins in the human diet will produce all of the following results, except:
A. body's defences against infections will weaken
B. production of hormones needed by the body will be impaired
C. conversion of heat by the body cells into energy, which sustains life, will be impaired
D. body's growth will be impaired

487. Fats and carbohydrates are an essential part of our food because they:
A. form new tissues
B. provide energy
C. strengthen the bones
D. contain essential vitamins

488. The centre for regulation of food intake in man is located in the:
A. Medulla B. Hypothalamus
C. Cerebellum D. Cerebral cortex

489. Milk in its natural form has a certain amount of sugar. This sugar is called:
A. sucrose B. lactose
C. fructose D. glucose

490. Potato is a rich source of:
A. Vitamin C B. Vitamin D
C. Vitamin A D. Calcium

491. Name the hormone which increases hunger for more appetite:
A. H_3H B. Orexalogin
C. Appetin D. Orexis

492. Which mineral is NOT dissolved when green vegetables are cooked?
A. Potassium B. Calcium
C. Sodium Chloride D. Iron

493. Source of vitamin C is:
A. milk B. egg
C. citrus fruit D. carrot

494. The lowest fat percentage is found in the milk of:
A. buffalo B. goat
C. cow D. camel

495. Which of the following has maximum protein?
A. Gram B. Pea
C. Soyabean D. Pigeon pea

496. Which of the following hormones of the human body regulate the blood calcium and phosphate?
A. Glucogan
B. Growth hormone
C. Parathyroid hormone
D. Thyroxine

497. The metallic ion found to be in the chlorophyll (chloroplast) is:
A. iron B. magnesium
C. zinc D. cobalt

498. The source of the oxygen produces during photosynthesis is:
A. water B. CO_2
C. chlorophyll D. mesophyll cells

499. The centre for DNA finger print and diagnostic is located at:
A. Hyderabad B. Bengaluru
C. New Delhi D. Chennai

500. Which of the following is called the suicide bags of the cell?
A. Lysosomes B. Ribosomes
C. Nucleosomes D. Golgibody

ANSWERS

1	2	3	4	5	6	7	8	9	10
B	D	D	A	A	C	A	A	C	A
11	**12**	**13**	**14**	**15**	**16**	**17**	**18**	**19**	**20**
D	B	D	A	B	D	D	C	B	D
21	**22**	**23**	**24**	**25**	**26**	**27**	**28**	**29**	**30**
B	B	C	B	B	B	D	C	C	B
31	**32**	**33**	**34**	**35**	**36**	**37**	**38**	**39**	**40**
C	C	A	D	C	B	C	C	B	C
41	**42**	**43**	**44**	**45**	**46**	**47**	**48**	**49**	**50**
D	B	D	D	B	C	B	C	C	B
51	**52**	**53**	**54**	**55**	**56**	**57**	**58**	**59**	**60**
D	C	B	B	C	B	C	B	B	B
61	**62**	**63**	**64**	**65**	**66**	**67**	**68**	**69**	**70**
A	A	C	C	D	A	B	A	B	B
71	**72**	**73**	**74**	**75**	**76**	**77**	**78**	**79**	**80**
D	C	A	B	A	C	A	B	A	D
81	**82**	**83**	**84**	**85**	**86**	**87**	**88**	**89**	**90**
D	B	C	D	B	A	B	D	D	D
91	**92**	**93**	**94**	**95**	**96**	**97**	**98**	**99**	**100**
C	B	A	A	C	A	D	B	A	A
101	**102**	**103**	**104**	**105**	**106**	**107**	**108**	**109**	**110**
B	A	B	D	D	D	A	D	B	D

111	112	113	114	115	116	117	118	119	120
B	A	B	A	A	B	A	B	C	D
121	**122**	**123**	**124**	**125**	**126**	**127**	**128**	**129**	**130**
D	A	B	D	A	A	A	A	D	A
131	**132**	**133**	**134**	**135**	**136**	**137**	**138**	**139**	**140**
A	D	C	D	A	A	B	A	B	A
141	**142**	**143**	**144**	**145**	**146**	**147**	**148**	**149**	**150**
B	C	C	A	C	B	B	A	A	A
151	**152**	**153**	**154**	**155**	**156**	**157**	**158**	**159**	**160**
C	C	C	C	C	A	C	B	C	B
161	**162**	**163**	**164**	**165**	**166**	**167**	**168**	**169**	**170**
A	B	A	C	A	A	A	B	D	A
171	**172**	**173**	**174**	**175**	**176**	**177**	**178**	**179**	**180**
C	B	A	B	D	D	B	C	B	C
181	**182**	**183**	**184**	**185**	**186**	**187**	**188**	**189**	**190**
B	C	B	D	B	C	A	D	A	D
191	**192**	**193**	**194**	**195**	**196**	**197**	**198**	**199**	**200**
D	C	B	A	A	D	C	A	A	D
201	**202**	**203**	**204**	**205**	**206**	**207**	**208**	**209**	**210**
D	B	D	B	B	C	B	B	C	D
211	**212**	**213**	**214**	**215**	**216**	**217**	**218**	**219**	**220**
B	C	D	C	B	C	C	C	A	B
221	**222**	**223**	**224**	**225**	**226**	**227**	**228**	**229**	**230**
D	B	C	D	D	D	B	D	B	D
231	**232**	**233**	**234**	**235**	**236**	**237**	**238**	**239**	**240**
B	B	B	B	B	B	D	C	B	B
241	**242**	**243**	**244**	**245**	**246**	**247**	**248**	**249**	**250**
D	A	A	D	C	D	D	D	A	B
251	**252**	**253**	**254**	**255**	**256**	**257**	**258**	**259**	**260**
B	C	A	B	A	B	A	A	A	B
261	**262**	**263**	**264**	**265**	**266**	**267**	**268**	**269**	**270**
C	C	B	B	A	B	C	B	C	A
271	**272**	**273**	**274**	**275**	**276**	**277**	**278**	**279**	**280**
D	A	C	B	A	D	C	B	A	B
281	**282**	**283**	**284**	**285**	**286**	**287**	**288**	**289**	**290**
B	A	D	D	A	B	C	A	C	D
291	**292**	**293**	**294**	**295**	**296**	**297**	**298**	**299**	**300**
B	B	A	D	C	A	B	C	C	A
301	**302**	**303**	**304**	**305**	**306**	**307**	**308**	**309**	**310**
A	B	C	C	D	A	C	A	C	A

311	312	313	314	315	316	317	318	319	320
C	B	D	C	D	B	D	D	C	B
321	322	323	324	325	326	327	328	329	330
D	C	B	C	B	C	D	B	D	B
331	332	333	334	335	336	337	338	339	340
A	A	C	B	D	C	C	D	C	A
341	342	343	344	345	346	347	348	349	350
D	B	B	A	B	C	D	C	C	C
351	352	353	354	355	356	357	358	359	360
B	C	A	A	B	C	B	B	A	D
361	362	363	364	365	366	367	368	369	370
C	B	C	C	A	C	C	A	B	A
371	372	373	374	375	376	377	378	379	380
B	D	A	A	B	A	B	C	B	A
381	382	383	384	385	386	387	388	389	390
A	A	D	B	A	A	D	A	D	A
391	392	393	394	395	396	397	398	399	400
B	A	D	A	C	B	D	A	C	B
401	402	403	404	405	406	407	408	409	410
A	A	B	A	A	A	C	D	D	B
411	412	413	414	415	416	417	418	419	420
D	D	D	B	D	A	D	D	B	A
421	422	423	424	425	426	427	428	429	430
D	A	A	C	D	A	C	C	A	C
431	432	433	434	435	436	437	438	439	440
B	B	B	D	A	A	B	D	A	B
441	442	443	444	445	446	447	448	449	450
D	D	A	B	B	D	A	D	D	C
451	452	453	454	455	456	457	458	459	460
B	B	A	B	C	C	B	D	C	C
461	462	463	464	465	466	467	468	469	470
D	B	B	B	D	C	A	C	C	A
471	472	473	474	475	476	477	478	479	480
C	B	A	B	B	B	A	D	C	D
481	482	483	484	485	486	487	488	489	490
A	C	A	A	C	C	B	B	B	A
491	492	493	494	495	496	497	498	499	500
D	D	C	B	C	C	B	A	A	A

●●●

CHAPTER

6

Yoga and Health

Concept of health and diseases

According to the World Health Organisation (WHO) the state of health is defined as a state of complete physical, mental, social and spiritual well-being and not merely an absence of disease or infirmity. It is clear from this definition that health and ill-health are not two discrete entities as commonly understood but health should be conceived as a continuous function indicating the state of well being.

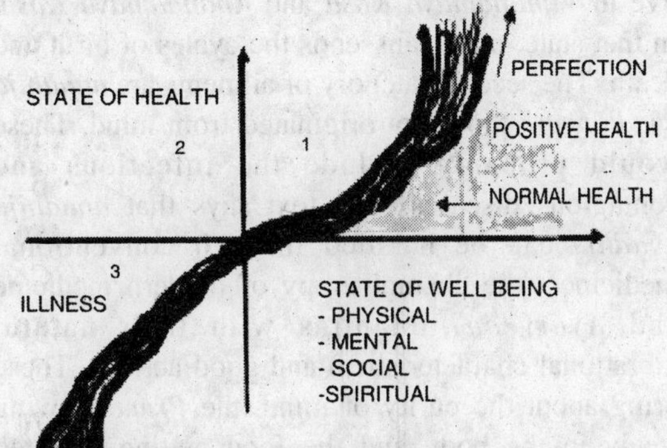

In the diagram, the 3rd quadrant 'the region of ill-health' represents what normally we designate as 'Sickness'. Below this, man acts instinctively and is akin to animal man. Coming to the first quadrant, the region of 'normal health' the state of normal man is indicated. As he moves along the line further up, he becomes healthier featured by the dormant faculties expressing more vividly in man. This is shown as the region of 'positive health', the next region after the human spectrum. In this state, the limitations of normal man namely the strong urges of thirst, hunger, fear and sex are reduced greatly and are fully under control. In the concept of Sri Aurobindo, the new faculties of deeper perceptions of the world beyond the five senses emerge in this phase of superhuman existence. Further growth leads man to unfold even deeper layers of consciousness and widen the spectrum of his knowledge to move towards divinity or 'perfection'. In this march towards perfection, Yoga is a systematic conscious process for accelerating the growth of a human being from his animal level leading ultimately to divinity. It is a systematic methodology for an all-round personality development—physical, mental, intellectual, emotional and spiritual components of man. Thus, Yoga in its general methodology for the growth of man to divine heights includes techniques useful for therapeutic applications in making man healthier.

Concept of disease

In *Yoga-Vasistha* which is one of the best texts on Yoga, the essence of Yoga is beautifully portrayed thus, *'manahprasamanopayah Yoga ityabhidhiyate' – Yoga is called a skilful technique to calm down the mind*. It is *(Upayah)*, a skilful subtle process and not a brutal, mechanical gross effort to stop the thoughts in the mind.

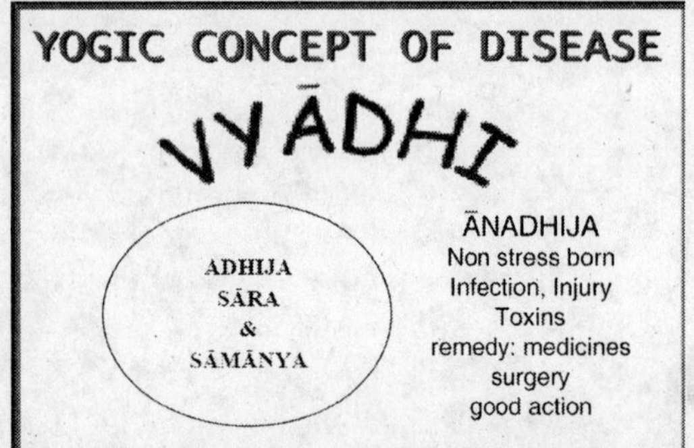

In *Anandamaya kosa* a man is healthiest with perfect harmony and balance of all his faculties. At *Vijnanamaya kosa* there are movements but they are channelized in the right direction. As such, it is in the Manomaya level the imbalances start, say the Yoga texts. Likes and dislikes have come to play at this level. The liking of Gulab Jamun in a diabetic may lure him to eat the same against the doctor's advice. Thus going against what is right causes imbalances. These imbalances amplify themselves resulting in mental illnesses called *'adhis'* – at this stage there are no symptoms at the physical level. Prompted by the perpetual growth of desires these mental diseases concealed in us, begin to manifest themselves externally and gradually they percolate to the physical frame. Preponderance of *Ajnana* (Ignorance about one's real state of bliss) leads one to perform wrong actions such as eating of unwholesome food, living in unhealthy dwellings, association with wicked, evil thoughts, inflict injuries etc. These breed physical diseases called *Vyadhis* or the secondary diseases.

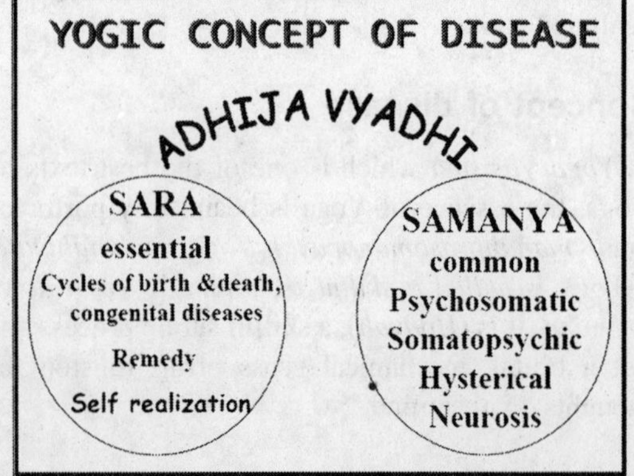

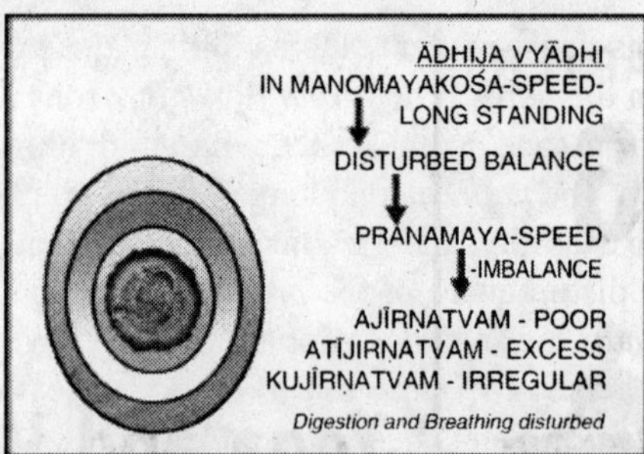

The *Adhis* (primary diseases) are two-fold *Samanya* (ordinary) and *Sara* (essential). The former includes the diseases incidental to the body while the latter is responsible for rebirth to which all men are subject. The *Samanya* are normally produced during the interactions with the world. These may be termed as psychosomatic ailments. When dealt with by suitable techniques and congenial atmosphere, *adhis* of the ordinary type will vanish. Along with it are destroyed the physical ailments *i.e.* the *vyadhis* caused by these *adhis* is *adhija vyadhayah.* The subtler *adhis* of the essential type *(Sara)* which cause the birth of the physical body can be destroyed only by the realization of the causal states of mind and a corresponding ability to live in *Vijnanamaya Kosa* and *Anandamaya Kosa.* In that state, man transcends the cycles of birth and death. The second category of ailments are *anadhija vyadhayah*—those not originated from mind. These would probably include the infectious and contagious diseases. The text says that *anadhija vyadhis* can be handled through conventional medicines (the chemotherapy of modern medicine and *Ayurveda*), Mantras with their natural vibrational characteristics) and good actions. These bring about the purity of mind, the *Prana* flowing freely in the body and the food getting digested better and assimilated properly allowing the diseases to vanish.

Psychosomatic illness

Among the two types of *adhis* described the *Samanya* (ordinary) type corresponds to the modern psychosomatic ailments. When the mind is agitated during the interactions with the world at large, the physical body also follows in its wake. These agitations cause violent fluctuations in the flow of *prana* in the *nadis*. The *prana* flows in wrong paths flying from one to the other without rhythm and harmony. The *nadis* can no longer, in this condition, maintain stability and steadiness, but quiver. Due to these disturbances of the *prana* and unsteadiness in the *nadis* the food does not get properly digested. These arise *kujirnatvam* (wrong digestion), *atijirnatvam* (over-digestion) and *ajirnatvam* (non-digestion). When this improperly digested food settles down in the body amidst such commotion it results in ailments of the psychosomatic type. Contained in this process of generation of psychosomatic ailments is the method for treating such ailments.

Genesis of ill health according to Patanjali Yoga Sutra

Genesis of existential disorders (Ill Health) in modern medicine and that in *Patanjali Yoga Sutra* has remarkable similarities. Only when predisposing factors (one's hereditary characteristics) interact with precipitating factors (critical incidences taking place in one's life) the existential disorders arise. This is the reason why anyone of the two sets of factors cannot create any disorders, singly. For example, hereditary characteristics, howsoever impactful, cannot produce a psychosomatic disorder even if both the parents have been afflicted by the same particular disorder, unless these hereditary characteristics are coupled with critical incidences. As well, even if critical incidences befall a person, he may not show any ill-effect of the same, so long he has a sound hereditary constitution. Great men in human history have refused to cave-in to great many sufferings and critical incidences taking place in their life. In the *Patanjali's* metaphysics, *Klesas* are considered as hereditary in nature while *Environment* denotes the occurrence of critical incidences in one's life. *Chittavrittis* denote aberrant mental functions, arising out of an interaction between predisposing factors and precipitating factors.

Klesas (afflictions) are considered as the very root cause of all existential disorders, in general, and that of psychosomatic disorders, in particular. *Klesas,* in interaction with internal environment (psychophysical strengths and weaknesses) and external environment (acquired mental complexes prejudices and temperamental aberrations), produce *chittavrittis,* the mental functions of pathological nature. If one starts identifying himself/herself with these *chittavrittis,* the *psychic stage* of stress starts getting expressed. If no remedial measures are adopted, one goes to the *psychosomatic* stage of stress. Here, enduring impact of newly developed psychosomatic disorders is exhibited. If remedial measures are not availed, the next stage of stress namely *somatic stage* ensues. *Samsakaras* (impressions) get established further if further aggravation is not arrested. Thus, the *organic stage* of stress is reached. The treatment approach for stress-borne disorders, therefore, should include (*i*) adopting positive life style changes (Environment) and (*ii*) adopting appropriate Yoga practices like *Kriya Yoga* (P.Y.S.II:1) and *Okaram Amin/Amen* would be helpful immensely. Best treatment effects are seen at the *psychic stage,* next best effects are evidenced at *psychosomatic stage* and the least but sure impact is seen at the *somatic* and *organic stages* of stress if Yoga practices are adopted and practiced regularly.

Concepts of triguna and panchakosa vis-a-vis holistic health

Concept of triguna

Human beings have always striven to achieve a total health and an invincible personality, bereft of any disturbances and aberrations whatsoever. There seems to be a compartmentalized approach to personality in psychology: Freud emphasizes childhood experiences as the basis of personality development an individual. Adler, Fromm and Harney speak about the social determinants as vital for one's personality. Erikson and Allport advocate achieving certain abilities. Maslow speaks of need hierarchy while Rogers speaks of one's movement from *true self* to *ideal self* in developing individual personality. Being holistic itself Yoga has a holistic view on personality.

Samkhya Darsana, popularly known as theoretical Yoga, has conceived the idea of three bodies viz. Gross *(Sthula sarira),* Subtle *(Suksma sarira)* and Causal *(Karana sarira).* Yoga has a premise that whatever affects gross body also 'affects' subtle body and causal body. Therefore, a balanced & meaningful material life may lead one to spiritual life. Systematic Yogic pursuits are available as per one's personality make-up. *Rajasika* person can opt for *Karma Yoga, Sattvika* person can go for *Bhakti Yoga* and *Tamasika person* can opt for *Karma Yoga* and *Jnana Yoga.* One can work with one's *Tamas guna* so as to transcend the same towards *Rajas guna* and then towards *Sattva guna,* so as to ultimately go beyond all *gunas* before reaching out to the *gunatita/niruddha* state.

Dr. Indrasen has said, *"Indian concept of personality analyses its normal make-up, discovering and devising the conditions of its growth and delineating the quality and character of its highest growth. In simple words, it speaks about what man is, what he can become and how he can become that."*

Taittiriya Aranyaka, however, conceives the concept of five body-sheaths: (*i*) *Annamaya kosa* (gross body-sheath), (*ii*) *Pranamaya kosa* (functional body-sheath), (*iii*) *Manomaya kosa* (emotional body-sheath, (*iv*) *Vijnanamaya kosa* (intellect body-sheath), and (*v*) *Anandamaya kosa* (Bliss body-sheath). All these body-sheaths coexist in a perfect interdependence amongst themselves with a complete harmony in a perfectly healthy individual.

According to *Tattiriya Aranyaka,* one has to do a complete justice with all these *Kosas* through appropriate practices. The *Panchakosa* concept holds a human individual as a composite whole with all five *kosas* as being coherent in a perfect harmony, in a truly healthy individual. All *kosas* are needed to be nourished by adopting a holistic approach to Yoga practice. *Astanga* Yoga, practiced in its holistic spirit, would nourish all the *kosas* holistically endowing us with a holistic personality in the process.

It is only in the case of therapeutic setting that we try to perceive the disturbance in one or more particular *kosas* and recommend practices to be practiced predominantly for the particular *kosas.* For instance, for treating disturbances at *Annamaya kosa,* we can recommend *Asana, Yuktahara* (proper and balanced *Sattvika food*) etc.; for disturbances at *Pranamaya kosa, Pranayama* and other such practices are recommended; for treating problem of *Manomaya kosa,* the practices prescribed are *Pratyahara* and experiential way of Yoga practices; for disturbance at the *Vijnanamaya kosa* the practices of *Dharana* & *Dhyana* can be recommended and for *Anandamaya kosa, Dhyana* techniques of transcendental nature, may be practiced.

Concept of panchakosa and positive health

Taittiriya Upanishad gives the concept of *Panchakosas* and their development. *Kosa* means layer of existence. The existence of human beings has been described in *Ananda Valli* of *Tattiriyopanishad* having five layers in *Brahmananda.* It says that starting from *Annamaya kosa* and reaching the *Anandamaya kosa,* our existence has 5 layers or sheaths called *kosas* (see figure).

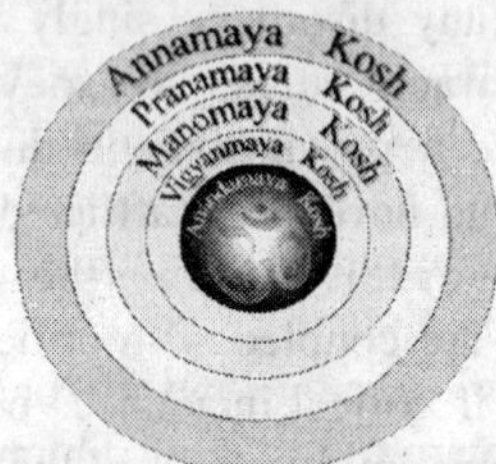

Fig. : *Pancha Kosa*

The gross body that we see is *Annamayakosa.* The subtler body made of *pranika* energy is called as *Pranamayakosa* or vital sheath. The third *kosa* is *Manomayakosa* or mental sheath which comprises one's feelings and emotions. The fourth one is *Vijnanamayakosa.* The *Vijnanamayakosa* is the highest state of *buddhi* or *viveka.* It is the perfect discriminatory knowledge or understanding. It does not prove anything on the basis of logic or empirical evidence, but through insightful discrimination. The fifth is *anandmayakosa* or sheath of bliss. Its characteristics are creativity, joy and bliss. Let us examine these sheaths in detail.

Annamayakosa: the food sheath

Literal meaning of *'Anna'* is food. However, as the lowest level of existence, *Annamayakosa* refers to the world of physical existence. Everything that we experience through our *Indriyas* (sense organs) is part of physical layer.

Physical layer is complete in itself. Beings in their physical world consume food. Ultimately, the physical existence of beings gets devoured by the matter itself. The physical body, the outer most part of our existence is termed as the *Annamayakosa* or Food Sheath. It has emerged from the essence of food assimilated by the father and nourished in the womb by the food taken by the mother. It continues to exist because of food consumed and ultimately, after death, goes back to fertilize the earth and becomes food. The substance of the physical structure, rising from food, existing in food and going back to become food, is naturally and most appropriately termed the food sheath. The food we eat gets transformed into muscles, veins, nerves, blood and bones. If proper exercise and proper diet is given the *Annamayakosa* develops well. The signs of healthy development are fitness, agility, stamina and endurance. A person having these qualities can easily master motor skills and has good eye hand co-ordination. Food taken is transformed into various nutritious elements and makes us grow physically. Regular eating habits, right kind of food, all types of exercises and games, jogging, running, walking and *asanas* facilitate the development of *Annamayakosa.*

Pranamayakosa: the vital sheath

The *Pancha Pranas,* which are corresponding to the five physiological systems described in *Ayurveda,* represent the vital sheath. These activities which support the body take place as a result of the air that we breathe in. As long as this vital principle exists in the organisms, life continues. *Pranayama* and breathing exercises improve the quality of *Pranamayakosa.* Hence, it is termed as the vital sheath. The five *Pranas* that comprise this sheath include the following:

(*i*) *Prana* (related to faculty of perception): It controls the perceptions of the fivefold stimuli received from the external environment through the five sense organs.

(*ii*) *Apana* (the faculty of excretion): All things thrown out of body or rejected by the body such as septum, perspiration, urine, faeces, etc. are expressions of *apana.*

(*iii*) *Samana* (the faculty of digestion): Digests the food collected in the stomach.

(*iv*) *Vyana* (the faculty of circulation): The power by which the nutrients resulting from the digested food are properly conveyed to the various limbs of the body through the blood stream.

(*v*) *Udana* (the faculty of thinking): The capacity in an individual to raise his thoughts from their present level so as to conceive a possibility of or appreciate a new principle or idea—the capacity of self-education. These five faculties gradually weaken as people advance in age. The Vital Sheath controls and regulates the food sheath. When the *pranas* do not function properly, the physical body is affected. The signs of healthy development of *Pranamayakosa* are enthusiasm, ability to use voice effectively, suppleness of body, perseverance, leadership, discipline, honesty and nobility.

Manomayakosa: the mind sheath

Manomaya is composed of *manas* or mind. It includes thinking, feeling and willing. The mind along with the five sensory organs tastes, (tongue), smell (nose), vision (eyes), hearing (ear), and touch (skin), is said to constitute the *Manomayakosa* or "mind-sheath". It is the cause of diversity. Man's bondage is caused by the mind, and liberation, too, is caused by that alone. The *Manomayakosa* is the mental faculty that receives all the sensory inputs, interprets them as good or bad and desires the good. This *kosa* is much more powerful than the preceding two *kosas* and governs them and is, in turn, governed by the two *kosas* superior to it. It is thus central to human existence. Many modalities of treatment like aroma, music, colour, placebo therapy, shamanism work in this *kosa.* Homeopathic medicines in the higher potencies also influence this *kosa.* The mind regulates the *Pranamayakosa* or Vital Sheath. For example, when the mind is upset due to some shock, the functions of *pranas* and the body are affected. Mind interprets the impressions of sense organs. It stores good and bad memories of the past. It is possible to increase the strength of mind by regular prayer, making resolutions and keeping them up. There is a deep relationship between mind, intellect and body. For the development of *Manomayakosa* study of good literature including poems, novels, essays and articles is useful.

Vijnanmayakosa: the intellect sheath

Vijnanamaya is composed of *Vijnana*, or intellect, the faculty which discriminates, determines or wills. It is the sheath composed of more intellection, associated with the organs of perception. This intellect sheath cannot be the supreme Self for the following reasons; it is subject to change, it is insentient, it is a limited thing, it is not constantly present.

The mind *(manas)* is that which receives the external stimuli through sense organs and communicates the responses to the organs of action. Though the stimuli received through the five sense organs are distinct and different from one another, an integrated experience of them is brought about by the mind. The intellect *(buddhi)* is the discriminating and discerning process which examines and judges the stimuli received. It also communicates to the mind its decision about the type of responses to be executed. The mind associates the impressions with pleasantness or unpleasantness based on memory. The intellect however, with its capacity to think, takes a rational decision which may not be liked by the mind but is ultimately beneficial to the person. The mind is the storehouse of all memories and knowledge. This storehouse of experience is the guiding factor in man's actions. The mind can also be described as the seat of emotions and the intellect is to examine the areas in which they operate. The mind has the capacity to travel only to the 'realms known' but the intellect, besides remaining in the realms known, can further penetrate into the 'realms unknown' to investigate, contemplate and comprehend new discoveries.

Anandamayakosa: the bliss sheath

It is considered blissful, because, whatever be the condition in which we are in our waking and dream states, once we reach, all of us experience relatively the same undisturbed peace and bliss due to the cessation of agitation experienced by us when we are awake or dreaming. The Bliss Sheath controls the intellect. When all the other *kosas* are well developed we experience harmony between the inner Self and the outer world. This harmony gives us a sense of joy and bliss. The five sheaths are like the layers of clothes worn by a person which are totally different from the wearer. So too, the *Atma* or the real Self is distinct and separate from the five outer layers.

Laghu Yoga Vasistha on health and diseases

Laghu Yoga Vasistha, a *HathaYogic* treatise, says that in the event of a disturbed *Manomayakosa* (mind) the *Pranamayakosa* gets disturbed. Consequently, the *Nadis,* through which *prana* flows, get disturbed. It results into *prana* getting more and more disturbed. The food taken in such a disturbed state would get turned into 'poison' for want of various digestive juices getting depleted due to the ensuing stress. There arise three types of problems, viz. indigestion, non-digestion and over digestion. The remedies recommended are service to the sages, chanting of mantras, not keeping late hours at night and such other measures that help mind becoming calm and *prana* getting restored to its normal function.

Pancha-kosa Viveka of *Taittiriya Aranyaka* denotes the holistic view of human organism wherein the inter-dependence of body, *prana,* mind, intellect and inner bliss has been indicated. One has to transcend all these levels of existence, through certain Yoga practices, before attaining the Self realization.

Potential causes of ill health

According to Yoga, causes of sickness or ill health are generally noted as impurities on the level of mind, body and speech. Your own speech can create distress in you as well as other people around you. Even distress or discomfort should be treated as an illness. Body, mind and spirit are like a tripod – even if one aspect isn't functioning properly, our life will not be balanced and that will lead to ill health. Yoga (a component of *Ayurveda*) is that link which creates a harmony by aligning all the three components (body, mind and spirit) into one. This harmony, in turn exists to support life.

Patanjali Yoga Sutras reflect that root cause of ill health is mostly mental. The *sutra* PYS-I: 31 indicates – *Duhkha-daurmanasya-angamejayatva-svasa-prasvasa-viksepasahabhuvah* (PYS, 1.31). This means pain and misery, mental depression, tremors of the body parts and disturbances of inhalation and exhalation are the accompaniments of disturbances of *Chitta.* The disturbances of *Chitta* are internal and many of these are not easily perceptible. But their presence can be inferred from accompanying external symptoms. These are enumerated in the present *sutra.* One or more of these will always be present. When any *Chitta-viksepa* is there, the presence and even intensity of the latter can be adjudged from the degree of activity of these external concomitant symptoms. Since these *sahabhuvah* (accompaniments) are the results of *Chitta-viksepas,* certain techniques, which can control the former, will be helpful in removing latter also. The first two *sahabhuvah* are somewhat mental, yet they will have effect on the body, which would, therefore, serve as easy means for the detection of the hidden and subtler *Chittaviksepas.* The latter two are direct changes occurring in the body and easily noticeable. *Duhkha* means both physical pain as well as mental misery. The latter may often produce the former or at least lead to physical discomfort. Such bodily pains or discomforts can be easily detected by gestures of very frequent readjustment of posture of the person.

Vyadhi (physical disease) is considered as one of the nine obstacles *(antaraya)* to integrative oneness of Yoga *(samadhi).* Maharsi Patanjali (Yoga Sutra 1.30) enumerates manifest symptoms such as *duhkha* (mental or physical pain), *daurmanasya* (sadness or dejection), *angamejayatva* (anxious tremor) and *svasa-prasvasah* (respiratory irregularities) as concomitant expressions of mental disturbances (Yoga Sutra 1.31). These *antarayas* are one of the major causes of disintegration *(vyadhi)* according to Gharote, an eminent Yoga expert of *Kaivalyadhama.* He has described *Samadhi* as the ideal state of health which is disturbed by the *chittaviksepa* (disturbances in mind) due to the *klesas* and *antarayas.* He has further stated that mind is responsible for bondage and liberation as well as happiness and unhappiness. According to him the purpose of Yoga is to lessen the impact of these factors *(klesatanukaranam)* and promote the state of integration *(Samadhi bhavanam).* Maharsi Patanjali gives us a clue to control the mental agitation by advising us to concentrate on slow and deep flow of respiration to still the mind (*pracchardana-vidharanabhyam-va pranasya* – Yoga Sutra 1.34). He also advises concentration on a painless inner state of luminosity to produce stability and tranquillity (*visoka va jyotismati* – Yoga Sutra 1.36).

Patanjali has also explained the primary causation of stress based disorders through concept of *panchaklesa* (psychological afflictions). These are *avidya* (ignorance of the ultimate reality leading to bodily identification), *asmita* (a false sense of identification), *raga-dvesa* (addiction and aversion), *abhinivesa* (clinging on to life for fear of death), (*avidyasmitaragadvesabhiniveah klesah* – Yoga Sutra II.3). *Avidya* as the root cause enables other *klesas* to manifest in different forms from time to time. They may be dormant, attenuated, manifest, or overpowering in their causation of pain and suffering. (*avidya ksetram-uttaresam prasuptatanu-vicchinnodaranam* – Yoga Sutra II.4).

From the Yogic viewpoint of disease, it can be seen that psychosomatic, stress related disorders appear to progress through four distinct phases. These can be understood as follows:

- **Psychic Phase:** This phase is marked by mild but persistent psychological and behavioural symptoms of stress like irritability, disturbed sleep and other minor symptoms. This phase can be correlated with *Vijnanamaya* and *Manomayakosas.* Yoga as a therapy is very effective in this phase.
- **Psychosomatic Phase:** If the stress continues there is an increase in symptoms, along with the appearance of generalized physiological symptoms such as occasional hypertension and tremors. This phase can be correlated with *manomaya* and *pranamayakosas.* Yoga as a therapy is very effective in this phase.
- **Somatic Phase:** This phase is marked by disturbed function of organs, particularly the target, or involved organ. At this stage one begins to identify the diseased state. This phase can be correlated with *pranamaya* and *annamayakosas.* Yoga as a therapy is less effective in this phase and may need to be used in conjunction with other methods of treatment.
- **Organic Phase:** This phase is marked by full manifestation of the diseased state, with pathological changes such as an ulcerated stomach or chronic hypertension, becoming manifest in their totality with their resultant complications. This phase can be correlated with the *annamayakosa* because the disease has become fixed in the physical body. Yoga as a therapy has a palliative and quality of life improving effect in this phase. It does also produce positive emotional and psychological effects even in terminal and end of life situations. Often, however, the early stages of the disease process are overlooked and the final stage is seen as an entity unto itself, having little relationship to one's living habits and patterns. This is because modern medicine only looks at the physical aspects and neglects effects of *pancakosa* and *trisarira* on health and disease.

One of the major Indian concepts of disease causation is the imbalances of *tridosa.* This is found in numerous classical texts of Yoga and *Ayurveda* like *Siva Svarodaya, Susruta Samhita, Charaka Samhita* and *Tirumandiram.* According to the Dravidian poet-saint Tiruvalluvar, disease results from *tridosa* (*vata, pitta, kapha*) imbalance. *Vata* is the energy of the body that moves like the wind and causes flow in the body. It may be related to the nervous system as well as joints that enable us to move. Pitta is related to bilious secretion and is the cause of heat in the body. It is the energy of catabolism that is essential for digestion. *Kapha* is the glue that holds everything together and is the energy of anabolism helping generative and regenerative processes. As they move out of balance, they affect particular areas of our bodies in characteristic ways. When *vata* is out of balance—typically in excess—we are prone to diseases of the large intestines, like constipation and gas, along with diseases of nervous system, immune system, and joints. When pitta is in excess, we are prone to diseases of the small intestines, like diarrhoea, along with diseases of the liver, spleen, thyroid, blood, skin, and eyes. When *kapha* is in excess, we are prone to diseases of the stomach and lungs, most notably mucous conditions, along with diseases of water metabolism, such as swelling. Practice of Yoga at dusk relieves *kapha*, practice at noon relieves *vata* and practice in morning relieves *pitta* disorders.

According to *Sivasvarodaya*, a classical text on *Svara Yoga*, disease develops when *svara* (smooth and regular air flow) in the nostrils do not adhere to their fixed timings and days. Normally *svara* flows in the nostrils in a certain pattern according to phases of the lunar cycle. It is also said that in case a disease develops due to erroneous functioning of *svara*, then a correction of that malfunctioning can cure that disease. The use of different techniques is also advocated for changing *svara* to eliminate various disorders.

Yoga Vasishtha, a great text of Yoga describes causation and manifestation of disease in a very logical way. It attributes all psychic disturbances and physical ailments to the five-fold elements *(pancha mahabhuta)* in a manner similar to other systems of Indian medicine. *Samanya adhijavyadhi* are described as those arising from day-to-day causes while *Saradhijavyadhi* is the essential disease of being caught in the birth-rebirth cycle that can be understood in modern terms as congenital diseases. The former can be corrected by day-to-day remedial measures such as medicines and surgery whereas the *Saradhijavyadhi* doesn't cease until knowledge of the Self *(atmajnana)* is attained. The Guru Stotra from the *Visvasaratantra* also takes a similar view in saying that the ultimate 'wisdom of the Self' gained through the Guru destroys karmic bondages from many births (*aneka-janma-samprapta-karma-bandha-vidhayine atmajnanapradanena tasmai srigurave namah:* Guru Stotra, verse 9).

Yoga Vasishtha gives an elaborate description of the mechanism by which psychosomatic disorders occur. Mental confusion leads to agitation of *prana* (life force) and haphazard flow along *nadis* resulting in depletion of energy and/or clogging up of these channels of vital energy. This leads to disturbance in the physical body with disturbances of metabolism, excessive appetite and improper functioning of the entire digestive system. Natural movement of food through the digestive tract is arrested giving rise to numerous physical ailments. We need to remember that this text is many thousands of years old whereas the concept of psychosomatic disorders in modern medicine has only been realized and accepted in recent times. Our ancient seers had great inner vision and it is up to us to coin their dreams and understand the great message they have left for humanity.

Yoga Maharsi Swami Gitananda Giri, founder of Ananda Ashram at Pondicherry has written extensively about the relationship between health and disease. He says, "Yoga views the vast proliferation of psychosomatic diseases as a natural outcome of stress and strain created by desire fostered by modern propaganda and abuse of the body condoned on all sides even by religion, science, and philosophy. Add to this the synthetic "junk food" diet of modern society and you have the possibility of endless disorders developing…even the extinction of man by his own ignorance and misdeeds". He explains the root cause of disease as follows. "Yoga, a holistic, unified concept of oneness, is *advaitam* or non-dual in nature. It suggests happiness, harmony and ease. Disease is created when duality or *dvaitam* arises in the human mind. This false concept of duality has produced all conflicts of human mind and the vast list of human disorders. Duality (disease) is the primary cause of man's downfall.

Tiruvalluvar has emphasized the link between overeating and disease by saying, "the one who eats on an empty stomach gets health while with the greedy glutton abides ill-health". He also warns us that those who eat beyond the level of hunger will suffer from untold hardships. He advises all doctors to look for the disease, then look for its root cause and finally search the remedy for the underlying cause.

Yoga understands that physical ailments that are not of a psychosomatic nature can be easily managed with surgery, medication, prayers, and lifestyle modifications as required. Various Yoga techniques may also be used to help correct the physical ailments and restore health with regeneration, recuperation and rehabilitation as necessary. Accident prevention is an important benefit of a Yoga life, for better alertness, reflexes and physical condition enables one to prevent accidents as well as avoid getting traumatized both physically and mentally by such occurrences. In addition to its preventive and restorative capabilities, Yoga also aims at promoting positive health that will help us to tide over health challenges that occur during our lifetime. Just as we save money in a bank to tide over financial crisis, so also we can build up our positive health balance to help us manage unforeseen health challenges with faster recovery and recuperation. This concept of positive health is one of Yoga's unique contributions to modern health care as Yoga has both a preventive as well as promotive role in the healthcare of our masses. It is also inexpensive and can be used in tandem with other systems of medicine in an integrated manner to benefit patients.

Yogic principles of healthy living (ahara, vihara, achara, vichara)

"Health is wealth" is an established fact. To live a healthy life entails to do healthy things and follow a healthy lifestyle. The modern world is facing a pandemic of lifestyle disorders that require changes to be made consciously by individuals themselves. Yoga places great importance on a proper and healthy lifestyle. Its main components are:

1. ***Achara-better mental health through right achara (daily routines)*** – Yoga stresses the importance of healthy activities such as exercise and recommends *asana, pranayama* and *kriyas* on a regular basis. It is advisable to keep up with the right routines. It is of utmost importance to stick to timing of work, meals, exercise and sleep. Sun is a good example of *Achara.* Cardio respiratory health is one of the main by-products of such healthy activities.
2. ***Vichara-better intellectual health through right vichara (thoughts)*** – Right thoughts and right attitude towards life are vital for our well-being. A balanced state of mind is obtained by following the moral restraints and ethical observances (yama-niyama). As Mahatma Gandhi said, "there is enough in this world for everyone's need but not enough for any one person's greed".
3. ***Ahara***–"Annam Brahma" – Food is Brahman. Yoga emphasizes need for a healthy, nourishing diet that has an adequate intake of fresh water along with a well-balanced intake of fresh food, green salads, sprouts, unrefined cereals and fresh fruits. It is important to be aware of the need for a *sattvika* diet, prepared and served with love and affection.
4. ***Vihara – "better emotional health through vihara"***– Proper recreational activities to relax body and mind are essential for good health. This includes proper relaxation, maintaining quietude of action speech - thoughts and group activities wherein one loses the sense of individuality. Karma Yoga is an excellent method for losing the sense of individuality and gaining a sense of universality. Active creative hobbies release pent up emotions and recharges the mind. Activities such as gardening, playing a musical instrument, singing songs or poetry, drawing and painting or hobbies which one likes would help create joy. Nature walks to garden, sea shore, near a lake or river side or a hill top in the morning or evening time in sunshine could also rejuvenate body, mind and soul. Simple playful activities like playing or throwing ball/ring to each other or play dough ball where laughing and giggling may happen playing such games regularly could also help rejuvenate body and mind and soul. Playing with children or involving in children's activities can also help relax and rejuvenate. After long and hard physical and mental work conscious relaxation practices of Hatha Yoga including savasana or nispandabhava would help relax and rejuvenate oneself. Conscious relaxation would also include good quality of sleep where body should be able to comfortably relax and mind should be quiet and calm.

Yogic diet (Ahara)

Dieting is catching up among the affluent, even in India – for better looks, of course; much less for sound health. High calorie junk foods are shunned. A struggle between the palate and the desire to slim down continues. The big dairy business of the U.S.A. is collapsing.

The scare of colon cancer has cut down the beef consumption drastically. The vegetarian food is spreading fast. Natural food consumption, buying farm food or organic food though more expensive, is becoming the fashion of the day. But on the other hand, aggressive commercials are trying to prevent this 'turning of tables'.

Research has shown that a balanced vegetarian diet/food can reverse coronary diseases and even the cholesterol deposits can be drastically reduced.

The Yogic concept of food takes into consideration the total dimension of human existence. Apart from the atoms and molecules of which our gross physical body is made, we all possess *prana,* mind, intellect, emotions and the spiritual dimension featured by freedom. Yoga is the process by which we bring an integration of the entire personality at all these levels. If the stamina of the body is to be developed, the *prana* should be brought to a nice balance, the mind should be calmed down, the emotion should be stabilized and the intellect should be under total control. A *'Balanced Diet',* therefore, according to Yoga, is that diet which restores balance at all levels. Only such diets could aid in a holistic way of living and development of personality.

Let us see how the ancient sages arrived at the concept of healthy diet and describe their general characteristics.

Classification of Foods

Yoga classifies food into 3 categories (similar to the classification of human beings) into predominantly Tamasika, Rajasika and Sattvika food.

Tamasika foods

Yatayamam gatarasam puti paryusitam ca yat ucchistamapi camedhyam bhojanam tamasapriyam (B.G.17.10)

That which is stale, tasteless, stinking, cooked overnight, refuse and impure is the food liked by the Támasiks.

Yatayamam and Gatarasam (cold food devoid of taste and essence):

One Yama is 3 hours. Food that gets cold is stale. In these days of canned foods, preserved fruits, stored vegetables and refrigeration facilities, almost a substantial majority of us has come to love stale foods. Ancient Indian writings on diet did not include taking a diet containing preservatives, insecticides, emulsifiers, artificial colourings and other chemicals.

Puti (foul-smelling): Men of inertia have a natural liking for stinking food that has intolerable smell for others.

Paryusitam (Stale): Food cooked overnight or kept for days together comes under this category. In south India, there is a peculiar appetite for taking rice that has been kept soaked in water through the previous night. The next morning it becomes both stale and tasteless (*gatarasam*). Some in north India like old rotis. We can include all the fermented drinks which the Tamasika people love to drink under this category.

Ucchistam (Leftover): That which is leftover by others, is commonly liked by the Tamasika persons.

Amedhyam (impure): Impure and filthy food *i.e.* that which is not fit for human consumption.

Those foods which are 'dead', partially spoiled, which have lost their essence, which have been processed a great deal, which have been preserved in some way having no spark of life about them, or which lack the vitality of food, are the ones liked by the *Tamasika.* The innate personality structure of the Tamasika is reflected in their liking for such foods. Hence, all such foods are classified as Tamasika foods. These foods may add 'matter' to the physical body, may nourish the grossest aspect of the body but they create a feeling of heaviness and lethargy.

Due to external circumstances like busy work schedule, high-tech advertisements etc. even when a Sattvika man resorts to such diets (as canned foods, etc.), mentioned above. Energy and vitality are almost absent in such foods and hence the functioning gets sluggish and diseases of degeneration and accumulation of excessive toxic matter are likely to occur leading to illness like obesity, arthritis, hardening of the arteries, etc.

When food is spoiled, its chemical structure breaks down, and because of the acidity that results, some nutrients are destroyed. Rather than being useful, they may break down into products which cannot be used by the body, but must be excreted. In the mean time, they are under circulation and may act as irritants to the nervous system as well as to the other cells, tissues and organs. Eating Tamasik food makes one lethargic. One may vacillate between an irritating restlessness and a tendency to fall asleep.

Fermentation is essentially a process of decomposition, especially when it is poorly controlled and overdone. Alcoholic drinks, especially the poorer quality ones, belong to this category.

Meat is also likely to be Tamasika especially when it is not fresh. Once the animal cells die, the process of degeneration and decay begins. Most marketed meat is not fresh. Unless this process is carried out carefully with a total knowledge of what is happening, the food is likely to be Tamasika.

The way in which the animal lives and grows may also affect its properties. Animals that are sluggish, heavy and unhealthy, are more likely to yield a Tamasika food. Wild game and fish freshly killed and properly prepared were not regarded by the ancient Indians as detrimental. The effects of such fresh, wholesome meat were said to be *Rajasika.*

Rajasika Foods

Foods that are katu (bitter), amla (sour), lavana (saline), ati usna (steaming hot), tiksna (burning), are the ones liked by Rajasika.

That which stimulates the nervous system, speeds up metabolism and activates, is called Rajasika. *e.g.:* coffee, tea, tobacco. Green chillies and pepper are considered Rajasika but dried red chillies tend to be more Tamasika. High quality wines are Rajasika.

These Rajasika foods will energise but not in the sense of lending a clear balanced energy. They tend to stimulate and push the organism to increase its speed and to indulge more in physical activity, sensual pleasures and comforts. Spiced and cooked to perfection food with lots of rich sauces, tempts one to eat more and leads the attention to the savour of the food and away from internal signals.

It is recognised that a pushing, aggressive worldly kind of activity is appropriate for rulers, for the military forces and for those who concern themselves with political matters - who deal in the area of domination, forcefulness and warfare. In fact, in some of the Indian traditions, the castes which performed such roles – the Rajputs (literally "son of the King"), were expressly permitted to take meat and wine, whereas the Brahmana, who is not a ruler, but a scholar, teacher, and a spiritual seeker, has always been forbidden these Rajasika foods.

Such a diet, no doubt, creates in an individual brilliant energies and keeps all vigorous men restlessly striving to fulfil their uncontrolled passions and desires; hence, in their final reactions, they lead the eater towards a life productive of 'Pain, grief and disease'.

Sattvika Foods

ayuh sattvabalarogya sukhapritivivardhanah
rasyah snigdhah sthirah hrdyah aharah sattvikapriyah (B.G 17.12)

Those foods which increase the *ayuh* (Life and vitality), *Sattva* (purity), *Bala* (Strength stamina), *Arogya* (health), *Sukha* (happiness) and *Priti* (cheerfulness and good appetite), are termed Sattvika. These foods are *Rasyah* (savoury), *Snigdhah* (oleaginous), *Sthirah* (substantial), *Hrdyah* (agreeable) and are liked by the *Sattvika.*

In contrast to Tamasika and Rajasika foods, foods which are fresh, wholesome, natural, of good quality, yet mild in spices, neither over nor undercooked, are experienced as lending a calm alertness and at the same time a state of quiet energy. Such foods are called Sattvika. They are said to nourish the consciousness. They not only provide nourishment for the body, but they do not adversely affect the overall energy state. They add vitality to the total system by bringing a perfect, harmonious balance of energy states in the food itself. They don't pull energy from the body or weigh it down; they don't make it heavy; neither do they irritate nor push it beyond its capacity. Rather, they provide a precise balance of nourishment and create no undue waste. Such foods are the ones which are most likely to be experienced as *Sattvika*. They are the ones which are likely to give the body lightness, alertness, energy and create a clear consciousness.

Sattvika foods give strength from within. In contrast Rajasika foods supply strength to the muscles and give a feeling that one's energy is coming from the food, one has eaten. Fresh fruits, wholesome grains and the fresh milk of a cow are Sattvika foods. Raw milk just drawn from a healthy cow is considered ideal. If, however, it is kept for sometime, then it is to be heated to its boiling point before it is consumed. Milk of buffalo is considered more Rajasika since it is heavier and more fattening. Any milk which becomes sour or spoiled, of course tends to acquire a Tamasika property.

In describing the natural taste of particular types of food that is accepted and liked by good men of spiritual urges (Sattva), it is said that they like only such diets which increase the vitality *(Ayuh)*, and not sheer bulk; which supplies the energy for meditative purposes *(Virya);* which increases and unfolds the secret strength (*Bala*) to resist temptations for sense-objects; which provides good health (*arogya*) so that they may not fall ill and suffer a break in their regular *sadhana*. Such people will have a natural inclination to take food which will augment joy (*Priti*) and inner cheerfulness (*Sukha*). In short, such creative men, by their own choice, enjoy only food that is pure and wholesome.

Integrated approach of Yoga for management of health

The disturbances in the *Manomayakosa* percolates into the physical layer *(Annamayakosa)* through the *Pranamayakosa.* Hence, in the treatment of these psychosomatic ailments it becomes mandatory to work at all these levels of our existence to bring about the quickest results. The integrated approach, thus, consists in not only dealing with physical sheath, the relief of which could at best be temporary as is happening with the drugs used in modern medicine to treat diseases of the psychosomatic type like asthma, diabetes mellitus, hypertension, etc. it also includes using techniques to operate on different sheaths of our existence. The large number of Yoga practices available in the texts of Yoga and *Upanishads* are adopted to balance and harmonise the disturbances at each of the five *kosas* and tackle this type of complex psychosomatic ailments. Each activities relating to different *Kosas* are given below which can be used to ensure an integrated personality management.

A. Practices at Annamayakosa (the physical layer)

A healthy Yogic diet, *kriyas,* loosening exercises and *Yogasanas* are used to operate at the *Annamayakosa* level and to remove the physical symptoms of the ailments.

(*i*) ***Kriyas*** – These are Yogic processes described in Hatha Yoga to cleanse the inner organs of our body. They bring about the following effects (*a*) Activating and revitalising the organs, (*b*) Toning up their functions, (*c*) Desensitization, and (*d*) Development of deep internal awareness. Among the major *kriyas* enumerated in the texts of Yoga, simplified versions of a few *kriyas* like catheter *neti, jala neti, kapalabhati, agnisara, vamanadhauti (kunjal kriya),* etc. are used extensively.

(*ii*) ***Physical exercises and movements – sithilikarana vyayama :*** Very simple physical movements to mobilise and activate the affected parts of the body are used. Some easy physical exercises are adopted to fulfil the needs of the particular ailments to (*a*) loosen the joints, (*b*) stretch and relax the muscles, (*c*) improve the power, and (*d*) develop stamina.

(*iii*) ***Yogasanas – postures:*** Yogasanas are physical postures often imitating the natural positions of the animals meant to make the mind tranquil. Through these postures, the physical revitalization and deep relaxation and mental calmness are achieved.

B. Practices at Pranamayakosa (the layer of prana)

Prana is the basic life principle. *Pranayama* is a process for gaining control over *Prana.* The five manifestations of *Prana* and the corresponding most comprehensive definition of *Pranayama* in the human system are described in *Pranopanishad.* Also the conventional *Pranayama* through regulation of breath is described therein.

Through the practice of proper breathing, *Kriyas* and *Pranayama* we start operating on the *Pranamayakosa.* Suitable types of *Pranayama* and breathing help to remove the random agitations in *pranika* flows in the *Pranamayakosa.* Thus, the ailments are handled at this *Pranamayakosa* level.

C. Practices at Manomayakosa (The mental layer)

(*i*) *Dharana and dhyana:* A direct operation on this level is made possible by the last three limbs of *Astanga Yoga* of Patanjali – *Dharana, Dhyana* and *Samadhi.* The culturing of mind is accomplished by focusing the mind *(Dharana)* initially on some object or image, followed by relaxed dwelling of the mind in a single thought *(Dhyana)* for longer and longer durations leading ultimately to super-consciousness *(Samadhi).* A progressive habituation allows the mind to remain relaxed during the period of meditation *(Dhyana).* The benefits of Transcendental Meditation, a simple standardised technique, are numerous, interesting and noteworthy. Its application to treat many psychosomatic ailments has become popular.

(*ii*) *Emotion culture:* To handle and gain control over the basic cause for mental agitations, we use the Yoga techniques that control our emotions. A devotional session containing Prayers, Chants, Bhajanas, Namavalis, Dhunas, Stotras etc., help to build a congenial atmosphere to evoke, recognise, attenuate and dissipate the emotions. Thus, control over emotions is obtained through the devotional session. The emotional imbalances and upsurges are eliminated by such control.

D. Practices at Vijnanamayakosa (The layer of wisdom)

As Bhrgu reports to Varuna about this wonderful discovery, the master is happy but he says "Please move on. You have just a few steps to go ahead, you are in the right direction." Now through intense long tapas, Bhrgu realises that it is all the *Vijnana* (knowledge) from which the entire creation has happened and that could be the final reality.

Vijnanamayakosa is the fourth layer of our existence. We all have two minds. For *e.g.,* when the *Manomayakosa* said that "It is a beautiful rose, I want to have it" and you started instructing your hands to pick up the flower, the inner mind said "Sorry, you cannot pluck that flower; it does not belong to you; it is from the neighbour's garden" and you stopped the action. This conscience within that continuously guides us to do a thing or not to do a thing is the *Vijnanamayakosa.* It is this component of the mind that has developed in human race greatly that differentiates man from animals.

Bhartrihari brings out this point as to how the higher faculty, the *Vijnanamayakosa* continuously guides the *Manomayakosa* to get mastery over the basic instincts which are eating, mating, fearing and sleeping. Hence in man we know that, even these basic instincts are all psychological. For example, we have lost the cyclical behaviour as in animals who get into reflex oestrus cycles (heat) for sexual behaviour. This freedom element which is inbuilt in a human being, guides him to discriminate what is "good and bad", "right and wrong", "useful and not useful" to move towards long term *sukha* (happiness). Thus, *Vijnanamayakosa* is the discriminating faculty.

A basic understanding is the key to operate from *Vijnanamayakosa. Upanishads* are the treasury of such knowledge which is the redeemer of all miseries and obsessions. It is the lack of that inner *Jnana* which is responsible for many wrong habits, agitations, etc. The Happiness Analysis – *Ananda Mimamsa* of the *Taittiriya Upanishad* handles the most fundamental problem relevant to all living creatures. The analysis systematically leads the reader to that substratum from which *Prana* and mind emerge – the *Anandamayakosa.* It helps the person to change his attitude of greed and deep attachment to material possessions and enjoyments towards the realisation that happiness is within and 'each one of us' in our causal state is *'ananda'* embodied. As a result, man's outlook in life changes. Knowledge burns the strong attachments, obsessions, likes and dislikes which are the basic reasons for the agitations of mind. The *sara* type of *adhis* can only be removed by this knowledge *(atma-jnana* or *Self-realisation).*

E. Practices at Anandamayakosa (the layer of bliss)

Varuna now directs the son to go back to tapas and this time Bhrgu never returns. The master goes to check why the son has not come back. He was surprised to see that Bhrgu is completely engrossed in deep *Ananda* (bliss). There is no individual 'I' of the *Vijnana* or *Manomayakosa* that can report to the father about his realisation. Bhrgu is now established in the knowledge of the final truth that *Ananda* is the basic stuff of this universe from which everything has been created.

This is called *Anandamayakosa* – the bliss layer of our existence. This is the most subtle aspect of our existence which is devoid of any form of emotions; a state of total silence – a state of complete harmony, and perfect health.

While in *Manomayakosa* the creative power predominates, in *Vijnanamayakosa* it is the power to discern and discriminate. Bliss is embodied in *Anandamayakosa,* the highest stage of evolution in the manifested existence. It is the subtlest among the five layers of existence. In his journey towards the Ultimate, man crosses these *kosas* of existence one by one. Through analysis called *'Panchakosa-viveka'* (knowing through experience, one's five *kosas* of existence) and the associated practices called *'tapas'* man transforms himself by gradually getting relieved from the bondages and constrictions of each *kosa*. This is one of the methods of reaching the ultimate goal enumerated and described in the *Upanishads.*

To bring the bliss of our causal body *(Karana sarira)* called *Anandamayakosa* in all our actions is the key for a very happy and healthy life. This also brings our innate healing powers to effect, a complete cure of our ailments. The techniques used come under the heading *Karma Yoga,* the secret of action.

The secret lies in maintaining an inner silence, equipoise at the mental level as we perform all our actions. Normally we get upset, or excited over things which we do not like or we like. But we have to learn to maintain equipoise *(samatva).* The next step is to have a deep silence and a blissful awareness in the inner subtler layers of our mind while we are in action.

This is accomplished by self awareness, constant drive to change oneself and auto-suggestions. To recognise that 'I am getting tensed' is the first step. Correct by withdrawing to the inner compartment of total bliss, peace and rest. Remember this by repeated inner silence several times in the day. Retain a smiling relaxed face during all the Yoga practices.

Kosa	*Stage*	*Actions*
Annamayakosa	Organic body	Download movies, Upload family pictures to facebook, parties on weekends
Pranamayakosa	Energy body, vitality	Sports, Attend Yoga workshops for health purpose
Manomayakosa	Psychic body, thoughts and feelings	Help people, participate in social activities (not parties)
Vijnanamayakosa	Intellectual body, spiritual discrimination and wisdom	Seeking knowledge
Anandamayakosa	Body of joy, pure consciousness and bliss	State of blissful being, Body is still within awareness.

Multiple Choice Questions

1. What is the meaning of the word 'sara' in vatsara?
   A. All B. Purity
   C. Element D. Complete
2. What is the meaning of word 'vari' in varisara?
   A. Vayu B. Jal
   C. Aakash D. Agni
3. Which chakra provides calmness, pleasure and stoicism to a person?
   A. Swathisthana B. Anahata
   C. Ajna D. Manipura
4. What is meaning of word 'vahnisara'?
   A. Vayu tatva B. Jala tatva
   C. Agni tatva D. Aakash tatva
5. The main aim of vyaghra kriya is:
   A. To strengthen respiratory system
   B. To purify alimentary canal
   C. To purify small intestine
   D. To carry out undigested food
6. By practice of which pranayama vata doshas get eliminated?
   A. Suryabhedi B. Nadishodhan
   C. Ujjayi D. Murchha
7. By practice of which asana pranashakti gets stabilized?
   A. Bhadrasana
   B. Matsayendrasana
   C. Mayurasana
   D. Gomukhasana
8. Which type of doshas get eliminated by practice of ujjayi pranayama?
   A. Vata doshas B. Pitta doshas
   C. Kapha doshas D. Both A and B
9. Which of the following statement is true about suryabhedi pranayama?
   A. It prevents ageing
   B. It eliminates vata dosha
   C. It removes intestinal worms
   D. All of the above
10. Which kriya is useful in elimination of kapha doshas?
    A. Dhauti B. Vasti
    C. Nauli D. Neti
11. Which asana is related to vasti kriya?
    A. Utakatasana B. Singhasana
    C. Mandukasana D. Siddhasana
12. Which mudra enchances blood circulation in body?
    A. Shunya mudra B. Prana mudra
    C. Vayu mudra D. Apana mudra
13. By regular practice of vasti kriya which type of dosha borne diseases get eliminated?
    A. Vata B. Pitta
    C. Kapha D. All the above
14. Which of the following statement is correct regarding benefits of shitkari pranayama?
    A. It purifies blood B. It quenches thirst
    C. It removes acidity D. All of the above
15. Which of the following statement is correct regarding benefits of shitali pranayama?
    A. It eliminates insomenia
    B. It eliminates spleen disorders
    C. It eliminates throat disorders
    D. All of the above
16. Which of the following statement is not correct?
    A. Practise of moolbandha changes the direction of vyana vayu
    B. Practise of moolbandha changes the direction of apana vayu
    C. Practise of moolbandha removes mental disorders
    D. Practise of moolbandha eliminates asthma and arthritis
17. The regular practice of which asana helps a person to cultivate the habit of early rising?
    A. Kukkutasana B. Makarasana
    C. Kurmasana D. Kagasana

18. Which pranayama is not suitable for kapha dominant individuals?
A. Murchha B. Bhastrika
C. Shitli D. Shitkari

19. By regular practice of which pranayama a person can control his hunger and thirst?
A. Murchha B. Brahmri
C. Shitli D. Shitkari

20. Which pranayama is useful for pitta dominant individuals?
A. Shitli B. Shitkari
C. Nadisodhan D. Suryabhedi

21. Pitta dominant individuals should avoid regular practice of which kumbhaka?
A. Ujjayi B. Shitli
C. Nadishodhan D. Surya bhedi

22. Which kriya increases memory power?
A. Nauli B. Trataka
C. Kapalbhati D. Neti

23. Which mudras eliminate allergy problem?
A. Linga, Sankha B. Surya, Prithvi
C. Prithvi, Prana D. Apana, Gyana

24. By the practice of moolbandha _____ vayu changes its direction and starts flowing towards manipura chakra?
A. Samana B. Prana
C. Apana D. Vyana

25. Which pranayama helps in maintaining concentration and mental peace?
A. Sahita B. Bhastrika
C. Kevali D. Suryabhedi

26. Which yogic kriya helps in maintaining balance of vata, pitta and kapha in the body?
A. Asana B. Pranayama
C. Bandha D. Mudra

27. To maintain regular concentration of chitta is known as:
A. Dharana B. Samadhi
C. Pratyahara D. Dhyana

28. An easy way to change a disturbed mind to a peaceful mind is:
A. Dharana B. Yoga nindra
C. Surya namaskara D. Samadhi

29. Which yogic practice removes the ignorance of individual and provides wisdom?
A. Pranayama B. Asana
C. Trataka D. Bandha

30. During the practice of which mudra mulabandha occurs naturally?
A. Mahamudra B. Mahabandha
C. Mahabheda D. Khechari

31. Which of the following is not a part of niyama?
A. Socha B. Santosha
C. Aprigarha D. Ishwarpranidhana

32. Which of the following pranayama can be performed during travelling?
A. Ujjayi B. Bhastrika
C. Shitli D. Shitkari

33. Which vayu is called as reserve energy bank?
A. Udana B. Vyana
C. Samana D. Prana

34. Which vayu is strengthened by fasting?
A. Udana B. Prana
C. Samana D. Vyana

35. Which of the following should be practised to gain stability of the body?
A. Shatkarma B. Bandha
C. Asana D. Mudra

36. Which of the following methods are used during practice of cyclic meditation?
A. I.R.T. B. D.R.T.
C. Q.R.T. D. All of the above

37. Regular practise of which mudra prevents falling and whitening of hairs?
A. Manduki B. Ashwini
C. Tadagi D. Yoni

38. Which of the following elements belong to kapha dosha?
A. Earth, fire B. Earth, water
C. Fire, water D. Air, earth

39. The qualities of enthusiasm and progress develops by awakening of which chakra?
A. Anahata B. Visuddhi
C. Manipura D. Muladhara

40. At the death of human which vayu takes away causal body from gross body?

A. Prana B. Udana
C. Samana D. Vyana

41. Out of seventy two thousand nadis how many nadis are considered important in the text 'Shiva Samhita'?

A. 12 B. 14
C. 16 D. 18

42. By gaining control over which vayu a yogi gets success in attaining 'laghima'?

A. Samana B. Prana
C. Udana D. Apana

43. Which elements are associated to sweet taste?

A. Earth, fire B. Earth, water
C. Fire, air D. Earth, air

44. When _____ is less and ____ is more in body, the insomnia disorder occurs.

A. Kapha, Pitta B. Pitta, Kapha
C. Vata, Kapha D. Vata, Pitta

45. In the balanced state what is the ratio of vata, pitta and kapha in body?

A. 1 : 2 : 4 B. 2 : 4 : 1
C. 1 : 4 : 2 D. 4 : 2 : 1

46. In which type of samadhi the sadhaka withdrawls himself from worldly objects and concentrates his mind?

A. Asamparagyata B. Sampragyata
C. Vicharanugata D. Anandanugata

47. To concentrate mind on Brahma is known as:

A. Shradda B. Samadhana
C. Shama D. Dama

48. Which of the following statement is incorrect?

A. Rajas guna becomes nil in susuptavastha
B. Tamas guna becomes nil in susuptavastha
C. Rajas guna remains as minute fraction during svapnavastha
D. All of the above

49. Which of the following statement is not correct?

A. Rajas guna becomes nil in nindravriti
B. Tamas guna becomes nil in nindravriti
C. There is a percept of destitution in ahavritti
D. All of the above

50. Match the correct:

(*a*) Heya 1. Reason of sorrow
(*b*) Hetu 2. Way to Salvation
(*c*) Haana 3. Form of Sorrow
(*d*) Haanopaya 4. Form of Salvation

	(*a*)	(*b*)	(*c*)	(*d*)
A.	3	1	4	2
B.	3	4	2	1
C.	2	4	1	3
D.	1	3	2	4

51. Who is known as the founder of yoga?

A. Maharishi Gheranda
B. Matseyandranath
C. Gorakshanath
D. Maharishi Patanjali

52. Which dosha get suppressed in hemant (late autumn) ritu?

A. Vata B. Pitta
C. Kapha D. Both A and C

53. Which dosha get suppressed in grishma (summer) ritu?

A. Vata B. Pitta
C. Kapha D. Both B and C

54. In which season pitta dosha is dominant?

A. Garishma B. Sharad
C. Shishira D. Varsha

55. The reason of vaikarika nindra is more _____ and less _____ in the body?

A. Pitta, Kapha B. Kapha, Pitta
C. Vata, Pitta D. Pitta, Vata

56. According to ayurveda how many total seasons are there?

A. 3 B. 4
C. 6 D. 7

57. In dakshinayana the sun is:

A. Towards tropic of capricorn
B. Towards equator
C. Towards tropic of cancer
D. None of these

58. The line – 'Aatu Rasa Vikara Parsabddama' is related to:

A. Yoga B. Fast
C. Fruits D. Swasthavrita

59. In which season kapha is accumulated in the body?
A. Winter
B. Late autumn
C. Spring
D. Summer

60. In which season consuming of sattu is unsafe?
A. Summer
B. Winter
C. Spring
D. Late autumn

61. Much spicy food which takes more time to be digested is known as:
A. Tamasic food
B. Sattvic food
C. Rajasic food
D. None of these

62. Which type of food is the main cause of diseases?
A. Rajasic food
B. Tamasic food
C. Sattvic food
D. Hot food

63. Which of the following statement is correct?
A. Consuming cloying food is pitta annihilator
B. Consuming cloying food is kapha creator
C. Consuming cloying food is vata annihilator
D. All the above

64. The meaning of 'prajalapta' is:
A. Over eating
B. Talkativeness
C. Feeble minded
D. Over sleeping

65. The therapy done by water is known as:
A. Hydropathy
B. Heliotheraphy
C. Pathology
D. Waterpathy

66. The meaning of word 'mita' in mitahara is:
A. One time
B. Two times
C. Food
D. Limited

67. According to Ayurveda, how much part of stomach should be left empty for space during taking meal?
A. One-third
B. One-fourth
C. Half
D. None of the above

68. The water charged in which colour of bottle is useful for person suffering from chronic skin disease?
A. Blue
B. Green
C. Red
D. Yellow

69. The therapy done with the help of sun rays is known as:
A. Heliotherapy
B. Mesotherapy
C. Solartherapy
D. Heat-therapy

70. The feeling of ahamkara, desire, jealousy, anger in a person are eradicated by awakening of which chakra?
A. Anahata
B. Muladhara
C. Manipura
D. Swasthisthana

71. According to Maharishi Patanjali by doing which type of karmas a person attains Kaivalya?
A. Shukla karma
B. Krishna karma
C. Shukla-krishna karma
D. Ashukla krishna karma

72. 'Tapo davindava sahnama'– line is described in which text?
A. Shiva Samhita
B. Patanjali Yoga Sutra
C. Bhagavad Gita
D. Yoga Sudhakara

73. What is the meaning of the given line? - 'Tapo davindava sahnama'.
A. Tapa and davindava are same
B. To bear davindava is tapa
C. To bear tapa is davindava
D. Tapa is attained easily by means of davindava

74. Which of the following is not a type of vihit karma?
A. Prayaschita karma
B. Nisidha karma
C. Kamya karma
D. Nemitika karma

75. Practise of mudras strengthen mainly which kosha?
A. Pranamaya kosha
B. Manomaya kosha
C. Anandmaya kosha
D. Both A and B

ANSWERS

1	2	3	4	5	6	7	8	9	10
C	B	D	C	D	A	B	C	D	A
11	**12**	**13**	**14**	**15**	**16**	**17**	**18**	**19**	**20**
A	B	D	D	D	A	A	A	C	B
21	**22**	**23**	**24**	**25**	**26**	**27**	**28**	**29**	**30**
D	B	A	C	C	B	D	B	A	A
31	**32**	**33**	**34**	**35**	**36**	**37**	**38**	**39**	**40**
D	A	B	C	D	D	A	A	C	B
41	**42**	**43**	**44**	**45**	**46**	**47**	**48**	**49**	**50**
B	C	B	A	D	B	B	A	D	A
51	**52**	**53**	**54**	**55**	**56**	**57**	**58**	**59**	**60**
B	B	C	D	A	C	A	D	A	D
61	**62**	**63**	**64**	**65**	**66**	**67**	**68**	**69**	**70**
C	A	D	B	A	D	B	B	A	D
71	**72**	**73**	**74**	**75**					
D	B	B	B	D					

●●●

CHAPTER

7

Therapeutic Yoga

Yoga is the science of life and the art of living. It is the common sense answer to overall physical and mental fitness. Basically Yoga is a system of physical and mental self improvement and final liberation, that people have been using for thousands of years. Yoga arose in the age of the Vedas and Upanishads. **It is India's oldest scientific, perfect spiritual discipline.** Yoga is a method of training the mind and developing its power of subtle perceptions so that man may discover for himself the spiritual truths on which religion, beliefs and moral values finally rest. It is realization of our hidden powers. Swami Shivananda said, "He who radiates good, divine thoughts does immense good unto himself and to the world also". **Yoga is science of life, it offers us simple, easy remedies and techniques and methods of health and hygiene to assure physical and mental fitness with a minimum of time, effort and expense.**

Yoga in other term Preksha Dhyan invented by prominent Jainacharya Mahaprajna is such an uncomplicated, easy to learn technique of meditation. It comprised of the following—

(*i*) Kayotsarga (Total relaxation)

(*ii*) Antaryatra (Internal trip)

(*iii*) Svash preksha (Perception of breath)

(*iv*) Sharir preksha (Perception of body)

(*v*) Chaitanya-kendra preksha (Perception of psychic centers)

(*vi*) Leshya dhyan (Perception of psychic spectrum)

(*vii*) Perception of the present moment

(*viii*) Perception of thoughts

(*ix*) Self-discipline

(*x*) Bhavna (counter-vibrations)

(*xi*) Anupreksha (contemplation)

(*xii*) Concentration.

Yoga is one of the most ancient metaphysical sciences, which investigates the nature of soul and, through its discipline, awakens the super-conscious mind of the man which unites the moral being with the immortal supreme spirit. Yoga leads to balance and also provides both a philosophy and a religion. The real joy of life appears when we can unify nature and culture, wealth and poverty, movement and stillness, attachment and detachment. Yoga can serve both the individual and society. **Yoga is neither a sect nor an ideology but a practical training of mind and body.** Broadly speaking, it has three main outcomes : it makes us more aware of our natural wisdom, it strengthens the body's ability to recover from illness or injury; it teaches us how to co-operate with others. Yoga teaches us truth through mind and body rather than theory, it brings about deep change of attitude. The entire thrust of our life is to devote total attention to every action and, at the same time, to trust in the power of sacred.

Eight stages of Patanjali Yoga are:

(*i*) **Yama:** The universal moral laws.

(*ii*) **Niyama:** Personal moral roots of conduct.

(*iii*) **Asan:** Yogic postures.

(*iv*) **Pranayama:** Acquiring and controlling prana or energy, by means of the breath.

(*v*) **Pratyahara:** The withdrawl of the senses from the outer environment.

(*vi*) **Dharana:** Concentration.

(*vii*) **Dhyana:** Meditation.

(*viii*) **Samadhi:** Enlightenment.

Yoga is also a technique for achieving purest form of self-awareness, devoid of all thoughts and sensations. Today some kind of reconstruction of thought is necessary to understand clearly what the great Yoga teachers of the past have taught. Patanjali, the systematiser of Yoga, has explained the thoughts through Yogasutra. In the Gita and Upanishads we find a broader and positive expression of Yoga. Our ancient masters through Yoga teach us an art of living a life for eternally blissful experiences of even flow of happiness by removal of miseries and sufferings of our limited life. The term Yoga means a systematic practice and implementation of mind and body in the living process of man to keep harmony within self, within the society and with nature.

Kundalini Yoga is a systematic and integrated practice for body and mind and its thrust to make a man creative. By a new method, which is wholly safe, one can get the Kundalini power aroused in minutes. Hence this method is called the simplified Kundalini Yoga, abbreviated to "SKY". Kayakalpa is the culmination of Kundalini Yoga and its objective is to enable the practitioner to postpone the ageing process and death. In all sky centers in India, Malaysia, Singapore, South Korea, Japan and USA, Kayakalpa Yoga is now being taught at regular intervals. These two yogic practices are very important in karma Yoga, the world religion.

Benefits of Yoga

At the physical level Yoga and its cleansing practices have proven to be extremely effective for various disorders. Yoga is beneficial as follow:

(*a*) **Increasing flexibility:** Yoga has position that act upon the various joints of the body including those joints that are never really on the "radar screen" let alone exercised.

(*b*) **Increasing lubrication of the joints, ligaments and tendons:** The well researched Yoga positions exercise the different tendons and ligaments of the body. Surprisingly it has been found that the body which may have been quite rigid starts experiencing a remarkable flexibility in even those parts which have not been consciously work upon.

(*c*) **Massaging of all organs of the body:** Yoga is perhaps the only form of activity which massages all the internal glands and organs of the body in a thorough manner, including those such as prostate—that hardly get externally stimulated during our entire lifetime. Yoga acts in a wholesome manner on the various body parts. This stimulation and massage of the organs in turn benefits us by keeping away disease and providing a forewarning at the first possible instance of a likely onset of disease or disorder. One of the far-reaching benefits of Yoga is the uncanny sense of awareness that it develops in the practioner of an impending health disorder or infection. This in turn enables the person to take pre-emptive corrective action.

(*d*) **Complete detoxification:** By gentle stretching muscles and joints as well as massaging the various organs, Yoga ensures the optimum blood supply to various parts of the body. This helps in flushing out of toxins from every nook and cranny as well as delayed ageing, energy and remarkable zest of life.

(*e*) **Excellent toning of the muscles:** Muscles that have become flaccid, weak or slothy are stimulated separately to shed excess flab and flaccidity.

Attitude training in Yoga therapy

Most of the Asanas and Pranayams are classified as if they are for particular physical or mental problems. For example matsyendrasan Asana is good for a diabetic patient or savasana is good for controlling high blood pressure. As a matter of fact, only Asanas or Pranayam is not going to help if it is done in a mechanical pattern or form. There are other factors, which are playing a major role in recovery process. The Yoga therapist must and should impart the technology and philosophy of this science while providing the training to their patients. The traditional poses are not at all suitable to the needs of the men of this age where our life style is completely different from those of the old days. It is more important to teach more simplified versions as Yoga is nonspecific when it comes to effective and positive results, especially if other factors are not incorporated, for example, diet, routine, positive attitude, openness to accept the changes and learning new healthy habits etc. These other factors are:

(*i*) **Awareness:** A person who is practicing Yoga as a therapy must understand the reason for this practice. It is not important that the pose should be perfect in order to get its benefit but more important is the awareness of the body and attitude.

(*ii*) **Concept:** The concept of pose and Pranayam must be explained and should be very clear before its practice. The scientific explanation is a must.

(*iii*) **Commitment:** There has to be a commitment from both the sides—the therapist and the practitioner. There must be a mutual understanding that one is there to explain and teach and the other is there to learn, recover and gain.

(*iv*) **Dedication:** Quite often people are taking up Yoga as an experiment. Sometime when all other doors are closed, people come to Yoga practice and expect a miracle or instance change or recovery. Just as there is a big difference in allopathic medicines and herbal medicines, likewise there is a big difference between other holistic physical training and Yoga. Once the person feels some positive results, he has to practice on a regular basis as a routine. Once a week, one hour practice is not going to help.

(*v*) **Trust and faith:** Just as a patient trusts his doctor or any other health practitioner, in the same way there has to be a faith and trust in whatever the patient is practicing during Yoga therapeutic sessions. It is very important that a good relation is maintained during the treatment and follow up sessions.

(*vi*) **Attitude:** Often, people who believe in other faiths or religions are not ready for certain Yoga practices when it comes to the philosophy and devotional practices for relaxation and meditation. The attitude is that "I want to learn Yoga but I do not want to learn philosophy, I am here to learn only poses and breathing." In other words, "I want to learn swimming but without getting wet. It is very important far a therapist to provide the scientific explanations with spiritual support. All Yoga practices are based on the laws of the nature. It is very true that the science of Yoga was developed in India and majority of Hindu people practice that. The base is of Hindu, Jainism and Buddhism faith—but as a way of life. All Hindu, Buddhist and Jains scriptures and literature are explaining Yoga. One has to have some sort of knowledge of Bhagwat Gita, Preksha Dhyan, Patanjali Yoga Sutra, Health Yoga Pradipika and such texts.

Here the intention is not to teach the religion but the philosophy behind the practice. If certain techniques are practiced with a certain attitude then it helps, more than a mechanical practice *e.g.*, chanting of OM as an universal sound. Many attitudes are cultivated while practicing any pose. Each and every move can provide a space to learn a certain attitude if explained and developed during its regular practice. It could be from gross to the subtlest level, that will help the practitioner in the long run to change his life style and in cultivating healthy habits.

HEALTH MANAGEMENT THROUGH NATUROPATHY

(I) Cure of heart disease by Naturopathy

Millions of people in the world suffer from the diseases of the heart and blood vessels. The heart which is muscular pump, keeps the blood circulation continuous. But when there is a break down of this complicated mechanism, blood supply to a part of the body may be affected leading to what is known as heart attack. But with naturopathy the following cardiovascular diseases can be cured : Coronary Thrombosis-sudden blocking of one of the arteries.

Arteriosclerosis—hardening of arteries.

Degenerative heart disease—gradual decay of blood vessels due to excessive smoking of tobacco. Hypertensive heart disease straining of blood vessels due to high blood pressure. This leads to hardening of blood vessels, hence diminishing the supply of blood.

High blood pressure (Hypertension)—Blood pressure remains high leading to disorder like lack of strength, bad temper, visionary troubles, tiredness, headache, coldness of hands and feet.

Nature cure

- Routine-mudpack
- Specific-full massage (reverse direction), neutral spinal spray, ice massage to spine.

(II) Diabetes

Diabetes a very old disease, has a common feature—excessive accumulation of sugar in blood, due to malfunctioning of pancreas. The general prevalent method of treating the diabetic patient is to inject insulin to compensate what could be produced by the pancreas. The yogic treatment restores the normal functioning of the pancreas and other endocrine glands. The chemistry of the body becomes normal leading to a healthy body.

Nature cure

- Routine-enema, mudpack
- Specific-full massage, partial massage to abdomen, cold abdomen pack, cold hip bath.

(III) Cancer

Cancer has affected millions in the entire world. It is the fobia of the disease which causes more suffering than the caner itself. In cancer, floating starved non-functional cells group together and manifest themselves as tumours, ulcers and cancer.

Nature cure

- Routine-enema, mudpack, cold spinal spray/ bath, wheat grass juice therapy, grape diet.
- Specific-full massage, steam bath, under water massage, cold circular jet.

(IV) Obesity

Obesity is becoming a common health hazard and leads to many other diseases like coronary heart disease, high blood pressure, diabetes, psychosomatic disorders and a shorten life span. **The main cause of obesity is excessive eating**. The best method to control weight is to reduce the intake of protein, carbohydrates and fat and increase the supply of mineral and vitamins and also increase exercises.

Nature cure

This method of cure involves body purification. The method lightens the body and makes it free from toxins and morbid matter which in turn results in problem free weight loss. The procedures are :

Full body dry friction - for 10 minutes daily.

Enema (colon irrigation) - with luke warm water, alternate days.

Steam bath - 20 minutes, twice in a week.

Hot foot bath - 20 minutes, 5 days per week.

ROLE OF YOGA IN HEALTHY LIVING

Yoga is a subject of science of high order, which carries in it the mystery of conservation of health and transformation of life. A complete expression of life is possible only through Yoga. Yogasana, pranayam, meditation develops faith in a person, chiefly because it is half a therapy. It is common saying that confidence is half the cure. The concept of Ashtanga Yoga proposed by Mahrashi Patanjali with different aspects have enormous contribution towards healthy living as out lived here:

1. Yama

Under this include different aspects such as Ahimsa, Satya, Asteya, Brahmacharya and Aparigraha. Through this first step of Astanga Yoga one turns to more ideal in his day to day life. With this he discharges his duties towards society in a more orderly manner.

2. Niyama

The major components under this include Shauch, Santosh, Tapa, Swadhyaya, Ishwarpranidhan. Practice of this aspect of Yoga turns a person, more disciplined and orderly. With this one can overcome the deformities of personal senses. In fact the reformation of personal actions for us is the basic foundation of healthy living.

3. Asanas

Having achieved the perfection over the guideline of Yama and Niyama only then one must commit for the practice of Yogasanas. Without this the Yoga practices is ineffective. For various Yogasanas body is flexed for an specific posture regularly at a given time for a given purpose. This exerts special effect on different body joints, muscles, heart, digestive system, endocrine glands, lungs & nervous system. This revives the normal functioning of respective organs and body system. At present time special significance to Yogasana is direct relation to healthy living.

4. Pranayama

Pranayama is a highly sophisticated procedure of Yoga, where by one achieves a total control over the vital force which governs the proper functioning of body's life process. Pranayama helps to tone-up the most vital activities of the body, such as respiratory system, cardio-vascular system. In addition, it strengthens the body immunity which is extremely important for maintaining the quality of life and healthy living.

5. Pratyahara

The real purpose of this Yoga practice is to drive the body's consciousness inwardly and focus at a pleasant thought or a point of auspicious feeling. In a daily life the practice of such yogic terms helps to achieve a high order of quality life.

6. Dharana

For the purpose of achieving the spiritual excellence, this type of yogic exercise, called Dharana carries special significance. It is mainly for the reason that Dharana itself means to focus on a solitary point through flow of thought. Continuity of this state is termed as - Dhyana, which is the final objective of Yoga practice for healthy living.

7. Meditation

Meditation acts as a powerful tonic. It is a mental and nerving tonic as well. The holy vibrations penetrate all the cells of the body and cure the diseases of the body. Those who meditate save doctor's bills. The powerful, soothing waves that arise during meditaion exercise a benign influence on the mind, nerves, organs and the cells of body. The divine energy freely flows like Tailadhara (flows of oil from one vessel to another) from the feet of the Lord to the different systems of the Sadhakas.

Considerable changes take place in the mind, brain and the nervous system by the practice of meditation. New nerve-currents, new vibrations, new avenues, new grooves, new cells, new channels are formed. The whole mind and nervous system are remodeled. You will develop a new heart, a new view of mind, new sensations, new feeling, new mode of thinking, acting and a view of the universe (as God in manifestation). The fire of meditation annihilates all foulness due to vice. Then suddenly comes knowledge or divine wisdom, which directly leads to final emancipation.

Real peace and Ananda (bliss) manifest only when Sankalpas get extinguished. When you fix the mind on the supreme energy even for five minutes Sattva guna is infused into the mind. Vasanas (impression) are thinned out and the force of sankalpa become less and less.

You will feel peace and bliss during the five minutes. You can compare this Ananda from meditation with the transitory sensual pleasures. You will find that this Ananda from meditation is a million times superior to sensual pleasure. Meditate and feel this Ananda. Then you will know its real value. You will get the full Ananda of the divine glory only when you merge deep into silent meditation. When you are on the border land of divinity of God, when you are at threshold of God, when you are in the outer skirts, you will not get the maximum peace and bliss.

8. Samadhi

Samadhi is provided to super normal healthy person.

ROLE OF ASANAS, PRANAYAMA & MEDITATION IN COMMON DISEASES

Anaemia

- **Pranayama:** Ujjayi (energy-renewing Pranayama), Nadi-Sodhana (alternate breathing).
- **Asanas:** Paschimottanasans (stretching the back and legs), Ardhamatsyendrasana (Simplified version of the Yogi Matsyendra Posture), Sarvangasana (Shoulder-stand), Sirshasana (Head-stand), Savasana (Complete Relaxation Posture).
- **Diet:** Change over to foods rich in iron and Vitamin-B juice of wheat sprouts (grass), uncooked Juices or soups of leafy vegetables, fresh fruits, germinated corn and beans, pulses etc.

Arthritis

- **Pranayama:** Rhythmic breathing, Nadi-Sodhana (alternate breathing).
- **Asanas:** Trikonasna (triangle posture), Padmasana (The lotus Position), Salabhasana (The Locust Posture), Dhanurasana (The Bow Posture), Vakrasana (Spinal Twist), Viparitakarani (The Inverted posture), Savasana (Complete Relaxation Posture).
- **Diet:** Avoid sours and masala food. Eat light vegetable foods. Take alkaline content fruits like sweet lemon and orange, pineapple etc.
- **Meditation:** Silent meditation for 20 minutes.

Asthma

- **Pranayama:** Rhythmic breathing, Nadi-Sodhana (alternate breathing without retention of the breath).
- **Asanas:** Vakrasana (Spinal Twist), Paschimottanasans (stretching the back and legs), Viparitakarani (The Inverted posture), Savasana (Complete Relaxation Posture).
- **Diet:** Avoid milk and milk product, non vegetarian food, eat fruits and vegetables in season and cooked rather than raw vegetables.
- **Meditation:** Silent Meditation for 15-30 minutes.

Constipation

- **Pranayama:** Bhastrika (bellows)
- **Asanas:** Uddiyana (Rising of the diaphragm), Trikonasana (triangle posture), Vakrasana (spinal twist), Paschimottanasans (stretching the back and legs), Sarvangasana (shoulder-stand), Supta-Vajrasana (The Supine Pelvic Posture).
- **Diet:** Include food with flares and roughage in daily diet. Plenty of raw vegetable, fruits, whole wheat chapaties etc. should be taken.

Diabetes

- **Pranayama:** Rhythmic breathing, Nadi-Sodhana (alternate breathing without retention of the breath).
- **Asanas:** Uddiyana (Rising of the diaphragm), Paschimottanasans (Stretching the back and legs), Ardhamatsyendrasana (Simplified version of the Yogi Matsyendra Posture), Sarvangasana (Shoulder-stand), Savasana (Complete Relaxation Posture).
- **Diet:** Avoid starchy food, eat more fibers and protein content food, restrictions should be followed.

Exhaustion

- **Pranayama:** Rhythmic breathing, Nadi-Sodhana (alternate breathing without retention of the breath).
- **Asanas:** Halasana (The Plough posture), Vakrasana (Spinal twist), Paschimottanasans (Stretching the back and legs), Sarvangasana (Shoulder-stand), Matasyasana (The fish posture), Sirshasana (Head-stand), Savasana (Complete Relaxation Posture)

Haemorroids

- **Pranayama:** Rhythmic breathing, that revitalizes the nervous system.
- **Asanas:** Uddiyana (Rising of the diaphragm), Viparitakarni (The Inverted Posture), Sarvangasana (Shoulder-stand), Matsyasanas (The fish posture), Shirsasana (Head-stand), Savasana (Complete Relaxation Posture).
- **Diet :** Only light easily digestable food with plenty of fibrous materials should be taken.

Headaches

- **Pranayama:** Rhythmic breathing, Nadi-Sodhana (alternate breathing).
- **Asanas:** Viparitakarani (The Inverted posture), Savasana (Complete Relaxation Posture).
- **Diet:** Easily digestable food.

Heart Trouble

- **Pranayama:** Rhythmic breathing, Nadi-Sodhana (alternate breathing).
- **Asanas:** Depending on the case Uddiyana (Rising of the Diaphragm), Trikonasana (Triangle Posture), Sirshasana (Head-stand), Savasna (Complete Relaxation Posture).
- **Diet:** Avoid foods containing fats and cholesterol. Eat more vegetable and fruits. Take light vegetarian meals.
- **Meditation:** Silent meditation for 20-30 minutes.

High blood pressure

- **Pranayama:** Rhythmic breathing, nadi-sodhna (alternate breathing, without retention of the breath).
- **Asanas:** Padmasana (the lotus position), Viparitakarani (the inverted posture), Savasana (complete relaxation posture).
- **Diet:** Consume less salt and fat. Eat 10 vegetables more.
- **Meditation:** Silent meditation for 20 minutes.

Indigestion

- **Pranayama:** Bhastrika (Bellows), Nadi-Sodhana (alternate breathing).
- **Asanas:** Uddiyana (Raising of diaphragm), Bhujangasana (The Cobra Position), Salabhasana (The Locust Posture), Dhanurasana (The Bow Posture), Trikonasana (Triangle Posture), Paschimottanasana (Stretching the back and legs), Sarvangasana (Shoulder-stand), Savasana (Complete Relaxation Posture).
- **Diet:** Include food with flares and roughage in daily diet. Plenty of raw vegetable, fruit whole-wheat chapaties etc. should be taken.

Liver Ailments

- **Pranayama:** Rhythmic breathing, Nadi-Sodhana (alternate breathing).

- **Asanas:** Uddiyana (Raising of diaphragm), Baddha Konasana (Yoga-Mundra, feet jointed), Mayurasana (The Peacock Posture), Paschimottanasana (Stretching the back and legs), Vipritakarani (The Inverted Posture), Savasana (Complete Relaxation Posture).
- **Diet:** Take liquid diet for a period and gradually change over to our usual. Eliminate fatty food and alcohol from diet.

Low Blood Pressure

- **Pranayama:** Rhythmic breathing, Bhastrika (Bellows).
- **Asanas:** Siddhasana (Posture of the Ac), Halasana (The Plough Posture), Paschimottasana (Stretching the back and legs), Sarvangasana (Shoulder-stand), Sirshasana (Head-stand), Savasana (Complete Relaxation Posture).

Obesity or Overweight

- **Pranayama:** Bhastrika (Bellows), Ujjayi (energy-renewing Pranayama), Kapala bhati (breathing that revitalizes the body).
- **Asanas:** Uddiyana (Raising of the diaphragm), Pachimottanasana (Stretching the back and legs), Trikonasana (Triangle Posture), Vakrasana (Spinal Twist), Sarvangasana (Shoulder-stand), Sirshasana (Head-stand), Dhanurasana (The Bow Posture).
- **Diet:** Restriction in diet are unavoidable, if reduction in weight is desired. Reduce drastically the intake of foods containing high proportion of carbohydrate and raw vegetables should form a major part of daily diet.

Sinus Trouble

- **Pranayama:** Nadi-Sodhana (alternate breathing), Surya Bhedana.
- **Asanas:** Viparitakarni (The Inverted Posture), Savasana (Complete Relaxation Posture).

Tuberculosis

- **Pranayama:** Rhythmic breathing, Nadi-Sodhana (alternative breathing).
- **Asanas:** Viparitakarani (The inverted Posture), Sarvangasana (Shoulder-stand), Sirshasana (Head-stand), Savasana (Complete Relaxation Posture).
- **Diet:** Take rich protein diet.
- **Meditation:** Silent meditation for 15-30 minutes.

Anxiety

- **Pranayama:** Kapalabhati (breathing and revives the body), Nadi-Sodhana (alternative breathing). Kumbhaka (retention of the breath).
- **Asanas:** Suptavajrasana (The Supine Pelvic Posture), Ardha-Matsyendrasana (Simplified version of the Yogi Matsyendra Posture), Trikonasana (Triangle Posture), Dhanurasana (The Bow Posture), Sarvangasana (Shoulder-stand), Savasana (Complete Relaxation Posture).
- **Meditation:** Japa, Ajapa silent meditation for 15-30 minutes.

Depression

- **Pranayama:** Rhythmic breathing, Surya-Bhedana (breathing that revitalizes the nervous system), Bhastrika (Bellows).
- **Asanas:** Vakrasana (Spinal Twist), Bhujangasana (The Cobra Position), Salabhasana (The Locust Posture), Halasana (The Plough Posture), Paschimottanasana (Stretching the back and legs), Sarvangasana (Shoulder-stand), Savasana (Complete Relaxation Posture).
- **Meditation:** Silent meditation for 15-20 minutes and antara mouna.

Fatigue

- **Pranayama:** Rhythmic breathing, Nadi-Sodhana (alternative breathing), Ujjayi (energy-renewing Pranayama).

- **Asanas:** Halasana (The Plough Posture), Paschimottanasana (Stretching the back and legs), Ardha Matsyendrasana (Simplified version of the Yogi Matsyendra Posture), Sarvangasana (Shoulder-stand), Matsyasana (The fish posture), Sirshasana (Head-stand) Savasana (Complete Relaxation Posture).
- **Meditation:** Silent meditation for 15-30 minutes.

Nervousness

- **Pranayama:** Rhythmic breathing, Nadi-Sodhana (alternative breathing).
- **Asanas:** Yoga-Mudra (The Symbol of Yoga), Vakrasana (Spinal Twist), Salabhasana (The locust Posture), Halasana (The Plough Posture), Mayurasana (The Peacock Posture), Viparitakarni (The Inverted Posture), Savasana (Complete Relaxation Posture).
- **Meditation:** Silent meditation for 15-30 minutes.

Frustration

- **Pranayama:** Rhythmic breathing, Nadi-Sodhana (alternative breathing), breathing that purifies.
- **Asanas :** Baddha Konasana (Yoga-Mudra, feet jointed), Halasana (The Plough Posture), Vakrasana (Spinal Twist), Sarvangasana (Shoulder Stand), Savasana (Complete Relaxation Posture).

Note: Above is a short list of various Pranayama, Meditation and Asana exercises corresponding to different disorders and illnesses, both functional and organic. It is absolutely essential to ensure the guidance of a properly trained and experienced expert, able to adapt these exercises, based on long experience of Yoga, to the needs of the individual.

NATUROPATHIC TECHNIQUES FOR HEALTHY LIVING

Naturopathy is a unique therapeutic system where the natural measures and sources are employed to keep a person hale and hearty. The basic concept of naturopathy is that a man is an integral component of nature and he is made up of five basic elements earth, water, fire, ether and air. In a state of imbalance of these elements the morbid matters start accumulating in the body and a person turns sick. Under naturopathy mud, water, air steam, sun-rays are employed to treat a patient. Under naturopathy body's in built power or immunity is toned-up to reconstitute healthy living through following technique:

1. Food and nutrition

For an ideal life style balanced diet plays a vital role. As we know there are four major aspects of health; physical, mental, social and spiritual. All these major aspects must be built-up for achieving an ideal health. The purpose of food is not to satisfy the hunger or the taste of tongue. Instead of this the purpose of diet must be to offer nutrition to body along with toning-up the mental spiritual health. This is significant since the body, mind and the inner conscience all the three are the strong pillars of health. Until all the three are healthy one can not term it as a complete health.

In the ancient Indian literature the food has been classified under three major categories, Sattvika, Rajasika and Tamasika. It is mentioned that those who desire for a good physical, mental and spiritual health, they must go for sattvika diet. Those who look for the two aspects of health *i.e.*, physical and mental only, they must opt for Rajasika diet. With pure food mental rejuvenation is ensured, it means that it helps to control body's functional components *i.e.*, Indryas. Further, pure food helps to generate mental concentration. The most suitable food is that which offers vitality to the body, reduces destructive forces, provides desired body temperature, must be digestable, non-stimulant and promotes memory, longevity strength, courage, mercy and co-operation.

All type of synthetic and confectionery food products, salt, alcoholic drinks, meat products, hydro peroxides used for food processing, plastic wares, pesticides. Chemical fertilizers and food, cosmetics, toilet products and various chemicals which come under the direct contact with the body may cause diseases on prolonged use.

The sprouted food and fresh eatables carry with them a higher percentage of enzymes, vitamins and essential minerals. Enzymes play a vital role in the biological process of digestive system. Moreover, it helps in providing essential portions for the regeneration of body cells, enzymes and also purifies the vital body fluid; blood. The cooked food entirely lacks the enzymes; as a result the body runs into enzymes deficiency. Enzymes are the key factor for health and longevity. Enzymes are present essentially in the sprouted and uncooked food material.

Life promoting food includes fresh unripe fruits, fresh green vegetables, sprouted cereals, wheat aqueous extract; milky Juice of sprouted seeds etc. Such biologically live food stuffs, contain high quality and partially digested carbohydrates, dextrose, sucrose lactobacilli, Saccharomyces proteins, fat, Vitamin-A, thiamine, riboflavin, niacin, pyridoxine, B-12 biotin, pantothenic acid, folic acid, choline, inosital, Para amino benzoic acid, vitamin–A, B, C, D, E, K, G, L, M and W all sorts of vitamins, Calcium, Phosphorus, Sulphur, Sodium, Magnesium, Chlorine, Iron, Manganese, Copper, Iodine, Zinc, Chromium, Molybdenum, Boron, Cadmium, Silicon etc. Such major mineral elements and those enzymes which participate in biological reactions, for combating physical and mental disorders and for maintenance of normal health.

Life supporting food items carry clinical importance in fighting against common ailments. Leading scientists related to Bionutrition such as Dr. Vigmor and other Biochemists have investigated the role of micro-nutrition for the management of various chronic disorders such as cancer, eczema, intestinal disorders, paralysis, arthritis, anemia, asthma, psoriasis, posrosis etc. With this it may be inferred that food of biological origin especially vegetable, non-cooked or sprouted cereals may built up the deteriorating physical and mental health of entire world. This may not be possible with other expensive therapies.

All types of fast food lack vital elements *e.g.*, Vitamin A, B, C, E, Calcium, Phosphorus and Iron. Due to the deficiency of the essential nutrients the persons who consume the fast food, turn highly irritable, pain in their calf muscles hand and feet, breathlessness, lack of concentration, heart and kidney disorders, lack of interest in studies, body imbalance, indigestion etc. several such clinical symptoms. Due to the presence of excess salt, sugar and several synthetic chemicals the fast food turn extremely poisonous and toxic. As a result the symptoms of liver, kidney disorders, hypertension and diabetes start appearing.

2. Hydrotherapy

1. **Steam bath:** Mild steam bath is extremely useful for various ailments, such as joint disorders, respiratory problems, oedema, asthma, obesity, apart from this it relieves liver disorders, hysteria, nephritis and prevents kidney failure.
2. **Neutral-full tub immersion bath:** Under massage during full immersion tub bath stimulates the functional activity of kidney and lungs which stimulates body's immunity. It relieves blood circulatory problems. More over it tones up the mental capacity and heart's strength.
3. **Hot full tub immersion bath:** It stimulates excretion of toxic wastes including uria, uria acid, ammonia, amino acid etc. It relives serious clinical problems such as ascites, oedema, respiratory congestion, pneumonia sciatica, arthritis, psoriasis, cystitis etc.
4. **Sauna bath:** The special feature of sauna bath is the use of hot and dry flow of air over the body. Due to this the blood capillaries get dilated and their oxygen retention capacity increases. Due to the hyper-thermic effect the melanin cells get activated.
5. **Hipbath:** It suits to relieve constipation, indigestion, prostrate gland's disorders, ulcer, insomnia, anemia etc.

6. **Hot hipbath:** It is useful to relieve inflammation of colon, urinary bladder, uterus prostate gland neuralgia, sciatica and spondilitis.
7. **Spinal bath:** Cold spinal bath acts as nervine tonic and general tonic. It tones-up the entire spinal nervous system.
8. **Hot-cold fermentation:** Different body parts are sequentially exposed to hot and cold treatment. Thus employing various techniques of hydrotherapy it is possible to prevent various ailments, keep healthy and thus avail an ideal healthy life.

3. Chromotherapy/Heliotherapy

Sun is the Atman of world. Sun controls the biological clock. The sun rays are indispensable not only for conservation of health but also for maintaining a healthy daily routine.

The infra rays exert the temperature regulation effect. Where as the ultra violet rays exert the physio-chemical and physio-biological effect and thus regulate the blood pressure. When sun rays belong to 0.4 μ to 0.65 μ wave length they turn useful to mankind, as during sunrise, where it tones up blood vessels. Such rays divert the blood flow towards skin and thus nourishes it. This activates the sensory nervous system, expands the constricted cells, regulates the peripheral resistance and thus lowers blood pressure. The sun rays of low density, as during morning and evening stimulates melamine formation and controls the synthesis.

4. Airings or 'Air bathing'

This means that once every so often one removes the clothing, allowing the pores to breath freely. This is extremely good for the body and improves the exterior tone of the neurovegetative system so that the body develops a wonderful power of resistance.

5. Fasting

Fasting for one day in even ten or twelve days, even one is in good health, purifies the body and thus can prevent the inception of diseases.

PHYSIOLOGICAL EFFECT OF ASANAS AND PRANAYAMA

Yoga is great ancient discipline, it is recognized as one of the most important and valuable gifts of our culture. The modern era, with the development of Science and Technology provides man more comfort for his basic necessities. But with these comforts only today the world is looking for solutions to solve the menacing problems of unhappiness, restlessness, conditional imbalance etc. Now the time has come to think of change in attitude and take a new dimension to solve the problems. There is the importance of Yoga and spiritual lure. Yoga is the gift of our Rishi culture, is a science and art of pure life style. Yoga offers man a conscious process to solve his problems. Yoga helps the man to evoke the hidden potentialities of man in a systematic and scientific way by which man becomes a full individual. All his faculties physical, mental, intellectual and emotional–developed in a harmony and integrated fashion to meet the all-round challenge. At the modern technological era, with its hectic speed the specialty of the yogic process is that the faculties get sharpened in time with the spiritual progress of man.

Yoga refers to a science, which helps to receive an ideal body build-up, mental elegance and excellence of consciousness. Yoga refers to an utmost height of physical, mental and spiritual health. Yoga refers to a science of total transformation of life. Yoga is an experiment for expression of truth of life. Yoga is the scientific process of transition of mind to a state of thoughtless sub-consciousness. Yoga is the philosophy of enjoying a life filled with comfort and pleasure. With Yoga practice each and every part of the body is affected with positive responses. Yoga and Asanas practice leads to flexibility, stability and functional integrity of nerves, muscles, vessels and blood capillaries. Asanas exert influences particularly over the heart, lungs, spinal cord and endocrine glands.

Yoga asanas impart physical and mental health over the body by controlling, regulating and balancing the effect over the sympathetic and parasympathetic nervous system. Through regular practice of Yoga normal physiological activities of nervous system, flexibility and contractibility of muscles vital capacity of lungs, blood circulation etc such biological processes are toned-up.

SPECIFIC EFFECT OF YOGASANA ON DIFFERENT SYSTEMS

1. Digestive system

Regular practice of Yogasanas activates the contractibility and physiological activity of stomach. Secretion of gastric Juices and hormones is increased. This helps to normalize the digestive processes. Through various studies it has been observed that by Yogasanas the peristaltic activity of intestines is increased. Moreover the absorbing capacity of Villi of small intestine is promoted by asanas. As a result of which adequate amount of nutrients are absorbed and desired supply of nutrition is made available to respective part of the body.

Yogasanas help to regulate these body processes, which thereby control gastric disorders, such as constipation, indigestion and acidity chiefly Yogasans, which cause positive effects on digestive system include Udar Shakti Vikasak Kriya, Padmasana, Vajrasana, Ardhayamatsayendrasana, Gomukhasana, Dhanurasana etc.

2. Respiratory System

A regular practice of deep Pranayama, Shavasana helps to regulate inspiration and expiration, which, in turn, provides adequate amount of oxygen in the body. Oxygen gets attached to blood and circulates the entire body.

A regular practice of Pranayama helps to prevent the infestation of bacterial infection in the lungs, more specifically the apical region of lungs. Especially the saprolactic bacteria are prevented, which subsequently cause T.B. Apart from this, the practice of finer techniques of pranayama, helps to relieve pulmonary disorders, such as bronchitis, pneumonia etc.

Effects on Endocrine Glands

It has been revealed through extensive researches that various meditative asanas, especially, Padmasana, helps to regulate endocrine secretion of serotonin and dopamine. In such persons in whom there is more secretion of adrenaline and cortisone, meditative asanas such as Padmasana helps to control such secretions. This helps to control serious disorders, such as high B.P., stress and anxiety. Thus, every asana regulate one or the other endocrine gland and thus offers physical and mental health and alleviate disorders.

Hyperactivity of parasympathetic nervous system results into aggressiveness and criminal behaviours in a person. On the other side, hyperactivity of sympathetic nervous system leads to inferiority complex and down with undue terror. With the result of Yogasanas the activity of both these nervous systems are well regulated and balanced, which leads to progressive growth and development of the person.

Effects on Muscular System

A regular practice of Yogic Asanas and Yogic processes tones up muscles and offers flexibility. It normalizes the physiological activities of muscles. Moreover, at minute levels it reconstitutes any damage to muscles. Yogasana accelerates the oxygen supply to blood and thus promotes the normal catabolism of glycogen to release desired level of energy. This helps to regulate the lactic acid level in blood and energy based different metabolic processes continue in a normal manner.

Effect of Yogasanas on Circulatory System

Regular practice of Yogasana promotes purification and circulation of blood in different systems of the body. An accelerated blood flow during Yoga practice helps to deplete various harmful deposits, such as cholesterol in the blood vessels. Thus Yogasanas helps to prevent various disorders related to cardiovascular system.

Physiological Effects of Pranayama on Respiratory system

The concept of pranayama is often mistaken for deep breathing. In the later situation, movement of breath is fast and forceful. There is no time for the cells to get soaked in the inhaled oxygen. In pranayama, the movements are so slow that there is adequate time for every alveoli to soak in oxygen.

1. The respiratory system is geared to aerate the internal atmosphere.
2. The venous return is much better due to phasic changes in breathing. The pulmonary vascular bed relaxes to accommodate more inflow of oxygen and blood. Better diffusion of gases occurs.
3. Elasticity of the lungs and the entire respiratory tract is maintained to a ripe old age.
4. The haemoglobin/oxygen saturation is enhanced during kumbhaka, as there is enough time for saturation.
5. The vital capacity, inspiratory volumes are increased. The dead space is reduced. The residual volume is decreased as more complete exhalation is performed.
6. The alveoli are exercised, which promotes excellent excretion of toxins and gases.
7. Due to more efficient changes in blood gases, proper maintenance of pH is achieved. This is the most important requisite, for better cellular function.
8. The ventilation of sinuses is made excellent, promoting good drainage.
9. The healthy movement of diaphragm massages the abdominal organs, improving their blood supply and aiding the venous drainage to the thoracic, cavity.

Physiological Effects of Pranayama on Digestive system

The flow of breath in sitali pranayama stimulates the taste buds. In other types, the salivary glands get rest.

1. The proper return of lymph and venous blood improves the digestive, absorptive and eliminating functions of the abdominal organs.
2. Constipation is relieved. The Stomach is massaged. The intestines are contracted and reflex expansion promotes excellent blood flow and venous return.
3. The liver and gall bladder are massaged, improving their function.
4. Due to reduction in sympathetic tone, acid secretion diminishes, relieving stress-related peptic disorders.

ROLE OF YOGA IN CORONARY HEART DISEASE

Coronary heart disease is the commonest cause of the cardiovascular disability and death. This pathological state includes "Arteriosclerotic Coronary Arterty Disease" and "Ischemic heart disease". The heart functions as the pumping station for the supply of blood to the whole body, whereas "Coronary arteries" which come out of the aorta, supply the blood and feed the heart muscles themselves. The main coronary arteries lie on the surface of the heart and small arteries penetrate into the cardiac muscle mass. The 'left coronary artery' supplies mainly the anterior part of the left ventricle, whereas the "right coronary artery" supplies most of the left ventricle.

The fresting coronary blood flows in the human being averages approximately 225 ml per minute, which is about 4 to 5 percentage of the total cardiac output. During extra work period the heart increase its cardiac output as much as four to five folds, and it pumps the blood against a higher than normal arterial pressure. Consequently the work output of the heart under severe conditions may increase as six to eight folds. The coronary blood flow also increases four to five folds to supply the extra nutrients needed by the heart.

Coronary Heart disease is a condition in which the heart muscle receives an inadequate amount of blood because of an interruption on its blood supply.

Depending on the degree of interruption, symptoms can range from a mild chest pain to a full scale heart attack. Generally, the symptoms manifest themselves when there is about a 75 per cent narrowing of coronary artery lumen. The underlying causes of this disease are many and varied. Two of the principal ones are "Atherosclerosis" and "Coronary artery spasm".

CAUSES

Atherosclerosis

Atherosclerosis (Something called 'hardening of the arteries') is a situation characterized by thickening of the arterial wall with:

Large number of smooth-muscle cells.

Deposits of cholesterol and other substances in the portion of the vessel wall closest to the lumen.

The mechanism that initiates this thickening is not clear, but it is known that cigarette smoking, high plasma cholesterol concentration, hypertension, diabetes and several other factors increase the incidence and the severity of the atherosclerotic process. The extra muscle cells and various deposit in the wall bulge into the lumen of the vessel and increase resistance to flow. This is usually progressive, often leading ultimately to complete occlusion. Acute coronary occlusion may occur because of:

Sudden formation of blood clot on the roughened vessel surface,

(*a*) The breaking off of a fragment of blood clot or fat then loges downstream, completely blocking smaller vessel, or

(*b*) A profound spasm of the vessel, smooth muscle.

Coronary Artery Spasm (CAS)

CAS is a condition in which the smooth muscle of a coronary artery undergoes a sudden contraction, resulting in vasoconstriction. It typically occurs in individuals with atherosclerosis and may result in chest pain during rest, chest pain during exertion, heart attacks and sudden death. Although the causes of coronary artery spasm are not well known, smoking, stress and alcoholism are said to be the triggering agents.

SYMPTOMS

The most common symptom is angina, where the patient suffers recurrent chest pain of effort, which normally does not produce pain, such as walking on level ground or climbing a flight of stairs. This is due to poor circulation of blood and oxygen to the heart muscle.

Unstable angina is the condition where the patient suffers chest pain, which is difficult to stabilize with drugs. Rhythmicity is lost. In unstable angina, the pain occurs at rest (Prinzmetal's angina), which means that the blood flow to the heart is grossly reduced. Emergency bypass surgery may be required.

Yet another manifestation of underlying ischemia is occasional chest pain often overlooked as being due to wind, giddiness, or the presence of hypertension.

Yogic Management

Yoga insists that prevention is better than cure. Asanas relieve angina pain very quickly. Asanas and pranayama practiced regularly keep CHD at bay, each of the different practices contributing in its own way.

When the process of atherosclerosis advances, the blood vessels are narrowed beyond a critical degree. So strokers, heart attacks and malfunctioning of all organs occur. Thus, the elasticity of the blood vessels is lost and pressure rises in the blood vessels. Asanas maintain the elasticity of tissues and prevent changes in pressure.

Yoga is the wonderful solution to all circulatory problems. It works by keeping the two gates of the body—the circulatory system and the respiratory system—clean. Regional circulation (blood flow to each organ) reduces, as one grows older. There is a fall in perfusion pressure, dampening the flow of blood to vital organs.

Effect of Standing Asanas

Standing poses strength the cardiac reserve. No lactic acid is formed and hence fatigue of the muscle does not occur. Lung capacity can be increased by standing poses. As the various returns are higher, varicose veins do not occur and the pumping efficiency of the heart is higher; Endurance is built up. All standing poses alternatively increase and decrease the flow of blood to the other organs like the liver, spleen, kidneys.

Effect of Forward Bending Asanas

Forward bends stretch the posterior surface of the abdominal organs. Forward bends soothe the nerves and improve the function of the sympathetic nervous system.

Forward bends bring down the heart rate and pulse. Since the body is parallel to the floor, gravity does not affect the heart and blood flows to both extremities without strain. The sympathetic nervous system is given a tremendous boost of energy so that when these poses are completed one feels extremely energetic and refreshed. Forward bends trend to close the chambers of the heart.

Effect of Back-Bending Asanas

All back bends stretch the cardiac vessels, so that blood flow increases and blocks cannot occur. It is precisely for this reason that patients with coronary ischemia are taught back bends and no forward bending asanas initially.

The massaging force literally breaks down the molecules of obstruction in the arteries. This natural outcome is called 'physiological bypass'. The quality of contraction of a muscle fibre is directly proportional to the initial length of the muscle. As all back bends stretch the thoracic organs, venous return is enhanced. It improves coronary blood flow.

The flow of blood to the frontal lungs is greatly increased in all back bending asanas. Elasticity of the tissues is maintained so that the vital capacity of the lungs does not decrease with age. Because of increased blood flow to the lungs, oxygen uptake is stimulated. There will be no areas of hypo perfusion in the lungs of a yogi.

A healthy lung leads to a healthy heart. If the lungs perform efficiently with excellent intake of oxygen, the myocardium gets the benefits as the oxygen rich blood flow into the heart.

Effect of Inverted Asanas

Inverted poses drain all the venous blood from all organs, revitalizing them with fresh blood. An important effect of inverted poses is on the vasculature of the legs. The constant strain of gravity and the effort needed to pump the blood upward to the heart is removed and rest is given to the entire musculature and nerves of the leg. So, varicose veins do not occur. The small muscles inside the calf, which continuously pump the lymph up the body, get rest.

Practice of inverted postures re-establishes the blood flow to the heart and penetrates to the level of the microcirculation. The coronary cells cannot die prematurely. The cerebral nerves are rested in this pose and one feels soothed with revitalization of the centers in the brain that control the heart.

Pranayama

As a deep inhalation is done, enhanced venous return occurs along with better lymphatic drainage. The rhythmic up and down movement of the diaphragm massages the abdominal organs, increasing their circulation and efficiency. Blood flow changes in the kidneys, permitting better filtering action of water and solutes.

Changes in coronary flow occur during paranayama, allowing more blood to flow into the coronary vessels. The input of healthy blood into the lungs increases, allowing better uptake of oxygen and build up of adenosine triphosphate (ATP) molecules at the cellular level, which is the source of energy to the cell. Blood flow in the brain can change with pranayama where a prolonged exhalation soothes the neurons by increasing the blood flow. Quietening of the mind during pranayama is very beneficial to cardiac patient, reducing stress on the sympathetic nerves.

Relaxation of the nervous system allows excellent perfusion of blood with the coronaries relieving oxygen starvation of tissues. Angina vanishes rapidly after pranayamic practice. It is the only science that delivers oxygen directly without strain and facilitates storage at the cellular level.

Suggested Practices

- **Asanas:** 1. Breathing practices, 2. Uttkatasana, 3. Bhujangasana, 4. Makrasana, 5. Padmasana, 6. Savasana
- **Pranayama:** 1. Sectional breathing, 2. Nadi Sodhan, 3. Ujjayi pranayama
- **Meditation:** Silent meditation for 20-30 mints.
- **Diet:** Avoid foods containing fats and cholesterol. Eat more vegetables and fruits. Take light vegetarian meals.

YOGIC MANAGEMENT OF DIABETES

Introduction

Diabetes is a disease of the prosperous and in wealthy countries. It is one of the major health problems. Dietary sugars and starch are broken down to glucose by the process of digestion and this glucose is the major fuel for the various processes, organs and cells of the body. Glucose metabolism is under the control of the harmone insulin, which is secreted by the pancreas, a large gland behind the stomach. When this gland becomes stressed or exhausted, the hormone insulin becomes deficient in quantity or sensitivity. As a result, the blood sugar level becomes high and uncontrolled, then patient suffers from Diabetes.

Type I: Insulin Dependent Diabetes Mellitus (IDDM) or Juvenile onset

In this type of diabetes the hormone insulin is completely or almost completely absent from the islets of langerhans and plasma, and insulin treatment is essential. It is called insulin dependent diabetes because of compulsory periodic insulin administration, to control the rise of blood-glucose level. It can occur at any age, though it most commonly occurs during younger age.

Type II: Non-Insulin Dependent Diabetes Mellitus (NIDDM) or Maturity Onset

This type of diabetes is much more common than juvenile onset and most often occurs in people who are over 40 and over weight. Since it occur in the later stage in life, it is termed as maturity onset diabetes. In this condition of diabetes the hormone insulin is often present in plasma at near-normal or even above normal level and additional insulin is not required to sustain life and to maintain normal blood glucose level. Patient with this type of diabetes produces little or excessive insulin in their pancreas, it either is not enough for proper function or is not being produced quickly enough to influence glucose levels in the blood effectively. This happen probably due to defects in molecular machinery that mediates the action of insulin on its target cells. That is why this diabetes is called non- insulin dependent diabetes mellitus.

Causes

Yogic science recognizes two interrelated causes of diabetes. Firstly long term devitalzaticm and sluggishness of the digestive process due to dietary abuse, overeating, obesity and lack of exercise. High intake of sugar and carbohydrate rich diet is especially implicated. If a person takes a large amount of sugar, sweets or chocolates etc. then his pancreas is ready to respond by pouring out a large amount of insulin to rapidly manage the rocketing blood sugar level without incident.

However, if such a sugar-rich diet is eaten every day, the pancreas is being called upon constantly to secrete enormous amounts of insulin, and it begins to get tired and become depleted. Insulin production in response to sugar stimulation becomes increasingly inadequate. As a result, the blood remains saturated with sugar for long periods of time, it is then only a matter of time before diabetes is diagnosed. This usually occurs when the patient attends the doctor for investigation of one of the symptoms of high blood sugar *e.g.* an excessive thirst or urination, a resistant skin or urinary infection or failing eyesight.

The second causative factor is that diabetes is stress related. The stress and frustrations of modern sedentary man largely manifest on the mental and emotional planes, unlike our ancestors who had to wage a physical battle for survival. Nevertheless, the adrenal glands are in a constant state of activation, spilling the "stress hormone" adrenaline into the blood stream. This is a potent stimulus to the body to mobilize glucose into the blood. In this way a constant heavy burden of worries and an anxieties imposes a constant demand for insulin secretion, which can ultimately precipitates especially in conjunction with a sugar.

Symptoms

The most marked symptoms are polyuria and polydipsia. The patient may pass lot of urine in 24 hours. The urine is clear and of low specific gravity (1002-2004) and osmolatity. The osmotic effect of increased levels of blood glucose causes more thirst and hunger. These classified symptoms, however, are not the normal presentation.

Sometimes the patient suffers a frozen shoulder and this can be a manifestation of diabetes. Lethargy, weight loss and easy susceptibility to infections, particularly of the skin (like a simple boil or fungal infection) excessive hunger, craving for sweets and sweating are some of the other symptoms.

Normally, the fasting level of blood glucose is less than 90 mg/dl and the post prandial (2 hours) level is less than 120 mg/dl. If the post-prandial sugar level is between 150 and 200 mg, the condition is labelled as an impaired tolerance, and if above 200. It is frank diabetes.

Yogic Management of Diabetes

Yogasana is ideally suited for both types of Diabetes Mellitus. In Insulin Dependent diabetes Mellitus, asanas help to prevent an increase in insulin required over the years. In NIDDM, asanas help to normalize blood sugar due to the high intensity workout. Yogic exercises can either be of high or low intensity, depending on the clinical condition. Young active diabetics can be made to practice very intense asanas in a dynamic manner, which will increase the cellular activity of the muscle, which needs more sugar. The advanced asanas require a lot of energy and this helps normalize blood sugar but, if the person is obese, asana practice is difficult and it is easier to reduce weight by other means and then take up Yoga.

The single advantage of the asana system is that the internal organs, which are directly affected by the geometric shape of the asana itself. Even an elderly diabetic can practice it without any danger.

The force of arterial flow can be increased and directed to any organ, which is of immense use in the diabetic state. In standing poses, the skeletal muscles increase their uptake of sugar. Hence, the tissues retain insulin sensitivity. Capillary changes are easily prevented by Yoga as the action is on the vessel wall.

Yoga is microcellular in its action. At the internal organs are massaged, sensitivity to insulin and uptake of sugar are enhanced. Twisting poses squeeze the intestines and massage them. Hence, stagnation of colonic contents due to autonomic dysfunction cannot occur. Asanas also pressurize the pancreas in an effort to improve the secretary status. The massage of the pancreas by forward bends and twisting helps to release more insulin in response to food.

Backward bends, being very strenuous, help to reduce blood sugar. Backbends improve blood supply to all abdominal and pelvic organs. This ensures healthy cellular integrity and due to the massage no deposit are formed. Forward bends increase the gastric fire and help healthy digestion of food. This prevents fluctuations of sugar levels in a diabetic. Burning up of excess sugar is promoted by the stimulation of gastric fire.

Pranayama definitely increase the natural immunity of body and vital capacity of lungs. Pranayama is highly valuable for improving oxygen perfusion to tissues. As it also removes stress on the system, progression of blockage is arrested. Oxygen delivery to the tissue is systematic and sure. Tissue hypoxia never occurs. Sympathetic and parasympathetic stabilization prevent autonomic dysfunction.

It is very useful for all complication of the diabetic state particularly cardiac autonomic dysfunction, retinopathy and peripheral arterial occlusive conditions.

Simplified Yogic Practice Chart For Diabetic Patient

- **Asanas:** Ardha matsyendrasana, Trikonasana, Vakrasana, Bhujangasana, Dhanurasana, Matsyasana, Savasana.
- **Pranayama:** Vibhaga; Nadishodhan; Bhramari.
- **Meditation:** Silent Meditation for 15-20 minutes.
- **Diet:** Avoid starchy Food, eat more Fibers and Protein content. Food restrictions should be followed.

YOGIC MANAGEMENT OF HYPERTENSIVE PATIENT

Hypertension or high blood pressure is the most common disease affecting the heart and blood vessels. There is an agreement at large that blood pressure of 120/80 is normal in a healthy adult. Borderline high blood pressure is defined as diastolic pressure between 85 and 90 mild high blood pressure is diastolic pressure between 91 and 104 and moderate high blood pressure is diastolic pressure between 105 and 115 severe high blood pressure is diastolic pressure of 116 or higher. Isolated systolic hypertension is systolic pressure greater than 160 in those whose diastolic pressure is less than 90.

Hypertension could be caused by an increase in cardiac output or in total peripheral resistance or both. In reality however the major abnormality in most cases of well-established hypertension is increased total peripheral resistance caused by abnormally reduced arteriolar lumen for more than 95 per cent of the persons with hypertension. The cause of hypertension is known and in that condition it is called 'essential hypertension'. The remaining percentage is secondary hypertension which has an identifiable underlying cause such as kidney diseases, adrenal hyper secretion etc.

Psychological, physiological and environmental factors are only three of the many factors that lead to high blood pressure. A common misconception is that ageing causes hypertension. It doesn't always though the universal average for the onset of hypertension in the late thirties. Overweight people and those who are tense and excitable are especially susceptible to hypertension; emotional conflicts are also a cause.

The cells of the kidneys secrete the hormone rennin which is influenced by sympathetic stress, the stress faced by the body and the mind. Hence rennin secretion may well be under mental influences. Rennin reacts with a chemical known as angiotensinogen and this sets off a series of chemical changes producing an end product known as angiotensin which causes vaso-constriction and elevated blood pressure. This situation is also influenced by the hormone aldosterone which retains salt and water through the kidneys aggravating the condition.

The normal blood pressure under resting conditions should be 120/80 mm of mercury. Both the systolic and diastolic pressure can be affected. Both have to be made normal with treatment. The level at which the systolic pressure should be treated is 140 mm and the diastolic 90 mm. Pressure of 130 to 135 mm systolic and 85 to 88 diastolic are labelled as high normal. Systolic pressure is the measurement made when the heart is contracting and the muscle pushes out blood from the ventricles and in the process presses on the coronary arteries reducing its own blood supply. Hence if the diastolic pressure remains above 90 mm coronary artery filling will be jeopardized.

This sympathetic stress is reduced, the diastolic pressure is reduced and coronary filling is normalized. High blood pressure is a serious condition and requires prompt attention because it is an underlying factor that brings about other cardiovascular and renal disorders like stroke heart disease, kidney trouble and hardening of the arteries. The pressure can remain stable or fluctuate. The latter is a dangerous can produce a stroke high blood pressure works insidiously. It affects the heart and blood vessels and then indirectly other organs. When blood vessels get constricted, the heart must work harder and a time comes when its own coronary arteries can no longer nourish the heart then heart disease develops. Similarly hypertension affects the brain and kidneys resulting in stroke and uraemia both fatal conditions.

Yoga is an excellent means of treating high blood pressure. As hypertension begins in the mind Yoga is of prime value. However, weight loss is essential for yogic management to be of use and only dynamic exercises can reduce weight. Yoga can be practiced side by side with weight-reducing exercises as Yoga alone can prevent vascular complications due to its massaging effect on the arteries. Asanas make the arteries and capillaries elastic and allow more blood to flow into various areas resulting in better relaxation of those tissues.

The sympathetic nervous system is always set on higher level of charge in hypertensive. By the practice of Yoga the tone of sympathetic discharge is brought down. Savasana relaxation is like sleep. It is conscious sleep. In sleep the nervous system recoups itself, the same happens in Yoga. There is yet another difference. In sleep the subconscious mind is still active and the nerves are still tense. In Yoga every part of the nervous system is kept passive and the relaxation of the nerves is far better.

The state of nerves in a hypertensive is one of overuse and decreased excitability. Excitabilities means the ability to transmit an impulse. In a hypertensive the nerves are exhausted and overstrained. As the excitability of the nerve is inversely proportional to the degree of activity, Yoga restores the elasticity of the nervous system. A proper sleep pattern is essential for all particularity for a hypertension patient. The delicate biorhythm in the body which influences the neuro-endocrine circuit should never be upset.

Forward bends are the linchpin of yogic management without which the pressure never normalizes. Fluctuations of blood pressure are controlled by these poses. When these posses are practiced the thoracic cage is brought parallel to the ground and the heart slows down as there is no strain to push the blood against gravity to the brain. With the heart rate slowing the cardiac output also slows. These poses increase in the tone and the excess sympathetic tone is reduced. There is then a decrease in the tone of the vasomotor centre in the brain (which controls the tone of the arteries) and blood pressure drops.

Setu bandha, sarvangasana rests the brain and again the cortical centers are rested and the mind is kept at its root. The lift of the diaphragm and lungs and the emotional centre on the heart which occurs in this asana stabilizes the blood pressure. Savasana with normal inhalation and prolonged exhalation stabilizes the sympathetic nervous system. The longer exhalation relaxes the sympathetic nerves and the BP is controlled.

Pranayama greatly influences the circulatory system. With each inhalation and exhalation the output of blood flow to the body varies. This changes the blood pressure. In prolonged inhalation (never done by normal people) the right ventricular (RV) output increases and left ventricular (LV) output falls. In exhalation the reverse occurs. Due to the increase in duration of inhalation and exhalation significant pressure changes can occurs. The emphasis on inhalation or exhalation depends on blood pressure being high or low. The overdrive of the sympathetic nervous system is most amenable to reduction by the practice of pranayama. The elasticity of the aorta and major blood vessels is well maintained.

The steady rhythmic breathing helps control the autonomic system. As the breathing rate reduces the stress on the body is reduced. The hibernative state removes the accumulated stress. All this happens over a period of time.

Useful Yoga Practices

- **Asanas:** 1. Ardhakati chakrasana, 2. Garudasana, 3. Ardhamatsyendrasana, 4. Bhujangasana, 5. Usthrasana, 6. Savasana
- **Pranayama:** 1. Sectional breathing, 2. Nadishodhan pranayama, 3. Brahmari ,
- **Diet :** Consume less salt and fat. Eat leafy vegetables more.

OBESITY, CAUSES, COMPLICATIONS AND YOGIC MANAGEMENT

Obesity is spreading like an epidemic not only in the developed countries but also in the developing countries, all are facing this problem a like. Why there is this sudden increase in the incidence of obesity? There are several theories to explain this. However given the facts that obesity leads to several complications it must be considered the condition to be treated with utmost priority. While there are several facts to the problem of obesity. It is clear that obesity is associated with shortening of life span and complications which make life difficult for the individual.

It is also commonly believed that obesity often result from endocrine disturbances but in fact that is exceedingly rare apart from hyper insulinism. Crushing disease and occasionally myxoedema, frotlich's syndrome is due to hypothalamic and not due to pituitary dysfunction. The obesity which so commonly starts after the pregnancy or the menopause has probably little or no endocrine connection.

Causes

(*i*) **Psychogenic Obesity:** Studies of obese patients show that a large proportion of obesity results from psychogenic factors. Perhaps the most common psychogenic factor contributing to obesity is the prevalent idea that healthy eating habits requires three meals a day and that each meal must be filing. Many children are forced into this habit by over-solicitous parents and the children continue to practice it throughout life.

(*ii*) **Genetic Factors in Obesity:** The genes can direct the degree of feeding in several different ways including (*i*) a genetic abnormality of feeding centre that sets the level of nutrient storage high or low, and (*ii*) abnormal hereditary psychic factors that either watch the appetite or causes the person to eat as a release mechanism.

(*iii*) **Genetics-Leptin:** It is widely accepted that leptin – a naturally occurring hormone that controls the appetite - may be one of the causes of obesity. When full fat cells release the hormone leptin, it curbs appetite. If leptin production is hindered, the fat cells are unable to signal that they are full, and weight gain occurs. Research into leptin is only just beginning although the leptin–obesity link appears to have been disproved by some initial studies.

(*iv*) **Genes-Hormones:** A small minority of cases of obesity can be explained by glandular or hormonal problems. One such problem is clinical hypothyroidism, where there is not enough thyroid hormone to control normal rates of metabolism. In Crushing's syndrome also where the production of the corticosteroid hormones is abnormal sex hormones can also affect obesity. In women, the balance of female sex hormones determines body fat level during adolescence, pregnancy and the menopause. Changes in energy intake desire for food and specific cravings occur at various stages of the menstrual cycle. Some women appear to be more susceptibly than others to hormonal changes and many overweight woman cite pregnancy as the time when their problem started.

(*v*) **Illness and /or Drugs:** Some illness can lead to obesity or a tendency to gain weight. So far we have dealt with an excess of energy/calories, in but lack of calories out is also one of the major causes of weight gain and obesity. Lack of physical activity caused by watching too much TV, or playing too many computer games is strongly associated with obesity levels especially in young people.

(*vi*) **Childhood over nutrition:** The number of fat cells in the adult body is determined almost entirely by the amount of fat stored in the body during early life. The rate of formation of new fat cells is especially rapid in obese infants and it continues at a lesser rate in obese children until adolescence thereafter the number of fat cells remains almost constant throughout the life. Thus, it is believed that overfeeding children, especially in infancy and to a lesser extent during the older years of childhood, can lead to lifetime obesity.

Complication of obesity

(*i*) **Osteoarthritis of knees:** In almost any obese individual some degree of osteoarthritis of the knees is inevitable so that they develop pain in knees by the age of 50 and walk with a wadding gait.

(*ii*) **Varicose veins:** Torturous veins in the legs result from damage to their directly related with obesity and it has been documented that a weight reduction brings the blood pressure down without the use of drugs.

(*iii*) **Hiatus hernia:** A large accumulation of fat in the abdominal cavity pushes the uppermost part of stomach into the thorax through the diaphragmatic aperture. This can lead to symptoms such as heartburn and sour regurgitation.

(*iv*) **Breathlessness:** An average obese individual is all time carrying an extra load of fat of about 15-20 kg. For this reason alone one can become breathless while climbing up stairs. However, this is not all. The extra fat has its own blood supply and in this way puts some demand on the heart. There is an associated increase in blood pressure. All these factors may lead to a mild heart failure; which also may contribute to the breathlessness experienced by obese individuals. Weight reduction may reduce the symptoms.

(*v*) **Sleep Apnea:** A grossly obese individual who has about 20 kg extra fat in the body has about 300-400 gms. extra fat in the tissues of the throat and back of tongue. Snoring is a common problem. In these individuals; when they sleep, the tongue falls back and closes the throat. A chocking sensation results which awakes the patient from sleep. There are almost 20-50 awakenings per night with the result of that the individual becomes sleep-deprived and feels drowsy in the daytime. Of late 'CPAP therapy' has been developed for such sufferers. It is given using a machine which delivers positives pressure breathing a tube fitted in the mouth. The person has to sleep with the gadget put on with the tube in his mouth and tied securely to the head.

(*vi*) **Coronary heart Disease:** Both sudden death and clinically documented heart attacks are more common in obese people especially males while females suffer from coronary heart disease.

(*vii*) **Diabetes—(NIDDM):** It is not unusual to see an obese person becoming a diabetic. In fact obesity is always associated with insulin resistance lack of affectiveness of insulin—the blood sugar lowering hormone

(*viii*) **Back Problems:** Since the enlarges protuberant abdomen changes the way a person stands it deforms the backbone and leads to what is known as spondylolisthesis. Once acquired the wrong posture cannot be corrected unless the excess of body fat is got rid of.

Management of Obesity

Diet management

This is probably the only way available to reduce body weight in obese persons. If we take into account the daily calorie consumption as around 2200-2400 cals and the fact that IG of fat produces 9 Cals then it can be calculated that a totally fasting individual will lose around 50 G of fat per day. When the obvious weight loss is much more than this it is due to the loss of water and electrolytes and which is soon regain once normal diet is resumed.

Yogic management

In Yoga thereby we practice asanas not only for the sake of burning extra calories, but also to develop body awareness to understand the language of our body the way it works and what suits it best. From this understanding we can modify or adjust our diet and lifestyle to suit the needs of our body and mind. Even though the aim of Yoga is not just reduction of weight this is bound to happen as an outcome of our increased self-awareness.

Surya Namaskar (salutation to the sun) is most important for the treatment of obesity. Surya Namaskar is a complete practice itself because it is a combination of asana, pranayama, mantra and meditation. This practice has a unique influence on the endocrine and nervous system helping to correct metabolic imbalance that cause and perpetuate obesity. Being a dynamic practice it is also an excellent exercise equated to cycling, jogging or swimming. The best asanas for obesity are the Pawanamuktasana. Series for the digestive system which help to remove extra fat from the abdomen hips and thighs and activate the energy in the lower pranic centers. These practices are very good for strengthening the abdominal muscles which are usually very flaccid in the obese patient. It also helps to burn the extra fat tissue of the momentum which is fold of peritoneum in the abdomen very rich in fat tissue.

The practices from the shakthi bandha series are also effective in reducing obesity. Kriyas like jaladhauti, shankha, prakshalana etc. and asanas like halasana, paschimottanasana, dhanurasana, sarvangasana, matsyasana, padhastasana, Yogamudra massage the abdominal organ and to release the power of the manipurak chakra the source of willpower and self-assertiveness (which is often weak in the obese patient) and that governs all our metabolic processes. The pranayama practices recommended for obesity are also the more dynamic forms which stimulate the metabolism they include bhastrika, kapalabhati and suryabhedi which are performed along with balancing practices like nadi shodhan, ujjayi, sheetali and sheetkari are relaxing cooling practices which influence different hypothalamic centers which give control over thirst and the feeling of satisfaction with healthy quantities and qualities of food.

Useful practices

- **Suryanamaskar**
- **Asanas:** Parivart, Trikonasana, Paschimottanasana, Usthrasana, Ardhamatsyendrasana, Yoga Mudra, Dhanurasana, Navasana, Halasana, Sarvanagasana, Matsyasana.
- **Pranayama:** Suryabhedi, Ujjayi, Nadisodhan.
- **Kriya :** Bhastrika, Kalpalabhati.
- **Meditation:** Silent meditation 15-20 minutes.

EFFECT OF SURYA NAMASKAR ON DIFFERENT SYSTEM OF BODY

Surya Namaskar practice interacts with the physical organs of the body directly, by applying pressure, massaging, stretching and generally toning up and supporting internal tissue structures. This aids the eliminative functions as well as stimulating nervous energy. It enhances our wellbeing.

Respiratory System

In Surya Namaskar a deep rhythmic breathing process is synchronized with each movement, which completely empties the lungs of all, traces of stale gas and refills them with fresh, clean, oxygenated air. All the pockets of the lungs are expanded stimulated and then cleaned. The oxygen content of the blood is increased, which improves the overall vitality and oxygenation of the cells and tissue of the body and brain. Sluggishness and lethargy are rapidly overcome. This practice is also good for the prevention of diseases such as tuberculosis, which develop in the little used, stagnant regions of the lungs.

Circulatory System

The regular practice of Surya Namaskar improves flow of blood, to speeds up the elimination of morbid matter and introduces fresh oxygen and nutrient of all the cells, and general circulation is improved. The cardiac muscles are strengthened. Microcirculation to the heart is increased and reducing the chances of heart attack. Sluggish circulation, cold hands and feet, blood vessel diseases and general fatigue can also be eliminated. The circulation of lymph, which is prime importance in fluid balance and in combating infections, is toned, the body gains an increased resistance to infections, and a better ability to heal.

Digestive System

The alternate stretching and compressing movements of Surya Namaskar tone the whole digestive system by thoroughly massaging all the abdominal viscera. This not only enhances elimination but also increases the digestive fire, promoting a healthy appetite, and complete and rapid assimilation of food.

Skin

The skin is the important and Largest body organ and apart from holding the body together serves to regulate body temperature, as well as excreting waste matter through **perspiration.** When there is an excess of poisonous matter in the blood, it comes out through the skin in the form of boils, rashes and pimples. As Surya Namaskar produces perspiration, speeds up circulation and enhances the elimination of wastes through the digestive and urinary systems, it cleanses and endows the practitioner with a clean, glowing complexion, which is an important sign of health. Many skin disease caused by subcutaneous toxin deposits, such as pimples and eczema, can be removed. Bad odours from the body are eliminated, and the overall circulation of blood to the skin is improved. When Surya Namaskar is practiced in the early morning hours while facing the rising sun, ultraviolet light rays are absorbed through the skin. At sunrise, these rays are at their greatest intensity and are thought to be very beneficial for healthy as well as being responsible for vitamin D production.

Nervous System

In the twelve movements of Surya Namaskar, the spinal column is systematically stretched and compressed to the maximum extent, stimulating circulation in the whole spinal cord, and all nerve plexuses. Surya Namaskar tones nerve flows by stimulating internal organs. It stretches organs. It stretches nerves, work on the spine and enhances prans, which activates brain centers. The whole nervous system is activated and seems to wake up.

The Endocrine System

The endocrine glands are the most vital and mysterious of all systems of the body. They play an overall role in the coordination and integration of all physiological process and yet very little are actually known about them. The main function of the endocrine glands is the production and secretion of hormones, chemical substances are released into the bloodstream and carried throughout the body to act upon particular organs.

Pituitary Gland

The pituitary gland is master gland of human body. It has many hormonal secretions, which control the body's growth and development, by increasing the flow of blood to the head and through its effects on the nervous system. Surya Namaskar stimulate the hypothalamus, which regulates the pituitary action. The practice of Surya Namaskar thereby has a direct and beneficial effect on this vital centre and the whole body.

Pineal Gland

The pineal gland is situated in the brain. Yogic Science states that it has a vital function and acts as connecting link between the different levels of awareness above and beyond the physical plane. Surya Namaskar plays an ideal role in the maintenance of this important gland.

Pancreas

The Pancreas is located behind the stomach at the level of the solar plexus. Parts of this important gland produce the hormone insulin, which controls the body's ability to store and utilize sugar. Surya Namaskar compresses the abdominal organs, which press onto the pancreas especially during backward bending in bhujangasana.

Multiple Choice Questions

1. Regular practice of which asana makes a person tolerant?
   A. Kukutasana B. Virasana
   C. Dhanurasana D. Mayurasana
2. Regular practice of which asana prevents the loss of the nectar secreted by bindu chakra?
   A. Dhanurasana B. Matseyendrasana
   C. Mayurasana D. Kurmasana
3. Sankhaprakshalan kriya should not be performed by the person suffering from which of the following disease?
   A. Heart B. High blood pressure
   C. Epilepsy D. All of the above
4. Which of the following pranayama should not be performed by patient of epilepsy?
   A. Suryabhedi B. Nadishodhan
   C. Shitli D. Ujjayi
5. The disorders of heart and lungs arise due to deterioration of which vayu?
   A. Prana vayu B. Apana vayu
   C. Udana vayu D. Vyana vayu
6. Which of the following asana destroys the intestinal worms?
   A. Salabhasana B. Gomukhasana
   C. Chakrasana D. Kukkutasana
7. Which of the following kriya activates nervous system?
   A. Vatsara B. Varisara
   C. Agnisara D. None of these
8. The patients of cervical spondylitus should not perform which type of asana?
   A. Backward bending asana
   B. Forward bending asana
   C. Left bending asana
   D. Right bending asana
9. Practise of which kriya is useful in curing leprosy?
   A. Gajakarni B. Kunjal
   C. Vamana D. Dhauti
10. Which asana is best for diabetic patient?
    A. Chakrasana
    B. Ardha matsyendrasana
    C. Gomukhasana
    D. Mandukasana
11. Which asana is useful in maintaining shukra dhatu in body?
    A. Sarvangasana B. Mandukasana
    C. Shirshasana D. Halasana
12. Practice of which asana is useful in curing hernia?
    A. Bhadrasana B. Sarvangasana
    C. Vajrasana D. Utkatasana
13. Which mudra should not be performed by patients of low blood pressure?
    A. Mahamudra B. Mahabheda mudra
    C. Kaki mudra D. Ashwini mudra
14. Which kriya is useful in eliminating diabetes disease?
    A. Neti B. Dhauti
    C. Vasti D. Nauli
15. Regular practice of which asana checks the process of ageing?
    A. Gomukhasana B. Makarasana
    C. Sarvangasana D. Kurmasana
16. Which asana purifies blood?
    A. Salabhasana B. Gomukhasana
    C. Mayurasana D. Mandukasana
17. Which mudra is useful in eliminating obesity and heaviness of body?
    A. Prana B. Gyana
    C. Linga D. Surya
18. Which mudra is useful in treatment of paralysis and arthritis?
    A. Shunya mudra B. Prana mudra
    C. Vayu mudra D. Apana mudra
19. Which mudra is useful in treatment of skin and blood disorders?
    A. Varuna mudra B. Surya mudra
    C. Prana mudra D. Vayu mudra

20. Which asana is best for patients of thyroid?
A. Gomukhasana B. Shirshasana
C. Mandukasana D. Sarvangasana

21. Which asana cures naval displacement?
A. Sarvangasana B. Mayurasana
C. Supta-vajrasana D. Vajrasana

22. Which asana is best for people suffering from phobia?
A. Mayurasana B. Singhasana
C. Makarasana D. Salabhasana

23. By regular practice of which asana the digestive fire is stimulated so much that it can digest even the poision?
A. Mandukasana B. Garurasana
C. Mayurasana D. Matsayasana

24. Which asana is best for people suffering from gas problem and acidity?
A. Uttkatasana B. Kurmasana
C. Pawanmuktasana D. Makarasana

25. Which pranayama helps in eliminating mental tension?
A. Brahmri B. Bhastrika
C. Kevali D. Plavini

26. People suffering from which disorder should not perform suryabhedi pranayama?
A. Ulcer B. Low blood pressure
C. Asthma D. All of the above

27. Which pranayama purifies blood?
A. Ujjayi B. Sahita
C. Shitli D. Shitkari

28. Which pranayama is useful for people suffering from low blood pressure?
A. Shitli B. Shitkari
C. Nadishodhan D. Suryabhedi

29. Which pranayama should not be peformed by patients of high blood pressure and heart?
A. Shitli, Murchha
B. Shitkari, Suryabhedi
C. Ujjayi, Bhastrika
D. Nadishodhan, Murchha

30. Regular practise of which pranayama kills the intestinal worms?
A. Shitli B. Shitkari
C. Sahita D. Suryabhedi

31. Which pranayama removes the acidity?
A. Nadishodhan B. Suryabhedi
C. Shitli D. Ujjayi

32. Which kriya should not be performed by patients of heart and high blood pressure?
A. Kunjal B. Vasti
C. Neti D. All of the above

33. Which pranayama is useful for the diabets?
A. Bhastrika B. Brahmri
C. Suryabhedi D. Shitli

34. Which pranayama is useful for patients of thyroid?
A. Ujjayi B. Shitli
C. Shitkari D. Bhastrika

35. Which bandha should not be performed by patients of high blood pressure and hernia?
A. Moolbandha B. Jalandharabandha
C. Uddiyanabandha D. Mahabandha

36. Which mudra removes the ear disorders?
A. Prana B. Vayu
C. Surya D. Shunya

37. Practise of Jalaneti kriya removes the disorders related to which organ?
A. Nose B. Ear
C. Eye D. All of the above

38. Which mudra is useful for the patients of high blood pressure?
A. Surya mudra B. Kaki mudra
C. Gyana mudra D. Pashini mudra

39. Which asana is useful for people suffering from high blood pressure and mental fluctuations?
A. Kurmasana B. Uttan kurmasana
C. Mayurasana D. Shavasana

40. Serotonin level in the body is increased when _______ is done?
A. Asana B. Mudra
C. Trataka D. Meditation

41. Which pranayama should not be performed by patients of heart and high blood pressure?
A. Murchha B. Shitli
C. Brahmri D. All of the above

42. Which pranayama is useful for high blood pressure patients?
A. Ujjayi B. Suryabhedi
C. Sahita D. Bhastrika

43. Which of the following statement is not correct?
A. Heart patients should not perform matsyendrasana
B. Matsyendrasana eliminates disorders of excretory system
C. Matsyendrasana strengthens the digestive system
D. Matsyendrasana strengthens the respiratory system

44. Practise of meditation lowers the level of which harmone in human body?
A. Serotonin B. Kortisol
C. Endorphin D. Thymosin

45. Practise of meditation increases the level of which of the following?
A. DHEA B. GABA
C. Endorphin D. All of the above

46. To control the diseases by fasting is which type of therapy?
A. Laghana B. Satabhana
C. Savedana D. Sanehana

47. The disorders caused by natural agents are known as:
A. Aadhibhoutika B. Aadhidehika
C. Daruna D. Devabalaja

48. Arthritis is mainly:
A. A vatta generated disorder
B. A pitta generated disorder
C. A kapha generated disorder
D. Both B and C

49. Down's syndrome is ________ disease.
A. sex-linked B. autosomal
C. helminthic D. viral

50. The causative agent of trachoma is:
A. virus B. bacterium
C. bacteroid D. chalmydia

51. Mumps is a viral disease that causes inflammation of:
A. parotid gland B. sublingual gland
C. submaxillary gland D. infraorbital gland

52. In polio, the legs get paralysed and atrophied due to:
A. obstruction of muscles
B. degeneration of bones
C. death of some muscles
D. shrinkage of muscles

53. In sickle-cell anaemia, death occurs when lethal genes are present in:
A. homozygous dominant state
B. homozygous recessive state
C. codominant condition
D. heterozygous state

54. Haemophilia is caused by:
A. extra autosome
B. extra sex chromosome
C. gene mutation in sex chromosome
D. gene mutation in autosome

55. The disease not prevented by DPT is:
A. Diphtheria B. Pertussis
C. Poliomyelitis D. Tetanus

56. Which of the following is not a causative agent of diarrhoeal diseases?
A. *Shigela* B. *Traponema*
C. *Campylobacter* D. *Escherichia*

57. Albinism is a:
A. deficiency disease
B. hereditary disease
C. degenerative diseases
D. sex-linked disease

58. Which of the sexually transmitted diseases is correctly matched with its pathogen?
A. Urethritis *Bacillus anthracis*
B. Syphilis – *Treponema pallidum*
C. Gonorrhoea – *Entamoeba*
D. Soft sore – *Bacillus brevis*

59. Albinism is a congenital disorder resulting from the lack of the enzyme:
A. catalase B. fructokinase
C. tyrosinase D. xanthine oxidase

60. A bacterial eye disease is:
A. glaucoma B. trachoma
C. xerophthalmia D. protanopia

61. Congenital diseases:
A. are present at birth
B. are deficiency diseases

C. spread from one individual to another
D. occur during life

62. Cancer cells are damaged by radiations while others are not because cancer cells are:
A. starved
B. different in nature
C. undergoing rapid divisions
D. None of the above

63. Which type of cancer affects lymph nodes and spleen?
A. Carcinoma B. Sarcoma
C. Leukaemioa D. Lymphoma

64. Haemophilia is a genetic disorder, in which:
A. blood fails to clot at an injury
B. there is delayed coagulation of blood
C. blood clots in blood vessels
D. blood cell count falls

65. Mental retardation in man, associated with sex chromosomes abnormality, is usually due to:
A. reduction in X complement
B. increase in X complement
C. moderate increase in Y complement
D. large increase in Y complement

66. A metastatic cancerous tissue is termed 'sarcoma' if the disorder is in:
A. immune system B. epithelial cells
C. fibroblasts D. circulatory system

67. Schuffner's dots are seen in RBCs of man due to the disease:
A. kala-azar B. filariasis
C. malaria D. diabetes

68. Colour blindness, in which all colours are perceived as gray, is termed:
A. chromasia B. dichromasia
C. monochromasia D. All of these

69. Which of the following diseases is due to an allergic reaction?
A. Skin cancer B. Hay fever
C. Enteric fever D. Goitre

70. If a person shows production of interferons in his body, the chances are that he has got an infection of:
A. typhoid B. measles
C. malaria D. tetanus

71. Dengue is transmitted by:
A. *Culex* B. *Male Anopheles*
C. *Female Anopheles* D. *Aedes*

72. Human Immuno-deficiency Virus (HIV) has a protein coat and a genetic material which is:
A. single-stranded DNA
B. single-stranded RNA
C. double-stranded RNA
D. double-stranded DNA

73. A pregnant woman, who has got amniocentesis test done, finds an extra barr body in her embryo. The syndrome, which is likely to be associated with the embryo is:
A. Down's syndrome
B. Patau's syndrome
C. Edward's syndrome
D. Klinefelter's syndrome

74. The disease, in which a thick tough membrane stops the passage of air through the throat, is:
A. tetanus B. pertussis
C. tuberculosis D. dephtheria

75. The blood cancer is known as:
A. leukemia B. thrombosis
C. haemolysis D. haemoophilia

76. Which of the following pairs of diseases is caused by a virus?
A. Typhoid, tetanus B. AIDS, syphilis
C. Rabies, mumps D. Cholera, tuberculosis

77. In which of the following diseases, the man has an extra-X chromosomes?
A. Bleeder's disease
B. Down's syndrome
C. Turner's syndrome
D. Klinefelter's syndrome

78. Diphtheria is caused by:
A. poisons released from dead bacterial cells into the host tissues
B. poisons released by living, bacterial cells into the host tissues
C. excessive immune response by the host's body
D. poisons released by virus into the host tissues

79. Immune deficiency syndrome could develop due to:
A. Defective liver
B. Defective thymus
C. AIDS virus
D. Weak immune system

80. Toxin produced by tetanus affects:
A. voluntary muscles
B. involuntary muscles
C. both voluntary and involuntary muscles
D. jaw bones

81. Diseases of the heart, joints and nervous system are called:
A. communicable diseases
B. degenerative diseases
C. deficiency diseases
D. allergies

82. Myocardial infarction means damage to the:
A. brain
B. heart
C. kidneys
D. lungs

83. Match the following:

(*a*) Diabetes mellitus		1.	Inflammation of joints
(*b*) Arthritis		2.	Alkaptonuria
(*c*) 45+XY or XX		3.	Insulin deficiency
(*d*) Autosomal gene mutation		4.	Down syndrome

Codes:

	(*a*)	(*b*)	(*c*)	(*d*)
A.	3	1	4	2
B.	3	2	1	4
C.	4	3	1	2
D.	4	1	3	2

84. Treatment of ______ was discovered by Louis pasteur.
A. rabies
B. polio
C. mumps
D. measles

85. Rheumatic heart is characterised by damage to ______.
A. a trioventricular valves
B. sinuaricular valves
C. both of the above
D. None of these

ANSWERS

1 B	2 B	3 D	4 A	5 A	6 D	7 C	8 A	9 A	10 B
11 B	12 C	13 C	14 D	15 D	16 C	17 D	18 C	19 A	20 D
21 C	22 B	23 C	24 C	25 A	26 A	27 C	28 B	29 C	30 D
31 C	32 A	33 A	34 A	35 C	36 D	37 D	38 B	39 D	40 D
41 A	42 A	43 A	44 B	45 D	46 A	47 B	48 A	49 B	50 D
51 A	52 D	53 B	54 C	55 C	56 B	57 B	58 B	59 C	60 B
61 A	62 C	63 D	64 A	65 B	66 C	67 C	68 C	69 B	70 B
71 D	72 B	73 D	74 D	75 A	76 C	77 D	78 B	79 C	80 A
81 B	82 B	83 A	84 A	85 A					

●●●

CHAPTER

8

Applications of Yoga

YOGA IN EDUCATION

What is Yoga Education?

Yoga on one hand concentrates on keeping man healthy and on the other hand, it is a cohesion with physical development and good habits to keep human body healthy. Education as thought by Mahatma Gandhi is 'drawing out of the best in child and man—body, mind and spirit'. This concept of education is practicable through 'Yoga Education'.

Intricacy in day-to-day happenings is disturbing mental peace of human beings on large scale therefore man is in the guest of mental peace. A man therefore either visits temples very frequently to seek peace or tries to put himself comfortable in natural surroundings. The study of yoga education gives him right direction for healthy mental set up. The study of yogasanas alongwith meditation has now become most important part of physical education. In almost all religions viz. Hindu, Boudha, Jain, Sikh, Yoga is now treated as a source of meditation. Yoga is thought to be not the property of those who wish to seek the existence of God through highest degree of spiritual development. To a common man the study of yoga has become an instrument of keeping mental faculty on right lines. The daily practice of some asanas has become the need of the hour to get relief from the tension of day happenings.

The doctors on large scale are advising to take medicines to cure diseases but according to many doctors the root cause of physical disorder is a mental disturbance. A mentally well set up patient immediately responds to medicines prescribed by doctors. Therefore, doctors prescribe some sort of physical exercise even after they cure the diseases. It is now supposed on wider scale that the diseases like blood pressure and some primitive heart troubles can be cured with a strong healthy mind. Mental tolerance is very necessary to cure physical disorders. The best medicine for headache may perhaps be a tension free life. Only medicines may not be proper cure for headache.

Very recently Yoga Education has got a great impetus throughout the world with different objectives. In Britain Richard Hitleman tried to use yoga as a means for beauty culture whereas in Australia Roma Blaue thought and practised yoga to redress mental stress only. The syllabus of yoga education is therefore a syllabus containing topics on physical education and health education. Yoga education concentrates on physical exercise for physical fitness and for strong and healthy mind, it keeps relation with 'Pranayam', 'Meditation' and 'Asanas'.

From Prayer to Raj Yoga Meditation

Yoga believes in uniting human self or human soul with the supreme soul *i.e.*, God. The process goes on as the linking of mind with God. Human mind is not free. It is a reservoir with all worldly desires, aptitudes, interests and greediness but if directed properly becomes torch bearer to enlighten human beings to know the supremacy of God.

Prayers of God Almighty are many a times too much superfluous. It may a praise of God on surface level. These surface level prayers cannot be treated as full concentration of mind. They are mostly followed as a habitual practice without much knowledge about the supreme soul. But it has also got its importance. In Ganesh festival and in Durgapuja festival many persons participate in collective prayer or 'Arati' without much devotion and very little knowledge of the meaning of the verse which they sing collectively. It is the first stage in yoga education.

Meditation is superior to simple prayers. Meditation means 'to think'. Thinking is the power of the mind but mind is so occupied with different and controversial thoughts that if proper track is not found out it revolves only on worldly aspirations and attractions. It is through yoga only that it seeks its right pavement. Human body including brain is a matter. Brain is the controlling authority of human body. The detachment of self from human body is the subject matter of spiritual development. The supreme soul is the abode of highest qualities. By conscious efforts and concentration the human mind regains the power and establish relationship with param Atma *i.e.*, supreme soul.

B.K. Jagdish Chander Hassija in his book entitled 'Raj Yoga Meditation' (Publisher–Brahma Kumaris Ishwariya Vishwa Vidyalaya, Mount Abu, Rajasthan) considers 'Raj Yoga Meditation' as the highest type of meditation. According to him 'Raj Yoga Meditation' is awareness of the metaphysical self and absorption of one's mind in loveful and purposeful consciousness of God and concentration on Him and on His divine attributes. He says The name 'Raj-Yoga' is significant. The word 'Raja' means the king, the soverign or The supreme. This yoga is called Raj Yoga because it is the supreme or the highest yoga, being true and most effective.

Another reason for calling it 'Raj Yoga' is that it relates mainly to Mind and Mind is considered as the king that rules the sense organs and the body. Moreover, the term Raja Yoga also implies that even such a person as a king, who is very busy and has so much to do, can practise it, and it does not involve act of austerities or penances or of renouncing one's household. This is different from another yoga, also called Raj Yoga, for in this yoga, there is no need to practice breath control, physical postures, or use a mantra or an image nor does it require one to stop all thoughts, but to stop only wordly or negative thoughts and to concentrate Mind on God.

Relationship of Yoga-Education with Value Education

The values to be inculcated through yoga education is concentration and strengthening of mind. Wordly attractions through the use of scientific advancement becomes the part of temporary satisfaction. Too much joy and too much sorrow is the cause of discomfort of human life. Both physical and mental well being is essential for human happiness.

All family relations may cause unhappiness to human beings but relation with supreme soul is the source of eternal peace and happiness of mankind. The values so collected through yoga education have very close and permanent bearing on value education.

Swami Vivekanand, the great educator of mankind defined education "as the manifestation of perfection already in man." Entire Vedanta Philosophy and Science of human development is enshrined in this definition. The aim of all education undoubtedly is the attainment of human excellence and perfection. Education should be the instrument to convert human raw material to excellent characterised product *i.e.*, culturing the qualities of head, heart and hand. In practical life this has to be translated in the qualities of truthfulness, self confidence, tolerance, love, integration of body, mind and intellect. These are the steps leading to unfoldment of perfection already in man. Truly educated and cultured men alone can meet the challenges with the help of positive thinking. The process of value based education is the system to develop the yogic conscience.

The education as is obtained today is not aimed at character building with the result that we find highly educated men with power and service machinery but their command fail miserably while tackling problems in the right way. Hence, we are in need of men and women with character, integrity, dedication and dignity of labour.

Yoga, the ancient science of India, is conscious process for gaining mastery over the mind and thereby grow better from the animal level and ultimately towards perfection itself. If yoga and present education system work together it could master the information of the subject as well as master the mind of the individual. Character building is possible there and then only.

The mandatory and systematic introduction of yoga techniques and its right presentation can certainly go a long way in resconstructing the lost values in our country.

Objectives of Yoga Education with Reference to Value education:

1. To develop the mind for tolerance.
2. To develop the mind to think positively.
3. To know the relationship between body, soul and universal entity.
4. To know that physical fitness is not only the way to sound personality.
5. To know basic procedure regarding the methods of yogic practice.

Aims of Education

All round development of individuals is possible through education. Among it intellectual, mental and functional development is expected. Though cognitive and conative domains are developed through today's educational system, affective domain cannot receive its proper place. That is the reason of paucity of national attitude, and social consciousness among students. If moral, social and spiritual values are exchanged through the media of subject content, emotional development will easily be possible.

Following are the chief aims of educations:

1. Knowledge
2. Understanding
3. Application
4. Skill
5. Interest and Aptitude
6. Appreciation
7. Incalcation of human values.

NEP 1986 prepared value based curriculum. It also made clear and fixed particular values alongwith objectives while teaching particular units.

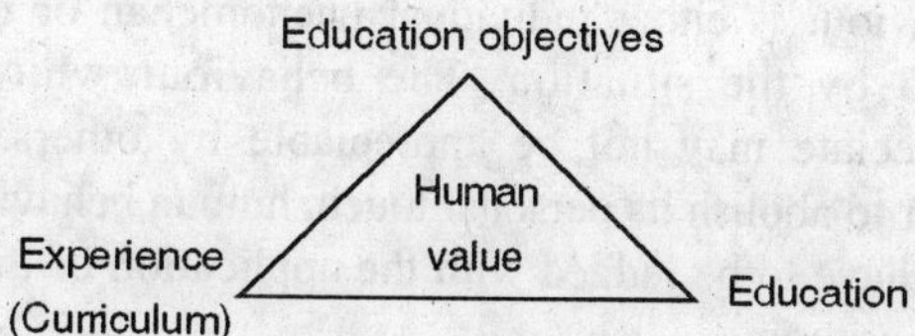

Lesson Planning: In value based teaching, human values are to be fixed first and then learning experiences are arranged in the teaching of a particular unit. It is then only, expected objectives can be achieved and value based teaching can be carried out. In existing teaching learning process, stress is only on to provide information, therefore other objectives remain untouched. For this curriculum and planning will have to be re-orientated. Curriculum will have to be restructured and value based curriculum will have to be put to practice.

Concept of value: Though meaning of value is originally related to economic value, philosophers like, Rudaullh Lotse, Albrace Richel in nineteenth century attached more extensive meaning to value. It is in this broad sense, we today use the term value as 'Literary value', 'Democratic value', 'Life value' and 'Education value' in our day-to-day speaking and writing.

In life process man accepts good things and avoids bad things. It is not human living to act neutrally and in the light of witness only. Acceptable and non acceptable, good and bad are the nature of values. Values are established and they are practicable. They can be achieved.

Chilana studied Indian culture and observed that Indian culture is based on the values viz kind heartedness, self control, universal brotherhood, honesty, respect to others and faith. Due to deterioration of these values, new values like indiscipline and destructive mentality came into existence. He suggested to include these values in curriculum and called it value based curriculum.

Criteria to fix value: It has not been yet stated how to fix the criteria to decide the values. Dr. Gawande put forth the following four criterion. It is very difficult to decide whether a particular human behaviour is value based or not because human behaviour is either individual phenomenan or it is ruled by the situation. The behaviour which I appreciate may not be appreciable by others. In order to abolish its personal touch, human behaviour will have to be judged with the application of these four criteria.

Criteria

1. Individual progress should be achieved through expected behaviour.
2. Expected behaviour should be conducive to society.
3. Expected behaviour should be conducive to a nation.
4. Expected behaviour need to be accepted on international level.

If human behaviour fulfills all these criteria then alone it is human value. If a particular human behaviour satisfies only one or two criteria it cannot be called human value. Therefore, if any behaviour satisfies all the four criteria then only it is called human value.

Distinction Between Value Education and Moral Education

1. The concept of value education is more extensive in comparison with the concept of moral education. Moral education is a constituent of value education.
2. Value education is developmental and it is based on expected values on the contrary moral education is static and it is based on the ideals of society.
3. In value education, all round development of human is considered whereas in Moral Education only ideals of individuals with its relation to society are considered.
4. Value education is scientifically based but it cannot be said with determination whether moral education is so based scientifically. It is so because in Moral Education customs, faiths and traditions are reared and sometimes reflect the religion.
5. Value education consists all the component parts like individual, society, nation, environment and universe etc. but in moral education only relation between individual and society is emphasised.

In Moral education each society fixes its own ideals and it is the endeavour of the society to keep these ideals stable. Therefore individual's behaviour is restricted to individual and society. There is a great impact of religion on society and therefore religion is reflected in individual's behaviour. We preserve it in the name of customs and culture. But in value education the changes in human behaviour are studied in its new perspective and propagated through various medias.

Progressive Outlook of Value Education

Generally, society is found of preserving customs and these customs are sometimes treated as culture of the society. Many customs and traditions are based on religion. Religion is originated in consideration with the prevalent situation. Though idea about emancipation in many religions is the same, the ways in each religion are different. Individual's behaviour according to each religion therefore differs. Individuals tries to safeguard the behaviour. We call it culture. The sanskars (experiences) are transmitted from one generation to other generation. These are the ideal behaviour patterns of society. As there are so many religions and different sects within a religion, individuals are free to decide their ideal behaviour within religion and within sect of each religion. If we try to mould the public through religious and moral education, there is possibility of religious and cultural struggle in a secular country like India. Religious and moral education is possible in a country where only one religion is dominant.

Society is dynamic and values that are created in political, economic and social fields are subject to changes in these fields. An individual and society exist by the assimilation of these value. Society thus becomes dynamic. *e.g.*, the rising of twenty first century is the gift of science age. Society has to accept behaviour and thoughts in consonant with the age of science. This is the accepted behaviour of an individual. E.g. Moon is not a God but a planet. We proved it by scientific existence. The said behaviour is favourable to science age and also expected for individual progress and progress of society. We call such behaviour as value oriented behaviour, e.g. Small pox is a disease and it does not exist due to divine anger. A patient becomes normal by medical treatment. We therefore take preventive measures or if there are symptoms of disease we approach to doctor for medical treatment. This behaviour is expected from society. It is based on scientific outlook and favourable to a nation. An individual therefore gets free from the disease and his individual progress becomes possible. In the aforesaid behaviour, four criteria are properly followed and therefore it is value oriented behaviour.

Definitions of Human Value

(i) **Rokeach:** Value is defined as enduring belief, a specific mode of conduct or end state of existence alongwith continum of importance.

(ii) **Kluchhohn:** Value is a conception of desirable and not something desired.

(iii) **Shaver:** Values are standard and principles for judging worth.

Human value is an academic behaviour through which progress of individual, society, nation and international understanding are created. Education aims in all round development of human beings, therefore Cognitive, Conative and Affective domains are taken to task at learning levels for individual progress. By exchange of subject information, development in cognitive domain is easily possible. Application of skills, which is conative domain is also possible but emotional development or affective domain is related to fixing of human values and its preservation. Until emotional feelings does not exit, an individual cannot achieve wisdom. This important part is neglected through curriculum.

Thus, inculcation of value education is for emotional development. It is through this that we establish men of character, responsible citizens and sensitive personality of individuals. In individual so described discharges the responsibility of both rights and duties. It is in this sense that value education becomes indispensible for human all round development.

Dr. Eknath Gawande therefore defines value education in the following words:

Definition : When human values are inculcated through curriculum to trancend to cognitive, affective and psychomotor level for conducive development of individual, society, national and international understanding, it is called value education.

Among various objectives of value education, to produce men of character is chief among them. The salient features of characterisation are—(*i*) Honesty, (*ii*) Adventure, (*iii*) Pleasantness, (*iv*) Controlled and sensitive nature. Men of character have faith in their performances, therefore they speed up their work.

According to Chilan, Indian culture is superior because it is based on pity, self control, honesty, honour, faith and universal brotherhood. If these value are included in the curriculum, emotional development can be achieved.

Dr. Kothari tried to emphasise the value viz., democracy, socialism, equality of all religions. He attached great importance to achieve skills through science and technology and also balanced development of human values. National Education Policy 1986 studied Indian background and came to the conclusion that religious education is not possible in India as India is a country with many religions. N.E.P. 1986 therefore advocated the concept of value education, giving extensive meaning to the term moral education. N.E.P. also tried to raise the levels of cognitive, conative and affective domains. Conscious efforts to make changes through formal educational system should be done and for this curriculum at secondary school level is the best media to do so, was its view. Knowledge, skill and emotion developed through the curriculum media transforms the right attitudes, interests and liking among students. Afterwards the constituents become the integral part of personality and thus creates value based personality.

Components of Value Education

1. Moral Education
2. Environmental Education
3. Population Education
4. Human rights and duties
5. Health Education
6. Indian Culture
7. Physical Education
8. Yoga Education
9. History of India's freedom movement.

The above-mentioned component parts should be included in curriculum and it should be so farmed as would give justice to various learning experiences through the media of subject units. Value education thus will not be treated as an independent subject in curriculum but it will lead to integrated development through effective value based curriculum.

CONCEPTS AND NATURE OF SELF DEVELOPMENT

Self development is to educate and sensitize the young mind with values like that of the desirable human virtues such as honesty, tolerance, justice, forgiveness, patience, sharing, humanity, self-control, contentment, love for the environment and good citizenship.

Swami Vivekananda has said that education is not the amount of information that is put into the brain running riot there, but it is the assimilation of ideas. He also said that education should give us character that would make us flower into the best of humans – full of love, Self-confidence, Self-reliance, fearlessness, compassion and a spirit of service like that in a Buddha, a Christ or a Ramakrishna. To Swamiji education meant transformation of life from instinctual to intellectual level. He was thus advocating the essence of the Vedic values in our education which leads to Self development.

A man is known by his character. As a living being in this world, man is distinguished by the fact that he possesses character. Each person is unique because of the character that he represents. In a way the character is regarded as his 'Self'

The Self can manifest itself in various forms. One can be mild and modest; or one can be arrogant and overbearing. One can be devoted to noble pursuits or one can be obsessed with narrow self-serving pursuits. The reason why we are endowed with character is not to be confined only to human virtues and human limitations. Beyond all such things our character consists in the actualization or manifestation potential divinity that is within everyone of us. To cultivate this divine quality, to raise our ordinary human existence to the godliness we all represent ***is the motto of life.***

How do we strive to attain this divinity?

Man is an admixture of three different elements—*animality, humanity* and *divinity.* The link element of humanity must be perfected to reach closer to divinity. For that the primary effort has to be in the direction of curbing all one's animal propensities. The result will be attainment of true human character. From that stage there may be the beginning of a transition to divinity. There are various ways prescribed by ancient sages to attain that divinity:

- truthfulness the acid test of which we find in the story of *Satyakama.*
- the ideal of plain living as opposed to abundance and luxury.

- an attitude of happiness and service to others.
- natural respect to the elderly and eminent.
- honesty, integrity and scruple.
- ability to restrain oneself from malice, avarice, envy, animosity and violence.
- modesty to save oneself from undue over estimation.

One must have the supreme wisdom to understand that a man may lose everything he possesses, he may even become a destitute, but can regain a lot. This cannot be said of his character. When one's character is lost it can never be recovered.

Bhartirhari, brother of King *Vikramaditya* wrote three outstanding treatises—*Niti-satakam, Vairagya-satakam* and *Sringara-satakam.*

He made penetrating observations of human character in *Niti-satakam.* In about 64 shlokas he has described human character in all its aspects and broadly divides men into three categories *i.e.,* the **good** and the **noble** who lead an honest and regulated life while most of the time doing good to others; the second group consists of those who are self-centered, pleasure seekers, helping others only when compelled, who abide by laws not by nature but for fear of punishment; the third group are the most dangerous one called demons in human form—extremely selfish, totally bereft of all values, vicious and intolerant, ready to grab everything for themselves at the cost of others.

Role and function of values in Self-development

The conduct of each citizen should be so conditioned and regulated that the result is collective good at its maximum. This has been the central theme of classical Indian thought about the State and the society. Swami Vivekananda who wanted every member of the society to give up weak mentality, attain mental and moral strength, work for the unity of the country, rise above petty interests, eradicate superstitions and above all have the highest regard for women.

The following are the roles and functions of values in Self-development:

- Inculcation of national spirit—we Indians should know what great luck it means to be born in this country. India that is Bharat carries special meaning derived from the etymology—it means the land of illumination of mind.
- The pursuit of self interest has to be consistent with self enlightenment. Also it needs to be balanced with social responsibility.
- A responsible person must learn to pay due regards to all forms of the work howsoever arduous or low paid. A job done is after all equivalent to service rendered to others. Hence no work should be looked down upon or avoided as demeaning.
- No society can progress unless all its members get seriously engaged in producing wealth—tangible as well as intangible, material as well as cultural. And part of what they appropriate as their wages or profit ought to be given back to the cause of the society. Payment of taxes is legal responsibility. But compulsory charity is a virtue in itself. Preservation of environment and biodiversity supported by compassion for all living creatures is also necessary.
- One should also learn to distinguish between one's essential material needs and undue abundance that feeds nothing but one's greed. Again being envious of other people's affluence does no good; it only adds to one's misery.
- A responsible citizen, above all, should be a good human being. The qualities of goodness are inherent in man. They need to be elicited and the more they are elevated, the greater is the manifestation of divinity in man. A society with qualities such as conscientious citizens practicing social values (respect for the elderly and women) and abjuring violence and demanding justice for everybody can claim to be an ideal society.

- We do not need anything much higher than our natural tendency to feel angry against misdeeds done by others particularly when they hurt our interests. But true morality requires that we do not make selfish distinctions between others and ourselves. We have to be equally conscious to evils outside and those within. This is not something desired from our animal nature; it arises from our higher nature. It is the aim of value education to help develop this higher nature.
- We must distinguish between the laws that regulate our external conduct and the rules that take care of our inner Self. Here we come across the constant interaction between mind and intellect, desire and reason. Out of it comes a higher rationality that guides men to self-perfection.

Contribution of Yoga towards Self development

The ultimate goal of Yoga is to verify the development of the Self, which has all the characteristics of divinity in potential form. Yoga (especially the *Astanga Yoga*) is the ladder to reach the highest in one's journey to Self-realization. Maharsi Patanjali through his *Astanga Yoga* seeks to prepare one to attain that Selfhood. He delineates the principles of *Yama* and *Niyama* which perform social observances and personal restraints respectively and which lead to Self-control. The five *yamas* are: non-violence *(Ahimsa) i.e.* non-injury to others by thought, word or deed; the practice of speaking the truth *(Satya)*; non-covetousness (*Asteya* and *Aparigraha*), which enables oneself to shun jealousy and possessiveness.

Self-control is the virtue of those endowed with divine nature, which is instrumental to the cultivation of many other such virtues such as fearlessness, purity of heart, charity, austerity, straight-forwardness, non-violence, truth, freedom from anger, renunciation, tranquility, aversion to fault-finding, compassion, freedom from avarice, modesty, steadiness, vigour, forgiveness, fortitude and freedom from malice and excessive pride. At the same time it curbs vices like arrogance, pride, anger, harshness, and ignorance, the marks of those endowed with demoniac nature.

Everybody has to practise self discipline to some extent in order to live in a society. The more one may control one's senses and mind, the better it is. Human life is a journey towards perfection. Man is basically an animal, and all the animal instincts are in him. But he is a rational animal. By means of rationality, he may elevate himself to humanity. The endeavour will be then to rise to divinity and from that level to Supreme Consciousness — the ultimate goal.

Self discipline is a key to success in our development from the mundane to the spiritual. It endows an individual with power that enables us to perform our duties, without being distracted by the passions or emotions that may impede our ways towards our journey to higher pursuits. The impediments often appear in the form of anger, greed, power or position. It generates in us the strength and competence to discern and disseminate between what is and what ought to be.

A self-disciplined person thus can easily discriminate between the *'Sreyass'* (desirable) and the *'Preyas'* (desired). This quality of the individual is, 'what we in Yoga psychology call *Vijnanamaya kosa* or *Buddhi* or *Viveka.*

Pratyahara means the control of senses and sense organs from their objects. Our senses are going out to reach the world — the objects of enjoyment. There are five objects of our senses, namely, sight, taste, sound, smell and touch. One has to control the sense and sense organs. The turbulent senses carry away even intelligent people. Only those whose senses are under control attain stable wisdom *(vase hi yasyendriyani tasya prajna pratisthita, Gita 11.61)*

Constant thought of the sense objects leads to attachment, a particular kind of fondness towards the objects. From attachment grows desires for them. But not all such desires are fulfilled. When there is an obstruction, anger results from non-fulfilment of desires. Out of anger a man does wrong and cruel deeds. Delusion follows anger, one loses reason, the power of discrimination and becomes unfit for the human goals.

Gita as well as *Patanjali Yoga* speak about two methods for restraining the mind—***practice and dispassion***—(*Abhyasa* and *Vairagya*). Success and excellence in every field require regular practice. Practice is to be adhered to for a long time, without break, adhered to with regard, with great confidence. Yogic practices such as *'Asana'* and *'Pranayama'* are therefore the purpose of controlling the mind. There are various postures in which one can sit still for a long time. Control of the movements of the vital force can be achieved by means of *Pranayama,* by regular and systematic breathing. One begins by controlling the breath, as the easier way of getting control of the vital force.

A balanced, disciplined way of life is necessary for Yoga. Too much of food or no food, too much of sleep such extremes are detrimental to Yogic practices. Moderation is necessary — moderation in food and recreation, moderation in sleep and wakefulness, temperate attitude in action — even for practical, professional life much more so for spiritual.

There are three stages in Yoga:

(*i*) The first is concentrating the mind upon an object.

(*ii*) When the mind has become strong and does not waver much then it is meditation.

(*iii*) Higher stage is total absorption leading to the realization of Ultimate Reality.

To avoid the danger of concentrating the mind upon an object and then being unable to detach it at will, the Gita advises combination of practice and detachment. (6.35) So also says Patanjali Yoga Sutra 1.12.

It is easier for the dispassionate one to concentrate the mind. The calmer we are, the better it is for us to work. When we let loose our feelings we waste much energy, shatter our nerves, disturb our minds, and accomplish very little work. It is the calm, forgiving, equable, and well balanced mind that does the greatest amount of work.

Essentials for Self development

- Physical fitness,
- Core human values,
- Personal hygiene,
- Managing stress,
- Emotional balancing, and
- Spiritual evolution.

Holistic approach to Self development

To manage a state of balance at all these layers of the Self as mentioned above would sound to be too idealistic and less practical. But it can be made possible. It is practicable. For that just one set of practices would not suffice. One has to make a concerted effort. This means a highly integrated approach is the need. Such an approach is very well known as 'holistic approach', an approach that efficiently and successfully addresses issues at all the segments of the personality. Thus all-round Self-development can be a possibility.

You can do that. All of us can do that. Many have done it successfully.

First of all, some kind of understanding is necessary to set the ball rolling. Without the basic points clarified, we cannot go much far. This has been suggested by Patanjali in his *Yogasutra.* The sage has bought out the scheme of *'Astanga Yoga'*—an eight-pronged treatment of the Self so as not to leave even a single aspect of the total persona unattended. From gross physical existence to the pure consciousness, Patanjali has a method to suggest upgrading each one of them. It is just that a rough diamond has to be polished so that it can shine. And practising the same in a systematic manner development of you as an individual can be vertical. This should encourage you.

Practice of *Yama* can be quite useful in managing mental and emotional stress. This can enhance mental and physical health.

Niyamas should be managing the personal hygiene, mental satiation and spiritual realignment.

The effect of *Asanas* practised by using bodily muscles and joints thus relaxing the body, does not remain to the body plane alone, but essentially affects the mental and emotional layers as well.

Pranayama has an approach ranging from subtle to the gross areas of the body.

Pratyahara, Dharana, Dhyana and *Samadhi* are for completing the process of internalization.

This brief account is to show that Patanjali's approach is a 'holistic' approach where the totality of the Self is taken into account. No issue of an individual is ignored.

(In addition to the above scheme, science of *Hatha Yoga* has certain cleansing processes *(suddhikriyas)* to detoxify the body from within).

It may also be clear to us that just one set of practice will not be able to successfully dealing with all the issues revealing at various layers of you. Hence an integrated approach is well-justified. This is a rational and sound approach for total Self-development.

The concept of values and value education

The Sanskrit term for values is dharma or *Sadachara.* Dharma is described as 'the set of values that sustains the creation without which the very existence of it would be threatened'. *Sankaracharya* defined dharma as the values that sustained human beings and helped them to enjoy happiness both in this mundane as well as in the spiritual world.

Thus education in India meant not merely intellectual cramming of information into the brain but the application of them into one's life so that life became better at individual, social, secular and spiritual levels. Education was a life-transformer. The education, according to Upanishads, is the one that liberates *"Sa Vidya ya vimuktaye'* is the aphorism which defines the goal of education according to ancient Indian scriptures.

Thirst for knowledge

Education was called Vidya, *i.e.,* acquisition of knowledge, which was compulsory for every one after he attained the school-going age. Social milieu created this thirst for learning. In the Chhandogya Upanishad the famous Satyakama, a boy of school-going age, tells his mother *Jabala,* 'Mother, I want to go and study under a teacher. Let me know my ancestry (so that I may tell the teacher if asked). The ancient system was to live with an enlightened teacher and to learn all he could teach. This was called the Gurukula system.

Knowledge at two levels: Para and Apara

What were the subjects a student learnt? We read in the Mundaka Upanishad the teacher recounting the subjects: all the four Vedas, the science of phonetics, civil engineering, grammar, etymology, poetry and astronomy. This is only the lower knowledge *(apara-vidya).* Quite distinct from this is the higher knowledge, *(para-vidya)* 'through which one realizes one's own imperishable Self'.

Thus, the Vedic system of education conceived knowledge at two levels—one about the things concerning the world of senses *i.e.,* almost all known sciences, humanities, arts and crafts of the times. The second, about Brahman, the divinity which is the non-material stuff of all creation, the so called material which was not matter but infinite and immortal pure consciousness. It is from *Brahman* that all this creation has come, in *Brahman* it lives, and to *Brahman* it returns during dissolution. It is this *Brahman* again that is the soul of man and of all beings. Every student has to learn this at the higher stage of education called *Para Vidya.* Education was considered not enough if the student knew only about sciences, arts, engineering or technology. True, this knowledge gave him control over the things and powers of nature. But power without a control-system cannot be safely put to use. What is this control system in man which can make him apply his knowledge only to useful purposes and never otherwise? It is his character and culture, which he acquires through *Para Vidya,* the higher knowledge. The higher knowledge teaches that one Universal Soul permeates all beings, that the individual soul is a part of this Universal Soul, and hence the individual and the collective are not separate entities but one whole. Hence for a man with right knowledge, love of fellow beings would come as naturally as breathing to the lungs, because he feels that all beings and himself are one in the Universal Self. We know that all limbs are interlinked through the body and any harm to one limb would harm the other limb too. Thus love, compassion and service to humanity flow as a natural character of a really educated man. This constitutes his wisdom. He imbibes these 'values' from a good education.

Values through education

Thus the 'science of spirituality', which one may call *Para Vidya,* is the power to check and control that comes to men and by which all his powers derived from the knowledge of science and technology are canalized only to the welfare of humanity. Person with such wisdom would never use an atom for destruction, or wealth for enslavement of others, or army for destruction of innocent people. This is the value-system derived through a complete education comprising the *para* and the *apara vidyas.*

Concentration

We know what important role the concentration of mind plays in mastering the various subjects of study. The more the power of concentration, the deeper is the observation, the greater is the knowledge gained and the quicker is its achievement. Hence concentration of mind is a great value stressed in education. Arjuna, the great archer-prince in the Epic Mahabharata, is asked to shoot the eye of a bird sitting on a far off tree. He shoots successfully only when he does not see anything else but only the bird's eye. Real concentration cuts off all other objects of sense except the one under observation. Swami Vivekananda's life abounds in examples wherein we see his marvellous power of studying volumes of books by reading them only once and that too with a lightening speed.

Chastity

Concentration can come only to a pure mind. Purity of mind means a mind free from desires and distractions. Desires are of two categories – gross and subtle. Gross ones are those concerning enjoyments of sense pleasures and the subtle ones are for name, power and position. The sex enjoyment is the leader in the 'gross' category. Therefore, to control the sex desire is equivalent to controlling all other desires. Hence the purity of mind much depends on how much the student can observe chastity. The Indian education suggests various methods to sublimate the sex desires through proper attitudes of respect and worshipfulness towards the member of the opposite sex. Through meditation on the Divine Self, on one's own and others, the identification with one's physical body is replaced by the feeling of Oneself called the Atma, which is beyond all sex and form. This, aided by healthy engagements in duties, deep studies and contemplation, enables the student to remain established in chastity to a great degree. Chastity heightens the grasping and retention of knowledge, as well on the creation of knowledge. Thus concentration and assimilation of ideas are the main features of education. It dispenses with the huge equipments – note books, text books and what not!

Truthfulness

Now comes another value considered very significant in our lives. That is truthfulness. We read in the Taittiriya Upanishad that after the completion of education, the teacher advises the outgoing student thus: 'Speak the truth, practice dharma, never deviate from study, help the teacher through wealth in his/her mission of diffusion of knowledge, and become a householder and beget good progeny. Also give with sincerity *(sraddhaya deyam).*' Truthfulness means straightforwardness in thought, word and deed. It means to think noble relevant thoughts. Thus the speech of the truthful has the strength of his whole personality behind it. Therefore, it cannot fail to produce its results. Truthfulness results in fulfilment without fail, says the Yoga Sutra. In fact, in realizing the highest knowledge, truthfulness occupies the highest place. 'He that speaks truth always is sitting on the lap of God, as it were', says Sri Ramakrishna. The speech of a truthful person unfailingly produces its effect, *i.e.,* it impresses its purport on the heart of the hearer, brings succour to his distressed mind through an uttered benediction, and brings fearlessness to the speaker himself!

From truthfulness come honesty, punctuality, cleanliness, orderliness, simplicity etc. Truthfulness is the guard against all duplicity, cunningness and hypocrisy. It saves the student from many a false step. It makes him work hard to get sound knowledge rather putting up an appearance of it! It gives him an inner urge to confess his failures to the teacher and thus get corrected. A true student will be humble to accept and apologize when he is wrong. This great quality attracts the love and solicitation from the teacher.

Tapas

We also give an important place for austerity in education. 'Know *Brahman* through *tapas*', says the Taittiriya Upanishad. The practice of truthfulness, as discussed earlier, is itself a great austerity. *Satyam tapah,* says the *Mahanarayana* Upanishad. Indeed, it is so! Sri Ramakrishna, the perfect Avatara, also says, 'Truthfulness is the austerity for the Kaliyuga (the present age).'

What is austerity and its purpose? Austerity, called *tapas*, literally means 'burning' or 'melting by heating.' The mind of a student has to be ridden of lethargy, lust, distracting thoughts, and spurious whims and fancies and when this is done, the mind, like a molten metal, can take the mould of the teacher. It can assimilate the real purport of the words of the teacher. The student remains receptive to the teachings of the Guru. The student's mind takes, as it were, the shape of the Guru's enlightened mind. Sri Ramakrishna used to sing a song in Bengali, 'Mother, I will cast you into the mould of my mind and will take out your Image from it.'

Training the body to be strong and efficient; following the principle early to bed and early to rise and thus controlling sleep to minimum; practicing simplicity in clothing and bedding; moderateness in eating and drinking; forbearing calmly when one is ill or punished for one's wrong – all these practiced as a necessary part of education will constitute *tapas* and will help make the student efficient and strong.

A taste for exercises

Sublimation of lower impulses takes place through cultivating higher tastes like reading noble literature, singing devotional music, creating, edifying art forms, healthy and hard exercises like gymnastics, games and sports, long trekking, swimming, running and so on. A taste for training the body should be cultivated even from boyhood.

Pure love

Love is a value which every youth is fascinated with but almost all mistake it for lust, which is selfish and jealous and results in misery. Educators should put the youth to serve the poor, the afflicted and the needy. Then they would experience that the students should be taught without any expectation of gratitude or obligation as a return should never be entertained. Love cannot be bartered for money or for favours. In love, there should be no place for lust, envy, rivalry or restrictions. It is all freedom and joy. All intimate relations between young people should be based on a pure love like unto a father, mother, sister, brother or a child.

Love of music

This is another value that can sublimate the lower emotions very easily. Greek educationists advocated music as a compulsory subject in education. The writer knows the case of a college student who had a book of songs which he had learnt to sing in his student days in his school. Once when he was very depressed in his college hostel, being far away from his home, just by singing a few songs from the book he overcame his depression as if through a psychiatric treatment! Music can thus be a private psychotherapist accompanying to a student all the twenty-four hours all his life!

Prayer

Another sterling value is prayer. Vedic seers prayed and prayed in the *Rigvaidika* and *Samavaidika* hymns called Sukta. Great saints like Jayadeva, Kabir, Surdas, Mirabai, Nanak, Chaitanya, Sri Ramakrishna and his band of apostles all would go into ecstasy through prayers. The elevating literature of prayer can teach great philosophical thought.

There is a great universal prayer in the Vedas which should be repeated by all students - irrespective of race, gender, caste or colour. That is the Gayatri Mantra which runs thus: 'We meditate *(dhimahi)* on the adorable spiritual effulgence *(varenyam bhargoh)* of the Divine Creator *(savituh)* who projects the three worlds – the gross, subtle and the causal (represented by *bhuh, bhuvah, svah*). May He enlighten our intellect!' The individual intelligence imbibes the cosmic intelligence through such a prayer when practiced regularly. Practice means chanting at regular intervals – at least at morning and evening hours, simultaneously meditating on its meaning. Indian education teaches this prayer to every student to arouse the dormant powers of understanding in him or her. In the past ten years there is a sudden interest awakened in the public in this country towards this mantra. Numerous schools, colleges and public prayer places have regular chanting of this mantra which augurs well.

Sraddha

This is another value whose place in education can never be over-emphasized. *Sraddha* in a student is not only his faith in his teacher but it is also an indomitable "will" to acquire knowledge at any cost. Sraddha is Self-confidence. It is faith in the unfailing cosmic power behind one's individual Self. It can face failures with smiles, and renew further efforts with fresh hopes. One with *Sraddha* is ever resourceful. No obstacle is too big for him to overcome. *Sraddha* is capacity to shoulder any responsibility with efficiency and sacrifice. *Sraddha* is, as it were, the philosopher's stone that can convert any obstacle into a stepping stone to success.

Wisdom, the goal

Wisdom and not mere knowledge is considered the goal of all education. Wisdom is to know what is permanent and what is not and to reject the latter. In the early stages of the student this is possible only by emulating the ideal characters in the milieu in which the student finds himself. For example, in the Indian context contemplating on the lives of Rama, Krishna, Buddha, Mahavira, Christ, Nanak, Chaitanya, Ramakrishna and Vivekananda can help in cultivating this wisdom. A reverence to all religious leaders cultivated during student life can narrow down the gap between the various socio-religious communities in this country. Religious harmony is a sweet fruit of the tree of wisdom. I recall here an experience.

In the state of Arunachal Pradesh, the tribal boys pray in R.K. Mission's hostels daily before the picture of several prophets, all of equal size and decorated on an altar. The pictures are Sri Ramakrishna, Holy Mother, Swami Vivekananda, Jesus, Buddha, Nanak and Zoroaster. It has been observed that, after a few years in these schools, students feel and say, 'We belong to all religions because we are from the Ramakrishna Mission.' The point to note here is that they are taught the 'harmony of religions'! This liberal attitude is one of great value that our education has to inculcate in all students of our country to strengthen its social and religious fabric.

Yoga and value development

In order to develop values we have to confront the reality that it represents. This calls for self-discipline in the form of self-control, self-knowledge and inward concentration. This kind of self-discipline, in due course, brings about transformation of one's consciousness which is what Yoga aims at.

Yoga is thus, the connecting link between values and reality. Yoga transforms value experience into mystic experience. Yoga gives us the power to go beyond values and realize the ultimate reality which they symbolize. Without Yoga, values remain mere dreams of poets and preachers. For many people Yoga means nothing more than some postural exercises. But true Yoga is an inner discipline for the transformation of consciousness through self-knowledge, self-control and self-directed activity.

Though there are special forms of Yoga for this transformation such as *Jnana Yoga, Bhakti Yoga, Raja Yoga* etc. yet any work, any activity, can be done as Yoga. Education—both teaching and learning—can be done as Yoga. Pursuit of art can be done as Yoga. Pursuit of science can be done as

Yoga. Social service can be done as Yoga. Indeed, one's whole life can be converted into Yoga.

Pursuit of values and quest for the ultimate reality are both manifestation of man's innate evolutionary urge at two planes of existence—the empirical and the spiritual. Such a view transforms education between the secular and the sacred, and makes one's life a ceaseless striving for higher degrees of knowledge and happiness. Such a holistic view alone can make life meaningful, harmonious and peaceful. This is the integral philosophy of life that the world is very much in need of now.

The lower needs connected with man's physical existence, such as the need for food, clothing, shelter, etc. are called 'basic needs' or simply 'needs'. The needs higher to these constitute values. Of many different types of values prevailing in human society some have permanent utility. They are called 'eternal' because they are universal and can orient us towards higher purpose of life, which progressively outgrow conflicts and lead us to equality and peace. We must therefore try to locate those eternal values without which the existence of human society will be in danger. Based on this premise we can say that value based education is that type of training or education which 'makes the person aware of the higher purposes of life—individual or cosmic, material as well as spiritual.'

In ancient India as we learn from history, the guiding forces in individual and social life were the religious or scriptural injunctions that enshrined higher values. Yoga Sutras of Maharsi Patanjali and the Upanishads speak about our such values.

The term Yoga has its verbal root as *yuj!* (*yuj* in Sanskrit means joining, *yujyate anena iti Yogah*). Yoga is that which joins. What are the entities that are joined? In the traditional terminology it is joining of *jivatma* with *paramatma* the individual Self with the Universal Self. It is an expansion of the narrow constricted egoistic personality to an all pervasive, eternal and blissful state of REALITY.

Patanjali Yoga is one among the six systems of Indian philosophy—known as *Sad-darsanas.* One of the great Risis (Seers), Patanjali, compiled the essential features and principles of Yoga (which were earlier interspersed in Yoga Upanishads) in the form of '*Sutras*' (aphorisms) and made a vital contribution in the field of Yoga, nearly 4000 years ago (as dated by some famous western historians). According to Patanjali, Yoga is a conscious process of gaining mastery over the mind.

The scope of Yoga as portrayed in the Bhagavadgita and the Upanishads is far more comprehensive. As Swami Vivekananda puts it "It is a means of compressing one's evolution into a single life or a few months or even a few hours of one's bodily existence". In general, there is a growth process due to interactions with nature in all creation. But it may take thousands and millions of years for this natural growth; that is the long, instinctive way in animals. Man, endowed with discrimination power, conscious thinking faculty, the Mind *(Buddhi)* and well-developed voluntary control systems, aspires to accelerate his growth. Yoga is that systematic conscious process which can compress the process of man's growth greatly.

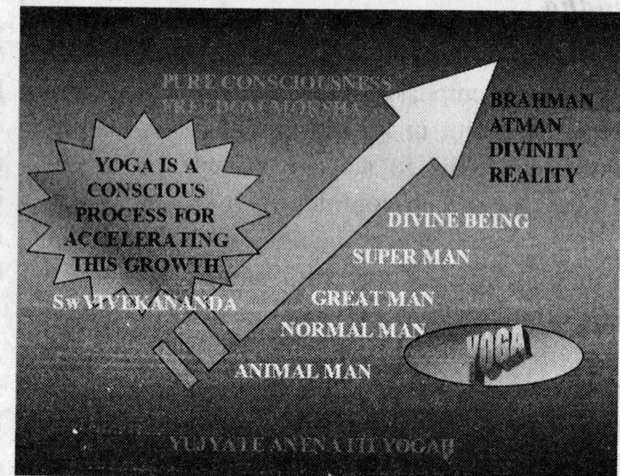

Sri Aurobindo emphasizes an all-round personality development; at the physical, mental, intellectual, emotional and spiritual levels. He means by Yoga a methodical effort towards self-perfection by the development of the potentialities latent in the individual. It is a process by which the limitations and imperfections can be washed away resulting in a super human race.

Thus, Yoga is a systematic process for accelerating the growth of a man in his entirety. With this growth, man learns to live at higher states of consciousness. Key to this all-round personality development and growth is the culturing of mind.

The main thesis we have been trying to establish is this: Value orientation must be supported by Reality orientation. Values have no value in themselves. It is the reality behind the values that gives them power. Values must be rooted in reality.

Values according to *Patanjali Yoga* and *Hatha Yoga*

Speaking the truth, loving all, compassion, honesty, sincerity, respect, helping the needy, charity etc. are some of the universal values for all human beings at all times. These are not different from the values recommended by Yoga.

Yogic set of values

Yogic set of values comes from at least two sources:

(*i*) Yoga of Patanjali, and

(*ii*) Hatha Yogic texts.

Types of values in general and according to Patanjali's Yoga and Hatha Yoga.

(i) Yoga of Patanjali

Yoga of Patanjali gives a set of values under the name of the *Yamas*. The set of Yamas are well-known to the students of Yoga. Yoga firmly holds that these are universal values. Every social human being must follow them without any compromise.

There is no leniency to be shown for an aspirant Yogi as regards these practices. A prospective Yogi must integrate these with life.

The word Yama means social observances, restraining the Self, to act or behave carefully, to think twice or even thrice before you commit any one of these. Think of the consequences that they may beget. According to the consequences, you will feel either good or bad. Thus it depends on you how would you like to feel. Good or bad. The choice is yours.

You might want to know what Patanjali says about the Yamas. He says something special. Let us consider.

Jati-desa-kala-samayanavacchinnah sarvabhaumah mahavratam Yoga Sutra 3.31

These five *Yamas* are to be applied in life without any exception since these are of highest significance. These are to be practiced without any consideration of time, place, person and the like.

You cannot say that to one person or animal you will be kind and not to others. This will not do. You should not say that to someone or at particular time you will speak the truth and not to others on other times. Does this make sense to you? Yes, I guess what you are thinking. How is it possible to speak truth all the time? Don't you bother at this moment yet?

What are the components of *Yama?*

Yamas of Patanjali are: *Ahimsa* (non-violence), *Satya* (truthfulness), *Asteya* (non-stealing), *Brahmacharya* (celibacy, meditation on brahma) and *Aparigraha* (non-acquisitiveness).

Let us have a little bit of clarity on each of these Yamas.

Ahimsa: Non-violence, not to cause harms to any living being by any deed or thought. It is so since the same animal or human being can retaliate in the same manner or even with more severity. The peace will be missing. Safety will be missing.

Satya: You certainly feel good when somebody speaks truth to you. Similar is the case with someone else to whom you speak the truth. For example, if you bunk the school for a day and the same is brought to the notice of your parents/guardians, it is expected that you speak the truth. Accept the mistake. This will make the things easier. Otherwise you will have a heavy burden on your heart and mind and also relation will spoil. Moreover, people will hardly believe you. The similar set of criteria applies to all the other practices of *Yama* as well.

Asteya (non-stealing): To grab or snatch away something not belonging to me. I have no right to claim on something which is not legitimately owned by me. This is not socially or morally acceptable.

Brahmacharya (celibacy or devotion to Supreme Providence): This word has two shades of interpretation. (*i*) not to enter into physical relationship with opposite gender out of wedlock. (*ii*) to develop and maintain a deep and sincere feeling of devotion towards Brahma (the Supreme Lord).

Aparigraha (non-accumulation, non-acquisition, not to have hoarding tendency, not to accumulate too many material objects which are not essential for living): Hoarding is a covert means to deprive someone else who might be in need of the same badly.

(ii) Hatha Yogic texts

There are number of texts which espouse the lessons of values. We shall limit our discussion only on the text of **Hathapradipika. Ch.vi,** (The Lonavala Yoga Institute, Lonavala, 2011) which describes values and related topics quite well. This text has narrated a number of values which are to be followed by everybody.

One is equipped with certain strong points as well as weak points. All of you possess some divine qualities and also certain dark areas. By default, this is common to all of us. In the first place one should create 'awareness' as regards to this aspect of one's personality which subsequently will help re-organizing dominance of these qualities on the required lines.

We are briefly outlining some of these personal values in the following lines:

The positive values (qualities) are: forgiveness, respect, generosity, and wisdom.

The negative aspects are: jealousy, envy, criticism, falsehood (it is opposite to *Satya*), anger and violence (opposite to *Ahimsa*).

There is another way to look at these values which is as follows:

Hatha Yoga divides these into three broad classes, namely, *Sattvika, Rajasika* and *Tamasika.*

'Sattvikabhava'

Forgiveness, compassion, generosity, respect are some of the *Sattvikabhavas.*

An individual with *Rajasika Bhava* is often engaged in activities, tending to have a control over the people around his/her, and is deeply attached with and attracted towards family especially the wife, children and property. Such a person has a tendency to reign over people, and often interested in attaining the result of goal without any consideration about the means to be applied in the attainment of goal.

Some of the *Tamasika* values are falsehood, envy, lethargy and other negative aspects as indicated above.

You want to raise a question. These human traits are not covered under *Yama* and *Niyama.* So why should we discuss about them?

You have a point. These do not appear in *Yama* and *Niyama.* These also are important human values. We cannot ignore them.

The text of *Hathapradipika* suggests that one will do well by reducing the negative qualities or values by practice of Yogic techniques. Yogic techniques will help a person to promote the positive qualities.

Thus to consider these among values is necessitated.

Development of the Self cannot be possible without taking these into consideration.

The text says that *Sattvikabhavas* are divine virtues *(daivi gunas).* You should keep on enhancing them.

Some *Rajasikabhavas* are to be used carefully, with lot of judiciousness. Inappropriate use of *Rajasikabhavas* can bring disturbance in one's Self. Also there can be disturbance in social setup.

Tamasika features are always to be conquered upon, for these can only cause damage to the individual as also to the society at large.

INTERNAL YOGA

Swami Vivekananda enunciated that concentration and detachment are the principles of true education to achieve the goal of total development. This is what *Patanjali* portrayed in his second sutra while defining the term Yoga.

Yogah chitta vritti nirodhaha

Yoga is total control over mental modifications. It is a capacity to concentrate which helps to overcome the haphazardness of the mind developing the skill to vanquish them totally and remain silent. Thus the fundamental part of education is to achieve the mastery. ***Yoga vasishtha*** an important yogic scripture defines yoga as:

Manah Prasamano payah yogah ityabhi dheeyate

To meet out the demand of modern life-style full of speed and stresses development of an all-around personality is mandatory. Internal yoga is what Sri Aurobindo suggested. This then brings a four-fold consciousness—civic sense, patriotic urge, service zeal and spiritual aspiration to make man a holistic and an able component of the society in which he lives. This approach towards a total growth of man forms the basis of a holistic vision of education.

The integrated personality development comprises of the following components:

(a) Personality development at the physical level

An ideal body essentially means a proportionate body with all the muscles relaxed in formal state. It is soft like a flower flexible to the core. Instantaneously it can acquire diamond like hardness too. All the organs and systems in the body with least abnormality is the first feature of good personality at the physical level. The chronic and acute ailments are thus absent in such a body.

The second aspect of personality development at the physical level is to make the body work more efficiently by using the energies in the most controlled fashion. At resting periods metabolic rate is normal and during normal activities just the necessary amount of energy is used by the body. The body sets all the necessary strength to deal with the critical situation.

This stamina of harnessing the inner vital energies and training the different organs and systems to work in such co-ordination can be effectively accomplished by yogic practice. It is in this area of application of YOGA that specialists in physical culture, wrestlers, sportsmen and dancers are keenly interested and thus practise yoga.

(b) Personality development at mental level

The power of imagination, *i.e.*, the **creativity** and steadfastness or **will power** are the two aspects of the mind which come under this head of personality development. It has been seen that yogic practice enhances the creative power of man. Hence many musicians, poets, film artists, engineers and technologists have been attracted to yoga.

Will power is an essential requirement for all persons to accomplish any work however insignificant or great the task is. Yoga by its systemic and conscious process of calming down the mind erases the weaknesses and builds the will power within. Such a powerful mind possesses tremendous energy to combat any given situation. Thus bravery becomes a part of the personality. Therefore challenges are being turned into opportunities successfully.

(c) Personality development at Intellectual level

In the modern area of science, a sharp intellect and the faculty of reason play a key role in the scheme of education. Thinking and perceptive analysis are now valued more in the learning process. The children are taught right from the primary stage to think logically and scientifically. The capacity to analyze and correlate relevant information forms the function of the intellect. Concentration with precision is the need of the hour.

However the enhanced power of a sharp intellect associated with powerful concentration has bound man to the whirlpool of its strong clutches. His worries and attachment do not release him. The development of personality at the intellectual level should not only sharpen the intellect but also must provide mastery over the dominating power of the sharpened intellect.

Swami Vivekananda rightly emphasized that Concentration and Detachment as the two vital parts of education. One should not only learn to dwell deep in any subject but also should learn to come out of it. It is again YOGA that can bring this comprehensive development of the intellect. Hence YOGA is attracting the attention of intellectual community too.

(d) Personality development at Emotional level

Our emotions control our behaviour especially at crucial junctures. The challenges of the modern era pose a great threat to the emotional faculty of man probably stronger than ever. Yet the culturing of our emotional faculties finds no place in the whole scheme of education. Man finds himself lost amidst the struggle of life unable to overcome his emotional conflicts and turmoil. The result is deep unrest, agony and thereby the emergence of psychosomatic ailments.

Yoga trains us to:

- systematically sharpen and sensitize our emotion,
- consciously expand and diffuse the over tones of emotions.

Thus YOGA offers a fine tool for the development of the emotional personality of a man.

(e) Personality development at Spiritual level

A man may have very sturdy physique, amazing creative power, a powerful intellect and highly sensitized emotional grasp, yet may have no idea of spiritual happiness. He may not possess inclination towards the spiritual dimension. According to *Kathopanishad,* generally we are so structured that we always seek things outside. The senses grasp the things around them predominantly, the objects of the world outside. But the real happiness, knowledge and the secret of solution to all the problems lies within us. Hence Kathopanishad suggests every man to unravel the mysteries that lie within him.

Such knowledge shall make our lives more comfortable and enjoyable. This knowledge shall help bringing up our children to perpetuate and sustain in the society striving to set patterns of behaviour, etiquettes and so on. The inner search begins the quest for reality and bliss.

Paranchi khaani vyatrinat paribhuhu

Svayambhuhu tasmat paran pashyati naantaraatman

Kaschit dheeraha pratyagaatmaana maikshatha

Avrutta chakshuhu Amrutattva micchan.

This is a stage where a person marches towards spirituality. It is this inward look or an inner awareness which helps us to work upon the subtler layers of the mind and unfold them. Yoga is not only a process for leading man towards his hidden personality by bringing mastery over the body, mind, intellect and emotional faculties but also a powerful tool to manifest those hidden potentials.

The process of development of personality is a continuous function of one's growth and the enfoldment of perfection in him. This growth of the individual is coupled with the emergence of the five fold consciousness enunciated earlier. Yogic techniques provide many more benefits besides the advantage of stress and anxiety free tendency. Sri Aurobindo emphasizes that Yoga provides an all-round personality development at physical, mental, intellectual, emotional and spiritual levels.

Srimad Bhagavad Gita says that repeated cogitation and looping of thoughts is the prime reason to make a personality sick and weak. This features mental and emotional imbalances which later on lead to physical illnesses. Hence there arouse the need of a study which could reveal a gauge of progressive improvements occurring in the physical, mental, emotional layers of a prisoner. Prisoners countenance life as a compulsion, wherein they lead a life full of trauma in continuous cogitation of past events.

YOGA FOR STRESS MANAGEMENT

CONCEPT OF STRESS

Stress from the modern perspective

Stress is a normal response of the body towards the situations which seem difficult to manage. Actually, our body has various psycho-biological systems which regularly work for the sake of our survival. For this purpose, a constant monitoring of our internal and external environment is done by our brain. In routine, we face many difficult situations which are perceived as a threat to our well-being and survival. In order to cope with those situations our body's psycho-biological systems take automatic corrective actions. For example, in the extreme heat, sweat glands in our body start producing sweat in order to bring the body temperature back to normal. Similarly, in situations of danger, we become more alert and pay more attention to the clues which may help in finding solution to the problem. These responses are the autonomic responses generated by our body and mind to such situations. In routine, these autonomic responses help us in our well-being and in our survival. But sometimes, there are situations which are too difficult to be handled in the routine way. In order to adjust with such situations our body and mind have to work extra; and as a result certain responses take place in our body and mind. These responses which occur within our body and mind to tackle the difficult situations, are called 'stress' response. Thus, stress is the psycho-physiological responses which take place in the person to tackle a difficult situation.

For example, if we hear a very loud noise and sense any kind of danger, psychological and physiological responses would immediately start taking place. Psychologically, our mind would become extra alert. We would try to figure out what the noise means to us. Our thinking becomes focused and we try to find the solutions/ways to protect ourselves from the perceived danger. On the biological level, our glands start working and produce hormones which help us get extra energy to fight with or flight from that situation. During stress, both body and mind reach an altered state *i.e.*, it is different from normal homeostatic conditions.

Stress (psycho-physiological responses) takes place in the difficult situations, called 'stressor'. In simple words, we can also say that stress is the general psycho-physiological response of a person to a stressor. In this sense, any object, situation or event which causes stress can be called the stressor. It can be any pleasant or unpleasant change in the environment like marriage, arrival of a new member in the family, promotion, death of someone in the family or of a near and dear one, an ill-tampered boss, a break in relationship etc. It can be any simple sensory input or physical demands like extremes of cold, heat, disease conditions, exercise etc. or it can be major catastrophic events like earthquake, flood, riots, or any other social situations, which are perceived harmful, dangerous and exceeding our personal resources. The only thing which underlies stress is that the stressor demands coping.

Here, one thing very important is that the stressor depends upon the threat perception about the situation. Only those situations which are perceived as difficult can become stressor. The situations which are perceived not too difficult do not act as stressor. A marriage or a promotion in job may become stressor for the person who perceives that the responsibilities/changes associated with them (marriage or the promotion) are too difficult to cope with. This implies that a situation may act as stressor for one person while the same may not be stressor for another person. Therefore, marriage or promotion will be perceived by one person as difficult situation, while the same may be perceived by another person an opportunity to grow. Similarly, one student may perceive the examination as a progressive tool. But another student may perceive the examination as a threat, and for her/him the examination will become stressor. Thus, stress is not caused by the situation, rather it is caused by the perception about the situation.

Further, the degree of stress would depend upon how much threat is being perceived by the individual in the situation. Same situation may create different amount of stress in different persons. For example, the marriage, promotion or examination may produce mild stress in one person; while in another person, these may create severe stress. Thus, we can say that perception plays an important role in stress; and also cause individual differences in the responses.

The stressor may not always be real. Sometimes it is imaginary or is an anticipated object/situation. For example, a person employed in a good job may be unnecessarily stressed to think that one day she/he may have to quit the job. Similarly, a person may imagine that others do not like her/him and may become stressed. In these cases, the situations are not real or actually present, but are only imaginary situations or an unseen future which may cause stress in the person stressed.

From the above discussion, it is clear, that stress is a dynamic state of the body. In this state, several changes take place within us and prepare our body and mind to tackle the danger which is perceived to be inherent in the situation. For example, suppose we are having a walk. Suddenly we hear gun-shots and find ourselves in a dangerous situation. Immediately, our endocrine system becomes active; our blood pressure and heart rate increase; our digestion becomes slow; and we become highly alert and focused. All these responses occurring within us help our body and mind to cope with the danger. The increase in the heart rate and blood pressure facilitate the pumping of important chemicals into different parts of body and especially the muscles. Slow digestion would help our body to divert the blood supply to the muscles of legs and/or arms which in that situation require it more. Similarly, high alertness helps us to analyze even small clues and take fast decisions. Overall, these changes prepare us in our responses to fight or to flight.

Type of stress

There are two types of stress: eu-stress and distress (figure):

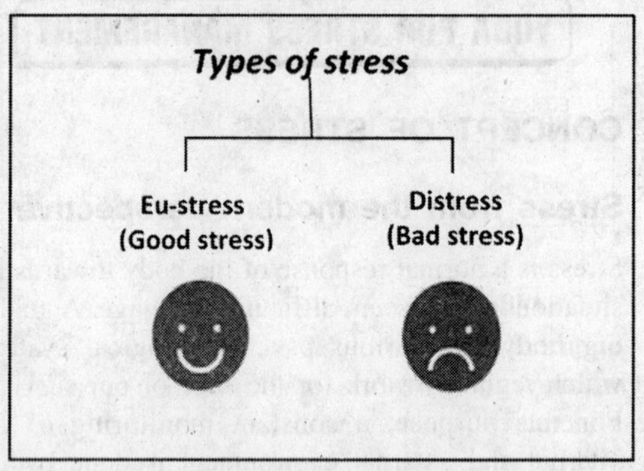

Fig.: *Types of stress*

Eu-stress is good or a pleasant form of stress. It is caused by pleasant stimuli or events like marriage, promotion, birth of a child in the family, sitting for the competitive examination etc. It is related to successful handling of a difficult situation. It is a healthy stress as it leads to better performance and better opportunities leading towards growth and development. It motivates the person to work better like getting a good score or rank in an examination or performing better in job.

Distress is a bad or harmful stress which is caused by undesirable, unpredictable and uncontrollable factors which are perceived too difficult to be managed. It may also be caused by prolonged and/or severe stress like prolonged financial troubles or continuous heavy work-load. This type of stress is characterized by worry, fear of failure etc. Chronic distress may result into various psychological and physiological problems. It is important to understand that eu-stress, if not managed properly, can convert into distress.

Relationship between stress and performance

We can see that consequences of the stress make it good or bad. If the stress is of mild degree, it is manageable and gives us pleasure then it is eu-stress. If the stress is severe, chronic and unmanageable; then it is distress. There is relationship between the stress and performance (see figure).

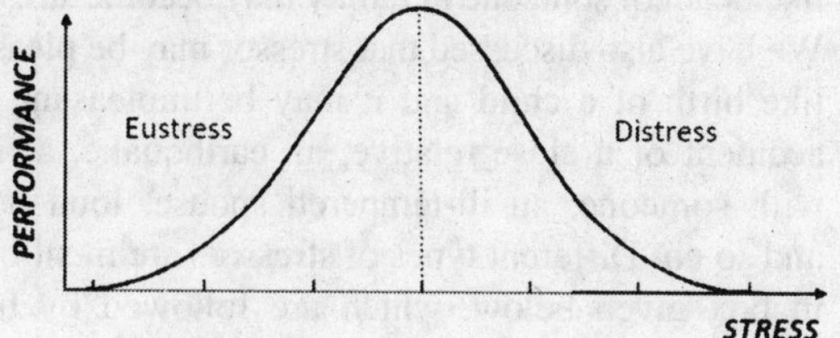

Fig.: *Stress and performance*

Figure shows that mild stress becomes eu-stress and enhances the performance. But as the degree of stress increases it gets converted into distress and negatively affects the performance. There is a relationship between the degree of stress and the level of performance. The performance increases with the increase in stress upto certain level. After this, as the stress increases the performance starts decreasing.

Physiology of stress

The autonomic nervous system is important for stress. During stress, sympathetic nervous system gets activated to cope with the situation. As a result, a number of hormonal and other physiological changes take place in response to the stressor. These changes provide us strength to fight or to run away from the stressor. Once the stressor disappears, the parasympathetic nervous system of the body takes over. As a result our hormone levels return to normal; body starts to calm down; blood pressure becomes normal; heart rate falls and muscles relax.

The physiology of stress can be understood from the work of Hans Selye, an eminent endocrinologist. Hans Selye coined a term 'general adaptation syndrome (GAS)' for body's responses to the stressors. The GAS implies that during stress, a massive bodily activity takes place within a person. This activity helps in adapting to the stressor, hence the name. According to Hans Selye, responses of the body occur in three stages: (*i*) the alarm reaction, (*ii*) the stage of resistance, and (*iii*) the stage of exhaustion.

The stage of **alarm reaction** is basically the emergency responses of the body which are generally regulated by sympathetic nervous system. For example, during stress, muscle tone decreases; and heart rate and blood pressure increase. These responses prepare our body to cope with the stressor here and now. Thus the alarm reactions prepare us to face the threat.

The **stage of resistance** begins if the stressor continues to be present. In this stage, the body starts resisting the effects of continuing stressors mainly with the help of hormonal responses such as cortisol, adrenalin etc. These hormones provide our body more fuel to cope with the stressor. They help us to resist the stressor for a long time; and help us to adapt to the situations. As a result, the efficiency of the person increases. But it depletes our recourses as our body has limited resources. Due to the reduced resources at hand, the body at this stage cannot face other stressors. Therefore, if some other stressor occurs during this period, the body cannot cope with the new situation (figure). Thus, the phase of resistance leads towards adaptation but results in the depletion of the energy available, as a result the person becomes incapable of resisting new stressors. If this stage continues for long, then comes the stage of exhaustion.

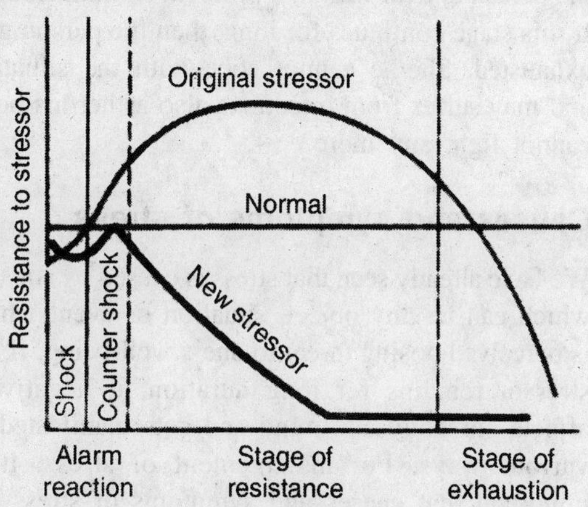

Fig.: *Selye's general adoption syndrome*

In the stage of exhaustion the resources of the body are exhausted. As a result, the person is unable to respond to the continuing and also to the new stressors. The person may not be able to fight off the infections. As a result of her/his diminished immunity, she/he may fall sick and may even die.

The following example can further clear the GAS syndrome. Suppose, a person meets an accident. The person is initially shocked. Immediately the alarm reactions start taking place within the body. There may be an increase in heart rate and blood pressure. The pulse rate also may not be normal. Hormonal changes also take place within the body. These changes provide extra fuel and energy to the body which will enable the person to deal with the situation. In this case, the person would call a doctor or call someone for help to take her/him to hospital. Thus the alarm reactions prepared the person to cope with the stressor of accident-injury. If the injury is not much, the situation becomes normal and the stress will be over at this stage of alarm reaction. But if the injury proves to be serious and requires prolonged hospitalisation, then the person may remain in the state of prolonged physiological changes. This is the phase of resistance. In this stage, the physiological changes will help the person to adapt to the situation but will reduce her/his bodily resources. In this phase, if some other problem takes place in the family, then it will be difficult for the person to deal with that problem simultaneously. If this stage continues for long, then the person gets exhausted. She/he cannot cope with the situation and may suffer from infections also as her/his body cannot fight any more.

Causes and symptoms of stress

We have already seen that stress is caused by stressor which can be any object, situation or event which is perceived posing threat to one's well-being. If the stressor remains for long duration, it negatively affects our body and mind and gets manifested in various ways. For management of stress, it is important that causes and symptoms of stress are identified. In this section, we will discuss what may cause stress and what may be the symptoms of stress.

(a) Causes of stress

There may be numerous stressors and it is difficult to identify them. *A stressor can be mild or strong.* A mild stressor like traffic jam or a strong stressor like death of someone in family may become stressor. We have also discussed that stressor may be pleasant like birth of a child and it may be unpleasant like accident of a close relative, an earthquake, a fight with someone, an ill-tempered spouse, loud noise and so on. Different types of stressors are mentioned in box given below, which are followed by brief description as under:

Stressors
○ Physical conditions
○ Physiological states
○ Psychological conditions
○ Personal life events
○ Social conditions
○ Working place related conditions.

Box: *Sources/conditions of stressors*

- *Physical conditions* which are present in the external environment can cause stress in a person. High altitude, tough geographical conditions, extreme temperature, natural calamities like flood, earthquake, man-made disasters, riots, war etc fall in this category.
- *Physiological states* such as fatigue, old age, puberty, pregnancy and pathological conditions of any disease are important causes of stress. You might have noticed that during these conditions tolerance and resistance get reduced and the person may then undergo stress even as a result of mild conditions.
- *Psychological conditions* such as frustrations, conflicts, pressures, lack of tolerance, high aspirations, unrealistic goals, negative attitude, emotional turmoil etc. may also cause stress in a person. Emotional stressors are important psychological stressors. There are several emotional stressors. Charlesworth and Nathan state that emotional stressors are found in different combinations in different persons. Each individual has a unique set of emotional stressors. One person may become stressed on being late on an

appointment but may not be much affected by her/his financial resources; while another person may be anxious due to insufficient financial resources but may not be affected by being late on an appointment. Psychological conditions are very important for stress. A person who has less tolerance can become easily stressed. Similarly our frustrations also may make us more prone to stress.

- *Personal life events* such as wedding, divorce, death of someone, new arrival, accidents, personal financial problems etc. may also become stressor for a person. The people who are undergoing personal problems in life become easily stressed even by small conditions.
- *Social conditions* such as family structure and relationship within the family are some social conditions which may become stressor. Social stressors involve interactions with other people. The social stressors vary from person to person. For example, attending a party or social functions may become stressor for a person who likes to stay at home while for an outgoing person, staying at home may become stressor. Social support also is important for stress. A person who has support of the family, has good relations with the family members is less likely to undergo stress; while a person without any social support may get easily stressed. Similarly, *social environment* such as tough competition, discrimination, fast-paced life, political turmoil, imbalances in society etc. can produce stress in a person.
- *Working place related conditions* such as exploitation by the employer, irregular working hours, problems related to transfers and promotion, relationship with colleagues and the behaviour of a boss etc. may become stressor to a person. Job-contents also may be source of stress. Work-related stressor also differ from person to person.

(b) Symptoms of stress

Identifying stress is an important step in stress management. Prolonged stress negatively affects the body and mind and may get manifested in physiological, emotional, cognitive/intellectual, behavioural and work-performance related symptoms. The following symptoms help us to identify that the person is undergoing stress.

- *Physiological symptoms:* Prolonged stress gets reflected in physiological symptoms like headaches, backache, pain in neck and shoulders, sweating specially over nose and palm, palpitations, pounding heart, breathlessness, tight muscles etc. A stressed person may feel fatigued and dizziness. She/he may have sleeping problems like over-sleeping or insomnia and may have digestive problems as constipation, diarrhoea, nausea. As the person has less immunity, she/he becomes prone to infections like colds and flu. She/he would be more susceptible to accidents.
- *Intellectual or cognitive behaviour:* Stress shows itself in intellectual or cognitive behaviour also. Poor concentration, memory problems, inability to make decisions or making hasty decisions, loss of sense of humour, lack of logical thinking, negative thinking are some of the symptoms which indicate that the person is undergoing stress.
- *Emotional behaviour:* Stress is manifested in the emotional behaviour too. In stress, the person experiences anxiety and fear. She/he becomes restless for no apparent reasons. Her/his behaviour may be marked by frequent mood swings, sadness, discontentment, hostility, irritability, aggression, impatience and unhappiness. The person may lose the zest for life and confidence. She/he may be having worries about health and may experience difficulty in relaxing. Overall a lack in sense of well-being prevails in the person.
- *Physical and social behaviour:* Stress can be identified with the help of behavioural

symptoms also. Sometimes, the person may indulge in unnecessary increased spending. Her/his physical appearance may be unkempt appearance coupled by poor hygiene. Nail-biting, addictions, substance abuse are some of the behaviours which indicate the presence of stress.

During stress, social behaviour also gets affected. The person may face problems in relationships due to her/his impulsive behaviour. She/he may lose temper more easily causing problems in interpersonal behaviour. This may be seen in the work place also in form of absenteeism, poor time management, over-working, failure to delegate, fall in usual standards etc. The person may be irritable with colleagues resulting in poor inter-personal relationships. Her/his efficiency to perform tasks may go down.

Consequences of stress

We have seen that stress may be good (eu-stress) or bad (distress). It is the consequences which make the stress good or bad. Mild stress acts as eu-stress and is beneficial for performance. It motivates the person to acquire skills which are needed to cope with stressor and thus helps in her/his personality development.

It is the severe and chronic stress which is harmful and leads to several physical and psychological problems. According to American Psychological Association, stress becomes dangerous when it interferes with our ability to live a normal life over an extended period. Dealing with relationship problems, death of the spouse, severe financial problems, unemployment etc are such problems which may make us tired, irritable and unable to concentrate. Stress can also damage our physical health.

We have studied in earlier sections that in order to deal with the stressor, certain psychophysiological changes occur within our body. These changes prepare us person to cope with the stressor. However, if the stressor remains for long then the body also have to remain in the altered state for longer time which may be harmful for the person. In this section, we would like to study the adverse effects of stress which are given below:

(i) Impairment in cognition

A person perceives threat in the stressor. This threat perception may affect his/her sensory input, memory, attention, decision-making capacity etc. Under chronic stress, the memory and concentration get reduced. The person may suffer from forgetfulness. She/he may misunderstand the normal things. For example, examination is a stressor for some students. Such students during examination may not read the instructions properly or may misinterpret the questions or may forget the answers. Similarly, during stress we are so focused on the problem that we may ignore various clues which could help in finding the solution. In stress, we may not be able to see the problem from different angles. This happens due to narrowed down attention and the rigidity in our perception during the stress.

(ii) Inappropriate emotional reactions

Prolonged stress may affect one's emotional reactions. If a person remains in stress for a long time, her/his emotional responses may not be appropriate and she/he may continue to experience negative unpleasant emotions, such as fear, anger, anxiety etc. even after the stressor has disappeared.

In addition to this, if negative emotions remain unexpressed, this may lead to helplessness and depression. Prolonged stress may make the person pathologically over-sensitive or insensitive. In over-sensitivity, the person intensely responds to those stimuli which may not be evoking responses otherwise. For example, even a phone-call may make a person scared. A needle-prick which otherwise does not provoke any reaction in normal situations, may cause much pain. In the case of insensitivity, the person remains unaffected by the sufferings of self and the others. For example, during examination a student may become indifferent to the pain of her/ his ailing family member.

(iii) Lowering of work efficiency and performance

Prolonged stress may adversely affect the efficiency of a person. It may hinder the efforts to tackle the situation. Due to stress, quality of work also suffers. A person under constant stress, may commit several mistakes and may not perform well. For example, examination jitters may lead the student to perform poorly despite adequate preparation. A speaker may find it difficult to speak properly and start stammering in a debate. Or in a situation of intense danger, we may become rooted to the ground and unable to take self-defense. All these examples show that the efficiency and performance gets negatively affected by the stress.

(iv) Problems in social behaviour and interpersonal relationships

Social relations also may suffer due to stress. A person under stress may avoid social contacts. We have discussed that stress gives rise to negative emotions. Due to this, a persón may experience irritability and hostility towards others, which may break relationships. For example, a husband who is being harassed by the boss may easily lose temper at home. As a result, there may be frequent fights at home. This would also adversely affect her/his interpersonal relationships. Social problems such as divorce, drug-addiction, murders could be the result of stress.

(v) Lowering of resistance to new stressors

Prolonged stress lowers the resistance of body. During stress, body's ability toward off attacking viruses gets diminished and the person becomes more prone to infections. In previous section, we have discussed that our body's coping resources are limited. If these resources are utilized for long, the same may not be available to tackle other situations. It is generally found that physiologically, a person may develop resistance to one disease but may become prone to other disease. Coleman quotes an example from the work of Selye in which mice were exposed to extreme cold. These mice developed increased resistance to cold but became unusually sensitive to X-rays. Similarly, a person who remains in constant stress, becomes psychologically weak. Coleman gives the example of soldiers, who are strong enough to combat in the battle field; they can face any bad news related to the battle, but may not face bad news from home.

(vi) Health problems

Stress affects physiological and psychological well-being of a person. People who remain under severe stress may develop physiological and psychological problems. Now medical science also is recognizing that stress can increase the risk of several diseases.

Severe and chronic stress makes our body and mind weak. It may induce pathology in organs and systems of our body. Various psycho-somatic diseases like peptic ulcers, migraine, backache, diabetes, high blood pressure, heart attack, brain strokes may be the result of chronic and severe stress. Chronic stress remains a major cause of psychological problems like maladaptive behaviour, anxiety disorders, depression, suicide, delinquency, imbalanced personality etc. In extreme cases, stress may cause death even.

In modern times, we are witnessing a rapid increase in psycho-somatic diseases like diabetes mellitus, high blood pressure, heart attack, brain strokes and post-traumatic stress disorder (PTSD). Various psychological problems like depression, anxiety-related disorders, addiction, suicide etc. are on the increase in modern times. These happenings can be explained by the facts that in modern times, the life is full of stress. Complexities of modern life are pushing many of us towards intense stress. Each stress leaves its traces on mind and body and causes irreversible wear and tear and pathology in body and mind. If a person remains in stress for long time, our body and mind become weak and dysfunctional and give rise to psycho-somatic and psychiatric diseases.

Stress from a Yogic perspective

Stress, from a Yogic perspective, can be seen little differently. We should remember that Yoga is basically a mind-controlling discipline; and in Yoga, the facts of life have been discussed in relation to mind and behaviour. From Yogic perspective, stress can be seen as a mental state of unhappiness and emotional instability.

According to Patanjali, a person's original state is a stress-free state. This state is devoid of any tension. In this state, *chitta* (mind) remains calm and relaxed; and unaffected by external events. This is the ideal state. However, this original tension-free and blissful state becomes emotionally unstable due to various *klesas* namely *avidya* (wrong knowledge), *asmita* (I-ness), *raga* (liking or attachment to worldly possessions), *dvesa* (disliking and negative emotions) and *abhinivesa* (fear of death).

According to Patanjali Yoga Sutra (P.Y.S. 2.3), the main cause of this emotional instability is *avidya.* (ignorance). Due to *avidya*, non-eternal worldly things are mistaken as eternal (P.Y.S. 2.5). Impure things are mistaken as pure and pain-giving things are mistaken as happiness-giving. Due to *avidya*, the mind becomes externally oriented and tries to seek happiness through worldly possessions. This makes the mind unstable and gives rise to the stress.

In *Bhagavad Gita,* the state of mental instability has been discussed in detail. In fact, stress is the main theme of *Bhagavad Gita.* According to *Bhagavad Gita*, stress starts with our attachment and desire for worldly things. In life we have so many desires. These desires make us emotionally unstable and negatively affect our cognition. According to *Bhagavad Gita*, constant thinking about objects leads to attachment with the objects, attachment leads to lust (strong likes and dislikes), lust leads to anger; anger leads to delusion; delusion leads to loss of memory; loss of memory leads to loss of intelligence (aviveka or loss of discriminating ability); and ultimately one gets destroyed (BG: II:62-63).

Dhyayato visayan pumsah sangastesupajayate/

Samgat samjayate kamah kamat krodho' bhijayate//

Krodhat bhavati sammohah sammohat smrtivibhramah/

Smritibhramsad buddhinaso buddhinasat pranasyati//(BG: II:62-63)

In Yogic texts, we find references of various symptoms of emotional instability. Patanjali (P.Y.S. 1.31) mentions that pain, depression, shaking of body and unrhythmic breathing are the symptoms of mental instability. In *Bhagavad Gita* also, we find the indication of the symptoms of stress when Arjuna says that he feels that the limbs of his body are quivering; mouth is drying up, whole of his body is trembling; hair are standing erect, his bow *Gandiva* is slipping from his hands and the skin is burning; he is unable to stand up; he is forgetting himself; his mind is feeling and he sees the misfortune (Bhagavad Gita, 1. 28-30). All these symptoms indicate that Arjuna was under grave stress.

How does stress take place in a person?

The answer to this question, may be given with the concept of *Panchakosa.* We have discussed the concept of *Panchakosa* in detail in the previous Unit on "Yoga and Personality Development". From that section, you may recall that the real identity of the person is the 'Self'. This 'Self' is covered by a series of five sheaths, namely, *annamaya kosa, pranamaya kosa, manomaya kosa, vijnanamaya kosa* and *anandamaya kosa.* Each *kosa* affects other *kosas* which are in close contact and also gets affected by them.

With reference to stress, *manomaya kosa* is more important. Stress is primarily related to *manomaya kosa.* Chronic worries, anxiety and tension cause disturbance in the *manomaya kosa.* Thus, stress originates in *manomaya kosa.* From *manomaya kosa* it spreads to other *kosas* and adversely affects them. On one hand, stress in *manomaya kosa* adversely affects *pranamaya kosa* and *annamaya kosa;* and on the other hand it negatively affects *vijnanamaya kosa* and *anandamaya kosa.* When stress reaches *pranamaya* and *annamaya kosa* from the *manomaya kosa,* diseases in the body take place; and when stress affects the *vijnanamaya* and *anandmaya kosa,* psychological disorders take place.

How do psycho-somatic disorders develop?

Psycho-somatic disorders are the result of stress. These seem to develop in the following four phases:

1. Psychic Phase
2. Psychosomatic Phase
3. Somatic Phase
4. Organic Phase

- **Psychic phase** is marked by mild but persistent psychological symptoms of stress like irritability, disturbed sleep and other minor symptoms. This phase can be said to be related with *vijnanamaya* and *manomaya kosas.* Yoga as a therapy can be effectively used in this phase.
- **Psychosomatic phase** occurs if the stress continues for long. In the psychosomatic phase, there is an increase in symptoms. In this phase, psychological symptoms of earlier phase are accompanied by physiological symptoms, such as occasional hypertension, tremors, weakness. In this phase, the disease has progressed from the *manomaya* to the *pranamaya kosa.* Thus, both *manomaya* and *pranamaya kosas* are affected. Yoga can be effectively used in this phase also.
- **Somatic phase** is a more advanced stage of disease. At this phase, the disease takes a direction and gets manifested with its symptoms. The adverse effects of stress are visible on several organs and systems of body. The functioning of many organs, particularly the targeted organ get disturbed like heart or cardio-vascular system, pancreas, or any other organ or system may become dysfunctional. In this stage, *pranamaya* and *annamaya kosas* are affected as disease has progressed from *pranamaya* to the *annamaya kosa* also. Yoga in this phase may need to be used with other methods of treatment.
- **Organic phase** is the final stage of disease. In this stage, the disease is fully manifested with pathological changes in the targeted organ of the body. For example, the heart or pancreas may become completely dysfunctional. The person may experience the complications of diabetes mellitus or chronic hypertension. In this phase, the disease has finally settled into the *annamaya kosa.* In this phase, Yoga as a therapy has a palliative effect; it can reduce the pain and can improve quality of life.

Yoga as a way of life to cope with stress

We have studied that stress is essentially associated with life. Wherever there is life, there is stress. Life without stress is probably not thinkable. The crematorium is the only place which is stress-free but it is without life. The essence is that we cannot avoid stress. But we can definitely manage it. Therefore, it is important that we know how to manage it. There are ways by which stress can be managed. Yoga is one of them. Udupa has found that Yoga can immensely help in prevention of stress-related diseases by successfully managing the stress.

Yoga is viewed in several ways. Some people consider Yoga as a set of *asanas* (physical postures), *pranayama* (breathing techniques) and meditation. Some consider Yoga as a prescribed course consisting of physical exercises. And for some people it is a way of life. Again for some people, it is a spiritual discipline which is aimed at spiritual evolution. Here in the next section, we shall focus on Yoga as the life style for healthy living.

Yoga, as a life style, is based on certain principles which are beneficial for healthy living. These principles are found in philosophy of various schools of Yoga such as *Jnana-Yoga, Raja-Yoga, Karma-Yoga* and *Bhakti-Yoga* and are enshrined in traditional texts of Yoga like *Patanjali Yoga Sutra, Bhagavad Gita, Hatha Yoga Pradipika, Gherand Samhita, Hatha Ratnavali etc.*

Yogic principles are universal in nature and can be adopted by all human beings irrespective of time, place, age, gender, profession or race. These principles are related to every aspect of life and treat the person as a whole. The Yogic principles bring about harmony between body and mind. At the physical level, they focus on strength, stamina, and endurance and at mental and emotional level they are concerned with concentration, right knowledge, calm, peace, happiness. Yogic principles of healthy living can be put into the following categories:

- *Ahara* (Food)
- *Vihara* (Relaxation)
- *Achara* (Conduct)
- *Vichara* (Thinking)
- *Vyavahara* (Behaviour)

These principles are discussed in detail as under:

Ahara (food)

Ahara is a Sanskrit word which means food. Food is a biological need essential for one's survival. Modern medical science considers the food as necessary from physical point of view. It focuses on intake of calories and also on various components of food such as proteins, carbohydrates, fat, minerals, and vitamins. However, Yoga views food differently. It considers the food as necessary for the nourishment of both, the body and the mind.

In this context, the Yogic concept of *'mitahara'* is very relevant. *'Mitahara'* puts emphasis on proper quality and quantity of food and also includes proper state of mind, when food is eaten.

In Hatha Yoga *Pradipika* (1.58), *'mitahara'* is defined as agreeable and sweet food, leaving one fourth of the stomach free, and eaten as an offering to please 'The Lord Siva' (Swami Muktibodhananda, 1993).

According to the concept of *mitahara,* food should be of good quality; it should be freshly cooked, nutritious and be close to its natural form. It should be nourishing to the body and the mind. It should not be very spicy that agitates the mind. Regarding the quantity of food, *mitahara* does not specify any specific amount. Rather it says that half of the stomach should be filled with food; one quarter of the stomach should be filled with water and remaining one quarter should be left empty for circulation of air. It implies that stomach should never be overloaded. It also implies that quantity of food would depend upon requirements of an individual. Therefore, a young person would require more food than an elderly person. Similarly a physically active person needs food in more quantity as compared to the person who is doing desk job and leading sedentary life. *Mitahara* emphasises that food should be eaten in a positive state of mind with full concentration on food. The state of mind is very important while taking food. We all know if we eat the food while talking to someone on phone or reading a book or newspaper, or when we are angry, then we do not relish the food rather we inadvertently just swallow it down; and if asked suddenly, we cannot tell about the taste of the food; all foods seem similar. Thus we see that *mitahara* not only takes care of the needs of our body as also of our mind because mind and body are mutually and reciprocally related.

Food is important for managing stress. There is a relationship between food and stress. We have already seen that our body needs more resources to cope with a stressor; it consumes more energy and there is more wear and tear in body. If we do not eat proper food, our body requirements will not be met; as a result body will become weak and would not be able to deal with the situation. Therefore, it is necessary that we eat proper diet as signified by *'mitahara'*; it would strengthen our body and consequently our mind will be calm and cool; and thus, help us to manage stress.

Vihara (relaxation)

Vihara is a Sanskrit word. It means the activities for the purpose of recreation and relaxation. Relaxation is paramount to leading happy and long life. It really sustains our life. Our busy schedule demands that we make ourselves relaxed by good creative activities. For this purpose *asana, pranayama,* and *meditation* or some games can be made part of our daily routine. These activities would help to relax our body and mind; and also channelise our energies in a positive way and rejuvenate us physically and mentally. Some of these physical activities will make us strong enough to face the challenges of life and help us to manage stress in a better way. For example, a student, who spends all her /his time on studies only, may have difficulty in concentrating on the subject. If she/he spends some of her/his time on some good hobbies like music, painting, playing games, or reading a good book, it will give her/him some needed rest and enable her/him to perform better. In this context relaxation practices like *Yoga-nidra, savasana* also can relax our body and mind. *Svadhyaya* (reading good literature) and having good company too give us relaxation physically and mentally.

If we develop good hobbies and engage ourselves in worthwhile activities, it will give rest to the tired body and mind and refuel them with fresh energy enabling us to deal with the difficulties of life. Keeping a time-table which allows time for activities for relaxation is a good step in this direction.

Achara (conduct)

Achara means right conduct that includes self-discipline, positive attitude, positive emotions and principles in life. Yogic principles advocate that a person should develop positive attitude towards oneself and others. The positive attitude calms down the mind and makes the environment friendly which helps us manage the stress in a better way. With positive attitude half the battle of stress is already won. If we have negative attitude, then we will remain more tensed and would not be able to work properly. Therefore, it is necessary that we work with positive attitude. Yoga guides us to develop the positive attitude of friendliness, compassion, equanimity. These attitudes bring about happiness and make the person tension-free.

In Yogic philosophy, we find the principles of *yama* and *niyama*. The *yama* and *niyama* guide us how to conduct ourselves. We have discussed *yama* and *niyama* in previous Unit. You know that the *ahimsa* (non-violence), *satya* (truthfulness), *asteya* (non-stealing), *brahmacharya* (right conduct) and *aparigraha* (non-acquisitiveness) are the five principles of *yama;* and *saucha* (cleanliness), *santosa* (satisfaction with what one has), *tapah* (austerity), *svadhyaya* (study of good literature and self-introspection) and *Isvarapranidhana* (dedication and surrendering to the Supreme power) are the five principles of *niyama.*

The *yama* and *niyama* help us in managing stress. Not practising *yama* produces stress in a person. For example, if a person tells a lie, she/he would have to tell so many lies in order to prove it right. She/he will remain under constant tension because of the fear of getting caught. Her/his conscience and guilt feeling also would make her/him more stressed. Contrary to it, if the person speaks the truth it would save her/him from the stress caused by fear and the guilt feeling. We can lead a tension free life if we are contented in our life and are not in the rat-race. We can lead a happy life if we are non-violent and not harming in any way. Our body and mind will be strong if we follow the austerity in our life. In other words, we can say that principles under *yama* and *niyama* protect us from unnecessary stress. Practising *yama* and *niyama* would bring about harmony within us and the society.

Vichara (thoughts)

Vichara is a Sanskrit word meaning thought/thinking. Thinking is an important attribute of our being human. It is the force that guides and controls our actions. Right thinking will guide our actions in right directions while wrong thinking will give a wrong direction to our actions. It is our thoughts that can make heaven out of hell and hell out of heaven. It is necessary that we develop a right perspective and acquire right knowledge about things. This would give our thoughts a right direction. In addition to that, our thinking should be positive. Positive thinking creates joy while negative thinking makes us unhappy. We can never be happy if we have negative thoughts about ourselves and people around us. The negativity about our own self will make us uncomfortable and negativity for others will destroy our interpersonal relations. If we think positively about ourselves we shall have more self confidence, which will lead to have high self esteem. This will give us hope and energy, improve our performance and protect us from undue worries. Yogic philosophy proposes that our thoughts should be pure. Yogic practices of *antaranga Yoga* like *dharana, dhyana* or meditation help us in purifying our thoughts.

Vyavahara (Behaviour)

Vyavahara refers to behaviour or actions. Our actions are resultant and/or the reflection of our emotions and thinking; therefore, we need to act cautiously. Yogic philosophy professes that we should choose the right modes to achieve our goals. We should have control on our actions and should always try to act rightly. Our actions should not be impulsive; and should not be hurting to ourselves and others. Our deed, good or bad, repay us in the same kind. We will get the results according to our deeds *(karma)*. The right actions develop peace within and protect us from stress.

For stress management, the principles of *'niskama karma'* and *'karmasu kausalam'* also are very relevant. According to *'niskama karma'*, (doing action without expectation of the fruits) and we should perform our duties with full dedication without worrying for the results. This principle implies that we should not aspire for the results of our action. Do these as a part of your duty only. It is our expectations which make us sad or happy. If our expectations are not fulfilled then we become stressed. If we act without expectations, we will not be tensed even in the situations of adverse results. Therefore, *niskama karma* protects us from stress.

Another principle *'karmasu kausalam'* states that we should perform our acts with skilfulness. It is a known fact that skills increase the efficiency and self confidence. If we are skilled then we would be better equipped to deal with the struggles in life and will remain relatively stress-free. Thus, *'karmasu kausalam'* establishes that we should strive for enhancing our skills.

Yogic practices for stress management

By now you must have realized that Yoga can play an important role in stress management. We can manage stress effectively by stretching our body and also by relaxing our body and mind. A strong body can withstand the effects of stress; while relaxation helps to relieve the symptoms of stress. It refreshes the body and the mind; and helps to replenish the energy which has been consumed by stress. Yoga works both ways. It strengthens as well as relaxes the body and mind. In this section we will discuss those Yogic practices which help to strengthen and relax the body and the mind.

Asana

Asanas are good for body and mind. During stress, the endocrine system is the most affected system in our body. Therefore, the practices that work on our endocrine system are good for managing stress. The most effective *asanas* for this purpose are *Hastottanasana, Padahastasana, Trikonasana, Ustrasana, Ardha-matsyendrasana, Sarvangasana, Matsyasana, Bhujangasana* and *Savasana.* These *asanas* strengthen the glands and regulate their functions. By doing so, these *asanas* enable the body to effectively deal with the stress. Additionally, the relaxing *asanas* like *Makarasana* and *Savasana* give the required rest to body and mind and help to reduce the impact of stress.

Pranayama

Pranayama is a Yogic practice which is very effective for coping with stress. It has a calming effect on body and mind. You must be knowing that *Pranayama* is a breathing technique by which *prana* (vital life force) is controlled and regulated. *Pranayama* is not merely a physiological respiratory process, rather it is psycho-physical in nature. It works on body and mind both. *Pranayama* maintains a harmony between body and mind. It helps to develop balance between parasympathetic and sympathetic nervous systems of the body, brings emotional control and pacifies the mind. *Pranayama* when performed with bandha regulates the functioning of endocrine glands. It especially rejuvenates pituitary and pineal glands. Of late, modern medical system has recognised the health benefits of *Pranayama* for prevention and management of psycho-somatic disorders.

Pranayama consists of three phases: (*i*) *puraka* (regulated inhalation), (*ii*) *rechaka* (regulated exhalation), and (*iii*) *kumbhaka* (regulated retention of breath). *Puraka* involves slow, deep and prolonged inhalation as per the capacity. *Rechaka* involves slow, deep and prolonged exhalation in a regulated way; and *kumbhaka* involves retention of breath. *Kumbhaka* can be performed in two ways: (*i*) by holding the breath inside after *puraka,* and (*ii*) by holding the breath outside after *rechaka.*

In the *Patanjali Yoga Sutra, Pranayama* has been discussed for spiritual evolution. Later on, the Hatha-Yogic traditional texts like *Hatha-Yoga Pradipika, Gheratha Samhita, Hatha Ratnavali, Goraksa Samhita* discussed about the *Pranayama* in detail.

There are several kinds of *Pranayama*, but *Nadi-sodhana Pranayama* and *Bhramari Pranayama* have been considered effective for the purpose of managing stress.

Nadi-sodhana Pranayama is also known as *Anuloma-viloma Pranayama. Gheranda Samhita* (5.34) states that the practice of *nadi-suddhi pranyama* removes the blockages from the *nadis,* purifies them and facilitates the free flow of *prana* (given in Saraswati, Swami Niranjanananda). *Nadi-sodhana Pranayama* is soothing to the mind and body. It stimulates parasympathetic system; improves blood supply to brain; and provides sufficient oxygen to the nerve cells of body. It is beneficial in several health conditions and especially in stress-related disorders. *Bhramari Pranayama* reduces blood-pressure and is beneficial in cases of insomnia. Its practice relieves tension and anxiety; and reduces anger.

Yoga-nidra

Yoga-nidra is a method of relaxation. *Yoga-nidra* means a sleep with awareness. It is a Yogic technique of inducing us into conscious sleep for making our body and mind relaxed. In ordinary sleep, we take rest unconsciously without any control, while in *Yoga-nidra,* rest is taken in a state of consciousness.

The process of *Yoga-nidra* involves body awareness, breath awareness and image visualisation. In *Yoga-nidra,* the awareness is consciously withdrawn from the external world and then is taken inside. *Yoga-nidra* is an efficient and effective means for rejuvenation than the normal sleep state. It is so effective that an hour's *Yoga-nidra* can give us the benefits which could be derived from four hours' ordinary sleep. By *Yoga-nidra*, 'psycho-somatic imbalance' is restored (Swami Satyananda Saraswati, 1998).

Yoga-nidra helps to reduce stress. It brings balance among various systems of body and helps in managing stress-related problems. It is good for prevention of stress-related disorders and can also be used for the management of alexithymia (dysfunction in emotional awareness) asthma, cancer and colitis and peptic ulcer and cardiovascular diseases (Swami Satyananda Saraswati, 1998).

Antarmauna

Antarmauna also is a Yogic technique of relaxation. In Sanskrit language, *antar* means inner and *mauna* means silence. Thus, it is related to maintaining inner silence.

Antarmauna also takes the person away from external world and relaxes the body and the mind. By *antarmauna*, we come to know about our inner world which consists of thoughts and emotions. Actually, we are so externally oriented that we do not know about our own inner thoughts, feelings and emotions. This external orientation makes us stressed. We can be relaxed, if we can keep ourselves away from these stimuli. This we can experience in our daily life also.

We might have observed that our anger disappears if we maintain silence for few minutes. *Yoga-nidra* does the same. The silence during *antarmauna* takes us away from external world. It starts our inward journey. *Antarmauna* is relaxing to our body and mind and also effective for dealing with the stress.

Meditation

Meditation is a well-known Yogic practice which is suited to various purposes. As probably you know that in meditation, we practise to withdraw our attention from different objects or ideas of the mundane world and focus it on a single idea/object instrumentally for some time.

Dhyana, according to Patanjali, is step towards spiritual evolution. Swami Satyananda Saraswati explains that when attention is focused on a particular object or an idea and it remains there without any interruption for longer time, then it is called *dhyana. Dhyana* in simple words, can be defined as an effortless sustained single-pointed concentration. In *dhyana*, there is no break in concentration.

The meditation is practised in a comfortable and relaxed sitting position. In that position the attention is focused on a particular part of body or on the breathing or on an idea for some time.

There are variety of meditation techniques which have been designed to induce relaxation in body and mind.

Meditation is very effective for stress-reduction. It can reverse the stress-response by activating the parasympathetic nervous system. During meditation, our heart rate and breathing slow down, blood pressure becomes normal and our hormonal secretion gets normalized.

Cyclic meditation for stress management

Yoga is simply a conscious and systematic process for the complete physical, mental, intellectual, emotional, and spiritual development of a human being. In short, it is a methodical approach to self-perfection. In practice it is a technique for calming down the mind to its subtle and more sensitive layers by releasing stress and sharpening the faculty of action and understanding.

The three cardinal principles of Yoga are:

(*i*) Relaxation of all the groups of muscles;

(*ii*) Slowing down of the breath; and

(*iii*) Calming of the mind.

Four main streams of Yoga techniques could be identified. They utilise the four major faculties in man—*intellect, emotion, will-power,* and their executive capacities in Action through the sensory and motor organs.

Stress according to Yoga is imbalance. Imbalance is misery. At the mental and physical levels, it is excessive speed and thus a demanding situation which causes pain and leads to ailments and diseases. Imbalances at the emotional level manifest as upsurges which are caused by strong likes and dislikes. At the psychological level the imbalances lead to conflicts and often manifest as petty and narrow ego-centric behaviour. Lack of holistic knowledge and a balanced outlook, at the subtle levels are responsible for imbalances found at gross levels.

The Yogic way of management of stress, is totally holistic, and is based on an understanding of the concept of stress, as presented earlier. It is not enough, to work at the physical level *(annamaya kosa)* alone to reduce stress, but it is essential to bring a balance at all the other levels, *pranamaya, manomaya* and *vijnanamaya kosas* too. This is the total approach used in Yoga.

The stress accumulated at the body level as stiffness of joints and spasms of muscles can be released by the practice of *Yogasanas* which are congenial postures of the body to help in calming down the mind. Slow movements help in combating the rush from within. Rhythmic breathing and the breath-slowing process of *Pranayama* bring a balance at the *pranika* level.

Retaining awareness and relaxation throughout the practice help to gain a mastery over the mental processes and thus eliminate imbalances at the *manomaya kosa.* Keeping our goal of achieving a happy, peaceful, healthy, and efficient life and to promote harmony in the surroundings we prevent ourselves from getting into the rat race and mad rush of accumulating affluence and losing the very purpose of inner poise, tranquility and calmness. We then learn to work the right way, free of tension. Thus, a holistic approach of Yoga will be the right answer to the challenges of stress.

By using the technique of Yoga, we learn to expand our horizons, increase our capacities and manifest our dormant potentialities. The Bhagavad Gita (5-23) portrays: He who is able to withstand, in this very life before casting off this body, the rush (speed) of lust and anger alone is the accomplished one and he alone is a happy man.

The people who achieve this state enjoy serene peace and bliss deep within. Those attuned to the illumination of total knowledge within and actively engage themselves for the good of all beings, enjoy the very process of serving others, says the Gita. Further, the process for achieving this goal is to learn the three cardinal principles of Yoga, **"Relax the body, slow down the breath, calm down the mind".**

Crystallising these principles and techniques which Yoga offers Dr. H.R. Nagendra of S-VYASA University has developed very effective programmes for the management of stress. These programmes are presented under the four heads:

1. Instant Relaxation Technique (IRT)
2. Quick Relaxation Technique (QRT)
3. Deep Relaxation Technique (DRT)
4. Self-Management of Excessive Tension (SMET)

These courses have been conducted at various business houses, factories, industries, educational institutions, management development institutions in particular and for the common public in general, over the last 10 years. The participants of the course have experienced great calmness of the mind and body as well as deep relaxation during the programme. Preliminary investigations have shown the efficacy of the course in handling stress effectively.

Stimulation-relaxation combine—the core

In understanding stress we have been looking at one segment of the population of the world namely the highly developed sector, for whom issues such as the usefulness, advantages as well as the problems and challenges of scientific progress and technological advancements, are at the fore-front. The fast, sensitive, sharp mind of modern man is demanding its physical system to cope with its rush. Unable to meet the challenge, the physiological system is collapsing and problems of hypersensitivity and stress are on the ascent.

But in another part of the world (the undeveloped and underdeveloped regions), hypoactivity, laziness, drowsiness, lethargy, constriction and stagnation are the characteristic features and problems. The challenge is one of procuring food, shelter and clothing — the basic necessities of life. It is due to lethargy that the development of the underdeveloped takes a very long time. A resistance to act or change: laziness, also called *Tamas* — or the hypo-active phase. Many people in the villages are so lazy that even hunger cannot drive them to be active.

Timma is a well-built youth of our village. But he is extremely lazy. He would work for a day or two in a week. Even though his wife and four children are all hungry, he remains unperturbed.

He would rather starve with his family than go to work.

Though lethargy is a characteristic feature of village life, modern man also is not free from it.

High calorie food and increased comfort levels have made the modern man exert less and less, physically, and as such a sedentary lifestyle has become a common feature among executives.

This is TAMAS at the physical level though they are hyper-active at the intellectual level.

Lethargy is not only at the physical level. It can also be at the mental level. A resistance to think is common even in many educated people. They prefer taking up some mechanical work, rather than use their intellect in creating things in the work-place.

John had his say with his father. Though his parents wanted him to continue his college and complete his MBA for which they were prepared to pay, John refused. He did not want to study any further. The thought of using his thinking faculty was too much for him. He hated maths!

Soon after school, he took up carpentry. While machines have replaced manual labour; calculators and computers in the modern age have reduced the necessity for thinking. This has led to mental lethargy in most of the working class in the developed countries, too.

In both the hyper and hypo-active phases, there is an imbalance. In both, work creates tensions. In the hypo-active phase, it is 'the bliss of ignorance' which stabilises that stage of laziness and lethargy. An inability to work and a resistance to think creates stress when one is forced to work manually or to think actively. In the hyper activity cases, it is the high ambitions and strong desires which make them develop an attachment to work and think. The very process of working or thinking with attachments and ambitions is tiresome and creates stress.

Whatever problems we find at the global level, hyper-activity in the developed parts and hypo-activity predominantly in the undeveloped, are also the two-fold problems at the individual level. In fact, both these aspects are found in each part of the globe and in each mind but they may be in different proportions. For example, during sleep even the hyper-active mind is drowsy, lazy and lethargic. Man does not want to get up early in the morning. Similarly, a lazy village man will also have times of excitement and over-activity during the day. Thus, each mind is featured by both these facets of hyper and hypo-activity.

A remedy to one may not be a remedy for the other. For example, the relaxation posture *Savasana* can be a fine solution to hyper activity. But that would only enhance *Tamas* in lazy people! Stimulations or desires can be good for lazy people, but they are the causative factors for stress in the hyper active man. So what is the way out? The solution is contained in, the most profound and the shortest of the *Upanishads*, the *Mandukya Upanishad.* It contains this two-fold process of *Sadhana.*

When the mind gets to a state of lethargy, stimulate and awaken it; as if starts speeding up and distractions set in, calm it down again.

Thus, it is a series of successive stimulations and relaxations that can solve this complex problem of the mind. It is using this STIMULATION — RELAXATION combine, that the present course has been designed and developed. Each stimulation helps to end the stagnation, open the constrictions and then the release of stimulation brings relaxation. After the relaxation continues for a while, the system reaches a saturation level often leading to stagnation or drowsiness. It is then that we need to stimulate ourselves again. Successive stimulations and relaxations one after the other thus help to release stress at deeper and deeper levels.

Stimulations in this course are provided by various Yoga techniques like *Asanas, Pranayama*, etc. The basic frame of *Yogasanas* acts as a skeleton on which to build the flesh and nerves to give it a shape. Breathing and *Pranayama*, awareness and meditation feeling and sensing, sound response, etc. are woven harmoniously into the practice.

The two major problems in *sadhana* are that the mind is either drowsy and sleepy or hyperactive with distraction. When we activate the system, the stagnation is shattered which may lead to distractions. Calming of distractions is the remedy. But again it may lead to subtle stagnation which has to be recognized to make further progress. Devoid of distractions and featured by wakefulness, if the mind gets steadied, it is the right state to stay in without further disturbance.

YOGA AND PERSONALITY DEVELOPMENT

Personality is a central theme of the disciplines of Yoga and psychology. Personality refers to persistent patterns of a person's behaviour. It tells about the unique characteristics of a person. You are aware that in modern psychology personality has been explained in various ways. For the convenience of understanding, these theories of personality have been divided into four broad categories, namely, type and trait theories, psycho-analytical theories, learning theories, and humanistic-existential theories. Modern psychology recognises body and mind as the two entities of a person. In order to understand mental processes and behaviour of an individual, modern psychology takes the help of various concepts like ego, self and consciousness. However, in Yoga philosophy, personality has been viewed differently. Yoga views the person more deeply over and above physical body and mind; it has added a third entity called self (*atma*). In Yoga, the concepts of ego, self and consciousness have different connotations. Concepts of *Panchakosas* and *gunas* are very relevant in the context of understanding and development of personality.

You can understand the above paragraph if you look around and observe how your friends and family members behave; how they interact with one another; how they express their feelings and emotions; how they react or respond to a given situation or event. Each one of your friends behaves differently. One who is short tempered, reacts furiously; the other keeps cool, no matter what happens.

Have you noticed that when your friend is aggressively provoked by his/her hostile feelings or emotions, his breathing shortens, muscles contract, and hands and legs tremble? This is to prove that even though an emotion is a mental function, it has inseparable connection with the gross physical body and all the processes therein.

It means that an individual is an indivisible unit. For the sake of convenience, we should continue to say that, it is body, it is mind and so on. This is called an integrated approach to personality. In Yoga philosophy, in its entirety, it comprises five sheaths, called *Panchakosa*, which are described as under.

Panchakosa

The concept of Panchakosa adopts a multi-dimensional approach to the understanding of personality and explains the person in an extensive manner. The concept of Panchakosa is mentioned in the *Taittiriya Upanishad.*

The word, *Panchakosa* comprises two words: *pancha* and *kosa. Pancha* means five; and *kosa* means body or sheath or layer. Thus, *Panchakosa* literally means five bodies or five sheaths. According to the concept of *Panchakosa*, the 'self' — the divine spirit — is the real identity of a person. It constitutes the inner most core of a person. This real identity is encased in a series of five *kosas* (sheaths), named respectively from the outermost to the innermost as: *Annamaya kosa:* (physical or gross body), *Pranamaya kosa* (energy body), *Manomaya kosa* (mental body), *Vijnanamaya kosa* (wisdom body), and *Anandamaya kosa* (bliss). The absolute reality can be discovered through the experience of the 'self' (Saraswati, 2004). 'Self' is difficult to be accessed as it lies at the innermost core. This has been graphically shown in figure below.

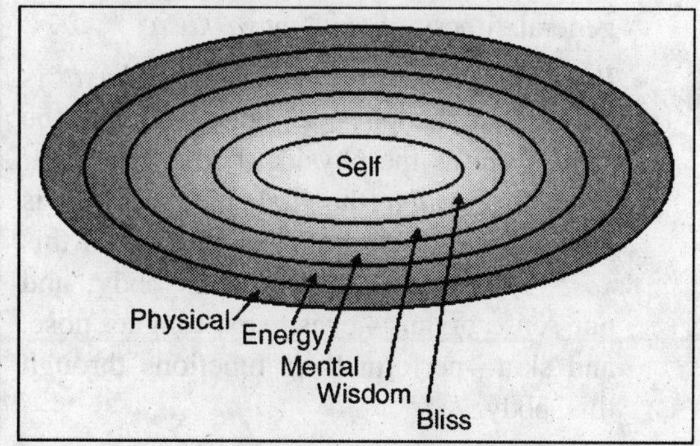

Fig. : *Five kosas (sheaths) and the 'self'*

These kosas represent functioning of a person at different levels. They carry different levels of awareness; and are arranged successively from the grosser to increasingly more subtle awareness. Here, *annamaya kosa* is the grossest body; while *anandamaya kosa* is the most subtle body of awareness. Each sheath covers and obscures the more subtle awareness of the body which is interior to it. This implies that a person functions at various levels of awareness. It is important for you to note that all *kosas* exist in a fixed order, but they are interrelated and form one entity. Therefore, the practices that benefit one *kosa* will benefit other *kosa* also, and 'Self' can be accessed by working on all these bodies.

- ***Annamaya kosa:*** *Annamaya kosa* is the outer-most body. This part is mainly nourished by the food (*anna*) which we take;

hence is called *annamaya kosa.* This body functions on physical plane. It represents the physical body which is measurable by physical means. This *kosa* is constituted by the organs and systems of our body which we can understand with the help of anatomy and physiology. It is essential that we keep this body healthy since only a healthy physical body can facilitate functioning of other *kosas* (bodies or sheaths). Internal cleansing practices (*satkarma*) and *yogasanas* are main practices for development of physical body. *Asanas* are an effective means to attain flexibility, relaxation, strength, toning, balance and general fitness of *annamaya kosa.*

- ***Pranamaya kosa:*** *Pranamaya kosa* is encased in the physical body and has the same form as the physical body. This *kosa* consists of *prana* (the vital energy) which is crucial for life. We are alive because of this *kosa.* Life is derived from this body; and our sense organs—eyes, ears, tongue, nose, and skin—perform their functions through this body.

  Pranamaya kosa is the basis of our physical body. We all know that without *prana,* the physical body becomes lifeless. This *kosa* is constituted by *nadis, chakras* and various types of *pranas* (*Udana, Prana, Samana, Apana* and *Vyana*). *Prana* (energy) flows through the *nadis* (energy-channels). It is said that there are 72,000 *nadis* but the prime *nadis*, are *Pingala, Ida* and *Susumna nadi*. *Pranamaya kosa* can be approached through *pranayama*. Our physical sheath is affected by this kosa. This body is the link between *annamaya kosa* (physical body) and *manomaya kosa* (mental body).

- ***Manomaya kosa:*** It lies interior to the *pranamaya kosa* (energy body). This *kosa* is concerned with our emotional and cognitive behaviour which includes feelings, emotion, instincts, desires and various needs like security and protection from danger. Our emotions such as love, hate, fear, sadness, anger, disgust all are related to this *kosa.*

  In addition to this, *manomaya kosa* also consists of *manas, ahamkara,* memory and lower levels of *buddhi* or intelligence. The empirical knowledge, thinking and reasoning — both inductive and deductive — are part of this kosa. Here, buddhi (intelligence) may yield to the pressure of emotions and habits; or it may make decision independent of the impulses or past programmes.

  Our responses to the inputs received by the senses are controlled by this *kosa* only. *Manomaya kosa* helps *'manas'* (mind) to reach better decisions with rational thinking in handling day-to-day activities. At this level, one tends to draw conclusions on the basis of evidence and reasoning in day-to-day life. In short, it can be said that *manomaya kosa* is concerned with our functioning at emotional level as well at lower levels of buddhi.

  This *kosa* is very significant as most of our day-to-day activities are governed by *manomaya kosa.* If a person is impulsive, cannot control her/his emotions, then the person needs to work on this *kosa* to improve on emotional dimension of her/his personality.

  This *kosa* is the link between *pranamaya kosa* (energy body) and *vijnanamaya kosa* (intellectual body). This *kosa* or body can be studied by focusing the attention inward on the working of mind. By regulating the breath, mind can be brought into focus. Meditation and devotional sessions can be used to develop this *kosa.* This *kosa* can be made healthy by expressing our negative emotions like anger, hate, fear etc. and also through constructive channels such as music, sports and games, stories, articles etc.

- ***Vijnanamaya kosa:*** It lies interior to the *manomaya kosa.* It consists of higher levels of 'buddhi' which is related to power of discrimination and true understanding about the self. This *kosa* does not give into the passions of the other bodies. This is a realm of pure *buddhi*. This level is beyond thinking and reasoning. At this level, *buddhi* remains unaffected by emotions, habits, sense-impressions, perceptions or personal gains and egoism. It is governed by wisdom and *viveka* (which discriminates between right and wrong). If a person is able to discriminate between right and wrong, then the person can be said to be working at the level of the *vijnanamaya kosa.*

The *vijnanamaya kosa* establishes the link between *manomaya kosa* (mental body) and *anandamaya kosa* (bliss body). We can access this *kosa* by working upon three lower *kosas* by removing their blockages and reducing our identification with them. Another way is by doing good activities and by associating ourselves with the people who are working at higher levels like thinkers, joyous people, yogis etc. Exploring new avenues, learning more, and accomplishing good deeds etc. help to develop it. This *kosa* may be developed by analysing and understanding the problems in Yogic way.

- *Anandamaya kosa: Anandamaya kosa* is the most subtle body. It remains in the most intimate contact with pure spirit or the *'atma'* which is the true reality of all of us. *Anandamaya kosa* reflects the blissful state of the 'self' characterised by an ineffable experience of peace, love and ecstasy. This *kosa* can be functional in people who are dominated by selfless love. A person, functioning at this level, remains in a state of joy. She/he does not get affected by external stimuli or events or things. The individual at this stage remains in a perfect state of mental equipoise — transcending even the Buddhi. Rationality or empirical experience have no meaning for an individual in the bliss state.

  We are generally not able to access this *kosa* because we are entangled in the lower levels of functioning and are associated with other outer *kosas.* This *kosa* can be accessed by practising joy in all circumstances and by doing *niskama karma.*

If we think deeply we find that all the five bodies are important for a holistic personality. If we want to develop the 'self' — the core of the personality — all bodies need to be integrated and given enough care and attention. In Section 1.4 of this unit, we shall discuss various dimensions of holistic or integrated personality. You can see that the concept of *Panchakosa* represents all those dimensions and emphasizes the integration of all five bodies for development of a holistic personality.

Gunas (attributes): sattva-guna, rajas-guna and tamas-guna

Yoga also describes an individual human being on the basis of *'gunas'* or attributes.

Example: Consider the following example: Students are given an assignment and are told that the one who gets the highest marks will receive cash reward. One student is attracted by the cash reward, but does nothing and keeps on postponing the work on the assignment. Another student starts working on the assignment due to the cash reward attached to it. Some other student works on the assignment because she thinks that working on the assignment is her duty. She works for her inner satisfaction and happiness and not for the sake of cash reward.

How do we explain the above kinds of behaviour? The answer to this can be given in terms of the *gunas.*

Let us discuss the concept of *gunas* in detail.

'Gunas' may be described as the qualities or the tendencies within a person which determine and explain the personality and behaviour of a person. There are three *gunas – sattva, rajas* and *tamas.* Together they are known as *tri-guna.* These *gunas*

get reflected in our mental states and manifest behaviour.

The concept of *gunas* is mentioned in the **Atharvaveda.** It has been described in detail in the *Bhagvad Gita* and *Samkhya Darsana.*

According to *Samkhya Darsana, Prakriti* (nature) is composed of *tri-gunas—sattva, rajas* and *tamas.* Patanjali also defines *sattva, rajas* and *tamas gunas* as illumination, action and inertia respectively in the following verse:

prakasa-kriya-sthitisilam bhutendriyatmakam bhogapavargartham drisyam P.Y.S. 2.18

The Bhagvad Gita also defines these *gunas* in the similar way. According to the Bhagvad Gita, *sattva* is stainless (pure), luminous, and healthy. It is attached to happiness and knowledge (Bhagvad Gita, 14.6). Rajas is passion and arises due to attachment with worldly things. It binds an individual to the fruits of her/his actions (Bhagvad Gita, 14.7). *Tamas* is inertia which arises from ignorance (Bhagvad Gita, 14.8).

On the basis of above description, we can simply say that *sattva* is associated with such qualities as brightness, kindness, intelligence, love, compassion for others etc. All these qualities reflect the 'selflessness' and egolessness within the person. Rajas can be said to be associated with activity, energy, passion, desires etc., whereas *tamas* is characterized by laziness, dullness, heaviness, ignorance, etc.

In the above **Example,** the first student who is attracted by the cash reward, but does nothing and keeps on postponing the task is dominated by *tamasika guna.* The student who immediately starts working on the task due to the cash reward attached to it is dominated by *rajas guna.* The third student who works for her inner satisfaction and happiness is dominated by the *sattvika guna.*

On the basis of the dominance of the above *gunas*, an individual's personality can be categorised in three broad groups namely, *sattvika* personality, *rajasika* personality, and *tamasika* personality. These are the three types of personalities according to Yoga.

- **Sattvika personality** is dominated by *sattvika guna* and has inherent desire to be good and caring. Here, behaviour is motivated by moral strength, respect for humanity, non-violence, meditation, kindliness, silence, self-control, and purity of character. Forgiveness, patience, love and compassion for others, cool, altruistic behaviour etc. are some of the qualities of *sattva guna*. According to the Bhagvad Gita (14:11), an individual endowed with *sattva guna* becomes illuminated by wisdom. A *sattvika* person becomes attached to happiness and can discriminate between right and wrong (Prabhupada, 1986). Renunciation and detachment are the characteristics of the personality of a person dominated by *sattva.* If a person works for others without his/her own interest, we can say that she/he is dominated by this *guna*. Saintly persons are an example of this type of personality.

  If you look around in the society, you will find many great personalities who do lot of social work. They selflessly serve disabled people, socially discarded women and children, children who have no parents and relatives to take care of. These are acts of pure love and compassion. Those who do such kind of work have no self interest. They are just a few or handfuls. They can do so since they have predominance of *sattva guna*.

- **Rajasika personality** is dominated by action. According to the Bhagvad Gita (14.12), a *rajasika* person becomes passion-oriented with desires and intense endeavour. Such a person gets attached to the activities which would lead to expected results (Prabhupada, 1986). The attachment with self-interest gives the person a distorted picture of right and wrong. Enthusiasm, interest, activity are some of the attributes of this *guna*. A person dominated by *rajas* remains active. This type of personality can be seen in the people who are always active to fulfil their desires. A person who is always aspiring and tirelessly working to fulfil those aspirations can be said to have a *rajasika* personality. People with high achievement, motivation and with a vibrant attitude are the examples of this type of personality.

- **Tamasika personality** is dominated by inertia (Bhagvad Gita, 14.13). This kind of person is characterised by inactivity, heedlessness, delusions, lack of enlightenment. Tamas produces ambiguity, idleness and fantasy. Tamasika person derives happiness from self-delusion and miscomprehension. Procrastination, laziness, gossiping, day-dreaming, harming others, being revengeful etc. are some other characteristics of this *guna*. This kind of person remains aloof and does not care for others. A person who spends most of the time in gossiping, always sits idle and does not do anything worthwhile is an example of this type personality. Criminals or people who harm others are also examples of this personality type.

The above categorisation is based mainly on the dominance of a single *guna*. But, in real life, pure *sattvika, rajasika,* or *tamasika* personalities are a rare phenomenon. Generally people have the combination of two or more *gunas* and are dominated by more than one guna. In that case, personality can be put into different categories such as *sattvika-rajasika, rajasika-tamasika,* etc. Individual difference can be explained by the variations in the degree of the *sattva, rajas,* and *tamas* within these combinations.

As a matter of fact, we all have *sattva, rajas* and *tamas* within us, which are reflected in different kinds of our mental states, tendencies, and actions at different times. We have *sattvika* tendency when we are helping others without our own interest. We are driven by *rajasika* tendency when we are doing our work in school, college, office or in home for expected results. Similarly, we show *tamas* when we are sleeping or while away the time.

Dimensions of integrated personality

Personality development in an individual is a process that involves patterns of changes or movements that begin at the conception and continues throughout his/her life span. Development is a multi-dimensional process that consists of evolution of personality on several dimensions. It is a multi-directional process characterised by both growth and decline. During infancy, childhood, adolescence and early adulthood, growth is the centre-stage of all development. However, as the person grows into middle and late adulthood, maintenance and regulation become more important and are more sought after.

You might have seen that some people in your neighbourhood are physically strong, but are weak in grasping basic arithmetic or even alphabets. This is an uncomfortable state of personality. You might have also come across certain highly intelligent students or teachers who quickly lose their temper on just drop of a hat. So also a contra example is available. A physically weak student is extraordinary in his studies. Even though it will be a rare thing to find a person who is very good in all dimensions, yet the discussion on an integrated personality would essentially comprise all these unusually recognised aspects.

Not mere development of an integrity in a person, but maintenance of the same could be quite challenging for all of us.

Personality development is a multi-dimensional phenomenon. There are several dimensions which need to be integrated. Absence of any one dimension makes one's personality incomplete and lop-sided. For a holistic personality, the following dimensions are required to be integrated (see figure below):

- Physical dimension
- Intellectual/Cognitive dimension
- Emotional dimension
- Social dimension
- Spiritual dimension

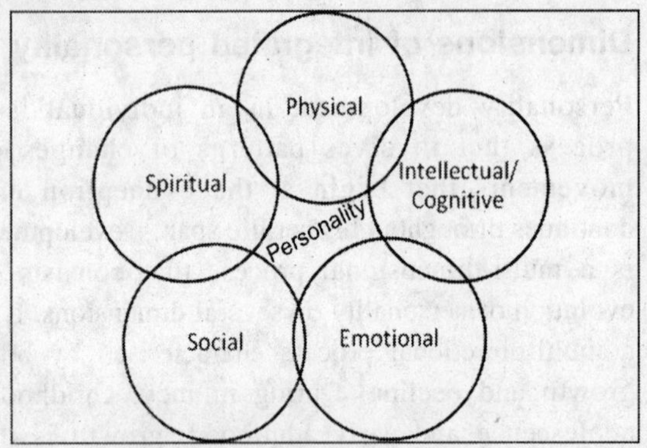

Fig.: *Dimensions of personality*

Each dimension has specific activities and processes which undergo certain changes. These changes normally take place in an orderly sequence, though there may be variations in their rate. It is important to note that all dimensions of personality are overlapping, inter-dependent, and intricately interwoven. A purely compartmentalized approach is not at all possible. These are studied separately for the purpose of better understanding only.

Physical dimension

Physical dimension is mainly concerned with the development of body from anatomical and physiological point of view. Changes in height, weight, and motor skills, development of brain, hormonal changes, cardiovascular changes etc. — all are parts or aspects of the physical development. The physical dimension is concerned with physical health and fitness of body. It gets reflected in healthy functioning of the body where different systems of body work in a coordinated way.

For a holistic personality, a person requires to be physically fit and healthy. This dimension to certain extent is determined by biological inheritance but can be developed by *asana* and *pranayama* and healthy food also.

Emotional dimension

The emotional dimension involves development of skills for management of emotions including feelings and attitudes. Emotions may be positive such as state of happiness, joy, contentment, love, kindness, compassion etc. They may be negative also, such as state of hate, anger, fear, sadness, jealousy etc. It is important that positive emotions are developed to the maximum; and negative emotions are controlled and expressed in a proper way. It is equally important that a person is emotionally stable. There should not be frequent and rapid mood swings. Thus we can say that emotional stability, development of positive emotions, proper expression and channelization of negative emotions lie in this domain. The development of this dimension is reflected in appropriate emotional reaction towards a given situation.

This dimension is generally the most neglected area in real life, though it is of paramount importance for a holistic personality. We can find the traces of this neglect in our disproportionate emotional behaviour. In mega cities, often we witness the increasing incidents of road-rage. Murders are being committed in a fit of rage on petty issues even for the sake of ₹ 20, 50 or 100. Is this behaviour normal? Are these emotions appropriate? You will agree that they are not appropriate. They are the emotional outbursts arising out of the negligence in management of our emotions. It is happening because the person is not able to control the emotions. A holistic personality requires that we develop positive emotions, sublimate negative emotions, and express them in a proper way.

In order to do this, it is necessary that we effectively manage our emotions. This area falls in the domain of emotional intelligence which is related to management of emotions in an intelligent way. An emotionally intelligent person explores her/his emotional behaviour. This exploration helps in gaining personal insight into the way how one feels and behaves. It also helps in learning new healthy ways to deal with ups and downs of life.

In emotional management, Yoga can play a crucial role. *Yama, niyama, pranayama, pratyahara, dhyana* (meditation) are the Yogic practices which facilitate the development of this dimension.

Cognitive, intellectual dimension

Cognitive or intellectual development is related to mental abilities and mental processes, such as perception, learning, memory, thinking, language, concept-formation, reasoning, decision making, problem solving, creative activities etc. Due to the development of this dimension, we are able to acquire new skills and knowledge about the facts and environment around us and perform various mental tasks like analysing, synthesising, evaluating etc. Cognitive development enables us to develop right perspective about the concepts, things or situations.

A nurturing environment is essential for cognitive development. Developing the habit of reading good literature (*svadhyaya*) is a healthy way to cognitive development. Various other Yogic practices such as *pratyahara, dharana* and *dhyana* (meditation) also facilitate it by enhancing concentration and memory.

Social dimension

The social dimension of personality is concerned with social skills. This dimension includes inter-dependence, harmony with others, behaving according to rules and norms of the society, developing healthy and caring relationships with those around us etc. A person may be called socially developed if she/he conforms to the social norms and can bring balance between her/his social and personal life. The development of this dimension gets reflected in the feeling of association with other people and participating in community activities.

Social dimension is an important aspect of personality as it brings harmony in society. Lack of social development may cause severe problems in society. Many of the social problems like divorce, quarrels in the family, drug-addiction, rebellious behaviour, act of terrorism are the result of lack of social development. Therefore, it is essential that this dimension is developed. For this, a person needs to develop social skills and take interest in the community work.

Social dimension is closely related to emotional dimensions. A person who cannot control her/his negative emotions may not have good interpersonal relationships. Social dimension of personality can be taken care of by developing positive attitude towards others and controlling our negative emotions.

Spiritual dimension

Spiritual dimension of personality includes knowing the 'self' or more appropriately realizing the 'self', having a sense of right and wrong (moral values) and understanding meaning and purpose of life. It also includes integration of values with actions. The actions of spiritually developed person would match with her/his beliefs and values (respect for human life, honesty, equality, integrity, simplicity etc.).

Spirituality is an important dimension of personality; and is increasingly being identified as a vital part of psychological well-being. Humanistic psychologists like Carl C. Rogers, A. Maslow and Fritz Pearl put much emphasis on human values. According to them, spiritual emptiness and affluence of materialism are major reasons of mental health related problems.

For a holistic personality, spirituality is essential. We may be intelligent, may have high status in the society, may have good physical appearance, but if we do not have universal human values, then we may not be feeling fully satisfied in life and may sometimes perceive life as a meaningless journey. This is due to the lack of spirituality. Therefore, for a holistic personality, spiritual growth is essential.

Here, it is important for you to know that spirituality and religion are two different concepts. Many people consider spirituality and religion as one and the same thing. This is a wrong notion. Spirituality is a universal concept and revolves around ethics, morality and knowing about the 'true self'. Religion is different; it may be one of the several means to achieve spirituality, but cannot be called as spirituality in itself.

Spiritual development can be achieved by self-analysis, introspection, proper alignment of thought pattern, adopting moral values in day-to-day life. Contemplation on certain questions (like, who am I? or what is meaningful in my life?) can develop an awareness about the self and develop a sense of purpose and direction in life resulting into spiritual growth. Being tolerant of the opposites and contradictions that exist within one's world also can be helpful in attaining spirituality. A spiritually grown person develops a sense of peace within.

It very probably be so since they can look at the opposites in life with complete sense of objectivity. It means acceptance of life in its entirety. You also actually do the same. How? You accept cycles of day and night. Don't you? Even though these are opposites just like black or white. Similar is the case as regards happiness and sorrow, pain and pleasure etc. Then, you may ask what is the difference between the spiritually evolved person and you? It is 'awareness' that makes the difference; and, moreover, the acceptance of the existence of these opposites.

YOGA FOR INTEGRATED PERSONALITY DEVELOPMENT

Yogic practices, if applied in a right way are very useful in developing an integrated personality. In this section, we will discuss the role of Yogic attitudes and Astanga Yoga for developing a holistic personality.

Yogic attitudes for personality development

Attitudes are crucial to one's personality. The attitudes influence our cognition and prepare us to behave in a particular way. They are accompanied by emotions and feelings.

Attitudes can be both positive and negative. Positive attitude prepares an individual to behave in a positive way, while negative attitude brings negative proneness in one's behaviour. Simply put, our behaviour is the reflection of our attitudes. Hostility reflects the negative attitude, while friendliness reflects the positive attitude. A person with negative attitude may find faults in other persons, objects, and situations; while, the person with positive attitude would see the strengths in those persons, objects, and situations.

You have seen that a boss goes along very well with certain employees, while with some other employees, he always has strained relation. It is a matter of attitude.

Yoga emphasises on adoption of positive attitudes which we call Yogic attitudes. We may define Yogic attitudes as mental predispositions which have been recommended by the Yogic philosophy to respond consistently in a positive manner toward a given person, object or situation. In simple words, Yogic attitudes can be considered as bhavas (internal affective orientation) which guide us as to 'how to approach persons, objects and events in life'. Yogic attitudes develop in a person a positive perspective about various situations and events happening around her/him.

Patanjali in the following *sutra* emphasises the positive attitudes of friendliness, compassion, gladness and indifference respectively towards happy, sad (suffering), virtuous and vicious people and events.

maitri-karuna-muditopeksanam sukha-duhkha-puny-apunya-visayanam bhavanatas chitta-prasadanam (P.Y.S. 1.33).

'In relation to happiness, misery, virtue and vice, by cultivating the attitude of friendliness, compassion, gladness and indifference respectively, the mind becomes purified and peaceful'.

The above aphorism (*sutra*) shows us the way to sublimate our negative emotions into positive ones. In day-to-day life, a person may have negative attitudes. She/he may be jealous of the successful people. A student may be jealous of the students who got better grades. A person may be indifferent towards the suffering of others. We may become indifferent to good people and get angry with vicious people. All these behaviours show the negative attitude. Patanjali stressed that we should have positive attitudes. Thus, jealousy towards happy people can be replaced by friendliness, and indifference and disgust for miserable people can be replaced by compassion. Indifference and jealousy towards virtuous people can be replaced by gladness and the disgust towards vicious people can be replaced by indifference. These positive *bhavas* bring happiness within and also help in our social, emotional and spiritual development.

Nevertheless, Yoga puts general emphasis on adopting positive attitude in life which can be developed with *Vairagya bhava* (detachment), *Samatva bhava* (equanimity), *Sakshi bhava* (witnessing as an observer), *Niskama bhava* (action without expectations), *Kartavya bhava* (dutifulness), *Egolessness* and *Sraddha* (faith).

If a person wants not to be emotionally involved in a given task or situation, then she/he should work with faith and sense of duty. This would help her/him in developing a right perspective and help her/him in taking right decisions. This would also protect the person from emotional turmoil and also help in her/his social and spiritual development.

Patanjali's Astanga Yoga for personality development

Astanga Yoga is a Yogic system that has been devised by Maharsi Patanjali in order to control the mind. *Astanga Yoga* was enunciated basically for spiritual development, but it is also very relevant to attain holistic personality. *Astanga Yoga,* if adopted properly would help in physical, intellectual, emotional, social and spiritual development of a person.

It consists of eight components; therefore, it is known as *Astanga-Yoga* (eight-limbed Yoga). The components/limbs mentioned in *Astanga Yoga* are: *Yama, Niyama, Asana, Pranayama, Pratyahara, Dharana, Dhyana* and *Samadhi*. These eight components have been further divided into two parts known as *Bahiranga Yoga* and *Antaranga Yoga. Bahiranga Yoga* consists of *Yama, Niyama,*

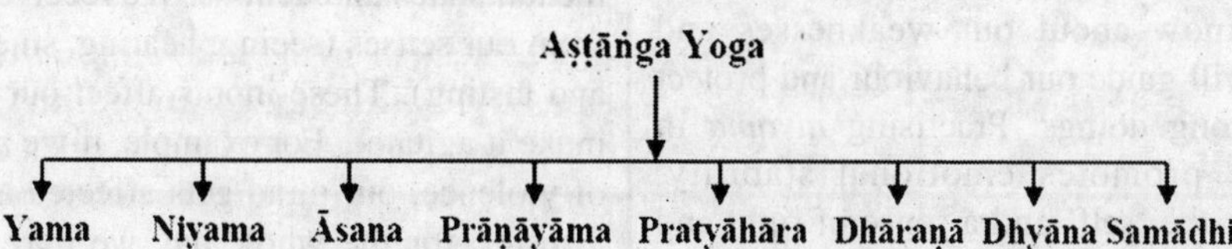

Fig. : *Limbs of Astanga Yoga*

Asana, Pranayama and *Pratyahara;* while *Antaranga Yoga* consists of last three limbs—*Dharana, Dhyana* and *Samadhi.*

Yama: *Ahimsa-satya-asteya-brahmacharya-aparigrahah-yamah* (P.Y.S. 2.30).

Yama can be interpreted as self-restraints or the social code of conduct, which are to be followed in social life. *Ahimsa* (non-violence), *Satya* (truthfulness), *Asteya* (non-stealing), *Brahmacharya* (continence) and *aparigraha* (non-acquisitiveness) are *yamas.*

Yamas are very important. They tell us how we should behave in our social life. *Ahimsa* means not harming others in any manner—through intention, speech or action. Truthfulness means we should be truthful and honest in our thoughts and actions. *Asteya* means non-stealing which is opposite to stealing. *Asteya* includes not taking or using the things belonging to others without their permission. *Brahmacharya* means exercising control in our sexual behaviour. *Aparigraha* means that we should not accumulate or hoard things property/wealth etc, which are not required. If we analyse them in depth, we would find that the behaviour guided by these principles will help to control our emotions, promote our relations and would also lead towards spiritual path.

We all know that social problems like murders, corruption, theft, polygamy, rape etc. are caused by the violent tendencies, dishonesty, untruthfulness, greed, hoarding, stealing and sexual urges. If we exercise control on these, the society will be peaceful and our interpersonal relations will be good. In addition to this, yamas also bring emotional balance and mental peace and lead us to the spiritual journey. Thus, with the help of *Yama,* emotional, social and spiritual development is facilitated.

Niyama: *Saucha-santosa-tapah-svadhyaya-isvara-pranidhanani-niyamah* (P.Y.S. 2.32).

Five niyamas are: *Saucha* (purity cleanliness), *Santosha* (contentment), *Tapah* (austerity to discipline body mind), *Svadhyaya* (study of self by introspection and studying scriptures), and *Isvara-pranidhana* (surrender to God). *Niyama* can be viewed as observances or code of conduct in personal life.

The *niyama* of *saucha* implies that our body and our surroundings should be clean and mind should be pure. *Santosha* means that we should be contented with what we have in life and should not hanker after more and more; such cravings would lead to frustrations in life. The *niyama* of *tapah* implies that we should discipline our body and mind by developing a habit of austerity; it will protect us from unnecessary extravagance for satisfying never-ending desires. *Svadhyaya* means the study of self and study of scriptures. It can be promoted by introspection and self-analysis. By *svadhyaya* we can develop an insight into our behaviour, to know about our weaknesses and strengths. This will guide our behaviour and protect us from our wrong doings. Practising *niyama* in day-to-day life promotes emotional stability, knowledge about the 'self' and a sense of right and wrong; thus facilitating emotional, intellectual and spiritual development of oneself.

Yama and *niyama* put together, thus, help to promote social, emotional, intellectual and spiritual development of an individual.

Asana: *Sthira-sukham-asanam* (P.Y.S. 2.46).

Patanjali defines *asana* as the steady and comfortable position (of the body). He does not talk about any specific *asanas.* It is the *Hatha Yoga* tradition in which various body-postures have been suggested by the proponents of *Hatha Yoga. Asana* helps to regulate the *pranika* flow in the body facilitating the functioning of various systems and organs of the body. Thus, *asanas* help to promote physical development. Alongside, they also help regulation of emotions by working upon autonomic nervous system.

Pranayama: *Tasmin sati svasa-prasvasayor-gativicchedah pranayamah* (P.Y.S. 2.49).

Pranayama means control and regulation of breathing process. Practising *Pranayama* helps in physical development by improving capacity and functioning of lungs. They help in emotional development by activating the parasympathetic system of the CNS (Central Nervous System). The activation of parasympathetic system makes a person relaxed.

Regular practice of *pranayama* makes a person energetic and relaxed. Thus *pranayama* works not only at physical level, it also helps in emotional management. Our negative emotions like anger can be effectively managed by *pranayama.*

Pratyahara: *Sva-visaya-asamprayoge chitta-svarupanukara ivendriyanam pratyaharah* (P.Y.S. 2.54).

Patanjali, in the above *sutra,* defines *pratyahara* as withdrawal of senses from their respective objects and experiences. It is related to control of senses.

Actually, our senses play a crucial role in our mental states and actions. We receive various inputs from our senses (seeing, hearing, smelling, touching and tasting). These inputs affect our mind and may make it agitated. For example, if we see a movie full of violence, our mind gets affected accordingly. As a result, for the whole day we may not be able to focus on our work as the violent scenes of the movie are disturbing us again and again. This kind of situation would not have aroused, had we not seen that violent movie. So in order to control the mind, sensations are to be withdrawn. This withdrawal (*pratyahara*) protects us from emotional turbulences which are caused by continuous worldly inputs. However, it is not always possible to stop the inputs. In that case, *pratyahara* can be exercised by taking right inputs from our senses. The right selection of our inputs would protect our mind from undesirable states. Thus, *pratyahara* helps in emotional management.

Pratyahara can be done with the help of self-analysis and introspection. During introspection and self-analysis, we focus our attention within. It helps to make an inward journey. It makes the person aware of her/his strengths and weaknesses and leads her/him towards self-improvement. Thus, *pratyahara* helps a person in her/his emotional, intellectual and spiritual development.

Dharana: *Desabandhas-chittasya dharana* (P.Y.S. 3.1).

Dharana means fixing up of mind on a particular object as Patanjali says in the above *sutra.*

Dharana helps to improve concentration and stabilizes the mind. Thus, it helps in emotional, intellectual and spiritual development.

Dhyana: *Tatra pratyayaikatanata dhyanam* (P.Y.S. 3.2).

Dhyana means an unbroken or uninterrupted flow of *chitta* towards the object of contemplation. In simple words, it is the prolonged *dharana.* The practice of *dhyana* promotes the concentration and may lead towards emotional, intellectual and spiritual development in a person.

Samadhi: *Tadevarthamatra-nirbhasam svarupa-sunyamiva samadhih* (P.Y.S. 3.3).

Samadhi is that state of *dhyana* in which the subject-object distinction is submerged. It is the final stage of Yoga. *Samadhi* leads to the state of self-realization. In this state, the object of *dhyana* becomes more vivid and the awareness about one's own existence disappears. In this state, all emotions go away, and the individual is led towards inner peace, happiness and complete bliss. It is an increased state of concentration. In this state, mind appears as if not functioning but it is not blank. This state is characterised by the increased level of consciousness about the 'self'. *'Samadhi'*, therefore, would certainly contribute to emotional, intellectual and spiritual development of one's personality.

Dharana, dhayana and *samadhi,* together called *'Samyama'* are beneficial for one's intellectual, emotional and spiritual development.

Table: *Astanga Yoga and corresponding developmental dimensions of personality*

Limbs of Astanga Yoga	Developmental Dimensions of Personality
Yama	Emotional, Social and Spiritual Development
Niyama	Emotional, Intellectual and Spiritual Development
Asana	Physical and Emotional Development
Pranayama	Physical and Emotional Development
Pratyahara	Emotional, Intellectual and Spiritual Development
Dharana, Dhyana and Samadhi	Emotional, Intellectual and Spiritual Development

Traditional texts especially *HathaYogic* texts such as *Gheranda Samhita, Hatha-Pradipika, Hatha-Ratnavali* etc. claim about the beneficial impact of all Yogic practices. Further scientific studies are needed to support these claims. Various theoretical and empirical researches have been conducted in order to investigate the role of Yoga for developing various aspects of personality. Majority of the studies supports the claims made in the Yogic texts.

INTELLIGENCE

Today terms like IQ (Intelligence Quotient), EQ (Emotional Quotient), SQ (Social Quotient) are commonly used. In fact, you hear these concepts not just in academics but you can be very familiar using these terms in day-to-day life. Let us first try to understand what exactly is meant by Intelligence?

Intelligence is usually considered as a complex concept involving the ability to:

Learn which includes all kinds of informal and formal learning via any combination of experience, education and training;

Pose problems which includes recognizing problem situations and transforming them into more clearly defined problems;

Solve problems which includes solving problems, accomplishing tasks, creating, fashioning products, and doing complex projects.

People have different levels of intelligence. Psychologists working in the field of intelligence, traditionally focused on measurement of intellectual differences and individual differences using various tests, called the intelligence test. With the help of such tests, Terman introduced the concept of Intelligence Quotient or IQ. Let us now try to understand the concept more clearly.

What is intelligence quotient (IQ)?

The best-known Binet adaptation, created by Stanford University's L.M. Terman in 1916, is the **Stanford-Binet Intelligence Scale.** Terman introduced the term **intelligence quotient (IQ),** which is a numerical value given to scores on an intelligence test (a value of 100 corresponds to average intelligence).

The score on Stanford-Binet intelligence test will give the mental age (MA) of the child or adult.

The mental age is then divided by the chronological age (CA), which is the biological age in years, of the person and multiplied by hundred.

The result is the index of Intelligence called the intelligence quotient.

$$IQ = MA/ CA \times 100$$

Any person will reach the maximum IQ at about the age 18. It is possible to have a slight increase of IQ until one is about 30 years of age. Increase depends upon favourable conditions such as higher education or challenging learning experiences. Studies have shown that one's IQ changes very little after 30 years of age. Instead it may go down slightly with advanced age. It has also been shown that there are no differences in the average IQ of men and women or people from different racial backgrounds.

The Stanford-Binet is designed to measure this ability in four areas: verbal reasoning, abstract/visual reasoning, quantitative reasoning, and short-term memory.

Facets of intelligence

Actually research has shown that there are seven facets of intelligence, which sometimes are called the seven types of Intelligence. These are the following:

- **Musical Intelligence** which is the ability to learn, perform and compose music.
- **Kinesthetic Intelligence** which is the ability to use one's physical body expediously.
- **Logical-Mathematical Intelligence** which is the ability to learn higher mathematics and the ability of a person, to handle complex and logical arguments.
- **Linguistic Intelligence** which is the ability of a person to communicate well, perhaps both orally and in writing, perhaps in several languages.
- **Spatial Intelligence** which is the ability to know where you are relative to fixed locations.
- **Interpersonal Intelligence** which is the core capacity to notice distinctions in others moods, temperament, motivations and intentions etc.
- **Intrapersonal Intelligence** is the capacity to understand the internal aspects of oneself. The ability of a person, to sense other's feelings and be in tune with others feelings and have empathy with.

It is the ability to access to one's own feeling and life, one's range of emotions, and the capacity to make discrimination among the range of emotions as a means to guide and understand one's behaviour. A person with good intrapersonal intelligence has an effective model of himself consistent with a description constructed by careful observers. The person's ability to know, your own body and mind, which may be termed as self awareness.

Concept of intelligence according to Yoga and the practices for IQ development

We all are aware that we have senses through which we obtain knowledge of the external world. They are called *Jnanendriyas* and we perform action through these organs — hands, legs, speech organs, excretory organs and genital organs. They are called the *Karmendriyas.* There are four functional manifestation of the entity called the *Antahkarana.* We have understood that the grossest function is of the random mind. The mind jumps from one subject matter to another. Concentration helps us to channelize these energies which get wasted in a random thinking. When the dam, for example is constructed, channels and control valves are arranged, the whole water becomes useful for irrigation and for generation of electricity. Similarly the energy of our *Chitta* has to be properly channelized to make use of it effectively. But in its gross form of *Manas,* it cannot be done as it jumps randomly. The whole effort in education is to develop power of intelligence, power of discrimination, logical mind, analytical mind, discriminative mind. From diversity to unity is the key essence of intelligence. That is called the Buddhi. The right brain is more related to the emotions and intuition. Now what is Intelligence? The ability to do a work; not to do the work; or do it in a new way or different way is the key essence of intelligence. This is the feature of what we call our consciousness — the *Chaitanya.* Using the consciousness or the Chaitanya, we have brought about wonderful scientific revelations. This is possible mainly by the special feature of consciousness called intelligence — a discriminative faculty to decipher things in a logical manner. For example, in the case of photoelectric effect, after years and years of the discrimination and in-depth research, scientists found that light can travel as particles as well as waves and, thus, the dual nature of light was unravelled. This is possible because of logic, discrimination power, connecting one to another, finding the reason. When we channelize our energies, we bring the whole thing into a single subject. We bring in a connection between one thought and the other which unravels the subject. In the same way all related thoughts are brought together and that is the dimension related to intelligence.

Therefore, let us all develop this intelligence which is the key essence of cognitive development of human beings. Intelligence differentiates us from animals as the Sloka says *"ahara-nidra-bhaya-maithunanca samanyam etat pasubhir naraanam".* There are four features that are common for both animals and human beings: the Food, the Sleep, the Fear and the Procreation. As human beings we are endowed with higher faculty. This *Buddhi* (intellect) is unique in humans, without which we are no better than animals (*Buddher vihinah pasubhih samanah*). It is the Buddhi, in fact, that characterizes us as human beings and if we don't use our Buddhi, we are equivalent to animals. So let the Buddhi prevail in us. Let the discrimination power grow in us.

Development of intelligence

We have understood that, in the grossest form, the random mind jumps everywhere and moves from one subject to another. But in concentration, the mind has to stay on a single subject. The energies are all wasted in the random mind. But once you come to the level of concentration, the energies are channelized. The channelized energies will start giving all the dividends. Such channelized energy can bring harmony in the society. This is possible through proper innermost development. The inner development is related to the three modes of human nature or *Gunas* — *Tamas* (lethargy), *Rajas* (Active and aggressive) and *Sattva* (goodness). Intelligence should be used to develop the *Sattva* within us. When *Sattva* is predominant, we become selfless and service oriented. Use techniques to see that harmonization takes place, aesthetic energization takes place. Intelligence in itself is a pure power which if not used judiciously, can be used to develop an atomic nuclear power which, can devastate or if properly channelized, can transform our lives for the betterment of humanity. We have witnessed the horrors of atomic nuclear explosion in Hiroshima. So let us develop IQ and use it in the right direction.

Yoga practices for IQ development

1. *Breathing Practices*

(*a*) *Baddhakonasana* Breathing

(*b*) *Setubandhasana* Breathing

(*c*) *Navasana* Breathing

(*d*) *Prasarita Padahastasana* Breathing

2. *Sithilikarana Vyayama*

(*a*) *Spinal Stretch*

(*b*) *Pada Sanchalana*

(*c*) *Situps* from Standing (2 Types)

(*d*) Uthita *Ardha Sirsasana* Breathing

(*e*) Butterfly Stretch

(*f*) *Prasarita Padahastasana* Stretch

3. *Yogasanas*

(*a*) *Parsva Konasana* (both sides)

(*b*) *Gomukhasana*

(*c*) *Sarvangasana*

(*d*) *Ardha Sirsasana/ sirsasana*

(*e*) *Baddhakonasana*

(*f*) *Parsvottanasana*

4. *Pranayama*

(*a*) *Surya Anuloma Viloma*

5. *Kriyas (Satkarma)*

(*a*) *Kapalabhati* (Right Nostril)

6. *Meditation*

Creativity

According to Guilford, the term *creativity* is characterized by originality, flexibility and fluency of ideas. Creativity is producing something of value. Creativity is the driving force that turns dreams into reality. Creativity happens when we are in a curious, receptive, open, and humble state of mind. Creativity happens when boundaries are removed, or at least, extended. Creativity plays with the (seemingly) impossible and is the spice of life.

Creativity is an attribute skill of the mind, which has three primary steps:

1. **Imagination:** The first step in creativity is to imagine. This initial step is about letting your imagination go wild and dreaming up as many ideas. This step is about freeing your brain to dream up lots of ideas. Ideas need to be first caught and then refined.
2. **Critique:** The second step in creativity is to critique the ideas imagined in the first step. Brainstorming and collecting the input from a diverse group of people is an excellent way to critique ideas. Brainstorming gathers a mix of broader ideas and different perspectives which will stimulate idea generation and improve the idea. A good brainstorming environment occurs where negative criticism is suspended and there exists a non-judgemental attitude. Each new person added to the brainstorming process creates exponential new possibilities and relationships.
3. **Enactment:** The third step is enactment of the idea. Creativity is more than just using your imagination. After critical thinking and improvement of the idea, we need to enact the idea into a valuable product or creation. This stage of enactment combines real life skills to turn your ideas into success.

There is a concept called Creative Discontent which holds that Creativity is the natural evolution of things driven by a sense that things can always be or be done better.

Physiology and creativity

Physiology has an important effect on innovation and imagination potential. It can have a very positive or very negative impact on imagination. Fatigue and stress stunt imagination. Good sleep makes for an alert brain which is imagination's best friend. Negative stress like worry lowers your level of concentration, and stifles your imagination. It can also lower your ability to critique ideas and plan them. Positive stress, like deadlines and the excitement of new ventures and creations, heightens the senses and improves imagination. Alcohol and drugs are depressants which slows your body's cognitive and motor functions. Good nutrition can play an important role in improving creativity.

Research has shown that exercises enhance cognitive functioning. However, it may be noted that excessive exercise can cause fatigue which can have the debilitating effect of depressing arousal and creativity.

Creativity traits: Creativity traits includes Fluency, Flexibility, Originality, Elaboration, Curiosity, Imagination, Complexity, Risk Taking, Discipline, Fortitude and attention to purpose.

Creativity: the Eastern Concept

What is Creativity? How is it different from intelligence? What are the uses of creativity? We will try to understand these in this part of the Unit. Creativity and Intelligence are facets of our mind. In this creation; everything is in the form of seed. For example, the seed of the mango predetermines the type, quality, taste, size and colour of the mangoes. So the diverse manifestation or expression outside is all contained in the potential form in the seed. So creativity is to create from potential to the kinetic or the manifestation from one to many. In the beginning, for the creation the Lord told that I am one; I am going to become many. *Bahu syam prajayeta iti* ... I am going to create many. In the same way that power is also within us by which we will be able to create newer and diverse things. This is Creativity. *nava-navonmesasali manah.*

Creative mind is that which has the power to bring out newer things. Each time you go to a dream world, you have a new dream that is coming up; each time you are creating the world of your own. The dream you had yesterday will not be repeated today or tomorrow. Very rarely you have the same type of dream. So there is creativity in the dream world. The dream is a new world of your own. It is the creation of your mind. Everyone has their own *Svapna Prapancha* or dream fantasies. Some dreams are very fascinating and enjoyable. But some dreams can be terrific and frightening.

Difference between intelligence and creativity

It is important to understand the difference between Buddhi — the intelligence, and creative power. It is Buddhi or Discrimination power that takes us deep into the subject matter. The manifestation of this intelligence and creativity are found in the left and the right lobes of our brain respectively. Though there is no exact fixed functions of the right and the left brains, they are little overlapping with one another. Predominantly we can say that the right brain is creativity and the left brain is intelligence. Fine arts, Music, Dance, Drama, Painting, Sculpture, Aesthetic they all belong to the category of creativity. The right brain activity, intuition is yet another dimension of that creativity, whereas the left brain essentially is a logical brain.

Silence is the source of creativity

Creativity is the power within us to manifest that which is in the seed form. From the potential to the manifest. How can this happen? The mind has to be calmed down to go into a single thought. So from that single thought emerges the whole gamut of this multiple (thousands and millions) of thoughts. What is that inner state of oneness that creates everything? That is what our Yoga Scriptures tell us emphatically that we all possess that immense potential inside us called Anandamaya Kosa. But it is in the potential form. Its manifestation comes outside in the form of dreams, in the form of multiplicity, in the form of the thoughts in different directions.

How to fathom creativity?

As silencing the mind is the source of creativity, Patanjali has codified, collected and summarized and edited all those techniques that were available earlier to him. The process of meditation is to calm down the mind to see that the whole thing starts manifesting. So calming of mind is the key essence to tap the subconscious. Yoga Vasista also talks about *Manah Prasamana Upayaha Yogaha*, which means Yoga is a process by which you calm down the mind, silence the mind, tranquil the mind and take the mind to the deep silence and there we have all the creativity which can blossom up. That which is deep within us has to be brought to the surface for manifestation. That is what a creative mind does.

Invariably the creativity starts blossoming up when you face challenges. Archimedes was to find out whether there is adulteration of gold in the crown. The King gave him 15 days of time and said that he has to find out this without cutting or mutilating the crown. With the inner anxiety, the rush and inner zeal to find the answer, he entered into the bath tub. While taking a bath, he noticed the water level moving as he lowered and raised himself. He was so excited that he leaped up and ran naked through the streets of Syracuse shouting 'Eureka,' meaning, 'I've found it. Archimedes found that the crown was a mixture of gold and silver, which was bad news for King, and even worse news for the King's craftsman! A great innovation came up with dharana or focusing on a single thought.

Creativity development — Yogic approach

We wish to bring creativity in our education system among our students. We have now-a-days very simple techniques to invoke creativity. Here are some simple questions.

Show 5 and 1 is equivalent to 4

One of the student came and wrote — IV.

Show 2 and 1 is equivalent to 21.

Another girl told — this is 2, this is 1 = 21

There can be hundreds of such simple activities, which can be good or can stimulate creativity.

Yogic practices for creativity development

1. *Breathing Practices*

(*a*) Sectional Breathing — (Abdominal)

(*b*) Sectional Breathing — (Thoracle)

(*c*) Sectional Breathing — (Clavicular)

(*d*) Sectional Breathing — (Full Yogic Breathing)

2. *Sithilikarana Vyayama*

(*a*) Alternate legs

(*b*) *Padasanachalana*

(*c*) Tiger Stretch (Prabheda)

(*d*) Baby Walk

(*e*) *Makarasana* Cycling

(*f*) Clap Jumping

3. *Yogasanas*

(*a*) *Virasana*

(*b*) *Ardha Chandrasana*

(*c*) *Yoga Mudrasana*

(*d*) *Karnapidasana*

(*e*) *Dhanurasana*

(*f*) *Chakrasana*

4. *Pranayama*

(*a*) *Nadi Suddhi*

(*b*) *Sitali*

(*c*) *Sitkari*

5. *Bandhas and Mudras*

(*a*) *Chin Mudra*

(*b*) *Chinmaya Mudra*

(*c*) *Adi Mudra*

(*d*) *Brahma Mudra*

6. *Kriyas*

(*a*) Agnisara

7. *Meditation*

Anger is an emotional state that varies in intensity from mild irritation to intense fury and rage. Like other emotions, it is accompanied by physiological and biological changes; when you get angry, your heart rate and blood pressure go up, as do the levels of your energy hormones, adrenaline and non-adrenaline.

Anger can be caused by both external and internal events. You could be angry at a specific person (such as a co-worker or supervisor) or event (a traffic jam, a cancelled flight), or your anger could be caused by worrying or brooding about your personal problems. Memories of traumatic or enraging events can also trigger angry feelings.

Expressing anger

The instinctive, natural way to express anger is to respond aggressively. Anger is a natural, adaptive response to threats; it inspires powerful, often aggressive, feelings and behaviours, which allow us to fight and to defend ourselves when we are attacked. A certain amount of anger, therefore, is necessary to our survival.

On the other hand, we can't physically lash out at every person or object that irritates or annoys us; laws, social norms, and common sense place limits on how far our anger can take us.

People use a variety of both conscious and unconscious processes to deal with their angry feelings. The three main approaches are expressing, suppressing, and calming. Expressing your angry feelings in an assertive—not aggressive—manner is the healthiest way to express anger. To do this, you have to learn how to make clear what your needs are, and how to get them met, without hurting others. Being assertive doesn't mean being pushy or demanding; it means being respectful of yourself and others.

Anger can be suppressed, and then converted or redirected. This happens when you hold on your anger, stop thinking about it, and focus on something positive. The aim is to *inhibit* or *suppress* your anger and convert it into more constructive behaviour. The danger in this type of response is that if it isn't allowed outward expression, your anger can turn inward—on yourself. Anger turned inward may cause hypertension, high blood pressure, or even depression.

Unexpressed anger can create other problems. It can lead to pathological expressions of anger, such as passive-aggressive behaviour (getting back at people indirectly, without telling them why, rather than confronting them head-on) or a personality that seems perpetually cynical and hostile. People who are constantly putting others down, criticizing everything, and making cynical comments haven't learned how to constructively express their anger. Not surprisingly, they aren't likely to have many successful relationships.

Finally, you can calm down inside. This means not just controlling your outward behaviour, but also controlling your internal responses, taking steps to lower your heart rate, calm yourself down, and let the feelings subside.

Outcomes of anger

Life has its ups and downs, even during a single day our emotions may seem like riding on a veritable roller coaster.

In the Yoga Sutra, Patanjali says, "Pain and suffering that has not yet manifested can and is to be avoided".

Anger can be the result of hurt pride (ego), of unreasonable expectations, or of repeated hostile fantasies. Besides getting our way, we may unconsciously use anger to blame others for our own shortcomings, to justify oppressing others, to boost our own sagging egos, to conceal other feelings, and to handle other emotions (such as when we become aggressive or when we are afraid).

Anger is feeling mad in response to frustration or injury. You don't like what has happened and usually you'd like to get revenge. Anger is an emotional-physiological-cognitive internal state; it is separate from the behaviour it might prompt.

Direct behavioural signs

Following are the symptoms/signs of a person in an anger state:

- *Assaultive:* physical and verbal cruelty, rage, slapping, shoving, kicking, hitting, threatening with a knife or gun, etc.
- *Aggression:* overly critical, fault finding, name-calling, accusing someone of having immoral or despicable traits or motives, nagging, whining, sarcasm, prejudice, flashes of temper.
- *Hurtful:* malicious gossip, stealing, trouble-making.
- *Rebellious:* anti-social behaviour, open defiance, refusal to talk.

Direct verbal or cognitive signs

- Open hatred and insults: "I hate your guts;" "I'm really mad;" "You're so damn stupid."
- Contempt and disgust: "You're a selfish SOB;" "You are a spineless wimp, you'll never amount to anything."
- Suspicious: "You haven't been fair;" "You cheated!"
- Blaming: "They have been trying to cause me trouble."

- I don't get the respect I deserve: "They just don't respect the owner (or boss or teacher or doctor) anymore."
- Revengeful: "I wish I could really hurt him."

Thinly veiled behavioural signs

- Distrustful, sceptical.
- Argumentative, irritable, indirectly challenging.
- Resentful, jealous, envious.
- Disruptive, uncooperative, or distracting actions.
- Unforgiving or unsympathetic attitude.
- Sulky, sullen, pouting.
- Passively resistant, interferes with progress.
- Given to sarcasm, cynical humour and teasing.
- Judgemental, has a superior or holier-than-thou attitude.

Indirect behavioural signs

- Withdrawal: quiet remoteness, silence, little communication especially about feelings.
- Psychosomatic disorders: tiredness, anxiety, high blood pressure, heart disease. Actually, college students with high Hostility scores, had 20 years later, become more overweight with higher cholesterol and hypertension, had drunk more coffee and alcohol, had smoked more cigarettes, and generally had poorer health.
- Depression and guilt.
- Serious mental illness: paranoid schizophrenia.
- Accident-proneness and self-defeating or addictive behaviour, such as drinking, over-eating, or drugs.
- Vigorous, distracting activity (exercising or cleaning).
- Excessively submissive, deferring behaviour.
- Crying.

Indirect verbal signs

- "I just don't want to talk."
- "I'm disappointed in our relationship."
- "I feel bad all the time."
- "If you had just lost some weight."
- "I'm really swamped with work, can't we do something about it?"

Yogic management of anger

Yoga teaches us that any experience can point us to the Self. Instead of being a prisoner of anger, one can become its student. And our daily life provides us with ample "opportunities" to breathe in our upset and awaken our heart.

In the Bhagavad Gita, Chapter 2 verses 62 and 63 the Lord says:

> "When a man thinks of the objects, attachment to the object arises: from attachments desire is born; from desire anger rises; from anger comes delusion; from delusion the loss of memory; from loss of memory the destruction of discrimination; from destruction of discrimination a man perishes". Gita 2.62, 63.

When an object has charmed one to a point of deep attachment, and when fear of its being lost has started coming up in waves to disturb the individual, then, such an individual's attitude towards those that come between him and the object of his attachment is called 'anger.'

Anger, therefore, is only because of our attachment with an object, expressed as an obstacle that has come between us and the object of our desire.

The theme of the Vedas and the Upanishads is freedom of the human spirit; and their message is fearlessness, love and service. They explain every great event — social, political, or religious, the phenomena of the life itself, to an expression of the urge to freedom inherent in every organism — the struggle of the infinite caught up in a cell or in body. Hence their constant order to man is to wake up and march on: 'Arise! Awake! And stop not till the goal is reached!' as conveyed by Swami Vivekananda adopting the powerful words of the Kathopnishad: *'Uttistha jagrata prapya varan nibodhata'*.

Freedom is not giving a free flow to the senses and the mind. Generally, we think that freedom is to allow the senses to go wherever they want. Whatever the mind says, one starts doing it. Is it not a slavery to our senses and mind? Freedom is freedom from all bondages. What is this bondage or slavery? The tendency of the senses to go towards the sense objects is the slavery in which we are bound. Look at the slavery of the mind: right from the time we wake up and till we go to sleep, the mind is constantly busy, with no respite. We are drowned into surges of emotions. ***Kama, Krodha, Lobha, Moha, Mada, Matsarya*** are the six enemies of man (desire leading to greed, irritability to bursts of anger, miserliness, infatuation and delusion, ego showing as arrogance and the subtle jealousies. To overcome these, is the real freedom. Therefore, the unrestricted or free flow of the senses or the mind or emotions is slavery. Therefore, mastery over them is the real freedom.

Over the years, with such an attitude, you will see that not only do you get angry less often, but also each brush with an unpleasant situation provides a remarkable opportunity to know your subconscious mind in a better way. Every such insight brings you one step closer to the supreme goal — that is, enlightenment (perpetual Bliss).

Yoga Practices for Anger Management

1. *Sakti Vikasaka*

(*a*) *Anguli Sakti Vikasaka*

(*b*) *Bhujabhandha Sakti Vikasaka*

(*c*) *Jangha Sakti Vikasaka*

(*d*) *Kundalini Sakti Vikasaka*

(*e*) *Bhujangasana and Parvatasana*

(*f*) *Kaponi Sakti Vikasaka*

2. *Yogasanas*

(*a*) *Trikonasana*

(*b*) *Virabhadrasana-I*

(*c*) *Virabhadrasana-II*

(*d*) *Virabhadrasana-III*

(*e*) *Makarasana*

(*f*) *Virasana*

3. *Breathing Practices*

(*a*) Dog breathing

(*b*) Rabbit breathing

4. *Pranayama*

(*a*) *Chandra anuloma viloma*

(*b*) *Nadi Suddhi*

(*c*) *Sitali*

(*d*) *Nadi Suddhi with kumbhaka*

(*e*) *Chandra anuloma viloma*

5. *Kriyas*

(*a*) *Kapalabhati — left nostril*

6. *Bandhas and Mudras*

(*a*) *Uddiyan Bandha*

(*b*) *Sastanga Namaskara Mudra*

(*c*) *Agnisara*

(*d*) *Janusirsasana* with *jalandharabandh*

7. *Meditation*

EMOTIONAL QUOTIENT

Emotional Intelligence is a type of social intelligence that involves the ability to monitor one's own and others' emotions to discriminate among them, and to use the information to guide one's thinking and actions. Emotional Intelligence is knowing how you and others feel and what to do about it. It is both intrapersonal and interpersonal.

Intrapersonal

- **Self-awareness** — The ability to recognize and understand your moods, emotions and drives, as well as their effect on others.
- **Self-regulation** — The ability to control or re-direct disruptive impulses and moods and the propensity to suspend judgement and to think before acting.
- **Motivation** — A passion to work for reasons that go beyond money and status and a propensity to pursue goals with energy and persistence.

Interpersonal

- **Social skills** — A proficiency in managing relationships and building networks.
- **Empathy** — The ability to understand the emotional makeup of other people.

The causes of emotions — Eastern perspective

The mind carries on its different functions such as perception (*Manah*), memory (*Chitta*) and ego (*Ahamkara*). Mind, which is defined as a conglomeration of thoughts, responds to the input obtained through sense organs. For example, you see a big red flower; eyes send the image to the brain and the mind (manah) perceives it as a beautiful rose. Within the next fraction of a second your memory (chitta) deciphers that it as a very rare variety of rose which you wanted to see badly. The thought circulates in mind and chitta which soon goes on to make you feel "Oh, it is so beautiful, I like it, I love it, I want it". This component of the manomaya kosa in which this rapid recycling takes place and gathers momentum is called the 'Emotions' (Bhavana). This is characterised by feelings such as "likes or dislikes", "love or hate", backed by the heavy 'I' (the ego). It is this emotion that is the root cause of all human joy and distress. When the emotions become powerful, they start governing our actions. Going against the cosmic laws" leads to imbalances called Adhi or Stress. Long standing Adhis get pushed into pranamaya and annamaya kosa causing Vyadhis or psychosomatic ailments. Manomaya kosa is our mental and emotional library, the subtler layer of our existence. Hence the statement "You are what you think you are'!

Culturing the emotion

The most common difficulty of people with anger is that they are highly sensitive and reactive. It is these surges of highly excited states, repeated several times in a day that cause un-surmountable stress. We have seen how emotional conflicts, sensitivities and suppressions are a great hindrance to one's progress. Yoga helps one develop "Samatva", the equanimity of mind *i.e.,* the ability to maintain cool headedness under provoking situations. He needs to be wiser, and not drawn away by rage, anxiety, fear, depression or excitement. It is this equanimity of mind that goes a long way to strengthen the personality. A stable minded person is always considered wiser than an emotionally disturbed individual. Once this emotional stability is achieved via the practice of the inner peace and quietude, one can work more efficiently and handle one's own problems better without suppress them.

The challenges of the modern era pose a great threat to the emotional stability of man. Man looks lost amidst the atrocities of life, unable to overcome his emotional conflicts, blocks, and turmoil. The result is deep unrest, agony and psychosomatic ailments. To remedy the situation, we need an education, which can help us develop our emotions and culture these. But in the educational map, it seems to be the most neglected area. It is Yoga alone where culturing of emotions takes a centre stage. Yoga trains us to

(*i*) systematically sharpen and sensitize our emotions, and

(*ii*) consciously expand and diffuse the overtones of such sensitization. Thus, Yoga offers an effective tool for the development of stable personality of the individual.

The practice of Nadanusandhana, OM meditation, Bhajana sessions help in emotion culture.

CONCENTRATION

Concentration has been defined as "the ability to direct one's thinking in whatever direction one would intend." We all have the ability to concentrate for a small time. But at other times our thoughts are scattered, and our minds run from one thing to another. To deal with such situations, we need to learn and practise concentration skills and strategies. To concentrate, we have to learn a skill, and as with any other skill, this means practice repeated day after day until we achieve enough improvement to feel that we can concentrate when we need to.

Our ability to concentrate depends on

- commitment to the cause
- enthusiasm for the task
- skill at doing the task
- our emotional and physical state
- our psychological state
- our environment

Expanding your concentration span

People sometimes refer to a concentration span: this is the time we can concentrate on a specific task before our thoughts wander. In learning concentration skills, we apply aim to extend our concentration span-bearing in mind that we will have a different span for different tasks. It cannot be expanded to infinity! Most people find their level for most tasks round about an hour, but for some people and some tasks it will just be a few minutes, while for others it might be two or three hours. In this context, the following points needs to be borne in mind.

- *Barriers to concentrate:* The main barriers to concentrating are boredom, anxiety and day-dreaming. Thus in improving our concentration skills we need to counteract these barriers. The following three skills are basic to concentration: if you want to improve your concentration. Start by practicing them. They will be followed by further strategies which will allow you to build onto the basic skills.
- *Focused task:* According to modern psychology, the mind cannot remain fixated on any solitary object for any considerable period. Rather, it must in some way remain moving, although the boundaries of that movement can be constrained. For instance, one can remain 'concentrated' on a book to the exclusion of all external attentions, yet that concentration is dynamic in the sense that one's mind is engrossed in the lively fantasy of the story, or intellectual analysis of the subject matter.

  Similarly, one could be performing a very focused task, such as drawing or painting, building a highly detailed model, playing chess, rock-climbing, playing a musical instrument or bird-watching, yet the mind remains active, albeit contained within a very defined range of things.
- *Practice makes perfect:* Needless to say, the more skilled or adept one becomes in this 'restriction of the mental field' the more proficient one becomes at certain tasks. This mastery is exhibited by people who are at the forefront of all fields in life, be it sportspersons, artists, brain surgeons, or whatever you are.
- *Beyond focus:* But *according* to *Eastern psychology,* though concentration begins with this form of 'controlled' or 'contained' movement of the mind, it is possible to attain a further state wherein all mental movements stop. At this point, the mind becomes 'one' with the essential nature of the object of concentration, and, therefore, can go no further.

It is this state of lack of movement (completely stopping the mind, so-to-speak), yet with awareness (illumination), that the mind must first attain in order to be able to make the 'jump' from one plane (of consciousness) to the other — which is the next stage of Yoga, dhyana or meditation.

Patanjali described dharana as "the binding of the mind to a particular place" — simple and precise! Arjuna, the great warrior and leader of the Pandava army, complains to Lord Krishna in the Bhagavad Gita: "The mind is restless, turbulent and strong, as difficult to curb as the wind." — Gita 6.34. One of the biggest challenges throughout the ages has remained to keeping the 'making mind' quiet. Concentration is like a muscle — its ability increases with practice, and diminishes with disuse. So just as we have to perform regular physical exercises to keep the body strong and fit, we also have to work holistically with all the layers of our existence in order that it will be capable of being kept still and focused.

Yoga techniques for effective concentration

In Yoga, there are many effective techniques for concentration.

- Many Yoga practices are available to improve concentration and train the mind. For example, the repetition of mantras in *japa, ajapa* and *ajapa-japa* form, to visualizations, concentrations upon certain 'inner sounds' (laya), and the use of external concentration devices such as a *yantra* (geometric design).
- Focusing intently upon certain aspects of the body during Asana practice can also be a form of dharana.
- The Hatha Yoga Asanas, Kriyas and Mudras all contain a point to concentrate upon during their practice.
- The same is true for Pranayama, where certain points of concentration are used while controlling the breath, or in some cases, the breath itself is the point of concentration.

Yoga techniques for concentration development

1. *Breathing-stretch breathing*

(*a*) *Sasankasana* breathing
(*b*) *Pavanamuktasana* breathing (Alternate legs)
(*c*) *Pavanamuktasana* breathing (both legs)

2. *Asanas*

(*a*) *Vakrasana*
(*b*) *Garudasana*
(*c*) *Padahastasana*
(*d*) *Supta Virasana*

3. *Pranayama*

(*a*) *Bhramari*
(*b*) *Kriyas* (*Satkarma*)
(*c*) Right nostril *Kapalabhati*
(*d*) *Dharana* (On flower)
(*e*) *Dhyana* (On flower)

MEMORY

Memory is the capacity to retain and recall information about past and present incidents. Memory capacity is the ability to analyze and synthesize the assimilated information. The power of memory varies among individuals.

Simply put, memory is the mental activity of recalling information that you have learned or experienced. That simple definition, though, covers a complex process that involves many different parts of the brain. Memory can be short-term or long-term.

Short-term memory

In short-term memory, your mind stores information for a few seconds or a few minutes: the time it takes you to dial a phone number you just looked up or to compare the prices of several items in a store. Such memory is fragile, and it's meant to be; your brain would soon read "disk full" if you retained every phone number you called, every dish you ordered in a restaurant, and the subject of every Advertisement, you watched on TV. Your brain is also meant to hold an average of seven items, which is why you can usually remember a new phone number for a few minutes but need your credit card in front of you when you're buying something online.

Long-term memory

Long-term memory involves the information you make an effort (conscious or unconscious) to retain, because:

- it is personally meaningful to you (for example, information about family and friends);

- you need it (such as job procedures or material you're studying for a test);
- it made an emotional impression on you (a movie that had you riveted, the first time you ever caught a fish, the day your uncle died);
- some information that you store in long-term memory requires a conscious effort to recall;
- these are episodic memories, which are personal memories about experiences you've had at specific times;
- these are semantic memories (factual data, not bound by time or place), which can be everything from the names of the planets to the colour of your child's hair.

Another type of long-term memory is procedural memory, which involves skills and routines you perform so often that they don't require conscious recall viz. the motor or intellectual skill that you develop.

Areas of the brain important in the formation and retention of memory

- The hippocampus plays the single largest role in processing information as memory.
- The amygdala helps imprint memories that involve emotion.
- The cerebral cortex stores most long-term memory in different zones, depending on whether the information involves: language, sensory input, problem-solving, and so forth.
- In addition, memory involves communication among the brain's network of neurons, millions of cells activated by brain chemicals called neurotransmitters.

Stages of memory foundation and maintenance

There are three stages that the brain goes through in forming and retaining memories.

Acquisition—New information enters your brain along pathways between neurons. The key to encoding information into your memory is concentration; unless you focus on information intently, it goes in one ear and goes out through the other. This is why teachers are always nagging students to pay attention!

Consolidation—If you've concentrated well enough to encode new information in your brain, the hippocampus sends a signal to store the information as long term memory. This happens more easily if it's related to something you already know, or if it stimulates an emotional response.

Retrieval—When you need to recall information, your brain has to activate the same pattern of nerve cells it used to store it. The more frequently you need the information, the easier it is to retrieve it along healthy nerve cell connections.

The following Yoga practices help improve the memory through mind body coordination, calming the mind, preventing unnecessary thoughts, which Patanjali rightly describes "Chitta Vrtti Nirodah". This helps to eradicate the wrong impressions or Samskaras.

Yoga practices to improve memory

1. *Breathing exercise*

(*a*) Hands stretch breathing
(*b*) Ankle stretch
(*c*) *Bhujangasana*
(*d*) SLR breathing (Alternate legs)

2. *Asanas*

(*a*) *Padmasana*
(*b*) *Ustrasana*
(*c*) *Yoga Mudrasana*
(*d*) *Halasana*
(*e*) *Vajrasana*

3. *Pranayama*

Bhramari

4. *Kriyas (Satkarma)*

Kapalabhati; Alternate & both nostril

5. *Meditation;* silencing the mind with slow breathing

(For Practices refer to Guidelines to Practicum).

Multiple Choice Questions

1. All Humanistic theories share a view of personality that is focused on people's:
A. Internal perceptions or introspections
B. External observation
C. Cognitive learning
D. Tendency to grow

2. According to Eyesenck there are only three basic dimensions of personality namely:
A. Extraversion, agreeableness, conscientiousness
B. Extraversion, neuroticism, psychoticism
C. Conscientiousness, neuroticism, psychoticism
D. Psychoticism, extraversion, conscientiousness

3. Which of the following statements is correct?
A. In Rationalization we "make excuses" giving a reason different from the real one for what we are doing
B. Rationalization is not lying, we believe our explanations
C. Rationalization is a common mechanism we all use to bolster our self-esteem when we have done something foolish
D. All of the above

4. Which one of the following statements is not correct?
A. Intellectualization involves reasoning
B. In intellectualization, the intensity of the anxiety is reduced by a retreat into detached, unemotional, abstract language
C. Professionals who deal with troubled people may intellectualize in order to remain helpful without being overwhelmed by sympathetic involvement
D. Intellectualization is a form of projection

5. Which of the following statements of Alfred Adler, is the correct one?
A. He emphasised the importance of social factors in personality. He called attention to the importance of birth order
B. He suggested that children are spoiled by too much parental attention
C. First borns are 'dethroned' by a second child and second-borns, are competitive
D. All of the above

6. Match List-I with List-II and select the correct answer from codes given below the lists:

***List-I* (*Dimensions of personality*)**	***List-II* (*Explanation*)**
(*a*) Extraversion	1. Ranges from good natured cooperative, trusting at one end to irritable, suspicious, uncooperative at the other
(*b*) Agreeableness	2. Ranges from sociable talkative and enthusiastic at one end to sober, reserved and cautious at the other
(*c*) Conscientiousness	3. Ranges from well organised, careful and responsible at one end to disorganized careless and unscrupulous at the other
(*d*) Emotional stability	4. A dimension ranging from imaginative, witty at one end to down to earth, simple at the other
(*e*) Openness	5. A dimension ranging from poised, calm at one end to nervous, anxious at the other

Codes:

	(*a*)	(*b*)	(*c*)	(*d*)	(*e*)
A.	3	1	2	4	5
B.	2	1	3	5	4
C.	2	3	1	4	5
D.	1	2	3	5	4

7. Match list-I with List-II and select the correct answer from the codes given below the lists:

List-I (Aspect of personality)	*List-II (Level of consciousness)*
(*a*) Ego	1. All levels, but mostly preconscious
(*b*) Id	2. Mostly conscious
(*c*) Super ego	3. Unconscious

Codes :

	(*a*)	(*b*)	(*c*)
A.	2	3	1
B.	3	2	1
C.	1	2	3
D.	3	1	2

8. Consider the following statements:
1. The ego's task is to hold the id in check until conditions allow for satisfaction of its impulses.
2. The ego operates in accordance with the reality principle.
3. The ego directs behaviour so as to maximize pleasure and minimize pain.
4. The eternal struggle of ego with the id, is outside our conscious knowledge.

Which of the above sentences is correct?
A. 1, 2, 3 and 4 B. 2 and 4
C. 1, 2 and 3 D. 1 and 3

9. Which one of the following statements is correct about 'super ego'?
A. It is acquired from our parents and through experience
B. It is the final aspect of personality described by Freud
C. It represents our internalization of the moral teachings and norms of our society
D. All of the above

10. According to Freud's psychosexual stages of development fixation at anal stage, stemming from overly harsh toilet-training experiences may result in individuals, who:
A. Are excessively orderly or compulsive
B. Cannot leave any job unfinished
C. Strive for perfection and neatness in everything
D. All of the above

11. According to Freud, oedipus complex is:
A. A crisis of psychosexual development in which children must give up their sexual attraction to their opposite-sex parent
B. A tendency of aggression
C. Fixation
D. Desire to kill the parent of opposite sex

12. According to Freud:
A. All human beings pass through a series of discrete psychosexual stages of development
B. At each stage, pleasure is focused on a particular part of the body
C. Too much or too little gratification at any stage can result in fixation and can lead to psychological disorders
D. All of the above

13. .... theories of personality are concerned with the individual's personal view of the world, his self-concept and his push toward growth or self-actualization.
A. Humanistic B. Social
C. Psychoanalytic D. None of the above

14. Freud constructed a model of personality with:
A. Two interlocking parts
B. Three interlocking parts
C. Four interlocking parts
D. None of the above

15. Hardiness is a personality disposition, that is marked by:
A. Commitment B. Challenge
C. Control D. All of the above

16. Studies have shown that people who are not outcome oriented, experience:
A. Less strain
B. Less mental health problem
C. Less physical health problem
D. All of the above

17. Studies have shown that, smokers:
A. Exercise less and eat more
B. Eat less and exercise more
C. Do less exercise and less eating
D. Eat more and exercise more

18. Consider the following statements.
1. Stretching exercises increase the arousal level of the body.
2. Aerobic exercises have a calming effect.
3. Yogic asanas provide systematic stretching to all the muscles and joints of the body.
4. Yogic asanas massage the glands and other body organs.

Which of the above statements are correct?
A. 1, 2, 3 and 4 B. 1 and 2
C. 3 and 4 D. 1, 3 and 4

19. Which one of the following techniques is considered as helpful in resolving stress.
A. Transcendental meditation
B. Deep breathing
C. Zen
D. All of the above

20. Which one of the following statements is not correct?
A. Persons who have good sleep habits are able to resolve stress better.
B. The state of health includes only physical and mental well-being
C. Scheier and his colleagues have developed a measure to assess optimism.
D. Social psychological and spiritual well-being is also included in the state of health.

21. Which one of the following options presents the correct ascending order sequence of stressful life events that impair an individual's health?
A. Death of spouse, marital separation, personal injury, getting fired at work.
B. Personal injury, marital separation, death of spouse, getting fired at work.
C. Getting fired at work, personal injury, marital separation, death of spouse.
D. Marital separation, personal injury, getting fired at work, death of spouse

22. Which of the following factors determine who will become addicted to smoking?
A. Genetic B. Psychosocial
C. Cognitive D. All of the above

23. Which one of the following statements about the role of emotion in physical health is correct?
A. Failure to express our emotions can adversely affect the progression of cancer and other illness
B. Emotions can also lead to an increase in a person's blood pressure
C. Emotions play no role in physical health
D. Both A and B

24. Which of the following statements about time management as a behavioural coping technique is correct?
A. By using the method of time management, we can reduce the stressors in our lives
B. Time management is learning how to make time work for us instead of against us
C. Principle of time management is to balance work time and play time
D. All of the above

25. Consider the following statements.
1. Our biological system is equipped with some stress alarms that are essential for survival and allow one to function effectively in many situations.
2. Without undergoing stress, there can be no constructive and creative activity.
3. A certain level of stress is necessary to perform better in examinations.
4. Stress quite often increases our efficiency and makes us search for new coping resources.

Which of the above statements are correct?
A. 1, 2, 3 and 4
B. 2, 3 and 4
C. 2 and 4
D. 1 and 3

26. A young woman leaves home to escape parental domination, only to come back to receive parental protection; her attitude toward her parents is:
A. Ambivalent
B. Approach avoidance conflict
C. Vacillation-avoidance approach
D. None of the above

27. Stereotype is a tendency to:
A. Exhibit repetitive, fixated behaviour
B. Change and modify one self
C. Show abnormal attachment
D. Seek comfort in fantasy

28. Retrogressive behaviour is:
A. A form of regression
B. A return to behaviour once engaged in
C. A primitive kind of behaviour
D. All of the above

29. Which one of the following statements about defence mechanism is not correct?
A. Defence mechanisms provide a protective armour while we are earning more mature and realistic ways of solving our problems
B. Defence mechanisms give us time to solve problems that might otherwise overwhelm us
C. The person who depends upon defence mechanisms for protection may never be forced to learn more mature ways of behaving
D. Actions based on defence mechanisms always reach their goals and the resulting behaviour is tension-reducing

30. _____ is an internal state which can be caused by physical demands on the body or by environmental and social situations which are evaluated as potentially harmful, uncontrollable, or exceeding our resources for coping.
A. Stress B. Anxiety
C. Pain D. None of the above

31. _____ termed the body's response to stressors the general adaptation syndrome.
A. Sigmund Freud B. Hans Selye
C. William James D. None of the above

32. The alarm reaction, the stage of resistance and the stage of _____ are the three stages of the general adaptation syndrome.
A. Productivity
B. Overloading
C. Exhaustion
D. None of the above

33. If the stressor continues to be present, the stage of ____ begins, where in the body resists the effects of the continuous stressor.
A. Alarm reaction B. Exhaustion
C. Resistance D. None of the above

34. Adrenocorticotropic hormone is secreted in the blood stream by certain cells in the:
A. Pineal gland B. Pituitary gland
C. Parathyroid gland D. None of the above

35. Stressors are able to activate the nerve cells of the ___ so that more corticotropin releasing factor is sent to the pituitary gland, thus increasing secretion of ____ into the blood.
A. Thalamus, ACTH
B. Hypothalamus, ACTH
C. Hypothalamus, Thyroxin
D. None of the above

36. In the stage of exhaustion, the body's capacity to respond to both continuous and new stressors has been seriously:
A. Accepted B. Compromised
C. Rejected D. None of the above

37. The term ___ disorder is used when perceived stressors, viz., mental events increase the susceptibility of the body to disease.
A. Neurotic B. Mental
C. Psychosomatic D. None of the above

38. Treatment of psychosomatic disorders involves medical help for the physical problems, and at the same time ____ factors producing the stress.
A. Attention to the psychological
B. Transformation of the mental
C. Negligence of the psychological
D. None of the above

39. The origins of stress can be:
A. Physical B. Environmental
C. Social D. All of the above

40. Which set of disorders occur when perceived stressors increase the susceptibility of the body to disease?
A. Physiological B. Psychosomatic
C. Organic D. Cardiac

41. Match List-I with List-II and select the correct answer by choosing from the codes given below:

List-I (Concept)	*List-II (Explanation)*
(*a*) Personality Structure	1. Psychological reactions and motives that change dynamically over relatively brief periods.
(*b*) Personality Process	2. Stable and enduring qualities that define the individual and distinguish individuals from one another.
(*c*) Personality Development	3. People sometimes change and sometimes resist change or are unable to change accordingly.
(*d*) Psychopathology and Change	4. Everybody comes up to be an unique individual by adulthood.

Codes:

	(*a*)	(*b*)	(*c*)	(*d*)
A.	1	2	3	4
B.	2	3	4	1
C.	2	1	4	3
D.	4	1	2	3

42. What type of cell is responsible for the reproduction of other cells of the body?

(*a*) Blood cells (*b*) Stem cells
(*c*) Neurons (*d*) Basal cells

Codes:

A. (*a*) only
B. (*b*) only
C. (*c*) and (*d*) only
D. (*d*) and (*a*) only

43. Sleep disorders can be categorized as:

A. Paraphilias and Dysfunctions
B. Insomnia and Hypersomnia
C. Parasomnias and Dyssomnias
D. Serotonergic and Dopaminergic

44. Which of the following is not a diagnosable sleep disorder?

A. Somnambulism B. Somniloquy
C. Sleep terror D. Insomnia

45. Brief stress enhances the activity of immune system as evidenced by the action of _____.

A. macrophages B. T cells
C. B cells D. All of the above

46. Personality assessments in forensic settings use the following psychometric and behavioural measures:

(*a*) Galvanic Skin Response (GSR)
(*b*) Millon Clinical Multiaxial Inventory (MCMI)
(*c*) Continuous Performance Test (CPT)
(*d*) Sixteen Personality Factors Test (16 PF)

Codes:

A. (*a*) and (*b*) B. (*c*) and (*d*)
C. (*a*), (*b*) and (*c*) D. (*b*), (*c*) and (*d*)

47. Match List-I with List-II and select the correct answer by choosing from the codes given below:

List-I (Sleep phenomenon)	*List-II (EEG display)*
(*a*) Stage-1 sleep	(*i*) Single large –ve wave followed by large +ve wave
(*b*) Stage-3 sleep	(*ii*) Low voltage high frequency EEG signal
(*c*) Sleep spindle	(*iii*) Occasional presence of delta waves
(*d*) K-complex	(*iv*) Waxing and waning burst of 12-14 Hz wave

Codes:

	(*a*)	(*b*)	(*c*)	(*d*)
A.	(*i*)	(*iv*)	(*iii*)	(*ii*)
B.	(*ii*)	(*iii*)	(*iv*)	(*i*)
C.	(*iii*)	(*iv*)	(*i*)	(*ii*)
D.	(*iv*)	(*iii*)	(*ii*)	(*i*)

48. Emergent stage-I sleep is characterized by:

(*a*) sleep-spindle
(*b*) electromygraphic changes
(*c*) electro-oculographic changes
(*d*) K-complex

Codes:

A. (*a*) and (*b*) B. (*a*) and (*d*)
C. (*a*), (*c*) and (*d*) D. (*b*), (*c*) and (*d*)

49. Read each of the following two statements - Assertion (A) and Reason (R) and indicate your answer using codes given below:

Assertion (A) : The forgetting of a memory is caused by the disappearance of its engram over a period of time.

Reason (R) : Once the engram has disappeared, the memory no longer exists anywhere in the memory system.

Codes:

A. Both (A) and (R) are true and (R) is the correct explanation of (A)
B. Both (A) and (R) are true, but (R) is not the correct explanation of (A)
C. (A) is true, but (R) is false
D. (A) is false, but (R) is true

50. The following social factors play a role in educational settings:

(*a*) co-operation (*b*) competition
(*c*) peer influence (*d*) role modelling

Codes:

A. (*a*) and (*b*) only B. (*b*) and (*c*) only
C. (*c*) and (*d*) only D. All of the above

51. Deterioration Quotient (DQ) was first used in which intelligence test?

A. Benet-Simon Test
B. Galton-Cattell Test
C. Raven Progressive Matrices
D. Wechsler Adult Intelligence Test

52. The evidence that sleep is a biological motive comes from __________ in lengthy sleep deprived subjects.

A. rebound effect of slow wave sleep
B. rebound effect of REM sleep
C. insomnia
D. enhanced stage-I and stage-II sleep

53. Match the items of List-I with the items of List-II. Select the correct response from the answer codes given below:

List-I	***List-II***
(*a*) Latent learning	(*i*) Learning a response to terminate an aversive stimulus.
(*b*) Cognitive learning	(*ii*) Occurrence of learning is not evident in behaviour until later.
(*c*) Escape learning	(*iii*) A change in the way of processing informations as a result of experiences.
(*d*) Avoidance learning	(*iv*) Learning a response to avoid an aversive stimulus

Codes:

	(*a*)	(*b*)	(*c*)	(*d*)
A.	(*iii*)	(*ii*)	(*iv*)	(*i*)
B.	(*ii*)	(*iii*)	(*i*)	(*iv*)
C.	(*i*)	(*iv*)	(*ii*)	(*iii*)
D.	(*iv*)	(*iii*)	(*i*)	(*ii*)

54. Which of the following psychologists first empirically established that social stress distort physical health?

A. Selye
B. Lazarus and Folkman
C. Holmes and Rahe
D. Srivastava and Pestonjee

55. A psychotic disorder in which a person's functioning is not markedly impaired, whether is behaviour obviously odd or bizarre and free from hallucinations is called:

A. Schizo-affective Disorder
B. Schizophreniform Disorder
C. Delusional Disorder
D. Shared Psychotic Disorder

56. In which of the following disorders a person has two or more different personalities, and either of which is dominant at a time?

A. Dissociative amnesia
B. Split personality
C. Dissociative identity disorder
D. Schizophrenia

57. Which is not a characteristic symptom of Narcolepsy?

A. Cataplexy
B. Sleep paralysis
C. Nocturnal myoclonus
D. Hypnagogic hallucinations

58. Among the following concepts which are related to Alfred Adler's theory of personality?

1. Organ inferiority 2. Psychoticism
3. Archetypes 4. Masculine protest

Codes:

A. 1 and 4 B. 2 and 3
C. 1 and 2 D. 4 and 3

59. Mental grouping of similar objects, events or people is called:

A. Cognition B. Concept
C. Prototype D. Thinking

60. Which of the following are characteristics of Charismatic leaders?

1. Vision and Articulation
2. Risk taking behaviour
3. Volatile moods
4. Sensitivity to followers' needs

Codes:

A. 2, 3 and 4
B. 1, 2 and 4
C. 1, 3 and 4
D. 1 and 4

ANSWERS

1	2	3	4	5	6	7	8	9	10
A	B	D	D	D	B	A	A	D	D
11	**12**	**13**	**14**	**15**	**16**	**17**	**18**	**19**	**20**
A	D	A	B	D	D	A	C	D	B
21	**22**	**23**	**24**	**25**	**26**	**27**	**28**	**29**	**30**
C	D	D	D	A	A	A	D	D	A
31	**32**	**33**	**34**	**35**	**36**	**37**	**38**	**39**	**40**
B	C	C	B	B	B	C	A	D	B
41	**42**	**43**	**44**	**45**	**46**	**47**	**48**	**49**	**50**
C	B	C	B	D	A	B	B	A	D
51	**52**	**53**	**54**	**55**	**56**	**57**	**58**	**59**	**60**
D	A	B	C	C	C	C	A	B	B

●●●

CHAPTER 9

Practical Yoga

CONCEPT OF YOGIC PRACTICES

The term Yoga carries several technical meanings. One of its principal meanings is 'Yukti'. Yukti means technique, trick or skill for achieving the goal indirectly when the goal cannot be achieved directly. Yoga as Yukti can also be termed as a junction in order to feel the divine within us.

Yoga as Yukti involves many different processes which require proper training. So the techniques or practices (*i.e.*, yuktis) enjoined in yogic literature also go under the name of Yoga. Thus we get such terms as Laulika Yoga, Neti Yoga, Dhyana Yoga, Samadhi Yoga etc., for the individual yoga practitioner. When various such techniques or practices are systematized and formulated they are known as schools of yoga like Bhakti Yoga, Jnana Yoga, Karma Yoga, Hatha Yoga, Laya Yoga, Raja Yoga etc. All these schools of Yoga are only Yoga in the sense of so many techniques, Yuktis or Yogic practices.

The four major schools or streams of Yoga are:

(*i*) Karma Yoga – Path of Self Sacrifice
(*ii*) Bhakti Yoga – Path of Self Surrender
(*iii*) Jnana Yoga – Path of Self Analysis
(*iv*) Raja Yoga – Path of Self Control

The nature of all Yogic practices is psycho-physiological. Although every Yogic practice is psycho-physiological in nature, those practices which emphasis control of mental processes directly are more psychological. Some yogic practices of Hatha Yoga are more physical or physiological than psychological. Only these yogic practices which predominantly are physical or physiological in nature could be referred to as exercises. Rather, they should be understood in the sense of what is called the hygienic exercises. Some of the yogic exercises are Surya Namaskar, Asana, Pranayama, Mudras, Bandhas and Shat kriya.

TYPES OF YOGIC PRACTICES

Yogic practices begin to work on the outmost aspect of the personality. The physical body is the practical and familiar starting point for most of the people. When imbalance is experienced at this level, the organs, muscles and nerves no longer functions in harmony, rather they act in opposition to each other.

Yogic practices help to overcome these imbalances and create harmony in the body and mind.

In Bhagavad Gita **Yogeshwar Krishna** defines yoga as:

***"Samatvam yoga ucchyate"*—Equanimity of mind.**

***"Yogaha karmasu koushalam"*—Yoga is skill in action.**

Doing everything skillfully is also the main aim of Yoga. Yogic practices help in attaining the attitude of perfection in the mind.

The various types of Yogic practices from which everyone can get benefitted are:

(*i*) Yama and Niyama (Attitude Training Practices)

(*ii*) Asana (Steady Postures)

(*iii*) Pranayama (control of the breathing process)

(*iv*) Mudras and Bandhas (seal and lock for energy)

(*v*) Shat Karmas (six purification techniques)

(*vi*) Dhyana (Meditation)

BENEFITS OF YOGA PRACTICES

Physical Benefits

- Creates a toned, flexible and strong body.
- Improves respiration, energy and vitality.
- Helps to maintain a balanced metabolism.
- Promotes cardio and circulatory health.
- Relieves pain.
- Helps you look and feel younger than your age.
- Improves your athletic performance.

Mental Benefits

- Helps you relax and handle stressful situations more easily.
- Teaches you how to quiet the mind so you can focus your energy where you want it to go - into a difficult yoga pose, on the tennis court or golf course, or in the office etc.
- Encourages positive thoughts and self-acceptance.

Spiritual Benefits

- Builds awareness of your body, your feelings, the world around you, the needs of others.
- Promotes an inter dependence between mind, body and spirit.
- Helps you live the concept of "oneness."

ASANA

Asana is one of the most ancient yogic practices. It forms the base for almost all the other practices of Yoga, namely, Pranayama, Kriyas, Meditation, Bandhas and Mudras, etc. It plays a very important role in Yoga training from the beginning to the end.

We can trace the origin of yoga asana to the prehistoric times of ancient India namely the Indus Valley Civilization. The archeological findings at Mohenjo-Daro shows deities seated in Yogic postures.

Today asana are the most popular aspect of yoga. Some people even mistake that Yoga means only Asana. Obviously this is a gross misconception about Yoga.

Definition

The term Asana is derived from the Sanskrit root "Aas" means "To sit" or "Asi" means "To be".

Maharishi Patanjali has provided the definition of Asana alongwith its basic methodology as well as effect in the following aphorisms in his Yoga Sutra:

"Sthirasukham asanam"

Asana is a posture held firm or stable with comfort.

From the above aphorism of Patanjali, the two key characteristics of an Asana should be stability and comfort. In practical terms stability here signifies immobilisation or stability of the body and comfort denotes a harmonious peaceful and serene mental state.

Thus the above definition of Asana brings out the essentially of it. Contrary to the common motion among people asana is not only a practice involving the human body but also the human mind. The methodology or mechanism of Asana given by Patanjali throws more light in this respect.

Maharishi Patanjali also tells us about how an Asana can be done:

"Prayatnasaithilya ananthasamapattibhyam"

Effortlessness and Contemplation on the infinite.

Effortlessness or relaxation of effort is the first requirement. It may involve relaxation of all those groups of muscles in the body which are not at all required to participate for the performance of a particular asana. Further even those muscles which are involved in the maintenance of Asana are made to relax consciously to the maximum possible extend. That is the best result can be achieved from the Asana by slackening of effort that is by performing the Asana in a very relaxed manner.

Together with such slackening of effort one should also contemplate or meditate on some infinite entity. For instance, feel oneself as a part and parcel of an infinite mightily ocean or the infinite sky, and totally identified with it and merging into it. This process leads one to the oceanic feeling which is also called Meditation on the vast ocean.

Maharishi Patanjali defines the benefit of Asana as:

"Tato dwandya anabhighaatah"

Thereby the power of the opposite ceases to have any impact.

Rightly performed, Asana makes one immune to clash of the opposite's tensions strife, stress and conflicts in life. It helps to overcome the disharmonies in the body and help to restore perfect harmony in the working of the whole body especially the neuro-musculo-glandular tone. Moreover, it also helps to restore mental and emotional well-being.

This point has been emphasized in Hatha Yoga as well. The text Hatha Yoga Pradipika of Swatmarama says.

"Kuryat tad asanam sthairyam arogyam ca angalaghavam"

Perform Asana to bring about stability in health and suppleness of the body.

SCOPE AND LIMITATIONS OF ASANA

According to Yogic texts the number of Asanas runs into 84 lakhs. However they present the techniques of around a hundred Asanas or so. The texts also tend to differ in many minor points of detail in the techniques of these Asanas, but they are almost unanimous about the major benefits claimed for each Asana they describe. All of them recognize the worth of Asana in the restoration of health and their therapeutic utility.

The scope of Yogic Asana is so vast and all embracing that their limitations seem to fade into insignificance comparatively. Depending upon the anatomic limitations due to fat rigidity ageing process, illness etc., and one can choose the simplest from the vast array of Asanas with their modified variations to serve specific purposes of an individual. Asana take full advantage of the extreme range of movement made available due to the various types of joints in the body. Asana further takes advantage of the flexibility of the body itself and the gravitational aspects of human body. Some texts even prescribe use of ropes and various mechanical aids in the performance of specific Asana. This has encouraged some outstanding Yogis like Swami Kuvalayananda and B.K.S Iyengar to develop mechano-Yogic-procedures to make the performance of Asana within reach of even patients.

The basic limitations about Asana are:

(*i*) It cannot be fully understood with the help of only the exercise Physiology or Physical Education norms. So one cannot expect to achieve the fitness factors considered most important by modern sciences at present.

(*ii*) Lack of standardization of the techniques of specific Asana poor agreement among the experts on the basic principles underlying the concept and practice of Asana also put severe limitations in utilizing Asana appropriately in an objectively sound manner.

In spite of such limitations asana are found easier to learn and practice with least injury and maximum benefit.

RELAXATIVE ASANAS

These are the Asana that are designed to give complete relaxation to the entire musculature of the body. The two well-known relaxative Asana are Shavasana and Makarasana. They not only remove bodily fatigue they also remove mental strain and thereby brings about peace and clarity of the mind.

However it must be remembered that even the difficult Cultural Asana could and should become more and more relaxative with proper training and practice. Then only they can be called to be Asana according to the definition and procedure prescribed by Maharishi Patanjali.

Different types of Asanas

Asana also classified into different types they are:

- Front bending postures Eg: Paschimottanasana, Hastapadasana.
- Back bending postures Eg: Chakrasana, Bhujangasana.
- Twisting postures Eg: Ardha matsyendrasana, Pasasana.
- Hand balancing postures Eg: Kakasana, Kukkutasana.
- Standing postures Eg: Vrikshasana, Ekapadasana.
- Topsy-turvy postures Eg: Sarvangasana, Sirasasana.
- Lateral bending postures Eg: Ardhakati Chakrasana, Trikonasana.

ROLE OF ASANA IN YOGIC SPIRITUAL YOGIC CULTURE AND PHYSICAL CULTURE:

"Yoga is the unification of the individual psyche (JIVATMA) with the transcendental Self (PARAMATMAN)"—Yoga Yajnavalkya

Yoga was originally developed in ancient times as a spiritual discipline. Samadhi or becoming one with god was the main aim of yoga. Asana were profound for meditating on the divine comfortably as a Sadhana.

Jesus Christ says "the physical body (the sthula sharira) is the living temple of the lord".

Hence the spiritual culture of Asanas used is in order to obtain the divine realization within ourselves.

However Swami Kuvalayananda had developed a system of yogic physical culture which consisted of few Asana, Kriyas, Bandhas, Mudras and Pranayama etc., Asana form the major part of this system. It has proved to be ideal system of physical culture which can be followed even by ordinary people who do not believe in spiritual aspects of Yoga.

Further this Yogic physical culture system has been found extremely valuable even by the spiritual culturists.

The objectives of the Yogic physical culture according to Swami Kuvalayananda include:

(*a*) To secure the largest percentage of energy with minimum energy expenditure.

(*b*) To secure increase in the vital index.

(*c*) To develop a healthy nervous system.

(*d*) To take special care of endocrine glands.

(*e*) To take care of the heart and circulatory system including efficient micro-circulation in all the parts of the body.

(*f*) To develop the neuro-muscular system to the physiologically sound optimum level without taxing other systems in the body.

The physiological advantage sought through the Yogic physical culture system ensure at preserving and promotion of healthy and efficient functioning of various systems, organs tissues and cells in the body as a whole.

The Asana included in the Yogic physical culture are found to serve in the Yogic spiritual culture system as well. Here the spiritual aspects of these every Asana are emphasized more. Here the emphasize is made with a view to stimulate the Kundalini, to develop a well-trained nervous system to gain increasing control over the Pranic activities in the body, spiritual practices like repetition of mantra etc., the activities of spiritual culture are also required to study traditional texts and reflect on the spiritual implication contained in them with a devotional frame of mind.

SHAT KRIYAS

The Sanskrit word 'Kriya' literally means 'Action'. It has a technical meaning in Yoga. It means a purifying and reconditioning process. In Yoga it is specifically used for various cleansing processes.

The Yogic kriyas are the first and foremost important practices in Hatha Yoga. They are said to be cleanse the body internally. As Ashtanga Yoga emphasis on Yama and Niyama, Hatha Yoga emphasis on cleaning process that is Kriyas, in belief of the healthy and clean body can only have healthy and clean Mind. The Yogic Kriyas or cleansing practices are six in number hence called Shat-Karma (six-actions). These practices are not taught or even referred to in most schools of Yoga for several reasons. Firstly the practices look difficult, sometimes revolting, and un-natural and are definitely not as easy as standing on your head. There is some risk of harm to the Learner if something goes wrong.

Keeping all this in mind, most Yoga teachers conveniently overlook these practices. However, it cannot be forgotten that these practices are a part of traditional Hatha Yoga. In fact there they are mentioned as pre-requisites. It is believed that these practices cleanse the body and prepare it for Hatha Yoga. It is as if you are cleaning up your house first before re-decorating it. Surely you will not bother beautifying a dirty house. Cleanliness comes first and hence the importance of kriyas.

The term Shat Karma or Shat Kriya means 'six actions'. The ancient Rishis considered them as essential to the practice of Yoga: "In Yoga, control of the body starts with the cleansing processes known as the Kriyas, the first step to eliminate poisonous substances accumulated in the system".

Those cleansing processes are powerfully and profoundly purifying, acting at all levels of 'being'. When the body is purified, then one is trained in concentration. These six actions or Shat Karmas are the foundation of the Asanas and meditative practices of Hatha Yoga.

The six Kriyas are:

"Dhautir-vastis-tatha netir, tratakam, naulikam tatha;

kapal-bhatis-c-aitani, sat-karmani samacaret!!

(GS, I:12)

The body is cleaned with the help of the six following processes:

(*i*) *Dhauti*—cleanses the upper Gastro Intestinal Tract (GIT) upto the stomach.

(*ii*) *Basti*—cleanses the lower Gastro Intestinal Tract (GIT) especially the rectum.

(*iii*) *Neti*—cleans the upper nasal tract from the throat to the nostrils.

(*iv*) *Trataka*—cleanses the eyes and improves the eyesight.

(*v*) *Nauli*—tones up the abdominal muscles and viscera.

(*vi*) *Kapalabhati*—cleans the lower respiratory tract and activates the brain cells.

They help to balance Tridoshas (three humors) and also help to prevent various psychosomatic disorders. They are supposed to bring about purification of Nadis. Purification of the Nadis is considered as a necessary preparation for the practice of Pranayama.

Some Yogis believe that Kriyas are not necessary for the purification of the Nadis. They hold the view that Pranayama can bring about the cleansing of the Nadis as well as restoration of health. So they have prescribed a special kind of Pranayama done through alternate-nostrils known as NADISHODHANA PRANAYAMA OR ANULOMA-VILOMA PRANAYAMA.

Dhauti

It cleanses various openings or cavities in the body, using water, rubber or catheter tube and muslin cloth. The different types of Dhauti are:

(*i*) *Vaman Dhauti*—It is used for washing the stomach by stimulating the vomiting reflex.

(*ii*) *Vastra Dhauti*—It is used for cleansing and massaging the stomach and food-pipe using a long strip of cotton cloth.

(*iii*) *Danda Dhauti*—Dhauti means washing and massaging the food pipe and stomach with stick or catheter tube and water.

Vaman Dhauti

- Prepare 2 to 3 litres of lukewarm saline water
- Drink 2 to 3 litres of this water as possible and as quickly as possible in a standing position.
- Lean forward and tickle the throat using index, middle and ring finger.
- Try to give vomiting sensation and vomit completely.
- Perform the practice until you feel that most of the water has come out.

Vastra Dhauti

- 'Vastra' means 'cloth' and 'Dhauti' means 'cleansing'.
- Sterilize the cotton cloth with the given measurement (twenty two feet length × two and half inches width).
- Fill a mug with lukewarm water.
- Place one end of the cloth in mouth and then begin swallowing it.
- When the majority of the cloth except for the portion being held by you has gone inside the stomach perform the Nauli Kriya by churning the abdomen in both directions.
- The cloth should then be brought out slowly and carefully.

Danda Dhauti

- Prepare 2 to 3 litres of lukewarm saline water.
- Drink 2 to 3 litres of this water as possible and as quickly as possible in a standing position.
- Take a rubber tube (Danda) about 1 cm in diameter and about a meter long.
- Slowly place the thin and tapered end of the tube in the back of the throat and push it down the esophagus into the stomach.
- It reaches the stomach, slowly bend forward.
- Perform a flapping action of the abdominal wall to help push the water out.

Benefits of Dhauti

- Relieves problems of upper GIT (Gastritis, acidity).
- Cleanses roughages from the stomach.
- Helps to activates appetite.
- Reduces Kapha disorders (Obesity, Asthma)
- It improves the strength of the body and growth.
- It heals tumors, enlarged spleen, liver and common fever.
- Balances the Pitta Dosha.

Contra-indication

- Patients of Peptic ulcer, Coronary Heart diseases should avoid this practice.
- Hypertension, heart diseases, stroke or generally illness should be avoid this practice.

Basti

It cleanses the colon through neuromuscular control.

The different types of Basti are:

(*i*) *Jala Basti*—Contraction and relaxation of anal sphincter in order to clean lower intestine through water is called Jala Basti karma.

(*ii*) *Sthala Basti*—Contraction and relaxation of anal sphincter in order to clean lower intestine through wind or air is called Sthala Basti karma.

Jala Basti

- Jala Basti means "Yogic enema with water".
- Prepare ½ to 1 liter of lukewarm water.
- Fill water in colon through anus (enema).
- Practice of Nauli may be done for better result.
- Hold water in colon for few minutes.
- Finally try to evacuate filled water completely.

- After evacuation, it is traditionally taught to perform Mayurasana or Padma Mayurasana to further evacuate the colon completely as the pressure exerted stimulates further peristalsis and any water that may remain inside is thrown out.

Sthala Basti

- Sthala Basti means "Dry yogic enema".
- Take up a squatting position such as Utkatasana.
- This technique may be done, by sucking the air into the bowels, by performing Ashwini Mudra.
- The air is held in the colon for sometime and then expelled out through the anus.
- Nauli Kriya may be done while holding the air in the colon for better results.

Benefits of Basti

- Basti cleans the colon by removing the gas and other accumulated waste material from the colon.
- Relieves constipation.
- Cool down the body and strengthen abdominal visceral organs.
- Reduces Vata disorders.
- The body becomes light and active.
- Old stool and gas is expelled.

Contra-indication

- Hernia and Severe piles patient should be avoid this practice.

Neti

Neti cleanses and acclimatizes the nasal passages.

The different types of Neti are:

(i) *Jala Neti*—Nasal irrigation done with water.

(ii) *Dugdha Neti*—Nasal irrigation done with milk.

(iii) *Ghrta Neti*—Nasal irrigation done with ghee.

(iv) *Sutra Neti*—Nasal irrigation done with thread or rubber catheter.

Jala Neti

- Jala Neti means cleansing the nasopharyngeal tract with water.
- Prepare warm saline with 10 grams of salt per litre of lukewarm water.
- Insert the nozzle of the pot into your right nostril.
- Keep your mouth open and breathe freely through your mouth.
- Tilt your head slightly forward and sideward to the left, so that the water from the pot enters the right nostril and comes out through the left by gravity. Allow the flow till the pot is empty.
- Repeat the same on the left side.

Sutra Neti

- Check which nostril is flowing freely and perform the neti.
- Sutra neti means cleansing the nasopharyngeal tract with thread.
- Insert the blunt end of a thin soft rubber catheter or cotton thread from the front horizontally into the nostril that is open.
- Insert your right index and the middle fingers through the mouth and catch the tip of the catheter at the back of your throat.
- Remove the catheter through the mouth so that the thick end of the catheter pulls all the mucus into the throat and spit it.
- Repeat on the opposite side.

Benefits of Neti

- All the five special sensory organs (Jnanendriyas) are purified and activated by the Neti Kriya.

- It is a good preventive measure against cold, cough, sinusitis, hysteria, epilepsy, migraine and depression.
- Removes mucus and dust particles from the nasal passages and the sinuses.
- Neti, in general, purifies most structures in the head and neck.
- Vision becomes more subtle.

Caution

- Neti Kriya is to be followed by few rounds of Kapalabhati, so as to keep the nasal passages clear of any stagnant water that may cause problems later.

Nauli

Nauli is the isolation and the manipulation of the abdominal recto muscles to stimulate the healthy functioning of the abdominal organs.

The different types of Nauli are:

(*i*) *Madhyama Nauli*—It is the technique of compression and relaxation of the abdominal muscles at the centre of the abdomen.

(*ii*) *Vama Nauli*—It is the technique of compression and relaxation of the abdominal recti muscles to the left side of the abdomen.

(*iii*) *Dakshina Nauli*—It is the technique of compression and relaxation of the abdominal muscles to the right side of the abdomen.

(*iv*) *Nauli Chalana*—It is the technique of compression and relaxation of the abdominal muscles in clockwise and anticlockwise direction.

Pradakshina Nauli : Nauli chalana in the clockwise direction.

Apradakshina Nauli : Nauli chalana in anticlockwise direction.

Practice of Nauli

- Stand with feet separated by about three feet.
- Perform Uddiyana Bandha in the standing position. With a mock inhalation, contract the abdominal muscles and compress them in the centre. This is Madhyama Nauli.
- Then compress the muscles on the left (Vama Nauli) and then on the right side (Dakshina Nauli). The muscles right to left and right to left in a circular motion.
- Do not strain.
- When finished slowly stand up back in the Samastithi asana with deep breathing and relax for some time.

Benefits of Nauli

- Nauli purifies and strengthen the vital organs.
- It helps in removing most of the abdominal ailments.
- The functions of liver, pancreas and spleen as well as the kidneys are activated by Nauli.
- It massages and tones the muscles of the entire abdominal area.
- It stimulates appetite, digestion, assimilation, absorption and excretion in the digestive tract.

Contra-indication

- Persons suffering from High BP, peptic or duodenal ulcers, hernias or serious digestive disorders should avoid this practice.

Trataka

Trataka is a technique of gazing to cleanse the eyes. The different types of Trataka are:

(*i*) *Jyothi Trataka*—Gazing a candle light.

(*ii*) *Urdhava Mukha & Adho Mukha*—Gazing the movement of hand downward and upward respectively.

(*iii*) *Vama, Dakshina & Ubhaya Jatr Trataka*—Gazing the movement of the hand towards left, right and gazing the shoulder respectively.

(iv) *Brumadhya Trataka*—Gazing on the bindu point of concentration.

(v) *Nasarga Trataka*—Gazing on the nose region.

Benefits of Trataka

- Trataka helps to correct weakness of the external ocular muscles.
- Helps to improve eyesight.
- Helps develop the power of concentration to an almost unlimited degree.
- Improves memory.
- Helps those suffering from insomnia and mental tension, if practiced before going to bed at night.

Kapalabhati

Kapalabhati is breathing at the speed of 120 breaths per minute through abdominal strokes to cleanse the entire respiratory passages as well as to stimulate blood circulation throughout the body.

(i) Chandra Anuloma Kapalabhati

(ii) Surya Anuloma Kapalabhati

(iii) Chandra Bhedana Kapalabhati

(iv) Surya Bhedana Kapalabhati

(v) Both nostril variation

(vi) Alternate nostril variation

Practice of Kapalabhati

- Sit in comfortable crossed leg position with back straight. Hands resting on knees in either Chin or Dhyana Mudra. Face to be relaxed.
- To start forcefully expel all of the air from the lungs while pushing the abdominal diaphragm upwards.
- The expulsion is active but the inhalation is passive.
- Inhale deeply through the nostrils, expanding abdomen and exhale with the forceful contraction of abdominal muscles.
- The air is pushed out of lungs by contraction of the diaphragm.
- Gradual practice will lead to do 120 strokes per minute.
- It cleanses the entire respiratory passage.

Benefits of Kapalabhati

- Kapalabhati cleanses the lungs and entire respiratory system.
- The blood is purified and body gets an increased supply of oxygen to all cells.
- Digestion is improved.
- Abdominal muscles are strengthened.
- Prepare the mind for meditation.
- Energizes the mind for mental work.
- Activates the brain cells.
- Stimulates the abdominal organs.

Contra-indication

- Persons suffering from heart disease, high blood pressure and Hernia should avoid this practice.

There is also Jala Kapalabhati which is more similar to Jala Neti Kriya they can be classified as Vyutkrama Kapalabhati and Seetkrama Kapalabhati.

Other important Kriyas are:

(i) *VARISARA*—It is a process of cleaning the whole alimentary canal with water. Some call this a Sankhapraksalana. One drinks water to the capacity and practices Nauli Chalana to enhance the peristaltic movement and evacuate the water without it being absorbed by the intestines. When modified for therapeutic purposes one uses saline water added with salt and practices some poses including forward bending, backward stretching, twisting, lateral bending and pressing of abdomen.

(ii) *VATASARA*—It is the process of subjecting the internal mucosa of the whole alimentary canal to the current of air swallowed by mouth and evacuated through the lower passage. It has been observed that when the stomach is filled with air, it reduces the gastric acidity.

(*iii*) *VAHNISARA OR AGNISARA*—It is practiced with holding the breath after deep exhalation. The abdomen is retracted and protruded repeatedly, keeping the abdominal muscles tight throughout the performance. One repeats this process several times as may be found necessary.

Kriyas are commonly used as remedial measures in yogic therapy. But, originally, Kriyas are meant to assist and prepare one's body for the mastery of Pranayama. Practical experience with Kriyas will convince one and all the kriyas make the practice of Pranayama quite easy.

Precautions

(*i*) Swami Kuvalyananda and Dr. SL Vinekar refer to these kriyas as procedures for Naso-Pharyngeal Hygiene, Gastric Hygiene, Intestinal Hygiene, Colon Hygiene etc. from this it is obvious that the instruments and materials utilized in kriyas needed to be properly sterilized, free of germs and pathological substances and properly handled with due care and caution.

(*ii*) All the Kriyas must be practiced with due guidance of the Guru until mastery is obtained.

TECHNIQUES OF ASANAS

Savasana

- Lie down on the back.
- Spread the legs a little apart.
- Keep the hands by the sides of the body, palms facing upwards.
- Keep the head in a relaxed position.
- Close the eyes.
- Feel the movements of the abdominal wall.
- Do small inhalations and exhalations.
- After some time, discontinue breathing (*i.e.* don't breathe at all).
- Just keep the body motionless.
- Maintain this passive pose for fifteen to twenty minutes.
- Come out to active state slowly and carefully.

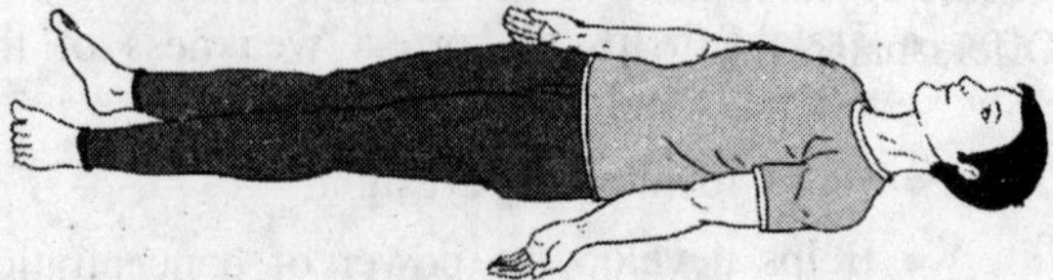

Fig. : *Savasana*

Benefits

'Chittavisranti-karakam' which brings mental calmness. Also provides rest to a tired body.

Niralambasana

- Lie prone (on the belly) on the floor.
- Spread the legs apart.
- Keep the elbows on the ground.
- Rest the face on the palms.
- Keep eyes shut.
- Feel the flow of breath at the tip of nose.

Benefits

Nice for realigning the lumber and cervical parts of spine.

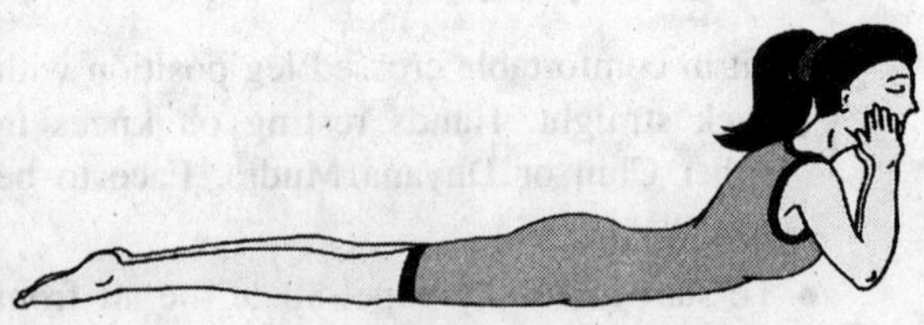

Fig. : *Niralambasana*

Sukhasana *(Hathapradipika)*

- Sit on floor with legs crossed.
- Keep the spine upright.
- Place the hands on the respective knees.

- Close the eyes.
- Focus on the flow of breath.
- It suits well for meditation.

Benefits

Cheers up the mind. Good to develop concentration. Offers balance to body.

Fig.: *Sukhasana*

Vajrasana

- Sit on the floor with the legs extended: Step 1.

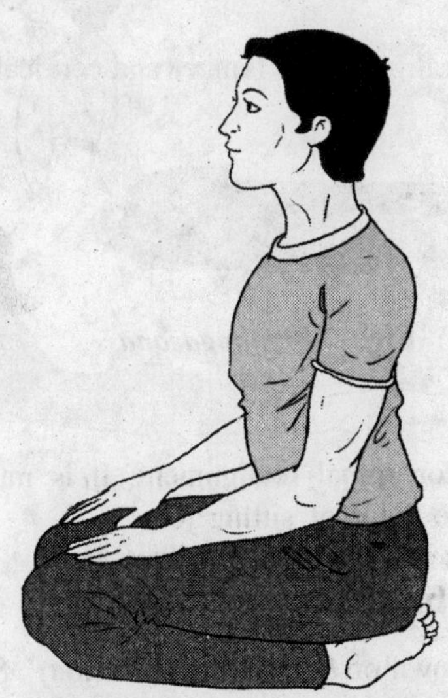

Fig.: *Vajrasana*

- Fold one leg at knee and keep the foot under the bottom: Step 2.
- With the support of hands, shift the body weight carefully on the folded leg and then fold the other leg in the same manner.
- Knees may be kept together.
- Keep the spine straight.
- Close the eyes and sit stable: Step 3.

Benefits

Offers suppleness to ankles, shanks, calves, hamstrings and knees. Avoid doing this if there is severe pain in the knees.

Parvatasana

- Sit with legs crossed.
- If possible, sit in Padmasana.
- Raise both hands slowly above the head.
- Touch the palms.
- Stretch hands upwardly with force.
- Keep breathing.
- After some time bring down the hands.
- Repeat the same for several times.

Fig. : *Parvatasana*

Benefits

Stretches the shoulder joints, ribs and spine. Brings right alignment to spine.

Viparitakarani

- Lie down on ground in supine posture: Step 1.
- Lift both legs up to make an angle of 40-50 degree: Step 2.
- With a small jerk raise the bottoms and waist up.
- Quickly give support to the bottoms with both hands.
- Then raise legs still higher.
- Legs are a bit tilted over the head.
- Maintain the pose for some time: Step 3.
- Breathe normally.
- Lower the bottoms and legs on ground slowly and carefully.
- Repeat this for a few number of times.

Fig. : *Viparitakarani*

Benefits

Promotes circulation to head region. Spine is inverted which helps autonomic nervous system to rejuvenate. Veins in legs are rested. People having high blood pressure should avoid this Asana.

Bhujangasana

- Lie down on ground in prone lying position (belly on ground).
- Keep the legs at comfortable distance.
- Now place the palms under the shoulders.
- Press the floor with hands.
- Raise the nose, chin, shoulders, chest, abdomen and lower abdomen.
- Take all the body weight on hands.
- Keep the elbows straight.
- Breathe freely and deeply as much as possible.
- With each inhalation and exhalation lumber spine will contract and expand.
- Stay for quite some time in this position.
- Return and take rest.
- Repeat this for a number of times.
- Each time shift the position of palms back and forth.

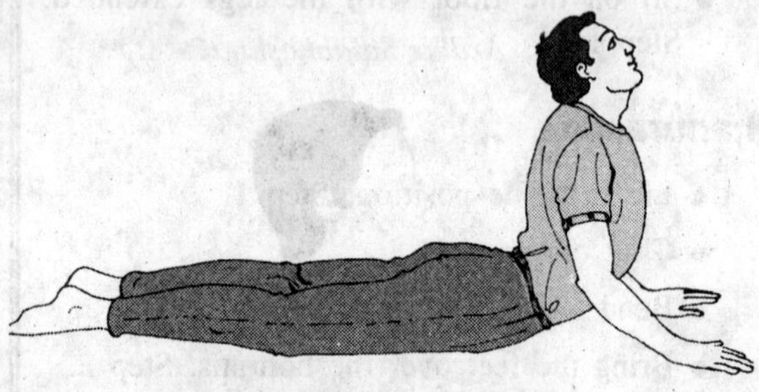

Fig. : *Bhujangasana*

Benefits

Very good for spinal realignment. It is must for those who do a lot of sitting job.

Ardhasalabhasana

- Lie down on belly (prone position) : Step 1.
- Place the chin on ground.

- Place the palms by the sides of the body.
- Strain one leg firmly.
- Lift the leg straight towards the sky: Step 2.
- Don't tilt the leg.
- Don't bend at knee.
- Press the ground with fists to support the leg.
- Breathe as the body demands.
- Don't hold breath.
- Lower the leg after some time.
- Do the same with opposite leg.
- Repeat for several times.

Benefits

Nice for waist region, hamstrings and lower abdomen.

Pics Step 1, Step 2.

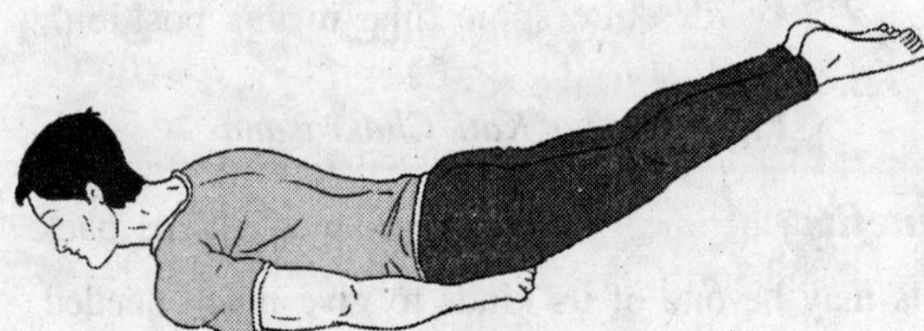

Fig. : *Ardha Salabhasana*

Dhanurasana

- Lie in prone position: Step 1.
- Chin on ground.
- Bend both legs at knees.
- Bring the feet over the bottoms: Step 2.
- Firmly catch hold of the ankles: Step 3.
- Give a strong pull to lift the legs up: Step 4.
- Keep hands straight.
- Make sure that all body weight falls on belly.
- Keep breathing.
- Do not hold breath.
- Before fatigue sets in, unwind.
- Repeat this for a few cycles.
- This could be a demanding practice.

Fig.: *Dhanurasana*

Benefits

Quite good for spinal complaints. Promotes abdominal health. A very refreshing practice.

Ardhamatsyendrasana

- Sit on ground.
- Spread both legs in front: Step 1.
- Fold the right knee and place it on ground.
- Keep the right foot outside the left hip: Step 2.
- Now fold the left knee and bring it in front of the face: Step 2.
- Place the left foot outside the right knee: Step 2.
- Turn the right hand outside the left knee and catch the left foot: Step 3.
- Left hand will go around the trunk and hold the right thigh or place it on ground.
- Turn the face towards the extreme left.
- Do breathe.

- Hold the position for some time.
- Do the same by interchanging the legs and hands.

Fig. : *Ardhamatsyendrasana*

Benefits

Balancing the body pose. For trunk it is highly refreshing. So also good for the belly and hip joints.

Ardha-Kati-Chakrasana

- Stand on both feet: Step 1.
- Keep feet together.
- Stand straight.
- Raise right hand up so that arm touches the right ear.
- Stretch the hand upwardly: Step 2.
- Then lean the head and right hand at the left side: Step 3.
- Do a lot of exhalation so that head and shoulders are coming down towards the ground easily.
- Repeat the same at the opposite side as well for equal number of times.

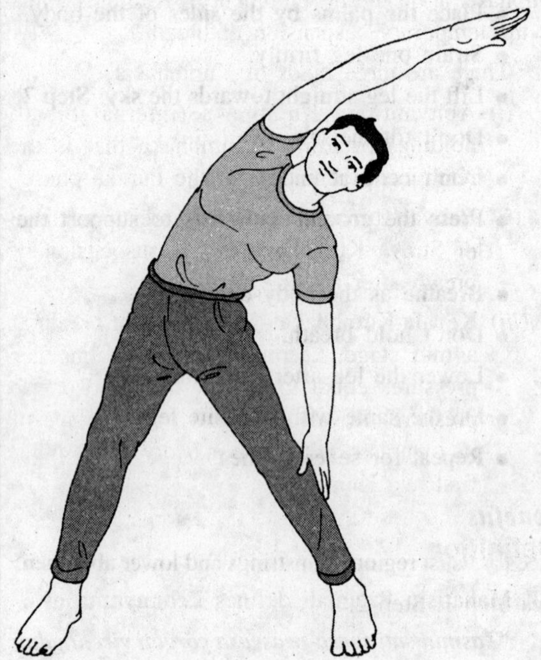

Fig. : *Ardha Kati Chakrasana*

Benefits

This may be one of its kinds to give much needed lateral bending to the spine. Stretches the sides of the abdomen and ribs.

PRANAYAMA

Pranayama is a Sanskrit word meaning "restraint of the Prana or breath". The word is composed of two Sanskrit words, Prana, life force, or vital energy, particularly, the breath, and "Ayama", to suspend or restrain. It is often translated as control of the life force (Prana). When used as a technical term in yoga, it is often translated more specifically as "breathe control". Pranayamas are of primary importance in yoga. Some yogis feel that no other practice is necessary for attaining the purification of body and mind. Pranayama, by itself is sufficiently capable of eradicating all toxins.

Pranayama essentially constitute a volitional (conscious) control of breathing. In Pranayama the emphasis is on the development of Kumbhaka that is the temporary suspension of breath.

There are three kinds of Kumbhaka:

(*i*) Abhyanthara Kumbhaka (internal breath holding) or Puraka Kumbhaka that is the retention of breath after the Puraka phase.

(*ii*) Bahya Kumbhaka (external breath holding) or Sunya Kumbhaka that is suspension of breath after a full expiration.

(*iii*) Kevala Kumbhaka - suspension of breath at a mid stage, keeping the intra pulmonary pressures equal to that of the atmospheric pressure. Kevala Kumbhaka takes place of its own as result of the mastery of the other first two Kumbhakas.

Definition

Maharishi Patanjali defines **Pranayama** as ***"Tasmin sati svasa-prasvasa yorgati vicchhedah pranayama".***

Asana having completed cessation of inhalation and exhalation (Kevala Kumbhaka) is called as Pranayama.

According to Hatha Yoga School, Pranayama is

"Breath holding is practiced systematically so that Pranic currents travel effortlessly upward through the Sushumna-Nadi situated in the spine".

The benefits of **Pranayama** according to **Maharishi Patanjali** are:

"Tatah kshiyate prakashah aavaranam"

Thereby the covering of the inner light disappears.

"Dharanasu cha yogyatee manasah"

The mind develops fitness for higher practices such as concentration.

Now the body and mind are fit to go into the state of Meditation on the divine as self realization is obtained.

According to Hatha Pradipika, the eight varieties of Pranayamas are:

1. *Surya Bhedana*—Sun Cleaving Breath
2. *Ujjayi*—Victorious Breath
3. *Sitkari*—Hissing Breath (Cooling Breath)
4. *Sheetali*—Beak Tongue Breath (Icing Breath)
5. *Bhramari*—Sound of Bee Breath
6. *Bhastrika*—Bellows Breath
7. *Murchha*—Fainting or Swooning Breath
8. *Plavini*—Floating Breath

Their techniques differ from each other with reference to the Puraka and Rechaka phases. All these Pranayamas are also called Kumbhakas. Even though Kumbhaka is a key to the technique of Pranayama, for an average man of health, the practice of breath holding or Kumbhaka is not recommended. A man of average health can get all benefits of Pranayama by following the Puraka and Rechaka phases of different Pranayamas. By doing so, we can get the benefits of Pranayama in the long run without any complications or risks inherent in the practice of Kumbhaka aspects of Pranayama technique.

Different phases of Pranayama

Basically there are four phases in the practice of Pranayama. They are:

1. *Puraka*—Controlled inspiration.
2. *Antara Kumbhaka*—Controlled suspension of breath after inhalation.
3. *Rechaka*—Controlled expiration.
4. *Bahira Kumbhaka*—Controlled suspension of breath after exhalation or Shunyaka.

Safety Measures and Precautions

According to Hatha Yoga Pradipika and other texts on yoga, carelessly practiced Pranayama can lead to various complications and disorders. It can also wreck one's health both physically and mentally. Therefore, one earnest practitioner of Pranayama should take proper measures of safety and precautions.

1. First of all fully understand the need, significance and various risk-factors

associated with the techniques from teachers, having insight, experience and also consult a physician to ensure the safety of one's health and well-being.

2. Master a selected routine of Asana, specifically one Meditative Asana like Padmasana, Siddhasana or Vajrasana.
3. Master some of the Kriyas that will cleanse the respiratory passages, the alimentary track and stimulate blood circulation in the body.
4. First master the Puraka and Rechaka phases with 1 : 2 ratios without undue strain.
5. Master the technique of different Pranayama without the Kumbhaka phase that is only the Puraka and Rechaka phases of Pranayama initially.
6. Later include the Sunyaka phase of Pranayama.
7. Do not practice the application of the three Bandhas for the internal Kumbhaka as it can lead to serious problem indulged in without the supervision of an experienced yoga teacher.
8. Apply Jalandhara Bandha, Jihva Bandha and closure of nostrils as and when you start the mild practice of internal Kumbhaka.
9. Diet regulation, adequate sleep, correct psychological attitudes etc. have been prescribed to reduce the risk factors considerably. Tradition SUGGESTS SURRENDERING TO THE WILL OF THE ALMIGHTY GOD in this connection if your belief system permits you to do so. This can aid you profoundly if anything goes out of control by mistake and carelessness.
10. Regulate your practice according to your chosen objectives like treatment, physical culture, spiritual culture etc. Avoid purposeless approach. For an average man of normal health who wishes to maintain sound physical and mental health needs only the Puraka and Rechaka phases of Pranayama according to Swami Kuvalyananda.

Significance of Shat Kriyas and Pranayamas in Yogic curriculum

Kriyas constitute the preparatory cleansing processes that aids in the mastery of Pranayama techniques. Pranayama, on the other hand cleanses, fortifies and develops the body and mind for the advanced practices of Yoga like awakening of the Kundalini, higher meditational practices etc., both Kriya and Pranayama goes hand in hand with each other, supplementing each other. Thus both are for reconditioning of the psychophysiological mechanism of man.

Practice of Pranayama

- Practice of *Pranayama* can bring in extraordinary benefits if practised regularly for long period of time.
- Consistent practice keeps one cheerful, energetic, mentally calm, balanced and focused. Stress can be effectively managed. Anxiety can be considerably reduced. One remains highly spirited.
- Practice of *Pranayama* is done while sitting in cross legged posture, if possible *Padmasana*. Or else *Sukhasana* or *Siddhasana*.
- The place should have clean air flow but it should not be windy.
- Room should be well-ventilated.
- Atmosphere should be pleasant.

Deep Breathing

(*a*) Sit upright on floor by crossing legs.

(*b*) Keep hands on knees.

(*c*) Close the eyes.

(*d*) Steadily take air in and keep on filing up the lungs to the maximum level but don't overdo.

(*e*) Then start exhaling slowly as much as possible.

(*f*) In the beginning, do this for five to six minutes.

(g) Then as you make progress, do this for ten to fifteen minutes.

(h) This will enhance the capacity of the lungs muscles so that other techniques of *Pranayama* can be taken up smoothly.

Fig. : *Deep breathing*

Anuloma-Viloma

(a) Sit straight on ground.

(b) Keep eyes shut.

(c) Gently plug the right nostril with the right thumb: Step 1.

(d) Inhale through left nostril and then exhale through right.

(e) Then again inhale through right to exhale through left.

(f) Inhale and exhale to the possible limit.

(g) Breathe in and out smoothly.

(h) Try to follow a simple ration of 1 : 1 between inhalation and exhalation time. It means that, inhale for 10 seconds and exhale also for 10 seconds.

(i) As the practice progresses, inhale for 10 seconds and exhale for 20 seconds.

(j) While inhaling, chest will expand and spine will extend, but while exhaling, belly will contract. Watch this closely.

(k) One inhalation and one exhalation make one cycle. Do as many cycles as possible.

(l) In the original version of this technique, holding of breath is suggested which we have omitted for convenience of the beginners.

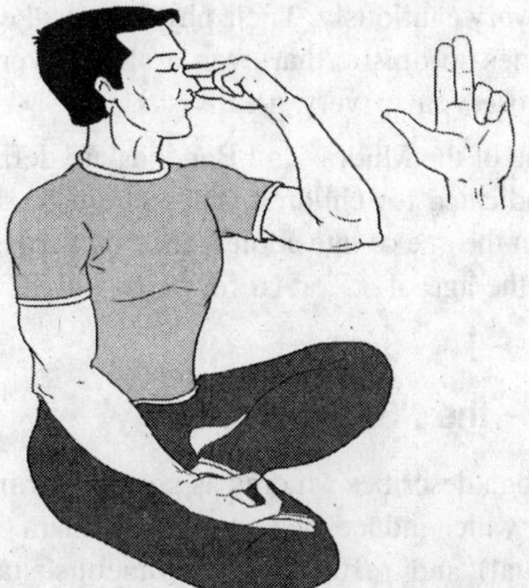

Fig. : *Anuloma-Viloma*

BANDHAS AND MUDRAS

The Sanskrit word Mudra means "a seal for energy". It denotes positions which close the body apertures. Bandha means "a lock for energy", bondage, joining together, fettering or catching hold. It also refers to a posture in which certain organs or parts of the body are gripped, contracted and controlled.

For Eg. When electricity is generated, it is necessary to have transformers, conductors, fuses, switches and insulated wires to carry the power to its destination; otherwise the current would be wasted.

And so when Prana is made to flow in the yogi's body by the practice of Pranayama, it is equally necessary for him to employ Bandhas to prevent the dissipation of energy and to carry it to the right places without damage. "Without the Bandha, the Pranayama practice, and the flow of Prana can injure the nervous system".

Bandhas and Mudras are a special feature of Hatha Yoga. Most of them consist of certain neuro-muscular locks and involve changes in the internal pressure to a very high degree. They directly influence the tone of the visceral organs, glandular secretions, endocrine glands and also the vital nerve plexuses.

Though these practices look very innocent, easy and harmless, the Mudras and Bandhas have to be restored very cautiously. Their physiological effects are at times so drastic that even a slight over dose may expose you to very great risks.

Some of the Mudras and Bandhas are definitely contra-indicated for children. They could be started only from the age of late adolescence onwards. That is, from the age of 15 or 16 for boys and 12 or 13 for girls.

Mudra - the "Seal for energy"

Hatha Yoga describes Mudras as gestures or mental attitudes, which induce the state of Pratyahara (Sense withdrawal) and results in spontaneous state of meditation.

"Mudra yati klesam iti mudra"

Mudra is that which removes pain and sorrow.

"Mudam rati iti mudra"

That which brings about happiness is called Mudra.

"Nasti mudrasamanam kinchit siddhidam kshitimandale"

There is nothing in this world like Mudras for giving success.

Hatha Pradipika prescribes practice of Mudra as follows: One should practice the Mudras with all efforts in order to arouse the Goddess Kundalini sleeping at the base of Sushumna nadi.

Yogis texts describe supernatural powers that can be got with the practice of Mudras. However, they also warn that Mudras are difficult to accomplish without the blessings and guidance of a Guru.

Classification of Mudra

According to **Yogamaharishi Dr. Swami Gitananda Giri,** Mudras can be classified as follows:

Hatha Mudras, Prana Mudras, Hastha Mudras, Pada Mudras, Mukha Mudras, Chakshu Mudras, Kaya Mudras, Jnana Mudras, Mano Mudras, Pratya Mudras, Dharana Mudras, Shanti Mudras, Shakti Mudras, Siddha Mudras and Puja Mudras.

Mudras may also be classified as:

- Kriya Mudra E.g: Simha Mudra, Bhujangini Mudra, etc.,
- Asana Mudra E.g: Yoga Mudra, Viparita Karani Mudra, etc.,
- Pranayama Mudra E.g: Chin Mudra, Shanmuki Mudra, etc.

Bandha - the "lock for energy"

Bandhas are necessary for the practice of Pranayama, Bandha means energy lock. These locks are essential while doing the Kumbhaka that is retaining the air inside or outside of the lungs. If Kumbhaka or retention is done without Bandhas, it may have a very negative effect on the digestive system, excretory system, nervous system, brain etc.

Bandhas can be defined as those Mudras that are applied as a part of various phases of Pranayama.

The three Bandhas thus applied during Pranayama are:

1. Jalandhara Bandha or Chin Lock
2. Mula Bandha or Anus Lock
3. Uddiyana Bandha or Abdominal Lock

Application of these three Bandhas is essential in the advanced training of Pranayama technique in Hatha Yoga. However, Swami Kuvalyananda has cautioned against the use of all the three bandhas by the yoga-sadhakas, as when practiced wrongly the internal pressure changes brought about by these bandhas may lead irreparable damages.

Swami Kuvalyananda also prescribed the adoption of Jalandhara bandha while performing the Kumbhaka phase of Pranayamic training to prevent various complications. He rather advocates the simple adoption of Puraka-Rechaka phases of Pranayama to derive the advantages of Pranayama devoid of risks.

JALANDHARA BANDHA

The first Bandha the Sadhaka should master is Jalandhara Bandha, Jala meaning a net, a web or a mesh, we may assume as the net of Nadis (energy channels) and the word "Dhara" means to stop or to hold the flow of the fluid (Amrut), flowing through the nadis. It also means "Glottis lock".

Steps for Practice

1. Sit in Padmasana or in any comfortable meditative posture.
2. Bend your neck a little forward (Performing the mayura mudra).
3. Slowly place firmly your chin on chest (jugula knotch) doing the swallowing action (Apraksha mudra) so that when you practice Pranayama with Kumbhaka, the inside retained air must not come out.
4. While returning, slowly raise your chin and straighten your neck.

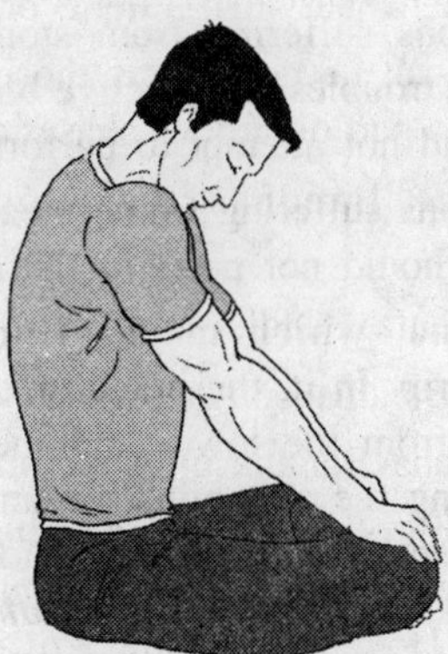

Benefits

- This Bandha influences our vocal organs directly.
- The solar plexus is situated at the center. According to Yoga, it is the seat of the digestive fire (jatharagni), which burns food, and creates heat. The lunar plexus is in the center of the brain and creates coolness. By performing jalandhara bandha, due to the lock of the nadis around the neck, the cool energy of the lunar plexus is not allowed to flow down or to be dissipated by the hot energy of the solar plexus. In this way the elixir of life is stored. And life itself is prolonged.
- The bandha also presses the ida and pingala channels and allows the prana to pass through Sushumna Nadi. The Jalandhara Bandha clears the nasal passages and regulates the flow of blood and Prana (energy) to the heart, head and the endocrine glands in the neck (thyroid and para-thyroid).
- If pranayama is performed without Jalandhara Bandha, pressure is immediately felt in the heart, brain, eye-balls and in the inner ear. This may lead to dizziness. It relaxes the brain and also humbles the intellect (manas, buddhi and ahamkara).

Precautions

1. Those having complaint of neck pain or spondilitis should not practice it.
2. Persons suffering from breath related problems or high or low blood pressure, should practice the Bandhas under the supervision of the experts in the field of Yoga.
3. During Pranayama, the Bandha is to be observed after Puraka. Rechaka is to be practiced after Kumbhaka, by releasing the Bandha. Rechaka should not be observed while being in the Jalandhara bandha.

UDDIYANA BANDHA

The Uddiyana Bandha is enumerated among the three bandhas and ten mudras. Uddiyana means "upward" or "fly up lock"; Bandha means bonding.

The Gheranda Samhita says about the Uddiyana Bandha as "Of all the Bandhanas, this is the best. The complete practice of this makes emancipation easy".

"Even an old person can become young when [Uddiyana Bandha] is done regularly", says the *Hatha Yoga Pradipika*.

Steps for Practice

1. Stand erect.
2. Spread out the legs. The distance between two legs should be 15" to 18".
3. Lean forward, place hands on the thighs or knees and now exhale fully, hold the breath out.
4. Expand the chest so that the abdomen would be drawn in and you will feel that the upper portion of the abdomen is being pulled towards the ribs.
5. After pulling it completely maintain for 5-10-15-20 seconds (according to your capacity). Now return.
6. Now slowly relax the abdomen and stand erect after inhalation.

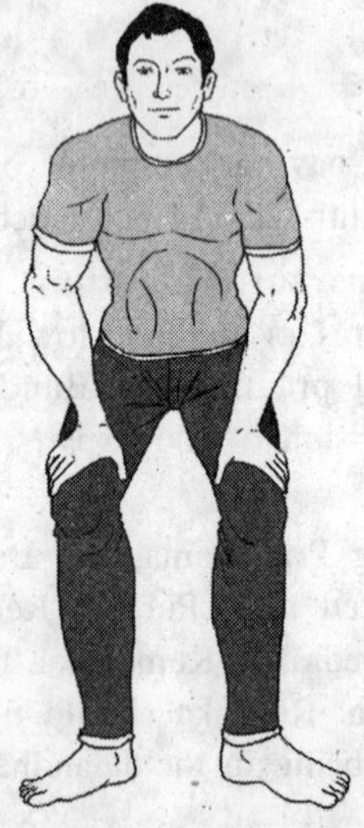

Benefits

- Removes constipation, invigorates digestion pressurizes the navel plexes, and help to make retention of breath stable.
- Strengthens the abdominal muscles and diaphragm.
- Massages abdominal viscera, the solar plexus, the heart and lungs.
- Increases gastric fire; Improves digestion, assimilation, and elimination and purifies the digestive tract of toxins.
- Stimulates blood circulation in the abdomen and blood flow to the brain.
- Stimulates and lifts the energy of the lower belly (Apana vayu), to unite it with the energies localized in the navel (Samana vayu) and heart (Prana vayu).

Precautions

1. The waist should not lean much while bending forward.
2. The chest should be expanded, shoulders bent a little.
3. The legs should not be bent more at the knees.
4. Do not keep the abdomen tight. Let it relax.
5. Exhale fully (completely).
6. Always practice Uddiyana on an empty stomach.
7. Persons suffering from stomach ailments, heart troubles or defective blood circulation should not attempt to perform the Bandha.
8. Persons suffering from diseases like hernia too should not perform this Bandha.

Uddiyana, which means flying up, is an abdominal grip. In it, the prana or energy is made to flow up from the lower abdomen up into the thorax, pulling the abdominal organs back and up towards the spinal column. It is said to be *the lion that kills the elephant named death.*

MULA BANDHA

In Sanskrit, Mula means "root," and Bandha translates as "lock" or "binding." The action of Mula Bandha is a lifting of the root muscles, or pelvic floor muscles. This exercise, called Kegels in the medical community, has many benefits. It can help prevent incontinence and strengthen the vaginal walls after childbirth. It may also help stabilize the spine and improve posture. It means "Anal lock".

Contraction of the anus is known as Ashwini Mudra. Ashwini Mudra indicates the movement a horse makes with its rectum during evacuation of the bowels. In the *Gherand Samhita* it is said to contract and relax the anal aperture again and again. This is called "Ashwini mudra".

When Mula Bandha is initially practiced, there is a tendency to control the two areas, *i.e.* the perineum and the anus. Mula Bandha takes place in the center of the body, neither in the front nor back. Then Mula Bandha chakra is directly contracted.

Steps for Practice

1. Sit on the floor in a comfortable, cross-legged position. If possible, place the heel of one foot at the perineum, right between the anus and the genitals. This placement will help you identify the muscles to be engaged.
2. Actively engage the pelvic floor muscles by pulling them upwards toward the spine.
3. Hold the contraction for five counts. Then slowly release the muscles for five counts.
4. You can practice Mula Bandha in conjunction with Yoga breathing, or Pranayama, by slowly contracting the pelvic floor while inhaling for five counts, and then slowly releasing the muscles while exhaling for five counts.

Benefits

- The practice of Mula Bandha reactivates the areas in the brain controlling this region of the body, bringing the neuronal circuits responsible for its control into the sphere of CONSCIOUSNESS. Controlled systematic contraction of the perineal body/cervix produces heat in the subtle body, and this awakens the potential of Kundalini.
- Mula Bandha focuses on the muscles that form a sling in the pelvis from the pubis to the coccyx. These muscles support the upper part of the vagina, the uterus, the bladder, the rectum, and the prostrate. They also surround the sphincters of the urethra, vagina, and rectum, which can help protect against leakage.

The Physical Effects of Mudras and Bandhas

Out of the several mudras mentioned in Hatha-Yoga texts, Jalandhara, Uddiyana and Mula Bandha are essential to Pranayama. They help to distribute energy and prevent its waste through hyper-ventilation of the body. They are practiced to arouse the sleeping Kundalini and direct its energy up through the Sushumna channel during Pranayama. Their use is essential for experiencing the state of Samadhi.

The performance of Mudras and Bandhas in conjunction with Pranayama (breath and energy control) affects the whole body as follows:

(*i*) They harmonize the efficient functioning of the endocrine system: Jalandhara Bandha directly influences the pituitary, pineal, thyroid, parathyroid, thymus; Uddiyana Bandha directly influences the adrenals and pancreas; Mula Bandha directly influences the gonads and the perineal body/cervix (which are said to be vestigeal endocrine glands). All Bandhas have an indirect effect on the pituitary, pineal and brain.

(*ii*) As a result of the direct effect that Bandhas have on the endocrine glands, certain biorhythms in the body are also regulated. For example, both Mula Bandha and Uddiyana Bandha are extremely useful in stabilizing menstrual periods.

(*iii*) All Bandhas, when performed correctly, lower respiration rate, inducing calmness and relaxation.

(*iv*) Blood pressure is decreased.

(*v*) Heart rate is lessened.

(*vi*) Alpha brainwave production, an index of profound relaxation, is increased, indicating slowing of nervous activity.

(*vii*) Sympathetic activity in the body is decreased, a further index of relaxation.

(*viii*) Confused and/or crossed neurological circuits in the brain are reordered, in effect for 'retraining the brain'.

(*ix*) The digestive system is toned, massaged and revitalized via pressure on the internal organs.

(*x*) Harmony in the activity of the neuro genital system occurs as a result of reflex action via the nervous system.

MEDITATION (DHYANA)

Dhyana seems to be considered an essential process in yoga for the attainment of real emotional stability and integration of personality. This process of Dhyana has to be practiced in a very relaxed way to attain the beneficial results claimed for it.

On the other hand Dhyana is the stage of meditative trainings that lead to Samadhi.

Meditation is the work of consciousness aimed at the conscious development along the path to Perfection and to the Mergence with the Creator. Meditation is practiced at three stages of the Patanjali's scheme.

(*i*) At the dhyana stage adepts among other things learn how to expand consciousness in the subtlest and the most beautiful that exists in the world of matter. By means of such attunement a person establishes in sattva guna. (And through working with Yidam they may immediately come in contact with the Fiery manifestation of Divine Consciousness and experience Samadhi).

(*ii*) At the dhyana stage adepts work at increasing the "mass" of consciousness and at obtaining power in subtlety. So that at the next stage their efforts will be focused upon interaction of individual consciousness with Consciousness of the Universal God and upon merging with Him in His Fiery Aspect as well as in the Infinity of the "trans-mirror realm".

(*iii*) At the dhyana stage the meditative work is especially effective if it is performed at special "places of power" — areas on the Earth's surface that have an energetic impact on human beings. Among the variety of them only those should be chosen that makes the expanding of consciousness in the subtlest eons. A correctly selected subsequence of such places ensures that the most complex tasks of correct "crystallization" (*i.e.*, quantitative growth) of consciousness will be solved easily and with little efforts.

For the same purpose one can meditate during athletic exercises, as well as practice winter swimming and "meditative running".

The structure of the human organism responsible for meditation is the lower "bubble of perception", the principal part of which is Anahata Chakra, supplied with energy by the complex of three lower Chakras. This is why success of the work at this stage depends on the level of purity and development of the entire system of seven chakras, which is combined into one complex by the meridians that have been mentioned above.

From the very beginning of meditative training until the absolute Victory of Merging with the Primordial Consciousness one should always remember that a person's main merit is measured by the level of development of his spiritual heart. This is by what a man can merge with God. This is why it is the spiritual heart that a man should develop and keep pure in every possible way. What was said above allows us to take it not as a nice figure of speech or a metaphor, but as a quite practical knowledge and a guide to action.

The steps of the ladder of a spiritual ascent that we are discussing now are meant for teaching one how to position consciousness into Anahata first, then to ensure the growth of the Anahata within the body and after that beyond it — within the "cocoon", within Earth and then beyond Earth in the highest eons.

This is how we can grow ourselves as Love. God is Love; this is why one can merge with Him only after becoming a Great Love, a Great Soul of Love (Mahatma). And there are no other ways of developing Divinity of oneself, except for those fundamental steps that we are describing here.

The usual preliminary procedures of yoga help bring in a balanced working of body and mind. As long as the body and mind are under strong divergent pulls and are in a highly imbalanced state. Dhyana should not be resorted to. One should resort to the practice of Dhyana only when the body and mind are a bit stabilized.

"Tatra pratyaya ekatanata dhyanam"

Meditation is the state when there is a steady and continuous flow of attention and concentration on that point, place, region or object.

One key meaning of the term 'Yoga' itself is 'Dhyana' according to the Sanskrit, Lexicon *Amarkosha. Quoting Hatha Pradipika.* ***Swami Kuvalayananda*** *says the Dhyana us 'seeing' one's mind with one's own mind.*

"Dhyanam nirvishayam manah"

That is emptying the mind of sensual perceptions and objectives is Dhyana.

The process if Dhyana usually begins with the mastery of a selected meditational Asana with certain cerebro-ocular mudras like Shambhavi-mudra or unmani-mudra, or khechari-mudra etc. Fixation of gaze on a point is common in all these cerebro-ocular mudras. If such a cerebro-ocular mudra is maintained in a meditative posture for some time, a few seconds only in the beginning, customary images get automatically eliminated. It has to be noted that every meditational posture requires its practitioner to fix his gaze in a particular way.

According to the instructions of Patanjali and yogic tradition, the correct practice of Asana the process of ANATHA SAMAPATTI or MAHAHRIDANUSANDHANA or PRANADHARANA assumes central significance. If these processes in the practice of the Meditational Asanas is taken to its logical end, this can lead to relaxed way to Dhyana.

Benefit of Dhyana

- It lowers oxygen consumption.
- It decreases respiratory rate.
- It increases blood flow and slows the heart rate.
- Increases exercise tolerance in heart patients.
- Leads to a deeper level of relaxation.
- Good for people with high blood pressure as it brings the B.P. to normal.
- Reduces anxiety attacks by lowering the levels of blood lactate.
- Decreases muscle tension (any pain due to tension) and headaches.
- Builds self-confidence.
- It increases serotonin production which influences mood and behaviour. Low levels of serotonin are associated with depression, obesity, insomnia and headaches.
- Helps in chronic diseases like allergies, arthritis etc.
- Reduces Pre-menstrual Syndrome.
- Helps in post-operative healing.
- Enhances the immune system. Research has revealed that meditation increases activity of 'natural-killer cells', which kill bacteria and cancer cells.
- Also reduces activity of viruses and emotional distress.

Modern Derived Meditation Techniques And Its Classifications

Although the goal of meditation is same (calmness and peace), there are different ways of reaching it. The *Vijnana Bhairava Tantra* presents 112 meditation techniques. These include several variants of breath awareness, concentration on various centres in the body, non-dual awareness, chanting, imagination and visualisation and contemplation through each of the senses. Basically in the form of a dialogue between lord Shiva and his wife Parvati this text discusses 112 meditation techniques which can be used for realizing our true self. Recently, Lajpat Rai has complied all these 112 meditation techniques. Here, an attempt has been made to describe the well-known derived meditation techniques.

Transcendental Meditation (TM)

Transcendental meditation is a form of mantra meditation which is introduced by Maharsi Mahesh Yogi. Transcendental meditation is practised for 15-20 minutes in the morning and evening, while sitting comfortably with the eyes closed. TM involves mental chanting of a particular *mantra* with awareness. During this technique, the individual's awareness settles down and experiences a unique state of restful alertness. As the body becomes deeply relaxed, the mind transcends all mental activity to experience the simplest form of awareness, Transcendental Consciousness, where consciousness is open to itself.

Vipassana Meditation

Vipassana, which means to see things as they really are, is one of the ancient techniques of meditation. It was discovered by Gautama Buddha more than 2500 years ago and now popularized by Mr. S.N. Goenka. In *Vipassana* meditation the meditator, sitting in a comfortable position, initially observes his own breathing and thereafter, observes sensations and feelings in various part of the body with an attitude of witness. *Vipassana* is a way of self-transformation through self-observation. It focuses on the subtle interconnection between mind and body, which can be experienced directly by disciplined attention to the physical sensations that form the life of the body, and that continuously interconnect and condition the life of the mind. It is this observation-based self-exploratory journey to the common root of mind and body that dissolves mental impurity, resulting in a balanced mind full of love and compassion.

Zen Meditation

Zazen-Zen meditation is a fundamental part of both the Soto and Rinzai Sects of Zen Buddhism. The aim in this form of meditation is the ultimate state of enlightenment called *Satori*. This technique involves concentration. There are three types in this type of meditation. In the first type, the meditator concentrates on his breathing, counting the breaths or without counting. In second type of meditation, the meditator has to solve koans or say non-logical riddles. In third type of meditation, the meditator just sits and breathes in a prescribed manner without any aids or concentrating on his breath.

Ananda Marga Meditation

In this technique, the meditator has to repeat a sacred *mantra* given by the *guru*, with intense concentration. This meditation is practiced and propagated by the *Ananda Marga* organization. The technique consists of two important steps. First, the meditators sit in comfortable relaxed position and withdraw the attention inwards by ignoring the external stimuli and paying attention to their breathing. Then they silently repeat the two lettered personal *mantra* with their breathing.

Brahmakumaris Raja Yoga Meditation

This meditation technique is preached and practiced by *Brahmakumaris Isvariya Visvavidyalaya.* During this meditation, aspirants sit in a comfortable position with their eyes open, and with effortless gaze fixed on a *jyoti* (light–representing supreme consciousness). At same time, they actively generate positive thoughts about the Universal force pervading all over, as light and peace.

Cyclic Meditation

Cyclic Meditation (CM) is devised by Dr. H.R. Nagendra, the founder, Vivekananda Yoga Anusandhana Samsthana. The concept has taken from *Mandukya Karika.* Cyclic meditation involves a combination of gentle yogic stretching performed with awareness and with very slow movements followed by relaxation. This cycle repeats for three times and ends in deep relaxation and silence. The combination of stimulation and relaxation takes one to the deeper layers of relaxation.

1902 (Yoga)–67-II

Om Meditation

Om meditation involves mental chanting of Om with awareness. The practitioner has to sit in meditative posture and chant Om mentally with awareness. The chanting should be very slow and the silence between the two Omkaras has to be experienced. If there are any distractions, chanting should be made faster and after some time once again chanting should be done slowly. Finally, this process leads to a state of Ajapa (no repetition) which is a state of bliss, deep silence and peace.

Sahaja Yoga Meditation

The Sahaja Yoga meditation technique is discovered and propagated by Mataji Nirmala Devi. The process of Sahaja Yoga is spontaneous and natural. It is a technique to awaken the *Kundalini shakti* which lies in the sleeping state at the base of the spine (muladhara chakra) of each human being. Sahaja Yoga is the state of self-realization produced by cleansing of chakras and *Kundalini* awakening and is accompanied by the experience of thoughtless awareness or mental silence.

Sudarshana Kriya Meditation

Sudarshana Kriya is developed by Sri Sri Ravishankar, founder of art of living foundation. The Sudarshan Kriya incorporates specific natural rhythms of breath to release stress and bring the mind to the present moment. It involves practice of ujjayi followed by bhastrika pranayama. After pranayama, one has to chant OM for three times and feel the vibrations. Finally, chanting of so ham mantra leads to silence and deep relaxation.

Preksa Meditation

This is also an ancient meditation technique practiced in Jainism. *Preksa* means to perceive and realize the subtlest aspects of one's own self, 'to see the Self'. *Preksa* is derived from the *Sanskrit* word "*Pra + iksa*" which means to observe carefully. Basically, it sums up the perception of body, psychic centers, breath and observation of mind. In *Preksa Dhyana*, no thought is forcefully stopped Instead, the art of merely observing the thought process without forming any reaction or attachment is developed. By doing so, thoughts themselves cease to appear.

Yoga Nidra

Yoga-nidra (yogic psychic sleep) is a meditative technique, derived from ancient *tantra* popularized by Bihar School of Yoga (BSY). Yoga-*nidra* is described as a systematic method of inducing complete physical, mental and emotional relaxation, while maintaining awareness at deeper levels. *Yoga-nidra* is performed in *savasana* and it consists of progressive relaxation and rotation of awareness all over body, resolve, and visualization of some images of nature and *tantric* abstract symbols.

Qigong Meditation

Qigong, is a practice of aligning breath, movement, and awareness for exercise, healing, and meditation. With roots in Chinese medicine, martial arts, and philosophy, qigong is traditionally viewed as a practice to cultivate and balance qi (chi) or what has been translated as "intrinsic life energy". Typically a qigong practice involves rhythmic breathing coordinated with slow stylized repetition of fluid movement, a calm mindful state, and visualization of guiding qi through the body.

Metta Meditation (loving-kindness meditation)

Metta is loving-kindness, good will, close mental union and active interest in others. It is one of the ten *paramis* of the *Theravada* school of Buddhism, and the first of the four sublime states (*Brahmaviharas*). This is love without clinging (*upadana*). The cultivation of loving-kindness (*metta bhavana*) is a popular form of meditation in Buddhism. In the Theravadin Buddhist tradition, this practice begins with the meditator cultivating loving-kindness towards themselves, then their loved ones, friends, teachers, strangers, enemies, and finally towards all sentient beings.

All these meditation techniques are derived within the last 200 years. The scientific literature shows differences in the results of these meditation techniques. The differences in results among meditation techniques could be related to the method and principle involved. Hence, it would be helpful if we look at the all the meditation techniques based on the traditional yoga texts. All the above mentioned techniques have been classified into two meditative states mentioned in the yoga text as given in the Table.

Table. *Classification of meditation techniques*

Sl. No.	*Meditation Technique*	*Meditation Type*
1.	Transcendental Meditation (TM)	*Dhyana*
2.	Vipassana Meditation	*Dhyana*
3.	Om Meditation	*Dhyana*
4.	Ananda Marga Meditation	*Dharana*
5.	Cyclic Meditation (CM)	*Dharana*
6.	Zen Meditation	*Dharana*
7.	Brahmakumaris Raja Yoga Meditation	*Dharana*
8.	Preksha Meditation	*Dharana*
9.	Sudarshana Kriya Meditation	*Dharana*
10.	Sahaja Yoga Meditation	*Dharana*
11.	Yoga Nidra	*Dharana*
12.	Metta Meditation (loving-kindness)	*Dharana*
13.	Qigong Meditation	*Dharana*

SURYA NAMASKARA (SUN SALUTATION)

Surya means 'sun' and namaskara means 'salutation' or 'bowing down'. It consist of 12 postures. The regular practice of *surya namaskara* helps improve blood circulation throughout the body and maintain health, and thereby helps one to remain disease-free. Postures practised during *surya namaskara* act as a good link between warm-ups and *asanas*. *Surya namaskara* should preferably be done at the time of sunrise. It can be done any time on an empty stomach. However, morning is considered to be the best time for it. Adolescents should start doing *surya namaskara* daily to have healthy body and mind.

Let us perform *surya namaskar* by following the steps given below:

1. Stand erect with legs together and hands by the sides of the body. Bring both the arms to the chest with palms together in the prayer posture. *(Namaskarasana).*

1

2. Inhaling, raise both the arms above the head. Stretching bend the trunk backwards. *(Hastottanasana).*

2

3. Exhaling, bend the trunk forward and place the hands on the floor besides the feet and forehead near the knees. *(Padahastasana).*

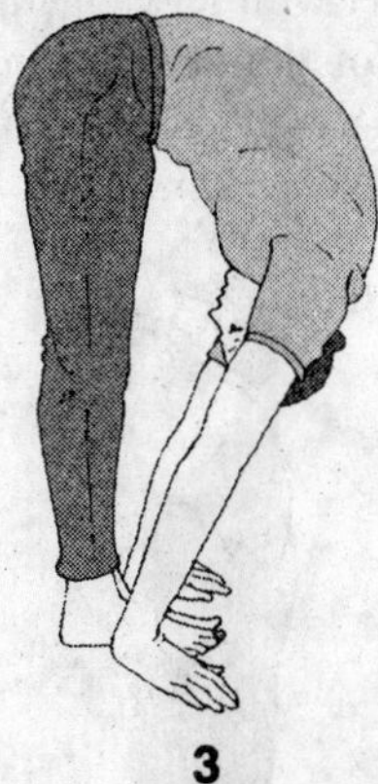

3

4. Inhaling, stretch the right leg backward and bend the left leg at the knee. Tilt the head backward and, look up while arching the spine. *(Ashwasanchalanasana)*

4

5. Stretch the left foot backward by the side of right foot, lower your head and move buttocks upwards. Keep arms and legs straight and heels on the floor. *(Parvatasana)*

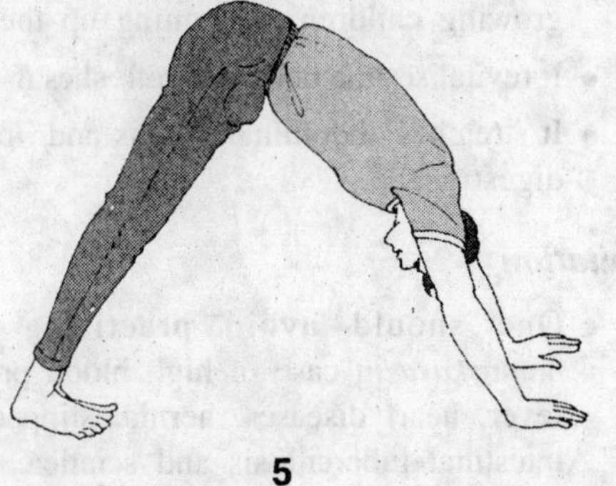

5

6. Lower the knees, chest and chin to the floor. Keep the hips slightly up. The toes, knees, chest, hands and chin should be touching the floor. *(Ashtanga namaskara).*

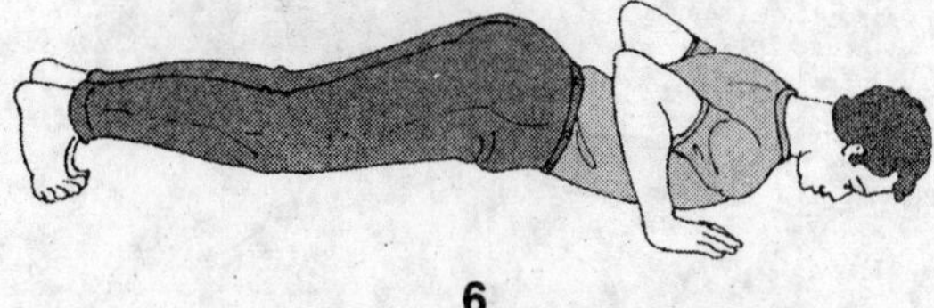

6

7. Lower the hips. Raise the head and torso upto the navel region. Bend the head backwards. *(Bhujangasana)*

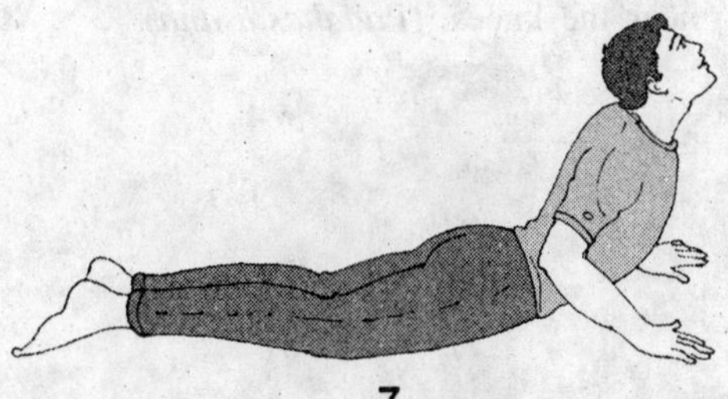

7

8. Lower the head and trunk to the floor, now raising the buttocks and straightening the arms, bring feet towards the head. Head should be between the arms. Come to the postion 5. *(Parvatasana)*

8

9. By bending the right leg, bring it to the front between the hands. Take the left leg behind with knee touching the floor. Keep palms on both the sides of the right foot and head tilted backward and back arched. Look up. *(Ashwasanchalanasana)*

9

10. Exhaling, bring the left leg forward and keep it by the side of right leg. Keep the hands on the floor on sides of the feet and head near the knees. *(Padahastasana)*

10

11. Inhaling, raise both the arms above the head and bend the trunk backwards. *(Hastottanasana)*

11

12. Come to the erect and straight position. Join both palms in prayer posture. *(Namaskarasana)*

12

Benefits

- It helps to increase strength, endurance and flexibility.
- It regulates all the systems of the body.
- It improves concentration.
- It helps in removing excess fat.
- It helps in constipation and improves blood circulation in the body.
- It energises the body.
- It helps in increasing the height of the growing children and toning up the body.
- It revitalises the body and refreshes the mind.
- It stretches abdominal organs and improves digestion.

Limitation

- One should avoid practising *surya namaskara* in case of high blood pressure, fever, heart diseases, hernia, slipped disk, intestinal tuberculosis and sciatica.

Multiple Choice Questions

1. Which of the following is also known as mahadhauti kriya?
A. Antar dhauti B. Bahiskarita dhauti
C. Danta dhauti D. Danda dhauti

2. Which of the following asana is done by lying down flatwise?
A. Shavasana B. Makarasana
C. Markatasana D. Sarvangasana

3. What is the meaning of word 'tadagi'?
A. Snake B. Water pot
C. Mountain D. Deer

4. Which place is most suitable for bahiskrita dhauti kriya?
A. Pond B. Lake
C. River D. Both A and B

5. During the practice of ujjayi pranayama, through left nostril one should do:
A. Puraka B. Rechaka
C. Both the above D. None of the above

6. In the position of which of the following asana the pranayama can be performed?
A. Shavasana B. Trikonasana
C. Kukkutasana D. None the above

7. Which type of asana should be done before practice of varisara kriya?
A. Forward bending asana
B. Backward bending asana
C. Both the above
D. None of the above

8. Regular practice of which mudra makes entry of the consciousness into causal body?
A. Shambhavi B. Pashini
C. Khechari D. Shaktichalini

9. Which asana is prohibited for females?
A. Vajrasana B. Shirshasana
C. Chakrasana D. Shidhasana

10. Vyaghra kriya should be performed:
A. Daily
B. Once in a week
C. Twice in a week
D. Only when there is requisite

11. Vyaghra kriya can be practiced at a gap of .... after meal.
A. One hour B. One and half hour
C. Two hours D. Three hours

12. During practice of varisara dhauti kriya salt water is used because:
A. Body do not easily absorb salt water
B. Salt water carry out wastes from body easily
C. Salt water is warm
D. Salt water maintains temperature of body

13. Agnisara kriya can not be performed in the position of which asana?
A. Bhadrasana B. Vajrasana
C. Sukhasana D. Siddhasana

14. During the practice of uttanmanduka asana one should concentrate on:
A. Muladhara chakra
B. Swathisthana chakra
C. Manipura chakra
D. Anahata chakra

15. Ujjayi pranayama is useful because:
A. It removes kapha dosha
B. It removes epilepsy
C. It increases consciousness level
D. All of the above

16. Pratyahara is related to which asana?
A. Mayurasana B. Kurmasana
C. Bhadrasana D. Siddhasana

17. Murchha pranayama can not be practiced in the position of:
A. Padmasana B. Swastikasana
C. Sukhasana D. Gomukhasana

18. Agnisara kriya can be practiced in _______ position.
A. Sitting B. Standing
C. Sleeping D. Both A and B

19. Which is the best season to perform varisara dhauti kriya?
A. Summer B. Winter
C. Spring D. Rainy

20. Which kriya should be performed after varisara dhauti kriya?
A. Kunjal B. Vatsara
C. Jalaneti D. Both A and C

21. After how much time of practice of sankhaprakshalana kriya one should take bath?
A. 1 hour B. 2 hours
C. 3 hours D. None of the above

22. Vatsara dhauti kriya should always be performed in sitting position because:
A. Intestines get purified
B. Air easily passes into stomach
C. Air can not enter into intestines
D. More air passes into digestive system

23. Which pranayama should not be performed daily by introvert persons?
A. Shitkari B. Shitli
C. Murchha D. Ujjayi

24. Which mudra is performed during practice of Singhasana?
A. Tadagi B. Shambhavi
C. Bhujangini D. Manduki

25. Practise of pratayahara makes a sadhaka:
A. Introvert to extrovert
B. Extrovert to introvert
C. Introvert to ambivert
D. None of the above

26. Which mudra is best for students and scholars?
A. Gyana mudra B. Prana mudra
C. Surya mudra D. Prithvi mudra

27. Which pranayama is considered best for spiritual development?
A. Murchha B. Bhastrika
C. Nadisodhana D. Kevali

28. Which of the following statements is incorrect?
A. Practise of asanas eliminates rajas guna
B. Practise of asanas eliminates tamas guna
C. Practise of asanas strengthens digestive system
D. None of the above

29. Which asana purifies all the seventy-two thousand nadis?
A. Siddhasana B. Bhadrasana
C. Shirshasana D. Vajrasana

30. By regular practice of which asana a person becomes good orator and judicious?
A. Murchha B. Kevali
C. Bhramari D. Ujjayi

31. Surya bhedi pranayama is recommended to do in ______ season.
A. Summer B. Rainy
C. Spring D. Winter

32. During practice of surya bhedi pranayama puraka (inhalation) should be done through:
A. Right nostril B. Left nostril
C. Both nostril D. Mouth

33. Which is the third posture of suryanamaskara?
A. Padahastasana B. Bhujangasana
C. Parvatasana D. None of the above

34. Which kriya is recommended to do after jalaneti?
A. Sutraneti B. Kunjal
C. Nauli D. Kapalbhati

35. Which asana is recommended to do after shirshasana?
A. Chakrasana B. Sarvangasana
C. Kurmasana D. Shirshasana

36. Which asana leads us to liberty?
A. Gomukhasana B. Bhadrasana
C. Vrikshasana D. Siddhasana

37. Which mudras eliminates melancholy and anxiety?
A. Gyana, Prana B. Gyana, Surya
C. Surya, Prana D. Prana, Prithvi

38. Which mudra helps in maintaining shukra dhatu in body?
A. Mahabheda mudra
B. Maha mudra
C. Vajroli mudra
D. Kaki mudra

39. Which kriya is recommended to do before practise of uddiyana bandha?
A. Vatsara
B. Varisara
C. Agnisara
D. Vahnisara

40. Which asana is recommended to do after practice of matsyasana?
A. Dhanurasana B. Halasana
C. Nokasana D. Gomukhasana

41. Which season is best to begin the practice of pranayama?
A. Spring and winter
B. Autumn and shishira
C. Summer and rainy
D. Summer and winter

42. To withdraw the senses from objects is called as:
A. Samadhi B. Dharana
C. Pratyahara D. Dhyana

43. Which is the ninth step during practise of surya namaskara?
A. Uttanasana
B. Ashwa-Sanchalasana
C. Hasta Uttanasana
D. Bhujangasana

44. The main objective of shatkarma is:
A. To strengthen the panch-kosha
B. To strengthen the panch-tatva
C. To eliminate the tri-dosha
D. To purify the blood

45. Salt water is used during practice of jalaneti kriya because:
A. Salt water is virus destroyer
B. Salt water do not cause infection when enter into trachea
C. Salt water matches with the tonicity of cells and blood
D. Cells of body can easily absorb salt water

46. Which mudra is performed by placing the ring finger at the base of thumb and pressing it by thumb?
A. Prana B. Shunya
C. Surya D. Apana

47. Which mudra is performed by placing tips of middle and ring finger to the tip of thumb?
A. Vayu B. Apana
C. Surya D. Prana

48. Which is the second step during surya namaskara?
A. Hastapadasana
B. Hasta-Uttanasana
C. Parvatasana
D. Pranamasana

49. Which asana should not be performed daily by newly married persons?
A. Siddhasana B. Mayurasana
C. Bhadrasana D. Gorakshasana

50. How many total postures are there in suryanamaskara?
A. 10 B. 11
C. 12 D. 14

51. Sankatasana should be performed daily because:
A. It increases concentration
B. It strengthens the body
C. It is helpful in awakening kundalini
D. All of the above

52. Which of the following statements is not correct about bhadrasana?
A. It helps in awakening of muladhara chakra
B. It activates the digestive system
C. It keeps the mind peaceful and calm
D. Ashwini mudra and shambhavi mudra occurs naturally while practicing bhadrasana

53. Ujjayi pranayama can be performed while:
A. Walking B. Standing
C. Sitting D. All of the above

54. Which of the following nadi is present inside sushumna nadi?
A. Vajrini nadi B. Brahma nadi
C. Chitrni nadi D. All of the above

55. What does 'Vipasyana' means?
A. To percept the real nature of objects
B. To do yoga in adverse condition
C. To do yoga in favourable condition
D. To attain the siddhis

ANSWERS

1	2	3	4	5	6	7	8	9	10
B	B	B	C	B	A	D	C	D	D
11	**12**	**13**	**14**	**15**	**16**	**17**	**18**	**19**	**20**
D	A	C	C	A	B	A	D	C	D
21	**22**	**23**	**24**	**25**	**26**	**27**	**28**	**29**	**30**
C	C	D	B	B	A	A	D	A	B
31	**32**	**33**	**34**	**35**	**36**	**37**	**38**	**39**	**40**
D	A	A	D	D	D	A	C	C	B
41	**42**	**43**	**44**	**45**	**46**	**47**	**48**	**49**	**50**
A	B	A	C	C	C	B	B	A	C
51	**52**	**53**	**54**	**55**					
D	D	D	B	A					

●●●

CHAPTER

10

Methods of Teaching Yoga

TEACHING & LEARNING

Teaching is a part of the educational process which involves the following factors:

(*i*) *Teaching* - A process involving methods

(*ii*) *Learning* - A process of adjustment through action

(*iii*) *Teacher* - A person who directs the process

(*iv*) *Student* - A person who adjusts himself through the action

(*v*) *Subject or Activity* - Content of learning

(*vi*) *Environment* - Class or situation in which the whole process is conducted.

The Terminology

Education is a process of growth, development and adding something new to one's experiences. There are two phases involved in the educational process namely teaching and learning.

Teaching consists of 'Organization and conduct of learning experience' by the teacher.

Learning is an adjustment of the whole organism by the student to a new situation created by the teacher.

Teacher is a person who stimulates learning in the student by organizing and guiding certain experiences of the individuals under his leadership. He is essentially an educator who 'leads out' all that is best in the student.

Student is a person who desirous of adjusting his whole organization to a new situation organized and guided by the teacher.

Methods are techniques or procedures used by the teacher through which an interaction between teacher and student takes places.

The Scope of Teaching-Learning

The purpose of teaching is to induce change in the student. There can be no teaching unless learning takes place. The teacher merely arranges the environment for learning and stimulates and guides the students' activity in that environment. It is the student who learns and each student has to do his own learning. Teaching serves to bring the student into a learning environment and enhance the efficiency of the learning process.

Teaching is a science in the sense that it involves logical and systematic arrangement based on certain principles. Teaching is also an art, meaning that it cannot be reduced to a formula. Teaching as an art requires sensitivity to factors affecting the student and his environment for learning and which must be suitably modified according to his needs.

The whole educational process involving teaching-learning centers round the most important factor – the student.

Methods of Teaching

During the process of teaching several methods have been tried over many years and we find that they fall into two main categories:

(*i*) Instructional methods used in the classroom for teaching theoretical subjects.

(*ii*) Methods used for teaching practical skill on the fields or in gymnasiums.

The classroom methods are variously named the lecture method, the recitation method, the project method, the laboratory method, the dramatic method and the group discussion method. The methods for teaching skills or physical activities, however, have not been properly categorized. Each method used in the classroom situation has many implications for teaching physical activities and skills, but they cannot be directly applied to teaching physical activities and skills. Even in respect of classroom teaching, no single method or pattern could serve as the best method for all teaching situations. The method of teaching yogic practices comes closer to that of physical activities rather than theoretical subjects.

Traditionally, there have been two approaches towards successful teaching: the first is a teacher-centered approach and the second a student-centered approach.

The teacher-centered approach was the main method in the past, even in Yoga. But today scientific thought focuses its attention on and emphasizes the student-centered approach.

So naturally, the principles and concepts which underlie the methods are expected to involve this student-centered approach, the main emphasis of which is due consideration of the needs of the students.

Methods of teaching must be compatible with the goals sought or the outcomes expected. The purpose of any method is to create learning in the student. The teacher should know how a particular method he uses affects the student's learning ability. The following are some of the basic methods of teaching:

Lecture Methods

It is perhaps the oldest method used for formal teaching. It is valuable in organizing large fields on material, separating a particular type of information for immediate use, presenting new information and synthesizing information from a wide variety of sources.

It is more useful with mature students having a high degree of auditory perception since it involves problems of attention, voice level, clarity, use of rest period and vocabulary level.

The lecture has considerable use in teaching yogic practices. It may be used in presenting any type of information related to particular activity in the perspective of yoga in general. When extensive lecture is necessary for the achievement of a specific goal, the students should be able to hear the teacher clearly. A lecture can be stimulating interesting and motivating to the students if the teacher prepares it properly.

The lecture method proves of greater advantage when combined with other methods. The use of visual materials is of considerable help in aiding students to retain the content of the lecture.

When using the lecture method the teacher should also be aware of the limitations of this method, which may be mentioned as follows:

(*i*) It is a teacher-centered activity and may encourage lack of participation on the part of the students.

(*ii*) Many student lack ability to earn by this method.

(*iii*) It may lead teachers to ignore more effective methods.

(*iv*) The attention span of more immature students is too short to benefit from a long lecture.

Response-to-Instruction Method

In this method the teacher gives precise instructions which precede, follow or are concurrent with a demonstration and all students respond to the instructions of the teacher in the same way.

There is very little attention paid to the individuals. The emphasis is on the subject matter of activity that is introduced. This method has a formal approach. An information approach with this method is more favourable in teaching such activities where there is some variation in the performance of individuals. This method can be profitably used after due attention to problems of individuals.

Individualized Instructional Method

It is based on the principle that learning is highly individualized. In this method attempts are made to provide by different means for individual differences within the pattern of the group structure.

Directed-Practice Method

Assignments for extra practice of selected yogic practices out of class hours enhance skill and performance levels of the students. Necessary introduction alongwith the preliminary practice of selected yogic exercises like Sirasasana, Uddiyana, Kapalabhati, Nauli, Purificatory processes etc. may be done in the class and the efficiency could be developed through out-of-class practice. The students should be encouraged to do out-of-class practice and the teacher may check the results during subsequent classes and give additional suggestions for further practice. Obviously, the success of this method depends upon motivation of the students and their rapport with the teacher.

Project Method

The aim of this method is to enable the students to put into practice what they have learned in the class. It may also be of help for students to learn related information. When the time is short in the regular schedule the projects such as preparing note-books on the yogic practices undergone, collection of related material from various sources, preparing models and the exhibits of the yogic practices, planned observations of seminars, conferences, competitions related to yogic activities as well as visits to different well-known yoga centers represent valuable help to teaching under this method.

Demonstration Method

Demonstration refers to non-competitive type performances with emphasis on skill and form. Demonstrations are of value, if properly directed to both performer and viewer. The Demonstration method describes the organization of the teaching of the class with the sole purpose of public demonstration when concluded. Demonstration method as a technique for the use of the class has some disadvantages. The scope of learning is restricted. It utilizes existing talent rather than developing new skills. However, the demonstration method serves as an excellent group method.

Unfortunately, there appears to be no simple formula for selecting the best methods. This depends on the conditions available, such as time, space and equipment. The teacher should have the skill to use a particular method and adapt it to prevailing conditions so that the students receive proper orientation and understanding of the technique and purpose of the method. In other words, a method should always be considered as a means to an end and not the end in itself. The method should allow for individual differences and in itself. The method should allow for individual differences and stimulate both creativity and independent thinking in the students. In Yoga, the teaching method has to be eclectic, drawing upon useful vital contributions from several exiting methods.

Factors Influencing the Method

The following factors govern the selection of particular method or combination of methods:

Content

We have already seen that the method of teaching depends upon the nature of the subject and that the practical subject requires a different method from the theoretical subject. Even different practical skills require different methods. We know also that the method of teaching skills in Physical Education comes closer to the teaching of yogic practices due to the similarity of content.

Previous Background and Experience of the Student

The method of teaching differs according to the previous experience of the students. Progressive skills cannot be taught to those who have not already mastered basic skills. The teacher can save time and energy by enquiring about students' previous experience in the skill to be learned.

The Teacher

Efficiency of method depends on the teacher who uses it. Method itself is neither good nor bad. It turns out to be good in the hands of an able teacher. The teacher does influence the method selected. The teachers have the following qualities which are all reflected through the chosen method:

(*i*) A genuine interest in communication.

(*ii*) Love of the work of teaching.

(*iii*) A willingness to share interest and experiences with others.

(*iv*) An ability to put him or herself in the position of the student.

(*v*) The capacity for understanding expressed in an open, authentic way without blaming or condemning the students.

(*vi*) An attractive personality.

(*vii*) The ability to set a good example through lifestyle and behaviour.

(*viii*) A sense of professional responsibility towards the students.

(*ix*) A pleasant, yet commanding voice.

(*x*) The awareness that, "The person in the teacher is more important than the method".

Suitable modification in the method depending upon the needs of student and the time framework are possible only when the teacher is conscious of the situation he is handling.

The art of teaching on the part of the teacher depends on the suitable modifications in the teaching method routinely used.

Facilities

Availability of facilities greatly influences the teaching method. It becomes more efficient with the necessary facilities. In the absence of required facilities the teacher sometimes feels insecure, tense and is unable to give of his or her best. These facilities could be in the form of an adequate space, necessary equipment and congenial atmosphere. For example, if there is no hall for teaching Asanas and the class is required to be conducted on the open ground, the teacher will face the problem of introducing Asanas in the lying position. If there are no water facilities available, purificatory processes or kriyas will have limitations for teaching. If the atmosphere is noisy, introduction of meditation techniques will be found difficult.

Scientific Principles

An effective teaching method depends on the knowledge of important principles of anatomy, physiology, psychology, pedagogy and yoga so that the teacher may be flexible in modifying the method. These principles also provide sound base for selection and formulation of methods.

SOURCES OF TEACHING METHODS

The teacher should be well acquainted with the variety of important principles drawn from education, yogic discipline, psychology of learning, anatomy and physiology in order to formulate good teaching methods.

Yogic Principles

(*i*) Yogic practices are not 'exercises' as we understand the exercise. The exercise is generally applied to vigorous physical movements. Since Yogic practices do not involve vigorous movements, any kind of violent action should be avoided during yoga practice.

(*ii*) The nature of yogic practices is varied and involves different mechanisms through which the results of particular yogic practices are obtained. The Asana, Pranayama, Bandhas, Mudras, Kriyas and Meditation do not use the same channels for bringing the result of the practices.

(*iii*) Asana – one of the most important and best known of the yogic practices — are 'static stretching procedures'. They should be performed slowly and smoothly in order to influence the tonic system rather than the phasic one.

(*iv*) The position in a particular asana should be comfortably maintained for some time with least effort. Effortless performance and relaxing as much as possible during the final position are the chief characteristics of the technique of Asanas.

(*v*) Pranayamic practices are very different in purpose and technique from the 'Breathing exercises'. They are supposed to increase oxygen uptake. However, they are considered of little value in the literature of Physical Education.

(*vi*) Yogic practices should not lead to undue fatigue. If there is fatigue it should be overcome by the practice of relaxation in savasana.

(*vii*) All yogic practices should be performed according to one's own capacity and without competition with others.

(*viii*) All yogic practices should lead to peace of mind.

(*ix*) Any yogic routine should begin with psycho-physical relaxation, centering one's attention as one would in prayer, or actual recitation of some prayers.

Psychological Principles

(*i*) Interest is the best motivation for learning. The teacher should teach in such a way that students maintain their interest and motivation to learn.

(*ii*) Activity is necessary for learning. Learning is a process of experience. Unless the student is involved in the experience of activity he/she may not be able to learn. Therefore practice is essential, especially for motor-learning or skill-learning. Again it is not mere practice but the correct practice that is important. Complex motor skills require more repetitions of correct practice.

(*iii*) All learning has a neural basis. Unless proper neuromuscular coordination is formed one cannot expect further developments in any motor skills.

(*iv*) For efficient learning the material to be learnt must be within the range of experience and abilities of the learner. Learning is highly individualized and results in progressive changes in behaviour. The ability to learn depends upon the innate capacity and previous experiences of the student. All individuals do not learn at the same rate.

(*v*) Learning of motor skills is hastened if the performer is able to grasp an intellectual understanding of the nature of the task before beginning the practice.

(*vi*) Regular practice of an activity resulting in pleasure and satisfaction contributes to the most effective learning.

(*vii*) Occasional short periods of rest between the practice periods produce superior results in learning motor skills. Brief rest period prevent fatigue in the muscles and efficiency of the muscles is not decreased.

Anatomico-Physiological Principles

1. Age and Sex are the two important factors determining the anatomico-physiological conditions which need to be considered in the teaching-learning process of motor activities. There are anatomical differences between the male and the female. One of the main differences to be taken into account is the structure. Women are considered to be weaker in structure generally than men. This means that both bones and ankles are not as strong and their bodies have more fatty

tissue. The male body is composed of 41.8% of the body weight of muscle, while the female body has 35.8%. The distribution of fatty tissue is 18.2% of the body weight in males and 28.2% in females. Hence this gives men more muscular strength than women.

2. The muscle strength is proportionate to the amount of fat to muscle tissue. The more fat there is obviously the less efficient are the muscles. Reduction in the fat therefore, contributes to building of muscle strength.
3. The abdominal wall can also be weaker in women from a mechanical point of view. Women's abdominal organs are not firmly situated and the abdominal tone is often lost through childbirth, miscarriages or other reproductive problems.
4. There are differences also in the proportions of the different segments of the spinal column. Specially in the lumbar region which affects performance of physical movements. The shorter lumbar and thoracic regions in the female sometimes produce a more pronounced shortening of lower back muscles resulting in lordosis. The lumbo-sacral angle is also different: 138 in female and 133 in male.
5. The tone of the muscles influences to a considerable extent the posture and functions of the bodily organs of an individual. Muscle tone is a sort of sustained contraction of the muscle fibres. Cultivation of improved muscle tone implies relaxation of undue tensions as well as increase of tone of habitually slack muscles. It is accompanied by an increased awareness of the entire body. One becomes aware of undue tensions in the body and learns to relax more and more when one is attempting to regain proper tone. Improvement of muscle tone brings corresponding improvement in equilibrium, circulation and neuro-glandular activity. Static stretching of the muscles contributes to the proper development of muscle tone.
6. Abdominal muscles pay an important role in holding the abdominal viscera in place. The tone of the abdominal muscles governs the efficient functioning of the organs situated in the abdominal cavity.
7. Muscle efficiency is lost during long periods of inactivity, especially, if the activity is caused by illness. Under such circumstances any physical activities demanding exertion should be introduced slowly and cautiously.
8. Fatigue is not confined exclusively to the particular muscles exercised. But it spreads through the body as a whole to some degree. Hence to remove the fatigue relaxation of the whole body is desirable.
9. The equilibrium of the body involves muscular co-ordination and proper functioning of the semi-circular canals of the internal ears, the eyes, the receptors in the skin and nerve endings in muscles and ligaments around joints.
10. Minimum expenditure of energy is the criterion of simplicity and efficiency in any activity. Vigorous movements consume more energy, while static activities consume less energy.
11. The theory and practice of warming up needs consideration when one engages in vigorous, dynamic and jerky activities. It is not relevant in static activity.
12. The centre of gravity in female bodies is lower than in males. This should be taken into consideration in practices involving stability and balance.

Educational Principles

1. Learning depends upon impressions received by the necessary receptors. Five senses represent the avenues of learning. Therefore the presentation of a specific practice or skill should involve as many senses as possible to form an adequate image of the practice.

However, the most important cues in practice come from audio-visual aids. Motor learning is perceptual, cognitive, rational, thoughtful and involves mental as well as physical aspects of learning. The ideas must be translated into muscular action. There are individual differences in effectively utilizing various kinds of sensory information. Some individuals have remarkable ability to organize visually presented information quickly. Others synthesis information and analyses the situation, hence appear to respond more slowly.

Visual demonstration of the practice is one of the most effective way to enhance the learning of a motor skill. However, the learning is hastened if the student is able to grasp an intellectual understanding of the nature of the task before the beginning of the practice and is given sometime to integrate the initial cues from observing the demonstration and listening to instructions. Brief, clear descriptions of the activity with repeated demonstrations and pointing out likely faults bring good results.

2. At the preliminary stages, 'Over learning' through repeated practice is necessary. The emphasis should be on aiming at right or correct practice. This can be done by specific instructions.

   Instructions may also be divided into those offered before the performance of the activity, those which accompany performance and those by way of information or corrections at the end of the performance of the activity. Formal instructions are best suited during the initial phases of the learning process. Initial instructions prevent the student from adopting incorrect habits that might later have to be unlearned.

   Students should be instructed in the positive way of performing the activity rather than being informed initially what to avoid. However, best performance comes when individuals are informed both what to do and what to avoid.

   This helps in learning the activity by eliminating possible errors as well as increasing such positive aspects as ease, comfort, efficiency, lowering of tension during performance and speed in some respects.

3. Adequate time should be allotted for actual practice without which learning cannot be effective. The practice period should be divided into informal practice and supervised practice in a group.

4. The 'Principle of Progression' is vital to learning. It means performance of any activity from "simple to complex" and from "known to unknown".

   This principle rests upon a sound neuro-muscular basis. Complex motor learning requires an order of pre-requisites, a background of specific attainments. The learning of co-ordinated movement patterns is dependent upon the possession of sufficient amount of fundamental physical abilities such as muscular strength, flexibility, muscular endurance and cardio-respiratory endurance. This obvious relationship is sometimes ignored, but effective learning is possible only when this relationship is kept in mind.

   The whole programme of activities should therefore be planned and conducted in the light of the principle of progression.

5. Effective learning takes place through the use of the Whole Method, Part Method or a combination of Whole and Part Methods. The combination method is also called Progressive Part Method or Repetitive Part or Continuous Part Method. The use of any of these methods depends on the degree of complexity of the activity.

   (*a*) The Whole Method consists in presenting the activity in its entirety without any division. If the activity to be learnt is not complex and the learner is mature, the whole method is suitable.

(b) The Part Method is based on analysis of the purpose and of identifying a logical sequence of parts for presentation from simple to complex. The part method is better if the student is immature and/or the activity complex.

(c) Progressive Part Method is more often used than the part method. In this method a part is learned, paired with the second part and the two practiced together. Then the third part is practiced and three parts practiced as a whole until the entire activity is constructed.

Methods of presentation may stress formal instructions or informal suggestions. But the fundamental basis of all methods is the nature and need of the students, including their individual and group characteristics in learning. The nature of educational objectives and the type of activities used in the programme also dictate the choice of methods.

6. The teacher's interest and attitude towards the students determines to great extent adequate learning. There is a need on the part of the teacher to inspire the student to accurate and satisfactory performance. If the student is not performing correctly he should be shown the points where he/she makes mistakes in a positive way that encourages self-correction.
7. Learning does not take place unless there is some way for the performer to assess his/her relative success or failure. Although it is necessary to correct faulty performance, too many corrections at a time can confuse. The teacher should correct the most important fault first. Most corrections should be in the form of positive suggestions.
8. Immediately after the ideal demonstration of the activity the opportunity to try out and practice the activity should be provided for the students.
9. The teacher should encourage students to ask any questions related to the activity, listen to what each person has to say and try to understand his problem. Never discourage or ridicule even a trifling question. It may add to new thinking on the part of the teacher. Give a suitable answer to his satisfaction and/or use the question to open a discussion in the class as a whole if necessary.

Sociological Principles

Utility Value : The idea of utility need not necessarily be interpreted in the light of activities involved in earning a living alone. Many activities and experiences are of real practical use in helping the person to live happily and successfully that are not of any immediate vocational significance. Yogic practices may not necessarily be of vocational value but they are certainly of immediate practical use for a person of any age and sex in maintaining good health and physical fitness together.

ESSENTIAL QUALITIES OF A GOOD YOGA TEACHER

1. Must be a good learner and ready to also learn through the process of teaching.
2. Must have a strong self-introspective ability.
3. Must be disciplined and dedicated towards the cause of Yoga.
4. Must have a sound knowledge of the Yoga principles and techniques alongwith an understanding of the precautions, contrain-dications etc. that are involved.
5. Must have an understanding of the wholistic nature of Yoga physiology, philosophy and psychology.
6. Must posses a strong desire for spiritual evolution.
7. Must be willing to learn from all situations and not have an, "I know it all!" attitude.
8. Must possess a sense of empathy for others.
9. Must be willing to sublimate their own EGO.

10. Must have a good sense of humour and be able to laugh at themselves without reservation.
11. Must be able to motivate others by self-example and lead the way as a true Yoga Acharya.
12. Must learn from their mistakes and be ready to correct themselves when they have made such mistakes.
13. Must have devotion to the Guru who has guided them to the level of becoming a teacher themselves. Guru Droha or treachery to one's Guru is considered the worst sin.

20 GENERAL INSTRUCTIONS FOR YOGA TEACHERS

1. Choose a natural setting with some trees, plants in an open area or a roof top. If in a hall, please open the windows to improve the ventilation.
2. Make sure that all the mats are in a line and well organized. Discipline at all levels is an important aspect of Yoga.
3. Make sure there is an adequate supply of water during the class. Proper hydration is to be maintained at all times.
4. Try to keep the teacher student relationship in a traditional form as a Guru Kula atmosphere. Without such a relationship real teaching cannot occur.
5. Give proper advice on the comfortable Yoga dress to be worn for the class. Cultural aspects must be understood with regards to the dressing.
6. Make sure that you have already clearly explained the necessity of having an empty stomach before performing any of the Yoga practices.
7. Try to have the classes in the morning and emphasize the importance of facing the morning sun while doing the practices.
8. Help the students to become aware of what they are doing and what is happening with every movement in the class. Becoming aware of how unaware we are is the first step to be emphasized.
9. Clarify the right and left confusion that tends to occur during the practices.
10. Suggestions for a healthy diet and life style should be given as appropriate. The importance of stopping the negative habits must be emphasized as much as possible.
11. Try to give a detailed view of the practices that are being taught. For e.g. when teaching the Surya Namaskar, make sure that you explain the concepts of the Usha Shakti, names of the sun with their meaning, importance of breath-movement coordination etc. The cultural understanding should also be developed at all times.
12. Yoga is a way of life and not just a few techniques. It is important to discuss the principles such as the Yama-Niyama when appropriate.
13. Stress upon the importance of the three R's. Regularity, rhythm and repetition that have been so nicely explained by Amma. Daily practice should be encouraged.
14. It is important to help them understand how to make life more meaningful by paying attention to the process of transforming oneself from the lower animal to the Divine states of existence. Change is the only constant as Amma always says and the Panchakshara of Om Namahshivaya is a very good Japa in this regard.
15. This is a slow and steady process. Don't rush them into any of the practices without adequate preparation and don't over stretch them as it may cause a negative reaction. Pay attention to the students at all times.
16. Give them an understanding of the various paths of Yoga, the different traditions, the types of Sadhakas and the importance of Guru Bhakti and Guru Dakshina (gratitude

to the Guru) in the evolutionary process. Shraddha or faith in the Guru and their wisdom is essential for all students.

17. Slowly and steadily make the mind ready for the internal practices of Dharana and Dhyana with proper step by step guidance. The awareness of the flow of Prana in the different practices can make the student ready for the inner experiences that occur later. Om Japa and the chanting of Mantras can help make the process more internal.
18. The Sanskrit names are essential to understand the essence of the practice and so make sure you give the names and their relevance.
19. Relaxation is very important and the teacher must guide the student in a slow and step-by-step manner during the relaxation.
20. Swamiji and Amma have given us great examples of how to live the Yogic life and teach for all types of students in all situations. We should learn from them and follow their great examples.

CONSIDERATIONS IN TEACHING A PRACTICAL CLASS

- Prepare yourself and be well read up on the topic to be taught.
- Assess the level of the student and start from their present level.
- The first rule of Yoga and medicine is Ahimsa - do no harm!
- Start the class with a period of quiet sitting and a group prayer.
- Gentle warming up practices such as the Jathis are a useful way to prepare the students physically and mentally for further practices.
- Gently work the students into the different Yoga practices such as the Kriyas and Asanas with emphasis on breath and body movement coordination.
- Don't make the students to hold the postures to long at the beginning.
- The progression in each practice should be ideally from the:
  - first step of going in and out of the posture in tune with the breathe cycle,
  - the second step of holding the posture for a short period,
  - the third step of holding it for a longer duration of time.
- Make the class lively with some Yoga jokes and have a sip of water in between the practices to hydrate the tissues.
- Introduce the breathing practices to develop a proper breathing pattern and encourage the use of complete Yogic breathing (Mahat Yoga Pranayama) from the beginning.
- Introduce the Pranayama practices in a step by step manner and go from a short breath cycle to a longer one with time. Use of Bandhas is to be brought in later when trying to hold the breath for longer periods of time.
- The importance of Mudras can be taught at the appropriate time with proper examples to understand the flow of energy in the body. Sparsha Mudras are an excellent tool to help students to understand the power of Mudras.
- Relaxation is the most important time in the class as the benefits of the practices done in the class settle down in the body in a healthy manner at that time. Don't neglect this vital period of rest, relaxation and recuperation.
- Make mentions of the Yogic philosophy and psychological aspects as well as the benefits of the practices at different intervals in the class. Repeat the concepts many times as students tend to drift off and may not catch the concepts if mentioned just once.
- Be open to questions and answers in the class but don't let them disturb the general rhythm, better to have a time allocated for the questions at the end of the class.
- End the class with a group prayer and motivate the students to be regular as that is one of the most important aspects of Yoga Sadhana.

CLASS MANAGEMENT

Students rarely cause trouble when they are interested and when suitable lesson content is presented in a competent and stimulating fashion. One essential thing in reducing the problem of control to a minimum is to create an atmosphere of natural freedom, friendliness, mutual help and understanding. These qualities in a class should emanate from the leadership of the teacher. This develops social consciousness in students and an awareness of their responsibility to the group.

The students or participants of Yoga may be grouped under the following headings:

- Beginners
- Experienced or advanced
- School children
- Special attention Groups

(*a*) *Beginners Group.* This group may involve persons of all ages, males and females, young and old and special individuals who are making their first acquaintance with yoga. They need a general background of yogic discipline and motivation to continue with yoga.

(*b*) *Experienced or Advanced Group.* This group may consist of persons who have some experience with yoga and wish to advance further to gain more varied and deeper experience. Their expectation is to acquaint themselves with a greater number of yogic practices and indulge in subtler and higher practices intensively.

(*c*) *School Children.* This is a select group ranging from the age of 6 years to 18 years and commands largest percentage of the society. School children need exposure to the field of yoga based on their immediate needs of their age and temperament.

(*d*) *Special Attention Groups.* These individuals can vary on the basis of age like children and adults; on the basis of sex like males and females: on the basis of age and sex like boys and girls; on the basis of individual problems of health, abnormality or handicaps. All these individuals need special attention which is possible in a homogeneous group but not in a heterogeneous group.

Dealing with Difficult Students

The following techniques are useful in dealing with inattentive, talkative or difficult students.

1. Individual students who are disturbing the class may have their attention directed by pausing during instruction, glancing in the direction of the particular student, calling his or her name and asking a question, or if the disturbance is troubling the rest of the class, it should also be pointed out that they are preventing others who are paying attention and working well from hearing the instructions. Alternately, the class can be switched to another activity.
2. It may help to separate people who talk perpetually but if these students continue to cause disturbance after a few warnings, they should be sent out of the class for a short period. However, it is important to bring the person back soon in the class and to let him or her know that improved behaviour is expected.

In addition, the teacher will have more control if he or she avoids being too familiar with older students. Be friendly but maintain your dignity and social distance. Remember that you are their teacher.

Also never allow yourself to become antagonistic towards a student. Your effectiveness in helping him will depend upon your patience and understanding.

Seating Arrangement

The organisation of the class may have any suitable form of seating either in lines, rows, a semi-circle or small circle. Consider that each student needs about 40 square feet and arrange your room accordingly.

It is preferable if the floor is covered with a carpet but if this is not possible the floor should be clean and each student should use his own mat. In either case it is desirable that the mat or carpet is covered by a clean sheet of cloth of 6 feet × 3 feet.

The seat of the teacher should be such that the teacher is visible to every student. If the group is large a platform is necessary for the teacher to be visible. In a small group a semi-circle is more suitable as it allows every student to see the teacher clearly. When a platform is used, a revolving one is ideal.

The hall or room where the class is conducted should be well ventilated. It should be well lit so that not only is the class able to see the teacher but the teacher should have a clear view of the class when he is teaching from the platform and while moving about for teaching and answering questions.

The practice room or hall should be as quiet as possible and free from any disturbance.

Instructions

Learning of a particular yoga practice depends upon precise instructions by the teacher. Formal instructions are best suited during the initial stage of learning the practice. Instructions could be divided into those that are given verbally before the beginning of the yogic practice, those which accompany performance of the activity individually or by the group and those that are extended by way of information or corrections after the completion of the activity. Initial instructions prevent the student from adopting incorrect habits which might have to be unlearned later. Practical instructions guide the students for correct and efficient performance.

The following guidelines can help the teacher convey instructions clearly:

(*i*) Be sure that you have the attention of everyone in the class before any instructions are given.

(*ii*) When a long explanation is needed it is best to have the class sit down and if necessary closer to the teacher.

(*iii*) Make your instructions brief, perfectly clear and spoken slowly and distinctly.

(*iv*) The instructions should be given for only one thing at a time.

(*v*) Try to use different words and expressions to catch the attention of the students. For example, if students do not understand the first time, use different words in repeating the instructions.

(*vi*) Describe the technique and procedure of any activity before the students are actually asked to practice.

The Audio-Visual Aids

The progress of science in various fields has developed techniques that have made knowledge widely available. These radically alter our systems of communication. The use of computers, for example, has reduced the need for man-power in the area of teaching. Several groups of students in different locations can be served from a single source which can show the same programme to many different groups. There are many revolutionary possibilities opening up the field of communication through such media as television, video, satellite etc. This is a new phase in our history and these media have immense possibilities for teaching an enormous number of people.

Although sophisticated audio-visual aids are not always within the reach of the teacher, it is necessary to realize the importance of these aids in the learning process. A teaching aid provides quick information about the subject matter to the students. It gives the teacher a better opportunity of conveying the meaning of what he is saying. It helps the students at all levels to grasp the important points in a class situation. It helps to make the lesson interesting and students are more receptive. Hence it is a very important aspect of teaching method. The response of the students is the best way to judge whether the aid is effective or not, but even if the teacher cannot tell this in advance he should, nevertheless, know the basic principles of preparing and using the aids.

The various teaching aids which are mostly used include blackboards, bulletin boards, pictures of all kinds, diagrams, sketches, drawings, charts, models, projected devices such as filmstrips, slides, motion pictures and recordings, video-cassettes and television.

Visual demonstration is one of the most effective aids to enhance the learning of a motor activity. There is individual difference related to the manner in which various kinds of sensory information are effectively used by the students. Some students have remarkable ability to quickly organize visually presented information. It is desirable that the teacher himself should give the demonstration of a particular yoga practice. The teacher can communicate with his students better through the demonstration staged by him. At the same time he should verbally explain clearly the fundamental principles underlying the yoga practice. Any practice by the students must be preceded by visual demonstration to be effective.

Discussion

A small question-answer session is very helpful at the end of the lesson to evaluate the outcome and remove any difficulties on the part of the students.

The following hints will be useful in conducting a question-answer or discussion session.

(*i*) Encourage the students to ask their questions or address their comments to the group for discussion.

(*ii*) Never discourage or ridicule any student's question or contribution whatever small it may be.

(*iii*) Try to draw all students into discussion rather than a few who are always ready to talk.

(*iv*) It is wise to limit the discussion to a few important points.

(*v*) The teacher is expected to know more than the students on the points of discussion. If the teacher is not prepared to answer any question or does not know any point he should not hesitate to say so, and should say that he will find out the answer and explain that at the next meeting.

(*vi*) Remember that young children are not mature enough to participate in a group discussion so a different approach is necessary in encouraging them to share their experience.

(*vii*) Exercise some control over the time spent on questions. Steer the discussion to important and relevant questions. Do not sacrifice valuable time on those points that are not important.

Extra-Class Practice

Once the yoga practice is introduced and techniques explained to the students, it is desirable that they are encouraged to practice on their own at home. All kinds of motivation for the practice at home should be given and they should be assured of all help for correction, modification, improvement from the teacher when they meet next.

LESSON PLANNING

We have seen earlier that the purpose of teaching is to cause desirable change in the student. Successful planning is necessary on the part of a teacher in order to fulfil this purpose. A plan of each lesson should therefore be prepared.

The advantages of a written lesson plan are:

(*i*) It helps the teacher to organize his thinking.

(*ii*) It increases the teacher's confidence and prevents him or her from losing direction during the lesson.

(*iii*) It helps the teacher to keep the teaching procedure and objectives in minds.

(*iv*) It ensures availability to necessary materials and saves last minute rush to provide adequate arrangements and anxiety caused by such a situation.

(*v*) It serves as a aid for future plans.

Essentials of a Good Lesson Plan

1. It should be prepared shortly before use.
2. It should be specific and detailed.
3. It should take cognizance of individual differences.
4. It should include (*a*) statement of objectives of the lesson; (*b*) statement of activities and experiences with instructional points; (*c*) a list of materials needed; (*d*) description of method and procedures to be used; (*e*) provisions for linking previous and future plans; (*f*) provisions for comments by the teacher after the lesson.

Whatever the type of method selected for teaching it should be compatible with the purpose or desired outcome and the best among available methods to bring the desired outcome. It should be adapted to the activity to be taught. It should also be feasible taking into consideration time, space and equipment available. The teacher should have the skill to use a particular method. Proper orientation and understanding of the technique and purpose of the method should be given to the students.

The immediate goal of any yogic lesson is to introduce a particular yoga practice and its correct technique and give the feel of that practice of the participants of the lesson so that they are motivated to continue further practice and derive maximum benefits. In order to attain these objectives the yogic lesson should be properly planned and executed.

Here are some guidelines for conducting yoga lessons successfully

1. *Setting the Atmosphere.* A yoga class should begin with a calm and quiet atmosphere. It may start with a short prayer or with a prayerful mood. As far as possible some meditative pose may be recommended for this purpose. The students are asked to take their seats in a suitable formation. The quiet sitting or prayerful mood creates suitable internal environment in the students conducive to the yoga lesson.
2. *Introduction to the Practice.* The main part of the lesson starts with the introduction of the yoga practice. This introductory part may be divided into two sections. The first part may be devoted to verbal instructions with the back-ground of the practice containing as much information about the practice as possible. This part is specially intended to create interest and motivation among the students. Depending upon the knowledge of the teacher about the practice and his/her skill in presenting the information, the teacher can make this more interesting and motivating.
3. *Demonstrating Practice.* The second part may be devoted to the ideal demonstration of the yoga practice as a whole. Although it is possible to take the help of Audio-visual aids like pictures, sketches, filmstrips etc., it is more impressive, practical and desirable that the demonstration is staged by the teacher himself. As far as possible this demonstration should be most efficient, faultless and complete so that an overall image of the practice is presented to the students. As compared to the presentation of a particular yoga practice through an audio-visual means, when the teacher himself demonstrates the practice the students can relate personally to the teacher and identify more closely with the practices shown. There is more appreciation and respect for the teacher generated through live demonstration.
4. *Analysing the Practice.* The whole demonstration of the yoga practice may be useful in forming an overall general picture. But it may not be enough to get into the detailed stages of the technique which requires analysis of that practice. The insight into the proper technique is gained only by analysing the practice is more essential when the technique is difficult. When the practice is simple a demonstration as a whole would be sufficient and the analysis may not be

necessary. When the practice is analysed and demonstrated in parts, it is desirable to supplement it with a brief and clear description about the technique, bringing to the notice of the students salient points of the practice. These salient points should include hints about do's and don'ts.

5. *Students' Individual Practice Time.* When students see a technique demonstrated, they naturally want to try it out themselves. So allot some time for the students to try it on their own individually and to find out for themselves how successfully they are able to practice it. While students are practicing the teacher should watch their performance and find out their difficulties, mistakes and deviations from the correct and ideal performance of the practice. He should correct the most obvious mistakes of those students who are practicing in a way that is detrimental to them and then point out common mistakes that are committed generally. A repeat demonstration of the practice as a whole and in parts should be given to ensure that the point of the corrections has been understood by everyone.

6. *Group Practice.* After getting the feel of the practice and becoming conversant with the technique the teacher may ask the whole group of students to perform the practice together under the guidance of the teacher in a formal manner. Collective participation in the group will give an idea to the individual about his performance in relation to the performance of others.

7. *Correcting Mistakes.* Performance in the group by the students helps the teacher to locate any performance that has deviated from normal and which needs correction. This saves the time of the teacher in checking every individual's performance. He can concentrate on the particular students who are not performing the technique properly. He can suggest necessary modifications in the performance of the students or suggest some lead-up practices in case of particular individuals, if necessary. Yoga practices being essentially individualistic, when they are performed by the group, individual capacities should be taken into consideration.

8. *Giving Instructions.* In the group practice when directions are used, it should be remembered that their purpose is to suggest different stages of practice to be undergone in succession by the group. The commands or instructions should, therefore, have a very slow rhythm so that the jerky motions in response to brisk instructions are avoided and due respect is given to the individual capacities. The emphasis should be on an informal way of performance rather than a formal one.

9. *Repeat Demonstration.* The performance of the yoga practice by the group should be followed by pointing out the lacunae still remaining in the performance of some individuals, suggesting proper corrections and avoiding the mistakes committed by the individuals and elaborating on some points which need clarification or explanation.

10. *Repeat Practice.* The group should then repeat the practice of the technique.

11. *Repeat Demonstration.* The teacher should demonstrate and clarify the main points again.

12. *Rest Periods.* After the group practice is over the students may be given rest in the form of Shavasana—the yogic way of relaxation.

When more than one yoga practice is introduced, it is desirable that Shavasana is practised at the end of the lesson and sometimes even after some yoga practices during the lesson, if necessary.

Before the end of the lesson the teacher would do well to sum up points considered as important for the correct and efficient performance of yoga practices. He could also induce students to ask any questions related to the practice so that there is a good imprint the introduced yoga practice on the memory of the students.

To sum up the precise steps in the conduct of a yogic lesson, the whole process includes –

1. Creating an environment suitable for the lesson by a prayer or prayerful mood.
2. Establish the concept of yoga practice by verbal introduction.
3. Giving the complete picture of the yoga practice through whole demonstration.
4. Analysing the whole performance into suitable parts or stages.
5. Allotting time for getting the feel of the practice by individuals.
6. Group practice under the guidance and supervision of the teacher.
7. Detection and correction of the mistakes in the performance.
8. Giving instructions with emphasis on the salient points analysing the performance again.
9. Giving complete demonstration with clear explanation of the various stages involved in the practice.
10. Again practice by the group.
11. Again providing complete picture of the whole practice by demonstration, discussion, modifications when necessary, lead up practices for weaker students.
12. Giving complete rest in Shavasana at the end.

Success of the teacher lies in how best he utilizes the above steps in his lesson, Remember, "Teaching is what you make it".

The above mentioned ideas or considerations relate to the yoga lesson where new practice is introduced. But a yoga lesson could also be a practice session. Previously introduced practices are undergone during such a lesson. There would obviously be some different between the two types of yoga lesson. The main purpose of the first type of lesson would be to teach new practice with all details of its technique. The second type, on the other hand emphasizes the continuing practice of those techniques already learnt, so that the original techniques are not forgotten and their appropriate health benefits are derived. In the practice type of yoga lesson.

(*i*) There are groups of yogic practices undergone.

(*ii*) The practices are meaningfully chosen from amongst the known techniques.

(*iii*) There is some sequence based on the principle of progression.

(*iv*) As far as possible variety of the groups of yogic practices are chosen for giving maximum benefits through stretching's, relaxation, breathing techniques and meditation.

The practice lesson should also follow the pattern given earlier, where the lesson begins with a calm and quiet mood and ends with general relaxation with Shavasana or meditation, so that the ultimate experience is given to the participants in the lesson.

A yoga lesson could be also a mixture of the above two types. After having conducted a practice lesson for sometime, the teacher could switch to the introduction of the new practice along a similar pattern to the one discussed earlier.

Emphasis in advanced groups in practice session could be on a meditative mood throughout the lesson or more time could be devoted to practice of meditation at the end.

METHODS OF TEACHING YOGASANAS

MEANING OF YOGA: As you all vividly know the word yoga means 'unity' or 'oneness'. On a more practical level, yoga is channel of balancing and harmonizing the body, mind and emotions. This is possible through regular practice of Asana, Pranayama, Mudra, Shat karma and meditation etc.

MEANING OF ASANA: Asana mean a state of being in which one can remain physically and mentally steady, calm, quiet and comfortable. According to Hatha Yoga Pradipika – By practicing Asanas, one can attain steadiness of body and mind, freedom from disease and lightness of limbs. According to Yoga Sutra – *Sthiram sukham asanam* means a position which is comfortable and steady. However it is found that asana means certain specific body positions which open the energy channels and Psychic centre. As mentioned in the yogic scriptures that there are 84,00,000 Asanas exists. Our great rishi's and yogi's modified and reduced the number of Asanas to few hundred which is known today. It is very difficult to perform all the Asanas by all. Of these few hundred, it's sufficient to practice a few Asanas which is most suitable to a particular practitioner. Regular practice of yoga brings the maximum benefit.

TEACHING ASANAS TO THE BEGINNERS: There is a group of Asanas that should be performed by those who have never practiced Yogasanas before, who are infirm in any way, weak or sick and who are therefore unable to perform the most difficult practices. This group consists of elementary techniques designed to prepare the mind and body. The major Asanas of this group consists of Pawana muktasana series. In Sanskrit these practices are referred to as "Sukshma Vyayama". The word 'Pawan' means wind or Prana and 'Mukta' means release and 'asana' means pose. Therefore pawana muktasana also means a group of Asanas that remove any blockages that prevent the free flow of energy in the body and mind. It is very useful as a preparatory practice as it opens up all the major joints and relaxes the muscles of the body. This group of Asanas can be practiced by all beginners or advanced, young or elderly people suffering from minor ailments. Because of its simplicity, it should be taught to all beginners. These practices are divided into three parts such as:

Part-I: Anti-rheumatic group: These groups of Asanas are very good for those with rheumatic arthritis and related ailments. These exercises consist of toe-bending, ankle rotation, half butterfly, full butterfly and hip rotation, hand bending, wrist bending, wrist joint rotation, elbow bending, shoulder socket rotation and neck movement.

Part-II: Digestive/Abdominal group: This group of Asanas is concerned specifically with strengthening the digestive system. The practices are raised legs pose (uttana padasana), legs rotation (chakra padasana), cycling (pada sanchalanasana), leg lock pose (supta pavana muktasana), rocking and rolling, sleeping abdominal stretch pose (supta udara karshanasana) and boat pose (navasana).

Part-III: Shakthi Bhandha Asanas: These groups of Asanas are concerned with improving the energy flows within the body and breaking down neuro-muscular knots, especially in the pelvic region whose energy tends to stagnate. The practice consists of pulling the rope, dynamic spinal twist, churching the mill, rowing the boat, chopping the wood, salutation in sitting pose and abdominal stretch pose.

On regular practice of all the above three parts the beginners should taught the next stage of Asanas. Asanas can be classified into three groups as follows:

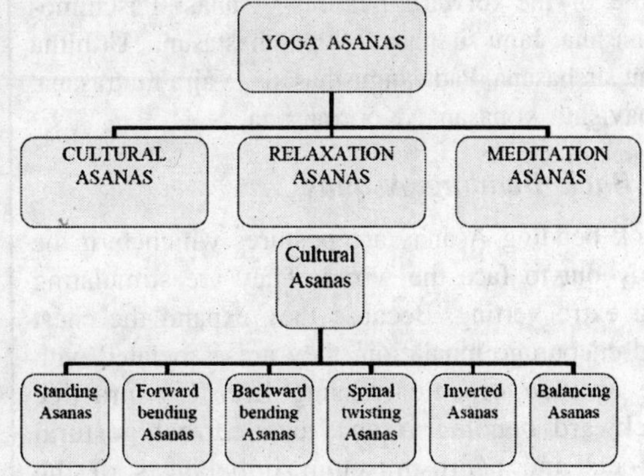

I. Cultural Asanas can be classified as follows

1. Standing Asanas

This series of asana has a stretching and strengthening effect on the back, shoulders and the leg muscles. They are particularly useful for those who spend a lot of time sitting down or who have stiffness or pain in the back. They improve posture, balance and muscular co-ordination. Some of the standing Asanas include: Natarajasana, Vrikshasana,

Tadasana, Utkatasana, Garudasana, Trikonasana, Parivritta Trikonasana, Parswa Konasana, Veera Bhadrasana, Ardha Chandrasana, Pada Uttanasana.

2. *Forward Bending Asanas*

Forward bending Asanas loosen up the back, maintaining good health and increasing vitality. These practices move the spine into the position known as the primary curve, the shape it takes in the womb.

During a forward bending asana each of the vertebrae is separated, stimulating the nerves, improving circulation around the spine and nourishing the spinal cord. This has a positive impact on the organs of the body generally and on the brain specifically.

This group of Asanas is also very important for making the back muscles supple and strong, compressing and massaging the abdominal organs, including the liver, kidneys, pancreas and intestine and stretching the leg muscles. The followings are some of the forward bending Asanas: Paschimottanasana, Janu sirshasana, Pada hastasana, Utthitha janu sirshasana, Pada angusthasana, Vajra mutrasana, Upavishta konasana, Koormasana.

3. *Back Bending Asanas*

Back bending Asanas are postures which turn the body out to face the world. They are stimulating and extro verting. Because they expand the chest and encourage inhalation, they are associated with the attitude of embarrassing life. The practice backward bending Asanas can correct postural defects and neuro-muscular imbalances of the vertebral column.

These Asanas help to circulate, purify and enrich the blood in the back region. This series of Asanas create a negative pressure in the abdomen and pelvis, helping neuro-circulatory toning of all the related organs and also massage the abdomen and pelvic organs.

The followings are some of the backward bending Asanas: Bhujangasana, Laghu Vajrasana, Salabhasana, Dhanurasana, Sedhu Bandhasana, Chakrasana, Ushtrasana.

4. *Spinal Twisting Asana*

Spinal twisting asana are important for spinal health. The twist imposed on the spine and the whole trunk exercises the muscles, make the spinal column more flexible and stimulate the spinal nerves. It also has a strong influence on the abdominal muscles, alternatively stretching and compressing them as the body twists from one direction to the others. The followings are some of the spinal twisting Asanas: Meru vakrasana, Ardha matsyendrasana, Parivritti janu sirshasana, Bharadvajasana, Pashasana, Privritta trikonasana, Privritta parshva konasana.

5. *Inverted Asanas*

Inverted Asanas reverse the action of gravity on the body; instead of everything towards the feet, the orientation shift towards the head. Similarly on the emotional on the Psych level inverted Asanas turns everything upside down, throwing a new light on the old pattern of behaviour and being. Generally these practices improve health, reduce anxieties and stress and increase self confidence. These Asanas encourage a rich supply of blood flow to the brain and nourishing the neurons and flushing out the toxins. Blood and limb, accumulated in the lower limbs and abdomen, are drained back to the heart, then circulated to the lungs, purified and re-circulated to all parts of the body. This process nourishes the cells of the whole human organisms. They enrich blood flow and also allows the pituitary gland to operate more efficiently. The followings are some of the inverted Asanas: Bhumi pada uttasana, Vipareeta karani asana, Sarvangasana, Padma sarvangasana, Halasana, Sirshasana, Oordhwa padmasana.

6. *Balancing Asanas*

Balancing Asanas develops the cerebellum, the brain centre that controls how the body works in motion. These Asanas induce physical balance, stilling unconscious movements. This group of practice develops a balanced mind and a more matured outlook on life. It also balances the novel system and removing stress and anxiety. At the beginning these Asanas may be difficult to perform however the body is very adoptable and progress will quickly be made with few weeks of regular practice. The following are some of the balancing Asanas: Garudasana, Natarajasana, Vatayanasana, Bakasana, Kukkutasana, Hansasana, Mayurasana.

II. Relaxation Asanas

The relaxation Asanas should be performed before and after the asana session and at any time when the body become tired. The followings are some of the important relaxation Asanas: Shavasana (corpse pose), Advasana (reversed corpse pose), Makarasana (crocodile pose), Jyestikasana (superior pose) and, Matsya Kridasana (flapping fish pose).

III. Meditation Asanas

The meditative Asanas needs to hold the body in a steady position without conscious effort. It is essential to remain awake and alert while going to various stages which lead to successful meditation. Initially most people will find it difficult to sit in one asana for a long time. However, through regular practice of the pre meditation posture, the legs and hips will become flexible enough comfortably maintain a steady posture. The followings are some of the Asanas prescribed for meditation. They are Padmasana, Bhadrasana, Siddhasana and Vajrasana.

GENERAL NOTE FOR THE YOGA PRACTITIONERS

The following practice notes should be thoroughly understood before teaching and practicing yoga.

Breathing: Always breathe through the nose unless specific instructions are given.

Awareness: Awareness has many connotations, in this context, it may be understood as consciously noting the physical movement, the postures itself, breath control and synchronization, mental counting, sensations in the body, movement of Prana, concentration on an area of the body or chakra and most important, any thoughts or feelings that may arise during the practice of Asanas. This awareness is essential in order to receive optimum benefits from the practices.

Relaxation: Shavasana may be performed at any point during asana practice, especially when feeling physically or mentally tired. Shavasana should also be practiced on completion of the Yogasanas programme.

Sequence: After completing shat karma, asana should be practiced, followed by Pranayama, pratyahara, dharana and then meditation.

Counter pose: The concept of counter pose is necessary to bring the body back to a balance state. It is important that the asana practice should be structured so that backward bends are followed by forward bends and vice-versa.

Time: Asana may be practiced at any time of the day after meals. The best time, however is the 2 hrs before and including sun rise. This period of day is known in Sanskrit as Brahmamuhurta and is most conducive to the higher practice of yoga.

Place: Practice in a well-ventilated room where it is calm and quiet. Asanas may also be practiced outdoors but the surrounding be pleasant, a beautiful garden with trees and flowers.

Blanket: Use a folded blanket of natural material preferably white in colour for the practice of Asanas.

Clothes: During the practice of Asanas it is better to wear loose, light and comfortable clothing. During the practice of Asanas spectacles, watches and jewelleries should be removed.

Bathing: Try to take a cold shower before starting Yogasanas.

Emptying the bowels: Before commencing the Asanas programme the bladder and intestine should preferably be emptied.

Diet: There are no special dietary rules for asana practitioners, although it is better to eat natural food and in moderation. At meal time it is advised to half fill the stomach with food, 1/4th of water and leave the remaining 1/4th empty. Eat only to satisfy hunger and not so much that a feeling of heaviness or laziness occurs. Eat to live rather than live to eat. Food which causes or gas in the digestive system, which are heavy, oily and spicy should be avoided, especially when Asanas are practiced with a spiritual aim.

No straining: Never exert undue force while doing Asanas.

Age: Asanas may be practiced by people of all age groups, male or female.

Contra-indication: People with fractured bones or who are suffering from chronic ailments should consult a yoga teacher or doctor before commencing Asanas.

Termination of Asanas: If there is excessive pain in any part of the body the asana should be terminated immediately and if necessary medical advice shout.

SHATKRIYAS: THE SIX PURIFICATORY ACTIONS

The term Shat Karma or Shat Kriya translates as 'six actions', each 'action' has several practices. Each one is powerfully purifying, profoundly cleansing at all levels of 'being' and induces self-study (Swadhyaya) that subtly alters aspects of the manipulative ego-personality. The ancient Rishis considered them as essential to the practice of Yoga as they have manifold, wondrous result and are held in high esteem. These Kriyas have powerful effects within both the physical and energy bodies (Koshas) and have a dynamic impact on the Doshas. Therefore, the aims of Hatha Yoga and of the Shat Kriyas are to cleanse the internal organs and thereby create harmony between the major Pranic flows, Ida and Pingala, and attaining physical and mental purification and balance. They help develop immunity by eliminating the toxins and stimulate the mind by removing lethargy (Tamas). Stimulates vitality and helps in retardation of ageing, increasing the awareness.

These Kriyas are listed in Shloka 12 of Gheranda-Samhita, (a classic text of Hatha Yoga).

Dhautir-vastis-tatha Netir, Tratakam, Nauli

Kapal-bhatis-c-aitani, Sat-karmani Samacaret

Which means, "The body is cleaned with the help of the six following process".

1. Dhauti–Cleanses the upper GIT up to stomach.
2. *Basti*–Cleanses the lower part of GIT, especially the rectum.
3. *Neti*–Cleanses upper nasal tract from nostrils to throat.
4. *Nauli*–Cleanses abdominal organs, strengthens and tones abdominal muscles.
5. *Kapalabhati*–Refreshes, activates brain cells cleaning the respiratory tract.
6. *Trataka*–Strengthens and tones the eyes, improves eye sight.

When Shat Karmas are used in the very beginning, it unplugs the repression of cultural conditioning, open up the energy channels, activate the energy centers, and also unburden the physical body of accumulated obstructions and toxins.

Shat Karmas are NOT simply physical cleansing exercises; rather they utilize specific body mechanics in order to remove emotional and mental blockages and hindrances. They affect the physical body, energy body, mental/emotional body, the creative thought processes and pathways of embodiment in a positive way.

They are meant to wake us up and remove obstacles. They are not designed to be used exclusively, but rather are preparatory activities intended to be integrated with the other practices such as Yama / Niyama, Asana, Dhyana, Pranayama, and the rest of the Yoga practices capable of creating a profound synergy and synchronicity (of body, nature, breath, mind, and spirit).

These Kriyas create space in the human temple for living spirit -- they detoxify the body, the blood stream, the nervous system, brain, Nadis, mind, thought patterns, and negative tendencies. By opening up these pathways, less distracting energetics are present and more positive, healing, and evolutionary creative energy is able to flow. The Kriyas thus serve as power synergists in the purification of the body-mind, its activation, and integration.

Precautions

- They look difficult, revolting, unnatural and are definitely not easy.

- There is some risk of harm to the learner if something goes wrong.
- These powerful techniques should never be learned from books or taught by inexperienced people. According to tradition only those instructed by a Guru may teach others.
- It is essential to be personally instructed as to how and when to perform them according to individual needs.

Hatha Yoga Pradipika Chapter 2 verse 21 – 36, explains the technique, benefits and the precautions of the Shat Karmas

21: "When fat or mucus is excessive, Shatkarma; the six cleansing techniques, should be practiced before (Pranayama). Others, in whom the Doshas, *i.e.* phlegm, wind and bile are balanced, should not do them.

22: Dhauti, Basti, Neti, Trataka, Nauli and Kapalabhati; these are known as the six cleansing processes.

23: These Shatkarma, which effect the purification of the body, are secret. They have manifold, wondrous results and are held in high esteem by eminent Yogis.

24: A strip of wet cloth four Angulas wide (*i.e.* 7–8 cms) and fifteen hand spans (*i.e.* 1½ m) in length is slowly swallowed and then taken out, as instructed by the Guru. This is known as Dhauti (internal cleansing).

25: There is no doubt that coughs, asthma, diseases of the spleen, leprosy and twenty kinds of diseases caused by excess mucus are destroyed through Dhauti Karma.

26: Sitting in Utkatasana, navel deep in water, insert a tube into the anus and contract the anus. This cleansing with water is called Basti Karma.

27: Enlargement of the spleen and all diseases arising from excess wind, bile and mucus are eliminated from the body through the practice of Basti.

28: By practicing Basti the appetite increases, the body glows, excess Doshas are destroyed and the Dhatu, senses and mind are purified.

29: Insert a soft thread through the nose to a length of one hand span so that it comes out of the mouth. This is called Neti by the Siddhas.

30: Neti cleanses the cranium and bestows clairvoyance. It also destroys all diseases that manifest above the throat.

31: Looking intently with an unwavering gaze at a small point until tears are shed is known as Trataka by the Acharyas (teachers).

32: Trataka eradicates the eye of all diseases, fatigue and sloth and closes the doorway to creating those problems. It should be carefully kept secret like a golden casket.

33: Lean forward, protrude the abdomen and rotate (the muscles) from right to left with speed. This is called Nauli by the Siddhas.

34: Nauli is foremost of the Hatha Yoga practices. It kindles the digestive fire, removing indigestion, sluggish digestion, all disorders of the Doshas and brings about happiness.

35: Perform exhalation and inhalation rapidly like a bellows (of a blacksmith). This is Kapalabhati and destroys all the mucus disorders.

36: By the six Karmas (Shatkarma) one is freed from excesses of the Doshas. Then Pranayama is practiced and success is achieved without strain.

TYPES OF THE SHAT KARMAS

DHAUTI—Types of Dhauti: (HYP describes Vatsara Dhauti only; the other Dhauti practices are described in the Gheranda Samhita.)

- ANTAR DHAUTI (internal): Vatsara (wind), Varisara (water), Danda (stick), Vaman (Kunjal), Bahiskrita (anal cleaning).
- DANTA DHAUTI (teeth), Jihva (tongue), Karna (ear), Kapalrandhra (frontal sinuses), Kapal (head), Chakshu (eyes), Danta (teeth).
- HRID DHAUTI: Vastra (cloth), Danda (stick), Vaman (Kunjal).

- MOOLA SHODHANA (base purification).

BASTI—Active enema process

- Jala Basti (Water is sucked into the colon through the anus and expelled)
- Sthala Basti (Air is sucked in this case)

NETI—Nasal irrigation technique (Neti destroys Kapha-Doshas, and is said to bestow clairvoyance (Divya Drishti)

- Jala Neti (passing warm saline water through the nose)
- Sutra Neti (passing a soft thread through the nose)
- Ghrta Neti (passing ghee through the nose)
- Dugdha Neti (passing of milk through the nose)

TRATAKA—A Yogic exercise for the eyes, it involves steady and continuous gazing at a point of concentration.

- Antara Trataka, (internal) and
- Bahira Trataka (external)

NAULI—In this the abdominal muscles are isolated and churned.

- Dakshina Nauli (when muscles are isolated to the right)
- Vama Nauli (left)
- Madhyama Nauli (middle)

KAPALABHATI—Detoxification technique of Yoga

- Vatakrama Kapalabhati (similar to Bhastrika Pranayama)
- Vyutkrama Kapalabhati (sucking water in through the nose and expelling it through the mouth)
- Seetkrama Kapalabhati (in through mouth and out through nose).

PRANAYAMA: EXPANDING THE MOTHER ENERGY

The Art and Science of Control and Expansion of The Mother Energy of The Universe that Holds Everything Together.

We can absorb Prana directly from the sun, through the breath, water, earth, other people, food and cultivating healthy emotions and high thinking.

CLASSIFICATIONS OF PRANAYAMA

1. *Adhama or Yoga Pranayamas (Tamas)*

—Correction of breathing difficulties
—Cleansing of the respiratory system
—Toning up the nervous system
—Strengthening the mind

Examples: *Vibhaga Pranayama, Bhastrika, Sheetali Pranayamas.*

2. *Samyama or Madhyama Pranayamas (Rajas)*

—Sensory control
—Sensory withdrawal
—Concentration
—Meditation

Examples: *Bhramari, Pranava and Savitri Pranayamas*

3. *Shakti or Uttana Pranayamas (Sattvas)*

The Uttanas are the higher Pranayamas that are useful in the arousal of Kundalini Shakti *Eg: Ujjayi* and *Surya Bhedana*

Kevala Khumbaka or Nirguna.

Adham Pranayama
Low Chest Breathing

Adhyam Pranayama
High Chest Breathing

Madhyam Pranayama
Mid Chest Breathing

Mahat Yoga Pranayama
Complete Breath

VIBHAGA PRANAYAMA: SECTIONAL BREATHING

HATHENAS: ASANAS AND KRIYAS TO OPEN THE LUNGS BY FORCING AIR INTO ITS BRONCOPULMONARY SEGMENTS

HINTS FOR CONDUCTING A LESSON ON MEDITATION

"Meditation is a mental device that limits stimulus input by directing attention to a single unchanging or repetitive stimulus". Throughout recorded history it has been used to alter state of consciousness. It forms a part of religious practices. Recently Meditation has been used for therapeutic purposes rather than as a religious practice. Meditation can be used as a noncultic practice.

The technique of Meditation is related to the biofeedback techniques and to the relaxation methods.

Characteristics of Meditation

1. During meditation one gets profound rest for the body and mind, Oxygen consumption can be lowered during 20-30 minutes of meditation to a degree which can be reached after 6-7 hours of sleep.
2. Heart and respiratory rates typically decrease.
3. There is a shift to parasympathetic dominance.
4. There is a lowering of anxiety at this time.
5. During Meditation EEG shows an alert-drowsy pattern with high alphas and occasional theta wave patterns as well as unusual pattern of swift shifts from alpha to slower (more sleep - like) frequencies and then back again.
6. Meditation has been physiologically termed as 'wakeful, hypometabolic state'.
7. When practiced regularly it appears that Meditation alters behaviour suggesting number of beneficial changes.

Cautions

Meditation has its limitations. All persons cannot practice meditation even for 20 to 30 minutes. Overdose of meditation for such persons can be dangerous. The theory of "More the better" cannot be applied here.

Release of certain emotions that is difficult to handle may occur with prolonged meditation. In a person with an adverse psychiatric history, the beginning of meditation has been known to precipitate psychotic episodes. Even in relatively stable people, it is probably unwise to introduce prolonged sessions of meditation. To avoid such difficulties meditation should be practiced in moderation. It would be beneficial to start the practice of meditation after some amount of practice in stretching like Asanas, rhythmic breathing like Pranayama and relaxative technique like Shavasana.

It is doubtful whether meditation can really be ever taught effectively. In fact the state of meditation results out of the background prepared through variety of means contributing to a "meditative mood" which lasts not too long.

The Method of Teaching Meditation

The method of teaching meditation, therefore, requires creating an atmosphere of tranquility through pleasant voice and simple techniques leading to a meditative mood. All the yogic practices contribute to the building up of the meditative mood. Rather than introducing mechanical technique of meditation the participants be brought to "meditative mood" and left there for a comfortable time, the time being determined by the individual according to his capacity.

It is therefore, desirable that meditation should be introduced along with the group of yogic practices rather than as an isolated technique, so that it becomes more beneficial and less harmful. It should be remembered that in the hierarchy of yogic practices meditation occupies a higher position than other practices. However, all yogic practices are complementary to each other and each practice contributes to similar effects on a greater or a lesser scale. Stable, comfortable and erect sitting with head, neck and trunk in a vertical line and regulated breathing facilitates the practice of meditation.

Self Evaluation by the Teacher

When the teacher continually teaches the same activities in the same manner the teaching loses its interest within a very short time.

TEACHING YOGA TO CHILDREN

Nowadays, there is a lot controversy about introducing sex education in the schools. Why not instead, introduce non-controversial and highly desirable yoga education in the schools? In Vedic India, yoga education was a part of ashram life. If we introduce yoga in schools, we will surely produce many rishis and Vivekanands. Present day school education is stress-oriented and plagued by the burden of bulky school bags and stress generating examinations. Examination time is stressful not only to the students, but also to the parents and family members. Children need to relax and be happy. But, it is all stress because of high demands on them. Yoga is the best means to prevent as well as manage stress. Yoga is not "job education" but "self education". It is an ideal tool for holistic development of our body, mind and soul. Children are malleable and imitative and childhood is the most critical period of growth and development. Hence, school life is the most appropriate time for achieving excellence through yoga. Yoga can be used to improve not only physical health and physiological functions, but also concentration, memory, will power and discipline at the school level. Children do not need high metaphysical, philosophies, but common sense basic concepts of yoga.

In the elderly, body is rigid and health problems start appearing. Hence, yoga practice should include easy performing non-straining asanas, non-taxing pranayams, meditation and relaxation. At the college level, yoga training can be research oriented. School children are quite flexible and they can take to asanas like ducklings to water. Primary school children can enjoy suryanamaskar and AUM chanting. Children need to be taught how to concentrate. At high school level, meditation (dhyana) and self study and introspection (swadhyay) can effectively control the negative emotions and restlessness of mind. If dhyana is difficult, dharana (concentration) can be developed by conscious breathing, tratak and nasikagra mudra. This will help in developing awareness in every

1902 (Yoga)–71-II

action. The result will be desirable effect on children's emotional health and studies. Nadishuddhi with breath awareness and AUM chanting can effectively reduce the stress levels of children.

Violence is in the air. Terrorists are having a field day. Cinema glorifies violence. And we give our children water pistols and guns as toys! Emphasizing yam-niyam will inculcate virtues that will make children peaceful, humane and happy. It is clear that yoga will make our children physically strong, emotionally balanced, mentally peaceful and spiritually advanced. Thus, yoga is the best answer for children's psychological problems and all round development.

Teaching Yoga to Women

From the yogic point of view, childhood and postmenopausal periods of women are not different from men. On the other hand, the periods of adolescence (11-18 years), womanhood (19-45 years) and menopause (46-56 years) are unique to women.

During the adolescent period, there is increase in the production of female sex hormones resulting in profound physiological and psychological changes. Girls may experience mood swings and are vulnerable to sexual abuse if they are ignorant.

Hence, the emphasis should be on understanding (jnan yoga) and moral-ethical values (yam-niyam). Regular yoga practice will be of great help to cope with the situation. Relaxation techniques like shavasan and slow rhythmic breathing should be emphasized. Abdominal (adham) breathing, mool bandh, ashwini mudra, agnisar kriya and vipareetakarani are good for pelvic health.

For antenatal and postnatal care, abdominal breathing, shavasana and non-taxing asanas can be used to improve general health and reduce the pregnancy-related complaints. Regular practice of yoga will go a long way to reduce the incidence of surgeries and load on our healthcare delivery system.

Post-menopausal women may have the feeling of loss of womanhood and general emptiness. Disciplined yogabhyas is an ideal way to improve personality and general well-being to manage such cases.

For the Yoga Teacher

Rather than a teacher, you should be a guru, an acharya. Guru is an accomplished one, an expert in the field. Acharya is one who teaches by his personal example. Acharya is the best teacher because he inspires while good teacher explains and a bad teacher complains. Vedic India was on top of the world in every field—science, philosophy, art and craftmanship. This was because of the gurus, acharyas and rishis (seers, mantr drishtas) who, as nishkamakarmayogis, worked selflessly for the benefit of humanity.

Nowadays, teachers are devoid of noble thoughts and attitudes. They work for their salary and lack commitment, noble qualities and dedication to their work. Come exams and they go on strike! How can such teachers inspire the students?

As a yoga teacher, you should be an acharya, a guru and strive to become a rishi. Then you can impart knowledge of material sciences (apara vidya) as well as the spiritual knowledge (para vidya / brahm vidya). Spiritual background will help students to do better in material sciences as well and they will progress in their profession.

In Vedic India, gurukul system of education gave equal importance to material as well as spiritual knowledge. Treat all students equal, irrespective of social or economic status. Remember that the great Yogeshwar Krishna and his buddy, humble Sudama (Kuselan) studied together in the same gurukul.

As a role model, you should strictly observe yogic codes of conduct (yam-niyam) and embrace a simple and intellectual life that is based on regular self-appraisal (swadhyay). If you are blessed with these qualities you will be able to produce distinguished citizens who will be an asset to the society.

Multiple Choice Questions

1. Schools should cater to Individual differences to:
   A. narrow the gap between individual students
   B. even out abilities and performance of students
   C. understand why students are able or unable to learn
   D. make individual students feel exclusive
2. School Based Assessment:
   A. Dilutes the accountability of Boards of Education
   B. Hinders achieving Universal National Standards
   C. Helps all students learn more through diagnosis
   D. Makes students and teachers non-serious and casual
3. "Readiness for learning" refers to:
   A. general ability level of students
   B. present cognitive level of students in the learning continuum
   C. satisfying nature of the act of learning
   D. Thorndike's law of Readiness
4. A teacher has some physically challenged children in her class. Which of the following would be appropriate for her to say?
   A. Wheel-chaired bound children may take help of their peers in going to hall.
   B. Physically inconvenienced children may do an alternative activity in the classroom.
   C. Mohan why don't you use your crutches to go to the playground.
   D. Polio afflicted children will not present a song.
5. Learning disabilities may occur due to all of the following except:
   A. Cerebral dysfunction
   B. Emotional disturbance
   C. Behavioural disturbance
   D. Cultural factors
6. An inclusive school:
   A. Is committed to improve the learning outcomes of all students irrespective of their capabilities
   B. Differentiate between students and sets less challenging achievement targets for specially abled children
   C. Committed particularly to improve the learning outcomes of specially abled students
   D. Decides learning needs of students according to their disability
7. Gifted students:
   A. Need support not ordinarily provided be the school
   B. Can manage their studies without a teacher
   C. Can be good models for other students
   D. Cannot be learning disabled
8. The following are the steps in the process of problem solving except:
   A. Identification of a problem
   B. Breaking down the problem into smaller parts
   C. Explore possible strategies
   D. Anticipate outcomes
9. A teacher should:
   A. treat errors committed by students as blunders and take serious note of each error
   B. measure success as the number of times students avoid making mistakes
   C. not correct students while they're trying to communicate ideas
   D. focus more on lecturing and provide a foundation for knowledge
10. Which of the following cognitive verbs are used to analyse the information given?
    A. Identify
    B. Differentiate
    C. Classify
    D. Describe

11. Understanding Human Growth and Development enables a teacher to:
A. gain control of learners' emotions while teaching.
B. be clear about teaching diverse learners.
C. tell students how they can improve their lives.
D. practice her teaching in an unbiased way.

12. Which one of the following is true?
A. Development and learning are unaffected by socio-cultural contexts
B. Students learn only in a certain way
C. Play is significant for cognition and social competence
D. Questioning by teacher constrains cognitive development

13. Which one of the following is true about the role of heredity and environment in the development of a child?
A. The relative contributions of peers and genes are not additive
B. Heredity and environment do not operate together
C. Propensity is related to environment while actual development requires heredity
D. Both heredity and environment contribute 50% each in the development of a child

14. A PT teacher wants here her students to improve fielding in the game of cricket. Which one of the following strategies will best help his students achieve that goal?
A. Tell students how important it is for them to learn to field
B. Explain the logic behind good fielding and rate of success
C. Demonstrate fielding while students observe
D. Given students a lot of practice in fielding

15. A teacher wishes to help her students to appreciate multiple views of a situation. She provides her students multiple opportunities to debate on this situation in different groups. According to Vygotsky's perspective, her students will ______ various views and develop multiple perspectives of the situation on their own.
A. internalize B. construct
C. operationalize D. rationalize

16. Which of the following would be the most appropriate way to encourage disadvantaged children to attend school regularly?
A. A child collector employed by the school, must bring children from homes everyday
B. Paying ₹ 5 per day to attract children
C. Opening residential schools
D. Not allowing children to attend school may be made a legally punishable offence

17. The best way to avoid gender discrimination in a school may be:
A. formation of a rule to shun gender discrimination in the school and enforce it strictly
B. selection of more boys than girls for a music competition
C. metacognition of their gender-biased behaviours by teachers
D. recruitment of equal number of male and female teachers

18. Learning disabilities are generally found:
A. more often in children belonging to rural areas as compared to urban areas
B. in specially those children whose paternal relatives have such problems
C. in children with average to superior IQ
D. more often in boys as compared to girls

19. Assessment for learning takes into account the following *except*:
A. mistakes of students
B. learning styles of students
C. strengths of students
D. needs of students

20. Which of the following characteristics is the hallmark of the problem-solving approach?
A. The problem is based on only one principle/topic
B. There is an implicit hint given in the problem statement
C. The problem is original
D. There is usually one approach for getting the right answer

21. Learners who demonstrate an earnest desire for increased knowledge and academic competence are said to have a:
A. Work-avoidance orientation
B. Mastery orientation
C. Performance-approach orientation
D. Performance-avoidance orientation

22. A teacher can make problem-solving fun for students by doing all the following *except*:
A. providing open ended material
B. giving time for free play
C. providing endless opportunities for creative thinking
D. expecting perfection from the students while they are trying to do things by themselves

23. Critical pedagogy firmly believes that:
A. the teacher should always lead the classroom instruction
B. the learners need not reason independently
C. what children learn out of school is irrelevant
D. the experiences and perceptions of learners are important

24. Learners display individual differences. So a teacher should:
A. insist on uniform pace of learning
B. provide a variety of learning experiences
C. enforce strict discipline
D. increase number of tests

25. A teacher never gives answers to questions herself. She encourages her students to suggest answers, have group discussions and adopt collaborative learning. This approach is based on the principle of:
A. active participation
B. proper organization of instructional material
C. setting a good example and being a role-model
D. readiness to learn

26. Which of the following is a teacher-related factor affecting learning?
A. Mastery over the subject-matter
B. Proper seating arrangement
C. Availability of teaching-learning resources
D. Nature of the content or learning experiences

27. A school gives preference to girls while preparing students for a State level solo-songs competition. This reflects:
A. Gender bias
B. Global trends
C. Pragmatic approach
D. Progressive thinking

28. The emphasis from teaching to learning can be shifted by:
A. focusing on examination results
B. adopting child-centered pedagogy
C. encouraging rote learning
D. adopting frontal teaching

29. Inclusive Education:
A. includes teachers from marginalized groups
B. celebrates diversity in the classroom
C. encourages strict admission procedures
D. includes indoctrination of facts

30. According to Kohlberg, a teacher can instill moral values in children by:
A. giving strict instructions on 'how to behave'
B. giving importance to religious teachings
C. laying clear rules of behaviour
D. involving them in discussions on moral issues

31. Young learners should be encouraged to interact with peers in the classroom so that:
A. the teacher can control the classroom better
B. they can learn answers to questions from each other
C. the syllabus can be covered quickly
D. they learn social skills in the course of study

32. Human personality is the result of:
A. only heredity
B. upbringing and education
C. interaction between heredity and environment
D. only environment

33. Individual attention is important in the teaching — learning process because:
A. children develop at different rates and learn differently
B. learners always learn better in groups
C. teacher training programmes prescribe it
D. it offers better opportunities to teachers to discipline each learner

34. When a child gets bored while doing a task, it is a sign that:
A. the child needs to be disciplined
B. the task may have become mechanically repetitive
C. the child is not intelligent
D. the child is not capable of learning

35. In the context of education, socialization means:
A. always following social norms
B. creating one's own social norms
C. respecting elders in society
D. adapting and adjusting to social environment

36. Which of the following is a principle of development?
A. All processes of development are not inter-connected
B. It does not proceed at the same pace for all
C. Development is always linear
D. It is a discontinuous process

37. Human development is divided into domains such as:
A. physical, spiritual, cognitive and social
B. physical, cognitive, emotional and social
C. emotional, cognitive, spiritual and social-psychological
D. psychological, cognitive, emotional and physical

38. A teacher, because of his/her democratic nature, allows students to sit all over the class. Some sit together and discuss or do group reading. Some sit quietly and read themselves. A parent does not like it. Which of the following may be the best way to handle the situation?
A. Parents should request the principal to change the section of their ward
B. Parents should show trust in the teacher and discuss the problem with the teacher
C. Parents should take away the child from that school
D. Parents should complain against the teacher to the principal

39. 'Mind mapping' refers to:
A. a plan of action for an adventure
B. drawing the picture of a mind
C. researching the functioning of the mind
D. a technique to enhance comprehension

40. Learning can be enriched if:
A. more and more teaching aids are used in the class
B. teachers use different types of lectures and explanation
C. due attention is paid to periodic tests in the class
D. situations from the real world are brought into the class in which students interact with each other and the teacher facilitates

41. The term 'curriculum' in the field of education refers to:
A. overall programme of the school which students experience on a day-to-day basis
B. evaluation process
C. text-material to be used in the class
D. methods of teaching and the content to be taught

42. "Development is a never ending process." This idea is associated with:
A. Principle of continuity
B. Principle of integration
C. Principle of interaction
D. Principle of interrelation

43. Which one of the following is correctly matched?
A. Emotional Development – Maturation
B. Physical Development – Environment
C. Cognitive Development – Maturation
D. Social Development – Environment

44. Which one of the following is the main objective of teaching?
A. To develop thinking power of the students
B. To give information related to the syllabus
C. To dictate notes to the students
D. To prepare students to pass the examination

45. Which of the following statements regarding "Memory Level of Teaching" (MLT) is incorrect?
A. Memory is the initial stage of teaching
B. Memory Level of Teaching mainly depends on the prevailing socio-economic conditions
C. MLT includes the habit of rote memorization of facts and bits of information
D. MLT enables the learner to retain and also reproduce the learnt material whenever required

46. Which of the following statements regarding "Understanding Level of Teaching" (ULT) is incorrect?
A. Morrison is the main proponent of ULT
B. It is 'memory plus insight' as it goes beyond just the memorizing of facts. It focuses on the mastery of the subject
C. Cultural materialism is also a primary determining factor of ULT
D. It provides more and more opportunities for the students to develop the intellectual behaviour

47. Which of the following statements regarding 'Reflective Level of Teaching' (RLT) is incorrect?
A. Hunt is the main proponent of RLT
B. It is problem-centred teaching
C. The students are assumed to adopt some sort of research approach to solve the problem
D. The teacher assumes the primary place and the pupil occupies the secondary place

48. Which of the following is not one of the advantages of "Lecture Method"?
A. It is economical as it can cover large audience in less time
B. It promotes social cohesion among the pupils
C. It is useful for stimulating further learning
D. It has the flexibility for adapting the lecture according to time and equipment available

49. Which one of the following is not one of the advantages of 'TV or Video Presentation' as a teaching method?
A. Many important personalities and experts are brought to the classroom through videopresentation
B. This method is specifically useful for adult learners
C. It promotes a sort of nativism among the learners
D. Illustrated lectures and demonstrations can be supplemented by other teaching aids such as slides, models, specimens, etc.

50. Which one of the following is not one of the advantages of 'Team Teaching Method'?
A. It helps in sharing the best faculty by more students
B. It involves optimum use of teaching techniques and devices
C. It improves the teaching quality
D. It affects the socio-economic conditions of the pupils

51. Which one of the following is not one of the advantages of 'Group Discussion Method'?
A. It flattens out the ideological differences of the pupils
B. It can be planned where there is certainty about the conclusions and objectives. The discussion is guided by the trainer in an appropriate sequence

C. It promotes communication and interaction within a group around a topic or problem presented to the group
D. It can also be unplanned where the topic presented for discussion is without any opening statement and discussion that follows is entirely spontaneous

52. Which one of the following is not one of the advantages of the "Case Study Method'?
A. It provides opportunity to the participants to critically analyze the problem and express reasoned opinions
B. It promotes gender-sensitivity among the pupils
C. It enhances decision–making and problem-solving skills
D. It ensures active participation, which may lead to innovative solutions

53. Which one of the following is not one of the functions of 'Evaluation'?
A. Feedback
B. Motivation
C. Ideological indoctrination
D. Better guidance

54. Who among the following is considered a proponent of the Wardha Education System?
A. Sri Aurobindo
B. S. Radhakrishnan
C. J. Krishnamurti
D. Mahatma Gandhi

55. Who among the following was the main proponent of the Kindergarten system of education?
A. Froebel B. Rousseau
C. Maria Montessori D. John Dewey

56. Which of the following is not one of the "Projected Visual Aids"?
A. Slides
B. Bar Chart
C. Handheld Projector
D. Video Projector

57. Which of the following is an independent variable in teaching-learning process?
A. Student B. Institution
C. Teacher D. Parents

58. Who has the least chance of becoming an effective teacher?
A. One who has no interest in teaching
B. One who is a strict disciplinarian
C. One who neglects teaching
D. One who knows his subject well

59. Good teaching is best reflected by:
A. Attendance of students
B. Number of distinctions
C. Meaningful questions asked by students
D. Pin-drop silence in the class

60. A teacher of class VI in a co-educational school would observe perceptible differences between boys and girls in which of the following development?
A. Physical B. Intellectual
C. Social D. Moral

61. Which of the following approach views learning as an active mental process of acquiring, and using knowledge?
A. Constructivist B. Behaviouristic
C. Humanistic D. Social learning

62. 'Give me a dozen of healthy children, I can make them doctor, judge, beggar or even a thief'. This statement illustrates which one of the following learning theories?
A. Classical conditioning
B. Gestalt
C. Field theory
D. Behaviourism

63. After teaching a content, a teacher finds that the students are able to work with action verbs namely appraise, criticize and judge. Thus, objectives have been achieved at which of the following level?
A. Analysis level B. Synthesis level
C. Evaluation level D. Application level

64. According to Piaget, use of charts, graphs and diagrams is a useful strategy for teaching children at the:
A. Sensorimotor stage
B. Preoperational stage
C. Concrete operational stage
D. Formal operational stage

65. Which one of the following was of the view that anything that can be learned by direct experience can also be learned from observation. Models are most effective if they are seen as having respect, competence, high status or power. Thus, in most cases, teachers can be highly influential models.

A. Kohler B. Bandura
C. Thorndike D. Skinner

66. Building meaning by connecting what is to be learned with established words or images is use of:

A. Mnemonic strategies
B. Premack principle
C. Scaffolding
D. Assisted learning

67. A group of children learn a lot of arithmetical skills by way of completing a project on 'celebration of festivals'. This is a kind of:

A. informal learning
B. incidental learning
C. formal learning
D. non-formal learning

68. Which of the following do you consider most important to prevent classroom discipline problems?

A. Close monitoring of student's behaviour
B. Establishing rules and procedure
C. Creating stimulating classroom environment
D. Reward students for good behaviour

69. Which of the following is an objective related to the affective domain?

A. Students can paint a picture
B. Students can write a letter
C. Students can draw a graph
D. Students can value honesty

70. Which of the following would be more useful to eliminate routine misbehaviour of students in the classroom?

A. Removing potential trouble makers from class
B. Use of non-verbal cues
C. Ignoring and moving along
D. Providing token reinforcers as rewards

71. Which of the following techniques/procedures is most useful to promote creativity in children?

A. Simulation
B. Experimentation
C. Symposium
D. Brain-storming

72. When teaching, a teacher periodically tests her students to monitor their progress. She uses the results of such tests to identify areas where she may need to change or modify her instruction. The type of assessment used by her is called:

A. Normative B. Formative
C. Summative D. Diagnostic

73. Which of the following is the major obstacle to ensure achievement of high academic standards from disadvantaged students?

A. Belief that not every student is capable of mastering challenging content and skills
B. Non-availability of sufficient instructional materials aligned with the school curriculum
C. Providing students substantial autonomy to determine what they learn and how they will learn it
D. Providing a variety of individual, small group and large group activities

74. According to Article 21A of the constitution:

A. it is mandatory to provide free and compulsory education to children upto the age of 14 years
B. education is a fundamental right of children between the age of 0-14 years
C. education of children upto the age of 6 years is not a responsibility of the state
D. education is a fundamental right of children between the age 6-14 years

75. The procedures used by teachers to identify difficulties of learners in various fields of learning are part of:

A. placement assessment
B. formative assessment
C. diagnostic assessment
D. summative assessment

ANSWERS

1	2	3	4	5	6	7	8	9	10
C	C	B	C	D	A	A	B	C	B
11	**12**	**13**	**14**	**15**	**16**	**17**	**18**	**19**	**20**
B	C	A	D	A	C	C	B	D	B
21	**22**	**23**	**24**	**25**	**26**	**27**	**28**	**29**	**30**
C	D	D	B	A	A	A	B	B	D
31	**32**	**33**	**34**	**35**	**36**	**37**	**38**	**39**	**40**
D	C	A	B	D	B	D	B	C	D
41	**42**	**43**	**44**	**45**	**46**	**47**	**48**	**49**	**50**
A	A	D	A	B	C	D	B	C	D
51	**52**	**53**	**54**	**55**	**56**	**57**	**58**	**59**	**60**
A	B	C	D	A	B	C	A	C	A
61	**62**	**63**	**64**	**65**	**66**	**67**	**68**	**69**	**70**
A	D	C	C	B	A	B	B	D	B
71	**72**	**73**	**74**	**75**					
D	B	A	D	C					

●●●

YOUR SPACE